Pro Linux System Administration

James Turnbull, Peter Lieverdink,
Dennis Matotek

Contributors: Sander van Vugt, Donna Benjamin
Lead Editors: Michelle Lowman, Frank Pohlmann
Technical Reviewer: Jaime Sicam
Editorial Board: Clay Andres, Steve Anglin, Mark Beckner, Ewan Buckingham, Tony Campbell,
    Gary Cornell, Jonathan Gennick, Michelle Lowman, Matthew Moodie, Jeffrey Pepper,
    Frank Pohlmann, Ben Renow-Clarke, Dominic Shakeshaft, Matt Wade, Tom Welsh
Project Manager: Kylie Johnston
Copy Editors: Ami Knox, Nicole Flores
Associate Production Director: Kari Brooks-Copony
Production Editor: Elizabeth Berry
Compositor: Kinetic Publishing Services, LLC
Proofreaders: April Eddy, Dan Shaw
Indexer: BIM Indexing & Proofreading Services
Artist: Kinetic Publishing Services, LLC
Cover Designer: Kurt Krames
Manufacturing Director: Tom Debolski

Distributed to the book trade worldwide by Springer-Verlag New York, Inc., 233 Spring Street, 6th Floor, New York, NY 10013. Phone 1-800-SPRINGER, fax 201-348-4505, e-mail orders-ny@springer-sbm.com, or visit http://www.springeronline.com.

For information on translations, please contact Apress directly at 2855 Telegraph Avenue, Suite 600, Berkeley, CA 94705. Phone 510-549-5930, fax 510-549-5939, e-mail info@apress.com, or visit http://www.apress.com.

Apress and friends of ED books may be purchased in bulk for academic, corporate, or promotional use. eBook versions and licenses are also available for most titles. For more information, reference our Special Bulk Sales–eBook Licensing web page at http://www.apress.com/info/bulksales.

The source code for this book is available to readers at http://www.apress.com.

To Ruth, who continues to make it all worthwhile,
and my family, who have always supported me
—James Turnbull

To Donna, Pixel, and Mustafa
—Peter Lieverdink

To Bianca and my children, Ziggy and Anika, plus the pets
—Dennis Matotek

Contents

PART 1 ■■■ The Beginning

PART 2 ■ ■ ■ Making Linux Work for You

About the Authors

JAMES TURNBULL manages the Computer Emergency Response Team (CERT) at the National Australia Bank. He is also a member of Linux Australia, which included sitting on the Executive Council in 2008, and on the committee of Linux Users of Victoria.

He is a contributor to a number of open source projects and regularly speaks on topics related to writing, systems administration, and open source technologies.

He is the author of three books:

- *Pulling Strings with Puppet: Systems Administration Made Easy* (Apress, 2008), which explores the Ruby-based Puppet configuration management tool

- *Hardening Linux* (Apress, 2008), which focuses on hardening Linux bastion hosts including the base operating system, file systems, firewalls, connections, logging, testing your security, and securing a number of common applications including e-mail, FTP, and DNS

- *Pro Nagios 2.0* (Apress, 2006), which covers enterprise management using the Nagios open source tool

PETER LIEVERDINK was born in a small Dutch country town. He owns a pair of clogs, but has never eaten tulips or lived in a windmill.

On his 22nd birthday, Peter moved to Australia and briefly worked in an office cubicle. He now runs his own business, Creative Contingencies Pty, Ltd. The business depends on open source software for infrastructure and development as well as daily office tasks.

Peter specializes in web application development and helping other businesses implement open source solutions using Linux on both desktops and servers.

DENNIS MATOTEK was born in a small town in Victoria, Australia, called Mildura. As with all small towns, the chronic lack of good, strong coffee in Mildura drives the young to search further afield. Dennis moved to Melbourne where good, strong coffee flows through the city in a river called the Yarra. However, it was in Scotland during a two-year hunt for one of them fierce, blue-faced, part-smurf Scotsmen that Dennis was introduced to systems administration.

Scotland, on the technological edge, had 486DX PCs and a VAX. On arriving back in Melbourne, after staying awake for 24 hours at an airport minding his bags, Dennis was given a job interview—jobs in those days fell down like snow from the sky.

Since that time, Dennis has stayed predominately in Melbourne working with IBM AS400s (iSeries) for six years and mainly Linux for nine years. Dennis also wrote and directed some short films and plays. He has a lovely LP (life partner) and a little boy called Zigfryd and a new little girl called Anika, whom he misses terribly when at work, which is most of the time.

Oh, and he never did find one of those Scotsmen.

About the Technical Reviewer

JAIME SICAM occasionally works as an IT instructor and consultant. Prior to his hiatus from working full time, he indulged himself as one of the system administrators in the engineering team of Defender Technologies Group.

Jaime takes pride in being part of DOST-ASTI (Advanced Science and Technology Institute) on Bayanihan Linux. His team advocated the use of open source software for the computing needs of government agencies, schools, and small and medium-size enterprises in the Philippines. He enjoys technology, road trips, and keeping up to date on news of the Utah Jazz.

Acknowledgments

Kylie Johnston for her immense patience, organization, and good humor during the project management process

Our excellent copy editors—Ami Knox and Nicole Flores

Our production editor—Liz Berry

Michelle Lowman for her guidance and advice as editor

Frank Pohlmann for agreeing to the whole thing

Donna Benjamin for her excellent artwork and feedback

The team at Apress

Introduction

Information technology plays a critical role in business success. Investment in technology can increase productivity. It can provide access to new markets—for example, via the Internet. So understanding information technology and how it can serve your business is important.

You also need to understand the cost of the technology that your business relies on and how to make the best use of it. Today, one of your potential technology choices is free and open source software, or FOSS, which does not require license fees or maintenance charges and represents a serious and cost-effective alternative to commercial software.

This book is designed to guide the small business entrepreneur into the world of free and open source software. We will show you how to use open source software and how it brings low-cost and first-class information technology within reach of all businesses, even the smallest startups. The book explains how to install and configure open source software and how to tap into the global community that creates and supports FOSS.

From providing a basic file server for the office to setting up a web server, building your own IT systems puts you in control of your business. Whether you want to manage your own systems or just understand them better so you know what your support professionals are doing, this book is for you.

Linux and Free and Open Source Software

Linux is one of the most famous pieces of FOSS software. Linux, also sometimes called GNU/Linux, is a computer operating system, like Microsoft Windows or Apple Mac OS X. Unlike these other operating systems, Linux is free. Linux users also have the freedom to contribute to its development because the software source code is open and accessible to study and modification. In addition to this, Linux users are also free to share this software with others.

Linux was originally developed by Finnish programmer Linus Torvalds. First released in 1991, it has since grown to encompass an army of developers, tens of thousands of applications and tools, and millions of users.

Linux, however, is no longer just in the realm of the hobbyist enthusiast. Linux servers now run mission-critical applications in establishments like banks, manufacturing companies, and government organizations, and form the backbone of many media and Internet-based concerns.

What makes Linux different? Well, Linux is built with a collaborative development model. Linux, and the software that runs on it, is created by volunteers and by the employees of companies, governments, and organizations from all over the world. Some of the biggest companies in the world develop and use open source software including IBM, HP, Oracle, and Sun. Whole organizations have also built and developed products and support infrastructure around Linux and open source software.

Many of the principles behind FOSS are derived from the scientific principles of transparency. The openness and transparency of the code and development process means that open source software is not only contributed to by a variety of people but also audited at all levels. The free and open source community treats software just like any other information and believes people have the right to have full control over that information. You should be free to share it with anyone you wish in much the same way you are free to share recipes with your neighbors.

None of this impacts the day-to-day reality of running your business, but it is the philosophy that means FOSS exists. The practical reality of open source software is the freedom to run a huge variety of software in your business and modify or customize it for your own needs. Your information technology needs will grow as your business grows, and the real strength of FOSS lies in its scalability. You don't need to buy new licenses for every new machine you buy for a new staff member or for every additional CPU core in a server.

■**Note** Some people get confused between software and operating systems. An *operating system* is a collection of programs that controls how the computer operates. It knows how to talk to a printer or to another computer and to write information to your hard drive. Red Hat Enterprise Linux or Microsoft Windows Server 2007 are examples of operating systems. In comparison, software or application software can be something like a word processor or web browser. It requires the underlying operating system to function but performs some separate function. You can run a computer operating system without any software, but you cannot run a computer without any operating system.

WHAT DO YOU MEAN BY FREE?

FOSS software is free software for which the source code is available and is subject to one of a series of licenses. These licenses mandate that the software be freely available and not sold as a commercial product. The most commonly used license is the GNU General Public License (GPL). The GPL gives people who receive a copy of GPL-licensed software permission to reproduce, change, or distribute the work as long as any resulting copies or changes are also bound by the same GPL licensing scheme or with terms no more restrictive than those of the original license. An example of GPL-licensed software is the Firefox web browser.

Other open source licenses include LGPL, or GNU Lesser General Public License, Apache License, MIT license, and Artistic License. Most of the time though, you won't need to care about licenses and, more important, you won't need to *pay* for licenses!

There are some excellent references on FOSS licensing, but one of the best is an article by Mark Webbink, Senior Vice President and General Counsel of Red Hat, Inc., that is available at http://www.groklaw.net/article.php?story=20031231092027900. You can also find a mostly complete list of licenses and an explanation of their terms and conditions at the Free Software Foundation (FSF) website—http://www.fsf.org/licensing/licenses/.

Why Do You Need a Linux Server?

There are lots of good reasons to install a Linux server. Linux has all the features of similar commercial operating systems like the Microsoft Windows Server platform. For example:

- *Customer care*

  Free and open source software can help you communicate more effectively with your customers and be more responsive to their needs. After all, it is the quality of the relationships with your customers that really drives your business forward. E-mail has become the lifeblood of small business communication. FOSS lets you access features usually reserved for companies running mainframe mail servers and integrated communication suites. Productivity and database tools will help you professionally interact with colleagues, suppliers, and customers, and build and maintain those critical contacts more effectively.

- *Business efficiency*

  Having your own Linux server will help you to secure your computer network, keep it up and running, and protect your critical business information, like accounts and intellectual property. Spending less time and money on technology issues frees you to spend more time focusing on your business and your employee's productivity.

- *Secure and stable*

  Choosing Linux guarantees you have access to the most up-to-date software to keep your desktops and servers current with the latest versions and security patches, enhancing the safety and reliability of your network. There is no need to pay extra or upgrade to get full functionality software or access new features.

- *Nimble and responsive*

  From a development point of view, you can be at the edge of technological innovation. You are able to participate in leading development projects and help design systems that are right for your organization. From embedded devices to mainframes, Linux has the software you can use. You are not tied to the release cycle of some other organization, which means you are in control of your business and its future direction.

- *Freedom to grow*

  Access premium business software without paying for premium software licenses. This gives you the freedom to redirect licensing fees for software into customized services to meet the needs of your business or new hardware that delivers functionality you may not have otherwise been able to afford. Free and open source software will save you money and offer you unlimited flexibility and scalability for future growth.

What Does This Book Expect You to Know?

Well, most importantly, you don't need to know anything about Linux! We'll teach you everything you need to know about installing and configuring Linux servers and the applications that run on them.

In writing this book, we've assumed you know a little about computing. We've assumed you have

- Some familiarity with Microsoft Windows and its concepts

- Some exposure to networking including concepts like IP addresses

---

■**Note** Where possible, we've tried to direct you to links and resources that will help you extend your knowledge or provide more information on a particular topic.

What You Will Learn in This Book

This book is not about running your business; it is about running the computer systems that will support your business by helping you manage the information flow that is unique to your enterprise.

E-mail, web, and file servers as well as desktop computers and printers are essential tools for business. Open source software gives small businesses the opportunity to turn these tools into an efficient business system, not just a jumble of techno-tools.

Each chapter in this book looks at a different component or tool that will allow you to manage and support the technology in your business.

Part 1: The Beginning

In this part, we will teach you the Linux basics: how to install, how to configure, and how to manage Linux systems.

Chapter 1

We'll introduce you to some Linux distributions and how to choose an appropriate one for your needs.

Chapter 2

We take you through installing Linux, using two commonly used distributions, Red Hat Enterprise Linux and Ubuntu Server.

Chapter 3

This is a general guide to interacting with a Linux server and the basics of how to use Linux.

Chapter 4

You'll learn about users and groups and how to create, delete, and manage them.

Chapter 5

You'll learn about starting and stopping your server and managing the services and applications you're going to run on it.

Chapter 6

We'll explain networking with Linux including IP addressing and using a firewall to secure your Linux servers.

Chapter 7

You'll gain an understanding of packages, packaging, and package management. You'll understand how to install, manage, and remove software on your Linux server.

Chapter 8

You'll learn about disks, storage, and how to use and manage a variety of storage configurations including RAID on your Linux server.

Part 2: Making It Work for You

In this part, we'll show you how to put your newly gained knowledge to use by installing and configuring the services needed to run your business. We'll also show you how to keep them in optimum condition and how to automate system management and deployment.

Chapter 9

This chapter introduces many of the "plumbing" concepts like DHCP, DNS, and NTP that will tie together your Linux-based environment.

Chapter 10

We'll show you how to run your own mail server, manage mail boxes for your organization, allow remote access to e-mail, and protect your organization from spam and viruses.

Chapter 11

In this chapter, we demonstrate how to run your own web server, configure the useful MySQL database engine, and install and manage your own web applications.

Chapter 12

We'll teach you how to do file sharing and print serving with Linux—services that are compatible and can be used with Microsoft Windows servers and desktops! Included is an introduction to a free document management system that rivals Microsoft's SharePoint application.

Chapter 13

Using simple tools, we'll show you how to back up and recover your Linux servers and protect your organization's data from a disaster. This includes a backup server that is freely available, robust, and flexible enough to back up servers on your whole network.

Chapter 14

We'll introduce you to the concept of the virtual private network (VPN), which allows you to securely connect together remote users and remote offices across the Internet, via dial-up or across private links. With Linux, you can build VPNs without expensive products like Cisco ASAs or commercial firewall products.

Chapter 15

Microsoft Exchange, Novell GroupWise, and similar collaboration tools are becoming more and more important for sharing and managing information. We'll introduce you to a free and open source equivalent that will allow your users to collaborate and manage information in your environment.

Chapter 16

In this chapter, you'll learn about directory services and protocols that allow you to store and provide user information to other tools to authenticate users or provide address books and directories. This serves as a free alternative to Microsoft's Active Directory services.

Chapter 17

We'll show you how to manage the performance and capacity of your Linux servers and how to ensure they run efficiently and perform well.

Chapter 18

You'll learn about logging and log data, a useful source of information to manage your servers, and how to use simple monitoring tools that can notify you when something stops working or goes wrong.

Chapter 19

In this chapter, you'll learn how to quickly, easily, and automatically install servers, including servers and desktops, and how to use tools to automatically configure and manage them.

Chapter 20

Last, we'll introduce you to Linux virtualization: a free, cheap, and "green" way to deploy virtual servers.

Downloading the Code

The source code for this book is available to readers at http://www.apress.com in the Downloads section of this book's home page. Please feel free to visit the Apress website and download all the code there. You can also check for errata and find related titles from Apress.

Contacting the Authors

James Turnbull:
 info@james-turnbull.net
 http://www.james-turnbull.net

Dennis Matotek:
 book@ownenergy.net.au
 http://www.ownenergy.net.au

Peter Lieverdink:
 apress@cafuego.net
 http://cafuego.net

PART 1

■ ■ ■

The Beginning

CHAPTER 1

■■■

Introducing Linux

By James Turnbull, Peter Lieverdink, Dennis Matotek

You've decided to run your business on free and open source (FOSS) infrastructure? Congratulations and welcome to the world of Linux and open source software! This chapter will take you through the first steps into implementing that infrastructure. We cover choosing a platform or distribution, choosing appropriate and supported hardware, and finding the software you need. We also provide you with the location of some resources to help you support your Linux environment. Then, in Chapter 2, we'll show you how to install your first Linux hosts.

Linux Distributions

What is a Linux distribution? Well, in simple terms it is a collection of applications, packages, management, and features that run on top of the Linux kernel. The kernel is what all distributions have in common (it is sometimes customized by the distribution maintainers), but at their core they all run Linux.

■**Note** So what's a kernel, you ask? Don't panic, we'll fill you in. The *kernel* is the core of all computer operating systems and is usually the layer that allows the operating system to interact with the hardware in your computer. The kernel contains software that allows you to make use of your hard disk drives, network cards, RAM, and other hardware components. In the Linux world, the kernel is based on code originally developed by Linux's founder, Finnish developer Linus Torvalds. The kernel is now maintained by a community of open source developers, and changes go through a software life-cycle process. Your distribution will come with a version of that kernel, and like Windows or other operating systems it can be updated and upgraded to provide new features or fix bugs.

The world of Linux distributions may at first seem a little confusing. You are probably thinking, "If they are all 'Linux,' why are there so many different names, and which do I choose?" You may have heard names like Red Hat, Fedora, Debian, and the more oddly titled Ubuntu (it's a Zulu word that loosely translates as "humanity toward others"!). In this section, we'll explain what a distribution is, describe the ways in which they differ, and suggest some strategies for selecting the right distribution for you.

Distributions differ in several ways, and three of the most important are

- Purpose
- Configuration and packaging
- Support model

First, different distributions are often designed for different purposes and provide different user experiences. Some distributions are designed as servers, others as desktops, and some are designed to perform particular functions, for example, as embedded systems. The majority of Linux installations still tend to be servers. While more Linux desktops are appearing, the numbers do not yet challenge Windows and Apple OS X dominancy of the desktop market.

The second major difference between distributions is in their configuration. While some distributions keep all their configuration settings and files in the same locations, others vary this. Additionally, the process of installing and updating applications (which are usually installed by a *package*) is not consistent across distributions. Many distributions use different application installation and management tools (generally called *package management tools*). This can be confusing and can make administration difficult if you have an environment with differing distributions. In Chapter 19, we'll talk about configuration management tools and how to overcome these sorts of issues.

The third difference is that distributions also have differing support models. Some, like Debian, CentOS, and Fedora, are maintained by a community of volunteers. Others, like Red Hat Enterprise Linux and Ubuntu, are maintained and supported by a commercial vendor. The software is still open source, but you can pay for support and maintenance. Most commercial Linux vendors support themselves through the sale of maintenance and support services.

Let's look at some of the available choices; this won't be a comprehensive list, but we'll cover most of the major popular distributions and then present some reasons for selecting particular platforms. We'll also group together some of the like distributions, particularly focusing on distributions derived from two major distributions: Red Hat and Ubuntu (itself a derivation from the Debian distribution).

■**Note** So how can one distribution be "derived" from another distribution? Well, open source software means that the source code is available to developers. Developers can pick and choose the features they want in a distribution and potentially create their own distribution. Many of the major distributions appeared because a developer or group of developers decided to create their own version of another distribution. These new derivations often have their own branding and features. Some remain close to the parent distribution, and others follow their own path.

Red Hat Enterprise Linux

Red Hat Enterprise Linux (http://www.redhat.com/rhel/) is a popular commercially supported Linux platform. It comes in a number of versions, the two most common being Red Hat Enterprise Linux (also known as RHEL) and Red Hat Enterprise Linux Advanced Platform (RHELAP). The major difference between the versions is the number of CPUs supported, with RHEL supporting up to two CPUs and RHELAP supporting an unlimited number.

Red Hat platforms are commonly used by corporate organizations as server platforms due to the dedicated support and service levels available from the vendor. Red Hat, and most distributions based on it, make use of the Red Hat Package Management (RPM) packaging system.

At the time of writing, RHEL costs start at approximately US$350 dollars a year for basic support and range up to US$1,300 dollars for premium support. Its more advanced cousin, RHELAP, ranges in cost from US$1,500 to US$2,500 per year depending on the level of support desired. These costs provide you with technical support and any needed patches or updates to the distribution.

Red Hat used to be run by a community of volunteers too until the distribution became so important to the technical infrastructure of commercial organizations that people were happy to pay for guaranteed support. Their original volunteer community still lives on as the Fedora Project.

CentOS

CentOS (http://www.centos.org/) is a derivation of the Red Hat Enterprise Linux platform. Based on the same source code, it is available at no charge (and without Red Hat's support). People who wish to make use of the Red Hat platform and its stability without paying for additional support commonly use it. It employs the same packaging system, RPM, and many of the same administration tools as the Red Hat product.

The Fedora Project

The Fedora Project (http://fedoraproject.org/) is a distribution jointly run by the community and Red Hat. It is a derivative of Red Hat Enterprise Linux and provides a forward development platform for the product. Sponsored by Red Hat, Fedora is a testing ground for many of Red Hat's new features. As a result, it is occasionally considered by some to be too edgy for commercial use. Many of the features introduced in Fedora often make their way into the new RHEL releases. Fedora also makes use of RPM packages and many of the same administration tools used by RHEL.

Debian Linux

The Debian Linux distribution (http://www.debian.org) is a free community-developed and community-managed distribution with a diverse and active group of developers and users. It was started in 1993 and built around a social contract (http://www.debian.org/social_contract). The Debian distribution strives toward freedom, openness, and maintaining a focus on delivering what users want.

The Debian distribution is well known for the *dpkg* packaging system and the availability of nearly 23,000 applications and tools for the distribution.

Ubuntu

Initiated by South African technologist and entrepreneur Mark Shuttleworth, the Ubuntu operating system (http://www.ubuntu.com/) is free and based on the Debian Linux platform. It is community developed, and upgrades are released on a six-month cycle. Commercial support is also available from its coordinating organization, Canonical, as well as third-party support providers. It comes in different flavors to be used as desktops or servers. Some pundits believe the ubiquitous nature and stability of Ubuntu heralds the increased use of Linux as a desktop platform. Many people consider Ubuntu one of the easiest Linux platforms to use and understand, and much of its development is aimed at ease of use and good user experience. Ubuntu makes use of Debian's packaging system and a number of its administration tools.

Gentoo

The Gentoo distribution (http://www.gentoo.org/) is another community-developed platform. It is notable because it provides the option to compile the entire distribution from source code on your hardware. This allows you to customize every option to suit your particular hardware combination but can take a considerable time to complete. Gentoo can also be installed in a precompiled form for those with less technical skill who don't wish to compile everything. Gentoo is also well known for its frequent use as a platform for MythTV, an open source media center application similar to Microsoft Media Center. Gentoo makes use of a packaging system unique to the platform called Portage.

■**Tip** You can learn about the myriad of distributions available in the Linux world at DistroWatch (http://distrowatch.com/).

So Which Distribution Should You Choose?

Selecting a particular distribution should be based on your organization's budget, skills, and requirements. Our broad recommendation, though, is that you choose either a Red Hat–derived distribution or Ubuntu (a Debian-based distribution) or Debian. All of these are well supported by the organizations and communities that maintain them.

■**Tip** Online you'll find a useful automated quiz for selecting an appropriate Linux distribution available at http://www.zegeniestudios.net/ldc/index.php and an article on the topic at http://wiki.linuxquestions.org/wiki/Choosing_a_Linux_distribution.

With the exception of Red Hat Enterprise Linux, which requires a support contract to receive updates and patches, all of the distributions we've discussed are available free of charge. You can download and install them without having to pay a license fee.

■**Note** You can get the Red Hat Enterprise Linux software for free and install it without having to pay a license—only trouble is you will not be able to get any updates without a support agreement, which can leave you with a buggy and insecure host.

Several of the distributions we've discussed have commercial support, and if your technical skills are not strong, it is worth considering such a distribution, such as Red Hat Enterprise Linux or Ubuntu (with support provided by Canonical, their coordinating company). You should also remember that technical support may be available from a local provider. For example, a number of IT companies and systems integrators provide Linux support, and there are frequently small-to-medium companies in the IT support business that could also provide relevant support services.

■**Tip** You can find a listing of local support providers for Ubuntu Linux via Ubuntu Marketplace at `http://webapps.ubuntu.com/marketplace/`.

If you don't wish to pay for the third-party or vendor-provided commercial technical support, you might want to choose from a number of distributions that are noted for their large active communities where you can find support and assistance. Ubuntu support resources in particular have grown in recent years due to the many newcomers to Linux who have adopted that distribution.

Lastly, don't discount your own personal experience. Explore the distributions yourself. Try out LiveCDs, install a few of the distributions, and get a feel for the various administration tools and interfaces. Your own feelings about which distribution suits you and is the easiest for you to work with shouldn't be underestimated.

So Which Distributions Does This Book Cover?

As we have discussed, two popular choices are Red Hat, or derivatives like CentOS and Fedora, and Ubuntu and other related distributions. We've chosen to cover a Red Hat–derived distribution and Ubuntu, a Debian-derived distribution. We've chosen these because they represent good examples of the two major families of distributions. They also allow us to demonstrate the major configuration options and styles, package management tools, and associated administrative techniques used by a broad swathe of the available Linux distributions.

Specifically, this book covers the material needed to implement applications and tools on

- Red Hat Enterprise Linux or a Red Hat–based distribution like CentOS or Fedora

- Ubuntu or other Debian-based distributions

When providing specific examples, we've chosen to demonstrate using Red Hat Enterprise Linux 5 and Ubuntu LTS Server version 8.04.

■**Note** LTS is an abbreviation for "long term support." The Ubuntu project updates its server and desktop releases every six months. The Ubuntu project guarantees that an LTS release will be supported, for example, bugs fixed and security issues patched, for a period of five years after its release.

Each chapter will provide examples of configuration for each distribution and document any differences between the distributions such as the location of configuration files or the names of packages.

Picking Hardware

Detailed analysis on choosing appropriate hardware is beyond the scope of this book. We generally recommend you purchase hardware with sufficient reliability and support to meet your organization's requirements. If you need to rely on your infrastructure 24/7/365 and require high levels of availability, you should purchase hardware with redundant features, such as backup power supplies. You should also purchase appropriate support capabilities such as spare parts and onsite, phone, or online support.

■**Note** Another option is to purchase a dedicated or virtual server from a service provider like Rackspace (`http://www.rackspace.com`) or Linode (`http://www.linode.com`). Companies like these provide Linux servers hosted on the Internet with a variety of configurations and distributions available. You usually pay a monthly or yearly rental charge. You can then remotely connect to your server to install or configure it. Some companies also provide already installed and preconfigured hosts for a variety of purposes. We'll also look at using hosted and virtual services in Chapter 20.

Supported Hardware

In addition to purchasing the right hardware, you should take into account some important selection and performance considerations. The most important consideration is that not all hardware is supported by the Linux operating system. While rare, some hardware components (for example, some wireless network cards) lack drivers and support on some or all Linux platforms.

You should confirm that whatever hardware you purchase is supported by the distribution you have selected. Most distributions have Hardware Compatibility Lists (HCLs) you can use to verify your hardware is supported. Here are some of the currently maintained HCL sites:

- `https://hardware.redhat.com/` (relevant for Red Hat, CentOS, and Fedora)
- `https://wiki.ubuntu.com/HardwareSupport/` (Ubuntu)
- `http://kmuto.jp/debian/hcl/wiki/` (Debian, but also relevant for Ubuntu)
- `http://www.linuxquestions.org/hcl/index.php` (generic listing)

There are also many large-scale hardware vendors that provide systems with OEM Linux software. You can choose from companies such as Dell, HP, and IBM to provide hardware guaranteed to work with a specified list of supported Linux distributions.

Note We'll discuss a variety of specific performance issues in later chapters when we look at particular applications and tools.

Getting the Software

Where do you start with installing your first host? First, you need to get a copy of the software you require. There are a number of ways to acquire the base operating system software. Some distributions sell CD-ROMs and DVDs, and others offer ISO images to download (and some do both!). Other distributions also offer installation via network or the Internet.

Note We'll look at processes for automated, network-based provisioning of servers in Chapter 19.

Here is a list of some of the sites where you can get CD-ROMs and DVDs:

- http://www.ubuntu.com/GetUbuntu/
- http://www.debian.org/distrib/
- http://www.centos.org/modules/tinycontent/index.php?id=15
- http://www.gentoo.org/main/en/mirrors2.xml
- https://www.redhat.com/apps/download/
- http://fedoraproject.org/get-fedora

Once you have downloaded the required software, you can burn an ISO to CDs or a DVD. The following URLs describe how to burn ISO files onto CDs and DVDs:

- http://pcsupport.about.com/od/toolsofthetrade/ht/burnisofile.htm
- http://www.petri.co.il/how_to_write_iso_files_to_cd.htm
- https://help.ubuntu.com/community/BurningIsoHowto

Or if you already have media available, you can just get started with your installation in Chapter 2.

Getting Support

Finding help and support for your Linux distribution varies greatly depending on the distribution. If you've chosen a commercial distribution, you can contact your vendor to get the support you need. For noncommercial distributions, you can log tickets or review documentation at your distribution's site.

Additionally, never underestimate the power of search engines to find solutions to your problems. Many people worldwide use Linux and may have experienced the same issue you have, and posted or written about solutions.

For specific distributions, the following sites are most useful:

- *Red Hat*: https://www.redhat.com/apps/support/
- *CentOS*: http://bugs.centos.org/main_page.php
- *Fedora*: http://fedoraproject.org/en/get-help
- *Debian*: http://www.debian.org/support
- *Ubuntu*: http://www.ubuntu.com/support
- *Gentoo*: http://www.gentoo.org/main/en/support.xml

Check the sites of other distributions for their support mechanisms. Other useful sites include

- *LinuxQuestions.org*: http://www.linuxquestions.org/
- *LinuxHelp*: http://www.linuxhelp.net/
- *Linux Selfhelp*: http://www.linuxselfhelp.com/
- *ReallyLinux*: http://www.reallylinux.com/

Summary

In this chapter, we've introduced you to some varieties of Linux, including the two distributions this book focuses on:

- Red Hat Enterprise Linux
- Ubuntu

We've also discussed some of the reasons to choose a particular distribution, how to choose some appropriate hardware, and where to get some basic support for your choice of distribution. In the next chapter, we'll show you how to install both of the distributions that this book covers.

■■■

Installing Linux

By James Turnbull, Peter Lieverdink, and Dennis Matotek

In this chapter, we're going to take you through the process of installing a host with Red Hat Enterprise Linux (RHEL) and a host with Ubuntu Server. We'll show each distribution's installation process using the graphical installation tools and detail the options available during installation. We're going to perform the base installation and also install the packages needed to run a basic web, mail, and DNS server. Don't worry if you don't know what these functions are at the moment—we explain web servers in Chapter 11, mail in Chapter 10, and DNS in Chapter 9.

■**Tip** We recommend you read the whole chapter, including the sections covering the Red Hat and Ubuntu installation processes, to gain the best understanding of installing Linux hosts.

We'll start by installing a Red Hat–based distribution in the "Red Hat Enterprise Linux Installation" section. While the screenshots in this section are specific to RHEL, the installation processes for CentOS and Fedora are derived from RHEL and operate in a very similar fashion. So if you've chosen either of these distributions, you should be able to recognize easily the installation process of these distributions from our explanation. You'll find this is true of most configuration and management of Red Hat–derived distributions.

If you have chosen Ubuntu, you will find a full explanation of the Ubuntu installation process in the "Ubuntu Server Installation" section. Ubuntu is derived from Debian, but it has a different installation process. The configuration and options are closely aligned, though, and by following the Ubuntu installation process you should be able to recognize the installation process for Debian and other Debian-derived distributions.

■**Note** If you want use the CD/DVD-based installation process and the graphical installers provided, then you will need to install on a host with a monitor, a keyboard, and preferably a mouse. These peripherals will allow you to interact with the installation tool effectively. We'll describe how to do an *unattended* or *headless* (without a monitor) installation in Chapter 19.

We will also expand on the potential installation options in Chapter 7, when we look at installing software on Linux, and in Chapter 19, when we examine methods of automating installations and builds.

■**Caution** Distributions change, and installation screens and options change with them. Don't panic if the screenshots presented in this chapter don't exactly match the ones you see during installation. Generally, most installation options and steps remain similar between releases.

LiveCDs and Virtual Machines

Before we begin our first installation, we'll cover two other options for getting to know Linux on a host that may be useful to try before committing to build a physical server: LiveCDs and virtual machines. These methods allow you to explore a Linux distribution and how to use it with a minimal investment of time and infrastructure.

LiveCDs

LiveCDs are versions of distributions that you can run on your computer from a CD or DVD. They load themselves into memory without the need to install any software on your computer. This means you can try a distribution on your computer and then remove the CD and reboot to return to your existing operating system, making it very easy to explore and test Linux distributions and software without changing anything on your computer. You can find out more about LiveCDs at `http://en.wikipedia.org/wiki/Live_CD`.

You can find popular distributions such as the following in LiveCD format:

- Ubuntu: `https://help.ubuntu.com/community/LiveCD`

- Fedora: `http://fedoraproject.org/wiki/FedoraLiveCD`

- Debian: `http://debian-live.alioth.debian.org/`

You can also find a full list of the many LiveCDs available at `http://www.livecdlist.com/`.

Virtual Machines

You can also run your Linux distribution on a virtual machine. *Virtual machines* are software implementations of hosts that run just like physical hosts. You can run multiple virtual hosts on a single physical host. Examples of virtualization applications and servers include VMware (`http://www.vmware.com/`), VirtualBox (`http://www.virtualbox.org/`), and open source alternatives like Xen (`http://www.xen.org/`), among others. You can also purchase virtual hosts from hosting companies.

Note In this chapter, we demonstrate how to install Linux hosts. Our instructions detail the steps to install "bare metal" hosts rather than virtual hosts. The differences between bare metal installs and virtual installs are relatively minor. One of the differences with virtual hosts is that you can install your host directly from an ISO image, rather than having to burn an ISO image to CD/DVD first and load it into the CD/DVD drive. Virtual host installations also make building and rebuilding your host easier, and you can perform functions like creating point-in-time backups of different kinds of hosts.

You may also wish to take advantage of premade *virtual appliances*, which are virtual images of Linux distributions that you load with your virtualization software. They are already installed and configured, and the appliances are usually created with a particular purpose in mind, like a VoIP server, file server, or mail server. You can view the lists of appliances available at these sites:

- `http://www.vmware.com/appliances/`: Virtual appliances for VMware
- `http://virtualappliances.net/`: Ubuntu virtual appliances for a variety of virtualization engines
- `http://jailtime.org/`: Virtual appliances for Xen

Note We'll cover Linux virtual machines in more detail in Chapter 20.

Red Hat Enterprise Linux Installation

Let's start by installing a Red Hat Enterprise Linux host. We will make a few assumptions here:

- You are using a Red Hat Enterprise Linux ISO from the Red Hat website (`https://www.redhat.com/apps/download/`), and you have burned it onto a CD.
- You are building just a basic mail, DNS, and web server.
- You are installing on a fresh server without any previous operating system.

First, put your installation media (usually a CD or DVD) into your host and power it on.

Note If you were building a virtual machine, you'd build instead from the raw ISO. A virtual machine usually includes a "virtual DVD," where you would mount the installation ISO to boot from.

After loading your installation media and starting your host, you'll see the Red Hat installation splash screen shown in Figure 2-1.

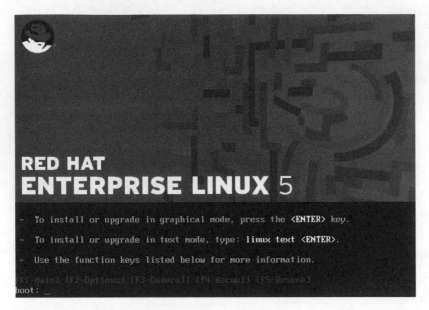

Figure 2-1. *The Red Hat Enterprise Linux splash screen*

From the splash screen you can initiate the installation, via either a graphical interface or a text-based installation mechanism. For this walk-through, we're going to use the graphical interface.

Additional options are available via the function keys. The F1 key returns you to the main menu. The F2 key shows you the installer's additional boot options that can be passed to Red Hat, including testing your installation media, checking your memory, and adding additional disk drivers. You can also prompt Red Hat to initiate a network-based installation, as we'll discuss in Chapter 19.

The F3 key shows general help and describes some options you can pass if you are having issues installing Red Hat. The F4 key describes some of the options you can pass to the kernel to customize your installation.

Lastly, the F5 function key shows the rescue mode options. Rescue mode assumes you already have Linux loaded, and it allows you to boot and potentially repair or rescue a broken Linux installation. You will boot into a rescue prompt that allows you to mount disks, edit configuration files, and access other useful utilities. You can find out more about rescue mode at `http://www.redhat.com/docs/manuals/enterprise/RHEL-5-manual/Installation_Guide-en-US/` `s1-rescuemode-boot.html`.

For now, though, just press Enter to move on to the next stage of the installation. On the next screen you are prompted to check your installation media. This check will scan your CD or DVD for errors. If you wish, you can skip this process and continue.

In Figure 2-2, the "anaconda" installer process that will install the host has been started. The anaconda application is the software that installs RHEL, and it runs in the X Window System—also known as simply X—but it also has a command-line mode. X is the graphical user interface used commonly on Linux; we'll talk a bit more about it in Chapter 3. You will first be shown the Release Notes, and you can then click Next to progress to the next screen.

Figure 2-2. *The Red Hat Enterprise Linux graphical installer*

■**Tip** The Release Notes tell you what has changed between this version and the last version. If you were upgrading your host, it would be a good idea to read and understand the implications of any changes documented in the Release Notes.

In the next few screens you will select your host's basic requirements, such as the language the host will use and the keyboard layout. In Figure 2-3 we have selected the language used in Australia; you should select the language relevant to you.

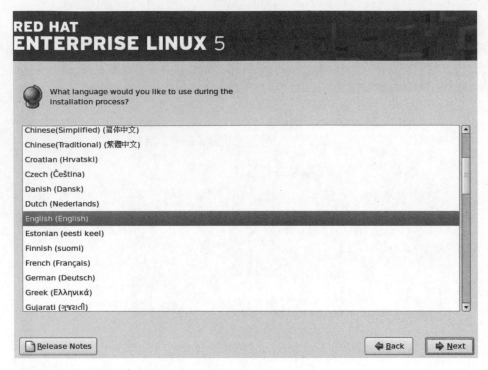

Figure 2-3. *Selecting the language to use during installation*

The keyboard mapping affects the default layout of your keyboard keys. In Figure 2-4 we selected the keyboard layout for our particular keyboard.

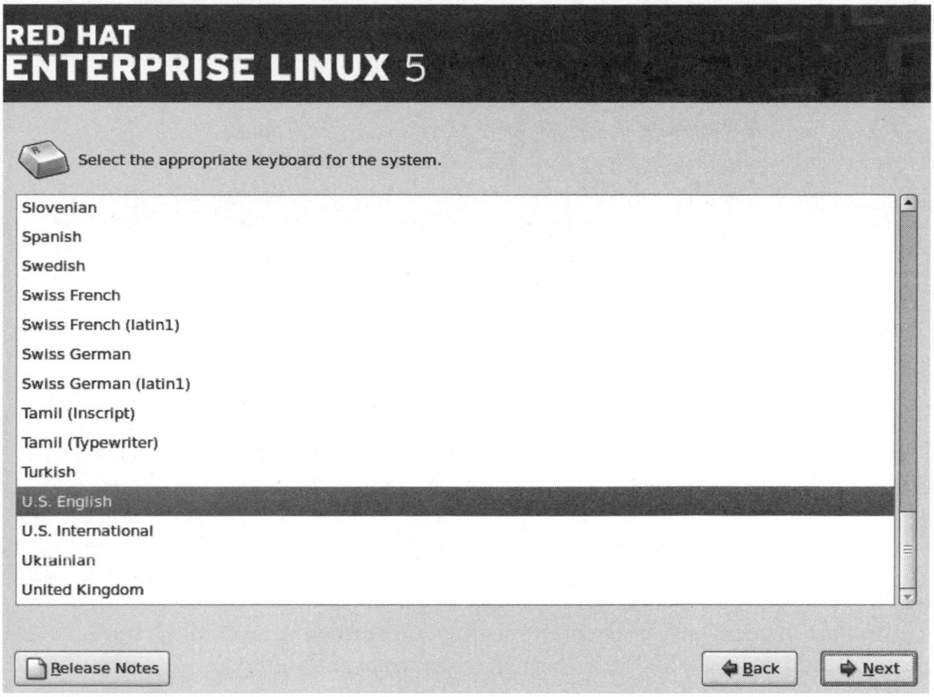

Figure 2-4. *Selecting the desired keyboard layout*

Tip If you use the Gnome desktop (more on desktops in Chapter 3), you can change your keyboard options by opening the Applications menu (the main menu on the panel), clicking the System Settings tab, and selecting the Keyboard application. On the command line you can run the `system-config-keyboard` command.

On the next screen we need to input the Red Hat Installation Number. When you purchased your Red Hat subscription, you were provided an Installation Number. If you've purchased a subscription and can't find the Installation Number, you can go to the Red Hat Support website and find it there: `https://www.redhat.com/wapps/support/protected/subscriptions.html`. Figure 2-5 shows the Installation Number entry screen.

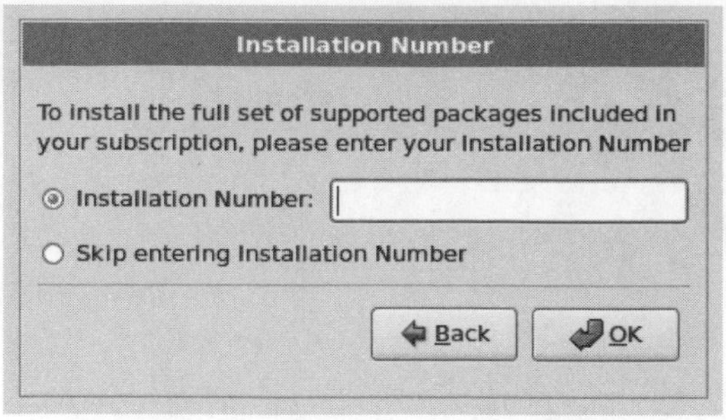

Figure 2-5. *Enter your Installation Number here.*

Note If you don't want to pay for a subscription, a distribution like CentOS, Fedora, or Ubuntu may be a better choice, rather than running Red Hat Enterprise Linux without having the patches and updates available to your host.

We will assume that you have a subscription and have entered it. If you don't have a subscription, you can still continue and either provide the number at a later date or use the Red Hat Enterprise Linux server without access to any updates until you purchase the subscription. We recommend that you purchase a subscription so you can get the latest patches and security fixes for your host.

Caution The next few steps can be dangerous. If you are installing on a host that has an existing operating system or important data, you can lose all existing data and the operating system may become unusable. Please proceed with appropriate caution and a necessary backup regime if needed.

Next, after the Installation Number screen, you will likely receive a warning informing you that you are about to create a new partition table. On brand-new hosts, this is normal and something you want to do, so select Yes to continue. If your host has had an operating system previously installed on it, or if you are sharing this host with another operating system such as Microsoft Windows, this next step may not be desired and this is your opportunity to quit the process. If you think you will destroy valuable data from a previous install, select No and exit the installation.

Note If you are overwriting an existing installation of RHEL or installing a virtual machine, you won't see the aforementioned warning.

You can see the partition initialization process in Figure 2-6.

Figure 2-6. *Initializing a drive by creating a new partition table*

Having created the new partition table, you move on to creating the partitions for your system. Partitioning a disk is like slicing a cake: you can choose how big each "slice" of disk should be, depending on the appetite of the slice's consumer. For example, if your system has a website and that website has pretty extensive logging, you may choose to divide the disk so that you have more room in the partition that holds your web data and logging files. If you are running a file server instead, you will reserve more of the disk for user data rather than web data or logging.

■**Note** We'll explain a lot more about partitions and how to customize and change your disks and storage in Chapter 8.

You will see that the hard disks available to you are listed, and you can select the disks you want to use. In our case, we have only one disk available to us, so we just select the default "Remove linux partitions on selected drives and create default layout" option. We also select the "Review and modify partitioning layout" option so we can see the resultant layout of the default settings. Figure 2-7 shows the options we are selecting.

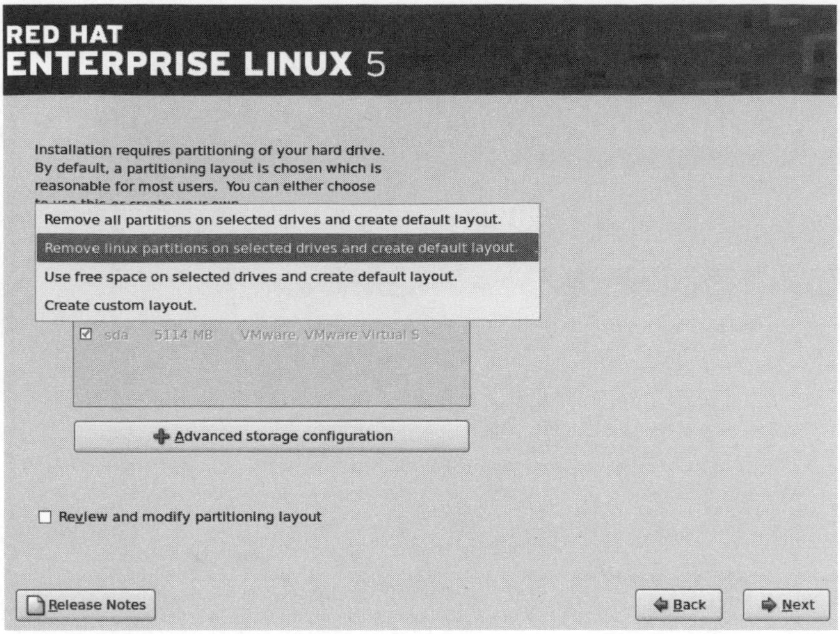

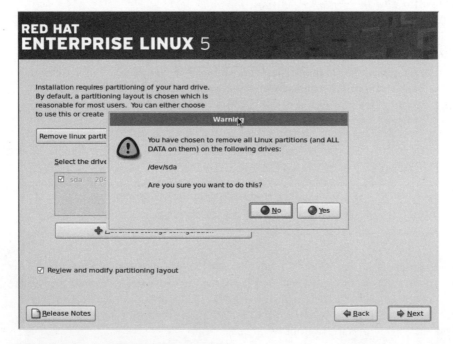

Figure 2-7. *Selecting the partitioning layout*

You will now see another warning, this time telling you that you are removing all the Linux partitions from the drive and asking if you would like to proceed (see Figure 2-8). Select Yes.

Figure 2-8. *Removing partitions warning*

Finally, Figure 2-9 shows the layout of our partitioning scheme.

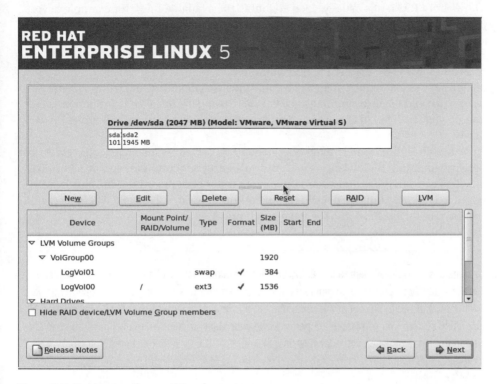

Figure 2-9. *Reviewing the partition layout*

As you can see, the default is to use logical volume management (LVM) to create one group with two logical volumes.

■Note LVM allows you to manage disk volumes and extend, shrink, and change the size of your disk partitions on the fly. The LVM software allows the administrator to change the disk layout, add new disk storage, or remove and repurpose disk storage to another part of the system without having to rebuild the system and reformat the underlying disks. We'll talk about LVM in detail in Chapter 8.

By default, the first volume is called swap. The swap volume is disk space used to hold data that overflows from RAM. It is usually sized at double the available RAM; for example, if you have 512MB of RAM you would have a 1GB swap disk. The second volume is called the root or / volume. This partition holds all of your host's data and applications. Although it is not clearly shown in Figure 2-9, there is also a 100MB partition called /boot. The /boot partition holds the Linux kernel and some code required to boot your host.

If you had any special requirements, you could alter this default structure and create new partitions, or you could delete everything and start again using the installer's partition manager. We will go into greater detail in Chapter 8 about how to carve up one or several drives for various purposes.

The next screen is the Grand Unified Bootloader (GRUB) loader installation screen. A *boot loader* is the program that the BIOS runs just after you start your computer, and it is installed into the first 512 bytes of the primary hard drive (the master boot record or MBR) by default. GRUB is used to load the Linux kernel when your computer is turned on; you will first encounter it when you reboot your host and see the menu it provides at startup.

■**Note** In some cases you may wish to install the boot loader in another partition. For example, you can run a host with the ability to *dual boot*, meaning the host can boot into two or more different operating systems, like Windows and RHEL, but not at the same time. In this instance, your MBR could be overwritten by the other operating system and you would temporarily lose your ability to boot your Linux host. You can see the GRUB menu that appears when you boot your host in Figure 2-20 later in this chapter. You can find a guide that explains dual booting at http://apcmag.com/the_definitive_dualbooting_guide_linux_vista_and_xp_stepbystep.htm.

In the screen in Figure 2-10, you select where you would like to install your boot loader. We have chosen the only disk available to us, /dev/sda.

■**Note** You can use a variety of disk types as your storage hardware. The different disks get different names. Figure 2-10 shows the drive /dev/sda, where s stands for SCSI or SATA. An IDE disk would be prefixed with h (e.g., /dev/hda). The latest kernel versions, however, use newer IDE drivers that name IDE disks as /dev/sd* to make things more consistent.

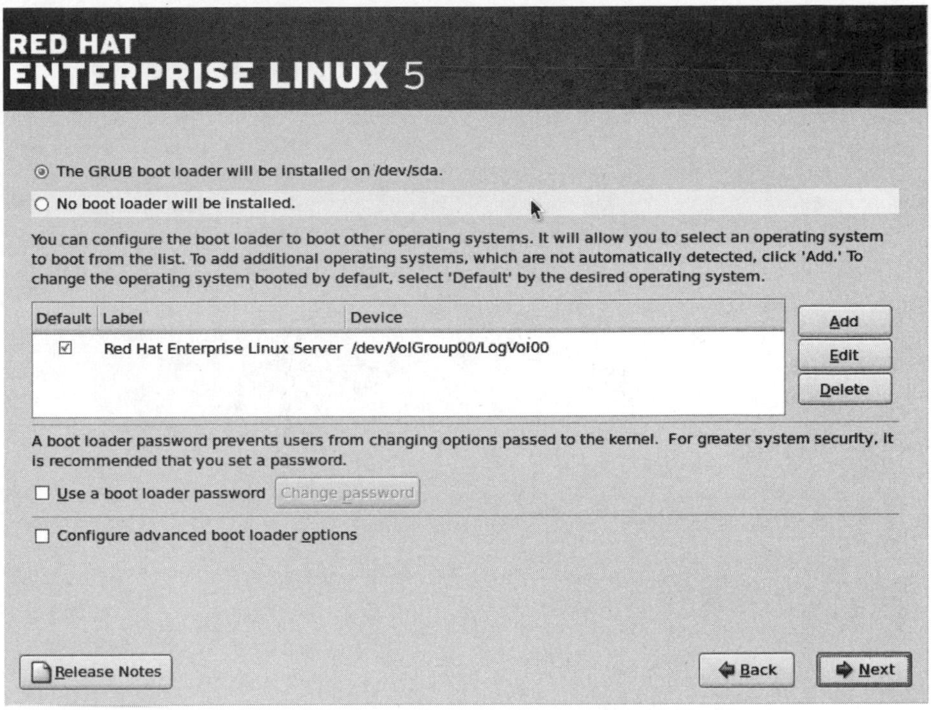

Figure 2-10. *Installing the boot loader on* `/dev/sda`

You could also set a password for your boot loader, which offers protection against changes being made to your boot options. For example, if someone wanted to make a change to the GRUB boot menu, that person would need to provide the correct password before being allowed to make any change. This is often a good idea for hosts that are co-located in a data center where there is ready access to the host, or in other places with poor physical security.

■**Caution** Physical security for your Linux hosts is important—you don't want anyone to steal your costly physical asset (and your data!). You should store your host in a locked cabinet or rack, or in a room to which you can control access. If you are hosting your server in a co-lo or data center, then you should ensure the location has appropriate physical security controls to protect your hosts.

The advanced boot loader configuration options allow you to specify where the boot record is installed, change the drive order, and set some legacy options like Force LBA32. If you need to pass any kernel parameters during boot-up, you can also add them here. Generally, you won't ever need to change any of these options, so we are just going to select the defaults.

You can see in Figure 2-10 that the default operating system we will boot is selected and it's Red Hat Enterprise Linux Server.

After installing the boot loader, you are now ready to configure the network. The next screen (see Figure 2-11) shows our networking configuration.

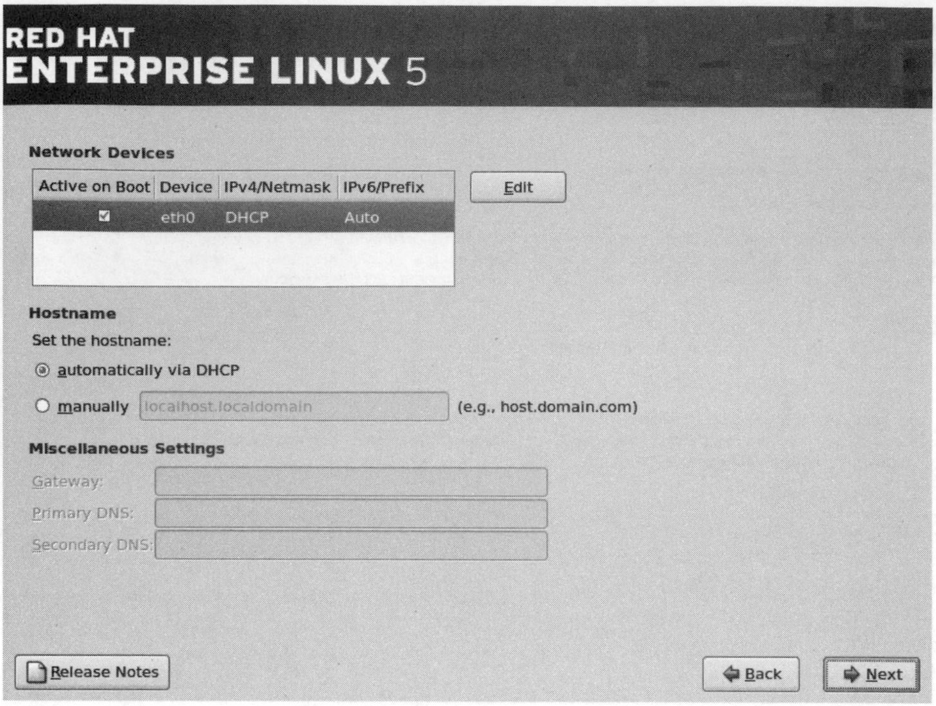

Figure 2-11. *Network settings*

The most important configuration item here is your IP address, which is the network address of your host that allows other hosts to find and communicate with it.

■**Tip** You can read about IP addresses and addressing at http://en.wikipedia.org/wiki/IP_address and http://computer.howstuffworks.com/question549.htm.

There are generally two ways to assign an IP address on your network. The first is by directly specifying each host's IP address during configuration. These are called *static addresses*. The second method uses a networking service called Dynamic Host Configuration Protocol (DHCP). DHCP uses a server located on your network to assign IP addresses to hosts when they request them. The DHCP server tracks these addresses and ensures there are no conflicts. You may already have a router that is capable of DHCP (as most ADSL modem/routers are) on your network. In the next screen, you could select the DHCP option and get an IP address automatically.

■**Note** We'll show you how to configure your own DHCP server in Chapter 9.

For the purposes of this installation, however, we are going to add a static IP address by selecting Edit to set the IP address. We've specified an address suitable for our network in Figure 2-12; you should enter a configuration appropriate for your environment. Select OK when you are done.

■**Tip** Figure 2-12 shows a check box for IPv6, which is another, newer form of IP addressing that isn't in wide use yet. You can read about IPv6 at `http://en.wikipedia.org/wiki/IPv6`. Most Linux distributions also support this new form of addressing.

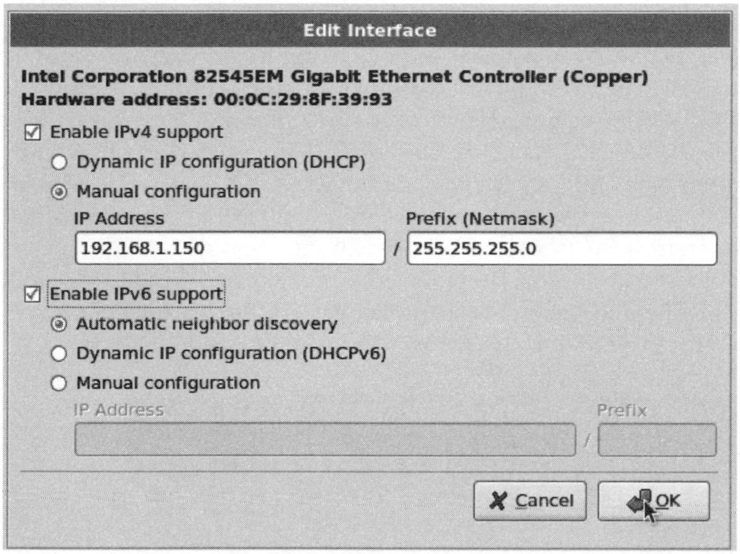

Figure 2-12. *Setting the IP address*

After setting your IP address, you now need to add a name for your host, or a *hostname*. It is a trend in small startups to name hosts after favorite TV characters, bands, or mythical creatures. While this is fun, it soon becomes annoying when you have multiple hosts in multiple geographical locations doing particular jobs. Our hostname is au-mel-rhel-1, as we prefer the descriptive naming standard *region-city-OS type-number*. As another example of a descriptive naming format, if you have a file server in the United States with an IP address ending in 155, you could choose us-ny-fileserver-155. The main thing is to be descriptive rather than naming your host "Brittany" or "Thor."

■**Note** You can choose any naming standard you like that suits your environment. Our preference is for a descriptive naming convention.

You also need to specify a default gateway and one or more Domain Name System (DNS) name servers. The default gateway is the route all traffic passes along before leaving your network. It will be either a modem/ADSL gateway or a physical router that connects your network to the Internet or other private networks. The primary and secondary DNS name servers are special servers that resolve IP addresses to fully qualified domain names.

■**Tip** Specifying a primary and a secondary DNS server adds redundancy to your network. If one server doesn't respond, your host will try the other server.

Every time your host goes to a website, it uses both the default gateway and DNS server to find out how to get there. For example, if you type www.google.com in your browser's address bar, your host will first find the DNS server, which may or may not be on your network. If it is not on your network, your host will use the default gateway to reach it. Your host then will ask the DNS server the IP address of www.google.com, and the DNS server will answer with something like 74.125.19.104. Your host will then again use your default gateway to leave your network and fetch the web page provided by www.google.com. In general terms, your DNS server is a map, and your default gateway is the first street you take to find what you want.

In Figure 2-13 we have chosen the appropriate settings for our network. We will talk about these services and their settings in much greater detail in Chapter 9 when we explain how to set your own DNS servers and manage your own routers.

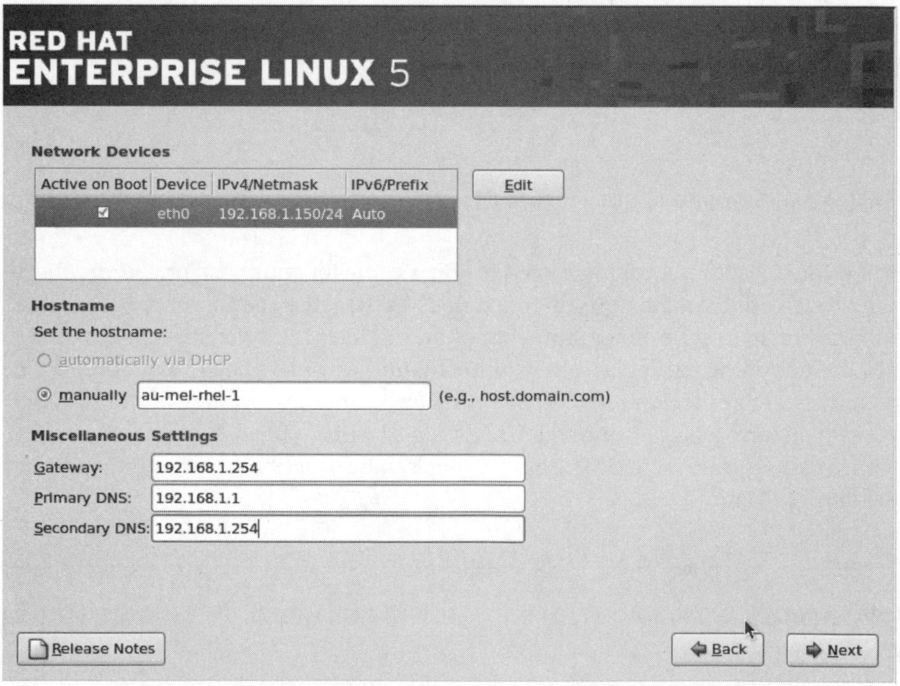

Figure 2-13. *Hostname, default gateway, and DNS settings*

The next screen is a good test to see if you know where you live in relation to other people on the planet. Use your mouse to point to your closest major city's yellow dot to set the right time zone, or select your region from the drop-down list. In Figure 2-14 we have chosen Melbourne, Australia.

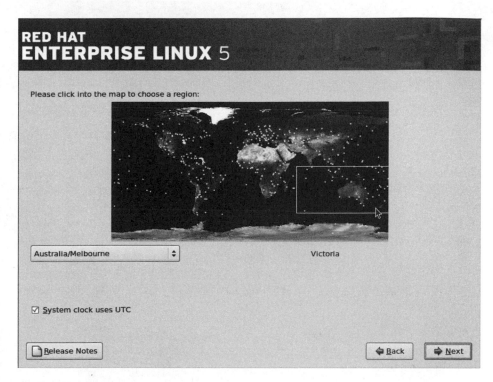

Figure 2-14. *Choosing your location*

Next, as shown in Figure 2-15, you are asked for the root password. In Linux the root user is the superuser who has access to the whole system, much like the Windows Administrator in the Windows OS.

■Tip We will discuss the root user in more detail in Chapters 3 and 4.

This password should be complex and consist of a combination of upper- and lowercase characters, numbers, and special punctuation keys like the following: @!%#*. It should also be at least eight characters long.

■Tip You can read about the characteristics of a good password at http://en.wikipedia.org/wiki/Password_strength.

Store this password somewhere safe. You could store it on an encrypted USB key using a password-safe program such as the open source product KeePass (http://keepass.info/), for instance.

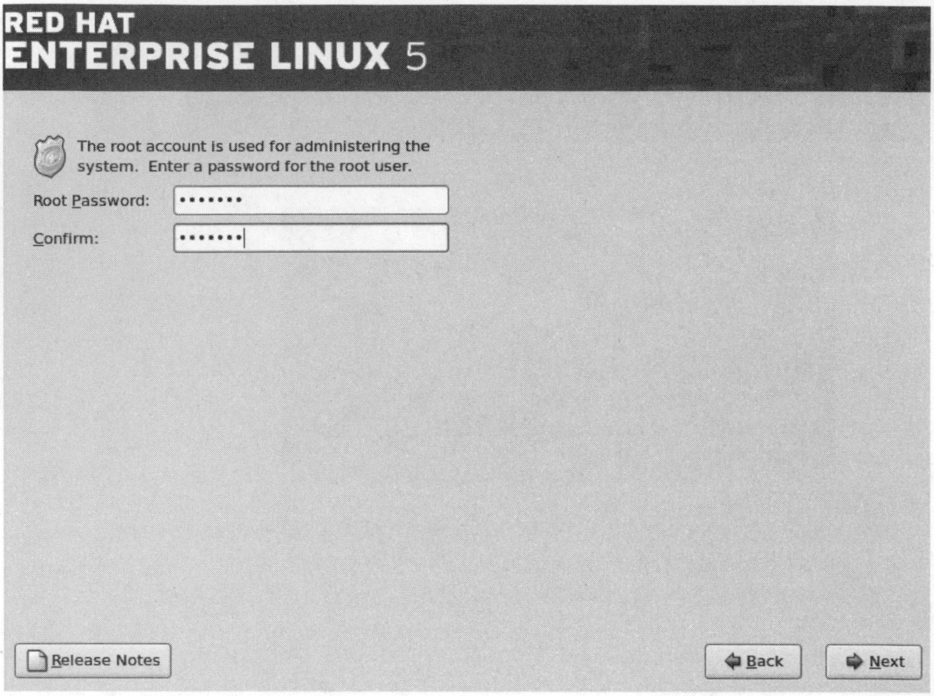

Figure 2-15. *The root password*

With all the preliminaries out of the way, you can now get down to selecting the packages you wish to install on your host. You're going to install packages appropriate for a host running web, DNS, and mail servers. The RHEL installation process is highly granular, and you can select the functions and applications to install by specifying roles for your host, right down to individual applications. Figure 2-16 shows some of the potential roles for our host:

- *Clustering*: A member of a cluster of hosts
- *Software Development*: A host being used to develop software and write code
- *Storage Clustering*: A member of a cluster that provides clustered storage
- *Virtualization*: A host that runs virtual machines
- *Web server*: A traditional web server

As you can see, we have deselected all the defaults and selected the Web server and Customize now options. Selecting the Customize now radio button allows us to drill down further and select individual applications.

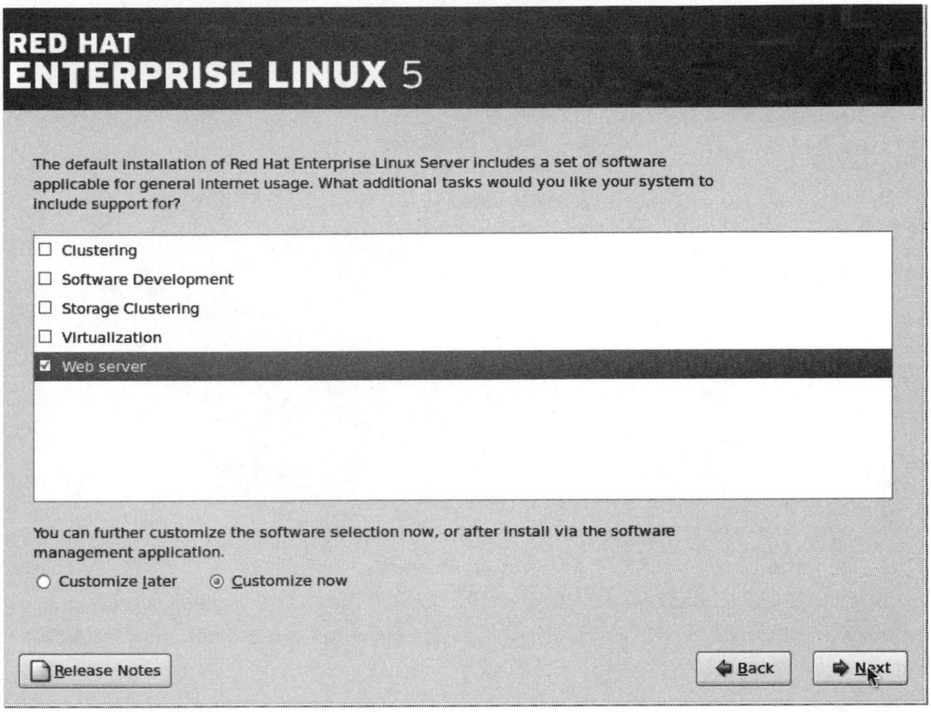

Figure 2-16. *Selecting packages*

The next page shows all the different package groups you can select to install. When you see an Optional packages button, you can click that to fine-tune the packages. Use the left frame to select the types of groups you are interested in (applications, development, etc.), and use the right frame to select the groups. In Figure 2-17 we have opened the Servers tab and chosen to install a DNS name server, a mail server, and the MySQL database.

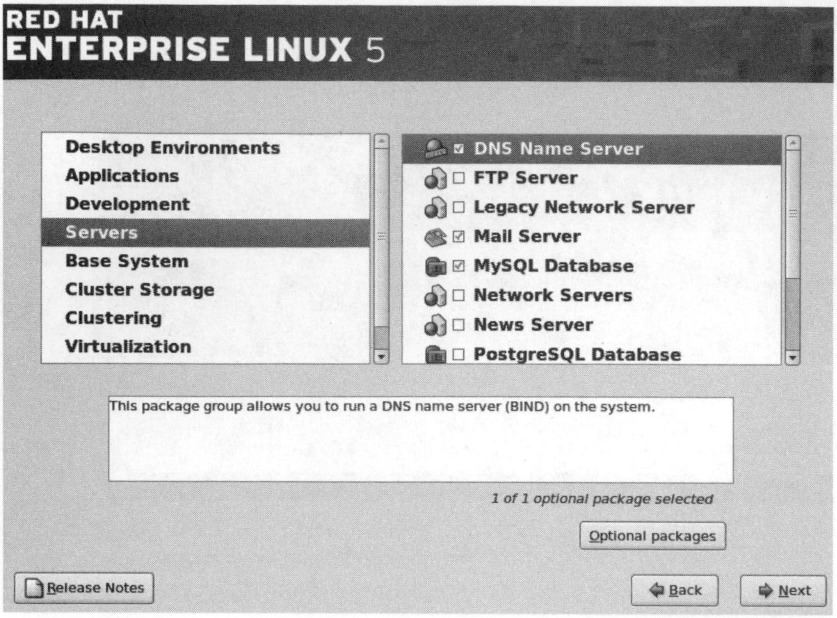

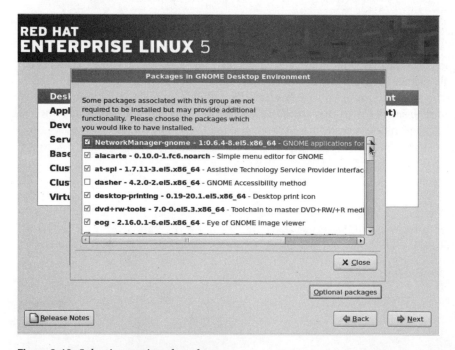

Figure 2-17. *Selecting from the Servers list*

If you click the Optional packages button for the MySQL database, you will see 11 other packages (some of which are shown in Figure 2-18) you can select or deselect, depending on your personal preference.

Figure 2-18. *Selecting optional packages*

You are almost ready to start writing your installation to disk. In the first step of this process, the installation program will check for package dependencies. This analysis scans the packages you've chosen to install and identifies any additional packages that need to be installed to support your choices.

Once this check is completed, the installer will then make sure you have enough disk space to install your package selections. Finally, you will be presented with an installation readiness screen like the one shown in Figure 2-19.

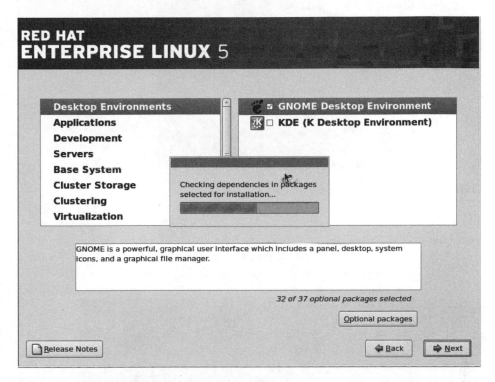

Figure 2-19. *Ready to install*

Once the installation has initiated, you will see a progress bar indicating the status of the installation. The installation process itself may take several minutes depending on the number of packages you have chosen to install.

Once the installation is finished, the CD/DVD will eject and you will be presented with a reboot screen. Simply click Reboot to restart your host.

After the reboot, you will see the GRUB menu screen (remember, this is the boot loader you installed earlier), which allows you to choose the operating system to boot into. You don't have to do anything on this screen, because in a few seconds it will select the default and begin to boot your new host. If you press any key during this countdown process, loading will be interrupted and the complete GRUB menu will display (see Figure 2-20).

Figure 2-20. *Booting your new host*

After GRUB has completed, you will be presented with a Red Hat splash screen. You're probably wondering, "What's it doing now?" To view the steps involved in your host's boot process, click Show Details. You can see all the processes the system runs as it starts up and whether they have successfully started, as shown in Figure 2-21.

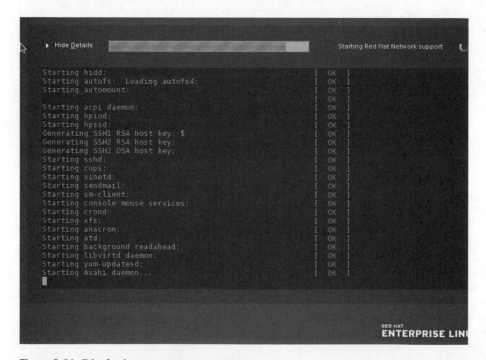

Figure 2-21. *Displaying system startup status*

■**Note** For a detailed explanation of the boot process, see the "Boot Process" section in Chapter 5.

If you chose the default package options, you will have installed an application called "firstboot." Since this is the first time you have booted this host, the firstboot application will start and you will be asked a series of questions about your host and how you want to configure it. You will also be given the opportunity to register with the Red Hat Network (RHN).

First, you will see the Welcome screen shown in Figure 2-22. Click Forward to proceed.

Figure 2-22. *The Welcome screen*

You are then asked to read and agree to the licensing agreement. Select "Yes, I agree" if you agree to abide by the license or "No, I do not agree" if you don't. If you don't agree to the license, you are given the option to reread the license or terminate your installation; you will not be able to continue to use your host until you agree to the license.

After the license agreement screen, you will be prompted to configure your host's firewall. Most Linux distributions configure and install a host-based firewall that uses the Netfilter firewall (also known as the `iptables` firewall after the command used to configure the firewall). We recommend you enable this firewall on all of your hosts.

For the moment, we'll just configure the firewall to allow TCP packets on port 22 so we can remotely connect to the host using a secure protocol called Secure Shell (SSH). We'll talk more about SSH in Chapters 3 and 6, and more about firewalls in Chapter 6. You can see our firewall configuration in Figure 2-23.

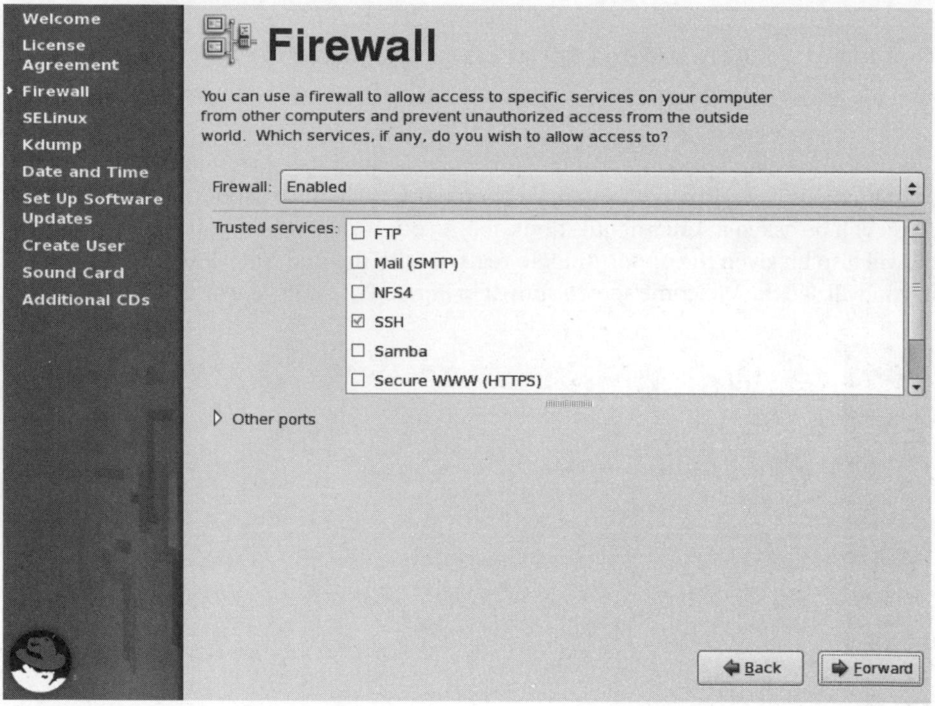

Figure 2-23. *Configuring your firewall*

On the next screen you will be prompted to configure the SELinux mode for your host. SELinux applies a security control called mandatory access control (MAC) to objects like files, processes, and information. SELinux was developed by the US National Security Agency "to enforce the separation of information based on confidentiality and integrity requirements to provide system security" (http://www.nsa.gov/selinux/index.shtml).

What does SELinux do? Well, traditional Linux security follows a concept called discretionary access control (DAC). With DAC, normal users can create objects and give these objects permissions (which you'll see more of in Chapters 3 and 4). Permissions allow reading, writing, or executing of objects on your host by particular users and groups. These objects, such as files and applications, can interact with one another based on these permissions.

With MAC provided by SELinux, a set of security policies work on the system level, and these control all objects on the system and how and if those objects interact with each other. So, for example, MAC provided by SELinux will prevent the Apache web server from accessing files belonging to the Postfix mail server, even if the web server was compromised and had gained root access to your host. These two processes will be logically separated by the security policy, so that if one is compromised, the other is not automatically compromised as well.

Since you are just starting out with your new host, set the mode to Permissive (see Figure 2-24), which means you will be informed of any issues that might arise from your security policy without that policy actually being enforced. It gives you the opportunity to fine-tune your host until you are ready to deploy it. After trying out this new host, you should set the security policy to Enforcing before moving your host into production to make the system more secure.

■Note You can read about how to implement SELinux on Red Hat at http://www.redhat.com/docs/
manuals/enterprise/RHEL-5-manual/Deployment_Guide-en-US/ch-selinux.html.

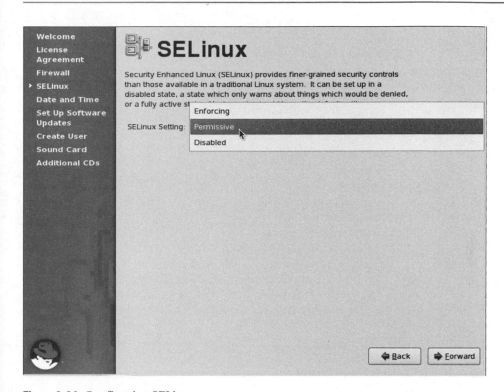

Figure 2-24. *Configuring SELinux*

■Note You don't have to use SELinux on your hosts, and if you don't wish to, you can disable it by selecting Disabled, as you can see in Figure 2-24. Not all Red Hat–derived distributions run SELinux by default, so
you may not need to do this on all platforms.

On the next screen, you will set the date and time, which is usually done using a protocol
called Network Time Protocol (NTP). NTP sets the time by connecting to time servers located
on the Internet (so you'll need to be connected to the Internet for this to work) that are connected to very accurate clocks. Your host will poll these time servers for the time. It will usually
poll three servers (the quantity and specific time servers to poll are configurable), and then it
uses an algorithm to decide the most accurate time based on the responses and the time zone
your host is in.

You enable NTP by selecting the Enable Network Time Protocol option on the Network Time
Protocol tab. Red Hat has some time servers available for you to use, and they are automatically
configured for you. If you want to add your own, you can use the Add, Edit, or Delete button.

The advanced options area of the Date and Time screen provides two options, as shown in Figure 2-25: "Synchronize system clock before starting service" and "Use Local Time Source." Disable your Local Time Source if you have a particularly unreliable hardware clock.

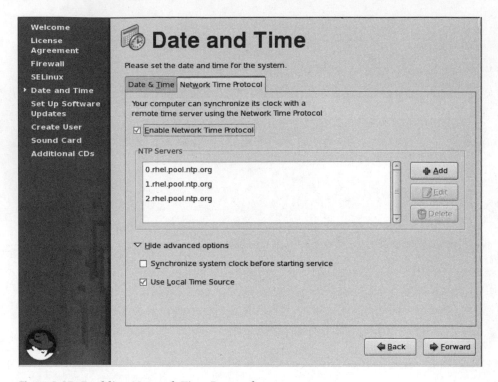

Figure 2-25. *Enabling Network Time Protocol*

■Note You can read more about NTP and the time servers at `http://www.ntp.org`. We'll also discuss NTP in more detail in Chapter 9.

After the installation process tries to contact the NTP servers (provided you have an Internet connection), you will be asked to set up software updates provided by Red Hat. These updates are available only via your RHN subscription (recall that RHN is the software update service you receive as part of your purchase of the Red Hat Enterprise Linux license). This option will work only if you have an appropriate subscription for your host. If so, select "Yes, I'd like to register now" as shown in Figure 2-26 and click the Forward button.

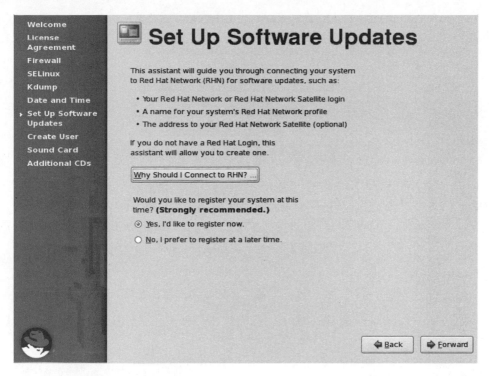

Figure 2-26. *Selecting software updates*

Next, you will choose where you get your updates from. You can choose Red Hat Network hosted by Red Hat either via the RHN portal, or via an RHN Satellite server or a Proxy server. The Satellite and Proxy servers are part of Red Hat's provisioning and management suite of applications. They allow you to set up a distributed network for managing patches and updates, and download updates only once and then distribute them to multiple sites and hosts. It is unlikely you will need to purchase one of these servers when you are starting out, but if you have multiple sites and numerous hosts, you may want to investigate their use; you can read more about these products at http://www.redhat.com/red_hat_network/ and http://www.redhat.com/docs/manuals/satellite/Red_Hat_Network_Satellite-5.1.1/html/Proxy_Installation_Guide/s1-intro-proxy.html.

■**Tip** Red Hat's Satellite server product has a free equivalent called Spacewalk (https://fedorahosted.org/spacewalk/), which is available with distributions like Fedora Core and CentOS. Spacewalk is an upstream development version of Satellite server and contains newer features, but it could be more unstable than RHN Satellite server.

As you can see in Figure 2-27, we have selected the default, which is to get our updates from RHN directly. If you use a Proxy server to connect to the Internet from your network, you can click the Advanced Network Configuration button and provide the details you require to use it there.

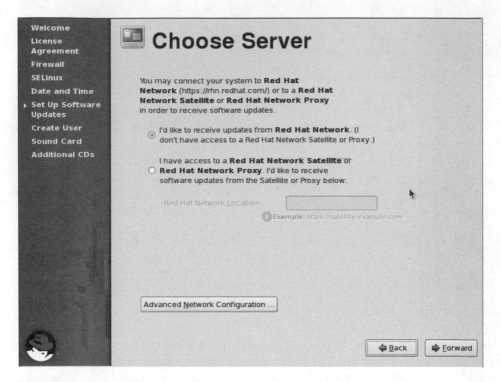

Figure 2-27. *Selecting the source of our software updates*

■Tip We'll discuss RHN and updating our host in more detail in Chapter 7. You will need to have your Red Hat login ID and password and also a subscription available for this new host. If you don't have one, you can register on the Red Hat website (`https://www.redhat.com/wapps/ugc/register.html`), and you can purchase the subscription online from the Red Hat website (`https://www.redhat.com/wapps/store/catalog.html`). Your subscription enables you to download security patches and other applicable software from Red Hat.

You are next asked to enter your Red Hat login ID and password, which are the same ones you use to access the RHN website. After you enter your credentials, click Forward to continue. Your login and password will be verified, and if they are correct you will be allowed to continue.

Next, you define a descriptive system name (preferably the hostname) to identify the host to RHN. You can see that we entered the hostname au-mel-rhel-1 in Figure 2-28. Make sure you have the "Send hardware profile" and "Send package profile" options checked to make the best use of your subscription and allow Red Hat to provide any updates for your system. Clicking Forward will allow you to review your details prior to sending the information to RHN.

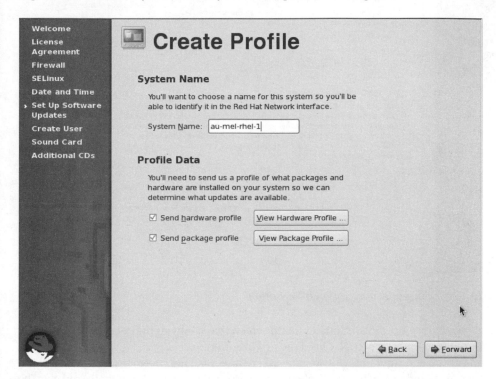

Figure 2-28. *Setting the system name for RHN*

You now have a chance to review your subscription information, as you can see in Figure 2-29. If you don't have a subscription, you will see an error message of Code 91. You can check your subscription with Red Hat and purchase an extra subscription for your new host if required.

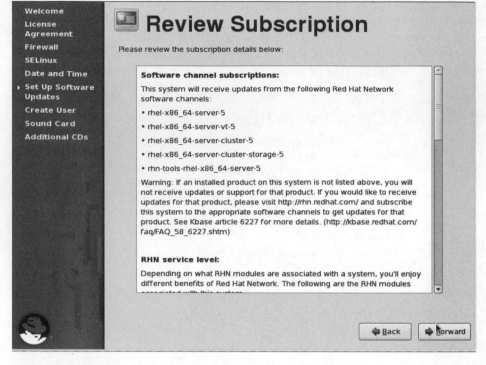

Figure 2-29. *Reviewing your subscription information*

Next, you will see the Finish Updates Setup screen that confirms the successful subscription of your host to Red Hat's RHN. Click Forward to continue.

Having set up your updates, you are now asked to set up a new user for your host. In this instance, we are going to create a user called `jsmith`. We will enter `jsmith`'s details and give the user a password. On this screen you can also potentially configure network authentication. *Network authentication* allows you to store users' details and the access they are entitled to in a remote host. This means that instead of needing to manage users and credentials on all your hosts, you can configure them once on this remote host and use them on all your hosts. Another example of network authentication is Microsoft Windows Active Directory.

If you have any network authentication infrastructure set up, you can enter the details after you click the Use Network Login button. In the network login section you are able to select other authentication types like Kerberos, LDAP, Smart Card, SMB, or Winbind, and make use of user information stored in databases like NIS and LDAP. If any of these terms are not familiar to you, don't panic—we will discuss them later in Chapter 16. For now, let's use the details shown in Figure 2-30.

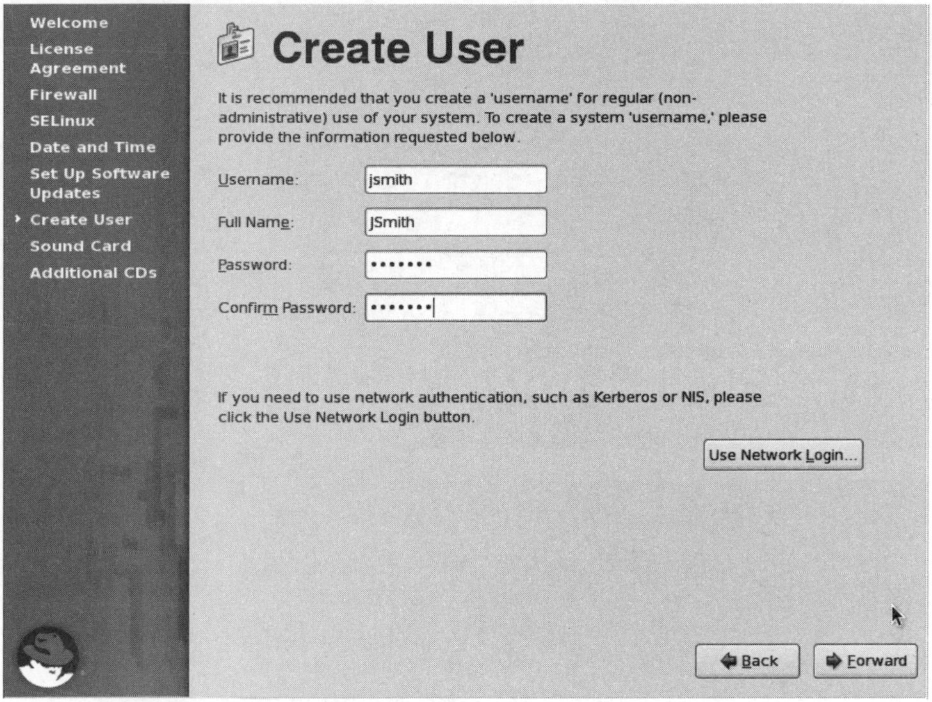

Figure 2-30. *Creating your first user*

Unless you are setting up a desktop system, we recommend ignoring the sound card setup. This is a legacy screen from when sound cards cost hundreds of dollars and were considered flashy on your new system. Nowadays, sound cards are given away on motherboards for free.

You can also ignore the Additional CDs section. Again, this is more or less a legacy screen, from when Internet connections were hopelessly slow and getting software on CDs was the only option you had.

Now your system installation is complete and you are presented with the screen shown in Figure 2-31.

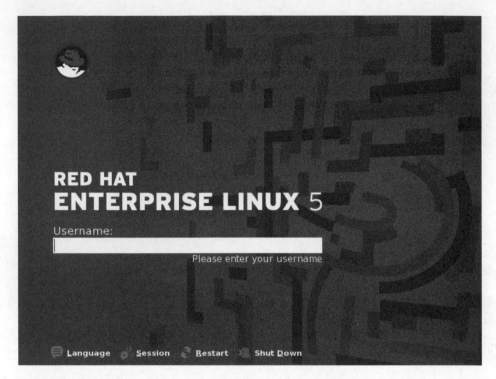

Figure 2-31. *Installation is complete and the system is ready to use.*

From here, you can move on to the next chapter, where we will introduce you to Linux and how to start using your new host. Alternatively, you can continue reading this chapter to learn how to install Ubuntu.

Ubuntu Installation

Ubuntu comes in two flavors: desktop and server. The desktop version is designed to be deployed as a desktop and the server version for your server hosts. In this section, we'll demonstrate how to install the server version. Installing Ubuntu Server is a very similar process to installing a Red Hat Enterprise Linux server. The main concepts are the same: choose the language and keyboard layout, choose the way you want to partition your disk, and then select the packages you want to install.

To install Ubuntu, we're going to download an ISO file from the Ubuntu website that contains much of the data we need to complete the installation. In this exercise we'll use the full-size CD from http://www.ubuntu.com/getubuntu/download.

Note Ubuntu and Debian make good use of net installers, providing installation flexibility. A *net installer* is a small version of the operating system usually provided as an ISO file that you can burn to a CD and boot from. It contains a simple kernel and the distribution's installer. The net installer provides your host with the basics it needs to boot and start the installation process, and any additional software or applications are then downloaded from online repositories. This means you need to be connected to the Internet to install a new host. It can also mean that installing a complete 4GB operating system may take a long time on a standard ADSL2, but using a net installer can be a great way to load a smaller system. We will explore net installs further in Chapter 19, when we look at ways to provision multiple systems.

We will make a few assumptions here:

- You are using an Ubuntu 8.04 LTS Server Edition ISO from the Ubuntu website (http://www.ubuntu.com/getubuntu/download), and you have burned it to a CD. You can find out more about burning ISO files to CD/DVD here: https://help.ubuntu.com/community/BurningIsoHowto.

- You are building just a basic mail, DNS and web server, like we did with the RHEL install.

- You are installing on a fresh server without any previous operating system.

After you place the CD in the CD drive and power on the host, you are presented with a selection of languages to use for the install. As shown in Figure 2-32, we chose English.

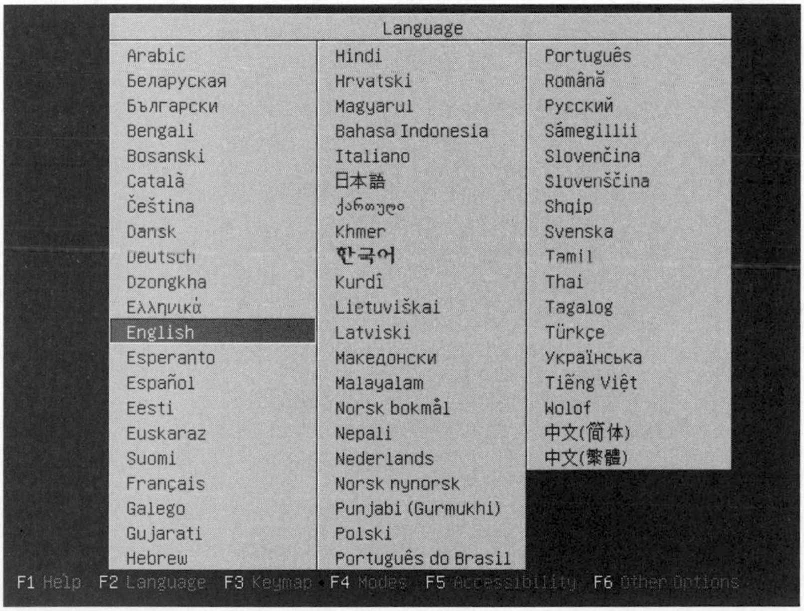

Language		
Arabic	Hindi	Português
Беларуская	Hrvatski	Română
Български	Magyarul	Русский
Bengali	Bahasa Indonesia	Sámegillii
Bosanski	Italiano	Slovenčina
Català	日本語	Slovenščina
Čeština	ქართული	Shqip
Dansk	Khmer	Svenska
Deutsch	한국어	Tamil
Dzongkha	Kurdî	Thai
Ελληνικά	Lietuviškai	Tagalog
English	Latviski	Türkçe
Esperanto	Македонски	Українська
Español	Malayalam	Tiếng Việt
Eesti	Norsk bokmål	Wolof
Euskaraz	Nepali	中文(简体)
Suomi	Nederlands	中文(繁體)
Français	Norsk nynorsk	
Galego	Punjabi (Gurmukhi)	
Gujarati	Polski	
Hebrew	Português do Brasil	

F1 Help F2 Language F3 Keymap F4 Modes F5 Accessibility F6 Other Options

Figure 2-32. *Selecting the language of the install*

The next screen (see Figure 2-33) presents a similar set of options to the RHEL installation screen. F1 brings up a comprehensive help system that explains how to use the installer and how to deal with special hardware. F2 and F3 allow you to change the language and keyboard mapping. F4 is unused on the server disk, but it allows you to choose different installation types on the desktop installer disc. F5 allows you to change the display to high-contrast mode and initialize screen readers or Braille displays. Finally, F6 provides you with an option to manually edit the boot command.

On this screen, you can also test to see if the CD has any defects and then go into rescue mode, which we will cover in Chapter 8.

The Test memory option does not boot Linux at all, but starts a utility called memtest86. This utility repeatedly writes blocks of data to your RAM and then reads them back, to see if the contents have changed. If you are experiencing random crashes or system lockups, testing the RAM to make sure it is seated properly and not damaged is one of the first things you should do.

If you select "Boot from first hard disk," the system will read the master boot record and boot your system as if there were no CD present. We'll talk about this boot process in more detail in Chapter 3.

Choose the Install Ubuntu Server option by pressing Enter, and your installation will begin.

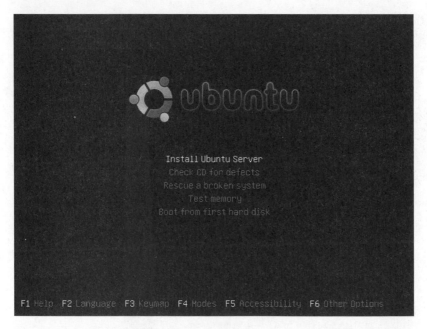

Figure 2-33. *Ubuntu Server splash screen*

Next is the first of your installation choices: the language you wish to use throughout the installation (see Figure 2-34). This will also be the default language for the final system.

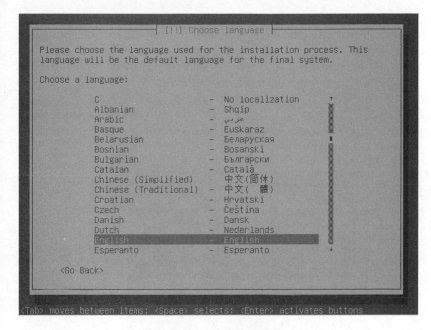

Figure 2-34. *Choosing the language for installation*

You are then asked to select your region. This is the geographical location in which the server you are installing is located. In Figure 2-35 we've selected Australia.

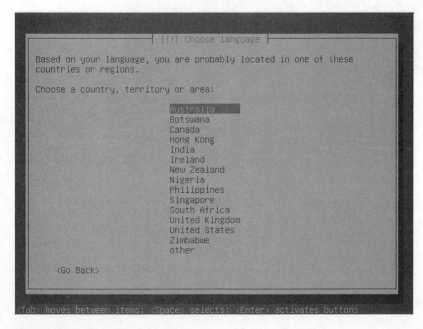

Figure 2-35. *Selecting your region*

Next, you select the keyboard and keyboard layout preference. As mentioned earlier, the keyboard layout is the keyboard mapping you are using. Different regions will have different mappings, so choose the one that best fits your area and language. Choosing Yes here, as shown in Figure 2-36, leads to a further series of questions and answers through which Ubuntu attempts to work out what type of keyboard you are using by having you press different keys.

Select No to save time and directly tell the installation what kind of keyboard you are using. The default here will work for most installations, but feel free to select the one most appropriate to your area. Figure 2-36 begins a series of screenshots that show the keyboard selection.

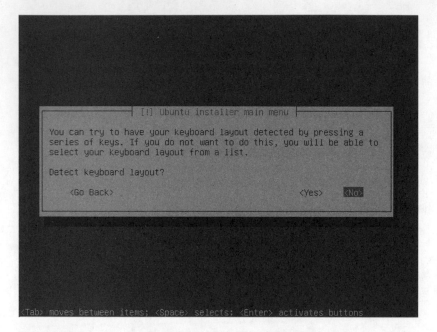

Figure 2-36. *Ubuntu attempts to detect your keyboard.*

After selecting No, the screen in Figure 2-37 appears, where you select the origin of the keyboard. We will pick USA and continue on.

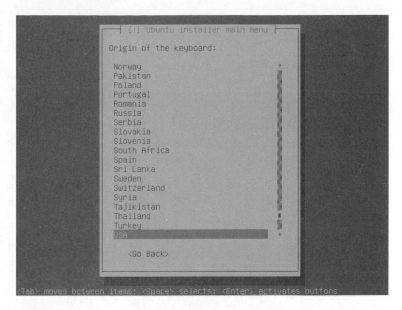

Figure 2-37. *Selecting the origin of your keyboard*

In Figure 2-38, we select the keyboard layout for USA that will give us the standard key mapping for Australian computers.

■**Tip** You can change the keyboard settings at any time after the installation is finished.

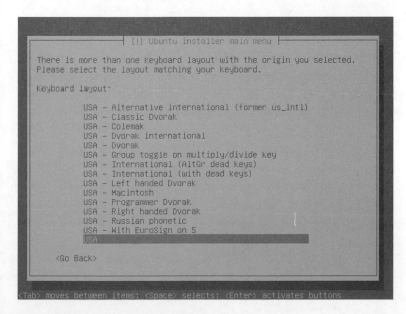

Figure 2-38. *Selecting keyboard layout*

The Ubuntu installation now takes a break to explore your hardware and discover more information about the target host. After this process is completed, you will be prompted for the hostname of your new host. As shown in Figure 2-39, we entered au-mel-ubuntu-1 here as it ties in with the naming standard discussed in the RHEL installation section.

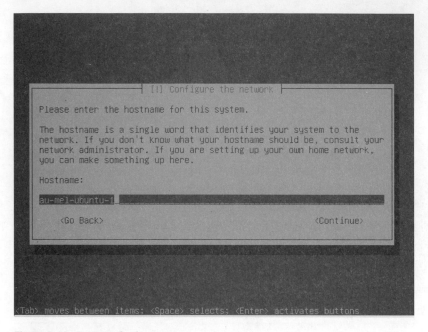

Figure 2-39. *Setting the hostname*

■**Tip** If you are using a net install ISO, you will be asked to provide the location from which to retrieve the applications you want to install. These locations, called *archive mirrors*, are the online repositories for Ubuntu software. Pick your closest geographic region; in our case, we would pick Australia.

You will next be asked to specify your time zone by selecting your nearest capital city. This is so you can use the right time zone information for setting your host's internal clock. We chose Melbourne, as you can see in Figure 2-40.

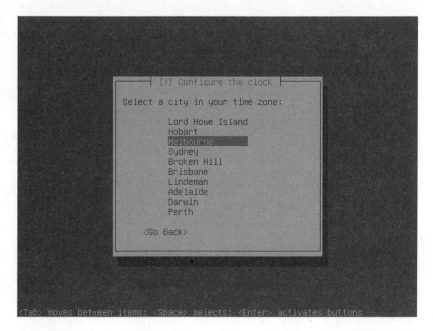

Figure 2-40. *Selecting your time zone*

Next, you need to partition your host. This partitioning occurs in much the same way described in our example RHEL installation. You can divide your disks into partitions of differing sizes depending on the requirements of your host. Again, as in the RHEL installation, you are prompted to either select one of several default partitioning options or customize your own using the partitioning tool.

- *Guided - use entire disk*: This option asks you to select a hard disk, which will be completely erased. The system then creates a root partition and a swap partition.

- *Guided - use entire disk and set up LVM*: This option also erases all data. It then creates a small boot partition and uses the rest of the disk for a root and swap volume in LVM.

- *Guided - use entire disk and set up encrypted LVM*: This option is identical to the previous, except the LVM data is all encrypted. You are asked to provide a password. Note that you need to input this password at boot time, so this option is not suitable for a remote or headless server. If you lose the encryption password, you will not be able to retrieve your data.

- *Manual*: This option opens the partition editor and allows you to manually configure partitions, software raid, encryption, and LVM. This is the option you should choose if you have a preexisting Windows installation you want to resize.

For our example host we are interested in using the "Guided - use entire disk and set up LVM" option. This uses the entire hard disk available to us and makes use of logical volume management (LVM). As described in the RHEL installation section, LVM is a powerful way to manage your partitions and disks, and gives you greater flexibility to make changes to your partition layout later.

■Note We'll discuss LVM in more detail in Chapter 8.

Figure 2-41 displays our default partition choices.

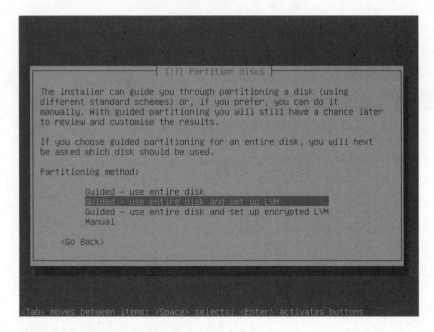

Figure 2-41. *Choosing LVM to partition disks*

Next, select the drive you wish to perform this partitioning on. We are given only one disk to select, as you can see in Figure 2-42.

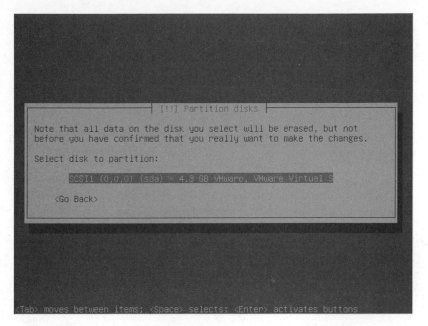

Note that all data on the disk you select will be erased, but not before you have confirmed that you really want to make the changes.

Select disk to partition:

SCSI1 (0,0,0) (sda) - 4.3 GB VMware, VMware Virtual S

<Go Back>

Figure 2-42. *Choosing the disk to partition*

■**Caution** If the disk already contains partitions, you will be prompted to overwrite them. If you are confident that you want to do this, then specify Yes and continue. Selecting Yes here will destroy any existing data you may have if you are installing over a previous system. If you are not confident, then specify No. Alternatives to this include repartitioning your host using a tool like PartitionMagic (http://www.symantec.com/norton/partitionmagic), installing on a hard disk that doesn't already have data on it, or installing on a virtual machine.

The next screen (see Figure 2-43) lets you confirm that you wish to write the partition information to the selected disk. The partition information needs to be written to disk before LVM can be configured. Select Yes and go to the next screen.

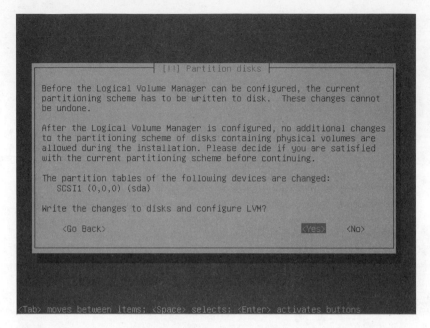

Figure 2-43. *Writing partition information to disk*

You will now be shown the LVM partition layout, which will show a small amount for swap space and the rest for the root or / partition. When we confirm this layout by selecting Yes, the LVM partitions shown in Figure 2-44 are created and formatted.

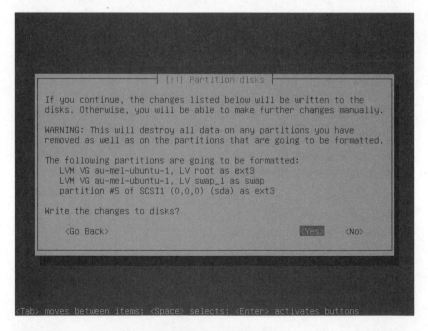

Figure 2-44. *Writing LVM partition changes to disk*

■**Note** Swap space is additional storage on your hard disk drive that is used for "overflow" data from RAM. If you find your host frequently using all of your swap space or frequently swapping, then you probably need to tune your host and most often add more RAM. We'll talk about swap space in more detail in Chapters 8 and 17.

At this stage of the installation, Ubuntu will start installing the base package requirements needed to get the rest of the operating system installed. If you are using a net install, this may take some time depending on your Internet connection. You will be presented with a progress bar similar to the one shown in Figure 2-45.

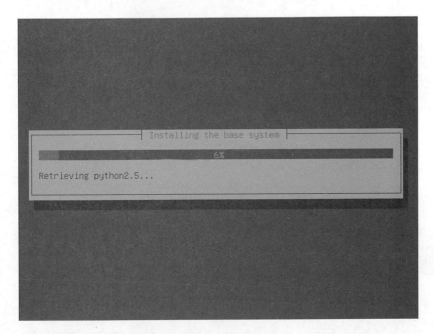

Figure 2-45. *Installing base system requirements*

Next, you are asked to create a user for this host. In Chapter 4 we will discuss user administration in greater detail, but it is important to know that the Ubuntu distribution disables the root user account by disabling its password. The root user is like the Windows Administrator and has access to everything on the host. In Ubuntu, instead of setting the root user's password like we did in the RHEL installation, users use a special command called sudo to access all the same privileges as the root user. We'll talk more about the sudo command in Chapter 4.

In Figure 2-46 you enter the full name of your new user.

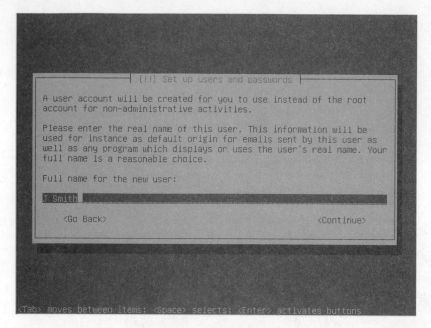

Figure 2-46. *Entering the full name of a new user*

In the next screen (Figure 2-47), you set the username for your new user.

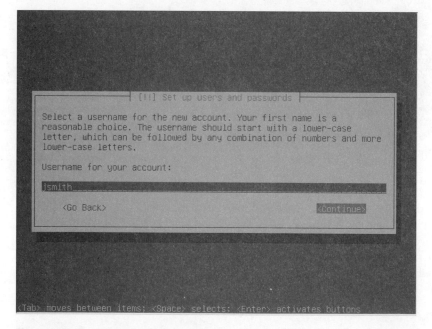

Figure 2-47. *Entering the username for the new user*

Finally, you set the password for your user, as shown in Figure 2-48. Again, as we discussed in the RHEL installation section, we recommend implementing a strong and complex password. You will be asked to verify that password.

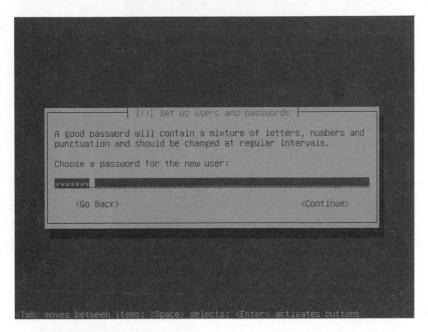

Figure 2-48. *Setting the user's password*

Next, you are asked for information about any Proxy servers you may need to use to access the outside world. We will ignore this for the moment and continue.

You are then asked what applications you would like to install on your host via the selection of application groups. We chose DNS, LAMP server (Linux, Apache, MySQL, and PHP), mail (Postfix), and OpenSSH, as you can see in Figure 2-49. When you are ready, select Continue.

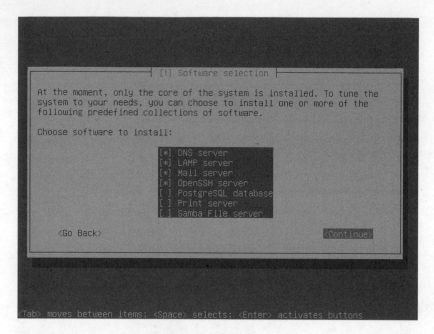

Figure 2-49. *Selecting applications for your host*

In this particular installation, because of the applications you have chosen to install, you are asked a series of questions to help Ubuntu configure or secure your chosen applications. Every time you install new applications on Ubuntu that require input to be configured, you will be prompted to answer similar questions.

As you can see in Figure 2-50, you are first asked to provide a password for the MySQL database root user. This is the master password for your MySQL installation and you should enter a secure and complex password. You will be asked to confirm this password by entering it again.

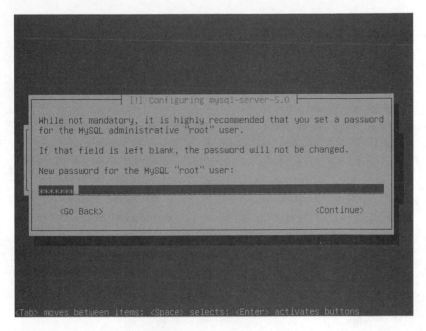

Figure 2-50. *Setting the MySQL root password*

Once you have provided this password, you are then asked to describe your mail server configuration. The screen in Figure 2-51 shows the configuration options, with each option briefly described. We will just choose the default, Internet Site.

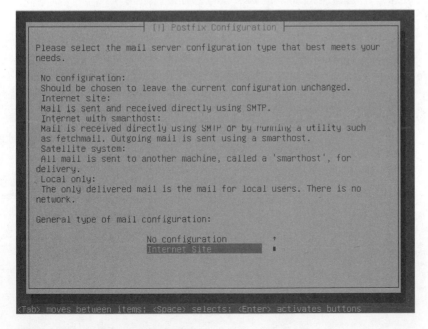

Figure 2-51. *Configuring the mail server*

We will explain how to configure and secure mail services in Chapter 10. Selecting the default here will provide a basic and secure configuration for sending and receiving mail for your domain.

Next, you provide the domain name for your mail server (see Figure 2-52). You should enter the domain name of the host for now, and we'll explain other potential options in Chapter 10.

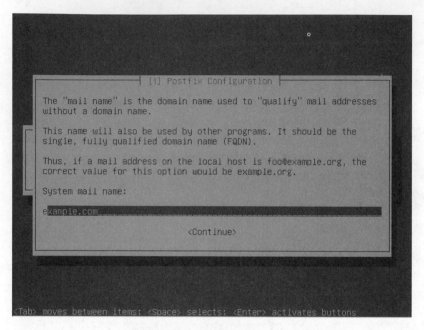

Figure 2-52. *Setting the mail server domain name*

After confirming your computer clock is set to UTC, as shown in Figure 2-53, your installation is nearly complete. UTC is used by your host to convert time into its local time using time zone information.

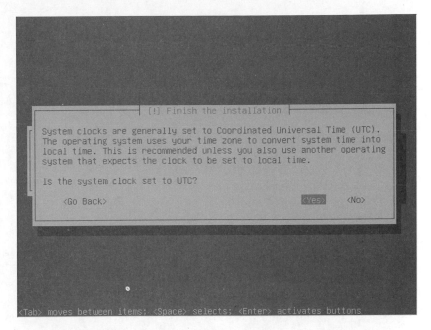

Figure 2-53. *Setting the clock to UTC*

Installation is now complete and Ubuntu will notify you of this, as you can see in Figure 2-54.

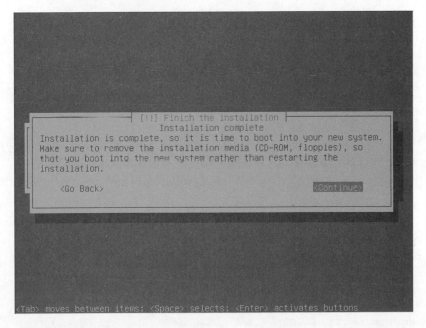

Figure 2-54. *Installation is complete.*

The CD or DVD will eject automatically, and after you remove it from the drive you can select Continue. Your system will now reboot and you will be presented with a login prompt (see Figure 2-55).

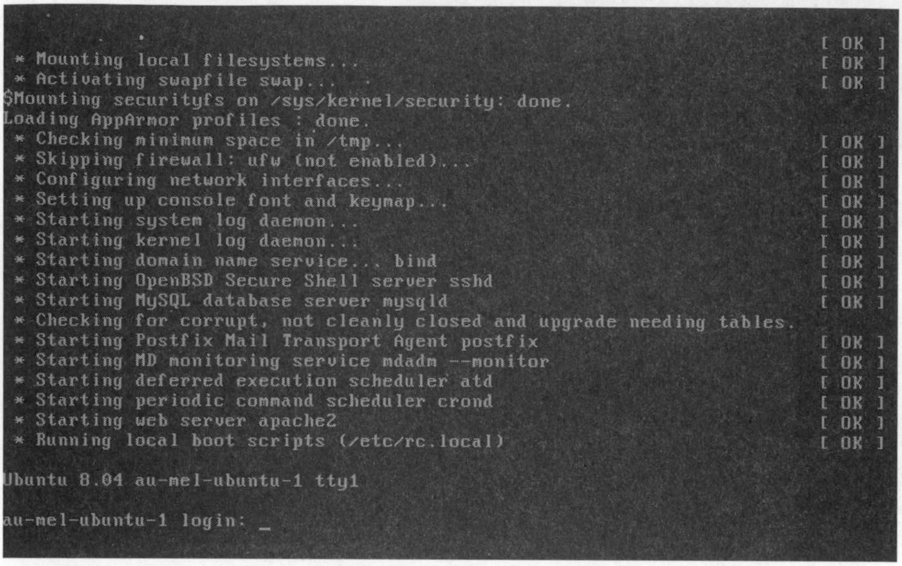

```
    .         .
* Mounting local filesystems...                                    [ OK ]
* Activating swapfile swap...                                      [ OK ]
$Mounting securityfs on /sys/kernel/security: done.               [ OK ]
Loading AppArmor profiles : done.
* Checking minimum space in /tmp...                                [ OK ]
* Skipping firewall: ufw (not enabled)...                          [ OK ]
* Configuring network interfaces...                                [ OK ]
* Setting up console font and keymap...                            [ OK ]
* Starting system log daemon...                                    [ OK ]
* Starting kernel log daemon...                                    [ OK ]
* Starting domain name service... bind                             [ OK ]
* Starting OpenBSD Secure Shell server sshd                        [ OK ]
* Starting MySQL database server mysqld                            [ OK ]
* Checking for corrupt, not cleanly closed and upgrade needing tables.
* Starting Postfix Mail Transport Agent postfix                    [ OK ]
* Starting MD monitoring service mdadm --monitor                   [ OK ]
* Starting deferred execution scheduler atd                        [ OK ]
* Starting periodic command scheduler crond                        [ OK ]
* Starting web server apache2                                      [ OK ]
* Running local boot scripts (/etc/rc.local)                       [ OK ]

Ubuntu 8.04 au-mel-ubuntu-1 tty1

au-mel-ubuntu-1 login: _
```

Figure 2-55. *Booting to the console screen*

You will notice that Ubuntu does not boot to a graphical user interface (GUI) but to a console screen. This is because the default Ubuntu Server installation does not install a GUI. We'll talk more about using the command line vs. a GUI in Chapter 3.

You now have a usable mail, DNS, and web server running the Ubuntu distribution that is ready for you to customize further for your environment.

Troubleshooting

Every now and then an installation will fail for some reason. Most commonly this happens due to defective installation media; less often it happens due to unsupported or defective hardware.

If there is a problem with the installation media, you may see read errors being logged or the installer may display an error stating it was unable to read a file. You should check the installation CD or DVD for scratches. If you created the CD or DVD from an ISO file, it might be worth writing a new disc at a lower speed. Media problems usually recur at the same step in the installation process.

Network installations can also fail if the connection is interrupted, so check that cables are plugged in and your Internet connection is working.

The less common type of failure is caused by hardware not being supported. For example, if an installation kernel does not support the disk controller, the installer will be unable to access hard disks. If this happens, check which kernel version is included on the installation disc and verify that it in fact supports your hardware. A newer version of your distribution, with support for more and newer hardware, might be available.

Nonreproducible crashes at random points in the installation usually indicate a hardware problem, and the most common problems are bad RAM or overheating. You can run a RAM tester like `memtest86` (http://www.memtest.org/), and you should verify that the CPU and case fans are working properly.

Diagnostic Information

If you need additional diagnostic information while you are installing, you can access a limited shell and some logging information from the installation process. You can use these to further diagnose any problems you might have.

On an RHEL host, the ALT+F2 key combination will give you access to a limited shell, ALT+F3 gives the installation log, ALT+F4 gives the system messages, and ALT+F5 gives miscellaneous messages. ALT+F7 returns to the installation GUI.

On Ubuntu, ALT+F2 and ALT+F3 each give access to a limited shell. ALT+F4 provides verbose installation progress and logs for the installer. The ALT+F1 combination switches back to the installer interface.

Restarting Your Installation

After a problem, you should normally restart installation from the beginning. Because files from the previous installation attempt might still be present on disk, it's best to have the installer reinitialize the partitions and start from scratch.

Troubleshooting Resources

Don't be afraid to make use of the communities that exist around most Linux distributions if you run into trouble. Chances are someone else has experienced the same problem you have and has documented the resolution. Here are some resources to try:

- Red Hat: https://www.redhat.com/apps/support/

- Fedora: http://forums.fedoraforum.org/forumdisplay.php?f=6

- Ubuntu: http://ubuntuforums.org/forumdisplay.php?f=333

Summary

In this chapter, we stepped through the process of installing two of the popular Linux distribution choices:

- Red Hat Enterprise Linux

- Ubuntu Server

We also explained what you might do if something goes wrong during installation. In the next chapter, we will give you a rundown of the basics of how to use your new Linux host.

■ ■ ■

## CHAPTER 3

Linux Basics

By James Turnbull

In Chapter 1, we talked a little about what Linux is and where it came from, and in Chapter 2 we installed our first Linux host. In this chapter, we're going to introduce you to some basic Linux concepts and skills. Some people find Linux intimidating because of what looks like arcane commands with strange switches and mysterious options. We'll decode some of the arcane commands you'll need to know and demonstrate these commands and their functions.

This chapter focuses on getting started, logging in, and working with and navigating the command line and the file system. We're also going to introduce some basic Linux concepts: users, groups, packages, services, the file system, and how to work with files and directories. In the chapters that follow, we'll expand on these concepts and introduce you to the key activities you'll need to know in order to operate and administer your Linux hosts.

In this chapter, we'll mostly talk about commands running on the command line. This gives you an introduction to using the command line and will help get you comfortable with operating on it. This is not to say that there isn't a broad array of graphical administration tools available for Linux. If you're more comfortable in a graphical, Windows-like environment, you can still easily and effectively find mechanisms to administer your Linux hosts. For most command-line tools we're going to show you, there is a graphical equivalent.

■**Note** This chapter is a broad introduction to Linux. It won't make you an expert. Rather, it'll prepare you to take the first steps to deploy your Linux infrastructure.

Getting Started

If you haven't already installed a Linux host, the easiest way to try out Linux commands prior to tackling a Linux install is to try a LiveCD. *LiveCDs* are Linux distributions on a CD or DVD. To use a LiveCD, you need to download an image, in the form of an ISO file, of your selected LiveCD and burn that image to a CD or DVD. Following are some URLs that describe how to burn ISO files onto CDs and DVDs:

- http://pcsupport.about.com/od/toolsofthetrade/ht/burnisofile.htm
- http://www.petri.co.il/how_to_write_iso_files_to_cd.htm
- https://help.ubuntu.com/community/BurningIsoHowto

Once you have burned your LiveCD, you can then insert the disc into your computer and reboot. Most computers will detect the LiveCD and offer you the option of booting from the CD or DVD.

■**Note** If your host doesn't offer you the option to boot from CD/DVD, you may need to adjust your BIOS settings to change your boot order so the CD or DVD is booted before your hard drive.

The LiveCD will load and present you with a working Linux distribution that you can experiment with. By default, this does not install anything to your host, and your original configuration will be available when you remove the CD/DVD and reboot your computer.

LiveCDs are available for a variety of distributions. Some good distributions to try using their LiveCDs include

- *Ubuntu*: You can find LiveCDs, called Desktop CDs, for Ubuntu at `http://releases.ubuntu.com/`.

- *Fedora*: You can find a LiveCD for Fedora (called Fedora Desktop Live Media) at `http://fedoraproject.org/en/get-fedora-all`.

- *CentOS*: Available for the latest CentOS 5 release is a LiveCD from one of the mirror sites listed at `http://isoredirect.centos.org/centos/5/isos/i386/`.

■**Tip** There is a comparison list of some of the available Linux LiveCDs available at `http://en.wikipedia.org/wiki/Comparison_of_Linux_LiveDistros`.

Logging In

After your Linux host or LiveCD boots, you will be presented with a login prompt: either a command-line or GUI login prompt.

In Figure 3-1, you can see a typical command-line login prompt for an Ubuntu Linux host, and in Figure 3-2, you can see the graphical login for a Red Hat Enterprise Linux host.

■**Note** Don't panic if your initial screens differ slightly from these, as some minor changes do appear between versions.

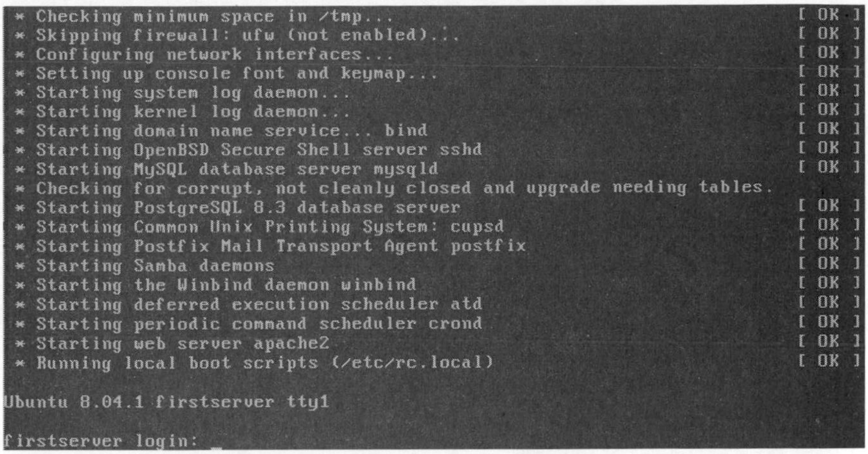

* Checking minimum space in /tmp... [OK]
* Skipping firewall: ufw (not enabled)... [OK]
* Configuring network interfaces... [OK]
* Setting up console font and keymap... [OK]
* Starting system log daemon... [OK]
* Starting kernel log daemon... [OK]
* Starting domain name service... bind [OK]
* Starting OpenBSD Secure Shell server sshd [OK]
* Starting MySQL database server mysqld [OK]
* Checking for corrupt, not cleanly closed and upgrade needing tables.
* Starting PostgreSQL 8.3 database server [OK]
* Starting Common Unix Printing System: cupsd [OK]
* Starting Postfix Mail Transport Agent postfix [OK]
* Starting Samba daemons [OK]
* Starting the Winbind daemon winbind [OK]
* Starting deferred execution scheduler atd [OK]
* Starting periodic command scheduler crond [OK]
* Starting web server apache2 [OK]
* Running local boot scripts (/etc/rc.local) [OK]
Ubuntu 8.04.1 firstserver tty1
firstserver login:

Figure 3-1. *Command-line login prompt*

RED HAT
ENTERPRISE LINUX 5
Username:
Please enter your username
Language
Session
Restart
Shut Down

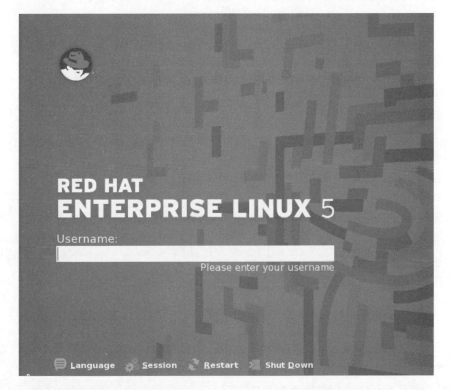

Figure 3-2. *Graphical login prompt*

At either login prompt you need to supply your username and a password or similar form of authentication. (Like Windows, Linux can also use smartcards or tokens or other mechanisms to authenticate users.)

If you just installed a Linux host, you'll have been prompted to create a user, and you can make use of that user to log in now. If you're testing Linux with a LiveCD, you may see a default username and password that you will be prompted to log in with, or you may even be automatically logged in. For example, the Ubuntu LiveCD has a default username of ubuntu with a password of ubuntu, and it usually automatically logs you in. If you don't see a default username and password, you may need to check the LiveCD's online documentation, or you may be prompted to create a username and a password.

Once your host has verified your access, then you'll be logged in, and depending on your configuration, your host will either display a command-line or a GUI desktop environment.

Linux vs. Microsoft Windows

The title of this section might sound a bit like we're about to present a pro wrestling match. However, it's more about the similarities between Linux and Microsoft Windows (hereafter just Windows) than their differences. Windows and Linux are both operating systems, and while different in many technical aspects, they share a lot of the same concepts. They may use different names for some of these concepts; for example, Windows calls a user's personal information, configuration, and disk space a *profile*, while the Linux world has a similar concept referred to as a *home directory*. In general, however, the overall concepts remain the same. As a result, we're going to examine these similarities to help you leverage some of your existing knowledge about Windows as a means of understanding related concepts in Linux.

In this book, we're going to look at how to interface with your Linux host. There are two principal interfaces: the GUI desktop and the command line. We'll explore both of these interfaces in this book.

The GUI Desktop

Both Linux and Windows have graphical user interfaces. Windows (unless you've got a problem) boots into a GUI interface, and from inside this interface you can open command-line windows. Unlike Windows, Linux can boot to either a GUI interface or the command line. Once you're booted up, you can also switch between these two modes, and we'll discuss how to do that in the section "The Command Line" later in this chapter and in some more detail in Chapter 5.

On Linux the GUI interface is a combination of several applications. The basic application is called the X Window System (you'll also see it called X11 or simply X). The X application provides an underlying "windowing" environment.

■**Note** You won't need to worry about installing or managing X. Your distribution will generally install this for you if you install a GUI desktop. If you don't install a GUI desktop, for example, if you are installing a server, X will not be installed, and you'll generally interact with Linux through the command-line interface. An example of a distribution that doesn't load a GUI by default is the Ubuntu Server distribution we installed in Chapter 2.

On top of X you then add a desktop environment to provide the "look and feel" and desktop functionality such as toolbars, icons, buttons, and the like. There are two major desktop environments popular on Linux: Gnome and KDE. Most distributions have one of these desktop environments as their default; for example, Gnome is the default desktop environment on the Debian, Ubuntu, Red Hat, and Fedora distributions, and KDE is the default on Ubuntu derivative Kubuntu and on SuSE.

■**Tip** In keeping with the flexibility of Linux, you can change the default desktop environment to KDE on all of these distributions.

In Figure 3-3, you can see the default Gnome desktop on an Ubuntu distribution.

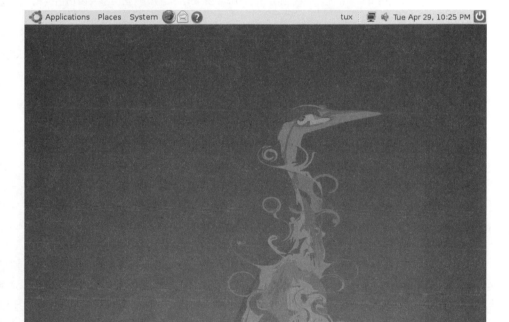

Figure 3-3. *Ubuntu Gnome desktop on the Hardy Heron release*

The Command Line

In the Linux world, the command line is one of the most powerful tools available to you. In this book, a lot of focus is going to be on the command line. This is where at least some of your administration tasks are going to occur, and it's important to be able to understand and make use of the command line. Indeed, in some cases you will not have a GUI environment available. If your GUI environment is not functional, you will need to be able to administer your hosts using the command line. The command line also offers some powerful tools that can make your administration tasks faster and more effective.

■**Note** This is not to say we're going to ignore the GUI. We'll also show you how to administer your Linux host using GUI tools.

Let's take a look at the Linux command line. You can access the command line in one of several ways. If your host has booted to a command-line prompt, as you can see in Figure 3-1, you can simply log in and use the prompt.

From inside the Gnome or KDE GUI interface, you have two options. The first is to use a virtual console—a kind of Linux management console that runs by default on most Linux distributions. Or you can launch a terminal emulator application like the Gnome Terminal or Konsole.

■**Note** A *terminal emulator* is a tool that emulates a text terminal inside another application. For example, when you start a *command prompt*, or *command-line shell*, in Windows, you've started a Windows terminal emulator.

To launch a virtual console from inside a Gnome or KDE GUI, use the key combination Ctrl+Alt and one of the F1 through F6 keys. Each of the windows that can be opened is a new virtual console. Six virtual consoles are available, and you can cycle through these consoles using the Alt+F1 to F6 keys or back and forth through the windows using the Alt+left arrow or Alt+right arrow keys. Each terminal is independent and separate. To return to your GUI, you use Alt+F7.

■**Tip** If you are not running a GUI interface, the virtual consoles are still available to you, and you can use the Alt+F1 to F6 keys and the Alt+left arrow and Alt+right arrow keys to navigate them.

You can also launch a terminal emulator. In Gnome, for example, you click the Applications menu, open the Accessories tab, and select the Terminal application. This will launch the Gnome Terminal application, as you can see in Figure 3-4.

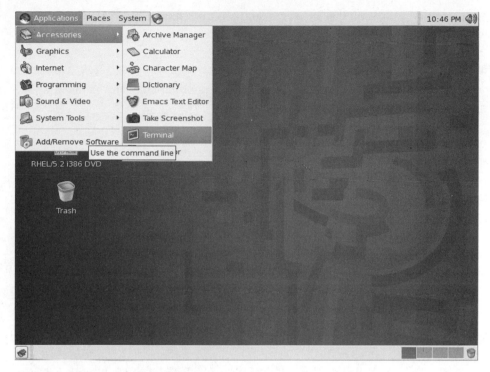

Figure 3-4. *Launching the Gnome Terminal application*

On KDE, things are slightly different. On earlier versions of KDE, you can launch the Konsole application by clicking Applications, opening System Tools, and selecting the Konsole application. On KDE version 4 and later, you launch Konsole by clicking Applications and then System, and selecting the Konsole application.

Shells

What command line is presented to you depends on what shell is running for your user. *Shells* are interfaces to the operating system and kernel of your host. For example, the command line on a Windows XP host is also a shell. Each shell contains a collection of built-in commands that allow you to interact with your host (these are supplemented by additional tools installed by your distribution).

A variety of shells are available, with the most common being the Bash (or Bourne-again) shell that is used by default on many distributions, including the popular Red Hat, Ubuntu, and Debian distributions.

■**Note** We talked more about some specific distributions in Chapters 1 and 2.

We're going to use the Bash shell for all of our examples in this chapter, because it is most likely the shell you'll find by default.

Command-Line Prompt

After you have logged in to your Linux host, you should see a prompt that looks something like this:

```
jsmith@au-mel-rhel-1 ~$
```

So what does this mean? Well let's break it down:

user@*host directory*$

On most Linux distributions, the basic prompt is constructed from the username you're logged in as, the name of the host, the current directory, and the $ symbol, which indicates what sort of user you are logged in as.

■**Tip** You can customize your prompt to include additional information, add or change colors, or implement a variety of other options. Find more information at `http://tldp.org/HOWTO/Bash-Prompt-HOWTO/`.

In our case, `jsmith` is the name of the user we are logged in as; the @ symbol comes next and is followed by the name of the host we are logged into, i.e., `jsmith` at au-mel-rhel-1.

■**Note** This part of the prompt looks like an e-mail address, for a good reason. This is how e-mail began— people with login accounts on connected Unix machines sending each other messages. The @ symbol was first used for this purpose in 1971! You can read about it at `http://openmap.bbn.com/~tomlinso/ray/ firstemailframe.html`.

Next you see a ~ symbol, which is an abbreviated method of referring to your home directory. On a Linux host, most users have a special directory, called a *home directory*, which is created when the user is created. Like a Microsoft Window's user profile, the user's preferences and configuration files and data are stored in this directory. Any time you see the ~ symbol used, it indicates a shortcut that means home directory. We talked about home directories earlier, and they roughly equate to a combination of the Windows concept of the Documents and Settings profile and the `My Documents` folder. You would usually find home directories under a directory called `/home`.

■**Note** Linux is a multiuser operating system where multiple users can log on multiple times and work simultaneously. Like Windows, users can have their own environment, storage, access controls, and permissions.

Lastly, you see the $ symbol. This symbol tells you what type of user you are; by default all normal users on the host will have $ as their prompt. There is a special user, called root, whose prompt uses the # symbol:

```
root@au-mel-rhel-1 ~#
```

The root user is the superuser. On Windows, we'd call this user the Administrator. Like the Administrator user on Windows, the root user can control and configure everything. So if you see the # symbol, you know you are logged in as the root user.

In some distributions, you can log in as the root user, and you'll usually be prompted to specify a password for the root user during installation. Other distributions, most notably the Ubuntu distribution, disable the root user's password. On Ubuntu, you are assumed to never use the root user, but rather a special command called sudo. The sudo command allows you to run commands with the privileges of the root user without logging in as that user. We'll talk about the sudo command in Chapter 4. To use the sudo command, you simply type **sudo** and the command you wish to run. You will usually be prompted for your password, and if you enter the correct password, the command will be executed.

```
$ sudo passwd root
```

This command would change the password of the root user, which is one method of enabling of the root user on Ubuntu.

The root user is all-powerful and can do anything on your host. As a result, it can be easy to accidentally make a mistake that could delete data or disrupt your applications and services when logged in as the root user. Thus, for security and safety reasons, you should never log in as the root user. We'll discuss other ways to administer your host without using the root user later in Chapter 4.

■**Note** In recent years, other security controls have been introduced that help reduce the reliance on the root user and provide more granular security controls. These controls include tools like SELinux and AppArmor, which we briefly discussed in Chapter 2.

Typing Your First Command

Now it's time to try entering a command. A command could be a binary executable (like a Windows executable or EXE file), or the command might be provided as part of the shell. Let's type a command called whoami and execute it by pressing the Enter key:

```
$ whoami
jsmith
```

The whoami command returns the name of the user you are logged in as. You can see our host has returned jsmith. This tells us we're logged in to our host as the user jsmith.

Each shell contains a series of built-in commands and functions to help you make use of the command line. Let's try one of these now. We start by running the whoami command again. This time, though, we make a spelling error and type the wrong command name:

```
$ whoamii
```

We then press the Enter key to run the command and find that Bash has returned the following response:

```
-bash: whoamii: command not found
```

So what happened? Well, Bash is telling us that no command called whoamii exists on the host. We can fix that. Let's start by correcting the command. We can bring back a previously typed command by using the up arrow key. Do that now, and you can see the previous command has returned to the command line:

```
$ whoamii
```

Bash usefully has what is called *command history*, which keeps track of a number of the previous commands typed. Bash allows you to navigate through these commands by using the up and down arrow keys.

You can also move the cursor along the command line to edit commands using the left and right arrow keys. Move to the end of the command using the arrow keys and delete the extra i, leaving you with

```
$ whoami
```

Now press the Enter key, and you will see the result on the command line:

```
jsmith
```

This time the corrected command, whoami, has again returned the name of the user who is logged in.

THE PATH

When Linux informs you it can't find a binary or command, it may be that you have misspelled the name of the command, or it could be that it can't find that particular command. Like Windows, when executing commands, Linux searches a list of directories to try to find that particular command. By default most distributions set a default path, usually containing the typical locations that contain executable binaries. Most of the time you won't need to set your path; the default path will be suitable. If you want to change the path, you'll need to update an environmental variable called $PATH. We'll talk about environmental variables in Chapter 5.

Remote Access

In the last two sections, we've talked about the GUI desktop and the command line. In both cases, we've assumed that you are logged on to your host locally (i.e., sitting in front of a screen and keyboard typing commands directly into the host). But in a lot of cases, people access Linux hosts remotely. This is particularly true for Linux hosts running as servers that might be hosted in a data center or in another geographical location, or stored in a rack or cabinet. In many cases, these hosts don't even have screens or keyboards attached and are only accessible via a network.

With Linux, it is very easy to remotely connect to these hosts so you can administer and manage them. You can use a number of different methods to do this remote connection. These include a desktop sharing protocol like Virtual Network Computing (commonly called VNC), Remote Desktop Protocol (RDP), which is often used to provide remote access to Windows hosts, and the extensively used Secure Shell (SSH).

Using SSH

We're quickly going to look at using SSH to provide remote command-line access to a Linux host. You can also access your GUI desktops with SSH, but we'll talk about that in Chapter 9.

SSH is both an application and a secure protocol used for a number of purposes but primarily for remote administration of hosts. On Linux hosts, SSH is provided by an open source version of the application called OpenSSH (see http://www.openssh.com/).

SSH connects over TCP/IP networks in a client-server model. Your connecting host is the client. For example, if you are connecting to a remote host from your laptop, your laptop is the client. The host you are connecting to is called the server and receives and manages your connection.

Remote connections using SSH are encrypted and require authentication, either a password or public key cryptography. To make an SSH connection, you need to know the IP address or hostname of the remote host. A connection is then initiated on the client and connects to the server via TCP on port 22 (you can change this port, and we'll talk about how to do that in Chapter 9).

■**Note** You have probably encountered IP addresses and hostnames before, but you might not have come across ports. *Ports* are communications endpoints used by services like SSH. Port numbers range from 0 to 65535 with some commonly known ports being 80 for HTTP, 25 for SMTP, and 21 for FTP. Ports between 1 and 1023 are generally reserved for system services, while ports 1024 and higher (also called *ephemeral ports*) are more arbitrarily assigned. We'll go into more detail on this in Chapter 6.

After the initial connection, the client is then prompted by the server for a username and authentication credentials like a password. If the user exists on the server and the correct credentials are provided, the client is allowed to connect to the server.

On most distributions, Secure Shell is installed as one of the default applications, and a server is started by default. This Secure Shell server or Secure Shell daemon (servers are also called *daemons* in the Linux world) allows remote connections to be made to the command line or GUI of your host.

You can use SSH via the command line or from one of a number of clients. Via the command line, client connections are made using a command called ssh. Most Linux and Unix-like operating systems (Mac OS X, for example) have SSH installed and have the ssh command available. To use the ssh command, you specify your username and the host you'd like to connect to separated with the @ symbol, as you can see in Listing 3-1.

Listing 3-1. *SSH Connections*

```
$ ssh jsmith@us-ny-server-1.example.com
Password:
```

In Listing 3-1, we've connected to a host called us-ny-server-1.example.com as the user jsmith. We've then been prompted to input our password. If we have entered the correct password, we will be logged in to the command line of the remote host.

■**Caution** In reality, if you run this exact command, it won't work, as the host us-ny-server-1.example.com doesn't exist. If you want to test this, you'll need to specify an actual live host.

There are also a variety of SSH clients or terminal emulators available, for example, the popular and free PuTTY client (available from http://www.chiark.greenend.org.uk/~sgtatham/putty/) that runs on Windows (and also on Linux).

SSH clients allow you to run text terminals to the command lines of your Unix or Linux hosts from your GUI interface. You can see the PuTTY client's configuration screen in Figure 3-5.

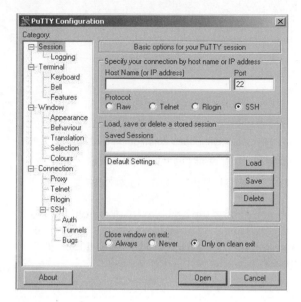

Figure 3-5. *The PuTTY Client*

Using a GUI client like PuTTY is very simple. As with the command line, you need to specify the hostname (or IP address) and port of the host to which you wish to connect. With a client like PuTTY, you can also do useful things like save connections so you don't need to input your hostname again.

If you intend to keep your desktop environment running Windows, we recommend you download a client like PuTTY. This will to allow you to remotely connect to and administer your Linux hosts from an environment that you're comfortable in. Mac OS, being Unix based, comes with an SSH client built in.

■**Tip** SSH clients also exist for operating systems like Windows Mobile, Symbian, and the Apple iPhone, allowing road warriors to connect to their Linux hosts while on the go!

Getting Help

So how do you get help on your Linux host? You're probably thinking, "I can't use the F1 key, right?" Well, actually you can. In both Gnome's and KDE's GUI interfaces, the F1 key will bring up help text for that interface. But on the command line, there are also a wide variety of tools designed to tell you how things work, help you find the command you want, and then explain the options available for that command.

The easiest way is to check the command or application's man page (short for manual page). A man page tells you what the command can do, what options are available, and a variety of other information about it. You can access the man page by typing **man** and the name of the command whose man page you wish to view, as you can see in Listing 3-2.

Listing 3-2. *The* man *Command*

```
$ man ls
```

The man command will return a document that describes the ls (or list) command and its various options.

■**Note** The ls or list command lists the files and directories on your host. We're going to show you quite a bit more about files with the ls command later in this chapter, so stay tuned.

If you are struggling with a command, its man page is the first place you should look for help. Not all commands have man pages, and you'll get an error message if the man page of a particular command does not exist. In this case, it is often useful to try adding the --help switch to a command, as you can see in Listing 3-3.

■**Note** *Switches* are command-line options you can add to particular commands. They are specified using a dash (-) or two dashes (--) and the single-letter abbreviation or name of the switch, for example, -l or --name.

Listing 3-3. *The* --help *Switch*

```
$ ls --help
```

■**Tip** Also available via the man command is a good introduction to Linux in general. To view this introduction, use the command man intro.

You can also search all of the man pages on a host for a keyword using the -K option.

```
$ man -K user
```

This would search all man pages for the keyword user and return a list of all man pages containing the term. You will then be prompted to view each page that is returned, skip a page and go to the next page, or quit the search.

This search can be a little slow because your host usually has a lot of man pages, so there are two simpler search commands available that may offer a shortcut to what you are looking for: whatis and apropos. The whatis command searches a summary database of commands that is available on most Linux distributions for a complete word match as follows:

```
$ whatis useradd
useradd(8) - create a new user or update default new user information
```

The whatis search has returned the useradd command and included a brief description of what the command does.

The apropos command also searches the whatis database but searches for strings rather than complete words.

```
$ apropos whoam
ldapwhoami(1) - LDAP who am i? tool
whoami(1) - print effective userid
```

The apropos search has searched the whatis database for all references to the string whoam and returned a number of commands and functions that contain this string.

There are also some additional useful commands that can tell you about commands on your host. The info command, for example, sometimes provides more verbose explanation of a command's function and options; try info ls to read about the ls command in more detail.

Users and Groups

Linux is multiuser operating system. This means it allows multiple users to connect simultaneously via multiple command-line or GUI sessions. Linux controls access to the host and its resources via user and group accounts. Users are also created for particular systems components and used to run services; for example, if you install a mail server, a user called mail might also be created that is used with this service, or a user called lp (for line printer) may exist to control printer resources.

Linux also relies on *groups*, which are collections of like users. Users can be members of one or more groups and are usually placed in a group so they can access some kind of resource. For example, all the users who need to access the Accounts Payable system might be added to a group called accounts.

■**Tip** Your user and group information is primarily contained in two files: /etc/passwd holds your user information, and /etc/group holds your group information. We'll talk more about these files in Chapter 4.

Users and groups are important, and we're going to explain how they work and how to create them in Chapter 4. Conceptually, users and groups operate in much the same way as they do on a Windows host. Each user has an account that is usually secured with a password. When most general users are created, a home directory analogous to a Windows profile is also created. This home directory provides users with a place to store their data and is also the default location for many applications to store their user-specific configuration. Users also belong to groups, as they do on Windows, which provide them with access to additional resources or services.

Services and Processes

On a Windows host, a lot of background activities and server applications run as *services*. Services can be started and stopped and often have to be restarted when an application is reconfigured. These services are usually controlled via the Services manager available in the Control Panel. On Linux hosts, the concept of services also exists. Services, also called daemons, run many of the key functions on your host.

Like on a Windows host, each service or daemon is one or more processes running on your host. These processes have names; for example, the Secure Shell daemon we discussed earlier usually runs as a process called sshd. Other common daemons include master (the Postfix mail server), httpd (the Apache web server), and mysqld (the MySQL database server). Some of these processes may be running by default on your host together with a number of other processes that perform a variety of system and application functions.

In Listing 3-4, we've used the ps command with the -A flag (for all) to list all the processes currently running on our host.

Listing 3-4. *The ps Command*

```
$ ps -A
PID TTY          TIME CMD
    1 ?        00:00:07 init
    2 ?        00:00:10 migration/0
    3 ?        00:00:00 ksoftirqd/0
    4 ?        00:00:00 watchdog/0
    5 ?        00:00:03 migration/1
    6 ?        00:00:00 ksoftirqd/1
    7 ?        00:00:00 watchdog/1
    8 ?        00:00:00 events/0
    9 ?        00:00:00 events/1
   10 ?        00:00:00 khelper
   11 ?        00:00:00 kthread
....
```

In Listing 3-4, you can see a truncated list of the processes running on our host. This list was generated using the ps command with the -A (or all) option. Each process running on the host is listed in order of its Process ID (PID), represented in Listing 3-4 by the left-hand column. PIDs are used to control processes, and we'll use them when we look at starting and stopping processes in Chapter 5. The most important process on your host is called init. The init (or initialization) process is the base process on Linux hosts that spawns all other processes on a host. This master process always uses PID 1 and must be running for your host to be functional.

There is another useful command that can tell you which processes are running on your host and which are consuming the most CPU and memory. This command is called top, and we run it in Listing 3-5.

Listing 3-5. *The top Command*

```
$ top
```

The top command starts an interactive monitoring tool that updates every few seconds with the top running processes on your host. You can see a snapshot of the top command's output in Figure 3-6.

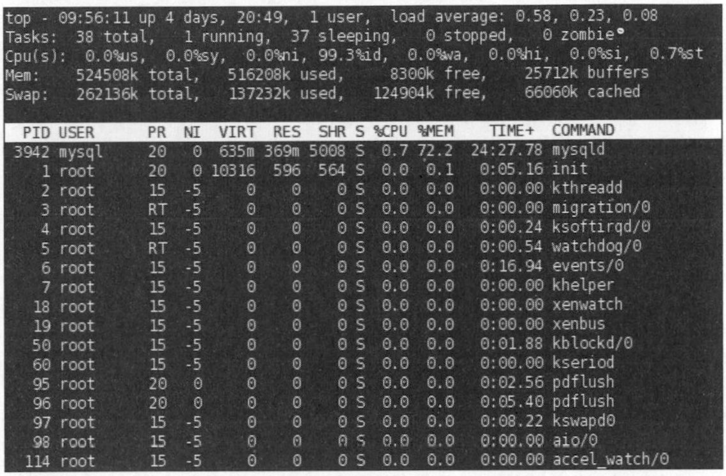

```
top - 09:56:11 up 4 days, 20:49,  1 user,  load average: 0.58, 0.23, 0.08
Tasks:  38 total,   1 running,  37 sleeping,   0 stopped,   0 zombie°
Cpu(s):  0.0%us,  0.0%sy,  0.0%ni, 99.3%id,  0.0%wa,  0.0%hi,  0.0%si,  0.7%st
Mem:    524508k total,   516208k used,     8300k free,    25712k buffers
Swap:   262136k total,   137232k used,   124904k free,    66060k cached

  PID USER      PR  NI  VIRT  RES  SHR S %CPU %MEM    TIME+  COMMAND
 3942 mysql     20   0  635m 369m 5008 S  0.7 72.2 24:27.78 mysqld
    1 root      20   0 10316  596  564 S  0.0  0.1  0:05.16 init
    2 root      15  -5     0    0    0 S  0.0  0.0  0:00.00 kthreadd
    3 root      RT  -5     0    0    0 S  0.0  0.0  0:00.00 migration/0
    4 root      15  -5     0    0    0 S  0.0  0.0  0:00.24 ksoftirqd/0
    5 root      RT  -5     0    0    0 S  0.0  0.0  0:00.54 watchdog/0
    6 root      15  -5     0    0    0 S  0.0  0.0  0:16.94 events/0
    7 root      15  -5     0    0    0 S  0.0  0.0  0:00.00 khelper
   18 root      15  -5     0    0    0 S  0.0  0.0  0:00.00 xenwatch
   19 root      15  -5     0    0    0 S  0.0  0.0  0:00.00 xenbus
   50 root      15  -5     0    0    0 S  0.0  0.0  0:01.88 kblockd/0
   60 root      15  -5     0    0    0 S  0.0  0.0  0:00.00 kseriod
   95 root      20   0     0    0    0 S  0.0  0.0  0:02.56 pdflush
   96 root      20   0     0    0    0 S  0.0  0.0  0:05.40 pdflush
   97 root      15  -5     0    0    0 S  0.0  0.0  0:08.22 kswapd0
   98 root      15  -5     0    0    0 S  0.0  0.0  0:00.00 aio/0
  114 root      15  -5     0    0    0 S  0.0  0.0  0:00.00 accel_watch/0
```

Figure 3-6. *The top process-monitoring command*

■**Note** Many of the processes whose name starts with k are not real processes, but kernel threads. These threads are a special kind of service that performs management tasks in the core of the operating system, the kernel. If your host runs the KDE GUI, some of these processes may also be KDE-related. You can tell them apart because kernel processes always run as the root user, while KDE processes rarely do, unless you log in to a KDE desktop as the root user.

Packages

Applications in the Microsoft Windows world are usually installed by running a binary application and following an installation process. Some applications also come with uninstallers that remove them if you no longer require them. In some cases, you may instead use the Add or Remove Programs tool in the Control Panel to add or remove applications.

In the Linux world, *package managers* are the equivalent of the Add or Remove Programs tool. A package manager contains a collection of prepackaged applications, for example, the Apache web server or the OpenOffice suite. These prepackaged applications are, not surprisingly, called *packages*. Applications bundled as packages contain the required binaries, supporting files, and often configuration files as well, and are ready to be run straight after being installed.

In Chapter 7, we're going to extensively cover two of the commonly used package management systems: RPM and Deb. These are used by distributions based on the Red Hat and Debian distributions, respectively. So Red Hat Enterprise Linux, CentOS, the Fedora Project, and SuSE are distributions that all use RPM. Distributions that use Deb include Ubuntu, Debian, and a number of others.

Files and File Systems

Now let's look at Linux files and the file system. We're going to start by using a command called pwd, or print working directory.

```
$ pwd
/home/jsmith
```

The pwd command allows you to orient yourself in the file system by identifying our working or current directory. From here you can navigate the file system; start by changing the directory to the root directory using the cd, or change directory, command, as you can see in Listing 3-6.

Listing 3-6. *Changing Directories*

```
$ cd /
/$
```

In Listing 3-6, we've moved from our current directory to /, which is called the *root directory*. The root directory is the base of the directory tree. The Linux file system is a single directory tree. This means that, unlike Windows, Linux has a single hierarchal directory structure. Instead of multiple drives, for example C:\ and D:\, with separate directory trees beneath them, all drives, partitions, and storage are located off the root, or /, directory.

How does this work? When you boot a Windows host, it detects attached drives and assigns them drive letters. In comparison, Linux drives and devices are *mounted* (this can occur automatically when you boot, or you can do it manually). These mounted drives and devices appear in the file system as subdirectories.

■**Note** We'll discuss more about storage and mounting devices in Chapter 8.

With the cd command, you can traverse to other directories and subdirectories. Linux calls the steps you take to traverse the file system a *path*. There are two types of paths—absolute and relative. The absolute path always starts with a slash symbol (/) representing the root directory and specifies the definitive location of the place you are describing; for example, /home/jsmith/ is an absolute path.

Relative paths allow you to specify a location relative to your current location or starting point. For example, the command

```
$ cd foobar
```

attempts to change from the current directory to a directory called foobar. If no such directory is present, the cd command fails.

There are also a couple of symbols that are often used with relative paths:

```
$ cd ..
```

The .. indicates that we wish to traverse up one level on the directory tree (if we're already at the top, we won't go anywhere at all).

We can also traverse in other ways through the directory tree using this mechanism, as you can see on the following line:

```
$ cd ../foo/bar
```

In this instance we have

1. Traversed up one directory level as indicated by the `..` notation

2. Changed into a directory called `foo` in the next level up

3. Then changed into a directory called `bar` under the `foo` directory

---

■**Note** If you're used to the Microsoft Windows command line, you may notice that the slash separating directories is a forward slash, or /, rather than a backslash, or \. This does take a little getting used to, but you'll soon be acclimatized!

We can also refer to relative objects in a directory using the following construct:

```
$ ./make
```

The addition of the `./` in front of the command executes the `make` command in our current directory.

Which directories you can traverse to depends on their permissions. Many directories only allow access to specific users and groups (the `root` user can go anywhere). If you try to change to a directory to which you don't have suitable permissions, you will get an error message:

```
$ cd /root
-bash: cd: /root: Permission denied
```

■**Note** We will talk about permissions in the "Permissions" section later in this chapter.

So now you know how to move around in your directory tree. But where is everything located on your host? Most Linux distributions adhere to a very similar directory structure. This is not to say all distributions are identical, but generally speaking, files and directories are located in a logical and consistent model. You can see the typical directory structure under the root directory in Table 3-1. Each entry has a brief description of each directory.

Table 3-1. *Linux Directory Structure*

Directory	Description
/bin/	User commands and binaries.
/boot/	Files used by the boot loader. (We talk about boot loaders in Chapter 5.)
/dev/	Device files.
/etc/	System configuration files.
/home/	User's home directories.
/lib/	Shared libraries and kernel modules.
/media/	Removable media is usually mounted here (see Chapter 8).
/mnt/	Temporary mounted file systems are usually mounted here (see Chapter 8).
/opt/	Add-on application software packages.
/proc/	Kernel and process status data is stored in here in text-file format.
/root/	The root user's home directory.
/sbin/	System binaries.
/srv/	Data for services provided by this host.
/tmp/	Directory for temporary files.
/usr/	User utilities, libraries, and applications.
/var/	Variable or transient files and data, for example logs, mail queues, and print jobs.

■**Note** Not every distribution will have every one of these directories (and others might have additional directories), but generally this list is accurate.

Let's look at some of the key directories under the root (/) directory that are listed in Table 3-1. The first, and one of the most important, is /etc/. The /etc/ directory, named for etcetera, is where most of the important configuration files on your host are located. You'll be frequently working with files located in this directory as you add applications and services to your hosts.

Next, the /home/ directory contains all of the home directories for users (except the root user—whose home directory is usually /root/). The /tmp directory is where you'll commonly find temporary files. In a similar vein is the /var directory, in which transitory data such as logs are stored. You'll often look at log files contained in the /var/log/ directory that have been created by applications or via the host's syslog (or system logger) daemon. These log files contain a wide variety of information about the status of your applications, daemons, and services.

■**Tip** Many distributions also try to standardize their directory structure in line with Linux Standard Base (LSB). LSB is an open standard that is an attempt to provide standards for the Linux operating system. You can find details on the LSB at http://www.linux-foundation.org/en/LSB.

Let's take a closer look at files and directories and how to work with them. Start by changing to the root, or /, directory:

```
$ cd /
```

Now you're at the root directory, and you want to see what is contained in that directory. To do this, you use the `ls`, or list directory, command, as you can see in Listing 3-7.

Listing 3-7. *Listing the Contents of a Directory*

```
$ ls
bin dev etc lib lost+found mnt proc root sys usr
boot home  lib64  media opt sbin srv tmp var
```

In Listing 3-7, you can see the `ls` command has returned a list of files and directories that are in the root directory. You'll see it looks pretty close to the list in Table 3-1.

By default, `ls` lists all files in a directory, but you can limit it to displaying a single file name or several file names by listing that file on the command line like so:

```
$ ls foobar
```

This command would display any file or directory called `foobar`. We could also use the wildcard or asterisk symbol to select files.

```
$ ls foo*
```

This would return any file called `foo` plus any files that started with `foo`, such as `foobar`, as well as the contents of any directories whose name starts with `foo`. Specifying the asterisk symbol alone lists all files and all directories and their contents.

■**Tip** You'll see a lot more of the * symbol, as it is used on Linux much like it is on Windows. It indicates a wildcard that is used to substitute for one or more characters; for example, you've just seen `foo*`, which means anything starting with `foo`. A single character is matched using the ? symbol; for example, specifying `?at` would match `cat`, `mat`, `bat`, etc. Collectively, this activity is called *globbing*, and you can read about its use in Linux shells at `http://www.faqs.org/docs/abs/HTML/globbingref.html`.

You can also list files in other directories by specifying the directory name:

```
$ ls /usr/local/bin
```

This would list all the files in the `/usr/local/bin` directory.

You don't see a lot of details about these files and directories in Listing 3-7, though. It only shows a list of names. To find out some more information about this list, you can add switches to the `ls` command, as you can see in Listing 3-8, to reveal more information.

Listing 3-8. *Getting More Information from* ls

```
$ ls -la
total 192
drwxr-xr-x  25 root  root   4096 2008-07-22 12:47 .
drwxr-xr-x  25 root  root   4096 2008-07-22 12:47 ..
-rw-r--r--   1 root  root      0 2008-07-15 20:47 .autofsck
drwxr-xr-x   2 root  root   4096 2008-05-18 04:11 bin
drwxr-xr-x   6 root  root   3072 2008-05-25 21:57 boot
drwxr-xr-x  14 root  root   4100 2008-07-19 12:26 dev
drwxr-xr-x 116 root  root  12288 2008-07-22 12:47 etc
drwxr-xr-x   7 smtpd smtpd  4096 2008-05-02 12:00 home
drwxr-xr-x  12 root  root   4096 2008-05-17 18:14 lib
drwxr-xr-x   8 root  root   4096 2008-06-06 10:19 lib64
drwx------   2 root  root  16384 2007-06-11 16:01 lost+found
drwxr-xr-x   2 root  root   4096 2007-06-11 16:14 media
drwxr-xr-x   4 root  root   4096 2007-06-12 11:28 mnt
...
```

In Listing 3-8, the l and a switches have been added to the ls command. The l switch, which is an abbreviation of long, uses a long listing format, which as you can see shows a lot more information. The a switch tells ls to list all files and directories, even hidden ones.

Tip Hidden files are prefixed with a full stop or period (for example, the .autofsck file in Listing 3-8) and are often used to hold configuration and history information or as temporary files.

You can see a full list of the available switches for the ls command by reading the command's man page—just enter man ls.

So what does the long listing format tell you about your files and directories? In Listing 3-8, each item has a small collection of information returned about it. In Listing 3-9, you can see a subset of that listing showing one file and one directory, which we're going to examine in more detail.

Listing 3-9. *File Listing Subset*

```
-rw-r--r--  1 root  root     0 2008-07-15 20:47 .autofsck
drwxr-xr-x  2 root  root  4096 2008-05-18 04:11 bin
```

Each line of the listing contains seven pieces of information about each object:

- Unix file type
- Permissions
- Number of hard links
- User and group ownership

- Size

- Time and date

- Name

Some of the information contained in the listing also introduces some key Linux concepts, such as permissions and users, groups, and ownership. We're going to take advantage of this introduction to not only explain each item, but also explore some of the broader concepts they represent.

File Types and Permissions

The file type and permissions are contained in the first ten characters, the section resembling -rw-r--r--. This potentially intimidating collection of characters is actually quite simple to decipher: the first character describes the type of file, and the next nine characters describe the permissions of the file.

File Types

Almost everything on the Linux file system can be generally described as a file. The first character of the listing tells us exactly what sort of file. A dash (-) here indicates a regular file that might contain data or text, or be a binary executable. A d indicates a directory, which is essentially a file that lists other files. An l indicates a symbolic link. Symbolic links allow you to make files and directories visible in multiple locations in the file system. They are much like the shortcuts used in Microsoft Windows.

Table 3-2 lists the file types available.

Table 3-2. *File Types*

Type	Description
-	File
d	Directory
l	Link
c	Character devices
b	Block devices
s	Socket
p	Named pipe

We'll cover the other types here briefly. Most of the types you won't regularly need, but they will appear occasionally in later chapters. The b and c file types are used for different types of input and output devices (if you look in the /dev directory, you will see examples of these device files). Devices allow the operating system to interact with particular hardware devices; for example, many distributions will have a device called /dev/dvd that represents a DVD drive attached to the host.

■**Tip** You'll learn more about devices in Chapter 8 when we show you how to load a CD or DVD on your host.

Lastly, sockets and named pipes are files that allow interprocess communications of varying types. They allow processes to communicate with each other. You'll see some sockets and named pipes later in the book.

Permissions

The next nine characters detail the access permissions assigned to the file or directory. On Linux, permissions are used to determine what access users and groups have to a file. Controlling your permissions and access to files and applications is critical for security on your Linux host, and frequently in this book we'll use permissions to provide the appropriate access to files. Thus it is important that you understand how permissions work and how to change them.

There are three commonly assigned types of permissions for files:

- Read, indicated by the letter r
- Write, indicated by the letter w
- Execute, indicated by the letter x

■**Note** There are two other types of permissions, sticky and setuid/setgid permissions, represented by t or s characters, respectively. We discuss these in the sidebar "Setuid, Setgid, and Sticky Permissions" later in this chapter.

Read permissions allow a file to be read or viewed but not edited. If it is set on a directory, the names of the files in the directory can be read, but other details, like their permissions and size, are not visible. Write permissions allow you to make changes or write to a file. If the write permission is set on a directory, you are able to create, delete, and rename files in that directory. Execute permissions allow you to run a file; for example, all binary files and commands (binary files are similar to Windows executables) must be marked executable to allow you to run them. If this permission is set on a directory, you are able to traverse the directory, for example, by using the cd command to access a subdirectory. The combination of the read and execute permissions set on a directory thus allows you to both traverse the directory and view the details of its contents.

Each file on your host has three classes of permissions:

- User
- Group
- Other (everyone else)

Each class represents a different category of access to the file. The User class describes the permissions of the user who owns the file. These are the first three characters in our listing. The Group class describes the permissions of the group that owns the file. These are the second set of three characters in our listing.

■**Note** Groups in Linux are collections of users. Groups allow like users to be collected together for the purpose of allowing access to applications and services; for example, all the users in the Accounting department can belong to the same group to allow them access to your Accounts Payable application. We'll talk about groups in Chapter 4.

Lastly, the Other class describes the permissions that all others have to the file. These are the final set of three characters in the listing.

Figure 3-7 describes these classes and their positions.

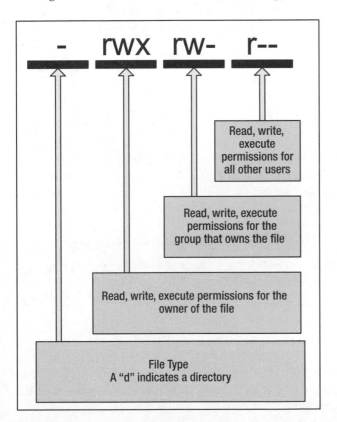

Figure 3-7. *File permission breakdown*

■**Note** A dash in any position means that particular permission is not set at all.

You can see a single file in Listing 3-10 whose permissions we're going to examine in more detail, and then you'll learn how to make some changes to those permissions.

Listing 3-10. *Permissions*

```
-rw-r--r--  1 root  root      0 2008-07-15 20:47 myfile
```

In Listing 3-10, we have a file, as indicated by the dash (-) at the beginning of the listing. The file is owned by the root user and root group. The first three permissions are rw-, which indicates the root user can read and write the file, but the dash means execute permissions are not set, and the file can't be executed by the user. The next three permissions, r--, indicate that anyone who belongs to the root group can read the file but can do nothing else to it. Lastly, we have r-- for the last three permissions, which tell us what permissions the Other class has. In this case, others can read the file but cannot write to it or execute it.

Now you've seen what permissions look like, but how do you go about changing them? Permissions are changed using the chmod (change file mode bits) command. The key to changing permissions is that only the user who owns the file or the root user can change a file's permissions. So in Listing 3-10, only the root user could change the permissions of the myfile file.

The chmod command has a simple syntax. In Listing 3-11, you can see some permissions being changed.

Listing 3-11. *Changing Permissions*

```
# chmod u+x myfile
# chmod u-x,og+w myfile
# chmod 654 myfile
```

In Listing 3-11, we've changed the myfile file's permissions three times. Permission changes are performed by specifying the class, the action you want to perform, the permission itself, and then the file you want to change. In our first example, you can see u+x. This translates to adding the execute permission to the User class.

■Note The execute permission is usually set only on files that are executable in nature such as scripts and binaries (a.k.a. applications or programs) and on directories.

After our update, the permissions on our file would now look like this:

```
-rwxr--r--  1 root  root      0 2008-07-15 20:47 myfile
```

You can see the addition of the x to the User class. So how did chmod know to do that? Well, the u in our change represents the User class. With chmod, each class is abbreviated to a single letter:

- u: User
- g: Group
- o: Other or everyone
- a: All

After the class, you specify the action you'd like to take on the class. In the first line in Listing 3-11, the + sign represents adding a permission. You can specify the - sign to remove permissions from a class or the = sign to set absolute permissions on the class. Lastly, you specify the permission to the action, in this case x.

You can also specify multiple permission changes in a single command, as you can see in the second line of Listing 3-11. In this second line, we have the change u-x,go+w. This would remove the x, or execute, permission from the User class and add the w, or write, permission to both the Group and Other classes. You can see we've separated each permission change with a comma and that we can list multiple classes to act upon. (You can also list multiple permissions; for example, u+rw would add the read and write permissions to the User class.)

Thus the second line in Listing 3-11 would leave our file permissions as

```
-rw-rw-rw-   1 root  root      0 2008-07-15 20:47 myfile
```

With chmod, you can also use the a class abbreviation, which indicates an action should be applied to all classes; for example, a+r would add read permissions to all classes: User, Group, and Other.

We can also apply the permissions of one class to another class by using the = symbol:

```
# chmod u=g myfile
```

On the previous line, we've set the User class permissions to be the same as the Group class permissions.

You can also set permissions for multiple files by listing each file separated by space like so:

```
# chmod u+r file1 file2 file3
```

As with the ls command, you can also reference files in other locations like so:

```
# chmod u+x /usr/local/bin/foobar
```

The previous line adds the execute permission to the User class for the foobar file located in the /usr/local/bin directory.

You can also use the asterisk symbol to specify all files and add the -R switch to recurse into lower directories like so:

```
# chmod -R u+x /usr/local/bin/*
```

The chmod command on the previous line would add the execute permission to the User class to every file in the /usr/local/bin directory.

The last line in Listing 3-11 is a little different. Instead of classes and permissions, we've specified a number, 654. This number is called *octal notation*. Each digit represents one of the three classes: User, Group, and Other. Additionally, each digit is the sum of the permissions assigned to that class. In Table 3-3, you can see the values assigned to each permission type.

Table 3-3. *Octal Permission Values*

Permission	Value	Description
r	4	Read
w	2	Write
x	1	Execute

Each permission value is added together, resulting in a number ranging from 1 and 7 for each class. So the value of 654 in Listing 3-11 would represent these permissions:

```
-rw-r-xr-- 1 root root 0 2008-08-14 22:37 myfile
```

The first value, 6, equates to assigning the User class the read permission with a value of 4 plus the write permission with a value of 2. The second value, 5, assigns the Group class the read permission with a value of 4 and the execute permission with a value of 1. The last value, 4, assigns only the read permission to the Other class. To make this clearer, you can see a list of the possible values from 0 to 7 in Table 3-4.

Table 3-4. *The Octal Values*

Octal	Permissions	Description
0	---	None
1	--x	Execute
2	-w-	Write
3	-wx	Write and execute
4	r--	Read
5	r-x	Read and execute
6	rw-	Read and write
7	rwx	Read, write, and execute

In Table 3-5, you can see some commonly used octal numbers and the corresponding permissions they represent.

Table 3-5. *Octal Permissions*

Octal Numbers	Permissions
600	rw-r--r--
644	rw-r--r--
664	rw-rw-r--
666	rw-rw-rw-
755	rwxr-xr-x
777	rwxrwxrwx

■**Tip** The chmod command has some additional syntax for changing permissions, and you can read about them in the command's man page.

Lastly, there is an important concept called *umask* that you need to also understand to fully comprehend how permissions work. The umask dictates the default set of permissions assigned to a file when it is created. By default, without a umask set, files are created with permissions of 0666 (or read and write permissions for the owner, group, and others are all set), and directories are created with permissions of 0777 (or read, write, and execute for the owner, group, and others). You can use the umask command to modify these default permissions. Let's look at an example:

```
# umask 0022
```

Here we've specified a umask of 0022. This looks familiar, doesn't it? Yes, it's a type of octal notation; in this case, it indicates what's not being granted. So here we would take the default permissions, for example 0666, and subtract the 0022 value, leaving us with permissions of 0644. With a umask of 0022, a new file would be created with read and write permissions for the owner of the file and read permissions for the group and others. Newly created directories would have permissions of 0755. Another commonly used umask is 0002, which results in default permissions of 0664 for files and 775 for directories. This allows write access for the group also, and this umask is often used for files located in shared directories or file shares.

On most hosts, your umask is set automatically by a setting in your shell. For Bash shells, you can usually find the global umask in the /etc/bashrc file, but you can also override it on a per-user basis using the umask command.

■**Tip** The umask command can also set umasks using alternative syntax. We've just described the simplest and easiest. You can find more details in the umask man page.

SETUID, SETGID, AND STICKY PERMISSIONS

There are two additional types of permissions, setuid/setgid and sticky, that are also important to understand.

The setuid and setgid permissions allow a user to run a command as if he were the user or group that owned the command. So why might this be needed? Well, this allows users to execute specific tasks which they would normally be restricted from doing.

A good example of this is the passwd command. The passwd command allows a user to change her password. To do this, the command needs to write to the password file, a file that has restricted access. By adding the setuid permission, a user can execute the passwd command and run it as if she were the root user, hence allowing her to change her password.

You can recognize setuid and setgid permissions by the use of an s or S in the listing of permissions. For example, the permissions of the passwd command are

```
-rwsr-xr-x 1 root root 25708 2007-09-25 17:32 /usr/bin/passwd
```

You can see the s in the execute position of the User class, which indicates that the passwd command has the setuid permission set.

On most distributions, setuid/setgid permissions are used sparely to allow this sort of access. They are used sparely because you generally don't want one user be able to run applications as another user or to have particular elevated privileges (another way to do this is through the su and sudo commands, which we're going to describe further in Chapter 4). As they could also potentially be abused and represent a security exposure, they should not be used indiscriminately. In this book, you may see one or two applications that use setuid/setgid permissions.

Sticky permissions are slightly different and are used on directories (they have no effect on files). When the sticky bit is set on a directory, files in that directory can be deleted only by the user who owns them or the root user, irrespective of any other permissions set on the directory. This allows the creation of public directories where every user can create files but only delete their own files. You can recognize a directory with sticky permissions from the t in the execute position of the Other class. Most frequently it is set on the /tmp directory:

```
drwxrwxrwt  4 root root  4096 2008-08-15 03:10 tmp
```

In octal notation, setuid/setgid and sticky permissions are represented by a fourth digit at the front of the notation, for example, 6755. Like other permissions, each special permission also has a numeric value: 4 for setuid, 2 for setgid, and 1 for sticky. So to set the sticky bit on a directory, you'd use an octal notation like 1755. If no setuid/setgid or sticky permissions are being set, this prefixed digit is 0 like so:

```
# chmod 0644 /etc/grub.conf
```

Links

Let's take another look at the example from Listing 3-9:

```
-rw-r--r--  1 root  root     0 2008-07-15 20:47 .autofsck
drwxr-xr-x  2 root  root  4096 2008-05-18 04:11 bin
```

In our listing, after our file type and permissions is the number of hard links to the file. *Hard links* are references that connect your file to the physical data on a storage volume. There can be multiple links to a particular piece of data. However, hard links are different from the symbolic links we introduced earlier (indicated by a file type of l), although both linkages are created with the same command, ln. We'll talk about the ln command later in this chapter in the section "Linking Files."

Users, Groups, and Ownership

Next in our listing is the ownership of the file. Each object is owned by a user and a group; in Listing 3-9, the objects are owned by the root user and root group. We briefly discussed user and group ownership when we looked at permissions. We explained that only the user who owns a file could change its permissions, and that groups were collections of users. Groups are generally used to allow access to resources; for example, all users who need to access a printer or a file share might belong to groups that provide access to these resources. As we discussed earlier in this chapter, on Linux hosts a user must belong to at least one group, known as the *primary group*, but can also belong to one or more additional groups, called *supplementary groups*.

You can change the user and group ownership of a file using the chown command. Only the root user has authority to change the user ownership of a file (although you can assume this authority using the sudo command we discussed earlier in the chapter and will cover in more detail in Chapter 4).

In Listing 3-12, we show some examples of how to use the chown command to change user and group ownership.

Listing 3-12. *Changing Ownership*

```
# chown jsmith myfile
# chown jsmith:admin myfile
# chown -R jsmith:admin /home/jsmith/*
```

In Listing 3-12, we've got three chown commands. The first command changes the user who owns the myfile file to jsmith. The second command changes the ownership of the file's user and group, the user to jsmith and the group to admin, the owner and group being separated by a colon, :. The third and last command uses the -R switch to enable recursion. The command would change the owner of every file and directory in the /home/jsmith directory to jsmith and the group to admin.

Note Also available is the chgrp command. It allows an unprivileged user to change the group of a file. The user can only change the group ownership to a group of which that user is a member. You use it like chgrp *groupname file*.

Size and Space

Next in our listing you see the size of the object on the disk. The size of the file is listed in bytes (a thousand bytes is a kilobyte, or K). We can also display sizes in a more human-readable format by adding the -h switch like so:

```
$ ls -lh
-rw-rw-r-- 1 jsmith jsmith  51K 2008-08-17 23:47 myfile
```

On the previous line, you can see that the myfile file is 51 kilobytes in size.

In a listing, the size next to the directory is not its total size but rather the size of the directory's metadata. To get the total size of all files in a directory, you can use the du, or disk usage, command. Specify (or change to) the directory you want to find the total size of and run the command with the -s and -h switches. The -s switch summarizes the total, and the -h switch displays the size in a human-readable form.

```
$ du -sh /usr/local/bin
4.7M    /usr/local/bin
```

The du tool has a number of additional switches and options that you can see by reviewing its man page.

In addition to the size of files and directories, you can also see the total disk space used and free on your host using another command, df. This command displays all of your disks and storage devices and the free space present on them. You can see the df command in Listing 3-13.

Listing 3-13. *Displaying Disk Space*

```
$ df -h
Filesystem                           Size  Used  Avail  Use%  Mounted on
/dev/mapper/VolGroup00-LogVol01      178G  11G   159G   6%    /
/dev/sda1                            99M   37M   58M    39%   /boot
tmpfs                                910M  0     910M   0%    /dev/shm
```

We've executed the command and added the -h switch, which returns human-readable sizes. It shows our current file systems and their used and free space, as well as percentage used. There are additional options you can use with the df command, and you can review these in the command's man page. We'll revisit the df and du commands in Chapter 8.

Date and Time

The penultimate and ultimate items in our listing are the date and time the file was last modified (known as *mtime*) and the name of the file or directory. Linux also tracks the last time a file was accessed (called *atime*) and when it was created (called *ctime*). You can display the last accessed time for a file by listing it with the -u switch like so:

```
$ ls -lu
```

You can list creation dates by using the -c switch like so:

```
$ ls -lc
```

■**Note** We will revisit atime in Chapter 17.

If you want to know the actual time and date on the current host, you can use the useful and powerful date command. Using date on the command line without any options will return the current time and date like so:

```
$ date
Tue Aug 19 13:01:20 EST 2008
```

You can also add switches to the date command to format the output into different date or time formats; for example, to display Unix epoch time (the number of seconds since January 1, 1970), you would execute the date command like so:

```
$ date +%s
1219116319
```

Here we've used the + symbol to add a format and then specified the format, in this case %s, to display epoch time. You can see additional formats in the date command's man page. You can also use the date command to set the time. Type **date** and then specify the required date and time in the format **MMDDhhmm[[CC]YY]**. You can find out more about Unix epoch time at http://en.wikipedia.org/wiki/Unix_time.

■**Note** This is just one way to set the time, and we'll discuss other more effective methods such as NTP in Chapter 9.

Working with Files

So in the course of exploring our simple file listing, we've covered a lot of concepts, introduced you to some Linux commands, and taught you how to perform a few key administrative tasks. Leading on from these tasks, we're going to finish this chapter by covering how to view, edit, search, copy, move, and delete files. You'll need to know how to handle all these tasks in order to administer your Linux host.

Reading Files

The first thing you're going to learn is how to read files. Many files on Linux hosts, especially configuration files, are text-based and can be read using some simple command-line tools.

■**Note** Always remember that in order to read a file, you must have read permissions to that file. This means you need to own it or belong to a group that has read permissions to the file, or the file has read permission set for the Other class.

The first of these tools is cat. The cat command is so named because it "concatenates and prints files." In Listing 3-14, you can see the use of the cat command on a text file.

Listing 3-14. *Using the cat Command*

```
$ cat /etc/hosts
# Do not remove the following line, or various programs
# that require network functionality will fail.
127.0.0.1               localhost.localdomain localhost localhost
::1            localhost6.localdomain6 localhost6
```

In Listing 3-14, we've outputted the /etc/hosts file to the screen. The /etc/hosts file contains the host entries for our Linux host (like the \WINDOWS\System32\services\etc\hosts file under Windows) that match hostnames to IP addresses. But the cat command is a pretty simple tool and just outputs the text directly. If the file is very large, the text will keep outputting and scrolling down the screen, meaning if you wanted to see something at the start of the file, you'd need to scroll back.

■**Tip** You can scroll a virtual console up and down via the Shift+Page Up and Shift+Page Down key combinations.

To overcome this issue, we're going to look at another command called `less`.

■**Note** You can try the `cat` command on the `/etc/passwd` and `/etc/group` files to see a full list of the users and groups on your host.

The `less` command allows you to scroll through files, both backward and forward, a screen at a time. Each time a page is displayed, you will be prompted as to how you'd like to proceed. We run `less` by specifying the name of the file like so:

```
$ less /etc/services
```

From inside the `less` interface, you can scroll through the file. To go to the next page, you use the spacebar, and to advance one line at a time, you use the Enter key. To scroll backward, you can use the B key. You can also scroll using the arrow keys, and to quit the `less` command, you use the Q key.

■**Note** There are additional ways to navigate files using `less` that you can see by reviewing the command's `man` page.

In addition to navigating through files, it is also possible to search a file or files for specific information. To do this, we can make use of the very powerful `grep` command. The `grep` command allows you to search through a file or files for a string or pattern (using regular expressions) and return the results of that search.

■**Note** The word *grep* has become a commonly used term in IT for searching, much like the term *google* has for using an online search engine. In 2003, the Oxford English Dictionary added the word *grep* as both a noun and a verb (e.g., "John grep'ed his mailbox to find the e-mail").

In Listing 3-15, you can see a very simple grep search for the string localhost in the file /etc/hosts.

Listing 3-15. *Introducing grep*

```
$ grep localhost /etc/hosts
127.0.0.1               localhost.localdomain localhost localhost
::1             localhost6.localdomain6 localhost6
```

To use grep, you specify the string you're searching for, in this case localhost (grep is case sensitive, so it will only find this lowercase string), and then the name of the file you're searching in.

■**Note** You can make grep case insensitive by adding the -i switch to the command.

By default, grep returns those lines in the file that contain the string we're searching for. You can also search for more than one file by using the asterisk symbol, as we have demonstrated for other commands earlier in this chapter, for example:

```
$ grep localhost /etc/host*
$ grep localhost /etc/*
```

The first command would search all files starting with host* in the /etc/ directory, and the second would search all files in the /etc/ directory. Both searches are for the string localhost.

You can also recursively search down into lower directories by adding the -r switch like so:

```
$ grep -r localhost /etc
```

■**Tip** On Ubuntu and Debian hosts, the rgrep command automatically recurses into directories.

You can also specify more complicated search terms, for example, multiple words, like so:

```
$ grep "local host" /etc/hosts
```

You can see we've specified the words *local* and *host* with a space between them. In order to tell grep these words are grouped together and have them parsed correctly, we need to enclose them in quotation marks. The quotation marks are used often on the command for a number of commands to protect input from being inappropriately parsed. In this case, we're searching for the exact string "local host", and grep has returned no results because the string is not present in the /etc/hosts file.

The grep command is capable of much more than these simple examples. You can use grep to do complex regular expression searches in files, for example:

```
$ grep 'J[oO][bB]' *
```

This would find the strings JOB, Job, JOb, or JoB in all files in the current directory (remember, grep is case sensitive by default, so our regular expression has explicitly specified upper- and lowercase variations). Regular expressions allow you to do some very powerful searching across your host.

Let's look at some other useful regular expression searches using grep.

```
$ grep 'job$' *
```

In the previous line, we've searched all files in the current directory for strings ending in job. The $ symbol tells grep to search for the text at the end of strings.

You can use the ^ symbol to in turn search for strings starting with a particular string like so:

```
$ grep '^job' *
```

This would return any string starting with job. There are a myriad of other regular expressions that you'll find useful for employing frequently.

■**Note** Regular expressions, or regexes, are a formal language used to identify strings of text; for example, a regular expression might identify all the references to the string job in a file. A variety of very similar regular expression languages are used by tools like grep and by programming languages, for example, Perl. The syntax of most regular expression languages is very similar, but occasionally they have subtle differences. You can read about regular expressions further at http://en.wikipedia.org/wiki/Regular_expression. We also recommend picking up a book such as *Mastering Regular Expressions* by Jeffrey Friedl (O'Reilly, 2006) to help you learn about regular expressions.

Searching for Files

We've shown you how you can read a file, but what if you need to find the location of a file? A number of commands and tools on a Linux host allow you to find files in much the same way as the Windows Search function works. In Figure 3-8, you can see the Gnome search function.

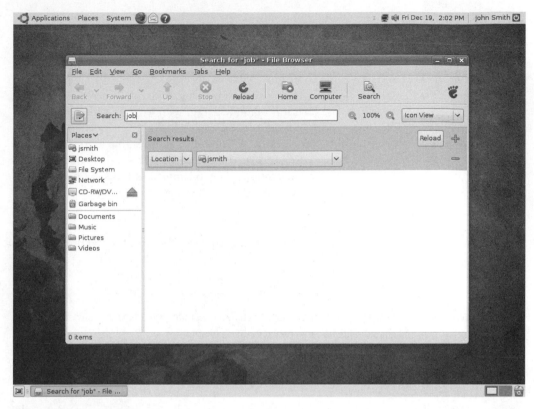

Figure 3-8. *Gnome search function*

On the command line, you can also search for files using the find command. Let's use the find command to search for a file called myfile in the /home directory:

```
$ find /home/ -type f -iname myfile*
```

The find command is very simple to use. First you specify where you are searching, in this case in the /home/ directory. You can also specify / for the root (and thus search the whole directory tree), or any other location that you can access.

■**Note** If you don't have permission to search a particular directory, you'll get an error message indicating that your search has been denied.

Next, we've specified two options, -type and -iname. The first option, -type, specifies the type of file we are searching for; in this case, a normal file is represented by f. You can also specify d for directories or s for sockets, for example (see the man page for all the possible types you can search for). The -iname option searches for a case-insensitive pattern, in this case, all files starting with myfile. These options are just a very small selection of the possible search options; you can also search by owner, group, permissions, date and time of creation or modification, and size, among others. The find command will then search the specified location and return a list of files that match the search criteria.

You could also use the find command to locate files and directories that aren't owned by any user or group. These often exist if a user or group has been deleted and the associated files not reassigned or removed with that user or group. We'll talk more about this in Chapter 4. Using the following find command, you can list all files in this state:

```
# find / -nouser -o -nogroup
```

This command, run as root, will search the whole directory tree for any files that don't belong to a valid user or group.

■Tip There are some other search-related commands you might want to look at, including locate, whereis, and which. You should read their man pages for more information.

Copying Files

In addition to viewing files, one of the most common actions you'll need to take while administering your host is to copy a file. The first thing to understand about copying files is that, like reading files, you need to have appropriate permissions in order to copy. To copy a file, you will need two permissions: read permissions on the file you are copying and write permissions on the destination you are copying to.

To copy a file, use the cp command (short for copy). In Listing 3-16, you can see a simple cp command.

Listing 3-16. *Copying Files*

```
$ cp /home/jsmith/myfile /home/jsmith/yourfile
```

In Listing 3-16, we've copied the file /home/jsmith/myfile to /home/jsmith/yourfile. You need to be a little bit careful with the cp command. By default, the cp command will copy over existing files without prompting you. This can be bad if you already have a file with the same name as the one you are copying to. You can change this behavior by adding the -i switch. The -i switch enables interactive mode, where you are prompted with a yes or no question if the file you are copying to already exists. You answer y to overwrite or n to abort the copy.

■**Note** On Red Hat, Fedora, and CentOS, the -i switch for the cp, mv, and rm commands is automatically set on by aliasing each command; for example, cp -i is aliased to cp. You can do this on other distributions using the alias command; see http://www.ss64.com/bash/alias.html for more details.

If we didn't have permission to read the file, we'd get an error like this:

```
cp: cannot open `/home/jsmith/myfile' for reading: Permission denied
```

We'd get a similar error if we cannot write to the target destination:

```
cp: cannot stat `/home/jsmith/yourfile': Permission denied
```

You can also do a few more things with cp. You can copy multiple files, using the asterisk symbol as follows:

```
$ cp /home/jsmith/* /home/jsmith/backup
```

The target on the previous line, /home/jsmith/backup, has to be a directory, and we're copying all files in the /home/jsmith directory to this directory.

You can also select a subset of files:

```
$ cp -i /home/jsmith/*.c ./
```

On the previous line, we've copied all the files with a suffix of .c to the current directory (using the ./ shortcut). We've also added the -i switch to make sure we're prompted if a file already exists.

You can also copy directories and their contents using cp by adding the -r switch.

```
$ cp -r /home/jsmith /backup
```

The previous line copies the /home/jsmith directory and all files and directories beneath it to the /backup directory.

■**Caution** When using the -r switch, be careful to not use the *.* wildcard like you might on Windows. When used on Linux, the .. directory will also be copied recursively, which probably is not your intent!

Lastly, when copying files using the cp command, some items about the file, such as dates, times, and permissions, can be changed or updated. If you want to preserve the original values on the copy, you can use the -p switch.

```
$ cp -p /home/jsmith/myfile /home/jsmith/yourfile
```

WORKING WITH DIRECTORIES

In addition to files, you can also manipulate directories. To create a directory, use the `mkdir` command. You must have write permissions to the location you're creating the directory in. If you want to copy directories and recursively copy their contents, you can do this with the `cp` command by adding the `-r` switch.

You can also move directories using the `mv` command in the same way as you can with files.

Lastly, if you want to delete a directory, use the `rmdir` command. The `rmdir` command will only remove empty directories (i.e., directories with no files in them).

The `cat` command we examined earlier can also be used to copy files using a command-line function called *redirection*.

```
$ cat /home/jsmith/myfile > /home/jsmith/yourfile
```

The use of the > symbol sends the output from one command to the command or action on the other side of the > symbol. In this case, the output of the `cat` command is redirected into a file called `yourfile`. If this file doesn't exist, it will be created. If it does exist, its content will be overwritten.

■**Caution** Be careful when using redirection, as your target file will be overwritten without warning.

You can also append to files using the same mechanism:

```
$ cat /home/jsmith/myfile >> /home/jsmith/yourfile
```

Using the >> syntax will append the output from the `cat` of `myfile` to the end of `yourfile`. If `yourfile` does not exist, it will be created.

■**Tip** Redirection can be used by many other commands as well to direct output from one command to another. It is also closely linked to another Bash capability called *piping* (see the sidebar "Piping and Other Bash Tips and Tricks").

PIPING AND OTHER BASH TIPS AND TRICKS

You've had a quick look at the Bash command line and some of the things you can do with it. This includes using redirection with the > or >> symbols to redirect output from one command to another. This concept can be extended using the |, or pipe, symbol. Piping passes the output of a command to another command, for example:

```
$ cat /etc/passwd | grep ataylor
```

In the previous line we've outputted the contents of the /etc/passwd file and then piped the result to the grep command to search for the term ataylor. This would output any line or lines containing the term ataylor. You can pretty much do this with any command that accepts input on the command line. Some useful commands that could be used with piping are sort (sorts input in a variety of ways), uniq (generates a unique list), and wc (counts lines, words, etc.). You can read about these commands in their man pages.

You can also take redirection a step further and redirect multiple times or use piping and redirection together. Let's look at an example:

```
$ cat *.txt | sort | uniq > text
```

In this example we've asked the host to output all files with a suffix of .txt, sort them alphabetically, delete duplicate lines (using the uniq command), and then output the result to a file called text (which would be created if not present and overwritten if present).

You can also redirect input as well as output:

```
$ grep accounts < /etc/group > matched_accounts
```

In the previous example, we've directed the file /etc/group into the grep command using the < symbol. We've then told grep to search for the term accounts and used the > symbol to direct the output of this command into a file called matched_accounts.

Another useful trick is the ability to run multiple commands on a single command line by separating each with a semicolon:

```
$ ./configure; make; make test
```

This command line would run the configure script in the current directory and then the make and the make test commands. The commands would run in sequence, one after the other.

These are just some very simple examples of the power of the Bash command line and redirection and piping. A lot more Bash capabilities are revealed by reviewing Bash's man page, man bash, or having a look at one of the many Bash tutorials online such as http://www.hypexr.org/bash_tutorial.php and http://tldp.org/LDP/Bash-Beginners-Guide/html/, or checking out the Bash reference manual at http://www.faqs.org/docs/bashman/bashref.html.

Moving and Renaming Files

Moving files around in Linux is pretty straightforward. Using the mv command, you can move a file or directory from one location to another. In order to move a file, you must have write permissions to the file and write permissions to the location you want to move it to.

Listing 3-17 demonstrates how to move a file.

Listing 3-17. *Moving Files*

```
$ mv -i ~/myfile /home/bjones/yourfile
```

The command in Listing 3-17 moves a file called `myfile` from the home directory to `/home/bjones` and renames it to `yourfile`. The `-i` option again ensures we get prompted if the target file already exists. You can also rename files in place with the `mv` command:

```
$ mv -i ~/myfile ~/mynewfile
```

You can do the same for directories.

Deleting Files

Use the `rm` (remove) command to delete files. As with any host, deleting files should be done carefully and with thought. On Linux, however, unlike Windows, there isn't a quick and easy way to undelete files, so you need to be careful and take some precautions before you delete files. The first precaution is the use of the `-i` switch with the `rm` command. The `-i` switch enables interactive mode, which prompts you each time a file is deleted. You have to respond with a y or Y to delete the file or anything else to abort, as you can see in Listing 3-18.

Listing 3-18. *The* `rm` *-i Switch*

```
$ rm -i /home/jsmith/myfile
rm: remove regular file `/home/jsmith/myfile'? n
```

■**Tip** Many distributions alias the `rm` command to `rm -i` to force deletion checking. You can enter the command `alias` to see a list of all the current aliases on your host. You can create your own aliases too. For instructions, check the `alias` command's `man` page.

You can also delete directories and their contents recursively with the `-r` switch like so:

```
$ rm -r /home/jsmith/backup
```

This would delete the `/home/jsmith/backup` directory and all its contents.
    You can also override the `-i` switch using the `-f`, or force, switch like so:

```
$ rm -fr /home/jsmith/backup
```

This will also delete the backup directory and all its contents, but you will not be prompted to confirm the deletions. Be careful of using this switch and always be cognizant of where you are in the directory tree when you execute the command—the results of an inappropriate use of this command could be devastating!

■**Caution** Unlike Windows with its Recycle Bin, deleting files on Linux tends to be fairly permanent unless you have backups. Some methods are available to recover files, however, and you can read about them at `http://recover.sourceforge.net/unix/`. But none of these methods are recommended. You should always delete files with extreme care, and you should make sure you have an appropriate backup. This is particularly important when editing configuration files. Always back up files before you edit, move, or delete them.

Linking Files

On Linux hosts, you can also create links to files. Links can be used like Windows shortcuts but come in two forms—hard links and soft, or symbolic, links. Hard links are not like Windows shortcuts. They are actual references to the physical file. If you delete all hard links to a file, the file they reference is also deleted.

■Note Hard links can hence only be created on the physical partition or hard drive; you can't link to a file located on another drive or partition.

Soft, or symbolic, links are more like Windows shortcuts: if they are deleted, the original file remains and only the link is removed.

You create links with the `ln` command. Hard links are created by default, and soft links are created by adding the `-s` switch. There are a few ways the `ln` command can be used, but the simplest is to create a link to a target file like so:

```
$ ln -s /home/jsmith/myfile
```

The previous line would create a symbolic link called `myfile` to the `/home/jsmith/myfile` file. You can see other options you can use with the `ln` command by reviewing its `man` page.

Editing Files

Linux provides a wide variety of editing tools for files, including both GUI and command-line tools. In the GUI, you can find editors like `kate` or the simpler `gedit`. These are straightforward editors, but they are not word processors—much like Windows Notepad. Also, there are tools that allow you to edit files from the command line, like the popular `vim`, `nano`, `joe`, or bizarrely popular `emacs`.

We're going to start by taking a quick look at `vim`, which is a text editor that is an enhancement of an older Unix editor called `vi`. To edit a file, you run the `vim` command and specify the name of the file to edit.

```
$ vim ~/newfile
```

■Tip Some distributions also alias the `vim` command to `vi` to make it easier for people who are used to the older name.

This opens a file called `newfile` in your home directory. To insert some text into the file, type **i**, which is short for insert. You will see the word `-- INSERT --` appear at the bottom of the screen. This means you're in insert mode, which allows you to add to the file. You can now type in the file. Let's type in **hello jsmith**. You can also use the arrow keys to move around on the line and through the file. The Enter key can be used to add lines to the file.

> **Tip** You can use the `touch` command to create empty files. Simply enter `touch` and the file name you want to create to create an empty file, for example, `touch /home/jsmith/newfile`.

When you've done that, press the Esc key. The Esc key takes you out of insert mode (you will see the text `-- INSERT --` disappear from the bottom of the screen). You can now save what you've added to the file by entering the colon character (`:`) and the letters `wq` for a combination of `:wq`. This means write and quit. You could also just specify `w`, which would write but not quit. If you quit back to the command line, you can now view your file and see your typed text:

```
$ cat newfile
hello jsmith
```

> **Tip** You can find an introduction to `vim` at `http://blog.interlinked.org/tutorials/vim_tutorial.html`, or you can run `vimtutor` on the command line to start a `vim` tutorial.

A variety of GUI editors are also available. Some are simple in a similar style to the Microsoft Window's Notepad or WordPad applications, and others are fully fledged word processors and text editors.

An example of these is the Gnome default text editor, `gedit`. You can launch `gedit` in Gnome by clicking the Applications menu, opening the Accessories tab, and selecting the Text Editor application. This will launch the `gedit` editor, as you can see in Figure 3-9.

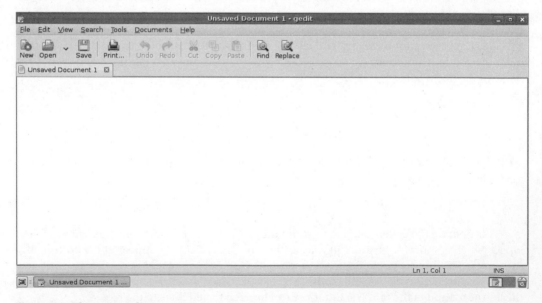

Figure 3-9. *The* gedit *editor*

Another example of these editors is kate (http://kate-editor.org/), which comes with the KDE GUI. In Figure 3-10, you can see a KDE desktop with kate open.

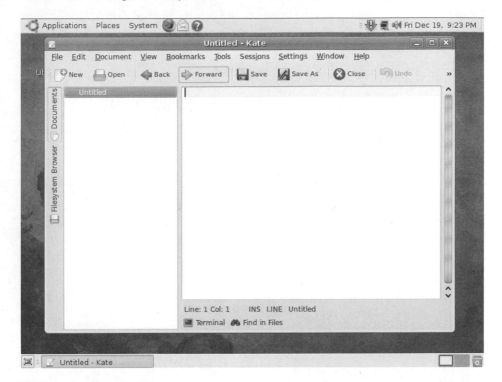

Figure 3-10. *The kate editor*

Summary

Well, what have you learned? First of all, Linux isn't that different from Microsoft Windows. It encompasses a lot of similar concepts and principles, and this will help you get started with Linux. Some of the key things you should take away from this chapter are the following:

- You can test out lots of things using LiveCDs without any risk to your existing hosts and data.

- Learn to use the command-line—it's useful and powerful (and sometimes you won't have a choice!). The Bash shell is especially powerful, and you'll find yourself wondering how you ever got by without a command shell.

- Learn a bit more about globbing and regular expressions—you'll find both useful and powerful tools in your arsenal when administering your hosts.

- Don't use the root user to administer your host. Instead, make use of the sudo command. More on the sudo command in the next chapter.

- Use the Linux man pages to find out more about each command. These are useful resources packed with information.

- Learn to use the `vim` editor (or another editor of your choice) to help you work with configuration files on the command line.

- Don't forget online resources or the Linux community if you need help. Lots of people use Linux, and someone may have found a solution to a problem you're having. Use Google or your favorite search engine to find these solutions.

In the next chapter, we'll cover more on users and groups and how to manage them on your hosts.

## CHAPTER 4

Users and Groups

By James Turnbull

Chapter 3 introduced Linux basics and the concepts of users and collections of users called groups. We explained how users and groups own files and objects. We also demonstrated how that ownership, in combination with permissions, controls access to those files and objects. Users and groups are also used to initiate and run processes.

In this chapter, we'll go into detail about how users and groups work, starting with what happens when you log in, and how to control some of that process. We'll demonstrate how to create users and groups, give you some more information about passwords, and explain the process by which Linux controls access to your host.

Among the topics we're going to talk about are the su and sudo commands. These commands let you run commands as other users, specifically the root user. Thus, these commands allow you to avoid logging in as the root user to perform administrative tasks. The su and sudo commands are critical to securely administering your hosts.

What Happens When You Log In

In Chapter 3, we talked about logging a user into a Linux host, and you saw some sample screens showing how you might enter your username and password. In this chapter, we're going to explain a bit more about what happens when you log in, and we'll begin to explore some of the options and security controls that you can manage as part of this process.

So what actually happens after you enter your username and password and before you are delivered to your command-line prompt or GUI screen? Well, this process varies slightly from distribution to distribution, but generally an application called login is executed and performs the following actions:

- Checks that the user and group exist and the user is allowed to log in
- Checks that the user is allowed to log in from a particular location (e.g., only some users can log in to the console, or the screen attached to a Linux host)
- Checks that the password is correct, and, if the password is incorrect, allows a specified number (usually three) of retries
- Checks that the password is valid and prompts the user for a new password if it has expired
- Sets environment variables like the user's home directory and path

- Starts the shell process
- Presents the user with a command-line prompt or GUI screen

In the sections that follow, we'll take you through these processes and explain how you can configure and change some of these steps to suit your environment. You'll start by learning how to create, delete, and manage users and groups.

■**Note** In this chapter, we demonstrate command-line user administration, but everything we show you is also available from a GUI tool if you prefer to administer your users and groups that way.

Working with Users and Groups

At the heart of managing access to your Linux hosts is the concept of users and groups. We introduced users and the collections of users called groups in Chapter 3, and you discovered they are much like the users and groups that exist on the Microsoft Windows platform.

You can organize users and groups on your host in two ways. One way is to add users and groups to each host in your domain; the other is to centralize your user administration on one or two authentication servers. In this chapter, we will explain the former, and in Chapter 16 we will explain the latter.

Like on Microsoft Windows hosts, everyone who needs to log in to your host will need a user created. Many applications, such as web and mail servers, will also require a user to be created. When they are started, these applications will then make use of that user's rights and privileges to access system resources like files, your network, or other aspects of your host.

Every user on your Linux host also needs to belong to at least one group but can belong to any number of additional groups as well. Groups are collections of users, gathered together because they are alike or require access to a particular resource. For example, all the users in your organization's sales department may belong to a group called sales. You might configure your host to ensure that only the users in the sales group have access to the sales department's applications and files.

■**Note** When applications are installed, they often install additional users and groups required to run those applications.

Users and groups are easy to create using two commands: useradd (to create users) and groupadd (to create groups). Additionally, two commands we can use to modify existing users and groups are usermod and groupmod. Lastly, to complete the life cycle, users and groups can be deleted with the userdel and groupdel commands.

■**Tip** Working with users and groups on Red Hat and Ubuntu is a very similar process that uses many of the same commands and options. We'll tell you about any minor variations between distributions.

Introducing sudo

Before we jump into explaining how to create users and groups, we want to discuss the sudo command, which we talked about a little in Chapter 3. The sudo command allows a user to run commands as if that person were signed in as the root user, Linux's equivalent of the Windows Administrator account. This ability is useful for three reasons:

- It increases security.
- It allows greater control of privileged commands.
- It provides you with a better understanding of who did what on your host.

■**Note** Another good reason to use sudo rather than the root user on Ubuntu is that Ubuntu doesn't enable the root user by default. You cannot sign on as the root user at all.

We're going to need sudo in this chapter because almost all of the commands used to manage users and groups require the privileges of the root user to run. For example, only the root user can create another user.

When you run the sudo command, it will prompt you to enter your password (to confirm you are actually who you say you are), and then you are allowed to make use of the sudo command for a period of 5 minutes on Red Hat and 15 minutes on Ubuntu. When this period expires, you will be prompted to reenter your password.

■**Tip** The first time you run the sudo command, it may also show you a warning to be careful with the power of the sudo command.

On Ubuntu, the sudo command is available and configured for the user you created when you installed Ubuntu. If you're logged in as that user, you can use the sudo command already. You can also enable sudo access for other users by adding them to the admin group. You can use the usermod command (which you'll see more of later in this chapter) to add a user to the group.

```
$ sudo usermod -G admin ataylor
```

Here we've used sudo and the usermod command to modify a user called ataylor. We've added the user to the admin group by specifying the -G option and the name of the group to add the user to. (Note that we've used the sudo command to do the user modification. The only user allowed to do this is the user you created when you installed the host, hence you must be logged in as that user to make this change.)

On Red Hat, the sudo command is not enabled by default, and you'll need to enable it. To do this, you need to use a command called visudo to edit the sudo command's configuration file, /etc/sudoers. To do this, you need to log on as the root user and run the visudo command.

```
# visudo
```

As you can see from the # command prompt, you're logging in as the root user and you're executing the visudo command. This opens an editing application that looks much like the vi or vim editor. Inside this file is the following line:

```
# %wheel  ALL=(ALL)       ALL
```

You need to uncomment the line and write and quit the file using the same commands you would with vim by typing the colon character, :, and w and q followed by Enter, or :wq. This enables any member of a group called wheel to use the sudo command. You can then add a user to the wheel group like so:

```
# usermod -G wheel ataylor
```

Again, you specify the group, wheel, with the -G option and the name of the user you want to add to the group last. Now the ataylor user can make use of the sudo command.

Creating Users

Now that you know how to enable and use the sudo command, we can start looking at users and groups. Let's begin by creating a new user using the useradd command, as shown in Listing 4-1.

Listing 4-1. *Creating a New User*

```
$ sudo useradd -m -c 'John Smith' jsmith
```

■**Note** In Listing 4-1, you can see we've prefixed the useradd command with the sudo command to avoid having to log on as the root user.

The useradd command has a number of options, and we're using just a couple in Listing 4-1. The first, -m, tells the host to create a home directory for the user. The format of the name and location of the home directory would usually resemble /home/*username*.

■**Tip** You can prepopulate the new home directory with, for example, generic configuration files. To do this, add files to the /etc/skel (short for skeleton) directory. When a new home directory is created (using the -m option), then all the files contained in this directory are copied to the user's new home directory.

The -c option adds a description of our new user. This description is stored in the /etc/ passwd file. All users have an entry in this file, and we'll examine this file and the /etc/group file that is used to store group data later in this chapter. Lastly, we've specified the name of our new user, jsmith.

By default, the new user will be created disabled and with no password set. You will need to change the user's password using the passwd command (which we'll cover in more detail later in this chapter).

Table 4-1 lists some other useful useradd command-line options.

Table 4-1. *Some useradd Command-Line Options*

Option	Description
-c	Add a description of the user
-d homedir	The user's home directory
-m	Create the user's home directory
-M	Do not create the user's home directory (Red Hat only)
-s shell	Specify the shell the user will use

The -d option allows you to specify the user's home directory. The -M option tells Red Hat–derived distributions not to create a home directory. This option highlights the major difference between creating users on Red Hat and Ubuntu distributions. On Red Hat–derived distributions, home directories are created automatically.

Ubuntu requires that the useradd command is executed with the -m option, otherwise no home directory is created.

■**Note** See the "adduser: An Alternative on Ubuntu" sidebar for an alternative method to create users on Ubuntu.

Lastly, the -s option allows you to specify a different shell from the default for the user.

■**Tip** We recommend you read the useradd command's man page for more detailed information on this command.

User Default Settings

Your new user will also be created with a variety of defaults (e.g., the setting for the user's shell). So where does the useradd command get these defaults from? On both Red Hat and Ubuntu distributions, the defaults are contained in the /etc/default/useradd file, and you can display the current defaults using the following command:

```
$ sudo /usr/sbin/useradd -D
```

Listing 4-2 shows a sample of this file.

Listing 4-2. *The /etc/default/useradd File*

```
$ sudo cat /etc/default/useradd
# useradd defaults file
GROUP=100
HOME=/home
INACTIVE=-1
```

```
EXPIRE=
SHELL=/bin/bash
SKEL=/etc/skel
```

This file is usually populated by default when your host is installed, but you can modify it to suit your environment. Table 4-2 shows the possible options you can include in the useradd file.

Table 4-2. *The /etc/default/useradd File*

Option	Description
SHELL	The path to the default shell
HOME	The path to the user's home directory
SKEL	The directory to use to provide the default contents of a user's new home directory
GROUP	The default group ID
INACTIVE	The maximum number of days after password expiration that a password can be changed
EXPIRE	The default expiration date of user accounts

Each option in the file controls a specify default; for example, the SHELL option specifies the default shell for the user. The HOME option specifies the directory in which all new home directories should be created. The SKEL option specifies which directory to use to populate the user's home directory, and as we discussed earlier, this defaults to /etc/skel. The GROUP option specifies the default group ID (GID) to use, and you generally won't ever change this. We'll talk a bit more about groups, membership, and GIDs in the sections that follow.

Lastly, two other options, INACTIVE and EXPIRE, control two different types of user account expiration. The INACTIVE value controls how long in days after a user's password expires that the user can reset his password. This allows you to specify that if a user's password expires, the user has a finite time to reset that password before he is marked inactive. The user would then require some interaction to re-enable it for access. A setting of -1 disables this setting, and a setting of 0 disables the account as soon as the password expires.

■**Note** We'll talk more about password expiration later in this chapter.

The EXPIRE option is useful for creating temporary accounts, as it specifies a date in the format YYYY-MM-DD on which the account will be expired and disabled. The EXPIRE default allows you to specify such a date for all accounts. You can also create an individual account on the command line using the following command:

```
$ sudo useradd –e 2009-09-15 temp_account
```

This command creates an account called temp_account that would be disabled on 09-15-2009.

You can change many of the default settings in this file by executing the useradd command with the -D option. Listing 4-3 shows you how to change the default shell for your new users, and Table 4-3 shows the additional options available for use with the -D option.

Listing 4-3. *Changing* useradd *Defaults with the* -D *Option*

```
$ sudo useradd -D -s /bin/bash
```

■**Tip** You can also change your default shell with the chsh command. Use chsh -l on Red Hat to see a list of all the available shells. On Ubuntu, you can see the list in the /etc/shells file.

Table 4-3. *The* useradd -D *Defaults*

Option	Description
-b path/to/default/home	Specifies the path prefix of a new user's home directory
-e date	Specifies the default expiration date
-f days	Specifies the number of days after a password has expired before the account will be disabled
-g group	Specifies the default group
-s shell	Specifies the default shell

Creating Groups

We mentioned earlier that every user must belong to at least one group. By default on most Linux distributions, including Red Hat and Ubuntu, when you create a new user, a new group with the same name as the user is also created. The new user is always the only member of this group.

■**Note** The creation of a unique group for each user is called a *user private group* (UPG) scheme. It is a flexible model for managing group permissions. You can read some details of UPG at http://www.centos.org/docs/5/html/5.1/Deployment_Guide/s1-users-groups-private-groups.html.

In our case, our first user, jsmith, would automatically belong to a group called jsmith. This group is called the *primary* group. Our user can also belong to other groups, and these additional groups are called *supplementary* groups.

So how do we tell what groups our new user belongs to? To check the details of a particular user, we can use the id command as shown in Listing 4-4.

Listing 4-4. *The* id *Command*

```
$ id jsmith
uid=1003(jsmith) gid=1003(jsmith) groups=1003(jsmith)
```

In Listing 4-4, we query our new user, jsmith, using the id command. But the command has returned some fairly cryptic information about uid and gid, the name of our user, and some numbers. So what exactly are these?

Each user and group is assigned a unique user ID (UID) and group ID (GID) when created. UIDs range from 0 to 65535, with the root user always having a UID of 0. GIDs also range from 0 to 65535, with the root user also always having a GID of 0.

If you run the id command for the root user, you can see the results on the following line:

```
$ id root
uid=0(root) gid=0(root) groups=0(root)
```

This shows the root user having a UID of 0 and a GID of 0.

■**Note** Each user and group on a host must have a unique UID and GID. A user or group cannot be created on your host with the same UID or GID as an existing user or group. Your operating system will automatically assign the numbers and prevent any conflicts.

Most distributions reserve ranges of numbers for particular types of users and groups. For example, the Red Hat distribution reserves the UID and GID ranges of 1 to 499 for "system" users and groups that run services—for example, a user running a database or web server. Ubuntu reserves the UID and GID ranges of 1 to 999 for the same purpose. So the very first new user created on a Red Hat host would have a UID of 500 and also a GID of 500. On Ubuntu, the first new user would have a UID and GID of 1000.

■**Tip** You can control the range of the UIDs and GIDs that are provided to users in the /etc/login.defs file. Edit the UID_MIN and UID_MAX range for UIDs and the GID_MIN and GID_MAX range for GIDs. It's unlikely you'll ever want to do this, but the option is there.

So in Listing 4-4 we've executed the id command for the jsmith user and displayed the user's UID of 1003 and GID of 1003 (with the name of the user and group in brackets after the UID and GID). The last field, groups, is where the primary and any supplementary groups are displayed.

You have two methods for adding your user to a group or groups. First, you can add the user to a group or groups upon creation with the useradd command. Second, you can modify an existing user and add groups using the usermod command.

On the following line, we're going to create a second user called ataylor and add her to some groups when we create her.

```
$ sudo useradd -m -c 'Anne Taylor' -G printing,finance ataylor
```

We have specified the -G option, which allows us to provide a comma-separated list of groups that we'd like our new user ataylor to join. The -G option allows our user to join additional groups other than her primary group, which is a unique group created when the user is created and shares her username. Here the user ataylor is a member of a unique UPG scheme primary group called ataylor, and we're trying to add her to the additional supplemental groups printing and finance.

If we execute that command now, however, it will fail because each of these groups needs to exist *before* we can add a user to them, otherwise we'll get an error message and the user will fail to be created. This is the error message that would be generated in such a scenario on Ubuntu:

```
useradd: unknown group printing
useradd: unknown group finance
```

On Red Hat, the error message is slightly different:

```
useradd: invalid numeric argument 'printing'
```

So in this case, we need to create our groups first, and we can do that with the groupadd command, as you can see in Listing 4-5.

Listing 4-5. *Creating New Groups*

```
$ sudo groupadd printing
$ sudo groupadd finance
```

Table 4-4 shows some command-line options available with the groupadd command.

Table 4-4. *The groupadd Command-Line Options*

Option	Description
-g GID	Sets the GID for the group. This must be a unique number.
-r	Creates a system group (with a GID inside the system GID range).

Use the -g option if you wish to override the autogenerated GID with a specific number. Available only on Red Hat, the -r option lets you create a system group and will ensure the group is assigned a GID within the range for system groups (e.g., on a Red Hat host between 1 and 499).

When we try to create the ataylor user, we succeed because the prerequisite groups now exist.

```
$ sudo useradd -m -c 'Anne Taylor' -G printing,finance ataylor
```

We can also add existing users to groups using the usermod command:

```
$ sudo usermod -a -G accounts ataylor
```

The usermod command is used to modify existing users. By specifying the -a (for append) option, the -G option, and the name of the new group to join (the group must already exist), we add the ataylor user to the accounts group.

■**Tip** You can change many of the aspects of a user with the usermod command, and we recommend reading its man page for further information.

Also available to manage groups is the gpasswd command, which allows you to delegate responsibility for managing groups and their memberships. You can assign a particular user rights to add or remove users to a particular group. For example, you could have someone on the sales team manage the membership of the sales group. You can read about gpasswd in more detail on its man page.

Deleting Users and Groups

In addition to creating and modifying users and groups, you will also want to be able to delete them. You can use the following two commands to do this: userdel and groupdel. The userdel command deletes users, and the groupdel command removes groups. Let's now delete the ataylor user we created earlier using the userdel command, as shown in Listing 4-6.

Listing 4-6. *Deleting a User*

```
$ sudo userdel ataylor
```

The userdel command deletes the user, but by default it doesn't delete the user's home directory. You can force Linux to delete the user's home directory using the -r option of the userdel command. This will delete the /home/*username* directory and all files in it, but it won't delete any files outside of this directory that might also belong to the user. The userdel command will also not delete a user who is currently logged in to the host.

Removing a user who owns files can be problematic. If you delete a user, then all the user's objects will no longer be owned by the user. You can identify these objects because the username will be replaced in the file listing with the former UID (the same applies for any deleted groups). As a result, if you create another user that uses the same UID or GID, that user will now own the deleted user's files. It's a very good idea to confirm the files and directories a user owns and work out what you are going to do with them prior to deleting the user. We'll show you how to assign ownership of files and directories later in this chapter. In light of this issue, it is sometimes better to disable a user rather than delete the user. But if you do decide to delete a user, you can run the command find / -user UID -o -group GID to find all the files associated with the user you have just deleted.

To delete a group, use the groupdel command and specify the name of the group to be deleted.

```
$ sudo groupdel finance
```

This command will remove the group from the host. It is important to note that the groupdel command won't delete the primary group of any user—for example, you couldn't delete the ataylor group before you deleted the ataylor user. If you want to delete a user's primary group, you must delete the user first. Like with users, deleting groups can leave files owned by those groups orphaned.

ADDUSER: AN ALTERNATIVE ON UBUNTU

Ubuntu ships with two additional user management utilities, adduser and addgroup. These provide easy-to-use and convenient alternatives to the useradd and groupadd commands. The normal way to run adduser is with the username of the new user you'd like to create. The utility will then ask you to provide additional information. For example, let's add an account for user Anne Taylor.

```
$ sudo adduser ataylor
Adding user `ataylor' ...
Adding new group `ataylor' (1001) ...
Adding new user `ataylor' (1001) with group `ataylor' ...
Creating home directory `/home/ataylor' ...
Copying files from `/etc/skel' ...
Enter new UNIX password:
Retype new UNIX password:
passwd: password updated successfully
Changing the user information for ataylor
Enter the new value, or press ENTER for the default
    Full Name []: Anne Taylor
    Room Number []:
    Work Phone []:
    Home Phone []:
    Other []:
Is the information correct? [Y/n] y
```

The adduser command asks for all the variables it needs, and it then calls the useradd command with the correct parameters in order to create the account. This means that even when you use the adduser command, the default useradd options you configure in /etc/default/useradd are still honored.

You can also use the adduser script to quickly add a user to a group, by running this:

```
$ sudo adduser username groupname
```

Both the user and group need to already exist on the host.

The adduser and addgroup scripts themselves can also be configured via the /etc/adduser.conf file. By default, they will create users of the specified name, put them in a group of the same name, create the home directory, and assign the lowest available user and group IDs.

Managing Users and Groups via the GUI

Both Red Hat and Ubuntu have graphical user interfaces (GUIs) for managing users and groups. On Red Hat the GUI tool is called User Manager and is launched by selecting System ➤ Administration ➤ Users and Groups (see Figure 4-1).

Figure 4-1. *Starting User Manager*

This very simple interface allows you to add, change, and delete users and groups, as shown in Figure 4-2.

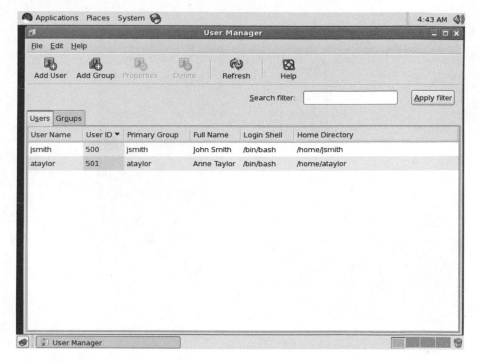

Figure 4-2. *The User Manager interface*

You add users by clicking the Add User button and groups by clicking the Add Group button. Lists of the users and groups currently on your host are contained in the two tabs. You can edit users and groups by selecting a user or group and then clicking the Properties button. You can configure all aspects of the user or group from this interface. To delete a user or group, select it and then click the Delete button.

On Ubuntu, the GUI user management tool is called Users Settings. You can launch it by selecting System ➤ Administration ➤ Users and Groups, as shown in Figure 4-3.

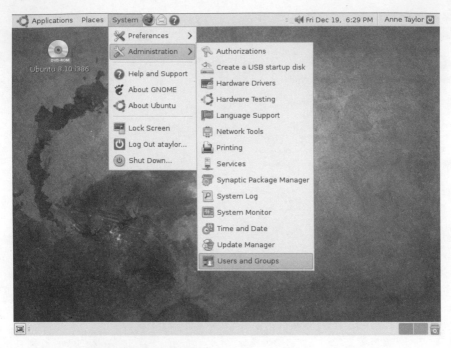

Figure 4-3. *Starting Users Settings*

Users Settings is a simple user manager that displays all the current users on your host (see Figure 4-4).

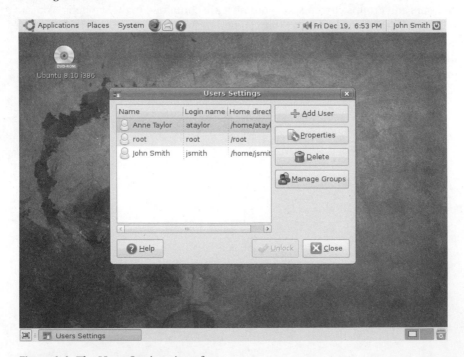

Figure 4-4. *The Users Settings interface*

To manage users, click the Unlock button, which initiates the graphical equivalent of the sudo command and prompts you for your password. If you successfully enter your password, you will be able to administer users and groups. You can add a user by clicking the Add User button, and you can delete a user by selecting the user and clicking Delete. You can edit user settings by selecting the user and clicking the Properties button. To manage groups, click the Manage Groups button.

■Note Remember, the Ubuntu Server version does not come with a GUI by default, and you should make use of the command-line tools provided. The Ubuntu Desktop release does come with the appropriate GUI tools, as it installs a GUI by default.

Passwords

Now that you've created a new user, you may want to set or change the user's password. To do this, you use the passwd command. The passwd command works one of two ways depending on who runs the command. If a normal user, like ataylor, runs the command, then she will be prompted to change her own password. You can see the passwd command in action in Listing 4-7.

Listing 4-7. *Changing Your Password*

```
$ passwd
Changing password for ataylor.
(current) UNIX password:
Enter new UNIX password:
Retype new UNIX password:
```

You type in your current password and then your new password. You'll be prompted to type the new password in twice to ensure it's correct. You'll also have to provide a suitable password. By default on most distributions, some basic password checking is performed to try to prevent you from providing a weak or easy-to-guess password. On most distributions these checks are generally as follows:

- Minimum password length of four characters
- Not a palindrome (i.e., the reverse of the last password)
- Not the same as the previous password with a case change (i.e., password to PASSWORD)
- Some basic similarity checking
- Some simplicity tests based on the length of the password and the combination of characters (all alpha, all numeric, etc.)
- Simple rotation checks (i.e., rotating letters in a password, such as ginger being changed to ingerg)

If you provide a password that isn't sufficiently complex, you'll be given an error message indicating what is wrong with your password. You will then be prompted to provide a more acceptable password.

Alternatively, if you are running the passwd command as the root user, you can change the passwords of other users as you can see in Listing 4-8.

Listing 4-8. *Changing Someone Else's Password*

```
$ sudo passwd jsmith
```

In Listing 4-8, the passwd command prompts you to provide a new password for the user jsmith.

■Tip It is important to note that as the root user you can override any warnings about bad passwords and change the user's password to a weak or easily guessable password.

Password Aging

Password aging allows you to specify a time period during which a password is valid. After the time period has expired, the user will be forced to choose a new password. This has the benefit of ensuring passwords are changed regularly and that a password that is stolen, cracked, or known by a former employee will have a time-limited value. Unfortunately for many users, the need to regularly change their passwords increases their desire to write down the passwords. We recommend you use a password age between 30 and 60 days for most passwords, depending on the nature of the host. More important hosts should have shorter password expiration periods (e.g., 30 days), while less critical hosts could have longer periods. Some organizations choose a single expiration period so the period is consistent for all users on all hosts.

Two ways exist to handle password aging. The first uses the command-line tool called chage to set or change the password expiration of a user account individually. Listing 4-9 shows this command.

Listing 4-9. *The chage Command*

```
$ sudo chage -M 30 ataylor
```

Listing 4-9 uses the -M option to set the password expiration period for the user ataylor to 30 days. After 30 days the user's password will be expired and the user will be prompted to enter a new password. Table 4-5 shows several of the other variables you can set.

Table 4-5. *The chage Command Flags*

Option	Description
-m days	Sets the minimum number of days between password changes. Zero allows the user to change the password at any time.
-M days	Sets the maximum number of days for which a password stays valid.
-E date	Sets a date on which the user account will expire and automatically be deactivated.
-W days	Sets the number of days before the password expires that the user will be warned to change it.
-d days	Sets the number of days since January 1, 1970, that the password was last changed.
-I days	Sets the number of days after password expiration that the account is locked.

■**Tip** You'll come across the date January 1, 1970, quite a few times in the Unix/Linux world. This date is also known as *Unix epoch* or *Unix time*. It is used to describe points in time and is measured in seconds since January 1, 1970 (e.g., 1229519557). You can find the Unix time on your host by using the command date +%s.

The first option, -m, allows you to specify the minimum amount of time between password changes. A setting of 0 allows the user to change the password at any time. The option -W specifies the number of days before a user's password expires that he will get a warning that the password is about to expire. The -d option is principally useful to immediately expire a password. By setting the -d option to 0, the user's last password change date becomes January 1, 1970, and if the -M option is greater than 0, then the user must change his password at the next login. The last option, -I, provides a time frame in days after which user accounts with expired and unchanged passwords are locked and thus unable to be used to log in.

If you run chage without any options and specify only the user, it will launch an interactive series of prompts to set the required values, as shown in Listing 4-10. The values between the brackets[ ] indicate the current values to which this user's password aging is set.

Listing 4-10. *Running chage Without Options*

```
$ sudo chage ataylor
Changing the aging information for ataylor
Enter the new value, or press return for the default
Minimum Password Age [0]:
Maximum Password Age [30]:
Last Password Change (YYYY-MM-DD) [2009-06-27]:
Password Expiration Warning [7]:
Password Inactive [-1]:
Account Expiration Date (YYYY-MM-DD) [2009-07-28]:
```

Users can also utilize the chage command with the -l option to show when a password is due to expire.

```
$ chage -l ataylor
```

The other method to handle password aging is to set defaults for all users in the /etc/login.defs file.

Listing 4-11 shows the controls available for password aging in /etc/login.defs.

Listing 4-11. *The* login.defs *Password-Aging Controls*

```
PASS_MAX_DAYS    60
PASS_MIN_DAYS    0
PASS_WARN_AGE    7
```

In Listing 4-11, we have set the maximum password age to 60 days using the PASS_MAX_DAYS option, allowing users to change their passwords at any time by setting the PASS_MIN_DAYS option to 0 and providing a warning to users that their passwords will expire seven days before the password expiration date using the PASS_WARN_AGE option.

Disabling Users

As the root user, you can also use the passwd command to disable and enable user accounts using the –l, or lock, option. For example, consider the following:

```
$ sudo passwd –l ataylor
```

The previous command would lock the ataylor user and prevent ataylor from logging into the host using her password. You can then unlock the user using the –u, or unlock, option.

```
$ sudo passwd –u ataylor
```

However, this potentially doesn't fully disable access to the host. Users could access the host through other authentication mechanisms such as public keys for remote access using SSH.

There is another way to totally disable access to the user that uses the usermod command with the --expiredate option:

```
$ sudo usermod --expiredate 1
```

This sets the account expiration date to January 1, 1970, and disables the account immediately. The user can now do nothing on the host.

Lastly, you can set the login shell to /bin/false on Ubuntu or /sbin/nologin on Red Hat. This doesn't lock a user out but disables the user's getting shell access.

```
$ sudo usermod –s /bin/false
```

■**Note** You can also set the user's shell to a command. For example, you could set the user's shell to the /bin/mail command, which is a small command-line mail reader. When the user then logs on, she can access only that command.

Storing User and Group Data

First, your host checks that your user exists and is allowed to log in. Linux distributions store details of users, groups, and other information in three files on your host: /etc/passwd, /etc/shadow, and /etc/group. You generally won't ever need to edit these files, as there are commands and tools that allow you to add, remove, and manage users and groups. It is useful, however, to know what information they contain.

■**Tip** If you use other forms of authentication such as NIS, LDAP, or Active Directory, which we'll look at in Chapter 16, then your host will usually query one of these authentication stores to confirm your user exists and is allowed to log in.

The first file, /etc/passwd, contains a list of all users and their details. Listing 4-12 shows examples of some passwd entries.

Listing 4-12. /etc/passwd *Entries*

```
root:x:0:0:root:/root:/bin/bash
daemon:x:2:2:daemon:/sbin:/sbin/nologin
```

Each entry can be broken into its component pieces, separated by a colon.

```
username:password:UID:GID:GECOS:Home Directory:Shell
```

The username is up to eight characters long and is case sensitive (though it's usually all in lowercase). The x in the next field is a marker for the password. The actual password is stored in the /etc/shadow file, which we will discuss in the upcoming "Shadow Passwords" sidebar.

Next is the UID and GID. As noted earlier, on a Linux host, each user account and group is assigned a numeric ID; users are assigned a UID and groups are assigned a GID. Depending on the distribution, lower-numbered UIDs and GIDs indicate system accounts and groups such as root or daemon. On Red Hat, system account UIDs and GIDs are those IDs lower than 500, and on Ubuntu those IDs are lower than 1000.

■**Note** As mentioned earlier, the root user has a UID and GID of 0. This should be the only user on the host with a UID and GID of 0.

The next item is the GECOS or comment field (see http://en.wikipedia.org/wiki/Gecos_field). This field usually contains data such as the name of the user, office locations, and phone numbers. If you have more than one item of data in the GECOS field, then a comma separates each data item.

The user's home directory comes next. As we described in Chapter 3, this is usually located in the /home directory (e.g., /home/jsmith).

The last item is the user's default shell. The shell, as we discussed in Chapter 3, is a command-line environment through which the user interacts with the host. Each shell is initiated by running a binary. For example, to start the Bash shell, the /bin/bash binary would be executed. This binary is specified in the /etc/passwd file. If the default shell points to a nonexistent file, then the user will be unable to log in.

The second line in Listing 4-12 uses the shell /sbin/nologin, which is a dummy shell that not only stops the user from logging it, but also logs the login attempt to the syslog daemon.

■**Note** The syslog daemon is the Linux logging server. It receives log entries from the operating system and applications and writes them to files, generally in the /var/log directory. We'll talk more about logging in Chapter 18.

This method is commonly used on Red Hat hosts to indicate that this user cannot log on. On Ubuntu hosts the shell /bin/false is used. Most users will have a shell entry that references the binary that launches their shell, for example, /bin/bash.

SHADOW PASSWORDS

You may have noted that no password appears in /etc/passwd but rather the letter x. This is because most (if not all) modern distributions use *shadow passwords* to handle password management.

Previously, passwords were stored as one-way hashes in /etc/passwd, which provided limited security and exposed usernames and passwords to brute-force cracking methods. *Brute-force cracking* is a method of attacking passwords where thousands or millions of different passwords are tried until a matching password is found. The /etc/passwd file was especially susceptible to this attack because its use by applications requires it to be readable by all users, or world readable. This was especially dangerous when a copy of a passwd file could be stolen from a host and brute-force-cracked offline. Given the weak security of this type of password when stored in the passwd file, a modern computer can crack simple passwords in a matter of minutes or harder passwords in just days.

Shadow passwords help reduce this risk by separating the users and passwords and storing the passwords as a hash in the /etc/shadow file. By default, MD5 hashes are used (although newer distributions support other hash types like Blowfish). These MD5 hashes are harder to break, and to further protect the passwords, the /etc/shadow file is owned by the root user, and root is the only user with access to the file. The next line shows a typical line from the shadow file:

root:1RwETwzjv$ifht7L/HiLCPR8Zc935fdO:13675:0:99999:7::::

You can also break down the shadow file into components, and like the passwd file, colons separate each component. The components of the shadow file are as follows:

- Username

- Password

- Date password last changed

- Minimum days between password changes

- Password expiration time in days

- Password expiration warning period in days

- Number of days after password expiration that account is disabled

- Date since account has been disabled

The username matches the username in the `passwd` file. The password itself is encrypted, and two types of special characters can tell you about the status of the user account with which the password field can be prefixed. If the password field is prefixed with ! or *, then the account is locked and the user will not be allowed to log in. If the password field is prefixed with !!, then a password has never been set and the user cannot log in to the host. The remaining entries refer to password aging, and we cover those in the "Password Aging" section.

On Linux hosts, information about groups is stored in the `/etc/groups` file. Listing 4-13 shows a sample from this file.

Listing 4-13. *Sample of the `/etc/groups` File*

```
root:x:0:root
ataylor:x:501:finance,printing
```

The `/etc/group` file is structured much like the `/etc/passwd` file, with the data separated by a colon. The file is broken into a group name, a password, the GID, and a comma-separated list of the members of that group.

```
groupname:password:GID:member,member
```

The password in the `group` file allows a user to log in to that group using the `newgrp` command. If shadow passwords are enabled, then like the `passwd` file, the passwords in the `group` file are replaced with an x and the real passwords are stored in the `/etc/gshadow` file.

LOGIN MESSAGES

Your login screen is the first thing users see. It's a good idea to put some important warnings and information in that login screen. To do this, you need to edit the contents of the `/etc/issue` and `/etc/issue.net` files. The `issue` file is displayed when you log in via the command line on the host's console, and the `issue.net` file is displayed when you log in to the command line via an SSH session. Most distributions use these files for this purpose, including both Red Hat and Ubuntu. These files can contain a combination of plain text and special escape characters that allow you to output colors, line feeds, and returns, for example.

You should also include a warning message stating that unauthorized access to the host is prohibited and will be prosecuted. You can use one of a series of escape characters in the files to populate the login screen with data from your host. We recommend you use a login message like the following:

```
^[c
\d at \t
Access to this host is for authorized persons only.
```

Unauthorized use or access is regarded as a criminal act
and is subject to civil and criminal prosecution. User
activities on this host may be monitored without prior notice.

The ^[c escape characters clear the screen, and the \d and \t escape characters display the current
date and time on the host, respectively. Other escape characters are available to you if you check the issue,
issue.net, and getty man pages.

In addition to the /etc/issue and /etc/issue.net files, the /etc/motd file's contents display
directly after a command-line login, and you may want to adjust them to include an Acceptable Use Policy or
similar information.

Configuring Your Shell and Environment

After a user has been authenticated and authorized, his shell is started. Most shells are highly
customizable, and many users eventually tweak every aspect of their shell environment to help
them work faster and more efficiently.

The Bash shell reads its initial configuration from the /etc/profile file. This file usually
contains references to other global configuration files and is used to configure Bash for all
users on the host except the root user. Finally, any configuration files in the user's home directory are processed. The .bash_profile and .profile files are most commonly used, and each
user will have these in his or her home directory.

■**Note** You can check the INVOCATION section of bash man page for a full listing of other configuration files.

Environment Variables

One of the main reasons for customizing your shell is to set environment variables. These
variables act as default options that are used by many applications. They can define characteristics like your preferred text editor, your preferred language, and the colors used when listing
files and directories with ls. You can also define your own variables for use with your own
scripts.

To get a full listing of all environment variables, use the env command. Table 4-6 lists the
most commonly customized variables.

Table 4-6. *Environment Variables*

Name	Used For
HOME	The user's home directory
LANG	Defines which language files applications should use
LS_COLORS	Defines colors used by the ls command
MAIL	The location of the user's mailbox
PATH	A colon-separated list of directories where shells look for executable files

Name	Used For
PS1	Defines the normal prompt
SHELL	The current shell
_	Contains the last command executed in this session

You can display the contents of an environment variable via the echo command. Prefix the name of the variable you want to display with $.

```
$ echo $PS1
\u@\h:\w\$
```

The preceding is a string of special escape codes that display the username \u, hostname \h , current working directory \w, and the final character \$ in the prompt. \$ displays a pound (#) symbol if the prompt is displayed as the root user and a dollar sign ($) otherwise. For a full listing of available escape codes, see the PROMPTING section of the bash man page.

You can change environment variables either by defining them in any of the Bash configuration files or by setting them from the command line. If we wanted to change our prompt to include a timestamp and have it break to give us more space to type commands, we could add the \T and \n codes:

```
$ PS1="[\T] \u@\h:\w\n\$ "
[12:50:59] jsmith@au-mel-ubuntu-1:~
$
```

■**Tip** You may have noticed that we sometimes use $ and sometimes not. The simple rule here is that if we are referring to the variable and prefixing it with $, then we're interested in the value of the variable (i.e., the contents of the variable). Without $, we're talking about the variable itself.

Another useful example is adding directories to your path. You can quickly prefix or suffix directories to your path. You can add a single directory to the start of the path like so:

```
$ PATH=/home/ataylor/scripts:$PATH
```

Here we've added the directory /home/ataylor/scripts to the front of the path and then included the existing path by separating it with a colon and specifying the $PATH value. This allows you to put binaries, scripts, or other applications in the path, which is searched every time you run a command or an application. In this case, when executing commands, Linux will look for the command first in the /home/ataylor/scripts directory before anywhere else on the host.

You can add a directory to the end of the path using the same basic construct:

```
$ PATH=$PATH:/home/ataylor/scripts
```

Then when you run a command, Linux will search all the directories in your path, and if a matching command or application isn't found, it will search your suffixed directory.

Any string of the type KEY=value is assumed to be an environment variable assignment by Bash. Making the variables uppercase is a matter of convention.

Of course, setting environment variables on the command line changes them only for the duration of your session. If you log off, they will revert back to the previous configuration. To make changes like this permanent, place them in the .bash_profile file located in your home directory, for example:

```
PATH=$PATH:/home/ataylor/scripts
export PATH
```

Here we've specified our new path and then used a special command, export, to propagate the change. Normally, changes to environment variables change only the current session or script in which they are being made. In order to use them in other sessions or scripts, you need to export them. To make a path or other environmental change for all users, add the changes to the /etc/profile file. This file is used by all users (except the root user; use the .bash_profile file in the /root directory to modify the root user's variables) to set values.

Tip You can find more information on configuring your Bash prompt at http://tldp.org/HOWTO/ Bash-Prompt-HOWTO/.

Command Aliases

The second reason for configuring your shell is to create command aliases. Aliases allow you to create shortcuts or set default options for often-used commands. A prime example is an alias for the rm command that many distributions enable by default and we discussed in Chapter 3.

When deleting a file with rm, you are not asked for confirmation unless you pass the -i option. By using an alias, you can have the shell execute rm -i each time you type rm, so you are always prompted for verification when deleting files. You create an alias via the alias command, and then create and delete a file.

```
$ alias rm='rm -i'
$ touch test
$ rm test
rm: remove regular file `test'? y
```

You can make an alias permanent by adding it to the .bash_profile configuration file in your home directory.

To get a listing of all aliases defined in your shell, run the alias command without any parameters.

```
$ alias
alias rm='rm -i'
alias v='ls -lt'
alias r='ls -lrt'
```

Here we've defined the interactive delete alias and two aliases that save us typing when listing a directory full of files sorted by their modification dates.

You should not define an alias with the same name as an existing command, unless you're setting default options. You will still be able to run the original command by specifying the full path to the executable, but it might create nasty surprises when you don't expect them (e.g., in automated scripts).

To delete an alias, use the `unalias` command. To remove our interactive delete we would use this:

```
$ unalias rm
```

To read more about aliases, see the `ALIASES` section of the `bash man` page.

The Bash shell is extremely powerful and flexible, and it can make everyday administration tasks very easy. If you want to know more about Bash and what you can use it for, see `http://www.tldp.org/LDP/Bash-Beginners-Guide/html/` and `http://tldp.org/HOWTO/Bash-Prog-Intro-HOWTO.html`.

Controlling Access to Your Host

You can control quite a lot of user characteristics, including when and how users can log in, what their passwords look like, and how often they have to change and reset their passwords. These controls are all checked when users log in to the host and are generally managed by a series of modules. These modules are collectively known as Pluggable Authentication Modules (PAM). Almost all Linux distributions, including Red Hat and Ubuntu, rely on PAM to control how and when users can interact with hosts.

In this section, we'll introduce you to PAM and how it works. You won't generally have to change much PAM configuration, but it is important to understand how it works.

■**Note** We'll talk a bit more about how PAM is used with other authentication mechanisms (e.g., Integration with Active Directory and LDAP) in Chapter 16.

PAM was originally designed by Sun Microsystems to provide a plug-in authentication framework. It has been heavily used and developed in the Linux world, and a large number of PAM modules exist to perform a variety of functions ranging from checking passwords to creating home directories. PAM modules were originally used to provide authentication and other services to applications that lacked authentication or a particular authentication capability. Later, as more sophisticated types of authentication became available, such as smart cards and one-time passwords (or tokens), PAM became a way to integrate and extend authentication mechanisms. Rather than having to rewrite each application for new authentication methods, all that is required is to add PAM support. PAM then takes care of the hard work of authenticating through a standard API.

Configuring PAM

Essentially PAM is a hierarchy of authentication and authorization checks that are performed when an application wants to perform some action. These checks are stacked together; for example, when logging in we check the user exists, then check that the user's password is valid, and then that the password hasn't expired. This stack is usually made up of multiple PAM modules, each of which performs some check function. Additionally, some checks must pass (e.g., your user must exist), and other checks may be optional. The best way to understand PAM is to examine some PAM configuration files.

On most Linux distributions, you have two possible locations to look for PAM configuration information. The legacy file /etc/pam.conf used to hold PAM configuration information on Linux distributions, but now it is generally deprecated and has been replaced by the /etc/pam.d directory. Most modern versions of Red Hat and Ubuntu use this directory to hold a collection of configuration files for PAM-aware services. The service shares the same name as the application it is designed to authenticate; for example, the PAM configuration for the passwd command is contained in a file called /etc/pam.d/passwd. These files are called *service configuration files*.

There are a variety of service configuration files—for example, when users log in to a host, we use an application called, appropriately, login. The login application is triggered when a user logs in, and inside the pam.d directory you'll find a file named login that contains the authentication configuration for the application. Similarly, you'll find a file called sshd that performs similar work for users who log in via an SSH connection.

Other common services that come with default PAM configurations and that you'll find in the /etc/pam.d directory are the passwd command and the cron scheduling daemon. Inside each of these files, you'll find the authentication configuration that these applications use.

■**Note** We'll discuss crontab and how to schedule jobs and actions in Chapter 5.

We're not going to look at each specific file, though, because most of these services rely on some common configuration for authentication. Red Hat and Ubuntu both have separate files that define the common authentication configuration. Many of the service files reference and include this common configuration. On Red Hat, this file is /etc/pam.d/system-auth, which is automatically generated when you install your host and is updated with a special command called authconfig. On Ubuntu, the same role is performed by four separate files: common-auth, common-password, common-session, and common-account. Let's look at the contents of the Red Hat system-auth file in Listing 4-14.

Listing 4-14. *The login PAM File*

```
#%PAM-1.0
# This file is auto-generated.
# User changes will be destroyed the next time authconfig is run.
auth        required      pam_env.so
auth        sufficient    pam_unix.so try_first_pass nullok
auth        required      pam_deny.so

account     required      pam_unix.so
```

```
password      required      pam_cracklib.so try_first_pass retry=3
password      sufficient    pam_unix.so try_first_pass use_authtok nullok md5 shadow
password      required      pam_deny.so

session       optional      pam_keyinit.so revoke
session       required      pam_limits.so
session       [success=1 default=ignore] pam_succeed_if.so service in crond quiet ➥
use_uid
session       required      pam_unix.so
```

The system-auth and the other service configuration files have four possible directives. Let's use a single line from Listing 4-14 to examine them in more detail.

```
auth          sufficient    pam_unix.so try_first_pass nullok
```

The first directive in our line is auth, which is the management group we're configuring. Four major management groups are available in PAM, and they represent the different portions of the authentication and authorization process that can be configured:

- auth: These modules perform user authentication, for example, checking a password.

- account: This management group handles account verification tasks, for example, confirming that the user account is unlocked or if only the root user can perform an action.

- password: These modules set passwords, for example, checking to ensure your password is sufficiently strong.

- session: These modules check, manage, and configure user sessions.

Usually one or more modules are assigned to each management group, and these modules are usually checked in the order they are specified, and each module will return either a success or failure result. A particular module might also be specified more than once in a PAM configuration. For example, in Listing 4-14 you can see that the pam_unix.so module is specified in all four management groups:

```
auth          sufficient    pam_unix.so try_first_pass nullok
account       required      pam_unix.so
password      sufficient    pam_unix.so try_first_pass use_authtok nullok md5 shadow
session       required      pam_unix.so
```

This indicates that the pam_unix.so module, which is the module that takes care of most standard Unix authentication functions such as entering a traditional password, can perform checks and functions for each management group. For example, it can confirm that the user's password is correct in the auth group and also confirm the user exists for the account group.

The next directive, sufficient, is called a *control flag*, and it tells PAM how to treat the result of the module. As mentioned earlier, some checks are more important than others. Control flags tell PAM what to do with the success or failure result and how that result impacts the overall authentication process. Table 4-7 lists the four PAM control flags.

Table 4-7. *PAM Control Flags*

Flag	Description
required	A required module must succeed for authentication to succeed.
requisite	If a requisite module fails, then authentication will immediately fail.
sufficient	Authentication immediately succeeds if the module is successful.
optional	The success or failure of the module doesn't impact authentication.

The required flag means the module result must be a success in order for the authentication process to succeed. If the result of this module is a failure, then the overall authentication is also a failure. If more than one module are stacked together, the other modules in the stack will also be processed, but the overall authentication will still fail.

The requisite flag also indicates that the module result must be successful for authentication to be successful. Additionally, unlike the required flag, the success or failure of this module will be immediately notified to the service requesting authentication, and the authentication process will complete. This means that if any modules are stacked together and a module with a requisite control flag fails, then the modules remaining to be processed will not be executed. In comparison, with the required control flag, the remaining modules in the stack continue to be processed.

The next control flag is sufficient. The sufficient flag means that the success of this module is sufficient for the authentication process to be successful or, if modules are stacked, for the stack to succeed. This is dependent on no other required modules processed prior to this module failing. If a sufficient module fails, however, then the overall stack does not fail.

The last control flag is optional. An optional module is not critical to the overall success or failure of the authentication process or the module stack. Its success or failure will not determine the success or failure of the overall authentication process.

The next directive, pam_unix.so, indicates what PAM module will be used and its location. If you specify a PAM module without a path, then the module is assumed to be located in the /lib/security directory. You can also specify a module from another location here by providing the path to it, as you can see in the following line:

```
auth        required     /usr/local/pamlib/pam_local.so id=-1 root=1
```

The last directives are arguments to be passed to the PAM module—in this case, we are passing the arguments try_first_pass and nullok to the pam_unix.so module. The try_first_pass argument tells the module to see if a password has already been received by the module, and if so, to use that password to authenticate. The nullok argument tells the module that it is OK to have a blank password. Most modules will ignore invalid or incorrect arguments passed to them, and the module will continue to be processed, though some modules do generate an error message or fail.

■**Tip** On Ubuntu you can find man pages for most PAM modules (e.g., man pam_unix will return the pam_unix man page). On Red Hat you can find documentation in the /usr/share/doc/pam-*version* directory. You can also find documentation at http://www.kernel.org/pub/linux/libs/pam/.

There is a last PAM function we need to mention: `include`. The `include` function allows you to include one PAM file in another. This is how our common configuration is included in specific service configuration files. To see this function, let's look at a snippet from the Ubuntu `login` PAM service configuration file in Listing 4-15.

Listing 4-15. *The Ubuntu* `login` *PAM Service Configuration File*

```
# Standard Un*x account and session
@include common-account
@include common-session
@include common-auth
@include common-password
```

Using the format `@include`, you can include other files in a PAM service configuration file. So `@include common-account` will include the content of the file `common-account` in the `login` file. Each module specified in that file will now be processed when the `login` file is used. The file is pulled in and parsed at the point at which it is included, and any modules in that included file are executed in order.

You can also use the `include` option as a control flag like so:

```
auth    include    system-auth
```

This will include all `auth` type lines from the file `system-auth`.

More About sudo

As discussed earlier in this chapter, the `sudo` command allows you to run some commands yourself with the privilege of another user, in most cases the `root` user. The command works much like the `RunAs` command in Microsoft Windows that allows a user to run a command as another user.

■**Note** Another command called `su`, also known as *substitute user* or *switch user*, allows you to change from one user to another without logging in and out. It is commonly used to change to the `root` user to perform some action. You can read about it through its `man` page. Note that `su` will not work if the `root` account is locked, as it is on Ubuntu. You can unlock the account by setting a password for the `root` user.

To use this command, you type `sudo` and then the command you want to execute. If you're allowed to run `sudo`, you'll be prompted to input a password, usually your own user password, and then the specified command will be executed as the `root` user. This allows you to perform the actions the `root` user can, like creating users, without actually having to sign in as the `root` user. You can see `sudo` at work in Listing 4-16.

Listing 4-16. *Using* sudo

```
$ sudo userdel ataylor
We trust you have received the usual lecture from the local System Administrator.
It usually boils down to these three things:
    #1) Respect the privacy of others.
    #2) Think before you type.
    #3) With great power comes great responsibility.
Password:
```

This rather intimidating message generally appears the first time you use the sudo command; afterward, you'll get the password prompt only.

The sudo command does not prompt you for a password each time it is used. After you enter your password, the sudo command gives you a grace period during which you are not prompted for your password. This period is 5 minutes on Red Hat and 15 minutes on Ubuntu. After this period, you will again be prompted for your password when you next run the sudo command.

On Ubuntu and Red Hat, the sudo command is installed by default. Ubuntu, in fact, doesn't even set a password for the root user; rather, you are encouraged to always use sudo to run privileged commands. Any member of the admin group on Ubuntu has access to run the sudo command. On Red Hat, we earlier configured it so that if you are a member of the wheel group, then you can run commands using the sudo command.

The sudo command is also highly configurable. You can specify exactly what commands, including grouping commands together as categories of commands, can be executed using the sudo command. You can configure the sudo command to allow users to execute all commands, some commands, or even to execute commands without prompting for their password (though this isn't recommended).

■**Tip** As you learned at the start of the chapter, you configure exactly what sudo can do by editing a file called /etc/sudoers using a special command called visudo. We'll talk more about this in the "Configuring sudo" section.

So what happens if you're not allowed to execute the sudo command? In Listing 4-17 we try to use the sudo command as the user ataylor, who doesn't have the correct authority to use the sudo command.

Listing 4-17. *Unauthorized* sudo

```
$ sudo useradd -m -c 'Illegal User' iuser
ataylor is not in the sudoers file.  This incident will be reported.
```

A failed attempt to use the sudo command will be logged by your host's syslog (or system logger) service, and then the message is sent to a file in the /var/log/ directory. On Red Hat–based distributions, you can see sudo command failures in the /var/log/secure file, and on Ubuntu they appear in the /var/log/auth.log file. A log message like this will be generated showing the date, time, user who tried to execute the sudo command, and unauthorized command the user tried to execute.

```
Sep  1 20:27:43 au-mel-rhel-1 sudo:      ataylor : user NOT in sudoers ; TTY=pts/1 ;
PWD=/home ; USER=root ; COMMAND=/usr/sbin/useradd -m -c 'Illegal User' iuser
```

These messages allow you to monitor for people attempting to perform inappropriate actions on your hosts, and can be used to detect attempted security breaches.

■**Note** In Chapter 18, we'll talk more about logging and how you can monitor for messages like the ones detailed in this section and send alerts or take some kind of action.

Configuring sudo

The sudo command checks the /etc/sudoers file for authorization to run commands. You can configure the sudoers file to restrict access to particular users, to certain commands, and on particular hosts.

Let's look at the /etc/sudoers file. First, you will need to use the command visudo to edit the /etc/sudoers file. The visudo command is a special editor designed to be used with the sudo command, and it is the safest way to edit the sudoers file. The command locks the file against multiple simultaneous edits, provides basic sanity checks, and checks for any parse errors. If the /etc/sudoers file is currently being edited, you will receive a message to try again later.

We'll start by looking at how we might allow our user ataylor to run the userdel command. We have added the content of Listing 4-18 to the sudoers file.

Listing 4-18. *Sample sudoers*

```
ataylor ALL=/bin/userdel
```

We can break down this line into its component parts.

```
username host = command
```

Listing 4-18 shows the user ataylor is allowed to, on all hosts (using the variable ALL), use the command /bin/userdel as if she were the root user. Any command you specify in the command option must be defined with its full path. You can also specify more than one command, each separated by commas, to be authorized for use, as you can see on the next line:

```
ataylor ALL=/bin/userdel,/bin/useradd
```

In the previous line, ataylor is now authorized to use the userdel and useradd commands as if she were the root user. All configuration lines in the sudoers file must be on one line only, and you can use \ to indicate the configuration continues on the next line.

A single sudoers file is designed to configure multiple hosts. Thus, it allows host-specific access controls. You would maintain your sudoers file on a central host and distribute the updated file to all your hosts.

■Note In Chapter 19 we talk about configuration management and how you could distribute this file to multiple hosts.

With host access controls, you can define different authorizations for different hosts, as shown in Listing 4-19.

Listing 4-19. *Using sudo Authorization on Multiple Hosts*

```
ataylor au-mel-rhel-1=/bin/userdel,/bin/useradd
ataylor au-syd-ubuntu-1=ALL
```

In Listing 4-19, the user ataylor is allowed to use only the userdel and useradd commands on the host au-mel-rhel-1, but on the host au-syd-ubuntu-1, she is allowed to use all commands as represented by the ALL option.

■Caution You should be careful when using the ALL variable to define access to all commands on a host. The ALL variable allows no granularity of authorization configuration.

You can be somewhat more selective with your authorization by granting access to the commands in a particular directory:

```
ataylor au-mel-rhel-1=/bin/*
```

This applies only to the directory defined and not to any of its subdirectories. For example, if you authorize access to the /bin/* directory, then you will not be able to run any commands in the /bin/extra/ directory unless you explicitly define access to that directory, like the configuration on the next line:

```
ataylor au-mel-rhel-1=/bin/*,/bin/extra/*
```

Sometimes you want to grant access to a particular command to a user, but you want that command to be run as another user. For example, say you need to start and stop some daemons as specific users, such as the MySQL or named daemon. You can specify the user you want the command to be started as by placing the username in parentheses in front of the command, like so:

```
ataylor au-mel-rhel-1=(mysql) /usr/bin/mysqld,(named) /usr/sbin/named
```

As you can imagine, lists of authorized commands, users, and hosts can become quite long. The sudo command also comes with the option of defining aliases. Aliases are collections of like users, commands, and hosts. Generally you define aliases at the start of the sudoers file.

Let's look at some aliases. The first type of alias is User_Alias, which groups like users.

```
User_Alias ADMIN = ataylor,jsmith
```

You start an alias with the name of the alias type you are using, in this case User_Alias, followed by the name of the particular alias you are defining, here ADMIN. Next you specify a list of the users who belong to this alias. You can then refer to this alias in a configuration line.

```
ADMIN=/bin/userdel,/bin/useradd, \
(named) /usr/sbin/named
```

In the previous line we have specified that the users in the alias ADMIN are able to use the commands userdel, useradd, and named.

The next type of alias you can define is a command alias, Cmnd_Alias, which groups collections of commands.

```
Cmnd_Alias USER_COMMANDS = /bin/userdel,/bin/useradd
```

You can use this alias in conjunction with the user alias just created.

```
ADMIN ALL=/bin/groupadd,USER_COMMANDS
```

Now all users defined in the alias ADMIN can use the command /bin/groupadd and all those commands defined in the command alias USER_COMMANDS on ALL hosts.

You can also specify an alias that groups a collection of hosts. The Host_Alias alias can specify lists of hostnames, IP addresses, and networks.

```
Host_Alias SERVERS = au-mel-rhel-1, au-mel-rhel-2, au-syd-rhel-1
```

You can combine this alias with the preceding ones you defined.

```
ADMIN SERVERS=USER_COMMANDS
```

Now all users specified in the ADMIN alias can run the commands specified in USER_COMMANDS on the hosts defined in the SERVERS alias group.

You can also negate aliases by placing an exclamation point (!) in front of them. Let's look at an example of this. First, you define a command alias with some commands you do not want users to use, and then you can use that alias in conjunction with a sudo configuration line.

```
Cmnd_Alias DENIED_COMMANDS = /bin/su,/bin/mount,/bin/umount
ataylor au-mel-rhel-1=/bin/*,!DENIED_COMMANDS
```

Here the user ataylor can use all the commands in the /bin directory on the au-mel-rhel-1 host except those defined in the DENIED_COMMANDS command alias.

Let's look at one of the other ways you can authorize users to use sudo. Inside the sudoers file, you can define another type of alias based on the group information in your host by prefixing the group name with %.

```
%groupname ALL=(ALL) ALL
```

You would then replace groupname with the name of a group defined on your host. This means all members of the defined group are able to execute whatever commands you authorize for them, in this case ALL commands on ALL hosts.

On Red Hat hosts, a group called wheel already exists for this purpose, and if you uncomment the following line in the /etc/sudoers file on your Red Hat host, then any users added to the wheel group will be able to use the sudo command to gain root privileges on your host. On Ubuntu this group is called admin rather than wheel.

```
%wheel ALL=(ALL) ALL
```

Additionally, the sudoers file itself has a number of options and defaults you can define to change the behavior of the sudo command. For example, you can configure sudo to send e-mail when the sudo command is used. To define who to send that e-mail to, you can use the option on the following line:

```
mailto "admin@au-mel-rhel-1.yourdomain.com"
```

You can then modify when sudo sends that e-mail using further options.

```
mail_always on
```

To give you an idea of the sorts of defaults and options available to you, Table 4-8 defines a list of the e-mail–related options.

Table 4-8. *Sending E-mail When sudo Runs*

Option	Description
mail_always	Sends e-mail every time a user runs sudo. This flag is set to off by default.
mail_badpass	Sends e-mail if the user running sudo does not enter the correct password. This flag is set to off by default.
mail_no_user	Sends e-mail if the user running sudo does not exist in the sudoers file. This flag is set to on by default.
mail_no_host	Sends e-mail if the user running sudo exists in the sudoers file but is not authorized to run commands on this host. This flag is set to off by default.
mail_no_perms	Sends e-mail if the user running sudo exists in the sudoers file but does not have authority to the command he tried to run. This flag is set to off by default.

The sudoers man page details a number of other options and defaults.

The sudo command itself also has some command-line options you can issue with it. Table 4-9 shows some of the most useful options.

Table 4-9. *sudo Command-Line Options*

Option	Description
-l	Prints a list of the allowed (and forbidden) commands for the current user on the current host
-L	Lists any default options set in the sudoers file
-b	Runs the given command in the background
-u user	Runs the specified command as a user other than root

The -l option is particularly useful to allow you to determine what commands the current user on the current host is authorized and forbidden to run.

```
$ sudo -l
Password:
User ataylor may run the following commands on this host:
   (root) ALL
```

The sudo command is complicated and, if improperly implemented, can open your host to security breaches. We recommend you carefully test any sudo configuration before you implement it and thoroughly explore the contents of the sudo and sudoers man pages.

WHO'S BEEN DOING WHAT?

Keeping track of what your users are doing is an important part of user management. In Chapter 18 we will talk about logging, and indeed one of the first resources you will use to keep track of the actions of your users is the content of your log files. But other commands and sources are also useful for keeping track of users and their activities.

The who command displays all users logged on to the host currently, together with the terminal they are logged on to. If users have connected remotely, the command shows the IP address or hostname from which they have connected.

```
$ sudo who
root      tty1         Jul  3 12:32
ataylor      pts/0          Jul  8 11:39 (host002.yourdomain.com)
```

You can modify the output of the who command, and you can see a full list of the options in the who man page. Probably the most useful command-line option is -a, which combines a variety of the command-line options to provide a detailed overview of who is logged in to your host, the login processes, and the host reboot and run-level details.

Also useful are the last and lastb commands, which display a record of when users last logged in to the host and a record of bad user logins, respectively. If you execute the last command without any options, it will print a report of the last logins to the host.

```
$ sudo last
root      tty1                              Sat Jul  3 12:32    still logged in
ataylor      pts/0          192.168.0.23      Sat Jul  3 14:25 - 14:26  (00:01)
reboot    system boot  2.4.20-28.8     Sat Jul  3 12:31          (4+05:40)
```

As you can see, the last command tells you that root is logged on and is still logged in. The list also shows the user ataylor, who logged in from the IP address 192.168.0.23 and stayed logged on for one second. The last entry shows a reboot entry. Every time the host is rebooted, an entry is logged that gives the time of the reboot and the version of the kernel into which the host was booted.

The lastb command produces the same style of report but lists only those logins that were "bad." In other words, it lists those logins in which an incorrect password was entered, or some other error resulted in a failure to log in.

> Related to the `last` and `lastb` commands is the `lastlog` command. The `lastlog` command displays a report that shows the login status of all users on your host, including those users who have never logged in. The command displays a list of all users and their last login date and time, or it displays a message indicating **Never Logged In** if that user has never logged in. Using command-line options, you can search records for specific users. Read the `lastlog` command's man page for further details.

Summary

In this chapter, you learned how to create users and groups from the command line or via the GUI interface. You also learned what happens when you sign on to your host, as well as about PAM and how to control access to your host.

The `sudo` command and how to use it to avoid the use of the `root` user to administrate your host was detailed. Additionally, we examined how to configure `sudo` to control who can access particular commands and how to report on `sudo` use. Lastly, we covered a bit about how to monitor your users' logins.

In the next chapter, we'll look at what happens when your host boots up and how to start, stop, and manage services.

CHAPTER 5

■ ■ ■

Startup and Services

By Dennis Matotek

In the last few chapters, you've learned how to install a Linux host, explored some basic Linux concepts, and been introduced to the concept of users and groups. This chapter is going to delve deeper into the workings of your Linux host and examine the way it operates "under the hood."

In this chapter, we'll look at what happens when your host starts up, or *boots*. We'll step through the process and show you how to start your host in a variety of modes and how to configure and modify the startup process. To demonstrate all of this, we'll take you through the process of how your host boots from the basic input/output system (BIOS) to login.

We'll also take you beyond the boot process and look at how your host starts and stops applications, system services, and other processes. Each distribution, Red Hat and Ubuntu, manages the addition, removal, starting, and stopping of these services slightly differently. We'll show you how to manage these services on each of these distributions and the nuances involved. You'll learn what services are, how to start and stop services, and how to see their status. Finally, we'll talk about how to make services start and stop automatically when your host boots or shuts down.

What Happens When Your Host Starts?

The boot process (*boot* is short for *bootstrap*) usually involves three separate but connected processes: the BIOS, the boot loader, and the loading of the operating system.

1. The BIOS initiates and checks your hardware.

2. The boot loader lets you select an operating system to load.

3. Lastly, your operating system is loaded and initiated.

These steps are not specific to Linux; you'll find most operating systems perform a similar set of functions and steps.

The BIOS

Let's look at what happens when you boot your host in a bit more detail. You may have noticed that when you turn on your host, it is common to hear a few beeps and whirrs and see some blinking lights on your front panel and keyboard. This is the first step of your host starting up, and this process is controlled by a small chip on the motherboard called the BIOS. The BIOS performs rudimentary system checks or power-on self-test (POST) operations on the availability of different bits of hardware attached to your system, like the memory, hard drives, keyboard, and video card. Depending on your BIOS, you can change different settings, but we will leave that to you to investigate at your leisure.

The BIOS will also poll other hardware such as hard drive controllers and initiate their onboard chips. Depending on your hardware, you may see the BIOS screen followed by information about devices the controller has found. You may be given an option to configure controllers or other hardware by pressing a certain key sequence (usually displayed on the screen when the hardware is initiated). This menu gives you the ability to manipulate the configuration of your host; for example, it allows you to set up RAID on a hard disk controller or troubleshoot problems with existing hardware configuration.

■**Caution** Changing some configurations can be dangerous, for example, incorrectly changing a RAID configuration could destroy your data, so use these menus with caution.

The BIOS also allows you to change the boot source for your host. The boot source is the media, for example, a hard drive, where your host looks for your operating system. The boot sequence setting allows you to boot from one of a number of sources: hard drives, CD/DVDs, or even USB keys. By default, your host will usually try to boot from an attached hard drive and, if configured, look for alternatives such as a CD/DVD drive or a USB key.

Every motherboard manufacturer has a different way of getting to the boot source menu, for example, by pressing Esc, Del, or a function key such as F1, F2, or F10. Usually a message appears on your screen indicating the appropriate key to press. From here a menu is usually displayed, and you can select the boot sequence you would like.

The Boot Loader

The BIOS uses the boot source setting to specify where to look for the next stage of the boot process: the boot loader. The BIOS uses a special section on your hard drive called a *master boot record* (MBR) to tell it what boot loader to start. The MBR is 512 bytes long and contains several pieces of information. Remember in Chapter 2 when we showed you how to partition the disk and installed the GRUB boot loader? The information about how your disk is portioned (i.e., how many slices, how big they are, and what they are called) is written to the MBR. This occupies the first 64 bytes of the record. Next, the installation process adds the GRUB boot loader to the record, and this loader takes up most of the remaining bytes.

Figure 5-1 displays a typical hard disk configuration, and you can see that it is divided into MBR and data partitions.

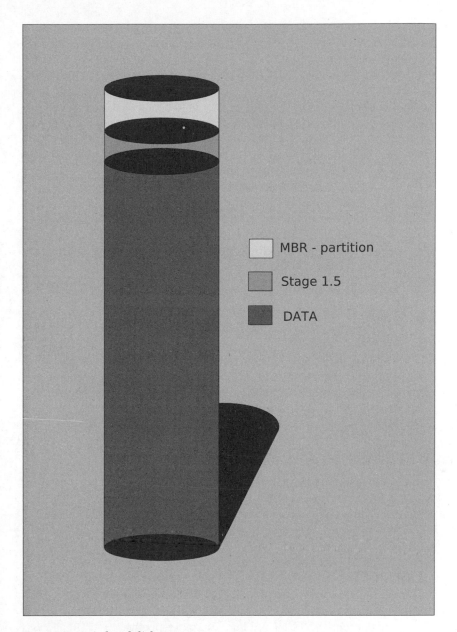

MBR - partition

Stage 1.5

DATA

Figure 5-1. *Your hard disk*

■**Note** For a good discussion on the structure of your hard disks, please see http://www.ranish.com/part/primer.htm.

Once the BIOS checks are complete, the BIOS reads the MBR on the boot source to look for a boot loader. If it finds one, the first stage of the boot loader process is launched. If it doesn't find one, your boot process will fail.

The GRUB boot loader process happens in three stages. Each stage initiates the next. The first stage the BIOS starts is called Stage 1. The sole job of this tiny stage code on the MBR is to load the next stage, Stage 1.5. Stage 1.5 loads the rest of the boot loader, called Stage 2, and displays a menu that allows you to choose which operating system to boot.

When Stage 2 is loaded, you will see the menu list of available kernels (and possibly other operating systems) to choose to boot into. Here you can also interact with the boot loader and pass different commands and variables to the booting kernel.

GRUB will boot the default kernel after a brief countdown. Pressing any key will stop the countdown, show you a more detailed menu of available options, and give you the opportunity to edit your boot configuration. Later in the "Using the GRUB Menu" section, we will explain these choices and how to manipulate them.

After picking the kernel you wish to boot into (or waiting until the default is loaded after the timeout), GRUB will now find the kernel binary and then load a special file called `initrd.img` into memory. This file contains the drivers your kernel needs to load to make use of the hardware of your host.

The Operating System

After loading `initrd.img`, GRUB completes and hands over control to the kernel, which continues the boot process by initiating your hardware, including your hard disks. Your operating system is started, and a special program called `init` is called that starts your services and brings your host to life. We'll take a look at `init` and how to manage services later in this chapter.

Understanding the GRUB Boot Loader

So let's now delve into what the boot loader is and what it does. We'll also look a bit at how you can configure it. We're not going to cover every detail of the boot loader, because you'll rarely need to change it, and most changes to it occur automatically, for example, when you install a new kernel package. But you should understand what it does and where it fits into your host's boot process.

In the Linux world, two main boot loaders exist: LILO and GRUB. The GRUB boot loader is the default for Red Hat and Ubuntu, so we will be concentrating on it here. GRUB, which stands for Grand Unified Bootloader, is a powerful multiboot loader. A *multiboot loader* can enable your host to boot into many different operating systems. Unlike Microsoft Windows or Mac OS X (and their boot loader tools—NTLDR and Boot Camp, respectively), GRUB allows you to boot multiple versions of Linux, Microsoft Windows, and Mac OS X on a single piece of hardware. This does not mean you can run them all simultaneously, like you can with virtual machine technology, but you can boot into them individually by selecting them from the GRUB menu at startup.

■**Note** LILO is a legacy boot loader used as the default boot loader on many older versions of Linux distributions. It is rarely seen today. For information on the LILO boot loader, please see `http://tldp.org/HOWTO/LILO.html`.

So how does GRUB work? GRUB uses four items to boot your system: a kernel file, the name of the drive, the partition number where the kernel file resides, and optionally an initial RAM disk.

GRUB is capable of booting in two ways. One is directly by finding and loading the desired kernel, and this is the way most Linux distributions are booted. GRUB also supports a method of booting, called *chain loading*; with this method GRUB loads another boot loader, such as the loader for Microsoft Windows, which then loads the desired operating system kernel. This allows GRUB to boot other operating systems using their own boot loaders.

Configuring GRUB

The GRUB boot loader is highly configurable, and its configuration is contained in the grub.conf configuration file. This file is located in different places on different distributions. On Red Hat, it can be found at /boot/grub/grub.conf (and the file is usually linked symbolically to /etc/grub.conf). On Ubuntu hosts, the file is called menu.lst and can be found at /boot/grub/menu.lst.

In Listing 5-1, you can see a typical grub.conf file for a Red Hat Enterprise Linux host.

Listing 5-1. */boot/grub/grub.conf*

```
#boot=/dev/sda
default=0
timeout=5
splashimage=(hd0,0)/grub/splash.xpm.gz
hiddenmenu
title Red Hat Enterprise Linux Server (2.6.18-92.el5)
        root (hd0,0)
        kernel /vmlinuz-2.6.18-92.el5 ro root=/dev/VolGroup00/LogVol01 rhgb quiet
        initrd /initrd-2.6.18-92.el5.img
```

Listing 5-1 shows the information GRUB requires to boot your Red Hat operating system. This is pretty similar to what you would see in a grub.conf file for an Ubuntu or other Linux host that uses GRUB. In the grub.conf file is listed each kernel (and hence operating system) available to boot. Configuration options specify which will load by default, and other options control the display and configuration of the menu.

Let's look at the file in Listing 5-1 in more detail. The first line, #boot=/dev/sda, is the boot device. It has been added here by the Anaconda Red Hat installer and is ignored by GRUB (as all lines beginning with # are comments and ignored).

■**Tip** In Linux configuration files, lines prefixed with the # symbol usually indicate comments, and these lines are skipped when processing your configuration files.

The second line, default=0, specifies which of the kernels (and therefore operating systems) is the default kernel to load. You can choose any operating system as the default operating system to load at boot time. If you have more than one kernel defined, GRUB reads them from top to bottom, with the first kernel being labeled 0, the next labeled 1, and so on. For example, if you wanted to load the third kernel in the configuration file by default, you would specify default=2.

■**Note** Numbering in the Linux operating system generally starts counting from 0 and not 1. The first partition on a disk is partition 0, as far as GRUB is concerned. A notable exception to this naming convention is device names: partition 0 on the first disk is /dev/sda1.

The third line is the timeout value, which specifies how long in seconds GRUB should wait before loading the default kernel. Remember that this count will be interrupted if you press any key during the boot process. The GRUB menu will then be displayed.

The fourth line is the location of the splash image, which provides the background picture to the GRUB menu. It is located by disk, partition, and then location in the file system; here (hd0,0)/grub/splash.xpm.gz indicates the splash.xpm.gz file located in the /grub directory on the first partition of the first hard drive, hd0,0 installed on our host.

The hiddenmenu instruction in the fifth line tells GRUB to hide its menu by default and instead initiate the countdown to loading the default kernel. Pressing any key will stop the timeout countdown and show the menu.

Next, you see the first of the kernel directives. Each kernel that is available to boot is listed here, the first kernel being 0, the second kernel 1, the third kernel 2, and so on (remember the default setting mentioned previously). In Listing 5-1 we only have one kernel listed. Each time you upgrade your kernel, usually by installing a new kernel package, another entry is added to this list, and generally an older kernel is also removed from the list and uninstalled.

■**Tip** We'll discuss installing and upgrading packages in Chapter 7.

Inside each kernel directive are a number of configuration variables. The first, title, signifies the start of a directive. This is also the title string shown on the menu screen for that kernel. The next option, root, specifies where to find the root partition for this kernel; if it is in the format of hd0,0, like our splash screen location, it is the first partition of the first hard drive installed in our host. If the root partition is specified as hd1,1, it would be the second partition of the second hard drive installed in your host. The location specified is where GRUB looks for the kernel it intends to boot. (GRUB's partition notation is different from Linux's partition notation; GRUB refers to the first disk as hd0 because it uses zero-based notation.)

The kernel option specifies the name of the kernel to load, its location, and how to load the kernel, and potentially passes options to the kernel to be processed. In Listing 5-1, we're loading a kernel with a version of 2.6.18, with its root located on an LVM volume group.

■**Tip** See Chapter 8 for more details of logical volume manager, or LVM.

Lastly, sometimes GRUB needs to know the location of a special file called initrd. This file is a tiny compressed file system that contains most of the drivers needed to use the host's hardware. Not all kernels need an initrd file; kernels that you have compiled yourself, for example, sometimes don't require an initrd file. You might, for example, compile a kernel if a later release of the kernel supported some new hardware or functionality you required. We recommend that you stick with the stock kernel provided by your distribution.

■**Note** You can find more information on defining kernels and kernel options to GRUB at http://grub. enbug.org/ and http://www.gnu.org/software/grub/manual/grub.html. You can also find information via the grub.conf man page.

Using the GRUB Menu

As we've described, when your host boots, it will boot into either the default kernel or operating system, or you can override it and display the GRUB menu. Once the menu is displayed, you will be presented with a list of boot options, and you can use the up and down arrows on your keyboard to choose the kernel you wish to boot. You can also edit the GRUB menu and change parameters, commands, and arguments before proceeding to boot into your chosen kernel.

For example, we could choose to boot into what is called *single-user mode*, or *maintenance mode*. This special mode, used when something is broken on your host, restricts access to the host to only one user: usually at the system console. This mode, which functions much like the Microsoft Windows Recovery Console, allows you to work with resources like disks and files without worrying about conflicts or other users manipulating the host. Let's look at booting into single-user mode now.

First, highlight the kernel you wish to boot into by using the up or down arrows on your keyboard. Press the E key to edit the highlighted kernel. You will see the configuration of that kernel, such as its location and parameters, displayed as in Figure 5-2.

Figure 5-2. *Booting to single-user mode, or maintenance mode, using the GRUB menu*

You'll see that the first line is highlighted, for example, root (hd0,0). As described previously when we outlined the grub.conf file, this is where GRUB expects its own root partition will be: on hard disk 0, partition 0. Using the up and down arrows, highlight the kernel /vmlinuz-2.x.x-x.el5 ro root line and press E again to edit that line.

You will see your cursor has been placed at the end of the kernel line where the settings rhgb and quiet have been specified. To boot into single-user mode, add the number 1 or the word single to the end of this line. In Figure 5-2, you can see that we have already added the word single to the end of the line.

Now if you boot the host, it will start in single-user mode, and you can perform required maintenance. The changes to the kernel line are not permanent, though, and the next time the host is booted, it will boot normally.

Using the GRUB menu, you can manipulate almost all of the configuration settings available; to find more detail of how to do this, go to http://www.gnu.org/software/grub/manual/grub.html.

Securing Your Boot Loader

Having such a versatile and configurable boot loader can have its drawbacks. One of those is security. An unsecured boot loader can be altered at boot time by any person with malicious intent. Many small offices will have their servers on or under a couple of desks rather than in a locked computer room, and these servers are therefore very susceptible to such attacks. We strongly suggest that you set a password on your boot loader and store it in a very safe place along with your other passwords.

■Caution You should always put your passwords somewhere secure like a safe or other secure, locked location. Sometimes it is also good to keep this somewhere offsite (as you would with offsite backups) so that if something happens to your site, you will not only be able to restore your data, but also have the right passwords handy to access your host. You should also have a backup of all passwords and tell someone you trust in your company where to find those passwords in case of an emergency.

GRUB provides the ability to set a password to the boot loader so that any changes to the preconfigured boot process requires the user to enter a password. First you have to generate an MD5 hash password, and then add that to the grub.conf file. To do this, you need to initiate GRUB's command-line manager using the grub command.

```
$ sudo grub
grub> md5crypt
Password: ************
Encrypted: $1$3yQFp$MEDEglsxOvuTWzWaztRly.
grub> quit
```

■Tip You can also use the grub-md5-crypt command to create this password.

Next, add this to your grub.conf file like so:

```
default=1
timeout=10
splashimage=(hd0,0)/grub/splash.xpm.gz
password --md5 $1$3yQFp$MEDEglsxOvuTWzWaztRly.
```

When your host next boots, you will notice that if you interrupt the boot process at the GRUB stage, you will be able to choose which kernel or operating system you would like to boot into. However, if you want to edit any of the GRUB configuration details, you are required to enter a password. To enter the password, you must press P and enter the password. You will then be able to edit the GRUB configuration as normal.

What Happens After You Boot?

So your host has found your kernel and booted it. Your operating system now starts to load, your hardware is initialized, disks are readied, IP addresses are assigned, and a variety of other tasks are performed. To do this, Linux runs the init program, which is tasked with initiating the operating system and its services.

> ■**Tip** The program `init` is the first process running on your host. If you looked at the process list on your host, you will notice that the `init` process has the process ID of 1.

The `init` tool is part a standard method for starting and stopping Linux and Unix hosts called SysV Init. SysV is a way of defining what state a host should be in at a particular point. SysV does this by using a concept called *runlevels*. Each runlevel contains a list of applications and services and an indicator of whether each should be started or stopped. So for example, during a normal boot of your host, the `init` tool knows what runlevel to set and then initiates all the required applications and services in that runlevel. Another example occurs when you shut down your host. When you tell your host to shut down, the `init` tool changes the runlevel to 0. This runlevel is configured so that all applications and services are stopped.

SysV has seven runlevels, ranging from 0 to 6, and each distribution uses different runlevels for different purposes. But some runlevels are fairly generic across all distributions. This includes runlevels 0, 1, and 6. You've already seen runlevel 0, which is used to shut down the host. Runlevel 1 is the single-user mode, or maintenance mode, that we described earlier in this chapter. Runlevel 6 is used when your host is being rebooted.

The runlevels on Ubuntu- and Red Hat–based hosts differ slightly. On Ubuntu, the remaining runlevels 2 to 5 all run in standard multiuser mode. *Multiuser* mode is the standard mode that most distributions start in, and all required services are usually set to be started by this runlevel.

In comparison, Red Hat generally starts in runlevel 5 if you have a GUI console installed or runlevel 3 for command line only. Red Hat has the following runlevels:

- *Runlevel 0*: Shuts down the host and brings the system to a halt

- *Runlevel 1*: Runs in single-user (maintenance) mode, command console, no network

- *Runlevel 2*: Is unassigned

- *Runlevel 3*: Runs in multiuser mode, with network, and starts level 3 programs

- *Runlevel 4*: Is unassigned

- *Runlevel 5*: Runs in multiuser mode, with network, X Windows (KDE, GNOME), and starts level 5 programs.

- *Runlevel 6*: Reboots the host

Configuring init

On most distributions, including Red Hat, the `/sbin/init` tool is configured using the `/etc/inittab` file. The `inittab` file specifies the default runlevel the system should use. It also details the other runlevels and where to find the list of applications to start or stop in each runlevel. The `init` tool uses a series of scripts and directories under the `/etc/rc.d` directory named `rc.x` where *x* is the runlevel; for example, the `/etc/rc.d/rc3.d` directory stores the applications in runlevel 3. Also described in this configuration file are virtual consoles (as we discussed in Chapter 3), accessible using the Ctrl+Alt+function key combinations.

You can learn more about how to edit the `inittab` file by reading the `inittab` man page:

```
$ man inittab
```

or by accessing the online version here: http://linux.die.net/man/5/inittab.

The inittab man page explains the syntax of the inittab file. Each line is comprised of the unique ID of the service being started, the runlevels the service will start at, the action to perform, and the command and any options to run, separated by colons. Any lines starting with # are regarded as comments.

```
id:runlevels:action:command -option -option
```

To change the default runlevel, which is the most common reason for editing the inittab file, you change the initdefault line. Here, the default runlevel is 5:

```
id:5:initdefault:
```

To change the default runlevel from 5 to 3, you replace the number 5 with 3 like so:

```
id:3:initdefault:
```

Your host will now boot to runlevel 3 and start all the programs associated with runlevel 3 when it next reboots.

The init program uses a series of scripts in /etc/rc.d to manage services and runlevels. These are listed in Table 5-1.

Table 5-1. *Scripts Used by init to Control Runlevels*

Script	Description
/etc/rc.d/rc.sysint	Initializes the system, and sets devices and other tasks.
/etc/rc.d/rc	Descends into the rcn.d directories and starts or stops init.d scripts listed there.
/etc/rc.d/rc.local	Local modifications required at boot time can be placed in this file.

The rc.sysinit script initializes things like swap, sets other devices, mounts file systems, and so on. This brings the host to a useful state where you can begin to run services on it. You should never edit and put new tasks into this file; you can use rc.local instead for this purpose.

The init passes the default runlevel *n* to /etc/rc.d/rc script, and the rc script will then descend into the /etc/rc.d/rcn.d directory and start or stop services there. We'll explain more about this in the "Managing Services" section. The /etc/rc.d/rc.local script is executed last of all, and you can include any special commands you would like to run at startup. These can be one-line commands that do certain tasks that you wish to perform when your host boots and which don't merit a full init script.

On Ubuntu and some newer versions of Fedora, the older system of SysV Init has been replaced by a new services management framework called Upstart. Upstart still calls the tool that starts services init, but instead of having an /etc/inittab file, it uses separate configuration files located in the /etc/event.d directory. The default runlevel is set in a file called rc-default in the /etc/event.d directory. We'll talk more about Upstart later in this chapter in the section "Upstart: A New Way."

■Tip If you want to change from Upstart to SysV Init on Ubuntu, you can do so by installing the `sysvinit` package. You can read about package installation in Chapter 7.

Moving Between Runlevels

How do we manipulate our host to run in different runlevels without rebooting? You can use the `telinit` or `init` command to switch between runlevels. First, work out what runlevel you are at now by using the `runlevel` command, which will return a message showing the previous and current runlevel, as shown in this example:

```
$ sudo runlevel
N 5
```

Here the previous runlevel is listed as N and the current runlevel as 5. If the previous runlevel is listed as N, the host doesn't have a previous runlevel (usually because its runlevel hasn't changed since it was booted).

Let's assume that your host boots into runlevel 5 by default. To switch it to runlevel 3, you can issue the command `telinit 3` (`telinit` needs to be run as the `root` user or via the `sudo` command). This will immediately run through the `/etc/rc.d/rc3.d/` directory and stop any programs undefined in that runlevel.

```
$ sudo telinit 3
```

We issue the `telinit` command to change the runlevel from 5 to 3. We issue the command again to change it back from 3 to 5:

```
$ sudo telinit 5
```

What has happened here is that first the `init` process has been sent the signal to move into runlevel 3 and therefore has descended into the `/etc/rc.d/rc3.d/` directory and terminated any processes that are not defined there. It will also start any processes that are defined to start at that runlevel that are not already started. The main thing you will notice here is that your X Windows session will cease, and you will be presented with the console. You will need to log back in and issue the `telinit 5` command. The `init` tool will again descend into the `/etc/rc.d/rc5.d/` directory, terminate any processes not defined there, and start any defined processes from `/etc/rc.d/rc3.d` that have not already been started. On Red Hat, you should now have a GUI X Window login presented to you.

Managing Services

In Chapter 3, we introduced you to the concept of processes and services. Each application and command you run creates a process. Some processes finish when the command completes, for example, listing the contents of a directory. Other processes are more long running and don't stop until you request them to do so or the host is rebooted. Some of these long-running processes run applications and services like mail and web servers or print or file services. These types of long-running processes are often called daemons. *Daemons* are processes that run in the background; that is, they are not required to be attached to a console. As we explained in

Chapter 3, each of these processes has a name; for example, sshd daemon or httpd, or apache for the Apache web server.

■**Note** All processes on Linux originate from a parent process. *Forking* a process involves a parent process making a copy of itself, called a child process. The originating parent usually exits and makes the init process the new parent. This means that processes can persist without requiring to be attached to a console or user session. When the parent process stops, so do all its children. For example, if you kill the init process on a host, you will stop all processes on the host. This is not a very good idea and will probably have unfortunate effects on a host. If you need to start and stop all services, you should use the commands we introduce in this chapter.

As we have explained previously, runlevels are used to group services so that when you boot our host to a particular runlevel, you can expect certain services to be available and others to be stopped. Services prescribed to start in the default runlevel are automatically started when your host boots. You can also start individual services at any other time. These services likewise can be stopped when your host exits a particular runlevel or when your host shuts down. You can also stop individual services manually at any time.

When the init program checks its default runlevel from the inittab file, it then uses the script called /etc/rc.d/rc to change between runlevels by giving the rc script the runlevel as an argument. It descends into the appropriate directory and starts or stops the services for that runlevel. The directory it chooses matches the runlevel desired. If the default runlevel is 3, the directory would be /etc/rc.d/rc3.d.

Once inside the appropriate directory, the rc script stops all the services prefixed with a K. It also starts all the services prefixed with an S. Services are started and stopped in sequence. You can examine what services will start in each runlevel by listing the contents of the /etc/rc.d/rcn.d directories (where *n* is a runlevel between 0 and 6). Let's look at part of the contents of the /etc/rc.d/rc3.d directory in Listing 5-2.

Listing 5-2. */etc/rc.d/rc3.d*

```
$ ls -l /etc/rc.d/rc3.d/
lrwxrwxrwx 1 root root 16 2008-04-29 06:58 K02httpd -> ../init.d/httpd
lrwxrwxrwx 1 root root 17 2008-04-29 07:31 K30postfix -> ../init.d/postfix
lrwxrwxrwx 1 root root 20 2007-11-09 04:48 K50netconsole -> ../init.d/netconsole
lrwxrwxrwx 1 root root 15 2007-11-09 04:46 K89rdisc -> ../init.d/rdisc
<snip>
lrwxrwxrwx 1 root root 19 2008-08-19 06:58 S08ip6tables -> ../init.d/ip6tables
lrwxrwxrwx 1 root root 18 2008-08-19 06:58 S08iptables -> ../init.d/iptables
lrwxrwxrwx 1 root root 17 2007-11-09 04:48 S80postfix -> ../init.d/postfix
```

You can see that all the files in the /etc/rc.d/rc3.d directory are symbolic links to individual init.d scripts, which are found in /etc/rc.d/init.d/ (as denoted by the l in the file type listing and the -> pointing to the referenced file). The individual scripts in the /etc/rc.d/init.d directory contain the instructions about how to start, stop, and return the status of each application or service.

All the symbolic links are prefixed with a *Knumber>* or *Snumber*. This orders the starting (S) and stopping (K) priorities of services in that runlevel and also instructs init to either send a start (S) or stop (K) argument to the respective init.d script. When init descends into these directories, first it stops those services defined with a K. Then it starts those defined with an S. It starts or stops these services in order of lower numbers to higher.

In Listing 5-2, you can see that the Postfix service will start after the iptables service because S08iptables is lower than S80postfix. (Postfix is an e-mail server we'll discuss in Chapter 10; iptables is a firewall we'll cover in chapter 6.)

This priority system is used to ensure services are started in the right order. For instance, in the example we've just cited, the iptables service starts before the Postfix service. This is because the iptables firewall protects our host from network attack, and we want to initiate our firewall before we initiate a network-facing service like Postfix. Another common example of priorities is that network-based services are started after the service that starts the network, simply because without a network you couldn't run network-based services.

In Listing 5-3, you see can see what /etc/rc.d/rc0.d (runlevel 0 or halt) will run when we halt our host.

Listing 5-3. */etc/rc.d/rc0.d*

```
[jsmith@au-mel-rhel-1 ~]$ ls -l /etc/rc.d/rc0.d/
total 276
lrwxrwxrwx 1 root root 17 Sep 15 03:50 K01dnsmasq -> ../init.d/dnsmasq
lrwxrwxrwx 1 root root 16 Sep 14 09:05 K01smartd -> ../init.d/smartd
lrwxrwxrwx 1 root root 22 Sep 14 09:05 K02avahi-daemon -> ../init.d/avahi-daemon
lrwxrwxrwx 1 root root 24 Sep 14 09:05 K02avahi-dnsconfd -> ../init.d/avahi-dnsconfd
lrwxrwxrwx 1 root root 16 Sep 14 09:02 K02dhcdbd -> ../init.d/dhcdbd
lrwxrwxrwx 1 root root 19 Sep 14 09:04 K02haldaemon -> ../init.d/haldaemon
lrwxrwxrwx 1 root root 24 Sep 14 09:04 K02NetworkManager -> ../init.d/NetworkManager
<snip>
lrwxrwxrwx 1 root root 18 Sep 14 09:00 K99cpuspeed -> ../init.d/cpuspeed
lrwxrwxrwx 1 root root 17 Nov 22 02:09 S00killall -> ../init.d/killall
lrwxrwxrwx 1 root root 14 Nov 22 02:09 S01halt -> ../init.d/halt
```

Your listing output may vary in content, as you may have different services installed on your host. In the list, every service is set to be stopped (denoted by the K), and only two services are set to start (denoted by the S): the killall and halt processes. So when we execute the telinit 0 command, either from the command line or when we shut down our hosts, the init process will go to /etc/rc.d/rc0.d and begin to stop the processes.

Managing Services on Red Hat

Managing services on Red Hat can be done using both a GUI tool and the command line. But let's start by looking at a Red Hat init script: take a look at the postfix script located in /etc/init.d. Let's look at the top of the script using the head command:

```
$ sudo head -n 5 /etc/init.d/postfix
```

This will show the first five lines of the /etc/init.d/postfix file, as you can see in Listing 5-4.

Listing 5-4. *RHEL Postfix Script*

```
#!/bin/bash
# postfix        Postfix Mail Transfer Agent
# chkconfig: 2345 80 30
# description: Postfix is a Mail Transport Agent, which is the program \
#              that moves mail from one machine to another.
```

On line 3 you see chkconfig: 2345 80 30. This information is used by a program called chkconfig to set up the symbolic links to the /etc/rc.d/rc2.d, /etc/rc.d/rc3.d, /etc/rc.d/rc4.d, and /etc/rc.d/rc5.d directories you saw earlier in this chapter. In this case, the Postfix script starts on runlevels 2, 3, 4, and 5 (as indicated by 2345), runs with a priority of 80, and stops with a priority of 30. The chkconfig command creates the symbolic links (often called symlinks) to the /etc/init.d/postfix script in the /etc/rc.d/rcn.d/ directories with the S80 and K30 prefixes. The #description line used by chkconfig is also important. Both the ckconfig and description definitions must be present, or an error will result. We explain how to use chkconfig later in this chapter in the "The chkconfig Command" section.

The rest of the contents of the postfix init script (which we've omitted from Listing 5-4) are the instructions used to start, stop, and sometimes query the status of the application or service managed by the script.

LSB AND INIT.D SCRIPTS

It should be noted that RHEL version 5 uses the pre-LSB standard for writing init.d scripts. These are already superseded and will be replaced with the LSB standard. Ubuntu 8.04 is already using LSB-compliant init.d scripts.

What's LSB? Short for Linux Standard Base, it is a set of standards agreed to by the various Linux distributions to make life easier for everyone using it, especially for those who develop on it. It seeks to make common standards for Linux configurations, file locations, package names, and other conventions. You can read more about it here: http://www.linuxfoundation.org/en/LSB.

In regard to init.d scripts, a new header syntax is required to make them LSB compliant. Here we list an example of a newer LSB-compliant init.d script for the Postfix program. The standard says that you must have the following keywords followed by a list of arguments, some denoted by a $ prefix. These $ arguments are reserved *virtual facilities*, which are described in the LSB specification. For instance, $local_fs means "all local file systems are mounted." So Required-Start prevents Postfix from starting unless all the file systems are mounted, the log service is running, the named server is running, the network is up, and the time has been synchronized. The others can be found here: http://refspecs.freestandards.org/LSB_3.1.0/LSB-Core-generic/LSB-Core-generic/facilname.html.

```
### BEGIN INIT INFO
# Provides:          postfix mail-transport-agent
# Required-Start:    $local_fs $remote_fs $syslog $named $network $time
# Required-Stop:     $local_fs $remote_fs $syslog $named $network
# Should-Start:      postgresql mysql clamav-daemon postgrey spamassassin
# Should-Stop:       postgresql mysql clamav-daemon postgrey spamassassin
# Default-Start:     2 3 4 5
# Default-Stop:      0 1 6
```

```
# Short-Description: start and stop the Postfix Mail Transport Agent
# Description:       postfix is a Mail Transport agent
### END INIT INFO
```

Other keywords are available too:

- `Provides`: Gives a brief indication what this service provides. This information is used by other services.

- `Required-Start`: Lists services that must be available for this script to start.

- `Required-Stop`: Indicates this service must be stopped before the services listed here are stopped.

- `Should-Start`: Defines a list of what services can be started, although not mandatory, before this service starts.

- `Should-Stop`: Indicates this service should be stopped, although not mandatory, before the services listed here.

- `Default-Start`: Defines the default runlevels the service should be run in.

- `Default-Stop`: Defines the default runlevels this service should not run in.

- `Description`: Gives a description of the service.

Starting and Stopping Services at Boot and Shutdown

So how do you actually manage the services on Red Hat hosts? There are two ways to turn on and off services: one is to use the command `chkconfig`, mentioned previously, and the other is to use the GUI Services Configuration program provided by Red Hat. Let's look first at the GUI Services Configuration.

GUI Services Configuration

You can start the GUI Services Configuration program in two ways: by running `system-config-services` from the command line or by selecting System ➤ Administration ➤ Services in the RHEL menu, as shown in Figure 5-3.

This opens the GUI program shown in Figure 5-4. It is simple to follow the process of turning on and off services using this program. You are told what runlevel you are currently at in this window. You have the ability to change the configuration of runlevel to 3, 4, 5, or all. You can change the runlevel you are editing by selecting from the Edit Runlevel menu.

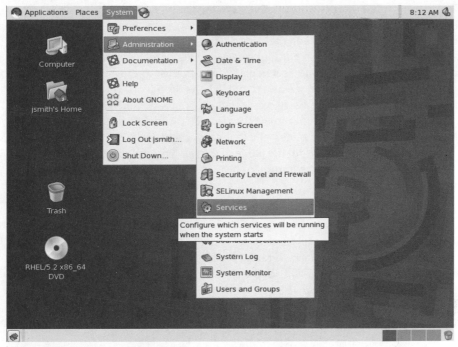

Figure 5-3. *Starting the GUI Service Configuration program*

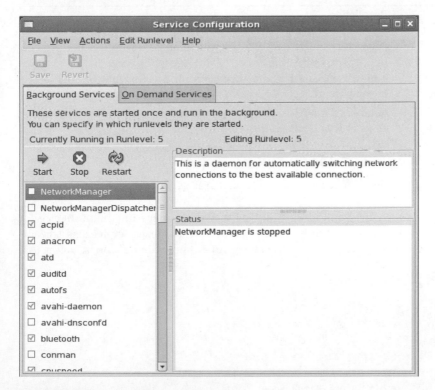

Figure 5-4. *Service Configuration program*

Notice in Figure 5-4 that there is a list of services in the left panel and a description and status window on the right. Our figure shows that NetworkManager is highlighted, and you are given a brief description of the service and the current status, stopped.

Simply select a check box next to a particular service name and click the start, stop, or restart icon to perform that action on the service. If you wish to stop the httpd daemon, for example, you would highlight that service and then click the Stop icon. You follow the same procedure with starting and restarting a service.

To delete the service from the current runlevel, you select it, and then use the Actions menu to delete the service. To add the service again, select the service and use the Actions menu to add the service. You will have to manually input the name of the service you wish to add.

To save your changes, click the Save button, or if you wish to revert your changes, click the Revert button.

The chkconfig Command

The other way to change service runlevels in Red Hat is to use the chkconfig command. You can use chkconfig to manage the scripts in /etc/init.d from the command line.

As briefly explained earlier, chkconfig uses the chkconfig headers in each init.d script to create the necessary symbolic links from the /etc/rc.d directories to the particular scripts in the /etc/rc.d/init.d/ directory. You can pass several options to the chkconfig command, and these are listed in Table 5-2.

Table 5-2. *chkconfig Options*

Option	Description
--list	Gives information pertaining to a service if that service is specified. Otherwise, all services are listed, with information given as to whether the service is started or stopped in each runlevel.
--add	Adds a service to chkconfig management. An entry in each runlevel is created according to the information found in the init script.
--del	Removes the service from chkconfig management. The symlinks in the /etc/rcn.d directories are removed.
--level	Manages services for particular levels combined with the name of the service and the setting you wish (e.g., chkconfig --level 25 httpd off).

We will now go through these options for you. To list all the services and their runlevels for your host, you need to pass the --list option to chkconfig. It will list each service against each runlevel and indicate whether it is on or off in that level. An example can be seen in Listing 5-5.

Listing 5-5. *chkconfig --list*

```
$ sudo /sbin/chkconfig --list
acpid    0:off  1:off  2:off  3:on   4:on   5:on   6:off
anacron  0:off  1:off  2:on   3:on   4:on   5:on   6:off
atd      0:off  1:off  2:off  3:on   4:on   5:on   6:off
auditd   0:off  1:off  2:on   3:on   4:on   5:on   6:off
autofs   0:off  1:off  2:off  3:on   4:on   5:on   6:off
```

As you can see in Listing 5-5, when you pass the `--list` option to chkconfig, it produces a long list of all the services it manages. You will also notice that the names have the same names as the init.d files found in the /etc/rc.d/init.d/ directory. This is because most packages that install daemons will run chkconfig as part of their install process for you.

If you intend to have the Postfix mail server added to the default runlevels according to the /etc/rc.d/init.d/postfix script, let chkconfig manage it for you by entering the following command:

```
$ sudo chkconfig postfix on
```

This turns the service on for the runlevels specified in the init.d script through chkconfig: 2345 80 30 by default. You can also manually specify with chkconfig the exact runlevels you wish Postfix to start in. For example:

```
$ sudo chkconfig --level 35 postfix on
```

This command will turn Postfix on at runlevels 3 and 5. When your host is rebooted, it will now start the Postfix service in either runlevel 3 or 5, but not in 2 or 4, unless specifically instructed to do so.

If you wish to turn a service off so it doesn't start when your host is restarted, you would issue the following command:

```
$ sudo chkconfig postfix off
```

This turns the service to off in all runlevels, meaning that the service will no longer start in any runlevel when the host is rebooted.

Starting and Stopping Running Services

You've just learned how to tell Red Hat to start and stop services when the host boots or shuts down, but how do you handle services that are currently running now? Let's say you've just updated your mail version and want to restart the service. There are two ways to do this: using the init scripts themselves and using the service command.

Using init Scripts

All of the scripts located in the /etc/init.d directory are generally executable (i.e., they have the executable or x permission set). Each script can also usually take one of the following arguments: start, stop, restart, reload, or status. To see how to restart the Postfix service, take a look at the following example:

```
$ sudo /etc/init.d/postfix restart
```

This will first stop and then start the Postfix mail server.

You can also use the following two commands to stop and then start the Apache httpd server:

```
$ sudo /etc/init.d/httpd stop
$ sudo /etc/init.d/httpd start
```

Lastly, most of the `init` scripts will give you usage information if you don't pass an argument, for example:

```
$ sudo /etc/init.d/postfix
Usage: /etc/init.d/postfix  {start|stop|restart|reload|abort|flush| ➥
check|status|condrestart}
```

The service Command

Red Hat–based distributions have another command that can also be used for starting and stopping running services: `service`. The benefit of using the `service` command is that it will start and stop an `init` script in the most predictable manner possible by stripping most of the environment variables and setting the current working directory to /. The following command line will reload Postfix (this will reread the configuration files, and the processes will restart as soon as they can):

```
$ sudo service postfix reload
Reloading postfix:                                      [  OK  ]
```

This automatically restarts the Postfix server after rescanning the configuration files. Any existing process is restarted once its current tasks are complete. This allows you to make changes to the configuration without greatly disrupting the Postfix mail server.

■**Tip** With Red Hat distributions, we recommend you try to use the `service` command.

Managing Services on Ubuntu

Both Ubuntu and Red Hat hosts follow the same SysV Init standard, but they differ slightly in their execution to achieve the same goals. In Red Hat, you have seen that you start and stop services using the `service` command, and you turn services on or off using either `chkconfig` or `system-config-services`. In Ubuntu, you use the `invoke-rc.d` command to turn on and off services and the `update-rc.d` command to manage services.

Ubuntu, however, is different from Red Hat in that it has adopted a newer `init` mechanism called Upstart. Upstart maintains backward compatibility and retains the ability to manage SysV Init scripts. We'll explain more about Upstart later in this chapter in the section "Upstart: A New Way."

Invoke-rc.d: Starting and Stopping Services

Let's first see just how these distributions are similar. Like Red Hat, Ubuntu hosts use the /etc/rc.d style directories to define what programs run in what runlevel, and the individual scripts are stored in /etc/init.d. Unlike Red Hat hosts, Ubuntu does not have an /etc/inittab file to manage the default runlevel, and directories that contain the symbolic links that determine what is started (and stopped) in each runlevel live in /etc. Ubuntu hosts don't use the `service` command to start and stop services, nor do they use `chkconfig` to manage the init scripts.

■**Note** Later versions of Ubuntu, from version 8.10 onward, have the `service` and `chkconfig` commands available (in a package called `chkconfig`).

On Ubuntu hosts earlier than version 8.10 (like our Ubuntu Server version 8.04), to start and stop services, you would run the `invoke-rc.d` command. As with Red Hat, you can also execute the individual scripts. All `init` scripts will have the `start` or `stop` options, but many also accept the `restart`, `reload`, and `status` options. If you were to try to start the Postfix program, you would issue the following:

```
$ sudo invoke-rc.d postfix start
```

If you wanted to then stop the Postfix service, you would initiate the following command:

```
$ sudo invoke-rc.d postfix stop
```

Or execute the individual script:

```
$ sudo /etc/init.d/postfix stop
```

■**Note** You can of course read the scripts yourself to find out what they do and what other arguments they accept.

Ubuntu: Turning Services On and Off

On Ubuntu, there is a useful text-based GUI called `sysv-rc-conf` to manage your services. The `sysv-rc-conf` program is a sister program to the Red Hat's `system-config-services`. It enables you to easily view what services are set to run at particular runlevels, and you can toggle them on an off for the next reboot. This command is not installed by default, so you will need to install it first.

```
$ sudo aptitude install sysv-rc-conf
```

■**Note** We'll delve into package management and ways to install software in detail in Chapter 7.

The `sysv-rc-conf` tool is a text-based GUI, but you can also use it on the command line by passing some arguments to it. The syntax is very similar to Red Hat's `chkconfig` command.

From the command line, you can list the services on your host by issuing the following:

```
$ sudo sysv-rc-conf -list
```

The output of this command is like the output from Red Hat's chkconfig --list command. You can also turn off services via the command line in much the same way as you would using chkconfig.

```
$ sudo sysv-rc-conf --level 35 postfix on
$ sudo sysv-rc-conf --level 35 postfix off
$ sudo sysv-rc-conf postfix on
$ sudo sysv-rc-conf postfix off
```

The sysv-rc-conf GUI is text based and quick and easy to use. You can see what it looks like in Figure 5-5.

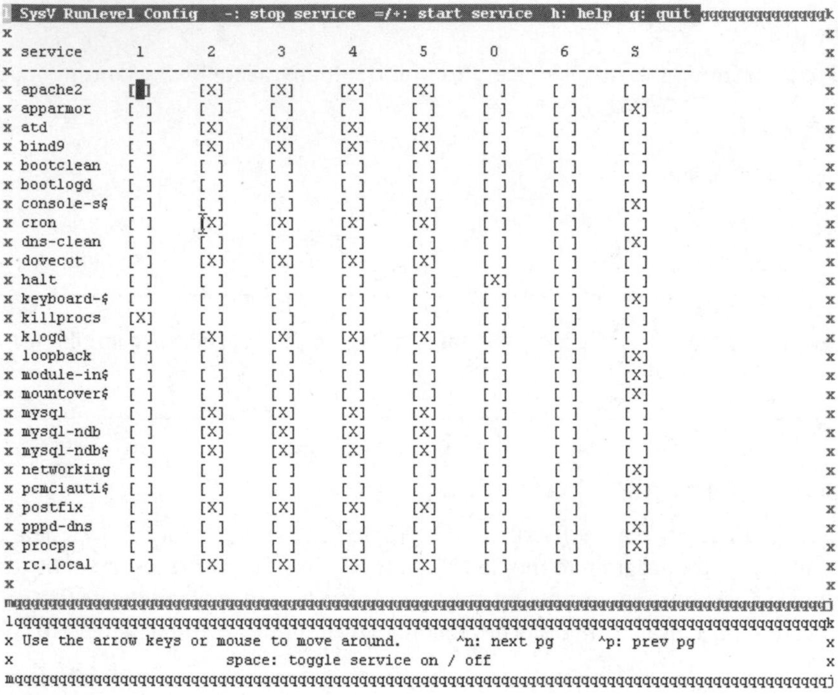

Figure 5-5. *sysv-rc-conf for managing services on Ubuntu*

To turn services on and off, you simply use the arrow keys to move the cursor to the service you wish to manage. Then use the space bar to toggle the X on or off depending if you want the service to run at that particular runlevel. You save and quit by pressing Q.

Update-rc.d: Turning On and Off Services on the Command Line

Managing services on Ubuntu on the command line is done via the update-rc.d command. Like chkconfig for Red Hat hosts, update-rc.d will create symbolic links into the /etc/rc?.d directories or remove them if instructed to do so. The update-rc.d command takes the options listed in Table 5-3.

Table 5-3. *update-rc.d Options*

Option	Description
start	Allows you to explicitly state the runlevels and startup sequence.
stop	Allows you to explicitly state the sequence and runlevels you wish to stop the service.
defaults	The update-rc.d script will create start symlinks with the default start sequence (S20) into runlevels 2, 3, 4, and 5 and stop symlinks into runlevels 0, 1, 6 with the stop sequence (K80).
remove	Removes the symlinks from each runlevel as long as the file /etc/init.d/*script-name* has already been removed. (See -f for more information.)
-n	Gives you a dry run of what would happen without changing anything.
-f	When used with the remove option, forces the removal of the symlinks from the /etc/rcn.d directories, even if /etc/init.d/*script-name* is still present.

Unlike the chkconfig information provided in the Postfix init.d scripts on the Red Hat host you saw earlier, update-rc.d does not require any particular information to be provided in the Ubuntu init.d scripts. The update-rc.d command will simply link init.d scripts into the /etc/rcn.d directories, usually with the defaults of runlevels 2, 3, 4, 5 and a start priority of S20, and runlevels 0, 1, 6 and a stop priority of K80.

From the command line, you can then issue update-rc.d to manipulate the services that run at particular runlevels. For example, to turn a service on with the Ubuntu defaults, you issue the following:

```
$ sudo update-rc.d postfix start defaults
```

With the defaults, as stated previously, the init.d scripts are symbolically linked to the /etc/rcn.d directories and given the standard start and stop priorities of 20 and 80.

You can specify the runlevels and priorities you wish your services to start on with the following:

```
$ sudo update-rc.d postfix start 23 40
```

Here we have set the service to start at runlevels 2 and 3 with a priority of 40.

To turn off the service in runlevel 2, issue the following:

```
$ sudo update-rc.d postfix stop 2
```

The preceding command will add a K80postfix symbolic link into the /etc/rc2.d directory.

To remove services from all runlevels, you would issue the following command:

```
$ sudo update-rc.d postfix remove
```

If the init.d script for the service you are trying to remove is still present in the /etc/init.d directory, which will be the case if you have not uninstalled Postfix, you will get an error unless you use the -f option. In this case, you issue the following:

```
$ sudo update-rc.d -f postfix remove
```

You are now probably beginning to understand why the LSB project we mentioned in the sidebar "LSB and init.d Scripts" earlier in this chapter is an important step to making Linux more user friendly. Both Red Hat and Ubuntu have different ways of achieving the same result, so the work on standardization is most welcome. Let's now look at the future of managing services on your Linux hosts.

Upstart: A New Way

As we pointed out earlier, Ubuntu does not use SysV to initiate its hosts. Newer versions of Ubuntu (since version 6.10) and versions of Fedora after version 9 use a new standard called Upstart. The idea behind Upstart is to create a comprehensive init process that can be used to start, stop, monitor, and respond to events on behalf of services on your Linux host. It is a reworking and expansion of the SysV Init paradigm; rather than outright replacing SysV Init, the designers have created Upstart to emulate SysV Init until everyone converts over.

We mentioned previously that SysV Init scripts are run by the init command in series, one after the other, based on their order in the appropriate /etc/rc.d directory. SysV Init relies on runlevels to determine what service is run on your host at startup. It does not take any interest in that service until it is time to shut the host down. Upstart, by comparison, only maintains the concept of runlevels for backward compatibility and brings forward a different focus to init by using events to decide what is run on your host.

The new init process under Upstart is an event-based daemon that uses event triggers to start or stop processes. An *event* is a change of state that init can be informed of. The event can be the adding of a peripheral device, like a USB memory stick being plugged in. The kernel can then inform init of this action by sending an event notice. This event in turn can trigger other jobs to be initiated or stopped depending on the job definitions under init's control.

Upstart collectively calls processes under its command jobs, and you interact with those jobs using the initctl command. Jobs can either be *services* or *tasks*. Services are persistent, like a mail server, and tasks perform a function and then exit to a waiting state, like a backup program. The definition files (or Upstart scripts) for jobs can be found under the /etc/event.d directory.

Listing 5-6 is what is called a *service job definition* for the logd daemon for Upstart. In this case, logd is a logging daemon that needs to write its output to the console. As logging daemon, it is important that if this gets stopped for some reason, it is good to get it to try to restart itself. Let's run through the major points here.

Listing 5-6. */etc/event.d/logd*

```
# logd
# This service is started automatically by init so that the output from
# other services can be logged.
description     "service logging daemon"
author          "Scott James Remnant <scott@ubuntu.com>"
stop on runlevel 0
stop on runlevel 1
stop on runlevel 6
console output
exec /sbin/logd
respawn
```

The stop on configuration option is an event definition signaling Upstart to stop logd when a runlevel 0 event is detected. This option works similarly for runlevels 1 and 6 as well. As you know, runlevels 0, 1, 6 are special runlevels that either shut down, reboot, or put your host into maintenance mode. The console output option directs the output of logd to the console. The exec option directs Upstart to the binary it should execute to run the logd daemon. Lastly, the respawn option directs Upstart to restart the job if it is stopped unexpectedly.

While Upstart is different from SysV and has no natural concept of runlevels, it has been made backward compatible with SysV Init scripts. Therefore, in /etc/event.d, you will see several rc? definition files. These help emulate the old-style SysV scripts by executing the /etc/init.d/rcn script. This will in turn run through the old /etc/rcn.d directory and start and stop services for that particular runlevel.

Because the old rcn.d directories are used, the service management tools we discussed earlier will still work fine with a system that uses Upstart.

Shutting Down and Rebooting Your Linux Host

There are several ways to shut down and reboot a Linux host both from the GUI and the command line. From the command line, to shut down the host you can issue the appropriately named shutdown command:

```
$ sudo shutdown -h now
```

This will begin to shut down the host and bring it to a halt (as we've specified the -h option in the example) immediately. What happens in the background is that the shutdown program tells init to change to runlevel 0. That immediately starts killing all the services and then runs two special programs: killall, which kills all remaining services that haven't been shut down normally, and halt, which unmounts file systems and powers off the host.

You can also set the host to reboot using the shutdown command, but this time giving the reboot option -r:

```
$ sudo shutdown -r -t: 5 "This host is being rebooted for maintenance"
```

■**Note** If you have mistakenly initiated a shutdown, usually the Ctrl+C key combination will cancel the scheduled shutdown.

Here you can see we have asked shutdown to reboot the host by passing the -r argument. We have also said that we want to give 5 minutes grace time by passing the -t: 5 argument. You can specify any length of time you require in minutes. Lastly, we have given a warning message outlining why the host is being rebooted. This message will be sent to all users currently logged on.

After 5 minutes, the shutdown program tells init to change to runlevel 6, where it performs the same actions as it does in runlevel 0 except it runs the reboot program instead of the halt program.

From the GUI, shutting down the host is easy. Click the System menu and then select the Shutdown option.

Scheduling Services and Commands with Cron

There is a last type of service management we need to show you: scheduling. You may already be familiar with the Microsoft Task Scheduler, which you can use to schedule tasks to be run once or repeated regularly on a given minute, hour, day, week, or month. The equivalent in Linux is called *crontab* (short for chronograph table). Its purpose is to submit tasks at set times according to the host's clock. *Tasks* can be any script or application that you desire. Commonly, you will find maintenance-type tasks in the crontabs. These can be scheduled to run nightly, weekly, or monthly and perform some kind of script, like one that deletes all files in the /var/log/httpd directory older than 2 months.

Cron jobs (the tasks that crontab performs) are defined in a series of scripts under the directories defined in the /etc/crontab file. These are referred to as *system cron jobs*. The lists of directories in the /etc/crontab file looks like this:

```
$ less /etc/crontab
SHELL=/bin/bash
PATH=/sbin:/bin:/usr/sbin:/usr/bin
MAILTO=root
HOME=/

# run-parts
01 * * * *  root  run-parts  /etc/cron.hourly
02 4 * * *  root  run-parts  /etc/cron.daily
22 4 * * 0  root  run-parts  /etc/cron.weekly
42 4 1 * *  root  run-parts  /etc/cron.monthly
```

You should not edit this file because, being the system crontab file, it is likely to be replaced with a new version each time crontab is updated. This means any changes will be lost. Plus you could cause other problems if you make a mistake. It does, however, provide a good example of the syntax of a crontab file.

■**Tip** When a single host is used to run a lot of virtualized servers, you should change the times cron jobs start on each virtual server to ensure they do not all start running at the same time. Having multiple virtual servers all start their daily cron tasks at the same time would impact system performance.

Listed at the top of the file are SHELL, PATH, MAILTO, and HOME environment variables, which we described in Chapter 4. Lines starting with # are comments and can be ignored. Further down the file, you can see five columns with either a number or *, a column with root, a column with run-parts, and lastly a directory listing.

The first five columns represent minute, hour, day of the month, month, and day of the week. Let's look at the last line:

```
42 4 1 * *  root  run-parts  /etc/cron.monthly
```

Here, 42 is the 42nd minute of the hour, the hour is 4 (with hours being based on a 24-hour clock), and 1 represents the first day of the month. So crontab will run the last line at 04:42 a.m. on the first day of every month.

■**Note** You can also specify the standard three-letter abbreviations for the months, days in the month, and days of the week columns, for example, `sun` for Sunday and `aug` for August, respectively.

Any column with an asterisk (*) in it means all values are valid and are not restricted as to when to run. Let's take our last line again:

```
42  4  1  *  3  root  run-parts  /etc/cron.monthly
```

Here we've changed the value in the day of the week column to 3. Our job would now run at 04:42 a.m. on the first day of the month and also every Wednesday.

■**Note** Day of the week starts with Sunday at 0 and goes through to Saturday at 6. When specified with a value in the day of the month column, days are cumulative. So a job will execute on all the days listed in the day of the month column and on every weekday listed in the day of the week column.

You can also specify automatically reoccurring jobs like so:

```
*/2  4  1  *  3  root  run-parts  /etc/cron.monthly
```

Here, instead of specifying an exact time to run, we have used the notation */2. This notation tells cron to run the job every time the number of minutes is cleanly divisible by 2. This allows you to do some powerful stuff. For example, you could use */4 in the hour column, and the job would run every other minute every fourth hour, like so:

```
*/2  */4  1  *  *  root  run-parts  /etc/cron.monthly
```

The use of the comma indicates a list of values, for example:

```
2  0,1,2,3,4  1  *  *  root  run-parts  /etc/cron.monthly
```

This would run the job at 12:02 a.m., 1:00 a.m., 2:00 a.m., 3:00 a.m., and 4:00 a.m.

You can also specify ranges of numbers like so:

```
2  0-4,12-16  1  *  *  root  run-parts  /etc/cron.monthly
```

Here the command would be run at 2 minutes past the hour between the hours of 12 a.m. and 4 a.m. and between 12 p.m. and 4 p.m.

The next column, `root`, represents the user that this program will run as. When you add your own cron jobs (or scripts), you can set this to be any valid user.

The `run-parts` option is the command that is being run. `run-parts` is a special command that will run any executable script within a specified directory. In this case, `run-parts` will change to the /etc/cron.hourly directory, /etc/cron.daily directory, and so on, and run the executable script it finds there.

Let's inspect one of the system cron directories, the /etc/cron.daily directory for example, and examine one of the scripts already present on the Red Hat host. These are system crons that will run once every day unless otherwise defined.

■**Note** You can edit the scripts in these crontab directories if you need to; however, any changes may be overwritten when your packages are updated. You can also add your own scripts in these directories to run them every hour, day, week, or month.

```
$ ls -l /etc/cron.daily/
-rwxr-xr-x 1 root root  379 Dec 19  2006 0anacron
-rwxr-xr-x 1 root root  118 Oct  1 00:06 cups
-rwxr-xr-x 1 root root  180 Oct 22  2007 logrotate
-rwxr-xr-x 1 root root  114 Jan 16  2008 rpm
-rwxr-xr-x 1 root root  290 Nov 26  2006 tmpwatch
```

Let's view one of these files, /etc/cron.daily/rpm, and see what is inside it.

```
$ less /etc/cron.daily/rpm
#!/bin/sh

/bin/rpm -qa --qf '%{name}-%{version}-%{release}.%{arch}.rpm\n' 2>&1 \
        | /bin/sort > /var/log/rpmpkgs
```

This daily executed script populates the /var/log/rpmpkgs file with a sorted list of all the RPM packages on your host.

■**Note** We'll discuss RPM packages further in Chapter 7.

Individual users can also create a crontab. You create and edit existing crontabs with the crontab -e command. If a crontab for your user does not exist already, this command creates a crontab file in /var/spool/cron/*username*.

The syntax used in a user's cron jobs is identical to that of the system crontab file you saw earlier, with one difference. You can only specify the user field in the system crontab file. Let's look at an example created by the user jsmith using the -l, or list, option for crontab.

```
$ crontab -l
*/2  *  *  *  *  [ -e /tmp/log ] && rm -f /tmp/log
```

You will see a list of all the cron jobs scheduled by this user. This is a simple series of commands that first check for the existence of a file called /tmp/log, and if it exists, remove it. It is set to run once every 2 minutes (*/2).

As a privileged user, you can view another person's cron by issuing the `crontab` command with the –u *username* option.

```
$ sudo crontab -u ataylor -l
1  2  *  *  *  /usr/local/bin/changeLog.sh
```

You can also edit another person's cron by issuing the same `crontab` command and the –u *username* -e options.

```
$ sudo crontab -u ataylor -e
```

This allows you to edit the crontab for the user.

You can also remove your crontab or another user's crontab by issuing the `crontab` command with the –r option.

```
$ sudo crontab -u ataylor -r
```

This removes `ataylor`'s crontab file: `/var/spool/cron/ataylor`.

Your host has a service that monitors the cron jobs and any changes to them. It also executes the individual jobs when they are scheduled. This service is called `crond` and can be started and stopped via an `init.d` script using the `service` command for Red Hat or the `invoke-rc.d` command for Ubuntu.

```
$ sudo service crond start/stop/reload
```

Summary

This chapter has explored how the host boots and the processes behind it like the `init` daemon. You have learned how to manage your services, how to start and stop them, and how to add and delete them from the different runlevels. You have also looked at the LSB project and got an overview of the new Upstart `init` daemon.

You should now be able to do the following:

- Describe the boot process for Linux.
- Use, configure, and secure GRUB.
- Describe `init` scripts, including those using the LSB standard.
- Start and stop services on Red Hat and Ubuntu.
- Turn services on and off for particular runlevels.
- Schedule tasks with crontab.

In the next chapter, we will show you how to configure your network, discuss firewalls, and introduce you to Linux security.

CHAPTER 6

■■■

Networking and Firewalls

By Dennis Matotek

So far we've shown you some of the basic features of Linux, but one of the most critical is networking. It is via networking that your host talks to other hosts and your applications communicate with your users and the world. In this chapter, we'll describe how to set up your host's networking and then how to protect that network from attackers using a firewall.

■**Note** A *firewall* is a series of rules that control access to your host through the network.

We'll teach you about how to configure your network cards or interfaces and how to give them IP addresses. You'll learn how to connect to other networks and how to troubleshoot your connections.

We'll also be looking at a software application called Netfilter that is a firewall common to all Linux distributions. You will learn how to manage a firewall and how to write firewall rules. To do this, we'll introduce you to Netfilter's management interface, `iptables`. Finally, we will also show you how you can use TCP Wrappers to secure daemons running on your host.

Once we've introduced the basics of network configuration, we'll also show you how to configure an example network that might suit your environment. By the end of this chapter, you should have the skills to be able to configure a suitable network for your environment.

Throughout this chapter, we'll be using networking terminology. We don't expect you to be a networking expert, but we have assumed you do have some basic knowledge. If you don't feel that you know enough, we recommend you check out these sites and tutorials:

- `http://handsonhowto.com/2007/lan101/`
- `http://www.w3schools.com/tcpip/default.asp`
- `http://compnetworking.about.com/od/workingwithipaddresses/l/blip.htm`
- `http://en.wikipedia.org/wiki/TCP/IP`

■**Note** `iptables` is used to protect your network services. You'll learn more about how to run network services like DNS and DHCP on your host in Chapter 9.

Introduction to Networks and Networking

Networks are made of both hardware and software. They vary in complexity depending on their size and the level of interconnectedness they require. In a small business you will probably have a simple network. You may have a web server and mail server, and you will probably have a file/print server (sometimes all these servers are actually one host). Undoubtedly, you will have a connection to the Internet, and you will probably want to share that connection with others in your organization.

The nature of your business and the work you do will heavily dictate how you choose to set up your network. A business that is starting out often has only one main server that pretty much does all the functions the business requires. It could be a DHCP, DNS, file, mail, and web server all rolled into one. Those familiar with Microsoft products would regard this as similar to a product like Windows Small Business Server. But as that business grows, it will probably begin to move some of these combined functions to its own hosts. Very few larger businesses would trust their entire company IT infrastructure to an individual host that has so many roles. This single point of failure should to be avoided where possible, but a small business rarely has the luxury of having a host for each service it wishes to provide.

■**Caution** If your business does have single points of failure, like many services on one host, backup and recovery become critical. Losing your data could be a disaster for your business, so you should always have backups and the ability to recover your hosts and data. See Chapter 13 for details of how to implement a backup and recovery strategy for your organization.

Then there are the interconnecting pieces of hardware you may require. If you are connecting users in your office to a single network, you will need cables, patch panels switches, and potentially a wireless access point that can create a wireless network.

■**Caution** Wireless networks are a useful and cheap way to spread your network. They don't require expensive cabling and switches, and your staff can be a bit more mobile in the office. They present some challenges, however. Wireless networks can allow attackers to connect and sniff your network if inappropriately secured, and they don't perform as well as wired networks (those with physical cables). For example, it is still much faster to transfer large amounts of data over wired connections rather than over wireless connections. If you're considering a wireless network for your business, we recommend you read the information at `http://en.wikipedia.org/wiki/Wireless_security`, `http://www.practicallynetworked.com/support/wireless_secure.htm`, and `http://www.us-cert.gov/reading_room/Wireless-Security.pdf`.

We're going to start by explaining how to configure networking on a single host and introduce you to the tools and commands you'll need to configure a broader network.

In order to show you how to configure a network, we're going to use an example network that we've created. You can see this example network in Figure 6-1.

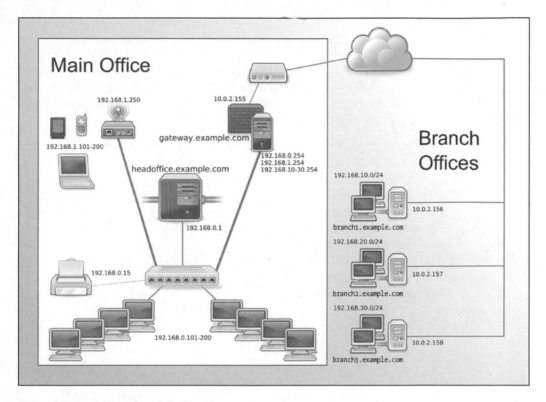

Figure 6-1. *Our example network*

Here is our complete network diagram. By the end of this chapter, this diagram will not be as daunting as it may appear now. We are going to take you through what the components of this are and how they are configured. We'll also explain what all those IP addresses are for and how we can block and move from one network to another.

In this chapter, we will show you how to configure elements of our example network. We will configure a firewall/router host we're going to call gateway.example.com. It has multiple IP addresses, one for every network it acts as a router for: 192.168.0.254 on our internal network, 192.168.1.254 on our wireless network, and an external IP address of 10.0.2.155.

We'll also configure a main server that we're going to call headoffice.example.com. It will have the IP address of 192.168.0.1 on our internal network. It'll route to other networks, like our wireless network, branches, and the Internet via the gateway.example.com host.

As you can see, we've divided the network into separate segments, and we have chosen different network addresses to show this. As we mentioned, our wireless network has the network address of 192.168.1.0/24 and is facilitated by a wireless access point with the IP address of 192.168.1.250.

Our branch offices each have a separate network address, and they range from 192.168.10.0/24 to 192.168.30.0/24. This gives us 254 possible nodes (or devices) in each branch office, with the ability to expand them if required.

We also have a local wired network, and this has the network address of 192.168.0.0/24. The main server, headoffice.example.com with IP address 192.168.0.1, will be able to communicate to the branch offices via the VPN networks we will establish from that host to those remote branches (we will explain VPNs in Chapter 14).

The desktops in our local wired network have been given a pool of addresses to use in a range of 192.168.0.101–192.168.0.200. This allows for 100 nodes and can be expanded upon if need be.

In reality, for a network of this size, we would probably have many more servers, and they would possibly be decentralized by placing servers in the branch offices. However, for the purpose of this chapter, we are going to concentrate on the scenario presented in Figure 6-2, in which you can see we have broken down our network into a smaller module.

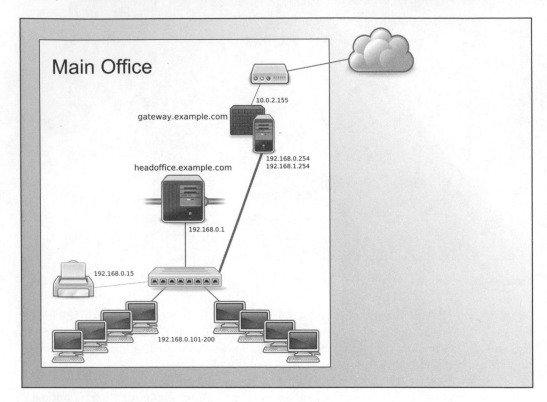

Figure 6-2. *The local wired network*

Here we can concentrate on building the principal servers for our office, gateway.example.com and headoffice.example.com.

We will show you how to set up a PPPoE connection on the gateway.example.com host to act as a firewall/router host to our ISP and the Internet.

■**Note** PPPoE is Point-to-Point Protocol over Ethernet, which is a method used for connecting from ADSL modems to the Internet.

Our main host, headoffice.example.com, will serve mail, web, and DNS services to the public (as we will show you in Chapters 9, 10, and 11).

We will use our gateway.example.com firewall host to accept and route traffic from the Internet through our internal network to our main host. The headoffice host will also provide DNS, DHCP, NTP, SMTP, IMAP, HTTP, and HTTPS services to our local network. We will also show you how to route traffic from our one host to another host in our network. Let's get started by looking at setting up our interfaces.

Getting Started with Interfaces

The first element of networking we're going to introduce to you is *interface*, or *network interface*. Each of the one or more network cards on your host will be a network interface. When we showed you how to install a distribution in Chapter 2 and configure a network, we were configuring an interface.

■Tip Interfaces are generally in two major states—up and down. Interfaces that are up are active and can be used to receive network traffic. Interfaces that are down are not connected to the network.

What kind of interfaces can you configure? Modern computer hosts nowadays can easily have more than one network card (or network interface) and sometimes have many hundreds of IP addresses (or IP aliases). An interface can have many aliases, or you can *bond* two or more interfaces together to appear as one interface.

IP aliases give you the ability to have multiple IP addresses on a single interface. The interface uses the same MAC address for all IP addresses. A bonded, or *teamed*, interface consists of two or more network interfaces appearing as a single interface. This can be used to provide greater fault tolerance or increased bandwidth for the interface. A bonded interface can also have many IP aliases. We will expand on this a little further on in the "Network Configuration Files for Red Hat" and "Network Configuration Files for Ubuntu" sections.

Each of your network interfaces will probably have at least IP addresses assigned to it. We'll start this introduction to interfaces by demonstrating a simple tool called ifconfig that can be used to view and change the status and configuration of your interfaces. The ifconfig tool is much like the ipconfig command on Microsoft Windows.

To display the status of all the interfaces on a host, use this command:

```
$ ifconfig –a
```

Running the ifconfig command with the –a option shows all interfaces on your host and their current status and configuration.

To make it easier to explore the configuration of an interface, you can also display a single interface, like so:

```
$ ifconfig eth0
Eth0    Link encap:Ethernet  HWaddr 00:0C:29:3F:69:60
          inet addr:192.168.0.1  Bcast:192.168.1.255  Mask:255.255.255.0
          inet6 addr: fe80::20c:29ff:fe3f:6960/64 Scope:Link
          UP BROADCAST RUNNING MULTICAST  MTU:1500  Metric:1
          RX packets:79 errors:0 dropped:0 overruns:0 frame:0
          TX packets:88 errors:0 dropped:0 overruns:0 carrier:0
```

```
        collisions:0 txqueuelen:1000
        RX bytes:19995 (19.5 KiB)  TX bytes:20765 (20.2 KiB)
        Base address:0x1078 Memory:ec840000-ec860000
```

This shows you the status for the network interface eth0. It has an IP address assigned to it, 192.168.0.1, and we explain that shortly. Every Ethernet network card has a unique hardware identifier that is used to identify it and communicate with other Ethernet devices. It's called a *Media Access Control (MAC) address* and it can be seen in first line of output (HWaddr 00:0C:29:3F:69:60 in this example).

The next line is an IPv6 address, here inet6 addr: fe80::20c:29ff:fe3f:6960/64, that is a *link-local* IPv6 address derived from the MAC address.

■**Note** See http://tldp.org/HOWTO/Linux+IPv6-HOWTO for more information on IPv6.

This can be used to communicate with other hosts using *stateless autoconfiguration*. Stateless autoconfiguration is used quite often by devices like PDAs and mobile phones and requires a less complicated infrastructure to communicate with other devices on the local network.

■**Note** See http://www.ipv6.com/articles/general/Stateless-Auto-Configuration.htm for more information on stateless autoconfiguration and IPv6.

The next line is the status of the interface. The state of the interface is currently UP. This means that the interface is active and can potentially receive traffic if it is properly configured.

The next option is MTU, or maximum transmission unit. The MTU is the maximum size in bytes of packets on your network; 1500 is the common default.

The rest of the information returned about the interface consists of statistical counters that can indicate possible problems, especially the packets that have been recorded in errors, dropped, and collisions. We will further discuss network troubleshooting later in this chapter in the "General Network Troubleshooting" section.

Let's take another look at the eth0 interface. This interface does not currently have an IP address assigned to it (we will demonstrate this shortly). But first, let's compare the previous output to what is displayed when eth0 is down:

```
  $ ifconfig eth0
eth0    Link encap:Ethernet  HWaddr 00:0C:29:3F:69:60
        inet6 addr: fe80::20c:29ff:fe3f:6960/64 Scope:Link
        BROADCAST RUNNING MULTICAST  MTU:1500  Metric:1
        RX packets:79 errors:0 dropped:0 overruns:0 frame:0
        TX packets:88 errors:0 dropped:0 overruns:0 carrier:0
        collisions:0 txqueuelen:1000
        RX bytes:19995 (19.5 KiB)  TX bytes:20765 (20.2 KiB)
        Base address:0x1078 Memory:ec840000-ec860000
```

You will notice that is the same except that the third line is missing an UP. This tells you that the interface is down and therefore no longer communicating. You can bring that interface up by issuing the following command:

```
$ sudo ifconfig eth0 up
```

Note There is also a simple alias for this command called ifup that you can use, like so: ifup eth0.

To bring down an interface, you would use the following:

```
$ sudo ifconfig eth0 down
```

Or you can use the alias command, ifdown:

```
$ sudo ifdown eth0
```

You can manually assign an IP address to an interface, or it is automatically assigned to your interface when your host or network service restarts. Say that our host has just been rebooted; the IP address we configured during the installation will now be attached to the eth0 interface. When we have an IP address assigned to the interface, the output of eth0 will look as follows:

```
eth0    Link encap:Ethernet  HWaddr 00:0C:29:3F:69:60
          inet addr:192.168.0.1  Bcast:192.168.1.255  Mask:255.255.255.0
          inet6 addr: fe80::20c:29ff:fe3f:6960/64 Scope:Link
          UP BROADCAST RUNNING MULTICAST  MTU:1500  Metric:1
          RX packets:99 errors:0 dropped:0 overruns:0 frame:0
          TX packets:92 errors:0 dropped:0 overruns:0 carrier:0
          collisions:0 txqueuelen:1000
          RX bytes:23534 (22.9 KiB)  TX bytes:22208 (21.6 KiB)
          Base address:0x1078 Memory:ec840000-ec860000
```

You can now see that eth0 has the IP address of 192.168.0.1 and that its status is UP.

The ifconfig command can also be used to add and delete IP addresses to and from an interface; here is how we could have added our 192.168.0.1 IP address to the eth0 interface:

```
$ sudo ifconfig eth0 add 192.168.0.1
```

We pass the ifconfig command three options: the interface we're working with, the action to take, and the IP address to use.

The ifconfig command can also be used to delete an IP address from an interface like so:

```
$ sudo ifconfig eth0 del 192.168.0.1
```

You can discover the other purposes for which you can use the ifconfig command by reading its man page.

The ifconfig command though is very simple. It can't do much more than what we've shown you, but it is useful as a quick tool to manipulate interfaces. In the next few sections, we're going to expand on how to configure interfaces and networks with both command-line and GUI tools. We will specifically focus on how to manipulate interfaces using another command, which is simply called ip.

■Note Changes to your interfaces using the `ifconfig` command are not persistent across reboots; when you reboot, you'll lose any changes. We will explain shortly how to permanently apply your changes to your host.

Configuring Interfaces from the GUI

Normally, you will have already configured at least one interface with an IP address during the installation process. As we described in Chapter 2, this address will be either of the following:

- A static IP address
- A DHCP-assigned IP address

Static IP addresses are manually configured addresses you use to give the host a specific IP address. This is usually how servers and other hosts for which you don't expect the IP address to change are configured. Addresses assigned via DHCP, or the Domain Host Configuration Protocol, are assigned from a pool of addresses. This is usually how desktops and client machines are configured because it is not so important for their IP addresses to stay the same.

There are a number of ways to edit an existing network interface, or add or delete a new interface. It is by far easier to use a GUI when you are beginning to use Linux. We will show you how to do this from both the GUI and later by using the work scripts themselves.

Configuring Networks with the Red Hat GUI

Red Hat hosts have a powerful user interface to manage your interfaces and network configuration. It is used to add IP addresses to your network interfaces, and manage your host's /etc/host file, DNS settings, and routes. *Routes* are the pathways that packets use to find other hosts in other networks. One of the main routes you may be familiar with is the default gateway, or default route.

■Note A *default route* is the destination of all network packets that your host cannot find for itself. Routers act as gateways between networks and are used to join separate networks together. If your default router cannot find the destination host, it will send the network packets off to its default route, and so on, until the final destination of the network packet is reached.

You can launch the GUI in two ways: one is by using the Services ➤ Administration ➤ Networking menu, as you can see in Figure 6-3, and the other is via the command line using the `system-config-network` command.

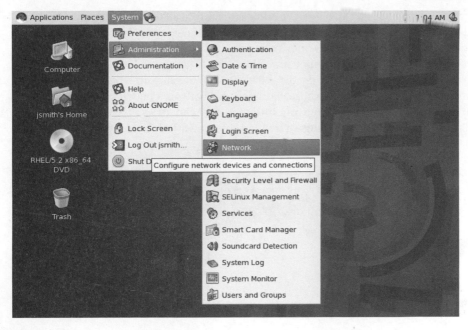

Figure 6-3. *Launching the Network Configuration tool on Red Hat*

This shows you the currently configured interfaces you have available. In Figure 6-4, you can see that we have one Ethernet device called eth0, and you can also see that is active. This is the networking device that is currently providing our network services.

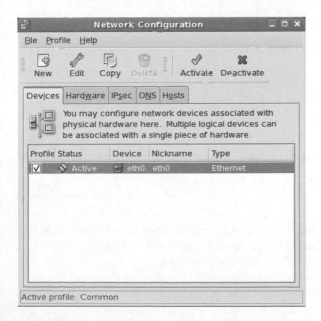

Figure 6-4. *Currently available network devices*

Through this window, you can choose to edit a currently available device or just make that device inactive. You can also choose to add a new device or delete the existing one.

On the Hardware tab, you can view information on the device drivers for the Ethernet card. The IPsec tab shows you IPsec information and allows you to configure IPsec tunnels on your interface. The DNS tab shows you DNS details and allows you to edit your DNS settings. Through the Hosts tab you can view and edit the hosts file associated with your network.

If your host has more than one network interface, you can add a new Ethernet device. Start by clicking the New button to bring up a comprehensive list of device types you can create, as shown in Figure 6-5.

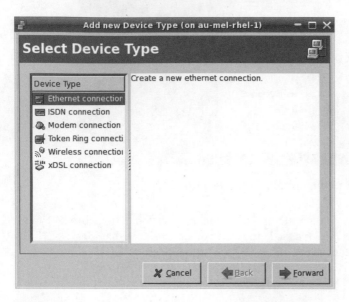

Figure 6-5. *List of possible network connections to create*

As you can see, you can create several different types of devices. Here we are going to focus on creating an Ethernet device.

■**Note** Later in the chapter, in the "Configuring Our Example Network" section, we will demonstrate creating an xDSL device to connect to the Internet.

In Figure 6-6, you see there are two possible Ethernet cards from which to choose. We already have a device configured, eth0, so we are going to choose the second device, eth1.

For every network card you have in your host (or virtual network cards if you are using a virtualized host like VMware), you will see a device listed here. If you do not see your device listed, you can always try to configure it using the Other Ethernet Card option, provided you know which drivers it requires to operate properly. Your kernel must be compiled with the correct driver for your card before it will work. You are presented with a list of Ethernet drivers that the kernel knows about. You should select the one that best matches your Ethernet device.

Figure 6-6. *Choosing the Ethernet device*

You will next be asked to provide either the IP address details of the interface or select how the interface intends to retrieve them. In Figure 6-7, you can see the options available to you.

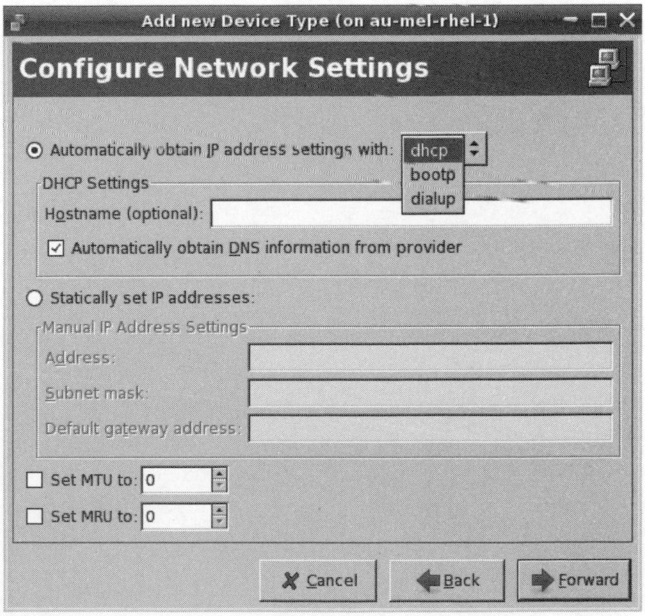

Figure 6-7. *Choosing the IP address provider*

You can choose from the following:

- dhcp
- bootp
- dialup

As we explained earlier, DHCP is a protocol whereby your interface can request to be assigned an IP address from a pool of available addresses. It requires that a DHCP server be available to issue it with an IP address. Many SOHO routers and DSL modems have built-in DHCP servers, and hosts on the network are automatically issued IP addresses by these devices.

■**Note** We'll look at DHCP and how you can run your own DHCP server in Chapter 9.

The BOOTP protocol is normally used for diskless workstations and enables the host to acquire an IP address and an operating system image. It will then use this image to boot the device. Thin clients (e.g., diskless workstations and service terminals like supermarket cash registers) don't have a hard drive from which to load their operating systems. Instead they use the BOOTP protocol to retrieve that image along with all the required network information.

The last option is dialup, which is used for dial-up modem connections via a Public Switched Telephone Network (PSTN) phone line. These sorts of connections are rarely used nowadays, as most organizations have DSL or other types of broadband connectivity.

You can also choose to enter your own address information, what we described earlier as a static IP address, as we have in Figure 6-8.

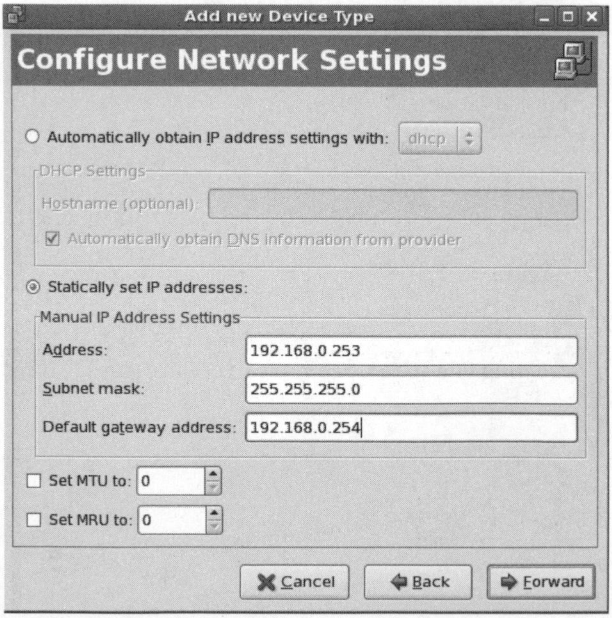

Figure 6-8. *Entering static IP address information*

Here we have added an IP address of 192.168.0.253. This address is from the example network we showed you in Figure 6-1. We have chosen an address from the list of available IP addresses we have marked as statically assigned as opposed to those that we have in our pool of addresses to be used by DHCP.

■**Note** See Chapter 9 for details on DHCP address pools.

After clicking the Forward button, you are presented with a summary of the options you have chosen. If you wish to apply these changes, click Apply; if you do not wish to do so, click Cancel.

If you click Apply, you will now see your new Ethernet interface appear in the list, as in Figure 6-9.

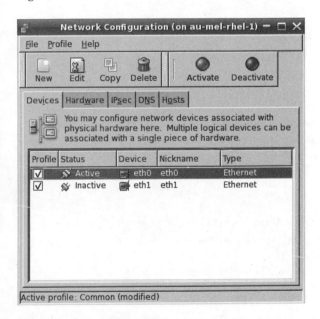

Figure 6-9. *The newly configured Ethernet interface*

You will see that your new device is inactive. Before you can make it active, you first have to save the configuration. You do that by selecting File ➤ Save, as you can see in Figure 6-10.

Figure 6-10. *Saving your configuration*

You will be shown an informational screen telling you that you may wish to restart your network services or reboot your host to activate your new devices. Linux can handle the addition of a new Ethernet device without the need for a reboot, and the GUI tool can restart your network service for you when you activate the new device.

You could also restart networking services via the command line as follows:

```
$ sudo /sbin/service network restart
```

To do so via the GUI, highlight your new device and click the Activate button; you will be presented with a screen showing the progress of the activation and then a screen showing both devices are active, as in Figure 6-11.

You now have two active Ethernet devices. You will want to make sure these devices are working, and we will explain how to do that shortly, but first let's investigate the other things you can do with this GUI tool.

In Figure 6-11, you can see that we have two active Ethernet devices, eth0 and eth1. We can edit configuration settings of these devices if we wish.

First let's look at our DNS settings. We talked about DNS briefly in Chapter 2, when we showed you how to install your host. DNS is used by hosts to match hostnames, like au-mel-ubuntu-1.example.com, to their associated IP address. It does this by sending a DNS query to a name server. The name server information is stored in the /etc/resolv.conf file.

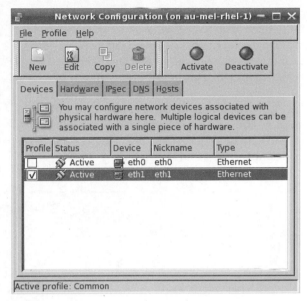

Figure 6-11. *Two active Ethernet devices*

Tip We'll look at DNS in more detail in Chapter 9.

In Figure 6-12, you see our DNS settings. These show our primary and secondary name servers.

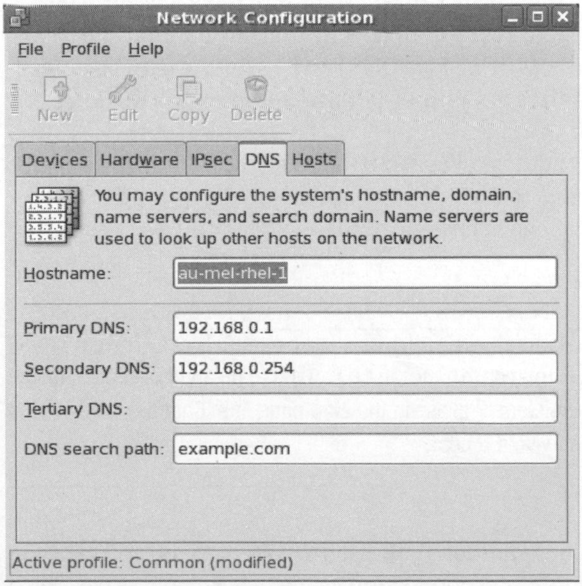

Figure 6-12. *Our DNS settings*

These settings are either provided manually or, as you'll see in Chapter 9, provided by the DHCP server. The servers are queried in preference of lowest to highest. Any changes need to be saved by selecting File ➤ Save from the menu as you saw previously in Figure 6-11.

The next setting we can change is the contents of our /etc/hosts file. This file is used when you want to give the name and IP address information of a particular host. For example, this would be appropriate in the event of the DNS service going offline, but you don't want your particular host to stop being able to communicate with another particular host. The drawback, however, would be that you have to maintain this information on this host if the addressing information changes. To add a host reference in your host file, you move to the Hosts tab, click the New button, and enter the information, like we have done in Figure 6-13.

Note You can also edit the /etc/hosts file to do this as well.

Figure 6-13. *Editing the hosts file information*

Here we have added the details of an Ubuntu host, au-mel-ubuntu-2. We have provided the IP address, the full hostname, au-mel-ubuntu-2.example.com, and an alias that can also be used to refer to it, au-mel-ubuntu-2. So now, if we lose DNS services for the network, our host will still be able to find the right IP address for au-mel-ubuntu-2—as long as we don't change the IP address of the Ubuntu host.

Using the GUI, you can also add an IP address alias. An IP address alias allows for more than one IP address to be assigned, or *bound*, to a single interface device. Unfortunately, IP address aliases do not support DHCP, so you have to statically assign IP addresses to each alias.

Note It is actually much easier to use the system-config-network tool to create an IP alias than to use the command line, but it is easier to add a nonpersistent IP alias via the command line. Changes made to the interfaces with the command-line tools will not survive a reboot.

To create an IP alias in the Network Configuration tool, open the Devices tab and click the New button to create a new device. Select Ethernet connection as the device type, as we did when we created our new eth1 device. Next, select the Ethernet card you wish to attach this IP alias to. For this example, we will choose the Ethernet card that has eth1 on it.

Next, you are asked to assign an IP address to your alias device. You can choose any that is available to you based on the same principle of not taking any from the DHCP pool. You need to add the default gateway and the netmask.

We talked about default gateways back in Chapter 2. The netmask is used for subdividing (called *subnetting*) a network into smaller segments. A netmask of 255.255.255.0 has 254 addressable nodes available to it compared to a netmask of 255.255.255.248, which has only 6 addressable nodes.

■**Note** You can read more about subnets at `http://en.wikipedia.org/wiki/Subnetwork`.

The default gateway is a host on the network that can route traffic to other networks such as the Internet.

In our example, we have chosen 192.168.0.23 and given the details shown in Figure 6-14.

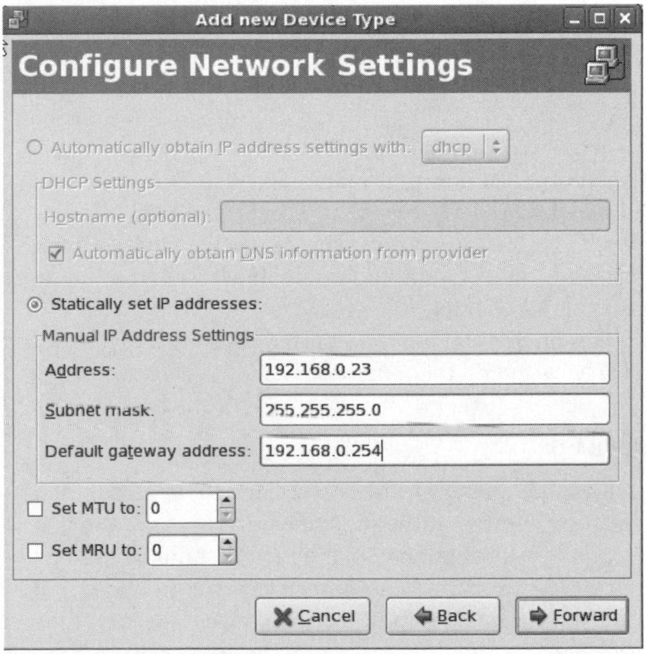

Figure 6-14. *IP alias configuration*

Lastly, let's look at adding routes to interfaces. To do so, go to the Devices tab in the Network Configuration tool and highlight one of the devices you have created. Once you've done this, click the Edit button. You will see a General tab, and next to that you will see the Route tab. Click the Route tab. As we have mentioned, routes are the pathways the host uses to find other hosts. To add a route for your interface, click the Add button. Have a look at what we have done in Figure 6-15.

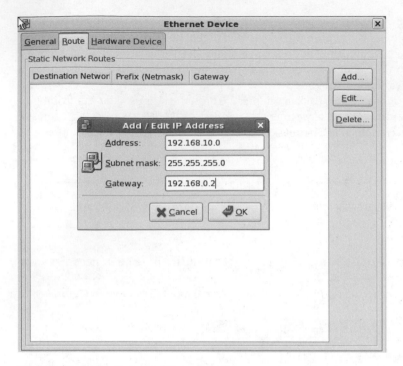

Figure 6-15. *Adding a route to our interface*

We have added a route to the 192.168.10.0/24 network via the 192.168.0.2 host for eth0. This creates three configuration files called route-eth0 in /etc/sysconfig/network-scripts, /etc/sysconfig/networking/profiles/default, and /etc/sysconfig/networking/devices. We explain more about viewing and adding routes via the command line later in the "Adding Routes and Fowarding Packets" section of this chapter.

All network device configuration files on Red Hat hosts are stored in the /etc/system/ network-scripts directory, and you can view or edit them there as well.

Configuring Networks with the Ubuntu GUI

Ubuntu hosts also have a GUI to configure your network interfaces. Their tool, network-admin, is designed to enable you to edit an existing interface rather than create a new one, and you cannot create a Point-to-Point Protocol (PPP) connection with it. PPP is commonly used to establish a direct connection between your network and your Internet service provider (ISP). You can use it to edit your /etc/hosts file, your DNS via the /etc/resolv.conf file, and your hostname by editing the /etc/hostname file.

The Ubuntu GUI is also not installed by default, and you will need to install it first. To do so, you can use the aptitude command:

```
$ sudo aptitude install gnome-network-admin
```

■**Note** We'll talk more about package installation in Chapter 7.

You start it by using the same menu path that you do in Red Hat, System ➤ Administration ➤ Network, or you can launch it from the command line with the network-admin command:

$ sudo network-admin

You need root privileges to alter your network settings. Notice in Figure 6-16 the Unlock button in the bottom panel of the Network Settings window. Upon clicking this button, you will be prompted for a password. The Unlock button runs the sudo command to grant you appropriate privileges to edit your network configuration.

Figure 6-16. *Unlocking the Ubuntu Network Admin tool*

You will automatically recognize that this looks like the Red Hat system-config-network interface. You will first see a list of different types of connection; for example, each wired connection is listed by connection type and interface.

You will also see the following tabs: General, where you can edit your host and domain names; DNS, for editing DNS configuration; and Hosts, where you can add hosts to the /etc/ hosts file.

By double-clicking the Wired connection item (or by clicking the Properties button), you can edit the connection's properties. This brings up a window similar to Figure 6-17.

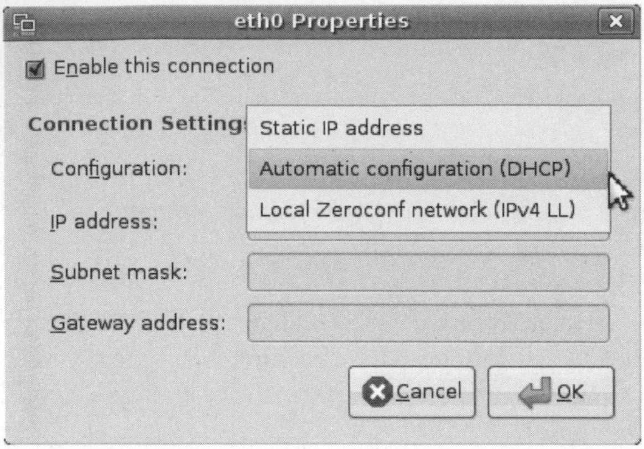

Figure 6-17. *Editing the Wired connection interface*

As seen in Figure 6-17, you can choose to have your host get its IP address from a DHCP server, or you can configure it to have a statically assigned one.

All configuration details for Ubuntu network devices are stored in the /etc/network/ interfaces file. You can also directly edit this file to add further configuration options. We will talk more about this in the next section.

Configuring Networks with Network Scripts

Both Red Hat and Ubuntu have their network configuration files stored in the /etc directory. Red Hat stores its files in a collection of network-related directories under /etc/sysconfig/ network-scripts, and Ubuntu stores its files under the /etc/networks directory.

Network Configuration Files for Red Hat

The Red Hat files relating to networking can be found under the /etc/sysconfig directory. The main places to find this information are

- The /etc/sysconfig/network file

- The /etc/sysconfig/network-scripts directory

- The /etc/sysconfig/networking directory

The /etc/sysconfig/network file contains general network information like HOSTNAME and default GATEWAY. The /etc/sysconfig/network-scripts directory contains all the startup and shutdown scripts for network interfaces. The /etc/sysconfig/networking directory contains device- and profile-specific files. These files are general copies of files in the /etc/sysconfig/ network-script directory and are created for you by the system-config-network tool.

Taking a look at the contents of the /etc/sysconfig/network-scripts directory, you will see the files shown in Listing 6-1.

Listing 6-1. *Files Found in* `/etc/sysconfig/network-scripts`

```
$ sudo ls /etc/sysconfig/network-scripts/
ifcfg-eth0  ifdown-ippp  ifup-bnep  ifup-sit
ifcfg-eth1  ifdown-ipsec  ifup-eth  ifup-sl
ifdown-ipv6  ifup-ippp  ifup-tunnel  ifdown-isdn
ifup-ipsec  ifup-wireless  ifdown-post  ifup-ipv6
init.ipv6-global  ifdown-ppp  ifup-ipx  ifdown-routes
ifup-isdn  ifdown-sit  ifup-plip  net.hotplug
ifcfg-lo  ifdown-sl  ifup-plusb  network-functions
ifdown  ifdown-tunnel  ifup-post  network-functions-ipv6
ifdown-bnep  ifup  ifup-ppp  ifdown-eth
ifup-aliases  ifup-routes
```

In Listing 6-1, you can see all the scripts that are used to configure your interfaces and bring them up or down. A variety of files are present.

The `ifcfg-eth?` files, like `ifcfg-eth0`, are configuration files for the Ethernet interfaces. The files with the naming convention of *ifaction-interface*, for example, `ifdown-ipsec`, are scripts that are used to control the state (i.e., bring the interface up or down).

Files like `network-functions` are scripts can that contain functions and variables. Other scripts can source the functions and variables from `network-functions` and use them in their scripts.

SOURCING FUNCTIONS AND VARIABLES FROM OTHER SCRIPTS

When you write a program in Bash, like in many languages, you can have a script that contains common functions, variables, and utilities that you wish to share with other scripts to save you having to rewrite the same code over and over again. For instance, say you have a function that handles errors from your program. For every script you create, you could rewrite the same error-handling function or instead write it into one script and *source* it, or import it, into another script.

If you named the error-handling script `errors.sh`, you can add the following line to your new script:

```
#!/bin/bash
. ./errors.sh
```

The first period (.), followed by a white space, is a shortcut for writing the `source` command. The `source` command will import the functions and variables from `errors.sh` into your current script. This saves you time and energy and avoids your having to duplicate all your functions in scripts.

Let's take a look at the configuration file for eth0, which is called `ifcfg-eth0`. You can see the contents of this file in Listing 6-2.

Listing 6-2. *The ifcfg-eth0 File*

```
$ sudo less /etc/sysconfig/network-scripts/ifcfg-eth0
# Intel Corporation 82545EM Gigabit Ethernet Controller (Copper)
DEVICE=eth0
BOOTPROTO=dhcp
HWADDR=00:0c:29:3f:69:56
ONBOOT=yes
TYPE=Ethernet
USERCTL=no
IPV6INIT=no
PEERDNS=yes
```

You can see a number of configuration options in the form of *option=argument*.

In Listing 6-2, you can see that to configure a Red Hat interface you will need to specify the device name like so: DEVICE=eth0. The boot protocol, BOOTPROTO=dhcp, is set to get its address from DHCP. The MAC address of the device is HWADDR=00:0c:29:3f:69:56, and this is the unique identifier assigned to this card. We also declare whether the interface will initialize at boot up by specifying ONBOOT=yes. The type of interface is declared by TYPE=Ethernet. Next, we declare whether users can start or stop the interface by using USERCTL=no. We don't want to initialize our interface with an IPv6 address, so we have explicitly declared IPV6INIT=no. We also have chosen to set PEERDNS=yes. When we declare PEERDNS=yes, we wish to modify the /etc/resolv.conf file with name servers provided by the DHCP server. If we set it to no, /etc/resolv.conf will remain unmodified when this interface is brought to an up state.

Table 6-1 lists the options you can use in your Red Hat interface files.

Table 6-1. *Network Configuration File Options, Red Hat*

Option	Description
DEVICE	The name of the device you are creating. This will appear in the interface listings.
BOOTPROTO	The protocol to use when the device starts up. The choices here are static, dhcp, and none.
ONBOOT	Whether the device is started when the host boots up.
NETWORK	The network address for this device.
NETMASK	The netmask for this device.
IPADDR	The IP address for this device.
USERCTL	Whether a user can start or stop the device. Choices are yes or no.
MASTER	The device to which this device is the SLAVE.
SLAVE	Whether the device is controlled by the master specified in the MASTER directive.
ETHTOOL_OPTS	Order-dependent options for ethtool. Useful for setting full duplex on devices capable of this, or speed and negotiation parameters.
DNS	DNS host's IP address (multiple addresses are comma separated). This will be added to /etc/resolv.conf if PEERDNS is set to yes.
PEERDNS	Setting that determines whether DNS hosts specified in DNS are added to /etc/resolv.conf. If set to yes, they are added. If no, they are not added.

What we will do now is use this information to show you how to set up a bonded Ethernet device. A bonded Ethernet device can also be referred to as a *trunk* device. Bonding allows you to use two or more Ethernet ports to act as one interface, giving you expanded bandwidth and some redundancy. In this way you can turn a 1GiB link into a 2GiB link for the one virtual interface.

So how would we do this feat? First we will edit the eth0 and eth1 configuration files we have created with the system-config-network GUI, as shown in Listing 6-3.

Listing 6-3. *The eth0 Slave Device Configuration*

```
$ less /etc/sysconfig/network-scripts/ifcfg-eth0
# Intel Corporation 82545EM Gigabit Ethernet Controller (Copper)
DEVICE=eth0
ONBOOT=yes
BOOTPROTO=none
USERCTL=no
SLAVE=yes
MASTER=bond0
```

This is a very simple configuration. We have specified the device we wish to control, eth0, and whether we would like it to initialize when we boot up our host by specifying ONBOOT=yes. The IP address for this bonded device will attach itself to the bond0 device, not to eth0 or eth1; therefore, we do not specify a boot protocol here and use the option BOOTPROTO=none, instead.

We also don't want users to bring this interface up or down, so we have set USERCTL=no. Next are the two options that add this device to a bonded configuration. The first, SLAVE=yes, declares that this device is to be a slave. Next, we declare to which master it belongs by specifying MASTER=bond0. The bond0 we are referring to is a device of the same name that we are about to create.

For interface eth1 (which is configured in the /etc/sysconfig/network-scripts/ ifcfg-eth1 file), we will mirror the copy and paste the details from eth0. Then we need to change the DEVICE=eth0 to DEVICE=eth1. The rest can stay the same.

Next we will create our bond0 device file. On Red Hat, the configuration details will be kept in a file called /etc/sysconfig/network-scripts/ifcfg-bond0. In Listing 6-4, you see what we need to create a bonded Ethernet device.

Listing 6-4. *Configuration for a Bonded Ethernet Device*

```
[jsmith@au-mel-rhel-1 ~]$ vi /etc/sysconfig/network-scripts/ifcfg-bond0
DEVICE=bond0
BOOTPROTO=none
ONBOOT=yes
NETWORK=192.168.0.0
NETMASK=255.255.255.0
IPADDR=192.168.0.1
USERCTL=no
TYPE=Ethernet
```

As you can see, it is very similar to a standard Ethernet device file. You need to specify the device name, bond0 in our example, and give it the appropriate network information like its IP address, network, and netmask information. Again, we want this device to be initialized at boot up, and we don't want users to be able to bring it up or down.

You will need to save these files in the /etc/sysconfig/network-scripts directory. Next thing you will need to do is inform the kernel that you have a new device ready for bonding.

For our example, we do this by adding the following line in the /etc/modprobe.conf file:

```
alias eth0 e1000
alias eth1 e1000
alias bond0 bonding
```

This tells the kernel that we have a bonding device that we want to call, bond0.

To enhance performance, we can add parameters to our bond device. We add these to the /etc/modules file:

```
bond0 mode=1 miimon=100
```

Mode 1 sets the interface bonding type to active backup. When the active interface fails, the other takes over. The miimon is how often the interfaces are checked for being active. In high-availability configurations, when miimon notices that one interface is down, it will activate the remaining interface(s).

Depending on your network and what kind of bonding you can implement given your network equipment, you can add other options here to give fault tolerance, redundancy, and round-robin features to your bonded device. For more information, please refer to the Red Hat manual here: http://www.redhat.com/docs/manuals/enterprise/RHEL-3-Manual/ref-guide/s1-modules-ethernet.html.

You can now use the insmod command to insert the module and create the alias like so:

```
sudo /sbin/insmod bond0
```

Alternatively you can reboot your host. When you issue either an ifconfig or ip addr show command, you should see the two Ethernet devices acting as one interface, in this case called bond0.

You can view your new bonded device by issuing the /sbin/ip addr show command, which will produce the following output:

```
2: eth0: <BROADCAST,MULTICAST,SLAVE,UP,LOWER_UP> ➡
mtu 1500 qdisc pfifo_fast master bond0 qlen 1000
    link/ether 00:0c:29:3f:69:56 brd ff:ff:ff:ff:ff:ff
    inet6 fe80::20c:29ff:fe3f:6956/64 scope link
      valid_lft forever preferred_lft forever
3: eth1: <BROADCAST,MULTICAST,SLAVE,UP,LOWER_UP> ➡
mtu 1500 qdisc pfifo_fast master bond0 qlen 1000
    link/ether 00:0c:29:3f:69:56 brd ff:ff:ff:ff:ff:ff
    inet6 fe80::20c:29ff:fe3f:6956/64 scope link
      valid_lft forever preferred_lft forever
5: bond0: <BROADCAST,MULTICAST,MASTER,UP,LOWER_UP> ➡
mtu 1500 qdisc noqueue
    link/ether 00:0c:29:3f:69:56 brd ff:ff:ff:ff:ff:ff
```

```
inet 192.168.0.1/24 brd 192.168.0.255 scope global bond0
inet6 fe80::20c:29ff:fe3f:6956/64 scope link tentative
    valid_lft forever preferred_lft forever
```

If you look at the interface description of eth0 and eth1, you can see that they are both set to SLAVE, and you can see that bond0 is set to MASTER. Neither eth0 nor eth1 have IP addresses associated with them. It is the bond0 interface that has the IP address associated with it.

If you wish to create device aliases for your interfaces on Red Hat hosts, you can do the following. As you know, all the configuration files of the devices you create must be stored in the directory /etc/sysconfig/network-scripts using a device file named something like ifcfg-eth1:1. Each device file ends with its device name. The ifcfg-eth1:n indicates that these files belong to the eth1 device. Each subsequent alias device on device eth1 will be incremented $n+1$.

An alias file looks like this:

```
DEVICE=eth1:1
BOOTPROTO=none
TYPE=Ethernet
USERCTL=no
IPV6INIT=no
PEERDNS=yes
NETMASK=255.255.255.0
IPADDR=192.168.0.22
GATEWAY=192.168.0.254
ONPARENT=no
```

You can see that the file looks very similar to a normal device file except that the DEVICE variable is defined as eth1:1. Here you will see that there is another variable called ONPARENT, and it is set to no. The ONPARENT variable is specific to alias devices and relates to the ONBOOT setting in a standard device file. It determines whether the alias device starts up when the parent device (in this case eth1), starts up. Setting this to no means that it will not start automatically when the parent device starts up.

The other way you can assign multiple IP addresses to an Ethernet device is to create a configuration file called a *range* file. This is a *clone* file that allows you to clone an Ethernet device, and it is slightly different from alias devices. A clone file can be used to specify additional options for an interface and does not create new devices, rather it modifies an existing device. To create a range of IP addresses, which has the same effect as creating many IP alias files, we create a file called /etc/sysconfig/network-scripts/ifcfg-eth0-range0. In that file we add the following options to add a range of IP addresses to the eth0 interface:

```
IPADDR_START=192.168.100.10
IPADDR_END=192.168.100.210
CLONENUM_START=10
NETMASK=255.255.255.0
```

As you can see, we are not specifying a DEVICE in this file. This is because it is extending our existing eth0 device file. This clone file will create a range of IP addresses on the eth0 device starting with 192.168.100.10 and ending at 192.168.100.210. The Ethernet clone devices will start at eth0:10 and end at eth0:210. (Starting at eth10 is not necessary. We could start at eth0:0 if we wished or at eth0:20.)

The other way to add an alias is to use a script to assign IP addresses when your host boots up. We can add something like this into our /etc/rc.d/rc.local script (this is the script that runs last in the startup sequence that we showed you in Chapter 5):

```
/sbin/ip addr add 192.168.0.24/24 brd 192.168.0.255 dev eth1
/sbin/ip addr add 192.168.0.25/24 brd 192.168.0.255 dev eth1
/sbin/ip addr add 192.168.0.26/24 brd 192.168.0.255 dev eth1
```

We will go on to explain the ip command shortly, but what this command will do is assign three IP addresses to the eth1 device when this host boots up.

___

■**Note** What's with the name eth0? It is actually an alias for the module name used by the kernel to control the device (*the driver* is a term that Microsoft Windows users will be familiar with). You can find the aliases for the Ethernet modules in /etc/modprobe.conf on Red Hat or in /etc/modprobe.d/aliases on Ubuntu. They are expressed like alias eth0 e1000. For detailed explanation of kernel modules in Linux, please read http://tldp.org/HOWTO/Module-HOWTO/.

___

Network Configuration Files for Ubuntu

Ubuntu has a similar directory for its network files in /etc/network. It contains the network files and scripts that are used by Ubuntu to set up your networking. As we described earlier, Ubuntu stores interface information in the file /etc/network/interfaces. It contains all the interface information for any configured interface.

An interface that uses DHCP can be as simple as the following:

```
# The primary network interface
auto eth0
iface eth0 inet dhcp
```

First we declare that eth0 is automatically started with auto eth0. Next, we declare the interface eth0 will use an IPv4 address, which it will get from a DHCP server, iface eth0 inet dhcp. If you were to configure other Ethernet cards, eth1 or eth2, you would also use the /etc/network/interfaces file.

The parameters you can use in your interface file can be seen in Table 6-2.

Table 6-2. *Ubuntu Parameters in* /etc/network/interfaces

Parameter	Description
auto	Brings up the interface at boot time
inet	Specifies IPv4 addressing
inet6	Specifies IPv6 addressing
ppp	Specifies the device is a PPP connection
address	Specifies the IP address

Parameter	Description
netmask	Specifies the netmask
gateway	Specifies the default gateway for that interface
dns-nameserver	Specifies the name server for that interface
post-up	Specifies action to run after interface comes up
pre-down	Specifies action to run before the interface comes down

In Table 6-2 you see most of the parameters available to you when setting up a network interface on Ubuntu. We will use some of these to set up a static network interface for eth0 in the /etc/network/interfaces file as follows:

```
auto eth0
iface eth0 inet static
address 192.168.0.10
netmask 255.255.255.0
gateway 192.168.0.254
dns-nameservers 192.168.0.1
```

Here we have set up our eth0 interface. We have set it to come up automatically when our host boots, auto eth0, and told our operating system it will have a static IP address assigned to it, iface eth0 inet static. We have given the eth0 interface the address 192.168.0.10 and a default gateway (default route) of 192.168.0.254. We have also specified the DNS server as 192.168.0.1, which is our internal network's primary name server.

We will now show you how they can be used in the following example. Using the interface file, we are going to create a bonded Ethernet device on our Ubuntu host.

The first thing we need to do is install an extra package:

```
sudo aptitude install ifenslave
```

This utility enables some simple round-robin load balancing across your slave interfaces and enables the attaching and detaching of the slave devices.

Next we need to append the following to our /etc/modules file:

```
bonding mode=0 miimon=200
```

This tells the kernel to load the bonding drivers in mode 0 with interface monitoring every 200 milliseconds. Mode 0 is a round-robin load-balancing configuration where packets are transmitted over each interface sequentially.

Now we need to configure the interfaces for bonding. To do this, we edit the Ubuntu /etc/network/interfaces file, adding the following:

```
# The primary network interface
auto bond0
iface bond0 inet static
address 192.168.0.10
netmask 255.255.255.0
gateway 192.168.0.254
dns-nameservers 192.168.0.1
```

```
post-up ifenslave bond0 eth0 eth1
pre-down ifenslave -d bond0 eth0 eth1
```

In the first line, `auto bond0`, we have declared here that the bond0 device should be loaded automatically at boot time. Next, in `iface bond0 inet static`, we have declared that the interface bond0 is an IPv4 statically assigned interface, meaning we are not going to use DHCP or another protocol to assign it an address. We then assign the IP address, netmask, gateway, and DNS servers using the key words `address`, `netmask`, `gateway`, and `dns-nameservers`, respectively. The next line allows us to specify a command after the interface come up. The `ifenslave` command, `post-up ifenslave bond0 eth0 eth1`, attaches eth0 and eth1 to bond0 after the bond0 device is up. Lastly, we can also specify a command before the interface comes down. We use `ifenslave` again to unattach the eth0 and eth1 devices from bond0 by issuing the –d option before we bring bond0 down as follows: `pre-down ifenslave –d bond0 eth0 eth1`.

And finally, like in Red Hat, we need to load the kernel modules to bring up the device. We will issue the following:

```
$ sudo modprobe bonding mode=0 miimon=200
$ sudo /etc/init.d/networking restart
```

We could have also rebooted our host. Now when we issue the following command, we see the following output:

```
$ sudo /sbin/ip addr show
2: eth0: <BROADCAST,MULTICAST,SLAVE,UP,LOWER_UP> ⇒
mtu 1500 qdisc pfifo_fast master bond0 qlen 1000
    link/ether 00:0c:29:94:bd:33 brd ff:ff:ff:ff:ff:ff
3: eth1: <BROADCAST,MULTICAST,SLAVE,UP,LOWER_UP> ⇒
mtu 1500 qdisc pfifo_fast master bond0 qlen 1000
    link/ether 00:0c:29:94:bd:33 brd ff:ff:ff:ff:ff:ff
7: bond0: <BROADCAST,MULTICAST,MASTER,UP,LOWER_UP> ⇒
mtu 1500 qdisc noqueue
    link/ether 00:0c:29:94:bd:33 brd ff:ff:ff:ff:ff:ff
    inet 192.168.0.10/24 brd 192.168.0.255 scope global bond0-=
    inet6 fe80::20c:29ff:fe94:bd33/64 scope link
        valid_lft forever preferred_lft forever
```

You can now see that the IP address 192.168.0.10 is attached to bond0, and both eth0 and eth1 are slaves to bond0: `<BROADCAST,MULTICAST,SLAVE,UP,LOWER_UP> mtu 1500 qdisc pfifo_fast master bond0`. You will also notice that all three devices have the same MAC address, `00:0c:29:94:bd:33`, which means they can all respond to Address Resolution Protocol (ARP) requests for that MAC address. We explain ARP a little further on in the "TCP/IP 101" section.

We have used the `ip` command many times in this chapter; now we'll move on to demonstrating how it can be used to alter network configurations.

Testing Network Configurations Using iptools2

Traditionally, on Linux hosts you can use the `ifconfig` command to manage your host's network interfaces and `route` to manage your routing tables. The `ip` command provided by the `IPtools2` package can be used for doing both these tasks. It is very useful in managing your interfaces and routes, especially in testing, adding, and deleting network settings. You can use the ip command to add IP addresses to an interface, remove an IP address, and bring an interface up or down. You can also use it to configure your network routes and routing tables.

The configuration changes made with the ip utility are not persistent across reboots. For a more permanent change, either use the GUI tools (system-config-network or network-admin) or directly edit the network configuration files for your relevant host, as we have shown you earlier in this chapter.

Why would you need the ip command then? Sometimes you don't want to permanently add an IP address to your interface, or your want to temporarily add a route when a certain script is running. You can use this tool to easily do both of these things.

Let's examine the ip command. The ip command has the following basic syntax:

```
ip [ OPTIONS ] OBJECT { COMMAND | help }
```

The guts of the ip command are the objects you can work on. The most common are link, address, and route. Table 6-3 describes these and the rest of the objects for this command.

Table 6-3. *Describing Objects in* ip

Object	Description
link	The network device
address	The address of the interface (IPv4 or IPv6)
neighbour	ARP or NDISC cache entry
route	Routing table entry
rule	Rule in the routing policy database
maddress	Multicast address
mroute	Multicast routing cache entry
tunnel	Tunnel over IP

The objects that you can work on with ip, such as the interfaces and the routing tables, allow you to manage many of your network needs. The *COMMAND* specified in the ip command syntax is the action you can perform on those objects. Each object type has its own set of legal commands that can be performed on it.

Let's take the object link, for example. You can use the up or down command to set the state of the link:

```
$ sudo /sbin/ip link set eth0 down
```

This command sets the eth0 device, link set eth0, to a down state. The link is the interface, and this command will set the state of our interface to down, much like the ifconfig eth0 down command you saw earlier. Here is the output of the ip link show command showing the link in a down state:

```
$ sudo /sbin/ip link show eth0
2: eth0: <BROADCAST,MULTICAST,UP,LOWER_UP> mtu 1500 qdisc pfifo_fast qlen 1000
    link/ether 00:0c:29:94:bd:3d brd ff:ff:ff:ff:ff:ff
    inet6 fe80::20c:29ff:fe94:bd3d/64 scope link
      valid_lft forever preferred_lft forever
```

You can see that eth0 is up in this instance by <BROADCAST,MULTICAST,UP,LOWER_UP>. We can take it back down by issuing the following and then viewing it again:

```
$ sudo /sbin/ip link set down eth0
$ sudo /sbin/ip link show eth0
2: eth0: <BROADCAST,MULTICAST> mtu 1500 qdisc pfifo_fast qlen 1000
    link/ether 00:0c:29:94:bd:3d brd ff:ff:ff:ff:ff:ff...
```

Now your interface is down, and no communications can take place using it. As you can see, neither state shows an IP address attached to the interface. We will attach one now to the eth0 interface. First, we bring the interface back up with /sbin/ip link set up eth0 (although you do not have to set the interface state to up). Then we add the IP address 192.168.0.120/24 to device eth0.

```
$ sudo /sbin/ip  addr add 192.168.0.120/24 dev eth0
```

Using ip to show the interface, you can see that the address 192.168.0.120 is now attached to the Ethernet interface eth0. The /24 gives the network mask of 255.255.255.0. You could choose /27 or .224 or /29 or .248 if you wish.

```
$ sudo /sbin/ip addr show eth0
2: eth0: <BROADCAST,MULTICAST,UP,LOWER_UP> mtu 1500 qdisc pfifo_fast qlen 1000
    link/ether 00:0c:29:94:bd:3d brd ff:ff:ff:ff:ff:ff
    inet 192.168.0.120/24 scope global eth0
    inet6 fe80::20c:29ff:fe94:bd3d/64 scope link
        valid_lft forever preferred_lft forever
```

■**Note** In the upcoming "Ping!" section, we will show you how to test that your interface is working using the ping command.

Next, we will delete the address from the interface. To do that we use the ip command with the addr object and the del command like so:

```
$ sudo /sbin/ip addr del 192.168.0.120/24 dev eth0
```

You must remember to add the correct network mask when deleting the interface; otherwise you will receive an error. When we now list the interface, the address is no longer shown.

```
 3: eth0: <BROADCAST,MULTICAST,UP,LOWER_UP> mtu 1500 qdisc pfifo_fast qlen 1000
    link/ether 00:0c:29:94:bd:3d brd ff:ff:ff:ff:ff:ff
    inet6 fe80::20c:29ff:fe94:bd3d/64 scope link
        valid_lft forever preferred_lft forever
```

■**Note** You may find it strange that IP addresses configured with the ip command will not appear when you run ifconfig. You will need to use the ip command to view any IP addresses you have created with this tool.

ETHTOOL

The `ethtool` command is used to further investigate and manipulate your interfaces. For example, you can change the link speed of your interface or your duplex settings.

You can see the settings your device is using by issuing the following command:

```
$ sudo ethtool eth0
Settings for eth0:
        Supported ports: [ MII ]
        Supported link modes:   10baseT/Half 10baseT/Full
                                100baseT/Half 100baseT/Full
                                1000baseT/Full
        Supports auto-negotiation: Yes
        Advertised link modes:  10baseT/Half 10baseT/Full
                                100baseT/Half 100baseT/Full
                                1000baseT/Full
        Advertised auto-negotiation: Yes
        Speed: 100Mb/s
        Duplex: Full
        Port: MII
        PHYAD: 0
        Transceiver: external
        Auto-negotiation: on
        Supports Wake-on: g
        Wake-on: d
        Link detected: yes
```

This shows the current settings of your eth0 device. If you want to change the duplex mode and speed, you would issue a command like the following:

```
$ sudo ethtool eth0 -s speed 1000 duplex half
```

Here we have changed the `speed` of the Ethernet card to 1000Mb/s and the `duplex` setting to `half` duplex. You can use other settings as well. For a greater understanding of the available settings, please read the man page for `ethtool`.

Adding Routes and Forwarding Packets

The other common thing you will do with the `ip` command is add routes to your host. Routes are the pathways your host should follow to access other networks or other hosts.

IP FORWARDING

Linux hosts generally have IP forwarding turned off by default. IP forwarding allows your host to act as a router, directing packets sent to it by hosts on your network to the destination host. If your host has IP forwarding turned on, your host will be able to forward packets from one interface to another or one network to another. This is a kernel-level function that can be turned on or off by editing the /etc/sysctl.conf file. This file allows you to configure kernel parameters at runtime. You can set many other parameters in the sysctl.conf file, including memory, swap, and other network-related kernel parameters that can be tweaked during runtime.

The kernel stores this kind of information in the /proc directory. For example, the IP forwarding setting is located in the /proc/sys/net/ipv4/ip_forward file. This file system is created by the kernel at boot up, and changes made directly to it are not persistent across reboots. If this is set to 0, IP forwarding is disabled, and your host will not pass on any packets not destined for it. If it is set to 1, IP forwarding will redirect those packets not destined for it to their destination host.

To make the setting persistent across reboots, you need to uncomment the following line in /etc/sysctl.conf, save the file, and then issue the sysctl -p command to load the changes into the kernel:

```
# Uncomment the next line to enable packet forwarding for IPv4
net.ipv4.ip_forward=1
```

You can also immediately turn on packet forwarding by echoing the number 1 into the file /proc/sys/net/ipv4/ip_forward like this:

```
echo 1 > /proc/sys/net/ipv4/ip_forward
```

This change is not persistent across reboots, but editing /etc/sysctl will make it permanent. For more information on sysctl.conf and the use of sysctl, please read the man pages.

We want to show you an example of how to add a route using the ip command. First, we'll explain what we want to achieve. We are on our main server host, which has the IP address 192.168.0.1—Host A in Figure 6-18. We have our firewall/router sitting on our network with the IP address 192.168.0.254 on interface eth0—Host B. Also on interface eth0 on our firewall host is the address 192.168.1.254/24. The network 192.168.1.0/24 is going to be our wireless network, which we will separate into its own subnet. There is a host with which we wish to communicate on that network with the IP address 192.168.1.220—Host C. Again this is made clear by Figure 6-18.

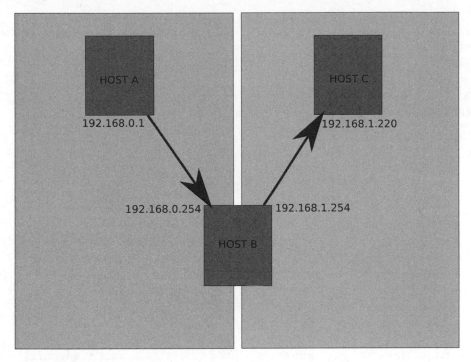

Figure 6-18. *Adding a route*

Host A and Host C are properly configured to route between the networks. In their routing tables, they send all requests destined for other networks via their default gateway. In this case their default gateway is the firewall/router, and the address of their default gateway is 192.168.0.254 and 192.168.1.254, respectively. Host A does not know that Host B has the 192.168.1.0/24 network attached to its eth0 interface, nor does Host C know that Host B has the 192.168.0.0/24 network attached to it.

Let's view the route table for Host A. By issuing the following command, we can list the route table of Host A:

```
$ sudo /sbin/ip route show
192.168.0.0/24 dev eth0  proto kernel  scope link  src 192.168.0.1
169.254.0.0/16 dev eth0  scope link
127.0.0.0/8 dev lo  scope link
default via 192.168.0.254 dev eth0  scope link
```

The route table shows us the networks that this host knows about. It knows about its own network, as shown with `192.168.0.0/24 dev eth0  proto kernel  scope link  src 192.168.0.1`. The network `169.254.0.0/16 dev eth0  scope link` is what is called a *local-link* network. It is used to get hosts to communicate with each other without the need for complex network services like DHCP and DNS.

The next line in the route output, `127.0.0.0/8 dev lo  scope link`, is for the loopback address network. Many services use addresses in this network range for interprocess communications, and this route is attached to the loopback device, `dev lo`.

Finally, you see the default route, default via 192.168.0.254 dev eth0 scope link. The default route points to the host on the network, which can handle the routing requests for hosts on its network. These are devices with usually more than one interface or IP address network attached to it and can therefore pass on the routing requests to hosts further along the routing path to the final destination.

Let's compare that route table with the one for Host B. Host B is our network router, so it should have more than one network attached to its interfaces.

```
$ sudo /sbin/ip route show
10.204.2.10 dev ppp0  proto kernel  scope link  src 10.0.2.155
192.168.0.0/24 dev eth0  proto kernel  scope link  src 192.168.0.254
192.168.1.0/24 dev eth0  proto kernel  scope link  src 192.168.1.254
169.254.0.0/16 dev eth0  scope link
default dev ppp0  scope link
```

First let's take a look at the default route on Host B. It indicates that anything it doesn't know about it will send out of dev ppp0. The device ppp0 is our PPP link to our ISP. The first line is related to that route. It shows us that the network 10.204.2.10 is reached via the device ppp0 and through the link src address of 10.0.2.155. The 10.204.2.10 host is in our ISP and is assigned to us by our ISP when we make our PPP connection.

We know that Host A and Host C are on different networks, and by themselves they cannot reach each other. For us to make a simple connection, like a ping connection, from Host A to Host C, the TCP/IP packets have to go through Host B. The ping command sends an ICMP echo request to the host specified on the command line. The echo request is a defined protocol that says to the requesting host what would in computer speak be "I'm here."

■**Note** Internet Control Message Protocol (ICMP) is a TCP/IP protocol that is used to send messages between hosts, normally error messages; but in the case of ping, it can also send an informational echo reply.

So let's see if we can reach Host C from Host A by issuing the ping command on Host A. (We explain ping in much greater detail further on in the chapter in the "Ping!" section.)

```
$ ping -c 4 192.168.1.220
PING 192.168.1.220 (192.168.1.220) 56(84) bytes of data.
64 bytes from 192.168.1.220: icmp_seq=1 ttl=64 time=1.79 ms
```

We have used the ping command, a way of sending network echoes, with the -c 4 option to limit the number of echo replies to 4. This is enough to confirm that we can reach our Host C from our Host A. That was relatively easy. Let's look at a slightly different scenario in which we have to add our own route. You can see a diagram of it in Figure 6-19.

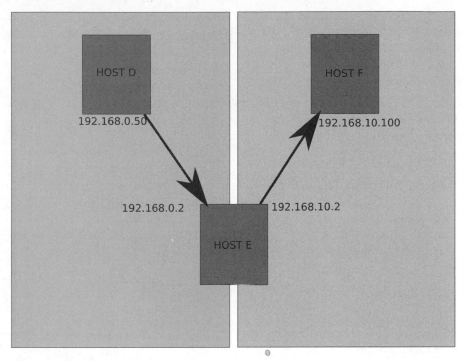

Figure 6-19. *Adding a route*

In this scenario, we will say that Host D is trying to reach Host F by passing through Host E. Host E has two Ethernet devices, eth0 and eth1. The device eth0 is attached to the 192.168.0.0/24 network with IP address 192.168.0.2, and eth1 is attached to the 192.168.10.0/24 network with IP address 192.168.10.2. Host D is on the 192.168.0.0/24 network with IP address 192.168.0.50. Host D has a default route of 192.168.0.254. Host F is on the 192.168.10.0/24 network with IP address 192.168.10.100. Host F has the default route 192.168.10.254.

Let's look at their route tables:

```
Host D
192.168.0.0/24 dev eth0  proto kernel  scope link  src 192.168.0.50
169.254.0.0/16 dev eth0  scope link
127.0.0.0/8 dev lo  scope link
default via 192.168.0.254 dev eth0  scope link


Host E
192.168.0.0/24 dev eth0  proto kernel  scope link  src 192.168.0.2
192.168.10.0/24 dev eth1 proto kernel  scope link  src 192.168.10.2
169.254.0.0/16 dev eth0  scope link
127.0.0.0/8 dev lo  scope link
default via 192.168.0.254 dev eth0  scope link
```

```
Host F
192.168.10.0/24 dev eth0  proto kernel  scope link  src 192.168.10.100
169.254.0.0/16 dev eth0  scope link
127.0.0.0/8 dev lo  scope link
default via 192.168.10.254 dev eth0  scope link
```

You can see that Host E contains the two interfaces with the two different networks attached. To get Host D to see Host F, we need to tell Host D to get to Host F via Host E. We do that by adding a route like this:

```
$ sudo /sbin/ip route add 192.168.10.0/24 via 192.168.0.2 dev eth0
```

Here we have to use the `ip` command combined with the `route` object to add a route to the 192.168.10.0/24 network from our Host D. We give the command the IP address of the host, 192.168.0.2, which is the router on our network for the destination network.

Now that Host D has the pathway to get to the 192.168.10.0/24 network, we should be able to ping Host F.

```
$  ping 192.168.10.100
PING 192.168.10.100 (192.168.10.100) 56(84) bytes of data.
64 bytes from 192.168.10.100: icmp_seq=1 ttl=64 time=1.24 ms
```

Now let's try to ping Host D from Host F. We use -c 4 to limit the number of pings that are sent to the destination host to four.

```
ping -c 4 192.168.0.50
PING 192.168.0.50 (192.168.0.50) 56(84) bytes of data.

--- 192.168.0.50 ping statistics ---
4 packets transmitted, 0 received, 100% packet loss, time 2999ms
```

Our hosts can't see each other when we ping from Host F to Host D. Why is that? It is because Host F knows nothing of the 192.168.0.0/24 network. We will send anything it doesn't know about to its default gateway. And because the default gateway of Host F isn't configured to know where to send packets to 192.168.0.50, it will send them off to its default gateway. Eventually these packets will die.

■**Note** Part of the TCP/IP protocol is a TTL—*time to live*—where after a period of time the packets are ignored and dropped by upstream routers. TTL is indicated by a number, usually 64 these days, but can be 32 or 128. As packets pass through each router (or *hop*), they decrease the TTL value by 1. If the TTL is 1 when it reaches a router and that router is not the final destination, the router will drop the packet and send a "TTL expired in transit" message using the ICMP protocol. You will see how useful this is shortly in the "MTR" section.

So how do we fix this? Well, we add a route to Host F telling it how to send packets to Host D via Host E.

```
$ sudo /sbin/ip route add 192.168.0.0/24 via 192.168.10.2 dev eth0
```

Now when Host F tries to ping Host D, we get the following result:

```
$ ping 192.168.0.50
PING 192.168.0.50 (192.168.0.50) 56(84) bytes of data.
64 bytes from 192.168.0.50: icmp_seq=1 ttl=64 time=1.24 ms
```

After adding the route to Host F, we can now reach Host D. Combining all this information, we can use these commands in a script to bring up an interface, add an IP address, and add a route.

```
#!/bin/bash

# bring up the interface
ip link set eth1 up

# add an address
ip addr add 192.168.10.1/24 dev eth1

# add a route
ip route add 192.168.100.1 via 192.168.10.254 dev eth1

# ping the host
ping 192.168.100.1 -c 4

# bring down the route, remove the address and bring down the interface.
ip route del 192.168.100.1 via 192.168.10.254 dev eth1
ip addr del 192.168.10.1/24 dev eth1
ip link set eth1 down

exit 0
```

We have used the same command to control our interface, bringing it up, adding an address, and then adding a route. We then brought it down again with the same command. This sort of script can be used to copy files from one host to another host or make any sort of connection.

Let's now move on to further explore how you can test your connections and troubleshoot your network using a few simple utilities.

General Network Troubleshooting

Things can go wrong on your network. Sometimes you aren't able to connect to services, or some part of your network is incorrectly configured. To identify and resolve these problems, you will need a set of tools. We will examine a variety of tools:

- ping: A command that sends packets between hosts to confirm connectivity

- tcpdump: A command that displays and captures network traffic

- mtr: A network diagnostic tool

- nc: The netcat, another network diagnostic and testing tool

Ping!

Probably the most common tool that people use for checking their network is a command called ping. You can ping a host or an interface to see if it responds. In the output response from issuing the ping command, you are shown the time it has taken for that response to come back. You can ping the other side of the world and receive a response in milliseconds. That is good. If you get response times in the order of whole seconds or a "host unreachable" message, that is bad. Of course, if the host you're pinging is on another continent or connected via a satellite link, ping times will be higher than if the host is sitting under your desk.

We just used the ping command to test our routes like this:

```
$  ping 192.168.0.50
PING 192.168.0.50 (192.168.0.50) 56(84) bytes of data.
64 bytes from 192.168.0.50: icmp_seq=1 ttl=64 time=1.24 ms
```

The ping command can take the following arguments. For other arguments, refer to the man page.

```
ping –c <count> –i <interval> –I <interface address> –s <packet size> destination
```

The ping command will send pings to a host indefinitely unless you either stop it, using Ctrl+C usually, or give it the number of pings to attempt using the -c *number* option.

You can also express the interval between pings as -i *number* (in seconds) and choose the interface you wish to use as the source address, specified by -I *IP address*. This is very handy if you have multiple interfaces and wish to test one of those. If you don't define an address, it will usually ping using the primary interface on the host, usually eth0. You can also specify the packet size, using -s *number of bytes*, which is useful for testing bandwidth problems or problems with MTU settings.

■**Note** As mentioned earlier in the chapter, MTU is the maximum transmission unit. It is used to limit the size of the packets to what the network devices on that network can handle. Normally it is set to 1500 bytes, but with jumbo frames it can be up to 9000 bytes. The MTU for most Internet devices is 1472.

One of the first things you can do to test your network is to use ping to ping the interfaces you have configured. If they respond to pings from your own host, they are up. They may not be configured properly, but at least they are working. You can do this like so:

```
$ ping 192.168.0.253
PING 192.168.0.253 (192.168.0.253) 56(84) bytes of data.
64 bytes from 192.168.0.253: icmp_seq=2 ttl=128 time=1.68 ms
```

Here we have sent a ping to the local IP address of our host, and we can see a series of responses indicating a connection has been made and the time it took. If we had received no responses, we would know something is wrong with our interface or network.

The next step is to ping another host on your network, like your default gateway or your DNS server (these two hosts are critical for your Internet communications).

```
$ ping 192.168.0.1
PING 192.168.0.1 (192.168.0.1) 56(84) bytes of data.
64 bytes from 192.168.0.1: icmp_seq=1 ttl=128 time=2.97 ms
```

If you can get there, you know that your host can reach other hosts. You would then ping a host outside your network, say www.ibm.com or www.google.com, and test its response:

```
$ ping www.google.com
PING www.l.google.com (150.101.98.222) 56(84) bytes of data.
64 bytes from g222.internode.on.net (150.101.98.222): icmp_seq=1 ttl=59 time=20.0 ms
```

When you experience problems connecting to hosts on the Internet, it can be for many reasons. There are instances where part of the Internet will go down because a core router is broken. In this situation, all your private network pings will return, but some pings to hosts on the Internet may not. If you don't get a response from one host on the Internet, try another to see if the issue is local or somewhere else down the line. Some remote networks will actively block ICMP traffic. These hosts will not respond to pings, and so you should check the response of other hosts before you panic. It is also handy in these situations to combine your investigations with other tools, one of which is mtr.

MTR

If you can ping hosts inside your network but can't ping hosts outside your network, you can use a tool like traceroute or mtr for troubleshooting. Both provide a similar service: they trace the route they use to get to the destination host. Both also use "TTL expired in transit" messages to record those hosts along the way. What do these messages mean? Well, as we have already explained, TTL is used to kill TCP/IP packets so they don't keep zinging around the Internet forever like some lost particle in the Large Hadron Collider. These commands take advantage of polite routers that send back "TTL expired in transit" messages when they kill your packet.

Let's take a look at an example. If we do a ping to www.ibm.com and set the TTL to 1, it gets to the first router along the path to whatever www.ibm.com resolves to. That first router looks at the TTL and sees that it is 1. It now drops the packet and sends the expired-in-transit message.

```
$ ping -t 1 -c 1 www.ibm.com
PING www.ibm.com.cs186.net (129.42.60.216) 56(84) bytes of data.
From 192.168.0.254 (192.168.0.254) icmp_seq=1 Time to live exceeded

--- www.ibm.com.cs186.net ping statistics ---
1 packets transmitted, 0 received, +1 errors, 100% packet loss, time 0ms
```

The mtr and traceroute applications use the packet sent back to discover the IP address of the router (as the TCP/IP packet containing the reply will hold this information). It then displays that information and sends the next ping, this time with the TTL set to 2. Once the ping reaches our destination, we should receive the standard echo response. Some routers are configured not to send these ICMP messages and appear as blanks in the trace output.

Have a look at the output from mtr. Here we have used mtr to trace the route between the host au-mel-rhel-1 and www.ibm.com using the following command:

```
$ sudo /usr/sbin/mtr www.ibm.com
                                   My traceroute  [v0.71]
au-mel-rhel-1 (0.0.0.0)                                    Thu Jan  8 17:38:23 2009
Keys:  Help  Display mode  Restart statistics  Order of fields  quit
                                                            Packets        Pings
  Host  Loss%  Last  Avg  Best  Wrst  StDev
 1. 192.168.0.254  0.0%   0.6   1.0   0.0   1.9   0.5  2.0
 2. loop0.lns10.mel6.domain.com  0.0%   9.1   8.5   7.9   9.1   0.5
 3. vlan13.cor2.mel6.domain.com  0.0%   9.2   9.7   8.0  14.5   2.4
 4. gi0-0-4.bdr1.mel6.domain.com  0.0% 201.7 202.0 201.0 202.9   0.7
 5. pos2-3.bdr1.syd6.domain.com  0.0% 168.2 169.1 168.2 169.5   0.5
 6. pos5-0.bdr1.lax1.domain.com  0.0% 201.1 200.8 200.1 201.5   0.6
 7. Gb3-2.GW1.LAX15.ALTER.NET  0.0% 169.1 168.4 167.7 169.1   0.6
 8. 01.XL3.LAX15.ALTER.NET  0.0% 168.0 169.1 167.6 172.2   1.9
 9. 02.XT3.STL3.ALTER.NET  0.0% 214.2 218.8 213.9 236.3   9.8
10. POS6-0.GW8.STL3.ALTER.NET  0.0% 247.7 247.3 246.7 247.7   0.4
11. ibm-gw.customer.alter.net  0.0% 216.5 216.4 215.5 217.0   0.5
12. ???
```

What the output from this command shows is that our first hop (each host/router we pass through is called a hop) is our firewall router. Next is the default gateway of our Internet connection at our ISP. As we pass through each hop along the way, we record information about our route. At the penultimate hop, we reach the IBM gateway. In the final hop, it appears that IBM has denied returning ICMP packets from inside their network, and mtr has printed ??? because it has not received the "TTL expired in transit" message.

TCP/IP 101

It's time to delve a little further into TCP/IP. You may be familiar with an IP address, but how does that fit in with the rest of TCP/IP? An IP address is used to find other hosts on the network and for other hosts to find you. But how does it do that?

You will be interested to know that when you initiate a TCP/IP connection (also known as a *socket*), a three-stage process gets that connection into an "established" state, meaning both hosts are aware of their socket to each other, agree how they are going to send data, and are ready to send that data. The first stage is the host initiating the socket by sending a packet, called a SYN packet, to the host it wants to start communications with. That host responds with another packet, known as a SYN, ACK packet, indicating it is ready to begin communications. The initiating host then sends a packet, another SYN, ACK packet, acknowledging that packet and telling the remote host it is going to begin sending data. When they have finished communicating, the connection is closed with a FIN packet. This is a basic overview of the process of TCP/IP communications.

The protocol it relies upon is made up of seven layers. Each of those layers has a special responsibility in the process of communicating data between hosts over the wire. In diagnosing your network, you will normally be interested in the layers 1, 2, and 3. You can see a description of these layers in Figure 6-20.

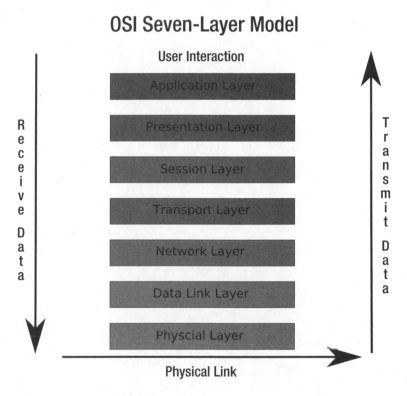

Figure 6-20. *The OSI layer model*

Layer 1 is the physical wire, and this is represented by the physical layer appearing at the bottom of Figure 6-20. When diagnosing network problems, it never hurts to jiggle the cables connecting your computer and the rest of the network. Also, when all else fails, you can try replacing cables. If cables are faulty, you will probably not see any lights on the switch/hub your host is connected to and the network card. Without these lights, your host will not be able to communicate to other hosts, so try to replace first the cable, and then the port it is connected to on the switch, and finally the network card.

Layer 2, the data link layer, provides the actual communication protocols across the wire. Problems encountered on this layer are rare. It is here that IP addresses get matched to MAC addresses by the use of ARP. When two hosts on the network have the same IP address and a different MAC address, your host might start trying to send data to the wrong host. In this case, the ARP table may need to be flushed, and the host with the incorrect IP address will need to be taken offline.

Layer 3 is the network layer. It is able to discover the routes to your destination and send your data, checking for errors as it does so. This is the IP layer, so it can also be responsible for IPsec tunneling. It is also this layer that is responsible for responding to your pings and other routing requests.

The tcpdump Command

You can't easily view communications at layer 1, but you can view them at layer 2 and layer 3 by using *packet-sniffing* software. One such application to view this detail is the tcpdump command-line tool. The tcpdump command, and those like it, can view traffic at the packet level on the wire. You can see the packets coming in and out of your host. The tcpdump command, when run without any expressions, will print every packet crossing the interface. You can use expressions to narrow the array of packets types it will show. See the man tcpdump page for more information.

■**Note** Another program you can try is called Wireshark. It has a very good GUI that allows you to easily filter traffic. It also has a command-line utility called tshark, which operates in similar fashion to tcpdump. You can see more about Wireshark here: http://www.wireshark.org/.

When you use the tcpdump command, the output appears as follows:

```
$ sudo /usr/sbin/tcpdump -i eth0
tcpdump: verbose output suppressed, use -v or -vv for full protocol decode
listening on eth0, link-type EN10MB (Ethernet), capture size 96 bytes
16:58:35.901825 arp who-has 192.168.0.254 tell 192.168.0.1
16:58:35.902941 arp who-has 192.168.0.254 tell 192.168.0.1
16:58:35.903145 arp reply 192.168.0.254 is-at 00:0b:cd:49:c0:7f (oui Unknown)
16:58:35.904845 IP 192.168.0.254 > 192.168.0.1.smtp: S 2737972828:2737972828(0) ➥
win 16384 <mss 1460,nop,wscale 0,nop,nop,sackOK>
16:58:35.917231 IP 192.168.0.1.smtp > 192.168.0.254: S 4235714640:4235714640(0) ➥
ack 2737972829 win 5840 <mss 460,nop,nop,sackOK,nop,wscale 4>
16:58:35.907176 IP 192.168.0.254 > 192.168.0.1.smtp: . ack 1 win 17520
16:58:35.922434 IP 192.168.0.1.smtp > 192.168.0.254: P 1:50(49) ack 1 win 365
16:58:36.101483 IP 192.168.0.254 > 192.168.0.1.smtp: . ack 50 win 17471
```

We have issued the command and told it to dump all the traffic that crosses the eth0 interface. We use the -i option to specify which interface to examine. In the output, we can break down the lines as follows:

timestamp source > destination : flags

In the preceding output, the first two lines contain information telling you what the command is doing, in this case, listening on eth0. The rest are actual packets crossing the wire. The first numbers of each line, for example, 16:58:35.901825, are timestamps.

```
arp who-has 192.168.0.254 tell 192.168.0.1
```

The first field (taking away the timestamp) is the protocol in the TCP/IP model. This is an ARP request, and ARP operates at the layer 2 (or data link layer) of the TCP/IP protocol stack. ARP is used to match up MAC addresses to IP addresses. You can see that 192.168.0.1 wants to know who has 192.168.0.254. There is an ARP reply that says that 192.168.0.254 is at MAC address 00:0b:cd:49:c0:7f.

Now that 192.168.0.1 knows where to send its packet, it tries to establish a socket by sending a SYN packet. The SYN packet carries the SYN bit set and has an initial sequence number of S 2737972828:2737972828(0).

```
IP 192.168.0.254 > 192.168.0.1.smtp: S 2737972828:2737972828(0) ➥
win 16384 <mss 1460,nop,wscale 0,nop,nop,sackOK>
```

The source and destination are described by 192.168.0.254 > 192.168.0.1.smtp, where .smtp is the port we are connecting to. That port maps to port 25. This is a connection being established to an SMTP mail server.

Let's look at the next part: S 2737972828:2737972828(0). The S after the source and the destination indicates that this is a SYN request and we are establishing a connection. Next are initial sequence numbers of the packets, 2737972828:2737972828(0). The sequence numbers are randomly generated and are used to order and match packets. The (0) after the sequence means that it is a zero-byte packet (i.e., it contains no payload).

The other flags, win 16384 <mss 1460,nop,wscale 0,nop,nop,sackOK>, provide other information in the communication like sliding window size, maximum segment size, and so on.

■**Note** For more information, see http://www.tcpipguide.com/free/
t_TCPMaximumSegmentSizeMSSandRelationshiptoIPDatagra.htm.

The next packet is the reply from 192.168.0.1.

```
IP 192.168.0.1.smtp > 192.168.0.254: S 4235714640:4235714640(0) ➥
ack 2737972829 win 5840 <mss 460,nop,nop,sackOK,nop,wscale 4>
```

This packet has the sequence number S 4235714640:4235714640(0). This is another randomly generated number, and the data payload is again zero, (0). Attached to this sequence is an ACK response, ack 2737972829. This is the original initial sequence number incremented by 1, indicating that it is acknowledging our first sequence.

The next packet is another acknowledgment packet sent by the originating host:

```
IP 192.168.0.254 > 192.168.0.1.smtp: . ack 1 win 17520
```

In this output, the dot (.) means that no flags were set. The `ack 1` indicates that this is an acknowlegment packet and that from now on, `tcpdump` will show the difference between the current sequence and initial sequence. This is the last communication needed to establish a connection between two hosts.

The last two packets are the exchange of data:

```
IP 192.168.0.1.smtp > 192.168.0.254: P 1:50(49) ack 1 win 365
P 192.168.0.254 > 192.168.0.1.smtp: . ack 50 win 17471
```

The mail server is sending a message to the client on 192.168.0.254, as indicated by `P 1:50(49) ack 1`. This is pushing, `P`, 49 bytes of data in the payload and is acknowledging the previous communication. The last communication is 192.168.0.254 acknowleging that packet, `ack 50`.

So now that you know how to see the communications between two hosts at the most basic level using packet-sniffing programs such as `tcpdump`, let's take a look at another useful tool, netcat.

■**Note** If you are interested in a deeper discussion of `tcpdump` and connection establishment, try this article: `http://www.linuxjournal.com/article/6447`.

The Netcat Tool

The other very useful tool you can use to diagnose network problems is the `nc`, or netcat, command. You can use this tool to test your ability to reach not only other hosts, but also the ports on which they could be listening.

This tool is especially handy when you want to test a connection to a port through a firewall. Let's test whether our firewall is allowing us to connect to port 80 on host 192.168.0.1 from host 192.168.0.254.

First, on host 192.168.0.1, we will make sure we have stopped our web server. For example, on Red Hat, we issue this command:

```
$ sudo /sbin/service httpd stop
```

We will then start the `nc` command using the `-l`, or listen, option on the host with the IP address of 192.168.0.1.

```
$ sudo nc -l 80
```

This binds our `nc` command to all interfaces on the port. We can test that by running another command called `netstat`:

```
$ sudo netstat -lpt
tcp    0    0 *:http    *:*    LISTEN  18618/nc    .
```

We launched the `netstat` command with three options. The `-l` option tells the `netstat` command to run and listen for network connections. The `-p` option tells `netstat` to display what applications are using each connection, and the last option, -t, tells netstat to look for TCP connections only.

The netstat command displays the programs listening on certain ports on your host. We can see in the preceding output that the program nc, PID of 18618, is listening for TCP connections on port 80. The *:http indicates that it is listening on all available addresses (network interface IP addresses) on port 80 (the :http port maps to port 80). OK, so we know our nc command is listening and waiting for connections. Next, we test our ability to connect from the host with the IP address of 192.168.0.254.

We will use the telnet command to make a connection to port 80 on host 192.168.0.1 as in the following example:

```
$ telnet 192.168.0.1 80
Trying 192.168.0.1...
Connected to 192.168.0.1.
Escape character is '^]'.
hello host
```

The telnet program allows us to test the connection between two hosts and send text to the remote host. When we type text and press Enter in our connection window, we will see what we have typed being echoed on the au-mel-rhel-1 host.

```
$ sudo nc -l 80
hello host
```

We now know our host can connect to the au-mel-rhel-1 host on port 80, confirming that our firewall rules are working (or too liberal as the case may be if we were trying to block port 80).

You Dig It?

dig is another handy tool for resolving DNS issues. If you use this tool in combination with others like ping and nc, you will be able to solve many problems. The dig command, short for domain information groper, is used to query DNS servers. Employed simply, the command will resolve a fully qualified domain name by querying the nameserver it finds in the /etc/resolv.conf file.

The /etc/resolv.conf file is used to store the nameserver information so your host knows which DNS server to query for domain name resolution. A /etc/resolv.conf file looks like this:

```
$ sudo cat /etc/resolv.conf
; generated by /sbin/dhclient-script
search example.com
nameserver 192.168.0.1
nameserver  192.168.0.254
```

First you can see that the resolv.conf file was generated by the DHCP client. The default search domain is example.com, and any hostname searches will have that domain appended to the end of the query. Next, we have the nameserver(s) we wish to query for our domain name resolution. These should be in IP address format. If the first nameserver is unavailable, the second will be used.

The dig command will query these nameservers unless otherwise instructed. Let's look at this query:

```
$ dig www.google.com

; <<>> DiG 9.5.0-P2 <<>> www.google.com
;; global options:  printcmd
;; Got answer:
;; ->>HEADER<<- opcode: QUERY, status: NOERROR, id: 46826
;; flags: qr rd ra; QUERY: 1, ANSWER: 5, AUTHORITY: 7, ADDITIONAL: 7

;; QUESTION SECTION:
;www.google.com.            IN      A

;; ANSWER SECTION:
www.google.com.    209821   IN      CNAME   www.l.google.com.
www.l.google.com. 92        IN      A       74.125.95.103
www.l.google.com. 92        IN      A       74.125.95.104
www.l.google.com. 92        IN      A       74.125.95.147
www.l.google.com. 92        IN      A       74.125.95.99

;; AUTHORITY SECTION:
l.google.com.      13489    IN      NS      g.l.google.com.
l.google.com.      13489    IN      NS      a.l.google.com.
l.google.com.      13489    IN      NS      b.l.google.com.
l.google.com.      13489    IN      NS      c.l.google.com.
l.google.com.      13489    IN      NS      d.l.google.com.
l.google.com.      13489    IN      NS      e.l.google.com.
l.google.com.      13489    IN      NS      f.l.google.com.

;; ADDITIONAL SECTION:
a.l.google.com.    75270    IN      A       209.85.139.9
b.l.google.com.    164012   IN      A       74.125.45.9
c.l.google.com.    127883   IN      A       64.233.161.9
d.l.google.com.    63971    IN      A       74.125.77.9
e.l.google.com.    46712    IN      A       209.85.137.9
f.l.google.com.    164012   IN      A       72.14.235.9
g.l.google.com.    42069    IN      A       74.125.95.9

;; Query time: 29 msec
;; SERVER: 64.5.53.6#53(64.5.53.6)
;; WHEN: Tue Apr  7 07:15:52 2009
;; MSG SIZE  rcvd: 340
```

In the ANSWER SECTION, you can see the www.google.com hostname will resolve to the DNS CNAME www.l.google.com, which has four possible IP addresses it will finally resolve to. The AUTHORITY SECTION tells us which nameservers are responsible for providing the DNS information for www.google.com. The ADDITIONAL SECTION tells us what IP addresses the nameservers in the AUTHORITY SECTION will resolve to.

IN A indicates an Internet address (or relative record). CNAME is used to alias hostnames. IN NS indicates a nameserver record. Numbers such as 92, 13489, and 75270, shown in the three sections in the preceding code, indicate how long in seconds the record is cached for. When they reach zero, the nameserver will query the authoritative DNS server to see whether it has changed.

At the bottom of the dig output, you can see the SERVER that provided the response, 64.5.53.6, and how long the query took, 29 msec.

You can use dig to query a particular nameserver by using the @ sign. You can also query certain record types by using the -t *type* option. For example, if we wanted to test our DNS server was working properly, we could use dig to find the IP address of Google's mail server.

```
$ dig @192.168.0.1 -t MX google.com

<snip>
;; Got answer:
;; ->>HEADER<<- opcode: QUERY, status: NOERROR, id: 12164
;; flags: qr rd ra; QUERY: 1, ANSWER: 4, AUTHORITY: 4, ADDITIONAL: 4

;; QUESTION SECTION:
;google.com.              IN      MX

;; ANSWER SECTION:
google.com.         557    IN  MX  10 smtp1.google.com.
<snip>
google.com.         557    IN  MX  10 smtp4.google.com.

;; AUTHORITY SECTION:
google.com.        73806  IN  NS     ns1.google.com.
<snip>
google.com.        73806  IN  NS     ns4.google.com.

;; ADDITIONAL SECTION:
ns1.google.com.     36427  IN  A      216.239.32.10
<snip>
ns4.google.com.     36427  IN  A      216.239.38.10

;; Query time: 1 msec
;; SERVER: 192.168.0.1#53(192.168.0.1)
<snip>
```

We could use this information and compare the response from other nameservers. If our nameserver has provided the same information, our DNS server is working correctly. If there is a difference or we return no results, we would have to investigate our DNS settings further. In Chapter 9, we discuss DNS and the dig command in more detail.

Other Troubleshooting Tools

The programs we've just discussed cover basic network troubleshooting. Many other networking tools are available to further help diagnose problems. We briefly touched on the netstat command, but there are a multitude of others. Table 6-4 lists some of the most common troubleshooting commands and their descriptions.

Table 6-4. *Other Handy Network Diagnostic Tools*

Tool	Description
netstat	This tool gives the status of what is listening on your host plus much more, including routes and statistics.
Host	Another tool to diagnose DNS servers. We'll show you how to use host in Chapter 9.
telnet	This tool allows you to make TCP connections to ports on remote hosts. You can test responses to commands from remote services.
openssl s_client	This is useful to test SSL connections as it can try to establish an SSL connection to a port on a remote host.
arp	This program queries and manages the ARP cache table, and allows you to delete ARP entries.

The list of useful tools in Table 6-4 is by no means exhaustive. However, armed with only a few of these tools, you can diagnose many common problems.

Netfilter and iptables

Many people now understand what a firewall is, as they have started to become mandatory on even the simplest of hosts. You may already be familiar with a firewall running on your desktop. These simple firewalls can be used to block unwanted traffic in and out of a single host, but that is all they can do.

Netfilter is a complex firewall application that can sit on the perimeter of a network or on a single host. Not only can it block unwanted traffic and route packets around the network, but it can also shape traffic. "Shape traffic?" you may be wondering, "What's that?"

Packet shaping is the ability to alter packets passing in and out of your network. You can use it to increase or decrease bandwidth for certain connections, optimize the sending of other packets, or guarantee performance of specific types of packets. This can be beneficial to companies that want to ensure VoIP calls are not interrupted by someone downloading some crazy frog ringtones.

How Netfilter/iptables Work

The iptables command is the user-space management tool for Netfilter. Netfilter was pioneered by Paul "Rusty" Russell and has been in the Linux kernel since version 2.4. It allows the operating system to perform packet filtering and shaping at a kernel level, and this allows it to be under fewer restrictions than user-space programs. This is especially useful for dedicated firewall and router hosts.

■**Note** The term *user-space program* refers to a tool used by end users to configure some portion of the operating system. In this case the internal operating system component is called Netfilter, and the user-space component, the command you use to configure Netfilter, is called `iptables`.

Packet filtering and shaping is the ability to change or discard packets as they enter or leave a host according to set of criteria, or rules. Netfilter does this by rewriting the packet headers as they enter, pass through, and/or leave the host.

Netfilter is a stateful packet-filtering firewall. Two types of packet-filtering firewalls exist: stateful and stateless. A *stateless* packet-filtering firewall examines only the header of a packet for filtering information. It sees each packet in isolation and thus has no way to determine whether a packet is part of an existing connection or an isolated malicious packet. A *stateful* firewall maintains information about the status of the connections passing through it. This allows the firewall to filter packets based on the state of the connection, which offers considerably finer-grained control over your traffic.

Netfilter is controlled and configured in the user space by the `iptables` command. In previous versions of the Linux kernel, other commands provided this functionality. In this chapter, we will frequently use `iptables` to refer to the firewall technology in general. Most Linux-based distributions will have an `iptables` package, but they may also have their own tool for configuring the rules.

Netfilter works by referring to a set of tables. These tables contain chains, which in turn contain individual rules. Chains hold groups of like rules; for example, a group of rules governing incoming traffic could be held in a chain. Rules are the basic Netfilter configuration items that contain criteria to match particular traffic and perform an action on the matched traffic.

Traffic that is currently being processed by the host is compared against these rules, and if the current packet being processed satisfies the selection criteria of a rule, the action, known as a *target*, specified by that rule is carried out. These actions, among others, can be to ignore the packet, accept the packet, reject the packet, or pass the packet on to other rules for more refined processing. Let's look at an example; say the Ethernet interface on your web server has just received a packet from the Internet. This packet is checked against your rules and compared to their selection criteria. The selection criteria include such items as the destination IP address and the destination port. For example, say you want incoming web traffic on the HTTP port 80 to go to the IP address of your web server. If your incoming traffic matches these criteria, you specify an action to let it through.

Each `iptables` rule relies on specifying a set of network parameters as selection criteria to select the packets and traffic for each rule. You can use a number of network parameters to build each `iptables` rule. For example, a network connection between two hosts is referred to as a *socket*. This is the combination of a source IP address, source port, destination IP address, and destination port. All four of these parameters must exist for the connection to be established, and `iptables` can use these values to filter traffic coming in and out of hosts. Additionally, if you look at how communication is performed on a TCP/IP-based network, you will see that three protocols are used most frequently: Internet Control Message Protocol (ICMP), Transmission Control Protocol (TCP), and User Datagram Protocol (UDP). The `iptables` firewall can easily distinguish between these different types of protocols and others.

With just these five parameters (the source and destination IP addresses, the source and destination ports, and the protocol type), you can now start building some useful filtering rules. But before you start building these rules, you need to understand how iptables rules are structured and interact. And to gain this understanding, you need to understand further some initial iptables concepts such as tables, chains, and policies, which we'll discuss next, along with touching a little on network address translation (NAT).

Tables

We talked about Netfilter having tables of rules that traffic can be compared against, possibly resulting in some action taken. Netfilter has four built-in tables that can hold rules for processing traffic. The first is the filter table, which is the default table used for all rules related to the filtering of your traffic. The second is nat, which handles NAT rules. Next is the mangle table, which covers a variety of packet alteration functions. Last of all is the raw table, which is used to exempt packets from connection tracking and is called before any other Netfilter table.

Chains

Each of the Netfilter tables, filter, nat, mangle, and raw, contain sets of predefined hooks that Netfilter will process in order. These hooks contain sequenced groupings of rules called *chains*. Each table contains default chains that are built into the table. The built-in chains are described in Table 6-5.

Table 6-5. *Built-in Chains*

Chain	Description
INPUT	Used to sequence rules for packets coming to the host interface(s). Found in the filter and mangle tables only.
FORWARD	Used to sequence rules for packets destined for another host. Found in the filter and mangle table only.
OUTPUT	Used to sequence rules for outgoing packets originating from the host interface(s). Found in the filter, nat, mangle, and raw tables.
PREROUTING	Used to alter packets before they are routed to the other chains. Found in the nat, mangle, and raw tables.
POSTROUTING	Used to alter packets after they have left the other chains and are about to go out of the interface(s). Found in the nat and mangle tables only.

Each chain correlates to the basic paths that packets can take through a host. When the Netfilter logic encounters a packet, the first evaluation it makes is to which chain the packet is destined. Not all tables contain all the built-in chains listed in Table 6-5.

Let's look at the filter table for example. It contains only the INPUT, OUTPUT, and FORWARD chains. If a packet is coming into the host through a network interface, it needs to be evaluated by the rules in the INPUT chain. If the packet is generated by this host and going out onto the network via a network interface, it needs to be evaluated by the rules in the OUTPUT chain. The FORWARD chain is used for packets that have entered the host but are destined for some other host (for example, on hosts that act as routers or software-based firewalls at the perimeter of your network or between your network and the Internet). You are able to create chains of your own in each table to hold additional rules. You can also direct the flow of packets from a built-in chain to a chain you have created, but this is only possible within the same tablespace.

■**Tip** Think of the hooks in the preceding explanation as a set of fishing hooks with different types of bait to catch different types of fish. When the fish that is swimming by is attracted to a certain bait, it is hooked, and its fate is then determined by what is at the end of the line the hook is on.

Policies

Each built-in chain defined in the filter table can also have a policy. A *policy* is the default action a chain takes on a packet to determine whether a packet makes it all the way through the rules in a chain without matching any of them. The policies you can use for packets are DROP, REJECT, and ACCEPT. When the iptables command is first run, it sets some default policies for built-in chains. The INPUT and OUTPUT chains will have a policy of ACCEPT, and the FORWARD chain will have a policy of DROP.

The DROP policy discards a packet without notifying the sender. The REJECT policy also discards the packet, but it sends an ICMP packet to the sender to tell it the rejection has occurred. The REJECT policy means that a device will know that its packets are not getting to their destination and will report the error quickly instead of waiting to be timed out, as is the case with the DROP policy. The DROP policy is contrary to TCP RFCs (Requests for Comment) and can be a little harsh on network devices; specifically, they can sit waiting for a response from their dropped packet(s) for a long time. But for security purposes, it is generally considered better to use the DROP policy rather than the REJECT policy, as it provides less information to the outside world.

The ACCEPT policy accepts the traffic and allows it to pass through the firewall. Naturally, from a security perspective, this renders your firewall ineffective if it is used as the default policy. By default, iptables configures all chains with a policy of ACCEPT, but changing this to a policy of DROP for all chains is recommended.

■**Caution** On remote hosts, make sure you have configured ACCEPT rules that allow you to connect before changing the policy to DROP.

This falls in line with the basic doctrine of a default stance of denial for the firewall. You should deny all traffic by default and open the host to only the traffic to which you have explicitly granted access. This denial can be problematic, because setting a default policy of DROP for the INPUT and OUTPUT chains means incoming and outgoing traffic are not allowed unless you explicitly add rules to allow traffic to come into and out of the host. This will cause all services and tools that connect from your host that are not explicitly allowed to enter or leave that host to fail.

Network Address Translation

Network address translation allows your private network IP address space to appear to originate from a single public IP address. It does this with the help of IP masquerade, which rewrites IP packet headers. NAT holds information about connections traversing the firewall/router in translation tables. Generally speaking, an entry is written into the translation table when a packet traverses the firewall/router from the private to the public address space. When the matching packet returns, the router uses the translation table to match the returning packet to the originating source IP.

Many years ago, each host on the Internet was given a public IP address to become part of the Internet and talk to other hosts. It was soon realized that the available addresses would run out if every host that wanted to be on the Internet was given its own public IP address. NAT was invented to be able to have a private address space appear to come from a single IP address.

When you have a single host, the traffic flow through your firewall will look something like Figure 6-21.

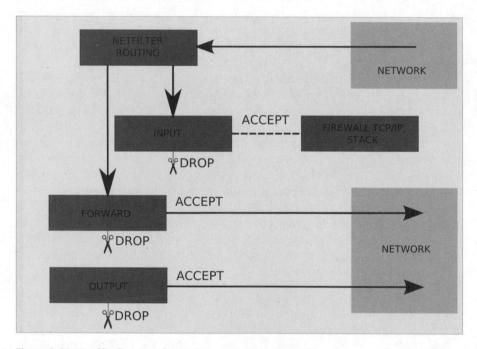

Figure 6-21. *Traffic flowing through a single host firewall*

When you have configured `iptables`, packets of traffic will come in through your firewall's interface. In Figure 6-21, traffic enters the hosts from the network. The network can be either the local network or the Internet. Each packet is immediately passed through the Netfilter program, and its next route is determined through your host. It does this based on the final destination address of the packet, if it is destined for the local host or if it is for another host.

If the packet is for another host and you have IP packet forwarding turned on (which we explained earlier in the "Adding Routes and Forwarding Packets" section), the packet will be sent to the forwarding chain. If you don't have IP forwarding turned on, or if you have policies and rules to deny forwarding of packets through your host, the packet will be dropped. Once in the FORWARD chain, if you have rules and policies to allow the packet to be forwarded on from your host, it will be allowed to pass through and out to the network.

If the final destination of the packet is the firewall itself, Netfilter routing passes it to the INPUT chain. Here, any packets that do not match the rules defined are dealt with by the default policy. If the packets do match a rule, an action can be specified in a target with the -j *target* option. If this target is ACCEPT, the packet continues to the IP stack, and the connection is allowed to be established and continue.

Traffic originating from the firewall and destined for some other host will be directed through the OUTPUT chain. If the rules and policies of the OUTPUT chain allow these packets to pass through to the network, they will go out of the configured interface. If not, they will be dealt with by the default policy.

Using the iptables Command

Now that you understand the concepts of packet flows in Netfilter, we'll show you how to use the iptables command to manage them. The iptables command allows you to do the following:

- List the contents of the packet filter rule set.

- Add/remove/modify rules in the packet filter rule set.

- List/zero per-rule counters of the packet filter rule set.

To effectively use the iptables command, you must have root privileges. The basic iptables command structure and arguments are as follows:

```
iptables -t table-name -command chain rulenumber paramaters -j target
```

Table 6-6 gives a rundown on the commands, shown in the preceding syntax *command*, we will be demonstrating and their description.

Table 6-6. *Command Options Available to the* iptables *Command*

Option	Description
-L	Lists the current rules of iptables you have in memory.
-D	Deletes a rule in a chain. The rule to delete can be expressed as a rule number or as a pattern to match.
-I	Inserts a rule into a chain. This will insert the rule at the top of the chain unless a rule number is specified.
-F	Flushes a chain. This will remove all the rules from a chain or all the rules in all the chains in a table if no chain is specified.
-A	Appends a rule to a chain. Same as -I except the rule is appended to the bottom of the chain by default.
-X	Deletes a chain. The chain must be empty and not referenced by any other chain at the time you wish to delete it.
-N	Creates a new chain. There can be no target already existing with the same name.
-P	Sets a default policy for a chain. Each built-in chain (INPUT, OUTPUT, FORWARD, POSTROUTING, etc.) has a default policy of either ACCEPT, REJECT, or DROP.

■**Caution** It is always a good idea when you are working with firewall rules to have access to a system console in the event that you make a mistake and block all your network traffic. Changing your firewall rules over the network, especially on remotely housed systems, can leave you in an awkward position if you make a mistake.

A large number of parameters, shown in the iptables command syntax as *parameters*, can be used to manipulate packets as they pass through your firewall. When we explained chains, we said they were like hooks. The parameters are the different types of bait that sit on the hook. Each parameter will attract packets depending on the information in the packet. It can be the source and destination addresses of the packet or the protocol. The packet can furthermore be matched to source or destination ports or the state the packet is in. The parameters can also be used to match packets, capture them, tag them, and release them.

The target argument, depicted by -j *target* in the iptables command syntax, is the action to be performed on the packet if it has been hooked. Common targets are ACCEPT, DROP, LOG, MASQUERADE, and CONNMARK. The target can also be another user-defined chain.

We want to now show you how to use the iptables command by running you through some examples.

The iptables command is common to both Ubuntu and Red Hat and operates in the same way. The following examples show how to manage Red Hat's iptables rule sets that are generated at installation. If you have an Ubuntu host, you are still advised to read this section, but expect different results from those shown.

Let's look at listing the contents of the iptables rule sets we currently have running. We do that by issuing the following command:

```
$ sudo /sbin/iptables -t filter -L --line-numbers
```

Here we are viewing the filter table. The -L option lists all the chains and their associated rules with line numbering, specified by --line-numbers, for each. The line numbering is important because, as has been mentioned, iptables runs through each rule sequentially starting from the first to the last. When you want to add a new rule or delete an old rule, you can use these numbers to pinpoint which rule you want to target. For our Red Hat hosts, we have selected a portion of the listed output in Listing 6-5.

Listing 6-5. *RH-Firewall-1-INPUT Chain*

```
Chain RH-Firewall-1-INPUT  (2 references)
num  target  prot  opt  source   destination
1    ACCEPT  all   --   anywhere  anywhere
2    ACCEPT  icmp  --   anywhere  anywhere  icmp  any
3    ACCEPT  esp   --   anywhere  anywhere
4    ACCEPT  ah    --   anywhere  anywhere
```

You will notice that we have shown the user-defined chain RH-Firewall-1-INPUT in this example. Red Hat hosts will have this chain created for you when you use the system-config-security tool or when you configure a firewall as part of your installation.

For Ubuntu users, iptables will be presented fresh without any predefined Ubuntu chains. Ubuntu has the default policy of ACCEPT on both the INPUT and OUTPUT chains, and DROP on the FORWARD chain in the filter table.

```
$ sudo /sbin/iptables -L
Chain INPUT (policy ACCEPT)
target  prot opt  source  destination

Chain FORWARD (policy DROP)
target  prot opt  source  destination

Chain OUTPUT (policy ACCEPT)
target  prot opt  source  destination
```

It is up to you to set the minimal rule requirements. However, you can create a similar Red Hat–like chain on an Ubuntu host by issuing the following command:

```
$ sudo /sbin/iptables -t filter -N Firewall-eth1-INPUT
```

This command creates a new chain using -N Firewall-eth1-INPUT in the filter table as denoted by -t filter. It does not have any rules associated with it yet, but by the end of this section you will be able to add and remove rules. We will proceed with using our Red Hat rule sets as an example, but you should know that the same rule sets can be applied to an Ubuntu host.

■**Note** You don't have to use the preceding naming standard for naming your chains. However, you will benefit from using something that makes sense to your configuration. Otherwise, the output of your iptables rules could look very messy and hard to diagnose for faults. You also don't need to create your own user-defined chains if you don't want to, but it will make reading your rules simpler if you do.

Referring back to Listing 6-5, which shows our RH-Firewall-1-INPUT chain, we now want to remove the esp rule from our RH-Firewall-1-INPUT chain in the filter table.

```
3    ACCEPT    esp  --  anywhere          anywhere
```

To do that we will use the name of the table, -t filter, and the chain we are working on, RH-Firewall-1-INPUT. We want to delete, using the -D command, the rule in position 3 like so:

```
$ sudo /sbin/iptables -t filter -D RH-Firewall-1-INPUT  3
```

We will now list our rules again, this time refining our output to just print the rules associated with the RH-Firewall-1-INPUT chain.

```
$ sudo /sbin/iptables -t filter -L RH-Firewall-1-INPUT --line-numbers
Chain RH-Firewall-1-INPUT (2 references)
num  target prot opt  source  destination
1    ACCEPT all  --  anywhere anywhere
2    ACCEPT icmp  --  anywhere anywhere icmp  any
```

```
3    ACCEPT  ah  --  anywhere  anywhere
4    ACCEPT  udp  --  anywhere  224.0.0.251  udp dpt:mdns
```

Now you will see that the rule matching the protocol esp has been removed and that the rule matching protocol ah has now moved up to the number 3 position. We'll now add the same rule back again by inserting the rule, using the -I command, into rule number 3 in the RH-Firewall-1-INPUT chain, matching on the protocol esp, as denoted by -p esp, and giving it a target of -j ACCEPT.

```
iptables -t filter -I RH-Firewall-1-INPUT 3 -p esp -j ACCEPT
```

When you look at the third line now in the RH-Firewall-1-INPUT chain, you can see that our rule has been inserted and has the target of ACCEPT.

```
Chain RH-Firewall-1-INPUT (2 references)
num target    prot opt source    destination
1 ACCEPT  all  --  anywhere  anywhere
2 ACCEPT  icmp  --  anywhere  anywhere  icmp  any
3 ACCEPT  esp  --  anywhere  anywhere
4 ACCEPT  ah  --  anywhere  anywhere
```

■Note Encapsulating Security Payload (ESP) and Authentication Header (AH) are protocols used for transmitting IPsec communications. You will learn more about them both in Chapter 14.

You can also flush your chains, which means removing all the rules from all the chains or all the rules from a specified chain. This can be used to clear any existing rules before you add a fresh set. You achieve this by issuing a command similar to the following:

```
$ sudo /sbin/iptables -t filter -F INPUT
```

Here we have flushed, as denoted by -F, all the rules from the INPUT chain in the filter table. If you now view the INPUT chain in the filter table, you will see there are no longer any rules associated with it.

```
$ sudo /sbin/iptables -L --line-numbers
Chain INPUT (policy ACCEPT)
num  target    prot opt source             destination

Chain FORWARD (policy ACCEPT)
num  target  prot opt source  destination
1 ACCEPT  all  --  anywhere  192.168.0.0/24  state  RELATED,ESTABLISHED
```

In this case, since we have a default policy of ACCEPT, clearing this chain does not affect the way our host operates. If we changed the policy to DROP, all inbound connections will be cut, making our host unusable for network-related tasks and services. This is because the policy determines what happens to packets that are not matched by any rule. If there are no rules in your chain, then iptables will use the default policy to handle packets accordingly.

We'll create the following chain again on our host:

```
$ sudo /sbin/iptables -t filter -N Firewall-eth1-INPUT
```

Here we have created the chain `Firewall-eth1-INPUT` instead of the Red Hat default of `RH-Firewall-1-INPUT`. We are now going to add a rule to it. For the rules in our `Firewall-eth1-INPUT` chain to be parsed, we need to add a rule in the `INPUT` chain that directs all the incoming packets to our host to the `Firewall-eth1-INPUT` chain.

```
$ sudo /sbin/iptables -t filter -A INPUT -j Firewall-eth1-INPUT
```

Here we have issued the command to append the rule that indicates all packets coming into our host with our firewall as the final destination, as you can see by `-t filter -A INPUT`, be sent to chain `Firewall-eth1-INPUT`, denoted by `-j Firewall-eth1-INPUT`, for further processing.

You can refine what you want to catch in your rules by adding other parameters. In the following incidence, we could match only on TCP traffic and send that to some target.

```
$ sudo /sbin/iptables -t filter -A INPUT -p tcp -j Firewall-eth1-INPUT
```

We can further refine our "bait" to attract different types of fish . . . er . . . packets. Showing the result of this command on the `INPUT` chain reveals the following:

```
$ sudo iptables -L INPUT --line-numbers
Chain INPUT (policy ACCEPT)
num  target       prot opt source              destination
1    Firewall-eth1-INPUT  all  --  anywhere              anywhere
```

We have now appended a rule, by specifying `-A`, to the `INPUT` chain that directs all traffic from all sources and destinations to our user-defined `Firewall-eth1-INPUT` chain. Since this is the only rule in the chain, it has been appended to the rule set in position number 1.

Lastly, we will now set a default policy on our `INPUT` chain. We will set this to `DROP` so that anything not matched by our rule set will be automatically "dropped to the floor." We achieve this by specifying the table name, specified by `-t filter`, the chain, denoted by `INPUT`, and the target, `DROP`.

■**Caution** This is one of those potentially dangerous commands that can drop all your network connections. Before you run this command, make sure you have access to a physical console just in case. Or you can use a model like the one described at `http://www.iptablesrocks.org/guide/safetynet.php`.

```
$ sudo /sbin/iptables -t filter -P INPUT DROP
```

When we now list the `INPUT` chain in the `filter` table, the default policy is shown to be `DROP`.

```
$ sudo iptables -L INPUT
Chain INPUT (policy DROP)
target       prot opt source              destination
Firewall-eth1-INPUT  all  --  anywhere              anywhere
```

It is good practice and a good habit to remember to apply the policy of DROP to all your chains. For firewalls to be most secure, a default policy of denial should be mandatory in all your chains.

Armed with these basic commands, you will be able to perform most functions on your chains and rule sets. There are many more features that you can add to your rules to make your firewall perform very complex and interesting routing. Please refer to the iptables man page for a complete list of tasks you can do.

Starting and stopping iptables is simple on Red Hat and slightly more complicated on Ubuntu unless you are using a firewall management tool like ufw, which will be discussed later in the chapter in the section "Other Firewall Configuration Tools."

On Red Hat, the command service iptables can take several arguments:

```
$ sudo /sbin/service iptables start|stop|restart|condrestart|status|panic|save.
```

The arguments status, panic, and save are unusual here. The status argument prints the current rule set in memory. The panic argument will flush all your rules and immediately set all policies on your default chains to DROP. This **will block every connection** trying to go into or come out of your host and should not be used unless there is a real need to panic!

The save argument tells iptables to save the current rule set to /etc/sysconfig/iptables so you can make your changes to the running rule set persistent.

Caution If you use the panic option, you will block all traffic to your host. If you are connected to the host remotely, via SSH or the like, your connection will also be dropped. If you don't have any other means of accessing the host, you will be locked out until you can either physically log in to the host and change the firewall rules or have someone else do it.

On your Ubuntu host, you can use the iptables-save and iptables-restore commands to retrieve and set your iptables rule sets. You may wish to put these rules into a file called /etc/networks/firewall and then call them from your /etc/network/interfaces file.

An example of this would be the following:

```
$ sudo /sbin/iptables-save > /etc/network/firewall
```

You would make any changes and additions to your rules. Then you could use the following in your /etc/network/interfaces file to activate your rules and save them again.

```
auto eth0
iface eth0 inet dhcp
    pre-up iptables-restore < /etc/network/firewall
    post-down iptables-save -c > /etc/network/firewall
```

Here we have a standard interface configuration for eth0. We use the pre-up command to activate the firewall rules before we bring up our interface. We then use the post-down command to save our rules once our interface has come down.

If you are using ufw on your Ubuntu host, you can use the invoke-rc.d command to stop and start ufw:

```
$ sudo invoke-rc.d ufw start|stop|restart
```

Here the invoke-rc.d is used to manage the ufw service. We talk about ufw a little later in this chapter in the section "Other Firewall Configuration Tools."

Further Reading

Netfilter and iptables are complex topics, and we recommend you read up further on them. For additional information about Netfilter and the iptables command, read its man page. Also available are some online tutorials:

- http://iptables-tutorial.frozentux.net/iptables-tutorial.html

- http://www.linuxtopia.org/Linux_Firewall_iptables/index.html

   Ubuntu also installs some iptables documentation on the local hard disk:

- /usr/share/doc/iptables/html/packet-filtering-HOWTO.html

- /usr/share/doc/iptables/html/NAT-HOWTO.html

And for more advanced topics, these may be of interest:

- *Designing and Implementing Linux Firewalls with QoS using netfilter, iproute2, NAT and L7-filter* by Lucian Gheorghe (PACKT Publishing, 2006)
- *Linux Firewalls: Attack Detection and Response with iptables, psad, and fwsnort* by Michael Rash (No Starch Press, 2007)

Explaining the Default Rules on Red Hat Hosts

As we explained earlier, Ubuntu does not come with any default firewall rules when you install your host. Red Hat, on the other hand, does. While we don't necessarily recommend all the rules Red Hat creates for you with its system-config-security tool, you can use this tool to create a reasonable firewall for your stand-alone hosts, and it provides an excellent overview of how iptables firewalls can be configured.

■**Note** Ubuntu readers should still find this section interesting, as we explain how Red Hat uses its user-defined chains. Ubuntu iptables management tools like ufw also create user-defined chains.

On Red Hat hosts, you can use the `service iptables status` command (this is the equivalent to using the `iptables -t` *tablename* `-L --line-numbers -n` command for each table on the command line) to get a list of the current rule set memory. Listing 6-6 shows the default Red Hat firewall configuration from our installation with no additional rules.

■**Note** Ubuntu users will find a set of similar files if they are using an `iptables` tool like `ufw`. In the `/etc/ufw` directory are `before.rules` and `after.rules` files that contain rule sets.

Listing 6-6. *Red Hat Default iptables Rule Set*

```
$ sudo /sbin/service iptables status
Table: filter
Chain INPUT (policy ACCEPT)
num  target        prot opt source               destination
1    RH-Firewall-1-INPUT  all  --  0.0.0.0/0            0.0.0.0/0

Chain FORWARD (policy ACCEPT)
num  target        prot opt source               destination
1    RH-Firewall-1-INPUT  all  --  0.0.0.0/0            0.0.0.0/0

Chain OUTPUT (policy ACCEPT)
num  target        prot opt source               destination

Chain RH-Firewall-1-INPUT (2 references)
num  target     prot opt source            destination
1    ACCEPT     all  --  0.0.0.0/0         0.0.0.0/0
2    ACCEPT     icmp --  0.0.0.0/0         0.0.0.0/0  icmp type 255
3    ACCEPT     esp  --  0.0.0.0/0         0.0.0.0/0
4    ACCEPT     ah   --  0.0.0.0/0         0.0.0.0/0
5    ACCEPT     udp  --  0.0.0.0/0         224.0.0.251  udp dpt:5353
6    ACCEPT     udp  --  0.0.0.0/0         0.0.0.0/0  udp dpt:631
7    ACCEPT     tcp  --  0.0.0.0/0         0.0.0.0/0  tcp dpt:631
8    ACCEPT     all  --  0.0.0.0/0         0.0.0.0/0  state RELATED,ESTABLISHED
9    REJECT     all  --  0.0.0.0/0         0.0.0.0/0  reject-with icmp-host-prohibited
```

You can see in Listing 6-6 that we have listed one table, `filter`, and that it contains the three built-in chains: INPUT, FORWARD, and OUTPUT. These all have the default policy of ACCEPT. You can also see that there is another chain, called RH-Firewall-1-INPUT, that has two other chains referencing it (2 references): INPUT and FORWARD. To get a grasp of what is occurring here, look at Figure 6-22, which shows how a packet would flow through the `filter` table with the preceding rule set.

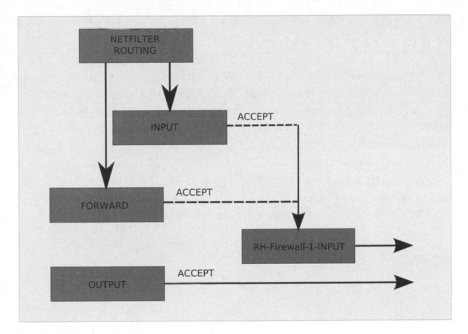

Figure 6-22. *Traffic flow through the* filter *table*

In Figure 6-22, you can see the way that packets will flow through the filter table. The Netfilter firewall program will route incoming IP packets to either the INPUT or the FORWARD chain depending on their destination address. The INPUT rule shown in Listing 6-6 says that it is to pass all packets, regardless of type, source, and destination, to the Firewall-1-INPUT chain. If the packets are destined for the firewall host itself, they will be passed to the INPUT chain and then automatically passed on to the RH-Firewall-1-INPUT chain.

If the incoming packets are destined for another host, and IP forwarding has been enabled on the firewall host, they are delivered to the FORWARD chain. The FORWARD chain in this instance only has one rule, that is to forward all packets to Firewall-1-INPUT. Once dealt with by that rule set, the packets will leave the host if they are allowed or be blocked if they are not.

Why point the INPUT and FORWARD chains to the RH-Firewall-1-INPUT chain? Red Hat intended INPUT and FORWARD to be treated the same way so they direct packets to the same rule set. The rule set in RH-Firewall-1-INPUT itself is quite small and only allows some very basic network services access. We could have had the same rules in both the INPUT and FORWARD chains and achieved the same effect.

The OUPUT chain is for packets originating on the actual firewall host destined for another host elsewhere. It is set to a default policy of ACCEPT. This allows the firewall host to initiate sockets of any protocol type with any other destination host.

Let's now look at the configuration files for iptables that you would expect to find on a Red Hat host (Ubuntu hosts don't have iptables configuration files until you create them). You can add and edit firewall rules directly from a file. You can use the iptables-save command, which will include any in-memory additions that are not yet reflected in the /etc/sysconfig/iptables file. Here, we'll quickly save the current iptables rules to a file and view its contents. The following will save the current rule set to a file called default-firewall_rules:

```
$ sudo /sbin/iptables-save > default-firewall_rules
```

On Ubuntu, you can use the same command to create a file of the current rule set.

▌Note You should not directly edit the /etc/sysconfig/iptables file. The file itself has the warning "Manual customization of this file is not recommended." This is because the file is created by the system-config-securitylevel application, and any changes you have made can easily be overwritten by it without warning.

Listing 6-7 shows the contents of the file default-firewall_rules. You can see this is a file created when you install your Red Hat host. It already has several entries, and we will take you through them. In Listing 6-7, we have added line numbers to help clarify our explanation of the file.

Listing 6-7. *default-firewall_rules File*

```
 1.  # Generated by iptables-save v1.3.5 on Fri Jan  9 04:02:33 2009
 2.  *filter
 3.  :INPUT ACCEPT [0:0]
 4.  :FORWARD ACCEPT [0:0]
 5.  :OUTPUT ACCEPT [0:0]
 6.  :RH-Firewall-1-INPUT - [0:0]
 7.  -A INPUT -j RH-Firewall-1-INPUT
 8.  -A FORWARD -j RH-Firewall-1-INPUT
 9.  -A RH-Firewall-1-INPUT -i lo -j ACCEPT
10. -A RH-Firewall-1-INPUT -p icmp --icmp-type any -j ACCEPT
11. -A RH-Firewall-1-INPUT -p 50 -j ACCEPT
12. -A RH-Firewall-1-INPUT -p 51 -j ACCEPT
13. -A RH-Firewall-1-INPUT -p udp --dport 5353 -d 224.0.0.251 -j ACCEPT
14. -A RH-Firewall-1-INPUT -p udp -m udp --dport 631 -j ACCEPT
15. -A RH-Firewall-1-INPUT -p tcp -m tcp --dport 631 -j ACCEPT
16. -A RH-Firewall-1-INPUT -m state --state ESTABLISHED,RELATED -j ACCEPT
17. -A RH-Firewall-1-INPUT -j REJECT --reject-with icmp-host-prohibited
18. COMMIT
```

In Listing 6-7 the first line, denoted by #, is a comment. Next, *filter denotes the table we are working with: :INPUT, :FORWARD, :OUTPUT, and :RH-Firewall-1-INPUT are chain declarations (lines 3–6). INPUT, FORWARD, and OUTPUT all have a default policy of ACCEPT. The [0:0] on lines 3–6 are byte and counter marks, which can be used to see how much traffic in volume has passed through that chain as well as how many packets have passed through it (you can use iptables -Z *chain* to reset these counters to zero if you wish).

Line 7 is our first rule in our INPUT chain in the filter table. If we wanted to create this line from the command line, we would issue the following:

```
$ sudo /sbin/iptables -t filter -A INPUT -j RH-Firewall-1-INPUT
```

■Note Remember, you can either use the `iptables` command to create each of your rules or save the current rule set to a file and make your edits to that with the view to restoring that file at a later date.

You have seen this earlier. What this does is direct all packets that are passed through the INPUT chain in the `filter` table to another chain called `RH-Firewall-1-INPUT`.

Notice in line 8 that all the packets that pass through the FORWARD chain are also directed to the `RH-Firewall-1-INPUT` chain.

As it stands, this is a pretty relaxed firewall because we have default policies of ACCEPT. Red Hat does tighten things up a little by making use of the REJECT target at the end of the `RH-Firewall-1-INPUT` chain. Let's now take a look at the rules in the `RH-Firewall-1-INPUT` chain. Lines 9–17 in Listing 6-7 are all rules relating to this. These are all parsed in order of first to last, but we want to show you the core rules of interest. First, let's start with the last, line 17:

```
-A RH-Firewall-1-INPUT -j REJECT --reject-with icmp-host-prohibited
```

This is a catch-all rule that should always be the last rule in this chain. Any rule placed after this rule will never be parsed, as all previously nonmatched packets are rejected by it. So when a packet traverses this chain and it is not matched to any rule, `iptables` rejects it with a nice administrative ICMP message. This is the equivalent of a REJECT default policy on the INPUT and FORWARD chain, since they both pass all packets to the `RH-Firewall-1-INPUT` chain. However, as explained earlier, it is definitely **not the same** as a default REJECT policy on the INPUT and FORWARD chain.

The next important rule is in line 16. This rule allows connections that belong to already established or to related traffic to be accepted.

```
-A RH-Firewall-1-INPUT -m state --state ESTABLISHED,RELATED -j ACCEPT
```

To explain this line, let's suppose we are going to initiate an outgoing connection to a DNS server on some remote host. As explained earlier, `iptables` remains aware of the states of each packet in, out, and through the firewall. When we initiate our DNS connection, our OUTPUT chain is first parsed to make sure we are allowed to make a connection to a DNS server. In our firewall's current state, there is a default policy of ACCEPT, and there are no rules to parse. We are allowed to initiate the socket (NEW state) to the remote host. The remote DNS server will send back a response to our socket initiation. All packets inbound are sent to the INPUT chain of the `filter` table. We parse the rules in that chain and are passed to the `RH-Firewall-1-INPUT` chain. We must have a rule in our `RH-Firewall-1-INPUT` chain to accept this incoming connection. If we had the rule `-A RH-Firewall-1-INPUT –p tcp,udp -m state –state NEW --dport 53 -j ACCEPT` in `RH-Firewall-1-INPUT`, `iptables` will accept it. Once the connection is established (ESTABLISHED state), our firewall allows the ongoing communication. Our firewall tracks the states of our connections and allows those that are ESTABLISHED or RELATED to continue.

NEW, ESTABLISHED, RELATED, AND INVALID STATES

The NEW connection state indicates a freshly initiated connection through which data has not passed back and forth. You must allow the NEW connection state, either incoming or outgoing, if you want to allow new connections to a service. For example, if you do not specify that the NEW connection state is accepted for incoming SMTP traffic on a mail server, remote clients will not be able to use the mail server to send e-mail.

An ESTABLISHED connection state indicates an existing connection that is in the process of transferring data. You need to allow ESTABLISHED connections if you want a service to be able to maintain a connection with a remote client or server. For example, if you want to allow SSH connections to your host, you must allow NEW and ESTABLISHED incoming traffic and ESTABLISHED outgoing traffic to ensure the connection is possible.

The RELATED state refers to a connection that is used to facilitate another connection. A common example is an FTP session where control data is passed to one connection, and actual file data flows through another one.

The INVALID state is branded on a connection that has been seen to have problems in processing packets: they may have exceeded the processing ability of the firewall or be packets that are irrelevant to any current connection.

■**Note** The state module is provided by the ipt_conntrack Netfilter kernel module, which should be loaded by default with most recent iptables releases. If it is not, you can load it with the insmod command: insmod ipt_conntack.

Line number 9, -A RH-Firewall-1-INPUT -i lo -j ACCEPT, is also important as it accepts any socket connections that originate from the loopback address (lo, or 127.0.0.1) to initiate any connections to itself (as 127.0.0.1 is nonroutable, it can only make connections to itself). This is important as many services and applications use the loopback address to send signals or make other connections to various ports on the loopback address.

Line 10, -A RH-Firewall-1-INPUT -p icmp --icmp-type any -j ACCEPT, allows ICMP connections involving such things as ping, traceroute, and others. These are used to convey information about the route or report on errors encountered as part of RFC 792 (http://tools.ietf.org/html/rfc792) and RFC 1122 (http://tools.ietf.org/html/rfc1122).

Lines 11 to 15 are added by Red Hat to facilitate different general networking requirements. Port 50 and 51 are used by IPsec, which is a secure encrypted transport tunnel. Port 5353 is for the Multicast DNS service, which allows hosts in the local network segment to answer special DNS queries (for more information, please see http://www.multicastdns.org). Lastly, port 631 is used by the Internet Printing Protocol (IPP) and by the CUPS printing service. We will be removing these services from our bastion firewall, as they are not the kind of services we want to be allowed (however, we will revisit IPsec connections in Chapter 14). For bastion hosts, it is especially important to turn off any unwanted rules and services.

```
-A RH-Firewall-1-INPUT -p 50 -j ACCEPT
-A RH-Firewall-1-INPUT -p 51 -j ACCEPT
```

```
-A RH-Firewall-1-INPUT -p udp --dport 5353 -d 224.0.0.251 -j ACCEPT
-A RH-Firewall-1-INPUT -p udp -m udp --dport 631 -j ACCEPT
-A RH-Firewall-1-INPUT -p tcp -m tcp --dport 631 -j ACCEPT
```

Finally, the COMMIT in line 18 is the instruction to commit the rule set for that table to memory and activate the rule set. Each table stanza should have a COMMIT; otherwise it will not be made active.

Configuring Our Example Network

There are some typical network scenarios that most networks subscribe to. They range in complexity and security needs. A network can be as simple as two computers joined together with a cross-over cable or as complex as a system that spans the globe with centralized data centers, disaster recovery sites, and thousands of servers all ticking away at a multitude of important tasks.

In the rest of this chapter, we are going to demonstrate how to configure the example network we introduced earlier. As we described at the start of this chapter, our network will consist of an Internet connection, a Linux firewall called gateway.example.com, and a main server called headoffice.example.com. We hope that by understanding how we build our simple network, you will learn how to build a firewall on any host and have a modular security plan that you can then add pieces to when needed.

Our Configuration

Here we'll introduce you to the components of the example network we outlined at the start of the chapter. Our simple network will consist of the following:

- One modem/router.
- One network switch/hub.
- One Linux firewall host called gateway.example.com.
- Two Ethernet cards, eth0 and eth1, for our Linux firewall. Our eth0 interface will have the PPP communications attached to it, and eth1 will be the internal private network interface.
- One main business server (combining mail, print, file, web) called headoffice.example.com.
- A set of desktops/workstations.

In our network, we're going to do a few things a little differently. With a home or small office connection, the ISP connection terminates on the modem and handles NAT translations for the network rather than a dedicated firewall, as we are configuring. For cable modem home and small office networks, you should be able to plug your Linux firewall host into your cable modem in our scenario.

In some cases, if your modem/router also includes a firewall, you will be able to configure that to bypass the need for a Linux firewall/router, if you so wish. Unfortunately, due to the large variances in devices you could employ and how they are configured, we cannot begin to show you all the ways this would be achieved. Please refer to the documentation supplied by your modem vendor.

In our scenario, the modem/router is in bridging mode, so the Internet connection from the ISP actually terminates on the Linux firewall host. Take a look at Figure 6-23, which shows once more the diagram of how the network will look.

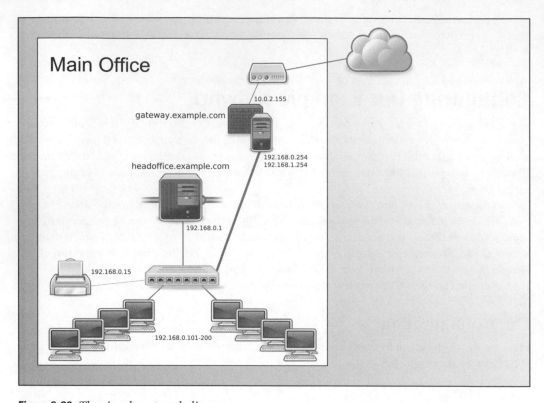

Figure 6-23. *The simple network diagram*

So what is bridging mode? *Bridging mode* means that the modem does not attempt to establish a Point-to-Point Protocol (PPP) link with your ISP. Instead it passes the connection packets from the WAN (the ISP or Internet side) through to whatever you have connected to the other side or LAN (in our case, a Linux host with a PPPoE daemon running on it). This daemon can then establish a connection with your ISP's network.

If your modem does support bridging mode, you will need to refer to the vendor documentation as to how to achieve this. If your modem currently supplies IP addresses and DNS facilities for your network, you will have to move these services onto your Linux host first, as your modem is will lose the DNS and DHCP services it currently provides.

■**Note** We cover DNS and DHCP in Chapter 9.

In bridge mode, your modem just forwards connections through to your Linux host without interfering—it provides no firewalling, no NAT/SNAT (source network address translation) addressing, no DNS, and no DHCP. For your Internet connection to terminate at your Linux host, you will need to add a PPPoE or PPPoA (Point-to-Point Protocol over Asynchronous Transfer Mode) connection. Your Linux host will then become the router/firewall for your network.

■**Note** In this networking example, we are using an IP address from the IPv4 private address range as our external public IP address, 10.0.2.155. An address in the 10.0.0.0/8 range will never normally appear as a public IP address and should not be used as your public IP address in your network. See `http://en.wikipedia.org/wiki/Private_network` for more information.

Setting Up a PPP Connection

On our gateway.example.com *bastion*, or *gateway*, host, which is another name for the router/firewall on the perimeter of a network, we will need to set up a PPP service. The PPP service makes a connection to your ISP, provides some authentication details, and receives the IP address provided to you by the ISP. This IP address can be either a static address, meaning it doesn't change, or a dynamic address, which means it is provided from a pool of addresses and will regularly change every few days. We are going to set up a PPP xDSL connection, which is a common way to connect to an ISP.

The most common way to set up an xDSL connection on Linux is to use the Roaring Penguin PPPoE client. To do so, first you will need to check that you have this client installed. On Red Hat, you need to install the `rp-pppoe` package. On Ubuntu, you have to install `pppoeconf`.

Let's take a brief look at how you go about setting up your PPP xDSL connections using Red Hat and Ubuntu.

With Red Hat, you can configure your PPP connection in two ways: from the command line using the `adsl-setup` command or from the Red Hat `system-config-network` GUI application.

With Ubuntu, you can use the `adsl-setup` command as you would on Red Hat, create a PPP connection in your `/etc/network/interfaces` file, or use the `network-admin` GUI.

xDSL Setup Using adsl-setup

Since it is common to both the Red Hat and distributions, we'll look at the `adsl-setup` command and guide you through some basic questions and answers regarding your connection. First, you are asked to enter your login name for your ISP account provided by your ISP supplier.

```
$ sudo adsl-setup
Welcome to the ADSL client setup.  First, I will run some checks on
your system to make sure the PPPoE client is installed properly...

LOGIN NAME

Enter your Login Name (default root): username@isp.com
```

Next, you are asked to provide the interface that the connection will be set up on. The PPP connection in this instance requires an Ethernet interface. Our modem is now bridging our PPP service from our ISP through to the equipment on our side of the modem. We will use our eth0 interface (as this is connected to the modem's hub) to be our interface in this instance.

INTERFACE

```
Enter the Ethernet interface connected to the ADSL modem
For Solaris, this is likely to be something like /dev/hme0.
For Linux, it will be ethX, where 'X' is a number.
(default eth0):  eth0
```

We are next asked if we want the link to come up on demand or be up continuously. This was much more of an issue with old dial-up modems and ISPs that charged for the time connected, not the just the amount downloaded. We will answer no.

```
Do you want the link to come up on demand, or stay up continuously?
If you want it to come up on demand, enter the idle time in seconds
after which the link should be dropped.  If you want the link to
stay up permanently, enter 'no' (two letters, lower-case.)
NOTE: Demand-activated links do not interact well with dynamic IP
addresses.  You may have some problems with demand-activated links.
Enter the demand value (default no): no
```

The next question involves DNS: do you wish to provide the name server to resolve your DNS request or allow the ISP to provide dynamic DNS, or do you not want this configuration to touch anything? In our case, we will not enter anything here, as in this instance we will want to configure our /etc/resolv.conf (our DNS configuration file) ourselves.

DNS

```
Please enter the IP address of your ISP's primary DNS server.
If your ISP claims that 'the server will provide dynamic DNS addresses',
enter 'server' (all lower-case) here.
If you just press enter, I will assume you know what you are
doing and not modify your DNS setup.
Enter the DNS information here:
```

You are now required to enter the password for your ISP connection. This is provided by your ISP. There will be nothing echoed to the screen, and you will be asked to reenter it.

PASSWORD

```
Please enter your Password:
Please re-enter your Password:
```

Next, you are asked if you would like normal users to be able to control the starting and stopping of the connection. We will say no, which means that we will have to start or stop the connection as the root user, using sudo or signing into the root account.

USERCTRL

```
Please enter 'yes' (three letters, lower-case.) if you want to allow
normal user to start or stop DSL connection (default yes): no
```

You are asked now if you would like to set up a firewall on your connection. We are not going to use the firewall settings provided as we will configure our own shortly, so we will choose 0 for this next question.

```
FIREWALLING

Please choose the firewall rules to use.  Note that these rules are
very basic.  You are strongly encouraged to use a more sophisticated
firewall setup; however, these will provide basic security.  If you
are running any servers on your machine, you must choose 'NONE' and
set up firewalling yourself.  Otherwise, the firewall rules will deny
access to all standard servers like Web, e-mail, ftp, etc.  If you
are using SSH, the rules will block outgoing SSH connections which
allocate a privileged source port.

The firewall choices are:
0 - NONE: This script will not set any firewall rules.  You are responsible
          for ensuring the security of your machine.  You are STRONGLY
          recommended to use some kind of firewall rules.
1 - STANDALONE: Appropriate for a basic stand-alone web-surfing workstation
2 - MASQUERADE: Appropriate for a machine acting as an Internet gateway
                for a LAN
Choose a type of firewall (0-2):  0
```

Lastly, you are asked if you wish to have the service started when your host boots up. This will set the interface ONBOOT option to yes in the configuration file.

```
Start this connection at boot time

Do you want to start this connection at boot time?
Please enter no or yes (default no):yes
```

You are now presented with the summary information, similar to what you see here. If the settings are to your liking, enter y.

```
** Summary of what you entered **

Ethernet Interface: eth0
User name:          username@isp.com
Activate-on-demand: No
DNS:                Do not adjust
Firewalling:        NONE
User Control:       no
Accept these settings and adjust configuration files (y/n)? y
```

This has now created an ifcfg-ppp0 file in the /etc/sysconfig/network-scripts/ directory. As we have explained previously, /etc/sysconfig/network-scripts is where Red Hat hosts store its network configuration files. Our ifcfg-ppp0 file looks similar to the Ethernet files you saw before, as you can see in Listing 6-8.

Listing 6-8. *ifcfg-ppp0 File on Red Hat*

```
$ sudo cat /etc/sysconfig/network-scripts/ifcfg-ppp0
USERCTL=yes
BOOTPROTO=dialup
NAME=DSLppp0
DEVICE=ppp0
TYPE=xDSL
ONBOOT=yes
PIDFILE=/var/run/pppoe-adsl.pid
FIREWALL=NONE
PING=.
PPPOE_TIMEOUT=80
LCP_FAILURE=3
LCP_INTERVAL=20
CLAMPMSS=1412
CONNECT_POLL=6
CONNECT_TIMEOUT=60
DEFROUTE=yes
SYNCHRONOUS=no
ETH=eth0
PROVIDER=DSLppp0
USER=username@isp.com
PEERDNS=no
DEMAND=no
```

This should be familiar; you can see that the file is different from the Ethernet configuration files but still has some of the same variables and syntax. We have TYPE=xDSL, a device name of DEVICE=ppp0, BOOTPROTO=dialup, and the PROVIDER and USER options set to the names you have just configured. For more information on all the variables, please read the man pppoe.conf page.

The password for our PPPoE connection is now stored in /etc/ppp/pap-secrets and /etc/ppp/chap-secrets, as shown in Listing 6-9. The password is stored in clear text, and we need to ensure it is suitably protected from casual snooping. To do this, we need to set secure permissions on these files.

```
$ sudo chown root:root /etc/ppp/pap-secrets /etc/ppp/chap-secrets
$ sudo chmod 0600 /etc/ppp/pap-secrets /etc/ppp/chap-secrets
```

Listing 6-9. *Password File for ppp0*

```
$ sudo cat /etc/ppp/pap-secrets
# Secrets for authentication using PAP
# client         server  secret                    IP addresses
"username@isp.com"     *      "myisp-password"
$ sudo cat /etc/ppp/chap-secrets
# Secrets for authentication using CHAP
# client         server  secret                    IP addresses
"username@isp.com"     *       "myisp-password"
```

Once you have created a PPPoE device on Ubuntu, you will see that the ppp section has been added to /etc/network/interfaces file:

```
iface ppp0 inet ppp
provider ppp0
auto ppp0
```

Here you can see that an interface called ppp0 is going to be created when the network is started, signified by auto ppp0. It is an IPv4 interface using PPP. Next, notice that the device information will be provided by the provider ppp0. The provider information is found under the /etc/ppp/peers directory. Ubuntu has appended the following information to the end of our /etc/ppp/peers/ppp0 file:

```
plugin rp-PPPoE.so eth0
user username@isp.com
```

The password information is stored here, in the /etc/ppp/chap.secrets file, and the contents are much like Listing 6-9.

xDSL Setup Using the GUI

We will quickly show you how to configure a PPPoE connection using the available GUI tools on both Red Hat and Ubuntu.

Red Hat

You can also use the system-config-network GUI to configure your xDSL PPPoE connection. As when you configure a new Ethernet connection, you click the New button, but this time you select xDSL connection, as shown in Figure 6-24.

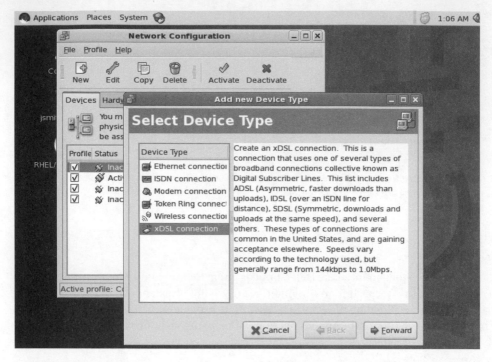

Figure 6-24. *Selecting xDSL connection*

Next add your details to connect to your ISP. You can use any name for the Provider name field. You will need to add your username and password for your ISP connection, as shown in Figure 6-25. Then click Forward.

You are now presented with a confirmation screen of the details you have entered. Clicking Apply will add the device to your configuration. You will need to save the configuration before you can activate it, but this is the same as what you would do for normal Ethernet devices.

If you wanted to edit the details of your connection, you would again highlight the device, ppp0 in our example, and then click the Edit icon. Next you can change any details by editing the device you just created (see Figure 6-26).

Figure 6-25. *ISP details*

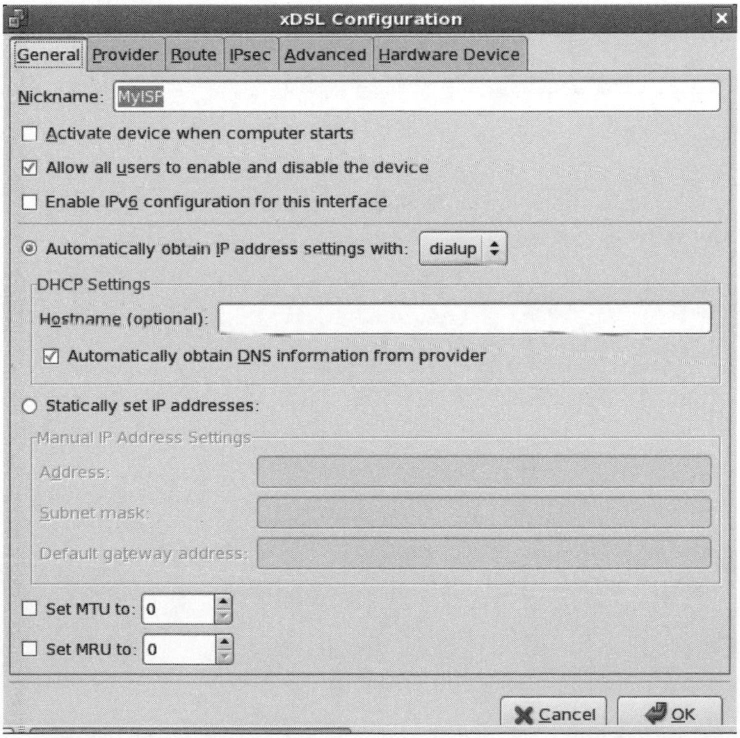

Figure 6-26. *Editing details*

Again, you must save the settings before your changes take place. Your host is now ready to make a connection to the Internet. It will try to connect automatically when your host starts up.

Ubuntu

On your Ubuntu host, you would use the Network Admin tool to create your device. You can see in Figure 6-27 there is a PPP device to be configured. Clicking the Properties button allows you to edit your settings.

Figure 6-27. *PPP with Network Admin*

Figure 6-28 shows the window that appears. This is where you add your username and password information for your ISP connection.

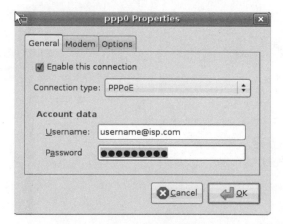

Figure 6-28. *Username and password details*

You now choose the device that you wish to attach this PPP device to. You can see our choice in Figure 6-29.

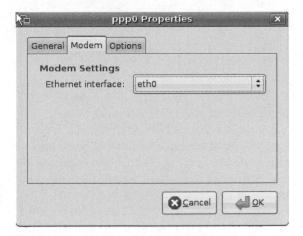

Figure 6-29. *Ethernet device for our PPP connection*

Lastly, you have some general options regarding your connections, as shown in Figure 6-30.

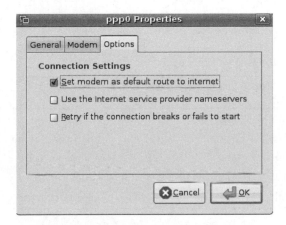

Figure 6-30. *PPP options in Network Admin*

We have chosen to set this device as our default route to the Internet. We have declined to use our ISP name servers and have unchecked the Retry if the connection breaks or fails to start check box option. Now that we have set up our PPP connections, we can move on to making them secure.

Setting Up the Bastion Firewall

In the previous section, we configured the ppp0 interface that will handle the PPP(oE) connection to our ISP. During that configuration, we were asked whether we would like a firewall configured with our connection, and we chose not to. We are now going to configure that firewall. In doing so, we expect that you will understand how to configure a firewall for not only a standard host, but also a gateway host. In reality, a gateway host is differentiated by its routing functions, but it still needs to have a standard firewall configuration for its own services. We will take you slowly through it by starting with configuring the `filter` table and then moving to the more fancy firewalling.

To be able to configure an adequate and secure firewall, you need to first consider what role your host will be playing in your network and the typical traffic you will be expecting to pass through your host. Firewalls are not features you "set and forget." They are dynamic and need to be changed as your business needs change. However, you can assume your firewall will need some basic rules to enable it to meet the requirements of your network by looking at the expected traffic flows.

Our firewall host will have two Ethernet network cards, which will handle different parts of the network. The device called eth0 will have the PPPoE device, ppp0, attached to it, which will handle all the Internet or public traffic. The device called eth1 will have the private network or LAN traffic. If you do not have two network interface cards on your firewall, you can still configure your firewall logically, separating eth0 and ppp0 devices in your `iptables` configuration.

In the upcoming two tables, Table 6-7 and Table 6-8, we list the expected traffic flow in respect to traffic flowing in and traffic flowing out of our host. Our main server will be the only host through which we allow traffic from the public network (the Internet) to our public hosts (192.168.0.1). This is because our main server will be our web server, mail server, and DNS server. These will therefore require access from the Internet. So when we plot our network traffic for our firewall gateway, we will need to map the connection we expect to make to 192.168.0.1. This data we collect now can also be used when we configure the firewall for our main server. Table 6-7 shows what traffic will be flowing out of our network.

Table 6-7. *Traffic Flowing Out of Our Network*

Interface	Source IP	Protocol	Source Port	Destination IP	Destination Port	Purpose
ppp0/eth1	192.168.0.1	TCP	Any	Any	25	SMTP
ppp0/eth1	192.168.0.1	TCP/UDP	Any	Any	53	DNS or domain
ppp0/eth1	192.168.0.1	TCP	Any	Any	123	Time or NTP
ppp0/eth1	192.168.0.0/24	TCP	Any	Any	22	SSH
ppp0/eth1	192.168.0.0/24	TCP	Any	Any	80, 443	HTTP or www

In Table 6-7, we have given a list of expected traffic that will flow out of our network, the destination details, and the purpose of that traffic. We know that the host 192.168.0.1 will be an SMTP, a DNS, an NTP, and an HTTP server, and that traffic will flow through our firewall. We have given all hosts in our private network the ability to initiate connections to any public hosts on ports 22, 80, and 443 as we see an immediate business need to do so. We can extend this list later as we discover more ports that our business requires.

■**Note** These ports that we speak of are like channel frequencies on a radio. They are predefined stations where your host can listen to certain traffic. There is a "station" for web traffic, and one for delivering mail. Like radio stations, these ports are not random but are assigned by an external body. The list of assigned ports can be found in the /etc/services file or here at the organization in control of their assignment: http://www.iana.org/assignments/port-numbers.

Without having the host in place, it is hard to confirm what is exactly happening "on the wire" (another way of referring to the actual traffic coming into the interface, eth0 in this case). We are making assumptions here based purely on what we expect our network to do, not what it could really be doing. Once the firewall host is in place, we will be able to further clarify and amend the traffic flow tables to better suit our network by analyzing our traffic with a packet sniffer (like tcpdump or Wireshark, discussed earlier). We can then use this information to set further Netfilter rules to log and block unwanted traffic we notice along the way.

Table 6-8 shows the opposite traffic flows to Table 6-7, as this is the traffic we expect to see coming into our network. This allows hosts in the public domain to initiate sockets to hosts in our private network. You don't see a long list here, as we are not offering many services to the public. We will allow public hosts the ability to initiate sockets to our DNS, SMTP, and HTTP services. Again, this list can grow according to our business needs.

Table 6-8. *Traffic Flowing into Our Network*

Interface	Source IP	Protocol	Source Port	Destination IP	Destination Port	Purpose
ppp0	Any	TCP	Any	192.168.0.1	25	SMTP
ppp0	Any	TCP/UDP	Any	192.168.0.1	53	DNS or domain
ppp0	Any	TCP	Any	192.168.0.1	80, 443	HTTP or www
eth1	192.168.0.0/24	TCP	Any	192.168.0.254	22	SSH
eth1	192.168.0.0/24	TCP/UDP	Any	192.168.0.254	53	DNS or domain

What is also evident from looking at Table 6-8 is that we will need to implement destination network address translation (DNAT) so that connections to ports on the public interface address are mapped to ports on our internal host (commonly referred to as *port mapping*). This is the more fancy firewalling, and we will cover it last.

Hosts on the public network, when trying to establish a socket with our web server for instance, will try to establish a socket to port 80 on our external or public address (10.0.2.155), since that is the address that has been given to them by DNS. They know nothing of our internal network and so don't know we actually serve our web pages from our 192.168.0.1 host, nor should they have to. The firewall host itself will not answer their requests, as it will not be running a web server at all. So to get around this, we will use our firewall to map (or route) those connections across to our 192.168.0.1 host. So a socket initiated by some public host to 10.0.2.155:80 will be internally port-mapped to 192.168.0.1:80 as if it were actually talking to 10.0.2.155.

■**Note** You could run your services on nonstandard ports if you wish. In the preceding example, if we had our www site being hosted on 192.168.0.1:8080, we could still map 10.0.2.155:80 to 192.168.0.1:8080. In this case, all sockets being initiated on port 80 will be mapped to port 8080 on our internal host.

Now that we have gathered some information about how we expect the network traffic to flow, we can begin to define our rules. In this example, we are using a Red Hat host to be our bastion firewall. As mentioned previously, the information presented here can equally apply to an Ubuntu host.

NAMING OUR CHAINS

In this chapter, we are going to create our user-defined chains and rule sets in a similar way to what you would find in a Red Hat host. For example, Red Hat defines its `INPUT` and `FORWARD` chain as `RH-Firewall-1-INPUT`. In our changes, we will use the naming convention `Firewall-nic-INPUT`, where *nic* is the network interface card (NIC) we are designing the rules for, like eth0, eth1, or ppp0. In this way, we hope to make our rule sets clear as to what traffic they affect.

When you install a Red Hat host and set up the firewall as part of the installation process, a set of `iptables` rules are generated for you. The user-defined chains are fundamentally a good idea and adequate for a stand-alone host. While the rules that they generate may not be what we require, the concept of defining our user chains in this way is good. However, these chains also become limiting when you have multiple NICs.

We can quickly view traffic in our `FORWARD` chain on device ppp0 if we have a chain named `Firewall-ppp0-FORWARD` and rules relating to that traffic placed under it. We have removed the `RH` prefix for this chain and others to make them less Red Hat–centric. The actual naming convention you choose to use is entirely up to you. However, your rule sets will be much clearer to read by others if you define your rules in a similar way.

Why didn't we choose Ubuntu's naming convention for our user-defined chains? Ubuntu does not create a rule set during the installation process and will be clean of any rules and user-defined chains. Tools like `ufw` also create user-defined chains, and you are free to follow that naming convention if you prefer. It doesn't matter which you choose as long as your rules are clear and easy to read.

We'll start with saving our current rule set to a file. Issuing the following command from the command line

```
$ sudo /sbin/iptables-save > firewall-20090101
```

saves the current `iptables` rules we have in memory to the file `firewall-20090101`.

We can restore a saved set of rules at a later date by issuing the following:

```
iptables-restore < firewall-20090101
```

This will reinstate our firewall rules from the file `firewall-20090101` and save the new firewall rules to `/etc/sysconfig/iptables`.

Creating Our Own Rules: The Basic filter Table

We now want to start editing and make our own firewall rules. We have looked at our network requirements and have seen the current state of our firewall rules. First, we'll save a copy of the current rules to a file, cull the undesirable rules, and begin to write our own set.

We need to create a file to hold our rule set. We will give the file a meaningful name:

```
$ sudo vi /home/jsmith/gateway.example.com-20090101
```

We can now edit the file /home/jsmith/gateway.example.com-20090101. We will add the following rule set to get started:

```
*filter
:INPUT DROP [0:0]
:FORWARD DROP [0:0]
:OUTPUT DROP [0:0]
:Firewall-eth1-INPUT - [0:0]
-A INPUT -j Firewall-eth1-INPUT
-A FORWARD -j Firewall-eth1-INPUT
-A Firewall-eth1-INPUT -i lo -j ACCEPT
-A Firewall-eth1-INPUT -p icmp --icmp-type any -j ACCEPT
-A Firewall-eth1-INPUT -m state --state ESTABLISHED,RELATED -j ACCEPT
-A Firewall-eth1-INPUT -j REJECT --reject-with icmp-host-prohibited
COMMIT
```

We have set a default policy of DROP on all our chains. We want all our chains to have the default stance of denial (according to the principle of allow by exception). We want to make sure that nothing is allowed unless explicitly specified in the firewall rules.

We now have a fresh filter table and have set the built-in chains' policies all to DROP. With the current configuration, our host will not be able to communicate with any other host. So let's begin with setting the rules for our firewall host.

We have a few things to consider now, such as the two interface devices eth1 and ppp0. Our eth1 device will be a private network interface, and ppp0 will be our public interface. We are going to separate our traffic into two spheres: one that deals with the internal private traffic and one that deals with the public external traffic.

We are concentrating traffic coming into our host. We have determined that we will need the following ports open on our firewall to our private network: SSH, which communicates on port 22 from our private network, and domain, which communicates on the TCP and UDP port 53, from both private and public networks. We require the loopback address to be able to initiate sockets back to itself, and we will allow ICMP packets to be answered. Any packet that is in a related or established state will also be accepted.

```
-A INPUT -i eth1 -j Firewall-eth1-INPUT
-A FORWARD -i eth1 -o eth1 -j Firewall-eth1-INPUT
-A Firewall-eth1-INPUT -i lo -j ACCEPT
-A Firewall-eth1-INPUT -p icmp -m icmp --icmp-type any ➥
-m limit --limit 3/s -j ACCEPT
-A Firewall-eth1-INPUT -m state --state RELATED,ESTABLISHED -j ACCEPT
-A Firewall-eth1-INPUT -s 192.168.0.0/24 -p tcp ➥
-m state --state NEW -m tcp --dport 22 -j ACCEPT
```

```
-A Firewall-eth1-INPUT -p tcp -m state --state NEW -m tcp --dport 53 -j ACCEPT
-A Firewall-eth1-INPUT -p udp -m state --state NEW -m udp --dport 53 -j ACCEPT
-A Firewall-eth1-INPUT -j REJECT --reject-with icmp-host-prohibited
```

What have we done now? Well, in our first line, we have directed all traffic that is incoming on eth1 to our `Firewall-eth1-INPUT` chain.

```
-A INPUT -i eth1 -j Firewall-eth1-INPUT
```

Next, we direct packets being forwarded through our host, coming in on interface eth1 and exiting our host back through eth1, to the `Firewall-eth1-INPUT` chain as well.

```
-A FORWARD -i eth1 -o eth1 -j Firewall-eth1-INPUT
```

We then allow the loopback address to initiate connections and allow ICMP packets, and we limit the amount that we accept to just three per second as specified by `-m limit –limit 3/s`. We will explain this further later in the chapter in the "Configuring Our Rules: Revisiting the filter Table" section.

```
-A Firewall-eth1-INPUT -i lo -j ACCEPT
-A Firewall-eth1-INPUT -p icmp -m icmp --icmp-type any ➥
-m limit --limit 3/s -j ACCEPT
```

We also want to allow `RELATED` and `ESTABLISHED` packet states to pass through to be accepted.

```
-A Firewall-eth1-INPUT -m state --state RELATED,ESTABLISHED -j ACCEPT
```

In the next line, we allow SSH connections with a source address from our private network, denoted by `-s 192.168.0.0/24`, to the firewall host. We could limit this to a single host if we chose by specifying `192.168.0.?/32` (where ? is the last octet of an IP address).

```
-A Firewall-eth1-INPUT –s 192.168.0.0/24 -p tcp -m state ➥
--state NEW -m tcp --dport 22 -j ACCEPT
```

We have also enabled DNS connections to our firewall host, specified here as `--dport 53`. We expect that any host can query our DNS server from either the private or public networks, so we have not specified any source or destination networks. DNS is actually served on both TCP and UDP protocols, so we have specified each on a separate line. We can specify the protocols on one single line by the separating them with a comma like so: `-p tcp,udp`.

```
-A Firewall-eth1-INPUT -p tcp -m state --state NEW -m tcp --dport 53 -j ACCEPT
-A Firewall-eth1-INPUT -p udp -m state --state NEW -m udp --dport 53 -j ACCEPT
```

We still want to reject anything that doesn't match these few rules and send an ICMP message informing services trying to make a connection.

```
-A Firewall-eth1-INPUT -j REJECT --reject-with icmp-host-prohibited
```

We have set our default policies for all our built-in chains to `DROP` including our `OUTPUT` chain. We wish to make sure our firewall can communicate to our private network, so we will now add the following rule:

```
-A OUTPUT -s 192.168.0.0/255.255.255.0 -d 192.168.0.0/255.255.255.0 -j ACCEPT
```

In this rule, we are using the source parameter, as specified by `-s 192.168.0.0/255.255.255.0`, and destination parameter, written here as `-d 192.168.0.0/255.255.255.0`, to restrict the hosts we can initiate connections to. We can of course use `-i eth1` and `-o eth1` instead of specifying the IP networks, which would be a looser restriction.

We will further restrict the OUTPUT chain later on in the "Configuring Our Rules: Revisiting the filter Table" section, to only allow the communications we want to be initiated by our firewall.

Let's stop here for a moment. If we review the current rules we have in our file, we can see we have the framework for any host firewall. We have default policies of DROP on all our built-in chains and have a set of rules that only allows the types of communication we want. We can copy and paste the following rules and use them as the basis of a firewall on any host in the future.

```
*filter
:INPUT DROP [0:0]
:FORWARD DROP [0:0]
:OUTPUT DROP [0:0]
-N Firewall-eth1-INPUT
-A INPUT -i eth1 -j Firewall-eth1-INPUT
-A FORWARD -i eth1 -o eth1 -j Firewall-eth1-INPUT

-A Firewall-eth1-INPUT -i lo -j ACCEPT
-A Firewall-eth1-INPUT -p icmp -m icmp --icmp-type any ➡
-m limit --limit 3/s -j ACCEPT
-A Firewall-eth1-INPUT -m state --state RELATED,ESTABLISHED -j ACCEPT
-A Firewall-eth1-INPUT -p tcp -m state --state NEW -m tcp --dport 53 -j ACCEPT
-A Firewall-eth1-INPUT -p udp -m state --state NEW -m udp --dport 53 -j ACCEPT
-A Firewall-eth1-INPUT -s 192.168.0.0/24 -p tcp ➡
-m state --state NEW -m tcp --dport 22 -j ACCEPT
-A Firewall-eth1-INPUT -j REJECT --reject-with icmp-host-prohibited

-A OUTPUT -s 192.168.0.0/255.255.255.0 -d 192.168.0.0/255.255.255.0 -j ACCEPT
COMMIT
```

To create the firewall we require for our headoffice.example.com host, all we need to do is add the rules to allow DNS, DHCPD, NTP, SMTP, IMAP, and HTTP services the ability to connect. We expand on these services in Chapters 9, 10, and 14.

headoffice.example.com Firewall

The host headoffice.example.com is our main server and has many services running on it for our internal office and public clients. We require mail services (SMTP and IMAP) and web services (HTTP and HTTPS) to be accessible from the public and private network. We will restrict DNS, DHCPD, and NTP to our internal private network only.

We will add the following to our basic rule set:

```
*filter
:INPUT DROP [0:0]
:FORWARD DROP [0:0]
```

```
:OUTPUT DROP [0:0]
-N Firewall-eth1-INPUT
-A INPUT -i eth1 -j Firewall-eth1-INPUT
-A FORWARD -i eth1 -o eth1 -j Firewall-eth1-INPUT

-A Firewall-eth1-INPUT -i lo -j ACCEPT
-A Firewall-eth1-INPUT -p icmp -m icmp --icmp-type any ➥
-m limit --limit 3/s -j ACCEPT
-A Firewall-eth1-INPUT -m state --state RELATED,ESTABLISHED -j ACCEPT
-A Firewall-eth1-INPUT -p tcp -m state --state NEW --dport 53 -j ACCEPT
-A Firewall-eth1-INPUT -p udp -m state --state NEW --dport 53 -j ACCEPT
-A Firewall-eth1-INPUT -s 192.168.0.0/24 -p tcp -m state ➥
--state NEW --dport 22 -j ACCEPT
-A Firewall-eth1-INPUT -p tcp -m state --state NEW --dport 25 -j ACCEPT
-A Firewall-eth1-INPUT -s 192.168.0.0/16 -p udp -m state ➥
--state NEW --sport 68 --dport 67 -j ACCEPT
-A Firewall-eth1-INPUT -s 192.168.0.0/16 -p tcp -m state ➥
--state NEW --sport 68 --dport 67 -j ACCEPT
-A Firewall-eth1-INPUT -p tcp -m state --state NEW --dport 80 -j ACCEPT
-A Firewall-eth1-INPUT -s 192.168.0.0/24 -p udp -m state ➥
--state NEW --sport 123 --dport 123 -j ACCEPT
-A Firewall-eth1-INPUT -s 192.168.0.0/24 -p tcp -m state ➥
--state NEW --dport 143 -j ACCEPT
-A Firewall-eth1-INPUT -p tcp -m state --state NEW --dport 443 -j ACCEPT
-A Firewall-eth1-INPUT -j REJECT --reject-with icmp-host-prohibited

-A OUTPUT -s 192.168.0.0/24 -d 192.168.0.0/24   -j ACCEPT
COMMIT
```

Here we have added rules to allow access to the services running on headoffice.example.com. DNS is allowed access via the following rules, accepting connections from both the private and public network:

```
-A Firewall-eth1-INPUT -p tcp -m state --state NEW --dport 53 -j ACCEPT
-A Firewall-eth1-INPUT -p udp -m state --state NEW --dport 53 -j ACCEPT
```

SSH is given access from within our local networks with this rule:

```
-A Firewall-eth1-INPUT -s 192.168.0.0/24 -p tcp -m state ➥
--state NEW --dport 22 -j ACCEPT
```

We are allowing mail access, SMTP, from all hosts with this rule:

```
-A Firewall-eth1-INPUT -p tcp -m state --state NEW --dport 25 -j ACCEPT
```

DHCP requires the following rules to allow access to the local network. You will notice that we are specifically allowing access to all our network subnets with the 192.168.0.0/16 netmask.

```
-A Firewall-eth1-INPUT -s 192.168.0.0/16 -p udp -m state ➥
--state NEW --sport 68 --dport 67 -j ACCEPT
```

```
-A Firewall-eth1-INPUT -s 192.168.0.0/16 -p tcp -m state ➡
--state NEW --sport 68 --dport 67 -j ACCEPT
```

HTTP and HTTPS access is granted via the following two rules. We are allowing access from all networks.

```
-A Firewall-eth1-INPUT -p tcp -m state --state NEW --dport 80 -j ACCEPT
-A Firewall-eth1-INPUT -p tcp -m state --state NEW --dport 443 -j ACCEPT
```

NTP, the Network Time Protocol, is allowed within our local network. We are careful here to make sure that we filter on the destination and source ports. We can do this because we know the port this UDP connection will use to communicate with each host, 123.

```
-A Firewall-eth1-INPUT -s 192.168.0.0/24 -p udp -m state ➡
--state NEW --sport 123 --dport 123 -j ACCEPT
```

Finally, in the list of rules we have added, we have the IMAP rule. IMAP is a mail protocol that we discuss later in Chapter 10, and here we are allowing only our internal network access to it.

```
-A Firewall-eth1-INPUT -s 192.168.0.0/24 -p tcp -m state ➡
--state NEW --dport 143 -j ACCEPT
```

This would create the rules necessary to get our headoffice.example.com host up and running. Now let's configure the gateway.example.com.

gateway.example.com Firewall

So what do we need to add to this host to turn it into a gateway firewall capable of distinguishing all sorts of packets from either ppp0 or eth1 and then route our packets through the appropriate interface? We need to add some more chains and add our nat table.

THE DIFFERENT PROTOCOLS

Netfilter or `iptables` filters traffic based on different protocols in the TCP/IP protocol stack. You can filter on protocols like TCP, UDP, AH, IPsec, PPPoE, STP, and many others.

You can get a good list of all the possible protocols in `/etc/protocols` along with their protocol numbers. In `iptables`, you can specify the protocol name, like `udp`, or a protocol number, like 17 (for UDP), when declaring a rule. In the following, we are filtering on UDP packets:

```
iptables -A INPUT -p 17 -m state --state NEW --dport 53 -j ACCEPT
```

If you do not specify a protocol, the default is to match all. You can also use ! to exclude a protocol by specifying your rule like this:

```
iptables -A INPUT -p ! udp -m state --state NEW -j ACCEPT
```

This rule accepts packets of all protocols except those using the UDP protocol in a `NEW` state. The following is a good reference on network protocols: `http://www.protocols.com/pbook/tcpip1.htm`.

Configuring Our Rules: The nat Table

We'll take a break from the filter table for a moment and look at the configuration we need in our nat table. The definition of the nat table has been described earlier in this chapter in the "Tables" section. The nat table will handle our IP masquerading and DNAT (port mapping) rules. We need to configure the following built-in chains: PREROUTING and POSTROUTING. The nat table will be used to route and alter the traffic coming in and out of our ppp0 interface. We will now add these lines to the file:

```
*nat
:PREROUTING ACCEPT [0:0]
:POSTROUTING ACCEPT [0:0]
:OUTPUT ACCEPT [0:0]
-A PREROUTING -i ppp0 -p tcp -m tcp --dport 25 -j DNAT --to-destination 192.168.0.1
-A PREROUTING -i ppp0 -p tcp -m tcp --dport 80 -j DNAT --to-destination 192.168.0.1
-A POSTROUTING -o ppp0 -j MASQUERADE
COMMIT
```

We only need a few rules to get it to work. Netfilter will load all the rules between the *nat and COMMIT lines and read them sequentially, just like it does in the filter table. For Netfilter to be able to use nat, you need iptable_nat to be loaded in the kernel. You can check to see whether it is loaded by issuing the following command:

```
$ sudo /sbin/lsmod |grep table
ip_tables              17029  2 iptable_nat,iptable_filter
```

Let's examine the way that the packets will flow through our host if we have NAT configured. In Figure 6-31, we have mapped the path that a packet might take in relation to the nat table.

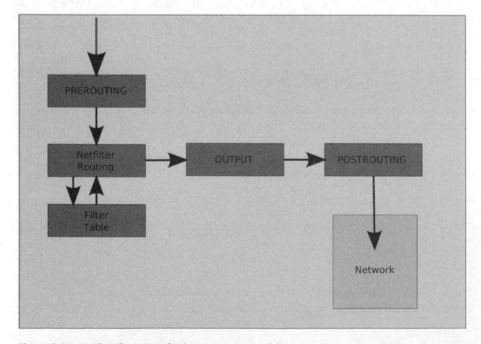

Figure 6-31. *Packet flow in relation to our nat table*

Packets will come in on our interface and be met by the PREROUTING chain. Here we can perform our DNAT operations (port mapping). Once they pass through this chain, the packets will be routed according to their final destination. They will be passed to the filter table and either forwarded through the FORWARD chain on or passed to the INPUT chain. Packets are then passed back out through the nat table OUTPUT chain, where any packets generated by the firewall can be changed (if needed). The POSTROUTING chain is where we MASQUERADE our packets so they appear to come from the public IP address. This address will be bound to the base IP address of the external interface. If you want to alias your external connection on the firewall, you have to use SNAT.

In the preceding example for our nat table, you can also see that we have created three chains (these are the default built-in chains for the nat table). You signify a chain by using :*chain-name*. So what happens to our traffic coming into our host can be broken down into parts.

In the first part, all traffic is directed to our PREROUTING chain and accepted, as denoted by PREROUTING ACCEPT. Next, all traffic coming in on interface ppp0, written here as -i ppp0, with protocol TCP, denoted by -p tcp, is flagged. Any of those packets that match protocol TCP, again written here as -m tcp, and destined for port 25, specified by --dport 25, on our ppp0 interface we want sent to the DNAT target, which will forward those packets to IP address 192.168.0.1; this is indicated by -j DNAT --to-destination 192.168.0.1. We treat traffic coming in on port 80 the same way.

The next line handles all traffic leaving our host via the ppp0 interface. After the packets have been routed, they make their last dash toward the wire through our POSTROUTING chain.

```
-A POSTROUTING -o ppp0 -j MASQUERADE
```

This is the final line in our nat chain. It says as traffic leaves our ppp0 interface, specified by -o ppp0, send packets to our MASQUERADE target extension, specified by -j MASQUERADE. What does this do? Well, as mentioned previously, this takes all the traffic leaving ppp0 and puts it into a nat table. The table records traffic going out of the interface. It records the original source IP and the destination IP. At this point, our firewall rewrites the packet so that the packet's source IP address is that of our public IP address and sends the packet off to its destination host. Packets responding to our connections come back through our firewall. We use the nat table to match our incoming packets to the originating hosts.

Configuring Our Rules: Revisiting the filter Table

Now that we have our basic filter rules in place and have the chains in our nat table configured, we will need to revisit our filter table to make sure the traffic flows correctly between the two. Packets need to find their way from one interface to the other. Traffic coming in on one interface and going out on the other will need to use our FORWARD chain.

We are going to create another set of chains for our filter table. These will handle all our traffic in and out of our ppp0, or public, interface. We will call them Firewall-ppp0-*chain   name*.

```
:Firewall-ppp0-INPUT
:Firewall-ppp0-FORWARD
:Firewall-ppp0-OUTPUT
```

The chain `Firewall-ppp0-INPUT` is going to handle all the traffic coming into our firewall from our ppp0 interface. We direct incoming traffic on ppp0 like this:

```
-A INPUT -i ppp0 -j Firewall-ppp0-INPUT
```

This chain is concerned with public (Internet) traffic destined for the firewall itself. We want to control this traffic differently from packets we are forwarding to other hosts, so we do not want to combine this with the `FORWARD` rule. We will create this rule instead:

```
-A FORWARD -i ppp0 -o eth1 -j Firewall-ppp0-FORWARD
```

Here we are going to make rules for traffic coming in on our public interface and forwarded out through our private interface, eth1. Finally we want to handle all traffic originating from our own firewall host differently from our built-in `OUTPUT` chain.

```
-A OUTPUT -o ppp0 -j Firewall-ppp0-OUTPUT
```

Let's take a look now at the complete rule set for the `filter` table. You can see we have added a few rules to our user-defined chains to allow the traffic we expect to see on our network.

```
*filter
:INPUT DROP
:FORWARD DROP
:OUTPUT DROP

:Firewall-1-INPUT
:Firewall-ppp0-FORWARD
:Firewall-ppp0-INPUT
:Firewall-ppp0-OUTPUT

-A INPUT -i eth1 -j Firewall-eth1-INPUT
-A INPUT -i ppp0 -j Firewall-ppp0-INPUT
-A FORWARD -i eth1 -o eth1 -j Firewall-eth1-INPUT
-A FORWARD -i eth1 -o ppp0 -j Firewall-ppp0-INPUT
-A FORWARD -i ppp0 -o eth1 -j Firewall-ppp0-FORWARD
-A OUTPUT -o ppp0 -j Firewall-ppp0-OUTPUT
-A OUTPUT -s 192.168.1.0/255.255.255.0 -d 192.168.1.0/255.255.255.0 -j ACCEPT

-A Firewall-eth1-INPUT -i lo -j ACCEPT
-A Firewall-eth1-INPUT -p icmp -m icmp --icmp-type any ➥
-m limit --limit 3/s -j ACCEPT
-A Firewall-eth1-INPUT -m state --state RELATED,ESTABLISHED -j ACCEPT
-A Firewall-eth1-INPUT -p tcp -m state --state NEW -m tcp --dport 22 -j ACCEPT
-A Firewall-eth1-INPUT -p tcp -m state --state NEW -m tcp --dport 53 -j ACCEPT
-A Firewall-eth1-INPUT -p udp -m state --state NEW -m udp --dport 53 -j ACCEPT
-A Firewall-eth1-INPUT -p tcp -j LOG --log-prefix "eth1_in_tcp_REJECT "
-A Firewall-eth1-INPUT -j REJECT --reject-with icmp-host-prohibited
```

```
-A Firewall-ppp0-INPUT -p icmp -m icmp --icmp-type any ➧
-m limit --limit 5/s -j ACCEPT
-A Firewall-ppp0-INPUT -m state --state RELATED,ESTABLISHED -j ACCEPT
-A Firewall-ppp0-INPUT -p tcp -m state --state NEW -m tcp --dport 53 -j ACCEPT
-A Firewall-ppp0-INPUT -p udp -m state --state NEW -m udp --dport 53 -j ACCEPT
-A Firewall-ppp0-INPUT -m limit --limit 5/s -j LOG --log-prefix "ppp0_in_REJECT "
-A Firewall-ppp0-INPUT -j REJECT --reject-with icmp-host-prohibited

-A Firewall-ppp0-FORWARD -m state --state RELATED,ESTABLISHED -j ACCEPT
-A Firewall-ppp0-FORWARD -p tcp -m state --state NEW -m tcp --dport 22 -j ACCEPT
-A Firewall-ppp0-FORWARD -p tcp -m state --state NEW -m tcp --dport 25 -j ACCEPT
-A Firewall-ppp0-FORWARD -p tcp -m state --state NEW -m tcp --dport 53 -j ACCEPT
-A Firewall-ppp0-FORWARD -p udp -m state --state NEW -m udp --dport 53 -j ACCEPT
-A Firewall-ppp0-FORWARD -p tcp -m state --state NEW -m tcp --dport 80 -j ACCEPT
-A Firewall-ppp0-FORWARD -p tcp -m state --state NEW -m tcp --dport 80 -j ACCEPT
-A Firewall-ppp0-FORWARD -p udp -m state --state NEW ➧
-m udp --sport 123 --dport 123 -j ACCEPT
-A Firewall-ppp0-FORWARD -j REJECT --reject-with icmp-port-unreachable

-A Firewall-ppp0-OUTPUT -p icmp -m icmp --icmp-type any -j ACCEPT
-A Firewall-ppp0-OUTPUT -m state --state ESTABLISHED,RELATED -j ACCEPT
-A Firewall-ppp0-OUTPUT -p tcp -m state --state NEW -m tcp --dport 53 -j ACCEPT
-A Firewall-ppp0-OUTPUT -p udp -m state --state NEW -m udp --dport 53 -j ACCEPT
-A Firewall-ppp0-OUTPUT -p tcp -m state --state NEW -m tcp --dport 80 -j ACCEPT
-A Firewall-ppp0-OUTPUT -j DROP
COMMIT
```

We'll break this down into pieces that are easier for you to digest. Let's look at what we have done to the Firewall-eth1-INPUT chain first:

```
-A Firewall-eth1-INPUT -i lo -j ACCEPT
-A Firewall-eth1-INPUT -p icmp -m icmp --icmp-type any ➧
-m limit --limit 3/s -j ACCEPT
-A Firewall-eth1-INPUT -m state --state RELATED,ESTABLISHED -j ACCEPT
-A Firewall-eth1-INPUT -p tcp -m state --state NEW -m tcp --dport 22 -j ACCEPT
-A Firewall-eth1-INPUT -p tcp -m state --state NEW -m tcp --dport 53 -j ACCEPT
-A Firewall-eth1-INPUT -p udp -m state --state NEW -m udp --dport 53 -j ACCEPT
-A Firewall-eth1-INPUT -p tcp -m limit --limit 5/s ➧
-j LOG --log-prefix "eth1_in_tcp_REJECT "
-A Firewall-eth1-INPUT -j REJECT --reject-with icmp-host-prohibited
```

This affects traffic forwarded from eth1 or coming in from our private network to the firewall. As explained earlier, we are allowing the loopback address to make any connection it likes. We are allowing ICMP traffic and any connection that is a state of ESTABLISHED or RELATED. We are also allowing connections to be initiated to our SSH server and our DNS server. We have covered all these before except for the -j LOG target, which is next:

```
-A Firewall-eth1-INPUT -p tcp -m limit --limit 5/s ➡
-j LOG --log-prefix "eth1_in_tcp_REJECT "
```

The syntax is iptables -t *table chain parameters* -j LOG --log-prefix *some string*. Any TCP traffic, captured by -p tcp, that has not been matched by any of the rules will be logged to the syslogd daemon (whose files can be found in /var/log/messages or /var/log/syslog). In this case, they will be prefixed with eth1_in_tcp_REJECT.

Here is an example of a message recorded in /var/log/messages on our Red Hat host:

```
Jan 17 00:02:23 localhost kernel: eth1_in_tcp_REJECT IN=eth1 OUT= ➡
MAC=00:0b:cd:49:c0:7f:00:02:2d:87:6e:0c:08:00 SRC=192.168.0.1 ➡
DST=192.168.0.254 LEN=52 TOS=0x00 PREC=0x00 TTL=128 ID=2178 DF PROTO=TCP ➡
SPT=1556 DPT=445 WINDOW=16384 RES=0x00 SYN URGP=0
```

After the date stamp, Jan 17 00:02:23, comes the hostname, localhost, and the program that issued the log, kernel. You can now see the string we prefixed the log with, eth1_in_tcp_REJECT. The very next rule is the rule to reject all packets, so we are recording what traffic is about to be rejected. Next you see the traffic detail. The IN and OUT indicate where the traffic is coming from. Notice after that the MAC addresses of the hosts involved and their SRC and DST (source and destination) IP addresses. Various other parameters are recorded including the source port, SPT, and destination port, DPT.

Last of all in this set of rules is the REJECT rule to reject all unmatched traffic. We have examined this rule previously.

Now we will explore how we deal with traffic coming in on the ppp0 public interface and destined for our firewall host itself. This traffic is directed through the INPUT chain routed to the Firewall-ppp0-INPUT chain.

```
-A Firewall-ppp0-INPUT -p icmp -m icmp --icmp-type any -m limit ➡
--limit 5/s -j ACCEPT
-A Firewall-ppp0-INPUT -m state --state RELATED,ESTABLISHED -j ACCEPT
-A Firewall-ppp0-INPUT -p tcp -m state --state NEW -m tcp --dport 53 -j ACCEPT
-A Firewall-ppp0-INPUT -p udp -m state --state NEW -m udp --dport 53 -j ACCEPT
-A Firewall-ppp0-INPUT -m limit --limit 5/s -j LOG --log-prefix "ppp0_in_REJECT "
-A Firewall-ppp0-INPUT -j REJECT --reject-with icmp-host-prohibited
```

Here we are allowing ICMP connections, and we have placed a limit (-m limit --limit 5/s) on how many we will accept in a second. This will help reduce our susceptibility to SYN flood attacks by limiting the rate that people can initiate ICMP connections. We are accepting anything that is in an established or related state. The only ports we will have open on our firewall are DNS for UDP and TCP protocols. It is not uncommon to have two DNS name servers in case one of them goes offline, and our firewall will act as one of those name servers. You can see that we are also limiting our logging of packets that will be rejected so that our logs are not flooded with bogus information, which can also lead to a system crash because the logs fill the disk.

DIFFERENT TYPES OF ATTACKS

There are different types of attacks that people can use to bring down your network. Some target the perimeter of your network, tying it up with bogus connections until it breaks and stops responding; these are known as Denial of Service attacks (DoS), for example, SYN flood attacks. Others will use the services you are running (like a mail or a web server) to bypass your perimeter security and launch an attack from within your network (e.g., virus attacks, Trojan attacks, script injection attacks).

While keeping your network secure is a constant process, you can do a few things to minimize your risks:

- Track security alert mailing lists for your hosts.

- Keep your hosts up to date with the latest security patches.

- Close off unwanted ports and services.

- Get to know your logs and learn to detect anything that looks odd.

- Review your security every six months at minimum to make sure it is still working properly.

Nothing connected to the Internet is 100% secure, but you can take measures that ensure your network isn't one of those with a well-known vulnerability. It doesn't take long for the script kiddies to find your host and try for common and preventable exploits.

Time to move on to the rule set that controls what can be forwarded across our interfaces from ppp0 to eth1. These rules need to exist to make any connection to the Internet possible. When we try to initiate a connection or socket on the Internet (going to a website, for instance), we send a SYN packet first (synchronization packet with a sequence number). This tells the web server we want to start a socket. It will send back a SYN, ACK packet, and iptables treats this packet as being in a NEW state. It is only after the connection is established with a further SYN packet with the sequence number incremented by 1 that the state is ESTABLISHED. So we need to allow NEW packets coming in on our firewall interface destined for somewhere within our network so that we can establish connections.

```
-A Firewall-ppp0-FORWARD -p icmp -m icmp --icmp-type any ➥
-m limit --limit 3/s -j ACCEPT
-A Firewall-ppp0-FORWARD -m state --state RELATED,ESTABLISHED -j ACCEPT
-A Firewall-ppp0-FORWARD -p tcp -m state --state NEW -m tcp --dport 22 -j ACCEPT
-A Firewall-ppp0-FORWARD -p tcp -m state --state NEW -m tcp --dport 25 -j ACCEPT
-A Firewall-ppp0-FORWARD -p tcp -m state --state NEW -m tcp --dport 53 -j ACCEPT
-A Firewall-ppp0-FORWARD -p udp -m state --state NEW -m udp --dport 53 -j ACCEPT
-A Firewall-ppp0-FORWARD -p tcp -m state --state NEW -m tcp --dport 80 -j ACCEPT
-A Firewall-ppp0-FORWARD -p tcp -m state --state NEW -m tcp --dport 443 -j ACCEPT
-A Firewall-ppp0-FORWARD -p udp -m state --state NEW ➥
-m udp --sport 123 --dport 123 -j ACCEPT
-A Firewall-ppp0-FORWARD -j REJECT --reject-with icmp-port-unreachable
```

It is for this reason that we allow the NEW connections to ports 25, 53, 80, and 443—all these relate to the traffic we want coming into our host, 192.168.0.1. It requires connections to be able to be established for mail on port 25, for DNS on port 53, and for web serving on ports

80 and 443. We wish to allow other hosts in our network to connect to mail, web, and time servers on port 123 and SSH on port 22 servers, so we require those to be accepted as well.

Lastly, we have the `Firewall-ppp0-OUTPUT` chain to handle all outbound traffic from our firewall host to the Internet. These are very simple rules as you can see:

```
-A Firewall-ppp0-OUTPUT -p icmp -m icmp --icmp-type any -j ACCEPT
-A Firewall-ppp0-OUTPUT -m state --state ESTABLISHED,RELATED -j ACCEPT
-A Firewall-ppp0-OUTPUT -p tcp -m state --state NEW -m tcp --dport 53 -j ACCEPT
-A Firewall-ppp0-OUTPUT -p udp -m state --state NEW -m udp --dport 53 -j ACCEPT
-A Firewall-ppp0-OUTPUT -p tcp -m state --state NEW -m tcp --dport 80 -j ACCEPT
-A Firewall-ppp0-OUTPUT -j DROP
```

We allow outbound ICMP traffic and anything in an `ESTABLISHED,RELATED` state. We are not rate limiting our own ICMP connections outbound. We are also allowing our firewall host to make connections with any DNS name server, and we want to allow communication with two web servers. We do this by specifying `--dport 53` and `--dport 80`, respectively. We allow port 80 outbound so that our host can receive updates for packages. You may wish to lock this down further by specifying particular hosts your firewall can connect to via the `--destination` parameter like so: `--destination myrepo.example.com -p tcp -m state --state NEW -m tcp --dport 80 -j ACCEPT`. This will allow outbound connections to myrepo.example.com only, where myrepo.example.com is an APT or a Yum repository under our control (you will learn more about Yum and APT repositories in Chapter 7).

Other Firewall Configuration Tools

After all this, you can see that Netfilter firewalls and their rules can become awfully complicated. So are there any tools that you can use to help you create your firewall configurations?

Well yes, there are. Red Hat hosts come with a tool you will have seen when you first installed your host. It is a simple firewall tool that can't be used to make firewall rules other than those in the `filter` table. You can access it by issuing the following command:

```
$ sudo system-config-security
```

Red Hat has some good documentation on using the tool here: `http://www.redhat.com/docs/manuals/enterprise/RHEL-4-Manual/sysadmin-guide/ch-basic-firewall.html`.

You have seen the rule set it provides earlier, and we recommend that you go over some of the Red Hat default rules and remove things you don't need (like allowing IPP and IPsec rules).

Ubuntu also has a tool for manipulating firewall rules from the command line. It is called `ufw` and is available from the `ufw` package.

■Tip We'll talk more about installing packages in Chapter 7.

Documentation for `ufw` is available here: `https://wiki.ubuntu.com/UbuntuFirewall`. This package uses commands like the following:

```
$ sudo ufw allow 80/tcp
```

This enables port 80 access via TCP. Commands can be stored in a script and run when the host starts up.

For more complicated scenarios, we suggest exploring another configuration tool called Shorewall. It is available for download from `http://shorewall.net/`, where you can also view the documentation for this tool. Shorewall is also available for Ubuntu and Fedora from the online repositories under the package name `shorewall`.

Shorewall allows for some complicated firewall rules that cover DNAT, SNAT, IPsec, dual WAN interface configuration and routing, and much more. It writes very clean `iptables` rules, meaning that it does not add anything by default, like Red Hat's `system-config-security` tool sometimes does.

■**Note** Another example of this sort of software is called Firestarter (`http://www.fs-security.com/`). For single host `iptables` configuration and brute-force attack detection, you can also look at using Advanced Policy Firewall (APF) and Brute Force Detection (BFD) from `http://www.rfxnetworks.com/apf.php` (not suitable for gateway firewall hosts).

There are also Linux distributions that are purposely built for firewalls. IPCop, an example of this type of distribution, can be downloaded and installed from `http://www.ipcop.org/index.php`. It has a web-based graphical configuration and is designed to be solely a firewall for SOHO businesses. This is not a Red Hat or an Ubuntu distribution. It has its own way of installing and updating packages, which is outside the scope of this book.

TCP Wrappers

Lastly, one of the other ways of securing your host is to use TCP Wrappers. If your network service is compiled with support for TCP Wrappers, you can use TCP Wrappers to further secure the services of your hosts. TCP Wrappers control access to the daemons running on your host, not to the ports, through a series of definitions in the /etc/hosts.allow and /etc/hosts.deny files.

The rules in hosts.allow take precedence over the rules in hosts.deny. If you are going to use TCP Wrappers, it is a good idea to set the following in hosts.deny:

```
ALL: ALL
```

This will set the default action of denial to all services unless specified in the /etc/hosts.allow file. The rules are read in order from top to bottom.

You would then add network services. For example, for our example network, we will allow network services by setting the following:

```
ALL: localhost ACCEPT
sshd: .example.com  EXCEPT .baddomain.com
```

These settings will first allow any localhost connections to be accepted. Many services require connections to services running on the loopback (localhost) interface, and these need to be accepted. Next, we are allowing the hosts on the example.com network to connect to our SSH daemon. Here also we are explicitly denying baddomain.com. For more information on configuring TCP Wrappers, please see the man page for hosts_options or hosts.allow and hosts.deny.

Summary

We have now completed a basic firewall for a bastion host. Along the way, we have demonstrated that you can use the filter table only to protect a stand-alone host on our network. You now know how to use NAT on your firewall so that your private network IP addresses are masqueraded behind a single public IP on your firewall.

This chapter covered how to do the following:

- Configure interfaces on our host.

- Configure a PPP connection.

- Configure your bastion firewall.

- Use NAT on your firewall.

- Port-map your connections.

- Secure your hosts.

- Use TCP Wrappers to secure your daemons.

In the next chapter, we will look at how to manage packages on a host. In that chapter, you will learn how to install, remove, and update software on your hosts.

CHAPTER 7

■■■

Package Management

By James Turnbull, Peter Lieverdink, and Dennis Matotek

In Chapter 2 you installed your first Linux host. As you learned in that chapter, a host can be installed with a variety of different applications, ranging from a bare-bones installation to one with every application and tool installed. But this isn't the end of the line for installing and managing applications. Once you've installed your host, you'll often need to add applications, upgrade and patch them, and sometimes remove them. This chapter explains how to do these tasks on both Red Hat Enterprise Linux and Ubuntu.

On Linux distributions, this sort of application management is called *package management*. This is because most applications available on Linux hosts have been made available as *packages*. Packages make it very easy to add and remove applications to and from your host. A package usually contains all the binaries, configuration files, and other supporting material required to install an application. The package also knows where these files need to be installed and usually if other packages also need to be installed to meet any prerequisites of an application. To make a comparison, a Linux package is much like a Windows installation or setup executable.

Packages are generally installed by an application control center called a *package manager*. Most Linux distributions come with a package manager, which usually has a set of command-line and graphical tools for managing packages, and a small database that records what has been installed.

By the end of this chapter, you'll have a good understanding of what packages are, how to install and remove them, how to find the right package for your needs, and how to install software from source code. We'll demonstrate all of these tasks using command-line tools as well as the available GUIs for the Red Hat and Ubuntu distributions.

■**Note** After the "Introduction to Package Management" section, this chapter is divided into sections covering installation on Red Hat, on Ubuntu, and from source code. You need to read only the section that relates to your chosen distribution. We also recommend you read about how to install software from source code. You won't often need to do this (and we recommend that you stick to using packages to manage applications), but it's a useful thing to know.

Introduction to Package Management

Different distributions have different ways of packaging their software. For instance, Red Hat Linux and CentOS use the RPM (Red Hat Package Management) package format, while Ubuntu uses the deb (short for Debian, the distribution Ubuntu was originally based on) format. Just as the package formats differ, so do the tools that you can use to manage them.

Each of these package types uses different tools to install and manage packages. On systems that use RPM packages, the basic package manager is called rpm, while on systems that use deb packages, it is called dpkg. Both are extremely powerful applications that allow you to manipulate software packages on your system. In addition to these basic package managers, there are applications that provide extra functionality such as network-based upgrading, package searching, and GUIs.

■**Note** Having different package formats and managers might seem strange—these are all Linux distributions, after all—but the reasons are mainly historical. When these distributions were originally created, the developers did not agree on how the package systems should work, so they created their own. Over the years, development on them has continued, and nowadays we have multiple different mature package systems and formats. Of course, if you use only one distribution, then you need to learn about just one type of package management.

Although all Linux distributions can contain thousands or tens of thousands of packages, broadly speaking these packages fall into three main categories:

- Application packages
- Library packages
- Development packages

Most *application packages* contain, as the name suggests, applications. These applications could range from a simple command-line editor to the whole OpenOffice productivity suite.

■**Note** OpenOffice is the open source equivalent of Microsoft Office. It contains a word processor, spreadsheet program, and presentation software, among other tools. It allows you to edit Microsoft Office documents and provides similar functionality to Microsoft Office.

Library packages contain files that are used by applications and the operating system to provide additional functionality. For instance, cryptography support is provided by the libssl package. Much like your community book library, Linux libraries are where applications can go to find the stuff they need without having to own it themselves. Because such libraries are often used by multiple applications, it makes sense to distribute them in a package of their own, rather than include a copy of each library with every application. If a library package is updated, all applications that make use of the library will now automatically use the updated version. The names of these packages often start with `lib`.

Development packages contain source code and header files that are required to compile software from source. These packages usually have names that end in `-dev` on Ubuntu or `-devel` on Red Hat. Most library packages have an accompanying development package, to allow for software development using these libraries. Generally, unless you are developing applications, you won't need to install these packages. But some applications do use them, and if you choose to compile applications from source and install them that way, you'll often require development packages to do this.

Because the package management tools used by Red Hat and Ubuntu are completely different, we cover each in its own section. We'll first cover package management on Red Hat and then on Ubuntu.

WHAT'S A PACKAGE?

Packages are designed to make managing applications easier. They are generally constructed from the source code of an application and have logic that tells your distribution where to put the application's binaries, files, and configuration. We're going to use two types of packages, RPMs and deb files. Both package types are archives that contain other files. So what's inside these packages? Packages contain data, metadata, and sometimes control files. The data is the files that will be installed. Control files contain descriptive information about the package, scripts for user interaction, and scripts that manage automated pre- or postinstallation tasks.

Package Management on Red Hat Linux

At the most basic level, the way applications are managed on Red Hat–based systems is via the Red Hat Package Management tool, or `rpm`. It is used on distributions like Red Hat Enterprise Linux, CentOS, Mandriva, and the Fedora Project. The `rpm` tool itself is designed for installing, manipulating, querying, and deleting packages on the local system.

■**Tip** You can identify RPM packages by their suffix of `.rpm`. Each RPM package is built using information contained in a `spec` file. The `spec` file contains metadata about what is in each package and describes the way the package should be installed on your system. We will talk a little bit about `spec` files and how to build your own packages later in this chapter.

The `rpm` tool provides the basic package management tasks like installing and removing packages, but it doesn't handle a variety of other tasks, such as retrieving dependency packages (i.e., packages you need to install alongside, or prior to, a particular package installation) from online repositories or the regular automation of package updates.

■**Note** Having worked with Linux for a long time, we can attest that managing a Linux system is now many times easier thanks to smart package management. In the old days, installing a package or updating an application could involve hours of hunting for *dependencies*, packages that should be on your system before you install and use another package. Before these managers arrived, you had to build all your applications from source code and deal with all the conflicts that arose. Nowadays it is much simpler. But, of course, if you really want to do so, you can always build from source—Linux is so powerful, it gives you that choice. We'll talk about building from source in the last section of this chapter.

To provide some of the functionality that rpm lacks, most Red Hat–derived distributions have some additional tools. Most of these tools assist by retrieving packages from repositories (where the packages are stored; most distributions have a number of repositories available online) and presenting them to be installed. These sorts of tools include Red Hat's Red Hat Network (RHN, which is Red Hat's commercial update service that we covered briefly in Chapter 2), Duke University's Yellowdog Updater Modified (Yum) or yum, and Mandriva's urpmi. In this section, we're going to focus on the tools provided as part of Red Hat Enterprise Linux, but the information contained within will also help with other Red Hat–based distributions like CentOS, Fedora, and Mandriva.

In the sections that follow, we'll take you through package installation via the GUI interface and the command line, and how to use the rpm tool itself to manage individual packages. We'll also show you how to configure your Red Hat Enterprise Linux host to use RHN and how to build your own RPM packages.

Getting Started

On Red Hat–based hosts like Red Hat Enterprise Linux, CentOS, and Fedora, the easiest way to manage your packages is via the desktop. You can access the GUI tools for this after logging in to your desktop.

Two programs on the desktop enable you to administer all the packages on your host and allow you to list, search, install, upgrade, or remove packages. They have the very basic names of Package Manager and Package Updater. You use Package Manager to list, search, install, and remove your packages, and you use Package Updater to update your packages from some remote repository.

For RHEL hosts, you will need to have a subscription to get the full value from both of these package management tools, and we explain in the next section how to connect to RHN.

■**Note** You might want to skip down to the "Red Hat Network (RHN)" section if you haven't already set up RHN. We also looked at RHN setup in Chapter 2 when we installed a Red Hat host.

For Fedora and CentOS hosts, you can use both tools without the need for a subscription.

You can find both package management tools by selecting Applications ➤ Add/Remove Software for the Package Manager program, or by selecting Applications ➤ System Tools ➤ Software Updater for the Software Updater program. Figure 7-1 shows how to find Software Updater from the Red Hat desktop.

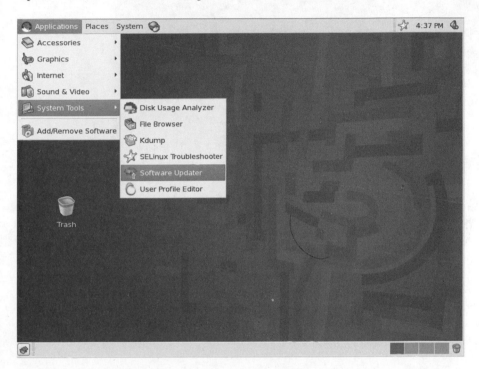

Figure 7-1. *Finding package management software on RHEL*

These tools are very easy to use, as we demonstrate in the next sections.

Package Updater Program

One of the first things you will notice when you log in to your Red Hat or Fedora GUI desktop is the update alert icon in the top-right corner of the window. If you have a valid subscription, this icon informs you of any security updates available to apply to your host. For our Red Hat host, as you can see in Figure 7-2, the icon informs us we have 36 updates available. To get this information, our host has contacted RHN or our online update repository and queried for any available updates. This feature allows us to update the packages on our host.

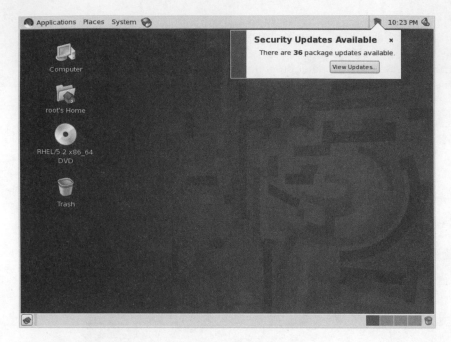

Figure 7-2. *Security alert shown after logon*

Clicking the alert icon brings us directly to the Package Updater for Red Hat Enterprise Linux, as shown in Figure 7-3. This is the same application you saw earlier that is available via the Applications menu. The application is called pup, and it is a graphical front end for installing updates via Yum (we explain Yum in greater detail in the "Yellowdog Updater Modified (Yum)" section).

To apply any updates to your host, you need to be a user with root privileges. You can gain access to root privileges by supplying the password when prompted and running the pup command under sudo, or by logging in and running updates as the root user. If you do not have root privileges under your current user, you will be prompted for the root password here.

In Figure 7-3, you can also see the packages that can be updated from RHN.

If an update requires a reboot of your host, you will see a circular arrow icon next to the update concerned, as shown in Figure 7-4. Being basically a new operating system, kernels, for example, require a reboot.

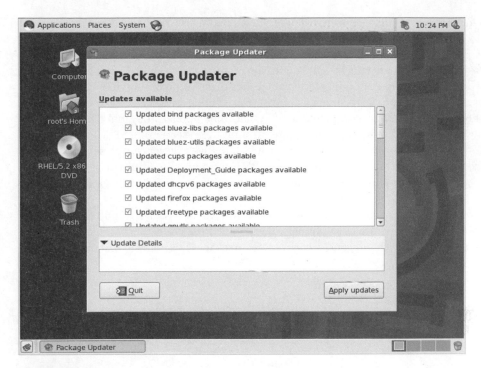

Figure 7-3. *Updates available*

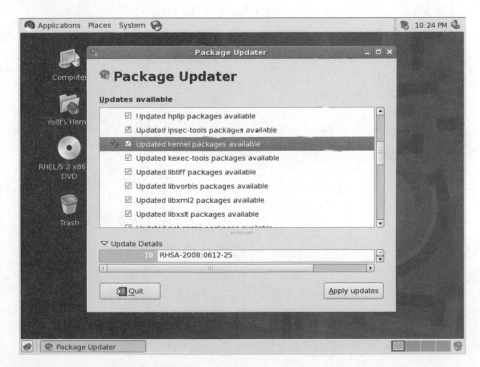

Figure 7-4. *A kernel update requiring a reboot*

Clicking the Apply updates button will upgrade all packages whose boxes you check. You can deselect any packages you do not wish to upgrade.

It is a good practice to understand what is being upgraded, and you should at least take note of the packages that are concerned. The reasons for this are twofold. First, Linux hosts are managed mainly by configuration files, and sometimes these configuration files can be overwritten by applying an update, resulting in your services failing. Second, if you are changing a production server, it is important to understand that some updates may make your applications behave differently. For example, if you are running a web server providing a web-based application, then updating or changing the version of the web server or web service could break or change the behavior of your application. It's important to read and understand the changes occurring with an update; this information is usually specified in the Update Details box.

The first time you apply updates to your system, you will be asked to import the Red Hat, Inc. release key. All RPM packages can be signed with a PGP/GPG key that acts like a signature for your host to verify the validity and security of any packages it is going to install.

■**Tip** PGP/GPG is a public key encryption tool. You can read about PGP/GPG at http://en.wikipedia. org/wiki/Pretty_Good_Privacy and http://en.wikipedia.org/wiki/Public-key_cryptography.

If the package you are updating doesn't match the PGP signature, it could be malicious or not from RHN. In Figure 7-5, we are asked to import the Red Hat key.

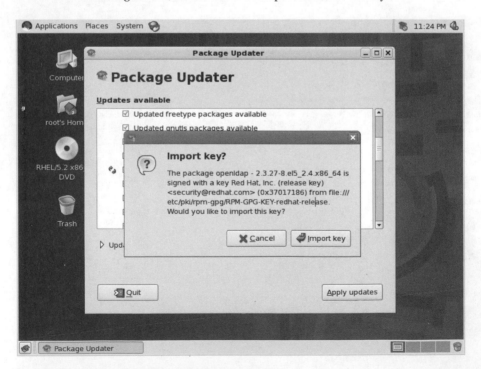

Figure 7-5. *Importing the Red Hat PGP key signature*

After you elect to import the key, the update process will begin downloading and installing the packages, as you can see in Figure 7-6.

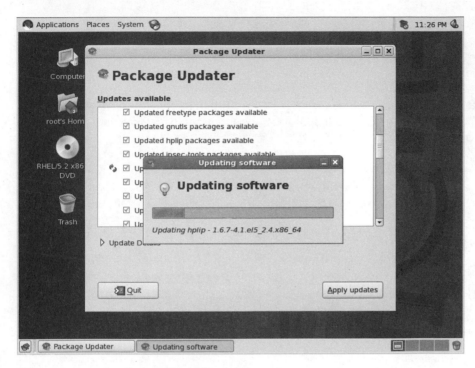

Figure 7-6. *Downloading and installing packages*

Once the process is complete, you may be asked to reboot. In this case, you have upgraded the kernel and your system will require a reboot if you wish to make use of that new kernel. You can choose not to reboot now and reboot the host at a more convenient time. If you choose to reboot, your host will begin to shut down and restart.

■**Note** If your host is a production server, make sure this is a good time to reboot and update, and tell your users or customers you are doing so. Otherwise, they may find themselves without whatever service your server provides without warning.

As you can see in Figure 7-7, the system is asking for a reboot.

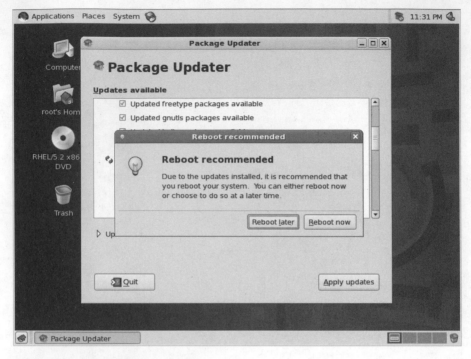

Figure 7-7. *Do you wish to reboot now?*

Because you installed a new kernel in this upgrade process, your /boot/grub/grub.conf file is rewritten with the new kernel set as the default. When your host restarts, it will now boot using the new kernel.

■**Tip** We discuss GRUB and the boot process in Chapters 2 and 5.

Your GRUB menu now presents two kernels for you to choose to boot into. As we explained, your newly installed kernel will be your default. You can see your choice of kernels in Figure 7-8.

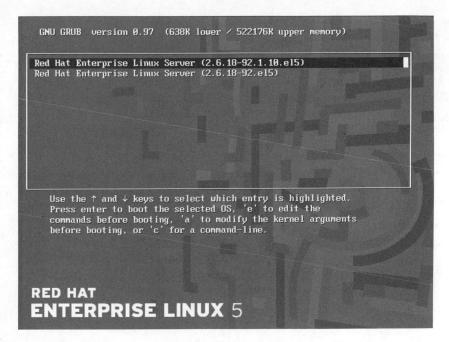

```
GNU GRUB  version 0.97  (638K lower / 522176K upper memory)

┌────────────────────────────────────────────────────────────────────────┐
│ Red Hat Enterprise Linux Server (2.6.18-92.1.10.el5)                   █ │
│ Red Hat Enterprise Linux Server (2.6.18-92.el5)                         │
│                                                                          │
│                                                                          │
│                                                                          │
│                                                                          │
│                                                                          │
└────────────────────────────────────────────────────────────────────────┘

     Use the ↑ and ↓ keys to select which entry is highlighted.
     Press enter to boot the selected OS, 'e' to edit the
     commands before booting, 'a' to modify the kernel arguments
     before booting, or 'c' for a command-line.


RED HAT
ENTERPRISE LINUX 5
```

Figure 7-8. *Choosing a kernel from the GRUB menu*

■**Note** There may be occasions when your new kernel does not behave in the manner you expect. Sometimes hardware stops working or applications fail for various reasons. You can use the GRUB menu to boot
into an older "known good" kernel until the problems are rectified.

Your host will boot into the default kernel unless you select an alternative within the timeout.
Interrupt the timeout by pressing any key and select from the menu the kernel you wish to boot
into by using the up and down arrows and the Enter key. Your host will now boot with all the new
package updates installed and applied.

Package Manager Program

We're now going to take a look at how to add and remove software using the Package Manager
application found under the menu Applications ➤ Add/Remove Software.

The application that this menu item runs is called pirut and, like its counterpart pup, it
is the graphical front end for Yum for installing, removing, updating, searching, and viewing
software packages on RHEL. It, too, requires root privileges and will prompt you for the root
user's password if you do not have these privileges.

In Figure 7-9, you can see that we have opened Package Manager, navigated to the List
tab, and selected the Available packages radio button to narrow down the list of packages
available to be installed. We have selected the nmap package, as indicated by the check in the
box next to it. When we click the Apply button, all selected packages will be installed (along
with their dependencies).

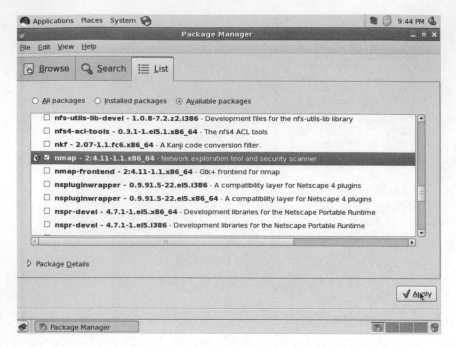

Figure 7-9. *Adding the nmap package using Package Manager*

After you click Apply to install the package, the confirmation dialog box shown in Figure 7-10 will appear.

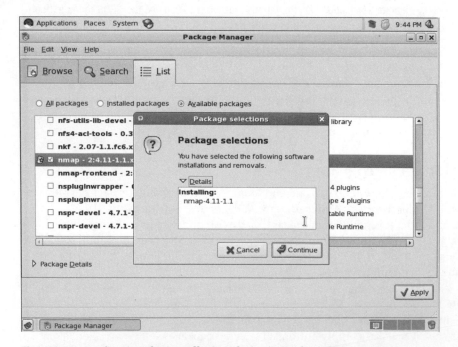

Figure 7-10. *Confirming the installation choice in Package Manager*

To remove an application using Package Manager, you simply use the Search tab to find Installed packages using the radio button and enter the name of the package to be removed in the search field. You can also remove packages using the List tab.

In Figure 7-11 we show that we have searched for the package nmap from the group of installed packages, and by deselecting the box next to the package we indicate that we wish to remove it. Clicking Apply will remove the application, and we'll get a confirmation screen similar to that shown in Figure 7-10.

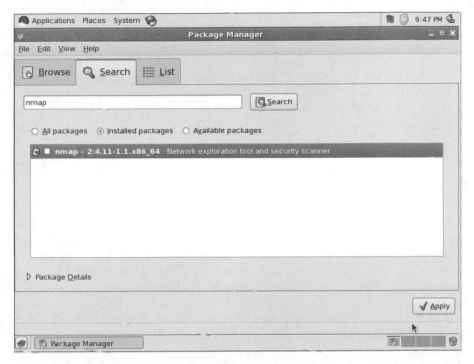

Figure 7-11. *Removing packages using Package Manager*

You can also use Package Manager to view installed packages, list available packages, and search for packages either installed on or available to your host. Package Manager offers a very quick and effective way to manage the packages on your host.

If you click the Browse tab, you will find that it is very similar to the dialog box available when you first selected the packages for your installation back in Chapter 2 (see Figure 2-17). As long as you have a valid subscription and a connection to the Internet, you will see the list of packages available to your host and a description of each package (otherwise, you will not see any information). Here you can select individual packages or package groups (e.g., Gnome Desktop or Office Productivity software groups) for installation or removal by checking the check boxes and clicking Apply.

■**Tip** You can use the command line to search for packages, update and add packages, or remove packages from your hosts. We'll talk about that in the "Yellowdog Updater Modified (Yum)" section later in this chapter.

Red Hat Network (RHN)

If you are using Red Hat Enterprise Linux, then you will want to configure RHN. This subscription-based service provides regular updates and patches for your Red Hat host. RHN offers a stable release cycle and the ability to budget costs associated with running your systems. It also gives you access to support from Red Hat's engineers as well as the comfort of having someone to call on if you encounter difficulty. To use the service, your hosts will need to be able to access the Internet.

■**Note** If you're not using RHEL, then you can skip this section.

With RHN, you can manage one system or thousands through the Red Hat web portal, `https://rhn.redhat.com`. The portal enables you to see the state of your systems and their status in relation to security patches, and it also enables you to download the software you have access to. In this section, we'll also show you how to manage your packages from the portal.

Before you can use RHN, you have to register your host with Red Hat. You may have already completed this step during the first boot of your host in Chapter 2, but we'll take you through it again just in case.

As we explained in Chapter 2, when you buy a Red Hat software subscription, you receive entitlements, and with each entitlement you are able to register one host to receive software updates and patches.

To register your system (if you haven't already done so during host installation in Chapter 2), you need to launch the Software Updater tool that we introduced earlier in this section. This will make a connection to RHN and check if your host has an active subscription. If you have a subscription, you will be presented with the Package Updater program. If not, you will be presented with a series of screens that enable you to register your host with RHN.

The first screen, shown in Figure 7-12, is a welcome screen giving brief information about registering for software updates.

The next window allows you to choose the location from which you source the updates. Here you can choose the Red Hat Network, or you can use an RHN Satellite server or an RHN Proxy server. These last two are part of the Red Hat provisioning suite of applications that is used if you have many hosts under management. We will choose RHN, as shown in Figure 7-13.

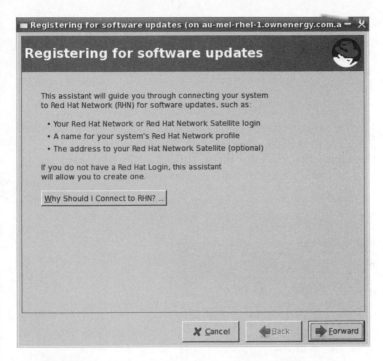

Figure 7-12. *First software updates registration window*

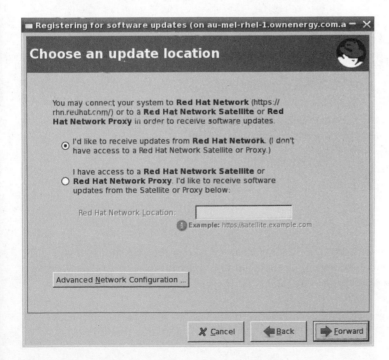

Figure 7-13. *Choosing the location of your updates*

You will now be asked to enter your username and password. This is the same username and password that you use to sign into your RHN web portal. You may already have a username and password previously registered, you may have created one while installing your host as described in Chapter 2, or you can create one now at `https://rhn.redhat.com`.

■**Note** Registering alone doesn't entitle you to updates—you still need to buy a software subscription and assign an entitlement to your host. The Red Hat site has instructions on how to do this.

In Figure 7-14 we have specified the username as `username`. You would put your RHN username here in its place.

Figure 7-14. *Entering your username and password*

Next, you will be given the opportunity to enter your system name and choose if you wish to send hardware and software information to Red Hat. This information is useful for getting the appropriate updates for your system, and we recommend you check these boxes as we have in Figure 7-15.

In Figure 7-16 you can see we are given an opportunity to review our subscription information. This will most likely be different from your own subscription information.

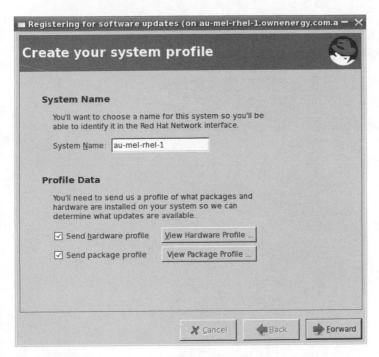

Figure 7-15. *System profile name and hardware and software information*

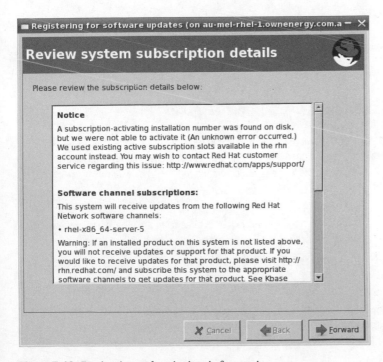

Figure 7-16. *Reviewing subscription information*

You will now be given confirmation that you have successfully set up your system for updates like in Figure 7-17. If you receive any errors about your activation not succeeding, you should contact Red Hat Support.

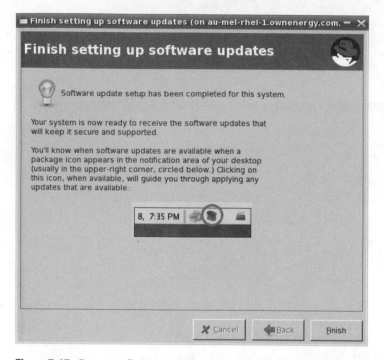

Figure 7-17. *Congratulations screen*

REGISTERING VIA THE COMMAND LINE

The alternative method to using the GUI is to use the command line to register your system. This is an example of how quickly you can achieve the same outcome by using the `rhnreg_ks` command. First, you can check the options available to you by passing the `rhnreg_ks` command the `--help` switch:

```
$ sudo rhnreg_ks --help
```

This will show all the options for you. The main options you are interested in are `username`, `password`, `profilename`, and `activationkey`. Using those options, you can see how easy it is to register your system from the command line. Here you should replace all the options enclosed in angle brackets `< >` with your own details.

```
$ sudo rhnreg_ks --username=<username> --password=<password> ➥
--profilename=<au-mel-rhel-1> --email=<sysadmin@yourdomain> ➥
--activationkey=<keyfromRHN>
```

Once registered, you can use the `https://rhn.redhat.com` web portal to manage all your software maintenance entitlements. You can see which systems have which packages and their current version. Your hosts can log in automatically and download important security patches for you and schedule package installs or deletions from inside the web portal.

Logging on to `http://rhn.redhat.com` and navigating to Systems, you can see that your new system is registered. Figure 7-18 shows that au-mel-rhel-1 is registered and that it has 37 errata and 51 packages available.

Figure 7-18. *RHN now records our system.*

Your host will now automatically poll RHN and determine if there are any updates to be installed for as long as you have a valid subscription (and a working connection to the Internet).

From the information in Figure 7-18, you can see that a number of errata packages are available for our host. You can get greater detail on these updates for your host by clicking the number (e.g., 37) in the Errata column, which links you to the Errata page. The Errata page gives a brief synopsis of each update and provides a link to the more detailed advisory (see Figure 7-19).

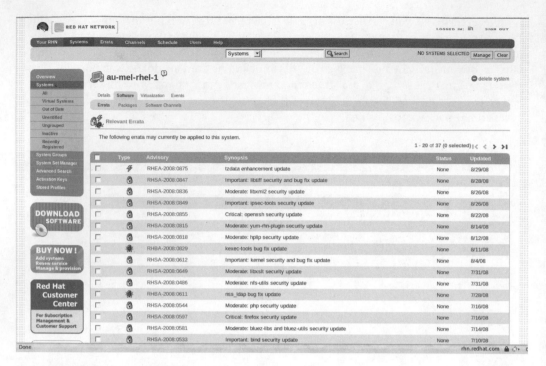

Figure 7-19. *RHN Errata page for our system*

Going back to the RHN page in Figure 7-18, notice the red exclamation point icon. That indicates to you which hosts require updates. As your host periodically checks in with RHN to see if it has any new updates, it also checks for any scheduled events (updates) to perform. You can use the RHN portal to schedule your host to update these errata packages, and they will be performed at the next check-in. If you click the exclamation point icon shown in Figure 7-18, you will be taken to the Confirm Errata Updates page. You will see a Confirm button at the bottom of this page, as shown in Figure 7-20.

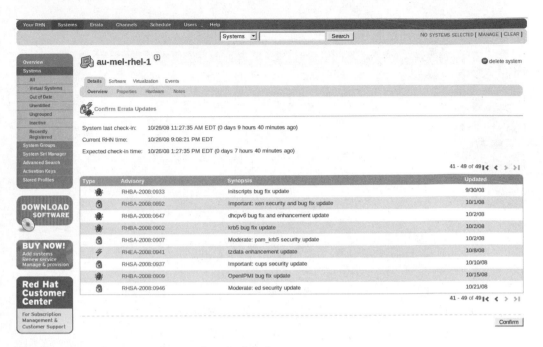

Figure 7-20. *Confirming updates to be scheduled*

■**Note** The process outlined in this section is not the only way to schedule your updates so that they are performed at the next check-in. You will see the red exclamation point icon on many RHN pages relating to your host. Those accompanied by the caption Update Now will automatically confirm and add these events to the schedule. All pending events for your host can be seen on the Events page for your system.

Clicking the Confirm button in Figure 7-20 will set the updates to Pending in the Scheduler. In Figure 7-21, you can see the updates are now in a Pending state on the System Software Errata page.

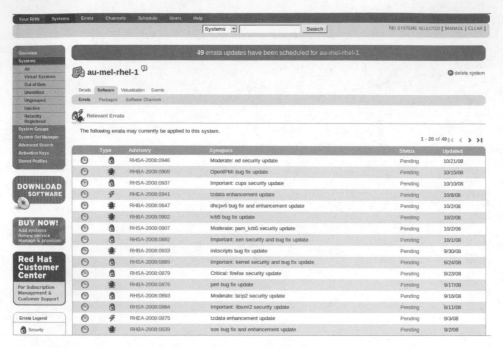

Figure 7-21. *Errata updates pending*

You can also cancel those update events by going to the System Events Pending page and selecting all or individual updates you wish to cancel. We are going to cancel all the pending events by clicking the Select All button and then the Cancel Events button, as shown in Figure 7-22.

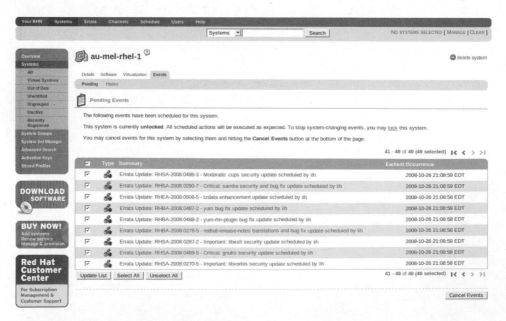

Figure 7-22. *Selecting events to be canceled*

After clicking the Cancel Events button, you will be taken to the confirmation page, where the updates you have selected are shown and the Cancel Selected Events button is available. By clicking the Cancel Selected Events button, you are confirming that you don't want those updates available to your host next time it checks in.

If you want to schedule the updates again, you can go to the System Software Errata page and select and confirm them again. In fact, you can schedule new packages to be installed on your host by going to the System Software Packages page and selecting any package you wish to install from the list on the Install New Packages page. For our host, there are almost 2,000 available packages that we could install.

To install a new package, you first navigate to the package you wish to install by using the alphabetical listing. For example, say you want to install nmap, a handy network-mapping tool. As shown in Figure 7-23, you can click the package you require and then click Install Selected Packages. That takes you to a confirmation page where, once it's confirmed, a new event will be added to the schedule.

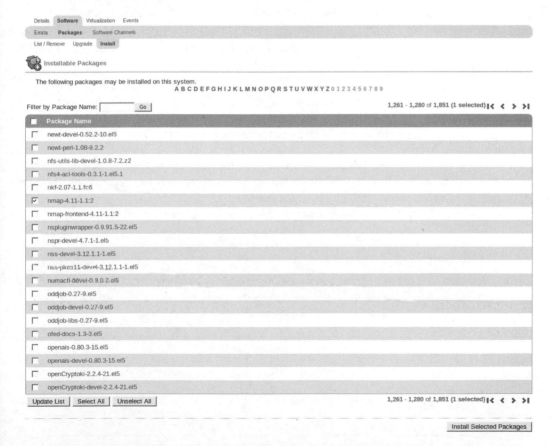

Figure 7-23. *Installing new packages via the RHN portal*

You are now likely beginning to see the beauty of managing your host via the RHN portal. We have updated our host and added new software to it without even logging on to it. It doesn't take long to think of the possibilities of managing thousands of hosts this way using the RHN portal. By dividing your hosts in groups, you can use the preceding actions for the group, and those updates or additional software installations will take place automatically to all the hosts within it.

Yellowdog Updater Modified (Yum)

For Red Hat–based distributions, one of the most common tools used to install, upgrade, or update a system is a command-line-based tool called Yellowdog Updater Modified (Yum). Yum provides the ability to search and find software available to your system on remote repositories. Repositories, as explained earlier, are collections of packages made available for your distribution by the distribution's vendor, interest groups, universities, and ISPs.

■**Note** Yum is available on Red Hat Enterprise Linux, Fedora, and CentOS, as well as other Red Hat–derived distributions. It is generally the default method for updating and maintaining the packages on those distributions via the command line.

Yum also has the ability to solve dependency issues by fetching the packages required to install any individual package. It uses a database to query what packages are installed on your host and then compares that to package lists provided by the repository. If you need an additional package or packages to meet any dependencies, then these are also downloaded and installed.

Yum is simple to use. On the command line, you simply type **yum** and one of a number of potential actions, such as **install**, **remove**, or **list**, and then potentially the name of the package or packages on which you wish to take action, for example:

```
# yum install nmap
```

■**Note** You need root privileges to run the yum command, either by being signed in as the root user or making use of the sudo command. We recommend using the sudo command, as we demonstrated in Chapter 4.

Table 7-1 lists the main options provided with Yum.

Table 7-1. *Options Available with Yum*

Option	Description
search	Allows you to search for packages available for download
list	Lists all the packages available for download
install	Installs a package or packages
check-update	Lists packages available for update
update	Updates the package specified or downloads and installs any available updates

Option	Description
remove	Removes a package or packages from your host
info	Provides package information about a package
provides	Tells you what package a particular file or feature belongs to
list updates	Lists all the packages with updates available only
list available	Lists all the available packages only
localinstall	Installs a locally downloaded RPM package
clean all	Cleans up downloaded package files that are no longer needed

Next, we'll look at each action and how we might use it.

Installing a Package with Yum

Let's get started with Yum by trying to install a package. In a normal situation, we would first search for the package to make sure it's available. We've chosen to install the nmap package (which, as mentioned previously, is a useful network-mapping and scanning tool). We will use the search option to see if the package is available, as you can see in Listing 7-1.

Listing 7-1. *Searching with Yum*

```
$ sudo yum search nmap
```

■**Note** Rather than using the root user in Listing 7-1, we're running yum using the sudo command, as demonstrated in Chapter 4.

In Listing 7-1, we've issued the yum command with the search option and then specified the name of the package we wish to search for. This produces a list of available packages that have nmap in their name. The yum command is not smart enough to know exactly what you're looking for, so it provides you with anything with nmap in the name.

You can also search for parts of the package name if you are unsure of the complete name. So, for example, you could type **yum search map** and get a list of all the packages with the pattern map in their description or name.

■**Tip** You can refine the list of packages by using the grep command we showed you in Chapter 3. For example, you could type yum search php | grep pear, and this will refine the list of the packages that are related to PHP by searching for the term pear and then displaying the resulting list of packages.

You can also use yum list see all the packages available from your repository, and you might also find yum grouplist useful to see the groupings of packages. Groups are a collection of individual packages that provide a certain application for convenience. So, for example, installing the KDE group will provide everything for running your KDE desktop, and installing the Text-based Internet group will provide the common packages needed to provide console access to web applications (e.g., the text-based browser Lynx and the mail client Mutt).

With that information, to install the nmap package we run the command in Listing 7-2.

Listing 7-2. *Installing the nmap Package*

```
$ sudo yum install nmap
$ sudo yum groupinstall 'Text-based Internet'
```

The first line will download and install a package called nmap, and the second will install all the packages in the group Text-based Internet. If any dependencies are required, they will also be downloaded, and you will be queried if you want to install them, too. If you don't install all the required dependencies, then you will not be able to install the package you require.

Updating Your Repositories

From time to time, your repository cache data will get out of date as new packages are added to and updated in the repository. It is a good practice to issue the command in Listing 7-3 to refresh your repository details before performing any package installation.

Listing 7-3. *Keeping Repositories Up to Date*

```
$ sudo yum check-update
```

Once the repository is updated, you can ask Yum to install any available updates by running the following command:

```
$ sudo yum update
```

You can also update one or more individual packages, as shown in Listing 7-4.

Listing 7-4. *Updating Packages with Yum*

```
$ sudo yum update nmap
$ sudo yum update nmap mutt
```

■**Note** You can upgrade from one version of a distribution to another using Yum (e.g., from Fedora 9 to Fedora 10). This isn't a recommended approach, however, as it can be risky and result in damage to your host. If you want to read further about this approach, please see http://fedoraproject.org/wiki/YumUpgradeFaq.

Removing Packages with Yum

You can also remove packages with Yum, as shown in Listing 7-5.

Listing 7-5. *Removing Packages with Yum*

```
$ sudo yum remove nmap
```

The remove option used in Listing 7-5 will leave a few files on your host, primarily configuration files, after the package has been removed. This means if you reinstall the package, you don't have to re-create your configuration. If you want to remove all files, you can use the erase option.

```
$ sudo yum erase nmap
```

Performing Additional Yum Tasks

You can do many other things with the yum command. Let's go through some other commands briefly.

The following command provides information about the package you're querying, such as its size, version, and installation status; a description of the package; and other useful information.

```
$ sudo yum info kernel
```

If you want to find what package provides a particular file, you could use the following.

```
$ sudo yum provides /bin/bash
bash-3.2-22.fc9.x86_64 : The GNU Bourne Again shell (bash) version 3.2
Matched from:
Filename    : /bin/bash
```

The preceding command tells you that the /bin/bash binary is provided by the bash package and describes the version and details about the package.

To see the list of updates available for your host, you would issue the following command:

```
$ sudo yum list updates
```

If your host is up to date, this command should produce no results.

Next, you can list all the packages that are available to be installed on your host by issuing the following command:

```
$ sudo yum list available
```

The preceding command lists all the available packages that are not already installed for your host from your repositories.

Finally, you can clean your cache directory (where Yum temporarily stores the packages you have downloaded). You would clear the cache if you needed to reclaim some disk space.

```
$ sudo yum clean all
```

The preceding command removes cached packages and headers contained in the /var/cache/yum cache directories.

Configuring Yum

The Yum application can be configured in a variety of ways. Yum has its configuration files stored under `/etc/yum.conf` and `/etc/yum.repos.d/`, and it stores state files in the directories `/var/lib/yum` and `/var/cache/yum`.

■**Note** State files tell Yum what is already installed on your host and also hold cached versions of downloaded packages. Be careful not to delete these directories, as you can easily corrupt your package database.

You will not normally need to make changes to the default `/etc/yum.conf`. An example of when you might want to change configuration is to add a proxy server that Yum should use when downloading packages. The defaults will generally suit most environments. A full list of the available configuration settings for Yum is available through the `yum.conf` man page.

```
$ man yum.conf
```

Though you will rarely change how Yum is configured, you may wish to add additional repositories to Yum from which you can download additional packages. The files defining what repositories are available to Yum are contained in the `/etc/yum.repo.d` directory. Let's look at a generic repository file:

```
$ cat /etc/yum.repo.d/myrepo.repo
[myrepo]
name=myrepo
baseurl=http://myrepo.mydomain.com/pub/linux/releases/$releasever/$basearch/os/
enabled=1
gpgcheck=1
gpgkey=http://myrepo.mydomain.com/linux/RPM-GPG-KEY-linux
```

Each of these options is explained in Table 7-2.

Table 7-2. *Options for Adding a Yum Repository*

Option	Description
`[repo-id]`	The `repo_id` is the unique name for the repository.
`name`	The `name` is a description of the repository.
`baseurl`	The `baseurl` is the URL to the repository. This is generally an HTTP URL, much like you would use in a web browser.
`enabled`	You can enable or disable the package by specifying 0 for disabled and 1 for enabled.
`gpgcheck`	This option tells Yum to check the GPG keys used to "sign" packages so that you can be sure the package hasn't been tampered with. Specifying 0 turns off checking and 1 indicates checking is on.
`gpgkey`	This is the URL where Yum should find the repository's GPG key.

In Listing 7-6, we have defined a new repository for a CentOS distribution.

Listing 7-6. *Adding a CentOS Repository in a Yum Repo File*

```
[source]
name=CentOS-releasever - Sources
baseurl=http://mirror.centos.org/centos/$releasever/os/SRPMS/
gpgcheck=1
enabled=1
gpgkey=http://mirror.centos.org/centos/RPM-GPG-KEY-CentOS-5
```

You can see that in the `baseurl` option we've specified a variable called `$releasever`. On Red Hat and CentOS, this variable defaults to the version of the `redhat-release` package. On Fedora, this variable defaults to the value of the `fedora-release` package. In both cases, this variable indicates the current version of your distribution. For example, for Fedora 9 the version would be as shown in Listing 7-7.

Listing 7-7. *Showing the Current Release of Your Distribution*

```
$ sudo yum info fedora-release
Installed Packages
Name        : fedora-release
Arch        : noarch
Version     : 9
Release     : 5.transition
Size        : 65 k
Repo        : installed
Summary     : Fedora release files
URL         : http://fedoraproject.org
License     : GPLv2
Description: Fedora release files such as yum configs and various /etc/ files ➥
that define the release.
```

This variable is a quick shortcut that enables us to specify a more generic URL. Yum uses this URL to find the right repository and substitutes the $releasever variable with the version of your distribution. For example, on version 5 of the CentOS distribution, the following:

```
http://mirror.centos.org/fedora/$releasever/os/SRPMS/
```

becomes this:

```
http://mirror.centos.org/centos/5/os/SRPMS/
```

Red Hat Package Management (RPM)

We've just looked at the yum command and how to use it to manage packages. In many ways, the yum command is just a wrapper around another command, rpm. The rpm command is the basic tool for manipulating the RPM files that contain your packages. While you may not often need to use the rpm command directly, it is important that you understand how it works.

To get an overview of the command, we recommend that you first read its man page.

```
$ man rpm
```

On rpm's man page, you can see the tasks the rpm tool can perform: query, install, upgrade, and remove packages.

Let's look at these options in more detail. Table 7-3 shows the major options you can pass to rpm and what they do. Each option has a number of flags that you add.

Table 7-3. *The Major* rpm *Options and Flags*

Options and Flags	Description
-q | --query	Allows you to query the RPM database and find information about installed packages on your host
-i | --install	Installs a local package on your host
-e | --erase	Removes a package from your host
-U | --upgrade	Upgrades an existing package or installs a package on your host if it is not already installed
-F | --freshen	Upgrades a package only if an earlier version is installed
-V | --verify	Verifies an installed package

Querying Packages

To begin, we'll look at querying the packages that are installed on your host, using the -q or --query option. To find out what is installed on your host, the rpm tool queries data stored in a database. This database is updated when packages are installed and removed.

Note The RPM database knows only your host's current state; it doesn't know what was removed yesterday or what the previous version of a package was. The record of what was installed, removed, or upgraded, or data about previous versions, is best obtained from your host's log files. You can see a log of the actions that the rpm command has taken in the /var/log/rpmpkgs file.

Let's now use rpm to examine the heart of the Linux operating system, the kernel. Supposed you are asked, "What kernels do we have installed?" To find the answer, you can use the rpm command, as shown in Listing 7-8.

Note You can also find the kernel you are currently using by issuing the uname -r command.

Listing 7-8. *Querying the Kernel Version*

```
# rpm --query kernel
kernel-2.6.18-92.el5
kernel-2.6.18-95.el5
```

Here we've run the rpm command with the --query flag and specified the name of the package we want to query, in our case kernel. You can see that this has produced a list of the kernels installed.

■**Note** You see more than one kernel in Listing 7-8 because you can have more than one kernel installed. This does not mean you have multiple kernels running at the same time; rather, you have multiple potential kernels you *could* run.

Those numbers at the end of each kernel installed are different versions. One is 2.6.18.92 and the other is 2.6.18-95. Both are for the Red Hat Enterprise Linux 5 system (.el5).

■**Tip** We discuss in Chapter 5 how you can select the kernel you want to boot.

What if you don't know the name of package you are looking for? Or what if you want to see all the packages installed? In those cases, you can use the command in Listing 7-9.

Listing 7-9. *Querying All Packages*

```
# rpm --query --all
```

This command, which uses the --query flag together with the --all flag, indicating that you are querying all packages, lists all the packages installed.

As you will see, this list can be quite long. Suppose instead you want to find only any package whose name contains php. You could then pipe that output through the grep tool, which searches the output for the string php, as you can see in Listing 7-10.

Listing 7-10. *Querying All Using Piping and grep*

```
# rpm --query --all | grep php
php-common-5.1.6-20.el5
php-cli-5.1.6-20.el5
php-5.1.6-20.el5
php-ldap-5.1.6-20.el5
```

■**Note** We cover the grep command and piping in Chapter 3.

Listing 7-10 shows that piping the output of the query to the grep command has reduced the list from thousands of packages to four packages with the string php in their name (an empty list would indicate there is no package installed with that string in its name).

Let's find out a bit more information about our kernel package. In Listing 7-11, we use the query option combined with the --info option to find out more information about one of our installed kernels.

Listing 7-11. *Getting Information About Packages*

```
# rpm -q --info kernel-2.6.18-92.el5
Name        : kernel                    Relocations: (not relocatable)
Version     : 2.6.18                        Vendor: Red Hat, Inc.
Release     : 92.el5                    Build Date: Wed 30 Apr 2008 ➥
04:10:41 AM EST
Install Date: Fri 15 Aug 2008 11:18:29 AM EST ➥
Build Host: ls20-bc2-13.build.redhat.com
Group       : System Environment/Kernel   Source RPM: kernel-2.6.18-92.el5.src.rpm
Size        : 82381879                     License: GPLv2
Signature   : DSA/SHA1, Thu 01 May 2008 07:42:12 AM EST, Key ID 5326810137017186
Packager    : Red Hat, Inc. <http://bugzilla.redhat.com/bugzilla>
URL         : http://www.kernel.org/
Summary     : The Linux kernel (the core of the Linux operating system)
Description :
The kernel package contains the Linux kernel (vmlinuz), the core of any
Linux operating system.  The kernel handles the basic functions
of the operating system:  memory allocation, process allocation, device
input and output, etc.
```

Listing 7-11 has produced a lot of information. Some of it may not mean very much to you initially, but let's look at some of the data. You can see the version number, who produced the package (in this case, Red Hat), and the dates when it was built and installed. You can also see what group the package is in, as each package on your host belongs to a group of like packages. You saw this when you installed your host in Chapter 2 and selected the packages you wanted as part of that process.

In addition, you can see the license the package is released under (in this case, the GPLv2 license), the size of the package and, most important, a description and summary of the package and some links to more information about the package.

Sometimes you will want to know what package installed a particular file or command. You can also use the rpm tool to query this information. For example, we have the /bin/bash command installed on our host, and we can find out what installed this command by using rpm as shown in Listing 7-12.

Listing 7-12. *Using query and whatprovides*

```
# rpm --query --whatprovides /bin/bash
bash-3.2-21.el5
```

Listing 7-12 tells us that the package Bash is responsible for the file /bin/bash, and it also informs us of the version number of the installed Bash package.

So now we know that Bash provided that file, but what other files on our system belong to the bash package? Armed with the information from --whatprovides, we can see what other files belong to the Bash package by using the `--query --list` options as shown in Listing 7-13.

Listing 7-13. *Using* `query` *and* `list`

```
# rpm --query --list bash
/bin/bash
/bin/sh
/etc/skel/.bash_logout
<snip> ...
```

Listing 7-13 displays a truncated list of all the files present in the bash package.

Installing Packages

The rpm tool is also used to install or upgrade packages. To install packages, you need to download the required RPM file and then use the rpm tool to install it on your host.

Note If you were using the yum command or the Add/Remove Package GUI tool, downloading the required RPM file would be done automatically. This is one reason it's better to use these tools rather than working with RPM files and the rpm command directly.

To demonstrate, let's download an individual RPM file using the wget command and install it.

Note The wget command is a network downloader (it can act like a web browser), and it can fetch files from websites, among other things.

In Listing 7-14, we download the files from the Nmap website and then list our directory to confirm that they are there. We are downloading two versions of the Nmap application so we can first show how to install the application and then how to upgrade to a newer version.

Listing 7-14. *Downloading Packages from the Internet*

```
$ wget http://mirror.centos.org/centos/5/os/SRPMS/nmap-4.11-1.1.src.rpm
```

In Listing 7-15, we use the command `rpm --install --verbose --hash` to install the RPM file.

Listing 7-15. *Installing Packages with rpm*

```
# rpm --install --verbose --hash nmap-4.11-1.1.src.rpm
Preparing...                ######################################### [100%]
1:nmap                      ######################################### [100%]
```

The `--install` option tells RPM to install the package, the `--verbose` option tells RPM to show us what it is doing, and the `--hash` option tells RPM to produce the hash marks (#) indicating the progress of the installation.

■**Caution** If you don't have other packages installed that Nmap depends on, then this installation will fail with an error message. This is another reason that using Yum or the GUI tools is much better for package management—they take care of installing and removing dependencies for you.

Removing Packages

With the `rpm` command, you can also remove applications from your host, as you can see in Listing 7-16.

Listing 7-16. *Removing Packages with* `rpm`

```
# rpm --erase nmap
```

The `--erase` option removes the `nmap` package completely from your system. Table 7-4 presents some other flags that you may find useful when erasing packages.

Table 7-4. *Extra Options for* `--erase`

Option	Description
`--noscripts`	Turns off all scripts associated with the package
`--nodeps`	Doesn't check dependencies before uninstalling
`--test`	Must be used in conjunction with `--vv`; shows what will be deleted when run

The first option shown in Table 7-4, `--noscripts`, tells RPM to remove the package without running any removal scripts associated with the package. This may leave some files from the package on your host. The `--nodeps` option removes only this package but leaves behind any dependencies. Lastly, the `--test` option allows you to do a trial run of the package removal. In combination with the `--vv` option, it shows what will be deleted when the command is run without actually deleting the package.

■**Tip** This section provided a very brief introduction to the `rpm` tool. We don't recommend you use it, however; rather, we suggest you make use of the GUI tools and the `yum` command introduced earlier in this chapter.

Building an RPM Package from Source

Why would you need to build a package from source? Well, sometimes you'll require a patch to the source, or perhaps you would like to build a more recent version of the package. If this is the case, you can take a couple of approaches.

Many packages have what are called *upstream* RPMs. Upstream RPMs are packages that contain a newer version of the application than the one shipped with your distribution. Frequently they are built by the developer of an application or another member of the application's development community. They will have newer patches of code or newer features that you may require, but they will be more edgy and could contain bugs and problems. These upstream RPMs will often be available on an application's website.

■**Caution** Upstream RPMs files can be built by anyone. They may not be stable, secure, or regularly maintained. You should exercise caution in using them.

The second approach is to download the source for the application you need to update and build your own RPMs. This sort of package creation goes beyond the scope of this book, but some excellent references are available online that can help you create your own RPM files:

- *Maximum RPM*: http://www.rpm.org/max-rpm-snapshot/

- *RPM Guide*: http://docs.fedoraproject.org/drafts/rpm-guide-en/

- *Packaging Software with RPM, Part 1*: http://www.ibm.com/developerworks/library/l-rpm1/

- *Creating RPMs*: http://pmc.ucsc.edu/~dmk/notes/RPMs/Creating_RPMs.html

It should be pointed out that creating your own packages from source can take some time depending on the complexity of the package you are trying to build and the number of dependencies it has. That is not to stop you from trying, but more to warn you about the sometimes long and treacherous road building your own packages can become.

Package Management on Ubuntu

Managing packages on Ubuntu servers is usually done using command-line tools, because the Ubuntu Server Edition does not install a GUI by default. In this section, we will first cover the command-line tools to manage packages. After that, we will look at a graphical package manager, Synaptic, that you can use if you have a GUI installed on your Ubuntu host.

The most common way to add software on Ubuntu hosts is to install packages from online software repositories via command-line tools. The distribution offers online software repositories containing over 22,000 ready-to-install packages. Over the years, several tools

have been created to help you add applications to your Ubuntu hosts from remote repositories. These tools provide the Ubuntu equivalent of Yum for Red Hat–based distributions.
We're going to look at two command-line tools:

- aptitude

- dpkg

These tools are both installed by default on Ubuntu hosts. The aptitude tool allows you
to install, remove, update, and search packages from online repositories. It is the preferred
way to manage packages, so we'll cover this tool in the most detail.

The dpkg tool is the base command-line tool used to install and remove packages. Aptitude uses dpkg internally to manage packages. We'll take only a brief look at dpkg because
you won't have much need to use it often.

Aptitude

You can work with the aptitude tool in two ways: interactively via menus and dialog boxes
or by passing it instructions via the command line. For beginning users, the easiest way is to
use aptitude's menu-based user interface. Let's start it up and have a look.

$ aptitude

After processing the package lists, aptitude presents its main window, as shown in
Figure 7-24.

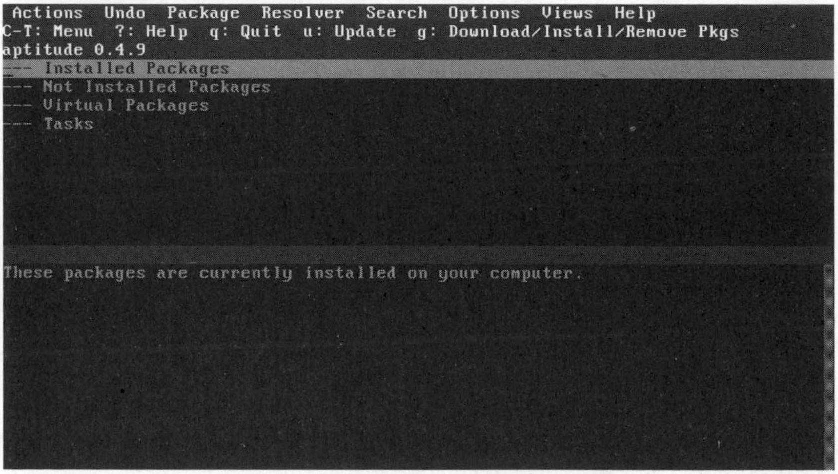

Figure 7-24. *The main aptitude screen*

The main screen consists of a menu bar, a command list, a window list, status information, the package list window, and an information window. Your cursor will first appear
in the package list window. You can move up and down the lists using the arrow keys and
expand a highlighted item by pressing Enter.

Press Enter to expand the Installed Packages list, then select and expand the base list,
and then expand the main list. You will see an alphabetical listing of the currently installed

packages in the main section. As you highlight a package, the package description is displayed in the information window. Switch to this window by pressing the Tab key, and then scroll up and down the information using the arrow keys. Press Tab again to switch back to the list window. In Figure 7-25, you can see we have highlighted the adduser package.

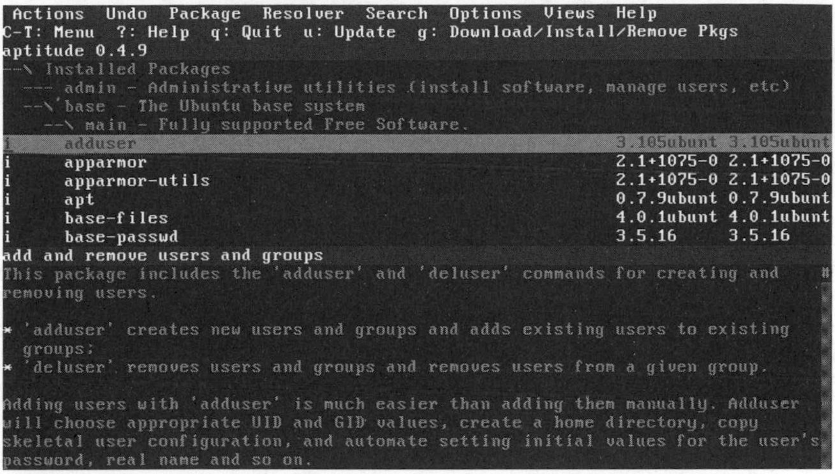

Figure 7-25. *Displaying the package description*

To display more detailed package information, scroll to highlight the package name and press Enter, as we have in Figure 7-26. You can now see information such as the dependencies, maintainer, and so on.

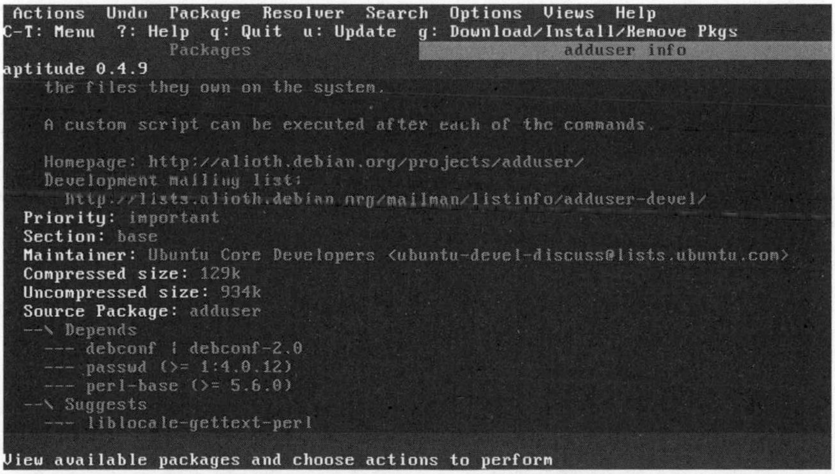

Figure 7-26. *Displaying detailed package information*

Press q to close the information window and return to the package listing.

Since scrolling through this listing is not fast, being able to search it is useful. Bring up the search dialog by pressing the forward slash (/) and entering the required search term. Let's look for the Ubuntu kernel package, called linux-image. As you type, aptitude will jump down the list to display the first matching package. You can see an example of this in Figure 7-27.

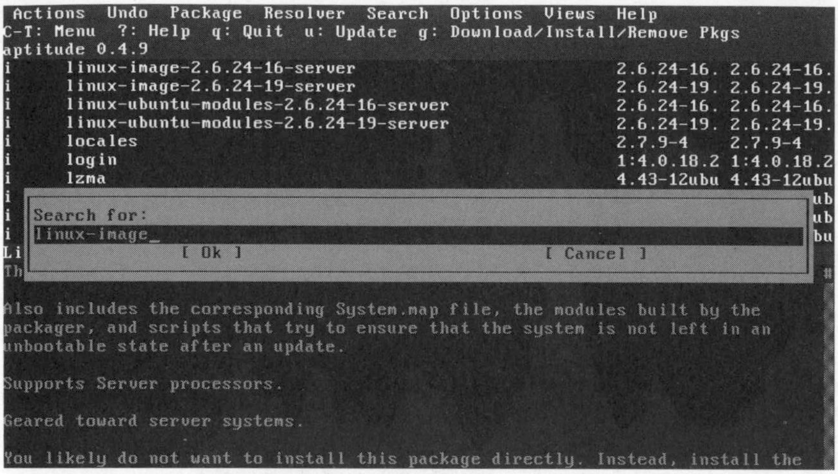

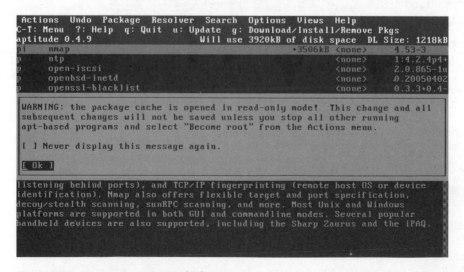

Figure 7-27. *Searching packages by name*

Press Enter to close the search dialog. To jump to the next matched package name, press n. If you keep pressing n, you will eventually find yourself in the listing of Not Installed Packages, which contains more kernels still. To display more package names on screen, you can toggle the information window by pressing D.

Let's now install a package. A small but helpful network utility is nmap, so we'll pick that. Use the find command to find this package in the listing, and then highlight it. To mark this package for installation, press the plus sign (+). You will see a warning dialog telling you that aptitude cannot install packages until you become the root user, as shown in Figure 7-28.

Figure 7-28. *root user warning dialog*

You can disable this warning from appearing in the future. You will notice there is a "Never display this message again" check box. First press Tab to jump to the check box, press the spacebar to check it, and then press Tab again to select the OK button and Enter to accept. To acknowledge this warning, press Enter.

■**Tip** If we had started `aptitude` via `sudo`, the warning dialog would not have appeared. However, making selections as a `non-root` user adds a layer of protection from mistakes. Since it is impossible to accidentally remove packages without being the `root` user, running `aptitude` as a `non-root` user and becoming `root` only to apply pending changes is a good idea.

Rather than installing the package immediately, you'll see that the package status has changed from `p` to `pi`. It is now marked for installation. This allows you to select any number of packages for installation—or removal—before applying the changes to your system.

You are going to install just the `nmap` application for now, but first you have to become the `root` user. To do this, press Ctrl+T to activate the Actions menu. Use the arrow keys to select Become root, press Enter, and `aptitude` will now run `sudo` for you. After you enter your password, it will restart itself with `root` user privileges. Although the package lists return to their initial collapsed state, the command to install your package was added to the internal to-do list.

To process your pending installation, press g. `aptitude` has found that the `nmap` package requires the `libpcre3` package to be present on the system, and thus it is automatically selected for installation (it is flagged with iA), as you can see in Figure 7-29.

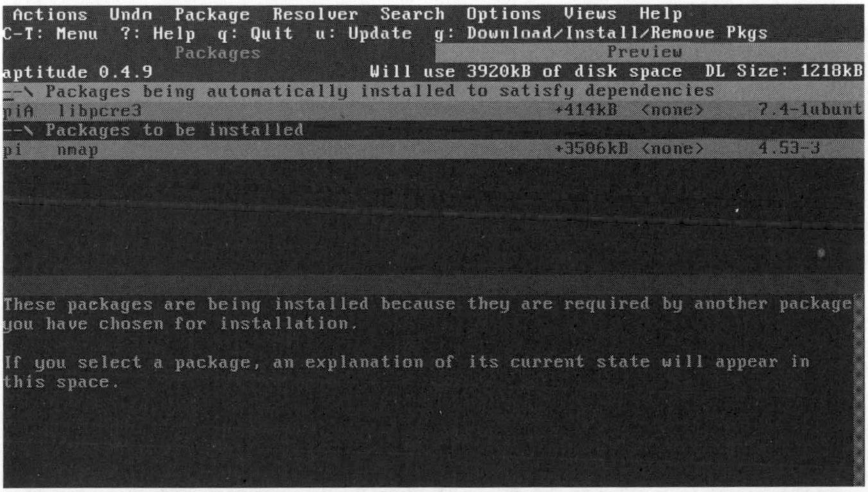

Figure 7-29. *Added package dependencies*

Confirm that you want this dependency to be installed by pressing g again, and `aptitude` will now download the required package files and install them. During this process, you'll be kept informed of what is happening (see Figure 7-30).

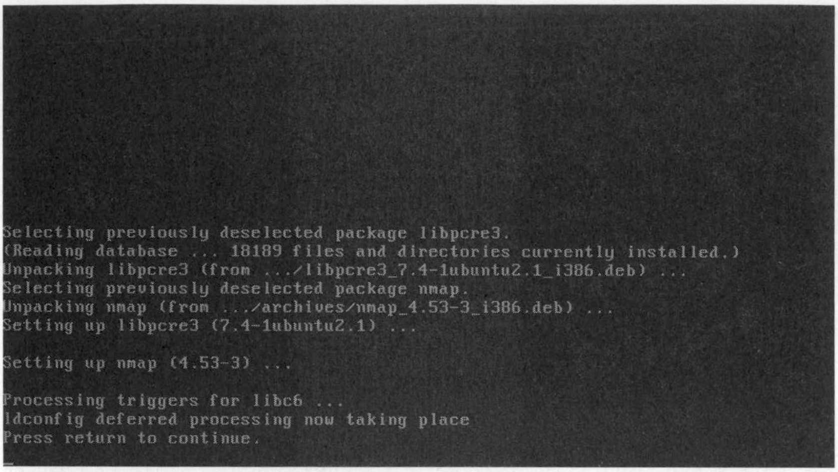

```
Selecting previously deselected package libpcre3.
(Reading database ... 18189 files and directories currently installed.)
Unpacking libpcre3 (from .../libpcre3_7.4-1ubuntu2.1_i386.deb) ...
Selecting previously deselected package nmap.
Unpacking nmap (from .../archives/nmap_4.53-3_i386.deb) ...
Setting up libpcre3 (7.4-1ubuntu2.1) ...

Setting up nmap (4.53-3) ...

Processing triggers for libc6 ...
ldconfig deferred processing now taking place
Press return to continue.
```

Figure 7-30. *Processing installation tasks*

After installation finishes, press Enter and you are back at the Aptitude menu. You will now learn how to remove packages by removing the nmap package you just installed. Search for it using the / key again, and press the hyphen (-) key to mark the package for removal. You'll see the desired package status character change from i to id. If you had customized configuration files and wanted to ensure these were removed as well at this stage, you could press the underscore (_) key to mark the package for purge; if you do so, you'll see the desired status change to p. In Figure 7-31, you can see that nmap is now set to id, as it is marked for deletion. To apply your queued changes, press g.

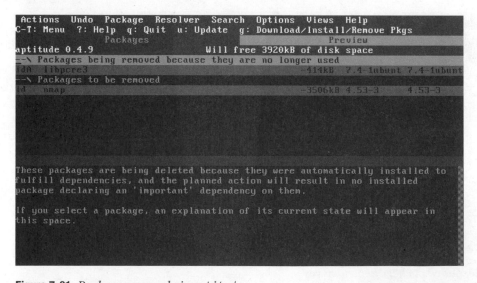

Figure 7-31. *Package removal via* aptitude

Because no more packages depend on libpcre3 and it was flagged as automatically installed, it is now automatically selected for removal (see Figure 7-32). Press g again to confirm and process the changes.

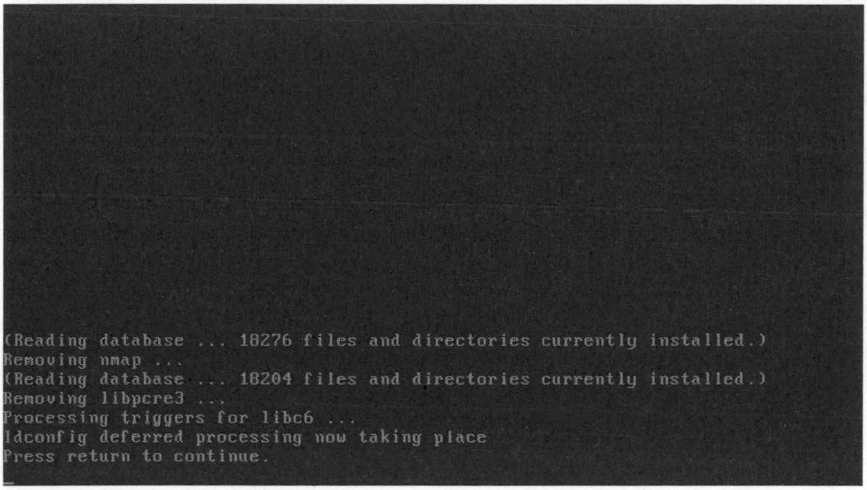

```
(Reading database ... 18276 files and directories currently installed.)
Removing nmap ...
(Reading database ... 18204 files and directories currently installed.)
Removing libpcre3 ...
Processing triggers for libc6 ...
ldconfig deferred processing now taking place
Press return to continue.
```

Figure 7-32. *Process pending removals*

For more information on the commands available in Aptitude, press the question mark (?) key. Figure 7-33 shows a listing of the available commands.

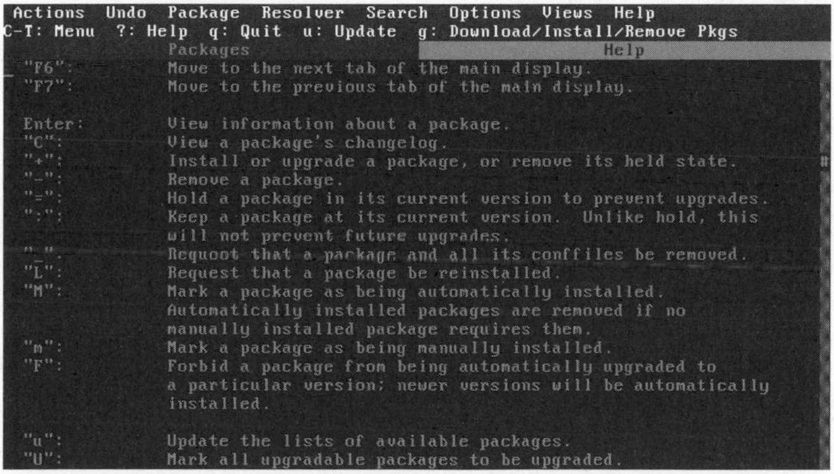

```
Actions  Undo  Package  Resolver  Search  Options  Views  Help
C-T: Menu  ?: Help  q: Quit  u: Update  g: Download/Install/Remove Pkgs
                  Packages                              Help
  "F6":           Move to the next tab of the main display.
  "F7":           Move to the previous tab of the main display.

  Enter:          View information about a package.
  "C":            View a package's changelog.
  "+":            Install or upgrade a package, or remove its held state.
  "-":            Remove a package.
  "=":            Hold a package in its current version to prevent upgrades.
  ":":            Keep a package at its current version.  Unlike hold, this
                  will not prevent future upgrades.
  "_":            Request that a package and all its conffiles be removed.
  "L":            Request that a package be reinstalled.
  "M":            Mark a package as being automatically installed.
                  Automatically installed packages are removed if no
                  manually installed package requires them.
  "m":            Mark a package as being manually installed.
  "F":            Forbid a package from being automatically upgraded to
                  a particular version; newer versions will be automatically
                  installed.

  "u":            Update the lists of available packages.
  "U":            Mark all upgradable packages to be upgraded.
```

Figure 7-33. *The aptitude command list*

You can exit the help listing by pressing q. You can then exit aptitude by pressing q again.

Noninteractive Mode

All this navigating and window switching might be user-friendly, but it's hardly quick. To this end, aptitude also has a command-line mode that does not use interactive menus, but instead takes action commands and package names as parameters. To demonstrate that using aptitude this way is just as handy as using the GUI, we will install the nmap package again. When using aptitude noninteractively, you need to run it as root for install and uninstall tasks. Take a look at how to install nmap again in Listing 7-17.

Listing 7-17. *Installing nmap with aptitude in Noninteractive Mode*

```
$ sudo aptitude install nmap
Reading package lists... Done
<snip>
The following NEW packages will be automatically installed:
  libpcre3
The following NEW packages will be installed:
  libpcre3 nmap
0 packages upgraded, 2 newly installed, 0 to remove and 0 not upgraded.
Need to get 0B/1218kB of archives. After unpacking 3920kB will be used.
Do you want to continue? [Y/n/?] y
Writing extended state information... Done
Selecting previously deselected package libpcre3.
(Reading database ... 18189 files and directories currently installed.)
Unpacking libpcre3 (from .../libpcre3_7.7-1ubuntu2.1_i386.deb) ...
Selecting previously deselected package nmap.
Unpacking nmap (from .../archives/nmap_4.53-3_i386.deb) ...
Setting up libpcre3 (7.7-1ubuntu2.1) ...
Setting up nmap (4.53-3) ...
Processing triggers for libc6 ...
<snip>
Writing extended state information... Done
Building tag database... Done
```

First, aptitude checks the package database to ensure the system is able to have packages installed; should there be packages that are partially configured or pending, it will tell you and abort this installation.

Next, aptitude notifies us that nmap has a dependency that will be installed as well and informs us of how much disk space will be used by these packages. Note that it tells us it needs to get 0 of 128KB of archives. Because we had previously installed nmap, the original package files are still on the machine. Now we can check to see that nmap is installed by executing the following from the command line.

```
$ nmap -v
Starting Nmap 4.53 ( http://insecure.org ) at 2008-08-31 16:05 EST
```

THE APT CACHE

When you install packages from the Internet, they are first downloaded to your computer and stored in a cache located at `/var/cache/apt/archives`. If you remove a package and then re-add it, it doesn't need to be downloaded all over again. Utilities are available that let you share such a cache across multiple computers, which is useful if you have a slow or expensive Internet connection. Examples of such utilities are `apt-cacher` and `apt-proxy`, both of which are available as packages.

We answer Y or accept the default by pressing Enter, and aptitude goes to work installing. It uses the dpkg command internally to handle this part. When done, it processes triggers that may be defined by the packages just added and rechecks the package status database to make sure everything succeeded. We then run the nmap command to check that it is indeed installed.

Removing Packages Using Aptitude

Listing 7-18 shows how to remove a package using aptitude. Again, like with dpkg, you can remove or purge a package. Removing, of course, removes everything but the configuration files from the host, while purging removes the package in its entirety.

Listing 7-18. *Removing Packages with aptitude*

```
$ sudo aptitude remove nmap
Reading package lists... Done
<snip>
The following packages are unused and will be REMOVED:
  libpcre3
The following packages will be REMOVED:
  nmap
0 packages upgraded, 0 newly installed, 2 to remove and 0 not upgraded.
Need to get 0B of archives. After unpacking 3920kB will be freed.
Do you want to continue? [Y/n/?] y
<snip>
Writing extended state information... Done
Building tag database... Done
```

If you want to also remove any configuration files, you can pass the extra --purge option to aptitude:

```
$ sudo aptitude remove --purge nmap
```

REPOSITORIES

Both Advanced Packaging Tool (APT) and Aptitude source packages from the online repositories. Repositories, as explained previously, are collections of packages maintained by the package maintainers for your particular distribution. Both of the tools we're going to look at use special configuration files called APT source files to define where they will go to find these repositories and what types of packages they want to have available.

APT and Aptitude use these source files to find information about tens of thousands of packages. The configuration information for your default repositories is usually stored in the `/etc/apt/sources.list` file, which is created during the installation of your host. Further repositories may also be defined in the `/etc/apt/sources.list.d/` directory.

Generally, separate repositories exist for different distributions, and within these distributions different repositories exist for each version of a distribution. A further set of repositories exists for different types of software. Sound complicated? Well, it isn't when you break it down. Let's look at the Ubuntu 8.04 release (codenamed Hardy Heron). If you have this release installed, you should see a line like the following in the `/etc/apt/sources.list` file:

```
deb http://archive.ubuntu.com/ubuntu hardy main restricted universe
multiverse
```

The repository definition starts with the repository type and a URL. The type indicates whether the repository contains binary packages or source code. A repository type of `deb` contains binary packages, and a type of `deb-src` contains packages containing the source code for applications. You generally won't need to ever use `deb-src` repositories unless you are creating backports (see the "Ubuntu Backports" sidebar). The URL points at the server that hosts the repository. The next field is the release, which for Ubuntu 8.04 is "hardy." You can find other releases of Ubuntu at `http://en.wikipedia.org/wiki/History_of_Ubuntu_releases`. Finally is a list of one or more sections that define which sets of packages you want to be available.

The packages are divided into these sections by license type and by support level. Ubuntu has four sections. First is "main," which contains all free software that is supported by Ubuntu's developer, Canonical. Packages not supported by Canonical directly are available from "universe" and supported by the wider Linux community. Proprietary (closed source but free-as-in-beer—see `http://en.wikipedia.org/wiki/Free_as_in_beer#beer`) software that is supported by Canonical lives in the "restricted" section. Finally, software that may be encumbered with patents or legal issues—like MP3 players or DVD player software—is available from "multiverse."

By not specifying one or more of these sections, you can restrict what types of packages to install on your host. For example, you may want to install only supported and free packages from Canonical, in which case your sources line might look like this:

```
deb http://archive.ubuntu.com/ubuntu hardy main
```

As an exercise, why not point your web browser to `http://archive.ubuntu.com/ubuntu` and see how a repository is laid out?

You can find out more about repositories and sections and how to set them up at `https://help.ubuntu.com/community/Repositories/Ubuntu`.

Updating Packages Using Aptitude

The other standard task of upgrading is accomplished by first updating the list of available packages (checking that you have the most current record of updated packages available from the repository) and performing the upgrade of packages that require upgrading on your host.

Listing 7-19 shows how to perform an update of the list of available packages. What happens here is that the `aptitude` program uses the list of repositories found in the `/etc/apt/sources.list` file (and any additional repositories contained in `/etc/apt/sources.list.d/`) and compiles a list of available packages for your host.

■**Note** We discuss repositories in more detail in the "Repositories" sidebar.

Listing 7-19. *aptitude Update*

```
$ sudo aptitude update
```

Now when you upgrade you have two choices: `safe-upgrade` and `full-upgrade`. `safe-upgrade` will not remove installed packages to upgrade the package being upgraded, which is sometimes required. Sometimes you may have to remove a third-party package in order to upgrade a second. With `safe-upgrade`, this package will not be upgraded to the newer version. In that instance, you must use `full-upgrade`, which will upgrade all installed packages by removing and installing any packages it needs to get the job done.

Listing 7-20 shows the syntax of each of these commands.

Listing 7-20. *Automatically Install Pending Package Upgrades*

```
$ sudo aptitude safe-upgrade
$ sudo aptitude full-upgrade
```

ADVANCED PACKAGING TOOL

Before Aptitude, the Advanced Packaging Tool (APT) suite of utilities provided most of the online package management functionality on deb-based distributions. These tools are still present, but some of the functionality they provide is not present in Aptitude or is not easily accessible, so it pays to get familiar with them. The commands that make up APT include `apt-get`, `apt-cache`, and `apt-file`. The `apt-get` command downloads, installs, and removes packages and source files. The `apt-cache` command searches package lists and displays package information. The `apt-file` command searches file content lists for which package provides a file.

The `aptitude` tool was written as a drop-in replacement for `apt-get`, so in all cases where you run `aptitude` noninteractively, you can replace it with `apt-get`. However, `aptitude` has more advanced algorithms for resolving package dependencies and conflicts, so we suggest you use `aptitude` whenever possible. For example, if you want to install the `nmap` package with `apt-get`, you use the following:

```
$ sudo apt-get install nmap
```

To find out information about a particular package using the `apt-cache` command, you use it like so:

```
$ sudo apt-cache showpkg nmap
```

To use the `apt-file` command to find out which package provides a specific file that is not yet installed on the system, you can use `apt-file` to search the package contents files provided by the repositories:

```
$ apt-file search /usr/sbin/foo
```

This requires an up-to-date contents listing on your system. If you think these contents may be out of date, you can update to the latest versions via the following:

```
$ sudo apt-file update
```

As an alternative, you can search the package lists online at `http://packages.ubuntu.com`.

Package Management with Synaptic

If you've installed the X Window System and Gnome on Ubuntu, you have another way of managing software installation. Ubuntu ships with `gnome-app-install` and `synaptic`, both of which allow you to add software, remove software, and manage repositories without needing to use the command line. However, `synaptic` itself is a front end or wrapper that uses apt and `dpkg` in the background for all its package operations.

You can skip this section if you don't want to install the X Window System on your server. Most servers sit in a rack without a screen or keyboard attached, so installing a large and complex desktop environment makes no sense. If you do want to add a full GUI, you should be able to install the `ubuntu-desktop` package for Gnome or the `kubuntu-desktop` package for KDE using `aptitude`. This will install X and Gnome or KDE for you.

When installation is complete, start the login manager via `sudo /etc/init.d/gdm start` or `sudo /etc/init.d/kdm start` and log in using your username and password.

You can start `synaptic` via the System ➤ Administration menu, as shown in Figure 7-34.

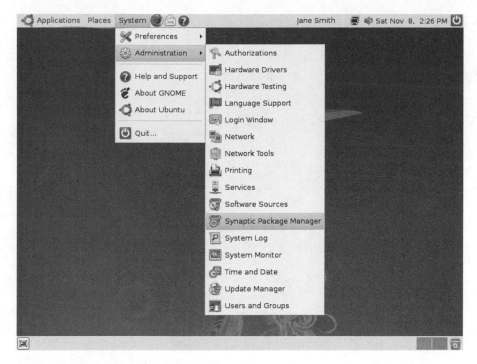

Figure 7-34. *Starting the Synaptic Package Manager*

Because synaptic needs to be started as the root user, it is initiated with the sudo command and you will be asked to enter your password. The first time it starts, you'll be shown a dialog with some notes to help you.

The layout of the application is straightforward. On the left, you have a listing of the same software sections you saw in aptitude. Below that are five buttons that allow you to display the packages filtered in different ways. Click each of them in turn to see how the list of sections changes.

Adding Software

Let's install nmap again, this time via Synaptic. We could scroll through the big, long list of packages in order to find nmap, but since there are—according to the status line down the bottom—24,948 packages, that might take a while. Instead, click the Search button and type **nmap** into the search field (see Figure 7-35). Note that you can search through more than just the name and description fields via the Look in listing. Leave the selection as Description and Name for now and click Search again.

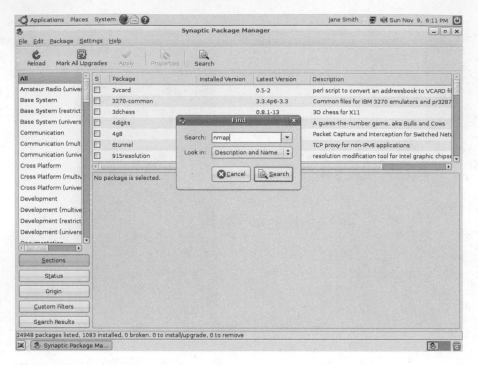

Figure 7-35. *Searching with Synaptic*

Synaptic will now list all packages with the string `nmap` in either the package name or description. You probably need to scroll down the list a bit to find the one you're after. Add it to the installation queue by clicking its check box and choosing Mark for Installation. Just like `aptitude`, `synaptic` will create an internal list of changes. It will not process this list until you click Apply, so you can search for all the software you want and install (or remove) it in a single operation. In addition, you'll see that the software sections on the left have changed into a list of searches you've performed. Whenever you do a search, `synaptic` will add that search as a filter to this listing, so you can quickly jump back to searches you've done previously. Note that this list persists only until you apply the pending changes.

Click Apply to process your list and install `nmap`. You'll be presented with a dialog that tells you about all packages that will be installed, removed, updated, or held back for this operation (see Figure 7-36).

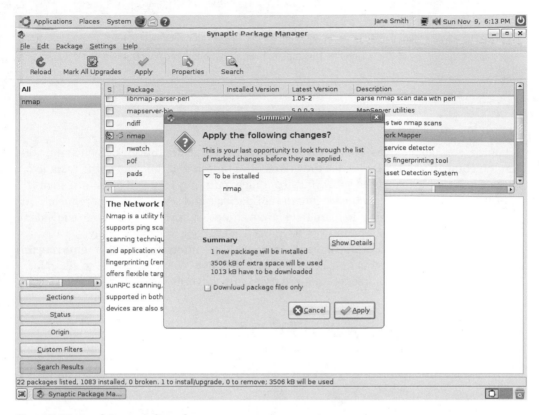

Figure 7-36. *Applying pending changes*

Click Apply again and a progress box will keep you informed of the installation status. When installation is complete, close the dialog (see Figure 7-37).

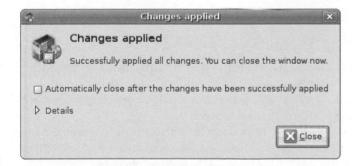

Figure 7-37. *Installation is complete.*

Like `aptitude` and `apt-get`, `synaptic` will automatically select any dependent packages that might be required by the software you're installing.

■**Note** The nmap application does not need to install the libpcre3 package this time, as it was installed earlier as a dependency of X and Gnome. This means it won't be automatically removed when we uninstall nmap.

Removing Software

Of course, you can remove software via Synaptic as well. The filter buttons down at the bottom left come in handy here—click the Status filter button and then select the Installed status. The list now changes to show you all packages currently installed on your system.

Click the darkened check box next to the apt package and select "Mark for removal." As you do this, you'll see a "Mark for complete removal" option as well. The latter is equivalent to the --purge option for dpkg. After you've marked apt for deletion, click Apply.

Synaptic will throw a warning at you (see Figure 7-38), informing you that removing this package may make the system unusable. You definitely don't want to do this, so click No. Synaptic has some basic protection that will try to stop you from doing things you generally should not be doing.

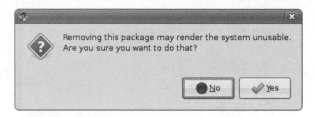

Figure 7-38. *Synaptic to the rescue!*

Find nmap in the installed software list, mark it for complete removal, and then click Apply to remove it.

Managing Repositories

Rather than managing the /etc/apt/sources.list file by hand, Synaptic provides you with an easy-to-use interface to enable, disable, or change repositories. To access it, choose Repositories from the Settings menu. You can also access this dialog by selecting System ➤ Administration ➤ Software Sources in the main Gnome menu bar.

On the tab that opens, Ubuntu Software, you can select an official mirror server to use and define which software sections you want to have available on your system (see Figure 7-39). Unless you have specific reasons not to, it's best to leave all these boxes checked.

The second tab, Third-Party Software, is where you add extra repositories. These extra repositories usually provide you with a deb line, which you can simply paste into the dialog and add to your collection of repositories (see Figure 7-40).

Figure 7-39. *Changing repository settings*

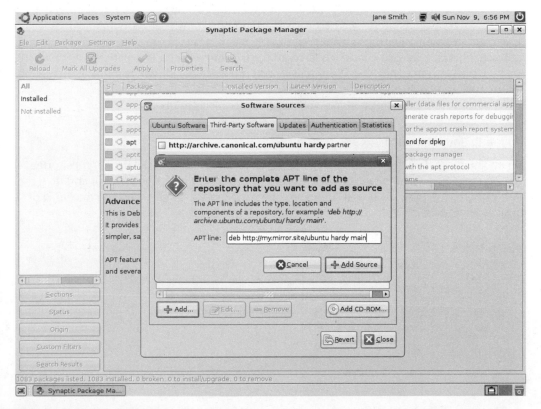

Figure 7-40. *Adding a third-party repository*

After you add this line, you can edit the entry, and you will then be allowed to add a custom description, as shown in Figure 7-41. Note that our example is a nonexistent repository, so you'll want to remove it again before closing `synaptic`.

Figure 7-41. *Adding a repository description*

Software updates generally go in their own repository, so it's especially important on a production server to keep the critical and recommended updates enabled on the Updates tab.

The other two tabs are Authentication and Statistics. The first allows you to import or remove encryption keys that may be used by any repositories you add, just like `apt-key` does on the command-line interface. These keys are an important way of verifying the packages you install are authentic. The Statistics option will, when checked, run the `popularity-contest` utility to submit a list of installed packages to the Ubuntu project. This listing is aggregated with submissions from all other Ubuntu users and is used to decide which applications should be shipped by default, among other things.

You can view collected statistics at `http://popcon.ubuntu.com/`.

Updating and Upgrading

When you close the repositories dialog, Synaptic will warn you that the list of repositories was changed and that it needs to update its internal package lists. Click Accept and then the Reload button. A progress box like the one shown in Figure 7-42 will keep you informed of download status.

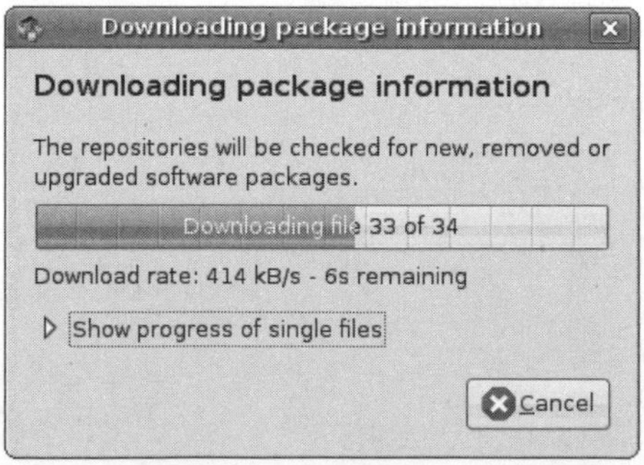

Figure 7-42. *Updating package listings*

Just like `aptitude update`, it will contact all repositories and download new listings of available packages. With these updated listings, it may well be that updates for already installed packages are now available. To find out, click the Status filter button and select the Installed (upgradeable) filter (see Figure 7-43).

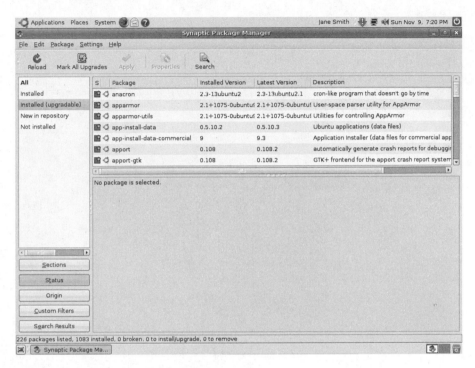

Figure 7-43. *Viewing available software updates*

We recommend that you install any updates when they become available. Keeping your software up to date means your host will be less vulnerable to bugs and malicious users. To install these updates, first click Mark All Upgrades and then Mark to confirm. Synaptic will then add all these updates to its internal task list. To process this list, click Apply and then confirm the list of pending changes.

Using Update Manager

Even when Synaptic isn't running directly, Ubuntu will let you know if any updates are available via a small red arrow icon in the top panel (see Figure 7-44).

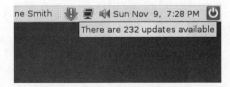

Figure 7-44. *Available updates notification*

Double-clicking the arrow icon will start Update Manager, which lists all available updates (see Figure 7-45).

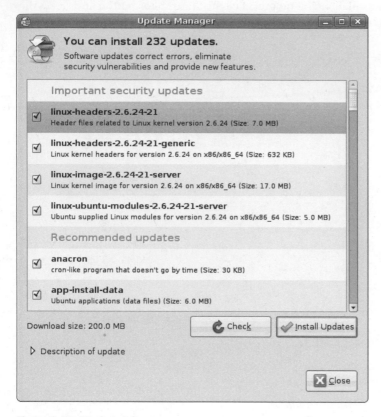

Figure 7-45. *Update Manager*

When you click Install Updates, Update Manager will start a copy of Synaptic, which will ask you for your password before downloading and installing the updated packages.

Using dpkg

The most basic package management tool on Ubuntu is dpkg (pronounced "dee-package"). The APT and Aptitude tools are both wrappers around dpkg, much like Yum is a wrapper around the rpm command.

■**Tip** We recommend you use Aptitude to manage your packages rather than dpkg. Aptitude takes care of dependencies and manages relationships between packages; the dpkg command does not.

The dpkg command allows you to list which packages are installed, install package files you had previously downloaded, and find out to which packages files on the system belong.

You can find all of the options (and there are many) that are available for dpkg by issuing the man dpkg command, as shown in Listing 7-21.

Listing 7-21. *The dpkg man page*

```
$ man dpkg
```

Table 7-5 lists some of the main options and flags for the dpkg command.

Table 7-5. *Options and Flags for dpkg*

Options and Flags	Description
-l | --list	Lists all installed packages on your host.
-p | --print-avail	Prints package information.
-c | --contents	Lists the contents of a particular uninstalled package.
-L | --listfiles	Lists the contents of an installed package.
-i | --install	Installs a package on your host.
-S | --search	Finds which package an installed file belongs to.
-r | --remove	Removes a package from your host. Leaves behind associated configuration files.
-P | --purge	Purges a package from your host. Deletes associated configuration files.

First, we'll get a list of packages that are already installed on our new Ubuntu system, as you can see in Listing 7-22.

Listing 7-22. *Listing Installed Packages*

```
$ dpkg -l
```

This produces the complete list of all the packages on our host. It is usually a very long list, but we can pipe the output from dpkg into the more command and display the output page by page (see Listing 7-23). We can then scroll through it at our leisure.

Listing 7-23. *Piping the dpkg -l Output to more*

```
$ dpkg -l | more
```

Notice in Listing 7-24 that dpkg lists output in four columns: status, name, version, and description.

Listing 7-24. *Viewing Results of dpkg -l*

```
$ dpkg -l | more
Desired=Unknown/Install/Remove/Purge/Hold
| Status=Not/Installed/Config-f/Unpacked/Failed-cfg/Half-inst/t-aWait/T-pend
|/ Err?=(none)/Hold/Reinst-required/X=both-problems (Status,Err: uppercase=bad)
||/ Name                  Version              Description
+++-====================-====================-==================
```

```
ii  adduser        3.105ubuntu1          add and remove users and groups
ii  apache2        2.2.8-1ubuntu0.3      Next generation, scalable, ➥
extendable web se
```

■Note Although is it not automatically clear from the output in Listing 7-24, the first three lines are in fact the status column.

Let's look at each of these columns for a moment. The status column actually consists of three states a package can be in:

- Desired status

- Current status

- Error

Usually, the status will be ii, which means the package is currently installed and will be upgraded if a newer version is available. Table 7-6 lists the most common status codes and their meanings.

Table 7-6. *The dpkg Status Codes*

Code	Meaning
ii	Package is installed and will install updates when available
hi	Package is on hold and installed but will not install updates
un	Package is not installed
rc	Package is not installed, but there are residual configuration files (usually means the package was removed)

The other columns speak for themselves. They contain the package name, the version (if the package is currently installed), and a short description.

You would usually not want a listing of everything, so let's limit the output to packages that provide the Linux kernel by passing a string for dpkg to match. The Linux kernel in Ubuntu goes by the name linux-image, which is different from RHEL, where it is just called kernel. Listing 7-25 lists all the linux-images installed on our host by using a glob string (meaning we catch all results with the string linux-image in them) by using the * symbol before and after the string we are targeting.

■Tip Glob strings are very useful methods for working with strings, especially strings like file names. You can read about using glob strings, known as *globbing*, at http://www.faqs.org/docs/abs/HTML/globbingref.html.

In this case, we are using *linux-image* (you should read a little about globbing and test the results returned when you use linux-image* and linux-image as your search string).

Listing 7-25. *Listing the Linux Kernel*

```
$ dpkg -l '*linux-image*'
Desired=Unknown/Install/Remove/Purge/Hold
| Status=Not/Installed/Config-f/Unpacked/Failed-cfg/Half-inst/t-aWait/T-pend
|/ Err?=(none)/Hold/Reinst-required/X=both-problems (Status,Err: uppercase=bad)
||/ Name           Version         Description
+++-=============-=============-=======================================
un  linux-image    <none>         (no description available)
un  linux-image-2. <none>         (no description available)
ii  linux-image-2. 2.6.27-16.30   Linux kernel image for version 2.6.24 on x86
ii  linux-image-se 2.6.24.16.18   Linux kernel image on Server Equipment.
```

Here you can see there are several linux-image packages, all with names based on the kernel versions they contain. This is so different kernel packages don't have the same name, thus allowing you to have multiple kernels installed. In addition, you'll find the linux-image package, which is a so-called virtual package. This package doesn't actually contain any files, but it does contain a link to the newest available kernel, so a normal upgrade always includes any available new Linux kernel package.

■**Tip** Because the default Linux terminal is only 80 characters wide and dpkg wants to display information for each package on a single line only, it is unable to display the full package name if this is longer than 14 characters. For many packages, this is not a problem, but the kernel packages have long names and so don't display completely. To work around this, you can override the terminal size for dpkg, so it will display more information, using an environment variable. To do this, prefix the command like so: $ COLUMNS=200 dpkg -l '*linux-image*'. This tells your host that your screen is 200 characters wide, so it displays more of all columns.

Examining Package Details

Let's have a look at some information about our kernel package using dpkg. Listing 7-26 shows the output of the dpkg -p command querying for information about one of our linux-image packages.

Listing 7-26. *Output of the dpkg -p Command*

```
$ dpkg -p linux-image-2.6.27-16-server
Package: linux-image-2.6.27-16-server
Priority: optional
Section: base
Installed-Size: 60524
Maintainer: Ubuntu Kernel Team <kernel-team@lists.ubuntu.com>
```

```
Architecture: i386
Source: linux
Version: 2.6.27-16.30
Provides: fuse-module, ivtv-modules, kvm-api-4, linux-image, linux-image-2.6, ➥
redhat-cluster-modules
Depends: coreutils | fileutils (>= 4.0), initramfs-tools (>= 0.36ubuntu6), ➥
module-init-tools (>= 3.3-pre11-4ubuntu3)
Pre-Depends: dpkg (>= 1.10.24)
Recommends: lilo (>= 19.1) | grub
Suggests: fdutils, linux-doc-2.6.24 | linux-source-2.6.24
Conflicts: hotplug (<< 0.0.20040105-1)
Size: 18447888
Description: Linux kernel image for version 2.6.24 on x86/x86_64
 This package contains the Linux kernel image for version 2.6.24 on
 x86/x86_64.

 Also includes the corresponding System.map file, the modules built by the
 packager, and scripts that try to ensure that the system is not left in an
 unbootable state after an update.

 Supports Server processors.

 Geared toward server systems.

 You likely do not want to install this package directly. Instead, install
 the linux-server metapackage, which will ensure that upgrades work
 correctly, and that supporting packages are also installed.
```

In addition to a description and version, each package also contains a contact e-mail for support and information about the disk space it uses when installed. The Depends section also details the packages it needs to be installed prior to the package itself being installed, which are called dependencies. Also shown in the Provides section is the functionality the package makes available to other packages.

Examining Package Contents

In addition to description information about packages, you can also query what files it installed and which directories it installed them to. You can find out the package contents using the dpkg -L command like so:

```
$ dpkg -L nmap
```

This returns a full list of the files installed by the nmap package.

■**Tip** An easy way to find out which commands are provided by a package is to list the files it installs to directories that hold executable applications. Make dpkg list the package contents and pipe the output to grep to limit the output to files and directories that contain the string bin, for example: dpkg -L <package name> | grep bin.

Performing a File Search

For files that are already present on the host, you can determine the package they belong to by using dpkg:

```
$ dpkg -S /usr/sbin/userdel
```

This command tells you what package provides the userdel command.

Installing Packages

All Ubuntu package files are made up of three parts: the package name, the package version, and the target architecture. For instance, version 2.17 of the foobar package for 32-bit Intel machines would be "foobar-2.17_i386.deb".

■**Note** The *target architecture* is the processor technology of your host, for example, i386 or x64.

After you obtain a package file for your Ubuntu version and architecture, you can install it using dpkg. Because packages contain files that need to be installed to privileged system locations (like /bin, /usr/sbin, etc.), the installation needs to be performed as the root user. On Ubuntu, you can use the sudo command discussed in Chapter 4 to perform the installation command as the root user:

```
$ sudo dpkg -i nmap_4.53-3_i386.deb
```

The dpkg command will keep you informed of progress during installation. Depending on the package, it may also ask you some questions about how you would like to configure the package. Don't worry, you can change the answers to these questions later.

Be careful when installing packages you manually download. If the package was not created for your Ubuntu version, other packages that it depends on may not be available in the correct version. Installing anyway might lead to an "unresolvable dependency" that can put your package system into an inconsistent state, where a package is partially installed and prevents further package management until the problem is solved. dpkg will warn you and not let you do this without forcing it to. A best practice is to always check if a package is available in the distribution itself before you download it from a third-party source.

Removing a Package

You have two different ways of removing an Ubuntu package: one is to remove the package, and the other is to purge the package from the system altogether. When you use the --remove option, you are removing everything except modified configuration files for that package from the host. When you use the --purge option, you are telling dpkg to remove everything installed by that package onto your host, including configuration files you modified yourself.

Why have the two methods? Because there are times when you want to completely remove everything and times when you want to remove something with the view of installing it again at some later stage.

Listing 7-27 shows both methods of deleting packages from a host with the dpkg command.

Listing 7-27. *Package Removal*

```
$ sudo dpkg --remove nmap
```

or

```
$ sudo dpkg --purge nmap
```

Compiling from Source

Although the list of packaged software is extensive, not everything is available as a convenient deb or RPM package. If a piece of software is not available in a packaged format, not even in a source package for backporting (see the "Ubuntu Backports" sidebar), you might need to build it from source.

UBUNTU BACKPORTS

Sometimes if a specific package version you need is not available, you may be told to create a backport. This might be the case if you are using an older version of a distribution or if a newer version of an application has not yet been packaged for your release. Creating a backport involves getting the source package from a newer (or older) release of Ubuntu and compiling it on your own machine. Backports are beyond the scope of this book, but some excellent references are available online from which you can learn how to use and create them. A good place to start is https://help.ubuntu.com/community/UbuntuBackports.

In this section we'll show you how to compile software from source and also give you some tips on how to keep such source installations manageable.

Building applications from source generally has three phases:

1. Configure the application.

2. Compile or make the application.

3. Install the application.

We'll take you through these three phases and use the nmap application again as our example. This time, rather than installing it from a package, we'll build the latest source at the time of this writing (version 4.76). First, let's grab the tarball from http://nmap.org/ using the wget utility.

```
$ wget -c http://nmap.org/dist/nmap-4.76.tar.bz2
```

■**Note** A *tarball* is a file (usually compressed) that contains a set of files and/or directories. The application used to create these tarballs is called `tar` (Tape ARchive), thusly named because it was initially used to write archives to magnetic tape. Tarballs have file extensions that normally indicate how the archive was compressed. Examples include `tar.gz` or `tgz` for `gzip` and `tar.bz2` or `tbz` for `bzip2` compression. You can see more information about `tar` on its `man` page.

■**Note** The `-c` flag tells `wget` to resume a partial download. This means it won't restart the download from scratch if it was interrupted for some reason. With the `-c` option, if the download fails, you can then just rerun the command and the download will resume from the point at which it stopped.

The `wget` command downloads files to the current directory, so we now have a tarball we can unpack. The extension tells us it was compressed using `bzip2`, so we need the `-j` flag to make `tar` use `bzip2` decompression.

```
$ tar xvjf nmap-4.76.tar.bz2
```

■**Tip** If you don't know what compression a tarball uses, you can find out by using the `file` command. Run `file <tarball>` and `file` will check the tarball for magic bytes, which indicate the file type. This list of magic bytes for thousands of file types is stored in `/usr/share/file/magic`. Once you know how the tarball was compressed, you can unpack it.

The `-v` parameter tells `tar` to be verbose and print the path of each file it extracts from the archive. If you know which files are contained within the archive, you might want to drop this parameter, so your terminal doesn't scroll with redundant information. As an added bonus, not printing file names means the extract operation completes a bit faster as well.

The tarball is now extracted, so we should change into the source directory and have a look around, to see which files are there.

```
$ cd nmap-4.76
~/nmap-4.76$ ls
```

In many cases the instructions for compiling and installing the application will be contained in a file called README or INSTALL. For `nmap`, there doesn't appear to be a README file, but there is an INSTALL file. By reading this file, we should be able to find the instructions for installing the application.

```
$ less INSTALL
```

We learn from this particular file that the installation documentation is online and not included in the tarball. We can refer to the `nmap`-specific online documentation at `http://nmap.org/book/inst-source.html` for detailed information. We'll use these instructions to compile and install the application.

But before we can compile our application, we need to install a compiler and its associated libraries and utilities. These are usually packaged, so we'll simply install them via the package system. Table 7-7 shows the required packages for Red Hat and Ubuntu.

Table 7-7. *Installing a Compiler and Essential Build Tools*

Distribution	Command
Red Hat	yum install gcc make
Ubuntu	aptitude install build-essential

Configure

With the compiler installed, we can now configure the sources for building. Most software is highly configurable, not just in terms of available features, but also in terms of installation location. To configure an application prior to building it, we use the configure command. In Listing 7-28, we run the configure command with the --help option to display all the options available to configure our application.

Listing 7-28. *Configuration Help*

```
~/nmap-4.76$ ./configure --help
'configure' configures this package to adapt to many kinds of systems.

Usage: ./configure [OPTION]... [VAR=VALUE]...

To assign environment variables (e.g., CC, CFLAGS...), specify them as
VAR=VALUE.  See below for descriptions of some of the useful variables.

Defaults for the options are specified in brackets.

Configuration:
  -h, --help              display this help and exit
      --help=short        display options specific to this package
      --help=recursive    display the short help of all the included packages
  -V, --version           display version information and exit
  -q, --quiet, --silent   do not print 'checking...' messages
      --cache-file=FILE   cache test results in FILE [disabled]
  -C, --config-cache      alias for '--cache-file=config.cache'
  -n, --no-create         do not create output files
      --srcdir=DIR        find the sources in DIR [configure dir or '..']

Installation directories:
  --prefix=PREFIX         install architecture-independent files in ➡
PREFIX [/usr/local]
```

■**Note** Note that in Listing 7-28 we've specified ./ in front of the configure command. This tells Linux to run the configure script it finds in the current directory.

The output goes on, but we'll stop here at the most important option, --prefix. This option determines where the software will be installed, and it's important this is a location that is not used by packaged software. Otherwise, you might end up in a situation where a file installed from source overwrites a packaged file. This would confuse the package system, and when you removed the package in question, your compiled file would be deleted.

Generally when you install applications from source, they are deployed in the /usr/local directory structure. This is usually the default option for --prefix (you can see this default in block brackets in Listing 7-28).

The other options to keep an eye out for are those that determine available features in the software. They determine whether third-party libraries should be checked for during configuration and used if present. These options are usually prefixed by --with- and --without-.

Armed with this new knowledge, we can now configure our nmap sources with default options, as you can see in Listing 7-29.

Listing 7-29. *Configuring Our Source Tree*

```
~/nmap-4.76$ ./configure –prefix=/usr/local
checking build system type... i686-pc-linux-gnu
checking host system type... i686-pc-linux-gnu
checking for gcc... gcc
<snip>
checking openssl/ssl.h presence... no
checking for openssl/ssl.h... no
configure: WARNING: Failed to find openssl/ssl.h so OpenSSL will not be used. ⮕
If it is installed you can try the --with-openssl=DIR argument
<snip>
checking if struct ip has ip_sum member... yes
configure: creating ./config.status
config.status: creating Makefile
config.status: creating nsock_config.h
<snip>                                    /                    \
          NMAP IS A POWERFUL TOOL -- USE CAREFULLY AND RESPONSIBLY
Configuration complete.  Type make (or gmake on some *BSD machines) to compile.
~/nmap-4.76$
```

The configure script checks our system for the presence of a compiler, required header files, and definitions of functions and data structures in these header files. We talked about header files and libraries at the start of this chapter and mentioned that you generally only need them when compiling software from source. In Listing 7-29, note that the script was unable to find the OpenSSL headers, so it will build nmap without support for OpenSSL. If we wanted support for OpenSSL, we would need to install the appropriate -devel or -dev package before configuring. For example, to install the OpenSSL headers on Ubuntu, we'd use the following:

```
$ sudo aptitude install libssl-dev
```

■**Note** If you are using a Red Hat–based distribution, you will install the `openssl-devel` package.

In some cases, you can still compile software without a header. The functionality related to those headers or libraries may just be disabled, as it is in Listing 7-29, but in other cases the configuration process may fail.

Compile and Make

When complete, the `configure` command writes a configuration header file and a special file called `Makefile`. The former contains code that instructs the compiler about available functions and libraries, and the latter contains the commands needed to build the software by the `make` command. The `make` command reads the `Makefile` and executes the commands and steps contained in there. We issue the `make` command to start building `nmap` in Listing 7-30.

Listing 7-30. *Compiling nmap*

```
~/nmap-4.76$ make
Makefile:262: makefile.dep: No such file or directory
g++ -MM -Iliblua -Ilibdnet-stripped/include -Ilibpcre  -Ilibpcap -Inbase ➥
-Insock/include main.cc nmap.cc targets.cc tcpip.cc nmap_error.cc utils.cc ➥
idle_scan.cc osscan.cc osscan2.cc output.cc scan_engine.cc timing.cc charpool.cc ➥
services.cc protocols.cc nmap_rpc.cc portlist.cc NmapOps.cc TargetGroup.cc ➥
Target.cc FingerPrintResults.cc service_scan.cc NmapOutputTable.cc MACLookup.cc ➥
nmap_tty.cc nmap_dns.cc traceroute.cc portreasons.cc nse_main.cc nse_nsock.cc ➥
nse_init.cc nse_fs.cc nse_nmaplib.cc nse_debug.cc nse_pcrelib.cc nse_binlib.cc ➥
nse_hash.cc nse_bit.cc  > makefile.dep
Compiling liblua
make[1]: Entering directory '/home/jsmith/nmap-4.76/liblua'
gcc -O2 -Wall -g -O2 -Wall  -fno-strict-aliasing   -DHAVE_CONFIG_H ➥
-DNMAP_NAME="Nmap" -DNMAP_URL="http://nmap.org" ➥
-DNMAP_PLATFORM="i686-pc-linux-gnu" -DNMAPDATADIR="/usr/local/share/nmap" ➥
-DNMAPLIBEXECDIR="/usr/local/libexec/nmap" -DLUA_USE_POSIX ➥
-DLUA_USE_DLOPEN -c -o lapi.o -c lapi.c
<snip>
changing mode of build/scripts-2.5/zenmap from 644 to 755
make[1]: Leaving directory '/home/jsmith/nmap-4.76'
```

If the `make` process completes successfully, the application is now built. If it fails, you'll generally receive an error message indicating why and hopefully some direction about how to fix it. There are a lot of reasons why building an application may fail—too many to detail here—but generally you'll probably have encountered a problem someone has found before. The issue you are experiencing may be detailed on the application's website—for example, in the installation documentation or in an FAQ section. Searching for the particular error message via Google may also point to possible solutions.

Install

Now that our nmap application has been compiled, we need to make it available to all users on the system, by installing it to the prefix location we chose earlier when configuring. The Makefile contains commands for this as well, and you can see the installation process in Listing 7-31.

Listing 7-31. *Installing nmap*

```
~/nmap-4.76$ sudo make install
[sudo] password for jsmith:
/usr/bin/install -c -d /usr/local/bin /usr/local/share/man/man1 ➥
/usr/local/share/nmap
/usr/bin/install -c -c -m 755 nmap /usr/local/bin/nmap
/usr/bin/strip -x /usr/local/bin/nmap
/usr/bin/install -c -c -m 644 docs/nmap.1 /usr/local/share/man/man1/
<snip>
ln -sf zenmap /usr/local/bin/xnmap
NMAP SUCCESSFULLY INSTALLED
```

We need to use sudo, because as a normal user we're not allowed to create new files under /usr/local. Again, make processes rules in the Makefile and executes the commands to install nmap and its associated files on the system. We can now run our newly installed application to make sure it all went OK, as shown in Listing 7-32.

Listing 7-32. *Running nmap*

```
nmap-4.76$ /usr/local/bin/nmap -V

Nmap version 4.76 ( http://nmap.org )
```

Uninstall

The tricky part of managing source installations comes when you want to remove them from the system. Some, but not all, contain deinstallation rules. For nmap we can invoke the following:

```
~/nmap-4.76$ sudo make uninstall
```

However, even that means we need to keep the configured sources lying about on our systems. This is less than ideal, as we need to track not only which software we installed from source, but also where we keep these sources. This is one of the reasons we recommend you avoid installing applications from source, but rather rely on packages to provide applications.

Summary

In this chapter, we looked at how Linux hosts manage software. You have learned how to manage installed packages, how to add and remove them, and how to change software repositories to make more software available.

You should now be able to check which packages are installed on your host and install and remove packages using the various package managers. You also learned how to update installed packages on your host, modify package repositories on your host, and perform a basic installation from source.

In the next chapter, we will look at setting up your storage for maximum reliability, and you will learn how to avoid and recover from hard disk problems.

CHAPTER 8

■ ■ ■

Storage Management and Disaster Recovery

By Peter Lieverdink

When you installed your first Linux host, you accepted all defaults when it came to setting up disks and partitions. Now that you have some basic systems administration knowledge, let's revisit the storage configuration and see how to change it to suit your needs. We'll look at various types of storage hardware and the ways in which you can use storage management software to your advantage. A critical part of any business is its data, so you need to make sure it is both safe and accessible and stays that way.

In this chapter, we will explain how to create and manage disk partitions and RAID, how to make your storage accessible to applications, and how to recover from a crash.

■**Note** In Chapter 13, we'll cover how to back up and restore your data.

Storage Basics

We're going to start by looking at how Linux handles storage. We'll do this by adding a variety of new disks, partitioning these disks, and then formatting and managing this storage.

Drives under Windows show up as a drive letter once you format them, but Linux works differently. It has no concept of drive letters, and formatting also doesn't work quite in the same way. Instead, drives and storage appear as devices, which can be partitioned. These partitions can, in turn, be formatted.

Let's start by looking at devices, which are the basic building blocks of Linux storage. We'll then move on to cover partitions and file systems.

Devices

We briefly touched on device files in Chapter 3. These files are the way Linux makes hardware devices, such as hard disk drives and DVD drives, accessible from within the operating system. Most—but not all—of the devices in a host are represented by files in the /dev directory.

The /dev directory is a special directory that's populated by a service called udev. When the host boots and the kernel detects a device, it tells udev, which then creates a representation of that device in the /dev directory. These device files are the way the kernel provides access to devices for applications and services.

There are several kinds of device files, but in this chapter we'll cover only the ones dealing with storage, which all fall into the category of *block devices*. This category covers hard disks, tape drives, CD and DVD drives, and even floppy drives. All types of hard disks—for example, ATA, Serial ATA, SCSI, and SAS—are represented by device files whose names start with sd, which stands for SCSI disk, as all these different types of drives are accessed as if they were SCSI drives.

■**Note** SCSI is an acronym that stands for Small Computer System Interface, a specification for how storage devices should be connected to and accessed by computers. You can read more about this specification at http://en.wikipedia.org/wiki/SCSI.

■**Note** On older kernel versions or with certain IDE controllers, ATA disks may be detected as /dev/hd? instead of /dev/sd?. This is nothing to worry about—simply use hd wherever we use sd.

You can see which disk devices are available on your host by listing them using the ls command, as in Listing 8-1.

Listing 8-1. *Listing Device Nodes*

```
$ ls -l /dev/sd*
brw-rw---- 1 root disk 8,   0 2008-12-19 20:24 /dev/sda
brw-rw---- 1 root disk 8,   1 2008-12-19 20:24 /dev/sda1
brw-rw---- 1 root disk 8,   2 2008-12-19 09:26 /dev/sda2
brw-rw---- 1 root disk 8,   5 2008-12-19 20:24 /dev/sda5
```

Listing 8-1 shows four block devices, or device nodes. They are readable and writeable by the root user and the disk group. Next, where normally the file size would be displayed, are two numbers separated by a comma. These are the device major number and minor number. The *major number* tells the kernel which device driver to use to access the device, and the *minor number* gives the kernel specific information about the device. Finally, the date and time the device file was last modified are shown.

The actual device file name consists of the prefix sd and a letter indicating which disk it belongs to. The first detected disk is sda, the second is sdb, the third is sdc, and so on. Finally, each partition on the disk gets its own device node as well, and the partition number is the final part of the name. This means that sda1 is the first partition on disk sda, sdb2 is the second partition on disk sdb, and so on. We'll discuss partitions shortly.

■Note Because device minor numbers can range from 1 to 255, and each disk needs 16 numbers, Linux can accommodate 16 hard disks with 16 partitions each, /dev/sda1 through /dev/sdp16, before it runs out of device nodes. You can find out more about device numbers and what they are used for at http://www. linux-tutorial.info/modules.php?name=MContent&pageid=94.

If you have a hardware RAID controller, it may name your array and any partitions differently. The RAID controller combines multiple disks into a Redundant Array of Inexpensive Disks (RAID). We'll talk more about RAID later on in this chapter. To find out what the device nodes for the RAID array are, you can list all block devices in the /dev/ directory with the following command:

```
$ ls -l /dev | grep ^b
```

This command will list only lines starting with b. It would, however, be more accurate to check the contents of the kernel internal log buffer. Whenever a kernel event occurs, it is added to the kernel internal log buffer. This buffer is then written to a log file by a logging daemon, and you can query it directly using the dmesg command.

```
$ dmesg |less
```

Most RAID controllers also use at least part of the kernel SCSI subsystem, and you can search for detected SCSI devices via the built-in search function in less. Enter /scsi inside the less window and press Enter to search for any lines containing the string scsi. You can press n to jump to the next match.

Partitions

After you add a disk to your host, you need to perform a few steps to make it usable. First, you need to create one or more partitions on that disk. The start of a disk must contain information about the way partitions are laid out, and to make the disk usable, you must create a partition even if you do not intend to split up the disk.

Generally, partitioning is a way of dividing a physical disk into multiple virtual disks, which you can then use independently, like splitting a disk into C:, D:, and E: drives on Windows. This way you can, for example, keep log and user data separate from the operating system, so logs or users cannot fill up your system disk and cause problems.

In Chapter 5 we mentioned the boot record, which is stored in the first 224 bytes of the disk. The information describing partition information is stored in the 64 bytes directly after the boot record. You can't store a lot of data in 64 bytes, so the number of partitions a disk could hold was originally rather limited.

PHYSICAL, EXTENDED, AND LOGICAL PARTITIONS

Partitions come in three flavors: physical, extended, and logical. This is because only a limited amount of partition information can be stored in the 64 bytes that are available. A partition needs 16 bytes of data to be described, so with information on four partitions, it's full!

As a workaround, the concept of an extended partition was invented. One of the four available physical partitions is marked as an extended partition, which then functions as a container for up to 15 additional logical partitions.

The 16 bytes describing every partition include information about the partition type, where on the disk it can be found, and whether it is bootable, though Linux doesn't care about the latter.

You can find more detailed information about partitions at `http://www.win.tue.nl/~aeb/partitions/`.

You can create and delete partitions using the `fdisk` utility. Let's start by having a look at what partitions are already there by listing the partitions on the first disk (see Listing 8-2). Because only the `root` user is allowed to read from and write to the raw disk device, you need to use `sudo`.

Listing 8-2. *Listing Partitions with `fdisk`*

```
$ sudo fdisk -l /dev/sda

Disk /dev/sda: 4294 MB, 4294967296 bytes
255 heads, 63 sectors/track, 522 cylinders
Units = cylinders of 16065 * 512 = 8225280 bytes
Disk identifier: 0x000c79c5

   Device Boot      Start         End      Blocks   Id  System
/dev/sda1   *           1          31      248976   83  Linux
/dev/sda2              32         522     3943957+   5  Extended
/dev/sda5              32         522     3943926   8e  Linux LVM
```

As you can see in the output of Listing 8-2, the installer created three partitions:

- A physical partition for the operating system
- An extended partition
- A logical partition for use with LVM

You don't want to modify your system disk, but let's say you bought a new hard disk and need to partition it, so you can start using it to store data. First, you need to check that the disk was detected by the operating system and what its device name is. The kernel prints information on all devices it detects when it boots up, and you can access that information via the `dmesg` command once you log in.

```
$ dmesg | grep sd
[    9.706404] sd 2:0:0:0: [sda] 8388608 512-byte hardware sectors (4295 MB)
[    9.706434] sd 2:0:0:0: [sda] Write Protect is off
[    9.706437] sd 2:0:0:0: [sda] Mode Sense: 5d 00 00 00
```

```
[    9.706486] sd 2:0:0:0: [sda] Cache data unavailable
[    9.706489] sd 2:0:0:0: [sda] Assuming drive cache: write through
[    9.706613]  sda: sda1 sda2 < sda5 >
[    9.709163] sd 2:0:0:0: [sda] Attached SCSI disk
[    9.709540] sd 2:0:1:0: [sdb] 16777216 512-byte hardware sectors (8590 MB)
[    9.709569] sd 2:0:1:0: [sdb] Write Protect is off
[    9.709572] sd 2:0:1:0: [sdb] Mode Sense: 5d 00 00 00
[    9.709617] sd 2:0:1:0: [sdb] Cache data unavailable
[    9.709620] sd 2:0:1:0: [sdb] Assuming drive cache: write through
[    9.709684]  sdb: unknown partition table
[    9.710185] sd 2:0:1:0: [sdb] Attached SCSI disk
[   15.739820] EXT3 FS on sda1, internal journal
```

By using grep to display only lines containing sd, you can limit the output to information about the SCSI disk subsystem.

■**Tip** Knowing how to interpret boot-up information can help you solve boot problems. You can find out more about dmesg at http://www.linfo.org/dmesg.html.

The system has detected two disks, sda and sdb. When it detected sda, it also found the partitions sda1, sda2, and sda5. The angle brackets around partition sda5 (<sda5>) indicate this is a logical partition. The other disk is new and has no partition table (sdb: unknown partition table), so let's create one.

```
$ sudo fdisk /dev/sdb

Device contains neither a valid DOS partition table, nor Sun, SGI or OSF disklabel
Building a new DOS disklabel with disk identifier 0xf541816d.
Changes will remain in memory only, until you decide to write them.
After that, of course, the previous content won't be recoverable.

The number of cylinders for this disk is set to 1044.
There is nothing wrong with that, but this is larger than 1024,
and could in certain setups cause problems with:
1) software that runs at boot time (e.g., old versions of LILO)
2) booting and partitioning software from other OSs
   (e.g., DOS FDISK, OS/2 FDISK)
Warning: invalid flag 0x0000 of partition table 4 will be corrected by w(rite)

Command (m for help): m
```

As you see, fdisk did not detect a partition table of any kind it recognizes, and it initialized a new DOS disk label, which is the partition table type used by Linux and Windows on x86 type hardware.

Press m to see a list of available options.

```
Command (m for help): m
Command action
   a   toggle a bootable flag
   b   edit bsd disklabel
   c   toggle the dos compatibility flag
   d   delete a partition
   l   list known partition types
   m   print this menu
   n   add a new partition
   o   create a new empty DOS partition table
   p   print the partition table
   q   quit without saving changes
   s   create a new empty Sun disklabel
   t   change a partition's system id
   u   change display/entry units
   v   verify the partition table
   w   write table to disk and exit
   x   extra functionality (experts only)
```

Let's quickly run through these options. The a option sets the bootable flag on a partition, and as we mentioned in the "Physical, Extended, and Logical Partitions" sidebar, Linux ignores this option.

The b option allows you to edit the BSD disklabel. This is an alternate way of partitioning a disk, which is used by BSD operating systems.

The DOS compatibility flag, which can be turned on or off with c, is used to ensure that disks with more than 1,024 cylinders can be used with Microsoft operating systems when partitioned under Linux. This option defaults to on, and there is no reason to turn it off.

You can delete partitions with the d option and list the types of partitions fdisk knows about via l. This option shows the hexadecimal identifiers that can be used with the t option.

To create a partition, use the n option, which will start a wizard to guide you through the creation process, as you'll see in a moment. To erase the current partition map and create a new empty one, use the o option. This is much quicker than individually deleting all partitions on a disk, so it can be a great time-saver.

To list the current partition table, press p. This lists the partition table as it exists in memory, not as it is on the disk.

If you made changes that you do not want to save, press q. This will quit fdisk without writing the modified partition table to the disk. When you use Linux on a Sun SPARC system, you need to use a different method of partitioning, which you can do via the s option.

Partitions also hold information about the type of file system they contain. The hexadecimal identifiers we got from the l option can be set using the t option.

If you want to display current partition sizes in sectors rather than cylinders, press u. The v option will check that the partition map is correct and display information about nonpartitioned space.

When you're happy with a new partition map, you can press w to save it to the disk. Finally, x allows you to access advanced fdisk options, such as changing the disk geometry and moving the data contained within a partition. We don't cover the use of any of these expert options.

Now press p to print the listing of partitions on the current disk. You'll see that it's empty. Normally, we recommend creating only a single partition on a data storage disk, but let's have some fun with this disk and create a few: one primary and two logical partitions.

Start by creating a primary partition, 2GiB in size. You can ignore the cylinder numbers. Just press Enter to accept the default value for the first cylinder, which will put this partition at the start of the disk. Next, enter +2G to indicate you want to create a partition that is 2GiB in size.

```
Command (m for help): n
Command action
   e   extended
   p   primary partition (1-4)
p
Partition number (1-4): 1
First cylinder (1-1044, default 1):
Using default value 1
Last cylinder or +size or +sizeM or +sizeK (1-1044, default 1044): +2G
```

Then add an extended partition, which spans the entire remainder of the disk. You'll make this partition number 4, so that there are free partition numbers left. You might need these if you want to divide partition 1 into multiple smaller partitions at some point in the future. When asked for the last cylinder, again press Enter to accept the default value.

```
Command (m for help): n
Command action
   e   extended
   p   primary partition (1-4)
e
Partition number (1-4): 4
First cylinder (245-1044, default 245): hit enter
Using default value 245
Last cylinder or +size or +sizeM or +sizeK (245-1044, default 1044):
Using default value 1044
```

Now that you have an extended partition, you can create logical partitions within it. Let's start with a 4GiB partition. As opposed to the primary or extended partition, these logical partitions will be automatically numbered.

```
Command (m for help): n
Command action
   l   logical (5 or over)
   p   primary partition (1-4)
l
First cylinder (245-1044, default 245):
Using default value 245
Last cylinder or +size or +sizeM or +sizeK (245-1044, default 1044): +4G
```

And finally, use the remainder of the extended partition by accepting the default value for the last cylinder.

```
Command (m for help): n
Command action
   l   logical (5 or over)
   p   primary partition (1-4)
l
First cylinder (732-1044, default 732):
Using default value 732
Last cylinder or +size or +sizeM or +sizeK (732-1044, default 1044):
Using default value 1044
```

Let's have a look at what we did and print the partition listing:

```
Command (m for help): p

Disk /dev/sdb: 8589 MB, 8589934592 bytes
255 heads, 63 sectors/track, 1044 cylinders
Units = cylinders of 16065 * 512 = 8225280 bytes
Disk identifier: 0x5ecec006

   Device Boot      Start         End      Blocks   Id  System
/dev/sdb1               1         244     1959898+  83  Linux
/dev/sdb4             245        1044     6426000    5  Extended
/dev/sdb5             245         731     3911796   83  Linux
/dev/sdb6             732        1044     2514141   83  Linux
```

You now have four partitions. By their start and end block numbers, you can see that partitions 5 and 6 are contained within the space used by partition 4.

By default, the partition ID (the type) created by fdisk is Linux. Linux itself doesn't generally care what the partition type is, but to make management easier, we recommend you change the type to match the intended use. We want to use /dev/sdb6 as the swap partition, so we'll change its type.

Type t to change the type, and then choose partition number 6.

```
Command (m for help): t
Partition number (1-6): 6
Hex code (type L to list codes): L
```

Here you will be presented with a long list of available partition types that you can choose from. The partition ID consists of two hexadecimal digits, but luckily you can get a listing of them and a description of each by pressing L. You're after "Linux swap," so you should pick ID 82. Table 8-1 shows the most common choices of partition types. You're likely to come across type c on USB keys that are used with Windows, Mac OS, and Linux systems.

Table 8-1. *Commonly Used Partition Types in Linux*

ID	Description
82	Linux swap/Solaris
83	Linux
da	Non-FS data (used for software RAID)
fd	Linux RAID autodetect (previously used for software RAID)
8e	Linux LVM
c	W95 FAT32 (LBA)
7	HPFS/NTFS

Enter 82 to pick the Linux swap partition type.

```
Hex code (type L to list codes): 82
Changed system type of partition 6 to 82 (Linux swap / Solaris)

Command (m for help): p

Disk /dev/sdb: 8589 MB, 8589934592 bytes
255 heads, 63 sectors/track, 1044 cylinders
Units = cylinders of 16065 * 512 = 8225280 bytes
Disk identifier: 0x8b1c93f9

/dev/sdb1            1         244    1959898+  83  Linux
/dev/sdb4          245        1044    6426000    5  Extended
/dev/sdb5          245         731    3911796   83  Linux
/dev/sdb6          732        1044    2514141   82  Linux swap / Solaris
```

At this point the new partition map exists only in RAM, as you have not yet saved your changes to the disk. To save and quit fdisk, press w. If you do not want to save these changes, quit fdisk by pressing q.

```
Command (m for help): w
The partition table has been altered!

Calling ioctl() to reread partition table.
Syncing disks.
```

The kernel reloads the partition map and creates new device nodes for your partitions. You'll see in the output from dmesg that the disk detection routine has run and found your new partitions. You can also check that their device nodes now exist on disk.

```
$ ls -l /dev/sdb*
brw-rw---- 1 root disk 8, 16 2008-11-28 16:32 /dev/sdb
brw-rw---- 1 root disk 8, 17 2008-11-28 16:32 /dev/sdb1
brw-rw---- 1 root disk 8, 18 2008-11-28 16:32 /dev/sdb4
brw-rw---- 1 root disk 8, 19 2008-11-28 16:32 /dev/sdb5
brw-rw---- 1 root disk 8, 20 2008-11-28 16:32 /dev/sdb6
```

Sometimes the kernel is not able to reread the partition table, which means you can't get access to the new partition device files until you have rebooted the host. This can happen if one of the partitions on the disk you were editing was still mounted. To avoid having to reboot, make sure no partitions on the disk you're partitioning are mounted. We'll cover mounting a bit later in this chapter.

■**Note** You can also make the kernel redetect partitions—without rebooting—by running the `partprobe` command.

Another utility to create and delete partitions is `parted`. Unlike `fdisk`, this utility allows you to edit the size and ordering of partitions. We recommend you don't go down the road of resizing partitions with `parted`, but rather use LVM. We will cover LVM in detail later in this chapter. For more information about `parted`, visit `http://www.gnu.org/software/parted/index.shtml`.

■**Caution** Resizing partitions can cause unrecoverable data loss. Always back up your data first!

GIBIBYTES VS. GIGABYTES

When a hard-disk manufacturer advertises its product, it wants the available storage space to seem as large as possible, so it calculates each gigabyte as 1,000 megabytes, which in turn is 1,000 kilobytes, which is 1,000 bytes.

However, because all calculations on computers are done via binary arithmetic, the actual multiplication value is 1,024. But if a storage manufacturer used that factor, its device would seem smaller when compared to the competition, so it doesn't.

To stop confusion between these ways of calculating sizes, new terms were coined for values using the 1,024 factor: kibibyte, mebibyte, gibibyte, and so on. They are indicated with KiB, MiB, GiB, and so forth. The Linux file system tools use the 1,024 factor, so if you purchase a 500GB disk, its size will always be less than 500GiB when viewed via Linux.

For more information, see `http://en.wikipedia.org/wiki/Gigabyte`.

File Systems

You've now created partitions, but you have not yet prepared them for use. The next thing you need to do is create a file system. In the Microsoft Windows world, this is known as formatting.

A file system is a bit like a library. It stores large amounts of data and has a catalog to ensure you can find what you're looking for. The layout of the aisles and shelves and the design of the catalog determine how long it takes to find and retrieve any particular piece of information. Creating a file system is like initializing the catalog and moving the shelves into an otherwise empty library.

Just as there is no optimal aisle and shelf layout for all libraries, there is no "best" file system for all uses. We won't go into a lot of detail, but let's look at some of the most commonly used Linux file systems. They are listed in Table 8-2 with their main features.

Table 8-2. *Linux File Systems and Their Main Features*

File System	Features
Ext2	Stable, general use, can be shrunk or expanded
Ext3	Stable, general use, quick recovery, can be shrunk or expanded
Ext4	New, general use, quick recovery, improves on ext3
XFS	Stable, general use, quick recovery, can be expanded online
JFS	Stable, general use, quick recovery

The ext2 and ext3 file systems generally perform better when you're storing many small files on them. They are a good choice of file system for an e-mail store, website store, or office file store, as these usually consist of many files that are up to several hundreds of kilobytes in size.

With lessons learned from ext3, a further advancement, ext4, has been developed. This file system has only recently become stable, and it offers some features not available in ext3, such as online defragmentation, better journal reliability, and faster file system checks. Ext4 is intended as an all-round file system with excellent performance.

If you need to store video, large images, or database files, the XFS file system is a good choice, as it performs much better than ext3, with files of up to several gigabytes in size. It offers some of the same advantages as ext4, but since XFS has been stable for longer, it is perhaps a better choice for server systems.

Lastly, JFS is considered a good all-round journaled file system that works well with files of varying volumes and sizes. It's also considered a light file system that doesn't use large amounts of CPU during heavy disk activity.

You can find an exhaustive list of file systems and comparisons of their features at http://en.wikipedia.org/wiki/List_of_file_systems and http://en.wikipedia.org/wiki/Comparison_of_file_systems.

Traditionally, Linux has used the ext2 (second extended file system) file system for data storage, and more recently ext3 has become the default. In case of a crash, ext2 has to scan the entire file system for problems before it can be mounted and used again. When a file system is only 2GiB, that doesn't matter, but with today's disks, file systems can be several terabytes in size, and checking them would take hours or even days, during which the data on the file system would be unavailable.

To combat this issue, the journaled file system was created. Ext3 and ext4 are such journaled file systems, and thus don't have the long recovery wait time that ext2 does. See the "Journaled File Systems" sidebar for more information.

JOURNALED FILE SYSTEMS

Imagine a library where a returned book causes the librarian to walk off to find an empty space on a shelf somewhere to put the book and then update the catalog, before returning to the front desk in order to process the next returned book. All the while, it's not possible for anyone to borrow a book.

With a book return chute, this problem can be solved. The librarian can process returned books when the library isn't busy with people checking out new books. And even if the books in the chute aren't processed before the library closes, they won't get lost. They will still be in the chute the next day.

A journaled file system works kind of like a library with a book chute. Any information that needs to be written to disk is put in the journal and then put in its final place on disk later, when the operating system has a spare moment. Similarly, if the machine crashes, data in the journal is not lost. The journal is simply processed—or replayed—the next time the file system is mounted.

Our metaphor breaks down here, though. In our file system library, people are allowed to borrow books from the return chute as well, and the librarian is allowed to ignore people who want borrow a book if the chute becomes too full.

Most modern file systems use journals, though some use the journal only for file metadata. For extra speed, some file systems allow you to store the journal on a separate device—for instance, on a solid-state drive (SSD). For more information about SSD devices, see http://en.wikipedia.org/wiki/Flash_drive.

Creating File Systems

The last partition you created earlier, /dev/sdb6, was a small one that you were going to use as a swap partition. The choice of file system for this one is easy, as there is only one swap file system format. Let's set it up first using the mkswap command, as shown in Listing 8-3.

Listing 8-3. *Setting Up Swap Space*

```
$ sudo mkswap /dev/sdb6
Setting up swapspace version 1, size = 2574475 kB
no label, UUID=96570203-0efd-4c18-8887-217d873a6051
```

You're using the mkswap utility to mark /dev/sdb6 as swap space. You can use the generated UUID to add an entry in the /etc/fstab file, which lists all file systems to be used on the host (see the "UUID" sidebar to find out what a UUID is). We'll come back to the /etc/fstab file later in this chapter. Technically speaking, you're not formatting the partition; rather, you're writing a small amount of information to indicate to the kernel that it can be used as swap space.

You can immediately activate the new swap partition via the swapon command. This command tells the kernel it can use the specified partition as swap space.

```
$ sudo swapon /dev/sdb6
```

This command will complete without printing anything, but you can check dmesg for information on what happened. Pipe the output into tail, to limit the number of lines displayed to the specified number.

```
$ dmesg | tail -n 1
[35980.499562] Adding 262136k swap on /dev/sdb6.
Priority:-1 extents:1 across:262136k
```

Another way of checking swap is seeing if the free command reports swap space. Specify the -m option to display sizes in megabytes.

```
$ free -m
                  total        used        free      shared     buffers      cached
Mem:                503         190         313           0          61          69
-/+ buffers/cache:               58         444
Swap:               255           0         255
```

The command reports a total of 255MB of swap space, which is indeed how much space you just added. We'll come back to the free command in Chapter 17, when we look at performance management.

UUID

You may have seen long, semirandom-looking strings of hexadecimal characters like "8d3564ba-92b0-4238-a56f-1c2a0ae85eb2" while installing software on Windows or in the URLs of some websites. These strings are Universally Unique Identifiers (UUIDs).

UUIDs provide a convenient and computationally cheap way of identifying information without the need to check if a generated ID is already in use. Because UUIDs are generated randomly or semirandomly, they are hard to guess and so can provide a little bit of security as well.

UUIDs are increasingly used on Linux as a way to distinguish components of RAID arrays, logical volumes, and file systems. You can read more about them at http://en.wikipedia.org/wiki/Universally_Unique_Identifier.

For your data partitions, start with your new 2GiB /dev/sdb1. You will format this as ext3 using the mkfs.ext3 utility, as shown in Listing 8-4. Apart from the journaling option, ext3 is identical to ext2. To create an ext2 file system, just run mkfs.ext2 instead.

Listing 8-4. *Creating an Ext3 File System*

```
$ sudo mkfs.ext3 /dev/sdb1
mke2fs 1.40.8 (13-Mar-2008)
Filesystem label=
OS type: Linux
Block size=4096 (log=2)
Fragment size=4096 (log=2)
122880 inodes, 489974 blocks
24498 blocks (5.00%) reserved for the super user
First data block=0
Maximum filesystem blocks=503316480
15 block groups
32768 blocks per group, 32768 fragments per group
```

```
8192 inodes per group
Superblock backups stored on blocks:
    32768, 98304, 163840, 229376, 294912

Writing inode tables: done
Creating journal (8192 blocks): done
Writing superblocks and filesystem accounting information: done

This filesystem will be automatically checked every 25 mounts or
180 days, whichever comes first.  Use tune2fs -c or -i to override.
```

When the command completes, take a moment to look at the output. You'll see the file system label is not defined. You could have specified a label using the -L parameter. This label would then allow you to refer to the partition by the label name, as opposed to the device name. You could, for instance, label the devices based on what they'll be used for.

You then see a series of statistics about the file system size and how storage space was allocated. See the "Blocks and Inodes" sidebar for a short explanation. Of note are the blocks reserved for the superuser and the superblock backups.

```
24498 blocks (5.00%) reserved for the super user
Superblock backups stored on blocks:
    32768, 98304, 163840, 229376, 294912
```

The superblock is part of the file system metadata. It contains information about the file system such as its size, the amount of free space in the file system, and where on the file system the data can be found. If a crash occurred and this superblock were damaged, you'd have no way of determining which parts of the file system contained your data. To help you in the event of such a problem, several backup copies of the superblock are maintained at well-known block numbers. We'll revisit recovery later in this chapter.

The reserved blocks for the superuser percentage exist so that a normal user cannot fill a file system to such an extent that the superuser (root) could no longer log in, or services running as the root user would be unable to write data to disk.

The 5% limit is historical and suitable, for instance, for the root file system, which is not normally larger than a few gibibytes. However, when you're using a 1TiB file system, this limit would equate to 50GiB of space that you could not use for storage of user data, so changing or removing it makes sense on data storage volumes.

You could have specified the -m 0 option for mkfs.ext3 to set this percentage of reserved blocks to 0 when creating the file system, or you can change this value later.

Finally, mkfs.ext3 tells you that you can change the automated file system check interval. By default, an automated file system check will occur whenever the mount count reaches 25—that is, the file system has been mounted 25 times—or each time it's mounted after 180 days without a check have passed. This is not the kind of behavior you want on your host, as such a check may take hours.

BLOCKS AND INODES

When you create a file system, the available disk space is divided into units of a specific size. These units are called *blocks* and by default they are 4KB in size.

A block can only hold one file or part of one file, so a 1KB file still uses up a whole block—and thus 4KB of disk space, wasting 3KB of storage space. Larger files are spread out over multiple blocks. If you are mainly storing files smaller than 4KB in size, you might opt to use a different block size for your file system.

Inodes are where most file systems store metadata such as creation and modification dates and permissions and ownership about a file or directory, as well as pointers to which blocks contain the actual file data. This means a file system can contain only as many files and directories as it has inodes. So, with a tiny block size and lots of files, you can run out of inodes before you run out of disk space. JFS does not have this limitation, as extra inodes are added automatically when needed. To read more about inodes, see http:// en.wikipedia.org/wiki/Inode.

Tweaking Ext2, Ext3, and Ext4 File System Options

To change ext2, ext3, and ext4 file system parameters after creation, you use the tune2fs utility. To get an overview of available options, first run the utility without any parameters. You can also pull up the entire manual via man tune2fs.

```
$ tune2fs
tune2fs 1.40.8 (13-Mar-2008)
Usage: tune2fs [-c max_mounts_count] [-e errors_behavior] [-g group]
    [-i interval[d|m|w]] [-j] [-J journal_options] [-l]
    [-m reserved_blocks_percent] [-o [^]mount_options[,...]]
    [-r reserved_blocks_count] [-u user] [-C mount_count] [-L volume_label]
    [-M last_mounted_dir] [-O [^]feature[,...]]
    [-E extended-option[,...]] [-T last_check_time] [-U UUID] device
```

Though it doesn't explicitly say so, the -l parameter lists current file system options. Let's run it on your new ext3 partition (see Listing 8-5).

Listing 8-5. *Displaying Ext2, Ext3, or Ext4 File System Options*

```
$ sudo tune2fs -l /dev/sdb1
tune2fs 1.40.8 (13-Mar-2008)
Filesystem volume name:   <none>
Last mounted on:          <not available>
Filesystem UUID:          f06da31f-ac2e-4e66-9f71-81373a36086e
Filesystem magic number:  0xEF53
Filesystem revision #:    1 (dynamic)
Filesystem features:      has_journal ext_attr resize_inode dir_index filetype
    sparse_super large_file
Filesystem flags:         signed_directory_hash
Default mount options:    (none)
Filesystem state:         clean
```

```
Errors behavior:            Continue
Filesystem OS type:         Linux
Inode count:                122880
Block count:                489974
Reserved block count:       24498
Free blocks:                477170
Free inodes:                122869
First block:                0
Block size:                 4096
Fragment size:              4096
Reserved GDT blocks:        119
Blocks per group:           32768
Fragments per group:        32768
Inodes per group:           8192
Inode blocks per group:     256
Filesystem created:         Thu Dec 18 16:24:16 2008
Last mount time:            n/a
Last write time:            Thu Dec 18 16:24:16 2008
Mount count:                0
Maximum mount count:        27
Last checked:               Thu Dec 18 16:24:16 2008
Check interval:             15552000 (6 months)
Next check after:           Tue Jun 16 15:24:16 2009
Reserved blocks uid:        0 (user root)
Reserved blocks gid:        0 (group root)
First inode:                11
Inode size:                 128
Journal inode:              8
Default directory hash:     tea
Directory Hash Seed:        18cbe84b-a400-4677-ab39-76659257aed9
Journal backup:             inode blocks
```

A lot of information is displayed, but of most interest to us are the file system UUID and state. The mount count, which is the number of times the file system has been mounted, and the check interval are listed here as well, though the interval is displayed in seconds, not days, as it was when we created the file system.

■**Note** We'll take a closer look at some of the file system features in Chapter 17 when we cover capacity planning and performance.

Let's first set the mount interval and maximum mount count to 0. You can still manually force a file system check at boot time if you want to, but this way you never get surprised by a sudden hour-long wait, when you had wanted to do a quick reboot. Also, set the reserved blocks percentage to 0, as you don't need reserved space on this partition.

```
$ sudo tune2fs -c 0 -i 0 -m 0 /dev/sdb1
tune2fs 1.40.8 (13-Mar-2008)
Setting maximal mount count to -1
Setting interval between checks to 0 seconds
Setting reserved blocks percentage to 0% (0 blocks)
```

Table 8-3 lists the options for tune2fs that you're most likely to use.

Table 8-3. *Commonly Used tune2fs Options*

Option	Function
-c N	Sets the number of mounts before a file system check is forced to N
-l	Lists the current file system options
-m N	Sets the reserved blocks percentage to N% of all blocks
-r N	Sets the number of reserved blocks to N
-j	Creates a journal on this file system (converts ext2 to ext3)
-L label	Assigns the label "label" to the file system
-O feat	Toggles the file system feature "feat" on or off

■**Note** We'll come back to the -O option and advanced file system features in Chapter 17 when we discuss performance and capacity planning.

The XFS and JFS File Systems

The XFS and JFS file systems were originally both proprietary and closed source. XFS was developed by Silicon Graphics, Inc., for its IRIX operating system, and JFS was developed by IBM for use on OS/2 Warp Server.

Both companies made their file system drivers open source some years ago and worked on integrating them into the Linux kernel, as Linux lacked a journaling file system at the time. The community enthusiastically embraced these newly open source file systems, as both offered new features and excellent performance. Now they are well accepted and supported on the Linux platform.

XFS

You already created an ext3 partition to store some small files on. Let's format your other partition using the XFS file system, so you can efficiently store large files as well. To this end, you use the mkfs.xfs tool. Since you didn't create an XFS partition when you first installed your host, the XFS utilities are not installed. They are provided by the xfsprogs package, so that is what you have to install. On Ubuntu you install them as follows:

```
$ sudo aptitude install xfsprogs
```

and on RHEL, you use the command

```
$ sudo yum install xfsprogs
```

After installing the package, you can create your file system using the default options, as shown in Listing 8-6.

Listing 8-6. *Creating an XFS File System*

```
$ sudo  mkfs.xfs /dev/sdb5
meta-data=/dev/sdb5              isize=256    agcount=8, agsize=122243 blks
         =                       sectsz=512   attr=0
data     =                       bsize=4096   blocks=977944, imaxpct=25
         =                       sunit=0      swidth=0 blks, unwritten=1
naming   =version 2             bsize=4096
log      =internal log           bsize=4096   blocks=2560, version=1
         =                       sectsz=512   sunit=0 blks, lazy-count=0
realtime =none                   extsz=4096   blocks=0, rtextents=0
```

As the file system is created, some information about its configuration is displayed. We'll make use of this information further in Chapter 17 when we look at performance and capacity planning.

All these options, which, for instance, control block size and journal size, can be set when the file system is created, but the mkfs.xfs tool will choose defaults based on the size of the partition it needs to format.

■**Note** XFS does not reserve 5% of its available space for the root user and also does not automatically force a file system check after a specific amount of time has passed.

JFS

To try out JFS, let's reformat the /dev/sdb5 partition with JFS instead of XFS. Just as with XFS, the JFS utilities are not installed by default, unless you created a JFS partition when you initially installed the host. These tools are provided by the jfsutils package. On Ubuntu you install them like so:

```
$ sudo aptitude install jfsutils
```

and on Red Hat like so:

```
$ sudo yum install jfsutils
```

Once you've installed the tools, invoke mkfs.jfs on the partition you want to format, as shown in Listing 8-7.

Listing 8-7. *Creating a JFS File System*

```
$ sudo mkfs.jfs /dev/sdb5
mkfs.jfs version 1.1.11, 05-Jun-2006
Warning!  All data on device /dev/sdb5 will be lost!

Continue? (Y/N) y
```

```
Format completed successfully.

3911796 kilobytes total disk space.
```

After you agree to destroy all data on the target partition, the file system is created. Just like with XFS, there is no reserved space and no forced file system check interval.

File Systems for Data Sharing

So far, we've covered file systems that are accessible only by Linux. If you need to transfer data between different operating systems—for instance, to your laptop or from a client's machine—you are likely to want to use a file system that can be accessed by Windows and Mac OS X as well as Linux.

The de facto standard for this purpose is the FAT file system, which was developed for MS-DOS by Microsoft. FAT comes in a few flavors. The latest version is FAT32, which supports disk sizes over 32GiB and file sizes of up to 4GiB.

To create a FAT32 file system, you use the mkfs.vfat utility. This utility is provided on both Ubuntu and Red Hat by the dosfstools package, so you need to ensure that dosfstools is installed.

After plugging in the USB drive you wish to format, check its device node name via the kernel log, as shown in Listing 8-8.

Listing 8-8. *Determining the Device Node for a USB Key*

```
$ dmesg
[   52.464662] usb 1-1: new high speed USB device using ehci_hcd and address 2
[   52.887506] usb 1-1: configuration #1 chosen from 1 choice
[   52.967324] usbcore: registered new interface driver libusual
[   52.981452] Initializing USB Mass Storage driver...
[   52.986046] scsi3 : SCSI emulation for USB Mass Storage devices
[   52.987804] usbcore: registered new interface driver usb-storage
[   52.987831] USB Mass Storage support registered.
[   52.988661] usb-storage: device found at 2
[   52.988687] usb-storage: waiting for device to settle before scanning
[   58.982976] usb-storage: device scan complete
[   59.350262] usb 1-1: reset high speed USB device using ehci_hcd and address 2
[   59.772402] scsi 3:0:0:0: Direct-Access     SanDisk  Cruzer
8.01 PQ: 0 ANSI: 0 CCS
[   59.789834] sd 3:0:0:0: [sdg] 15682559 512-byte hardware sectors (8029 MB)
[   59.792747] sd 3:0:0:0: [sdg] Write Protect is off
[   59.792754] sd 3:0:0:0: [sdg] Mode Sense: 45 00 00 08
[   59.792766] sd 3:0:0:0: [sdg] Assuming drive cache: write through
[   59.805772] sd 3:0:0:0: [sdg] 15682559 512-byte hardware sectors (8029 MB)
[   59.815884] sd 3:0:0:0: [sdg] Write Protect is off
[   59.815891] sd 3:0:0:0: [sdg] Mode Sense: 45 00 00 08
[   59.815894] sd 3:0:0:0: [sdg] Assuming drive cache: write through
```

```
[   59.816480]  sdg: sdg1
[   59.831448]  sd 3:0:0:0: [sdg] Attached SCSI removable disk
[   59.831942]  sd 3:0:0:0: Attached scsi generic sg7 type 0
```

In Listing 8-8, the SanDisk Cruzer USB drive was detected as /dev/sdg. Once you know which device node the USB drive is, you can create a primary partition of type c - W95 FAT32 (LBA), and you can then format this partition using mkfs.vfat. Use the -n option to label the partition and specify that you want a FAT32 file system via the -F 32 option.

```
$ sudo mkfs.vfat -n "USB Key" -F 32 /dev/sdg1
mkfs.vfat 2.11 (12 Mar 2005)
```

Other File Systems

A plethora of different file systems are available for Linux, so you might ask why we covered only three of them. Though many other file systems exist, we feel that most of them are not suitable or ready for use in a production environment. The foremost feature a file system needs to have is stability, and the file systems we covered offer this, as well as excellent performance. If you choose ext3, XFS, or JFS based on the type of data you are storing, you should see excellent reliability and speed. Choosing a faster but less stable file system for your server is not going to be of help if as a result you need to spend time restoring your data from backups once a month.

For a brief overview of other file systems supported by the Linux kernel, you can read the filesystems manual page.

■**Note** Linux can create NTFS file systems via the mkntfs tool in the ntfsprogs package. However, we recommend you don't use NTFS file systems to store data under Linux. We'll show you how to access NTFS partitions in Chapter 12, when we look at file sharing.

Using Your File System

You've now created partitions on your new disk, /dev/sdb, and you've formatted these partitions with the file system of your choice. However, before you can use the file system to store data, you need to mount it.

As we briefly explained in Chapter 3 and at the start of this chapter, file systems on Linux do not get assigned a drive letter. Instead, they are mounted as a directory, somewhere under the root file system or a subdirectory. In Chapter 3, we mentioned that the /mnt directory is commonly used as a place to temporarily mount file systems. Next, you'll create a directory called /mnt/data, and you'll use that for your new ext3 partition.

```
$ sudo mkdir /mnt/data
```

Mounting a partition is done via the mount command. You specify the file system type using the -t option, then the device file, and then the directory on which you want the file system to become available.

```
$ sudo mount -t ext3 /dev/sdb1 /mnt/data
```

If all goes well, the mount command will not print any information, but simply exit. To verify that the partition is now mounted, use the df command.

```
$ df
Filesystem              1K-blocks     Used Available Use% Mounted on
/dev/mapper/au--mel--ubuntu--1-root
                         3681680   638168   2857964  19% /
varrun                    257724       72    257652   1% /var/run
varlock                   257724        0    257724   0% /var/lock
udev                      257724      112    257612   1% /dev
devshm                    257724        0    257724   0% /dev/shm
/dev/sda1                 241116    25626    203042  12% /boot
/dev/sdb1                2080592    68680   1907056   4% /mnt/data
```

Our partition is listed at the bottom of the output, so the mount command has succeeded. We'll revisit df later in this chapter and explain in more detail what this output means.

You can also check for some more detailed information by examining the kernel log via the dmesg command.

```
$ dmesg
[692927.431902] kjournald starting.  Commit interval 5 seconds
[692927.440571] EXT3 FS on sdb1, internal journal
[692927.440583] EXT3-fs: mounted filesystem with ordered data mode.
```

The kernel detected an ext3 file system with an internal journal, and mounted it. It also started a kernel thread to flush data from the journal to the file system every five seconds—our librarian emptying the book chute.

If you change your working directory to the newly mounted partition, you can use ls to see if it contains anything:

```
$ cd /mnt/data
$ ls -l
total 16
drwx------ 2 root root 16384 2008-12-18 16:24 lost+found
```

Your brand-new file system contains a single directory called lost+found, which you didn't create! This is a special directory that exists on all ext2 and ext3 file systems—you'll see there is one in the root directory at /lost+found as well. This directory is used by Linux's file system repair tools, which we'll look at later in the "Recovering from Failure" section.

When you no longer need the file system, you can unmount it from your host using the umount command.

```
$ sudo umount /mnt/data
umount: /mnt/data: device is busy
umount: /mnt/data: device is busy
$ pwd
/mnt/data
```

umount is refusing to unmount the directory because it contains files or directories that are in use. In this case, it's because the current working directory is /mnt/data and our host can't unmount the device while we're in the directory. A device could be busy for many reasons, and it's not always clear which user or application has opened which files or directories. To help you find out, the lsof command lists open files and directories:

```
$ lsof /mnt/data
COMMAND   PID   USER    FD    TYPE DEVICE SIZE NODE NAME
bash    20932 jsmith  cwd    DIR  8,17 4096    2 /mnt/data
lsof    21352 jsmith  cwd    DIR  8,17 4096    2 /mnt/data
lsof    21353 jsmith  cwd    DIR  8,17 4096    2 /mnt/data
```

Apart from lsof itself, there is a bash process owned by the user jsmith. You can make this process stop using the directory by going back to your home directory. Type **cd** and the ~ shortcut for your home directory, and then check /mnt/data again using lsof.

```
$ cd ~
$ lsof /mnt/data
```

This time the lsof command has returned no open files and directories, and as the directory is no longer listed as in use, you can now safely unmount it:

```
$ sudo umount /mnt/data
```

■**Note** Unmounting a file system properly will set the Filesystem state flag you saw in the tune2fs output to clean, because it will ask the kernel to process the entire journal file and make sure all data is written to the disk. This prevents an automated file system check the next time your host boots.

When you run lsof as a non-root user, it will only list processes owned by that user. Someone else might still be using a file or directory on the file system you're trying to unmount. If umount keeps reporting the file system is busy, run lsof using sudo to check.

■**Note** If a mounted file system is being used by a system service, you will have to stop the service before you can unmount the file system.

Automating Mounts

You've probably noticed that your other partitions don't need to be manually mounted. When you started your host they were already mounted. This was done as part of the startup process. Each partition you want to mount automatically at startup needs to be listed in the /etc/fstab file. Listing 8-9 shows the one from our Ubuntu host.

Listing 8-9. *An fstab File*

```
# /etc/fstab: static file system information.
# <file system> <mount point>    <type>  <options>         <dump>  <pass>
proc            /proc            proc    defaults          0       0
# /dev/mapper/au--mel--ubuntu--1-root
UUID=e9e48791-dd89-4bf7-921e-f6d460f7ca24 /                       ext3 ➥
     relatime,errors=remount-ro 0        1
# /dev/sda1
UUID=74bce18f-6f8f-4f4c-be91-4ce38e2bff8e /boot                   ext3 ➥
     relatime        0       2
# /dev/mapper/au--mel--ubuntu--1-swap_1
UUID=83f01bff-2cc4-4f4a-abe1-0b9210c5dfa8 none                    swap ➥
     sw              0       0
/dev/scd0       /media/cdrom0    udf,iso9660 user,noauto,exec,utf8 0          0
/dev/fd0        /media/floppy0   auto    rw,user,noauto,exec,utf8 0         0
# /dev/sdb6
UUID=96570203-0efd-4c18-8887-217d873a6051     none                swap ➥
     sw              0       0
```

Each line in the file consists of six fields, separated by spaces or tabs. These fields specify how and where each file system is mounted, and what to do if a check is to be performed. All lines starting with a hash mark (#) are comments.

The file system field contains the device node name of the file system you want to be mounted. You can also substitute a file system label by specifying LABEL=label or the file system UUID, as in the example. By default, Red Hat uses device nodes or labels, and Ubuntu uses the UUID references, but both distributions support the use of either. We'll use UUID references, as they don't change even when disks are detected in a different order and thus might be named differently. Ubuntu places the original device node name in a comment on the line directly above. Next is the mount point, which is simply a directory anywhere on the file system. The mount point can be on a partition that was also mounted separately.

■**Tip** Keep in mind that entries in the /etc/fstab file are processed in order from top to bottom.

The file system type tells the system which type to expect. If this does not match, the mount will fail. You can specify a comma-separated list of types to try, as is the case with the DVD-ROM drive, /dev/scd0. This tries the udf DVD file system first and then iso9660, which is used by CD-ROMs.

Mount options are passed as a comma-delimited list as well. In our example fstab, you can see two different options being used for the ext3 file systems. The relatime option is used to increase file system performance, and we'll cover it in more detail in Chapter 17. The other option, errors=remount-ro, controls what happens if a file system error occurs. In this case, the file system will be immediately mounted in read-only mode. This prevents additional data corruption while keeping files available to services and users.

The other two possible values for error behavior are continue, which would cause the system to write a log entry but otherwise ignore the problem, and panic, which would cause the system to crash ungracefully. The default error behavior can also be specified in the file system itself via the tune2fs -e command.

Other mount options define access to files and directories on file systems that don't support Unix-style file permissions, like FAT32 and NTFS, or might tweak performance. Options for each supported file system can be found in the mount manual page.

The dump field contains a digit (0 or 1), which tells the system whether or not to dump some file system metainformation when a file system check is to be performed. This dump information can be used by the file system repair tools. We'll cover this in a bit more detail in the "Recovering from Failure" section later on.

Finally, the pass field is used to determine the order in which file systems should be checked. In our fstab file, the root file system is listed as 1, so it is checked first. After that the /boot file system would be checked. File systems with a 0 in this column are checked last. You can find longer descriptions of these fields on the fstab manual page.

To add your new partition, you will need to know its UUID. You can find this in the tune2fs listing, or you can use the blkid utility. If you run the latter without any parameters, it prints the UUID for all detected block devices, as shown in Listing 8-10.

Listing 8-10. *Displaying All UUIDs*

```
$ sudo blkid
/dev/mapper/au--mel--ubuntu--1-root: UUID="e9e48791-dd89-4bf7-921e-f6d460f7ca24"
    TYPE="ext3"
/dev/mapper/au--mel--ubuntu--1-swap_1: TYPE="swap"
    UUID="83f01bff-2cc4-4f4a-abe1-0b9210c5dfa8"
/dev/sda1: UUID="74bce18f-6f8f-4f4c-be91-4ce38e2bff8e" TYPE="ext3"
/dev/sda5: UUID="pahIPT-TRbM-NB5q-eRWm-GO0g-uOli-bf5mOi" TYPE="lvm2pv"
/dev/sdb1: UUID="f06da31f-ac2e-4e66-9f71-81373a36086e" TYPE="ext3" SEC_TYPE="ext2"
/dev/sdb5: UUID="7dd09ce2-cf34-4696-9cdd-eb5420c4f37e" TYPE="jfs"
/dev/sdb6: TYPE="swap" UUID="96570203-0efd-4c18-8887-217d873a6051"
```

To have it print the UUID for only a single device, pass the device node name as a parameter.

To mount your ext3 partition with the default mount options, add the following line to the /etc/fstab file:

```
UUID=f06da31f-ac2e-4e66-9f71-81373a36086e  /mnt/data  ext3  defaults  0  0
```

Note that you need to remove the quotes around the UUID as printed by blkid. If you want to use the device node instead, you can add this:

```
/dev/sdb1  /mnt/data  ext3  defaults  0  0
```

Now you can test this entry without the need to reboot. If you use the mount command and only pass the mount point as a parameter, it will check the /etc/fstab file for a matching entry and mount that, with the options specified in the file:

```
$ sudo mount /mnt/data
```

If the mount command exited without printing any errors, the fstab entry is correct and your file system will be automatically mounted each time you boot your host. You can double-check that the file system is mounted by running the mount command without any parameters, which will list all mounted file systems on the host, as shown in Listing 8-11.

Listing 8-11. *All Mounted File Systems*

```
$ mount
/dev/mapper/au--mel--ubuntu--1-root on / type ext3 (rw,relatime,errors=remount-ro)
proc on /proc type proc (rw,noexec,nosuid,nodev)
/sys on /sys type sysfs (rw,noexec,nosuid,nodev)
varrun on /var/run type tmpfs (rw,noexec,nosuid,nodev,mode=0755)
varlock on /var/lock type tmpfs (rw,noexec,nosuid,nodev,mode=1777)
udev on /dev type tmpfs (rw,mode=0755)
devshm on /dev/shm type tmpfs (rw)
devpts on /dev/pts type devpts (rw,gid=5,mode=620)
/dev/sda1 on /boot type ext3 (rw,relatime)
securityfs on /sys/kernel/security type securityfs (rw)
/dev/sdb1 on /mnt/data type ext3 (rw)
```

Alternatively, to add your XFS or JFS partition, create the mount point directory and add the correct UUID or device node name and file system type to /etc/fstab:

```
UUID=7dd09ce2-cf34-4696-9cdd-eb5420c4f37e  /mnt/other  jfs  defaults  0  0
```

■**Caution** A mistake in the fstab file might result in a system that cannot boot. If so, you may need to follow some of the steps discussed in the "Recovering from Failure" section or use single-user mode as described in Chapter 5 to boot and fix the error.

It's possible for the kernel not to have registered that the UUID on a file system has changed. If this happens, attempting to mount the file system by using the UUID reference would result in an error like this:

```
$ sudo mount /mnt/other
mount: special device /dev/disk/by-uuid/7dd09ce2-cf34-4696-9cdd-eb5420c4f37e
    does not exist
```

You can cause the UUID to be redetected and the correct symbolic link in /dev/disk/by-uuid to be created by restarting the udev service.

■**Tip** To avoid having to type long strings like UUIDs, install the gpm package and run the gpm utility so you're able to copy and paste in a terminal using the mouse. Selecting text copies it, and you paste via a middle click.

Checking File System Usage

When you start using a file system for data storage, you'll want to be able to keep an eye on the amount of available space. When a file system fills up, services that use it may refuse to start, stop working, or crash.

You can list space usage for an entire file system via the df command, which is usually used with the -h option. This option produces human-readable output with numbers in KiB, MiB, GiB, or TiB instead of blocks, as shown in Listing 8-12.

Listing 8-12. *File System Usage*

```
$ df -h
Filesystem          Size  Used Avail Use% Mounted on
/dev/mapper/au--mel--ubuntu--1-root
                    3.6G  618M  2.8G  19% /
varrun              252M   64K  252M   1% /var/run
varlock             252M     0  252M   0% /var/lock
udev                252M   80K  252M   1% /dev
devshm              252M     0  252M   0% /dev/shm
/dev/sda1           236M   25M  199M  11% /boot
/dev/sdb1           1.9G   35M  1.9G   2% /mnt/data
/dev/sdb5           3.8G  608K  3.8G   1% /mnt/other
```

The output shows you the total size, the amounts of space used and still available, and the percentage this equates to for each mounted file system. This command is quick, as it simply queries the file system metadata.

■**Note** To check the number of inodes, use the df -i command. Use this command when applications report that the disk is full, even if there is apparently a lot of free space left.

You can check the cumulative size of a directory and all the files it contains with the du command. This command needs to recursively scan files under the directory you're running it on, so it may take a long time to complete. We'll use the -h option again to give us human-readable output. By default, it will print the size for each subdirectory as well. To avoid this, we pass the -s option, so it shows us only the final total.

```
$ du -sh /etc
du: cannot read directory '/etc/lvm/backup': Permission denied
du: cannot read directory '/etc/lvm/cache': Permission denied
du: cannot read directory '/etc/ssl/private': Permission denied
3.7M    /etc
```

Because it scans directories, this command may encounter directories that you don't have permission to access. It cannot calculate the size of these directories, so the total that it reports is not correct in this case. To always get the correct total, you can run du as the root user:

```
$ sudo du -sh /etc
3.8M    /etc
```

This can be helpful when determining which directories to move to a partition of their own if a file system becomes full. An alternative solution would be to resize the file system, and we'll get to that shortly.

■**Tip** In Chapters 17 and 18, when we look at monitoring and logging, we'll cover how to automate file system monitoring.

RAID

Storing data on a hard disk is great to keep it accessible on your server, but when the disk fails, you lose your data. To combat this problem, you can use RAID.

RAID allows you to use multiple disks as if they were a single larger disk, with optional built-in redundancy. The three broad types of RAID implementations are as follows:

- Hardware RAID
- Fake RAID
- Software RAID

Hardware RAID uses specialized hardware controllers, often called *RAID controllers*, that manage RAID transparently from the operating system. Enterprise-level servers often come with these specialized hardware controllers. On such systems, you would usually configure RAID via the BIOS (which we discussed briefly in Chapter 5). Linux will then see a single RAID array, which you would use like a normal hard disk.

Fake RAID is a lesser form of hardware RAID used on smaller systems or desktop machines. Here the manufacturer may have added RAID functionality to the mainboard via a chip. We recommend you don't use fake RAID, as any RAID array created with this implementation would work only on a host sharing an identical controller. Its performance also depends on proprietary code provided by the manufacturer. These controllers can usually be configured to run as simple Serial ATA controllers, instead of RAID. A short listing of the most common fake RAID controllers is available at http://linux-ata.org/faq-sata-raid.html.

■**Note** If you have fake RAID set up with Windows and want to dual boot, you can still use most fake RAID arrays under Linux via the dmraid system. Disabling fake RAID would cause Windows to stop working, and you might lose your data.

The third RAID implementation type is via software contained in the Linux kernel. This system is called md or multiple disk. The md system usually performs much better than fake RAID, and md RAID arrays are transferable between hosts. In this section, we'll focus on using md RAID.

Types of RAID

There are several types—or levels—of RAID. The level you use depends on what is most important to you. The different levels offer a trade-off between available disk space, reliability, and speed. Table 8-4 lists the most commonly used RAID levels.

Table 8-4. *Commonly Used RAID Levels*

RAID Level	Functionality	Storage Capacity
RAID 0	Speed	N * size
RAID 1	Redundancy	N * size / 2
RAID 5	Redundancy, speed	N - 1 * size
RAID 6	Redundancy, reliability, speed	N - 1 * size
RAID 10	Redundancy, reliability, speed	N / 2 * size

You can find an exhaustive list and descriptions of RAID levels at http://en.wikipedia.org/wiki/Redundant_array_of_independent_disks.

It's common to use one hard disk as a spare as well. Should a disk in an array fail, its place can be immediately taken over by the spare disk.

■**Note** It's possible to run RAID without any spare devices, but you will then need to replace a failed device immediately, to avoid data loss.

Striping and Mirroring

The most basic way to use RAID is with two disks, which gives you the option to use either RAID level 0 or RAID level 1.

RAID 0, which is also known as *striping*, causes Linux to see the two disks as a combined disk of twice the size. When writing data to such a RAID array, parts of the data will end up on each of the disks. Since this is an operation Linux can execute simultaneously on both disks, writing to RAID 0 is faster than writing to a single disk. However, the drawback is that when one of the disks fails, arbitrary parts of files that were spread over both disks disappear. So you lose all your data.

■**Caution** Avoid using RAID 0 on a server or on any machine that holds nontransient data.

RAID 1, also known as *mirroring*, allows you to store only as much data on the array as a single disk holds. It stores identical copies of all files on both disks, so if one disk fails, you can still retrieve your data from the other. Since all data needs to be written to each disk, RAID 1 does not offer any improved write performance.

Figure 8-1 shows how files are stored on disk when using RAID 0 or RAID 1. On RAID 1, each disk contains a full copy of each file. On RAID 0, each disk contains only a partial copy of each file.

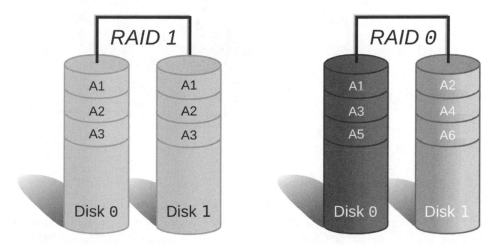

Figure 8-1. *RAID 0 and RAID 1 file storage*

When you have more disks to play with, you get more options to pick a RAID level that can give you improved performance as well as redundancy. The simplest extension is RAID 1+0 (RAID 10), which uses multiple RAID 1 mirrors as elements of a RAID 0 stripe. This way, all striped data is saved to at least two disks, which gives you the advantages of RAID 0 speed and RAID 1 redundancy. However, you can only store as much data as half the combined disk size. When disks are both large and cheap, and you have enough slots in your server to hold at least four disks, this might be a good option.

Processor to the Rescue

In order to get the best of all worlds—redundancy, storage size, and speed—you can call in the help of some processing power. RAID level 5 uses a minimum of three disks and gives you more efficient use of the available storage space and increased read and write speed. It accomplishes this by striping the data across multiple disks and also writing a checksum of each stripe to a different disk. Should a disk fail, the checksum can be used to reconstruct the data in the missing stripes.

The trade-off is that this approach uses processing power to calculate the checksums. When data is written to the array, a checksum needs to be calculated and stored on one of the disks. If a disk fails, the checksum can then be used in combination with the data on the remaining disks to recalculate the missing parts of the data. The faster your CPU, the faster this process is.

Figure 8-2 shows a simple diagram illustrating how data and checksum are split between disks. B1, B2, and B3 are parts of file B. Bp is a checksum. If disk 1 fails, B2 can be computed from B1, B3, and Bp, so when a replacement disk is added, its contents can be restored.

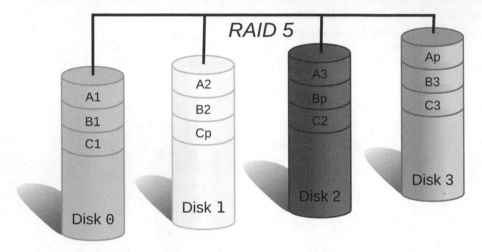

Figure 8-2. *RAID 5 stripe layout across multiple disks*

It's important to keep in mind that using RAID is *not* a substitute for creating regular backups. It will protect you from hardware failure, but not from intentional deletion. If you accidentally delete a file from the RAID array, it will be removed from all devices in the array. We'll cover data backup and recovery in Chapter 12.

Creating an Array

You want to protect the data on your host from disk failure, so you will want to use RAID on it. The most commonly used RAID levels on servers are RAID 1 and RAID 5, so in this section we will set up each of these. The one you use depends on the number of hard disks you have available. First, you need to make sure you have at least three disks and create identically sized partitions on all of them.

■**Note** If you do not have enough disks to use RAID, you can create multiple identically sized partitions on a single disk and use them as components in your RAID array. This will allow you to test RAID installation and management. Note that performance in this configuration will be quite slow, as data will need to be written to different parts of the same disk multiple times. It also doesn't provide much additional resilience against disk failures. If the single disk fails, then your RAID array will also fail.

On our example host we'll use sdb (so we should remove the file systems on that disk from the /etc/fstab file), and we'll add two identical extra disks, sdc and sdd. The partition type should be set to da - Non-FS data, as shown in Listing 8-13.

Listing 8-13. *Clearing the Partition Table and Creating a RAID Partition*

```
$ sudo fdisk /dev/sdb

The number of cylinders for this disk is set to 1044.
There is nothing wrong with that, but this is larger than 1024,
and could in certain setups cause problems with:
1) software that runs at boot time (e.g., old versions of LILO)
2) booting and partitioning software from other OSs
   (e.g., DOS FDISK, OS/2 FDISK)

Command (m for help): o
Building a new DOS disklabel with disk identifier 0x2bcf6dd1.
Changes will remain in memory only, until you decide to write them.
After that, of course, the previous content won't be recoverable.


The number of cylinders for this disk is set to 1044.
There is nothing wrong with that, but this is larger than 1024,
and could in certain setups cause problems with:
1) software that runs at boot time (e.g., old versions of LILO)
2) booting and partitioning software from other OSs
   (e.g., DOS FDISK, OS/2 FDISK)
Warning: invalid flag 0x0000 of partition table 4 will be corrected by w(rite)

Command (m for help): n
Command action
   e   extended
   p   primary partition (1-4)
p
Partition number (1-4):
Value out of range.
Partition number (1-4): 1
First cylinder (1-1044, default 1):
Using default value 1
Last cylinder or +size or +sizeM or +sizeK (1-1044, default 1044):
Using default value 1044

Command (m for help): t
Selected partition 1
Hex code (type L to list codes): da
Changed system type of partition 1 to da (Non-FS data)
```

```
Command (m for help): w
The partition table has been altered!

Calling ioctl() to re-read partition table.
Syncing disks.
```

Repeat this process for /dev/sdc and /dev/sdd. For these, you can skip the first step, the o command, which erases the current partition table.

Now that you have prepared your three disks, you can create the RAID array. For this you will need the RAID management utilities, which are provided by the mdadm package.

The command that manages all aspects of the RAID configuration is also called mdadm, and you can specify what it should do with your array via the mode option. To create an array, you need to specify create mode, which RAID level you want to use, and which partitions need to become part of the array. Listing 8-14 shows how to create a RAID 1 array.

Listing 8-14. *Creating a RAID 1 Array with a Hot Spare*

```
$ sudo  mdadm --create /dev/md0 --level=raid1 --raid-devices=2 /dev/sdb1 ➥
    /dev/sdc1 --spare-devices=1 /dev/sdd1
mdadm: /dev/sdb1 appears to contain an ext2fs file system
    size=1959896K  mtime=Mon Dec 29 19:04:24 2008
Continue creating array? y
mdadm: array /dev/md0 started.
```

As fdisk affects only the partition table, the file systems you created earlier are not affected at all and their data still exists on the disk. Since you won't use them anymore, you can tell mdadm to continue creating the array.

Creating or starting a RAID array will cause the md kernel modules to be loaded and display some status information. You can check the kernel log via dmesg, as shown in Listing 8-15.

Listing 8-15. *Kernel RAID Information*

```
$ dmesg
[58663.877141] md: bind<sdb1>
[58663.902844] md: bind<sdc1>
[58663.942803] md: bind<sdd1>
[58663.943742] md: md0: raid array is not clean -- starting background
    reconstruction
[58663.992313] md: raid1 personality registered for level 1
[58663.994631] raid1: raid set md0 active with 2 out of 2 mirrors
[58664.027163] md: resync of RAID array md0
[58664.027196] md: minimum _guaranteed_  speed: 1000 KB/sec/disk.
[58664.027224] md: using maximum available idle IO bandwidth (but not more than
    200000 KB/sec) for resync.
[58664.027543] md: using 128k window, over a total of 8385792 blocks.
[58705.830365] md: md0: resync done.
[58705.863620] RAID1 conf printout:
[58705.863646]  --- wd:2 rd:2
```

```
[58705.863700]  disk 0, wo:0, o:1, dev:sdb1
[58705.863716]  disk 1, wo:0, o:1, dev:sdc1
```

Because your new array was never synchronized, the kernel will start by ensuring the data on both disks is identical. It informs you it will perform the synchronization as fast as it can, but never slower than 1,000KB per second per disk and never faster than 200,000KB per second in total.

■**Tip** We'll show you how to change the synchronization speed in Chapter 17.

To check on the status of our RAID device, you can use the mdadm utility in query mode with the --detail option. This displays a wealth of information about the specified RAID device, as shown in Listing 8-16.

Listing 8-16. *Querying RAID Device Status*

```
$ sudo mdadm --query --detail /dev/md0
/dev/md0:
          Version : 00.90.03
    Creation Time : Tue Dec 30 11:13:43 2008
       Raid Level : raid1
       Array Size : 8385792 (8.00 GiB 8.59 GB)
    Used Dev Size : 8385792 (8.00 GiB 8.59 GB)
     Raid Devices : 2
    Total Devices : 3
  Preferred Minor : 0
      Persistence : Superblock is persistent

      Update Time : Tue Dec 30 11:21:03 2008
            State : clean
   Active Devices : 2
  Working Devices : 3
   Failed Devices : 0
    Spare Devices : 1

             UUID : 06b4cbbc:3838c8c8:9cc6715a:1cc4c6dd (local to host au-mel-ubuntu-1)
           Events : 0.4

    Number   Major   Minor   RaidDevice State
       0       8       17        0      active sync   /dev/sdb1
       1       8       33        1      active sync   /dev/sdc1
       2       8       49        -      spare   /dev/sdd1
```

Listing 8-16 displays the metainformation about the array, as well as a detailed status for each component. In case of our RAID 1 array, you can see /dev/sdb1 and /dev/sdc1 are both active and in sync. This means any data written to the RAID device is immediately written to both /dev/sdb1 and /dev/sdc1. If either of these devices should fail, our spare (/dev/sdd1) will be automatically activated and synchronized.

At boot time, your Linux host will invoke the mdadm utility. Depending on its configuration, the utility will scan either all partitions or defined disks for RAID superblocks. If it finds any, it will analyze them and try to assemble and start all RAID arrays. You can also explicitly define your RAID arrays in the mdadm configuration file, to ensure their device node names do not change. The configuration file to define your arrays in is /etc/mdadm.conf on Red Hat and /etc/mdadm/madadm.conf on Ubuntu. We've included a default mdadm.conf file from Ubuntu in Listing 8-17.

Listing 8-17. *Default mdadm.conf*

```
# mdadm.conf
#
# Please refer to mdadm.conf(5) for information about this file.
#

# by default, scan all partitions (/proc/partitions) for MD superblocks.
# alternatively, specify devices to scan, using wildcards if desired.
DEVICE partitions

# auto-create devices with Debian standard permissions
CREATE owner=root group=disk mode=0660 auto=yes

# automatically tag new arrays as belonging to the local system
HOMEHOST <system>

# instruct the monitoring daemon where to send mail alerts
MAILADDR root

# definitions of existing MD arrays

# This file was auto-generated on Tue, 30 Dec 2008 11:02:03 +1100
# by mkconf $Id$
```

This configuration file will cause the host to scan for arrays at boot time and create device nodes owned by the root user and disk groups, just like regular hard drives. It specifies that when mdadm is run in monitor mode, any e-mails about device failures are sent to the root user.

■**Note** We'll show you how to redirect all e-mail for the root user to a different address in Chapter 10.

Finally, there is a space to add the configurations for your RAID arrays. You'll add a definition for your RAID 1 array here. According to the mdadm.conf manual page, you need the following:

```
ARRAY /dev/md0 level=raid1 num-devices=2 spares=1 ➥
    UUID=06b4cbbc:3838c8c8:9cc6715a:1cc4c6dd devices=/dev/sdb1,/dev/sdc1,/dev/sdd1
```

Note that adding this array definition is not strictly necessary. mdadm will automatically detect and assemble the array even if you leave this array definition out of the configuration file.

We already mentioned that mdadm will send an e-mail to the root user if an event occurs. We'll show you an example later on, when we start failing devices in our array. To quickly check the state of all your RAID arrays, you can cat the contents of /proc/mdstat:

```
$ cat /proc/mdstat
Personalities : [raid1]
md0 : active raid1 sdd1[2](S) sdc1[1] sdb1[0]
      8385792 blocks [2/2] [UU]

unused devices: <none>
```

This will show you the status of all RAID arrays and all their components. The (S) after sdd1 indicates this device is being used as a spare.

THE /PROC FILE SYSTEM

You have likely noticed references to a directory called /proc in this chapter. This is a special directory that contains virtual files that provide a way of interacting with the kernel. For instance, you can get information about the host processor via cat /proc/cpuinfo.

Internal kernel variables are accessible via files under the /proc/sys directory. We'll come back to these in Chapter 17.

The /proc file system does not physically exist on disk, so it does not use any space, even though it appears to contain some very large files.

You can read more about the /proc file system at http://en.wikipedia.org/wiki/Procfs and http://www.redhat.com/docs/manuals/enterprise/RHEL-4-Manual/en-US/Reference_Guide/ch-proc.html.

If you have minimum of four hard disks, you can create a RAID 5 array instead. Doing so allows you to use the available storage space more efficiently and, in some cases, improve performance as well. To create a new RAID 5 array, you need to disassemble the RAID 1 array first. By stopping it, you release all devices it uses:

```
$ sudo mdadm --manage /dev/md0 --stop
mdadm: stopped /dev/md0
```

You can now use these devices for the new RAID 5 array. Take care to remove the entry added to the mdadm.conf file as well. You'll add a disk, /dev/sde, and create a single primary partition of type da on it.

When that's done, you can create a RAID 5 array with three active devices and one spare, as shown in Listing 8-18.

Listing 8-18. *Creating a RAID 5 Array*

```
$ sudo mdadm --create /dev/md0 --level=raid5 --raid-devices=3 --spare-devices=1 ➥
    /dev/sdb1 /dev/sdc1 /dev/sdd1 /dev/sde1
mdadm: /dev/sdb1 appears to contain an ext2fs file system
    size=1959896K  mtime=Mon Dec 29 19:04:24 2008
mdadm: /dev/sdb1 appears to be part of a raid array:
    level=raid1 devices=4 ctime=Tue Dec 30 11:13:43 2008
mdadm: /dev/sdc1 appears to contain an ext2fs file system
    size=1959896K  mtime=Mon Dec 29 19:04:24 2008
mdadm: /dev/sdc1 appears to be part of a raid array:
    level=raid1 devices=4 ctime=Tue Dec 30 11:13:43 2008
mdadm: /dev/sdd1 appears to contain an ext2fs file system
    size=1959896K  mtime=Mon Dec 29 19:04:24 2008
mdadm: /dev/sdd1 appears to be part of a raid array:
    level=raid1 devices=4 ctime=Tue Dec 30 11:13:43 2008
Continue creating array? y
mdadm: array /dev/md0 started.
```

Some of these devices were part of the previous RAID 1 array, and they still contain the old RAID superblock with array information. You want to create a new array, overwriting the old data, so answer Y. Because the old RAID 1 array was synchronized, all devices also contain a file system now, even though you had initially created only one on /dev/sdb1. You can check the array status again via /proc/mdstat.

```
$ cat /proc/mdstat
Personalities : [linear] [multipath] [raid0] [raid1] [raid6] [raid5] [raid4]
    [raid10]
md0 : active raid5 sdd1[2] sde1[3](S) sdc1[1] sdb1[0]
      16771584 blocks level 5, 64k chunk, algorithm 2 [3/3] [UUU]

unused devices: <none>
```

You now have a RAID 5 array with three active devices and one spare. Provided you have enough hard disks, you can grow the size of a RAID 5 array as well. This causes data to be shifted and checksums to be recalculated, so it will take some time to complete. You'll add a sixth disk, /dev/sdf, to your host, so you can grow the array and still have a spare device available. You also need to partition this disk as you did the others, with a single primary partition of type da. Then you can add the new device to your array and grow the array using mdadm in manage mode via the --add option, as shown in Listing 8-19.

Listing 8-19. *Expanding a RAID 5 Array*

```
$ sudo mdadm --manage /dev/md0 --add /dev/sdf1
mdadm: added /dev/sdf1
```

To add multiple devices in a single command, just list them all after the --add option. A quick check of /proc/mdstat now shows that both sde1 and sdf1 are listed as spares.

```
$ cat /proc/mdstat
Personalities : [linear] [multipath] [raid0] [raid1] [raid6] [raid5] [raid4]
    [raid10]
md0 : active raid5 sdf1[3](S) sdb1[0] sde1[4](S) sdd1[2] sdc1[1]
      16771584 blocks level 5, 64k chunk, algorithm 2 [3/3] [UUU]

unused devices: <none>
```

And now you can expand the array from three to four active disks with mdadm in grow mode. One of the spares will automatically be used for this. Part of this process is destructive, so if a power failure occurs while you're expanding the array, you might lose data. To prevent this, specify the --backup-file option. Be sure not to store this backup file in the /tmp directory, which is emptied on boot!

```
$ sudo mdadm --grow /dev/md0 --raid-disks=4 --backup-file=/root/raid-backup-file
mdadm: Need to backup 384K of critical section..
mdadm: ... critical section passed.
```

You can keep an eye on the progress via the /proc/mdstat file again:

```
$ cat /proc/mdstat
Personalities : [linear] [multipath] [raid0] [raid1] [raid6] [raid5] [raid4]
    [raid10]
md0 : active raid5 sdf1[3] sdb1[0] sde1[4](S) sdd1[2] sdc1[1]
      16771584 blocks super 0.91 level 5, 64k chunk, algorithm 2 [4/4] [UUUU]
      [=======>.............]  reshape = 35.8% (3008512/8385792) finish=22.2min
      speed=4022K/sec

unused devices: <none>
```

You now have four active devices and a single spare. The full new size of the array will not be accessible until the reshape has finished. As you can see, the reshape runs at a far slower rate than the RAID 1 resync.

■**Tip** Instead of rerunning the cat /proc/mdstat command manually, you can automatically run it at a specified interval via the watch command. Log in to a second console and run watch -n 5 cat /proc/mdstat to automatically run the command every five seconds. Exit watch by pressing Ctrl+C.

We'll revisit RAID and show you how to deal with disk failures in the "Recovering from Failure" section of this chapter. For more information about md RAID on Linux, you can visit http://linux-raid.osdl.org/index.php/Linux_Raid.

Next we'll show you how to make use of these RAID devices without the need to partition them.

Logical Volume Management

Using partitions to divide disks is all very well, but they are rather inflexible. Once you partition a disk, it's hard to resize the partitions or to add an additional one. Even if you do add disks and partitions, your data can become spread over a variety of locations and directories. This makes it harder to consolidate, back up, and manage your data, and it potentially makes it harder for your users to find their data. To overcome this issue, logical volume management (LVM) was created.

Rather than splitting a disk into a fixed number of partitions that are stored on a fixed area of the disk, LVM amalgamates one or more partitions or devices into a single logical volume group. You can then dynamically create, resize, and delete volumes in a volume group, removing the need to unmount volumes or reboot the system to update the partition map.

The LVM system has three layers. The bottom layer consists of physical volumes: disks, partitions, or RAID arrays. Physical volumes are used to create volume groups. A volume group can consist of one or more physical volumes. Finally, a volume group can contain any number of logical volumes, which are the LVM equivalent of partitions.

Both Ubuntu and Red Hat have a GUI that you can use to manage LVM. First, though, we'll take you through administering via the command line, starting with LVM volumes and groups.

Creating Groups and Volumes

If you want to use a partition with LVM, you need to set its type to `8e - Linux LVM` using `fdisk`. You can also use an entire disk or RAID array as storage for LVM. This is convenient, as you would not normally create partitions on a software RAID array. To use an entire disk with LVM, you need to erase its partition table first. You can do this by writing zeroes to the first sector, the first 512 bytes, of the disk using the `dd` command, for example:

```
$ sudo dd if=/dev/zero of=/dev/sdg bs=512 count=1
```

This command reads a single block of 512 bytes of data from `/dev/zero` and writes it to the first sector of `/dev/sdg`, thus erasing the boot record and partition map, which we know are stored there. You can read more about the `dd` utility on the `dd` manual page.

■**Caution** The `dd` command is a very powerful utility that writes to the raw block device, and it can easily destroy existing data. Use it with extreme care. It is sometimes also used to create backups of partitions or other block devices.

For our examples, we'll be setting up LVM on the RAID 5 array created earlier. The steps are identical when setting up LVM on RAID 1, individual partitions, or whole disks.

Each of these storage devices used by LVM is called a physical volume (PV). You can mark a device as such via the `pvcreate` command.

```
$ sudo pvcreate /dev/md0
  Physical volume "/dev/md0" successfully created
```

This command writes a small watermark to the start of the device, identifying it for use with LVM. You can list all such devices on the system via the pvs command.

```
$ sudo pvs
  PV         VG             Fmt  Attr PSize  PFree
  /dev/md0                  lvm2 --   23.99G 23.99G
  /dev/sda5  au-mel-ubuntu-1 lvm2 a-    3.76G     0
```

■**Note** You will get more detailed information about physical volumes if you use the pvdisplay command.

Recall that we chose to use LVM when we first installed the system. You can see now that it used the /dev/sda5 partition as a physical volume. The second column, labeled VG, refers to the volume group, which is the next layer in the LVM system.

You can list all volume groups on the system via the vgs command.

```
$ sudo vgs
  VG              #PV #LV #SN Attr   VSize VFree
  au-mel-ubuntu-1   1   2   0 wz--n- 3.76G     0
```

■**Note** You will get more detailed information about volume groups if you use the vgdisplay command.

There is one volume group, called au-mel-ubuntu-1, which was created by the installer. It spans one physical volume and contains two logical volumes. You can list these via the lvs command. There are currently two volumes, root and swap_1.

```
$ sudo lvs
  LV     VG              Attr   LSize   Origin Snap%  Move Log Copy%
  root   au-mel-ubuntu-1 -wi-ao   3.54G
  swap_1 au-mel-ubuntu-1 -wi-ao 224.00M
```

■**Note** You will get more detailed information about logical volumes if you use the lvdisplay command.

You can now add your physical volume to an existing group via the vgextend command:

```
$ sudo vgextend ubuntu-au-mel-1 /dev/md0
  Volume group "au-mel-ubuntu-1" successfully extended
```

And to check, you can display the physical volumes using pvs and vgs.

```
$ sudo pvs
  PV         VG             Fmt  Attr PSize  PFree
```

```
/dev/md0    au-mel-ubuntu-1 lvm2 a-    23.99G 23.99G
/dev/sda5   au-mel-ubuntu-1 lvm2 a-     3.76G    0
$ sudo vgs
  VG                #PV #LV #SN Attr   VSize  VFree
  au-mel-ubuntu-1    2   2   0 wz--n- 27.75G 23.99G
```

The new physical volume is now part of the au-mel-ubuntu-1 volume group. Adding the new physical volume to the group means it now has 23.99GiB of unallocated space.

The alternative would have been to create a new volume group and use your physical volume with that. You can still do so by removing /dev/md0 from the au-mel-ubuntu-1 group via the vgreduce command:

```
$ sudo vgreduce au-mel-ubuntu-1 /dev/md0
  Removed "/dev/md0" from volume group "au-mel-ubuntu-1"
```

It is now available to be used for a different volume group, which you create using the vgcreate command. You will assign the /dev/md0 device to the new raid-volume volume group. When this is complete, you can check that the new volume group exists using the vgs command.

```
$ sudo vgcreate raid-volume /dev/md0
  Volume group "raid-volume" successfully created
$ sudo vgs
  VG                #PV #LV #SN Attr   VSize  VFree
  au-mel-ubuntu-1    1   2   0 wz--n-  3.76G    0
  raid-volume        1   0   0 wz--n- 23.99G 23.99G
```

You now have a new volume group that you can use to create logical volumes. In preparation for later chapters, why don't we create a storage area for websites? With LVM, we can easily give each of these functions its own dedicated area on disk.

First, you need to create a logical volume, which you do via the lvcreate command. You need to specify a name, a size, and the volume group to create the volume in. You can then list it via lvs.

```
$ sudo lvcreate --name www --size 2G raid-volume
  Logical volume "www" created
$ sudo lvs
  LV     VG              Attr   LSize   Origin Snap%  Move Log Copy%
  root   au-mel-ubuntu-1 -wi-ao   3.54G
  swap_1 au-mel-ubuntu-1 -wi-ao 224.00M
  www    raid-volume     -wi-a-   2.00G
```

All that's left to do now is create a file system on the logical volume and mount it somewhere. To do so, you need the device node name for the logical volume. This is managed by a driver called device-mapper, which creates a device node entry for any volume you create.

A logical volume is accessible via /dev/mapper/<vgname>-<lvname>, which is symlinked from /dev/<vgname>/<lvname>. So for the new "www" LV, you can use /dev/raid-volume/www. As the website will likely consist of many smaller files, create an ext3 file system using the following:

```
$ sudo mkfs.ext3 /dev/raid-volume/www
```

You can use the volume as if it were an ordinary partition and add it to the /etc/fstab file, so it is automatically mounted on /srv/www when your host boots. For this, you can use either the device node name or the UUID of the file system just created. blkid will provide you with both. The /etc/fstab entry looks like this:

```
# /dev/mapper/raid--volume-www
UUID=c0f3d1ef-c201-4fae-bb35-6a21bfcafa0e  /srv/www  ext3  defaults  0  0
```

After you create the /srv/www directory and restart udev to have the new UUID detected and registered under /dev, you can mount it using the following:

```
$ sudo mount /srv/www
```

Expanding a Logical Volume

Thus far, using LVM has seemed just a more convoluted way of using your disks, but what if your website grew beyond 2GiB? Without LVM, you would need to create a partition on an unused disk, and then copy all data across and make sure /etc/fstab was updated. However, with LVM you can simply expand the logical volume and then resize the file system on it. If there was no space left in the volume group, you could add a physical volume to the group first.

You need to complete two steps to safely resize the file system contained in your logical volume. First, you need to resize the logical volume itself, and second, you need to resize the file system.

The volume can be expanded using the lvextend command. You need to specify either the new total size or the size increase you want, and the name of the volume. By prefixing the size parameter with +, you indicate you want the specified size added to the existing size.

```
$ sudo lvextend --size +2G /dev/raid-volume/www
```

To specify the new total size, you could also use the following:

```
$ sudo lvextend --size 4G /dev/raid-volume/www
  Extending logical volume www to 4.00 GB
  Logical volume www successfully resized
```

In this case, both approaches produce the same result: a logical volume 4GiB in size containing a 2GiB file system.

You now need to tell the file system about the new size of the device it is contained on, for which you use the resize2fs utility. You'll start with a 2GiB file system, as you can see in Listing 8-20.

Listing 8-20. *Resizing an Ext3 File System*

```
$ df -h /srv/www
Filesystem            Size  Used Avail Use% Mounted on
/dev/mapper/raid--volume-www
                      2.0G  135M  1.9G   7% /srv/www
$ sudo resize2fs /dev/raid-volume/www
resize2fs 1.40.8 (13-Mar-2008)
Filesystem at /dev/raid-volume/www is mounted on /srv/www; on-line resizing required
old desc_blocks = 1, new_desc_blocks = 1
Performing an on-line resize of /dev/raid-volume/www to 1048576 (4k) blocks.
```

The filesystem on /dev/raid-volume/www is now 1048576 blocks long.
$ df -h /srv/www
Filesystem   Size Used Avail Use% Mounted on
/dev/mapper/raid--volume-www
                    4.0G 137M 3.8G   4% /srv/www

And you now have a 4GiB file system.

XFS file systems can also be expanded while in use. You would again need to expand the logical volume first, and then expand the file system. For XFS you would use xfs_grow /srv/www. This command takes a mount point as a parameter, not a device node name. You can check the xfs_grow manual page for more information.

Shrinking a Logical Volume

In addition to expanding a file system, you can shrink one. To shrink a file system and a logical volume, you follow the previous steps in reverse and use the lvreduce command. Just make certain you do not shrink the logical volume to be smaller than the file system it contains.

■**Note** Unlike ext2, ext3, and ext4, the XFS file system cannot be shrunk.

Although it's a little bit more work to set up than simple partitions, LVM allows you to use your storage space in a far more flexible manner. Table 8-5 lists the LVM commands you'll most often use.

Table 8-5. *Basic LVM Commands*

Command	Used For
pvcreate	Labeling devices for use with LVM
pvremove	Removing the LVM label from a physical volume
pvdisplay / pvs	Displaying information on the specified device or all physical volumes on the system
vgcreate	Creating a new volume group
vgremove	Removing (deleting) a volume group
vgextend	Adding physical volumes to a volume group
vgreduce	Removing physical volumes from a volume group
vgdisplay / vgs	Displaying information about the specified group or all volume groups on the system
lvcreate	Creating a new logical volume
lvremove	Removing (deleting) a logical volume
lvextend	Increasing the size of a logical volume
lvreduce	Decreasing the size of a logical volume
lvdisplay / lvs	Displaying all logical volumes on the system or in a specified volume group

Managing LVM via a GUI

As briefly mentioned before, Red Hat-based hosts can manage LVM via a GUI, through the system-config-lvm tool. To be able to use this tool, you need to have installed the system-config-lvm package.

■**Note** The system-config-lvm GUI tool is not available on Ubuntu 8.04 LTS. However, it is available in the universe repository on newer versions of Ubuntu. If you use KDE on Ubuntu, you can also use the kvpm tool, which performs similar tasks.

You start the system-config-lvm application by selecting System ➤ Administration ➤ Logical Volume Management or from the command line by entering the following:

```
$ sudo system-config-lvm
```

Figure 8-3 shows the GUI.

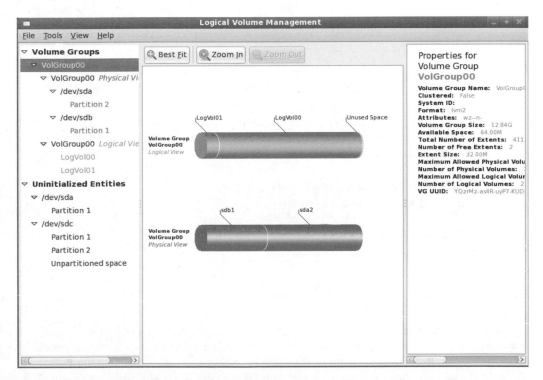

Figure 8-3. *The system-config-lvm application*

You have just added a new disk and created a single whole-disk partition on it using fdisk. You will initialize it, and then create a volume group and a logical volume. The disk will show up in the Uninitialized Entities menu in the left panel, as you can see in Figure 8-4.

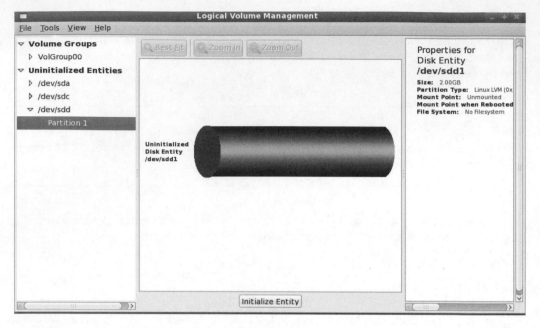

Figure 8-4. *New disks in the Uninitialized Entities menu*

In the right panel, you can see the properties of your new disk. To initialize the new disk (i.e., create a physical volume as you would with the pvcreate command), click the Initialize Entity button at the bottom of the middle panel.

Figure 8-5 shows the warning you are presented with that you are about to erase the /dev/sdd1 partition on the disk. If this is something you don't want to do, click the No button; otherwise, proceed by clicking the Yes button.

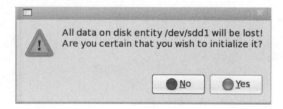

Figure 8-5. *Warning before erasing the partition*

The disk will be initialized and system-config-lvm will reload the LVM details. You will now see that the disk and partition have moved into Unallocated Volumes in the left panel. In the right panel, you will see that the properties have changed accordingly. As shown in Figure 8-6, you have three options to choose from in the middle panel: Create new Volume Group, Add to existing Volume Group, and Remove volume from LVM.

Now you'll create a new volume group. You could add to an existing volume group, and that will provide an extra 2GB of space for that group to use if you wanted. Create the new group by clicking Create new Volume Group.

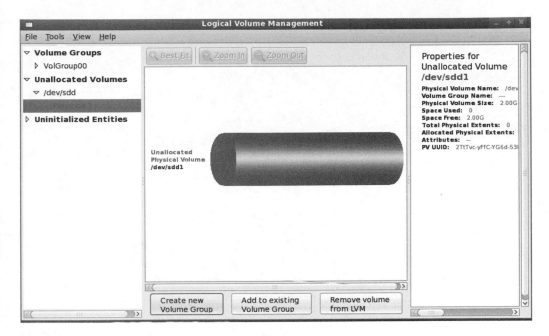

Figure 8-6. *Creating a new volume group*

In the screenshot in Figure 8-7, you are asked to provide some details like the volume group name, the size of the disk, and the physical extent size. Accept the defaults and give it the name VolGroup01. This will create a volume group with 2GB available.

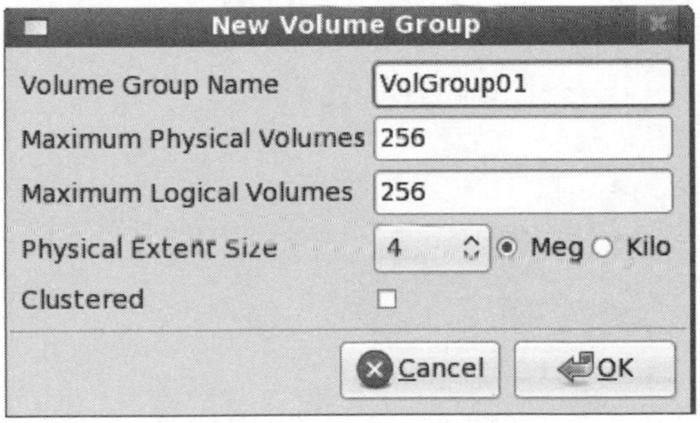

Figure 8-7. *Specifying the volume group name*

You can see in Figure 8-8 that the disk and partition have moved under Volume Groups in the left panel and are now ready to have the logical volume(s) created on them.

Next, you will create just one logical volume by selecting VolGroup01 Logical View and clicking the Create new Logical Volume button, as shown in Figure 8-8.

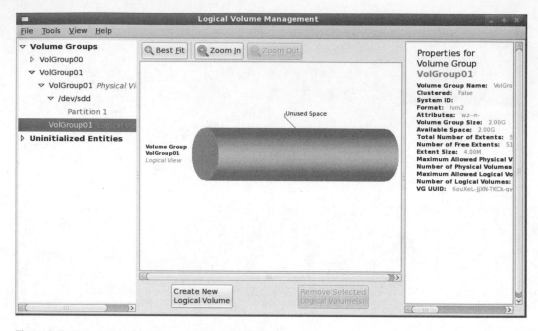

Figure 8-8. *Creating volume group VolGroup01*

In the Create New Logical Volume dialog box shown in Figure 8-9, you are asked to provide the details of our new logical volume. Give the volume the name wwwData, use the full 2GB available, add the ext3 file system to it, and finally mount it under the /srv/www directory.

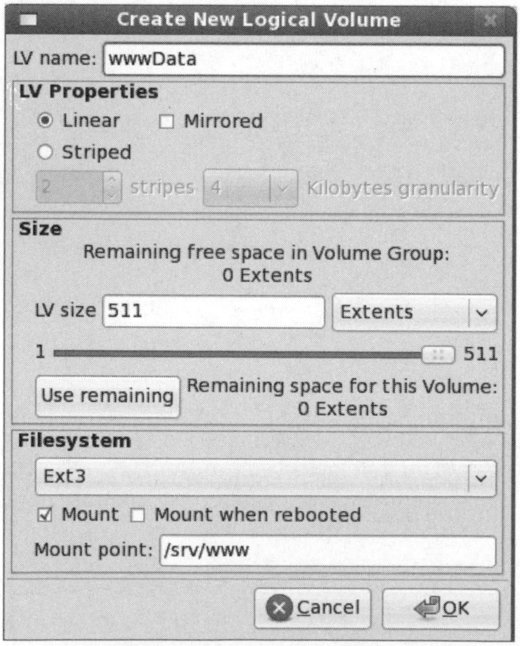

Figure 8-9. *Creating a new logical volume*

You are now asked if you wish to confirm the creation of the mount point (see Figure 8-10). This is where you will mount your new logical volume. Choose Yes and proceed. `system-config-lvm` will now create the mount point and format the logical volume with the ext3 file system.

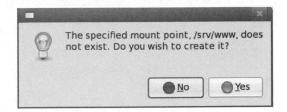

Figure 8-10. *Confirming creation of a new logical volume*

As you can see in Figure 8-11, a new logical volume called wwwData has been created. It is part of volume group VolGroup01, which is made up of the physical device /dev/sdd partition 1.

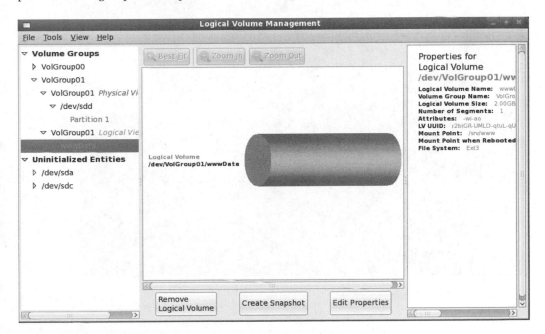

Figure 8-11. *The logical volume is now created.*

You can remove the logical volume or create a snapshot of it using the `system-config-lvm` tool. Removing the logical volume will destroy the data on that logical volume and you are given a warning before you proceed. If you remove a logical volume, you can create one or more new logical volumes in that volume group.

You can also use `system-config-lvm` to remove volume groups, but you must ensure that all logical volumes belonging to the volume group have been removed first.

Creating a snapshot of the logical volume creates a copy of the data at a point in time. You need enough disk space in the volume group to hold the data in the logical volume being snapped, as well as any new data that is written to the snapshot, for as long as it exists. This allows you to move a point-in-time copy of your data offline, so that you can take a backup or view or perform some kind of maintenance without impacting the existing logical volume.

■**Note** We'll talk more about LVM snapshots in Chapter 13 when we look at backup and recovery.

Recovering from Failure

If your host suffers a crash that leaves a file system in an inconsistent state, the system will automatically try to repair the problem at boot time. Figure 8-12 shows how the root file system on our host was automatically checked and the journal on /dev/sda1 was replayed after a crash.

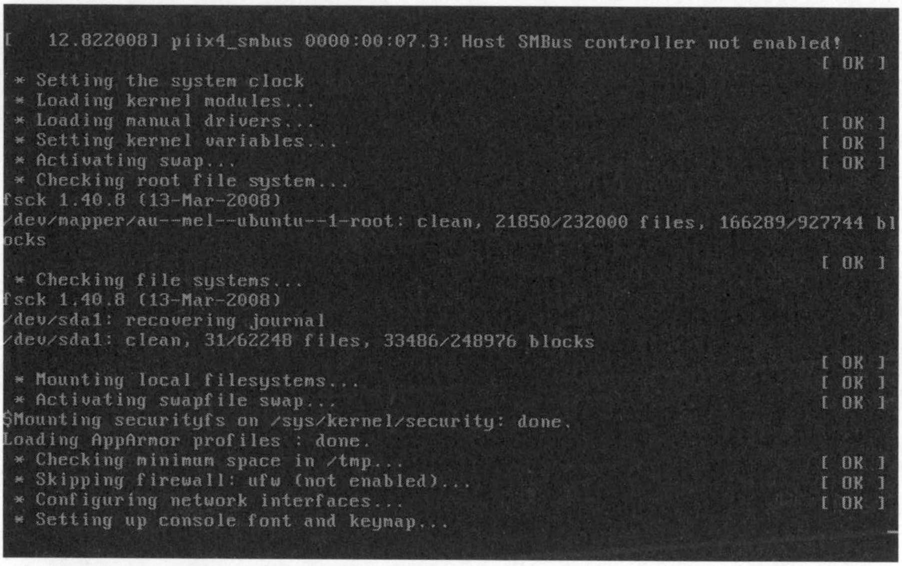

Figure 8-12. *Automatic file system recovery*

These automated recoveries will generally work, but on occasion the repair tools will find a problem they cannot fix automatically.

If this happens for the root file system, on which the repair utilities are stored, you will need to boot from your installation CD or DVD. You may remember from Chapter 2, the CD or DVD includes an option to boot in rescue or recovery mode. This mode boots to a minimal system running from the installation disc and drops you into a root shell. From this shell, you can then perform any steps needed to recover the file systems.

The simplest step is to run the appropriate file system checker. Table 8-6 details the system check and repair tools for the file systems you are most likely to use.

Table 8-6. *File System Check and Repair Tools*

File System(s)	Repair Tool
Ext2 and ext3	e2fsck
XFS	xfs_repair
JFS	jfs_fsck

To run these repair tools, you will need to make sure the file system you're checking is not mounted for writing. Repairing a file system that is mounted in read/write mode is guaranteed to destroy data, as the file system will be modified directly by the repair tool without the kernel knowing about it.

To check the file system, you pass the appropriate device node name as a parameter to the repair tool.

■**Note** When repairing the root file system by running a tool from the root file system itself, make sure to mount the file system read-only first.

If there is a problem on a file system that is not the root file system, the system will inform you that the file system could not be mounted and continue booting, as shown in Figure 8-13.

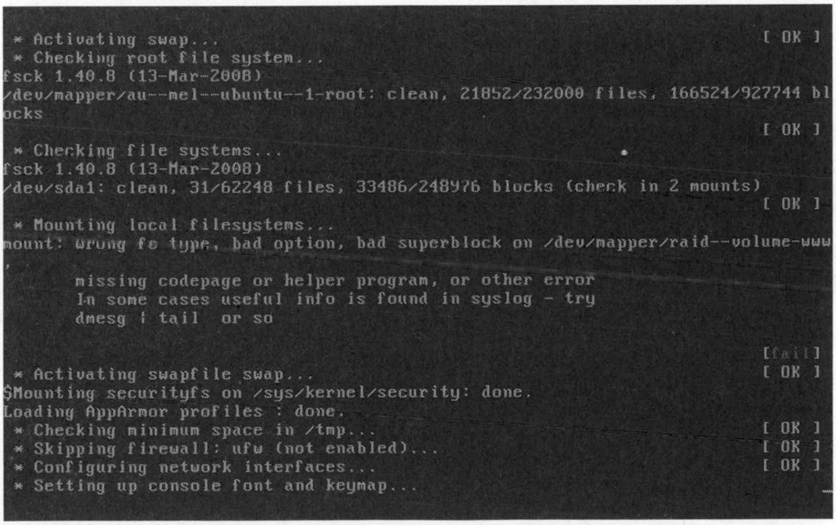

Figure 8-13. *A file system problem prevents an automatic mount.*

You'll also note that /dev/sda1 (/boot) will be automatically checked in two mounts. We didn't change this file system with tune2fs -c 0 earlier.

When boot completes, you can log in and run the repair tools. Listing 8-21 shows this process for the ext3 file system we created earlier. We pass the -p option to let e2fsck automatically repair problems that can be fixed without user intervention. If there are other problems, we generally answer Y to any questions to repair them. We're checking an ext3 file system in Listing 8-21.

Listing 8-21. *Repairing an Ext3 File System*

```
# e2fsck -p /dev/raid-volume/www
e2fsck 1.40.8 (13-Mar-2008)
/dev/raid-volume/www contains a file system with errors, check forced.
Pass 1: Checking inodes, blocks, and sizes
Pass 2: Checking directory structure
Pass 3: Checking directory connectivity
Pass 4: Checking reference counts
Pass 5: Checking group summary information
Block bitmap differences:  -(2--256) -520 -(32770--33024)
Fix<y>? yes

/dev/raid-volume/www: ***** FILE SYSTEM WAS MODIFIED *****
```

The e2fsck run found problems that it could automatically fix and repaired them.

On occasion there is a problem with the superblock for an ext2 or ext3 file system, which means the file system–checking tools cannot locate the file system metadata they need in order to repair the file system. For this reason, these file systems keep backup superblocks as well. You can use the dumpe2fs tool to display their location on the disk and then specify this location for e2fsck using the -b option, as shown in Listing 8-22.

Listing 8-22. *Finding Backup Superblocks*

```
# dumpe2fs /dev/raid-volume/www | grep Backup
dumpe2fs 1.40.8 (13-Mar-2008)
  Backup superblock at 32768, Group descriptors at 32769-32769
  Backup superblock at 98304, Group descriptors at 98305-98305
  Backup superblock at 163840, Group descriptors at 163841-163841
  Backup superblock at 229376, Group descriptors at 229377-229377
  Backup superblock at 294912, Group descriptors at 294913-294913
```

Once you know the location of a backup superblock, you can try running e2fsck and specifying the location of a backup superblock using the -b option.

```
# e2fsck -b 32768 -p /dev/raid-volume/www
e2fsck 1.40.8 (13-Mar-2008)
Pass 1: Checking inodes, blocks, and sizes
Pass 2: Checking directory structure
Pass 3: Checking directory connectivity
Pass 4: Checking reference counts
Pass 5: Checking group summary information
/dev/raid-volume/www: 11/131072 files (0.0% non-contiguous), 36947/524288 blocks
```

The e2fsck command can now run and repair the file system.

If there are problems and file data is found in inodes that e2fsck cannot place, this data will be stored in files in the lost+found directory on the file system you're checking. The file name is the inode number that the data is associated with. Although this doesn't tell you which files are no longer where they should be, you can inspect these numbered files manually and get some sense of which data might be missing.

If a lot of corruption occurred and there are many hundreds of files in the lost+found directory, it is probably better to restore your data from a backup.

Boot Loader Problems

If a problem occurs with a hard disk, the system may fail to boot altogether because the boot sector was corrupted. In this case, the boot loader cannot be started, and you'll see strange errors on the screen, like we showed you in Chapter 5.

These problems can be fixed by reinstalling the boot loader. The first step is to boot your installation CD or DVD in rescue or recovery mode and run a file system check from the root shell, as just shown. When the file system has been repaired, you can mount it.

```
# e2fsck -p /dev/sda1
# mount -t ext3 /dev/sda1 /mnt
```

We can now log in to the Linux installation on the mounted partition via the chroot (change root) command, which allows you to specify a different system root for your shell. By setting this new root to the mounted root file system, we effectively get a root shell on the system we're trying to recover.

Before we run chroot, we need to make sure we can access the device files and kernel interfaces via the dynamic /dev and /proc file systems. We can mount the existing ones on the root file system on which we will run chroot via a bind mount. A *bind mount* is a way of making a directory available in multiple locations on the system, without needing to use symbolic links. In this case, we can't use symbolic links, as they would point to a target outside the chroot, which is not accessible from inside the chroot itself.

```
# mount -o bind /dev /mnt/dev
# mount -o bind /proc /mnt/proc
```

When the bind mounts are done, we can chroot to the mounted root file system and run a Bash shell there. The prompt will look somewhat odd, as the Bash startup scripts will not be run.

```
# chroot /mnt /bin/bash
bash-2 #
```

Now that we have a shell, we can run the command to reinstall the boot loader on the first disk.

```
bash-2 # /usr/bin/grub-install /dev/sda
```

When that is done, we log out from the chroot and unmount the file systems in reverse order. If we don't unmount these, our fixed root file system cannot be unmounted, and a check will be forced again when we next boot up.

```
bash-2 # exit
# umount /mnt/proc
# umount /mnt/dev
# umount /mnt
```

We can now reboot the host using Ctrl+Alt+Delete, the reboot command, or the shutdown -r now command. Remove the installation media, so the host boots from hard disk.

Disk Failure

Sooner or later one of your hard disks will fail. When you're using RAID, this is no longer a problem, but you will need to take action to ensure the array is fully working again before the next disk fails. As you've seen earlier in this chapter, you can keep a disk marked as a spare, and that automates part of this process.

To simulate a disk failure, we'll use mdadm to tell the kernel that /dev/sdb1 has failed, as shown in Listing 8-23.

Listing 8-23. *Testing Our RAID Array*

```
$ sudo  mdadm --manage /dev/md0 --fail /dev/sdb1
mdadm: set /dev/sdb1 faulty in /dev/md0
```

The RAID subsystem now knows the device has failed. This is identical to what happens when the RAID drivers detect that an error has occurred on one of the devices in the array. Let's have another look at the /proc/mdstat file:

```
$ cat /proc/mdstat
Personalities : [linear] [multipath] [raid0] [raid1] [raid6] [raid5] [raid4]
    [raid10]
md0 : active raid5 sdf1[3] sdd1[2] sde1[4] sdc1[1] sdb1[5](F)
      25157376 blocks level 5, 64k chunk, algorithm 2 [4/3] [_UUU]
      [=======>.............]  recovery = 38.6% (3242368/8385792) finish=0.7min
      speed=120087K/sec

unused devices: <none>
```

The sdb1 disk is now marked as failed with (F), and sde1, which was our spare disk, is being brought up to date. We can check the system log to make sure the RAID monitor has picked up on these changes and acted appropriately. On RHEL this is /var/log/messages, and on Ubuntu it is /var/log/syslog:

```
Dec 31 12:53:52 au-mel-ubuntu-1 kernel: [68789.499377] raid5: Disk failure on
    sdb1, disabling device. Operation continuing on 3 devices
Dec 31 12:53:52 au-mel-ubuntu-1 kernel: [68789.532848] RAID5 conf printout:
Dec 31 12:53:52 au-mel-ubuntu-1 kernel: [68789.532857]  --- rd:4 wd:3
Dec 31 12:53:52 au-mel-ubuntu-1 kernel: [68789.532863]  disk 0, o:0, dev:sdb1
Dec 31 12:53:52 au-mel-ubuntu-1 kernel: [68789.532866]  disk 1, o:1, dev:sdc1
Dec 31 12:53:52 au-mel-ubuntu-1 kernel: [68789.532868]  disk 2, o:1, dev:sdd1
Dec 31 12:53:52 au-mel-ubuntu-1 kernel: [68789.532871]  disk 3, o:1, dev:sdf1
Dec 31 12:53:52 au-mel-ubuntu-1 kernel: [68789.561038] RAID5 conf printout:
Dec 31 12:53:52 au-mel-ubuntu-1 kernel: [68789.561044]  --- rd:4 wd:3
Dec 31 12:53:52 au-mel-ubuntu-1 kernel: [68789.561054]  disk 1, o:1, dev:sdc1
Dec 31 12:53:52 au-mel-ubuntu-1 kernel: [68789.561057]  disk 2, o:1, dev:sdd1
```

Dec 31 12:53:52 au-mel-ubuntu-1 kernel: [68789.561059] disk 3, o:1, dev:sdf1
Dec 31 12:53:52 au-mel-ubuntu-1 kernel: [68789.561168] RAID5 conf printout:
Dec 31 12:53:52 au-mel-ubuntu-1 kernel: [68789.561170] --- rd:4 wd:3
Dec 31 12:53:52 au-mel-ubuntu-1 kernel: [68789.561173] disk 0, o:1, dev:sde1
Dec 31 12:53:52 au-mel-ubuntu-1 kernel: [68789.561175] disk 1, o:1, dev:sdc1
Dec 31 12:53:52 au-mel-ubuntu-1 kernel: [68789.561177] disk 2, o:1, dev:sdd1
Dec 31 12:53:52 au-mel-ubuntu-1 kernel: [68789.561180] disk 3, o:1, dev:sdf1
Dec 31 12:53:52 au-mel-ubuntu-1 kernel: [68789.562910] md: recovery of RAID
    array md0
Dec 31 12:53:52 au-mel-ubuntu-1 kernel: [68789.562944] md: minimum
    guaranteed speed: 1000 KB/sec/disk.
Dec 31 12:53:52 au-mel-ubuntu-1 kernel: [68789.562948] md: using maximum
    available idle IO bandwidth (but not more than 200000 KB/sec) for recovery.
Dec 31 12:53:52 au-mel-ubuntu-1 kernel: [68789.562953] md: using 128k
    window, over a total of 8385792 blocks.
Dec 31 12:53:52 au-mel-ubuntu-1 mdadm: Fail event detectedon md device
    /dev/md0, component device /dev/sdb1
Dec 31 12:53:52 au-mel-ubuntu-1 mdadm: RebuildStarted event detected on
    md device /dev/md0
Dec 31 12:53:52 au-mel-ubuntu-1 mdadm: SpareActive event detected on
    md device /dev/md0, component device /dev/sdb1
Dec 31 12:53:52 au-mel-ubuntu-1 postfix/pickup[6687]: 5978A4550:
    uid=0 from=<root>
Dec 31 12:53:52 au-mel-ubuntu-1 postfix/cleanup[8457]: 5978A4550:
    message-id=<20081231015352.5978A4550@au-mel-ubuntu-1.example.com>
Dec 31 12:53:52 au-mel-ubuntu-1 postfix/qmgr[5280]: 5978A4550:
    from=<root@au-mel-ubuntu-1.example.com>, size=1023, nrcpt=1 (queue active)
Dec 31 12:53:53 au-mel-ubuntu-1 postfix/local[8459]: 5978A4550
    to=<root@au-mel-ubuntu-1.example.com>, orig_to=<root>, relay=local, delay=1.1
    delays=0.41/0.37/0/0.29, dsn=2.0.0, status=sent (delivered to command:
    procmail -a "$EXTENSION")
Dec 31 12:53:53 au-mel-ubuntu-1 postfix/qmgr[5280]: 5978A4550:
    removed
Dec 31 12:54:52 au-mel-ubuntu-1 mdadm: Rebuild80 event detected on
    md device /dev/md0
Dec 31 12:55:01 au-mel-ubuntu-1 kernel: [68858.893259] md: md0: recovery done.
Dec 31 12:55:01 au-mel-ubuntu-1 kernel: [68858.985655] RAID5 conf printout:
Dec 31 12:55:01 au-mel-ubuntu-1 kernel: [68858.985661] --- rd:4 wd:4
Dec 31 12:55:01 au-mel-ubuntu-1 kernel: [68858.985665] disk 0, o:1, dev:sde1
Dec 31 12:55:01 au-mel-ubuntu-1 kernel: [68858.985668] disk 1, o:1, dev:sdc1
Dec 31 12:55:01 au-mel-ubuntu-1 kernel: [68858.985670] disk 2, o:1, dev:sdd1
Dec 31 12:55:01 au-mel-ubuntu-1 kernel: [68858.985672] disk 3, o:1, dev:sdf1
Dec 31 12:55:01 au-mel-ubuntu-1 mdadm: RebuildFinished event detected
    on md device /dev/md0
Dec 31 12:55:01 au-mel-ubuntu-1 mdadm: SpareActive event detected
    on md device /dev/md0, component device /dev/sde1

Great! The monitor has picked up on the failure, activated the spare, started the rebuild, sent an e-mail, and completed rebuilding the array. The RAID system has acted to preserve our data and the array is still intact. All that's left for us to do is remove the failed disk from the array and then replace it. First, we'll invoke mdadm to remove the failed disk from the RAID array:

```
$ sudo mdadm --manage /dev/md0 --remove /dev/sdb1
mdadm: hot removed /dev/sdb1
```

The next step depends on your hard disk controller. If it supports hot-swapping of drives, you could unplug the broken disk and replace it with a new one. If not, you will have to shut down the host to physically replace the drive.

When you've installed the new drive and started the host, you will need to partition the new disk as you have the other disks in the array. The new disk will likely have the same device node name as the disk it replaces. When partitioning is done, you can add the new partition to the array via mdadm, as shown in Listing 8-24.

Listing 8-24. *Adding a New Device to a RAID Array*

```
$ sudo mdadm --manage /dev/md0 --add /dev/sdb1
mdadm: added /dev/sdb1
$ cat /proc/mdstat
Personalities : [linear] [multipath] [raid0] [raid1] [raid6] [raid5] [raid4]
    [raid10]
md0 : active raid5 sdb1[4](S) sdf1[3] sdd1[2] sde1[0] sdc1[1]
      25157376 blocks level 5, 64k chunk, algorithm 2 [4/4] [UUUU]

unused devices: <none>
```

The new disk was added as the spare, ready to take over if another disk fails.

It's possible that a problem might prevent a RAID array from automatically starting. If you are booting in rescue mode from CD or DVD, the array will likely not be detected and started either. If this happens, you can manually assemble the array. To re-create a RAID array from existing components, use mdadm in assemble mode. This will try to assemble the array from the components you specify. Check the mdadm manual page for more information.

Summary

In this chapter, you learned how to manage storage on Linux and how you can most securely and flexibly store your data by making use of RAID and LVM. You can now create partitions and file systems, as well as mount and unmount file systems manually and at boot time. You also learned how to set up software RAID and LVM, and resize volumes and file systems. In case of disk failure, you now know how to remove components from and add components to a RAID array, and you can repair file system errors.

In Chapter 9, we will show you how set up infrastructure services such as an SSH server, discuss how to manage the time on your hosts using NTP, and introduce DNS and DHCP.

PART 2

■ ■ ■

Making Linux Work for You

■■■

Infrastructure Services: NTP, DNS, DHCP, and SSH

By Peter Lieverdink

In the previous chapters, you installed your host and got to know your way around it. You then learned how to add and configure storage hardware. Now it's time to look at how to make the software work for you. In this chapter, we will cover the infrastructure services that help you manage the basics of your network.

We'll first describe how to keep the time on your systems synchronized, which is important because a lot of applications rely on your host having the correct time. In the process, we'll introduce you to the Network Time Protocol (NTP).

We'll also cover the Domain Name System (DNS), which is the glue that allows networks like the Internet to function by allowing hosts to find one another. We'll detail the components of DNS and how to set up and manage a DNS server.

We'll then discuss the Dynamic Host Configuration Protocol (DHCP), which is used to assign addresses and network configuration to your hosts. Using DHCP means you don't have to configure individual network settings for clients in your network; rather, this can be automatically provided. You'll learn about how to use DHCP and how to set up address allocation and pass network configuration information to your hosts.

■**Note** We'll look at other ways to automatically configure hosts in Chapter 19.

Lastly, we'll expand on the Secure Shell (SSH) service and show you how to easily access hosts and how to transfer files between hosts using SSH.

Network Time Protocol

We'll start by showing you how to keep all system clocks on your hosts synchronized. Though this might seem a trivial issue, having system clocks match means your log entries will all carry consistent timestamps. This in turn means you can easily correlate log entries from different hosts, should the need arise. Synchronized system clocks are also a prerequisite for the functionality we'll be enabling later. You can't simply rely on your host's motherboard's onboard clocks, as their quality varies a lot and some can run out of sync by as much as several minutes each day.

Time services are provided by a service called the Network Time Protocol (NTP). NTP servers provide synchronization services to a client that connects to them, and they also synchronize themselves with upstream time servers. The layers in this model are called *strata*, with the highest level, stratum 0, consisting of dedicated time hardware such as atomic clocks or satellite receivers. Servers connected to these stratum 0 time sources are called stratum 1 servers. Servers that synchronize off stratum 1 servers are stratum 2 servers, and so on.

■**Note** You can read more about NTP strata at `http://www.akadia.com/services/ntp_synchronize.html`.

You can make use of NTP servers in two ways. One is by running a client utility called ntpdate that synchronizes the system clock once. The other is to run an NTP service that automatically synchronizes whenever the system clock runs too far out of sync with the actual time. A lot of systems actually use both methods. If the system clock and atomic time differ too much, it can take a while for a system to synchronize with an upstream time server. To overcome this, the ntpdate utility is invoked and the clock is synchronized before the NTP service is started.

Let's have a look at the ntpdate utility first. On both Red Hat and Ubuntu it is provided by the ntpdate package. To update the system time, run the utility with the upstream server address as the only command-line parameter. It needs to be run as root, in order to be able to update the system clock.

```
$ sudo ntpdate pool.ntp.org
18 Jan 12:56:25 ntpdate[8695]: adjust time server 203.19.252.1 offset 0.089414 sec
```

The ntpdate utility connected to one of the pool.ntp.org servers and adjusted our system time by nine-hundredths of a second. By default, the utility is run on Ubuntu when a network interface is brought up by the DHCP client. To make sure the system clock remains synchronized, you can add an entry in /etc/crontab that runs ntpdate once every two hours. You redirect standard input and standard output to /dev/null, so you don't receive twice-hourly e-mails.

```
0 */2 * * *    root    /usr/sbin/ntpdate pool.ntp.org > /dev/null 2>&1
```

However, you'd need to install and maintain such a crontab entry on each of your hosts, and even then, depending on the quality of the hardware, the system clock can skew quite a lot over the course of two hours. You can ensure that the system clock is adjusted whenever it attempts to run out of sync by installing and running an NTP server on your host. This will keep your host synchronized and also allow you to use it to synchronize other hosts on your network.

The NTP server and some associated utilities are provided by the ntp package. You need to install it via yum install ntp on Red Hat or sudo aptitude install ntp on Ubuntu. When it starts, the ntpd service will read its options from the /etc/ntp.conf file and listen on UDP port 123. When you look at this configuration file, you can see it consists of two main sections: first is the actual time source configuration and second is the authorization configuration. We'll start with the reporting and time source configuration as shown in Listing 9-1.

Listing 9-1. *ntp.conf*

```
# /etc/ntp.conf, configuration for ntpd; see ntp.conf(5) for help

driftfile /var/lib/ntp/ntp.drift

# Enable this if you want statistics to be logged.
#statsdir /var/log/ntpstats/

statistics loopstats peerstats clockstats
filegen loopstats file loopstats type day enable
filegen peerstats file peerstats type day enable
filegen clockstats file clockstats type day enable

# You do need to talk to an NTP server or two (or three).
server ntp.ubuntu.com
```

The driftfile directive gives the server a place to store information about the idiosyncrasies of your local system clock. Over time, it will use this information to report the time more precisely between synchronization attempts, as the daemon knows how the local clock behaves.

Statistics reporting is not enabled by default, as the statsdir option is not enabled. However, if you were to uncomment that line, the next directive, statistics, would enable loopstats, peerstats, and clockstats reporting to files in /var/log/ntpstats.

loopstats collects information on the updates made to the local clock by the ntpd server. peerstats logs information about all peers—upstream servers as well as clients that use your server to synchronize. Finally, clockstats writes statistical information about the local clock to the log file.

The filegen directive tells the daemon which file you want this statistical information written to and how often the file needs to be changed. In our example, a new version of each of these files is created each day due to the type day directive.

Finally, the server option tells ntpd which upstream server to use for synchronization. To make sure your host stays in sync, it is generally a good idea to add multiple server directives with multiple different servers. We'll explain how to find these servers in a moment.

First let's quickly look at the next section in the /etc/ntp.conf file, which defines which hosts may access your NTP server. On Red Hat, this section is listed at the top of the file, as you can see in Listing 9-2.

Listing 9-2. *Access Control in ntp.conf*

```
# By default, exchange time with everybody, but don't allow configuration.
restrict -4 default kod notrap nomodify nopeer noquery
restrict -6 default kod notrap nomodify nopeer noquery
```

```
# Local users may interrogate the ntp server more closely.
restrict 127.0.0.1
restrict ::1
```

The restrict keyword is used to define access classes. The same access levels are defined for IPv4 and IPv6 clients here, by using the -4 and -6 parameters.

default is a wildcard keyword that matches all possible addresses. kod is used to slow down clients that exceed a defined rate limit, by sending a special response packet. We haven't defined such limits, so it's not used here. notrap rejects any control packets that get sent, while nomodify disallows attempts to modify the time on the server. nopeer ensures your server doesn't start using a connecting client as an upstream NTP server, and finally, noquery prevents your server from being queried for peer and other statistics.

The second set of restrict directives ensures that connections from the local machine can interrogate and reconfigure the NTP server. None of these prevent a client from synchronizing with your NTP server, though.

■**Note** You can find more information on NTP configuration and access control at http://www.cis.udel.edu/~mills/ntp/html/.

The Global NTP Server Pool

Many organizations run their own time servers and make them accessible to third parties. Microsoft and Apple run time servers that are used by default by their respective operating systems, and many Linux vendors do the same.

However, when you want to add extra servers to your own ntp.conf file, you will need to know their addresses. Luckily, there is an open source project that aims to provide a pool of local NTP servers for all continents. This project is called pool.ntp.org, and the participants are individual users and organizations that allow third parties to use their servers for synchronization.

The project provides DNS-based groups for various server strata and geographical locations—for instance, 1.pool.ntp.org is provided by stratum 1 servers, au.pool.ntp.org contains only servers located in Australia, and us.pool.ntp.org is provided by servers located in the United States. By adding a selection of pool.ntp.org servers, you are assured of always having up-to-date and nearby servers available for synchronization.

■**Note** You can read more about the project and join the pool at http://www.pool.ntp.org/.

We'll add a stratum 1 server and a local server to the server section in our /etc/ntp.conf file, as shown in Listing 9-3.

Listing 9-3. *Defining Extra Upstream NTP Servers*

```
server ntp.ubuntu.com
server 1.pool.ntp.org
server au.pool.ntp.org
```

With these servers added, we can restart our NTP server with sudo invoke-rc.d ntp restart on Ubuntu or sudo service ntpd restart on Red Hat. The server writes any status updates to the system logger; you can find them in /var/log/syslog on Ubuntu or in /var/log/messages on Red Hat. Listing 9-4 shows you the output of a server that is started and then synchronizes with upstream servers.

Listing 9-4. *ntpd Status in the System Log*

```
Feb  1 17:00:47 au-mel-ubuntu-1 ntpd[26855]: ntpd 4.2.2p4@1.1585-o Mon
    Jan  5 19:56:03 UTC 2009 (1)
Feb  1 17:00:47 au-mel-ubuntu-1 ntpd[26856]: precision = 1.000 usec
Feb  1 17:00:47 au-mel-ubuntu-1 ntpd[26856]: Listening on interface
    wildcard, 0.0.0.0#123 Disabled
Feb  1 17:00:47 au-mel-ubuntu-1 ntpd[26856]: Listening on interface
    wildcard, ::#123 Disabled
Feb  1 17:00:47 au-mel-ubuntu-1 ntpd[26856]: Listening on interface
    lo, ::1#123 Enabled
Feb  1 17:00:47 au-mel-ubuntu-1 ntpd[26856]: Listening on interface
    eth0, fe80::216:6cff:fe8e:d687#123 Enabled
Feb  1 17:00:47 au-mel-ubuntu-1 ntpd[26856]: Listening on interface
    lo, 127.0.0.1#123 Enabled
Feb  1 17:00:47 au-mel-ubuntu-1 ntpd[26856]: Listening on interface
    eth0, 192.168.0.1#123 Enabled
Feb  1 17:00:47 au-mel-ubuntu-1 ntpd[26856]: kernel time sync status 0040
Feb  1 17:00:47 au-mel-ubuntu-1 ntpd[26856]: frequency initialized -18.989
    PPM from /var/lib/ntp/ntp.drift
Feb  1 17:01:02 au-mel-ubuntu-1 ntpd[26856]: synchronized to 202.60.65.243,
    stratum 2
Feb  1 17:01:02 au-mel-ubuntu-1 ntpd[26856]: synchronized to 203.19.252.1,
    stratum 2
Feb  1 17:01:02 au-mel-ubuntu-1 ntpd[26856]: kernel time sync enabled 0001
```

We can also verify that our host is synchronized by querying the NTP server from the local host via the ntpq command, as shown in Listing 9-5. We use the -p option to list any peers we are connected to and the -4 option to resolve the hostname to an IPv4 address.

Listing 9-5. *Listing Connected Peers*

```
$ ntpq -4 -p localhost
     remote           refid      st t when poll reach   delay   offset  jitter
==============================================================================
+europium.canoni 193.79.237.14    2 u    5   64  377  350.024  -59.414   1.069
+fe1-1.mel-ii.bd 203.36.227.2     2 u   64   64  377   71.646  -48.217   1.993
*ns.tti.net.au   203.36.227.2     2 u    2   64  377   69.299  -58.937   1.630
```

You can now configure any of the other hosts on your network to use the bastion host as their upstream NTP server and make sure that they work via the ntpq command.

Domain Name System

In Chapter 2 we suggested using descriptive names for hosts. However, unless you provide some way of translating these names to the addresses the hosts are configured with, you cannot use these names to access the hosts remotely. On most computer systems, such name-to-address mappings are stored in a "hosts" file, as we explained in Chapter 3.

Once your network grows beyond more than a handful of hosts, though, making sure that all copies of this file remain synchronized becomes an effort, and you might want to consider implementing a Domain Name System (DNS) server.

■**Note** Before DNS existed, a single hosts.txt file was used. This file was maintained by the Network Information Center (NIC) and distributed to all ARPANET-connected machines via FTP.

This DNS server maintains lists of address-to-hostname (and vice versa) mappings and can be queried for such mapping by other hosts, or by users directly, using various utilities.

Root Servers

Somehow, a DNS server needs to know which host or hosts to query for the correct address. An apple.com DNS server has no idea about a google.com host, so how does our own DNS server know where to look?

The entire DNS structure is like a large upside-down tree. Each period in a domain name is like a branch in this tree. As you read a domain name from left to right, each period indicates a split to a lower level in the tree, which is closer to the root. These levels are called *zones*, and for each zone a domain is a part of, a query is done to find out what the name servers are for that zone. One of these servers is then queried in turn to obtain a DNS server for the next zone. The lowest-level zone—the one that all other zones are members of—is called the *root zone*. We indicate this zone with a single period. The next level consists of top-level domains (TLDs), including generic domains such as net, com, org, and edu, as well as country codes such as au, nz, uk, and us. Figure 9-1 shows a small part of this tree structure.

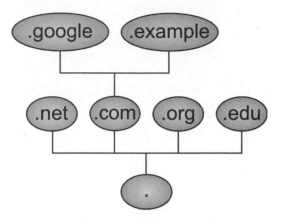

Figure 9-1. *DNS tree structure*

When writing a hostname or domain name, you usually leave off the trailing period for the root zone, but when you're dealing with DNS servers you should explicitly include it, as leaving it off may lead to unexpected results. The DNS information for these TLDs is stored in so-called root servers.

WHOIS

When an organization or person buys a domain, the root DNS servers need to know which DNS servers further down the tree know about the domain in question. The organization in charge of the .com domain is the Internet Corporation for Assigned Names and Numbers (ICANN), and it manages the registrars.

When you buy a domain from a registrar, you need to specify the name servers the domain is delegated to. The registrar then ensures that your DNS servers are added in the correct TLD zone, so third parties can use your DNS servers to look up hostnames on your domain.

You can obtain a listing of DNS servers for a given domain by querying the registrar's database directly. The tool used for this, whois, is handy for making sure DNS delegations are correct. On Red Hat it's provided by the jwhois package, and on Ubuntu it's provided by the whois package. Install the package and let's look at the delegations detail for the google.com domain, as shown in Listing 9-6.

Listing 9-6. *Using whois to Check Delegation Details*

```
$ whois google.com
[Querying whois.verisign-grs.com]
[whois.verisign-grs.com]

Whois Server Version 2.0

Domain names in the .com and .net domains can now be registered
with many different competing registrars. Go to http://www.internic.net
for detailed information.
```

```
Domain Name: GOOGLE.COM
Registrar: MARKMONITOR INC.
Whois Server: whois.markmonitor.com
Referral URL: http://www.markmonitor.com
Name Server: NS1.GOOGLE.COM
Name Server: NS2.GOOGLE.COM
Name Server: NS3.GOOGLE.COM
Name Server: NS4.GOOGLE.COM
Status: clientDeleteProhibited
Status: clientTransferProhibited
Status: clientUpdateProhibited
Status: serverDeleteProhibited
Status: serverTransferProhibited
Status: serverUpdateProhibited
Updated Date: 18-nov-2008
Creation Date: 15-sep-1997
Expiration Date: 14-sep-2011
```

```
>>> Last update of whois database: Sun, 01 Feb 2009 20:46:19 EST <<<
```

Here whois has connected to the VeriSign WHOIS server and retrieved some information about the domain, including the name of the registrar; the name servers it is delegated to; and creation, modification, and expiration dates.

Some registrars also provide contact details for the domain owner via whois. This is something to keep in mind when choosing a registrar to buy your domain from, as it's a relatively convenient way for spammers to collect e-mail addresses.

■**Note** Most registrars allow only a limited number of lookups per day from a specific address against their database, to discourage address harvesting.

Querying Name Servers

You will already be using the DNS server or servers run by your Internet service provider to look up addresses for hosts on the Internet. Typing **www.google.com** is a lot more convenient than having to remember 74.125.19.147 whenever you want to do a web search. The addresses for these DNS servers are stored in the /etc/resolv.conf file. We've included ours in Listing 9-7; yours will, of course, be different.

Listing 9-7. /etc/resolv.conf

```
$ cat /etc/resolv.conf
search example.com
nameserver 192.168.1.1
nameserver 192.168.1.254
```

When you visit a website or connect to a host via SSH, the application in question performs a host lookup using these DNS servers. These applications use a system library, which first checks your /etc/hosts file and then queries a name server only if needed.

The host Command

You can also query DNS servers manually. The DNS-related tools are provided by the bind-utils package on Red Hat and the dnsutils package on Ubuntu, so install them. Direct host or address lookups can be done via the host utility.

■**Note** You may be used to using the deprecated nslookup utility. The host command is its replacement.

You pass the hostname or address you want to look up and optionally the DNS server you want to query, as shown in Listing 9-8. If you leave off the DNS server, the utility will use one defined in /etc/resolv.conf.

Listing 9-8. *Querying a DNS Server with host*

```
$ host www.google.com 192.168.1.1
www.google.com is an alias for www.l.google.com.
www.l.google.com has address 74.125.47.99
www.l.google.com has address 74.125.47.147
www.l.google.com has address 74.125.47.104
www.l.google.com has address 74.125.47.103
```

In Listing 9-8, we've asked the DNS server running on 192.168.1.1 to look up an address for www.google.com, and it determined that is actually an alias, which in turn points at four different IP addresses.

Conversely, we can ask the server to look up the hostname for any of these IP addresses as well.

```
$ host 74.125.47.99
99.47.125.74.in-addr.arpa domain name pointer yw-in-f99.google.com.
```

That's a different hostname from www.l.google.com. Let's do a lookup on this new hostname, to see if it has the same address.

```
$ host yw-in-f99.google.com
yw-in-f99.google.com has address 74.125.47.99
```

It does, so it looks like this address has two names assigned to it.

The dig Command

Though host is useful, it does not generally provide enough information to help resolve any DNS problem you might have, especially when you run your own DNS servers. A more flexible utility is dig, which is also provided by the bind-utils or dnsutils package.

At its most basic level, dig also does name- or address-based lookups, but it provides additional information with each lookup. Let's do the same lookup we did in Listing 9-8, but use dig instead (see Listing 9-9).

Listing 9-9. *Querying a DNS Server with dig*

```
$ dig www.google.com
; <<>> DiG 9.5.0-P2 <<>> www.google.com
;; global options:  printcmd
;; Got answer:
;; ->>HEADER<<- opcode: QUERY, status: NOERROR, id: 40553
;; flags: qr rd ra; QUERY: 1, ANSWER: 4, AUTHORITY: 7, ADDITIONAL: 7

;; QUESTION SECTION:
;www.google.com.                        IN      A

;; ANSWER SECTION:
www.google.com.          497971  IN      CNAME   www.l.google.com.
www.l.google.com.        217     IN      A       66.249.89.99
www.l.google.com.        217     IN      A       66.249.89.104
www.l.google.com.        217     IN      A       66.249.89.147

;; AUTHORITY SECTION:
l.google.com.            27182   IN      NS      e.l.google.com.
l.google.com.            27182   IN      NS      g.l.google.com.
l.google.com.            27182   IN      NS      f.l.google.com.
l.google.com.            27182   IN      NS      a.l.google.com.
l.google.com.            27182   IN      NS      c.l.google.com.
l.google.com.            27182   IN      NS      d.l.google.com.
l.google.com.            27182   IN      NS      b.l.google.com.

;; ADDITIONAL SECTION:
e.l.google.com.          65980   IN      A       209.85.137.9
f.l.google.com.          65980   IN      A       72.14.235.9
g.l.google.com.          65981   IN      A       74.125.95.9
a.l.google.com.          152381  IN      A       209.85.139.9
b.l.google.com.          152381  IN      A       74.125.45.9
c.l.google.com.          26586   IN      A       64.233.161.9
d.l.google.com.          65980   IN      A       74.125.77.9

;; Query time: 29 msec
;; SERVER: 192.168.1.1#53(192.168.1.1)
;; WHEN: Wed Mar 11 15:39:55 2009
;; MSG SIZE  rcvd: 324
```

In Listing 9-9 you can see that `dig` outputs the query results in distinct sections. First comes some information about the command you're running, including whether or not the query succeeded. Next is the query section, which shows you what you actually sent to the DNS server. In this case, we are looking for an A record for the host www.google.com. An A record is one that maps names to addresses. We'll cover record types in more detail shortly.

The answer section holds the response to your query. In this case, it says that `www.google.com` is a `CNAME` record for www.l.google.com and that www.l.google.com has three A records assigned to it.

In the authority section, `dig` lists the authoritative name servers for this query. Here you can see that authoritative responses for the l.google.com zone can be obtained from no fewer than seven DNS servers, named a.l.google.com through g.l.google.com. `dig` provides us with the IP addresses of these seven servers in the additional section.

Finally, `dig` tells us how long the query took, which server was queried, when the query was run, and how much data it received.

The actual response data is displayed in five columns. This format is identical to the way Berkeley Internet Name Domain (BIND) defines domains internally, where records are defined using five fields and semicolons are used for comments. These five fields are the record name, the time until the data expires (better known as *time to live* or TTL), the record class (which is virtually always IN for Internet), the record type, and finally the data for this record.

You can use `dig` to query any DNS server for specific record types as well. Table 9-1 lists the most commonly used record types. We'll set up some of these later as well.

Table 9-1. *DNS Record Types*

Type	Used For
SOA	Defines a serial number and expiration information for the domain
A	Maps a hostname to an address
CNAME	Adds an extra name for an existing A record
MX	Specifies mail servers for the domain
NS	Specifies DNS servers for the domain
PTR	Maps an address to a hostname

Armed with this knowledge, you can now make use of the more advanced features of `dig`. We previously invoked it with just a hostname as parameter, but a full command usually looks like `dig @server name type`. In the case of our first example, the full explicit command would have been `dig @192.168.1.1 www.google.com A`.

■**Note** To use the `host` utility for the same kind of lookup, enter `host -v -t type name server`.

We found out the main DNS servers for the google.com domain via `whois` earlier. To check that these DNS servers are configured properly, we can query them for all records of the NS type in the google.com domain, as shown in Listing 9-10.

Listing 9-10. *Querying a DNS Server for a Specific Record Type*

```
$ dig @ns1.google.com google.com NS

; <<>> DiG 9.5.0-P2 <<>> @ns1.google.com google.com NS
; (1 server found)
;; global options:  printcmd
;; Got answer:
;; ->>HEADER<<- opcode: QUERY, status: NOERROR, id: 18249
;; flags: qr aa rd; QUERY: 1, ANSWER: 4, AUTHORITY: 0, ADDITIONAL: 4
;; WARNING: recursion requested but not available

;; QUESTION SECTION:
;google.com.                    IN      NS

;; ANSWER SECTION:
google.com.             345600  IN      NS      ns1.google.com.
google.com.             345600  IN      NS      ns3.google.com.
google.com.             345600  IN      NS      ns4.google.com.
google.com.             345600  IN      NS      ns2.google.com.

;; ADDITIONAL SECTION:
ns1.google.com.         345600  IN      A       216.239.32.10
ns2.google.com.         345600  IN      A       216.239.34.10
ns3.google.com.         345600  IN      A       216.239.36.10
ns4.google.com.         345600  IN      A       216.239.38.10

;; Query time: 178 msec
;; SERVER: 216.239.32.10#53(216.239.32.10)
;; WHEN: Wed Mar 11 17:15:16 2009
;; MSG SIZE  rcvd: 164
```

The above listing shows us that the ns1.google.com DNS server does indeed have information about four name servers for the google.com domain, so it appears to be configured correctly.

Zone Metadata

We mentioned earlier that one of the columns listed in dig results is TTL. This field defines how long DNS records are valid for, which allows your local applications to cache the results of a DNS lookup for a certain time. This way, there is no need to perform several DNS lookups (remember, one or more lookups are performed to find an authoritative DNS server first) for each connection you make, which speeds up the process of establishing network connections considerably.

The other important type is called SOA, for Start of Authority. This record contains metainformation about the zone. For instance, it includes a serial number so servers can check if the zone was changed, and it defines a contact e-mail for the server administrator as well.

Let's ask one of the Google servers for the SOA record of the google.com domain (Listing 9-11). We've left the authoritative and extra sections off the output.

Listing 9-11. *Querying a DNS Server for an SOA Record*

```
$ dig google.com @ns1.google.com SOA

; <<>> DiG 9.5.0-P2 <<>> google.com @ns1.google.com SOA
;; global options:  printcmd
;; Got answer:
;; ->>HEADER<<- opcode: QUERY, status: NOERROR, id: 32611
;; flags: qr aa rd; QUERY: 1, ANSWER: 1, AUTHORITY: 4, ADDITIONAL: 4
;; WARNING: recursion requested but not available

;; QUESTION SECTION:
;google.com.                      IN      SOA

;; ANSWER SECTION:
google.com.             86400   IN      SOA      ns1.google.com. dns-admin.google.com.
    2009031200 7200 1800 1209600 300
```

Listing 9-11 shows that the SOA record consists of seven fields, which define how other DNS servers interact with this zone. We'll come back to them later, but for now we'll mention the last item in the list, which is the *negative cache* TTL. This is used to prevent servers from continuously performing a lookup for a host that does not exist, or to cache a native response. In this case, a remote server is allowed to keep responding with "No such host" for 300 seconds after the initial query.

Running Caching DNS

Not all ISPs' name servers are equally reliable, and some can be slow, so why don't we run our own? A few DNS server software packages are available, but the most commonly used and well known is Berkeley Internet Name Domain (BIND).

■**Note** BIND is named after the place where it was developed, the University of California at Berkeley.

The software is provided by the bind package on Red Hat, and the basic configuration ships in the caching-nameserver package. The configuration interface is provided by system-config-bind. You install these via yum install bind caching-nameserver system-config-bind. On Ubuntu, these are provided by the bind9 package, which you add via sudo aptitude install bind9. The DNS server binary itself is called named.

The main configuration file shipped on Ubuntu is /etc/bind/named.conf, while on Red Hat the /etc/named.conf file is used. Listing 9-12 shows you the basic file that ships with Ubuntu.

Listing 9-12. *The Top of /etc/bind/named.conf in Ubuntu*

```
// This is the primary configuration file for the BIND DNS server named.
//
// Please read /usr/share/doc/bind9/README.Debian.gz for information on the
// structure of BIND configuration files in Debian, *BEFORE* you customize
// this configuration file.
//
// If you are just adding zones, please do that in /etc/bind/named.conf.local

include "/etc/bind/named.conf.options";
```

This file contains references to other files, which contain the actual configuration settings and (optionally) information about domains that are hosted locally. Comments in these configuration files are prefixed with a double slash (//) and all directives and blocks are terminated with a semicolon (;). We've included part of our named.conf in Listing 9-11.

The include directive tells named to read the specified file and process any directives it contains, including nested include commands. In this case, the named.conf.options file contains the options section, which affects the way named operates. This is the file you would edit to make changes to your configuration on Ubuntu (see Listing 9-13).

Listing 9-13. *Default named Options in Ubuntu*

```
options {
    directory "/var/cache/bind";

    // forwarders {
    //     0.0.0.0;
    // };

    auth-nxdomain no;    # conform to RFC1035
    listen-on-v6 { any; };
};
```

The directory directive determines the location named will use to look for files and also to write any files, if it's configured to do so. You can override this for individual files by specifying a full system path starting with /.

Forwarders are what named calls upstream DNS servers. If you want your caching name server to use only your ISP's name server or a set of other name servers, you can list their IP addresses in the forwarders block, each on a line by itself and terminated by a semicolon.

The next option, auth-nxdomain, is set to no. This controls how the name server responds to lookups for domains that it thinks do not exist, which means that your local DNS server will not claim to be authoritative if it cannot find information about a domain. This in turn means that a client can continue querying other DNS servers, if this one cannot find information about a domain.

Finally, the `listen-on-v6` option tells BIND that it should listen for queries on all available IPv6 addresses on all network interfaces.

To avoid the chicken-and-egg problem, a caching DNS server ships with a built-in listing of root servers. You can find them in `/var/named/named.root` on Red Hat and `/etc/bind/db.root` on Ubuntu. You can also use `dig` to obtain a current list of root servers, by querying a root server for all records of type `NS` in the "." zone.

```
$ dig @a.root-servers.net . NS > db.root.
```

Red Hat's default configuration file needs to be generated by running the `system-config-bind` tool once. Start it via System ➤ Administration ➤ Server Settings ➤ Domain Name System, as shown in Figure 9-2.

Figure 9-2. *Starting* `system-config-bind`

This tool needs to run as the `root` user, so enter the root password when you are asked.

When it is first run, it will detect that no `/etc/named.conf` configuration file exists and it will generate a default one for you when you click OK, as shown in Figure 9-3. Then the default configuration file is saved to disk and loaded in the BIND configuration GUI.

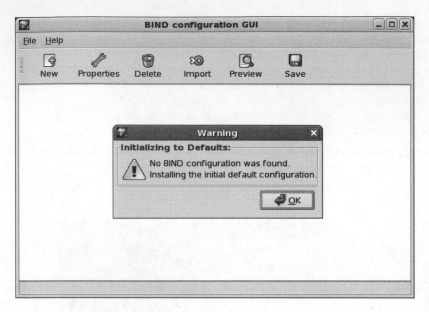

Figure 9-3. *Default configuration*

We're done, so we can close the BIND configuration GUI window. A basic /etc/named.conf file has been created for us. We've included the important part in Listing 9-14.

Listing 9-14. *Red Hat /etc/named.conf*

```
// Red Hat BIND Configuration Tool
//
// Default initial "Caching Only" name server configuration
//

options {
    directory "/var/named";
    dump-file "/var/named/data/cache_dump.db";
    statistics-file "/var/named/data/named_stats.txt";
    /*
    * If there is a firewall between you and nameservers you want
    * to talk to, you might need to uncomment the query-source
    * directive below.  Previous versions of BIND always asked
    * questions using port 53, but BIND 8.1 uses an unprivileged
    * port by default.
    */
    // query-source address * port 53;
};
```

The major difference between the Red Hat and Ubuntu files is the location you use to store data for named. The dump-file directive allows named to write transient data to a file when it exits. It can then reread this data when it is started again. The statistics-file defines where named writes statistical information about the types and number of queries it receives.

We can now start the name server via the sudo service named start command. On Ubuntu, the name server is started automatically when it is installed, but if it were not running we could start it via sudo invoke-rc.d bind9 start.

So that our new DNS server can be queried, we need to ensure the firewall is not blocking traffic. DNS defaults to using the UDP protocol on port number 53, but it will switch to the TCP protocol if responses contain a large amount of data. Add the appropriate rules to the correct Netfilter chain for your network layout.

```
$ sudo /sbin/iptables –t filter –A Firewall-eth0-INPUT -p udp --dport 53 -j ACCEPT
$ sudo /sbin/iptables –t filter –A Firewall-eth0-INPUT -p tcp --dport 53 -j ACCEPT
```

■**Note** Make sure to configure the firewall on the DNS host to permit outgoing DNS responses, too. We covered firewalls and iptables in Chapter 6.

We now have our own caching DNS server, which we can use to do lookups. We call it a *caching* DNS server because it keeps the answers to any queries we do, so the next time we perform the same query, it can respond immediately with the cached information.

To make sure it works, we will query it directly, as shown in Listing 9-15.

Listing 9-15. *Querying Our Local Caching DNS Server*

```
$ host www.google.com localhost
www.google.com is an alias for www.l.google.com.
www.l.google.com has address 74.125.47.99
www.l.google.com has address 74.125.47.147
www.l.google.com has address 74.125.47.104
www.l.google.com has address 74.125.47.103
```

We asked the DNS server running on localhost to look up the address for www.google.com and it responded, so it works!

With a working caching DNS, we can replace the nameserver entries in our /etc/resolv. conf file with nameserver 192.168.0.1 to use our own server. We can also add this DNS server to the resolv.conf files on any other hosts we have.

Authoritative DNS

The alternative to a caching DNS server is an *authoritative* DNS server. This means the server is an authoritative source of information for a zone. We can use one to provide DNS resolution for our local network, on which we'll use the example.com domain. We do this by defining two zones: one to provide mappings from name to address and one to provide reverse mappings, from address to name.

For security reasons, you should not use a caching DNS server to also provide authoritative DNS servers.

Rezoning

Zones are defined in zone files, much like the root zone file we mentioned earlier. Zone files always contain a header, also known as the SOA record. This header is optionally followed by DNS records that define services and hosts. We've included a sample zone file header in Listing 9-16.

Listing 9-16. *Zone File Header for the example.com Domain*

```
$ORIGIN example.com.
$TTL  86400
@   IN   SOA    example.com.    root.example.com. (
      2009013101  ; Serial
      604800   ; Refresh
      86400  ; Retry
      2419200  ; Expire
      3600 )  ; Negative Cache TTL
```

This header defines some metainformation about our zone that is used by caching DNS servers and also by any slave servers we may have defined. *Slave servers* are authoritative DNS servers that automatically retrieve their zone information from a master DNS server. You would use them to provide redundant DNS services, like your ISP does.

We've listed the fields from our zone header and their use in Table 9-2. In our example we've listed all times in seconds, but you can also use 1d instead of 86400 to indicate one day, or 4w instead of 2419200 to indicate four weeks.

Table 9-2. *Zone Header Fields*

Field	Use
$ORIGIN	Defines the start of the zone
$TTL	Time to live, which is the default expiration for records in this zone that do not have their own expiration time set
SOA	Start of Authority, which contains seven records of zone metadata
Master	Primary authoritative DNS server for this domain
Contact	E-mail address of the contact for this domain, with the at sign (@) replaced by a period
Serial	Defines the version of this zone file, used by slave name servers
Refresh	Defines how often slave servers should update their copy of this zone
Retry	Defines the interval between attempts to refresh a slave server
Expire	Defines how long a slave server is allowed to use any version of this zone file
Negative Cache TTL	Defines how long a failed lookup result may be cached

It's also worth noting that we're using a date-based serial number for the zone. The format is YYYYMMDDNN for the current year, month, and day, followed by a two-digit number. This allows us to easily see when the zone was last changed, while still allowing for 99 changes each day, and you can see in Listing 9-11 that Google uses this format. Alternatively, you can use a simple incrementing number as the serial number, which is what the system-config-bind utility on Red Hat does. The at symbol (@) in front of the SOA evaluates to the name of the current zone. We could have also typed **example.com.** in its place.

Forward Lookup Zones

On Ubuntu, as opposed to Red Hat, creating zones is a bit more labor intensive. You need to create zones files via a text editor and add their definitions to the /etc/named.conf.local file, whereas on Red Hat you can use the provided administration utility. We'll look at the manual way first.

We're going to store our forward lookup zone in a file called example.com.db. Because only the root user may write to the zone file directory, we start our editor using sudo.

```
$ sudo vim /var/cache/bind/example.com.db
```

Now, we simply copy and paste the zone header from Listing 9-17 into this file and save it. With the header done, we can start to add actual host and service records into this file.

You need two basic service record types to be present in your zone. One is the NS record, which defines which hosts act as DNS server for this domain, and the other is the MX record, which defines mail servers for this domain. Both records start with a blank field, as they do not define hostnames.

Listing 9-17. *Our Service Records*

```
        NS      ns.example.com.
        MX      10 mail.example.com.
```

The data for the MX record consists of a priority number and then the hostname that remote servers should try to deliver mail to. A properly configured remote mail server will work through a list of MX records, starting with the lowest priority number, and try to deliver e-mail. Note that we've specified a fully qualified domain name (FQDN; which is the hostname plus the full domain name) with a trailing period for these entries. If we'd left it off, the DNS server would assume we had defined hostnames only and would automatically append the $ORIGIN to the end of these records.

We've used the ns and mail hostnames in these definitions, but we've not yet defined these hosts in the zone file, so let's do that next (see Listing 9-18). Host-to-address records are called A records. We'll also add an A record for our current hostname.

Listing 9-18. *Creating A Records for Our Domain*

```
@    IN    A    192.168.0.1
ns   IN    A    192.168.0.254
mail    IN    A    192.168.0.1
au-mel-ubuntu-1    IN    A    192.168.0.1
```

We did not specify an FQDN in the host column for these records, so the DNS server will treat them as if they have $ORIGIN (example.com.) appended to them, which is exactly what we want. The @ symbol is replaced with the origin, too, so users will be able to access a host by going to just the domain as well.

You'll note both these names will now resolve to the same address. An IP address can have as many A records associated with it as you like. The other type or record in a forward zone is called a CNAME, also known as an alias. You might remember we found an alias when we looked up www.google.com earlier.

You use a CNAME when you want to associate a number of aliased names with a single host and still be able to change the address for that host without needing to then change a long list of A records. For instance, our host au-mel-ubuntu-1 needs to provide web and SQL services, and the mail server will also provide POP and IMAP access. We can create some CNAME entries to provide aliases that all point to the mail A entry (see Listing 9-19). In the future if we migrate mail services to a different host, we only need to change the A record and all CNAME entries will automatically point at the new address as well.

Listing 9-19. *Adding Some CNAME Entries*

```
gateway     IN    CNAME    ns.example.com.
headoffice     IN    CNAME    au-mel-ubuntu-1.example.com.
smtp   IN    CNAME    mail.example.com.
pop   IN    CNAME    mail.example.com.
imap   IN    CNAME    mail.example.com.
www   IN    CNAME    au-mel-ubuntu-1.example.com.
sql   IN    CNAME    au-mel-ubuntu-1.example.com.
```

We've also created CNAMEs called gateway and headoffice, which we will use when we set up a Virtual Private Network in Chapter 14. That's all we need for now. We'll save the file and create an accompanying reverse zone file, which will provide an address-to-name mapping.

Reverse Lookup Zones

In order to set up a reverse zone, you need to first find out what it is called. Unlike a forward zone, it has no domain name, but it does have a unique address range. To provide lookups for addresses, a special domain named in-addr.arpa. is used. This is essentially the root zone for reverse mappings.

Just like forward zones, you prepend the parts of your network address to this zone, with the most significant parts to the right. For our network of 192.168.0.x, this results in a 0.168.192.in-addr.arpa. reverse zone name.

■**Note** in-addr.arpa. zones are always prefixed with up to three quarters of a dotted quad. There is no standard way of having reverse zones for a subnet with fewer than 255 addresses.

We once again fire up our editor (as the root user) to create a new zone file.

```
$ sudo vim /var/cache/bind/192.168.0.db
```

The header in this file needs to be a bit different from our forward zone, as the zone name is different. Add in the contents of Listing 9-20.

Listing 9-20. *The Reverse Zone Header*

```
$ORIGIN 0.168.192.in-addr.arpa.
$TTL  86400
@  IN  SOA  ns.example.com.  root.example.com. (
        2009013101  ; Serial
        604800  ; Refresh
        86400  ; Retry
        2419200  ; Expire
        3600 )  ; Negative Cache TTL
```

With the header created, we can now start adding PTR records, which map addresses to names. Let's add one for our bastion host and one for our host on 192.168.0.254 and the mail A records, as shown in Listing 9-21.

Listing 9-21. *Adding PTR Records for Our Hosts*

```
1     PTR     mail.example.com
1     PTR     au-mel-ubuntu-1.example.com.
254   PTR     ns.example.com.
```

We save the reverse zone file and exit the editor. All that's left to do now is add the zone definitions for these two zones to /etc/bind/named.conf.local. We open this file and add in the definitions, as shown in Listing 9-22. Each zone directive block contains a reference to the file that defines the zone. By default, the server expects these in the directory specified in the main configuration file. Since we're the authoritative DNS server providing these zones, we need to set the zone type to master.

Listing 9-22. *Adding Zone Definitions*

```
zone "example.com" {
    type master;
    file "example.com.db";
};

zone "0.168.192.in-addr.arpa" {
    type master;
    file "192.168.0.db";
};
```

Then we save the file and quit the editor. We need to tell the server to reload its configuration, either by restarting the server via invoke-rc.d or service, or using the rndc utility. The latter is much faster and does not interrupt services, so let's do that.

```
$ sudo rndc reload
```

The name server should know about our new zones, and we can query it to check this. Let's start by looking up the address for ns.example.com, as shown in Listing 9-23.

Listing 9-23. *Testing Forward Name Resolution*

```
$ host ns.example.com localhost
Using domain server:
Name: localhost
Address: 127.0.0.1#53
Aliases:

ns.example.com has address 192.168.0.254
```

That works fine. Let's also check that the reverse zone works by looking up the name associated with the 192.168.0.1 address, as shown in Listing 9-24.

Listing 9-24. *Testing Reverse Name Resolution*

```
$ host 192.168.0.1 localhost
Using domain server:
Name: localhost
Address: 127.0.0.1#53
Aliases:

1.0.168.192.in-addr.arpa domain name pointer au-mel-ubuntu-1.example.com.
1.0.168.192.in-addr.arpa domain name pointer
    mail.example.com.0.168.192.in-addr.arpa.
```

That isn't quite right! The name server has appended the reverse zone name to the mail.example.com host. We know what usually causes this, though, so if we go and check the reverse zone file, we can see that we did indeed forget the trailing period at the end of the entry for mail.example.com.

We'll add the period now and increment the zone serial number. When we finish, we issue the sudo rndc reload command again. If we test the reverse resolution again, we can see the problem has been fixed.

Using system-config-bind on Red Hat

Adding and modifying zones on Red Hat works somewhat differently, as you can use the GUI tool to do this. Let's start it again and then add forward and reverse entries for our example. com and 0.168.192.in-addr.arpa zones. We then select New ➤ Zone, as shown in Figure 9-4.

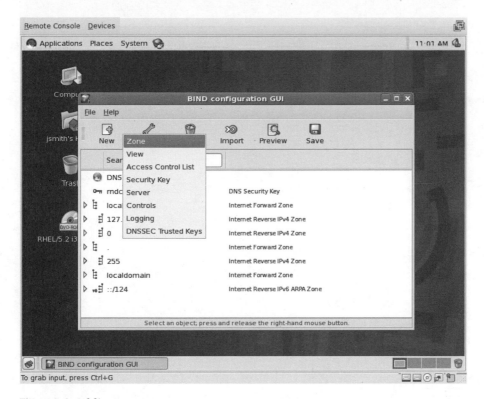

Figure 9-4. *Adding a new zone*

Next, we need to specify the class, origin, and type. We click OK for the default class and origin type, as shown in Figure 9-5, as we're creating an Internet Forward zone.

Figure 9-5. *Specifying the zone type*

When you accept the origin type, you need to enter the origin for the zone—its name. In this case, we enter example.com., as shown in Figure 9-6.

Figure 9-6. *Entering the zone origin*

The zone type is correct, so we click OK. We are then presented with the zone SOA properties dialog, as shown in Figure 9-7.

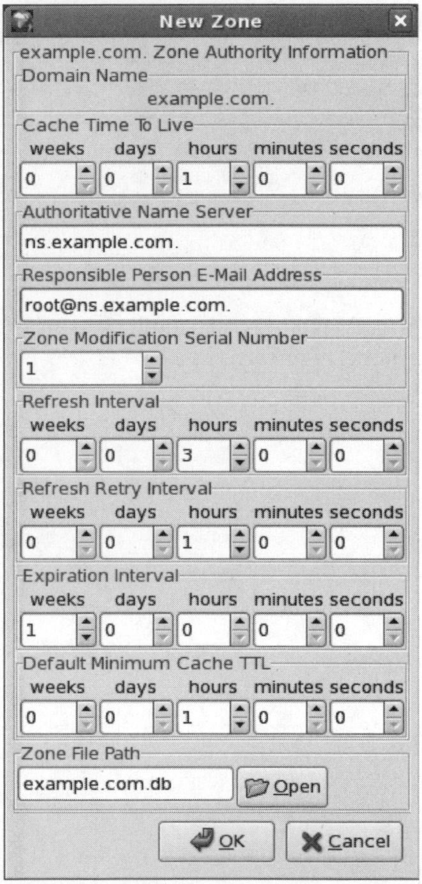

Figure 9-7. *Zone authority information*

As we discussed earlier, this sets the zone metadata and some slave server options. We set the authoritative name server to ns.example.com. and the responsible person to the root user at that host. The default expirations are all fine, so we do not need to change these. Finally, there is the zone file path, which is the file the zone will be stored as. On Red Hat that will be in /var/named, as you saw earlier.

Now that the zone has been created, we can start adding records to it. The NS record was done automatically when we created the zone, so we can add an MX record next. Right-click the example.com. zone and choose Add ➤ MX Mail Exchange, as shown in Figure 9-8.

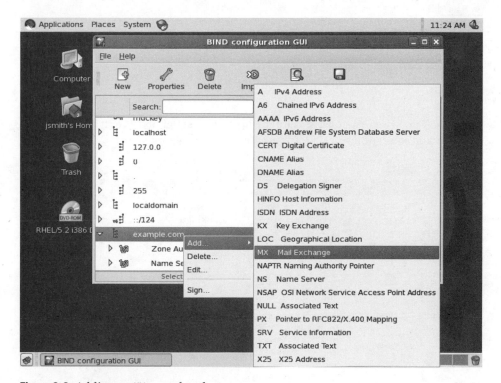

Figure 9-8. *Adding an MX record to the zone*

In the MX record dialog, we set the priority to 10 and enter the name of the mail server, as shown in Figure 9-9.

Figure 9-9. *Setting the MX record details*

All we have left to do is create A records for the hosts we just defined. We right-click the zone name again and select Add ➤ A IPv4 Address, as shown in Figure 9-10.

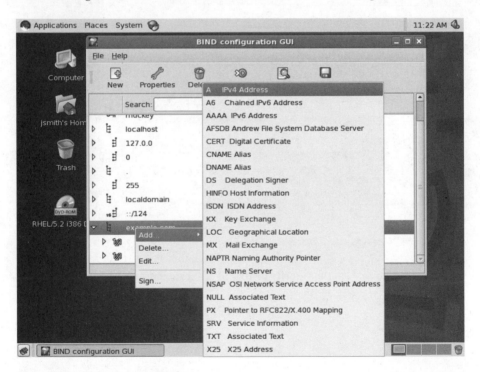

Figure 9-10. *Adding an A record*

In the next dialog, we add the FQDN and the address we want to be associated with this name, as shown in Figure 9-11. Note the Create Reverse Mapping Record check box. By ensuring this is checked, we let the `system-config-bind` tool automatically create and populate the associated reverse mapping zone.

Figure 9-11. *New A record details*

We click OK to add this A record to the zone. If we now look at the main window, we can see a 192.168.0 zone was added. When we click the arrow to open the zone, we can see a PTR record mapping 1 to ns.example.com. was created, as shown in Figure 9-12.

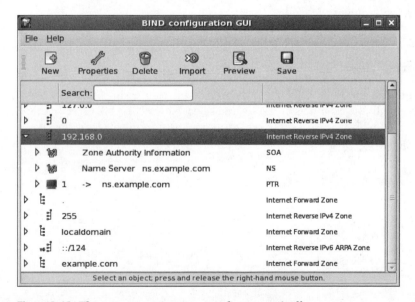

Figure 9-12. *The reverse zone was created automatically.*

We'll continue by adding A records for mail.example.com. and au-mel-rhel-1.example. com. to the forward zone now. Both of these will point at the 192.168.0.254 address.

When done, click Save. The system-config-bind tool will ask if you wish to create a backup of the current configuration and zone files and then replace them with the updated versions, as shown in Figure 9-13.

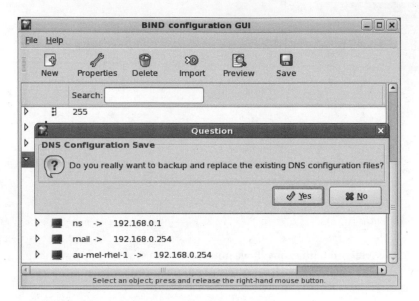

Figure 9-13. *Saving updated configuration files*

When you click Yes, the tool will automatically increment the serial numbers on the changed zones and tell the name server to reload its zones files. It's worth noting that the serial numbers it uses are simple incrementing numbers, not based on the date.

As done on Ubuntu, let's now add a few CNAME records to make accessing services a bit easier for users. We highlight the example.com. zone and select New ➤ CNAME Alias. In the Domain Name field, we add the alias we want to create, and in the Canonical Name field we add the FQDN of the host we're creating the alias for, as shown in Figure 9-14.

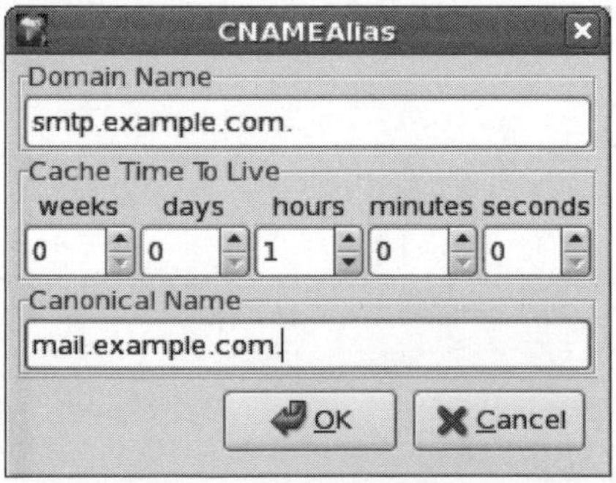

Figure 9-14. *Adding a CNAME record*

We'll also add in the CNAME records for pop and imap, both pointing at mail.example.com., and then add www and sql, pointing at au-mel-rhel-1.example.com. Finally, we add a CNAME called gateway that points at ns.example.com and a CNAME called headoffice that points at au-mel-rhel-1.example.com. We'll use these in Chapter 14 when we set up a virtual private network.

When done, we click Save to update the zone files and reload the server.

Security Considerations

We're now running the DNS server on the bastion host as both an authoritative and caching DNS server. Though the software can handle this fine, there are some security considerations. The main one of these is due to an attack known as *DNS cache poisoning*, which allows an attacker to make your caching DNS server hand out incorrect addresses, by making it perform a DNS lookup via getting a user to click a malicious web link or open an e-mail with an embedded link.

■**Note** You can read more about DNS cache poisoning at http://en.wikipedia.org/wiki/ DNS_cache_poisoning.

By hosting your own authoritative domain on a separate DNS server that does not query upstream servers, you can prevent such an attack from impacting the domain. This does not solve the problem, but it does minimize the impact on your infrastructure.

Adding a Slave Server

In order to provide reliable DNS services, virtually all domain registrars require you to enter a minimum of two DNS servers for any domain. It is, of course, possible to maintain multiple copies of all your zone files, but you can make use of the master/slave functionality in BIND to automate this process.

Let's add a slave server for our example.com domain, starting with Red Hat.

Red Hat

First, you need to tell your master server that the slave server is allowed to retrieve the zone file for your domain. Open the BIND Configuration utility on the master server and highlight the example.com zone, and then click Properties.

On the zone options screen, find the allow-transfer option in the list of all options on the right side, and then click the plus sign icon. Now highlight the allow-transfer option in the list of current options on the left and add the slave server IP address, as shown in Figure 9-15.

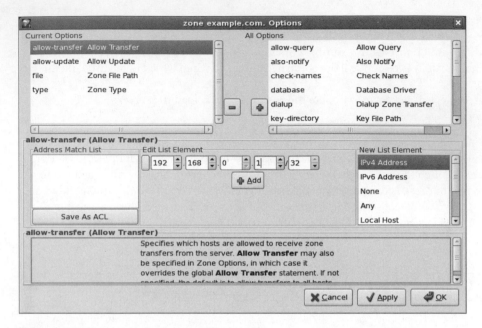

Figure 9-15. *Allowing a slave to transfer zone files*

Click Add to add the address to the match list. If you want to add more slaves, repeat this process for each one. Next, click OK to accept this change and return to the main screen. Save the configuration to apply your changes and reload the DNS server.

Next, you need to configure the slave. Open the BIND Configuration tool on the host that will be the slave server and select New ➤ domain. Accept the IN class and enter example.com. as the zone origin. For the zone type, choose slave, as shown in Figure 9-16.

Figure 9-16. *Adding a slave zone*

Click OK to accept and proceed to the next screen. Here you need to add the IP address for your master DNS server. Highlight IPV4 Address and enter the address, as shown in Figure 9-17.

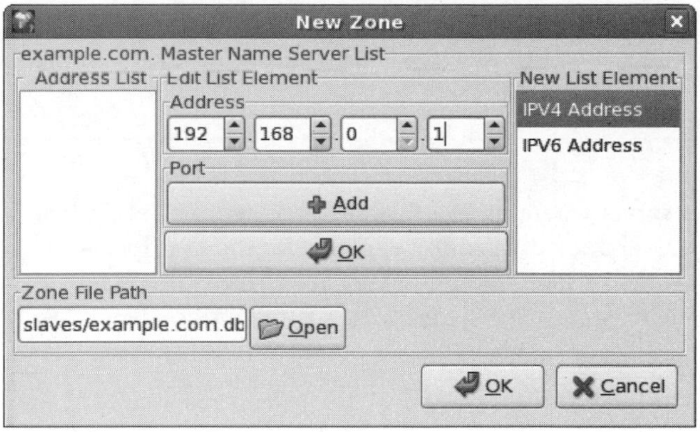

Figure 9-17. *Adding a master server*

When you've finished, click the OK button in the middle of the dialog to add the address to the listing on the left. Then click OK to accept this configuration. Finally, save the configuration and exit the utility.

BIND will now restart, and as it does it will retrieve the zone file from the master server. You can verify this via the /var/log/messages file.

Ubuntu

If you want to set up the master to allow transfers from slave hosts on Ubuntu, you need to change the zone definitions in /etc/bind/named.conf.local. You need to ensure the master server contacts the slaves when a zone is updated, and you do this by adding the notify yes directive. This means you don't need to wait until the slave reaches the zone expiration time, as any zone changes on the master server will be replicated to the slave immediately.

Next, you add an allow-transfer directive, which should contain the IP address of the slave server. We've included the new definition for the example.com zone in Listing 9-25.

Listing 9-25. *Adding Zone Definitions*

```
zone "example.com" {
    type master;
    notify yes;
    allow-transfer {
        192.168.0.2;
    };
    file "example.com.db";
};
```

When you've added the addresses for all slaves, save the file and then tell BIND to reload its configuration via sudo rndc reload.

■Tip To test the master configuration, you can use dig on the slave to simulate a zone transfer. Use the AXFR query type: dig example.com @192.168.0.1 AXFR.

The next step is to tell the slave server where to find the master. Open the /etc/bind/ named.conf.local file on the slave server and add a zone definition for the example.com domain. Set the zone type to slave. To make sure that the server can retrieve the zone data, you need to specify the address for the master server in the masters configuration block. We've included the configuration for our network in Listing 9-26.

Listing 9-26. *Slave Server Zone Configuration*

```
zone "example.com" {
    type slave;
    masters {
        192.168.0.1;
    };
    file "example.com.db";
};
```

When you've finished, save the configuration file and tell the slave server to reload it via sudo rndc reload. You can check the /var/log/syslog file to verify that the zone is being transferred, or you can query the slave server using host or dig to ensure the zone data is present.

Dynamic DNS

If your ISP is assigning your host a new random address each time you connect to the Internet, running your own authoritative DNS doesn't make a lot of sense. Your server's address will keep changing, and you will need to keep changing the delegation information in the WHOIS database.

An alternative solution is dynamic DNS, which is available from various providers on the Internet. With this solution, the dynamic DNS provider hosts DNS servers. A small client application runs on one of your systems and remotely updates host records on the DNS servers whenever your IP address changes. The TTL on these dynamic DNS services is low enough not to interrupt services like mail delivery. Of course, you can also use such a service even if your external IP address never changes.

There are various dynamic DNS providers, a nonexhaustive list of which is available at http://www.dmoz.org/Computers/Internet/Protocols/DNS/DNS_Providers/Dynamic_DNS. If you choose to outsource DNS hosting this way, the dynamic DNS provider you choose will provide you with DNS server details to enter in your registrar's registration form.

If you require dynamic updates, you should choose a provider that offers a client utility that works under Linux. A few of these utilities are available as packages in Ubuntu, such as ddclient or ez-ipupdate:

- *ddclient*: http://sourceforge.net/projects/ddclient/ and http://dag.wieers.com/rpm/packages/ddclient/

- *ez-ipupdate (source)*: http://www.ez-ipupdate.com/

For Red Hat, you will need to download the tarball for one of these tools and install it by hand, or find an RPM package created by a third party.

Dynamic Host Configuration Protocol

Now that we have naming of hosts sorted, it might be nice to have network addresses assigned automatically to some hosts, like workstations or laptops. The service used for this is Dynamic Host Configuration Protocol (DHCP). It consists of a server, which defines which addresses can be assigned to which clients, and a client, which requests addresses from the server and uses the response to configure the local network interface.

This is great for random machines that you may want to add to your network, where you don't really care what address is assigned to them. However, for servers, if you even use DHCP on them at all, you'll usually want static allocation. If a server's address changes unpredictably, you won't be able to use the services it provides.

Luckily, the DHCP server allows you to split your range of available network addresses into pools. Each of these pools can then be configured to be assigned to known hosts, or to unknown hosts. This way, it's possible to have visiting laptops assigned a random free address in a specific range.

Installing and Configuring

The DHCP server is provided by the dhcp3-server package on Ubuntu and the dhcp package on Red Hat. On Ubuntu, a sample configuration file is installed as /etc/dhcp3/dhcpd.conf. Red Hat uses the /etc/dhcpd.conf file, which is blank by default. However, it ships with the /usr/share/doc/dhcp-3.0.5/dhcpd.conf.sample file.

The configuration file consists of a set of global directives followed by one or more subnet definitions. Comments are prefixed with hash marks (#). We've included the global directives from the Ubuntu file in Listing 9-27.

Listing 9-27. *dhcpd.conf Global Settings*

```
ddns-update-style none;
default-lease-time 600;
max-lease-time 7200;
log-facility local7;
```

The first directive specifies that our DHCP server will not do DNS updates for addresses that it hands out. You'll see a bit later how to change this. The default-lease-time directive specifies how long a DHCP lease will be active if a connecting client does not specify a time. If it does specify a time, this time cannot be longer than max-lease-time. Both settings specify a time in seconds. Finally, the log-facility specifies how the system logger should handle log entries generated by the DHCP server. We'll show you how to configure the syslog side of things in Chapter 18.

Let's change this configuration somewhat to suit our own needs. As we don't expect to have many machines turn on and off every minute, we can increase the lease times as well. Let's set the default to six hours and the maximum to 24 hours.

```
default-lease-time 21600;
max-lease-time 86400;
```

With that done, we can add a subnet on which our DHCP server should hand out leases.

```
subnet 192.168.0.0 netmask 255.255.255.0 {
}
```

The DHCP server will check the network addresses assigned to the local network interfaces when it starts and automatically assign each subnet declaration to the correct network interface.

We can now add subnet-specific options within this configuration block. We'll start with options that define which address to use as the default route on our network and which host to use as the name server.

```
subnet 192.168.0.0 netmask 255.255.255.0 {
    option routers 192.168.0.254;
    option domain-name "example.com";
    option domain-name-servers 192.168.0.1;
    option broadcast-address 192.168.0.255;
}
```

Here we have defined which network settings should be sent to a client when it requests a lease. The router option specifies the default gateway to be used by the client. The domain-name option speaks for itself. In the domain-name-servers option, we can add one or more DNS server addresses, separated by spaces. The broadcast address is a special address on the network that is used to send requests to all hosts on the same network range, and we specify it via the broadcast-address option.

However, we have not yet specified any addresses that the DHCP server is allowed to hand out. We do this via the range directive.

```
subnet 192.168.0.0 netmask 255.255.255.0 {
    option routers 192.168.0.254;
    option domain-name "example.com";
    option domain-name-servers 192.168.0.1;
    option broadcast-address 192.168.0.255;
    option subnet-mask 255.255.255.0;
    range 192.168.0.101 192.168.0.200;
}
```

This tells the server that if a client requests a lease, it may assign any address from 192.168.0.101 through 192.168.0.200. We don't specify the full network range here, so that we have some addresses left to assign manually to servers or other hosts.

All that is left for us to do now is tell the DHCP server which network interfaces it should listen on. If we don't do this, it won't start. On Ubuntu, we can specify this by editing the /etc/default/dhcp3-server file and adding each interface on which we want the server to listen to the INTERFACES variable.

INTERFACES="eth0"

On Red Hat, we do this by editing the /etc/sysconfig/dhcpd file and adding each interface to the DHCPDARGS variable.

DHCPDARGS="eth0"

We save the file and then start the server using sudo invoke-rc.d dhcp3-server start on Ubuntu or sudo service dhcpd start on Red Hat.

When the server assigns a lease to a specific client, it records the client MAC address and the assigned lease to a file. Generally, it tries to reassign the same address to a client when it reconnects, even if more time than max-lease-time has passed. Of course, if the address isn't available because it has been assigned to a different client, the server will need to issue a different one.

Static Lease Assignments

Sometimes you want to be able to assign the same IP address to a host or device—for instance, a networked printer or a workstation that hosts a development website. You can manually edit the configuration on the client, but that means you need to log in to a client to make changes to the network configuration.

DHCP allows you to assign the same IP address to a host by matching it with the host's MAC address. If you make use of this, you can change address assignments to any host by simply editing dhcpd.conf, restarting the DHCP service, and waiting for a host to renew its lease.

Recall that you can obtain the MAC address for a host by running the ifconfig command. You can also run the arp command to list IP addresses and associated MAC addresses on the local network.

These configuration directives all go within the subnet block in the dhcpd.conf file. You start by defining a group, which you can give any name you like; here we've chosen "static."

```
subnet ... {
    group "static" {
    }
}
```

Next, you add a host definition. Each host is defined in a block of its own, within your group definition. The hardware ethernet option specifies the MAC address that will have the address specified with the fixed-address option assigned to it.

■**Note** You can find out the MAC address for a network interface via the ifconfig command.

This option can contain either an IP address or a resolvable FQDN. We'll use the FQDN, as DNS is working fine for us. It also means that if we want to change the IP address that is assigned to the host, but don't want to change its hostname, we only need to update the DNS zone file and not the DHCP server as well.

```
subnet ... {
    group "static" {
        host au-mel-ubuntu-2 {
            hardware ethernet 00:16:3E:15:3C:C2;
            fixed-address au-mel-ubuntu-2.example.com;
        }
    }
}
```

We set the use-host-decl-names flag to on. This ensures that the name we set on the host block—au-mel-ubuntu-2 in our case—will be sent to the DHCP client as the hostname it should use. If we did not set this, we would have to add a specific hostname option to each static host we define this way. Because we define it within the group, it does not apply to any configurations that fall outside this group.

```
subnet ... {
    group "static" {
        use-host-decl-names on;
        host au-mel-ubuntu-2 {
            hardware ethernet 00:16:3E:15:3C:C2;
            fixed-address au-mel-ubuntu-2.example.com;
        }
    }
}
```

Finally, we will want to make sure that the addresses we use for static DHCP leases never get assigned to clients the DHCP server doesn't know about. We can reserve some of our 100 addresses for this purpose by defining address pools. We'll first define a pool for hosts the DHCP server knows about. Again, these pool definitions go within the subnet block.

```
subnet ... {
    ...
    pool {
        range 192.168.0.101 192.168.0.150;
        deny unknown clients
    }
}
```

This reserves 50 addresses for use with hosts that need a static assignment. Next we'll define a pool for all other clients. On this pool we will also override the lease times, as visiting machines generally won't need an address all day long.

```
subnet ... {
    ...
    pool {
```

```
        range 192.168.0.101 192.168.0.150;
        deny unknown clients
    }
    pool {
        range 192.168.0.151 192.168.0.200;
        allow unknown clients;
        default-lease-time 7200;
        max-lease-time 21600;
    }
}
```

We have split our original range of IP addresses into two. To make sure the server doesn't think it's allowed to assign the same range twice, we comment out the original statement near the top of the file.

```
subnet ... {
    ...
    // range 192.168.0.101 192.168.0.200;
    ...
```

We can now restart the DHCP server. All that is left to do is make sure DHCP requests reach our server through the firewall. A DHCP client by definition does not have an IP address assigned yet, so it cannot send a packet to a specific network address.

What it does instead is broadcast a UDP packet to port 67 at the address 255.255.255.255, which is the broadcast address for the 0.0.0.0 network. The DHCP server knows to listen for these packets and will respond if it receives one. We thus need to configure the firewall on the DHCP server host to accept packets to port 67 at any address.

```
$ sudo /sbin/iptables -t filter -A Firewall-eth0-INPUT -p udp --dport 67 -j ACCEPT
```

We now have a DHCP server configuration that assigns specific reserved IP addresses to defined hosts and uses a different address range for other hosts. By having these hosts use a predetermined set of IP addresses, we can also regulate their access by setting firewall rules and changing server configurations to either grant or deny access based on the address a host is connecting with.

Dynamic DNS Updates

You might also want to assign fixed DNS names to specific hosts, regardless of which IP address they were assigned by the DHCP server. This allows you to refer to machines by name, even if their address changes. This is accomplished by setting up a cryptographic key that is shared by both the DNS and DHCP servers. The DHCP server will then contact the DNS server when it issues a new lease and update the associated A and PTR entries, if required.

Configuring DNS

On Ubuntu, we start by generating the key, and for this we will use the `dnssec-keygen` tool. We will specify the HMAC-MD5 algorithm with the `-a` option and a 512-bit key size via the `-b` option. The key name type we need to use is HOST, and we specify that with the `-n` option. Finally, we pass the key name we want to use.

```
$ dnssec-keygen -a HMAC-MD5 -b 512 -n HOST dynamic-update-key
Kdynamic-update-key.+157+05884
$ ls -l
-rw------- 1 jsmith jsmith  127 Feb 10 22:16 Kdynamic-update-key.+157+05884.key
-rw------- 1 jsmith jsmith  145 Feb 10 22:16 Kdynamic-update-key.+157+05884.private
```

The key that is generated is stored in the `Kdynamic-update-key.+157+05884.private` file.

```
$ cat Kdynamic-update-key.+157+05884.private
Private-key-format: v1.2
Algorithm: 157 (HMAC_MD5)
Key: 3PDRnypPtzJqpbQvbw/B7bhPuHqpUeOSdi95Z4Ez/IzhS61dzcK6MJ6CdFHkkegpTN1kmXOM6GggRNE
24aPmOw==
```

Note that your key file name will differ, as the key ID, which is the second set of numbers, will be different. We don't need the `Kdynamic-update-key.+157+05884.key` file for our current task.

We now need to add this key to the configurations for both `named` and `dhcpd`. We'll start with the former, on Ubuntu, by adding the key definition to the `/etc/bind/named.local.conf` file, as shown in Listing 9-28.

Listing 9-28. *Adding a Cryptographic Key to the `bind9` Configuration*

```
key dynamic-update-key {
    algorithm HMAC-MD5;
    secret "3PDRnypPtzJqpbQvbw/B7bhPuHqpUeOSdi95Z4Ez/IzhS61dzcK6MJ6CdFHkkegp➡
TN1kmXOM6GggRNE24aPmOw==";
};
```

The DNS server knows about the key, but we still need to tell it that clients that present this key are allowed to update specific zones. We do this by changing the zone definitions to include an `allow-update` directive, as shown in Listing 9-29.

Listing 9-29. *Allowing Zone Updates with a Key*

```
zone "example.com" {
    type master;
    notify yes;
    allow-transfer {
        192.168.0.1;
    };
```

```
    file "example.com.db";
    allow-update {
        key dynamic-update-key;
    };
};

zone "0.168.192.in-addr.arpa" {
    type master;
    notify yes;
    allow-transfer {
        192.168.0.1;
    };
    file "192.168.0.db";
    allow-update {
        key dynamic-update-key;
    };
};
```

We then reload the name server configuration via `sudo rndc reload`.

On Red Hat, you can add the key using the `system-config-bind` utility. Start it via System ➤ Administration ➤ Server Settings ➤ Domain Name System. Then highlight DNS Server and select New ➤ Security key.

All you need to do here is enter the name you want to give the key. When you click the New button, a key will be automatically generated. After that, click OK to add the key to your name server configuration, as shown in Figure 9-18.

Figure 9-18. *Creating a DNS security key*

Next, you need to change the zone definition to allow this key to perform updates. Select the zone (in our case, example.com) in the listing and then click the Properties button. In the options window, highlight `allow-update` in the All Options listing, and then click the plus sign to add it to the Current Options listing, as shown in Figure 9-19.

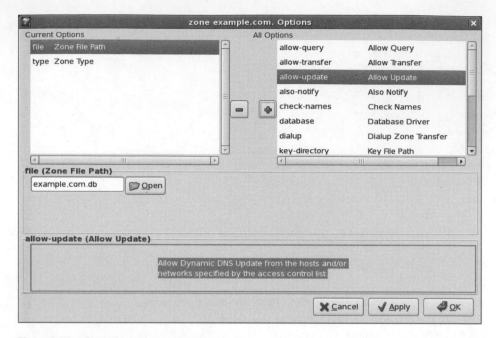

Figure 9-19. *Changing zone options*

Highlight the `allow-update` option in the Current Options listing, which will allow you to change its properties. You'll work from right to left this time. First, scroll down the New List Element listing, so you can highlight Named Key. Doing so shows the list of available keys in the Edit List Element listing. We've highlighted our new `dynamic-update-key`, as shown in Figure 9-20.

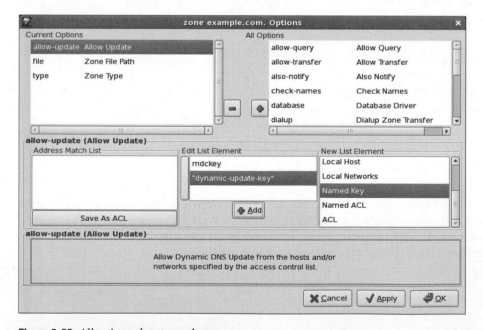

Figure 9-20. *Allowing a key to update a zone*

When you click Add, the `dynamic-update-key` is added to the Address Match List, as shown in Figure 9-21.

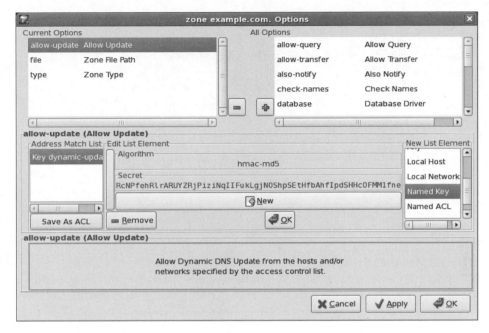

Figure 9-21. *Zone configuration is complete.*

Click OK to close this window. You'll get a warning informing you that the name server will not be able to update the zone file if it remains in the /var/named directory, as shown in Figure 9-22.

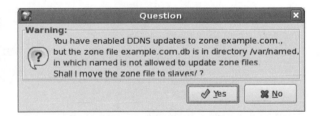

Figure 9-22. *Moving the zone file to a writeable directory*

This is a security consideration that prevents attackers from changing zones on disk, should they be able to compromise the DNS server. Of course, if your DHCP server is to update a zone, it will need to be written to, so you can instead store the zone file in the /var/named/slaves directory, which is writeable by the DNS server. Click Yes to accept this change.

Now you need to do exactly the same thing for the reverse zone. Open its properties window and add the `allow-updates` permission for the `dynamic-update-key`, just as you did for the forward zone. When you accept this change, you are again asked if you want to move the zone file to the slaves directory, which you should accept.

Write the updated zone files to disk by clicking Save and choosing to back up and replace the existing configuration files, as shown in Figure 9-23.

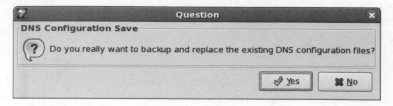

Figure 9-23. *Accepting and saving changes*

■**Tip** You can also use key-based authentication between master and slave DNS servers.

Configuring DHCP

The next step is to tell the DHCP server about this key as well, and to configure it so it sends DNS update requests to named when it hands out a new lease. We start by changing the ddns-update-style variable from none to interim. We also want a fairly low TTL on these dynamic DNS entries, so they don't remain active after a host disappears off the network. We'll specify an hour.

```
ddns-update-style interim;
ddns-ttl 3600;
```

Under that, still in the global configuration section, we add the key definition. It is important to use exactly the same key name used on the name server, or the updates will not work.

```
key dynamic-update-key {
    algorithm hmac-md5;
    secret
"3PDRnypPtzJqpbQvbw/B7bhPuHqpUeOSdi95Z4Ez/IzhS61dzcK6MJ6CdFHkkegpTN1kmXOM6Ggg➡
RNE24aPmOw==";
}
```

And finally we need to tell the DHCP server that we want to perform dynamic updates on the forward and reverse zones. We need to add a zone definition for each zone in the global section of the configuration file. We also need to specify which key should be used for updates and which DNS server the updates need to be sent to, as shown in Listing 9-30.

Listing 9-30. *Adding Zone Update Definitions in dhcpd.conf*

```
zone 0.168.192.in-addr.arpa. {
    key dynamic-update-key;
    primary 192.168.0.1;
}
```

```
zone example.com. {
    key dynamic-update key;
    primary 192.168.0.1;
}
```

We restart the DHCP server as well, and when that is done, the server-side configuration is complete. All that remains to do now is tell the DHCP clients to send a hostname string to the server when they ask for a lease. This hostname string will then be used to create the FQDN for the DNS entries.

To set it, we edit the file /etc/dhclient.conf on the client and add the send host-name option. On a host that we'd like to be named au-mel-rhel-2.example.com, we add the following:

```
send host-name "au-mel-rhel-2";
```

■**Note** The configuration in /etc/dhclient.conf is applied to all network interfaces. You can use the /etc/dhclient-eth0.conf file instead to apply it to the first interface only.

We can then run the dhclient utility to renew our address lease, as shown in Listing 9-31. This would also run automatically at boot time if we'd configured the host to use DHCP. If that is the case, and you want to manually renew a lease, you should first kill the running dhclient process.

Listing 9-31. *Obtaining a Lease with dhclient*

```
$ sudo dhclient eth0
Internet Systems Consortium DHCP Client V3.0.5-RedHat
Copyright 2004-2006 Internet Systems Consortium.
All rights reserved.
For info, please visit http://www.isc.org/sw/dhcp/

Listening on LPF/eth1/00:0c:29:7b:b1:77
Sending on   LPF/eth1/00:0c:29:7b:b1:77
Sending on   Socket/fallback
DHCPREQUEST on eth0 to 255.255.255.255 port 67
DHCPACK from 192.168.0.1
bound to 192.168.0.200 -- renewal in 7181 seconds.
```

We can check the system log on the server to see what happened. We've included a snippet in Listing 9-32. On Red Hat this log file would be /var/log/messages, and on Ubuntu it would be /var/log/syslog. We'll show you how you can redirect specific log messages to different files in Chapter 18.

Listing 9-32. *The DHCP Server Log*

```
Feb 11 11:23:15 au-mel-ubuntu-1 dhcpd: DHCPDISCOVER from 00:0c:29:7b:b1:77 via eth0
Feb 11 11:23:16 au-mel-ubuntu-1 dhcpd: DHCPOFFER on 192.168.0.200 to
    00:0c:29:7b:b1:77 (au-mel-rhel-2) via eth0
Feb 11 11:23:16 au-mel-ubuntu-1 named[5187]: client 192.168.0.1#46749: updating
    zone 'example.com/IN': adding an RR at 'au-mel-rhel-2.example.com' A
Feb 11 11:23:16 au-mel-ubuntu-1 named[5187]: client 192.168.0.1#46749: updating
    zone 'example.com/IN': adding an RR at 'au-mel-rhel-2.example.com' TXT
Feb 11 11:23:16 au-mel-ubuntu-1 named[5187]: journal file example.com.db.jnl does
    not exist, creating it
Feb 11 11:23:16 au-mel-ubuntu-1 dhcpd: Added new forward map from
    au-mel-rhel-2.example.com to 192.168.0.200
Feb 11 11:23:16 au-mel-ubuntu-1 named[5187]: zone example.com/IN:sending
    notifies (serial 2009020102)
Feb 11 11:23:16 au-mel-ubuntu-1 named[5187]: client 192.168.0.1#58073: updating zone
    '0.168.192.in-addr.arpa/IN': deleting rrset at '200.0.168.192.in-addr.arpa' PTR
Feb 11 11:23:16 au-mel-ubuntu-1 named[5187]: client 192.168.0.1#58073: updating zone
    '0.168.192.in-addr.arpa/IN': adding an RR at '200.0.168.192.in-addr.arpa' PTR
Feb 11 11:23:16 au-mel-ubuntu-1 named[5187]: journal file 192.168.0.db.jnl does
    not exist, creating it
Feb 11 11:23:16 au-mel-ubuntu-1 dhcpd: added reverse map from
    200.0.168.192.in-addr.arpa. to au-mel-rhel-2.example.com
Feb 11 11:23:16 au-mel-ubuntu-1 dhcpd: DHCPREQUEST for 192.168.0.200 (192.168.0.1)
    from 00:0c:29:7b:b1:77 (au-mel-rhel-2) via eth0
Feb 11 11:23:16 au-mel-ubuntu-1 dhcpd: DHCPACK on 192.168.0.200 to
    00:0c:29:7b:b1:77 (au-mel-rhel-2) via eth0
```

You can see the server received a DHCP request from a host with MAC address 00:0c:29:7b:b1:77. It then offered this host the address 192.168.0.200 and was told the host's name is au-mel-rhel-2. Next, you can see the name server adding an A and a TXT record for the au-mel-rhel-2.example.com FQDN. The TXT entry contains a checksum that is used to track whether a DNS entry was created by the DHCP server. If it is not present, the server will not change or remove the associated A entry.

The changes to the zone are then written to a journal file that is associated with the zone file created earlier. The actual zone file itself is not modified. After the forward zone is updated, it sends a notification to any slave servers that are configured for this zone. If we had any, this would trigger the slaves to transfer the updates zone file from the master.

Next, the same process is repeated for the reverse zone. When that is also done, the DHCP server allows the client to obtain the lease it offered and updates its internal leases file. We can quickly double-check that these new DNS entries work by performing a lookup via the host command.

```
$ host 192.168.0.200
200.0.168.192.in-addr.arpa domain name pointer au-mel-rhel-2.example.com.
$ host au-mel-rhel-2.example.com.
au-mel-rhel-2.example.com has address 192.168.0.200
```

Both lookups work, so we can now configure any other hosts on the network that we also want to have dynamically updated in the DNS server.

Manually Changing DNS Entries

Because these dynamic updates use a journal file, you need to perform an extra step if you want to manually change any DNS entries. If you simply change the zone file, these changes will be ignored because the data in the journal file will supersede it.

You can tell the DNS server you want to lock the zone journal files and reject any dynamic changes while you're editing a zone by issuing the `sudo rndc freeze` command before you start editing. When you're done editing the zone file, you can permit dynamic updates again by unlocking the zone via `sudo rndc unfreeze`.

THE INTERNET SUPERSERVER

Not all network services need to run all the time. For some of them, it would be handy to have a way of listening for traffic on a specific port number and start the service only when it is needed. Once a client disconnects, the service can be shut down again. Not all services support this, but if they do, it is a nice way to conserve system resources.

This "supervisor" functionality is provided by the Internet superserver. The latest and most feature-rich version of this software is provided by the `xinetd` package.

Each service that is managed by `xinetd` has its own configuration file snippet in the `/etc/xinetd.d` directory, and by default it will install configuration files for some very basic services, such as echo, which simply repeats any character you send to it. These services are not enabled until you edit their configuration files, though.

We'll show you how to add a service to `xinetd` in Chapter 19.

Secure Shell

Thus far, you've really only used SSH to connect from a workstation to a server, in order to make configuration changes or add new software. We'll now show you how you can get the most out of SSH. We'll set up key-based authentication, use `ssh` to copy files between hosts, and make use of tunnels to access remote services through a firewall.

When you connect to a host via SSH, you are asked to enter your password. This is fine if you need to type it once a day, but if you connect to remote hosts often, it can become time consuming, especially if you have a secure, long password.

SSH allows you to use key-based authentication instead. To make use of this, you create public and private keys and then copy the public key to the remote servers you want to connect to. When you connect, the remote host will verify that you have the private key that belongs to the public key component on that host. If you do, you are authenticated.

■**Note** The public and private keys are used to authenticate you. The connection encryption is provided by the SSH host keys, which are generated when the service is installed.

Creating and Distributing Keys

We'll start by creating a public/private key pair using the ssh-keygen utility. We can define the key type (two encryption algorithms are supported) and key size in bits, as well as the output file names to use. For the latter we'll use the defaults, and for the former we'll specify the RSA algorithm with the -t option and a 2,048-bit key using the -b option, as shown in Listing 9-33.

Listing 9-33. *Generating a New SSH Key Pair*

```
$ ssh-keygen -t rsa -b 2048
Generating public/private rsa key pair.
Enter file in which to save the key (/home/jsmith/.ssh/id_rsa):
Enter passphrase (empty for no passphrase):
Enter same passphrase again:
Your identification has been saved in /home/jsmith/.ssh/id_rsa.
Your public key has been saved in /home/jsmith/.ssh/id_rsa.pub.
The key fingerprint is:
8c:57:6d:26:ba:6c:47:98:55:25:ce:4d:50:51:f8:85 jsmith@au-mel-ubuntu-1.example.com
```

It is important to add a passphrase to your private key, as without one anyone who gets hold of your private key can use it to log in (without the need for a password) to any host that contains your public key.

Now that we have a key pair, we can copy the public part to a remote host. We need to store the public key in a file called authorized_keys in the .ssh directory in our home directory in order to be able to use it to log in. We can either add the key to that file by hand or use the ssh-copy-id utility to do this for us, like in Listing 9-34.

Listing 9-34. *Copying a Public SSH Key to a Remote Host*

```
$ ssh-copy-id au-mel-rhel-1.example.com
The authenticity of host 'au-mel-rhel-1.example.com (192.168.0.1)' can't be
    established.
RSA key fingerprint is 67:e3:50:bf:8c:2c:a0:d5:0c:e9:fc:26:3f:9f:ea:0e.
Are you sure you want to continue connecting (yes/no)? yes
Warning: Permanently added 'au-mel-rhel-1.example.com,192.168.0.1' (RSA) to the
    list of known hosts.
jsmith@au-mel-rhel-1.example.com's password:
```

Now we'll try logging in to the machine with the following:

```
$ ssh au-mel-rhel-1.example.com
```

Since we had not yet connected to au-mel-rhel-1 from the host we're logged in to, we're prompted to accept the remote SSH host key. The fingerprint that uniquely identifies this key is printed, so you can visually verify whether it matches with the key on the remote host.

■**Note** To obtain a host key fingerprint, you can use the ssh-keygen tool. In this case, use ssh-keygen -l -f /etc/ssh/ssh_host_rsa_key.pub to obtain the fingerprint for the host RSA key.

You'll note SSH assumes our username on the remote host is the same as the user we're logged in as locally. If this is not the case, we can copy the key to username@remotehost instead.

Next, we're prompted for the login password, since our key is not yet listed in the correct file on the remote host. Once we're authenticated, ssh-copy-id appends the public key to the correct file and asks us to test it. We do this by logging in to the remote host, as shown in Listing 9-35.

Listing 9-35. *Logging In Using an SSH Key*

```
$ ssh au-mel-rhel-1.example.com
Enter passphrase for key '/home/jsmith/.ssh/id_rsa':
Last login: Tue Feb 10 15:14:42 2009 from au-mel-ubuntu-1.example.com
[jsmith@au-mel-rhel-1 ~]$
```

This time, we were not asked for our login password on au-mel-rhel-1, which is exactly what we wanted. We can now check the .ssh/authorized_keys file on au-mel-hel-1 to make sure we haven't added extra, unexpected keys.

Using SSH Agent

However, we did still have to enter the password we set on the private SSH key. If you have to do this each time you want to connect to a remote host, it defeats the purpose of setting up key-based authentication. Enter the SSH agent, a small daemon that keeps unlocked private SSH keys in memory. Once we start it, we can unlock one or more private keys and add them to the agent. SSH can then use the agent to provide a private key and authenticate us to a remote host.

The way to tell SSH about the agent is by setting two environment variables, SSH_AUTH_SOCK and SSH_AGENT_PID. If these are set, ssh can communicate with the agent. The agent outputs shell code to set these variables when it starts, as you can see in Listing 9-36.

Listing 9-36. *Starting ssh-agent*

```
$ ssh-agent
SSH_AUTH_SOCK=/tmp/ssh-SZGGF11534/agent.11534; export SSH_AUTH_SOCK;
SSH_AGENT_PID=11535; export SSH_AGENT_PID;
echo Agent pid 11535;
```

If we then paste these lines into the shell, the variables will be set.

```
$ SSH_AUTH_SOCK=/tmp/ssh-SZGGF11534/agent.11534; export SSH_AUTH_SOCK;
$ SSH_AGENT_PID=11535; export SSH_AGENT_PID;
$ echo Agent pid 11535;
Agent pid 11535
```

Having to copy and paste these lines is a bit cumbersome, so instead we can use the eval shell function to make life a bit easier. This function executes any parameters passed to it as if they were commands. First, we'll stop the agent via ssh-agent -k, and then we'll restart it and set the environment variables in one fell swoop. The backquotes around the parameter cause it to be executed as a command by the shell. The output this command generates is then interpreted by eval.

```
$ ssh-agent -k
unset SSH_AUTH_SOCK;
unset SSH_AGENT_PID;
echo Agent pid 11535 killed;
$ eval `ssh-agent`
Agent pid 11541
```

All we need to do now is unlock the private key and add it to the agent.

```
$ ssh-add
Enter passphrase for /home/jsmith/.ssh/id_rsa:
Identity added: /home/jsmith/.ssh/id_rsa (/home/jsmith/.ssh/id_rsa)
```

We are able to connect to any host that contains the matching public key, without any further need to enter a password.

```
$ ssh jsmith@au-mel-rhel-1
Last login: Tue Feb 10 15:17:19 2009 from au-mel-ubuntu-1.example.com
[jsmith@au-mel-rhel-1 ~]$
```

■**Tip** You can tell multiple shells on the same host that you are using the agent by simply setting the SSH_AUTH_SOCK and SSH_AGENT_PID variables to the correct values in the shell.

Tweaking SSH Configuration

When all your SSH servers listen on the same port and you use a single key pair for all hosts, the default server configuration will suit you fine. If not (e.g., port 22 traffic might be firewalled or the remote username is different for each host), you might want to tweak the configuration for your server or client somewhat.

Basic Server Configuration

The server side of SSH reads its configuration from the /etc/ssh/sshd_config file. By default, it listens on port 22 on all available network interfaces. You can change this by changing the Port and ListenAddress options in the configuration file.

The Port option takes a single parameter, which is the port number you want the server to listen on. To have the server listen on multiple ports, you can add extra Port directives, one for each port number.

This also applies to the ListenAddress directive. As long as no such directive is present, the server will listen on all interfaces. When you add one, it will start listening on all defined ports on only the address specified. You can have it listen on multiple addresses by adding additional ListenAddress directives.

For instance, to make the SSH server on our bastion host listen on ports 22 and 2022 only on the internal network interfaces, we can add these directives to the configuration file:

```
Port 22
Port 2022
```

```
ListenAddress 192.168.0.1
ListenAddress 19.168.1.1
```

We can now tell the server to reload its configuration file via `sudo service sshd reload` on Red Hat or `sudo invoke-rc.d ssh reload` on Ubuntu. This will not affect current connections, so you can run this command remotely.

■**Caution** Make sure you do not reconfigure the SSH server to the point where you can no longer access it! If you're worried, do not log out after a configuration change. Try creating a new connection first, to ensure it still works.

The other basic server option we'll cover is designed to make your life easier when working with GUI applications on remote hosts. When the `X11Forwarding` option is set to `on` and you pass the `-X` parameter to the SSH client when you connect to such a host, you can run any graphical applications and their windows will be displayed on your local desktop. This feature takes advantage of the client/server modes of the X Window System by forwarding any connection attempts to an X server on the remote host through your SSH connection to the X server on your local host.

To force all users to use key-based authentication, you can add `PasswordAuthentication no` in the server configuration file. This will prevent everyone from being able to log in with a password. Note that if you lose your private key, you will no longer be able to log in to hosts with this option set.

You can find a full listing of all available server configuration options on the `man sshd_config` manual page.

Client Configuration

The SSH client can be configured globally for all users on a host and locally as well, specifically for each user. The global configuration file is `/etc/ssh/ssh_config` and the per-user file is `.ssh/config` in the user's home directory.

The most basic client configuration directives allow you to define which username and port number to use when you connect to a given host or all hosts. Each of these configuration blocks starts with a `Host` directive, which is followed by a hostname or a shortened alias if the section should apply to a single host only, or an asterisk if it should apply to all hosts.

For instance, we can easily customize our connection options for the bastion host by adding the following snippet to our `.ssh/config` file.

```
Host gateway
    Hostname au-mel-rhel-1
    Port 2022
    User ataylor
```

This configuration is used each time we use the `ssh gateway` command. It tells the client to connect to the au-mel-rhel-1 host on port number 2022 and log in as user `ataylor`. By adding these options in the client configuration file, we don't need to keep specifying the port number and login name on the command line.

Similarly, we can tell the client to use a different private key file when connecting to a remote host, by adding it using the `IdentityFile` directive. We'll generate a key pair to use for `ataylor` on the gateway host via `ssh-keygen -t rsa -s 2048 -f .ssh/gateway-ataylor`. Once done, we can tell the client to use this key for connections to the bastion host.

```
Host gateway
    Hostname au-mel-rhel-1
    Port 2022
    User ataylor
    IdentityFile ~/.ssh/gateway-ataylor
```

The final options we'll cover are designed to make your life easier when working on remote hosts. First, the `ForwardAgent yes` option allows you to tell a server that it should use the SSH agent on the originating host for authentication. This allows you to hop from host to host via SSH, without needing to enter passwords to start an SSH agent on each of these hosts.

So you don't have to keep adding the `-X` parameter to `ssh` in order to enable X forwarding, you can enable it on a per-host basis in the configuration file as well. For each host on which you want to remotely run GUI applications, add a `ForwardX11 yes` directive to automatically enable this option.

Tunneling

You can also use SSH to access protected services on remote hosts and networks without first setting up a VPN. If two sites share the same private network ranges, a VPN would not work, as the address ranges on both sides of the VPN would be identical. In this case, you can use SSH to forward connections from a local host to a remote address or vice versa. Such forwards act as a single-port tunnel.

You can do this each via command-line parameters, or you can define forwards for each host in your `.ssh/config` file. For instance, you could create an SSH tunnel that forwards connections to port 8080 on your local host to port 80 on a machine on the remote network. This way, you are able to access a remote website by browsing an address on your local network. You create a local forward by passing the `-L` option to the SSH client and specifying an optional local address followed by a mandatory local port as the start for the tunnel, and then a remote host and a remote port as the end for the tunnel, all separated by colons.

```
$ ssh -L 8080:192.168.1.12:80 ataylor@192.168.1.1
```

This command connects us to the host 192.168.1.1 as the user `ataylor` and sets up a tunnel that allows us to browse the website on the host 192.168.1.12 by visiting `http://localhost:8080` in our web browser. The connection will be forwarded over our SSH connection, and the web server on host 192.168.1.12 will see an incoming connection from the address 192.168.1.1.

■**Note** Accessing them via a tunnel may not work for all websites due to the way they are hosted. We will cover such name-based virtual hosting in Chapter 11.

Conversely, you can provide users on a remote host access to a service on your local network by creating a remote forward using the -R option. This option takes the same parameters as the -L option, but instead specifies an optional remote address and mandatory port number to listen on the remote host, followed by a local address and port number for the tunnel end point.

To allow a remote user to connect to a normally inaccessible SSH server on our local network, we can create a remote tunnel on port 2022 that forwards connections to port 22 on a host on our local network.

```
$ ssh -R 192.168.1.1:2022:192.168.0.15:22 ataylor@192.168.1.1
```

After we're logged on to the host 192.168.1.1 as user ataylor, we can SSH to port 2022 on the local host, which will then log us in to SSH on the host at 192.168.0.15.

For security reasons, the start of the tunnel will only ever bind to the loopback network interface, so users on different hosts on the network are not able to use the tunnel. We can change this behavior by adding the GatewayPorts directive to the SSH server configuration file. This option applies only to the starting point of the forward, so for local tunnels we add it on the local host, and for remote forwards we add it on the remote host.

To allow us to specify whether users on other hosts should be able to use a forward, we set the GatewayPorts option to clientspecified. If we do not specify an IP address for the forward starting point, it will be accessible only to local users, while it will be available to any users on the same network as the tunnel starting point if we specify an accessible address.

Since this requires quite a lot of typing, it's easier to define commonly used tunnels in the SSH client configuration file. We do this via the LocalForward and RemoteForward directives. Each of these takes two parameters, the forward starting address and port, separated by a colon, and the end point address and port, again separated by a colon.

We can add the forwards we used previously to our client configuration file:

```
Host gateway
    Hostname 192.168.1.1
    Port 22
    User ataylor
    IdentityFile ~/.ssh/gateway-ataylor
    LocalForward 8080 192.168.1.12:80
    RemoteForward 192.168.1.1:2022 192.168.0.15:22
```

Finally, the ForwardAgent yes option makes SSH configure the remote shell to use the SSH agent on your local host for any authentication. Provided your public key is available on all remote hosts, this allows you to hop from host to host without needing to reenter your password or starting a new ssh-agent instance on each intermediate host. This is an extremely useful option, so you may as well enable it for all users by adding it to the global section of the /etc/ssh/ssh_config file.

Performing Quick and Secure File Transfers

The SSH protocol allows for more than just remote logins. You can also use it to securely transfer files between hosts. One way is to use the scp command, which works just like cp, except the source or target files can be prefixed by a remote username and hostname, as shown in Listing 9-37.

Listing 9-37. *Using scp to Transfer a File to a Remote Host*

```
$ scp data.txt jsmith@au-mel-rhel-1:/tmp
data.txt                                        100% 3072KB   3.0MB/s   00:00
```

Because we had sent our public SSH key to au-mel-rhel-1 previously, scp was able to use the SSH agent to authenticate and we weren't asked for a password. We can log in to the au-mel-rhel-1 host and see the file data.txt is now in the /tmp directory.

We can also copy from a remote host back to a local host, by specifying a remote file path as the first parameter and a local file or directory second.

```
$ scp jsmith@au-mel-rhel-1:/tmp/data.txt /tmp
data.txt                                        100% 3072KB   3.0MB/s   00:00
```

We can even copy files or directories from one remote host to another remote host without logging in to either of them. For instance, on au-mel-ubuntu-1 we could run the following:

```
$ scp jsmith@au-mel-rhel-1:/tmp/data.txt ataylor@au-mel-rhel-2:/tmp
data.txt                                        100% 3072KB   3.0MB/s   00:01
```

SSH also provides a replacement for the FTP protocol. If you want to be able to interactively move files or directories, you can use the sftp command, as shown in Listing 9-38. Again, this command will use the SSH agent if present.

Listing 9-38. *Using sftp*

```
$ sftp jsmith@au-mel-rhel-1
Connecting to au-mel-rhel-1...
jsmith@au-mel-rhel-1's password:
sftp> cd /tmp
sftp> ls
data.txt         ssh-IWYooo5675
sftp> get data.txt
Fetching /tmp/data.txt to data.txt
/tmp/data.txt                                   100% 3072KB   3.0MB/s   00:00
sftp> quit
```

■**Tip** In combination with SSH port forwards, you can also easily copy files to hosts that aren't directly accessible. Note that scp uses the -P option to specify a port number, whereas ssh uses -p.

Summary

In this chapter, you learned about basic infrastructure services like NTP, DNS and DHCP. We've also shown you how to connect to remote hosts, to make system administration and maintenance easier. You should now be able to do the following:

- Set and keep the correct time on all your hosts.
- Create forward and reverse DNS records for all your hosts and have these records replicate to multiple DNS servers.
- Set up DHCP to automate address assignment and link it to DNS to automatically update relevant DNS records.
- Use ssh, scp, and sftp to easily and securely work on remote hosts and transfer files.

In the next chapter, we'll introduce you to mail services and teach you how to run your own mail server.

CHAPTER 10

■ ■ ■

Mail Services

By James Turnbull

One of the most common reasons to deploy a Linux host is to provide mail services including receiving and sending e-mail and retrieving e-mail via mechanisms like Internet Message Access Protocol (IMAP) and Post Office Protocol (POP3). In this chapter, we'll briefly explain how e-mail works, and we'll introduce you to the component parts of an e-mail solution, including

- *MTAs, or Mail Transfer Agents*: The servers that send and receive e-mail
- *MUAs, or Mail User Agents*: Clients through which your users send and receive e-mail
- *MDAs, or Mail Delivery Agents*: Tools that help you deliver e-mail to mailboxes

We'll also introduce you to some applications to perform these functions:

- *Postfix*: A Simple Mail Transfer Protocol (SMTP) e-mail server
- *Dovecot*: An IMAP and a POP3 server

The Postfix e-mail server will allow your users to send and receive e-mail both from internal users and externally, such as from the Internet. The Dovecot server provides IMAP and POP3 daemons. IMAP and POP3 are two different ways for your users to retrieve their e-mail from a mailbox located on your e-mail server (we'll explain those differences and why you might use one over the other).

We'll also show you how to protect your users from unsolicited e-mail or spam, and from viruses.

It is important to understand that this chapter explains basic mail services—sending, receiving, and managing e-mail. It does not include services like scheduling, calendaring, to-do lists, or other features of collaboration suites like Microsoft Exchange, Zimbra, and OpenExchange. We're going to talk about open source collaboration suites, which generally also include e-mail as well as these other features, in Chapter 15. If you feel you require those features, you may wish to skip to that chapter. However, we strongly recommend you also read this chapter to get an understanding of how e-mail works.

How Does E-Mail Work?

E-mail has become ubiquitous for personal and business communications. In many cases, it has completely replaced postal and fax services as communication tools. Most people don't need to worry beyond composing e-mails and clicking the Send button. In order to run your own mail server, however, you need to understand a bit more about the inner workings of e-mail. In Figure 10-1, you can see the typical e-mail life cycle.

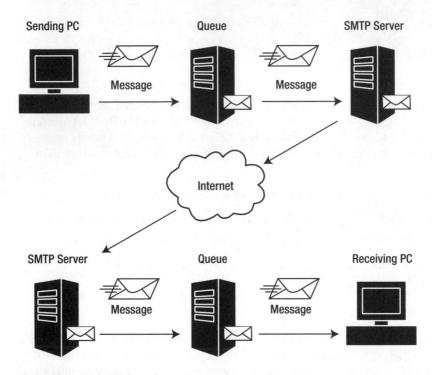

Figure 10-1. *E-mail life cycle*

What Happens When You Send an E-Mail?

E-mail is based around a protocol called SMTP (defined in RFC 5321: http://www.ietf.org/rfc/rfc5321.txt). Each e-mail has a series of headers that tell your mail server what to do with it and where to send it. So when users create a new e-mail, they address that e-mail. They add a recipient (or To field) and perhaps cc or bcc the e-mail to others. They then send the e-mail.

The user's e-mail client is configured with a server, and your client now contacts this server (on TCP port 25) and says "Hello! I have mail from this person to these people—please send it to them!" Actually, our client doesn't precisely say "hello," it says something pretty close—a command called EHLO (or more rarely HELO).

■Note There are a lot of names for e-mail servers. They can be called SMTP servers or SMTP daemons, but their proper name is Mail Transfer Agents. The client that sends e-mail is known in this nomenclature as a Mail User Agent. We'll also look at another component called the Mail Delivery Agent that can be used to deliver e-mail to a user's mailbox later in this chapter.

EHLO is an SMTP command that is part of SMTP's "language." Commands are how SMTP clients and servers (or MUAs and MTAs) communicate with one another. Originally, SMTP only had about ten words, or commands, in its language. In more recent times, an enhanced version of SMTP called Extended SMTP (ESMTP) has been created that adds many more useful commands to the language to provide features such as authentication and encryption.

■Note The HELO command we mentioned previously is an older form of the EHLO command. It's rarely used anymore, but all well-behaved mail servers should support it as a fallback in case your client is older and doesn't recognize EHLO.

In this case, the client is telling the server who it is, and in Listing 10-1 you can see a simple conversation in SMTP's "language."

Listing 10-1. *A Simple SMTP Conversation*

```
220 mail.example.com ESMTP Server
EHLO client.example.com
250 mail.example.com Hello client.example.com [192.168.0.100], pleased to meet you
```

The first line in Listing 10-1 is the server telling the client who it is, mail.example.com, and that it is an SMTP server that supports Extended SMTP (or ESMTP)

■Note You can see the line starts with a number in the format 2*xx*. These are response codes that the client and server exchange to indicate success or failure. If the line started with a number 5*xx*, your client and server would know this was an error code of some kind. You'll see more of these numbers later.

On the next line, the client says hello and tells the server who it is, client.example.com (the client generally identifies itself by its fully qualified domain name). Lastly, the server responds, acknowledges the connection, and returns the greeting.

Next, our actual e-mail is sent to the server. This starts with sending the sender and recipient details, what is commonly called the *envelope.*

```
MAIL FROM: <ataylor@example.com>
250 ataylor@example.com... Sender ok
```

Here the sender, ataylor@example.com, has used the MAIL FROM command. The server checks, returns the 250 response code, and indicates that this sender is allowed to submit e-mail. This acceptance can be based on a number of criteria, including a properly constructed e-mail address, and we'll talk about mechanisms like authentication later in this chapter.

Next, the server expects the RCPT TO command, or whom the e-mail is being sent to:

```
RCPT TO: <jsmith@example.com>
250 jsmith@example.com... Recipient ok (will queue)
```

Again, the acceptance of the address is dependent on criteria such as having a properly formed e-mail address.

Next, in our simple example, we need the content of the actual e-mail. The client sends a command called DATA to the server:

```
DATA
354 Enter mail, end with "." on a line by itself
Message-ID:
Date: Mon, 17 Aug 2009 12:29:26 +1100
From: Anne Taylor ataylor@example.com
To: John Smith jsmith@example.com
Subject: Email is cool

This is an email message.
.
250 SAA112345 Message accepted for delivery
```

The server responds with a request for the content of the e-mail and then a marker of a single period or full stop on a line by itself that indicates the end of the e-mail.

You can see we've passed some fairly default headers like the date, the To and From headers, the subject, and the content of the e-mail. We've specified the . marker, and the server has responded by saying that it has accepted the e-mail. Each e-mail is then submitted to a mail queue, processed, and then sent on by your server.

You can now continue to send e-mails by repeating the MAIL FROM command, or you can disconnect from the server using the QUIT command.

```
QUIT
221 Goodbye
```

This is a very simple scenario for sending e-mail. It's the most basic exchange of commands possible. Most of your normal e-mail sending will be a little more complicated when you factor in elements like encryption and authentication.

E-MAIL ADDRESSES

So what is acceptable as an e-mail address? What is a properly formed e-mail address? An e-mail address in its most basic form is a username and a hostname, domain name, or fully qualified domain name, separated by an @ symbol, for example, `jsmith@example.com`. The rules around what characters are allowed and the appropriate structure of e-mail addresses is often confusing. E-mail addresses can take many forms, and different e-mail servers or MTAs accept varying formats as valid. The MTA we're going to show you, Postfix, accepts e-mail addresses in a variety of formats. Postfix's e-mail address rewriting guide demonstrates some of the many e-mail address formats accepted: `http://www.postfix.org/ADDRESS_REWRITING_README.html`.

What Happens After You Send Your E-Mail?

After the server (or MTA) has received the e-mail from your client and places it in a mail queue, a whole new set of commands and steps get executed. First, the server needs to find out where to send the e-mail. To do this, the server takes the portion of the e-mail address to the right of the @ symbol. This is usually the fully qualified domain name, for example, example.com. The e-mail server then uses a DNS query to contact the remote domain and ask it where to send the e-mail.

■**Note** We discussed DNS in Chapter 9.

The e-mail server does this by querying a special kind of DNS record called an *MX record*. Querying the MX record returns one or more entries that tell your e-mail server where to send the e-mail, usually a specific host or IP address. If there is more than one e-mail server returned, a priority is also returned that tells your e-mail server which entry to use first, and then second, and so on.

■**Note** If the DNS query indicates that there isn't an MX record, your e-mail server will be unable to deliver the e-mail and will send you a message indicating this. This can often occur if your user has mistyped or specified an incorrect e-mail address.

The e-mail server then submits your outgoing e-mail to another queue, and from there it is sent on to the destination e-mail server. To do this, your e-mail server tries to connect, via TCP port 25, to each e-mail server returned by the MX query in the priority sequence the record specifies. The e-mail server then follows a submission sequence to see whether it can deliver your e-mail:

1. If an e-mail server responds, it will try to submit the e-mail.

2. If an e-mail server does not respond, your e-mail server will try the next server returned from the MX record in sequence.

3. If no e-mail servers respond, your e-mail server will usually queue your e-mail to try again later.

4. If, after continued failures, the e-mail still can't be delivered, the e-mail server will report failure to the user via an e-mail.

The destination server your e-mail server tries to send to could be the final destination of your e-mail. Or, it could merely be a gateway that your e-mail passes through onto one or more further e-mail servers until it finally reaches its destination. This depends on how the destination has configured its e-mail environment. Many environments have an Internet-facing e-mail gateway that receives mail and then internal e-mail servers that process internal mail. This configuration allows features like spam and virus filtering on your e-mail gateway that is different from what you may have on your internal servers.

Configuring E-Mail

We're going to show you how to create a basic e-mail server configuration that allows you to send and receive e-mail and helps protect your users from spam, viruses, and malware. We'll also make use of Transport Layer Security (TLS), a form of encryption that can be used to encrypt your e-mail, and talk about SMTP AUTH, which is a way to authenticate your users when they send e-mail.

We're going to use the headoffice.example.com host as our e-mail server, and our gateway.example.com will pass e-mail traffic through to that host as we described in our example network configuration in Chapter 6.

Our mail server will be called mail.example.com (which is a DNS CNAME we created in Chapter 9) and have an internal IP address of 192.168.0.1. You can see our example network in Figure 10-2.

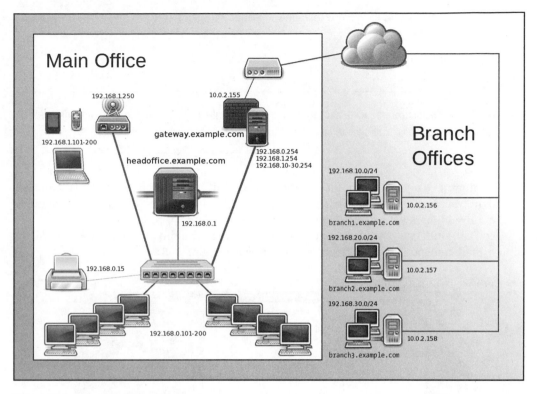

Figure 10-2. *Example network*

Installation

We're going to start by installing the packages we're going to need—the Postfix and Dovecot applications.

Red Hat Installation

On Red Hat Enterprise Linux, the default MTA is called Sendmail, but we're going to install Postfix and change the default MTA. We're going to do this because it is our experience that Postfix is much easier to understand, configure, and troubleshoot.

■**Note** There is a lot of argument over which MTA is best, and many are available including Sendmail, Postfix, Exim, and others. Our recommendation is to start with Postfix and see how you go. We think you'll find Postfix easy to use and that it meets all your needs.

First, let's see whether Postfix and Dovecot are already installed:

```
$ sudo rpm -q postfix dovecot
postfix-2.3.3.2
package dovecot is not installed
```

If one or more packages are not installed, we need to install them. We've done it here using the yum command:

```
$ sudo yum install postfix dovecot
```

■**Note** Some additional prerequisite packages can also be installed by either of these commands. We'll also install some additional packages later in the chapter to provide support for other functions.

We now need to tell Red Hat that Postfix is the default MTA. We do this using a command called the Mail Transport Agent Switcher, or system-switch-mail. It can be launched via the GUI or the command line using a command called system-switch-mail-nox.

You can launch the switcher from the GUI via the menu commands System ➤ Administration ➤ Mail Transport Agent Switcher as you can see in Figure 10-3.

Figure 10-3. *Launching the Mail Transport Agent Switcher*

You can see the Switcher's dialog in Figure 10-4.

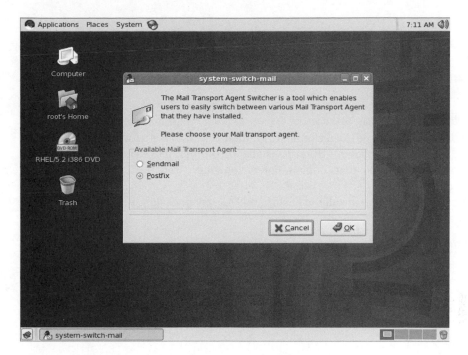

Figure 10-4. *The Mail Transport Agent Switcher dialog*

In the dialog box, select the Postfix MTA and click Okay. This will change the default MTA to Postfix, replacing the existing Sendmail MTA.

Or you can run the system-switch-mail-nox command on the command line:

```
$ sudo system-switch-mail-nox
```

You can see the command-line dialog in Figure 10-5.

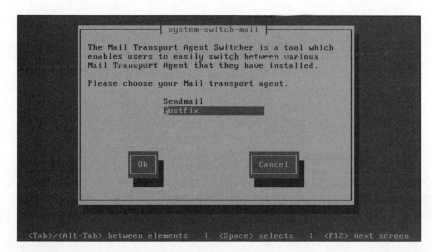

Figure 10-5. *The* system-switch-mail-nox *dialog*

> **Tip** If your host can't find these commands, you need to install the `system-switch-mail` and/or the `system-switch-mail-gnome` packages for the command line and GUI applications, respectively.

Ubuntu Installation

The Postfix MTA is the default MTA on Ubuntu distributions, and so it is usually already installed. Indeed, you saw in Chapter 2 that our Ubuntu installation prompted us to perform some basic MTA configuration. We'll revisit that configuration dialog shortly (see the "Editing Postfix Configuration" sidebar).

If not installed, we want to install the Postfix and Dovecot packages. Let's first check to see whether they are installed:

```
$ sudo aptitude show postfix
Package: postfix
State: installed
...
$ sudo aptitude show dovecot-common
Package: dovecot-common
State: installed
...
```

Here we have checked whether the `postfix` package and the `dovecot-common` packages are installed. If both are installed, you've already got what's needed.

If they are not installed, you can use the `aptitude` command to install them.

```
$ sudo aptitude install postfix dovecot-common dovecot-imapd dovecot-pop3d
```

Starting Postfix

After installation, it is very easy to start Postfix using the service management tools we introduced to you in Chapter 5. For Red Hat, you start Postfix using the `service` command:

```
$ sudo service postfix start
```

For Ubuntu, you use the `invoke-rc.d` command:

```
$ sudo invoke-rc.d postfix start
```

> **Tip** It is also important to restart Postfix after making configuration changes, and you'll see we mention that throughout the chapter. If you can't work out why something isn't working, a restart is often a good start to your troubleshooting.

You can confirm Postfix is started by checking its log files. Postfix logs its output to the system logger, or syslog, which in turn logs to files located on your host. You can find its log files in the /var/log directory. On Red Hat, we need to look in the /var/log/maillog file. On Ubuntu, Postfix sends all log messages to /var/log/mail.log. On Ubuntu, error and warning messages are also logged to /var/log/mail.err and /var/log/mail.warn files, respectively. It's a good idea to monitor these files for error messages. A good way to do this is with the tail command using the -f option, which monitors files in real time and scrolls down your screen as new log messages are added to the file:

```
$ sudo tail -f /var/log/maillog
```

When Postfix is started successfully, you should see the following log messages:

```
Jan  5 19:52:33 au-mel-rhel-1 postfix/postfix-script[31669]: starting the Postfix ➥
mail system
Jan  5 19:52:33 au-mel-rhel-1 postfix/master[31670]: daemon started -- version ➥
2.5.5, configuration /etc/postfix
```

Understanding Postfix Configuration

The majority of Postfix configuration is handled by two files, located in the /etc/postfix directory. These files are called main.cf and master.cf. The main.cf file contains a subset of the major configuration options you can use to customize Postfix. You can add any additional options you need to configure Postfix to this file. The master.cf file controls how clients connect to your server and how the services that make up the server are configured. Most of the time you won't change much in the master.cf file.

Let's start by taking a quick look at how each file is structured.

■**Note** Most distributions install preconfigured main.cf and master.cf files. These usually include extensive inline documentation describing each option.

Inside main.cf each option is structured as follows:

```
option = value
```

Options do not have to be placed in any order, and empty lines are ignored.

■**Note** Like most Linux configuration files, any lines starting with # are comments.

In Listing 10-2, you can see a sample of a typical main.cf file.

Listing 10-2. *The* `main.cf` *File*

```
# The command_directory parameter specifies the location of all
# postXXX commands.
#
command_directory = /usr/sbin
```

We'll talk about some of the configuration options in the `main.cf` file during this chapter; you can see a full list at `http://www.postfix.org/postconf.5.html`.

In the `master.cf` file, you can see a structured list of the daemons, services, and processes you can enable and configure in Postfix. In Listing 10-3, you can see some sample lines from this file.

Listing 10-3. *The* `master.cf` *File*

```
# service type  private unpriv  chroot  wakeup  maxproc command + args
smtp    inet    n   -    n    -   -    smtpd
submission inet n       -       n       -       -       smtpd
-o smtpd_enforce_tls=yes
-o smtpd_sasl_auth_enable=yes
```

Here two services are defined, `smtp` and `submission`. Each service is generally a daemon process that runs in the background and performs a specific function.

■**Note** Unlike many other services, Postfix isn't a single monolithic daemon but rather a collection of small processes that perform individual functions and communicate with each other. As such, when you start Postfix you may see a number of processes start rather than a single process.

In this case, the `smtp` service is the basic SMTP service that receives mail for your host on TCP port 25, and the `submission` service is an alternative service that listens on TCP port 567 and is sometimes used to receive e-mail from internal mail clients.

Next on the line, we define the type of service; here `inet` defines these as network-based services (i.e., services that run on your network interface). Other types of services also available include local Unix sockets and named pipes (see `http://en.wikipedia.org/wiki/Unix_domain_socket` and `http://en.wikipedia.org/wiki/Named_pipe`).

Next, we have a series of settings for each service. Each setting is specified on the line in sequence and separated with spaces. You won't need to worry about these settings for your basic configuration, but you can find more details of them at `http://www.postfix.org/master.5.html`.

Last, each service needs to have the command that starts the service specified together with any arguments to be passed to that command. In Listing 10-3, both services are started with the command `smtpd`, but the `submission` service has several options passed to the command. These are the same options available in the `main.cf` configuration file, and this allows us to configure a particular service in a way that varies from our main configuration. We'll look at how to pass these options to an individual service in the section "Combating Viruses and Spam" later in the chapter.

EDITING POSTFIX CONFIGURATION

There are three ways to edit your Postfix configuration files, most particularly the `main.cf` file:

- You can use the `postconf` command.

- On Ubuntu, the `dpkg-reconfigure` command can perform basic Postfix configuration.

- You can employ a text editor like `vim` or `gedit`.

We generally recommend the last option, using a text editor to edit your configuration files, but first let's quickly look at the other two options.

The `postconf` command is a special command that allows you to manipulate the `main.cf` file and display your existing configuration. The command also has some useful command-line options for debugging and displaying your configuration. For example, to display any configuration options that have been changed from the default (i.e., modified for your host), you can use the –n configuration flag.

```
$ sudo postconf -n
```

If you are looking for troubleshooting, you will be usually asked to provide the output of the `postconf` -n command. You can also display every configuration option and its default setting using the –d flag.

Lastly, you can use the command to actually edit your configuration files via the `-e` option like so:

```
$ sudo postconf -e 'inet_interfaces = all'
```

Here the `inet_interfaces` option (which controls which network interfaces Postfix binds itself to) has been set to a value of `all`.

On Ubuntu, you can use the `dpkg-reconfigure` command to configure the basic state of Postfix:

```
$ sudo dpkg-reconfigure postfix
```

This command offers you a selection of basic configuration models, for example, a basic Internet host that sends and receives e-mail. Another model uses a smarthost; in this case, e-mail is sent to an intermediate relay server. This model is often used in ISP environments where you are sometimes restricted from sending and receiving e-mail directly to port 25. This is designed to reduce spam volumes by preventing the sending and relaying of e-mail from compromised desktop hosts in DSL, ADSL, or cable networks. We'll discuss smarthosts in the "Smarthosting" sidebar later in this chapter.

A number of other configuration options are also set by the same utility. We don't recommend you use the utility though; instead, you should manually edit your configuration files using a text editor.

Always remember that after any Postfix configuration changes, you must restart the `postfix` service.

Initial Configuration

Despite all the rather complicated-looking configuration processes and options, Postfix is actually very easy to configure. A simple e-mail server, designed to send and receive e-mail for a domain, can be set up in minutes.

The first step is telling Postfix what domains it should be handling mail for. To do this, we update the `mydestination` configuration option in the `main.cf` configuration file by adding our domain to it, in this case example.com. We could make this change by editing the `main.cf` file directly and changing the option:

```
mydestination = mail.example.com, localhost.localdomain, localhost, example.com
```

We could also change it using the `postconf` command:

```
$ sudo postconf -e "mydestination = mail.example.com, localhost.localdomain, ➥
localhost, example.com"
```

On the previous line, we've added two items: our mail server and our local domain. Postfix now knows that if it receives mail destined to either of these, for example, ataylor@mail.example.com or ataylor@example.com, it should accept and process this e-mail.

■**Note** Postfix will only receive mail for users it knows about. Generally, this will be a user created on the host, but we'll briefly look at "virtual" users in the "Virtual Domains and Users" section later in this chapter. In some cases, Postfix knows about users on other e-mail servers and can be configured to forward mail to another host. But generally, if Postfix can't find a recipient for the e-mail (e.g., if an e-mail is sent to bjones@ example.com and Postfix doesn't know about this user), the e-mail will be rejected.

When we want Postfix to receive e-mail for other domains, for example, we want to receive e-mail from the example.net domain also, we'd add that domain to the `mydestination` option.

```
mydestination = mail.example.com, localhost.localdomain, localhost, example.com, ➥
example.net
```

The other entries, which will generally already be present, include `localhost`, which tells Postfix to process e-mail that is local to the host, for example, e-mail sent by a local process.

Next, we need to add our local networks to the `mynetworks` configuration option. This tells Postfix what IP address ranges to process e-mail for. In our case, we only care about the 192.168.0.0/24 and 192.168.1.0/24 ranges, which are our local wired and wireless network ranges. The 127.0.0.1, or localhost, address should already be present in the option:

```
mynetworks = 127.0.0.0/8, 192.168.0.0/24, 192.168.1.0/24
```

Or we can again use the `postconf` command to edit the option:

```
$ sudo postconf -e "mynetworks = 127.0.0.0/8, 192.168.0.0/24, 192.168.1.0/24"
```

Now we need to bind Postfix to the network interfaces we want it to listen on. In this case, we're going to bind to all network interfaces:

```
inet_interfaces = all
```

Or we could use the `postconf` command:

```
$ sudo postconf -e "inet_interfaces = all"
```

You can be more selective though, and if you wanted to only bind Postfix to a single interface, you could do so as follows:

```
inet_interfaces = eth0
```

■**Tip** If you're using IPv6, you can enable it by changing the `inet_protocols` option to `all`. By default, only IPv4 is enabled.

Finally, after making all the relevant changes, we need to restart Postfix. On Ubuntu, we would issue the following:

```
$ sudo invoke-rc.d postfix restart
```

And on Red Hat-derived distributions:

```
$ sudo service postfix reload
Reloading postfix:                                      [  OK  ]
```

■**Note** Every time you change a Postfix configuration option, you should restart Postfix.

In addition to restarting Postfix, you'll need to ensure TCP port 25 is open on your host to allow incoming connections. If you have the `iptables` firewall running, you'll need to create appropriate rules to allow access, for example:

```
$ sudo iptables -A INPUT -p tcp -m state --state NEW -m tcp --dport 25 -j ACCEPT
```

■**Tip** We talked about the `iptables` firewall, writing rules, and opening ports in Chapter 6.

Testing Postfix

We can now test to see whether Postfix is working by sending ourselves an e-mail. We are going to do this through a useful tool called netcat, or nc for short. The nc command is the Swiss Army Knife of network tools and can be used to create and manipulate TCP and UDP connections.

■**Note** There are others ways of sending a test e-mail (e.g., using the `mail` command from the command line), but the nc command allows you to view the SMTP commands and displays any error messages on the command line where you can see them.

We can use the nc command to script a session with our Postfix e-mail server, as you can see in Listing 10-4.

Listing 10-4. *A Scripted E-Mail Session with nc*

```
$ nc mail.example.com 25
220 mail.example.org ESMTP Postfix
ehlo example.com
250-mail.example.com
250-PIPELINING
250-SIZE 10240000
250-VRFY
250-ETRN
250-ENHANCEDSTATUSCODES
250-8BITMIME
250 DSN
mail from: jsmith@example.com
250 2.1.0 Ok
rcpt to: ataylor@example.com
250 2.1.5 Ok
data
354 End data with <CR><LF>.<CR><LF>
Subject: My first mail for my domain
This is a test.
Thanks
Mr Testing
.
250 2.0.0 Ok: queued as EEC04A0BA0
quit
221 2.0.0 Bye
```

In Listing 10-4, we've started by specifying the nc command, the e-mail server we want to connect to, and the port, 25, that we wish to connect to. Next, we've stepped through the SMTP commands needed to send an e-mail. In Listing 10-4, all the text in bold represents commands we've entered, and you will need to enter these to send your e-mail. Adjust the text to suit your environment, for example, replacing example.com with the name of your domain. The nonbolded text is the expected response from our e-mail server.

■**Note** You can see that each line is prefixed with the SMTP response code, for example, 250. You can see a full list of these codes at http://www.unixhub.com/docs/email/SMTPcodes.html.

We tell the server who we are with the EHLO command, and it responds with its own identity and a list of its available features. We then indicate to whom we want to send an e-mail and whom it is from. In our case, we're sending an e-mail to ataylor@example.com and from jsmith@example.com.

> ■**Note** We created these users in Chapter 4. If you are following along, you should substitute the names of users on your local host or create some new users to test your e-mail with.

We then tell our server we're sending the e-mail with the DATA command. We input our e-mail, marking its end with a period (.) and quitting.

> ■**Tip** As mentioned earlier, another way to send local e-mail from the command line is to use the mail command. This doesn't give us a diagnostic view of our server, but it is easier to use to send mail. To start the command, type **mail** on the command line together with the e-mail address you'd like to send e-mail to, for example, **mail root@example.com**. Entering the mail command on its own will open a very simple command-line mail client.

We can now check that our e-mail has arrived. In our case, we want to check whether the e-mail has been received by the user ataylor. By default, both Red Hat and Ubuntu use a mailbox format called *mbox* to store received e-mail. The mbox format has all of your e-mail held in a single file. But confusingly, while each distribution stores e-mail in mbox files, these files are stored in different locations depending on your distribution.

> ■**Note** See http://en.wikipedia.org/wiki/Mbox for more details of the mbox format.

On Ubuntu, a mailbox file named for the user is created in the /var/mail directory, for example, /var/mail/ataylor.

On Red Hat, each user has an mbox-format mailbox file contained in the /var/spool/mail directory. The file is named after the user, for example, /var/spool/mail/ataylor.

> ■**Note** On Ubuntu, /var/spool/mail is also a symbolic link to /var/mail.

Let's look inside one of these mbox files in Listing 10-5.

Listing 10-5. *An mbox File*

```
$ more /var/mail/ataylor
From jsmith@example.com  Mon Aug 11 05:02:26 2008
Return-Path: <jsmith@example.com>
Received: from mail.example.com (mail.example.com [127.0.0.1])
by mail.example.com (8.13.8/8.13.8) with ESMTP id m7AJ2QQK020858
for <ataylor@example.com>; Mon, 11 Aug 2008 05:02:26 +1000
Received: (from jsmith@example.com)
```

```
by mail.example.com (8.13.8/8.13.8/Submit) id m7AJ2Q2V020857
for ataylor; Mon, 11 Aug 2008 05:02:26 +1000
Date: Mon, 11 Aug 2008 05:02:26 +1000
From: jsmith <jsmith@example.com>
Message-Id: <200808101902.m7AJ2Q2V020857@example.com>
To: ataylor@example.com
Subject: My first mail for my domain
Status: O

This is a test.
Thanks
Mr Testing
```

In Listing 10-5, you can see the mbox file contains our e-mail, including all the headers and the content of the e-mail. Additional e-mails would be appended to this file. As a result, if you have a large volume of e-mail, these files can become unwieldy to manage, search, and back up.

ALIASES

When e-mail reaches your host, Postfix looks at the recipient to determine who to deliver it to. Some applications use recipients like the postmaster address (for example, errors from MTAs are usually sent to the user postmaster at your domain) and the `root` user. Since people do not generally log in as either of these users, this e-mail might never get seen. Postfix uses a function called *aliases* to allow you to redirect mail sent to these recipients to other users. Postfix uses a configuration option called `alias_maps` in the `main.cf` configuration file to specify a file that matches recipients to the user who will actually receive the e-mail. The default aliases file is usually `/etc/aliases`. Inside this file you'll find a list of users like so:

```
user1:user2
```

Here all mail for `user1` will be redirected to `user2`, with each username separated by a colon. You should check this file and ensure that both the postmaster and the `root` user's e-mail direct to an appropriate user. You can also send e-mail to a user at another host by specifying an external e-mail address, like `username@example.com`. A common pattern is to direct all e-mail for system users to the `root` user and then redirect the `root` user to someone who needs to see this e-mail, for example:

```
postmaster: root
operator: root
lp: root
root: ataylor
```

Here the `postmaster`, `operator`, and `lp` users' e-mail all redirects to the `root` user, whose mail in turn is redirected to the user `ataylor`.

After making any change to the `/etc/aliases` file, you need to run a command called `newaliases` to update Postfix with the changes.

```
$ sudo newaliases
```

Choosing a Mailbox Format

In addition to the potential to become a large and difficult-to-handle file, the default mbox format has another issue: the potential for file corruption. For example, if your MTA is delivering a message to your mbox file at the same time your MUA or mail client is deleting a message, there is the potential that your mbox file could become corrupted or return unpredictable results.

An alternative to mbox is the Maildir mailbox format. Rather than a single file, Maildir stores your e-mails in separate files under a directory. This allows multiple processes to interact with your mailbox without risking any conflicts or corruption. It's also easier to back up and restore.

The Maildir format is a directory, appropriately called `Maildir`, containing three subdirectories: `cur`, `new`, and `tmp`. You can see the listing of the Maildir-format directory here:

```
$ ls -l Maildir
total 168
drwxr-xr-x 2 ataylor ataylor 28672 2009-01-01 13:53 cur
drwxr-xr-x 2 ataylor ataylor  4096 2009-01-01 13:53 new
drwxr-xr-x 2 ataylor ataylor  4096 2009-01-01 13:53 tmp
```

E-mail messages are first delivered into the `tmp` directory and given a unique name (usually constructed from the current time, the hostname, and other pseudo-random characteristics). The e-mail is then moved into the `new` directory where they sit in a sort of "unread" status. When your MUA or mail client connects to the mailbox, it detects the e-mail in the `new` directory and then moves them to the `cur` directory.

■**Note** This sounds a little complicated, but it ensures that e-mail isn't corrupted or misplaced when e-mail is being delivered, read, sent, and deleted from your mailbox.

To use Maildir instead of mbox, we need to tell Postfix that we're using a different mailbox format. We're also going to change our default mailbox location from its existing location, either /var/mail or /var/spool/mail, to the user's home directory. To do both of these things, we're going to update a Postfix option called `home_mailbox` like so:

```
home_mailbox = Maildir/
```

or using the `postconf` command:

```
$ sudo postconf -e "home_mailbox = Maildir/"
```

The `home_mailbox` option tells Postfix the location of the user's mailbox, relative to the user's home directory, so that `Maildir/` translates to `/home/ataylor/Maildir`.

■**Note** The trailing / is important. It needs to be there, and it tells Postfix that the directory is a `Maildir` directory.

We also need to confirm that another option, `mailbox_command`, is blank. The `mailbox_command` option can specify an external command, for example, the mail processing tools like `procmail` or `maildrop`. These tools, called MDAs or mail filters, can perform actions on incoming mail as it is delivered to your mailbox. We'll talk a bit more about these applications in the "Mail Delivery Agents and Mail Filtering" sidebar later in this chapter. So we now set this option to a blank value.

```
mailbox_command =
```

or again using the `postconf` command:

```
sudo postconf -e "mailbox_command = "
```

Finally, we need to restart Postfix for all this to take effect, for example, on Red Hat:

```
$ sudo service postfix restart
```

Now, if we send another e-mail, you'll find a new directory created in the home directory of the recipient called `Maildir`. Inside this directory will be the `tmp`, `new`, and `cur` subdirectories, and inside the `new` directory will be your e-mail in a single file. You can use the `less` command to display the contents of this file, for example:

```
$ less /home/jsmith/Maildir/new/1231486748.M906603P5576.mail.example.com,W=8271:2,Se
From jsmith@example.com  Wed Aug 14 03:08:12 2008
Return-Path: <jsmith@example.com>
Received: from mail.example.com (mail.example.com [127.0.0.1])
by mail.example.com (8.13.8/8.13.8) with ESMTP id m7AJ2QQK020858
for <ataylor@example.com>; Wed, 13 Aug 2008 03:08:12 +1000
Received: (from jsmith@example.com)
by mail.example.com (8.13.8/8.13.8/Submit) id m7AJ2Q2V020857
for ataylor; Wed, 13 Aug 2008 03:08:12 +1000
Date: Mon, 11 Aug 2008 05:02:26 +1000
From: jsmith <jsmith@example.com>
Message-Id: <200808101902.m7AJ2Q2V0304567@example.com>
To: ataylor@example.com
Subject: My first email to my new Maildir mailbox
Status: O

This is also a test.
Thanks
Mr Testing
```

Here you can see that the individual `Maildir` file will contain an individual e-mail with all its headers.

■**Note** Each `Maildir` must be owned by the user it belongs to. For example, the `Maildir` directory belonging to the user `ataylor` must be owned and writable (with permissions of `0700`) only by that user. If needed, you can use the `chown` and `chmod` commands to change the ownership and permissions, respectively.

Although in this case Postfix automatically created the Maildir directory, it is usually a good idea to prepopulate your user's home directories with an empty Maildir directory. You can do this by adding an empty Maildir directory to the /etc/skel directory. You saw the /etc/skel directory in Chapter 4 and discovered that its contents are copied to the home directory of any newly created user.

To do the creation of a new Maildir directory on Ubuntu, there is a useful command called maildirmake.dovecot that can automatically create the Maildir structure.

```
$ sudo maildirmake.dovecot /etc/skel/Maildir
```

The command will also create the tmp, new, and cur subdirectories.

■Tip You can also create folders, for example a Sent folder, in your Maildir structure. Folders can be used to sort and store e-mail so that it is easier to find e-mails. Folders are subdirectories prefixed with a period (.); a Sent folder would have the structure /home/ataylor/Maildir/.Sent created by using the command maildirmake.dovecot /etc/skel/Maildir/.Sent. Be careful to avoid folder names containing spaces, like "My Personal Mail," as sometimes your mail client can get confused. You should use an underscore or dash to link the words together like so: "My-Personal_Mail."

On Ubuntu, there is another, potentially easier, way to create your Maildir directories and folders. To do this you can install a package called maildrop, which contains the maildirmake command, a more sophisticated version of the maildirmake.dovecot command.

On Red Hat, the same command, again called maildirmake, is also available if you install the maildrop package. This package isn't available directly from Red Hat, but you can download a compatible package from a third-party RPM repository.

```
$ sudo rpm -Uvh ftp://ftp.silfreed.net/repo/rhel/5/i386/silfreednet/RPMS/➥
maildrop-2.0.4-1.el5.i386.rpm
```

Here the package is for Red Hat Enterprise Linux 5 (see the el5 reference in the RPM name). We're downloading and installing it using the rpm command.

■Caution This is a third-party RPM repository, and the RPM is not supported by Red Hat. If you don't feel comfortable with this, you could also download the Courier Maildrop source from http://www.courier-mta.org/download.php#maildrop and create your own RPM using instructions from http://www.courier-mta.org/rpm.html and as we described in Chapter 7.

You can then use the maildirmake command to create the skeleton directory and any required folders.

```
$ sudo maildirmake /etc/skel/Maildir
$ sudo maildirmake -f Sent /etc/skel/Maildir
$ sudo maildirmake -f Trash /etc/skel/Maildir
```

```
$ sudo maildirmake -f Drafts /etc/skel/Maildir
$ sudo maildirmake -f Spam /etc/skel/Maildir
```

Here we've used the -f option of the maldirmake command to create folders. We specify the name of the folder we want created and the Maildir to create it in.

If you don't want to install the maildrop package, you can create the directories using the mkdir command as shown in Listing 10-6.

Listing 10-6. *Manually Creating* Maildir

```
$ sudo mkdir -p /etc/skel/Maildir/{cur,new,tmp}; chmod -R 0700 /etc/skel/Maildir
```

■**Note** In Listing 10-6 we've used a clever Bash shortcut and listed all three directories enclosed in brackets ({ }) and separated by commas. This technique, *brace expansion*, tells mkdir to create all three subdirectories. You can use this with a variety of other commands without needing to type the command three times. The −p option creates all the parent directories.

Listing 10-6 creates the Maildir and the required subdirectories, and changes the permissions on the resulting directories to 0700, hence allowing only the user who owns the Maildir to access it.

MAIL DELIVERY AGENTS AND MAIL FILTERING

Earlier in this chapter, we talked about MDAs. These tools sit between your MTA and the user's mailbox, and you can tell Postfix what MDA, if any, to use with the mailbox_command configuration option you saw earlier. When an MDA is specified in this option, Postfix will deliver e-mail to this MDA, and the MDA will deliver the e-mail to the user's mailbox.

During the delivery process, the MDA can perform a variety of actions; for example, it can look for a characteristic of an e-mail, like whom it is from, and redirect it to a specific mailbox folder. Many people use MDAs to sort e-mails from mailing lists into separate folders. MDAs are also used to sort e-mail based on headers added by other applications; for example, many spam filters add headers indicating whether an e-mail is spam or not. MDAs can read these headers and place e-mails into an appropriate folder—for example, into a spam folder. You can also use MDAs to generate out of office notices, forward particular e-mails to others, and perform a variety of other tasks.

You can also call other applications from some MDAs. For example, some people don't run spam filters in their MTA, instead running a spam filter with their MDA.

There are two popular MDAs: procmail and maildrop. Both are available on Red Hat and Ubuntu. We're going to show you how to configure and use both the procmail and maildrop MDAs in the "Using procmail and maildrop" section later in this chapter to help you deal with spam e-mail.

Extending Postfix Configuration

So far we've just touched on the basics of Postfix configuration that allow our local users to send and receive e-mail. However, Postfix has a lot of other facets to make your environment more secure and your user's experience better including the following:

- *Encryption*: To secure the transmission of both e-mail and the user credentials

- *Authentication*: To ensure only appropriate and authenticated users can send e-mail

Using Encryption

The Postfix MTA is able to encrypt e-mail transmission via an encryption protocol called TLS. TLS is a successor protocol to SSL and is commonly used for encrypting TCP/IP traffic. You've potentially used TLS before, though you probably didn't realize it, when connecting to a website using the Hypertext Transfer Protocol over Secure Socket Layer (HTTPS) protocol, for example, `https://www.gmail.com`. Many older HTTPS connections still use the older SSL protocol, but some connections have the newer TLS running underneath them.

TLS provides two key features for our e-mail communication:

- Prevents cavesdropping on our e-mail contents

- Encrypts communication between client and server and hence protects authentication

TLS and Certificates

TLS, like SSL, works using digital certificates and a type of cryptography called *public key encryption*. Public key encryption works with two keys: the public key is available publicly, and the private key is stored on the server and kept secret. Anything that is encrypted using the public key can be decrypted only with the corresponding private key.

■**Note** Digital certificates and public key cryptography are complicated topics. This is really only an introduction to give you the basics for using TLS. If you're really interested in the math behind this, we recommend this excellent book: *Practical Cryptography* by Bruce Schneier and Niels Ferguson (John Wiley & Sons, 2003).

When using TLS, the digital certificate is the server's public key and acts like an electronic driver's license. It identifies the server or the website you are connecting to. When you connect to an HTTPS website, what your browser is doing is accepting the site's digital certificate as evidence the site is who it says it is. Like driver's licenses, certificates have an expiry period and are valid only for a fixed period, usually 12 months.

Each digital certificate can also contain a reference to a Certificate Authority (CA). A CA is a mechanism that issues certificates and has a special certificate called a *root certificate* that is then used to validate the server certificate's veracity. To use the same license metaphor, the root certificate is like your state's department of motor vehicles. It is the place people go to check that you have a valid license and that you are who you say you are. These root certificates are usually bundled with the clients you use to connect to servers; for example, your web browser will have a collection of root certificates from well-known CAs.

So the basic flow for certificate-based encryption (in very simple terms) is as follows:

1. Your client connects to a server and asks for the certificate.

2. The server presents its certificate.

3. The client checks for a reference to a root certificate.

4. The client uses the root certificate bundled with it to validate that your certificate is genuine.

5. If your client trusts the certificate, a connection is initiated and is encrypted between client and server.

■Tip In some cases your client will tell you it isn't sure whether to trust the certificate and will prompt you to make a decision about whether you trust the server.

There are four types of certificates that you need to know about, and there are pros and cons with using each type:

- Certificates issued by a commercial CA
- Certificates issued by a noncommercial CA
- Certificates issued by a self-managed CA
- Self-signed certificates

Certificates from Commercial Certificate Authorities

Certificates from commercial CAs are issued by providers like VeriSign, thawte, or Go Daddy. These certificates generally require regular payment, for example, yearly or biannually. The prices vary depending on the type and number of certificates. The root certificates of most commercial CAs are bundled with clients like browsers, mail clients, and other tools that use SSL/TLS connections. Commercial CAs are usually regularly audited for security, and a certificate issued by them is generally assumed to be secure.

Certificates from Noncommercial Certificate Authorities

In addition to the commercial certificate providers are a small number of noncommercial providers. These providers don't charge for their certificates, but correspondingly their root certificates are not bundled with many clients. This means if you use these certificates for a website or to secure a service like SMTP, your client will most likely warn you that the validity and security certificates can't be determined.

The only way to overcome this is to manually add a noncommercial CA's root certificate to your clients. If you have a lot of clients, this can add a lot of overhead and maintenance to your environment. In many cases, for example, a website, you don't have access to the clients, and these errors may result in someone getting the message that his client cannot validate the certificate and hence not trusting your website. For example, this makes using noncommercial certificates for an e-commerce site problematic.

For more information see the CAcert website and wiki: `http://www.cacert.org/` and `http://wiki.cacert.org/wiki/`.

Certificates from Self-Managed Certificate Authorities

You can also create and manage your own certificates. These certificates are issued by a Certificate Authority that you create and manage yourself. As a result, the certificates don't cost any money, but they do have other issues. First, as it is your own CA, you can't expect others to trust your certificates. This leads us to the second issue: usability. Like the noncommercial certificates, the root certificate of your CA is not bundled with clients.

■**Note** In the case of noncommercial CAs, there are at least a small number of clients with their root certificate bundled. In the case of your own self-managed CA, the clients with your root certificates are ones you install it on yourself.

Hence, when your client attempts to validate certificates provided by your CA, an error message is generated indicating that the client does not trust the CA. To overcome this error, you need to install your CA's root certificate on the client. This is something you can do for clients you manage, for example, your internal desktops, but for others this isn't feasible.

■**Tip** In this model, you've got to secure and manage your own CA. This isn't overly complicated for a small number of certificates, but it does pose some issues and risks that we will discuss as we proceed.

Self-Signed Certificates

Self-signed certificates don't use a CA. They are signed by you and hence don't cost any money either. Like certificates generated by a self-managed CA, they are also generally not trusted and will generate a similar error message on your clients. Unlike those generated by a self-managed CA, you can't remove this error by adding a root certificate because you have no root certificate to add to the client. Self-signed certificates are generally used only for testing and rarely used in production environments.

Choosing a Certificate Type

The best certificates to use are those issued by commercial CAs. The key issue there is cost. A certificate from a commercial CA can cost $1,500 to $1,800 a year in some cases. This is a considerable expense just to secure your e-mail. As a result, if you don't want the expense of buying certificates, we recommend you create your own CA and issue certificates. If you have a limited number of clients, you can easily install your CA's root certificate in your clients. We'll show you how to do this in the next section.

> ■**Note** In general, if you're running a website for external customers that requires security, such as an e-commerce site, you should always buy a certificate from a commercial CA. We'll talk more about this in Chapter 11.

Creating Certificates for TLS

As we've discovered, for TLS to work we need two certificates: a server certificate and the root certificate from a Certificate Authority (either a commercial CA or your own CA). Let's start by generating our first server certificate. This first step is generating a server key and a certificate signing request (CSR). We would take these steps whether we were generating a certificate from a commercial or a self-managed CA.

The process creates our private key and a CSR. This CSR is then submitted to a CA, in our case our own CA, but also to a commercial CA. It is this signing process that allows a client to confirm the identity of a server certificate.

In Listing 10-7, we generate our key and the request using the openssl command that is part of the OpenSSL application. The OpenSSL application is an open source SSL implementation that allows Linux and other operating systems to encrypt and secure applications using SSL.

Listing 10-7. *Generating a Server Key and Request*

```
$ openssl req -new -newkey rsa:4096 -nodes -keyout mail.example.com.key ➥
-out mail.example.com.req
Generating a 4096 bit RSA private key
............................................................++
........................++
writing new private key to 'mail.example.com.key'
-----
You are about to be asked to enter information that will be incorporated
into your certificate request.
What you are about to enter is what is called a Distinguished Name or a DN.
There are quite a few fields but you can leave some blank
For some fields there will be a default value,
If you enter '.', the field will be left blank.
-----
Country Name (2 letter code) [GB]:AU
State or Province Name (full name) [Berkshire]:Victoria
Locality Name (eg, city) [Newbury]:Melbourne
Organization Name (eg, company) [My Company Ltd]:Example Pty Ltd
Organizational Unit Name (eg, section) []:
Common Name (eg, your name or your server's hostname) []:mail.example.com
Email Address []:postmaster@example.com

Please enter the following 'extra' attributes
to be sent with your certificate request
```

```
A challenge password []:
An optional company name []:
```

In Listing 10-7 we've used the openssl command to generate a private key using the RSA cipher and a CSR. To generate the key and the CSR, we use the req and the -new options. The -newkey rsa:4096 option generates an RSA private key that is 4096 bits long.

■**Note** Key lengths determine how secure your encryption is, but the longer the key, the more performance overhead required to encrypt your data. As a result, most keys used for websites are 1024 bits long. In our case, we're using the key to secure our e-mail server; we don't mind so much any performance impact on this server, so we're using a longer, more secure key for it.

We pass the -nodes option to tell the openssl command not to encrypt the new key, and the -keyout option tells the openssl command where to write the key, here to the mail. example.com.key file. The last option, -out, tells the openssl command where to write the request.

■**Tip** You can see more details about the openssl req options by entering man req.

You can then see the process of the new key being generated and then the request. During the request creation process, you will be prompted for some information about your new certificate. If you don't want to answer a specific query, you can type **Enter** to skip the field. You will be prompted for the two-letter country code, for example, US for the United States, GB for Great Britain, and AU for Australia.

■**Note** You can find a full list of country codes at http://www.iso.org/iso/english_country_names_ and_code_elements.

You will also be prompted for the state, municipality, and name of your organization and optionally an organizational unit in your organization. This data will be displayed in your certificate when a client or user queries it. It's a good idea to be specific and accurate here—especially if you are submitting your CSR to be signed by a commercial CA.

Next, and most importantly, we need to specify the common name of the certificate. This must be the exact hostname of the server that is going to use the certificate. If you specify an incorrect hostname, you will get an error about a mismatch between the server and certificate name. In our case, we specify mail.example.com, which is the fully qualified hostname of our e-mail server.

We then specify the e-mail address of the contact for the certificate, in our case postmaster@example.com.

Last, you are prompted for some extra attributes for the certificate. You don't need to worry about these, and you can type **Enter** to skip the fields.

This process will leave you with two files: `mail.example.com.key` and `mail.example.com.req`. We will keep these two files, as we'll need them later in this process.

The next step in the process is signing our CSR with a CA. If you're going to create your own CA, see the next section, "Creating Your Own Certificate Authority."

Otherwise, you need to provide the contents of the `mail.example.com.req` file that you would provide to your commercial CA, and it will then deliver a certificate to you. Your commercial CA will provide instructions as to how to provide your CSR file. Usually, you would cut and paste the contents of the CSR into a web page and submit it. The CA would then sign it and notify you when a signed certificate was available to download.

You can then take this certificate and use it in your Postfix installation, which we discuss in later in the "Configuring Postfix for TLS" section.

Creating Your Own Certificate Authority

Creating your own CA is an easy task. First, you create a directory to hold your CA and some subdirectories inside that directory. For example, we're going to put our CA in the `/etc/` directory for the moment:

```
$ sudo mkdir /etc/CA
$ sudo mkdir /etc/CA/{private,newcerts}
$ sudo chown -R root:root /etc/CA
$ sudo chmod 0700 /etc/CA/private
```

The `private` directory will hold the CA's private key, and the `newcerts` directory will contain a copy of each certificate the CA will sign. We also ensure the `root` user owns all the directories, and we secure the `private` directory so that only the `root` user can access it.

Next, you need to create a database to hold details of your signed certificates.

```
$ echo '01' | sudo tee  /etc/CA/serial
$ sudo touch /etc/CA/index.txt
```

> ■**Note** In the first line, we've echoed the number 01 to the `/etc/CA/serial` file. To do this, we've used a command called `tee`, which can read from standard output and then write to standard output and files. You can find more information in the `tee` command's man page.

The `serial` file tracks the last serial number of certificates issued through this CA, starting with the number 01. Each certificate issued by the CA has a unique serial number.

The `index.txt` file will contain a list of the certificates currently being managed by this CA. Next to each certificate will be a letter indicating the status of that certificate:

- R: Revoked
- E: Expired
- V: Valid

You also need a copy of the standard OpenSSL configuration file. There is a template file available on most distributions. This file, called openssl.cnf, is located in the /etc/pki/tls/ directory on Red Hat distributions and in the /etc/ssl/ directory on Ubuntu. Copy this file into your new CA directory:

```
$ sudo cp /etc/ssl/openssl.cnf /etc/CA
```

You need to make a small change to your openssl.cnf configuration file to set the default configuration options for your new CA. To do this, find the section in the configuration file that starts with

```
[ CA_default ]
```

Below this will be a configuration option called dir. Change this option to

```
dir = .
```

This tells OpenSSL to look in the current directory for directories and files needed to configure and sign certificates. This means when you sign a certificate, you must change your working directory to the CA directory, in our case /etc/CA.

■**Tip** Have a look at the default settings in the openssl.cnf file for your CA. It should show the default directories and files you've created for your CA; in our case, these are the private directory and the serial file.

Now you need to create a self-signed certificate and a private key for your CA.

```
$ cd /etc/CA
$ sudo openssl req -new -x509 -newkey rsa:4096 -keyout private/cakey.pem ➥
-out cacert.pem -days 3650 -config ./openssl.cnf
Generating a 4096 bit RSA private key
..................++++++
....++++++
writing new private key to 'private/cakey.pem'
Enter PEM pass phrase:
Verifying - Enter PEM pass phrase:
-----
You are about to be asked to enter information that will be incorporated
into your certificate request.
What you are about to enter is what is called a Distinguished Name or a DN.
There are quite a few fields but you can leave some blank
For some fields there will be a default value,
If you enter '.', the field will be left blank.
-----
Country Name (2 letter code) [GB]:AU
State or Province Name (full name) [Berkshire]:Victoria
Locality Name (eg, city) [Newbury]:Melbourne
```

```
Organization Name (eg, company) [My Company Ltd]:Example Pty Ltd
Organizational Unit Name (eg, section) []:
Common Name (eg, your name or your server's hostname) []:ca.example.com
Email Address []:postmaster@example.com
```

First, as we mentioned, we change our working directory to /etc/CA. Next, we're creating a key, this one also RSA and 4096 bits long. We store that key in the /etc/CA/private/cakey.pem file. We're also creating the certificate as self-signed because we don't have another CA to sign it. We specify the age of the certificate as 3650 days (or 10 years). We have specified some other options: -x509, which indicates the certificate is self-signed, and -extensions v3_ca, which specifies that we're creating a CA certificate. The last option, -config ./openssl.cnf, tells OpenSSL to use the configuration file we copied into this directory.

■**Tip** It's worth reading through the openssl.cnf configuration file to understand what other options are available to you.

You'll be prompted for a pass phrase or password for your CA private key. Choose a good password (see Chapter 4) and remember it. You'll need this password every time you create a new certificate. You'll also be prompted for some details about you and your organization, much like you saw earlier when creating the CSR.

You now have your own CA and can use it to sign certificates.

■**Tip** There is also a small application called TinyCA (http://tinyca.sm-zone.net/) that automates a lot of this process and provides a small graphical CA environment. You might find this tool easier to use than a manual process.

Signing Your Certificate with Your Certificate Authority

Now that you've created your CA, you can use it to sign your certificate request. This takes your CSR and signs it with your CA and outputs a signed certificate that you can use to configure Postfix for TLS. In Listing 10-8, we've signed our CSR.

Listing 10-8. *Signing Our Certificate Request*

```
$ cd /etc/CA
$ sudo openssl ca -out /root/mail.example.com.cert -config ./openssl.cnf ➥
-infiles /root/mail.example.com.req
Using configuration from ./openssl.cnf
Enter pass phrase for ./private/cakey.pem:
Check that the request matches the signature
Signature ok
Certificate Details:
```

```
        Serial Number: 1 (0x1)
        Validity
            Not Before: Jan  4 07:57:56 2009 GMT
            Not After : Jan  4 07:57:56 2010 GMT
        Subject:
            countryName              = AU
            stateOrProvinceName      = Victoria
            organizationName         = Example Pty Ltd
            commonName               = mail.example.com
            emailAddress             = postmaster@example.com
        X509v3 extensions:
            X509v3 Basic Constraints:
                CA:FALSE
            Netscape Comment:
                OpenSSL Generated Certificate
            X509v3 Subject Key Identifier:
                6F:A6:48:91:D5:3F:70:7B:E3:E2:AB:E5:F5:41:8A:F4:20:DA:31:6E
            X509v3 Authority Key Identifier:
                keyid:F7:0A:17:47:FA:0D:7B:C4:FA:63:0C:C9:FC:5B:49:1C:D5:C3:FF:1D

Certificate is to be certified until Jan  4 07:57:56 2010 GMT (365 days)
Sign the certificate? [y/n]:y

1 out of 1 certificate requests certified, commit? [y/n]y
Write out database with 1 new entries
Data Base Updated
```

In Listing 10-8, we've used the ca option to sign our request. The -out option specifies the signed certificate we're going to output, and the -infiles option specifies the CSR we want to sign (we've assumed our CSR file is in the /root directory). The last option, -config ./openssl.cnf, specifies our configuration file, which contains the default locations for our files and directories.

■**Tip** You can see the other options available with the openssl ca command by entering man ca.

You will then be prompted for the pass phrase you created for the CA's private key, the details of your certificate will be displayed, and then you will be prompted to sign the certificate and write its details to the CA's database. Answer y for yes to both questions.

At the end of the process, you will have a signed certificate, a private key, and a certificate request all located in the /root directory. Your certificate is valid for one year (you can override this period using the -days option to specify a different validity period).

■**Note** Be careful to keep track of all three files. They'll be needed in the next section.

You can examine the details of your certificate using the openssl command:

```
$ openssl x509 -in /root/mail.example.com.cert -noout -text -purpose | more
```

■**Tip** Keep ahold of your CSR. When you want to renew your certificate, after a year in our case, you can just resign this request using the command in Listing 10-8. This means you don't need to keep re-creating your CSR.

Remember, to avoid your clients indicating that your certificates are not trusted, you must install your root certificate in the relevant client, for example, the user's mail client! The CAcert site has instructions for installing its root certificate into a variety of clients at http://wiki.cacert.org/ wiki/BrowserClients. To install your certificate, replace its certificate with yours in the instructions.

MANAGING YOUR CERTIFICATE AUTHORITY

Managing a CA yourself poses two key issues: security and continuity. If your CA is compromised, anyone can create and sign certificates using your CA. Alternatively, if your CA is accidentally deleted, you will need to start from scratch to create new certificates and manage a new root certificate.

As a result, you should always

- Back up your CA.

- Ensure your CA is secure.

Backing up your CA is easy, and we'll discuss backups in Chapter 13. Securing your CA is a little harder. We recommend you actually store your CA on a separate host. Some people use a laptop or a PC that is kept locked up (again, make sure you back it up!) in a safe or locked room.

Configuring Postfix for TLS

Now, you have a certificate and a key, either a commercial certificate or one signed by your self-managed CA. You will also need the root certificate from either your commercial CA or your self-managed CA. If you've gone with a commercial certificate, your CA will generally provide a link to a downloadable root certificate. Otherwise, you should already have your CA's certificate at /etc/CA/cacert.pem.

Start by copying your files to somewhere suitable to configure Postfix. We're going to create a directory called tls under the /etc/postfix directory to hold our certificates and copy in our certificates:

```
$ sudo mkdir /etc/postfix/tls
$ sudo cp /root/mail.example.com.cert /etc/postfix/tls
$ sudo cp /root/mail.example.com.key /etc/postfix/tls
$ sudo cp /etc/CA/cacert.pem /etc/postfix/tls
```

Now that you have your certificates and key in place, you need to configure Postfix's `main.cf` configuration file. In Listing 10-9, you can see the options you need to add to your `main.cf` configuration file, and we'll walk you through each of these settings.

Listing 10-9. *Postfix TLS Configuration*

```
smtp_tls_security_level = may
smtpd_tls_security_level = may
smtpd_tls_key_file = /etc/postfix/tls/mail.example.com.key
smtpd_tls_cert_file = /etc/postfix/tls/mail.example.com.cert
smtpd_tls_CAfile = /etc/postfix/tls/cacert.pem
smtpd_tls_loglevel = 1
smtpd_tls_received_header = yes
```

The first two options in Listing 10-9, `smtp_tls_security_level` and `smtpd_tls_security_level`, specify when TLS is used. You can see they look very similar except for a difference in the initial prefix. One starts with `smtp` and the other with `smtpd`. Configuration options starting with `smtp` are used when Postfix is sending e-mail to another e-mail server. Options starting with `smtpd` are used when Postfix receives e-mail, for example, from a client. By specifying both `smtp_tls_security_level` and `smtpd_tls_security_level`, we are telling Postfix we want to potentially encrypt both incoming and outgoing connections.

The `may` value for both options enables a mode called *opportunistic TLS*. This basically means that if TLS is supported by the remote client or server, it should be used. Otherwise, plain text connections are acceptable. This is a sensible choice given that not all clients and servers support TLS, and restricting the server to encrypted connections would mean some e-mail servers could not send you e-mail.

The next three options, `smtpd_tls_key_file`, `smtpd_tls_cert_file`, and `smtpd_tls_CAfile`, specify the locations of our certificate, key file, and CA certificate.

The next two options, `smtpd_tls_loglevel` and `smtpd_tls_received_header`, control some informational characteristics of our connections. The first option controls how much logging of TLS connections Postfix will generate. Specifying 0 here disables logging, specifying 1 provides basic logging, while 3 and 4 produce the highest level of logging (and are not recommended unless you are troubleshooting). We recommend leaving it at 1 for day-to-day operations, and this will produce some brief information about the connection and any certificates used.

The `smtpd_tls_received_header` option will add headers to your e-mail message that provide some information about connections that use TLS.

After making the changes, you will need to restart the Postfix service.

```
$ sudo service postfix restart
```

Once restarted, you can test to see whether TLS is enabled using the same `nc` command we introduced earlier, as you can see in Listing 10-10.

Listing 10-10. *Testing Postfix with TLS*

```
$  nc mail.example.com 25
220 mail.example.com ESMTP Postfix
EHLO example.com
250-mail.example.com
```

```
250-PIPELINING
250-SIZE 10240000
250-VRFY
250-ETRN
250-STARTTLS
250-ENHANCEDSTATUSCODES
250-8BITMIME
250 DSN
```
STARTTLS
```
220 2.0.0 Ready to start TLS
```

In Listing 10-10, we have connected to our e-mail server and issued the EHLO command. The e-mail server has responded with the supported commands available. You'll see a new command listed here, STARTTLS. This tells us that Postfix is now offering TLS to clients and other servers. In Listing 10-10, we've then entered the STARTTLS command to tell Postfix we'd like to initiate an encrypted connection. Postfix responds to say it's ready to start an encrypted connection. This indicates that TLS is successfully set up and awaiting connections.

If you have issues with configuring Postfix TLS/SSL encryption, see the pointers and links in the upcoming "Getting Help for Postfix" section.

■**Caution** It is important to note a few issues about using Postfix TLS encryption to ensure the confidentiality of the content of your e-mails. Postfix sends e-mail to other servers but only encrypts it when the other server supports TLS. As not all servers support encryption, some e-mail may not be encrypted. The only way to ensure all your e-mail is encrypted is to make use of content-based encryption solutions like S/MIME (http://en.wikipedia.org/wiki/S/MIME), PGP (http://www.pgp.com/), and GnuPG (http://www.gnupg.org/).

Authentication

So now that we've got TLS configured, we can encrypt sessions between our clients and the server as well between our servers and other servers that support TLS. This leads us to the next stage of our Postfix configuration: authentication.

In its default configuration, your Postfix server will accept e-mail only from clients in its trusted networks as defined in the mynetworks configuration option, in our case the 192.168.0.0/24 and 192.168.1.0/24 networks. This prevents inappropriate users from using our e-mail server. E-mail servers without these restrictions are called *open relays*. An open relay allows anyone to send it e-mail, and the server will send it on. Spammers make extensive use of open relays to pollute the Internet with unwanted e-mail.

■**Caution** Open relays are highly problematic, and incorrect configuration that results in your server becoming an open relay can be greatly troublesome for your organization. Open relays generally get black-listed when they are detected. This blacklist process means the open relay's IP address is added to a list of servers from which e-mail will not be accepted. If your server is an open relay, even after closing the relay and fixing your server, it can be quite hard to remove yourself from these blacklists and allow your users to send e-mail. You should regularly test that your server isn't behaving like an open relay using a service like http://www.abuse.net/relay.html.

Postfix's configuration prevents your server behaving like an open relay by default. But, although this configuration stops open relaying, it leaves a security hole and creates a func-tionality gap.

Regarding the hole, anyone who can get an IP address on your network can send e-mail to your e-mail server. If an attacker compromises your wireless network, for example, she could make use of your e-mail server to send spam.

This configuration also leaves a functionality gap for mobile users. You almost certainly have users who travel, work from home, or have mobile devices like cell phones or PDAs. These users cannot make use of your e-mail server, because being mobile they don't have an IP address on your network. These users must rely on a service provider's e-mail server that allows relaying, an open relay, or VPN into your organization. Often this isn't an ideal situation.

With authentication, your users can send e-mail from anywhere as long as they are authen-ticated. It also means internal users on your trusted network need to provide authentication credentials before they will be allowed to send e-mail. This reduces the risk that someone can just jump onto your network and use your e-mail server.

Your authentication is in turn protected by the TLS encryption you've just configured, allowing your users to authenticate without the potential for their credentials to be exposed across the network.

■**Note** This is a good thing because people very commonly "sniff" networks using tools like tcpdump or Wireshark (both mentioned in Chapter 6). These people are "sniffing" for things like encrypted or exposed passwords to steal. With wireless networks, this is particularly easy, as an attacker doesn't even need to physically plug into your network.

SMTP AUTH and SASL

Authentication for e-mail servers is provided by a mechanism called SMTP AUTH. This is another SMTP command that prompts a user for a username and password before allowing him to send e-mail. That username and password can be provided via a variety of mechanisms including in plain text and in encrypted forms. Also available are mechanisms that support *one-time passwords* such as smart cards or tokens. What mechanisms are used very much depend on what mechanisms are supported by your client. The Microsoft Outlook client, for example, only supports a very small number of mechanisms, while the Mozilla Thunderbird supports a wider variety.

■**Note** You can learn about one-time passwords at `http://en.wikipedia.org/wiki/One-time_password`.

To confirm the user's credentials are valid, the `AUTH` command makes use of an authentication framework called Simple Authentication and Security Layer (SASL). SASL is much like PAM (which we looked at in Chapter 4), and it abstracts authentication. It allows multiple types of authentication to be hidden behind the SASL protocol. This means your e-mail server can check a variety of back-end services to validate that the user is allowed to send e-mail without needing to understand how to authenticate to those services.

These back-end services can include PAM (which can be used to allow users to authenticate with their Unix login and password), databases of users and passwords, and even user repositories like LDAP or Active Directory. Postfix doesn't have SASL built in. It relies on integration with other applications to provide SASL capabilities. We're going to use the Dovecot server to provide these SASL capabilities to Postfix.

If you've been following along with the example so far, you should have already installed Dovecot when we showed you how to install Postfix earlier in this chapter. If not, install it now using those instructions if you want to work through the upcoming instructions. Then you need to ensure Postfix supports SASL authentication with Dovecot. This can be done with the `postconf` command using the `-a` option:

```
$ sudo postconf -a
cyrus
dovecot
```

Here the `postconf` command has returned all the SASL authentication plug-ins supported by Postfix. We're looking for the `dovecot` entry. This support should be available on all recent versions of Red Hat and Ubuntu.

Configuring Dovecot for SASL

Now, we need to configure Dovecot's SASL support and start the Dovecot daemon. The Dovecot configuration file on Red Hat is located at `/etc/dovecot.conf` and at `/etc/dovecot/dovecot.conf` on Ubuntu. Both these files were created when we installed the Dovecot packages and contain sample configuration including a wide variety of documented options.

We're going to edit this file and set up Dovecot's SASL authentication service. We open the configuration file and look for the first option we want to edit: `protocols`. We first want to turn off all the services other than authentication. We do this by setting it to `none`.

```
protocols = none
```

■Note We'll come back to this option when we look at IMAP and POP3 and how to enable them in the "Configuring IMAP and POP3" section later in this chapter.

Next, we need to configure the authentication, or auth, service. To do this, find the auth default configuration option in the dovecot.conf configuration file.

You can see the auth service configuration options we're going to set in Listing 10-11.

Listing 10-11. *Configuring Dovecot auth*

```
auth default {
     mechanisms = plain login
     passdb pam {
     }
     userdb passwd {
     }
     socket listen {
       client {
         path = /var/spool/postfix/private/auth
         mode = 0660
         user = postfix
         group = postfix
       }
     }
}
```

The auth service consists of a series of directives enclosed in brackets ({ }). The service may be already partially configured in your existing dovecot.conf configuration file. You will need to ensure the configuration present in your existing configuration file matches that of Listing 10-11.

Let's look at each option. The first directive in the auth service is mechanisms, which specifies which authentication mechanisms that this Dovecot instance supports. By default, the PLAIN mechanism that accepts users and passwords in plain text is usually always enabled.

■**Caution** You should only use the PLAIN mechanism if you have TLS enabled; otherwise an attacker could steal your user's credentials from the network.

You can see the other types available to Dovecot in Table 10-1.

Table 10-1. *Dovecot Authentication Mechanisms*

Mechanism	Description
PLAIN	Plain text authentication.
LOGIN	A Microsoft authentication mechanism used in the Microsoft Outlook client.
CRAM-MD5	Encrypted password mechanisms. This has some support in mail clients.
DIGEST-MD5	Like CRAM-MD5 but with stronger ciphers. This has limited support in clients.
NTLM	Microsoft Windows–based authentication, generally only supported in Microsoft clients.
GSSAPI	Kerberos v5 support. This has limited support in clients.
ANONYMOUS	Supports anonymous logins. This is not recommended and not secure.
OTP	One-time password mechanism.
SKEY	One-time password mechanism.

■**Note** You can't specify an authentication mechanism that Dovecot is not configured to support. For example, without the correct supporting configuration, you can't specify the NTLM mechanism.

In Listing 10-11, we've also enabled the LOGIN authentication mechanism in case any of our users have a Microsoft client, but we're not going to enable any other types. The vast majority of clients will support PLAIN, and many others will also support the LOGIN authentication type. You can find a full list of mail clients and the authentication mechanisms they support at http:// en.wikipedia.org/wiki/Comparison_of_e-mail_clients#Authentication_support.

The next directive in Listing 10-11 controls the authentication store Dovecot checks to perform authentication. We've defined one authentication store: passdb pam. The passdb pam store is a password database that makes use of the PAM application to authenticate users against the local host's users. So for a user to authenticate to the host to send e-mail, he would need to have a user with a valid password created on the host.

When authenticating users, Dovecot then looks for a PAM service definition called dovecot in the /etc/pam.d directory. This file is installed when you install the Dovecot packages on your distribution. In Listing 10-12, we've shown the /etc/pam.d/dovecot file for Ubuntu.

Listing 10-12. *Dovecot PAM Service*

```
#%PAM-1.0

@include common-auth
@include common-account
@include common-session
```

You can see in Listing 10-12 that an authentication query to Dovecot uses the same PAM authentication check that a user logging on to the host would experience (as you saw in Chapter 4).

■**Note** See more information on password databases for Dovecot at http://wiki.dovecot.org/ PasswordDatabase and on PAM authentication for Dovecot at http://wiki.dovecot.org/ PasswordDatabase/PAM.

The next directive in Listing 10-11, userdb passwd, performs a user lookup to return some information about the user. It returns the user's UID, GID, and home directory among other information, and it retrieves this information from the /etc/passwd file.

■**Note** You can read more about the user database lookups at http://wiki.dovecot.org/UserDatabase.

The last directive in Listing 10-11 is the socket directive, which provides the connection between Postfix and Dovecot. The socket listens for authentication requests from Postfix and then returns the results. It does this by using a special type of file called a socket, which we briefly discussed in Chapter 3, that allows interaction between applications. This socket is located in a Postfix directory that stores files and sockets used by the daemon, /var/spool/ postfix/private/, and has a file name of auth. The mode, user, and group options control the permissions and ownership of the socket.

When the Dovecot daemon is running, you can see this file in the directory:

```
$ ls -l /var/spool/postfix/private/auth
srw-rw---- 1 postfix postfix 0 Jan  7 18:37 auth
```

After you have configured Dovecot, you'll need to start (or restart) it. For Red Hat, we start Dovecot using the service command:

```
$ sudo service dovecot start
```

For Ubuntu, we use the invoke-rc.d command:

```
$ sudo invoke-rc.d dovecot start
```

You can confirm Dovecot is running via syslog output, usually in the /var/log/maillog file on Red Hat and /var/log/mail.log file on Ubuntu. You should see an entry like the following:

```
dovecot: Jan 19 12:29:46 Info: Dovecot v1.1.7 starting up
```

Or, you can check that the Dovecot process is running:

```
$ ps -A | grep 'dovecot'
 7331 ?        00:00:00 dovecot
 7333 ?        00:00:00 dovecot-auth
```

Here you can see the dovecot and dovecot-auth processes running, indicating that Dovecot has started successfully.

On Red Hat, Dovecot logs to the /var/log/maillog file and on Ubuntu to the /var/log/mail.log file, and you can confirm it is running if you seeing a log entry like the following:

```
Jan  7 18:37:03 au-mel-rhel-1  dovecot: Dovecot v1.0.7 starting up
```

Configuring Postfix for SASL

Next, we need to configure Postfix to use the Dovecot SASL service we've just configured. Add the entries in Listing 10-13 to the main.cf configuration file.

Listing 10-13. *Configuring Postfix for Dovecot SASL*

```
smtpd_sasl_type = dovecot
smtpd_sasl_path = private/auth
smtpd_sasl_auth_enable = yes
smtpd_tls_auth_only = yes
smtpd_recipient_restrictions = permit_mynetworks, ➥
permit_sasl_authenticated, reject_unauth_destination
```

In Listing 10-13, we've used the smtpd_sasl_type option to specify that we're using Dovecot to perform our SASL authentication. The smtpd_sasl_path option specifies the location of the authentication socket relative to Postfix's spool directory, usually the /var/spool/postfix directory. This matches the Dovecot client socket we defined earlier in Listing 10-11. The smtpd_sasl_auth_enable option tells Postfix to enable SASL authentication.

The next option, smtpd_tls_auth_only, tells Postfix to only use authentication if TLS is enabled and running. This means the STARTTLS command needs to have been issued and an encrypted connection created between the client and server.

The last option, smtpd_recipient_restrictions, is one of Postfix's restriction lists. It tells Postfix what to allow or deny when the RCPT TO command is issued, for example, when an e-mail is received from a client. By default, as we mentioned earlier, Postfix will accept e-mail

- From clients whose IP addresses match the values in the mynetworks option

- To remote destinations that match the value of the relay_domains option, which defaults to the value of the mydestination option

- To and from the local host

We're going to adjust this default behavior by telling Postfix to also accept e-mails from users authenticated by SASL.

So first, we have the permit_mynetworks option, which maintains access for the networks in the mynetworks options. We then add the permit_sasl_authenticated option that tells Postfix to accept mail from SASL authenticated users. Lastly, in order for Postfix to receive e-mail and have a valid configuration, we must finish with a reject restriction, in this case the reject_unauth_destination option. This option rejects any e-mail not in accordance with the last two criteria we just established: to the specified remote destinations or to and from the local host.

■**Note** You can see a bit more about recipient restrictions at `http://www.postfix.org/`
`postconf.5.html#smtpd_recipient_restrictions`.

Testing Postfix Authentication

Now, once we've restarted Postfix, our SASL configuration should be active, and we can test
this. There are a number of ways we can test this now. The first is to configure a client to send
authenticated e-mail to our server. But since we haven't enabled a way for a client to browse
a mailbox yet, such as the IMAP or POP3 protocols, this isn't overly useful. Instead, we're
going to employ another method and make use of a new command called swaks to test our
authentication.

The swaks command is a more advanced version of the nc command to test our SMTP
server. The swaks tool can test a number of SMTP options, including encryption and authentication, that nc has trouble testing. You can download it from `http://jetmore.org/john/code/`
`#swaks`, or packages are available for Ubuntu.

On Ubuntu we install the swaks package.

```
$ sudo aptitude install swaks
```

Red Hat does not have a ready package, but you can download the tool from its website.

```
$ cd /usr/local/bin
$ sudo wget http://jetmore.org/john/code/swaks
$ sudo chmod 0755 /usr/local/bin/swaks
```

The swaks command is very easy to use, and you should read its man page to find details of
how to make full use of it.

To test the authentication, we need to know the username and password of a valid user on
our host, and we need to install some supporting modules required by the swaks tool to enable
authentication and encryption testing. On Red Hat, we need the following packages:

```
$ sudo yum install perl-Digest-SHA1 perl-Digest-HMAC perl-Net-IP perl-Net-DNS ➥
perl-Net-SSLeay
```

In Ubuntu, we need these packages:

```
$ sudo aptitude install libnet-dns-perl libnet-ssleay-perl libdigest-sha1-perl ➥
libdigest-hmac-perl  libnet-ip-perl
```

These packages provide SSL/TLS and SMTP AUTH support for swaks that allow us to test
Postfix's authentication.

In Listing 10-14, you can see a swaks session that tests SASL authentication.

Listing 10-14. *Using swaks to Test SASL*

```
$ swaks -tls -a -au ataylor -ap password -t jsmith@example.com -f ➥
ataylor@example.com
=== Trying mail.example.com:25...
=== Connected to mail.example.com.
```

```
<-  220 mail.example.com ESMTP Postfix
 -> EHLO localhost
<-  250-mail.example.com
<-  250-PIPELINING
<-  250-SIZE 10240000
<-  250-VRFY
<-  250-ETRN
<-  250-STARTTLS
<-  250-ENHANCEDSTATUSCODES
<-  250-8BITMIME
<-  250 DSN
 -> STARTTLS
<-  220 2.0.0 Ready to start TLS
=== TLS started w/ cipher DHE-RSA-AES256-SHA
 ~> EHLO localhost
<~  250-mail.example.com
<~  250-PIPELINING
<~  250-SIZE 10240000
<~  250-VRFY
<~  250-ETRN
<~  250-AUTH PLAIN LOGIN
<~  250-ENHANCEDSTATUSCODES
<~  250-8BITMIME
<~  250 DSN
 ~> AUTH LOGIN
<~  334 VXNlcm5hbWU6
 ~> YXRheWxvcg==
<~  334 UGFzc3dvcmQ6
 ~> cGFzc3dvcmQ=
<~  235 2.0.0 Authentication successful
 ~> MAIL FROM:<ataylor@example.com>
<~  250 2.1.0 Ok
 ~> RCPT TO:<jsmith@example.com>
<~  250 2.1.5 Ok
 ~> DATA
<~  354 End data with <CR><LF>.<CR><LF>
 ~> Date: Wed, 07 Jan 2009 21:11:10 +1100
 ~> To: jsmith@example.com
 ~> From: ataylor@example.com
 ~> Subject: test Wed, 07 Jan 2009 21:11:10 +1100
 ~> X-Mailer: swaks v20061116.0 jetmore.org/john/code/#swaks
 ~>
 ~> This is a test mailing
 ~>
 ~> .
<~  250 2.0.0 Ok: queued as 67972A0B92
 ~> QUIT
<~  221 2.0.0 Bye
=== Connection closed with remote host.
```

In Listing 10-14, we've initiated the swaks command with the -tls option, which tells swaks to use TLS encryption. Then we've specified the -a option, which enables authentication, and the -au and -ap options, which specify the username and password, respectively. Next, we've included the -t and -f options to specify whom the e-mail is to and from, respectively.

When the command is executed, you can see a connection is initiated, the STARTTLS command initiated, and an acknowledgement that TLS has been started. In the list of commands generated after the TLS connection, you can now see the AUTH command is available with two authentication mechanisms being offered: PLAIN and LOGIN.

The AUTH command is then initiated by the swaks command, and the username and password submitted. The LOGIN authentication mechanism was selected. The authentication succeeded, and the test e-mail was submitted. If the authentication mechanism had failed, Postfix would have kept trying authentication mechanisms, in our case LOGIN and then PLAIN, until one mechanism succeeds or all have failed. If all have failed, the client will receive an error message.

You can also confirm that the session has succeeded by checking the syslog log files for Postfix.

```
$ sudo less /var/log/maillog
Jan  7 21:11:11 au-mel-rhel-1  postfix/smtpd[12638]: ➥
connect fromlocalhost.localdomain[127.0.0.1]
Jan  7 21:11:11 au-mel-rhel-1  postfix/smtpd[12638]: setting up TLS connection from➥
localhost.localdomain[127.0.0.1]
Jan  7 21:11:11 au-mel-rhel-1  postfix/smtpd[12638]: TLS connection established ➥
from localhost.localdomain[127.0.0.1]: TLSv1 with cipher DHE-RSA-AES256-SHA ➥
(256/256 bits)
Jan  7 21:11:11 au-mel-rhel-1  postfix/smtpd[12638]: 67972A0B92: ➥
client=localhost.localdomain[127.0.0.1], sasl_method=LOGIN, sasl_username=ataylor
Jan  7 21:11:11 au-mel-rhel-1  postfix/cleanup[12643]: 67972A0B92: ➥
message-id=<20090107101111.67972A0B92@au-mel-rhel-1 .localdomain>
Jan  7 21:11:11 au-mel-rhel-1  postfix/smtpd[12638]: disconnect from ➥
localhost.localdomain[127.0.0.1]
Jan  7 21:11:11 au-mel-rhel-1  postfix/qmgr[12292]: 67972A0B92:
from=<ataylor@example.com>, size=562, nrcpt=1 (queue active)
```

Notice the TLS connection is established, the authentication initiated, and the e-mail sent.

If your authentication has succeeded, you've now got Postfix authentication running, your server can now be used by remote users, and your internal users can securely submit e-mail.

If you have issues with configuring Postfix authentication, see the pointers and links in the upcoming "Getting Help for Postfix" section.

SMARTHOSTING

As we mentioned earlier in the chapter, some ISPs block outgoing SMTP traffic. This is designed to help reduce spam. In addition, some SMTP servers are configured not to receive e-mail from certain types of networks, such as ADSL and those using dynamic IP addresses. If you cannot send outbound e-mail or some servers refuse connections from your server, this may be the issue. An easy way to check this is to see whether you can connect to an external MTA using a tool like swaks, or you can contact your ISP to find out if it restricts outgoing SMTP traffic.

If you are being blocked, you can overcome this with smarthosting. A smarthost is a relay server that receives and forwards your e-mail. Many ISPs offer smarthosts to their users.

There are two types of smarthost—unauthenticated and authenticated. Both types are specified with the relayhost configuration option in the main.cf configuration file (see http://www.postfix.org/postconf.5.html#relayhost) like so, where mail.isp.net is the hostname of your smarthost:

```
relayhost = mail.isp.net
```

This will tell your Postfix e-mail server to send all outgoing e-mail to mail.isp.net. This assumes that the smarthost will accept e-mail from you; for example, some ISP smarthosts are happy to accept e-mail from any IP address that the ISP manages.

Sometimes, however, your smarthost won't accept e-mail from you without SASL authentication. If so, you need to configure smarthost authentication. To do this, you need to configure SASL authentication where Postfix is a client rather than the server. Remember, when you configured it as a server, all the configuration options started with smtpd_, indicating it was for connections incoming to the server. Now you need to configure Postfix to be a client, and you use configuration options starting with smtp. To do so, set the following options in the main.cf file:

```
smtp_sasl_password_maps = hash:/etc/postfix/smtp_sasl_passwd
smtp_sasl_auth_enable = yes
smtp_sasl_mechanism_filter = plain, login
smtp_sasl_security_options = noanonymous
```

This configures SASL authentication for your server when it is a client. The smtp_sasl_password_maps option (see http://www.postfix.org/postconf.5.html#smtp_sasl_password_maps) specifies a database file containing a list of smarthosts and their required credentials. This is created by editing a file and using the postmap command to create a database from that file. The /etc/postfix/smtp_sasl_passwd file needs to contain the name of the smarthost and the username and password (separated by a colon) required to authenticate like so:

```
mail.isp.net     username:password
```

You need to make sure these files are readable only by the root user and have appropriate permissions to stop anyone viewing your passwords.

```
$ sudo chown root:root /etc/postfix/smtp_sasl_passwd
$ sudo chmod 0600 /etc/postfix/smtp_sasl_passwd
```

We then use the postmap command to create a database:

```
$ sudo postmap hash:/etc/postfix/smtp_sasl_passwd
```

A file called smtp_sasl_passwd.db is then created.

The remaining options are pretty simple. The `smtp_sasl_auth_enable` option turns on SASL authentication for Postfix as a client. The `smtp_sasl_mechanism_filter` option specifies what types of authentication mechanisms are supported by the smarthost, and the `smtp_sasl_security_options` option disables anonymous mechanisms.

After your configuration is updated, you will need to reload or restart Postfix, and you can then test to see whether your server can send SASL-authenticated e-mail to the smarthost. You can also specify more granular smarthosting with the transport option (see `http://www.postfix.org/transport.5.html`).

Getting Help for Postfix

Postfix is not only one of the easiest applications to configure, with a simple configuration model and lots of documentation, but also one of the friendliest to troubleshoot, with most error messages being descriptive and helpful.

■**Note** Not all MTAs are as easy to configure, and others have complex syntax and bewildering error messages. You'll find Postfix much easier to understand than some of the alternative MTAs.

You can find useful documentation at the Postfix home page (`http://www.postfix.org/`). This includes documentation (`http://www.postfix.org/documentation.html`), and how-tos and FAQs (`http://www.postfix.org/docs.html`).

There are some useful resources for specifically configuring and troubleshooting for SSL/TLS encryption and SASL. For encryption, you can find resources at `http://www.postfix.org/TLS_README.html`. For SASL, you can find a useful how-to at `http://www.postfix.org/SASL_README.html`, another for Ubuntu at `http://adomas.org/2006/08/postfix-dovecot/`, and a more advanced version at `http://www.lxtreme.nl/index.pl/docs/linux/dovecot_postfix_pam`.

You can also find some tips on running Postfix in a small office/home office environment at `http://www.postfix.org/SOHO_README.html`, and you might want to consider joining the Postfix mailing list at `http://www.postfix.org/lists.html`.

Remember that if you submit a question or a bug, you should include the following info:

- Your Postfix configuration (run `postconf -n`)

- Your platform (run `uname -a`)

- Any log messages generated (either in the `/var/log/mail.log` file on Ubuntu or the `/var/log/maillog` file on Red Hat)

Also available is an IRC channel called `#postfix` on the Freenode IRC server (`http://freenode.net/`) where you can seek assistance.

Combating Viruses and Spam

Now that you've got Postfix running with encryption and authentication, we're going to show you how you can defend your users and your organization from spam and viruses. We're going to look at two tools:

- *SpamAssassin*: An open source antispam tool

- *ClamAV*: An open source antivirus scanner and engine

We're going to integrate both these tools with Postfix and teach you how to use them.

Fighting Spam

Spam is unsolicited e-mail ranging from requests to help with myriad illegal financial transactions to offers for medicine that will enlarge portions of human anatomy. Spam is one of the biggest threats to the happiness of your users. Nothing is more irritating than coming to work to find a huge collection of spam e-mail and your actual e-mail buried. It is also a threat to your organization and users, as spam often hides phishing attacks (http://en.wikipedia.org/wiki/Phishing), virus distributions, and other types of malware attacks.

We're going to configure our Postfix server to reject some spam on its own and then introduce you to a popular antispam tool called SpamAssassin. SpamAssassin is a Bayesian spam filter (http://en.wikipedia.org/wiki/Bayesian_spam_filtering). *Bayesian spam filtering* in the simplest terms is a method that predicts the likelihood that the presence of a word, phrase, or other characteristic in an e-mail means that e-mail is spam.

Each e-mail is marked spam or not according to a numeric score calculated through a series of customizable tests or rules; by default, a score higher than 5.0 is marked as spam. Each rule either adds or subtracts from this score depending on the weighting of the rule. For example, a rule might check a particular characteristic of the e-mail, and if it matches, SpamAssassin might add 0.5 to the score assigned to that e-mail.

Bayesian spam filters also learn patterns from your users' incoming mail and can be trained by telling them which mail is spam and which is not, called *ham* by SpamAssassin (http://en.wikipedia.org/wiki/Spam_(food). The data from its learning is added to a database and used to make future analysis of incoming e-mail more accurate.

SpamAssassin runs as a daemon on your host, and e-mail is submitted to the daemon, analyzed, and then returned marked, via the addition of a new header, as either spam or not.

Configuring Postfix for Antispam

Before we configure SpamAssassin, we're going to tighten our Postfix configuration. To do this we add some configuration options to our main.cf configuration file. Most of these options reject e-mail that isn't compliant to the SMTP RFC, for example, by rejecting e-mail whose source address isn't a valid e-mail.

We're principally going to update the restriction lists we introduced when we were looking at Postfix authentication. Table 10-2 presents these restriction lists.

Table 10-2. *Postfix Restriction Lists*

Restriction List	Description
smtpd_client_restrictions	Restrictions when the clients connect
smtpd_helo_restrictions	Restrictions when the HELO/EHLO command is issued
smtpd_sender_restrictions	Restrictions when the MAIL FROM command is issued
smtpd_recipient_restrictions	Restrictions when the RCPT TO command is issued
smtpd_data_restrictions	Restrictions when the DATA command is issued

Restriction lists are triggered when particular events occur; for example, the smtpd_client_restrictions are checked when the client connects, and the smtpd_helo_restrictions are checked when the EHLO command is issued by the client.

In this case, we're going to add some options to the sender, recipient, and data restriction lists. First, add the smtpd_sender_restrictions options to main.cf like so:

smtpd_sender_restrictions = reject_non_fqdn_sender, reject_unknown_sender_domain

The reject_non_fqdn_sender option rejects e-mails where the sender mailing address is not in the proper format. This means the value passed by the MAIL FROM command must be in the form of a valid e-mail address, for example, ataylor@example.com. An address such as Anne Taylor or ataylor or Anne or anything else that you will not be able to respond to will not be accepted, and the e-mail is thereby rejected.

The reject_unknown_sender_domain option rejects e-mail where the domain of the sender has no DNS A or MX record. This is usually when the e-mail has been sent from a bogus domain, as is often the case with spam e-mail.

Next, we want to add another rejection criteria to our smtpd_recipient_restrictions option.

smtpd_recipient_restrictions = permit_mynetworks, permit_sasl_authenticated, ➥
reject_unauth_destination, reject_unauth_pipelining

Here we've updated our existing options (configured when we added authentication support to Postfix earlier in the chapter) to include the reject_unauth_pipelining restriction that rejects e-mails submitted using a special technique called *pipelining* without checking to see whether pipelining is supported. This is a common technique used by spam mailers to submit e-mail.

We're also going to add this same option to the smtpd_data_restrictions to catch spammers who use the same technique when the DATA command is issued.

smtpd_data_restrictions = reject_unauth_pipelining

Lastly, we're going to configure two options not related to restrictions lists that block some spam.

smtpd_helo_required = yes
disable_vrfy_command = yes

The first option, smtpd_helo_required, tells Postfix to deny connections from clients that don't send a proper EHLO and announce their name. The disable_vrfy_command option disables the

SMTP VRFY command. The VRFY command allows a sender to query the Postfix server and verify that an address exists. This is used by spammers to validate addresses and occasionally by hackers to harvest the names of users on your host prior to attacks.

■**Note** There are other restrictions you can enable, but these are the simplest, easiest, and least likely to restrict legitimate e-mail to your Postfix server. See http://www.postfix.org/uce.html for more details.

After making the changes, restart the Postfix daemon.

■**Note** It's a good idea to confirm that you can still send and receive e-mail after making your changes too.

Installing and Configuring SpamAssassin

To supplement our Postfix changes, we're going to install and configure SpamAssassin. We'll start by installing the required packages. On Red Hat, we need to install the spamassassin package and tell it to start the SpamAssassin daemon automatically.

```
$ sudo yum install spamassassin
$ sudo chkconfig spamassassin on
```

On Ubuntu, we need to install the spamassassin and spamc packages.

```
$ sudo aptitude install spamassassin spamc
```

Then we enable the SpamAssassin daemon by editing the /etc/default/spamassassin file and setting the ENABLED=0 option to the following:

```
ENABLED=1
```

■**Note** The SpamAssassin packages have some additional prerequisite packages that will also be installed on both Red Hat and Ubuntu when you install them.

We then need to start the SpamAssassin spamd daemon. On Red Hat, we use the service command:

```
$ sudo service spamassassin start
```

For Ubuntu, we use the invoke-rc.d command:

```
$ sudo invoke-rc.d spamassassin start
```

■Tip Like Postfix, it is a good idea to restart SpamAssassin after you make configuration changes.

Configuring Postfix for SpamAssassin

There are a number of different ways to integrate spam filters like SpamAssassin into your e-mail environment. One is to scan your user's incoming e-mail using an MDA before delivering them to the user. The spam filter then usually adds a header to the e-mail, which your MDA detects, and directs spam e-mail to a particular folder.

Another method is to analyze the e-mail while it is still inside the MTA. This allows us to pass the e-mail from Postfix's mail queue to SpamAssassin. The e-mail is then scanned and sent back to Postfix for delivery. A client or MDA can then make use of the results of that scanning, again a header added to the e-mail, to determine what to do with the e-mail. In Figure 10-6 you can see the proposed flow of e-mail through Postfix.

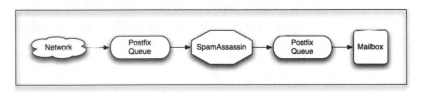

Figure 10-6. *SpamAssassin and Postfix filtering*

We're going to choose this latter method because it's a lot more efficient and scalable for most environments.

First, we update the `master.cf` file to send e-mail to SpamAssassin. To do this we adjust the `smtp` service in the `master.cf` file like so:

```
smtp    inet    n    -    n    -    -    smtpd
  -o content_filter=spamassassin
```

This adds the line `-o content_filter=spamassassin` (the `-o` should be indented with spaces to show it is a follow-on from the previous line). The `content_filter` option tells Postfix that we want all e-mail delivered to the `smtp` service to be sent to a filter called `spamassassin`.

We now need to define this filter. To do this, we add the filter to the bottom of the `master.cf` file. Define the filter like so:

```
spamassassin    unix    -    n    n    -    -    pipe ➡
  user=mail argv=/usr/bin/spamc -e /usr/sbin/sendmail -oi -f ${sender} ${recipient}
```

This creates a new service in the `master.cf` file, of the type `unix`, which is a Unix socket, and it calls another Postfix daemon called `pipe`, which delivers e-mail to an external command. In the next lines (again indented), we specify that external command.

We specify the user the command will run as `mail`, and then the command and arguments we're going to pass to that command. We're calling the `spamc` command, a binary that connects to the `spamassassin` daemon, submits our e-mail, and then receives the scanned results.

To the `spamc` command, we're passing the `-e` argument. This argument (which must be specified last on the command line) tells the `spamc` command what to do with the e-mail after it's been scanned. In this case, we're submitting it to the /usr/sbin/sendmail command, which is the Postfix command that delivers our e-mail back to Postfix to be delivered to the user.

We've also specified some options for the sendmail command. The –oi option tells the sendmail command not to stop processing e-mail when it finds a line with a single period (.) on it (remember our test e-mails earlier ended when a line with a period on it was sent). This is because the e-mail might have a line with a period on it that might not indicate the end of the e-mail. The -f ${sender} option makes sure the sender of the e-mail is sent on to Postfix. Lastly, the ${recipient} option contains the recipient of the e-mail so Postfix knows to whom to send the e-mail.

Testing SpamAssassin

To test SpamAssassin, let's send an e-mail using the swaks tool and examine the results.

```
$ swaks -tls -a -au ataylor -ap password -t jsmith@example.com -f ⇥
ataylor@example.com --body /usr/share/doc/spamassassin-version/sample-spam.txt
```

This command connects to your mail server and sends an e-mail to the user jsmith@example.com from the SASL authenticated user ataylor. We've also added the --body option to specify the contents of our e-mail. In this case, we're using a sample spam e-mail provided with the SpamAssassin package. The e-mail is located in the /usr/share/doc/spamassassin-version directory (substitute your SpamAssassin version for version, for example, 3.2.5). This sample spam is guaranteed to trigger SpamAssassin's spam filters and hence test our spam detection.

If we check in our Postfix logs, we can see this e-mail get received and processed as shown in Listing 10-15.

Listing 10-15. *Postfix Logs with SpamAssassin*

```
$ sudo less /var/log/mail.log
Jan 10 10:43:29 au-mel-rhel-1 postfix/smtpd[9599]: connect from ⇥
unknown[192.168.0.128]
Jan 10 10:43:29 au-mel-rhel-1 postfix/smtpd[9599]: A759D207EC: ⇥
client=unknown[192.168.0.128], sasl_method=LOGIN, sasl_username=ataylor
Jan 10 10:43:29 au-mel-rhel-1 postfix/cleanup[9608]: A759D207EC: ⇥
message-id=<20090109234329.A759D207EC@au-mel-rhel-1.example.com>
Jan 10 10:43:29 au-mel-rhel-1 postfix/qmgr[9596]: A759D207EC: ⇥
from=<ataylor@example.com>, size=492, nrcpt=1 (queue active)
Jan 10 10:43:29 au-mel-rhel-1 postfix/smtpd[9599]: disconnect from ⇥
unknown[192.168.0.128]
Jan 10 10:43:29 au-mel-rhel-1 spamd[5649]: spamd: connection from ⇥
localhost [127.0.0.1] at port 51641
Jan 10 10:43:29 au-mel-rhel-1 spamd[5649]: spamd: setuid to mail succeeded
Jan 10 10:43:29 au-mel-rhel-1 spamd[5649]: spamd: processing message ⇥
<20090109234329.A759D207EC@au-mel-rhel-1.example.com> for ⇥
mail:8
```

```
Jan 10 10:43:29 au-mel-rhel-1 spamd[5649]: spamd: identified spam (1003.6/5.0) ➥
for mail:8 in 1.6 seconds, 1304 bytes.
Jan 10 10:43:29 au-mel-rhel-1  spamd[5649]: spamd: result: Y 1003 - ➥
BAYES_05,GTUBE,MISSING_MID,scantime=1.6,size=1304,user=mail,➥
uid=8,required_score=5.0,rhost=localhost,raddr=127.0.0.1,➥
mid=<20090109234329.A759D207EC@au-mel-rhel-1.example.com>,➥
bayes=0.011644,autolearn=spam
Jan 10 10:43:29 au-mel-rhel-1 spamd[5363]: prefork: child states: II
Jan 10 10:43:29 au-mel-rhel-1 postfix/pickup[9594]: CCDA7207F2: uid=8 ➥
from=<ataylor@example.com>
Jan 10 10:43:29 au-mel-rhel-1 postfix/cleanup[9608]: CCDA7207F2: ➥
message-id=<20090109234329.A759D207EC@au-mel-rhel-1.example.com>
Jan 10 10:43:29 au-mel-rhel-1 postfix/pipe[9609]: A759D207EC: ➥
to=<jsmith@example.com>, relay=spamassassin, delay=0.17, delays=0.03/0.01/0/0.12, ➥
dsn=2.0.0, status=sent (delivered via spamassassin service)
Jan 10 10:43:29 au-mel-rhel-1 postfix/qmgr[9596]: A759D207EC: removed
Jan 10 10:43:29 au-mel-rhel-1 postfix/qmgr[9596]: CCDA7207F2: ➥
from=<ataylor@example.com>, size=812, nrcpt=1 (queue active)
Jan 10 10:43:29 au-mel-rhel-1 postfix/local[9613]: CCDA7207F2: ➥
to=<jsmith@example.com>, relay=local, delay=0.11, delays=0.06/0.01/0/0.03, ➥
dsn=2.0.0, status=sent (delivered to maildir)
Jan 10 10:43:29 au-mel-rhel-1 postfix/qmgr[9596]: CCDA7207F2: removed
```

In Listing 10-15, we've connected to our Postfix server, been authenticated, and submitted our e-mail. During the transaction the e-mail is submitted to SpamAssassin (see the lines with spamd—which is the SpamAssassin daemon).

```
Jan 10 10:43:29 au-mel-rhel-1 spamd[5649]: spamd: connection from ➥
localhost [127.0.0.1] at port 51641
Jan 10 10:43:29 au-mel-rhel-1 spamd[5649]: spamd: setuid to mail succeeded
Jan 10 10:43:29 au-mel-rhel-1 spamd[5649]: spamd: processing message ➥
<20090109234329.A759D207EC@au-mel-rhel-1.example.com> for mail:8
Jan 10 10:43:29 au-mel-rhel-1 spamd[5649]: spamd: identified spam ➥
(1003.6/5.0) for mail:8 in 1.6 seconds, 1304 bytes.
Jan 10 10:43:29 au-mel-rhel-1  spamd[5649]: spamd: result: Y 1003 ➥
BAYES_05,GTUBE,MISSING_MID,scantime=1.6,size=1304,user=mail,uid=8,➥
required_score=5.0,rhost=localhost,raddr=127.0.0.1,➥
mid=<20090109234329.A759D207EC@au-mel-rhel-1.example.com>,➥
bayes=0.011644,autolearn=spam
```

We can see our SpamAssassin daemon gets a connection from the server, changes our user to the mail user, and processes our e-mail message. It has returned a line indicating that the message is a spam e-mail, with a score of 1003.6 (significantly larger than 5.0 and hence spam). We can see a last line indicating that SpamAssassin is also learning from our mail with the message autolearn=spam.

This means our Bayesian database of information will take the characteristics of this e-mail and consider it spam. When future e-mails come in, this information will be used to weigh up whether future e-mail is spam or ham.

We can also look at our actual e-mail and see the details of the headers SpamAssassin has added:

```
$ cat /home/jsmith/Maildir/new/1231544609.V801I22129M888361.mail.example.com
Return-Path: <ataylor@example.com>
X-Original-To: jsmith@example.com
Delivered-To: jsmith@example.com
Received: by au-mel-rhel-1.example.com (Postfix, from userid 8)
id CCDA7207F2; Sat, 10 Jan 2009 10:43:29 +1100 (EST)
X-Spam-Checker-Version: SpamAssassin 3.2.5 (2008-06-10) on
au-mel-rhel-1.localdomain
X-Spam-Level: *****
X-Spam-Flag: YES
X-Spam-Status: Yes, score=1003.6 required=5.0 tests=
BAYES_05,GTUBE,MISSING_MID,AWL autolearn=spam
version=3.2.5
Received: from unknown (unknown [192.168.0.128])
by au-mel-rhel-1.example.com (Postfix) with ESMTPSA id A759D207EC
for <jsmith@example.com>; Sat, 10 Jan 2009 10:43:29 +1100 (EST)
Date: Sat, 10 Jan 2009 10:43:25 +1100
To: jsmith@example.com
From: ataylor@example.com
Subject: Test spam mail (GTUBE)
X-Mailer: swaks v20061116.0 jetmore.org/john/code/#swaks
Message-Id: <20090109234329.A759D207EC@au-mel-rhel-1.example.com>
```

We can see that SpamAssassin has added four headers:

- X-Spam-Checker-Version: The SpamAssassin version

- X-Spam-Level: The total score in asterisks

- X-Spam-Flag: Only present if e-mail is identified as spam

- X-Spam-Status: The spam status (No or Yes), the total the e-mail scored, and a list of the spam tests checked

Getting Help with SpamAssassin

Like Postfix, getting help with SpamAssassin is easy. Abundant documentation is available online as well as a helpful and extensive community. The best place to start when seeking help is the SpamAssassin home page at http://spamassassin.apache.org/. The page includes a wiki, FAQ, and documentation. You can also join the very active mailing list at http://wiki.apache.org/spamassassin/MailingLists, and you can submit bugs at https://issues.apache.org/SpamAssassin/index.cgi.

For broader discussions about Postfix and spam, you should read http://www.postfix.org/uce.html.

Remember that if you submit a question or a bug, you should include the following info:

- Your SpamAssassin and Perl version (run the `spamassassin` command with the `--version` option)

- Your platform (run `uname -a`)

- Any log messages generated (either in the `/var/log/mail.log` file on Ubuntu or the `/var/log/maillog` file on Red Hat)

Also available is an IRC channel called #spamassassin on the Freenode IRC server (`http://freenode.net/`) where you can seek assistance.

What to Do with the Spam?

If we have e-mail identified as spam by SpamAssassin, what do we do with it? Well in most cases, people put their spam e-mail into a separate folder to review and usually delete. Some people reject or delete any e-mail marked as spam, but we're always wary of that. Spam detection tools, including SpamAssassin, are not infallible, and false positives are sometimes generated. This means a legitimate e-mail can be marked as spam. If you delete your spam, you've lost this e-mail. Storing it in a folder for a period of time allows you to potentially find and retrieve these false positives.

We're going to use the first method and move our spam e-mail into a special folder in our `Maildir` for later review. To do this, we can use two main methods to leverage our newly acquired headers to move the e-mail to where we want it to go. These methods are

- MDAs like `procmail` or `maildrop`

- Mail client rules or filtering

Using procmail and maildrop

We talked about MDAs like `procmail` and `maildrop` in the "Mail Delivery Agents and Mail Filtering" sidebar earlier in this chapter. MDAs are e-mail filtering engines that sit between your MTA and your mailbox. Using these MDAs, you can create rules to process mail based on particular characteristics such as whom the mail is from or a header it contains. These rules can be set to work globally or on a per-user basis.

Choosing an MDA is very much a personal preference. Many people like `procmail`, and others prefer `maildrop`. We don't have a recommended preference and suggest you try both to find out which suits you.

■**Tip** There is also another MDA called Sieve that is often used with the Dovecot IMAP and POP servers. You can read about Sieve at `http://wiki.dovecot.org/LDA/Sieve`. Many people find it easier to use than `procmail` and `maildrop`, but it's less widely known, supported, and documented.

In this section, we'll demonstrate how to move your Spam e-mail to an appropriate folder using either tool. Start by installing both `procmail` and `maildrop`. On Red Hat, you issue this command:

```
$ sudo yum install procmail
```

There isn't a `maildrop` package for Red Hat, but you can use a third-party RPM (such as `ftp.silfreed.net/repo/rhel/5/i386/silfreednet/RPMS/maildrop-2.0.4-1.el5.i386.rpm`). You could also build an RPM from source (see `http://www.courier-mta.org/rpm.html`) as we talked about in Chapter 7.

Or, on Ubuntu, you can install both packages:

```
$ sudo aptitude install maildrop procmail
```

Now, create your Spam folder; in our case we'll do this for our `jsmith` user. On Red Hat and Ubuntu, we could use the `maildirmake` command from the `maildrop` package:

```
$ sudo maildirmake -f Spam /home/jsmith/Maildir
```

or use the more manual `mkdir` command:

```
$ sudo mkdir /home/jsmith/Maildir/.Spam/{cur,new,tmp}; ➥
chmod -R 0700 /etc/skel/Maildir/.Spam
```

Here we've created our Spam folder and given it appropriate permissions.

■Tip We could also add this folder to the `/etc/skel` directory to ensure it was added for each new user created.

We now need to tell Postfix to use an MDA to deliver our e-mail. To do this we have to update the `mailbox_command` configuration option from the `main.cf` file. Remember, when we showed you this command earlier, we set it to be empty, which disables the use of an MDA.

procmail

To use `procmail`, you update the `mailbox_command` as we demonstrate here:

```
mailbox_command = /usr/bin/procmail -a "$EXTENSION" ➥
"DEFAULT=$HOME/Maildir/" "MAILDIR=$HOME/Maildir/"
```

This tells Postfix to use the `procmail` command to deliver e-mail. We've added some options to tell `procmail` where to find our `Maildir`s. Without these options, `procmail` will try to deliver e-mail to an mbox file.

■Note You must have an alias for the `root` user to use `procmail`. Your alias must send e-mail for the `root` user to a real user as you saw in the "Aliases" sidebar. If you don't have this alias, `procmail` will fail.

After reloading Postfix, you can now try to deliver an e-mail to Postfix. Then you'll see in your syslog log file an entry indicating that `procmail` has delivered the e-mail.

```
Jan 11 13:07:40 au-mel-rhel-1 postfix/local[24520]: 899E5A1235: ➥
to=<jsmith@example.com>, relay=local, delay=0.07, delays=0.04/0.01/0/0.03, ➥
```

```
dsn=2.0.0, status=sent (delivered to command: /usr/bin/procmail ➥
-a "$EXTENSION" "DEFAULT=$HOME/Maildir/" "MAILDIR=$HOME/Maildir/")
```

When processing e-mail, procmail looks for instructions, also known as *recipes*, about what to do with your e-mail. It looks for these recipes in two files: /etc/procmailrc and files named .procmailrc located in the users' home directories. The /etc/procmailrc file contains global instructions that apply to all users, and the .procmailrc file allows individual users to configure specific instructions for themselves.

We will now add our procmail recipe to the global /etc/procmailrc file as you can see in Listing 10-16.

Listing 10-16. *procmail Recipe for Handling Spam*

```
:0:
* ^X-Spam-Status: Yes
.Spam/
```

This very simple script checks all incoming e-mail for a header called X-Spam-Status that contains Yes and moves any matching e-mail to the .Spam/ folder. The procmail command knows how to find the folder because we told it in the Postfix main.cf file that our user's mailboxes were contained in their home directories in a directory called Maildir. The trailing / is important because it tells procmail that it is delivering to a Maildir.

■**Tip** You could place this recipe in an individual .procmailrc file in the user's home directory (and consider including such a file in the /etc/skel directory to be added when new users are created) rather than set this globally if you'd prefer to limit this to selected users.

---

maildrop

To use the maildrop command instead, you would set the mailbox_command option to

```
mailbox_command = /usr/bin/maildrop -d ${USER}
```

This command tells Postfix to deliver e-mail to the maildrop command, and the -d option tells maildrop to run in a special mode called *delivery mode*. In delivery mode, the maildrop command runs as the user specified in the ${USER} variable, usually the user for which you're delivering mail. In this mode, the maildrop command only has the permissions of the user whose mailbox it is writing to, and this provides some security against an accidental or malicious use of the maildrop command.

You also need to add another option to the main.cf configuration file:

```
local_destination_concurrency_limit=1
```

This limits maildrop to delivering one e-mail at a time. This prevents issues when maildrop attempts to simultaneously deliver multiple e-mails.

■Note Like `procmail`, you must have an alias for the `root` user to use `maildrop`. Your alias must send e-mail for the `root` user to a real user as you saw in the "Aliases" sidebar. If you don't have this alias, `maildrop` will fail.

After you've reloaded or restarted Postfix, to load your new configuration, you can continue to configure `maildrop`.

Also like `procmail`, you need to tell the `maildrop` command that you're writing to a `Maildir`. Do this by creating a global `maildrop` recipe file called `/etc/maildroprc` and telling `maildrop` that you want to write to a `Maildir`. Create the `/etc/maildroprc` file and add the following to it:

```
$ sudo vim /etc/maildroprc
DEFAULT="$HOME/Maildir"
```

■Note On some distributions, this file might be added when the package is installed and hence may already exist.

This option tells `maildrop` where to find your user's mailboxes, and you can now try to deliver an e-mail. You can see the Postfix syslog showing the `maildrop` command delivering your message in Listing 10-17.

Listing 10-17. *Postfix Using the* `maildrop` *Command*

```
Jan 11 16:06:22 au-mel-rhel-1 postfix/local[15314]: DCD56207FC: ➥
to=<jsmith@example.com>, relay=local, delay=0.11, delays=0.06/0.01/0/0.03, ➥
dsn=2.0.0, status=sent (delivered to command: /usr/bin/maildrop -d ${USER})
```

Now that `maildrop` is delivering your e-mail, you can configure it to send spam to the appropriate folder. To do this, add a recipe to the `/etc/maildroprc` file as shown in Listing 10-18.

■Tip You could also specify the recipe in a file called `.mailfilter` (the `maildrop` equivalent to the `.procmailrc` file) in your users' home directories. This allows you to potentially be more selective about which users move e-mail to that folder.

Listing 10-18. *maildrop Recipe for Handling Spam*

```
if ((/^X-Spam-Status:.*Yes/))
{
to "./Maildir/.Spam/."
}
```

Listing 10-18 simply tests to see whether the X-Spam-Status header is set to Yes and if so sends the e-mail to the Maildir/.Spam folder.

■**Note** This barely scratches the surface of what procmail and maildrop are capable of achieving. It's well worth reading more on both tools to see what other things they are capable of doing.

You can find instructions and a tutorial about how to use procmail at http://www.ii.com/internet/ robots/procmail/qs/, http://lipas.uwasa.fi/~ts/info/proctips.html, and http://pm-doc. sourceforge.net/pm-tips.html. Or you can read procmail's man page.

Instructions and a tutorial about maildrop can be found at http://www.courier-mta.org/maildrop/ maildropfilter.html and http://www.courier-mta.org/maildrop/maildroptips.html. Or you can read maildrop's man page.

Using a Mail Client

Most mail clients are also capable of filtering e-mail based on the headers contained in them. Some clients are more sophisticated than others; for example, both Evolution and KMail allow users to perform antispam filtering on incoming e-mail. You can see the filtering interface of KMail, the default KDE mail client, in Figure 10-7.

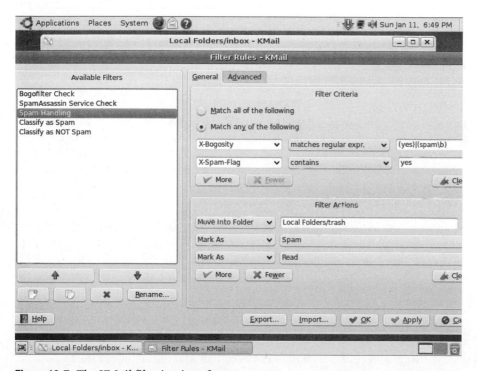

Figure 10-7. *The KMail filtering interface*

Other clients and interfaces that include suitable rules or filtering systems include the following (among others):

- Mozilla Thunderbird
- Microsoft Outlook
- Mutt

Antivirus

Viruses are malicious code designed to attack your hosts, steal your data, or compromise other aspects of your organization. While extremely rare on Linux distributions, some viruses have targeted Linux distributions. But we're not particularly worried about viruses attacking our Linux hosts via e-mail; instead, we're concerned with viruses that might spread via e-mail onto other, more susceptible, hosts such as Microsoft Windows desktops or be spread from your organization to other organizations.

We're going to introduce an application called ClamAV and show you how to integrate it with the SpamAssassin installation we've just configured. ClamAV is an open source antivirus engine much like similar tools from companies such as Symantec and McAfee. Unlike these commercial products, the ClamAV software and its update signatures are free.

■**Note** ClamAV uses special rules called *signatures* to scan your incoming e-mail for data that looks like a virus. Each signature contains information about a particular virus, for example, a string of data the virus file contains, that when found tells ClamAV a virus has been detected.

We're going to show you how to integrate ClamAV into SpamAssassin as a plug-in. SpamAssassin allows the use of plug-ins through which you can add additional capabilities and scanning techniques, such as virus scanning. This is also a quick and simple method of extending SpamAssassin without having to make significant changes to our configuration.

■**Note** There are other, more complex, ways of integrating ClamAV with SpamAssassin and Postfix, and you can read about some of them at http://www.falkotimme.com/howtos/spamassassin_clamav_procmail/index.php, http://www.section6.net/wiki/index.php/Setting_up_Postfix_Spamassassin_Amavisd_Clamav, and http://www.fatofthelan.com/articles/articles.php?pid=22.

Installing ClamAV

First, you need to install and configure the ClamAV scanner and its daemon, called clamd. You also need to install an update tool called FreshClam that automatically downloads and updates the virus signatures that ClamAV uses to detect viruses.

On Red Hat, the process of installing ClamAV is a little complicated because Red Hat does not ship the ClamAV product itself. To install ClamAV, you're going to add a well-known and trusted third-party RPM repository run by Dag Wieers. To do so, you need to install an RPM that adds support for this repository. You can see a list of appropriate RPMs at http://dag.wieers.com/rpm/FAQ.php#B2. In our case, we're going to install the appropriate RPM for Red Hat Enterprise Linux 5.

```
$ sudo rpm -Uhv http://apt.sw.be/redhat/el5/en/i386/rpmforge/RPMS/➡
rpmforge-release-0.3.6-1.el5.rf.i386.rpm
```

We can then install ClamAV from this repository, and some additional packages may also be installed as prerequisites.

You also need to install one other package, File::Scan::ClamAV, which allows you to integrate ClamAV with SpamAssassin as a plug-in.

```
$ sudo yum install clamav clamd perl-File-Scan-ClamAV
```

On Ubuntu, you install the clamav and clamav-daemon packages. Some additional packages may also be installed as prerequisites of these packages.

```
$ sudo aptitude install clamav clamav-daemon
```

The application File::Scan::ClamAV, which allows you to integrate ClamAV with SpamAssassin as a plug-in, isn't available as a package on Ubuntu. Instead, you can use a tool called CPAN (Comprehensive Perl Archive Network) to install this package on Ubuntu. CPAN is a collection of useful tools and applications written in a programming language called Perl.

To install the package, launch CPAN:

```
$ sudo cpan
```

After cpan is run, you will be prompted to configure the application:

```
Would you like me to configure as much as possible automatically? [yes]
```

Accept the automatic configuration process. You will see the configuration process execute and eventually be presented with a command prompt.

```
cpan[1]>
```

On this command line, type the following command to install the File::Scan::ClamAV package:

```
cpan[1]> install File::Scan::ClamAV
```

Here we've used the install command and the name of the package, and prefixed it with an option called notest. You may be prompted to connect to the Internet, and if so, answer yes to continue. The File::Scan::ClamAV package will then be installed.

Once all the relevant packages have been installed, you need to ensure the ClamAV daemon has been started. On Red Hat, you start the clamd service:

```
$ sudo service clamd start
```

> ■**Note** On Red Hat, when running SELinux, ClamAV does not correctly start. There are a couple of options to fix this. The first is to disable SELinux for ClamAV using the command `setsebool -P clamd_disable_trans=1`. Or you can update your SELinux policy using the `audit` command.

On Ubuntu, you start the `clamav-daemon` service and the `clamav-freshclam` service.

```
$ sudo invoke-rc.d clamav-daemon start
$ sudo invoke-rc.d clamav-freshclam start
```

Configuring ClamAV

You generally won't need to change any of ClamAV's configuration options, but you should know a bit about how it is configured. On Red Hat, the ClamAV daemon is configured via the /etc/clamd.conf file. The clamd.conf file configures the ClamAV daemon. The package installation process also creates a cron entry (in the /etc/cron.daily directory) for the FreshClam update tool that updates ClamAV's signatures once a day.

On Ubuntu, the ClamAV daemon is configured via the /etc/clamav/clamd.conf configuration file and the freshclam update daemon via the /etc/clamav/freshclam.conf configuration file. Rather than a cron job on Ubuntu, the FreshClam service is run as a daemon and will try to download any available signatures several times per day.

On both Red Hat and Ubuntu, running the ClamAV daemon will create a Unix socket file. This special type of file is used by SpamAssassin to communicate with the antivirus scanner. E-mail is submitted to the socket, scanned, and then returned to SpamAssassin with an assessment of whether it is a virus or not. This assessment is then added in the form of the X-Spam-Virus header to the scanned e-mail.

On Red Hat, this socket is located by default in /tmp/clamd.socket, and you can see a listing of it here:

```
$ ls -la /tmp/clamd.socket
srwxrwxrwx 1 clamav clamav 0 Jan 12 21:18 /tmp/clamd.socket
```

On Ubuntu, the socket is located in the /var/run/clamav directory and is called clamd.ctl.

> ■**Note** You'll need to know the location of this socket so you can tell SpamAssassin when to submit e-mails for scanning. You can adjust the location of this socket file in the clamd.conf configuration file.

Configuring SpamAssassin

Once you have ClamAV running, you need to integrate it into SpamAssassin. To do so, you need to create a plug-in. We're going to store our plug-ins in the /etc/mail/spamassassin directory, and it's going to consist of two files: clamav.cf and clamav.pm. The clamav.cf file is a SpamAssassin configuration file, and the clamav.pm file contains the code required for the ClamAV plug-in.

You can see the contents of the `clamav.cf` file in Listing 10-19.

Listing 10-19. *The* `clamav.cf` *File*

```
loadplugin ClamAV clamav.pm
full CLAMAV eval:check_clamav()
describe CLAMAV Clam AntiVirus detected a virus
score CLAMAV 10
```

In Listing 10-19, the `clamav.cf` file configures the ClamAV plug-in. It loads the plug-in and describes the special rule used to check for viruses. When the rule is triggered (i.e., when a virus is detected), the infected e-mail has a score of 10 added to it. This, being more than the default score of 5.0, automatically makes any detected virus a spam e-mail.

The `clamav-pm` file that our `clamav.cf` file loads is a SpamAssassin plug-in. You can see the content of the plug-in in Listing 10-20.

Listing 10-20. *The* `clamav.pm` *Plug-In*

```
package ClamAV;
use strict;

our $CLAMD_SOCK = "/var/run/clamav/clamd.ctl";   # change me
#our $CLAMD_SOCK = "/tmp/clamd.sock";   # change me
#our $CLAMD_SOCK = 3310;                     # for TCP-based usage

use Mail::SpamAssassin;
use Mail::SpamAssassin::Plugin;
use File::Scan::ClamAV;
our @ISA = qw(Mail::SpamAssassin::Plugin);

sub new {
  my ($class, $mailsa) = @_;
  $class = ref($class) || $class;
  my $self = $class->SUPER::new($mailsa);
  bless ($self, $class);
  $self->register_eval_rule ("check_clamav");
  return $self;
}

sub check_clamav {
  my ($self, $permsgstatus, $fulltext) = @_;
  my $clamav = new File::Scan::ClamAV(port => $CLAMD_SOCK);
  my ($code, $virus) = $clamav->streamscan(${$fulltext});
  my $isspam = 0;
  my $header = "";
  if(!$code) {
    my $errstr = $clamav->errstr();
    Mail::SpamAssassin::Plugin::dbg("ClamAV: Error scanning: $errstr");
```

```
    $header = "Error ($errstr)";
  } elsif($code eq 'OK') {
    Mail::SpamAssassin::Plugin::dbg("ClamAV: No virus detected");
    $header = "No";
  } elsif($code eq 'FOUND') {
    Mail::SpamAssassin::Plugin::dbg("ClamAV: Detected virus: $virus");
    $header = "Yes ($virus)";
    $isspam = 1;
  } else {
    Mail::SpamAssassin::Plugin::dbg("ClamAV: Error, unknown return code: $code");
    $header = "Error (Unknown return code from ClamAV: $code)";
  }
  $permsgstatus->{main}->{conf}->{headers_spam}->{"Virus"} = $header;
  $permsgstatus->{main}->{conf}->{headers_ham}->{"Virus"} = $header;
  # add a metadatum so that rules can match against the result too
  $permsgstatus->{msg}->put_metadata('X-Spam-Virus',$header);
  return $isspam;
}

1;
```

■**Note** The `clamav.cf` and `clamav.pm` files are also contained in the source code that accompanies this book, which can be downloaded from the Apress site. You can also copy and paste them from the following website: `http://wiki.apache.org/spamassassin/ClamAVPlugin`.

The `clamav.pm` file is a SpamAssassin plug-in written in the Perl programming language. You don't need to worry too much about most of the contents. You only need to change one line:

```
our $CLAMD_SOCK = "/tmp/clamd.sock";    # change me
```

Here you need to uncomment the line showing the location of your ClamAV daemon socket: `/tmp/clamd.sock` on Red Hat or `/var/run/clamav/clamd.ctl` on Ubuntu. Make sure you only have one line starting with `our $CLAMD_SOCK` uncommented and then restart SpamAssassin to enable the plug-in, for example, on Red Hat:

```
$ sudo service spamd restart
```

Testing SpamAssassin with ClamAV

Now that you've got the ClamAV plug-in enabled, you need to test to see whether your incoming e-mail is being scanned for viruses. To do this, use the `swaks` command again, as we demonstrate here:

```
$ swaks -tls -a -au ataylor -ap password -t jsmith@example.com -f ataylor@example.com
```

We've again used the swaks command to send an e-mail to jsmith@example.com.

■**Note** You would substitute the appropriate values for a user in your environment to test this.

This e-mail will be received and processed by your MTA and, based on your configuration, passed to SpamAssassin for analysis. The e-mail will be submitted to the user jsmith's mailbox, and you can then examine the contents of the e-mail's headers. In Listing 10-21, you can see the headers of the e-mail we've just sent.

Listing 10-21. *E-Mail Headers After SpamAssassin with ClamAV Scan*

```
Return-Path: <ataylor@example.com>
X-Original-To: jsmith@example.com
Delivered-To: jsmith@example.com
Received: by ubuntu-server.example.com (Postfix, from userid 8)
id 531F820814; Mon, 12 Jan 2009 23:40:21 +1100 (EST)
X-Spam-Virus: No
X-Spam-Checker-Version: SpamAssassin 3.2.5 (2008-06-10) on
au-mel-rhel-1.localdomain
X-Spam-Level:
X-Spam-Status: No, score=-1.4 required=5.0 tests=ALL_TRUSTED,AWL ➥
autolearn=ham, version=3.2.5
```

In Listing 10-21, you can see that a header called X-Spam-Virus has been added to the e-mail. The header in Listing 10-21 has a value of No. If a virus had been detected, the header would be marked Yes.

What to Do with an Infected E-Mail?

Like the X-Spam-Status header, you can use this header to process e-mail identified as containing a virus differently, for example, if you wanted to move all such e-mail to a separate folder called Viruses. You can do this using the procmail or maildrop commands you previously used to sort spam e-mail into a separate folder. To do this using procmail, you add a recipe like the following to your global /etc/procmailrc file or to the user's .procmailrc file:

```
:0:
* ^X-Spam-Virus: Yes
.Viruses/
```

To do the same with maildrop, you add the following recipe to the global /etc/maildroprc file or a user's .mailfilter file:

```
if ((/^X-Spam-Virus:.*Yes/))
{
to "./Maildir/.Viruses/."
}
```

Getting Help with ClamAV

You can find a variety of resources for troubleshooting ClamAV. You should start with the ClamAV home page (`http://www.clamav.net/`). On the same site, you'll find a variety of support resources available (`http://www.clamav.net/support/`), and you can join the ClamAV mailing list (`http://www.clamav.net/support/ml/`). You can find a list of current bugs at `http://www.clamav.net/bugs/`.

Remember, if you submit a question or a bug, you should include the following info:

- Your ClamAV version (run the `clamscan` command with the `--version` option)

- Your platform (run `uname -a`)

- Any log messages generated (either in the `/var/log/clamav/clamav.log` or the `/var/log/clamav/freshclam.log` file on Ubuntu, or the `/var/log/clamav/clamd.log` or `/var/log/clamav/freshclam.log` file on Red Hat)

Also available is an IRC channel called `#clamav` on the Freenode IRC server (`http://freenode.net/`) where you can seek assistance.

Configuring IMAP and POP3

Unlike what you've seen in most of the earlier sections of this chapter, your users aren't going to be directly accessing their e-mail via the command line. They will want to access it from an e-mail client on their local desktop. This is where an IMAP or a POP3 server comes into its own. These protocols represent two different methods of accessing mailboxes from a mail client or MUA. We're going to examine both methods, explain the pros and cons of each, and demonstrate how to configure and implement them in your environment.

IMAP

IMAP is used for accessing e-mail mailboxes from a remote client, like a desktop or laptop. Your client connects to the IMAP server, and you can read, manage, and delete any e-mail in your mailbox. You can also search messages, create and delete folders, and a variety of other management tasks.

POP3

POP3 is also used for accessing e-mail mailboxes from a remote client. E-mail is received and held in the users' mailboxes until they check their e-mail. When a user's e-mail client connects, all waiting e-mail is downloaded to the client and removed from the server.

What's the Difference?

The IMAP protocol acts much like a file server. Your e-mail stays on the server and can be read, deleted, and manipulated. POP3 is a store-and-forward mechanism. Each protocol offers advantages and disadvantages.

Advantages of IMAP:

- Allows users to access e-mail from multiple locations, not just their client. For example, IMAP allows webmail access.

- Protects your messages from accidental deletion.

- Centralizes e-mail, making backup and recovery easier.

Advantages of POP3:

- You don't need to be connected to the server (or indeed the network) to have access to your e-mail.

- Doesn't use any storage on your server—all mail is stored on your clients after retrieval.

Disadvantages of IMAP:

- You need to be able to connect to the server (and hence the network and/or Internet) to access your e-mail.

- Requires sufficient storage on your server.

Disadvantages of POP3:

- Mail is only present on the client and can't be accessed from elsewhere.

- Users can lose e-mail if they lose, damage, or rebuild their client desktop, laptop, etc., without sufficient backups.

- If users require e-mail to be backed up, a per-client backup and recovery strategy can be complex and difficult to implement.

Choosing Between IMAP and POP3

For the vast majority of circumstances, we recommend you use IMAP. The reasons for this are simplicity and ease of use. IMAP allows your users to roam with or without their client; for example, an IMAP server allows a user to have access to her e-mail via her laptop and a PDA device such as an iPhone or a Blackberry.

Your user's e-mail is also in a central location, which makes it easy for you to back it up (and recover it when one of your users inevitably deletes a vital e-mail). Additionally, with the cheap cost of storage, it is no longer an issue in most organizations to store e-mail centrally on a server or disk array.

The major caveat is that if your users cannot connect to the IMAP server, they will not be able to retrieve their e-mail. We consider the benefit of IMAP's other advantages outweigh the risk in this case.

In this section, we'll demonstrate how to configure IMAP in our examples. If you are interested in configuring POP3 instead, you can see some instructions, tips, and caveats at http://wiki.dovecot.org/POP3Server and http://wiki.dovecot.org/QuickConfiguration.

Introducing Dovecot

You've already been introduced to the Dovecot server because we're using it in our example as an authentication service for Postfix. There is some good news as a result. If you've been following along up to this point, you've already installed, started, and partially configured Dovecot. This means you have a limited number of steps you need to take to get it working now.

In this section, we're going to show you how to turn on IMAP, specifically the secure version of the IMAP protocol called IMAPS (with the *S* meaning *Secure*). This uses SSL encryption to protect both user authentication and the content of users' e-mail as it flows between the client and the server. The other main difference between IMAP and IMAPS is the TCP port they run on. The IMAP protocol runs on port 143, while the IMAPS protocol runs on port 993. You will need to specify this port number (and potentially tell your client to use SSL) in your mail client.

■**Tip** The POP3 protocol runs on TCP port 110, and its secure counterpart, SSL-POP3, runs on TCP port 995.

We're also going to configure Dovecot to find our local `Maildir` mailboxes. We don't need to configure authentication because we've already done it. The same authentication mechanism we enabled for Postfix, using the PAM authentication to check the local user's username and password, will work fine for IMAP connections.

Configuring Dovecot

The Dovecot server is configured using the `dovecot.conf` configuration file, as you discovered earlier in this chapter. On Ubuntu, this file is located at `/etc/dovecot/dovecot.conf`, and on Red Hat, the file is located at `/etc/dovecot.conf`. Let's start our configuration process by enabling the IMAPS protocol and specifying the location of the SSL certificates we're going to use. To make this easy, we're going to reuse the same certificates we created for our Postfix encryption.

First, we enable IMAPS by editing the `protocols` configuration option and changing it from `none` to `imaps` like so:

```
protocols = imaps
```

Next, we specify our SSL certificate and key files. To do this, we need to uncomment and update the `ssl_cert_file` and `ssl_key_file` options and add the location of our certificate and key.

```
ssl_cert_file = /etc/postfix/tls/mail.example.com.cert
ssl_key_file = /etc/postfix/tls/mail.example.com.key
```

The certificate and key files we're going to use are the same ones we used to provide Postfix's encryption. You could follow the same steps we followed in that section to create Dovecot-specific certificates, or you could even buy additional certificates specifically for Dovecot if you wish, but we don't feel this is necessary.

■**Note** Remember, your certificate is tied to a hostname, in our case mail.example.com. If you are running your Dovecot server on another host, you should create a new key and certificate with the hostname of the server running Dovecot. Additionally, as the certificate is tied to the hostname, you must specify this hostname (mail.example.com for this example) in your mail client rather than any other DNS name the host may be known as.

Next, we uncomment and change the `disable_plaintext_auth` option to yes.

```
disable_plaintext_auth = yes
```

This option disables any plain text authentication unless SSL is enabled and an encrypted connection is running. This protects our user's authentication credentials from attacks that might sniff or grab them off the network or Internet.

Finally, we're going to specify the location of our mailboxes using the `mail_location` option.

```
mail_location = maildir:~/Maildir
```

This tells Dovecot we're using `Maildir`s located in the user's home directory, or ~, and in the directory `Maildir`.

Now we need to restart the Dovecot server, and then we can test to see whether we can make a connection and retrieve our e-mail on Ubuntu, for example:

```
$ sudo invoke-rc.d dovecot restart
```

Testing Dovecot

Now that we've configured Dovecot, we can enable a client and test its access. We're going to configure a Mozilla Thunderbird client to test Dovecot.

■**Note** Mozilla Thunderbird is a popular open source mail client released by the Mozilla Foundation, which also developed the Firefox browser.

To configure the client, we first need to install it. On both Red Hat and Ubuntu, the required package is called `thunderbird`, and you should use your package management tool to install it.

Now, let's review what we need to know in order to configure our client:

- The name of our server
- Our username and password

We're going to launch the Mozilla Thunderbird mail client by selecting the menu options Applications ➤ Internet ➤ Thunderbird Email, as shown in Figure 10-8 (on Ubuntu, the application is launched from the same place but is called Mozilla Thunderbird Mail/News).

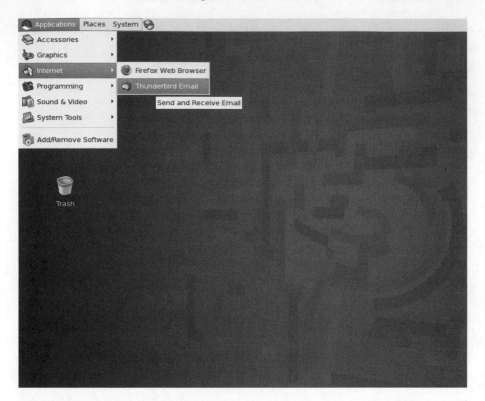

Figure 10-8. *Launching Mozilla Thunderbird*

If this is the first time you've launched Thunderbird, the Account Wizard will start. This wizard allows you to create a variety of new types of Thunderbird accounts. If the wizard doesn't run, you can create a new account by selecting the menu options Edit ➤ Account Settings and clicking Add Account.

We're going to configure a new e-mail account. We ensure this option is selected and click the Next button. On the next screen, we specify our name and e-mail address and click the Next button again.

On the following screen, we specify the type and name of our IMAP and SMTP servers (which Thunderbird calls the outgoing server). You can see this screen, populated with our example server mail.example.com, in Figure 10-9.

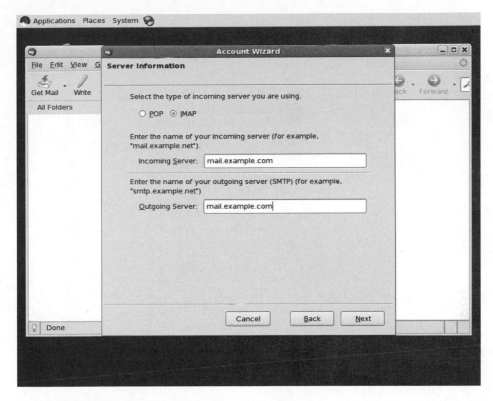

Figure 10-9. *Specifying server details*

Once we've specified our server details, we click the Next button.

The next screen prompts for the username; in our case, this is the name of a user that exists on our IMAP host. After we enter the name, we click the Next button.

On the next two screens, we specify a name for this account in Thunderbird. This is the name Thunderbird will call the account. We usually use the default, which is our e-mail address, and click the Next button. The last screen, shown in Figure 10-10, allows us to review the details we've entered to ensure they are correct.

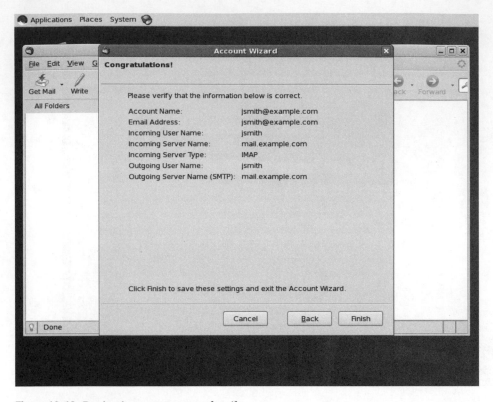

Figure 10-10. *Reviewing our account details*

The details are correct in our case, so we click the Finish button. If the details are incorrect when you reach this screen, you can use the Back button to go back and correct any details.

But our configuration is not quite complete because Thunderbird defaults to IMAP rather than IMAPS when configuring an account with the Account Wizard. So after we finish the wizard, we need to edit our account to use IMAPS. To do this, we select the Edit menu and the Account Settings option to launch a dialog that allows us to edit our account details. You can see that dialog in Figure 10-11.

We select the Server Settings tab and then the SSL radio button in the Security Settings box. Notice the port number changed to 993 to indicate we're making an IMAPS connection. We click the Okay button to complete configuration.

Now, if we click the Get Mail button, our client will connect to the mail.example.com Dovecot server on TCP port 993 and initiate an SSL encrypted connection. We are prompted to enter our password. When we authenticate successfully, any mail available in our mailbox will be displayed in Thunderbird, as you can see in Figure 10-12.

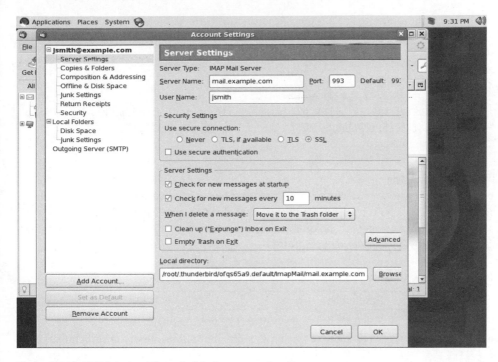

Figure 10-11. *Editing our Thunderbird account details*

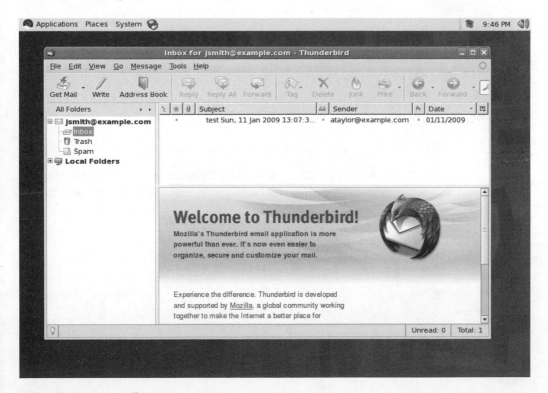

Figure 10-12. *Our mailbox*

You should also be able to see a record of your connection and authentication in the appropriate log file for your distribution: /var/log/maillog on Red Hat and /var/log/mail.log on Ubuntu, as you can see in Listing 10-22.

Listing 10-22. *Dovecot Authentication Log Entries*

```
Jan 14 22:13:53 au-mel-rhel-1  dovecot: imap-login: Login: user=<jsmith>, ➥
method=PLAIN, rip=::ffff:192.168.0.128, lip=::ffff:192.168.0.128, TLS
```

Troubleshooting Dovecot

If something doesn't work or you can't connect to your Dovecot server, then we recommend the first place you look is in the log files. You can make this process easier as Dovecot has some very useful debugging settings you can enable to get more verbose output if you are having an issue. Table 10-3 provides a list of these options.

Table 10-3. *Dovecot Debugging Options*

Option	Description
mail_debug	When set to yes, it shows more information about the mail process.
auth_verbose	When set to yes, it shows more information about the authentication process.
auth_debug	When set to yes, it shows debugging information about the authentication process.
auth_debug_password	If both auth_debug and this option are set to yes, the authentication mechanisms and password are displayed.

Turn on one or more of these options to see verbose debugging information. This information is sent to the syslog daemon and hence on to either your /var/log/maillog or /var/log/mail.log log files. The additional information should make it much easier to determine whether anything is wrong with your Dovecot installation.

■**Note** You must restart the Dovecot server after changing any of these options, and we recommend setting the options back to no after you've fixed any issues. Leaving debugging on can impact the performance of your Dovecot server.

Getting Help with Dovecot

A considerable amount of useful information is available to help you resolve any potential issues with Dovecot. The best place to start when trying to get help is the Dovecot home page at http://www.dovecot.org/. The site includes a comprehensive wiki (http://wiki.dovecot.org/) including a number of how-tos and examples for configuring Dovecot in variety of implementations. Also available are the Dovecot mailing lists (http://www.dovecot.org/mailinglists.html) and bug submission instructions (http://www.dovecot.org/bugreport.html).

Remember that if you submit a question or a bug, you should include the following info:

- Your Dovecot version (run the dovecot command with the --version option)

- Your platform (run uname -a)

- Any log messages generated (either in the /var/log/mail.log file on Ubuntu or the /var/log/maillog file on Red Hat)

Also available is an IRC channel called #dovecot on the Freenode IRC server (http://freenode.net/) where you can seek assistance.

Virtual Domains and Users

We've introduced the basics of providing e-mail to your users in this chapter. We're going to introduce you to a full e-mail and collaboration suite in Chapter 15, but here we'll discuss the ways you can extend the mail services we've introduced in this chapter.

The primary way you can extend Postfix and Dovecot is into virtual domains and virtual users. Up until now, we've assumed that the domain we're delivering mail for and the users who receive that mail are all physical instantiations. The domain we're accepting e-mail for is the domain the mail server belongs to, and our users actually exist on our mail server. With virtual domains and users, you can configure destinations and recipients for e-mail that aren't physical. We're not going to demonstrate these concepts, but we'll explain them and refer you to documentation that will allow you to extend what we've built in this chapter to do all of this.

Hosting virtual domains allows you to receive e-mail for additional domains. For example, say you currently receive mail for the domain example.com. Your company might also have the domains product.com and anotherproduct.com. You can configure Postfix to receive e-mail for these additional domains.

Virtual users are a similar concept. Thus far all our users have existed as actual Linux users, jsmith and ataylor, for example. Their mailboxes have been stored in the /home directory tree. With virtual users, your mail users don't need to be created as operating system users. Each e-mail address is mapped to a virtual user or a user contained in a database such as MySQL or LDAP. This reduces the need to create and manage large numbers of operating system users.

You can find a very complete how-to on configuring virtual domains and users with Postfix at http://www.postfix.org/VIRTUAL_README.html. You can find a more Ubuntu-specific guide at https://help.ubuntu.com/community/PostfixCompleteVirtualMailSystemHowto. You can also find instructions for extending Dovecot in a similar way at http://wiki.dovecot.org/VirtualUsers and on the Dovecot how-to page at http://wiki.dovecot.org/HowTo.

Summary

In this chapter, we introduced you to mail services on a Linux host that allow your users to send and receive e-mail from your organization. We discussed IMAP and POP3, protocols that allow your users to connect to your host and retrieve and manage their e-mail in mailboxes.

In the process, we've covered some important concepts:

- Protecting your users' e-mail and their authentication credentials via encryption

- Enabling SASL authentication to allow your users to safely and securely authenticate to your mail server to send and receive e-mail

- Making use of SpamAssassin to filter your e-mail and stop spam from reaching your users

- Using the open source ClamAV antivirus engine to check your user's e-mail for viruses and malware

- Using MDAs such as `procmail`, `maildrop`, or Sieve to filter your e-mail

- Implementing the Dovecot server to allow users to connect to their mailboxes and retrieve e-mail

In the next chapter, we'll introduce you to web services, and teach you how to run your own web server and provide your own web presence.

■■■

## CHAPTER 11

Web and SQL Services

By Peter Lieverdink

Now that you have e-mail services running, your clients can contact you. However, to complete your online presence, you will want to have a website as well. Not only that, but you could set up webmail for staff who want to access e-mail remotely, or a wiki so that staff can work cooperatively on projects.

In this chapter, you will learn how to set up the Apache web server and MySQL database server. Then you will install a content management system and a webmail application. Finally, we will show you how to make web browsing a faster and safer experience for your staff by protecting them via a web proxy.

Apache Web Server

Apache is probably the most widely used open source software today. It is used to host over 50% of all websites in existence[1] and is usually chosen for its maturity, stability, and flexibility. It is designed to be modular, so extra functionality can be added or removed by enabling or disabling modules. Packages are available for virtually all Linux distributions, so you can install it on your hosts via the package management system.

Installation and Configuration

Both Red Hat and Ubuntu install Apache version 2.2, but the packages are named differently. On Red Hat, you run `sudo yum install httpd`, while on Ubuntu you run `sudo aptitude install apache2-mpm-prefork`. Adding these packages will also cause some additional libraries to be installed.

You may have noticed that on Ubuntu some additional `apache2` packages are available. These packages provide a different internal engine that allows Apache to service specific kinds of web requests in a more efficient manner. We chose the `apache2-mpm-prefork` package because this engine allows us to add support for the PHP scripting language later. On Red Hat, these types of engines are all contained within the single `httpd` package, and we simply enable or disable them via a configuration file. To this end, we will also install the `system-config-httpd` package on Red Hat.

---

1. See http://news.netcraft.com/archives/web_server_survey.html.

■Note If you run a high-volume, high-traffic website that does not use PHP, you might consider changing to a different Apache engine or different web server altogether, such as lighthttpd or Tux. You can find a list of web servers at http://en.wikipedia.org/wiki/Comparison_of_web_servers.

We'll start by doing a basic configuration for Apache. Later on, we'll add some modules to extend functionality.

Red Hat

On Red Hat, you can use a GUI to configure Apache. To start it, select System ➤ Administration ➤ Server Settings ➤ HTTP. You will need to enter the root password to start the utility. This utility provides an easy-to-use interface that can change the basic settings in the /etc/httpd/conf/httpd.conf file.

You can set basic server information on the Main tab, as you can see in Figure 11-1. The server name and webmaster e-mail address are used by Apache when it displays default error pages. We'll enter values for our own host, au-mel-rhel-1.example.com and webmaster@example.com. The Available Addresses listing allows you to specify which IP addresses and port number you want Apache to listen for requests on. The default is to listen on port 80 on all addresses.

Figure 11-1. *Apache configuration GUI*

The next tab contains the definition for the default virtual host, which will service any requests that we haven't explicitly defined a custom virtual host for. See the "Virtual Hosts" sidebar for a short explanation of what a virtual host is. We'll come back to the Virtual Hosts tab shortly.

VIRTUAL HOSTS

A single Linux host running Apache can serve hundreds or thousands of websites, all with their own host-names. We call this *virtual hosting* because each of these sites isn't a single Linux host by itself. There are two kinds of virtual hosting: IP based and name based. Apache can provide both.

IP-based virtual hosting causes Apache to serve a web page from a specific directory, based on the IP address the request was received on. For each IP-based virtual host, the Linux host needs to have an IP address assigned to a network interface. This is done via aliases, as we discussed in Chapter 6. If you want to protect virtual websites with a security certificate, you need to use IP-based virtual hosts.

Name-based virtual hosting causes Apache to serve a web page for a specific directory based on the name of the site a remote user connected to. Any number of name-based virtual hosts can share a single IP address. The name of the site is determined by a special header that is sent in the request to the web server.

Next is the Server tab, as shown in Figure 11-2. This tab contains variables that define how the web server runs.

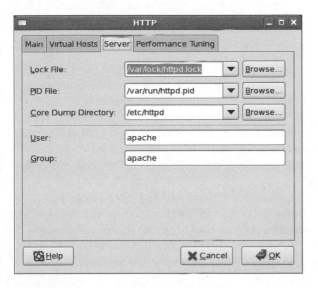

Figure 11-2. *Server process configuration*

The lock and pid files allow utility scripts to determine whether the web server is running, while the core dump directory specifies where memory will be dumped in case of a fatal web server crash.

Of more interest are the User and Group fields, which determine the account the web server will run as. It is important that these are not a user and group you use elsewhere on the system, as that might grant Apache access to files or directories it should not be able to see.

Finally, the Performance Tuning tab (see Figure 11-3) allows you to tweak some basic server limits.

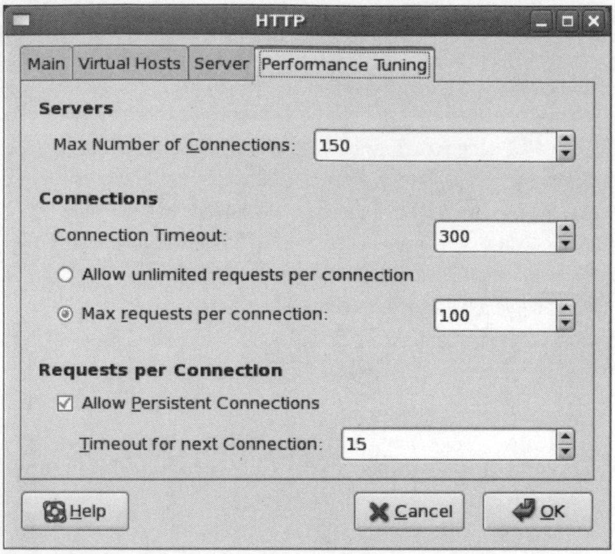

Figure 11-3. *Basic web server performance tuning*

The entry in the Max Number of Connections box determines how many concurrent connections this server will handle. Many web browsers make multiple connections to a web server, so they can download style sheets and images simultaneously. This means that the maximum number of connections does not equal the maximum numbers of users your server can handle. Each connection also uses a certain amount of system resources, such as RAM and CPU time, so it's important not to set this value too high.

The Connection Timeout setting specifies how long the server will wait for a client to tell it that data was received, or to send data. If nothing happens for 300 seconds, the server will close the connection.

Because some server modules may contain bugs that do not free used resources, we are able to tell the server to simply kill a process after it has served a specific number of connections. It will then be replaced by a new server process. The inaccurately named "Max requests per connection" setting controls how many requests a web server process may serve before it is replaced by a new process.

Finally, we can choose whether or not to enable persistent connections. When this is allowed, a client can request multiple files via the same connection. By not requiring both the server and client to set up a new connection for each file that is to be retrieved, you can improve speed and efficiency.

The "Timeout for next Connection" setting determines the number of seconds a connection may be idle before the server closes it. For now, let's leave all these values at their defaults and go back to the Virtual Hosts tab.

Select the Default Virtual Host and click Edit. The Virtual Host Properties dialog will open, as shown in Figure 11-4.

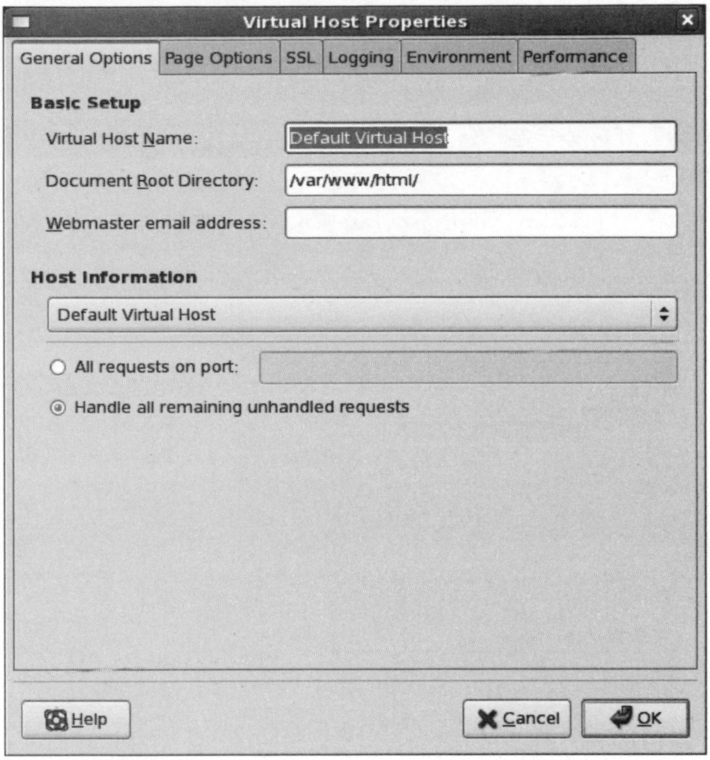

Figure 11-4. *Default virtual host settings*

The Virtual Host Name is a human-readable name you can set to make administration a bit easier. It does not impact the way Apache works at all. Of most interest on this screen is the Document Root Directory setting, as Apache serves files from this directory. You are able to override the webmaster e-mail address for this virtual host as well.

The Page Options tab (see Figure 11-5) allows you to specify which file is treated as the default home page in a directory. When a request is made to a directory, Apache will check for the existence of each file in the search list and send the first one it encounters to the browser.

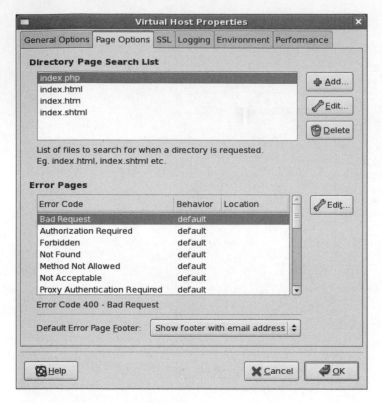

Figure 11-5. *Setting page options*

On this tab, you are also able to modify the default error behavior. Normally, Apache will display a standard error page if the server encounters an error. If you select Bad Request and then click Edit, you are able to have the server display a customized page or have it redirect the user to a different site altogether by specifying a URL, as you can see in Figure 11-6. This would allow you, for example, to redirect users to a search page if they request a file that the server cannot find. For now, leave this at the default behavior.

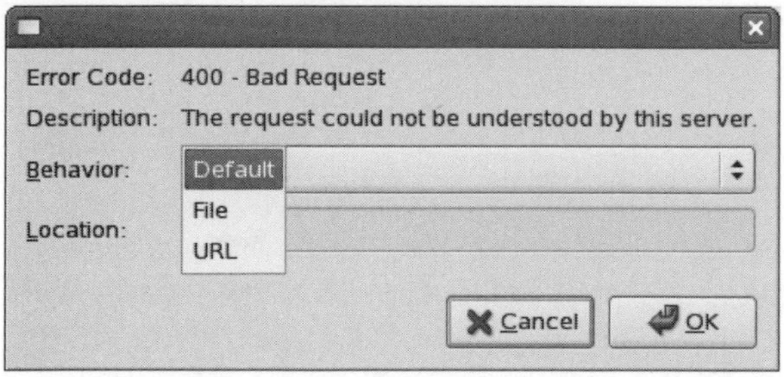

Error Code: 400 - Bad Request
Description: The request could not be understood by this server.
Behavior: Default
          File
          URL
Location:

Figure 11-6. *Changing error behavior*

The SSL tab allows you to configure encryption certificates for this virtual host. We'll come back to this later, when we configure a secure webmail site.

The Logging tab (see Figure 11-7) allows you to change which log files will be used to record access to the virtual host and any errors that may occur. If you have many virtual hosts, you might want them all to write their logs to different files, for processing by a log analyzer. You can change the amount of logging that occurs by adjusting the log level. We'll set this to Info instead of Debug, to keep the error log file size in check.

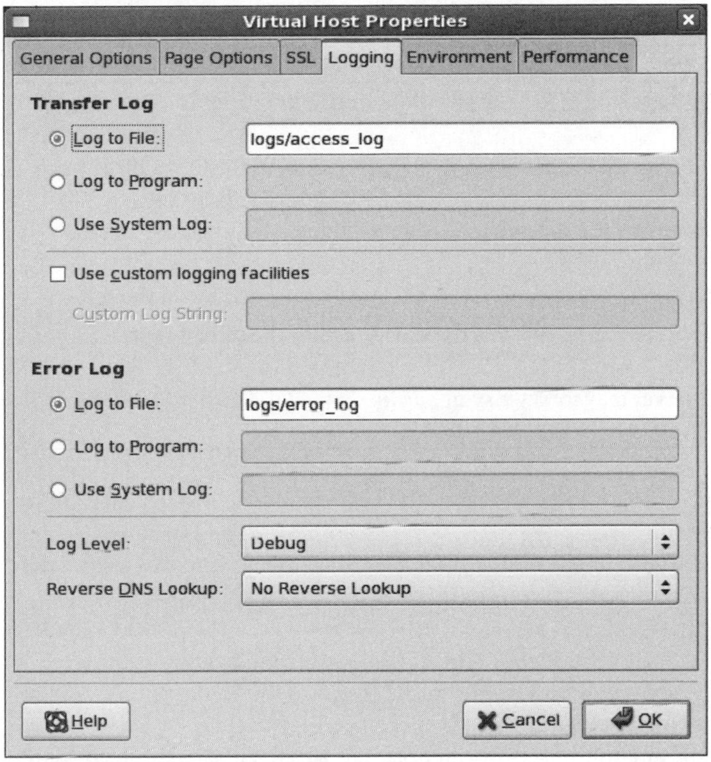

Figure 11-7. *Logging configuration*

Finally, the Reverse DNS Lookup option controls whether the logs contain just the remote IP address or the FQDN. If you specify No Reverse Lookup, just the IP address is logged. With Reverse Lookup specified, the server will query the configured DNS server and obtain the FQDN for the connecting client and log that instead. The last option, Double Reverse Lookup, causes the server to first look up the FQDN, and then also to look up that FQDN to see if it resolves back to the original IP address.

Because these lookups are slow, turning them on will adversely impact server performance, so leave this option set to No Reverse Lookup. Most log file analyzers can do DNS lookups much more efficiently.

The Environment tab allows you to pass environment variables from the startup script to the web server, so it can be accessed by CGI scripts. CGI stands for Common Gateway Interface, which is the protocol used to allow the web server to run applications when a browser requests a URL. These environment variables might include such things as a language or time zone setting. You can read more about CGI at http://en.wikipedia.org/wiki/Common_Gateway_Interface.

The incorrectly named Performance tab allows you to set web server–specific options for this virtual host and for specific directories it contains. These options determine which files the web server may serve, whether to execute CGI scripts, and even whether the options may be overridden via additional configuration files. The options on this tab enabled by default are listed in Table 11-1.

Table 11-1. *Virtual Host Default Options*

Option	Function
ExecCGI	Scripts are executed as applications and their output is sent to the browser.
FollowSymLinks	The server may follow a symbolic link and serve the file or directory it points to.
Includes	The server will process server-side include directives that can be embedded in pages.
IncludesNOEXEC	Server-side include directives may not execute scripts on the server.
Indexes	If no index page exists in a directory, display the directly contents in a listing.
SymLinksIfOwnerMatch	The server may follow a symbolic link only if the owner of the link is the same as the owner of the link target.

We won't make any other configuration changes to the default virtual host, so click OK to close the Virtual Host Properties dialog.

Let's set up a virtual host that will house our company website. We'll want this to be available as `http://www.example.com` and as `http://example.com`. Click the Virtual Hosts tab and then Add.

In the new Virtual Host Properties window, set the virtual hostname to www.example.com, the document root to /srv/www/www.example.com/html, and the webmaster e-mail to webmaster@example.com, as shown in Figure 11-8.

Next, specify that this will be a name-based virtual host. We'll make it accessible via all IP addresses on this server, so type * in the address field.

To allow the server to serve files from this site based on the hostname, you need to set the hostname to www.example.com. Remember, the Virtual Host Name field is just a label to help you find it in the list.

Finally, because you want this site to be available via the alias example.com as well, add it to the aliases list by clicking Add, entering the alias, and then clicking OK.

Figure 11-8. *Adding a www.example.com virtual host*

We'll leave the page options as they are, and we won't use SSL for this virtual host. On the Logging tab, set the log level to Error and ensure the server does not perform any reverse lookups. There is also no need to modify the environment options, but we will prevent the server from executing CGI scripts in the document root directory on this virtual host. To do this, click the Performance tab and then the Add button, to add settings for the new document root. In the listing, deselect the ExecCGI option, and select the option to allow you to override options via an .htaccess file, as shown in Figure 11-9.

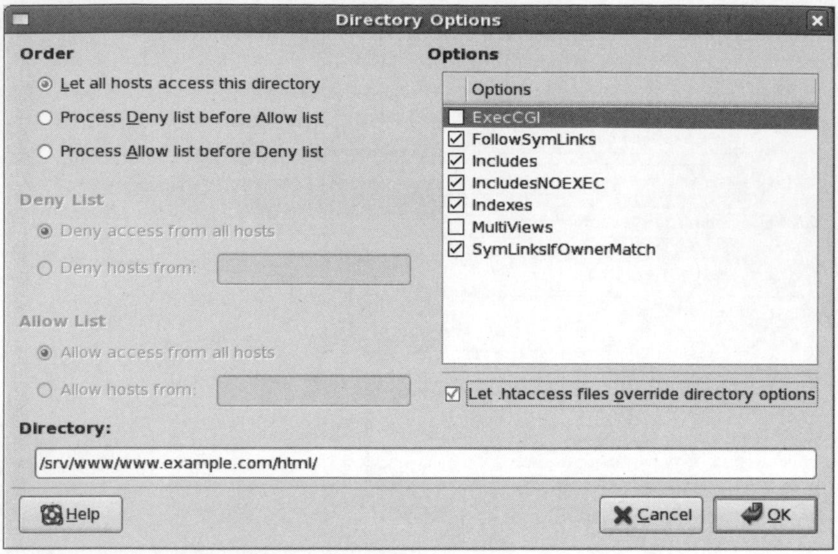

Figure 11-9. *Changing directory options*

Click OK to accept your changes and then click OK again to close the Virtual Host Properties dialog. Click OK yet again to close the HTTP configuration tool. When asked, answer Yes to accept the changes made.

All that is left to do now is ensure the document root directory exists, or an error will occur when you try to access the `http://www.example.com` site. We can create this directory with a single command, by passing the `-p` option to `mkdir`. This option will also create any parent directories that are required.

```
$ sudo mkdir -p /srv/www/www.example.com/html
```

On Red Hat, the web server is not started when it is installed, nor are the links set in the `init.d` directories. We'll need to do this manually, via `chkconfig`.

```
$ sudo chkconfig --level 2345 httpd on
```

Before we start the web server, we should also reconfigure the firewall to allow traffic to the port it uses. We choose System ➤ Administration ➤ Security Level and Firewall and check the box for the WWW (HTTP) option, as shown in Figure 11-10. Then we click OK to close the applet and Yes to apply our changes.

Figure 11-10. *Allowing web traffic through the firewall*

We can now start the server via the `service` command:

```
$ sudo service httpd start
```

and if we point a web browser at `http://localhost/`, we will see a generic welcome page.

Apache's module and slightly more advanced configuration is handled manually, by editing the main configuration file directly or by adding configuration file snippets into the `/etc/httpd/conf.d` directory, which is referenced by the main configuration file. We'll come back to module configuration a bit later, in the "Modules" section.

Whenever you make a configuration change, you need to tell Apache to reload its configuration files. Rather than stopping and starting the service each time, you can use `sudo apachectl graceful`, which tells the web server to reload its configuration files without dropping all active connections. You can also use `apachectl` to check the configuration files for mistakes by running `sudo apachectl configtest`. If you habitually do this, you will never cause a server crash due to a bad configuration directive.

Ubuntu

On Ubuntu, a GUI isn't available to manage Apache configuration settings, and the basic configuration has been divided among multiple files. The main file loaded by Apache on Ubuntu is `/etc/apache2/apache2.conf`. We've included the basic configuration directives from this file in Listing 11-1. This file contains directives that configure logging and performance, but it references additional files to configure virtual hosts, modules, and ports and IP addresses, as well as configuration snippets in the `/etc/apache2/conf.d` directory.

Listing 11-1. *Defaults in Ubuntu's apache2.conf File*

```
ServerRoot "/etc/apache2"
LockFile /var/lock/apache2/accept.lock
PidFile ${APACHE_PID_FILE}

Timeout 300
KeepAlive On
MaxKeepAliveRequests 100
KeepAliveTimeout 15

<IfModule mpm_prefork_module>
    StartServers          5
    MinSpareServers       5
    MaxSpareServers      10
    MaxClients          150
    MaxRequestsPerChild   0
</IfModule>

User ${APACHE_RUN_USER}
Group ${APACHE_RUN_GROUP}

AccessFileName .htaccess
<Files ~ "^\.ht">
    Order allow,deny
    Deny from all
</Files>

HostnameLookups Off
ErrorLog /var/log/apache2/error.log
LogLevel warn
Include /etc/apache2/mods-enabled/*.load
Include /etc/apache2/mods-enabled/*.conf
Include /etc/apache2/httpd.conf
Include /etc/apache2/ports.conf
LogFormat "%h %l %u %t \"%r\" %>s %b \"%{Referer}i\" \"%{User-Agent}i\"" combined
LogFormat "%h %l %u %t \"%r\" %>s %b" common
LogFormat "%{Referer}i -> %U" referer
LogFormat "%{User-agent}i" agent
ServerTokens Full

ServerSignature On
Include /etc/apache2/conf.d/
Include /etc/apache2/sites-enabled/
```

The default configuration on Ubuntu is mostly the same as on Red Hat; it's just the default file locations that differ, and the virtual hosting configuration is geared toward managing virtual hosts without a GUI.

The number of server instances to start is defined in a special block surrounded by IfModule tags. These tags allow you to set configuration variables if a specific module has been loaded into the server. In this case, the number of server instances will be set if the mpm_prefork_module is loaded. This section is conditional, because Apache would not recognize these variables if the mpm_prefork_module was not present, and it would exit with an error.

Also of note is the AccessFileName directive. It specifies the name of a file that may contain server configuration directives. This file is named .htaccess, and any web directory may contain such a file. The server will check if the file exists and process any directives it contains before attempting to serve files to a connecting client.

Directly below AccessFileName is a directive that prevents remote users from downloading any files whose name starts with the string .ht. This is needed because .htaccess files may contain information that could potentially be of use to an attacker.

The Order directive determines how access to these files is determined. The parameter allow,deny specifies that we will first list any hosts that are allowed to access the specified files and then all hosts that aren't. In this case, nobody is explicitly permitted to access these files and everybody is expressly denied access to them via the Deny from all directive. We'll come back to access restrictions a bit later on.

The first four Include directives cause Apache to process configuration information in the specified files. To load any modules that are enabled, the main configuration file includes mods-enabled/*.load. The configuration for these modules is then read from mods-enabled/*.conf. Because some automated installation scripts write information to the legacy file httpd.conf, it is included too. Finally, Apache loads information about which IP addresses and ports it should listen on from the ports.conf file.

ServerTokens specifies how much information Apache discloses to connecting clients about its version, the operating system it runs on, and the modules that are enabled. A setting of Full means it discloses everything via the Server header, which you can check using the HEAD utility. This utility is provided by the perl-libwww-perl package on Red Hat and libwww-perl on Ubuntu. This utility takes a URL as a parameter and will display any HTTP header lines it receives.

```
$ HEAD http://localhost | grep Server:
Server: Apache/2.2.8 (Ubuntu)
```

To change this, you can replace Full with Prod and tell Apache to reload its configuration file using sudo apache2ctl reload. If you then recheck the Server header, you can see the version number and operating system are no longer disclosed.

```
$ HEAD http://localhost | grep Server:
Server: Apache
```

The ServerSignature On directive causes Apache to append some basic server information on the default error pages that are displayed when a problem occurs.

Finally, any custom configuration snippets are loaded from files in the conf.d directory, and all virtual host information is read from the sites-enabled directory.

The default virtual host on Ubuntu is defined in /etc/apache2/sites-available/default and it defines /var/www as the basic document root directory. If you point a browser at http://localhost/ on Ubuntu, you'll see a terse "It works!" page.

To add virtual hosts on Ubuntu, you create a virtual host definition file in the /etc/apache2/
sites-available directory. You then make it available to Apache by running sudo a2ensite,
which creates a symbolic link in the /etc/apache2/sites-enabled directory.

Let's add a virtual host for www.example.com. We'll store it on the logical volume we created earlier. It helps to decide on a system for storing virtual hosts on disk before you start. As
the number of sites on your host grows, this will help make managing them easier.

To define the virtual host, we'll add the directives from Listing 11-2 in /etc/apache2/
sites-available/www.example.com.

Listing 11-2. *Our New Virtual Host Definition*

```
<VirtualHost *>
    ServerName www.example.com
    ServerAlias example.com
    ServerAdmin webmaster@localhost
    DocumentRoot /srv/www/www.example.com/html
    <Directory /srv/www/www.example.com/html>
        Options Indexes FollowSymLinks Includes IncludesNOEXEC SymLinksIfOwnerMatch
        AllowOverride All
    </Directory>
</VirtualHost>
```

As you can see, Apache uses HTML-like tags for its configuration sections. We start by
opening the VirtualHost tag and specifying that the definition will apply to all addresses. Next,
we specify the names we want this virtual host to reply for. Only a single ServerName can apply
to any given virtual host, but others can be added via ServerAlias. You can add extra aliases
with more ServerAlias directives.

The DocumentRoot directive specifies the directory from which this virtual host will serve
files. Once this is defined, you can use the Directory tag to specify options for this directory
and all files and directories it contains. You specify the same list as on the Red Hat machine. By
setting AllowOverride to All, you permit the server to modify these options with settings from
an .htaccess file. You could disallow this by setting AllowOverride to None. Finally, you close
the Directory and VirtualHost tags and save the file.

As opposed to on Red Hat, you need to explicitly enable this virtual host by creating a link
in /etc/apache2-sites/enabled to the configuration snippet just created. Luckily, you don't
need to do this manually via the ln command. Instead, the apache2-common package, which is
automatically installed with apache2, provides a handy utility called a2ensite to manage this
for you. You simply run it with the snippet's file name as a parameter.

```
$ sudo a2ensite www.example.com
Site www.example.com installed; run /etc/init.d/apache2 reload to enable.
```

You can now do as the script suggests, or use sudo apache2ctl graceful to manually
reload the server configuration. The init script runs the apache2ctl configtest command first,
to ensure the configuration files are valid before the server is restarted. It is a good practice to
do this, even if you use apache2ctl to reload the server configuration.

■**Note** Ubuntu contains the apachectl command as well, as part of the Apache legacy version 1.3 packages.

Access Restriction

We mentioned before that you can restrict access based on your host using the Order and Allow or Deny directives in .htaccess files. For instance, to allow hosts only on our local network to access the http://www.example.com site, we could create an .htaccess file at /srv/www/www.example.com/html and add the following directives:

```
Order allow,deny
Allow from 192.168.0.0/255.255.255.0
Deny from all
```

We tell Apache to first check for hosts that may access the site using our network address and netmask. Then we instruct it to deny access to everyone else using the all keyword. We could also deny access only to hosts on our other network by reversing the order of the parameters:

```
Order deny,allow
Deny from 192.168.1.0/255.255.255.0
Allow from all
```

First we reject access based on the host address, and then we accept everyone else.

The other way to restrict access to resources is by requiring users to enter a username and password. Many web applications manage this internally, but you can also have Apache manage a list of usernames and passwords, allowing you to protect specific directories without needing additional software.

First, we need to create a file that contains the usernames and passwords we want to use via the htpasswd utility. Normally, we pass the file name to use and the user to create as parameters, but if the file does not yet exist, we also need to pass the -c option.

```
$ sudo htpasswd -c /srv/www/www.example.com/htpasswd jsmith
New password:
Re-type new password:
Adding password for user jsmith
```

We can now add additional users without needing the -c option. If we want to not be asked for a password to use, we can set that on the command line as well, via the -b option.

```
$ sudo htpasswd -b /srv/www/www.example.com/htpasswd ataylor s3kr@t
Adding password for user ataylor
```

Next, we need to tell Apache to ask for authentication. We can do this in an .htaccess file, provided we are allowed to override the AuthConfig option, as shown in Listing 11-3. Since we have set AllowOverride to all, this will work fine.

First, we specify the authentication type we want to use via the AuthType directive, which in our case is basic. We then need to tell Apache which module will provide the basic authentication using `AuthBasicProvider`, which is `file`. Next, we need to tell Apache which file holds our authentication information via the `AuthUserFile` directive.

To help users determine what they're trying to access, we can specify a name for the protected resource via the `AuthName` directive. This name will be displayed to users when they are asked for credentials, as shown in Figure 11-11, so it helps to make this name fairly descriptive.

Finally, Apache needs to be told that access must be granted only if a user successfully authenticates. We do this by specifying `Require valid-user`.

Listing 11-3. *Authentication Configuration in an* `.htaccess` *File*

```
AuthType basic
AuthBasicProvider file
AuthUserFile /srv/www/www.example.com/htpasswd
AuthName "Restricted Area"
Require valid-user
```

If we now browse to `http://www.example.com`, our browser will ask us for a username and password, as shown in Figure 11-11.

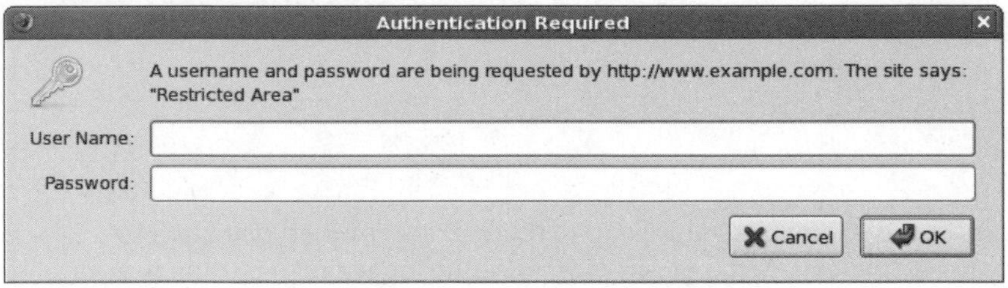

Figure 11-11. *Apache authentication*

We won't be granted access if we don't provide a valid username and password, but if we enter valid credentials Apache will let us view the site.

You can read more about host- and user-based access control on the Apache documentation site:

- `http://httpd.apache.org/docs/2.2/howto/access.html`
- `http://httpd.apache.org/docs/2.2/mod/mod_auth_basic.html`

Modules

Modules that provide extra functionality to Apache are enabled using the `LoadModule` directive, which specifies the path to the module file that should be loaded.

On Red Hat, extra modules are usually enabled by a configuration snippet in `/etc/httpd/conf.d` that is installed by the module package. When the server is restarted, it picks up these new files and processes their directives. To prevent such a snippet from being included, thus disabling the module, you can rename it so its file name no longer ends in `.conf`.

On Ubuntu, module packages add these snippets in the `/etc/apache2/mods-available` directory and then create links to them in the `/etc/apache2/modules-enabled` directory. These links can also be managed manually using the a2enmod and a2dismod commands, similar to a2ensite and a2dissite.

For instance, we will need the rewrite module to be enabled, so it can be used by a site we will install later. This module allows Apache to rewrite URLs on the fly. We can enable it by running sudo a2enmod rewrite and then reloading the server configuration.

Information on all included Apache modules and the functionality they provide is available at http://httpd.apache.org/docs/2.2/mod/.

Installing PHP Support

Many web applications are written in PHP, a scripting language developed by Rasmus Lerdorf. As your web browser requests a page from such an application, the web server processes the code in the page and displays the output to your browser. To be able to host these web applications, the web server needs to be able to understand and execute PHP code.

For some web servers this is handled via a CGI script, but on Apache you can add PHP support directly into the server by installing a module.

■**Note** You can read all about PHP at http://www.php.net/.

PHP itself is modular, so you can add functionality to PHP by installing additional packages. We'll set up a MySQL server shortly, so in order to have web applications use that, we need to add MySQL support in PHP. In addition, we'll install support for the commonly used GD graphics library, the mbstring string conversion library, and the IMAP mail protocol. The latter will allow us to also install and use PHP-based webmail applications.

On Red Hat, we can install all this via sudo yum install php5 php-mysql php-gd php-imap php-mbstring and on Ubuntu via sudo aptitude install libapache2-mod-php5 php5-mysql php5-gd php5-imap. PHP is enabled by default on Red Hat, but on Ubuntu you need to run sudo a2enmod php5 to enable it. To make PHP active, though, you should restart Apache on both systems.

File and Directory Permissions

When you're working with websites, you need write access to the document root directories where sites are installed. At the same time, the Apache user needs to not be able to write to the same directories, as that could allow anonymous web users to write files to your system, if they found a vulnerability in a website.

If multiple users will be managing sites, it's a good idea to create a group for this purpose. As long as the group in question has write permissions to the document root, any users you add to this group will be able to write to files and create directories.

■**Tip** Using a specific system group to manage websites also means you can allow members of this group to use the apachectl or apache2ctl commands via sudo without giving them full root access.

To ensure that files created by one user can be modified by another user in the same group, you need to set the umask so that any new files and directories created are writeable by the group. You also need to set the setgid bit, so that new files and directories will inherit ownership from the group that owns the parent directory, not the primary group of the user who happened to create the file or directory in question. We'll show you an example of this a bit later on, when we install some web applications.

■**Tip** More information and Apache documentation is available at `http://httpd.apache.org/`.

MySQL Database

Because many web-based applications use an SQL server to store data, we'll also show you how to install a MySQL server. Unlike Microsoft Access, MySQL consists of a server and a client part. The server provides data storage and retrieval, while the client can be any application that uses the server—a command-line utility, OpenOffice, or a library that is used by a website.

Installation

On both Red Hat and Ubuntu, the server component is provided by the `mysql-server` package. Install it via `sudo yum install mysql-server` and `sudo aptitude install mysql-server`, respectively. On Ubuntu, the installation process will ask you to enter a MySQL root user password, which is used to secure the MySQL root account. On Red Hat, you need to perform this step manually.

Red Hat

You'll need to make a few basic configuration changes on Red Hat. By default, the MySQL server listens for connections on all configured network interfaces and addresses. This is not very secure, so we'll limit it to the loopback interface only.

We open `/etc/my.cnf` in a text editor and add the following line under the `[mysqld]` section:

```
bind-address = 127.0.0.1
```

We also don't need it to use the old password format, so we can comment out the line that refers to these.

```
# old_passwords=1
```

Our new configuration file will look like Listing 11-4.

Listing 11-4. *Our New* `/etc/my.conf` *on Red Hat*

```
[mysqld]
datadir=/var/lib/mysql
socket=/var/lib/mysql/mysql.sock
user=mysql
```

```
# Default to using old password format for compatibility with mysql 3.x
# clients (those using the mysqlclient10 compatibility package).
# old_passwords=1
bind-address=127.0.0.1

[mysqld_safe]
log-error=/var/log/mysqld.log
pid-file=/var/run/mysqld/mysqld.pid
```

We can now start the MySQL server via the service command. When you first start the MySQL server, the default tables will be configured and you are reminded to set a root password, as in Listing 11-5.

Listing 11-5. *MySQL First Run on Red Hat*

```
$ sudo service mysqld start
Initializing MySQL database:  Installing MySQL system tables...
OK
Filling help tables...
OK
...
```

The server is now running, so we can set a root password and clean up the default tables. The server comes with a utility called mysql_secure_installation that will do this for us, so we don't need to manually run mysqladmin, like the startup script suggested.

```
$ sudo mysql_secure_installation

NOTE: RUNNING ALL PARTS OF THIS SCRIPT IS RECOMMENDED FOR ALL MySQL
      SERVERS IN PRODUCTION USE!  PLEASE READ EACH STEP CAREFULLY!

In order to log into MySQL to secure it, we'll need the current
password for the root user.  If you've just installed MySQL, and
you haven't set the root password yet, the password will be blank,
so you should just press enter here.

Enter current password for root (enter for none):
OK, successfully used password, moving on...

Setting the root password ensures that nobody can log into the MySQL
root user without the proper authorisation.

Set root password? [Y/n] y
New password:
Re-enter new password:
Password updated successfully!
Reloading privilege tables..
 ... Success!
```

By default, a MySQL installation has an anonymous user, allowing anyone to log into MySQL without having to have a user account created for them. This is intended only for testing, and to make the installation go a bit smoother. You should remove them before moving into a production environment.

Remove anonymous users? [Y/n] y
... Success!

Normally, root should only be allowed to connect from 'localhost'. This ensures that someone cannot guess at the root password from the network.

Disallow root login remotely? [Y/n] y
 ... Success!

By default, MySQL comes with a database named 'test' that anyone can access. This is also intended only for testing, and should be removed before moving into a production environment.

Remove test database and access to it? [Y/n] y
 - Dropping test database...
... Success!
 - Removing privileges on test database...
... Success!

Reloading the privilege tables will ensure that all changes made so far will take effect immediately.

Reload privilege tables now? [Y/n] y
 ... Success!

Cleaning up...

All done! If you've completed all of the above steps, your MySQL installation should now be secure.

Thanks for using MySQL!

Our server is now secured. It will not accept connections from remote hosts, and it will not allow users without MySQL accounts to connect. We can have it started automatically by adding its init script to the correct directories via chkconfig:

```
$ sudo chkconfig --level 2345 mysqld on
```

Ubuntu

On Ubuntu, the links in the correct init directories are created automatically and the server is started after the package is installed.

■Tip Also run `mysql_secure_installation` on Ubuntu, to tidy up the privilege tables and remove the test database.

Testing the Server

To check that the MySQL server is running, we can connect to it via the command-line client. We need to specify the `-u` option to specify a user to connect as. The `-p` option will prompt us for the associated password.

```
$ mysql -u root -p
Enter password:
Welcome to the MySQL monitor.  Commands end with ; or \g.
Your MySQL connection id is 11
Server version: 5.0.51a-3ubuntu5.4 (Ubuntu)

Type 'help;' or '\h' for help. Type '\c' to clear the buffer.

mysql> SELECT VERSION();
+--------------------+
| VERSION()          |
+--------------------+
| 5.0.51a-3ubuntu5.4 |
+--------------------+
1 row in set (0.00 sec)

mysql> \q
Bye
```

We are able to connect and run a query; the MySQL server is working fine. Note that the version string that is returned on your host may differ, depending on which MySQL server version is installed.

Basic Tuning for InnoDB

MySQL allows you to pick the way you want it to store your data on the disk by allowing you to specify what storage engine a database should use, as you create the database. If you don't modify the installation, it will use the MyISAM storage engine unless you explicitly pick another one when creating databases.

The MyISAM engine has been around for a long time, but it doesn't support such features as transaction support or foreign keys. Its ability to automatically recover from failure—such as a system crash—is also not fantastic, so we will set a different engine as the default for our server.

We'll configure our server to use the InnoDB storage engine unless otherwise specified. InnoDB supports transactions and foreign keys and is less likely to cause problems if we experience a system crash.

■**Note** You can read about the trade-offs between MyISAM and InnoDB at `http://tag1consulting.com/MySQL_Engines_MyISAM_vs_InnoDB`.

While we're switching over the default storage engine, we'll also make some changes to the server configuration that will improve performance. We'll adjust some variables that control how much RAM the SQL server can use, and how and how often it writes changed data to the disk.

HOW INNODB STORES DATA

InnoDB has a two-tiered storage design. When data in a table changes (e.g., because you run a query), InnoDB stores it in its transaction logs. When the transaction logs fill up, the MySQL server flushes these changed data records to the table files.

The reason for this is performance, just like with a journaling file system. By performing all these operations at once, the disk needs to spend less time jumping around looking for data at all other times.

When the MySQL server shuts down, it does not process these transaction logs, so they usually contain live data. This means they cannot be simply deleted and re-created in order to increase or decrease their size.

We will make a change to the size of the transaction log. The default of 5MB is rather small for systems these days. They fill up quickly, and this means the SQL server is continuously emptying these files, which degrades performance.

Before we change the InnoDB transaction log file size, we need to ensure the transaction log files no longer contain any live data. We can do this by forcing the server to process all entries in the transaction log and write them to the table files when we shut it down. This behavior is controlled by the variable innodb_fast_shutdown, which we can change on a running server by connecting to it as the root user and then running the query SET GLOBAL innodb_fast_shutdown=0, as shown in Listing 11-6.

Listing 11-6. *Forcing an InnoDB Transaction Log Flush at Shutdown*

```
$ mysql -u root -p
Enter password:
Welcome to the MySQL monitor.  Commands end with ; or \g.
Your MySQL connection id is 32
Server version: 5.0.45 Source distribution

Type 'help;' or '\h' for help. Type '\c' to clear the buffer.

mysql> SET GLOBAL innodb_fast_shutdown=0;
Query OK, 0 rows affected (0.00 sec)

mysql> \q
Bye
```

We can now shut down the MySQL server, and it will flush all pending changes from the transaction logs to the table files. That means we can safely move the existing files out of the way and change the transaction log file size. On Red Hat, we do this via `sudo service mysqld stop`, and on Ubuntu via `sudo invoke-rc.d mysql stop`.

The log files are called `ib_logfile0` and `ib_logfile1`, and they can be found in the `/var/lib/mysql` directory. We'll move both of these files out of the way, so the MySQL server can create new ones when we next start it.

```
$ cd /var/lib/mysql
/var/lib/mysql$ sudo mv ib_logfile* /root
```

■**Caution** Do not delete these log files until you've verified that the MySQL server works with its new configuration.

We can now edit the configuration file. On Red Hat, that file is `/etc/my.cnf`, while Ubuntu uses `/etc/mysql/my.cnf`. The file is relatively empty on Red Hat, so you can simply add in the configuration directives we'll give you. On Ubuntu, the file contains a large number of comments and configuration directives already. Where applicable, you should replace the values that are currently in the file with the ones we provide.

All changes we're making here go under the [`mysqld`] section. First, we'll change the default storage engine.

```
default-storage-engine  = InnoDB
```

Next, we'll change the way the InnoDB storage engine behaves.

```
innodb_log_group_home_dir = /var/lib/mysql
innodb_data_home_dir = /var/lib/mysql
innodb_data_file_path = ibdata1:10M:autoextend
innodb_log_file_size = 32M
innodb_log_buffer_size = 4M
innodb_log_files_in_group = 2
innodb_buffer_pool_size = 128M
innodb_flush_method = O_DIRECT
innodb_file_per_table = 1
```

We explicitly define where the InnoDB data and transaction logs are stored. Then we explicitly define the name and size of the default InnoDB data file. This `ibdata` file was created as 10MiB when you first started MySQL, so you should not change the values from what we show here.

We set the InnoDB transaction log file size to 32MiB and the in-memory log buffer to 4MiB. These values mean the server will use a bit more RAM, but it will need to access the disk less often, resulting in better performance. We tell the server it has two transaction log files via `innodb_log_files_in_group`.

Next, we need to assign some RAM for the server to use to keep table data and perform queries. This amount is controlled by the `innodb_buffer_pool_size` variable, and we've set it to

128MiB. This should be a reasonable amount on a modern server that runs MySQL as well as other services. If your server has less than 1GiB of RAM, you may want to lower this value.

We can tell the server not to cache any data in the operating system disk cache by setting `innodb_flush_method`. After all, the data is stored in the memory we've reserved for the InnoDB buffer pool. By specifying `O_DIRECT`, we prevent the system from keeping two copies of the data in RAM. Finally, setting `innodb_file_per_table` causes the server to store each table in each database as a separate file on disk. If we didn't specify this, all data would be appended to the ibdata file, which would grow without limit.

When data is not in RAM and needs to be written from disk, MySQL defaults to reading data one tiny 128-kilobyte chunk at a time. This saves on memory use but is very slow when many megabytes of data need to be read. We'll increase this chunk size via the `read_buffer_size` and `read_rnd_buffer_size` variables.

```
read_buffer_size = 1M
read_rnd_buffer_size = 1M
```

We'll also allow the server to perform very large queries, so larger amounts of data can be stored. The default is 1MiB; we'll change this to 16MiB.

```
max_allowed_packet = 16M
```

Finally, we'll enable the binary log by setting the `log_bin` variable. This will help us recover in case of a crash.

```
log_bin   = /var/log/mysql/mysql-bin.log
expire_logs_days = 14
max_binlog_size = 128M
```

We tell the server to automatically purge binary logs after 14 days. This means we should do a backup of the MySQL data at least every two weeks. (We'll cover how you can automate the backup process in Chapter 13.) Finally, we tell the server to start a new binary log file once the current one reaches a size of 128MiB. This prevents us from having to deal with enormous log files and also makes the process of purging old logs a bit easier, as the server won't need to remove a small part of a single huge log file.

On Red Hat, this log directory does not exist, so we create it and ensure the `mysql` user and group can write to it.

```
$ sudo mkdir /var/log/mysql
$ sudo chown mysql:mysql /var/log/mysql
```

We've now completed our basic MySQL server tweaks, so we can turn it back on via `sudo service mysqld start` on Red Hat or `sudo invoke-rc.d mysql start` on Ubuntu. To verify that the MySQL server is happy and has created the new InnoDB transaction log files, you can check the logs. On Red Hat, `mysql` writes to the `/var/log/mysqld.log` file; on Ubuntu, it uses the `/var/log/syslog` file.

Note that we have not tuned the MySQL server for high-end performance; we've just modified the basic configuration to give us better data integrity and to perform a bit better than it would normally. If you need extremely high performance or advanced features such as data replication across multiple servers, we suggest you read *High Performance MySQL, Second Edition* by Baron Schwartz et al. (O'Reilly Media, Inc., 2008).

Basic MySQL Administration

As you've seen already, MySQL has an internal list of users and passwords. This means that you need to know how to manage MySQL users, as you do not want all applications to connect to the MySQL server as root. We'll demonstrate how to create and remove databases and users via the command-line MySQL client.

Databases

Creating databases in MySQL is easy. You connect to the server via the command-line utility and issue the CREATE DATABASE statement, giving it the database name as a parameter, as shown in Listing 11-7. (Note that we've used uppercase in the SQL statements for clarity only; if you use lowercase, they'll still work fine.)

Listing 11-7. *Creating a New Database in MySQL*

```
$ mysql -u root -p
Enter password:
...
mysql> CREATE DATABASE `mydb`;
Query OK, 1 row affected (0.02 sec)

mysql> USE mydb;
Database changed
mysql> SHOW TABLES:
Empty set (0.00 sec)
```

We created a database called mydb, and then we switched to that database and checked whether it contained any tables. Note that we used backquotes to quote the database name. There is no explicit need to do so in this case, but database, table, and column names can sometimes contain a reserved character such as a hyphen. For instance, if you want to create a database called my-db, you need to use backquotes, otherwise MySQL would interpret my-db as subtracting the value in the db column from the value in the my column. Since neither of these columns exists, an error would be generated, as shown in Listing 11-8.

Listing 11-8. *The Importance of Proper Quoting*

```
mysql> CREATE DATABASE my-db;
ERROR 1064 (42000): You have an error in your SQL syntax; check the manual that
    corresponds to your MySQL server version for the right syntax to use
    near '-db' at line 1

mysql> CREATE DATABASE `my-db`;
Query OK, 1 row affected (0.00 sec)
```

With quotes, the database is created with the specified name.

■Tip When naming databases and tables, it's generally best to use only alphanumeric characters and the underscore character. Even then, proper quoting is a good habit.

We don't need this database, though, so we'll delete it again. We do this via the DROP DATABASE statement.

```
mysql > DROP DATABASE `my-db`;
Query OK, 0 rows affected (0.11 sec)
```

■Caution You cannot undo a DROP DATABASE command, not even if you run it within a transaction and then roll back. Make sure you create a backup before dropping data.

Users and Privileges

Privileges are managed via the GRANT statement. This statement takes a set of parameters that defines a set of operations a user on a given host is allowed to perform on a specific object. In practice, you usually just create a user who is allowed to perform all operations on a single database.

This means that each application that uses its own database gets its own MySQL login. If an application turns out to contain a bug that allows access to the database server, only the data used by that application is at risk.

We connect to the MySQL server as root and then create a user called jsmith, just like our host account, who can access all databases and tables and create new users. This way we do not need to keep using the MySQL root account.

```
mysql> GRANT ALL PRIVILEGES ON *.* TO `jsmith`@`localhost` IDENTIFIED BY 'secret'➥

    WITH GRANT OPTION;
Query OK, 0 rows affected (0.12 sec)

mysql > \q
Bye
```

The preceding code creates a user called jsmith who can connect from localhost only with the password "secret". The ALL keyword specifies the user has all privileges. We use the shorthand *.* to indicate all tables in all databases. We could limit access to tables in a single database called mydb by using mydb.* instead. Finally, we specify the GRANT OPTION, which gives this user permission to use the GRANT statement.

Let's log in as the user we just created and create a user with access only to the mydb database. We don't need to specify a MySQL user to connect as now, as we just created a MySQL user with the same name as our host account.

```
$ mysql -p
Enter password:
```

```
...
mysql> GRANT ALL PRIVILEGES ON `mydb`.* to `mydb`@`localhost` identified➡
    by 'passwd';
Query OK, 0 rows affected (0.00 sec)
```

We now have a user called mydb who can access only tables in the mydb database. Since we have no need for this user at the moment, we'll show you how to delete the user by removing mydb from the system.

```
mysql> DROP USER `mydb`@`localhost`;
Query OK, 0 rows affected (0.00 sec)
```

And since we also have no need for the mydb database, we'll remove that, too.

```
mysql> DROP DATABASE `mydb`;
Query OK, 0 rows affected (0.01 sec)

mysql> \q
Bye
```

Teaching SQL and MySQL administration skills is beyond the scope of this book, but these basic skills will allow you to set up most MySQL-based web applications by following their installation instructions. Many websites are dedicated to teaching MySQL skills, and the online manuals are also excellent sources of information:

- http://dev.mysql.com/doc/refman/5.0/en/index.html

- http://dev.mysql.com/doc/refman/5.0/en/grant.html

- http://dev.mysql.com/doc/refman/5.0/en/drop-user.html

■**Tip** A useful book for learning MySQL skills is *Beginning PHP and MySQL: From Novice to Professional, Third Edition* by W. Jason Gilmore (Apress, 2008).

Installing Websites

With a working web and SQL server, you can now install some web applications to enhance your online presence. In this section, we will show you how to install a few web applications on their own virtual hosts. We will not show you how to use these web applications, as most come with excellent documentation and a support community.

We'll start by creating a group called www to which we will add any users who need to be able to modify the website installations, and we'll add ourselves to that group. We can override the default umask for this group via the -K parameter.

```
$ sudo groupadd -K UMASK=0002 www
$ sudo usermod -G www jsmith
```

Once we log out and log back in, the group membership change will be active.

Next, we'll change the ownership and permissions of the /srv/www/www.example.com directory and any directories it contains, so the www group has full access to it.

```
$ sudo chgrp -R www /srv/www/www.example.com
$ sudo chmod u+rwx,g+srwx,o+rx /srv/www/www.example.com
$ sudo chmod u+rwx,g+srwx,o+rx /srv/www/www.example.com/html
```

Instead of the full permission string, we could have also specified octal mode 2775.

On Red Hat, we need to also tell SELinux that this new directory is used for web content.

```
$ sudo chcon -t httpd_sys_content_t /srv/www/www.example.com/html
```

If we omit this step, SELinux will prevent Apache from accessing any files in our new directory.

Web Presence

Of course, you will want your business to have a web presence, but not at the cost of having to learn HTML. To this end, we will install a content management system (CMS) to use as our website.

A CMS allows us to focus our energy on creating content and making it look good, while providing us with a framework that can save multiple revisions of pages, separates the web content from the graphic design, and manages access permissions for users and staff.

We will install a CMS called Drupal on the www.example.com virtual host. If you have a preference for another system such as Joomla! (http://joomla.org) or eZ Publish (http://ez.no), you can, of course, install it instead. We've chosen Drupal because it is mature, well supported, and easily extensible.

The software is available as a tarball from http://www.drupal.org. The latest version at the time of this writing is Drupal 6.10. We'll download it to our home directory using the wget utility.

```
$ wget http://ftp.drupal.org/files/projects/drupal-6.10.tar.gz
--11:07:45--  http://ftp.drupal.org/files/projects/drupal-6.10.tar.gz
Resolving ftp.drupal.org... 64.50.236.52, 64.50.238.52
Connecting to ftp.drupal.org|64.50.236.52|:80... connected.
HTTP request sent, awaiting response... 200 OK
Length: 1075558 (1.0M) [application/x-gzip]
Saving to: 'drupal-6.10.tar.gz'

100%[==============================================>] 1,075,558    382K/s   in 2.7s

11:07:48 (382 KB/s) - 'drupal-6.10.tar.gz' saved [1075558/1075558]
```

Next, we unpack the tarball. We can unpack it here and then move the required files and directories to the web root, or we can unpack it directly to the web root. We'll do the latter by telling tar to strip the first directory component from the archive and specifying a target directory using the -C option.

```
$ tar -xz --strip-components=1 -C➥
    /srv/www/www.example.com/html -f drupal-6.10.tar.gz
```

■**Tip** To find out which directories a tar archive contains, use the `-t` and `-v` options to display a list of files without extracting them (e.g., `tar -tvzf drupal-6.10.tar.gz`).

With the site content in the correct location, we can now point our web browser at `http://example.com/`. This will allow us to start the web-based installation process, as shown in Figure 11-12.

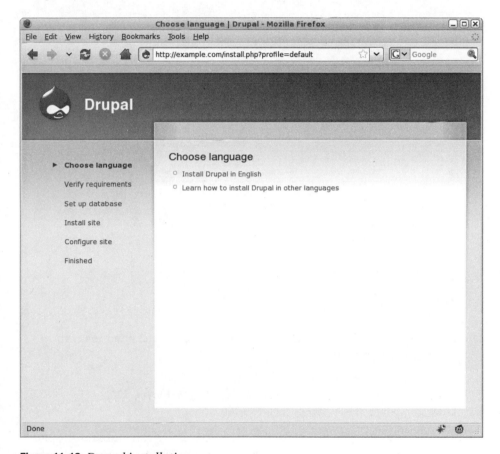

Figure 11-12. *Drupal installation*

To proceed, we click Install Drupal in English. The next page, shown in Figure 11-13, tells us that the installer needs us to create a file on the hard disk that it can write its settings to and a directory that it can use to store files.

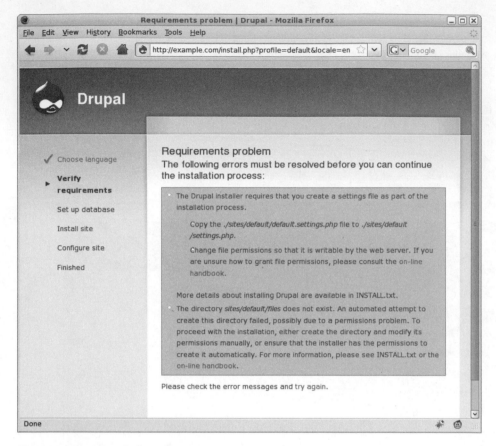

Figure 11-13. *Alert telling us that we need to create a writeable file*

We can resolve these issues by creating the required file and directory and giving them appropriate ownership and permissions.

```
$ cd /srv/www/www.example.com/html
$ cp sites/default/default.settings.php sites/default/settings.php
$ mkdir sites/default/files
```

We can manage write access to these locations in two ways: we can make the file and directory writeable by "other," or we can keep them writeable by our www group, but change the owner to the user the web server runs as. The second way will prevent any other users from overwriting the Drupal configuration file and storing data in the files directory.

On Red Hat, the web server runs as the apache user, and on Ubuntu it runs as www-data, so chown the file and directory as required.

```
$ sudo chown apache sites/default/settings.php
$ sudo chown apache sites/default/files
```

With these permissions changed, we can reload the page in our web browser. We're now taken to a page where we need to enter MySQL credentials. First, we'll create a database and user. It's a good practice to give the database the same name as the application that uses it and create a user of the same name. As long as you choose a secure password, this will not be a problem.

```
$ mysql -p
Enter password:
...
mysql> CREATE DATABASE `drupal`;
Query OK, 1 row affected (0.04 sec)

mysql> GRANT ALL PRIVILEGES ON `drupal`.* to `drupal`@`localhost` IDENTIFIED➥
    BY 'Fishao4h';
Query OK, 0 rows affected (0.20 sec)

mysql> \q
Bye
```

Now we can enter these details into the Drupal installer, as shown in Figure 11-14.

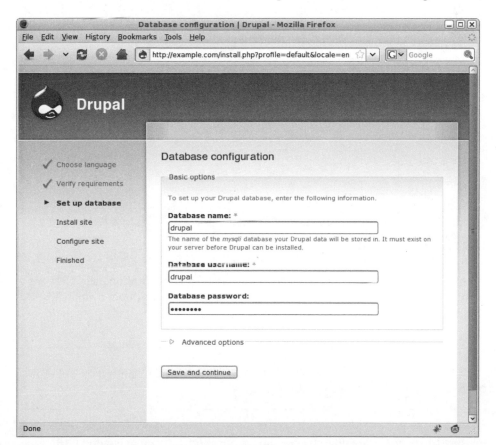

Figure 11-14. *Entering database details*

We click the Save and Continue button to begin the installation process, which will populate the database with the required tables and data. While this happens, a progress bar keeps us informed, as shown in Figure 11-15.

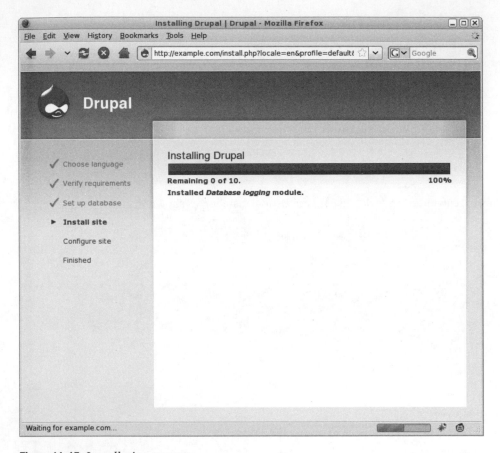

Figure 11-15. *Installation progress*

When installation is complete, we're taken to the basic site configuration page. Here we set the site name, create an administration user, and click Save and continue. Drupal finishes the configuration and asks us to visit our new website.

■**Note** Remember to change back the ownership of the `sites/default.settings.php` file when installation is complete, so Apache can no longer modify it.

From the main page, we are now able to manage our site, as shown in Figure 11-16.

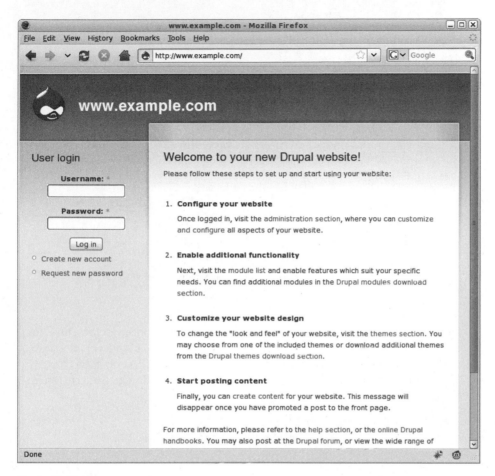

Figure 11-16. *Our new web presence*

A wealth of information about Drupal is available online at http://drupal.org:

- *Manual*: http://drupal.org/getting-started
- *Themes*: http://drupal.org/project/themes
- *Modules*: http://drupal.org/project/modules

Webmail

To provide remote access to e-mail for our users, we will install a webmail package on a virtual web host, which we'll call webmail.example.com. First, we need to add an IP address to our server and create an A entry for this address on the DNS server.

When you assign network addresses for hosts on your network, it is a good idea to reserve some addresses for virtual websites. We'll use the address 192.168.0.220.

■**Note** We explained how to add extra addresses to a network interface in Chapter 6 and how to add DNS hostnames and aliases in Chapter 9.

Next, we need to set up an IP-based virtual host in Apache that uses the `/srv/www/webmail.example.com/html` directory as the document root. We can't use a name-based virtual host because we want to protect our users' privacy with SSL. To this end, we'll create a certificate for Apache to use. This is done using `openssl` in exactly the same way as the certificate for the mail server:

```
$ openssl req -new -newkey rsa:4096 -nodes -keyout webmail.example.com.key➡
    -out webmail.example.com.req
```

■**Note** Don't forget to sign the server certificate using your CA, as we discussed in Chapter 10.

It would be good to store all virtual host–related files in one location, so create a directory called `/srv/www/webmail.example.com/ssl` and move the certificate and key you created into this directory. Make sure the Apache user account can read these files by setting the correct permissions using `chmod` and, if needed, the correct SELinux security context using `chcon` on Red Hat.

```
$ sudo chmod 0640 /srv/www/webmail.example.com/ssl/*
$ sudo chcon -R system_u:object_r:cert_t /srv/www/webmail.example.com/ssl
```

Red Hat

On Red Hat, you need to install SSL support for Apache first. This is provided by the `mod_ssl` package, which you can install via `sudo yum install mod_ssl`. Then you need to disable the default virtual SSL host that the module has enabled, as it will otherwise interfere with your configuration.

In a text editor, open the file `/etc/httpd/conf.d/ssl.conf` and comment out the `VirtualHost` directives on lines 81 and 228 by adding a hash mark in front of each:

```
# <VirtualHost _default_:443>
# </VirtualHost>
```

After saving these changes, restart Apache and start `system-config-httpd` via System ➤ Administration ➤ Server Settings ➤ HTTP.

Next, select the Virtual Hosts tab and click Add to add a new virtual host. Give your new virtual host a descriptive name and enter the correct document root and e-mail address (see Figure 11-17).

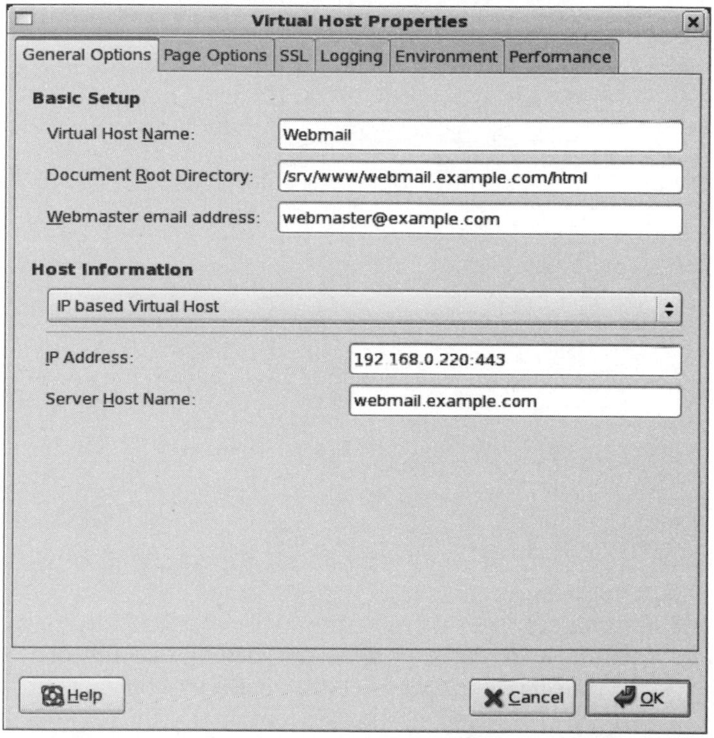

Figure 11-17. *Creating an IP-based virtual host on Red Hat*

Under Host Information, choose IP based Virtual Host and enter the IP address and port number this host should be available on and the hostname you want it to use. Then go to the Page Options tab and add index.php to the Directory Page Search List. This will ensure Apache will process and display the `index.php` file (if it is present) when a user accesses the website.

Finally, switch to the SSL tab and check the Enable SSL support box. This will enable the text fields that allow you to tell the server which certificates and keys to use.

Enter the full path to the Certificate File and Certificate Key File, as shown in Figure 11-18.

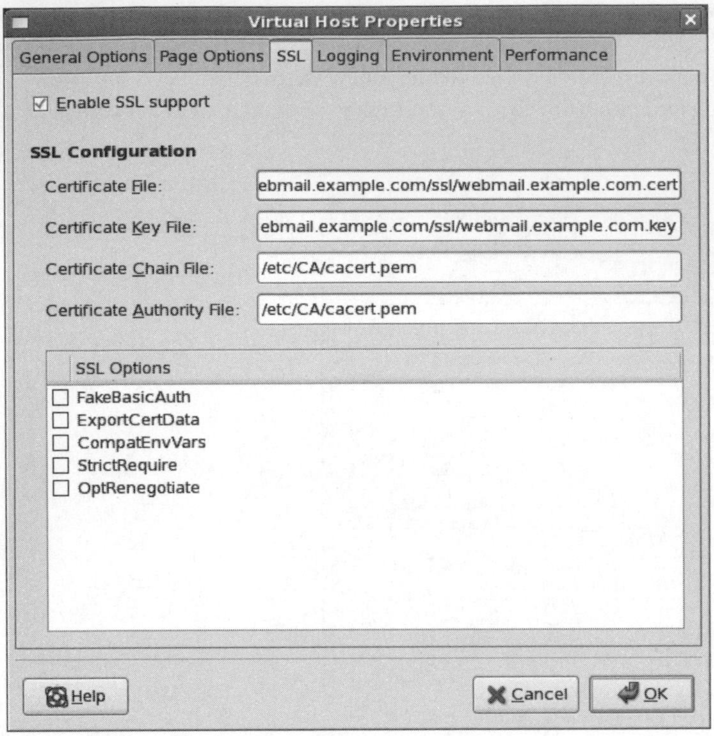

Figure 11-18. *Setting SSL properties*

If you purchase a commercial certificate from some providers, such as GoDaddy or InstantSSL, you will need to install a certificate chain file as well. This chain file contains the provider's signed certificate, and it is needed by a web browser to ascertain that the provider's signature on your own certificate is valid.

We don't have such a chain file for our self-signed certificate, but if we leave the Certificate Chain File field empty, Apache will refuse to start. To work around this issue, we can enter the location of our self-signed certificate in the chain file field. We also need to enter it in the Certificate Authority File field.

The virtual host is now configured, so you can accept these values and close the HTTP utility, saving your changes.

Finally, you need to enable access to SSL websites through your firewall by allowing traffic on TCP port 443. Then restart Apache.

Ubuntu

On Ubuntu, the SSL module for Apache is installed by default, but you do need to enable it via `sudo a2enmod ssl` before you can use it. Then you need to tell Apache you want it to listen for requests on the SSL port on the 192.168.0.220 address.

As you saw earlier, you can do this in the `/etc/apache2/ports.conf` file. To make sure Apache listens only on this port when the SSL module is loaded, we set the `Listen` directive inside an `IfModule` statement. To make sure Apache does not listen on port 443 on all addresses, we prefix the port number with the address, as shown in Listing 11-9.

Listing 11-9. *Conditionally Listen on the SSL Port*

```
<IfModule mod_ssl.c>
    Listen 192.168.0.200:443
</IfModule>
```

Next, we need to create the virtual host file, which we'll do in `/etc/apache2/sites-available/webmail.example.com.conf`. We'll again wrap the configuration inside an `IfModule` statement, so the SSL directives will not cause Apache to fail when the module isn't loaded.

We define our virtual host to run only on address 192.168.0.220, port 443, and set `ServerName`, `ServerAdmin`, and `DocumentRoot`. We also set some default options on the document root directory, as shown in Listing 11-10.

Listing 11-10. *Secure Virtual Host Configuration*

```
<IfModule mod_ssl.c>
  <VirtualHost 192.168.0.220:443>
    ServerName webmail.example.com
    ServerAdmin webmaster@example.com
    DocumentRoot /srv/www/webmail.example.com/html
    <Directory /srv/www/webmail.example.com/html>
      Options FollowSymLinks Includes IncludesNOEXEC SymLinksIfOwnerMatch
      AllowOverride All
    </Directory>
    SSLEngine on
    SSLCertificateFile /srv/www/webmail.example.com/ssl/webmail.example.com.cert
    SSLCertificateKeyFile /srv/www/webmail.example.com/ssl/webmail.example.com.key
    SSLCACertificateFile /etc/CA/cacert.pem
  </VirtualHost>
</IfModule>
```

To make sure all communication with this site is encrypted, we need to turn on SSL for this virtual host, which we can do via the `SSLEngine on` directive. Because we've included the directive within a `VirtualHost` block, this will turn SSL on only for this specific virtual host.

Finally, we need to tell the SSL engine which host certificate, host key, and CA certificate to use. When that is done, we can enable this virtual host using `sudo a2ensite webmail.example.com` and restart Apache.

Configuring SquirrelMail

We'll now show you how to set up the SquirrelMail web application on your new secure virtual host. SquirrelMail is just one of a variety of webmail applications available. You may have used others, such as RoundCube (`http://roundcube.net`) or the Horde Project's IMP (`http://horde.org/imp`).

SquirrelMail is available from `http://squirrelmail.org/` and the latest version at the time of this writing is 1.4.7. After downloading the tarball to your home directory, you can extract it to the correct directory.

```
$ tar -xz --strip-components=1 -C /srv/www/webmail.example.com/html➡
    -f squirrelmail-1.4.17.tar.gz
```

When you point your web browser at the new virtual host, you get an error, as Squirrel-Mail does not provide a web-based configuration process. The software comes with README and INSTALL files, though, which explain how to proceed.

```
$ cd /srv/www/webmail.example.com/html
$ less README
$ less INSTALL
```

You can follow the quick installation guide and skip the first three steps, which you've already completed. Next, you need to create directories for preferences and attachments. Because our web tree is a subdirectory of our virtual host directory, we can create these new directories under /srv/www/webmail.example.com/ as well, and not under /var as the documentation suggests. This has the advantage that when we do a backup, all data related to this virtual host is available in the same location, so we're unlikely to forget to back it up.

Create the directories data and attach in the virtual host directory and change their ownership as the INSTALL file suggests, so the Apache user can write to them.

```
$ cd /srv/www/webmail.example.com
$ sudo mkdir data attach
$ sudo chown apache:www data
$ sudo chgrp apache attach
$ sudo chmod 0730 attach
```

On Red Hat, you also need to change the SELinux label on these directories.

```
$ sudo chcon -t httpd_sys_content_t data attach
```

You can then continue with the next step, which is to run the configuration script.

```
$ cd /srv/www/webmail.example.com/html
$ ./config/conf.pl
```

You're now in the SquirrelMail configuration utility, as shown in Figure 11-19.

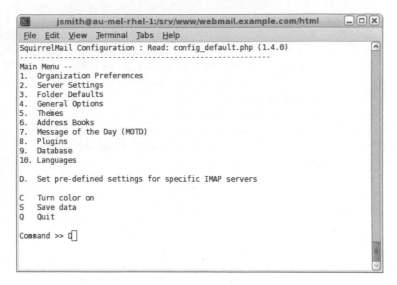

Figure 11-19. *SquirrelMail configuration*

Type **D** and press Enter. On the next screen, you need to load the default options for your
IMAP server (dovecot, in our case). Type in the name of the server and press Enter again. You
are shown the IMAP-specific options that are now set (see Figure 11-20).

Figure 11-20. *Choosing the IMAP server software*

Press Enter again to accept these settings and return to the main menu. (Pressing any other key will not, in fact, do anything.)

Next, you can change the mail server settings. We choose menu item 2, and since our web host is also our mail host, we don't need to make any modifications here. However, if we used different hosts for web and mail, we would change the host setting for both IMAP and SMTP. Return to the main menu by typing **r** and pressing Enter.

You still need to tell SquirrelMail about the data and attachment directories; you can do this via the General Options. Type **4** and then press Enter. Next, you set the data directory by typing **1**, followed by Enter. You can now enter the full path to the directory created earlier, as shown in Figure 11-21. When you're finished, press Enter.

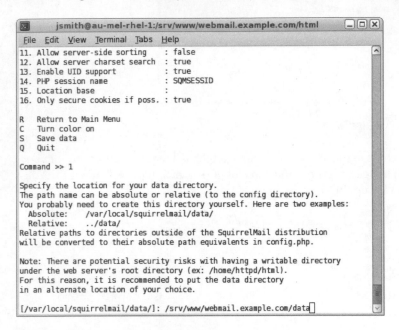

Figure 11-21. *Setting the data directory*

We set the attachments directory to /srv/www/webmail.example.com/attach by choosing option 2.

The basic configuration is done. Press r to return to the main menu, and then save the configuration by pressing s and then Enter. The utility will create a config.php file, and you can close it by pressing q.

When you reload the web browser, you are presented with the SquirrelMail login screen, as shown in Figure 11-22.

Figure 11-22. *You can log in to SquirrelMail from anywhere.*

Other Web Applications

We've shown you how to install two web applications in a virtual host of their own, which should provide you with a basic understanding of the process. We can't include installation guidance for all web applications here, but we can suggest some that you might find useful.

The phpMyAdmin tool provides a web-based interface to MySQL. It allows you to create databases and tables, import and export data, and manage users. You can download it from http://www.phpmyadmin.net/.

MediaWiki is a collaboration tool that runs Wikipedia (among other sites). You can download it from http://www.mediawiki.org/.

Moodle is a course or learning management system. It is used by many schools to provide web-based learning to their students. You can download it from http://www.moodle.org/.

SugarCRM is customer relationship management (CRM) software that can help you and your organization's salespeople manage clients and client relationships. You can download it from http://www.sugarcrm.com/.

Squid Cache

When multiple users in your office start browsing the web simultaneously, they can end up using quite a lot of bandwidth. To help minimize the impact of web browsing on other network users, you can install a cache or proxy server.

The most commonly used cache on Linux is Squid. When your browser is configured to use the cache, it keeps local copies of any files you retrieve from a website, so the next time the same file is accessed, it can be served from the local Squid cache instead.

The other mode of operation for Squid is as a *reverse proxy*, which sits in front of one or more web servers on the web server side of the connection. A reverse proxy is used when sites serve large amounts of content that doesn't change very often. By allowing the data that does not change to be cached by the reverse proxy, the load on the underlying web servers can be reduced. This kind of proxy is also known as a *web accelerator*. An example of a large website that uses Squid as web accelerator is Flickr (`http://www.flickr.com`).

Configuration

Squid is provided by the `squid` package. Install it via `sudo yum install squid` on Red Hat or `sudo aptitude install squid` on Ubuntu. Both distributions use the same configuration file for Squid, which is `/etc/squid/squid.conf`. Because this file can contain sensitive information (e.g., passwords), you cannot even view it without using `sudo`.

The default configuration file is well commented, so we won't go into great detail about most options. However, we will show you how to configure which address and port Squid should listen on, and how to configure it so your users are actually permitted to access the Web via the cache.

Squid listens on port 3128 on all network interfaces by default, though port 8080 is used commonly as well. The directive to modify the port in the configuration file is `http_port`. This directive allows you to specify a port number or an address and port number combination. If you want Squid to listen on multiple addresses and ports, you can add more `http_port` directives.

Because we're setting up Squid on the gateway host, we don't want it to listen for connections on all interfaces; users not on our local networks should not be able to access it. We thus need to add two `http_port` lines: one for the wireless network address range and one for the wired range.

```
http_port 192.168.0.254:3128
http_port 192.168.1.254:3128
```

Next, we need to tell Squid which ranges of IP addresses are allowed to connect to it and access websites. Squid uses access control lists (ACLs) for this. For each network range you want to control, you need to define an ACL. You then create rules that control access for each ACL. The configuration file contains a few basic ACLs, which we've included in Listing 11-11.

Listing 11-11. *ACL Definitions*

```
acl all src 0.0.0.0/0.0.0.0
acl localhost src 127.0.0.1/255.255.255.255
acl to_localhost dst 127.0.0.0/8
```

The `acl` directive tells Squid the rest of the line is an ACL definition. Next, we give the ACL a label, so we can refer to it later on. Then we specify the ACL type we're creating. Squid supports many types, but we'll be using only `src`, `dst`, and `port`, which control whether we're dealing with source addresses, destination addresses, or port numbers. Finally, we define the source, destination, or port using a string. To get a full list of ACL types, you can read through the ACL section on the Squid website at `http://www.squid-cache.org/Versions/v2/2.6/cfgman/acl.html`.

In our case, we've defined an ACL called `all` that encompasses all Internet addresses. The next ACL allows us to refer to all traffic originating on the local network interface as `localhost`. The third does the same, but for traffic *to* the local network interface.

Let's add in some ACLs for our network addresses. We can add these directly under the line that defines `to_localhost`.

```
acl wired src 192.168.0.0/255.255.255.0
acl wireless src 192.168.1.0/255.255.255.0
```

We've defined two new ACLs, one for the wired network range and one for the wireless range. We could have combined them by simply specifying the same label for both ACLs. However, giving them different names means we can give them different levels of access to the Web, should we want to.

Squid contains an ACL called `Safe_ports` that contains commonly used ports for web and FTP traffic. This way, you can control which ports on remote servers you want local users to be able to connect to. If a site you need to access runs on a nonstandard port, you can add the port number to the `Safe_ports` ACL and so permit browsers to connect to it.

```
acl Safe_ports port 80       # http
acl Safe_ports port 21       # ftp
acl Safe_ports port 443      # https
```

Now that we have defined all the ACLs we need, we can complete our configuration by defining access rules for these ACLs. Squid uses the `http_access` directive to determine whether a given ACL is allowed to use the cache. This directive has two parameters, an action and an ACL. These directives are processed in order, and processing stops when a rule matches.

The first rule prevents browsers from connecting to ports we haven't explicitly listed in the Safe_ports ACL.

```
http_access deny !Safe_ports
```

Next, `localhost` is permitted to connect and all other connections are rejected.

```
http_access allow localhost
http_access deny all
```

If no `http_access` rule matches, the opposite of the last seen action is applied. This is why it's important to always leave `http_access deny all` in place as the final rule; it means Squid will deny access unless it encounters a rule to allow access.

We should insert our new rules in between, as shown in Listing 11-12.

Listing 11-12. *Granting Access for Our Networks*

```
http_access allow localhost
http_access allow wired
http_access allow wireless
http_access deny all
```

Finally, we can change the directory on the disk that Squid uses to store its cached objects using the `cache_dir` directive. This is commented out, which means it will use the built-in default, as follows.

```
# cache_dir ufs /var/spool/squid 100 16 256
```

The preceding line tells Squid to store cache objects under the `/var/spool/squid` directory in `ufs` format. It will store a maximum of 100MiB of objects; after that, older objects will be expired from the cache and replaced by newer ones. The final two numbers control how many subdirectories Squid will create in the main cache directory. In this case, it will create 16 main subdirectories, each containing another 256 subdirectories.

This subdirectory schema came about because most file systems are quite slow at accessing directories containing a large number of files. For example, if each of the Squid subdirectories contained about 100 cached files, the total number of files in the cache would be over 400,000. If they were all stored in a single directory, each time one of these files was requested by a browser, the host would need to search through up to 400,000 entries in the directory inode, to find out where the data it needs is stored. By subdividing the cache, the number of inodes that need to be searched for any given file is much smaller, resulting in less performance degradation as the cache grows.

Since disk space is generally cheaper than bandwidth, we'll allow our cache to grow bigger.

```
cache_dir ufs /var/spool/squid 512 16 256
```

We save the configuration file and start Squid. On Red Hat, we should create the startup links via `chkconfig` first:

```
$ sudo /sbin/chkconfig --level 2345 squid on
```

We can now start Squid via `sudo service squid start` on Red Hat or restart it on Ubuntu via `sudo invoke-rc.d squid restart`. On Red Hat, the cache directory we specified will be created when Squid first starts. This already happened on Ubuntu, when we installed the package.

Client Configuration

All that is left for us to do is configure our web browser to use the proxy. In Firefox, we choose Edit ➤ Preferences, then select the Network tab, and then click the Settings button. We choose "Manual proxy configuration" and enter the address and port number for our proxy, as shown in Figure 11-23.

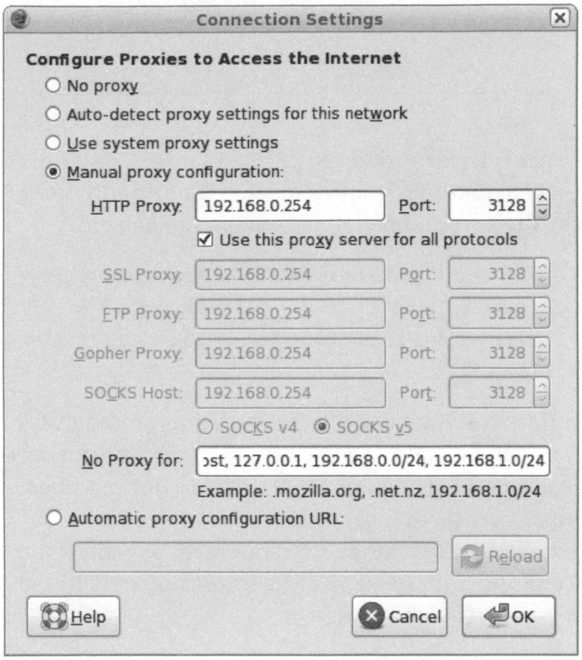

Figure 11-23. *Setting a proxy server in Firefox*

Also, we tell Firefox not to use the cache for any hosts on our local network by adding the two local network ranges, 192.168.0.0/24 and 192.168.1.0/24, in the No Proxy for list. We then close the network and Firefox settings and visit our favorite website. We can verify that the proxy is being used by looking at the Squid access logs, which are stored in /var/log/squid/access.log.

Transparency

If you don't want to make your users change their proxy settings in order to use the Squid cache, you can run Squid as a transparent proxy instead. A *transparent proxy* is one that has all outbound web traffic redirected to it via firewalling rules. Browsers accessing the Web don't know they're using a cache, and you don't need to explicitly configure any web browsers to use it.

To turn our current configuration into a transparent proxy, we have to make two small changes to the configuration file. For each http_port directive, we need to add the option transparent.

```
http_port 192.168.0.254:3128 transparent
http_port 192.168.1.254:3128 transparent
```

After restarting Squid, we add firewall rules on the gateway host. These rules should intercept all connections to remote websites and redirect them to our proxy instead. We want to change the destination address and port number on packets before the gateway sends them out to the Internet. This is a form of network address translation, and it is done by Netfilter in the nat table. Since we want to change the packet destination before anything else happens, we'll do this in the PREROUTING chain.

■**Note** We cover firewalls in Chapter 6.

To change the destination address of a packet, we need to use the DNAT target. This target requires the `--to-destination` parameter, which in turn requires a destination IP address with an optional port number. If we don't specify the port number, it will remain unchanged.

```
$ sudo iptables -t nat -A PREROUTING -i eth0 -d ! 192.168.0.0/16 -p tcp --dport 80➥
    -j DNAT --to-destination 192.168.0.254:3128
$ sudo iptables -t nat -A PREROUTING -i eth1 -d ! 192.168.0.0/16 -p tcp --dport 80➥
    -j DNAT --to-destination 192.168.1.254:3128
```

We specify the network device the traffic is coming in on via the `-i` option, so requests from the Internet to hosts on our own network are not affected. We also want to intercept only web requests, so we specify that we want our rule to match only TCP traffic to port number 80. Finally, this rule should only apply to hosts not on our local network, so we need to make sure traffic to local web hosts is not affected. We specify that the rule should match only if the destination address is not in the 192.168.0.0 through 192.168.255.255 address range via the `-d` option, which we prefix with an exclamation point to signify NOT.

■**Caution** If your transparent proxy host is not the gateway host, you should make sure it can access remote websites directly, without being redirected to itself.

Summary

In this chapter, we've shown you how to use your Linux host as a flexible web server with SQL support and how to make use of this by installing web services. You should now be able to do the following:

- Create and manage virtual websites.

- Add functionality to Apache via modules.

- Control access to sites based on hostname or username and password.

- Create and manage MySQL databases and users.

- Install and configure third-party web applications.

- Configure a web proxy to save on bandwidth costs and increase speed.

In the next chapter, we will expand the use of the server by adding file- and print-sharing capabilities.

CHAPTER 12

■■■

File and Print Sharing

By Dennis Matotek

One of the most common office functions is sharing and printing documents and files. In this chapter, we will show you how this can be done using Linux. Linux provides many ways to share information. It can share information with Microsoft Windows clients using an integration tool called Samba. It can also share documents between Linux (and other Unix) hosts using a tool called Network File System (NFS).

We're going to go beyond basic file sharing though and show you how Linux can be a platform for very cheap and very effective document management. In modern companies, sharing documents is an important function; however, document management—controlling documents from creation to publication—is vital as a part of the security and document control processes giving granularity that simple file system sharing cannot achieve. So we will also introduce you to the freely available KnowledgeTree, a document management system (DMS) that represents a comprehensive alternative to Microsoft's SharePoint application.

Lastly, we'll show you how to configure printing and print services on your Linux host. We'll demonstrate both how to print from your host and how to make your host act as a print server. Printing on Linux is very easy to implement, and both Red Hat and Ubuntu share a common toolset that makes it easy to implement and manage.

The ultimate aim of this chapter is to provide a comprehensive, modern, and secure data-sharing network. Samba will serve as our domain controller, providing access from our desktops to users' home directories and printer services. We will demonstrate the use NFS servers to mount file systems across our Linux hosts to share data between them. All documents in our office will be controlled via the DMS, bringing with it secure HTTP access, version control, and workflow practices. In this chapter, we will show you how this can be achieved.

File Sharing with Samba and NFS

File sharing is the ability to share documents between your users. Rather than everyone keeping company documents on their individual desktop computers and passing them via means such as e-mail, we centralize the documents in one place and allow our staff to access them in a controlled and secure way. The benefits of this are enormous, as it cuts down on the proliferation of multiple copies of one document on everyone's desktop and makes restricting access and backing up documents much easier. Certain applications require a file share before they can be accessed by desktop clients, and file sharing can be used for this.

On your Windows desktops, you will see a file share as a mapped network drive. A file share can be assigned when you log in to your host either via a domain controller that runs login scripts or manually when you require one. You can also mount file shares on your Linux desktop. Linux desktops can easily mount a Samba or an NFS share; however, they can't run Windows executable files without some modification.

■**Note** You may get some success running some Windows applications using software developed by Wine (`http://www.winehq.org`). This open source community works on integrating a selected group of Windows applications to run on Linux operating systems. There is also a supported version offered by sister organization CodeWeavers (`http://www.codeweavers.com`).

File sharing can be achieved in many ways using Linux, depending on your needs for access, security, and the clients that you have to support. Linux can provide a good platform for traditional file sharing, as it gives you the ability to mount a network drive on your client host. This allows for access to common data shared by a centralized file server host. The two main tools for achieving this are Samba for Microsoft Windows desktops and NFS for Linux or Unix hosts.

Samba can provide user authentication for file shares and printer services. NFS on its own does not provide any user authentication, but it can be integrated into a Kerberos domain for authentication. This is a complicated setup, and we will not attempt to cover it in this book.

Next, we give you an up-close look at Samba.

Samba

Samba is a file-sharing and printing service for Linux. It operates in the standard client-server model with a daemon accepting requests from network clients. It is based on the Common Internet File System (CIFS) and Server Message Block (SMB) protocols, the protocols that handle interhost communications of the file system on Microsoft products, making it compatible with Microsoft Windows desktop clients and Microsoft Windows domain services.

Samba servers can therefore be combined into a Windows domain to provide an integrated and cheap file-sharing solution. In addition, Samba is also capable of providing file and print services to your hosts, as either a domain controller or a file and print server.

SAMBA VS. MICROSOFT WINDOWS

Most organizations require a file server of sorts, and the main competition to Samba is your typical Microsoft Windows server. Microsoft Windows servers on a basic level are just file and print servers much like Samba servers. Microsoft currently does support an advanced centralized user management system in its Active Directory LDAP server, which is closely integrated into its file and print servers. Samba can achieve almost the same level of functionality at present with Samba and OpenLDAP. To get these benefits requires a little more effort to integrate them nicely. Depending on your environment, this may or may not be worth your effort.

Samba is soon to release its Samba 4 server, which will match a Microsoft Active Directory (AD) file and print server. Its close integration with OpenLDAP will allow easy setup of a single authentication server for file sharing, web access, and e-mail—some of the primary resources in a company today.

What we plan to do is show you how to set up a simple file and print server using Samba that will allow you to share documents with your co-workers. You will also learn how to set up a Samba domain server so your users can authenticate and get their user home directories mounted to their desktops, as well as how to set up a departmental share that you can also mount to your desktop.

First you need to install the software. Both Red Hat and Ubuntu require the same packages to get Samba up and running.

On Red Hat, you issue the following:

```
$ sudo yum install samba-client samba-common samba system-config-samba
```

On Ubuntu:

```
$ sudo aptitude install samba-client samba-common samba system-config-samba
```

The samba-common package may already be installed on your host, but requiring it to be installed will not cause any errors.

Once the packages are installed, you can start to configure Samba. Samba can be configured via a GUI or using a configuration file. Both Ubuntu and Red Hat store the configuration file for Samba in /etc/samba/smb.conf.

In our example configuration, we are going to set up our Samba host as a domain controller. It will share the user's home directories, a temporary directory called tmp, and a departmental file share called sales.

Authentication for those user accounts can be stored on the host itself, as we are about to demonstrate, or Samba can query an LDAP server for that information. Integration with LDAP for Samba is not an automatic configuration option, so it has to be manually set in your smb.conf file. We will show you both types in this chapter, even though we don't really discuss setting up an LDAP server until Chapter 16.

We are going to apply the following configuration file to our Samba server. We will take you through what each setting does shortly. First, let's move the existing configuration file to smb.conf.bak (sudo mv /etc/samba/smb.conf /etc/samba/smb.conf.bak). In Listing 12-1, you can see the configuration we wish to create and use for our Samba service (sudo vi /etc/samba/smb.conf).

Listing 12-1. *Samba /etc/samba/smb.conf File*

```
[global]

        workgroup = EXAMPLE
        server string = Samba Server Version %v
        netbios name = au-fileserver-1
#================ network info ===================
        interfaces = lo eth0
        hosts allow = 127. 192.168.
```

```
#================ logging ======================
        log file = /var/log/samba/%m.log
        max log size = 50


#================ domain info ===================
        domain master = yes
        domain logons = yes

        local master = yes
        os level = 33
        preferred master = yes

        security = user
        passdb backend = tdbsam

        logon path = \\%L\Profiles\%u
        logon script = %u.bat


#================ user administration ===============
        add user script = /usr/sbin/useradd "%u" -n -g users
        add group script = /usr/sbin/groupadd "%g"
        add machine script = /usr/sbin/useradd -n -c "Workstation (%u)" ➡
-M -d /nohome -s /bin/false "%u"
        delete user script = /usr/sbin/userdel "%u"
        delete user from group script = /usr/sbin/userdel "%u" "%g"
        delete group script = /usr/sbin/groupdel "%g"


#================ printing info ====================
        load printers = yes
        cups options = raw
        printcap name = cups


#================ services offered ===================
[homes]
        comment = Home Directories
        browseable = no
        writable = yes
        valid users = %S
        valid users = EXAMPLE\%S

[printers]
        comment = All Printers
        path = /var/spool/samba
        browseable = no
        guest ok = no
        writable = no
        printable = yes
```

```
[netlogon]
        comment = Network Logon Service
        path = /var/lib/samba/netlogon
        guest ok = yes
        writable = no
        share modes = no

[profiles]
        path = /var/lib/samba/profiles
        browseable = no
        guest ok = yes
        read only = no

[tmp]
        comment = temporary directory
        path = /tmp
        public = yes
        writable = yes
        printable = no

[sales]
        comment = shared sales directory
        path = /data/staff/sales
        readonly = yes
        public = no
        browseable = yes
        valid users = +sales
        write list = jsmith, bsingh
        force create mode = 0770
        force directory mode = 0770
        create mask = 0770
        directory mask = 0770
        force group = sales
        force user  = exbackup
```

The configuration file can be broken up into two sections, the [global] configuration options and then the specific configurations options, like [tmp], [home], and so forth. The [global] section, as the name implies, defines the configuration options that affect the whole server, and the specific configurations in [tmp] and [home] affect only those services they are trying to define.

Let's now go through the [Global] section. First you see the option workgroup. This option should be familiar to you if you are a Windows user. It is the workgroup name that will appear in your network neighborhood. A *workgroup* is a collection of computers sharing information. Usually, in a workgroup, the computers do not have central authentication, and each host in the workgroup takes care of its own authentication. In other words, you maintain a list of users with access to each host on each host.

Central authentication is achieved when one of the hosts in the workgroup becomes a primary domain controller (PDC). Hosts join the domain and then use the PDC to authenticate user access to their resources. If the host is not part of a domain, it can still share resources, but it will have to maintain its own authentication and access lists.

Setting the workgroup here does not make our host a PDC, just part of a workgroup. We have set this to our domain name, EXAMPLE.

```
workgroup = EXAMPLE
```

The next option is `server string`. The *server string* is the description that is displayed by your Samba service. The %v is a special variable that refers to the version of the Samba server. In ours, this will be 3.0.28 for Ubuntu or 3.0.28a for Red Hat.

Next you need to configure NetBIOS. NetBIOS is a local broadcast protocol that is used to handle connection information between hosts. NetBIOS information is used to match names to IP addresses in WINS servers, kind of like DNS. The NetBIOS protocol itself is used for a name service, session service, and datagram server. As you can see in Listing 12-1, we are setting the `netbios name` option to `au-fileserver-1`, and we will be able to use this NetBIOS name to refer to our host.

■**Note** If you are interested in a further explanation of NetBIOS, please read http://en.wikipedia.org/wiki/NetBIOS.

The next section deals with network interface and IP address access controls. Using the `interfaces` option, you can define which networks or network devices you want your Samba service to listen on; settings `lo`, `eth0`, `bond0`, and `192.168.0.1` are all valid depending on your network. If your host has multiple networks attached to the single interface, you can specify that the service only listen for connections on one of those networks.

For example, suppose our eth0 interface was configured with the following two IP addresses and networks: 192.168.0.1/24 and 192.168.10.1/24. If we started our Samba service and specified `interfaces = eth0`, our service will start on the 192.168.0.1 and 192.168.10.1 IP addresses and provide Samba service to the 192.168.0.0/24 and 192.168.10.0/24 networks. We might not want hosts on the 192.168.10.0/24 network to access this host. So instead of specifying eth0 as our interface, we would be more succinct and specify 192.168.0.1 instead. This tells Samba to only start services on the 192.168.0.1 address.

In our example, we are not concerned about the networks that access this host and want the Samba service to be available on our `lo` (loopback) device and eth0.

```
interfaces = lo eth0
```

■**Note** You can confirm this by using the `netstat -ltup` command, which will list the applications or services attached to your network interfaces.

You can further control access to your Samba service by specifying what hosts can access your service by using the `hosts allow` option. In our configuration, we specify the loopback network and the 192.168.0. network. The notations `127.` and `192.168.0.` are equivalent to specifying the network masks 127.0.0.0/8 and 192.168.0.0/24, respectively. Here you can also specify individual hosts by using their full IP address and exclude certain hosts by using the `EXCEPT` clause. For example, if we wish to allow access to all hosts on our 192.168.0. network except a naughty host with the address 192.168.0.15, we would use the following in `hosts allow`:

```
hosts allow = 127. 192.168.0. EXCEPT 192.168.0.15
```

You can also use fully qualified domain names (FQDNs) like headoffice.example.com or gateway.example.com to specify individual hosts. We don't show it here, but `hosts deny` allows you to list the hosts and networks you do not want to access this service.

We are going to have the networks 192.168.0.0 to 192.168.30.0 access this Samba service so we will specify the following:

```
hosts allow = 127. 192.168.
```

Next, we deal with logging information. First, we define the log file, which will be housed in the `/var/log/samba` directory. Each host will have its own log as signified by the variable `%m.log`. The `%m` is a special variable indicating machine name. We also tell Samba to roll over the logs once they get to 50K by specifying `log size = 50`. Samba will automatically roll over the log and create a new `%m.log.old` file. The log file for a host called desktop1 would be `/var/log/samba/desktop1.log`.

With the following, we define our domain information. As mentioned earlier, a domain allows for centralized authentication services for hosts that are joined to that domain. A domain requires a PDC or master, and there can be only one master in a domain. Those from a Windows background will already be familiar with this.

We are going to set the following:

```
domain master = yes
domain logons = yes
local master = yes
os level = 33
preferred master = yes
security = user
passdb backend = tdbsam
```

The `domain master = yes` line means this Samba server will try to act as the PDC. Having `domain logons = yes` indicates that we want to handle authentication requests from our domain.

The nmbd server provides the NetBIOS over IP naming services. For it to do so, it must become the master browser for the local workgroup broadcast network. Setting `local master = yes` means that our host will try to become that master browser (it does this by trying to win an election when the service starts). The `os level = 33` represents the chance, or desire, this host has at becoming the local master in those elections. The `preferred master = yes` line means that our host will force an election when it starts the nmbd service, giving itself the best chance to become the master browser.

■**Note** A *master browser* is a host responsible for collecting server announcements from other browsers on their network segments. The browsers provide a list of share resources to the clients. For further discussion about master browsers, please see `http://support.microsoft.com/kb/188001`.

The `security = user` setting, now the default of Samba servers, requires anyone connecting to our Samba services to have a valid user account and password on the host. Other options allow you to join other Samba servers in a domain or an AD domain; see the man page for details. The `passdb backend = tdbsam` indicates that we are using the local Samba password database for our authentication. Other valid options here are `smbpasswd` and `ldapsam` for providing authentication services. `tdbsam` points to a database file on the local host, `/etc/samba/passdb.tdb`. This file is owned by `root` and has the file permissions of 600 for security reasons.

Next, `logon path = \\%L\Profiles\%u` tells clients where their roaming profiles are stored. The `%L` refers to the NetBIOS name of the server, and the `%u` is the username of the user authenticating. If you don't want roaming profiles, this should equal an empty string (e.g., `logon path = " "`). The logon path must be accessible and writable by your users if they are to work. The profiles directory is normally in `/var/lib/samba/profiles` and should not be in the user's home directory on the server host. The `[profile]` share service defined further along in the configuration contains the details of this service. You can have individual startup scripts stored in your `netlogon` directory, which is also in `/var/lib/samba`. They are specified with the `logon script` directive, and the `[netlogon]` service is defined further on in the configuration file.

SAMBA VARIABLE SUBSTITUTIONS

All this %L stuff is becoming unbearable, right? Samba has some standard variable substitutions we will take a look at here. Following is a subsection of the available variables listed on the man page:

- %U: Session username (the username that the client wanted, not necessarily the same as the one it got).

- %G: Primary group name of %U.

- %S: Name of the current service, if any.

- %h: Name of Internet host that Samba is running on.

- %L: NetBIOS name of the server. This allows you to change your config based on what the client calls you. Your server can have a dual personality.

- %M: Internet name of the client machine.

- %D: Name of the domain or workgroup of the current user.

- %H: Home directory of the user given by %u.

We have not shown all the variables here; for the complete list of variables, please see the man `smb.conf` page.

Next in our configuration, we specify how we manage users on our host. These are the scripts that are run when we add, change, and remove users, groups, and machines on our Samba server. When we join a host to a domain, Samba will add a machine account for your host using the add machine script. Similarly, if we add users to our domain, Samba will use the add user script, and so forth.

```
add user script = /usr/sbin/useradd "%u" -n -g users
add machine script = /usr/sbin/useradd ➥
-n -c "Workstation (%u)" -M -d /nohome -s /bin/false "%u"
```

■**Caution** There are subtle differences between the options Red Hat accepts to add users and the way Ubuntu does. In the add machine script line just shown, you must remove the −M if you are using an Ubuntu host. In Red Hat, the −M option to useradd will instruct the command not to create a home directory for the new user. In Ubuntu, this specific option is not available, and home directories are not created by default.

If you wish, you can make sure that when users are created, they go into a certain group other than users depending on your needs. For this example, we would do so by changing the −g users in the add user script line to some other group, like −g staff. Also, if you are going to manage your user lists via LDAP, for example, you would use entirely different scripts. Those scripts are provided by the smbldap-tools package and look like this:

```
add user script = /usr/sbin/smbldap-useradd -m "%u"
```

In this instance, the smbldap-useradd script would take care of adding a user to our authentication service, where %u is the username.

SAMBA AND LDAP

If you have an existing LDAP server or plan to set one up later, moving your existing users to LDAP authentication will involve some effort if you want to make use of Samba as a PDC. If it is just acting as a file-sharing server, you can have it use LDAP simply by pointing passdb backend to your LDAP server.

```
passdb backend = ldap://ldap.example.com
ldap admin dn = cn=samba,ou=meta,dc=example,dc=com
ldap suffix = dc=example,dc=com
ldap user suffix = ou=People
ldap group suffix = ou=Group
ldap machine suffix = ou=Machines
```

If you already have an LDAP server, you will need to set up the ldap admin dn details to the appropriate distinguished name, or DN, and the proper ldap suffix, as well as specifying other details. We explain OpenLDAP in Chapter 16.

Next is the printing information. This is used in conjunction with the [printers] share service described later on in this section. The printcap name = cups line tells Samba to use CUPS as our printing service. The load printers directive tells Samba to load the printers configured in CUPS by default. The cups options directive is used for sending options to the CUPS server; raw is the default. Other options can be found in the CUPS man page.

Now it is time to look at the actual services Samba has configured in Listing 12-1. Samba considers some of the services, demarcated in sections beginning with the brackets [], to be "special": [global], [homes], and [printers] are special services. Samba treats these services differently from, say, [sales] or [tmp].

As you would expect, when Samba receives a file via the [printer] service, it deals with it differently from a file received via the [tmp] service. Samba has functions that are only associated with definitions in these "special" services. For example, the path definition in [printer] defines a spooling directory. When your printer spools your printout to this path via the [printer] service, Samba automatically passes it on to CUPS for printing. Setting the value for path in another service will not trigger this behavior.

When you define your own services, you use a set of directives that are common to special services and user-defined services. In Table 12-1, we have listed the directives that we will use in our example. You would use these directives to alter or create your own services.

Table 12-1. *Samba Service Directives*

Directive	Description
path	Defines the path of the share your are describing (e.g., /tmp).
browseable	Describes whether the share is visible in the browser list of shares.
comment	Gives a description of the share.
writable	Indicates the share can be written to, as opposed to being read-only.
readonly	Signifies the share is read-only.
printable	Allows spool files to be created and submitted to the share. Applies to printing only.
guest ok	Indicates no password is required for the share. Default is no. Also called public.
valid users	Specifies a list of users allowed to use this service.
write list	Specifies a list of users/groups that can read/write to a share regardless of the readonly setting.
force user	Assigns a default user to all connections to this share.
force group	Assigns a default group to all connections to this host.
force create mode	Forces Unix permissions on files that are created.
force directory mode	Forces Unix permissions on directories that are created.
create mask	Sets Unix permissions on files that are created.
directory mask	Sets Unix permissions on directories that are created.

You can use these service directives to define the path and access rights to your shares. There are many more directives available, and you can find a comprehensive explanation of them in the man smb.conf page.

As mentioned previously, the [homes] share is one of the special services. Samba checks user authentication details to find the path for the user's home directory (or it can create one if needed). The valid users setting for this service requires a connected and authenticated user specified by the client service name (a matching of the client and the service requested). The home directories are defined as writable but not browseable. To be browseable means a directory is listed in a browser list by the server. The browser list is like what you see in your network neighborhood browser.

The [printers] section is another one of the special services offered by Samba. We specify the spooling directory here, path = /var/spool/samba. Such a directory is not browseable, writable, or available to unauthenticated users (guest ok = no). However, printable means that clients will be able to write and submit spool files to the /var/spool/samba directory for printing.

The [netlogon] share is not classified as a special service in Samba, but it is a standard service in many default smb.conf files and is included by default in Ubuntu and Red Hat Samba packages. This service provides the logon scripts for individual users we specified earlier, logon script = %u.bat. For security reasons, the shared mode is set to no, and the directory is not writable. The shared mode, by default set to yes, allows shared mode to be enabled when opening a file. Also, guest ok is set to yes to allow users to access the logon scripts without being authenticated with a password.

The [profiles] directory is similar to the [netlogon] service. This is where clients can store their profiles, as in Application Data, My Documents, and other Windows client directories. They are stored under the /var/lib/samba/profiles/user directories as specified by the logon path = \\%L\profiles\%u directive.

■**Note** Storing roaming profiles can make logging in very slow across a network if there is a lot of data in the My Documents, Desktop, or Application Data directories. There are some tips to get around this problem here: http://wiki.samba.org/index.php/Samba_&_Windows_Profiles.

Remember also, if you want to forget about roaming profiles altogether, you can set logon path = ' '. This makes profiles on the local host.

Next we have a commonly configured directory. It is not set by default but is generally set up by administrators. The /tmp share allows for general file swapping between users. This is a volatile directory that is generally regularly cleaned out, so users should be warned not to use this to store important documents. This directory has very loose permission settings because generally we allow anyone access to it. The directory itself has a "sticky bit" set on it, meaning that you can delete only those files in the /tmp directory that belong to your user (see Chapter 3 for a discussion on directory permissions). It is also important not to place sensitive documents you don't want every user to see in this share. We have set the share to be available to guest clients, public = yes, and it is writable for all.

Lastly, we have set up a share called [sales]. This share is to be made available to our sales staff only. We have decided to put our staff shared documents into the /data/staff directory, and the sales directory will be under that. We have specified that it should be readonly by default. This stops unintended users writing to this directory. We have also denied public or guest users. It is browseable so it will appear in share browser lists for this Samba server. We have also specified here a valid users list, which is set to the sales group. The + indicates to Samba to look through the local Unix user/group lists. The people in the sales group will have readonly access to the [sales] share. We then specify exactly who we want to have read/write access, jsmith and bsingh. We could use group lists here as well. If we had a group called sales_admins, we could add write list = @sales_admins.

The last section ensures that files and directories are created with the correct ownership, group, and permissions. We don't want users owning their own documents throughout the directory tree and then having to get someone to change the permissions or ownership for them later when they want to share those documents with others. We want the owner to always be exbackup so that we will always be able to access the shares with our backup scripts, and we want the shares to have group ownership according to their departmental group. We want files to be readable and writable, and for directories we should give full access to the specified users and groups but no access for the general public.

```
force create mode = 0770
force directory mode = 0770
create mask = 0770
directory mask = 0770
force group = sales
force user  = exbackup
```

As you saw in Chapter 3, the permissions here are read, write, and execute/access on all files and directories. This might be too liberal for your requirements, but it gives you an idea how to use the permissions. You might want to create files with only 0660 permissions, which is entirely reasonable but might entail some administration overhead.

We now have a basic Samba configuration. You can add your own shares to this configuration as you see fit. There are several things we need to do now to the host to get it ready for users.

First, we need to create and change the file permissions on the directory /data/staff. We need to make sure that the appropriate groups can access the shares we have defined. Then we need to set up groups called sales and staff, if they don't already exist.

```
$ sudo mkdir -p /data/staff/sales
$ sudo groupadd -g 501 staff
$ sudo groupadd -g 502 sales
```

■Note These group IDs are arbitrary, and they may already be used on your host. You may wish to choose a different range for your network. On Red Hat, host values less than 500 are reserved for system accounts. On Ubuntu, host values less than 1000 are reserved for system accounts.

We need to change the permissions on the /data/staff and the /data/staff/sales directories. The group staff needs access to the /data/staff directory. The group sales needs access
to the /data/staff/sales directory.

```
$ sudo chgrp staff  /data && sudo chgrp staff  /data/staff
$ sudo chgrp sales /data/staff/sales
```

Now we have set permissions on those directories. We want to prevent general access to
the directories and only allow defined users and groups.

```
$ sudo chmod 750 /data && sudo chmod 750 /data/staff ➥
&& sudo chmod 770 -R /data/staff/sales
```

In the preceding examples, we are allowing access to anyone in the staff group to /data/
staff. We are then allowing anyone in the group sales access to read, write, and remove files
in the /data/staff/sales directory. People in the sales group will also be in the staff group.

We also need to create the Samba-specific shares if they haven't already been created and
assign them with the correct permissions.

```
$ sudo mkdir -p /var/lib/samba/netlogon && sudo mkdir -p /var/lib/samba/profiles
$ sudo chgrp staff /var/lib/samba/{netlogon, profiles} ➥
&& sudo chmod 770 /var/lib/samba/{netlogon, profiles}
```

Here we have created the two directories and then allowed the staff group access and read
permissions to those directories.

Adding Users to Samba

We have set up Samba in such a way that requires user accounts to be administered on
the Samba host. Samba provides a tool called smbpasswd to administer user accounts on your
Samba host. The smbpasswd tool uses the following syntax:

```
$ sudo smbpasswd [options] username
```

The main options we will be interested in are -a, to add a user, and -d, to disable a user.
We will add a user as follows:

```
$ sudo smbpasswd -a jsmith
New SMB password:
Retype new SMB password:
Added user jsmith.
```

We have added a new user called jsmith. There needs to be a Linux user account for the
user; otherwise, you will not be able to add the user. See here what happens when we try to
add bsingh:

```
$ sudo smbpasswd -a bsingh
New SMB password:
Retype new SMB password:
Failed to modify password entry for user bsingh
```

We will need to add `bsingh` to our Linux host before we add this user to our Samba server. One user we will have to add is `root`. The `root` user is required by Samba to add users and machine accounts when we are using it in PDC mode:

```
$ sudo smbpasswd -a
New SMB password:
Retype new SMB password:
```

Here we have added our `root` account. We will require it when we add our host to our domain. Unfortunately, `tbear` has just left the firm, and his Samba account needs to be disabled. To do that, we remove `tbear`'s details like so:

```
$ sudo smbpasswd –d tbear
Disabled user tbear
```

We will also have to remove him separately from our Linux user accounts and any groups he belonged to.

Now that we have this done, we can look at adding a Windows desktop to our domain server.

Adding a Host to the Domain

First, you will need to restart the Samba server to make sure your configuration is loaded. You do that using the `service` command on Red Hat or the `invoke-rc.d` command on Ubuntu:

```
$ sudo /sbin/service smb restart
$ sudo /usr/sbin/invoke-rc.d samba restart
```

If you experience any errors, you should check the logs that are available in the /var/log/ samba directory. The server daemon logs to /var/log/samba/smbd.log, and clients are logged to /var/log/samba/*client-name*.log. You should also check /var/log/messages or /var/log/ syslog for any error messages depending on whether you are running a Red Hat or Ubuntu host, respectively.

Now you need to log in to your Windows local administrator account. From there you can right-click the My Computer icon and select Properties. Select the `Computer Name` tab and then click the Network ID button. You have now started the Network Identification Wizard, as shown in Figure 12-1.

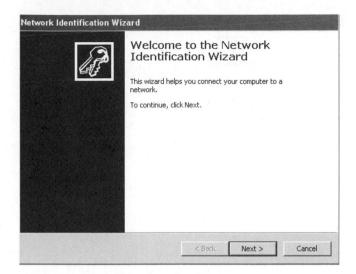

Figure 12-1. *Network Identification Wizard*

Select Next to continue on. You are then asked to describe the purpose of your computer as in Figure 12-2.

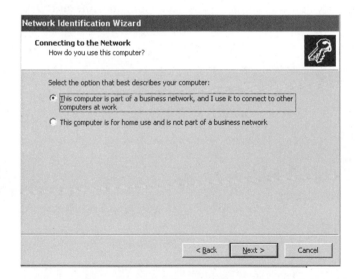

Figure 12-2. *Selecting the computer's main purpose in life*

This computer is part of a business network, so choose accordingly and click the Next button to continue. You are asked whether this company uses a domain; in this example, our company doesn't yet, but it will, so we specify Yes. If you select this option, you are then asked to have your information ready to join your domain.

Next, you add user account information, in this case, we use the information for jsmith. The wizard requires the username, password, and domain you wish to join, as shown in Figure 12-3.

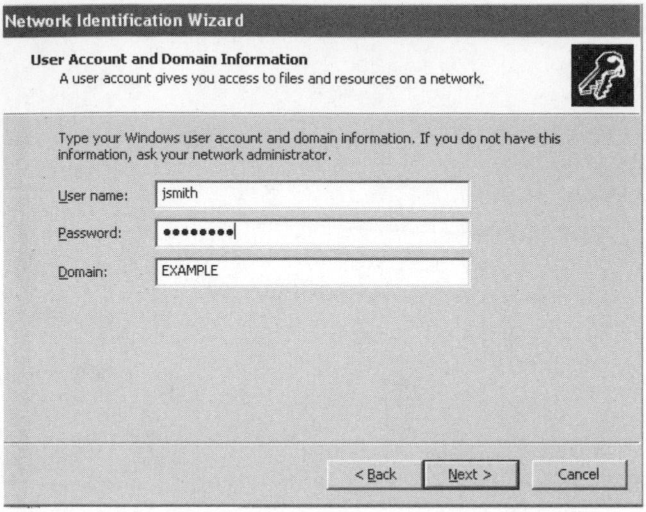

Figure 12-3. *User account information*

We have added the details for jsmith, and we want this user to join the domain EXAMPLE as we have specified in our smb.conf workgroup definition.

On the next wizard page, you need to enter a computer name and domain name and click Next again. We will use the computer name of desktop1 and the domain EXAMPLE, as you can see in Figure 12-4.

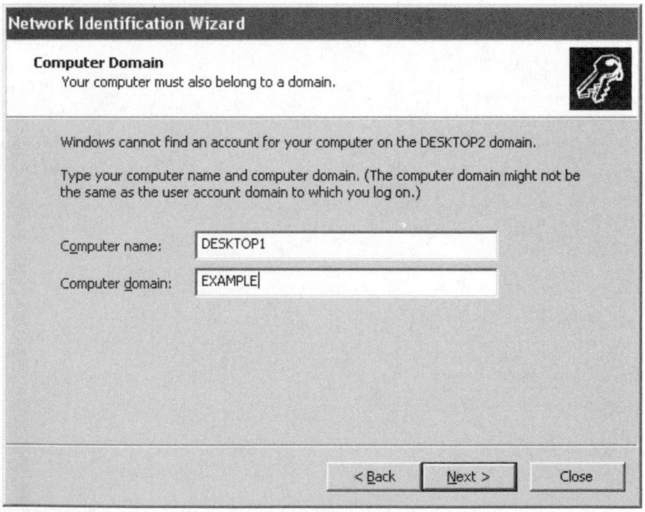

Figure 12-4. *Adding the computer name and domain*

Next you are required to enter the details of a user with the authority to join a host to a domain. In our case, that would be the root user using the Samba password we entered just before (see Figure 12-5).

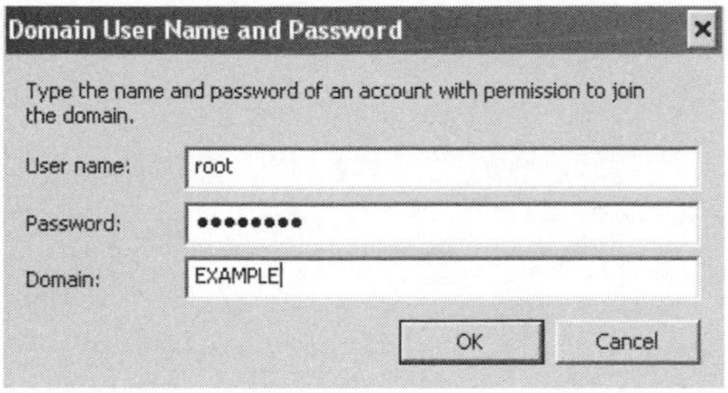

Figure 12-5. *Using the* root *user as the administrator*

Now depending on which user you are adding to your domain, you may see another window like Figure 12-6. It is asking us whether we want to add jsmith to the local computer that is joining the domain because an account does not exist for this user. We will decline to do so as she will only use the domain to log on to this host and does not need a local account. Your circumstances may differ, and you can add your users if you wish.

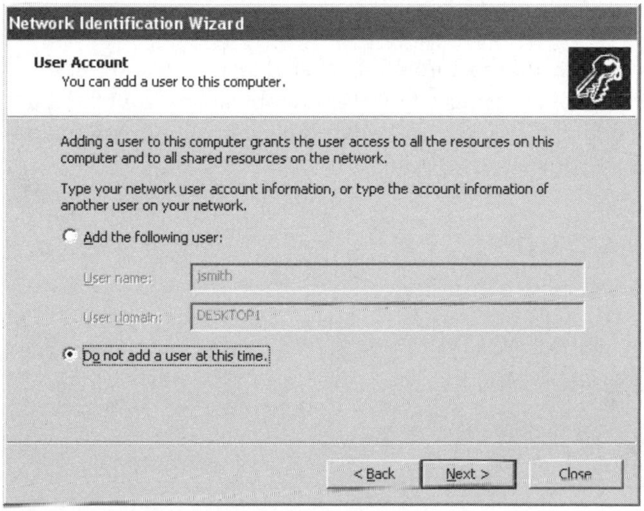

Figure 12-6. *Option to add users to the local host*

On successful completion of adding your host to the domain, you will receive a confirmation screen like that in Figure 12-7.

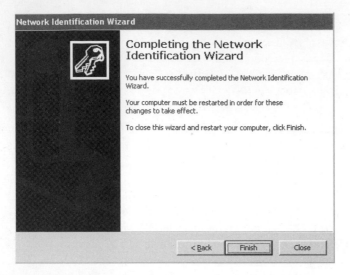

Figure 12-7. *Completion of the Network Identification Wizard*

You have now joined your host to the Windows domain. You need to log out and restart the Windows client before these settings will take effect. You are now able to use your Samba file shares as you would any other Windows file server. You will receive a domain logon screen and be able to store roaming profiles on your Samba server.

Required iptables Rules for Samba

Samba requires the following ports to be open in your firewall:

- UDP protocol on ports 137 and 138 for NetBIOS name services
- TCP protocol on port 139 for NetBIOS sessions
- The Microsoft-dn TCP port 445 for the Samba server

You would use the following commands to add them:

```
$ sudo /sbin/iptables -I Firewall-eth1-INPUT rule number -p udp ➡
-m state --state NEW -m udp --dport 137:138 -j ACCEPT
$ sudo /sbin/iptables -I Firewall-eth1-INPUT rule number -p tcp ➡
-m state --state NEW -m tcp --dport 139 -j ACCEPT
$ sudo /sbin/iptables -I Firewall-eth1-INPUT rule number -p tcp ➡
-m state –state -m tcp NEW --dport 445 -j ACCEPT
```

The INPUT chain specified should be the name you have defined in your iptables rules, and the *rule number* should be above any REJECT or DROP rule you may have.

■**Note** We discussed iptables in Chapter 6.

Mounting Samba Shares on Linux

Linux hosts can also mount Windows shares using the `mount` command and the `smbfs` type. However, some Linux distributions do not include the ability to read and write to NTFS shares, as Microsoft considers it a breach of their patent to do so. Ubuntu allows the ability to mount NTFS and FAT file systems, and you can find it in the `smbfs` package. To mount the Samba share on a Linux host, you would do something similar to the following:

```
sudo smbmount //au-fileserver1/data/staff /data/remote/ ➥
-o ip=192.168.0.1,user=jsmith,dom=EXAMPLE
```

This will mount the remote Samba share `/data/staff` under the `/data/remote` directory. You pass the IP address of the remote host, your username, and the workgroup or domain name. You will be asked to provide a password, and then the share should be mounted under the `/data/remote` directory. For more information on mounting Samba shares, read the `man mount.cifs` page.

Using the system-config-samba GUI

For simple and quick file sharing from a Linux host, you can use the `system-config-samba` GUI tool. This tool is available on both Red Hat and Ubuntu. It can't be used to set up complex Samba configurations, but it is handy for quickly setting up a few shares on your host.

Start the tool by selecting System ➤ Administration ➤ Samba, as you can see in Figure 12-8.

Figure 12-8. *Starting the Samba configuration tool*

■**Note** We have used the Ubuntu desktop to display the GUI, but it is exactly the same tool that is available on your Red Hat distribution.

As you can see in Figure 12-9, upon opening the tool, we automatically have the printer share available, and it is visible (i.e., browseable), and it has the share name print$.

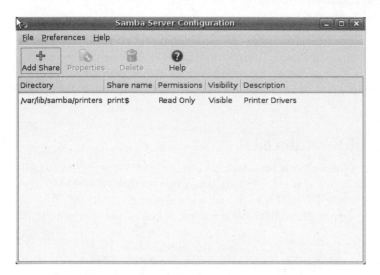

Figure 12-9. *The* system-config-samba *GUI*

You can change your Samba server setting by selecting Preferences ➤ Server Settings from the menu (see Figure 12-10).

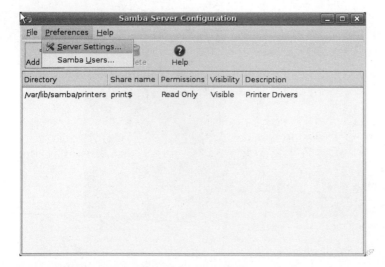

Figure 12-10. *Selecting the Server Settings menu option*

In this screen, you can set the workgroup name and the description. The Samba variables are available here, with %h indicating the hostname, as you can see in Figure 12-11.

Figure 12-11. *Basic server settings*

If you select the Security tab, you can choose the way your server will authenticate users. The Samba authentication modes of ADS (Active Directory Service), Domain, Server, Share, and User are available, as shown in Figure 12-12. In our case, we shall leave it at User.

Figure 12-12. *Security settings*

You can also fill in the details for your authentication server and Kerberos realm, if you have either. In Figure 12-12, we have selected to encrypt passwords, and we are denying guest accounts.

By selecting Preferences ➤ Samba Users, you can add user accounts. In Figure 12-13, you can see that there are two accounts already added to our host, the nobody account and the jsmith account.

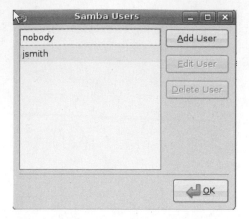

Figure 12-13. *User accounts for Samba*

User accounts must still be present on the Linux host before they can be added to Samba. We have just added Angela Taylor to our Linux host, and now we wish to add her to our Samba server. We click Add User and use the drop-down list for Unix Username to select her newly added account (see Figure 12-14).

Figure 12-14. *Adding the user* ataylor

Next, we fill out the Windows Username and the Samba Password fields, as you would expect. Figure 12-15 shows the details we have added for the user ataylor.

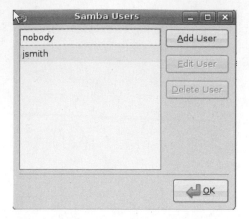

Figure 12-15. *The user details for* ataylor

Clicking OK saves the user into our Samba user database.

Next, you can move on to creating a Samba share. In the main window, click the Add Share button. You now see a Basic tab with share details like the one in Figure 12-16.

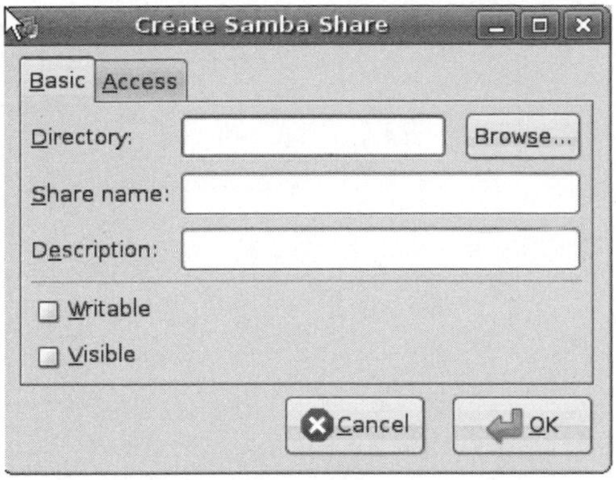

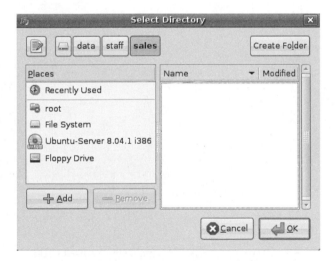

Figure 12-16. *Adding the basic share details*

Selecting Browse to add a directory brings up a familiar directory browser, allowing you to move to and select the directory you wish to share. We have chosen to share the /data/staff/ sales directory, as you can see in Figure 12-17.

Figure 12-17. *Browsing for a directory to share*

You can see in Figure 12-18 that we have chosen /data/staff/sales to be shared under the share name sales. We have made it writable and visible (visible is another way of indicating public or guest ok).

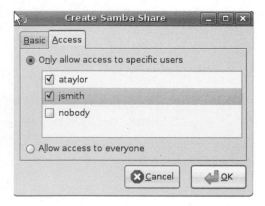

Figure 12-18. *Adding details of our sales share*

Next, click the Access tab to set the access permissions. You can see in Figure 12-19 that you can simply add specific users by clicking the radio button option Only allow access to specific users, or allow everyone by clicking the Allow access to everyone radio button option.

Figure 12-19. *Setting access permissions to our share*

Finally, in Figure 12-20 you can see the result of our efforts: we have a share called sales ready to be accessed by our desktop clients for the users ataylor and jsmith.

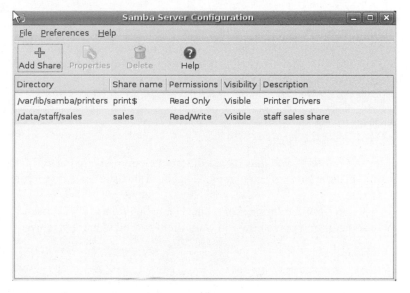

Figure 12-20. *Completed sales share configuration*

As we mentioned earlier, file sharing is excellent for distributing home directories to your client desktops, and Samba is an excellent tool for doing this. You can also distribute common directories used to share applications like databases files, as well as use shared folders to hold documents like word documents, spreadsheets, and other files.

■**Tip** As an alternative to shared folders, we're going to also show a document management system that can be used to manage your business documents. Document management systems provide granular security and version control that you don't get with shared or mounted folders and directories. We will introduce you to a DMS that could be a solution for you in the "Managing Documents" section.

Resources

For more information on setting up Samba, please see the following resources:

- `http://www.samba.org/samba/docs/man/Samba-HOWTO-Collection/`
- `http://www.samba.org/samba/docs/man/Samba-Guide/`

NFS Shares: Linux to Linux

Linux hosts can also mount shares from each other much in the same way that Samba does. Traditionally, this is achieved on Linux and Unix hosts via Network File System, or NFS. The latest version, NFSv4, has many advantages over previous NFS versions. Namely now it requires only one port, where before it required several, and prior to that you couldn't tell what ports it was going to use! This made it impossible to firewall, which of course made many security administrators immensely happy to deny its existence on their networks. It has learned from this and today is a respectable network citizen.

We will quickly show you how to share a file system, commonly called a *network mount*, between hosts. On Ubuntu hosts, you will need to install the nfs-kernel-server package. On Red Hat hosts, you will need to install nfs-utils.

NFS requires port TCP 2049 to be opened on your firewall. You would add it like so:

```
$ sudo iptables -I Firewall-eth1-INPUT -p tcp ➥
-m state --state NEW -m tcp --dport 2049 -j ACCEPT
```

You read about iptables in Chapter 6. You may have a different chain name to insert this rule into, and you may want to insert it into a particular place in your rule lists. Once done, you need to edit the /etc/exports file.

NFS reads its share instruction from the /etc/exports file. Here you add the directories you wish to share along with some options as to how you want them shared. You need to use the following syntax:

directory networknfs options,networknfs options

You select the directory you wish to share, the network to which you want it shared, and then several NFS options. Have a look at the one we are going to use:

```
/data/staff  192.168.0.2/255.255.255.255(rw,root_squash, subtree_check,fsid=0)
```

Here we are going to share the /data/staff directory to the host at 192.168.0.2/32. This IP address can also be an FQDN, like fileserver2.example.com, or a whole domain, like *.example.com.

Next, we set the following options: rw,root_squash, subtree_check,fsid=0. The first option allows the share to be readable and writable. The option root_squash means that the root user on the remote host has the UID/GID set to the anonymous UID/GID—which means this user loses her root powers over this share. This is to protect the network mount from being compromised by the remote root user. Next is subtree_check, which basically means that the NFS server will check the subtree of the file system when a request comes in for a file in the mounted share. How you set this depends on what kind of files exist on the share. The default is no_subtree_check. We have turned this on because files could be changed or renamed before they are accessed by the client. If this were a read-only file system, we would turn this off with no_subtree_check instead.

There are many other options that can be specified, and we suggest you read the man page for exports to get further details. To make these settings active, you need to run the following command:

```
$ sudo exportfs -a
```

This assumes that the NFS service is running. If it is not running, you can start it by issuing the following:

```
$ sudo /sbin/service nfs restart
$ sudo /usr/sbin/invoke-rc.d nfs-kernel-server restart
```

Now that the service has been restarted and the new network mounts have been defined, we will try to mount our share on our remote host. Let's see if our NFS mount is being served. You can use the showmount command to check your NFS shares by issuing the following:

```
$ showmount -e localhost
Export list for localhost:
/data/staff 192.168.0.2/255.255.255.255
```

You can see that the output shows our NFS mount and the host IP address that can connect to it. You could also use showmount -e *someotherhost* to view another host on your network.

On the remote host, 192.168.0.2, we need to issue the following command to mount the share /data/staff to /data/remote:

```
$ sudo mount -t nfs4 -o rw,intr,hard 192.168.0.1:/data/staff /data/remote
```

This will mount the /data/staff directory to the /data/remote directory on the remote host. You will notice that we have specified the share name, /data/staff, followed by the host to mount from, as indicated by the setting 192.168.0.1:/data/staff. This is because we are specifically requesting the directory that we have access to on that remote host; however, we could specify / if we wish, and we would mount all shares that we have access to.

We use the mount command to mount a file system of type nfs4. We have set the following options on that mount: read/write, interruptible (as specified by intr), and hard. The first is self-explanatory, the last two are not. NFS traditionally had the quirk that if the host sharing the file system had a hiccup, it would cause all hosts joined to it to be severely affected until that service was restored or the hosts rebooted. The intr, or interrupt, allows for NFSv4 operations to be interrupted while waiting for a response from the server. The hard option means that the file system will be treated like a local mounted file system. If it is set to soft, the alternative to hard, the file system would automatically be unmounted if it is idle for a period of time. For more information on mount options, please see the man page for mount.

To set this to automatically mount when our host is rebooted, we would add this to the /etc/fstab file:

```
192.168.0.1:/ /data/remote nfs4 rw,hard,intr,_netdev 0 0
```

Here we are accessing the NFS file system from host 192.168.0.1 and mounting the remote shares under the /data/remote directory. We are specifying the same options we did previously and adding one more. The _netdev option tells our host not to try to mount our file system until after our network devices are up. If this is not set, the host will fail to mount the file system and wait for ages until it fails and the attempt times out.

Now that you have explored the ways to share files from host to host and have seen how to set them so they are available when your host boots, it's time for us to show you another way to share documents and information using a document management system.

Resources

You can find more information about NFS here:

- http://nfs.sourceforge.net/nfs-howto/
- https://help.ubuntu.com/community/NFSv4Howto

Managing Documents

File sharing is an important part of distributing documents in your company. However, it does have certain limitations when it comes to tracking and versioning documents. Without excessive overhead in writing and checking permissions, you can't get great fine-grained control of who is accessing your documents. Also, you can't lock the file being edited, so two people can access the same file, make separate changes, and, when one user saves it back to the file share, destroy the other's work. There is still clearly a need for file sharing, but a better way to manage the documents in your business exists.

A DMS is designed to achieve five things:

- Securely share your documents with other staff members.

- Provide version control for documents so that previous edits are not lost.

- Require documents to be checked out so that two people can't edit the same document at the same time.

- Style the DMS to match your company's workflow for creating, reviewing, and publishing documents.

- Have a single entry point for all your document sharing without having to manage several file servers and their file shares.

With a good document management system, you would typically have a web portal that will become the central point for all access to your documents. This can be part of a secured intranet with remote offices accessing it via your private VPN links into your main office.

Using Document Management Systems

Your company doesn't need to be a large firm to have a good document management system. A little thought put into designing a DMS early on in your business will save you a lot of problems later as your business grows and your need to control documents becomes more evident. A good DMS helps not only with workflow, but also with securing your documents. Add to this version control of your documents, and you have greater security of the data you are sharing with your colleagues.

KnowledgeTree, an Open Source DMS

To demonstrate the capabilities of a document management system, we've chosen to look at a product called KnowledgeTree DMS (http://www.knowledgetree.com/). KnowledgeTree is a combination commercial and open source product. This means there is an open source community version of the product, which we're going to install, and a commercial version the KnowledgeTree company sells. The commercial version contains some additional features including a tighter integration with Microsoft Windows desktops and obviously comes with a support contract. For our purposes, however, the open source community version has sufficient features for our needs.

We also chose KnowledgeTree because the product itself is based on open source software. It makes use of the Apache web server and the MySQL database that we introduced in Chapter 11 and uses the open source language PHP. KnowledgeTree is distributed under the GPLv3 license.

In this section, we will show you how to install the KnowledgeTree application, add users, and change its SSL certificate. We will also show you how to check in and check out a document.

■**Tip** The KnowledgeTree website has a lot of useful documentation available at http://www.knowledgetree. com/resources.

You can download the KnowledgeTree product from http://www.knowledgetree.com/ try-now/knowledgetree_open_source_download. You will need to provide some basic information, and then you will be taken to the download site.

■**Note** KnowledgeTree is not packaged by any of the distributions we're using. We're downloading and installing the application from the company that makes it.

Once the file is downloaded, you need to change the mode on the file to make it executable so you can install the software.

```
$ sudo chmod 755  ktdms-oss-3.5.4a-linux-installer.bin
```

Installing KnowledgeTree

First you must create a place to install your application. As we have mentioned, this version of the installation package of KnowledgeTree will install a web server, Apache, a database server, MySQL, and the KnowledgeTree web application. Our directory will be housed in our /data directory in the /data/web/KT-DMS directory. We prefer to keep all our data for this host under the one /data directory. We create the directory with the following command:

```
$ sudo mkdir  p /data/web
```

■**Note** This host will store all your company documents. This should be on reliable hardware, with sufficient storage for your company's documents and other files.

Next you run the installer. This will install all the required software on your host. It will load the Apache web server and the MySQL database as well as the KnowledgeTree web application. It is a very friendly installation process, starting with the startup screen shown in Figure 12-21.

Figure 12-21. *KnowledgeTree welcome screen*

Moving forward, you are asked to accept the license. As mentioned, this is a GPLv3 license agreement. More information on what that means can be found on the GPL website's FAQ. In Figure 12-22, we are accepting the license.

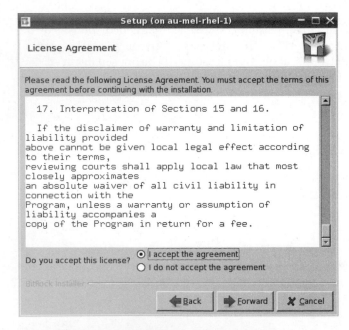

Figure 12-22. *Accepting the KnowledgeTree license*

Next you are asked where you wish to install the application. We are going to install it in the directory we have just created, /data/web/KT-DMS, as shown in Figure 12-23.

Figure 12-23. *Defining the installation directory*

You are then asked to choose the web server port you wish to run your service on. We will select port 80. If you are already running a web service on this host, you could choose port 8080, which is another common web server port. In Figure 12-24, we define our port.

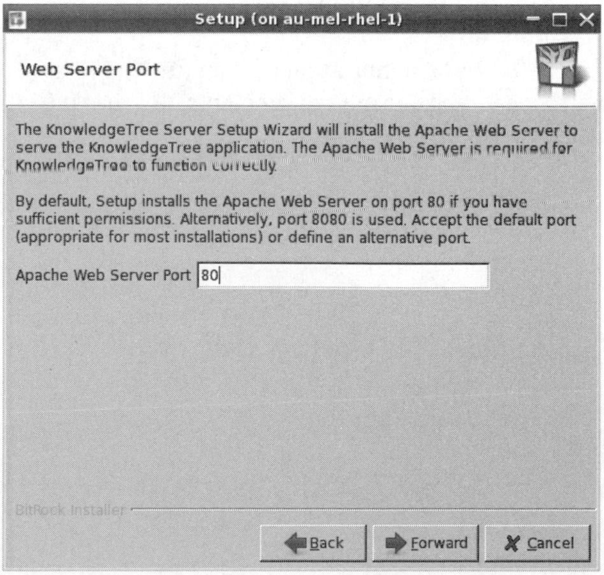

Figure 12-24. *Defining the web server port*

Next you are asked if you wish to enable SSL support for your web host. In Figure 12-25, we indicate that we most certainly do.

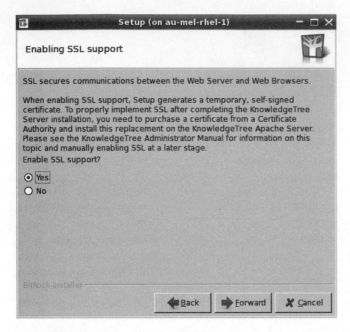

Figure 12-25. *Enabling SSL support for web services*

Now we will generate a SSL certificate to use with our host. In Chapter 10, you learned how to create your own certificates using your own Certificate Authority. We will create our own certificate after our installation has completed. In Figure 12-26, we are asked to provide the hostname and the number of days the certificate is valid for.

This will generate a self-signed certificate for the host dms.example.com (the "dms" here stands for document management system). Depending on your requirements, this may be adequate for your needs, and you won't have to generate your own certificates.

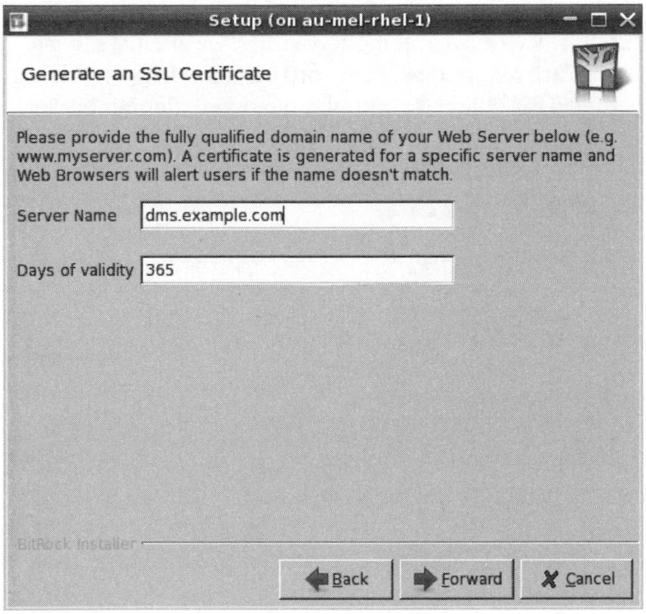

Figure 12-26. *Creating a self-signed certificate*

Next, you select the port that your MySQL server will listen on. Again, if you are already running a MySQL server on this host, you will have to choose a different port, like 3307. As you can see in Figure 12-27, we will use the standard 3306 for the purposes of this example.

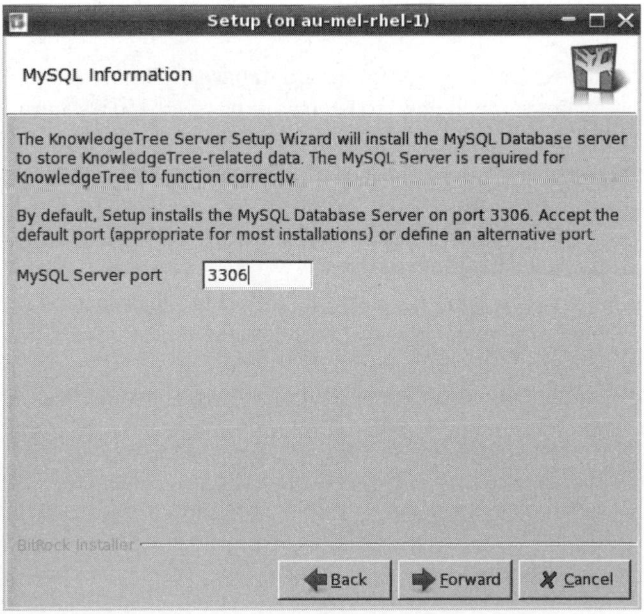

Figure 12-27. *Selecting the MySQL port*

Continuing on with configuring MySQL, you are now asked to define your root password for your database server (see Figure 12-28). As we have mentioned earlier, we are installing a completely new instance of MySQL and so are required to secure our installation by providing a root password. We have chosen another eight-character complex password. Remember to keep your password somewhere safe.

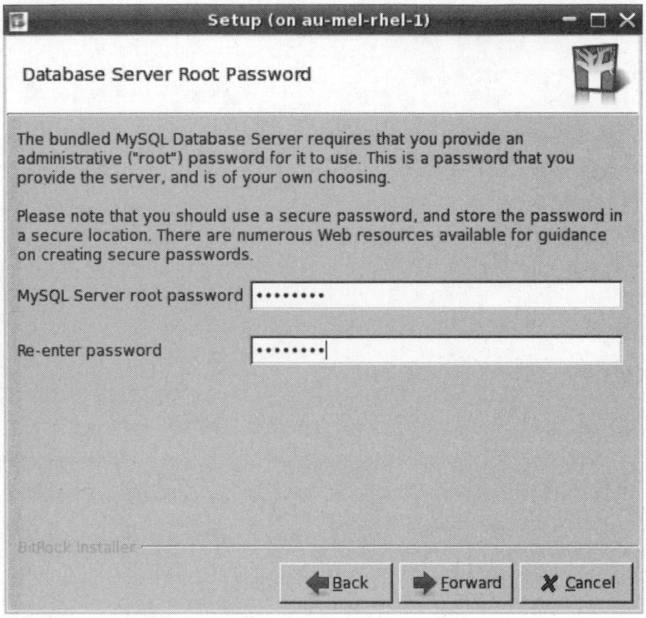

Figure 12-28. *Setting the MySQL password*

The KnowledgeTree installation will next create a user for your database. In Figure 12-29, we provide the password for that user. Again, you will need to keep your password in a secure and safe place.

This will create a password for the dms user account, which will have access to the dms MySQL database being created.

You are now asked if you would like to receive notifications from KnowledgeTree; select either Yes or No and click the Forward button.

Next is the End User License Agreement. If you are comfortable with this, please accept it and move on. If you don't accept the license, the installation will quit. Again, click Forward to continue.

Next, you are asked whether you want the Drop Box for Windows installed. The Drop Box for Windows allows you to drag and drop your documents from your desktop to KnowledgeTree. We declined the offer, as you can see in Figure 12-30, but you may wish to investigate the product for yourself.

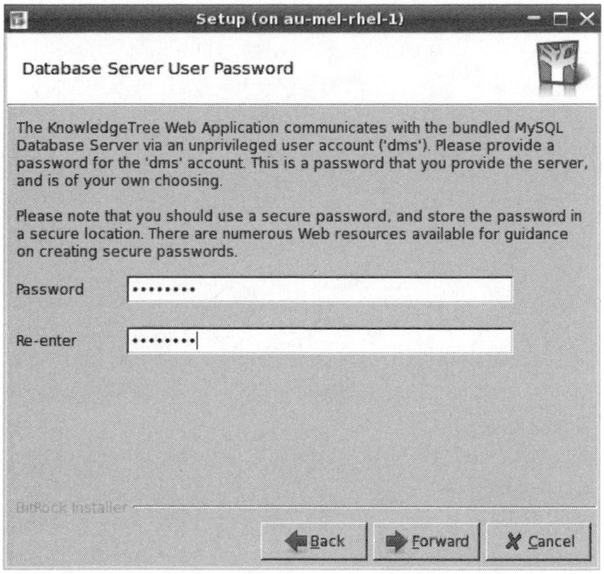

Figure 12-29. *Database server user password*

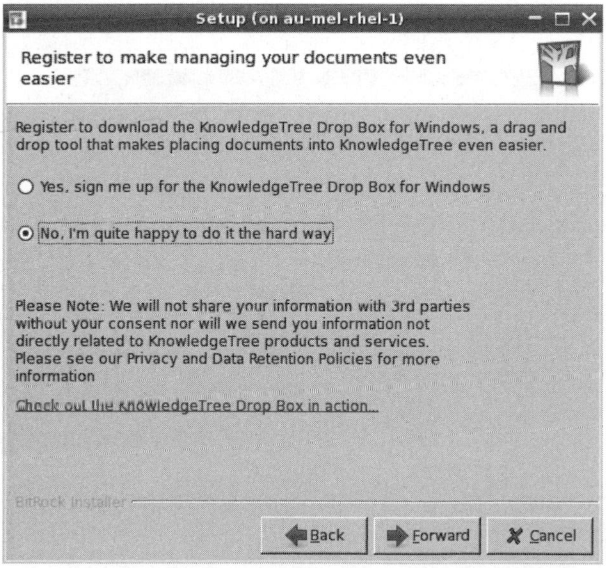

Figure 12-30. *Declining the offer of installing the Drop Box for Windows*

This brings you to the end of the questions and the start of the actual installation. Select Forward to proceed with the installation.

When you are shown the Ready to Install screen, click Forward again to begin the installation. Next, you can see the installation progress.

Once the installation is complete, you are given the opportunity to log in to your new DMS, as you can see in Figure 12-31.

Figure 12-31. *Success. Installation complete.*

Clicking Finish will complete the installation and launch your browser, which will display the KnowledgeTree login screen, as shown in Figure 12-32.

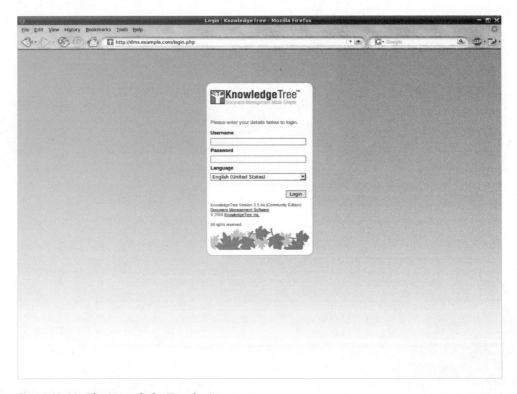

Figure 12-32. *The KnowledgeTree login screen*

Administering KnowledgeTree

Now you can begin administering your DMS application. You will be able to change the administrator password, add users, and set up the basics of your DMS.

The default username and password for KnowledgeTree are admin and admin, respectively. You will get the opportunity to change these shortly. Once signed in, you will see the layout shown in Figure 12-33.

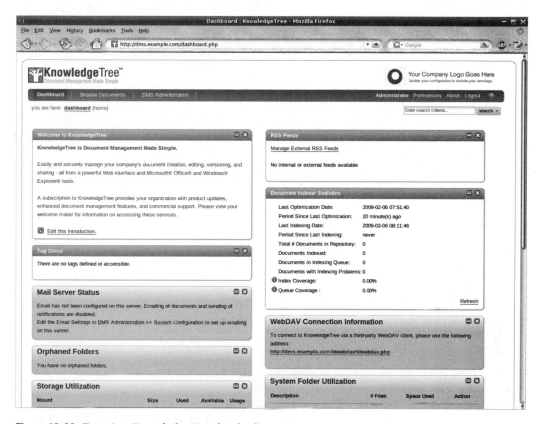

Figure 12-33. *Entering KnowledgeTree for the first time*

To change the password for the admin user, you need to click the Preferences link in the top-right corner after you sign on to bring up the window shown in Figure 12-34. Here you can change the password and set an e-mail address for the admin user.

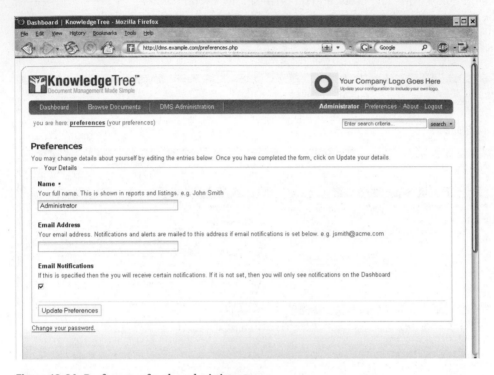

Figure 12-34. *Preferences for the administrator*

In Figure 12-34 you can also see the link Change your password. Click this link, and you are presented with a familiar screen to change a password (see Figure 12-35).

Next you can control the general administration for the site by clicking the DMS Administration link in the main menu. Here you can control how the DMS will work by defining workflows, document storage, and users and groups, as you can see in Figure 12-36.

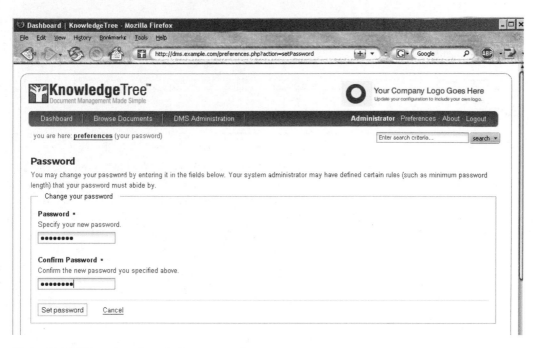

Figure 12-35. *Changing the admin password*

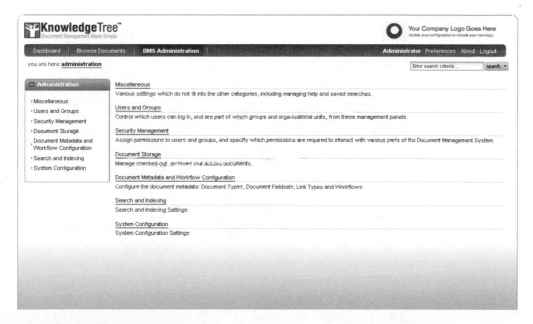

Figure 12-36. *DMS Administration tab*

Using the Users and Groups link, you can set up users and groups for the DMS. It is here that you can attach the DMS to your existing LDAP or AD server for user and password authentication if you have one.

■**Note**　We will explain LDAP servers in Chapter 16.

If you have an external authentication source, you can add a user by clicking the User Management link and selecting Add user from source from the window that appears. Alternatively, if you don't have an LDAP or AD directory server set up, you can add your users manually by again going to the User Management window. Figure 12-37 shows the Add a new user link in this window, and you can also see we have already added some users.

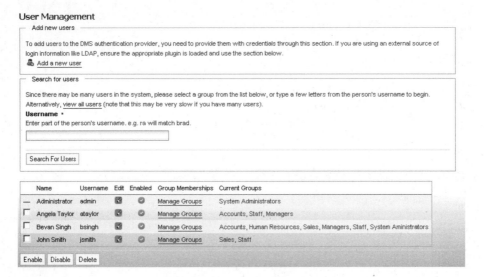

Figure 12-37. *User Management window in KnowledgeTree*

Now that you have user accounts, you can begin to develop your DMS to suit your company's needs. You may not require the full features of the DMS, but you might like to explore further roles, permissions, and workflows. How you do this is really an individual company decision. Before beginning to implement your DMS, we strongly suggest you read the KnowledgeTree documentation, especially this information: http://docs.knowledgetree.com/manuals/ag/organizational_hierarchy.html.

Working with Documents

We will briefly show you how you add and check out a document. Our DMS site already has some directories that we created. We have decided that all our company documents will be under the example.com directory. We chose that so that if we have a new business, we would add all its documents under its own tree. We have an Executive directory as well in which we can place all our sensitive documents that may relate to one or more companies.

To begin, we use the navigation menu to select Browse Documents, as shown in Figure 12-38.

Figure 12-38. *Browsing documents*

We are going to navigate into the `example.com` ➤ `Sales` directory to add a file from our desktop to the `Sales` directory. In the left-hand menu, you can see a big Upload Document button. When you click that button, you see a page to upload your document like the one in Figure 12-39.

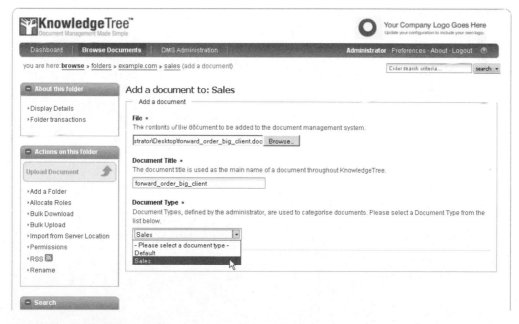

Figure 12-39. *Uploading a document into the Sales directory*

We are adding a document called forward_order_big_client.doc that we browsed to from our desktop. We can give a different name to the document if we wish, and we have selected a document type of Sales. A *document type* is a configurable item that holds metadata about the documents you are storing. The metadata is used to organize and find documents within your DMS. You create document types in the DMS Administration tab.

Note You can read more about creating document types at http://docs.knowledgetree.com/manuals/ ag/creating_effective_document_ty.html.

In Figure 12-40 you can see the document type metadata, which you can add to your document details. Some of this metadata is optional and some is mandatory, as signified by a red asterisk. You set this when you configure document types.

Figure 12-40. *Adding metadata to our document details*

We have saved our document, and we now navigate into the Sales directory and see it there, as shown in Figure 12-41.

Figure 12-41. *The document is now in the DMS.*

Now we will show you how to check out a document. To the right of the document is a check box to select it. When we check that box for our document, we can perform the functions in the buttons listed below it: Delete, Move, Copy, Archive, Download All, or Checkout.

We will check out the document, make a change to it, and then check it back in. We select the document by checking the box and clicking Checkout. In Figure 12-42, you can see that we are asked if we wish to continue with the checkout.

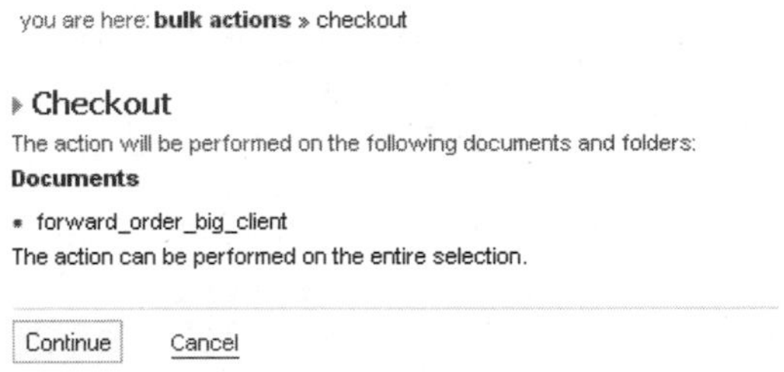

you are here: **bulk actions** » checkout

▶ Checkout
The action will be performed on the following documents and folders:
Documents

- forward_order_big_client
The action can be performed on the entire selection.

Continue   Cancel

Figure 12-42. *Checking out a document*

When you click Continue, you are presented with another page asking for a reason to check out the document. This reason is recorded against the document, and you as the administrator can use that information to find out when and why someone checked out a document. This is an audit trail that you may be required by law to keep on your documents or a way to investigate who did what and when.

In Figure 12-43, you see that we have included a simple reason to check out this document.

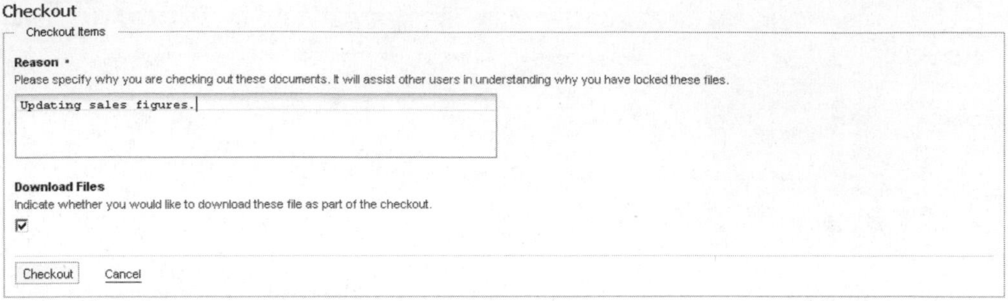

Checkout

┌─ Checkout Items ───┐
│   │
│ **Reason** *   │
│ Please specify why you are checking out these documents. It will assist other users in understanding why you have locked these files. │
│   │
│ ┌──┐   │
│ │ Updating sales figures.│   │   │
│ │   │   │
│ │   │   │
│ └──┘   │
│   │
│ **Download Files**   │
│ Indicate whether you would like to download these file as part of the checkout. │
│ ☑   │
│   │
│ [Checkout]   Cancel   │
└───┘

Figure 12-43. *Adding an audit trail for the document*

You are now given a zipped version of the document to speed up your downloading of larger documents. You can save this to the directory you wish to edit your document from or, depending on your compression software, you can open up the zipped document and begin editing your document. When you unzip your file, the document will be in the same directory structure as on your DMS. So the document in this instance can be found in the Root folder ➤ example.com ➤ Sales. We have made a minor change to the document and saved it back to our desktop again.

Now when we navigate back to the Sales directory, we will find the forward_order_big_ client.doc there. If we click the document, the menu on the right changes, and we are given the option to check the document in; in Figure 12-44, you can see the menu change. You also get to see some of the details for the document including the "This document is currently checked out by you" informational statement under Document Details.

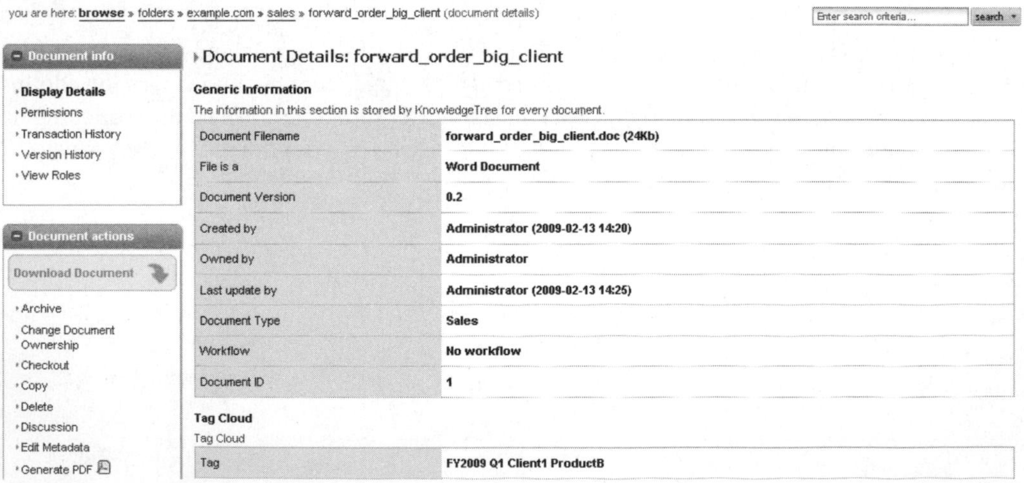

you are here: **browse** » folders » example.com » sales » forward_order_big_client (document details)   [Enter search criteria...] [search ▾]

Document info	
▸ **Display Details**	▸ Document Details: forward_order_big_client
▸ Permissions	**Generic Information**
▸ Transaction History	The information in this section is stored by KnowledgeTree for every document.
▸ Version History	
▸ View Roles	

Document Filename	**forward_order_big_client.doc (24Kb)**
File is a	**Word Document**
Document Version	**0.2**
Created by	**Administrator (2009-02-13 14:20)**
Owned by	**Administrator**
Last update by	**Administrator (2009-02-13 14:25)**
Document Type	**Sales**
Workflow	**No workflow**
Document ID	**1**

Document actions

[Download Document ➤]

▸ Archive
▸ Change Document Ownership
▸ Checkout
▸ Copy
▸ Delete
▸ Discussion
▸ Edit Metadata
▸ Generate PDF

Tag Cloud
Tag Cloud

Tag	**FY2009 Q1 Client1 ProductB**

Figure 12-44. *The checked-out document's details*

When you click the Check Document In button, you again browse for the file to be checked in (in our case, `forward_order_big_client.doc`); you are also asked whether it is a major or a minor version update and must fill in the mandatory Reason field to explain your changes. You can see this in Figure 12-45.

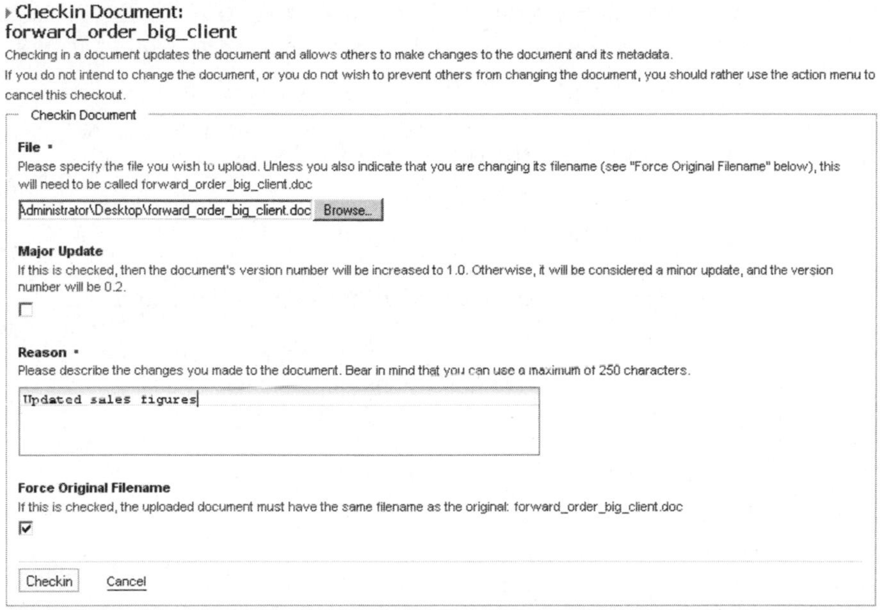

▸ Checkin Document:
forward_order_big_client

Checking in a document updates the document and allows others to make changes to the document and its metadata.
If you do not intend to change the document, or you do not wish to prevent others from changing the document, you should rather use the action menu to cancel this checkout.

```
┌─ Checkin Document ─────────────────────────────────────────────────────────────────┐
│                                                                                     │
│  File •                                                                             │
│  Please specify the file you wish to upload. Unless you also indicate that you are changing its filename (see "Force Original Filename" below), this │
│  will need to be called forward_order_big_client.doc                                │
│                                                                                     │
│  [Administrator\Desktop\forward_order_big_client.doc]  [ Browse... ]                │
│                                                                                     │
│  Major Update                                                                       │
│  If this is checked, then the document's version number will be increased to 1.0. Otherwise, it will be considered a minor update, and the version │
│  number will be 0.2.                                                                │
│  ☐                                                                                  │
│                                                                                     │
│  Reason •                                                                           │
│  Please describe the changes you made to the document. Bear in mind that you can use a maximum of 250 characters. │
│  ┌──────────────────────────────────────────────────────────────────────────────┐ │
│  │ Updated sales figures|                                                        │ │
│  │                                                                               │ │
│  └──────────────────────────────────────────────────────────────────────────────┘ │
│                                                                                     │
│  Force Original Filename                                                            │
│  If this is checked, the uploaded document must have the same filename as the original: forward_order_big_client.doc │
│  ☑                                                                                  │
└─────────────────────────────────────────────────────────────────────────────────────┘

[ Checkin ]    Cancel
```

Figure 12-45. *Checking the document back in*

You can now click the document again, and you will see that the version number has increased. You can also use the Document Info menu to get more information about the document; for example, clicking Version History displays the version details for the document, as you can see for our document in Figure 12-46.

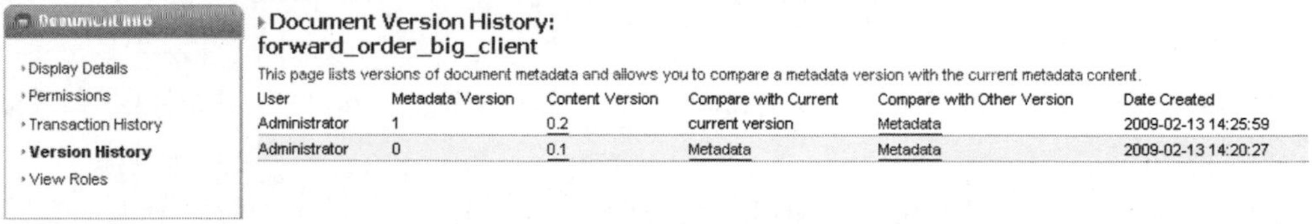

Document Info	▸ Document Version History: **forward_order_big_client**					
▸ Display Details	This page lists versions of document metadata and allows you to compare a metadata version with the current metadata content.					
▸ Permissions	User	Metadata Version	Content Version	Compare with Current	Compare with Other Version	Date Created
▸ Transaction History	Administrator	1	0.2	current version	Metadata	2009-02-13 14:25:59
▸ **Version History**	Administrator	0	0.1	Metadata	Metadata	2009-02-13 14:20:27
▸ View Roles						

Figure 12-46. *Version of our document*

We can use this page to see what our document looked like at version 0.1 or version 0.2. We can also compare metadata between the versions. If a change was made in version 0.2, we can easily roll back to version 0.1.

You can also use the Document Info menu to change permissions on the file, view the roles associated with the document, and view the transaction history to see who checked in and checked out the document over its life cycle.

You can see the advantages of having a DMS. You can set fine-grained permissions on the documents you have in your DMS and see how they have changed over their life cycle. You can also work with much more complex scenarios than the ones we have shown you here. Please see the KnowledgeTree website and view some of the webcasts there to learn the other features of this product: http://www.knowledgetree.com/resources.

Starting and Stopping the KnowledgeTree DMS

Starting and stopping the KnowledgeTree DMS is done by executing the dmsctl.sh command located in the root KnowledgeTree directory. In our case, it is situated in /data/web/KT-DMS. This command takes the start, stop, restart, and help arguments.

The script is actually an init script that can be added using the chkconfig command on Red Hat hosts:

```
$ sudo cp /data/web/KT-DMS/dmsctl.sh /etc/init.d/kt-dms
$ sudo chkconfig kt-dms on
```

Or the update-rc.d command on Ubuntu:

```
$ sudo update-rc.d kt-dms defaults
```

Securing KnowledgeTree with SSL

If you've been following along on your system as we've worked through KnowledgeTree to this point, your KnowledgeTree website is currently running unencrypted on port 80. We recommend that you add SSL to your site to ensure sensitive information like passwords and documents are protected. To do that, you have to change the configuration for the KnowledgeTree Apache server so that it uses your own SSL certificates and keys, as we'll demonstrate next.

In Chapter 10, we created a CA, or certificate authority, to sign our own SSL certificates. We will create a private key and a certificate request, and then sign that with our CA:

```
$ sudo openssl req -new -newkey rsa:2048 -nodes -keyout dms.example.com.key ➥
-out dms.example.com.req
```

We copy the request to the /etc/CA directory, and then sign the request with our CA:

```
$ cd /etc/CA
$ sudo openssl ca -out dms.example.com.cert -config ./openssl.cnf -infiles ➥
dms.example.com.req
```

We will now copy the dms.example.cert and the dms.example.key to the /etc/pki/tls/certs and /etc/pki/tls/private directories, respectively. This is the proper place for these files, even though we will not be using them directly in these directories. The dms.example.com.key needs to have secure permissions of 600, and the certificate should be readable, so we give it a permission of 644.

Instead of changing the Apache configuration file, /data/web/KT-DMS/apache2/conf/ssl.conf, we are going to change the files that this configuration file points to for the HTTPS service. The files of concern are

```
SSLCertificateFile   /data/web/KT-DMS/apache2/conf/ssl.crt/server.crt
SSLCertificateKeyFile   /data/web/KT-DMS/apache2/conf/ssl.key/server.key
#SSLCACertificateFile   /data/web/KT-DMS/apache2/conf/ssl.crt/ca-bundle.crt
```

We'll move those files (using the mv command) to *.orig so we don't destroy the originals. We then copy dms.example.key to /data/web/KT-DMS/apache2/conf/ssl.key/server.key and dms.example.cert to /data/web/KT-DMS/apache2/conf/ssl.crt/server.crt. There are two things we need to do now. First we need to add our certificate authority to the ca-bundle.crt file. Then we need to uncomment SSLCACertificateFile   /data/web/KT-DMS/apache2/conf/ssl.crt/ca-bundle.crt.

We have the file cacert.pem, which contains our certificate authority. We append that to the bottom of the ca-bundle.crt file like so:

```
$ sudo cat ca-bundle.crt >>  /data/web/KT-DMS/apache2/conf/ssl.crt/ca-bundle.crt
```

Then we need to issue $ sudo vi /data/web/KT-DMS/apache2/conf/ssl.conf and remove the # from the #SSLCACertificateFile   /data/web/KT-DMS/apache2/conf/ssl.crt/ca-bundle.crt line.

In the file /data/web/KT-DMS/apache2/conf/ssl.conf, we need to set ServerName and ServerAdmin to our settings as follows:

```
$ sudo vi /data/web/KT-DMS/apache2/conf/ssl.conf
ServerName dms.example.com:443
ServerAdmin webadmin@example.com
```

Finally, we need to restart the service for the changes to take effect:

```
$ sudo /etc/init.d/kt-dms restart
```

Once this is done, we restart the KnowledgeTree service and test our connection to the HTTPS service, https://dms.example.com.

Resources

For further reading on KnowledgeTree, please see the following:

- http://docs.knowledgetree.com/manuals/ag/ (Administrator Manual)
- http://docs.knowledgetree.com/manuals/ug/ (User Manual)
- http://wiki.knowledgetree.com/Main_Page

Print Servers

Setting up printer servers on Red Hat and Ubuntu is very easy. Both distributions use the same print server software to manage print services. We will show you how to set up the CUPS printer server, which is the de facto standard for Linux distributions and which also has a consistent GUI available across both Red Hat and Ubuntu.

CUPS also integrates nicely with Samba and makes printers available to your Samba domain. It is easy to turn your host into a print server that provides printer services to client desktops on your domain.

CUPS

CUPS is installed by default on Red Hat hosts and is also available on the Ubuntu distribution. Once it is installed, you can configure it via text files or by the web interface provided by CUPS.

We prefer to use the printer tools offered under both Ubuntu and Red Hat desktops. We will begin by showing you how to configure a new printer that is attached via USB to your host. You can then share that with other hosts in your network. To demonstrate this, we will then attach our printer that is being shared by our Samba server to a Windows client that is on our domain.

Installing Printer Management Tools and Configuring CUPS

You can configure your printers from the command line and by hand-editing your CUPS configuration files (though it's not recommended). It is much easier, however, to use the Printer configuration tools supplied by Red Hat and Ubuntu. For Red Hat, you need to have installed the `system-config-printers` package, and for Ubuntu, you need to have installed the `system-config-printer-common` and `system-config-printer-gnome` packages.

When you plug in your printer, the kernel will send an event notice to both Udev and HAL, or Hardware Abstraction Level manager. Udev is a user-space device management application, and HAL provides a consistent interface for the desktop programs. This means that applications like word processors can consistently know how to use a printer device, or a calendar can talk to a PDA using a consistent and defined set of rules.

DEVICE MANAGEMENT ON LINUX

What happens when you plug a device into your host? How does your system know what to do with it? When the kernel recognizes a new device, it will populate information in the `/sys` file system and then send an event to the message bus. Listening on that message bus are the Udev daemon, called `udevd`, and HAL, the Hardware Abstraction Level manager.

Udev, which is the user-space device manager for the Linux kernel, can be configured by a set of rules files. Udev keeps a database of all devices present on the system and reads its list of rules to look for any special instructions on how to handle a new device. If it finds a rule, it executes that rule; otherwise, it just creates a device file in `/dev` based on the type of device it is. A hard disk is assigned a device file like `/dev/hda`, or `/dev/sdb`, or an Ethernet card like eth1 or eth2. The same thing happens when a device is removed. The kernel will send an event to the `udevd` daemon and, depending on whether there is a corresponding rule matching that device, will perform some kind of action.

HAL is the software designed to free up desktop applications from having to know about underlying hardware information in order to use devices. HAL will provide to desktop applications information about available printers, PDAs, USB storage devices, and so forth so they can make use of these devices through defined APIs. This has two benefits. It makes accessing devices consistent, and it makes designing applications much easier.

On the whole you will not need to know much more about these, as they operate very much under the hood. You can read more about them, however, at the following sites:

- `http://www.redhat.com/magazine/002dec04/features/udev/`
- `http://www.freedesktop.org`

Let's look at what happens when we plug in an Epson USB printer on our Ubuntu host. To make sure everything is working properly, first we issue the `tail` command on the log to make sure our device has been picked up by the kernel:

```
$ sudo tail /var/log/syslog
Feb 18 21:27:16 au-mel-ubuntu-1 kernel: [ 2561.902999] usblp0: USB Bidirectional ➥
printer dev 10 if 0 alt 0 proto 2 vid 0x04B8 pid 0x0005
Feb 18 21:27:16 au-mel-ubuntu-1 kernel: [ 2561.903329] usbcore: ➥
registered new interface driver usblp
```

Here you can see that our host has recognized that we have attached a USB printer and has registered the device as `usblp`. We can check that the device exists by issuing `ls /dev/usblp`. Now we can be content that our device has been recognized and is ready to be added under the control of the CUPS printing service.

Configuring our printer device is now fairly simple. First, select System ➤ Administrator ➤ Printing from the desktop menu. This opens up the Printer configuration tool, which looks like what you see in Figure 12-47.

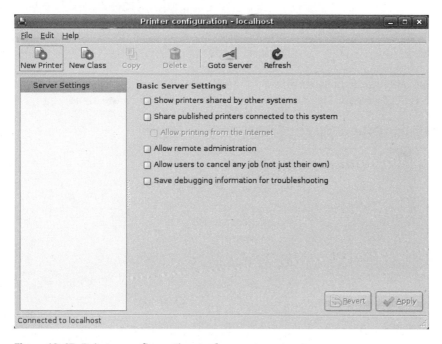

Figure 12-47. *Printer configuration tool*

As you can see, we have no printers set up yet. We will add a printer by clicking the New Printer icon, which brings up the window shown in Figure 12-48.

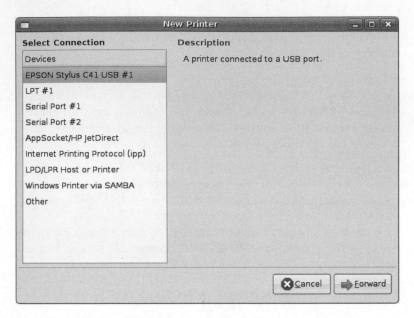

Figure 12-48. *Adding our printer*

You can see that our Ubuntu host has found our newly attached printer. We simply high-light the printer and click Forward. This brings up the window shown in Figure 12-49.

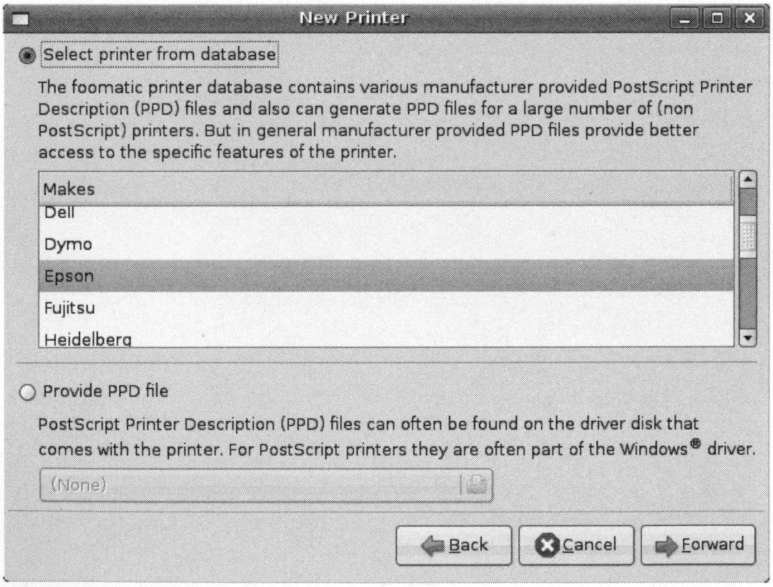

Figure 12-49. *Selecting a printer driver*

■**Note** Foomatic is a package that bundles various manufacturers' PPD files. These provide CUPS with the correct way to talk to your printer.

We have an Epson printer and are going to select Epson for our printer drivers. Clicking Forward brings up a window from which we choose a driver for our printer model (see Figure 12-50).

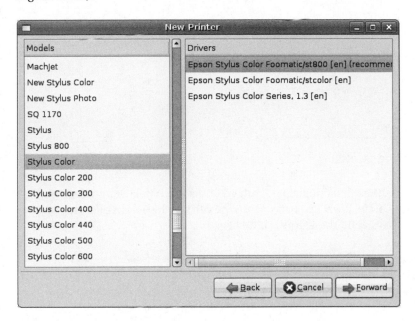

Figure 12-50. *Selecting the drivers for our printer*

The highlighted printer driver is the closest match for our printer.

Clicking the Forward button brings us to the window in Figure 12-51. Here we set the name, description, and location details of the printer, and then click the Apply button.

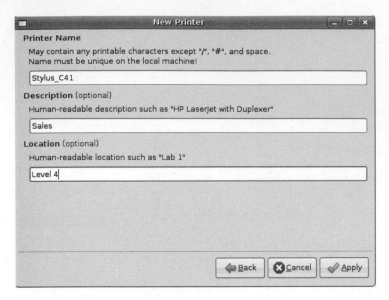

Figure 12-51. *Printer naming details*

You can see in Figure 12-52 that our printer is added under the Local Printers section. When we click Stylus_C41 in the Local Printers section, we can see the details of printer, as shown in Figure 12-53. We can edit these details if we like.

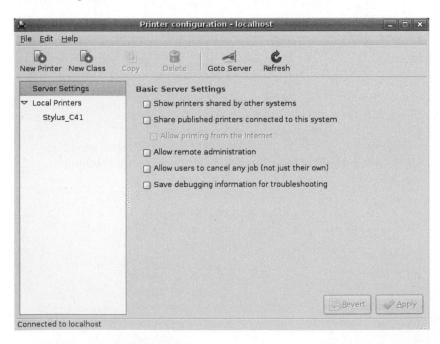

Figure 12-52. *Our printer is added.*

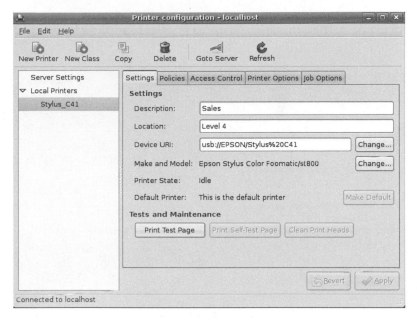

Figure 12-53. *Properties of our installed printer*

We can see that the description and location are what we just set in our print device. The device URI is made up of the type of interface and location of the printer. We can also run our test print from here using the Print Test Page button.

As you can see in Figure 12-54, you can set things like the state of the printer, enabled or not, and a few other settings by clicking the Policies tab.

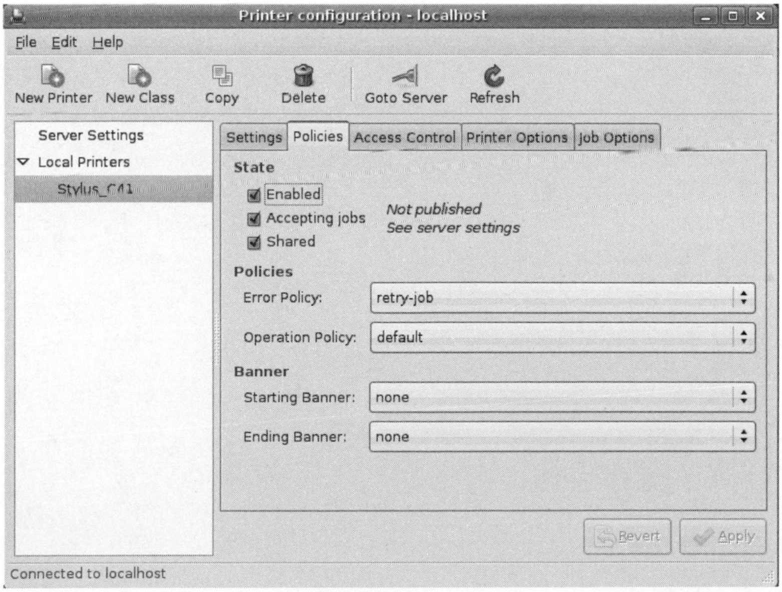

Figure 12-54. *Policies for our printer*

In Figure 12-55, you can see that we can set some security on our hosts to deny certain users from using the printer, via the Access Control tab. Users that you deny should have an account on your hosts for this to be effective.

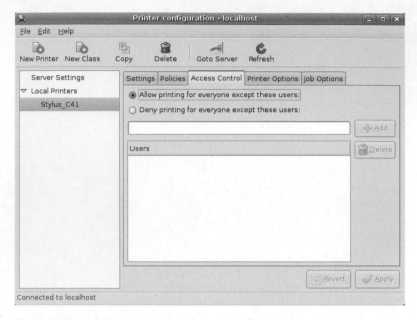

Figure 12-55. *Printer access controls*

On the Print Options tab, we can set the page size and the default resolution of our printer (see Figure 12-56).

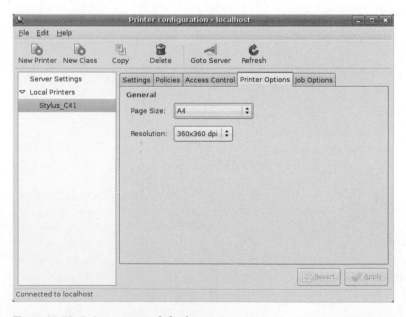

Figure 12-56. *Printer paper defaults*

Printer job options can be found on the Job Options tab, as you see in Figure 12-57, allowing you to set various job options.

We now have to select File ➤ Quit to exit the printer setup tool. We will restart the CUPS printer server to make sure our configuration is read.

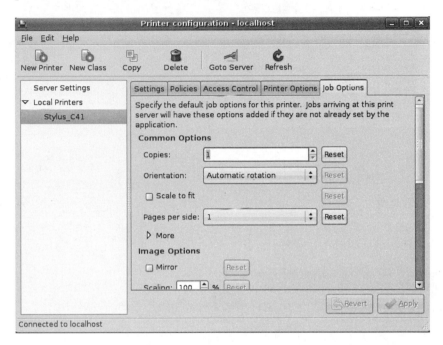

Figure 12-57. *Printer job options*

To restart, you use the now familiar service or invoke-rc.d command depending on your host distribution.

```
$ sudo /sbin/service cups restart
$ sudo /usr/sbin/invoke-rc.d cupsys restart
```

Samba and Print Services: Adding a Printer to Your Desktop

You have seen the [printer] service in your Samba configuration and the directives that Samba includes for printer services like those provided by CUPS. To make sure that Samba picks up any new printer you add, you need to confirm that you have set load printers = yes in your /etc/samba/smb.conf configuration file and restart your Samba server.

Now we will demonstrate adding a printer to our desktop that is being shared out by our Samba server. We have logged on to our EXAMPLE domain and will add the printer as we would any other network printer for the desktop. First we open the Printers and Faxes menu and click Add Printer.

In the dialog that appears, we select the radio button option A network printer, or a printer attached to another computer to add our printer (see Figure 12-58).

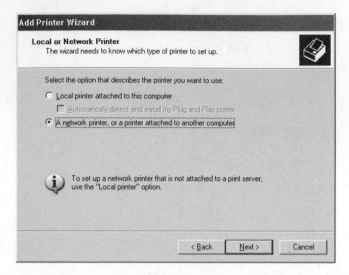

Figure 12-58. *Adding a network printer*

Next, we select Browse for a printer, as shown in Figure 12-59.

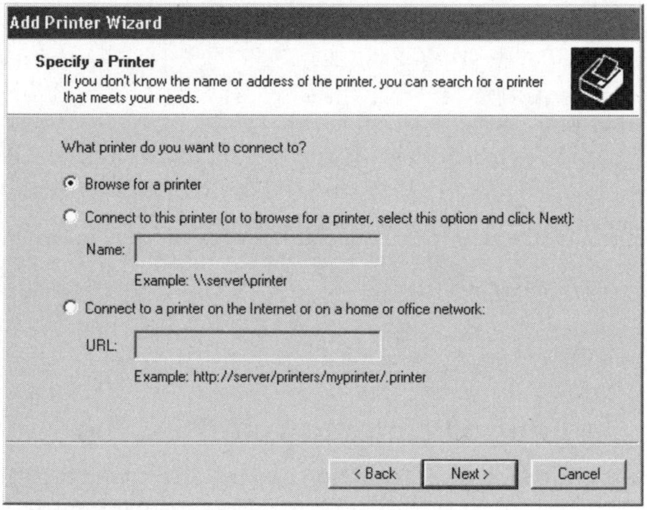

Add Printer Wizard

Specify a Printer
If you don't know the name or address of the printer, you can search for a printer that meets your needs.

What printer do you want to connect to?

⦿ Browse for a printer

○ Connect to this printer (or to browse for a printer, select this option and click Next):

 Name: [   ]

   Example: \\server\printer

○ Connect to a printer on the Internet or on a home or office network:

 URL: [   ]

   Example: http://server/printers/myprinter/.printer

  [< Back] [Next >]   [Cancel]

Figure 12-59. *Browsing for a printer*

Figure 12-60 shows the Epson Stylus printer attached to AU-FILESERVER-1, which we wish to use as our network printer.

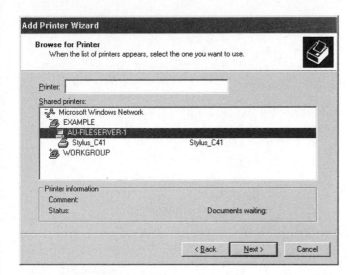

Figure 12-60. *Selecting our printer*

When you reach this point in the process of adding a printer, you will be asked to select printer drivers if you don't already have them installed. If there are no drivers available, you can always choose the Generic Text printer drivers for most printers, or go to the website for your printer and obtain the drivers from there.

We now have our printer attached to our host, ready for printing, as you can see in Figure 12-61.

Figure 12-61. *Installed printer ready to go*

We have now set up a printer that is shared via our Samba server.

Summary

In this chapter, we explored file- and print-sharing offerings from Linux. We have showed that the traditional methods of file sharing are via the Samba server and via the NFS server, depending on the clients you wish to serve. We introduced you to KnowledgeTree DMS, a great alternative to the traditional file-sharing methods. A DMS has many advantages over file sharing, since it offers finer-grained access control and versioning of documents, and allows you to implement company workflows. Finally, you learned how to set up the CUPS printing service and share it via your Samba server.

In this chapter, you learned how to do the following:

- Configure a Samba server to control a domain.

- Configure an NFS server to mount file systems between Linux hosts.

- Install and configure the KnowledgeTree DMS.

- Check out and check in a document in your DMS.

- Configure CUPS printer servers and attach them to a host in your domain.

In the next chapter, we will look at backup and recovery for your office.

■■■

## CHAPTER 13

Backup and Recovery

By Dennis Matotek

The ability to back up and restore data is critical in any organization. You need high-quality backups not only to restore deleted or overwritten data, but also in many cases for legal requirements you might have in your country (e.g., related to keeping tax or customer records).

We will begin this chapter by discussing disaster recovery planning (DRP) and business continuity management (BCM), giving you a grounding in these concepts. We will show you how to securely copy data from a remote host, whether it is on your network or on the other side of the world. We will then introduce you to the backup server Bacula and show you how to use it to save and restore your files. Also using Bacula, we will demonstrate how to back up and restore a database. Finally, we will discuss the Bat console, which is a GUI interface for Bacula.

By the end of this chapter, you should be able to do the following:

- Be aware of the requirements needed for DRP and BCM.

- Use the rsync command to securely copy data from one host to another and use a script to automate that process.

- Install and configure a backup server called Bacula.

- Manage your backups and create jobs within Bacula.

- Restore files to your host using Bacula.

- Configure and use the Bat console.

We'll start off with a general discussion on DRP.

Disaster Recover Planning

Of course, we all hope that nothing disastrous happens to our business, but it's important to prepare for any number of scenarios, just in case. There are two main categories of disaster: man-made disasters and natural disasters. An e-mail server going down for a day, causing vital, time-sensitive business matters to be missed, is a man-made disaster related to human error or mechanical malfunction that can have a process of recovery associated with it. On the other hand, an earthquake that destroys your office is a natural disaster that would require a completely different recovery response. Both scenarios can be planned for, depending on the likelihood of them occurring.

Disaster recovery planning (DRP) is all about recognizing, managing, and mitigating risk. It is part of an overarching process called *business continuity management* (BCM), or making sure a business can continue in the face of unknown adversity to at least a predetermined minimum level. BCM covers various aspects of your organization and should detail timelines that your business agrees upon for the restoration of particular services.

The following are questions to consider when formulating your organization's BCM and DRP strategy:

- Can we predict the most likely disruptions our business could face? What are the steps required to recover from them? What are timelines for expected recovery?

- What are the costs associated with mitigating the risks for and recovering from each potential event?

- Do we need a co-location where we can move our business?

- Do we need to rent extra equipment, such as power generators, in any potential crisis scenario?

- Who are the people and organizations that need to reached/communicated with in the event of disruption to the business? How should the disruption be communicated to the public?

- In the case of a large-scale catastrophic event, what are the points that determine whether continuation of the business can be achieved? Losses can quickly accumulate if key infrastructure or business assets are disrupted.

Developing BCM and DRP plans can be a complex process. Within your organization, you should have a BCM plan that contains the findings of risk analysis, business impact analysis, and crisis management investigations that can be signed off on by the major business units. Even small businesses can benefit from a semiformal arrangement, though the resources to develop a full BCM may not be required. For further information on BCM and DRP, we recommend the following resources:

- *Ready Business (U.S. Homeland Security)*: http://www.ready.gov/business/index.html

- *Australian National Security, Business Continuity Planning*: http://www.ag.gov.au/agd/www/nationalsecurity.nsf/Page/Information_For_BusinessBusiness_Continuity

- *Wikipedia, Business Continuity Planning*: http://en.wikipedia.org/wiki/Business_continuity_planning

- *Wikipedia, Disaster Recovery*: http://en.wikipedia.org/wiki/Disaster_recovery

- *Business Continuity and Disaster Recovery Checklist for Small Business Owners*: http://www.continuitycentral.com/feature0501.htm

- *Disaster Recovery Using Bacula*: http://www.bacula.org/en/rel-manual/Disast_Recove_Using_Bacula.html

In this chapter, we're going to focus on the process of backing up and restoring your data, which should be part of your organization's BCM and DRP plans. The next section covers backup strategies.

Backup Process

You have many different questions to think about when choosing a backup regimen. Answering these questions will give your company its backup strategy.

- What is it we are trying to back up?

- How often do we need to back up the data?

- How long do we want to keep the data backed up?

- Where should we store our backups and on what media?

The important thing here is to know your data. You need to know how often it changes and in what volume. You also need to know your storage media and how much data it can store, and for how long. Data volumes can be tricky things—without planning, you could have too much data to back up or not enough time to back up your data. In these situations, you may find yourself backing up data you don't need, or you may need to get different storage appliances for faster performance or larger backup volumes.

Data retention periods are also important to consider. You may need to keep your data for legal or tax purposes for specific periods of time, usually a few years. You may wish to keep client data for several years, and you may wish to keep other types of data for shorter periods of time. Depending on what you are backing up, there may be absolutely no point in keeping data on media with the aim to restore data that is months old; in such cases, you could look at shortening your backup cycles to free up that media.

Another thing to think about is scheduling. What time window do you have available to schedule backups in? You may be running 24/7 shops that leave very little time for offline backup regimens. You may have to perform *hot backups* (i.e., backups of live hosts at a moment in time), and you may not have much time to do this in. For scheduling, you may need to think in terms of daily, weekly, or monthly backup regimens.

Finally, you'll need to determine the type of backup you'll perform. In most backup regimens, you can break backups into three types: full, incremental, and differential. *Full* backups are definitive backups of data, and they will be the largest and longest backups performed. *Incremental* backups are backups of files and directories that have changed since the last backup (be it full, differential, or incremental). Incremental backups are smaller than full and differential backups, and they are normally much quicker to perform. *Differential* backups are backups of all changed files since the last full backup. These can be larger than incremental backups but are useful when doing restores, as you need only the full backup and the latest differential (if you are not running incremental backups at all). In scheduled backups, you may take one full backup every week with nightly incremental or differential backups.

With full, incremental, and differential backups, your restore operations are done in the following order: the last full backup is restored first, followed by the most recent differential backup, and then any subsequent incremental backups. If you are not using differential backups, then it is the last full backup followed by each subsequent incremental, from the oldest to the most recent.

■**Caution** In backup operations, you may restore unwanted, deleted files and directories along with good data. You should take care to examine what has been restored before proceeding.

Your network will have its own special backup requirements, and a plethora of hardware appliances and even online storage options are available for you to choose from. Hardware appliances can come bundled with different vendor software, or you can buy your hardware and run open source software to run your backups. The following are some hardware storage options:

- *Magnetic tapes*: Different types depending on the volume of your backups

- *Hard disks*: Different speed and volume options

- *Optical*: DVD/CD-ROM low-volume data backups

Online storage options may be useful for small volumes of data, unless you have a very fast Internet connection and low data-charge rates.

Network Backups

Our network is simple: we have one main host, headoffice.example.com, and hosts in remote branch offices that may have data we need to back up.

Figure 13-1 shows our network. (This is a variation on the diagram from Chapter 6.)

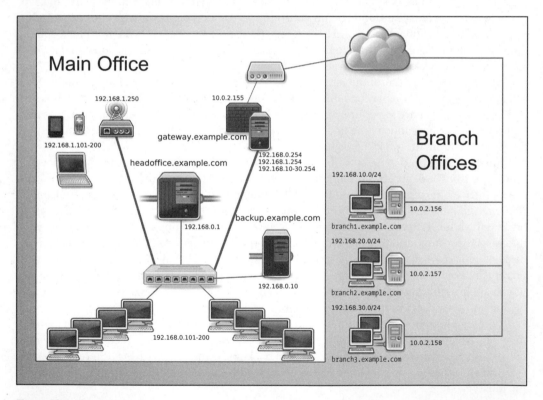

Figure 13-1. *Our network*

We are going to show you two methods of how we can back up our network. We will copy the data from the remote hosts to the headoffice.example.com central server. After copying these remote files, we can then back them up using a full-featured backup application that will reside on backup.example.com.

We have chosen to use a separate host to house our backup server. Ideally, you do not want your main server to also be your backup host because if you lose your main server, you also lose the ability to restore your backups. However, if you can't afford to buy an extra host, any backups are better than no backups, and you should then back up to external media such as DVDs or data tapes.

■**Note** Traditionally, Linux backups have been a combination of `tar`, `gzip`, `rsync`, `dd`, `cpio`, `dump`, `restore`, and `mt` commands in hand-rolled scripts. This approach is worthwhile for one or two hosts, but it can become unwieldy with a few cross-platform hosts. You might like to read the following guide for an explanation of the various Linux backup and recovery techniques: `http://www.ibm.com/developerworks/linux/library/l-roadmap8/`.

Using Rsync

We'll begin by showing you how to copy data from remote hosts securely and efficiently using a tool called rsync. This solution is designed for less complicated networks that don't require a full-blown backup plan. To do this, we're going to use rsync to securely copy data from host to host.

■**Note** The rsync tool is part of the Samba product suite (directly related to the Samba server project we covered in Chapter 12). The Samba community has taken rsync under their wing, though, and it is housed here: `http://rsync.samba.org/`.

The rsync tool can be used in a client/server configuration or a remote shell. When we talk about a "remote shell," we mean we can `rsync` between hosts over another transport mechanism like `ssh`, which will provide the rsync program with a remote shell (or command line) on the target host. It is because of this use of `ssh` that we can provide secure, efficient copying of data from hosts in hostile environments such as the Internet.

The rsync program is a fast and efficient way of copying data because it copies only data that has changed from an initial copy. After the initial rsync copy of the remote data to our host, any subsequent copy will be compared against what we already have. Rsync does this by sending a file list of the data it wants to copy to the receiving host. The file list includes the pathnames of the data we wish to back up and also the permissions, ownership, size, modtimes and, if specified, checksums of the files. This allows rsync to make a comparison of the files being copied and then copy only those that are different, making rsync very efficient when it sends data between hosts. It will also check the files being copied and copy only the portion of the data that is different in the file. For example, if a 1MB text file contains 990KB of the same data, rsync will copy only the 10KB that is different. Unfortunately, this can't be done with binary files (like JPEGs), because with binary files it is harder to differentiate any changes to the file.

As mentioned earlier, we can use rsync in a client/server model, where we run an rsync daemon on the target host that waits for rsync connections. These connections do not run over an encrypted session and therefore can be a security issue, so we are not going to discuss this method of using rsync further. In this chapter, we are going to describe using rsync with SSH to provide secure transport. This also means that we require only TCP port 22 to be enabled on our firewall rather than TCP port 873, which is required by the rsync daemon.

You can read more about setting up the rsync daemon in the following tutorials:

- http://sunsite.dk/info/guides/rsync/rsync-mirroring02.html

- http://everythinglinux.org/rsync/

Using Rsync over SSH

It is not uncommon to have a requirement to back up remote hosts outside your immediate network, across hostile environments like the Internet. In these situations, you can use rsync to remotely access those hosts via SSH and pull data off them, or make a backup. With the implementation of a simple Bash script, you can automate your backups by connecting to the remote host and copying the files back to your backup host. The first step is to set up an SSH connection to your remote host using SSH keys without a passphrase.

We introduced you to SSH communications in Chapters 3 and 9. Normally, you would create your SSH keys with a suitable passphrase, which you would use to authenticate your session when you signed on to a remote host. The reason we need an SSH key without a passphrase to make our connection is that we are going to run this script via crontab, which we introduced in Chapter 5, so we can regularly do the backup of our remote host without any user interaction. Not having a passphrase on our keys is a security concern, so we will take steps to mitigate any chance of them being abused a little later on.

First, we are going to create a new user, exbackup, to control these backups. Then we will generate our SSH keys.

```
$ sudo /usr/sbin/useradd -m -d /data/backups -u 525 -g adm exbackup
```

Here we have created a user called exbackup with a UID of 525 and default group of adm. We have added this user to the adm, or administrator, group because that group traditionally has access to read log files. The exbackup home directory is /data/backups, and that is where we will store all our backups. Next, we will sudo into the user's account and create our SSH keys.

```
$ sudo su - exbackup
$ mkdir .ssh  && chmod 700 -R .ssh && cd .ssh
$ ssh-keygen -b 2048 -t rsa -f exbackup
Generating public/private rsa key pair.
Enter passphrase (empty for no passphrase):
Enter same passphrase again:
Your identification has been saved in exbackup.
Your public key has been saved in exbackup.pub.
The key fingerprint is:
18:33:26:40:78:65:b5:b1:a8:17:5b:b6:32:05:0a:a4 exbackup@backup-1.example.com
$ ls -l
total 16
```

```
-rw------- 1 exbackup adm  3239 Feb 21 10:07 exbackup
-rw-r--r-- 1 exbackup adm  752   Feb 21 10:07 exbackup.pub
```

First, we issue sudo su - exbackup to change to the shell of exbackup. Then we create the
.ssh directory to store our keys in, and if that was successful (as signified by &&), we change the
permissions on the directory and change into that directory. We then use the ssh-keygen command to create our keys. We chose to make the key length 2048 bytes, -b 2048, and of type rsa
(you can choose rsa or dsa; these are encryption algorithms used to sign keys), and we called
the key exbackup. As the key was being generated, we were asked for the passphrase, and we
just pressed Enter twice. You can see that we have listed the contents of our .ssh directory
and we have the two keys, one private and one public, as indicated by the .pub suffix. We keep
the private one (exbackup) secured on this host, and we copy the contents of the public key
(exbackup.pub) to the authorized_keys file for the user on our remote host.

We need to now talk a little about security. Having passphraseless keys whizzing across
the Internet to your remote hosts is a potential security risk. The data will be encrypted to
prevent casual snooping, but a committed attacker could potentially use the keys as an access
point to attack your hosts. We could also create a security mechanism called a *chroot jail* on
our remote hosts, but this will limit our ability to access the rest of the host's file systems.

Tip For information on how to set up chroot jails, visit http://www.howtoforge.com/chroot_ssh_
sftp_debian_etch_p2 or http://howtoforge.org/chroot_ssh_sftp_fedora7_p2.

We could use passphrases with our keys and use a tool called key-chain to cache our passphrase for our connection, but we would have to enter the passphrase each time we rebooted
the host, which is not ideal. What we will do to make it slightly harder for an attacker is limit the
commands our SSH keys can be used for. On our remote hosts, we will create an executable file
called ssh_limiter.sh. When we log on to our remote host with our SSH key, this script will be
called, which allows only one command to be executed by anyone with this key.

You can limit what SSH can do by adding some options to the authorized_keys file.
authorized_keys is a file in the .ssh directory of the user on the remote host that holds copies
of the public keys authorized to make connections to our host. We create them in the home
directory of our user on our remote host. These options we can use to limit what our keys can
do include those shown in Table 13-1.

Table 13-1. *authorized_keys Options*

Option	Description
from	Limits where connections can come from. Takes domain, FQDN, and IP addresses.
command	Specifies the command to be executed whenever this key is used for authentication.
environment	Sets user environment if it is allowed by sshd.
no-agent-forwarding	Prevents SSH authentication agent forwarding.
no-port-forwarding	Prevents SSH port forwarding.
no-X11-forwarding	Prevents X11 forwarding.

Table 13-1 shows a subset of the complete options available. For more information, read the man page for sshd.

Let's use this information to create an authorized_keys file that we will send to our remote host. First, we'll copy the existing exbackup.pub key to a file called remote_authorized_keys. This creates a file containing the public key for the exbackup user.

```
$ cp exbackup.pub remote_authorized_keys
```

We'll also create a file called ssh_limiter.sh, and that will be the script we'll force our connection to run when we connect with the exbackup SSH key, as shown in Listing 13-1.

Listing 13-1. *Limiting the Commands ssh Can Do Using Keys*

```
$ vi ssh_limiter.sh
#!/bin/bash
# Command to be used by exbackup at example.com to limit what exbackup can
# do on a remote host.
# SSH2 stores the original command send by the remote host in a variable
# $SSH_ORIGINAL_COMMAND. We will use case to test and limit the commands
# we are running.

case "$SSH_ORIGINAL_COMMAND" in
  *\&*)
  echo "UNAUTHORIZED COMMAND"
  ;;
  *\;*)
  echo "UNAUTHORIZED COMMAND"
  ;;
  *\|*)
  echo "UNAUTHORIZED COMMAND"
  ;;
  rsync\ --server*)
  $SSH_ORIGINAL_COMMAND
  ;;
  *)
  echo "UNAUTHORIZED COMMAND"
  ;;
esac
```

In Listing 13-1, we are using the Bash scripting language to test the commands that are being presented by the ssh user. When we make an SSH connection to a host, the variable $SSH_ORIGINAL_COMMAND holds the command we wish to execute on our remote host. So if we make the following SSH connection:

```
$ ssh somehost@example.com ls -l /tmp
```

the variable $SSH_ORIGINAL_COMMAND will hold the value ls -l /tmp. When presented with a SSH key, we can now test that variable and decide if it's the kind of command we will accept this key to use. When we perform an rsync on our remote host, the variable will contain rsync --server <some other arguments for rsync>. We want to allow this and exclude anything else.

The case statement tests the variable $SSH_ORIGINAL_COMMAND to make sure it contains only the command rsync --server. First, we deny control commands &, ;, and |, which can be used to add other commands to the end of our intended command. If the command starts with rsync --server, then we accept it (the \ --server is making sure Bash escapes the <space>--). Anything else that may be passed as a command is denied by *. The case statement is ended by the esac statement.

We now need to edit our remote_authorized_keys file to add options for our key.

```
$ vi remote_authorized_keys
command="~/bin/ssh_limiter.sh",from="*.example.com",no-port-fowarding,no-X11-➥
forwarding,no-agent-forwarding ssh-rsa➥
AAAAB3NzaC1yc2EAAAABIwAAAgEAp7jGL2il3QKREVTpNWkdPqiEbG4rKdCLt/nx57PHkZvz➥
SGI64GlsclOzIz92PBN/ZjNb4Z1ZaOGS7UYQOg4SHKXsw5/VHchIN1k3p9Vwm9rZUiDg3azKr9J+R➥
+r9TDhwReyYtOQhR/j1aZf1gYS3+xRLs+bQb6UXVRrccygCFtxvrA2B5Kkgw2QJhctSlNRyi8XobUK➥
7kOs2Bw4zIY8hEZMRBFEibqi/diXPngWsMeo2UQQGICo6yXmgUKqiuQq1azdDuTbEstLS97/LdT➥
qWd9MNAsYk= exbackup@backup-1.example.com
```

Here we added the options to the remote_authorized_key file that will eventually be on our remote host. We specified the command to be run when we use the key and the hosts that can connect with it, and we limited the functions normally allowed with general users. Anyone connecting with this key will now be able to run only the ssh_limiter.sh script, which allows only the rsync command to be executed and only connections originating from the *.example.com domain. We could be more strict in the from= option if we wanted and put in the IP address of the host originating the connection.

We are going to set up our remote host with the username and directory mirroring what we previously did for exbackup. We need to make sure that the exbackup home directory on the remote host has an .ssh directory and that it has the permissions of 700 set on it. We will now copy the remote_authorized_keys file to our remote server using a normal user. First, we'll copy the remote_authorized_keys file somewhere we can access by the user jsmith; /tmp should be OK. We'll copy the ssh_limiter.sh file to /tmp, too.

Using jsmith, who has an account on the remote hosts with administrative sudo access, we do the following:

```
$ scp /tmp/remote_authorized_keys /tmp/ssh_limiter.sh➥
jsmith@branch1.example.com:~/
```

This securely copies the remote_authorized_keys file to the home directory of jsmith on the remote host. Now we issue the following series of ssh commands:

```
$ ssh -t jsmith@branch1.example.com 'sudo useradd -u 500 -g adm -m➥
-d /data/backups exbackup && sudo -u exbackup mkdir -p /data/backups/.ssh &&➥
sudo chmod 700 /data/backups/.ssh'
```

This sets up our exbackup user on our remote host. It also creates a directory called .ssh in the home directory and sets the permission of 700 on it, which is a requirement of SSH security. We would like to point out that we used sudo -u exbackup to make the directory, so it has the correct ownership permissions. The double ampersand (&&) indicates that we want to execute the next set of commands if the first set was successful. In this instance, we used ssh -t to submit our command. The -t tells ssh to force pseudo-tty allocation; otherwise our sudo call will refuse to run. A *pseudo-tty* is a pretend text terminal device we implement here so that sudo will work.

Next, we will copy the remote_authorized_keys file to its proper location, renaming it on the way and setting its permissions. We will also create the /data/backups/bin directory and move ssh_limiter.sh there.

```
$ ssh -t jsmith@branch1.example.com➡
'sudo mv remote_authorized_keys  /data/backups/.ssh/authorized_keys➡
&& sudo chown exbackup:adm /data/backups/.ssh/authorized_keys➡
&& sudo  chmod 600 /data/backups/.ssh/authorized_keys➡
&& sudo -u exbackup mkdir /data/backups/bin➡
&& sudo mv ssh_limiter.sh /data/backups/bin➡
&& sudo chown exbackup:adm /data/backups/bin/ssh_limiter.sh➡
&& sudo chmod 750 /data/backups/bin/ssh_limiter.sh'
```

In the preceding code, we used the backslash (\) to break up the lines; the backslash tells Bash that our command continues on the next line rather than to execute the line of code when we press the Enter key. As far as Bash is concerned, it could be all one line.

We again make our connection to branch1 forcing the pseudo-tty in ssh. The sudo command, unless used in conjunction with the –u <username> option, will create all the new files and directories with root being the owner. Therefore, we need to change the permissions and ownership of the directories and files we are creating. We also created a bin directory in the /data/backups directory, which is the home directory of exbackup. In the authorized_key file, we specified command=~/bin/ssh_limiter.sh, so our ssh_limiter.sh script needs to be copied to the bin directory with the appropriate permissions as well.

We are going to create a file on our remote host to test the rsync script we are about to show you. On our remote host, we will create a text file in the /tmp directory called /tmp/test_sync.txt and fill it with garbage text.

```
$ vi /tmp/test_sync.txt
fldjfsl
lfdsjfsla
fsdjfsl
fjsdl
fsjfs
fsl
fsa
23433
```

Here we created a file on remotehost.example.com and added random text to a file called /tmp/test_sync.txt. If you cat that file (cat /tmp/test_sync.txt), you will that see that it contains all that random text.

We are now going to test our backup of this file on the remote host using rsync and our SSH keys.

```
$ sudo su - exbackup
[sudo] password for jsmith:
$ rsync -av -e 'ssh -i .ssh/exbackup' remotehost.example.com:/tmp/test_sync.txt /tmp
receiving file list ... done
test_sync.txt
```

```
sent 42 bytes  received 194 bytes   472.00 bytes/sec
total size is 58  speedup is 0.25
$ cat /tmp/test_sync.txt
fldjfsl
lfdsjfsla
fsdjfsl
fjsdl
fsjfs
fsl
fsa
23433
Ldjas
```

We used the rsync command to perform a simple copy of the file test_sync.txt to our local /tmp directory. You can see that the file has been copied by using cat to display its contents. We will explain the details of the rsync command a little later.

Next, let's add some more lines to the file and sync it again.

```
$ vi /tmp/test_sync.txt
fldjfsl
...
<snip>
...
fsa
23433
ldjas
dfald
asd
12344556
```

We'll then save the file and do the rsync again.

```
$ rsync -av -e 'ssh -i .ssh/exbackup' branch1.example.com:/tmp/test_sync.txt /tmp
receiving file list ... done
test_sync.txt

sent 48 bytes  received 213 bytes   174.00 bytes/sec
total size is 77  speedup is 0.30
```

When we use the cat command on the /tmp/test_sync.txt file, on our local host you will notice that it contains the new changes to the file.

```
$ cat /tmp/test_sync.txt
fldjfsl
...
<snip>
...
fsa
23433
ldjas
```

```
dfald
asd
12344556
```

OK, so we can securely sync a file from a remote host without needing to use a password. Let's quickly test our ssh_limiter.sh script to check that it works as expected. Here we will test to see if we can use our key to ssh across to the remote host and run the top command.

```
$ ssh -i .ssh/exbackup remotehost.example.com top
UNAUTHORIZED COMMAND
```

Perfect—sending prohibited or unexpected commands elicits the UNAUTHORIZED COMMAND response. Now we can set up crontab scripts to regularly sync our remote host files down to our backup directory. Table 13-2 lists some of the options that can be used with rsync.

Table 13-2. *rsync Options*

Option	Description
-a	Archive, general-purpose option that copies recursively with these options: -rlptgoD.
-r	Recursively copy directories.
-l	Copy symlinks as symlinks.
-p	Copy permissions.
-t	Copy timestamps.
-g	Copy group permissions.
-o	Copy ownership permissions.
-D	Preserve device (character and block devices) and special files (fifo and named sockets).
--exclude	Exclude directories or file; can be patterns. An example is .svn/ to exclude .svn directories.
--include	Include directories or files; fine-tune the files you want to copy. Same syntax as --exclude.
-n, --dry-run	Dry run. Show what would happen but do not actually perform sync.

In general, you will primarily use the rsync command with the archive options set, which is –a. This is a bundled option that represents the following options: -rlptgoD. These options are –r, recursive; -l, copy symlinks as symlinks; -p, copy permissions; -t, copy mod times; -g, preserve groups; -o, preserve ownership; and -D, preserve devices and special files. These options are usually sufficient to archive your systems, but if you need to, you can add more options, which are explained in the rsync man page.

You will probably make use of the --exclude and --include options, which allow you to fine-tune the file or directory you wish to sync. You can also use --exclude-from=<file> and --include-from=<file> to list multiple selections of files or directories you wish to target.

Let's take a look at a typical script we can use to sync our remote hosts to our local host. On our remote hosts, we will have a directory called /data/staff/sales that we want to sync down to our local host, and then we will back that up with our backup application. We will have two remote hosts, branch1.example.com and branch2.example.com, and we will use rsync to sync the contents of their /data/staff/sales directory, except the /data/staff/sales/temp directory, which we want to exclude. We also want this script to be run by the exbackup user using the passphraseless key we have created.

First, let's set up the .ssh/config file that will handle all the SSH configuration we need. In that file, we will add the hostname, the IP address or FQDN name, and the user to connect with. We will also define the SSH key we will use in our connection.

```
$ cat .ssh/config
Host *.example.com
  User exbackup
  Identityfile ~/.ssh/exbackup
```

The preceding code adds the username exbackup with the identity file in ~/.ssh/exbackup to every ssh connection made to a host in the example.com domain space. It is the equivalent of specifying $ ssh -I ~/.ssh/exbackup exbackup@somehost.example.com.

The script that we will use to run the rsync between our hosts looks like Listing 13-2.

Listing 13-2. *The nightly_remote_sync.sh Script*

```
1. #!/usr/bin/env bash
2.
3. # This uses rsync to sync down remote files to the /data/backups/<hostname>
4. # directories.
5. # The rsync command we will use.
6. RSYNC='which rsync'
7. RSYNC_OPTS="-av "
8.
9. # Host list - Bash array
10. HOSTLIST='
11. branch1.example.com
12. branch2.example.com
13. '
14. # Back up directory on local host and source directory on remote host
15. BACKUP_DIR='/data/backups/'
16. SALES_DIR='/data/staff/sales'
17.
18. # excluded directory
19. EXCLUDED="temp/"
20.
21. # error function
22. error_check() {
23.   if [ $1 -eq 0 ] ; then
24.     echo "backup successful"
25.   else
26.     echo "backup failed: see error number: $1"
27.   fi
28. }
29.
30. # The rsync functions
```

```
31. get_sales() {
32.   ${RSYNC} ${RSYNC_OPTS} --exclude $EXCLUDED $HOST:$SALES_DIR  $BACKUP_DIR/$HOST➡
2>&1 > /dev/null
33. }
34.
35. # Bash for loop to go through each host and rsync the data.
36. for HOST in $HOSTLIST ; do
37.   get_sales
38.   error_check $?
39. done
40.
41. exit 0
```

The purpose of the script in Listing 13-2 is to sync files from one or more remote hosts to the /data/backups directory of the host the script is running on. This can be the local network's backup host, backup.example.com, where we will have installed proper backup software. This is just one approach among many to achieve this outcome.

Line 1 contains the call to set the environment as a Bash script. We could also use the traditional shebang (#!/bin/bash) to let Linux know we are running a Bash script.

Lines 2–5 are comments describing our script. Lines 6 and 7 set RSYNC variables, and lines 10–13 declare the list of hosts we wish to sync from. Lines 15–19 are more variables. The backup directory we will be directing our backups to is BACKUP_DIR='/data/backups'. The sales directory, SALES_DIR='/data/staff/sales', is the target directory we are backing up. The temp/ directory is the one we wish to exclude.

■**Note** The user exbackup must have read permissions on all the files and directories you wish to back up, and write permissions on the directories you are backing up to. You can look at using groups to achieve this.

Lines 22–28 are a Bash function that handles our error checking. If the script ends in anything other than a zero, then it fails; if it ends in zero, the script is successful. The error_check() subroutine or function takes the $? argument, the exit code from another function call, and tests it for a zero. We know that if everything goes well, rsync will exit with a zero; otherwise it exits with another error code. We can use this error-check function to test for the success or failure of any other function that exits with a zero on success.

The get_sales function declared in lines 31–33 describes the rsync function that calls the rsync command and syncs the /data/staff/sales directory to the /data/backups/<hostname> directory. In line 32 2>&1 >/dev/null directs the stdout and stderr (or standard out and standard error) to /dev/null. Note that /dev/null is a Linux black hole; if you send things to it, like stdout or stderr, they disappear into nothingness.

■**Note** When you run a program on Linux/Unix hosts, three standard special file descriptors are used: stdin (standard input), stdout (standard output), and stderr (standard error). When your program receives input, it can receive that input by attaching to the stdin file descriptor. Likewise, when it produces its output, it can write that to stdout. If there is an error in the program, it can write that to stderr. For more information on handling and redirecting stdin, stdout, and stderr, please visit `http://learnlinux.tsf.org.za/courses/ build/shell-scripting/ch01s04.html`.

Finally, lines 36–39 loop through each host in the host list with the `for` loop function and perform the `rsync` on each host. Then the script checks the error code of each to see if it is zero, and if so, it prints the success message.

■**Note** A good resource for learning more about Bash programming is located at `http://www.tldp.org/ LDP/abs/html/index.html`. Another reference is the book *Beginning the Linux Command Line* by Sander Van Vugt (Apress, 2009).

When we run the script from the command line, we get the following result:

```
exbackup@au-mel-ubuntu-1:~$ ./bin/nightly_remote_rsync.sh
backup successful
backup successful
```

■**Note** When you first run this script, you will be presented with SSH asking you to confirm the new key signature of the remote hosts. Type **yes** to confirm the signature and the script should proceed as normal from then on.

We will now put this script into a crontab file so we can run it on a regular basis. Recall that we discussed crontab files in Chapter 5. Let's create the file /etc/cron.d/example_nightly_sync and add the following:

```
# run the nightly rsync script at 5 minutes past 12 every morning.
MAILTO=jsmith@example.com
5       0       *       *       *       exbackup        ➥
  /data/backups/bin/nightly_remote_rsync.sh
```

Here we are setting the script to run every night at five minutes past midnight as the user exbackup. If there is an error, an e-mail will be sent to jsmith@example.com. This is a great way to sync up files from one host to another, but it is not really a great backup strategy. For instance, every night we sync over all the changed files, including mistakes. If they are not noticed early enough, then the mistakes are propagated to our backup host and we lose our good copy of data. When we use a proper backup strategy, the potential for losing our ability to restore good data is minimized.

A few backup tools have been developed around rsync:

- *BackupPC*: http://backuppc.sourceforge.net/

- *drsync*: http://hacks.dlux.hu/drsync/

- *Dirvish*: http://www.dirvish.org/

- *SystemImager*: http://wiki.systemimager.org/index.php/Main_Page

Next, we'll take a look at an open source backup server application called Bacula, which can back up both Linux and Microsoft Windows hosts.

Using Bacula

The cost of a commercial backup solution can be extremely high. Bacula provides a robust, reliable, customizable, and efficient open source backup service for Linux, Unix, and Windows desktops and servers. It works with most storage devices, DAT, LTO, and autoloaders, and it can also back up to disk. Bacula is easy to configure, secure, and upgrade, and it is a complete, free, and robust backup server.

Bacula works on the client/server model and requires a Bacula client installed on the target host to be backed up. The Bacula server itself requires two daemons to be running: the Director daemon and the Storage daemon.

The Director daemon controls what will be backed up, when it will be backed up, and the location to which it will be backed up. It also provides similar services for any restoration jobs that might need to take place. It has a configuration file that contains the details that control the running of the Director daemon itself, as well as the Storage daemon and the File daemon that run on the target host.

The Storage daemon communicates with the Director daemon and the File daemon running on the target host and controls the access to the devices where your data will be stored, either on disk or on tape. The Storage daemon controls access to the backup media, tape drives, and autoloaders. It can be configured to even write to DVDs.

The File daemon sits on the target host waiting for connections from the Bacula Director daemon. When it receives the instructions to start a backup, the target host gets a list of the files it is to back up. It then makes a direct connection to the Storage daemon and sends the backup data to the Storage daemon to be written to the backup media. The File daemon communicates what files have been backed up to the Director daemon, and that information is written to the Bacula catalog.

The catalog records the files that have been backed up, the location from which they were backed up, when they were backed up, and onto what media (or volume) they were backed up. This catalog is kept in an SQL database for future reference. Once the backup is complete, the Bacula program can verify the backup was successful by comparing what was written to the catalog and what was written to the tape.

When a restore operation is requested, Bacula will read the contents of the catalog and request that the appropriate media be loaded. It will then contact the target client and the Storage daemon, and they will begin the restoration process.

The backup and restore operations are referred to as *jobs* in Bacula. You can schedule backup and restore jobs in the Bacula Director configuration file, /etc/bacula/bacula-dir. conf. Each job is made up of a series of definitions, and these definitions can inherit a set of common definitions that can make your configurations easier to manage. Each job acts on a client that is the target host. The jobs back up on or restore from a *volume*, which refers to the storage media you are using (e.g., tape, DVD, or disk). These volumes can be grouped into *pools* and given common definitions concerning retention periods, usage, and rotation. The scheduler can, of course, manage the coordination of the jobs, clients, volumes, and pools to run a one-off operation or repeated ones.

You control Bacula operations via the bconsole, a terminal console program that you can use to run jobs and view the status of the Director, Storage, or File daemons. You can also use it to manage volumes, pools, and restore operations. It is simple to set up, and you can place it anywhere on the network.

■**Note** We will look at setting up Bacula's GUI console, Bat, in the "Introducing the Bat Console" section.

The Bacula server requires the following TCP ports open on your server:

- The Bacula Director daemon requires port 9101 (on the Bacula server only).
- The Bacula Storage daemon requires port 9102 (on the Bacula server only).
- The Bacula File daemon requires port 9103 (on any target host or client).

You add them with the following command on the backup server:

```
$ sudo /sbin/iptables -I Firewall-eth1-INPUT <rule-number> -p tcp -m state➥
--state NEW -m tcp --dport 9101:9103 -j ACCEPT
```

On the clients, you only need to open TCP port 9103.

Getting the Software

The SourceForge Bacula page (http://sourceforge.net/projects/bacula) provides rpm and deb packages of the latest releases for you to download. Most distributions are several versions behind the latest release. You can get the packages and tarballs here: http://sourceforge.net/project/showfiles.php?group_id=50727.

You install Bacula on Red Hat and Ubuntu hosts with the normal packaging tools as follows. Fedora hosts above FC8 require this:

```
$ sudo yum install bacula-client bacula-director bacula-storage bacula-console
```

For an RHEL host, you should download packages from SourceForge. There are some contributed RPMs here: http://sourceforge.net/project/showfiles.php?group_id=50727&package_id=213714. You also need to make sure that you have the MySQL server installed on your host, but you do not have to use that database server if you wish to use another on another host. Both are available via RHN, and you need to download the following packages:

```
bacula-mysql-2.4.2-1.el5.i386.rpm bacula-mtx-2.4.2-1.el5.i386.rpm
```

Make sure that /var/spool/bacula is created, and if it is not, create it with the mkdir command.

On Ubuntu, you have to use the following:

```
$ sudo aptitude install bacula-fd bacula-console bacula-director-mysql↪
bacula-sd-mysql
```

You will be asked to give a username and password for your MySQL service. This installs all the required packages and any dependencies, and creates the default configuration files in the configuration directory /etc/bacula. The bacula user is also created at this point. To get Bacula up and running, you will have to edit the following files in the configuration directory to access the Bacula management console: /etc/bacula/bacula-dir.conf, /etc/bacula/bacula-sd.conf, /etc/bacula/bacula-fd.conf, and /etc/bacula/bconsole.conf.

Before we configure anything in Bacula, we should explain the relationship these files have with each other. For the Bacula daemons to communicate with each other, they require the exchange of a set of passwords. Each Storage daemon (you can have more than one) and each File daemon (you will generally have more than one) must contain the name of the Bacula Director and the password it uses to verify itself. The password is set in two places for each daemon that wants to communicate with the Bacula Director.

Figure 13-2 shows the relationship between the configuration files and their common definitions.

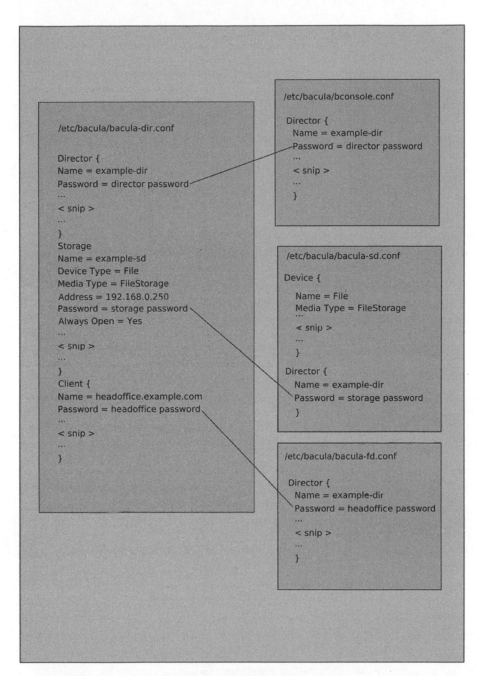

Figure 13-2. *Bacula common configuration file definitions*

As you can see in Figure 13-2, the Bacula /etc/bacula/bacula-dir.conf file for the Director will contain information for the Storage daemon, the Client daemon, and the bconsole program. You can also see that definitions of configuration objects, such as Storage, Pools, FileSets, and so forth, require the name of the object being configured and the definitions to be enclosed in curly brackets: {<*definition = value*>}. The definitions must be one per line.

You can also see in Figure 13-2 that in the Storage file, the Name and Media Type must match the Device Type and Media Type in the Device object definition in the Director file. The Director Name and Password in the Director object definition in the Storage file must match the storage password in the Storage section of the Director file.

When we define a client in our Director file, the password assigned to the client must be present in the File daemon configuration for that Director name. Also in Figure 13-2, you see that the bconsole program configuration file requires the name of the Director and the password for that Director before it will establish a connection.

We talked about MySQL servers back in Chapter 11. We are now going to create a database on that host to house our catalog. Along the way, we'll configure the MySQL host to be backed up. First, we need to create the correct accounts and the database on our MySQL host.

We will assume that the headoffice.example.com host has the MySQL database server installed and that we are running our backups from backup.example.com. We can, of course, house this database on the one host, headoffice.example.com, if we didn't have an extra host available to be the separate backup host. In that case, you should use localhost in the following examples where we have used backup.example.com. The other alternatives are to store a separate MySQL database server (or PostgreSQL, if you wish) on your backup host or to use a SQLite database on the backup host.

On the headoffice.example.com MySQL host, we will create a new database for Bacula and grant access to the user bacula from our backup.example.com host. We will then make sure that our backup.example.com host can connect to port 3306 on headoffice.example.com by making a change to the firewall. While we do that, we will also make sure that our Bacula File daemon is installed on headoffice.example.com and that we have firewall access for TCP port 9103 on that host from backup.example.com.

On headoffice.example.com we will do the following:

```
$ sudo mysql -u root -p
Enter Password:
...
mysql> CREATE DATABASE 'bacula';
Query OK, 1 row affected (0.00 sec)
mysql> GRANT  ALL PRIVILEGES ON bacula.* to bacula@backup.example.com➥
IDENTIFIED BY 'somepassword';
Query OK, 0 rows affected (0.00 sec)
mysql> FLUSH PRIVILEGES;
Query OK, 0 rows affected (0.00 sec)
mysql> \q;
Bye
```

On Red Hat hosts, you will find the SQL statements to create the database in /usr/lib/bacula/mysql. On Ubuntu, they will be in /usr/share/bacula-director.

To create the database tables for the Bacula database, we will run the following on the backup.example.com host:

```
$ sudo -u bacula /usr/lib/bacula/make_mysql_tables -h headoffice.example.com➥
 -u bacula -p
Creation of Bacula MySQL tables succeeded.
```

Running this script supplied by Bacula will create the necessary tables for our catalog. You can also see in that same directory that you will be able to use similar scripts to create the database and then assign the correct privileges if you want to.

We confirm that the database was created by running the following command:

```
$ sudo -u bacula mysql -h headoffice.example.com -u bacula -p -D bacula➥
-e 'show tables;'
```

This command connects to the MySQL database running on the headoffice.example.com host using the bacula username and password. -p prompts for a password, and -psomepassword is how you would submit the password on the command line (there is no space between -p and the password). Getting the output will do two things: confirm that our username and password are working correctly and that the script actually did create some tables.

■**Note** You can find additional information on using Bacula with MySQL at http://www.bacula.org/en/ rel-manual/Installing_Configurin_MySQL.html.

You will need to check that the /var/spool/bacula directory exists and is writeable by the bacula user. Other things to be aware of are that the /data/backups/bacula/FileStorage directory must exist and it must also be writeable by the bacula user, as should the /var/log/ bacula.log file.

Configuring Bacula

We'll now examine the configuration files that need to be defined for your Bacula server. As mentioned earlier, there are three files for dealing with the Bacula server itself and one for the management console. Let's start with the main file, the Director, at /etc/bacula/bacula-dir. conf.

bacula-dir.conf

The Director configuration file is the main file used by Bacula. In here, you define every aspect of the Bacula service: jobs, schedules, pools, and so on.

The Director {} section defines the directory itself:

```
Director {                          # define myself
  Name = example-dir
  DIRport = 9101                    # where we listen for UA connections
  QueryFile = "/etc/bacula/query.sql"
  WorkingDirectory = "/var/spool/bacula"
  PidDirectory = "/var/run"
  Maximum Concurrent Jobs = 1
  Password = "directorpassword"         # Console password
  Messages = Daemon
}
```

Here we have changed the Name and Password definitions. The rest are defaults and are fine. The Director port is sitting on 9101. The QueryFile directive points to /etc/bacula/query. sql and is a SQL file that contains various SQL statements that can be used to query the database. You could add your own SQL queries to this script, if you believe that Bacula doesn't have the information you are looking for.

Looking now at the JobDefs section, a default job or JobDefs can group similar backup job requirements together. For instance, our web servers can be in one JobDefs that defines their FileSet, Schedule, and Storage media, and mail servers can be defined in another. All the parts that you use to define a job can be put into the JobDefs.

```
JobDefs {
  Name = "DefaultLinux"
  Type = Backup
  Level = Incremental
  Client = headoffice-fd
  FileSet = "Linux"
  Schedule = "WeeklyCycle"
  Storage = File
  Messages = Standard
  Pool = Full
  Full Backup Pool = Full
  Incremental Backup Pool = Incremental
  Priority = 10
}
```

The preceding code is taken from the provided /etc/bacula/bacula-dir.conf. All of the definitions here can also be defined in the Job resource. First, we declare the JobDefs between the curly brackets {}. Next, we name the JobDefs as DefaultLinux. The Type of job can be Backup, Restore, Verify, or Admin. The Backup job type performs a backup, the Restore type performs a restore, the Verify type compares the contents of the catalog to the file system you have just backed up, and the Admin type can be used to perform catalog maintenance, if required.

The Level of backup required is not really required, but it must be specified either here in the JobDefs or in the Schedule. Any setting within the Schedule overrides the setting here. The value for Level can be Full, Incremental, or Differential. The full backup takes a backup of all files in the specified FileSet regardless of their backup history. The incremental backup will back up files changed since the last full backup. The differential backup will do a very similar job as the incremental, but it will back up *all* files changed since the last full backup. Let's discuss that a little more.

Whenever a differential or incremental backup is performed, the Bacula File daemon clients will check the file list for modified file timestamps and changed file timestamps, and compare them to the previous full backup. If the timestamps are different, then the files will be backed up by the incremental or differential backup process. However, what differentiates the differential from the incremental is that the differential backup merges all changed files into one backup since the last full backup. This means that although the backup may take up more space on your volumes (storage media), when you restore from the backups you will only need the last full backup and the most recent differential backup. If you had been using incremental backups, you would need the last full backup plus each incremental since the last full backup.

The other point we will make here is that if there is no full backup for this FileSet on this client for the retention time period, Bacula will upgrade your backup to a full backup automatically. We have left Level = Incremental in this JobDefs.

The Client directive here is set to bacula-fd. This is overridden by the Client {} definition but is needed by the configuration file. The client bacula-fd resource has to exist in the configuration file; otherwise an error will occur. We will leave this as is.

The FileSet = "Linux" directive defines the resource that describes the files we wish to back up for our hosts. The FileSet will be defined further on in our Director configuration file. In the FileSet, you can include and exclude directories and file names or types. You can also define both Linux and Microsoft Windows files to be backed up or excluded. The default the FileSet included here refers to a typical Linux file set.

Next is the Schedule resource we are assigning to the JobDefs, which defines when we should run this type of job. The default definition for the WeeklyCycle included in Bacula is a simple monthly full backup with a differential once a week. It also runs a nightly incremental backup from Monday to Saturday. We will alter this so that it runs another full backup every third week; we will cover how to do this shortly.

In the default JobDefs, we can also see that the Storage resource has been defined as File. This points to the name of the storage device defined by Name = File. We just explained that this points to our Storage configuration file, and our backups will go to a portion of hard disk we have set aside for backups, /data/backups/bacula/FileStorage.

Messages = Standard refers to the Messages resource. Here, you can set the way your messages are handled. They can either be written to a log or sent to an e-mail address.

The Pool = Full definition points the job to a particular pool of volumes where they are backed up. As mentioned earlier, volumes are groups of storage media. You might have a group for your daily backups, a group for your weekly backups, and a group for your monthly backups. In this instance, we have defined a default group, Full, for our backups. We have, however, defined Full Backup Pool = Full and Incremental Backup Pool = Incremental to make sure that the full and incremental backups go to the right media.

Lastly in our JobDefs we have Priority = 10. This setting helps prioritize jobs; the lower the number, the higher the priority Bacula will give to the job. Some settings in the JobDefs can be overridden by definitions in other areas, like in the Job, Schedule, and Client definitions.

```
Job {
  Name = "BackupCatalog"
  JobDefs = "DefaultLinux"
  Level = Full
  FileSet="Catalog"
  Schedule = "WeeklyCycleAfterBackup"
  # This creates an ASCII copy of the catalog
  RunBeforeJob = "/usr/libexec/bacula/make_catalog_backup bacula bacula"
  # This deletes the copy of the catalog
  RunAfterJob  = "/usr/libexec/bacula/delete_catalog_backup"
  Write Bootstrap = "/var/spool/bacula/BackupCatalog.bsr"
  Priority = 11                    # run after main backup
}

Job {
  Name = "RestoreFiles"
```

```
  Type = Restore
  Client = headoffice-fd
  FileSet = "Linux"
  Storage = File
  Pool = Default
  Messages = Standard
  Where = /tmp/bacula-restores
}

Job {
  Name = headoffice.example.com
  Client = headoffice-fd
  Enabled = yes
  JobDefs = "DefaultLinux"
}
```

The first two job definitions are standard in Bacula. We need the first job, named BackupCatalog, to back up our MySQL database, which holds the catalog. The second job definition is used by restore jobs. In the headoffice.example.com job, we have declared the Name and the Client (which we will define shortly), Enabled the job, and given it a JobDef. Most of the settings that can be assigned to a Job resource definition are defined through JobDefs = "DefaultLinux".

The remaining items we need to address are FileSet, Pool, and Schedule, and we need to set a Client. Let's look at the FileSet definition first. A FileSet describes what you want to back up on your hosts. You can declare as many as you like, and you can declare these file sets for Windows and Linux hosts. We are going to create a FileSet called Linux.

```
FileSet {
  Name = "Linux"
  Include {
    Options {
      Compression = GZIP
      Signature = SHA1
    }
    File = "/etc"
    File = "/var/lib"
    File = "/data"
    File = "/home"
  }
  Exclude {
    File = "/proc"
    File = "/sys"
    File = "/dev"
    File = "/data/backups/bacula/FileStorage"
  }
}
```

In this FileSet we first define the Name. This can be used in the JobDefs or Job resource definition. As you can see, we can divide the FileSet into two parts: the Include section and the Exclude section. In the Include section we have specified a couple of Options, Compression and Signature. These settings allow our backup data to be compressed with the gzip program and define the signature of either SHA1 or MD5. If we were using a tape drive that did hardware compression on the data as it was written to tape, we would not use the software compression here. With the signature, you can use either SHA1 or MD5, but MD5 (it is said) will add an extra overhead to each file saved in both data size and CPU time. The signature is stored in the catalog for use with verification of the file's contents and if they have changed. Next we define the files we wish to include in our backup. These are the /etc, /var/lib, /data, and /home directories. We chose /etc because it contains the main configuration files for our system, the /var/lib/ directory because some of our Samba and MySQL data will be stored there, and the /data and /home directories because that is where our user data will be stored.

We are also excluding some directories (or at least making sure that they will not be backed up by mistake): /proc, /sys, and /dev. These directories are nonpermanent and change at every boot of the host, so there is no point in saving them. The /data/backups/bacula/FileStorage directory is being excluded because that is where we are backing up to. There is no point making backups of backups here—if we did, our backups would double in size with every backup.

Our file lists can also be kept in a separate file that we include into the FileSet with the @ symbol. For example, say we have a Windows list like the following that we have saved to a file called /etc/bacula/windows.list:

```
File = "C:/"
File = "D:/"
```

In our FileSet we would include that file list like so:

```
FileSet {
  Name = "Windows complete"
  Include {
    Options {
      signature = SHA1
    }
    @/etc/bacula/windows.list
    Options {
      Exclude = yes
      WildDir - "C:/WINNT/TEMP"
      WildDir = "C:/winnt/temp"
      WildDir = "C:/WINDOWS/TEMP"
      WildDir = "C:/windows/temp"
      WildDir = "*/Cache/*"
      WildDir = "*/cache/*"
    }
  }
}
```

Here we have included the C: and D: drives on our Windows host via the @/etc/bacula/windows.list file. We are using the SHA1 signature for our catalog. We are also excluding some unwanted directories. We don't want any temp or cache directories, as these tend to hold lots of data that doesn't require backing up and can be quite large.

> ■**Note** You can find information on using Bacula with full Visual SourceSafe support on a Windows platform at http://www.bacula.org/en/rel-manual/Windows_Version_Bacula.html.

```
FileSet {
  Name = "Catalog"
  Include {
    Options {
      signature = MD5
    }
    File = /var/spool/bacula/bacula.sql
  }
}
```

This last FileSet has been defined in the BackupCatalog resource job. Next, we have the Schedule resources. A Schedule defines when a job should run. We can also describe the level of our backup (if it is declared in the Schedule, it overrides the setting in the Job or JobDefs resource). For the WeeklyCycle we are using, we need to change it slightly from the default. We want to take a full backup of our data bimonthly, so we change the Schedule to look like this:

```
Schedule {
  Name = "WeeklyCycle"
  Run = Full 1st 3rd sun at 23:05
  Run = Differential 2nd 4th 5th sun at 23:05
  Run = Incremental mon-sat at 23:05
}
Schedule {
  Name = "WeeklyCycleAfterBackup"
  Run = Full sun-sat at 23:10
}
```

As described in the Schedule named WeeklyCycle, we are running a full backup on the first and third Sunday of every month. We run a differential every second, fourth, and fifth Sunday, with an incremental nightly between Monday and Saturday. These date-time specifications are made up of several well-defined keywords, and it is easy to create complex schedules if you wish.

> ■**Note** You can read more about the terms you can use in the Schedule resource documentation at http://www.bacula.org/en/rel-manual/Configuring_Director.html.

Before we can run any backups, we need to create the Client resource. We do that by providing an Address, a Name, and a Password. The Name in the Client definition will match the Client defined in the Job resource. The Password must match the password defined in the File daemon configuration file. The Address can be the fully qualified domain name or the IP address. Our Client resource will look like the following:

```
Client {
  Name = headoffice-fd
  Address = headoffice.example.com
  Password = "headofficepassword"
  Catalog = MyCatalog
}
```

Let's now configure the Storage definition. Again, this will be within the Storage {} section of the bacula-dir.conf file. We will use this information in the bacula-sd.conf file soon.

```
Storage {
  Name = File
  Address = backup.example.com         # N.B. Use a fully qualified name here
  SDPort = 9103
  Password = "storagepassword"
  Device = FileStorage
  Media Type = File
}
```

This is the default configuration for the Storage section. We have changed only the Password and Address details. In Figure 13-1, you saw that the Name, Password, Device, and Media Type details should also be in the /etc/bacula/bacula-sd.conf file.

Next, we should add these details to the Bacula Director configuration file. The configuration for the catalog will begin with the Catalog definition.

```
Catalog {
  Name = MyCatalog
  dbname = bacula;
  user = bacula;
  password = "somepassword";
  DB Address = headoffice.example.com
}
```

The Name can be anything, and we will stick with the default MyCatalog. The dbname should be bacula, as should the user. The password is the password we created previously. The DB Address should be the address of the host the Catalog is on.

Pools, as described earlier, are media volumes that are grouped together to reflect their purpose. You could have pools of media in groups like monthly, weekly, daily, or archive, or even by things like web servers, database servers, and so forth. In the Pool definition, you specify things like retention policies, labeling formatting, and so on. We are using our hard disk as our storage device, so we won't have any physically different media to load in or rotate out like you do with tape media. Our main interest here will be retention, or how long we hold the data for before we wipe it.

In our `Pool` definition we will have the following:

```
Pool {
  Name = Default
  Pool Type = Backup
  Recycle = yes
  AutoPrune = yes
  Volume Retention = 365 days
}
Pool {
  Name = Full
  Pool Type = Backup
  Storage = File
  Maximum Volume Bytes = 500M
  AutoPrune = Yes
  Volume Retention = 6 months
  Recycle = Yes
  Recycle Oldest Volume = Yes
  Label Format = "Full-${Year}-${Month:p/2/0/r}-${Day:p/2/0/r}"
}
Pool {
  Name = Incremental
  Pool Type = Backup
  Storage = File
  Maximum Volume Bytes = 150M
  AutoPrune = Yes
  Volume Retention = 14 days
  Recycle = Yes
  Recycle Oldest Volume = Yes
  Label Format = "Incremental-${Year}-${Month:p/2/0/r}-${Day:p/2/0/r} "
}
```

We have defined two pools that both use the same `Storage` called `File`. The `Name` of the `Pool` will be used to reference the `Pool` in other resource definitions. Each has the `Pool Type` of Backup, which is currently the only available type, according to the Bacula documentation. We have set two different `Maximum Volume Bytes`, one at 500M and one at 150M. This will roll over the volume to the next available volume (or Bacula will create a new volume for us) when the volumes reach those size limits. This means that we will have small files to deal with, rather than one huge file containing all our backup data.

■**Note** With tape media, you probably won't set the `Maximum Volume Bytes` limit, as in general you will want the tape to hold as much as its capacity. If a volume is created with this limit, it will remain at that limit regardless of the setting in the `Pool` resource. You will have to update the volume itself to change this limit using the Bacula console.

In our Pool definition we have also set AutoPrune = Yes, which enables Bacula to delete backup details from the catalog once the Volume Retention period has expired. There are times when you would not want this to occur. For example, with archive backups—that is, when you wish to keep your data for as long as possible—you will not want the records of those backups to be deleted from the catalog. In this case, you would set AutoPrune to No, just to be safe.

■**Caution** Even if you have set your Pool to AutoPrune = No and Volume Retention = 10 years, your backup data will last only as long as the data on the tape lasts. Overwriting the data or corruption of the data will make restoring the data impossible, regardless of what the Bacula catalog says.

Volume Retention tells Bacula how long it should consider the data on the volume as current. We have set our pools to different values: we wish to keep the data in our full volumes for 6 months and in our incremental volumes for 14 days. You may want to consider longer retention periods. After this retention period has expired, Bacula considers the volume data to have expired and that data can be overwritten.

Setting Recycle = Yes in our Pool definition means that once the data on the volume is considered expired, that volume will become available again to the general pool, to be used for writing again. Setting Recycle Oldest Volume = Yes means the oldest volume will be used before any other volume when more than one volume is available. This has the obvious advantage of destroying any existing data on those volumes at the latest possible time, so you will still be able to restore from those volumes up until that time.

Last in our Pool resource is the Label definition. Bacula gives a name or label to volumes based on this format. Tapes from autoloaders with barcode labels are not automatically read into Bacula and need to be manually labeled when you add a new tape. In the case of tape media, a small section of data is written to the start of the tape, giving it the label name for that volume. Once a tape is labeled, Bacula will always know which tape is inserted into the tape unit. We are using "Full-" and "Incremental-" and adding the suffix "${Year}-${Month:p/2/0/r}-${Day:p/2/0/r}" to produce a labeled volume like Full-2009-01-01. For full details on the variable expansions available with Bacula, please visit http://www.bacula.org/en/rel-manual/Variable_Expansion.html#VarsChapter

---

■**Note** For a discussion on backup strategies in relation to managing your tapes and rotations using Bacula, go to http://www.bacula.org/en/rel-manual/Backup_Strategies.html.

The Console service gives the Director the ability to poll the File or Storage daemons and report on their status. This ability is verified by the password provided and requires the name of the Bacula service allowed to monitor it. In the Director configuration file, we have the following:

```
Console {
  Name = example-mon
  Password = "directormonpassword"
  CommandACL = status, .status
}
```

The messaging service is defined in the Director configuration and is a way for all communications from Bacula to be sent via the Director and not from the individual clients. When an incident occurs or a job completes, the messages are sent to the standard messaging service configured in the Director. The resource named Standard is defined in the Messages section and looks like the following:

```
Messages {
  Name = Standard
  mailcommand = "/usr/sbin/bsmtp -h mail.example.com -f \"\(Bacula\) %r\" -s \"Bacula:➥
%t %e of %c %l\" %r"
  operatorcommand = "/usr/sbin/bsmtp -h mail.example.com -f \"\(Bacula\) %r\"➥
-s \"Bacula: Intervention needed for %j\" %r"
  mail = root@localhost = all, !skipped
  operator = root@localhost = mount
  console = all, !skipped, !saved
  append = "/var/spool/bacula/log" = all, !skipped
}
Messages {
  Name = Daemon
  mailcommand = "/usr/sbin/bsmtp -h mail.example.com -f \"\(Bacula\) %r\"➥
-s \"Bacula daemon message\" %r"
  mail = root@localhost = all, !skipped
  console = all, !skipped, !saved
  append = "/var/log/bacula.log" = all, !skipped
}
```

Bacula uses the mailcommand and operatorcommand commands to send e-mail messages indicating the status of Bacula, either alerts or completion messages. It uses its own mailer binary, bsmtp, to send messages to the appropriate addresses. -f sets the From header, and -s sets the Subject header of the e-mail. You need to change the mail and operator settings to suit your environment by setting the e-mail address to the person responsible for administrating the Bacula server (in our case, admin@example.com). You can set operator type messages, such as "Please mount tape," to a different e-mail address compared to success/failure messages defined in the mail definition. We have also added the –h mail.example.com setting, which points to our mail server for the mailcommand and the operatorcommand commands.

In the next section, we'll look at the file we are going to configure to describe our Storage daemon.

bacula-sd.conf

Bacula stores the configuration details for the Storage daemon in the /etc/bacula/bacula-sd.
conf file. The Storage configuration file that is supplied by Bacula has many examples of different ways to configure your devices. You should use the file as a guide to setting up different
types of storage devices. In our Storage file we have the following:

```
Storage {
  Name = example-sd
  SDPort = 9103
  WorkingDirectory = "/var/spool/bacula"
  Pid Directory = "/var/run"
  Maximum Concurrent Jobs = 20
}
Director {
  Name = example-dir
  Password = "storagepassword"
}
```

In the file /etc/bacula/bacula-sd.conf, we have defined the Name of our Storage daemon,
example-sd. We could have other storage daemons on our network, so this name must be
unique. The Director section defines the Name of our Bacula Director and the storagepassword
we defined in the /etc/bacula/bacula-dir.conf. In the Device section, the Name matches the
Device in the Storage section of the Director configuration file. Media Type = FileStorage
matches in both the Director and Storage configuration files.

```
Device {
  Name = FileStorage
  Media Type = File
  Archive Device = /data/backups/bacula/FileStorage
  LabelMedia = yes;
  Random Access = Yes;
  AutomaticMount = yes;
  RemovableMedia = no;
  AlwaysOpen = no;
}
```

Here we have defined the device that our backups will be stored on. We don't have any
tape drives or autoloaders, so this will be a simple disk-based storage setup. We define where
on our host the backup files will be stored. In this instance, we are going to store them in the
/data/backups/bacula/FileStorage directory. We've left the other options at their defaults.

■**Note** You can read more on the configuration of the Storage daemon at http://www.bacula.org/en/
rel-manual/Storage_Daemon_Configuratio.html#StoredConfChapter.

```
Director {
  Name = example-mon
  Password = "directormonpassword"
  Monitor = yes
}
Messages {
  Name = Standard
  director = example-dir = all, !skipped, !restored
}
```

The Monitor, or Console, section in bacula-dir.conf defines the resource Director { ...
Name = example-mon ... }. This is used to monitor the resource and allows the Director to
get the status of the Storage daemon. It requires that the password be declared in the Director
configuration as well as here. The messages resource allows the Storage daemon to send informational messages via the Bacula Director daemon.

bacula-fd.conf

The very last thing we have to do before we can take a backup is install the bacula-fd software
on our headoffice.example.com host. Red Hat and Ubuntu hosts require bacula-common and
bacula-client, which will download any dependencies we may also need. Once these are
installed, we will edit the /etc/bacula/bacula-fd.conf file and add the following information.

```
Director {
  Name = example-dir
  Password = "headofficepassword"
}
FileDaemon {
  Name = headoffice-fd
  FDport = 9102
  WorkingDirectory = /var/spool/bacula
  Pid Directory = /var/run
  Maximum Concurrent Jobs = 20
}
Director {
  Name = example-mon
  Password = "directormonpassword"
  Monitor = yes
}
Messages {
  Name = Standard
  director = example-dir = all, !skipped, !restored
}
```

In the File daemon configuration script, we declare the Director {} stanza for connecting to the Bacula Director daemon. That requires the Name of the Director we are connecting
to and the Password we have defined in the Client resource for headoffice-fd. The FileDaemon
defines the Name, FDPort, and Maximum Concurrent Jobs settings. The Name setting must match

the `Name` in the `Client` resource, and the `FDPort` is set to the default TCP port of 9102. `Maximum Concurrent Jobs` defines the number of jobs that can connect to this host at any one time.

The `Director` and `Messages` sections are the same as described in the Storage file. They are used to allow the Director to get the status of the File daemon and define where to send messages if there is an error.

Testing the Syntax

We can now test the syntax of our `bacula-dir.conf` configuration file by issuing the following command:

```
$ sudo /usr/sbin/bacula-dir -t -c /etc/bacula/bacula-dir.conf
```

For the File and Storage daemons, we would issue this command:

```
$ sudo /usr/sbin/bacula-fd -t -c /etc/bacula/bacula-fd.conf
```

or this one:

```
$ sudo /usr/sbin/bacula-sd -t -c /etc/bacula/bacula-sd.conf
```

If neither command returns an error, we can start our service using either the `service` or `invoke-rc.d` command. Great! They're running, aren't they? You're right—how can we tell? We can use the `status` argument to see if they are running:

```
$ sudo /etc/init.d/bacula-dir  status
bacula-dir (pid 8774) is running...
$ sudo /etc/init.d/bacula-fd  status
bacula-fd (pid 8757) is running...
$ sudo /etc/init.d/bacula-sd  status
bacula-sd (pid 8738) is running...
```

bconsole.conf

We now have to set up the console so we can administer and monitor the backup service. The file that holds the configuration for our bconsole is called `/etc/bacula/bconsole.conf`.

Several consoles are available, and depending on your own preferences, you can set up either a GUI or a screen-based console. We'll first set up the screen-based console, and then we'll set up the GUI Bat console later in the chapter. In the `/etc/bacula/bconsole.conf` file, we define the following:

```
Director {
  Name = example-dir
  DIRport = 9101
  Address = backup.example.com
  Password = "directorpassword"
}
```

This has the same details (`Name`, port, `Address`, and `Password`) as the `Directory` resource in the `bacula-dir.conf` configuration file.

Managing Bacula with bconsole

After you configure Bacula, you can start the services by using the `service` or `invoke-rc.d` command, depending on your operating system. On Red Hat, you would issue the following to start the services:

```
$ sudo /sbin/service bacula-dir start
$ sudo /sbin/service bacula-sd start
$ sudo /sbin/service bacula-fd start
```

and on Ubuntu you would issue the following:

```
$ sudo /usr/sbin/invoke-rc.d  bacula-dir start
$ sudo /usr/sbin/invoke-rc.d bacula-sd start
$ sudo /usr/sbin/invoke-rc.d  bacula-fd start
```

We can now start the Bacula console program using the `bconsole` command like so:

```
$ sudo /usr/sbin/bconsole
```

First, we can list the current status of the Director by issuing the `status all` command. Issuing this command gives a detailed list of what is happening on Bacula Director, including the attached Storage daemons and File daemons.

To find out what the Director itself is doing, we use the `stat dir` command. This command gives an overview of the pending jobs, the current running jobs, and the jobs that have been completed. We access the console by issuing the following command.

```
$ sudo /usr/sbin/bconsole
Connecting to Director 127.0.0.1:9101
1000 OK: example-dir Version: 2.4.2 (26 July 2008)
Enter a period to cancel a command.
*stat dir
example-dir Version: 2.4.2 (26 July 2008) i386-redhat-linux-gnu redhat
Daemon started 04-Mar-09 07:59, 0 Jobs run since started.
 Heap: bytes=27,197 max_bytes=27,197 bufs=184 max_bufs=184

Scheduled Jobs:
Level           Type     Pri  Scheduled          Name                     Volume
===================================================================================
Incremental     Backup    10  04-Mar-09 23:05    headoffice.example.com   *unknown*
Full            Backup    11  04-Mar-09 23:10    BackupCatalog            *unknown*
====

Running Jobs:
No Jobs running.
====
No Terminated Jobs.
====
*
```

As you can see, we have no jobs completed and no jobs currently running. We have two jobs scheduled to run on March 4 at 23:05, one that backs up headoffice.example.com and one that backs up the catalog. Take some time to explore the bconsole a little more. For example, type **hand** and then press Enter to see a list of commands available to you on the command line. Table 13-3 lists the most useful commands.

Table 13-3. *Useful Bacula bconsole Commands*

Command	Description
run	Starts a job (a backup)
cancel	Cancels the current job
mess	Shows any current messages
restore	Manages restore jobs
label	Labels a tape or media volume
update volume	Allows you to update the properties of any particular volume
stat dir	Gets the current status of the Director daemon
stat client	Gets the current status of a File daemon
stat storage	Gets the current status of the Storage daemon
mount	Mounts a volume (e.g., loads a media volume into a tape drive)
unmount	Unmounts a media volume (e.g., unloads the tape from a drive)

■**Note** Another resource for useful commands is in the Bacula documentation at http://www.bacula. org/en/dev-manual/Brief_Tutorial.html.

You can run a job or a backup in two ways. One is to use the run command and press Enter. You are then presented with an easy-to-understand menu-driven way to submit your backup. The other is to place the commands directly on the command line like this:

```
* run job=headoffice.example.com level=full priority=7 yes
```

When we run the * stat dir command, we can see that our job is running.

```
Running Jobs:
 JobId Level   Name                                         Status
==================================================================
     2 Full    headoffice.example.com.2009-03-04_08.33.11 is  running
====
```

A new volume has been created, and the backup is restoring to it. If you type **mess** at the command line, you will receive any messages that are available about your job.

Now if we wanted to stop this job, we would use the cancel command with JobId 2 as an argument. You can see in the previous Running Jobs output the JobId to use.

```
*cancel jobid=2
```

The cancel command can be run without arguments and will automatically select the JobId for you (if only one job is running; otherwise, it presents a list to choose from). We have run the job again, this time without canceling it, and it has completed. When we do a stat dir in the Terminated Jobs section, we find the following.

```
JobId  Level    Files    Bytes    Status  Finished          Name
=================================================================================
    4  Full    1,198    12.60 M  OK      04-Mar-09 08:53  headoffice.example.com
```

The preceding output shows that we have a full save of the Linux FileSet for the host headoffice.example.com. You can see the number of files it holds and the data volume. Let's try to restore the /etc/hosts file using the restore command.

```
* restore
To select the JobIds, you have the following choices:
     1: List last 20 Jobs run
     2: List Jobs where a given File is saved
     3: Enter list of comma separated JobIds to select
```

The list of options to use here actually goes to 12, but we will use option 2 to find out the JobId (which we already know from the Terminated Jobs output to be 4).

```
Select item:  (1-12): 2
Automatically selected Client: headoffice-fd
Enter Filename (no path):hosts
+-------+------------+--------------+----------+----------+-----------+-----------+----------------+
| JobId | Name       | StartTime           | JobType | JobStatus | JobFiles | JobBytes |
+-------+------------+--------------+----------+----------+-----------+-----------+----------------+
| 4     | /etc/hosts | 2009-03-04 08:52:55 | B       | T         | 1198      | 12606355 |
+-------+------------+--------------+----------+----------+-----------+-----------+----------------+
```

Now that we know our JobId, we would then use option 3 to restore our hosts file, as follows:

```
Select item:  (1-12): 3
Enter JobId(s), comma separated, to restore: 4
You have selected the following JobId: 4

Building directory tree for JobId 4 ...   +++++++++++++++++++++++++++++++++++++++++
1 Job, 1,174 files inserted into the tree.
cwd is: /
$ cd /etc
cwd is: /etc/
$ mark hosts
1 file marked.
$ done
Bootstrap records written to /var/spool/bacula/example-dir.restore.1.bsr

The job will require the following
   Volume(s)                 Storage(s)                  SD Device(s)
```

```
====================================================================

   Full-2009-03-04          File                  FileStorage

1 file selected to be restored.

Using Catalog "MyCatalog"
Run Restore job
JobName:    RestoreFiles
Bootstrap:  /var/spool/bacula/example-dir.restore.1.bsr
Where:      /tmp/bacula-restores
Replace:    always
FileSet:    Linux
Client:     headoffice-fd
Storage:    File
When:       2009-03-04 09:07:47
Catalog:    MyCatalog
Priority:   10
OK to run? (yes/mod/no):yes
```

When selecting the files you wish to restore, you can use the ls and cd commands to list and change directories as you search for the files.

```
cwd is: /
$ cd /etc
cwd is: /etc/
$ mark hosts
1 file marked.
$ done
```

Here we have used the mark command to select the file we wish to restore after using the cd command to navigate through the backed-up file system. To select everything recursively in a directory, you can use the mark * command. When you are finished selecting the files you wish to restore, use the done command.

You are given a list of the media volumes required to perform this restore. You will have to load them if they are not already available to your backup host. Then you are given the rundown of the restore job you are going to run. Make a note of Where: /tmp/bacula-restores, as this is where your restored file will be found.

Looking at stat dir and the Terminated Jobs section, a complete restore will look like this:

```
JobId  Level   Files    Bytes   Status   Finished        Name
====================================================================
    5            1       274     OK       04-Mar-09 09:14  RestoreFiles
```

Now we can check that the file has been restored to the /tmp/bacula-restores directory:

```
$ sudo ls -l /tmp/bacula-restores/etc/
total 4
-rw-r--r-- 1 root root 274 2009-03-04 06:54 hosts
```

We could always use the `restore` command to restore to a different host and a different destination by changing the `Client` and `Where` options before we confirm that we want to run the restore job.

Backing Up Databases with Bacula

We now want to show you a more advanced scenario. We have a MySQL database running on our headoffice.example.com host. Currently it holds our Bacula catalog database, but it could also contain the KnowledgeTree DMS database that we created in Chapter 12 or any other databases we use. We are going to take a complete backup of that database server by dumping all of the databases on it. To do that, we will need to run the `mysqldump` command. But how can we do that at 4:00 a.m. and know when it has finished so we can take the copy? We will use a script that takes the dump and puts the dump file to disk, and then we will use Bacula to manage the execution of that script, monitor its successful completion, and execute the script again to manage the removal of the copied database file on the target host.

■**Caution** Make sure you have enough space on your host to handle the size of your database dump—you could find yourself in trouble if you run out of room. It is a good idea to dump this file into a separate partition so that if you do run out of space, it does not impact other processes on your host.

Bacula provides two instructions in the `Job` resource that we will take advantage of now: `Client Run Before Job` and `Client Run After Job`. As their names imply, these instructions can be used to run scripts on the target host. `Client Run Before Job` will execute the command or script on the target host and require a successful completion before it continues. If it does not succeed, the job will terminate and produce an error message. `Client Run After Job` also requires a successful completion of the script or command on the target host; otherwise it stops further processing for that job and submits an error message. Taking a look at the headoffice.example.com `Job` resource we defined earlier, we are going to change it as follows.

```
Job {
  Name = headoffice.example.com
  Client = headoffice-fd
  Enabled = yes
  JobDefs = "DefaultLinux"
  Client Run Before Job = "/usr/local/bin/mysql_backup start"
  Client Run After Job = "/usr/local/bin/mysql_backup stop"
}
```

The script `mysql_backup` must exist on our target host in the `/usr/local/bin` directory. This will now do two things. It will first run the `mysql_backup` script with the `start` argument before our backup job starts. This will run `mysqldump` and begin the dumping of our MySQL database. If that is successful, we will then proceed to back up the rest of our host as specified in the accompanying FileSet. If that is also successful, Bacula will run mysql_backup stop and the dump file will be deleted. We need to create the mysql_backup script ourselves. Listing 13-3 contains a good template you can use for this.

Listing 13-3. *MySQL Backup Script*

```
#!/bin/bash

USER='root'
PASSWD='mysqlrootpassword'

case $1 in
 start)
   mysqldump --opt --all-databases -u $USER -p$PASSWD➥
> /var/lib/mysql/backups/mysql.sql
        if [ $? -eq 0 ] ; then
          echo "backup successful"
        else
          echo "backup failed"
          exit 1;
        fi
 ;;

 stop)
   if [ -e /var/lib/mysql/backups/mysql.sql ] ; then
      rm -f /var/lib/mysql/backups/mysql.sql
        if [ $? -eq 0 ] ; then
          echo "removal of file successful"
        else
          echo "failed to remove file"
          exit 1;
        fi

   fi
 ;;
esac
exit 0
```

■**Caution** This script contains sensitive password information. We recommend you store this script carefully with the following permissions set: chmod 500.

On our target host, headoffice.example.com, we must make sure that the /var/lib/mysql/ backups directory is created and has sufficient space to take the MySQL dump file we will be creating.

We now run that from inside bconsole using the following command:

```
> run job=headoffice.example.com client=headoffice-fd yes
```

We can use stat client=headoffice-fd to view the progress of the job on the target host, and we can use stat dir to see the progress on the Bacula server. Also, any messages can be seen via the mess command or viewed in the Bacula log. Here is a completed job with a Backup OK termination code. As shown, Client Run Before Job and Client Run After Job have both succeeded.

```
05-Mar 07:21 example-dir: Start Backup JobId 12, Job=headoffice.example.com.➥
2009-03-05_07.21.41
05-Mar 07:21 example-dir: Recycled volume "Full-2009-03-04"
05-Mar 07:21 headoffice-fd: ClientRunBeforeJob: run command➥
"/usr/local/bin/mysql_backup start"
05-Mar 07:21 headoffice-fd: ClientRunBeforeJob: backup successful
05-Mar 07:21 example-sd: Labeled new Volume "Full-2009-03-04" on device➥
"FileStorage" (/data/backups/bacula/FileStorage).
05-Mar 07:21 example-sd: Wrote label to prelabeled Volume "Full-2009-03-04" on➥
device "FileStorage" (/data/backups/bacula/FileStorage)
05-Mar 07:22 headoffice-fd: ClientAfterJob: run command "/usr/local/bin/mysql_
backup➥
stop"
05-Mar 07:22 example-sd: Job write elapsed time = 00:00:49, Transfer rate = 262.7 K➥
bytes/second
05-Mar 07:22 headoffice-fd: ClientAfterJob: removal of file successful
05-Mar 07:22 example-dir: Bacula 2.0.3 (06Mar07): 05-Mar-2009 07:22:33
  JobId:                12
  Job:                  headoffice.example.com.2009-03-05_07.21.41
  Backup Level:         Full
  Client:               "headoffice-fd" 2.0.3 (06Mar07) i386-redhat-linux-gnu,➥
redhat,
  FileSet:              "Linux" 2009-03-04 08:50:13
  Pool:                 "Full" (From Job FullPool override)
  Storage:              "File" (From Pool resource)
  Scheduled time:       05-Mar-2009 07:21:25
  Start time:           05-Mar-2009 07:21:44
  End time:             05-Mar-2009 07:22:33
  Elapsed time:         49 secs
  Priority:             10
  FD Files Written:     1,200
  SD Files Written:     1,200
  FD Bytes Written:     12,738,605 (12.73 MB)
  SD Bytes Written:     12,872,793 (12.87 MB)
  Rate:                 260.0 KB/s
  Software Compression: 85.6 %
```

```
VSS:                    no
Encryption:             no
Volume name(s):         Full-2009-03-04
Volume Session Id:      4
Volume Session Time:    1236255409
Last Volume Bytes:      12,928,002 (12.92 MB)
Non-fatal FD errors:    0
SD Errors:              0
FD termination status:  OK
SD termination status:  OK
Termination:            Backup OK
```

You can now see how you can manage complex backups on the Bacula backup server. You can use Bacula to back up a complete file system, or you can target data directories only. If you are going to target data directories only, be sure to look at how you are going to rebuild your hosts in the event of a problem with the hosts.

Next, we're going look at using the Bat console to manage our Bacula configurations.

Introducing the Bat Console

Using a text-based console is a quick and easy way to set up and manage your Bacula services. Some people prefer a GUI, however, so Bacula created a nice, clean interface called Bat for managing Bacula Director.

You install Bat via the bacula-bat package for Red Hat, available from the http://sourceforge. net site, or the bacula-console-qt package for Ubuntu, available from the online repository. You will need to have the qt4 package installed as a dependency.

The configuration for Bat is exactly the same as the bconsole.conf configuration. It is stored in the /etc/bacula/bat.conf file.

```
Director {
  Name = example-dir
  DIRport = 9101
  address = backup.example.com
  Password = "directorpassword"
}
```

You can see that we have included the name of Bacula Director we wish to attach to as well as the address, port, and password required to access it. You can use Bat to manage more than one Director, and you add any additional Director configuration details here.

You start Bat from the Linux desktop menu, as shown in Figure 13-3.

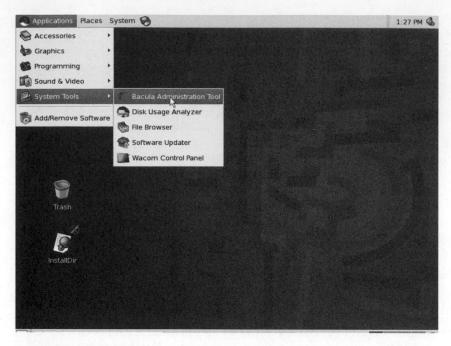

Figure 13-3. *Starting Bat*

You will be required to provide your password to gain administrative privileges. Bat then opens a screen like the one shown in Figure 13-4.

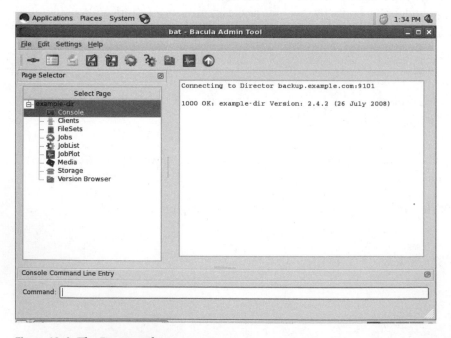

Figure 13-4. *The Bat console*

Figure 13-4 shows a clean and well-presented display of your Bacula service. On the left is the navigation menu and on the right is the result window. At the bottom of the screen is a Command text box that allows you to type Bacula commands directly into the console and see the results in the result window. All of the standard Bacula commands are accepted here.

In the left navigation menu you can see Clients, FileSets, and Jobs. Taking a look at the Clients window in Figure 13-5, you can see our headoffice-fd client is listed there, along with the details associated with that client, the File Retention and Job Retention policies, and so on.

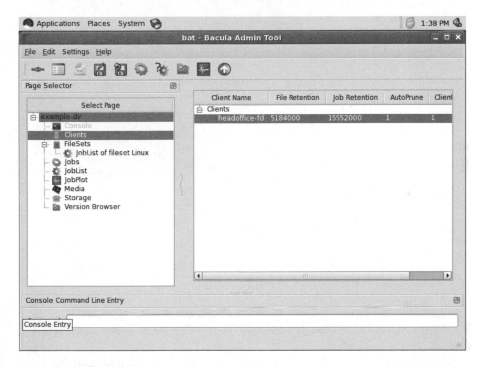

Figure 13-5. *Clients list*

You are able to use the mouse to interact with the Bat console. Right-clicking the mouse over a resource will bring up a list of options that you can select, as shown in Figure 13-6.

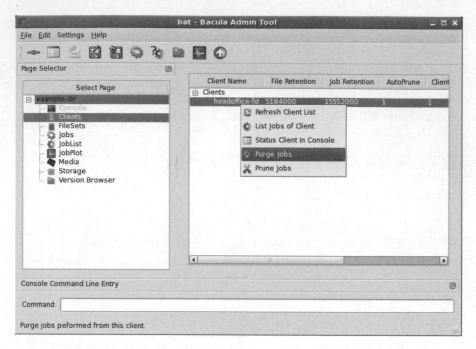

Figure 13-6. *Interacting with the Bat console*

In Figure 13-6, you can see that you can select several options when interacting with the Clients resource. Here we are selecting to purge all the jobs associated with the client headoffice-fd. This means that all the records associated with this client will be cleared from the database (but not actually deleted from the media itself).

Figure 13-7 shows that you can start a backup job from within the Bat console by right-clicking the job in the Jobs resource.

In the JobPlot window, you are able to see plotted data of the jobs that have run. This is useful for seeing trends in your backups. You can create different graphs of your data over varying time periods, so you can actively manage performance. In the Media section is a listing of the pools that have been set up and their status (see Figure 13-8).

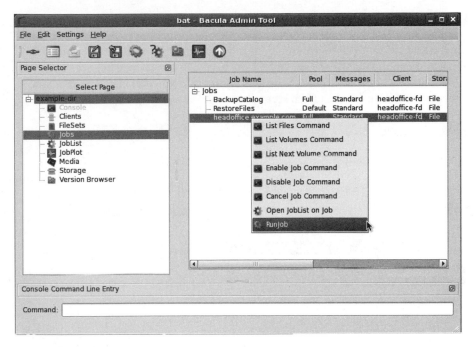

Figure 13-7. *Running a job*

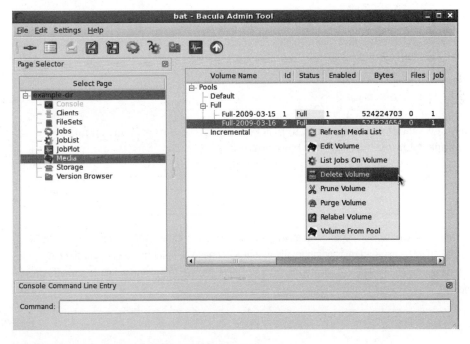

Figure 13-8. *Viewing pools in the Media section*

As you can see in Figure 13-8, we have one volume listed. It has been written to by the last job and its status is now Full. We have several options to select from here. If we were to select Delete Volume, we would remove the volume from the pool and delete all the records associated with that volume in the database.

Finally, you can view the details of the Storage resource, as shown in Figure 13-9. Again, by right-clicking you are able to select from several actions.

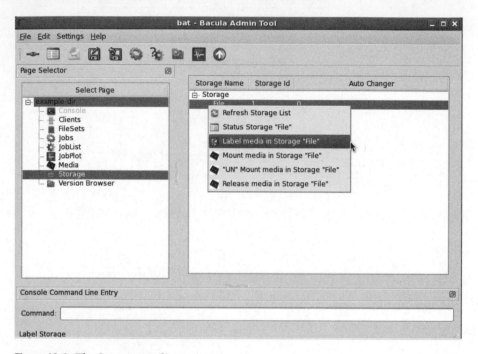

Figure 13-9. *The Storage media options*

You have several options to select from to act on storage resources. You can mount and unmount storage volumes and select to view the status.

As you can see, the Bat console is a comprehensive and intuitive tool to help you manage your Bacula configuration.

■**Note** In Chapter 19, we examine configuration management. We will extend this discussion on rebuilding your hosts in that chapter using a provisioning management tool called Cobbler and a configuration management tool called Puppet. These tools can be combined with Bacula server to provide a simple and effective recovery process.

Summary

In this chapter, we explored the backup options available to back up a single Linux host or hundreds of servers and workstations in a mixed environment. We introduced you to the software you can use to manage your backups, rsync and Bacula. You can combine them to securely back up remote hosts.

Later, in Chapter 19, we'll introduce automated provisioning systems that, combined with a backup regimen, allow you to quickly and efficiently recover your hosts.

In this chapter, we covered the following topics:

- Issues to consider when formulating a disaster recovery planning (DRP) and business continuity management (BCM) strategy

- How to back up remote hosts to a central host using rsync and SSH

- How to write a simple Bash script that can rsync your remote hosts regularly

- How to install and configure Bacula

- How to run a backup job with Bacula

- How to restore a file with Bacula

- How to do an advanced backup with Bacula of a MySQL database

- The Bat console, an advanced management GUI for Bacula

In the next chapter, we will show you how to manage your own VPN links and internetwork security.

CHAPTER 14

■ ■ ■

Networking with VPNs

By James Turnbull

In previous chapters, we talked about a lot of the services your organization might implement (e.g., e-mail and web services). We showed you a variety of ways to deliver those services to your users and customers, including over the Internet, and to mobile users and users located at other sites. Some services, however, are simply easier and safer to deliver locally (e.g., file and print services). If your users are not located locally, then you need some way of connecting them as if they were local. Enter the *virtual private network* (VPN).

A VPN is, in essence, a private network that runs over a public network. VPNs are often called *tunnels*, and they are used to secure and protect traffic you'd like to keep private over an otherwise public network like the Internet. VPNs can be initiated to and from network devices or to and from hosts. They can be made between two offices, for example, or from a client such as a desktop or laptop to an office. The traffic running over a VPN is usually encrypted and authenticated via a mechanism such as an SSL certificate, a password, or a two-factor authentication mechanism such as a token or smartcard.

In this chapter, we're going to show you how to install the required software (in our case, an open source VPN tool called OpenVPN) to create a VPN and how to configure and generate VPN tunnels.

Our Example Network

We're going to demonstrate a variety of VPN connections in this chapter, and we'll use the example network we created in Chapter 6 for our sample environment and network to configure. Figure 14-1 shows that network again.

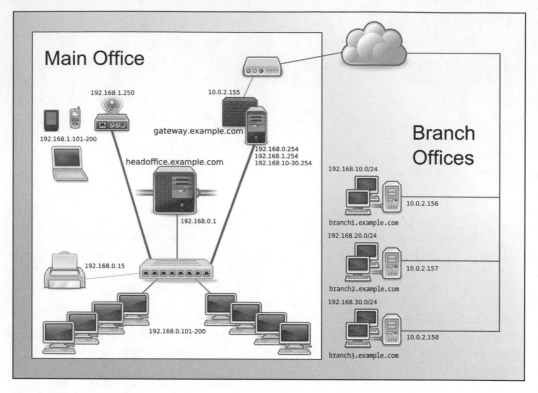

Figure 14-1. *Our example network*

Currently in our example network we have a head office with two main hosts:

- *gateway.example.com*: Our bastion host. It has an external IP address of 10.0.2.155 and an internal IP address of 192.168.0.254.

- *headoffice.example.com*: Our main head office server host. It has an internal IP address of 192.168.0.1 and external connections go out through the gateway host.

■**Note** We show how you can create these DNS CNAMEs (e.g., gateway and headoffice) in Chapter 9.

We also have three branch offices, each with its own internal and external IP address ranges:

- *branch1.example.com*: A branch office host with an external IP address of 10.0.2.156. The branch has an internal IP address range of 192.168.10.0/24.

- *branch2.example.com*: A branch office host with an external IP address of 10.0.2.157. The branch has an internal IP address range of 192.168.20.0/24.

- *branch3.example.com*: A branch office host with an external IP address of 10.0.2.158. The branch has an internal IP address range of 192.168.30.0/24.

Introducing OpenVPN

OpenVPN (http://openvpn.net/) is an open source SSL VPN application written by James Yonan that is available under the GNU GPL license. It works in a client/server model, with a server running on your host and clients connecting to the server and creating VPN tunnels.

■**Note** Other Linux-based VPN solutions are available, including IPsec implementations such as FreeS/WAN. You can find a fairly definitive list of other options at http://linas.org/linux/vpn.html.

OpenVPN runs on a variety of platforms including Linux, Solaris, Mac OS X, and Microsoft Windows. This allows you to connect a variety of clients to your Linux host; for example, you can connect a VPN tunnel from a desktop or laptop running Microsoft Windows. OpenVPN will even run on mobile devices running Windows Mobile or PocketPC and on devices like Apple's iPhone. You can use it to create VPN tunnels from these sorts of devices to allow you to securely access resources in your internal networks.

In the sections that follow, we will demonstrate how to install and set up OpenVPN in a variety of configurations.

Installing OpenVPN

You will need to install OpenVPN on both ends of your connection. For hosts, this means installing the OpenVPN server on both ends. If one end of your connection is a network device that supports connecting to OpenVPN, then you'll need to install the server only on the host that you will be using as the tunnel endpoint.

We're going to start by installing the server on our bastion host, gateway.example.com, which has the internal IP address of 192.168.0.254 and external IP address of 192.0.2.155, in the head office branch of our example network.

OpenVPN works on both Red Hat and Ubuntu, and it can be installed via a package. On Red Hat, you install the OpenVPN package from Dag Wieers's package repository (http://dag.wieers.com/rpm/packages/openvpn/). At the time of this writing, the latest version of OpenVPN is 2.09, and we're going to install that package. We also need one other prerequisite, a data compression library called lzo2.

```
$ wget http://dag.wieers.com/rpm/packages/openvpn/openvpn-2.0.9-1.el5.rf.i386.rpm
$ wget http://dag.wieers.com/rpm/packages/lzo2/lzo2-2.02-3.el5.rf.i386.rpm
$ sudo rpm -Uvh lzo2-2.02-3.el5.rf.i386.rpm openvpn-2.0.9-1.el5.rf.i386.rpm
Preparing...                ########################################### [100%]
   1:lzo2                   ########################################### [ 50%]
   2:openvpn                ########################################### [100%]
```

On Ubuntu, you install the openvpn package, and some additional prerequisites will generally also be installed.

```
$ sudo aptitude install openvpn
```

■**Note**   All examples in this chapter use OpenVPN 2.x and later; the examples won't work with OpenVPN version 1.x releases. If your distribution doesn't install a 2.x or later release, then you'll need to find and install a suitable version.

Starting and Stopping OpenVPN

OpenVPN runs as a service on your hosts. The openvpn package on both Ubuntu and Red Hat will install appropriate init scripts. You can start, stop, and restart the OpenVPN server using these scripts. On Red Hat, you use the service command to start the server:

```
$ sudo service openvpn start
```

and you use the chkconfig command to ensure it starts at bootup:

```
$ sudo chkconfig --add openvpn
```

On Ubuntu, you use the invoke-rc.d command to start and stop the server, and the update-rc.d command to ensure it starts when you boot up.

```
$ sudo invoke-rc.d openvpn start
$ sudo update-rc.d openvpn defaults
```

When you start the OpenVPN server, it will search the /etc/openvpn directory for any files suffixed with .conf and load any VPNs found in these files. For example, on our home office server, we might have the headoffice.conf and mobileuser.conf OpenVPN configuration files. When we start OpenVPN, these files will be automatically loaded and the server will attempt to start the specified VPNs.

Configuring OpenVPN

As we mentioned earlier, we need to configure OpenVPN on both ends of any connection. We're going to start our configuration by setting up the OpenVPN server on our bastion host in our head office, and then we'll configure connections to our branch offices. A connection between two offices like this is called a *static* or *point-to-point* VPN. Finally, we'll show you how to configure a client, such as a laptop or desktop, for a mobile user.

Our Proposed VPN Configuration

Let's quickly look at a network diagram of our proposed VPN tunnel configuration (see Figure 14-2). We're going to create tunnels between our head office branch and each of our branch offices.

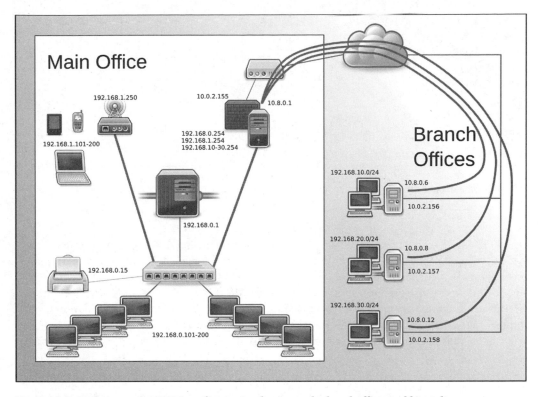

Figure 14-2. *Point-to-point VPN configuration between the head office and branches*

Configuring OpenVPN on Our Gateway Server

We've installed OpenVPN on our head office's bastion server, gateway.example.com, and now we're going to start configuring it. We start by telling OpenVPN a few basics about our configuration. We're going to create a file called gateway.conf in the /etc/openvpn directory, as shown in Listing 14-1.

Listing 14-1. *The gateway.conf Configuration File*

```
# Network configuration
dev tun
port 1194
proto udp
server 10.8.0.0 255.255.255.0
keepalive 10 120

# Logging configuration
log-append  /var/log/openvpn.log
status /var/log/openvpn-status.log
verb 4
mute 20
```

```
# Security configuration
user nobody
group nobody
persist-key
persist-tun

# Compression
comp-lzo
```

■**Note** We'll expand on the `gateway.conf` file with additional options as we go along.

In Listing 14-1 we've specified a number of options. The first of these options is `dev tun`, which tells OpenVPN we're going to configure a tun or tunnel device to run our VPN over, and we will create a virtual device, tun0, which will be used for the VPN connection. By specifying `dev tun` we're also creating a routed VPN. OpenVPN can create two types of VPNs: routed or bridged. In simple terms, a *bridged* VPN joins your networks together at the Ethernet level, while a *routed* VPN relies on TCP/IP networking to join your networks together. We're going to use routed VPNs because they are generally more scalable and better suited to our purposes.

■**Note** If you are interested in reading more about the differences between routed and bridged VPNs, you can find further information at `http://openvpn.net/index.php/documentation/howto.html#vpntype`.

Next, we've specified two options, `port 1194` and `proto udp`. These tell OpenVPN to listen for UDP traffic on port 1194 when making VPN connections. The firewall needs to be configured to allow traffic on this port to accept incoming connections.

■**Tip** If required, you can change the port and use TCP instead by changing these options to the required port and protocol.

Using the Netfilter firewall and the `iptables` command, you can ensure traffic passes through the appropriate port on your host, as you can see in Listing 14-2.

Listing 14-2. *OpenVPN Firewall Rules*

```
-A INPUT -i tun0 -p udp -m udp –dport 1194 -d 0/0 -j ACCEPT
```

Here we've added a rule allowing incoming UDP traffic to the tun0 interface on port 1194.
    Or, if you are using TCP instead, you use a rule like the following:

```
-A INPUT -i tun0 –p tcp -m tcp –dport 1194 -d 0/0 -j ACCEPT
```

■**Tip** The most common reason for a failed VPN configuration is due to a firewall issue. You should always check that your firewall rules allow access to this port by using the `tcpdump` or `nmap` command. We discuss firewall setup, rules, and troubleshooting in Chapter 6.

Next in Listing 14-1, the `server` option tells OpenVPN the IP address of the server and the pool of IP addresses available to our VPN clients. We've specified the default network, 10.8.0.0/24. By default, our OpenVPN server will take the address 10.8.0.1 and assign the remaining addresses to incoming VPN connections.

We've specified an option called `keepalive` that is used to keep our connection open. We specify the `keepalive` option and two values, 10 and 120. The value 10 indicates that OpenVPN will ping the connection every 10 seconds to check it is active. The value 120 indicates the time in seconds that OpenVPN will wait for a response. If no response is received within 120 seconds, then OpenVPN will assume the connection is down and notify us.

Then we've added some logging functions. The first is `log-append`, which tells OpenVPN to log to the `/var/log/openvpn.log` file. The second option, `status`, outputs a status file that shows current connections to a log file, in our case `/var/log/openvpn-status.log`. The third option, `verb`, tells OpenVPN how much logging to do. It ranges from 0 to 15, where 0 is no logging and 15 is maximum logging. A value of 4 generates sufficient logging to suit most purposes.

The next block of configuration options provides some additional security for our OpenVPN server. The first two options, `user` and `group`, allow us to specify a user and group for OpenVPN to run as. This drops any privileges (e.g., from the `root` user) the process has and ensures that if someone were to compromise the process, he would have limited privileges to exploit that compromise on your host. On Red Hat, you use the `nobody` user and the `nobody` group. On Ubuntu, we recommend you use the user `nobody` and the group `nogroup`.

```
user nobody
group nogroup
```

The next two options, `persist-tun` and `persist-key`, are related to this dropping of privileges. They allow OpenVPN to retain sufficient privileges to work with network interfaces and SSL certificates.

The last option in the file, `comp-lzo`, tells OpenVPN to use compression for VPN tunnels. This improves performance across the tunnel.

So we've configured the basics of our VPN, but is it now ready? Not quite yet—we have one more step: authentication.

Configuring OpenVPN Authentication

Authentication ensures that only authorized hosts can initiate VPNs and connect. OpenVPN allows a wide variety of authentication mechanisms including preshared keys, two-factor authentication such as tokens, and TLS/SSL certificates.

The most basic authentication is *preshared keys*, which are static keys generated on your host and then distributed to the host you wish to connect to. You can generate a static key with the `--genkey` option of the `openvpn` command like so:

```
$ sudo openvpn --genkey --secret /etc/openvpn/secret.key
```

This will create a file containing a key in a file called `secret.key` in the directory `/etc/openvpn`, the file name and directory being specified with the `--secret` option. You specify the location of this file in your OpenVPN configuration using the `secret` option.

```
secret /etc/openvpn/secret.key
```

You would then copy this file, preferably in a secure way such as via `scp` or SMIME- or GPG/PGP-encrypted e-mail, to the other host and add it to the client's OpenVPN configuration.

We're not going to use preshared keys, though, because they have some limitations. Their biggest limitation is that you can have only one server and client connection (i.e., you can connect only one host to each VPN tunnel). This isn't an ideal model if you have more than one host or office you want to connect—for example, it won't be effective to allow multiple mobile users to connect to your head office.

Instead, we're going to use certificates to secure the VPNs between our head office and branch offices. To use certificates, we need to create and sign them with a Certificate Authority (CA).

■**Note**   We discuss the CA process extensively in Chapter 10 (refer back there now if you like).

For your VPN tunnels, you can either purchase certificates or create and sign your own using a CA you have created and manage. We're going to show you how to create and sign your own using the CA we created in Chapter 10.

We first need to create a server certificate for the VPN server. You will remember the first step in the process of creating a new certificate is to create a certificate signing request (CSR) and a secret key. Let's do that now:

```
$ openssl req -new -newkey rsa:2048 -nodes -keyout gateway.example.com.key➡
-out gateway.example.com.req
```

We've generated a 2048-bit RSA key and created a CSR. You will be prompted to populate the required fields (State, City, etc.). You need to use the same values as your Certificate Authority. For the Common Name field, you should specify the fully qualified domain name of your server, in our case gateway.example.com.

We need to use our CA to sign our certificate, as shown in Listing 14-3.

Listing 14-3. *Signing Our Server Certificate*

```
$ cd /etc/CA
$ sudo openssl ca -out gateway.example.com.cert -config ./openssl.cnf➡
-infiles gateway.example.com.req
Using configuration from ./openssl.cnf
Enter pass phrase for ./private/cakey.pem:
Check that the request matches the signature
Signature ok
Certificate Details:
        Serial Number: 1 (0x1)
```

```
Validity
    Not Before: Jan  12 09:57:43 2009 GMT
    Not After : Jan  12 09:57:43 2010 GMT
Subject:
    countryName              = AU
    stateOrProvinceName      = Victoria
    organizationName         = Example Pty Ltd
    commonName               = gateway.example.com
    emailAddress             = postmaster@example.com
X509v3 extensions:
    X509v3 Basic Constraints:
        CA:FALSE
    Netscape Comment:
        OpenSSL Generated Certificate
    X509v3 Subject Key Identifier:
        8F:A6:48:91:D5:3F:70:7B:E3:E2:AB:E5:F5:41:8A:F4:20:DA:31:6E
    X509v3 Authority Key Identifier:
        keyid:F7:0A:17:47:FA:0D:7B:C4:FA:63:0C:C9:FC:5B:49:1C:D5:C3:FF:1D

Certificate is to be certified until Jan  12 09:57:43 2010 GMT (365 days)
Sign the certificate? [y/n]:y

1 out of 1 certificate requests certified, commit? [y/n]y
Write out database with 1 new entries
Data Base Updated
```

We first change into our /etc/CA directory and then run the openssl ca command to sign our CSR. This outputs a certificate signed by our CA. We now have two files, gateway.example. com.key (our private key) and gateway.example.com.cert (our certificate). We move these files to the /etc/openvpn directory.

```
$ sudo mv gateway.example.com.* /etc/openvpn
```

■**Note** In addition to the private key and certificate files, you have a CSR request file. It's worth hanging on to this for when your certificate expires. You can use this request again to create a new certificate, as we mentioned in Chapter 10.

We want to protect our certificate and key with the right ownership and some restricted permissions for our key.

```
$ sudo chown root:root /etc/openvpn/gateway.example.com.*
$ sudo chmod 0600 /etc/openvpn/gateway.example.com.key
```

We also need to create some *Diffie-Hellman parameters*, cryptographic parameters that enhance the security of our VPN session. (You can read about these parameters in more detail at http://www.rsa.com/rsalabs/node.asp?id=2248.) We can use the openssl command to create these.

```
$ sudo openssl dhparam -out /etc/openvpn/dh2048.pem 2048
Generating DH parameters, 2048 bit long safe prime, generator 2
This is going to take a long time
.....................................+..........................................
```

Here we've created a file called dh2048.pem in the /etc/openvpn directory. It's a 2048-bit DH parameter file, and we've specified the size using the 2048 option. We need to create a file with the same size as our certificates; as you can see from our earlier request generation, this is 2048.

Now we tell OpenVPN about our new certificates and the location of our CA certificate and our DH parameter file (see Listing 14-4).

Listing 14-4. *The gateway.conf Configuration File*

```
# Network configuration
dev tun
port 1194
proto udp
server 10.8.0.0 255.255.255.0
keepalive 10 120

# Certificate configuration
ca /etc/CA/cacert.pem
dh /etc/openvpn/dh2048.pem
cert /etc/openvpn/gateway.example.com.cert
key /etc/openvpn/gateway.example.com.key

# Logging configuration
log-append  /var/log/openvpn.log
status /var/log/openvpn-status.log
verb 4
mute 20

# Security configuration
user nobody
group nobody
persist-key
persist-tun

# Compression
comp-lzo
```

You can see we've added four options. The first is the ca option to specify the location of the CA certificate, in our case /etc/CA/cacert.pem. The next, dh, specifies the location of the Diffie-Hellman parameter file we created, in our case /etc/openvpn/dh2048.pem. Lastly, we've used the cert and key options to specify the location of our certificate and key files, respectively, in our case /etc/openvpn/gateway.example.com.cert and /etc/openvpn/gateway.example.com.key.

We can start our OpenVPN server as follows on Ubuntu:

```
$ sudo invoke-rc.d openvpn restart
* Stopping virtual private network daemon(s)...
  *   Stopping VPN 'gateway'                                       [ OK ]
* Starting virtual private network daemon(s)...
  *   Autostarting VPN 'gateway'                                   [ OK ]
```

You can see that we've restarted the OpenVPN server, and when it restarted it automatically started the VPN called "gateway." The VPN is named for the gateway.conf configuration file.

We are also able to see some log entries in the /var/log/openvpn.log file, as shown in Listing 14-5.

Listing 14-5. *The /var/log/openvpn.log Log File*

```
Fri Jan 30 00:36:32 2009 OpenVPN 2.1_rc11 i486-pc-linux-gnu [SSL] [LZO2]➥
[EPOLL] [PKCS11] built on Oct 15 2008
Fri Jan 30 00:36:32 2009 /usr/bin/openssl-vulnkey -q -b 2048 -m <modulus omitted>
Fri Jan 30 00:36:32 2009 TUN/TAP device tun0 opened
Fri Jan 30 00:36:32 2009 /sbin/ifconfig tun0 10.8.0.1 pointopoint 10.8.0.2 mtu 1500
Fri Jan 30 00:36:32 2009 UDPv4 link local (bound): [undef]:1194
Fri Jan 30 00:36:32 2009 UDPv4 link remote: [undef]
Fri Jan 30 00:36:32 2009 Initialization Sequence Completed
```

Listing 14-5 shows that the OpenVPN server has started, our interface tun0 was created, and our IP address of 10.8.0.1 was added and bound to the UDP port of 1194.

■**Note** Ensure you have the right firewall rules in place to allow VPN connections to your host—in this case, incoming connections on UDP port 1194 need to be accepted.

Our server is running, but we're still not quite done. We need to configure our clients, install the OpenVPN software, and create certificates for our clients to use to connect.

■**Note** Going forward in this chapter, we'll refer to two hosts. When a command needs to be run on a particular host, we're going to prefix it with the same of that host: gateway$ or branch1$.

Configuring OpenVPN on Our Branch Office Servers

First, we need to install the OpenVPN packages on our branch server, branch1.example.com. Follow the appropriate instructions for your distribution and set OpenVPN to start when your host boots, for example, on Red Hat:

```
branch1$ sudo chkconfig --add openvpn
```

and on Ubuntu:

```
branch1$ sudo update-rc.d openvpn defaults
```

■**Note** You can tell we're running the preceding command on the branch1.example.com host by the command prefix.

The next step is to create a certificate and key for each of our branch offices. We're going to create our certificate and key on the gateway.example.com host and sign it using the CA on that host. We'll start with one branch office, branch1.example.com.

```
gateway$ openssl req -new -newkey rsa:2048 -nodes -keyout branch1.example.com.key➥
-out branch1.example.com.req
```

We've generated a 2048-bit RSA key and created a CSR. You will be prompted to populate the required fields: State, City, and so forth. You need to use the same values as your Certificate Authority. For the Common Name field, you should specify the fully qualified domain name of your server, in our case branch1.example.com.

Then we use our CA to sign our certificate as we did earlier.

```
gateway$ cd /etc/CA
gateway$ sudo openssl ca -out branch1.example.com.cert -config ./openssl.cnf➥
-infiles branch1.example.com.req
```

Now we need to send our certificate and key as well as the CA certificate to the branch server. There are a number of ways you can do this, but you must do it securely—don't e-mail them, for example, as they can be readily intercepted. Take them on a USB key or DVD media and install them locally. Or if you are able to connect to the host, use the scp (secure copy) or sftp (secure FTP) command to send the files. These commands use an SSH connection to securely connect to another host and transfer files.

We're going to use the sftp command to connect to our branch office server and transfer the required files.

```
gateway$ sftp jsmith@branch1.example.com
Connecting to branch1.example.com...
jsmith@branch1.example.com's password:
sftp> put branch1.example.com.cert
Uploading /home/jsmith/branch1.example.com.cert to➥
/home/jsmith/branch1.example.com.cert
/home/jsmith/branch1.example.com.cert 100%    5881    12.0KB/s    00:03
```

We have connected to the branch1.example.com host and, using the put command, transferred the `branch1.example.com.cert` certificate file from its location, here the `/home/jsmith` directory, to the equivalent directory `/home/jsmith` on the branch1 host. You can use the cd command to change to an appropriate directory on the remote host where you want to write your files.

```
sftp> cd /tmp
```

You'll need permission to write to that location. You can use the lcd command to change the directory on the local gateway.example.com host if your files are located elsewhere.

We use the put command to also put the `branch1.example.com.key` and the `cacert.pem` CA certificate file onto the branch1 host. Now we're going to move our files to the `/etc/openvpn` directory and secure their ownership and permissions.

```
branch1$ sudo mv branch1.example.com.cert /etc/openvpn
branch1$ sudo mv branch1.example.com.key /etc/openvpn
branch1$ sudo mv cacert.pem /etc/openvpn
```

We want to protect our certificate and key with the right ownership and some restricted permissions for our key.

```
branch1$ sudo chown root:root /etc/openvpn/branch1.example.com.*
branch1$ sudo chown root:root /etc/openvpn/ca.cert
branch1$ sudo chmod 0600 /etc/openvpn/gateway.example.com.key
```

Next, we need to create a configuration file for our client. We're going to create a file called branch1.conf in our /etc/openvpn directory, as you can see in Listing 14-6.

Listing 14-6. *The branch1.conf Configuration File*

```
# Network configuration
dev tun
client
remote gateway.example.com 1194
keepalive 10 120

# Certificate configuration
ca /etc/openvpn/cacert.pem
cert /etc/openvpn/branch1.example.com.cert
key /etc/openvpn/branch1.example.com.key

# Logging configuration
log-append  /var/log/openvpn.log
status /var/log/openvpn-status.log
verb 4
mute 20

# Security configuration
user nobody
group nobody
```

```
persist-key
persist-tun

# Compression
comp-lzo
```

■**Note** If you're using Ubuntu, your group setting should be set to nogroup rather than nobody.

The file in Listing 14-6 is very similar to the gateway.conf configuration file, but we've specified some different options because of the host's role as a client. Again, we've specified dev tun for a routed VPN. We've also specified the client option, to indicate that this is a client, and the remote option, which tells OpenVPN where to connect our VPN tunnel. We've specified gateway.example.com and port 1194.

■**Note** OpenVPN must be able to resolve this host (i.e., it must be able to find an IP address for this host). If you don't have a DNS (you should), then you can specify an IP address directly in this option.

We've also specified the location of our CA certificate with the ca option and the location of our client's certificate and key using the cert and key options, respectively.

Starting OpenVPN on Our Branch Office Server

With the VPN configured on our server, we can now start OpenVPN on our client. For example, we use the following command on Red Hat:

branch1$ sudo service openvpn start

and this on Ubuntu:

branch1$ sudo invoke-rc.d openvpn start

Testing Our OpenVPN Tunnel

You can determine if your connection has worked in a number of ways, and we'll take you through them all. First, you should see some entries in the /var/log/openvpn.log file on the branch1 host. You should see similar entries to those in Listing 14-5, but you'll also see the negotiation process as our client connects to the server.

```
Fri Jan 30 18:51:35 2009 us=406059 [gateway.example.com] Peer Connection Initiated➥
with 10.0.2.155:1194
```

You should also see some entries on the gateway host in the /var/log/openvpn.log file showing the connection.

```
gateway$ less /var/log/openvpn.log
Fri Jan 30 18:50:19 2009 us=518613 10.0.2.156:1194 [branch1.example.com] Peer➥
Connection Initiated with 10.0.2.155:1194
Fri Jan 30 18:50:19 2009 us=518706 branch1.example.com/10.0.2.156:1194 MULTI:➥
Learn: 10.8.0.6 -> branch1.example.com/10.0.2.156:1194
```

In addition, you can see a new interface created on both the gateway and branch1 hosts, starting with tun. On the gateway host you can see a new interface called tun0 with an IP address of 10.8.0.1 (as mentioned earlier):

```
gateway$ ifconfig -a
tun0      Link encap:UNSPEC  HWaddr 00-00-00-00-00-00-00-00-00-00-00-00-00-00-00-00
          inet addr:10.8.0.1  P-t-P:10.8.0.2  Mask:255.255.255.255
          UP POINTOPOINT RUNNING NOARP MULTICAST  MTU:1500  Metric:1
          RX packets:0 errors:0 dropped:0 overruns:0 frame:0
          TX packets:0 errors:0 dropped:0 overruns:0 carrier:0
          collisions:0 txqueuelen:100
          RX bytes:0 (0.0 B)  TX bytes:0 (0.0 B)
```

On the branch1 host an interface, also called tun0, has been created with an IP address of 10.8.0.6 from the pool of addresses our server is offering:

```
branch1$ ifconfig -a
tun0      Link encap:UNSPEC  HWaddr 00-00-00-00-00-00-00-00-00-00-00-00-00-00-00-00
          inet addr:10.8.0.6  P-t-P:10.8.0.5  Mask:255.255.255.255
          UP POINTOPOINT RUNNING NOARP MULTICAST  MTU:1500  Metric:1
          RX packets:293 errors:0 dropped:0 overruns:0 frame:0
          TX packets:300 errors:0 dropped:0 overruns:0 carrier:0
          collisions:0 txqueuelen:100
          RX bytes:24612 (24.0 KiB)  TX bytes:25200 (24.6 KiB)
```

You can also see the route table on the branch1 host (using the ip command introduced in Chapter 6) has a route for our 10.8.0.0/24 network:

```
branch1$ ip route show
10.8.0.2 dev tun0  proto kernel  scope link  src 10.8.0.1
10.8.0.0/24 via 10.8.0.2 dev tun0
192.0.2.0/24 dev eth1  proto kernel  scope link  src 192.0.2.155  metric 1
192.168.122.0/24 dev vnet0  proto kernel  scope link  src 192.168.122.1
169.254.0.0/16 dev eth0  proto kernel  scope link  src 169.254.6.35
default via 192.0.2.2 dev eth1  proto static
default dev eth0  scope link  metric 1000
```

There is a route to the 10.8.0.1 host via the tun0 interface.

You'll notice that on both hosts a file called /var/log/openvpn-status.log has been created. This file contains a list of the current connections and is refreshed every 60 seconds. Let's look at this file on the gateway host.

```
gateway$ less /var/log/openvpn-status.log
OpenVPN CLIENT LIST
Updated,Fri Jan 30 20:37:15 2009
```

```
Common Name,Real Address,Bytes Received,Bytes Sent,Connected Since
branch1.example.com,10.0.2.156:1194,118186,117874,Fri Jan 30 18:50:19 2009
ROUTING TABLE
Virtual Address,Common Name,Real Address,Last Ref
10.8.0.6,branch1.example.com,10.0.2.156:1194,Fri Jan 30 20:37:14 2009
GLOBAL STATS
Max bcast/mcast queue length,0
END
```

You can see a connection listed from the branch1 host with an IP address of 10.0.2.156.

Lastly, you can use network tools to test your actual connection. Let's start by using the ping command on our gateway host to ping our branch1 host. We're going to ping the address used as the end of our VPN tunnel on the branch1 host, which we discovered earlier is 10.8.0.6.

```
gateway$  ping 10.8.0.6
PING 10.8.0.6 (10.8.0.6) 56(84) bytes of data.
64 bytes from 10.8.0.6: icmp_seq=1 ttl=64 time=0.800 ms
64 bytes from 10.8.0.6: icmp_seq=2 ttl=64 time=0.756 ms
64 bytes from 10.8.0.6: icmp_seq=3 ttl=64 time=2.26 ms
64 bytes from 10.8.0.6: icmp_seq=4 ttl=64 time=1.38 ms
64 bytes from 10.8.0.6: icmp_seq=5 ttl=64 time=1.17 ms
```

The preceding code shows us that the gateway host can see the branch1 host using ICMP and the 10.8.0.6 IP address on that branch1 host responds to ICMP traffic.

We can do the same thing from the branch1 host by trying to ping IP address 10.8.0.1 on the gateway host end.

```
branch1$ ping 10.8.0.1
PING 10.8.0.1 (10.8.0.1) 56(84) bytes of data.
64 bytes from 10.8.0.1: icmp_seq=1 ttl=64 time=10.02 ms
64 bytes from 10.8.0.1: icmp_seq=2 ttl=64 time=20.21 ms
64 bytes from 10.8.0.1: icmp_seq=3 ttl=64 time=10.19 ms
64 bytes from 10.8.0.1: icmp_seq=4 ttl=64 time=20.51 ms
64 bytes from 10.8.0.1: icmp_seq=5 ttl=64 time=10.17 ms
```

If both ends respond, then your VPN is up and you can use it to route traffic to and from your branch office to your head office.

If you now wish, you can repeat this configuration for any additional branch offices. For example, in our case we could add tunnels from the branch2.example.com and branch3.example.com offices.

Exposing Head Office Resources with OpenVPN

With our configuration so far, we can route traffic between our branch offices and our head office over our VPN tunnel. Let's take a look at how our head office and our branch offices now interact.

Currently, we have two paths from our branch offices to our head office. The first is across the 192.0.2.0/24 network that you saw in Chapter 6. This is our DSL or ASDL (or similar type) Internet connection between our offices and the Internet. Each individual office will generally have an individual Internet connection. We've used the 192.0.2.0/24 network as their IP address, but it's more likely that each office has an individual address acquired from the ISP.

This network is not secure, as it runs over the Internet. Unless we secure a particular application or protocol (e.g., in the way we used SSL/TLS in Chapter 10 to protect our SMTP and IMAP services), then an attacker could read our data from that network. Because of this potential security issue, across this connection we've instantiated our second path between these hosts, the 10.8.0.0/24 network that we are using for our VPN tunnels. Our head office is the OpenVPN server with an IP address of 10.8.0.1. Each branch office has an IP address from that range—for example, you've seen the 10.8.0.6 IP address assigned to the branch1.example.com office.

Currently through our VPN tunnel, however, we can reach only the IP address 10.8.0.1. This isn't much use to us because we can't access any of the resources available on the internal network (e.g., a file share on the headoffice.example.com host). We can test this from our branch office host by trying to ping the headoffice host:

```
branch1$ ping 192.168.0.1
```

We'll get no reply from these pings because there is no route to this network. To access these resources, we need to ensure two elements are in order: routing and firewall rules. We'll discuss these in the sections that follow.

Routing

We first need to configure our branch offices to route to the internal network of our head office. To do this, we tell our branch office that when it wants to route to the 192.168.0.0/24 network, it needs to go through the VPN tunnel to the gateway host. We do this as shown in Listing 14-7 by adding a line to the gateway.conf configuration file on the gateway host to push a route to our branch hosts.

Listing 14-7. *Push Route Added to gateway.conf*

```
push "route 192.168.0.0 255.255.255.0"
```

This line adds a route to all clients that connect to the OpenVPN server. For the new route to be pushed, we need to restart the openvpn service on both the gateway host and the branch office hosts.

If we look at the route table on our branch1 host, we can see a new route to the 192.168.0.0/24 network in our routes (in bold):

```
branch1$ route
Kernel IP routing table
Destination     Gateway         Genmask         Flags Metric Ref    Use Iface
10.8.0.5        *               255.255.255.255 UH    0      0        0 tun0
10.8.0.1        10.8.0.5        255.255.255.255 UGH   0      0        0 tun0
192.168.0.0     10.8.0.5        255.255.255.0   UG    0      0        0 tun0
192.0.2.0       *               255.255.255.0   U     0      0        0 eth1
169.254.0.0     *               255.255.0.0     U     0      0        0 eth1
default         192.0.2.2       0.0.0.0         UG    0      0        0 eth1
```

We can now ping this network from the branch1 host.

```
branch1$ ping 192.168.0.1
PING 192.168.0.1 (192.168.0.1) 56(84) bytes of data.
64 bytes from 192.168.0.1: icmp_seq=1 ttl=64 time=1.18 ms
64 bytes from 192.168.0.1: icmp_seq=2 ttl=64 time=1.31 ms
64 bytes from 192.168.0.1: icmp_seq=3 ttl=64 time=2.33 ms
64 bytes from 192.168.0.1: icmp_seq=4 ttl=64 time=1.25 ms
64 bytes from 192.168.0.1: icmp_seq=5 ttl=64 time=0.923 ms
```

You can see we're getting a response from the host 192.168.0.1 on our branch1 host. We are able to access anything that the firewall on the gateway host allows us to on the 192.168.0.0/24 network.

If the branch1 host is the default route for 192.168.10.0/24 (the local network at the branch1 site), then all our users in the 192.162.10.0/24 network will be able to access resources in the 192.168.0.0/24 network at our head office.

Note We're not going to tell our head office how to route to the internal networks of our branch offices, but this is also possible. Please visit `http://www.secure-computing.net/wiki/index.php/OpenVPN/Routing` for an example of this configuration.

Firewall

We also need to ensure the firewall rules on our gateway and branch hosts allow traffic to and from the relevant networks. On our gateway host, this involves forwarding IP traffic from our gateway host into the internal network and back, much like the configuration we created in Chapter 6 for forwarding our services from our bastion host, gateway.example.com.

First, we direct traffic that we wish to forward through our gateway host from the VPN tunnel interface tun0 through its own chain. We've called this chain `Firewall-tun0-FORWARD` like so:

```
-A FORWARD -i tun0 -o eth0 -j Firewall-tun0-FORWARD
```

We then need to create a rule set for this chain to allow our gateway host to forward particular traffic through the host, as shown in Listing 14-8.

Listing 14-8. *Some Sample iptables Rules for OpenVPN Routing*

```
-A Firewall-tun0-FORWARD -m state --state RELATED,ESTABLISHED -j ACCEPT
-A Firewall-tun0-FORWARD -p tcp -m state --state NEW -m tcp --dport 25 -j ACCEPT
-A Firewall-tun0-FORWARD -p tcp -m state --state NEW -m tcp --dport 53 -j ACCEPT
-A Firewall-tun0-FORWARD -p udp -m state --state NEW -m udp --dport 53 -j ACCEPT
-A Firewall-tun0-FORWARD -p tcp -m state --state NEW -m tcp --dport 80 -j ACCEPT
-A Firewall-tun0-FORWARD -p udp -m state --state NEW -m udp --sport 123 --dport 123➥
-j ACCEPT
-A Firewall-tun0-FORWARD -p tcp -m state --state NEW -m tcp --dport 443 -j ACCEPT
-A Firewall-tun0-FORWARD -p tcp -m state --state NEW -m tcp --dport 993 -j ACCEPT
-A Firewall-tun0-FORWARD -j REJECT --reject-with icmp-port-unreachable
```

We've created a variety of simple rules to allow traffic through the VPN tunnel and forward it into our internal network. We've forwarded SMTP, HTTP/HTTPS, and IMAP, among other protocols.

■**Note** You can use the instructions provided in Chapter 6 to add these rules to your gateway host.

VPN Connections for Mobile Users

OpenVPN is capable of more than just allowing point-to-point connections from your branch offices to your head office. You can also use it to allow mobile users to connect to your head office and access resources like file shares, printers, and applications. To do this, we need to set up another VPN tunnel on our gateway host and install OpenVPN on our clients. As we mentioned earlier in this chapter, OpenVPN can run on platforms including Linux, Microsoft Windows, Mac OS X, and others.

We're going to do a few things differently with our mobile users. We're not going to use certificates (although we could use them) to authenticate our client because the overhead of potentially generating a lot of certificates can be quite high.

■**Note** A tool that makes certificate management easier with OpenVPN is `easy-rsa`. It is available on Red Hat at `/usr/share/doc/openvpn-`*`version`*`/easy-rsa` and Ubuntu at `/usr/share/doc/openvpn/examples/easy-rsa`.

Instead, we're going to show you how to use PAM (which we introduced you to in Chapter 4) to authenticate your users. As a result of PAM's ability to plug in a variety of authentication mechanisms, we can use it to include authentication mechanisms such as the following:

- Local Linux users

- Two-factor authentication such as RSA tokens or smartcards

- Kerberos

- RADIUS

- IMAP (against an IMAP server)

- LDAP

We're going to show you how to configure basic local-user authentication—that is, your users will have a Linux user on the gateway host and they will be authenticated as if they were logging on to that host using the console or via SSH. Using PAM, you can easily extend this to other forms of authentication.

Configuring Our Mobile VPN

To start our configuration, we need a new .conf file. We're going to create one called mobile. conf in /etc/openvpn, as you can see in Listing 14-9.

Listing 14-9. *Mobile User's mobile.conf Configuration File*

```
# Network configuration
dev tun
port 1195
proto udp
server 10.9.0.0 255.255.255.0
keepalive 10 120

# Certificate configuration
dh /etc/openvpn/dh2048.pem
ca /etc/CA/ca.cert
cert /etc/openvpn/gateway.example.com.cert
key /etc/openvpn/gateway.example.com.key
plugin  /usr/lib/openvpn/openvpn-auth-pam.so passwd
client-cert-not-required
username-as-common-name

# Logging configuration
log-append  /var/log/openvpn-mobile.log
status /var/log/openvpn-status-mobile.log
verb 4
mute 20

# Security configuration
user nobody
group nogroup
persist-key
persist-tun

# Compression
comp-lzo
```

■**Note** We'll expand on this configuration later in this section when we look at configuring routing and related functionality on our client.

You can see that our mobile.conf configuration is very similar to our gateway.conf VPN tunnel. Let's focus on the differences. We've changed some networking configuration: we've used a different port, 1195, because our other VPN tunnel is bound to the 1194 port. We've also specified an additional IP subnet for our mobile users, 10.9.0.0/24.

We need to ensure we have suitable firewall rules in place for this subnet. First, we open the 1195 port for our tunnel on the tun1 interface (the interface number has incremented for our new tunnel).

```
-A INPUT -i tun1 -p udp -m udp –dport 1195 -d 0/0 -j ACCEPT
```

■Note Our interface is tun1 because we already have a tun0 interface. If you don't have another VPN tunnel, then your interface may be tun0. In iptables you can refer to all tun interfaces using the notation tun+.

We've specified the same certificate, key, and DH parameters, but we've added a new option called plugin. The plugin configuration option allows us to specify external plug-ins, in our case a PAM plug-in called openvpn-auth-pam.so that ships with the OpenVPN package.

On Ubuntu, the plug-in is located in the /usr/lib/openvpn/ directory. To ensure it functions correctly on Ubuntu, you'll also need to install an additional package:

```
$ sudo apt-get install libpam0g-dev
```

This package isn't needed on Red Hat. On Red Hat, the required plug-in is located in /usr/share/openvpn/plugin/lib and your plugin line would look like this:

```
plugin /usr/share/openvpn/plugin/lib/openvpn-auth-pam.so system-auth
```

We also need to specify the name of a PAM authentication file that OpenVPN will use to authenticate the VPN tunnel. On Ubuntu, we've specified the standard shadow password PAM authentication file, passwd, as the authentication mechanism to use. On Red Hat, we could specify the system-auth default PAM authentication file.

For other forms of authentication, you specify here an appropriate PAM authentication file for that mechanism. For example, to enable two-factor authentication, you might specify a file that uses the pam_rsa.so module (http://www.rsa.com/node.aspx?id=1177). This module allows you to integrate your authentication into an RSA SecureID server and use RSA tokens to authenticate users.

We've also specified two other options, client-cert-not-required and username-as-common-name, which disable the requirement for the mobile user to have a certificate and to use the username provided by the mobile user as if it was the Common Name of the certificate.

■Note Some people don't like disabling client certificates and in fact use both a username/password and a certificate.

We've updated the logging files to create new files for our mobile connection. We've also specified the user and group options (in this case, we've used the nogroup group on Ubuntu). Next, we need to restart our OpenVPN service to start our mobile VPN tunnel.

Configuring Mobile VPN Clients

You need to configure your clients to connect to the gateway, which you can do in a variety of ways depending on the client. A number of clients are available, ranging from the normal OpenVPN binary right through to sophisticated GUI clients. We'll provide a list of some of the available clients in this section, and we'll show you how to connect via OpenVPN.

The simplest client is the OpenVPN binary. To connect to the gateway, you need to have your server's CA certificate, but unless you want to use certificates, you don't need to create and send across client certificates.

If you're using the OpenVPN binary, you're also going to need to create a client configuration file. We'll call ours `mobileclient.conf` and store it in the `/etc/openvpn` directory on our client, as shown in Listing 14-10.

Listing 14-10. *The* `mobileclient.conf` *Configuration File*

```
# Network configuration
dev tun
client
remote gateway.example.com 1195
keepalive 10 120

# Certificate configuration
ca /etc/openvpn/ca.cert
auth-user-pass

# Logging configuration
log-append  /var/log/openvpn-mobile.log
status /var/log/openvpn-mobile-status.log
verb 4
mute 20

# Security configuration
user nobody
group nogroup
persist-key
persist-tun

# Compression
comp-lzo
```

You can see the options we've used previously with one addition and some minor changes. We've changed the remote port we're connecting on to 1195. We've also added the `auth-user-pass` option, which tells the client that we're going to use usernames and passwords rather than certificate authentication.

■**Tip** As mentioned earlier, you'd leave the `auth-user-pass` option in and add the `cert` and `key` options if you wished to use usernames/passwords as well as certificates.

Now, if we start OpenVPN on our client, it will connect to the gateway, prompting the user to enter appropriate credentials:

```
$ sudo /etc/init.d/openvpn restart
Shutting down openvpn:                          [  OK  ]
Starting openvpn:
Enter Auth Username:jsmith
Enter Auth Password:********
```

Notice the auth username and password prompts. We've entered the username of a user on the gateway host, jsmith, and his password.

The client will then connect and you should be able to see a new interface (tun1, in our case):

```
tun1      Link encap:UNSPEC  HWaddr 00-00-00-00-00-00-00-00-00-00-00-00-00-00-00-00
          inet addr:10.9.0.6  P-t-P:10.9.0.5  Mask:255.255.255.255
          UP POINTOPOINT RUNNING NOARP MULTICAST  MTU:1500  Metric:1
          RX packets:0 errors:0 dropped:0 overruns:0 frame:0
          TX packets:0 errors:0 dropped:0 overruns:0 carrier:0
          collisions:0 txqueuelen:100
          RX bytes:0 (0.0 b)  TX bytes:0 (0.0 b)
```

The interface has the IP address of 10.9.0.6 issued by the gateway host (remember, we set our mobile client VPN network as 10.9.0.0/24). You can then ping this IP address of the gateway host (in our case, 10.9.0.1) and vice versa back to 10.9.0.6:

```
$ ping 10.9.0.1
PING 10.9.0.1 (10.9.0.1) 56(84) bytes of data.
64 bytes from 10.9.0.1: icmp_seq=1 ttl=64 time=10.3 ms
64 bytes from 10.9.0.1: icmp_seq=2 ttl=64 time=10.64 ms
64 bytes from 10.9.0.1: icmp_seq=3 ttl=64 time=10.59 ms
64 bytes from 10.9.0.1: icmp_seq=4 ttl=64 time=10.73 ms
64 bytes from 10.9.0.1: icmp_seq=5 ttl=64 time=10.59 ms
```

If you don't use the OpenVPN binary as a client, then you have a variety of clients for various platforms available as noted in the "OpenVPN Clients" sidebar.

OPENVPN CLIENTS

A number of clients support OpenVPN on a number of platforms. The following short list is broken out by platform.

Linux

- *KVpnc (KDE)*: http://home.gna.org/kvpnc/en/index.html
- *network-manager-openvn Package (Gnome)*: http://packages.ubuntu.com/gutsy/network-manager-openvpn

Mac OS X

- *Tunnelblick*: http://code.google.com/p/tunnelblick/
- *Viscosity*: http://www.viscosityvpn.com/

Microsoft Windows

- *OpenVPN for Windows*: http://openvpn.se/

PocketPC

- *OpenVPN for PocketPC*: http://ovpnppc.ziggurat29.com/ovpnppc-main.htm

Mobile VPN Routing

Just as you can create a point-to-point head office to branch office VPN tunnel, you can also perform a variety of routing configurations between your client host and the gateway. In this case, you're going to not just help the client see hosts behind the gateway host, but also tell the client how to configure itself, especially its DHCP settings.

You'll also see how to force all traffic up through the VPN. This is a method commonly used to ensure a user's traffic goes only to your organization. For example, it is often used to ensure all user web traffic passes through your organization's proxy, thus ensuring it complies with your organization's acceptable use policy or similar standards.

First, let's allow our mobile user to see the 192.168.0.0/24 internal network at our head office. We do this by adding the push option to our mobile.conf configuration on the gateway host and use it to push a route.

```
push "route 192.168.0.0 255.255.255.0"
```

We also need to update the firewall rules on our gateway host, in much the same way as we added rules for the branch to head office tunnel. We add another chain for our mobile VPN tunnel.

```
-A FORWARD -i tun1 -o eth0 -j Firewall-tun1-FORWARD
```

We then need to create rules for this chain to allow our gateway host to forward particular traffic through the host, as shown in Listing 14-11.

Listing 14-11. *Some Sample* iptables *Rules for OpenVPN Routing*

```
-A Firewall-tun1-FORWARD -m state --state RELATED,ESTABLISHED -j ACCEPT
-A Firewall-tun1-FORWARD -p tcp -m state --state NEW -m tcp --dport 25 -j ACCEPT
-A Firewall-tun1-FORWARD -p tcp -m state --state NEW -m tcp --dport 53 -j ACCEPT
-A Firewall-tun1-FORWARD -p udp -m state --state NEW -m udp --dport 53 -j ACCEPT
-A Firewall-tun1-FORWARD -p tcp -m state --state NEW -m tcp --dport 80 -j ACCEPT
-A Firewall-tun1-FORWARD -p udp -m state --state NEW -m udp --sport 123 --dport 123➥
-j ACCEPT
-A Firewall-tun1-FORWARD -p tcp -m state --state NEW -m tcp --dport 443 -j ACCEPT
-A Firewall-tun1-FORWARD -p tcp -m state --state NEW -m tcp --dport 993 -j ACCEPT
-A Firewall-tun1-FORWARD -j REJECT --reject-with icmp-port-unreachable
```

We've created a variety of simple rules to allow traffic through the VPN tunnel and forward it into our internal network. We've forwarded SMTP, HTTP/HTTPS, and IMAP, among other protocols.

■**Note** You can use the instructions provided in Chapter 6 to add these rules to your gateway host.

We can also pass a variety of options to our client, for example, to help set DHCP options like DNS and WINS servers.

■**Note** We set up DHCP in Chapter 9.

Different types of clients (e.g., Linux and Microsoft Windows clients) require different methods to push down the required options. When passing options to a Microsoft Windows client, we can simply pass the required options along using the push option. For example, to push a DNS server IP address to the client, we do the following:

```
push "dhcp-option DNS 10.0.2.155"
```

Here we're telling OpenVPN to tell a Microsoft Windows client to push the DNS server 10.0.2.155 to its DHCP option.

In a Microsoft Windows environment, we can also push down a variety of other options, as shown in Table 14-1.

Table 14-1. *DHCP Options*

Option	Description
DOMAIN *name*	Sets the client's DNS suffix.
DNS *address*	Sets the DNS server address. Repeat to set secondary DNS servers.
WINS *address*	Sets the WINS server address. Repeat to set secondary WINS servers.
NBDD *address*	Sets the NBDD server address. Repeat to set secondary NBDD servers.
NTP *address*	Sets the NTP server address. Repeat to set secondary NTP servers.
DISABLE-NBT	Disables NetBIOS over TCP/IP.

On Linux and other hosts, you can't directly set these sorts of options using the push option. Instead, you need to tell OpenVPN to run scripts when the tunnel goes up and down. To do this, you use the appropriately named up and down options. We can add the following options to the mobileclient.conf on our VPN client:

```
up /etc/openvpn/tunnelup.sh
down /etc/openvpn/tunneldown.sh
```

Each option specifies scripts or commands that will be run when the VPN tunnel goes up and down. If we wished to set the DNS configuration of our client, we might use an up script, tunnelup.sh, like this:

```
#!/bin/sh
mv /etc/resolv.conf /etc/resolv.conf.bak
echo "search example.org" > /etc/resolv.conf
echo "nameserver 10.0.2.155" >> /etc/resolv.conf
exit 0
```

We could then use a down script, tunneldown.sh, to revert our configuration options, like so:

```
#!/bin/sh
mv /etc/resolv.conf.bak /etc/resolv.conf
```

■**Note** You need to transfer these scripts to the client yourself or use a configuration management tool, as we'll show you in Chapter 19.

Lastly, we can force all traffic from the client to the VPN. This is often used to force users to comply with some policy or standard, or to ensure all traffic is scanned for viruses and malware through a proxy or virus scanner.

There are some issues with pushing all traffic through your tunnel, though. Most notably, performance can be impacted by pushing traffic through the tunnel to your office and then onto the Internet. You will also need a proxy or NAT redirection for all the traffic generated by the client, as every protocol—not just web traffic—will need a means to connect.

To force all traffic up the VPN tunnel from the client, we add the following directive to the `mobile.conf` configuration file on our gateway host:

```
push "redirect-gateway def1"
```

If your VPN setup is over a wireless network and all clients and the server are on the same wireless network, you need to add to this directive:

```
push "redirect-gateway local def1"
```

You can see we've added the `local` option to the directive.

Troubleshooting OpenVPN

Troubleshooting OpenVPN requires you to take into consideration all elements of a connection: networks, firewalls, and OpenVPN itself. OpenVPN's extensive logging (you saw the `log-append`, `status`, and `verb` options earlier in the chapter) allows you to quickly see errors. Additionally, OpenVPN's error messages usually provide a clear and accurate indication of the actual problem.

But you also need to ensure you check that you have network connectivity and appropriate firewall rules, both `iptables` rules on your host(s) and potentially rules on any intervening network devices, to allow connections. You need to check that the connection is up, that firewall rules allow the VPN tunnel to connect, and finally that rules and routing exist that allow your traffic to flow across the VPN and to the intended destination.

■Tip Chapter 6 covers network and firewall troubleshooting.

The best place to start to look for troubleshooting help is the OpenVPN website (http://openvpn.net/). There you can find documentation, including a comprehensive HOWTO page (http://openvpn.net/index.php/documentation/howto.html) and an FAQ page (http://openvpn.net/index.php/documentation/faq.html). You can find OpenVPN's man page at http://openvpn.net/index.php/documentation/manuals/openvpn-20x-manpage.html. Also available is a mailing list you can join at http://openvpn.net/index.php/documentation/miscellaneous/mailing-lists.html. For more complex implementations, the OpenVPN developers provide commercial support, or you can turn to the book *OpenVPN: Building and Integrating Virtual Private Networks* by Markus Feilner (Packt Publishing, 2006) for help as well.

Summary

In this chapter, we've taken you through the process of configuring and managing VPN tunnels. We've introduced point-to-point tunnels, such as between a head office and remote branches. We have also explained how you can use VPN tunnels to allow your mobile users to securely and safely connect to resources at your head office or other locations. You've learned how to do the following:

- Configure VPN tunnels.
- Create and configure certificates for authentication.
- Make use of PAM to allow alternative forms of authentication.
- Configure your `iptables` firewall to allow VPN tunnels.
- Configure your networks and routing to allow users to traverse VPN tunnels and access resources.
- Configure networking options on your clients using OpenVPN.

In the next chapter, we'll discuss collaboration tools such as e-mail and calendaring.

CHAPTER 15

■ ■ ■

Collaborative Services

By Dennis Matotek

Collaboration servers, also known by the name *groupware*, are a combination of messaging services and document management services. Many organizations have a great need for people to be able to easily communicate, arrange meetings, exchange ideas, and write and share documents. Mail, shared mail folders, instant messaging, shared calendaring, shared task lists, shared documents, and shared workspaces are all combined to form one product, the collaborative service. The several offerings available range from free open source to closed source commercial applications that are all designed to run on Linux.

In this chapter, we show you how to install a Zimbra server. We chose to use this server over its rivals because of these key points:

- It is easy to install and configure.

- It has a complete feature set that will meet all your needs.

- The company responsible for Zimbra has an ongoing commitment to the open source community.

In your office, there is no reason why most of your staff can't use the Zimbra web interface or the free Zimbra desktop client to access your Zimbra server. It will cut down the effort required to support different e-mail clients, it will reduce your firewall complexity, and it will make management of your network and hosts easier. This means that you will not need to run IMAP and POP services, although these can also easily be accommodated if the need in your office requires it.

Additionally, in this sort of network environment, you can seriously look at reducing the Microsoft and Apple desktop count in your organization. As many client applications are web based, you can take advantage of this with Linux desktop hosts. Linux on the desktop is more than capable of running a web browser, and this will further drive down your costs. However, some people in your organization will still need a commercial desktop to run certain applications. As part of your strategy going forward, you could look at eliminating all software on your network that ties you to particular vendors.

In your office, you could run predominately Linux and open source software on your desktops, reducing your operating costs by tens of thousands of dollars per year (depending on the size of your business). In the end, anything that makes your operating costs leaner than your competitors' gives you a terrific advantage.

ALTERNATIVE COLLABORATIVE OFFERINGS

Following are a list of other available collaborative offerings you may wish to explore on your own:

- *Horde*: Entry-level groupware product that combines webmail access with calendaring (`http://www.horde.org/`).

- *Citadel*: Completely free mail and collaboration server. Not as fully featured as others that follow (`http://www.citadel.org/doku.php`).

- *OpenXchange*: Another open source fully featured collaborative server. Not licensed for commercial organizations without a fee (`http://www.open-xchange.com/`).

- *Scalix*: Another fully featured open source collaborative server. Has limited licensing for the community edition (`http://www.scalix.com/community/`).

- *Novell Groupwise*: Closed source fully featured collaborative service that can run on Linux and is offered by Novell. Commercial licensed product (`http://www.novell.com`).

- *Lotus Domino*: Another closed source collaborative service that can run on Linux and is offered by IBM. Commercial licensed product (`http://www-01.ibm.com/software/lotus/`).

Zimbra

As we have mentioned, we have chosen Zimbra to demonstrate collaborative services because of its full feature set, its company's commitment to open source community, and unlimited license for the community edition of the product. It is also a fine example of a core open source software technology being innovated to create a good product that is still true to its roots. Zimbra provides additional fee-based features that can be added to your server, including push e-mail to PDA and mobile devices and commercial support agreements.

Zimbra itself can be installed in several different operating scenarios. It can use an external authentication service like OpenLDAP. You can have many e-mail storage servers scattered around your network to help speed access to disparate geographic regions. Zimbra also allows for community members to create addition utilities called *Zimlets*; one of these Zimlets even allows you to manage your Samba domain from within the Administration Console provided by Zimbra.

■**Note** Zimlets are community-created add-ons that can add functionality to your Zimbra server. If you need some kind of functionality or mashup, you can create a Zimlet and then give it back to the community to enjoy.

Figure 15-1 shows a diagram of a complex Zimbra solution based on an illustration that appears in the *ZCS Administrator's Guide*.

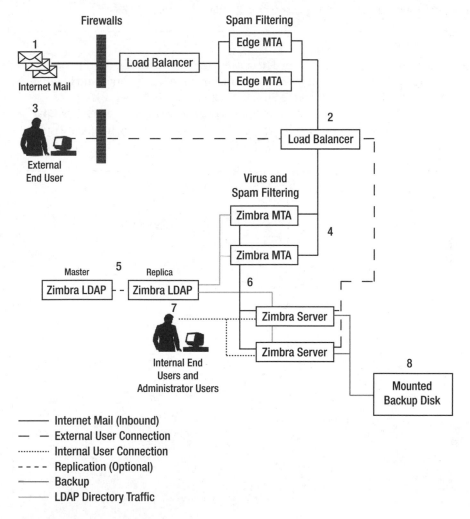

Figure 15-1. *A complex Zimbra solution*

As you can see, your e-mail systems can get quite complicated. In the diagram, you can see that this e-mail system has a lot of security and redundancy built into the design. E-mail coming into the company will flow into the edge MTAs that sit behind the firewall, and there we can do some preliminary spam and virus checking away from the internal e-mail servers. A load balancer distributes the user load across many Zimbra servers where our clients will be authenticated using the LDAP service, and e-mail is eventually delivered to the Zimbra servers where users can sign in to collect it.

We are going to take you through a stock standard installation. If you recall the office scenario we described in Chapter 6, we may have offices in other regions connected to our head office by a VPN. The installation we will describe here can be used in that situation without extra modification to our network or extra hardware. However, Zimbra is capable of much more complex configuration scenarios than we will describe here.

■**Note** We describe how to create our VPN connections in Chapter 14.

A single Zimbra server on a well-resourced host can handle as many as 500 to 1,000 clients. Once your company reaches this size, it is wise to allow for some redundancy and load balancing, because 500 people without access to e-mail can become a business risk.

Figure 15-2 shows our local office network. In this scenario, we only have one host that provides many services, which include DHCP, DNS, and mail. We are going to install Zimbra on our headoffice.example.com host.

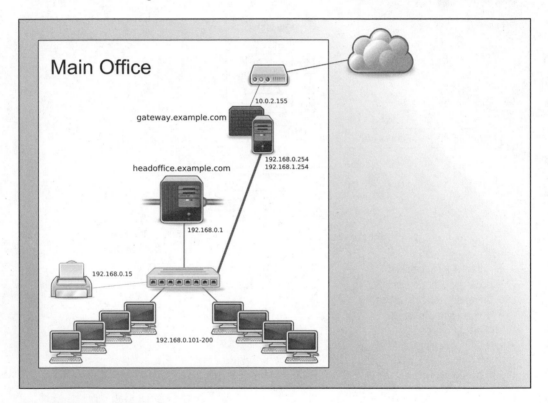

Figure 15-2. *Our network plan*

We will simply have one Zimbra server to provide all our e-mail services. In this case, we will be replacing the mail services we created in Chapter 10. The underlying MTA used by Zimbra is Postfix, so you can still use all the knowledge you gained on Postfix to understand how Zimbra works.

Installation of Zimbra

The Zimbra installation process is fairly easy to follow, and it is the same process whether your choice of host is Ubuntu or Red Hat, with minor exceptions we will detail shortly. It is a console text–based installation that asks a series of questions about what services you wish to install. The process takes about 20 minutes.

Prerequisites

Your system will need to meet a few prerequisites before you can install Zimbra. Zimbra installs into the /opt directory, and it requires over 5GB in /opt and at least 100MB in /tmp. You also need to have certain software installed on your host.

Ubuntu hosts have several requirements that differ from Red Hat hosts. On Ubuntu hosts, make sure the following are installed (any packages that are already installed will be ignored):

```
$ sudo aptitude install libidn11 libpcre3 libgmp3c2 libexpat1 libstdc++6 ➥
libstdc++5 libltdl3 perl
```

Red Hat requires the following packages to be installed:

```
$ sudo yum install sudo libidn fetchmail gmp compat-libstdc++ libstdc++ ➥
libtool-ltdl perl
```

It is important to know that these prerequisites may change over time. The installation process itself will check for any prerequisites, and if they are not present, you will be asked to install any missing packages before you can proceed. You can use either aptitude or yum to search for the missing packages.

The next thing to do is to turn off any existing services that may conflict with the services you are installing. You will need to turn off any SMTP, IMAP, POP3, HTTP, HTTPS, and LDAP services that are being served from your host. Make sure these services are not going to restart when your host reboots.

On your Ubuntu host, issue the following to stop these services:

```
$ sudo /usr/sbin/invoke-rc.d dovecot stop
$ sudo /usr/sbin/invoke-rc.d postfix stop
$ sudo /usr/sbin/invoke-rc.d apache2 stop
$ sudo /usr/sbin/invoke-rc.d mysql stop
$ sudo /usr/sbin/invoke-rc.d slapd stop
```

And to stop them starting on boot again:

```
$ sudo /usr/sbin/update-rc.d -f dovecot remove
$ sudo /usr/sbin/update-rc.d -f postfix remove
$ sudo /usr/sbin/update-rc.d -f apache2 remove
$ sudo /usr/sbin/update-rc.d -f mysql remove
$ sudo /usr/sbin/update-rc.d -f slapd remove
```

With your Red Hat hosts, use the following to stop the services:

```
$ sudo /sbin/service dovecot stop
$ sudo /sbin/service postfix stop
$ sudo /sbin/service httpd stop
$ sudo /sbin/service mysqld stop
$ sudo /sbin/service slapd stop
```

And to stop them starting on boot again:

```
$ sudo /sbin/chkconfig dovecot off
$ sudo /sbin/chkconfig postfix off
$ sudo /sbin/chkconfig httpd off
$ sudo /sbin/chkconfig mysqld off
$ sudo /sbin/chkconfig slapd off
```

Some of these services may not be present on your host, depending on the software you have installed. Please use the netstat command discussed in Chapter 6 to verify that these services have stopped. You can now continue on with the downloading and preparing of your hosts.

Downloading and Preparing the Hosts

You can get the Zimbra server from the Zimbra website. Use your Internet browser to download the compressed tarball or copy the link and use the wget command to download the package. All downloads are available from here: http://www.zimbra.com/community/downloads.html.

For this particular demonstration, we will be using our Ubuntu host. After the initial installation, the Zimbra application will act the same on either Red Hat or Ubuntu. You will notice on the Zimbra download website that different packages for different distributions are available. We will choose the one for Ubuntu 8.04 LTS (32-bit x86). Following is an example of how we would use wget to download a file from a URL:

```
$ wget http://h.yimg.com/lo/downloads/version/file
```

The *file* we have downloaded is in a compressed tar file. We need to use the tar program with the gzip flag, -z, to uncompress the downloaded package.

```
$ tar zxf zcs-5.0.13_GA_2791.UBUNTU8.20090206174622.tgz
```

The directory that is created is called zcs-5.0.13_GA_2791.UBUNTU8.20090206174622. We will now change into that directory and list its contents.

```
$ cd zcs-5.0.13_GA_2791.UBUNTU8.20090206174622/
$ ls
bin  data  docs  install.sh
packages readme_binary_en_US.txt
readme_source_en_US.txt  README.txt  util
```

Within this directory is a doc directory containing several helpful PDF files that are also available from the Zimbra website. The packages directory contains the individual packages we are going to install via the install.sh script.

Before we run the install.sh script, we will need to edit the /etc/hosts file to make sure we only have the following lines in our host:

```
127.0.0.1  localhost.localdomain localhost
192.168.0.1  mail.example.com
```

The host file is used to match hostnames to IP addresses. The reason we make these changes is because Zimbra sets the privileges of the MySQL user to only allow connections from the loopback address (127.0.0.1). If you do not set it this way, Zimbra will give a confusing installation error asking you to make changes to your hosts file.

You also see that we have added the hostname mail.example.com to the hosts file and assigned it the IP address 192.168.0.1. This host is already configured in our DNS zone file as headoffice.example.com, and we will need to make sure that mail.example.com also resolves to the 192.168.0.1 IP address.

We will also need to create MX records in our DNS service and set a CNAME for our mail host. If you are using a BIND DNS server like the one we set up in Chapter 9, you need to make sure that the MX records for your domain are pointing to the host you wish to use as your mail server. In the example.com zone file, you need to add the following:

```
mail    IN   CNAME   headoffice.example.com.
example.com.  IN  MX  10  mail
```

Our configuration changes have added a CNAME for the record mail to point to headoffice. example.com. There is already an A record for headoffice.example.com, which points to the IP address 192.168.0.1. The CNAME aliases hostnames to other records. We then use that record to set the MX record in our zone file to point to mail.example.com with a priority of 10. The MX signifies a mail exchange for a domain, and the priority allows you to have multiple MX records that you can preference with a lower priority number.

■Note You can view quick-start install information from http://www.zimbra.com/docs/ne/latest/single_server_install/.

Installing Zimbra

It is relatively easy to install Zimbra on your host. Having completed the prerequisites, you need to execute the install.sh script. This starts the text-based installation process and requires a few answers to some questions. The installation requires root user privileges and so should be run using the sudo command.

```
$ sudo ./install.sh
Operations logged to /tmp/install.log.5430
Checking for existing installation...
    zimbra-ldap...NOT FOUND
    zimbra-logger...NOT FOUND
    zimbra-mta...NOT FOUND
    zimbra-snmp...NOT FOUND
    zimbra-store...NOT FOUND
    zimbra-apache...NOT FOUND
    zimbra-spell...NOT FOUND
```

```
zimbra-proxy...NOT FOUND
zimbra-archiving...NOT FOUND
zimbra-convertd...NOT FOUND
zimbra-cluster...NOT FOUND
zimbra-core...NOT FOUND
```

When the installer starts, it begins by checking whether any Zimbra components are already installed. Ours is a fresh install, so we would expect to see that everything is listed as NOT FOUND.

Next, the installation checks for the prerequisites we should have installed earlier. If you have missed any, they will appear here, marked as MISSING, and you will have to install them before you can complete the installation.

```
Checking for prerequisites...
    FOUND: NPTL
    FOUND: sudo-1.6.9p10-1ubuntu3.4
    FOUND: libidn11-1.1-1
    FOUND: libpcre3-7.4-1ubuntu2.1
    FOUND: libgmp3c2-2:4.2.2+dfsg-1ubuntu2
    FOUND: libexpat1-2.0.1-0ubuntu1
    FOUND: libstdc++6-4.2.4-1ubuntu3
    FOUND: libstdc++5
    FOUND: libltdl3-1.5.26-1ubuntu1
Checking for suggested prerequisites...
    FOUND: perl-5.8.8
```

Now it is time to select the components of Zimbra you wish to install. You can configure different components of Zimbra on different hosts. For example, you can have your authentication services on several hosts and your mail stores also split out on different local or regional servers.

■**Note** For information on these advanced installations, please see the product overview in the *ZCS Administrator's Guide*: http://www.zimbra.com/docs/os/latest/administration_guide/2_ Overview%20System%20Architecture.3.1.html#1101622.

In this chapter, we are going to install the basic Zimbra server without the zimbra-proxy component. The zimbra-proxy service allows us to *proxy*, that is, to have these services running on another host, the IMAP and POP services. Since we don't plan to use IMAP or POP, we don't need this service at all.

Following are the packages we do want to install:

```
Select the packages to install
Install zimbra-ldap [Y]
```

This package is the authentication service that also holds the user configuration details in an OpenLDAP server. An advanced configuration may have many LDAP servers, one acting as a master and one or more as replicas.

```
Install zimbra-logger [Y]
```

This installs the Zimbra logging service, which provides some logging tools that enable syslog aggregation, reporting, and message tracing. To make use of the statistics section of the Administration Console, you must install this service.

■Note We'll talk more about syslog and logging in Chapter 18.

Install zimbra-mta [Y]

zimbra-mta installs a Postfix mail server used to send and receive mail as well as antivirus and antispam software.

Install zimbra-snmp [Y]

SNMP, which stands for Simple Network Management Protocol, can be used to monitor your host over a network. Zimbra (zimbra-ldap, zimbra-mta, and zimbra-core) also uses SNMP to monitor syslog and send SNMP traps.

■Note We discuss SNMP in Chapter 17. You can also read more about SNMP here: http:// en.wikipedia.org/wiki/Simple_Network_Management_Protocol.

Install zimbra-store [Y]

zimbra-store is the mail storage host service. In an advanced Zimbra configuration, you could have many zimbra-store servers in your network. These servers hold the messages and user data for your users. When you create a user, he is assigned to a mail store; and when that user signs in, he will be directed to that mail store from the web interface or POP/IMAP servers.

Install zimbra-apache [Y]

zimbra-apache will install the Apache server that will serve the web interface.

Install zimbra-spell [Y]

zimbra-spell component is used by the web client to do spell checking.

Install zimbra-proxy [N]

If you choose to install the zimbra-proxy service, you get the ability to deploy proxy IMAP and POP hosts on your network. These will route client IMAP/POP connections to the appropriate mail store.

```
checking space for zimbra-store

Installing:
    zimbra-core
    zimbra-ldap
    zimbra-logger
    zimbra-mta
    zimbra-snmp
    zimbra-store
    zimbra-apache
    zimbra-spell

The system will be modified.  Continue? [N] Y
Installing packages

    zimbra-core......zimbra-core_5.0.13_GA_2791.UBUNTU8_i386.deb...done
    zimbra-ldap......zimbra-ldap_5.0.13_GA_2791.UBUNTU8_i386.deb...done
    zimbra-logger......zimbra-logger_5.0.13_GA_2791.UBUNTU8_i386.deb...done
    zimbra-mta......zimbra-mta_5.0.13_GA_2791.UBUNTU8_i386.deb...done
    zimbra-snmp......zimbra-snmp_5.0.13_GA_2791.UBUNTU8_i386.deb...done
    zimbra-store......zimbra-store_5.0.13_GA_2791.UBUNTU8_i386.deb...done
    zimbra-apache......zimbra-apache_5.0.13_GA_2791.UBUNTU8_i386.deb...done
    zimbra-spell......zimbra-spell_5.0.13_GA_2791.UBUNTU8_i386.deb...done
Operations logged to /tmp/zmsetup.03102009-215512.log
```

You now have the packages installed on your host. The Zimbra installation process will next perform some postinstallation configuration.

```
Setting defaults...
        Interface: 127.0.0.1
        Interface: 192.168.0.1
```

This sets the network interface addresses for your host.

```
DNS ERROR - none of the MX records for mail.example.com
resolve to this host
Change domain name? [Yes] Yes
Create Domain: [mail.example.com] example.com
        MX: mail.example.com (192.168.0.1)


        Interface: 127.0.0.1
        Interface: 192.168.0.1
done.
Checking for port conflicts
```

If there are any mail or web services that are listening on the standard ports, like 80, 443, 110, 25, and so forth, you will be alerted to them here. You will need to shut down any existing mail and web services that should no longer be running.

Zimbra Postinstallation Configuration Menu

After you have selected the components of Zimbra you wish to install, you are presented with a menu that enables you to configure various aspects of your Zimbra server. It is here that you can set your passwords and also configure the Zimbra components. With this option-driven menu we will set a password for the Admin user, as indicated by the ******* symbols, for our Zimbra installation.

```
Main menu
    1) Common Configuration:
    2) zimbra-ldap:                          Enabled
    3) zimbra-store:                         Enabled
          +Create Admin User:                yes
          +Admin user to create:             admin@example.com
*******  +Admin Password                     UNSET
          +Enable automated spam training:   yes
          +Spam training user:               spam.syuqmdsha@example.com
          +Non-spam(Ham) training user:      ham.qiomilor@example.com
          +Global Documents Account:         wiki@example.com
          +SMTP host:                        mail.example.com
          +Web server HTTP port:     80
          +Web server HTTPS port:    443
          +Web server mode:          http
          +IMAP server port:         143
          +IMAP server SSL port:     993
          +POP server port:          110
          +POP server SSL port:      995
          +Use spell check server:   yes
          +Spell server URL:         http://mail.example.com:7780/aspell.php
          +Configure store for use with reverse mail proxy: FALSE
          +Configure store for use with reverse web proxy: FALSE

    4) zimbra-mta:                           Enabled
    5) zimbra-snmp:                          Enabled
    6) zimbra-logger:                        Enabled
    7) zimbra-spell:                         Enabled
    8) Default Class of Service Configuration:
    r) Start servers after configuration     yes
    s) Save config to file
    x) Expand menu
    q) Quit

Address unconfigured (**) items  (? - help) 3
```

As you can see, we select item 3, zimbra-store, under which is the Admin Password setting we want to specify. The menu that appears, shown here, allows us to navigate to the Admin Password option by selecting 4 and enter:

```
Store configuration

    1) Status:                              Enabled
    2) Create Admin User:                   yes
    3) Admin user to create:                admin@example.com
** 4) Admin Password                        UNSET
    5) Enable automated spam training:      yes
    6) Spam training user:                  spam.syuqmdsha@example.com
    7) Non-spam(Ham) training user:         ham.qiomilor@example.com
    8) Global Documents Account:            wiki@example.com
    9) SMTP host:                           mail.example.com
   10) Web server HTTP port:                80
   11) Web server HTTPS port:         443
   12) Web server mode:               http
   13) IMAP server port:              143
   14) IMAP server SSL port:          993
   15) POP server port:               110
   16) POP server SSL port:           995
   17) Use spell check server:              yes
   18) Spell server URL:              http://mail.example.com:7780/aspell.php
   19) Configure store for use with reverse mail proxy: FALSE
   20) Configure store for use with reverse web proxy: FALSE

Select, or 'r' for previous menu [r] 4
```

As you can see, once you are inside a nested menu, you can use the r key to return to the previous menu or use the numbers represented to choose your item. We select number 4, after which we are given the opportunity to add a password for the Admin user. A password is generated for you, as indicated by the string in the square brackets shown on the following line:

```
Password for admin@example.com (min 6 characters): [0aPFi_01Ta] somepassword123
```

or you can choose your own password as we have.

We select r to return to the main menu. Now we only needed to set the Admin user's password; we can configure the other options in the Administration Console.

```
Main menu

    1) Common Configuration:
    2) zimbra-ldap:                         Enabled
    3) zimbra-store:                        Enabled
    4) zimbra-mta:                          Enabled
    5) zimbra-snmp:                         Enabled
    6) zimbra-logger:                       Enabled
    7) zimbra-spell:                        Enabled
    8) Default Class of Service Configuration:
    r) Start servers after configuration    yes
    s) Save config to file
    x) Expand menu
```

```
  q) Quit

*** CONFIGURATION COMPLETE - press 'a' to apply
Select from menu, or press 'a' to apply config (? - help) a
```

Having configured the new password for our Admin user, we are ready to apply the change to the configuration. To do so, we type **a** and press the Enter key. Next, we are asked whether we want our configuration data saved to a file, SSL certificates generated, and various other things done.

```
Save configuration data to a file? [Yes]
Save config in file: [/opt/zimbra/config.11384]
Saving config in /opt/zimbra/config.11384...done.
The system will be modified - continue? [No] Yes
Operations logged to /tmp/zmsetup.03102009-215512.log
Setting local config values...done.
Setting up CA...done.
Deploying CA to /opt/zimbra/conf/ca ...done.
Creating SSL certificate...done.
Installing mailboxd SSL certificates...done.
Initializing ldap...done.
Setting replication password...done.
Setting Postfix password...done.
Setting amavis password...done.
Setting nginx password...done.
Saving CA in ldap ...done.
Creating server entry for mail.example.com...done.
Saving SSL Certificate in ldap ...done.
Setting spell check URL...done.
Setting service ports on mail.example.com...done.
Adding mail.example.com to zimbraMailHostPool in default COS...done.
Installing skins...
        steel
        beach
        sky
        zmail
        yahoo
        lavender
        bones
        bare
        lemongrass
        sand
        hotrod
        waves
done.
Setting zimbraFeatureIMEnabled=FALSE...done.
Setting zimbraFeatureTasksEnabled=TRUE...done.
Setting zimbraFeatureBriefcasesEnabled=TRUE...done.
Setting zimbraFeatureNotebookEnabled=TRUE...done.
```

```
Setting MTA auth host...done.
Setting TimeZone Preference...done.
Creating domain example.com...done.
Creating user admin@example.com...done.
Creating postmaster alias...done.
Creating user wiki@example.com...done.
Creating user spam.syuqmdsha@example.com...done.
Creating user ham.qiomilor@example.com...done.
Setting spam training accounts...done.
Initializing store sql database...done.
Setting zimbraSmtpHostname for mail.example.com...done.
Initializing logger sql database...done.
Initializing mta config...done.
Configuring SNMP...done.
Setting services on mail.example.com...done.
Setting up syslog.conf...done.

You have the option of notifying Zimbra of your installation.
This helps us to track the uptake of the Zimbra Collaboration Suite.
The only information that will be transmitted is:
        The VERSION of zcs installed (5.0.13_GA_2791_UBUNTU8)
        The ADMIN EMAIL ADDRESS created (admin@example.com)

Notify Zimbra of your installation? [Yes] Yes
Notifying Zimbra of installation via http://www.zimbra.com/cgi-bin/notify.cgi? ➥
VER=5.0.13_GA_2791_UBUNTU8&MAIL=admin@example.com

Notification complete

Starting servers...done.
Checking for deprecated zimlets...done.
Installing common zimlets...
        com_zimbra_date...done.
        com_zimbra_cert_manager...done.
        com_zimbra_ymemoticons...done.
        com_zimbra_phone...done.
        com_zimbra_url...done.
        com_zimbra_bulkprovision...done.
        com_zimbra_local...done.
        com_zimbra_email...done.
Finished installing common zimlets.
Initializing Documents...done.
Restarting mailboxd...done.
Setting up zimbra crontab...done.

Moving /tmp/zmsetup.03102009-215512.log to /opt/zimbra/log

Configuration complete - press return to exit
```

Now that you have completed your install of Zimbra, you need to start your service. You can do this in two ways: use the Zimbra script you will find installed in your /etc/init.d directory or issue su to change to the zimbra user and use the zmcontrol command to stop and start the service.

For Red Hat hosts, use

```
$ sudo /sbin/service zimbra stop|start|restart
```

For Ubuntu hosts, use

```
$ sudo /usr/sbin/invoke-rc.d zimbra stop|start|restart
```

■**Note** In Chapter 5, we explained how to start, stop, and add services to your host.

To start and stop Zimbra using the zmcontrol command, issue the following:

```
$ sudo su - zimbra
$ zmcontrol start|stop
```

The zimbra user can be used to control other aspects of your Zimbra service. You can get more information about the commands available to the zimbra user here: http://www.zimbra.com/docs/os/latest/administration_guide/A_app-command-line.13.1.html.

Firewall Changes

The firewall requirements for our Zimbra installation are very straightforward. We will only require access to our host to send and receive mail and HTTP/HTTPS access for users to retrieve their mail. Even the Zimbra desktop client and the push-mail-to-mobile clients transmit their communications over HTTPS. There is the special requirement for port 7071 to be open for the Administration Console, and this should be restricted to allow only local network connections with our host.

■**Caution** We recommend there be no direct connections from the Internet to the Administration Console for security reasons.

```
$ sudo /sbin/iptables -I Firewall-eth0-INPUT rule_number -p tcp -m state -state ➡
-m tcp NEW --dport 25 -j ACCEPT
$ sudo /sbin/iptables -I Firewall-eth0-INPUT rule_number -p tcp -m state -state ➡
-m tcp NEW --dport 80 -j ACCEPT
$ sudo /sbin/iptables -I Firewall-eth0-INPUT rule_number -p tcp -m state -state ➡
-m tcp NEW --dport 443 -j ACCEPT
$ sudo /sbin/iptables -I Firewall-eth0-INPUT rule_number -s 192.168.0.0/24 -p tcp ➡
-m state -state -m tcp NEW --dport 7071 -j ACCEPT
```

We showed you how to set up your firewall in Chapter 6. Here we open up ports 25, 80, 443, and 7071 using the iptables command. Firewall-eth0-INPUT and the *rule_number* may vary depending on the host you are working on.

If you decide that you would like to allow POP and IMAP access to your Zimbra host, you will have to allow those services through your firewall as well.

```
$ sudo /sbin/iptables –I Firewall-eth0-INPUT rule_number -p tcp –m state –state ➥
–m tcp NEW --dport 110 –j ACCEPT
$ sudo /sbin/iptables –I Firewall-eth0-INPUT rule_number -p tcp –m state –state ➥
–m tcp NEW --dport 993 –j ACCEPT
$ sudo /sbin/iptables –I Firewall-eth0-INPUT rule_number -p tcp –m state –state ➥
–m tcp NEW --dport 143 –j ACCEPT
$ sudo /sbin/iptables –I Firewall-eth0-INPUT rule_number -p tcp –m state –state ➥
–m tcp NEW --dport 995 –j ACCEPT
```

Next, we demonstrate how to use the Administration Console to provision users and define the service.

The Zimbra Administration Console

In this section, we are going to sign in to the Administration Console and begin setting up the rest of our service. You can find the Zimbra Administration Console with your browser using the HTTPS protocol and port 7071 by pointing your browser here: https://mail.example.com:7071.

Figure 15-3 shows the sign-in screen for the Administration Console. The username (in our case, admin@example.com) and password you set earlier is required here to gain access. Once inside, you will see the layout of the Administration Console, as presented in Figure 15-4.

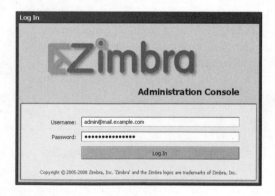

Figure 15-3. *Signing in to the Zimbra Administration Console*

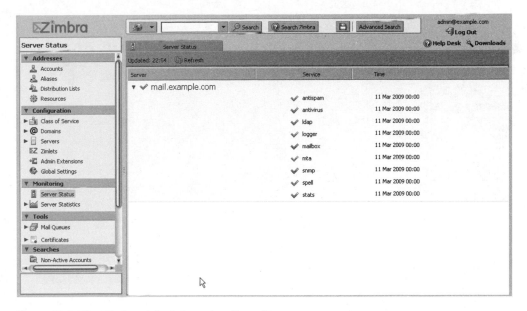

Figure 15-4. *The Zimbra Administration Console*

As you can see in Figure 15-4, you are presented with the server status whenever you first sign in. Notice that all our services are active in the main screen. On the left are the different parts of the server we can configure or inspect. Each time you selection one of the options on the left side, a new tab opens in the main screen. You can open several and then select the tabs you wish to currently work on. Zimbra uses a type of object called *Class of Service (CoS)* through which we can set default options for our service. These range from password options, mail hosts, and themes. We are going to create our own CoS to use with our domain example.com.

Creating a Class of Service

In Figure 15-5, you can see we already have a default CoS, and we are going to duplicate it.

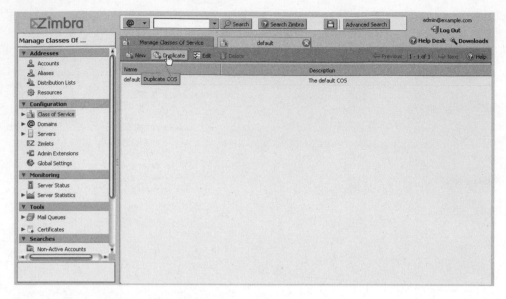

Figure 15-5. *Duplicating the default CoS*

Duplicating the default CoS allows us to copy some of the settings in the default CoS and change the ones we wish. Now look at Figure 15-6, which shows how we add some general details to describe the CoS.

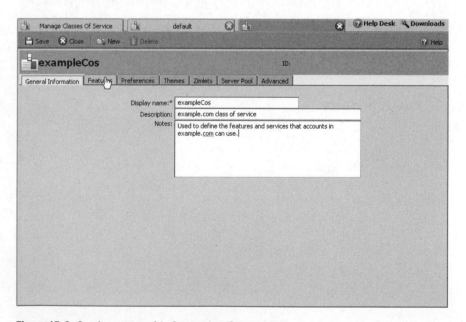

Figure 15-6. *Setting general information for our CoS*

In Figure 15-6, you can see that we have just filled out some general details, such as example-Cos for the Display name option, and so on. You can also see several other tabs, which we will go through in the remainder of this section.

The next tab after General Information is Features, and here we select what features we will give users in example.com access to.

In Figure 15-7, you can see how easy it is to select various features that can be accessed by the users using this CoS. These are available to the user via the web interface, and you use the mouse to select the check boxes to enable the features. We will select all the features, including those in General Features section (although we don't show this in the figure).

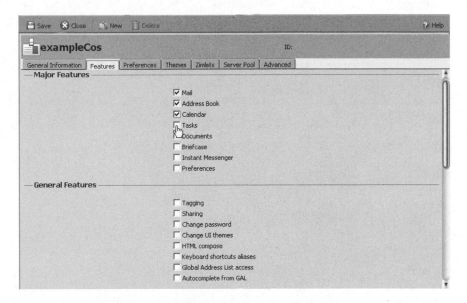

Figure 15-7. *Selecting features available to our users*

Next, we will add the preferences we want to use with our CoS. In Figure 15-8, you can see a subset of those we have selected.

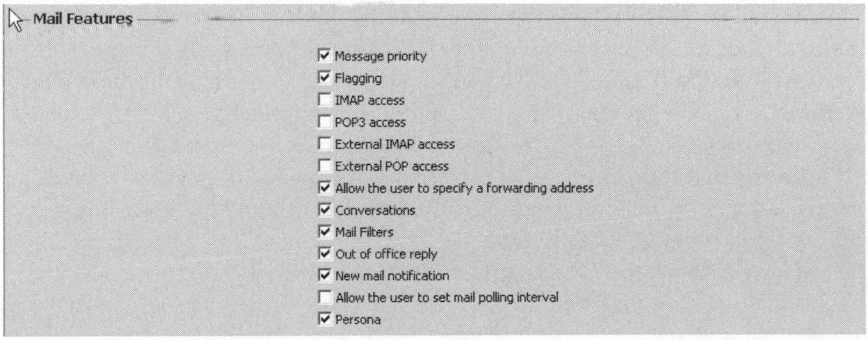

Figure 15-8. *Features selection*

The important thing to note in Figure 15-8 is that we are not allowing external IMAP or POP. The reason for this is we want everyone in our company to use the web interface and not use separate e-mail clients. This will make management of our desktops much easier and also reduce the complexity of our network, as we will now only require the HTTPS and SMTP ports to be open for our mail services.

In some companies, getting rid of e-mail clients may not be practical, as some people use their clients to do offline work that can't be achieved through a web interface. Zimbra does offer a desktop client in this case, and you can download it from here: http://www.zimbra.com/products/desktop.html. This client communicates with the Zimbra server over HTTPS, so it requires no extra configuration from a network perspective.

Still within the Preferences tab, we want to point out the way messages can be viewed in the web browser. In Figure 15-9, we are setting mail options, one of which is Group mail by.

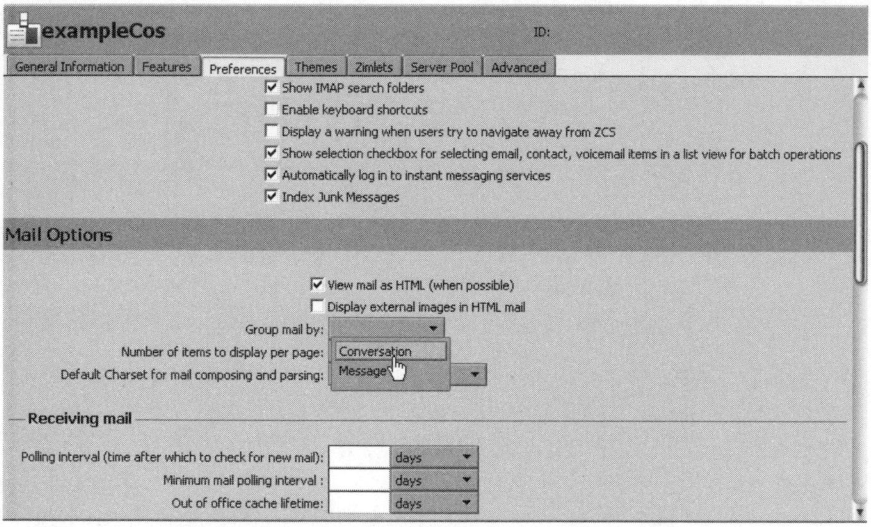

Figure 15-9. *The Mail Options section in the Preferences tab*

You might already be familiar with grouping e-mail by conversation (also known as a *threaded view*), as Google's Gmail does, for example. Instead of the traditional incoming messages appearing in your inbox and outgoing items in your sent folder, mail is grouped together by the conversation they belong to. So if you sent a mail to someone, and she replied, those messages will be grouped together and listed together in your message screen. We will show exactly what we mean later in the "Using Zimbra" section when we describe the web interface, but just be aware that this is where you can change the default behavior if you wish. Other settings available to you in the Preferences tab are default fonts, address book options, and calendar options.

The Themes tab lets you set the themes that are available to your users and specify whether they can change those themes. You may want to restrict this so that everyone has a consistent web interface experience, but that is up to you. In Figure 15-10, we show you what we have done.

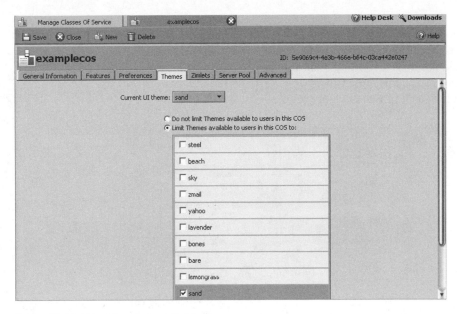

Figure 15-10. *Limiting the available themes*

Here we have limited the themes available to our users to just one: the sand theme, which is the default. You can also set the theme you are presently using by switching the Current UI theme option.

Zimlets, as we have explained earlier, are addition features that have been written either by Zimbra or community programmers to perform some extra functionality that can be used from the web interface. You can set the Zimlets available to your users in the Zimlet tab, as shown in Figure 15-11.

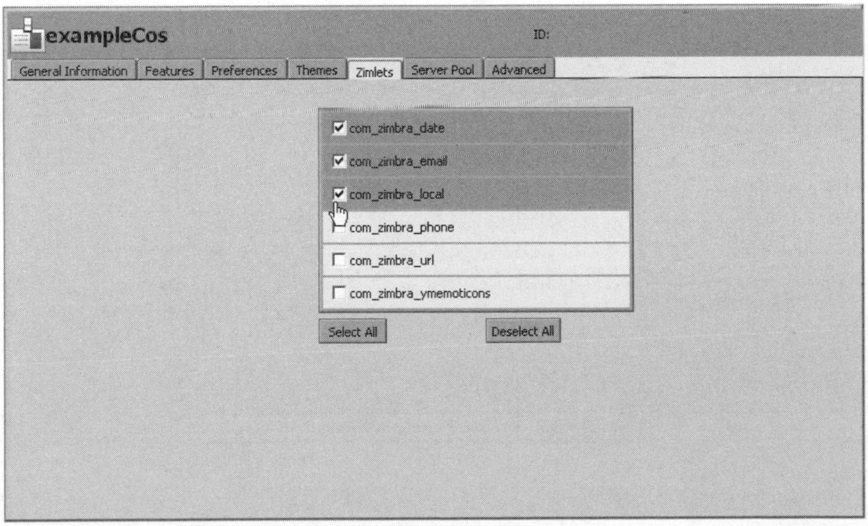

Figure 15-11. *Selecting available Zimlets*

Again, we select via check box those Zimlets we wish to make available. The ones you see in Figure 15-11 are installed by default with Zimbra, and so we will add them all.

Next tab is Server Pool. Here we can select the server we wish to attach our accounts to. In some cases you might have multiple mail storage servers on your network, and you may want specific people using a particular CoS to use a particular mail server. In our case, we only have one, which we select as shown in Figure 15-12.

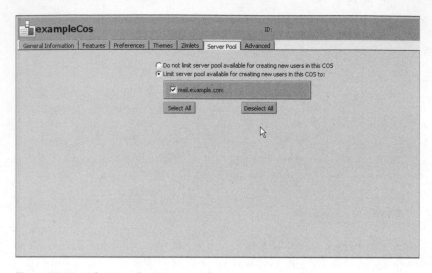

Figure 15-12. *Selecting the server pool*

The next tab is the Advanced tab. Settings found here include options for mailbox quotas, password control (length, complexity, aging), and e-mail retention policies. In Figure 15-13, you can see that we have set a mailbox quota via Account quota of 500MB and a stringent password control policy.

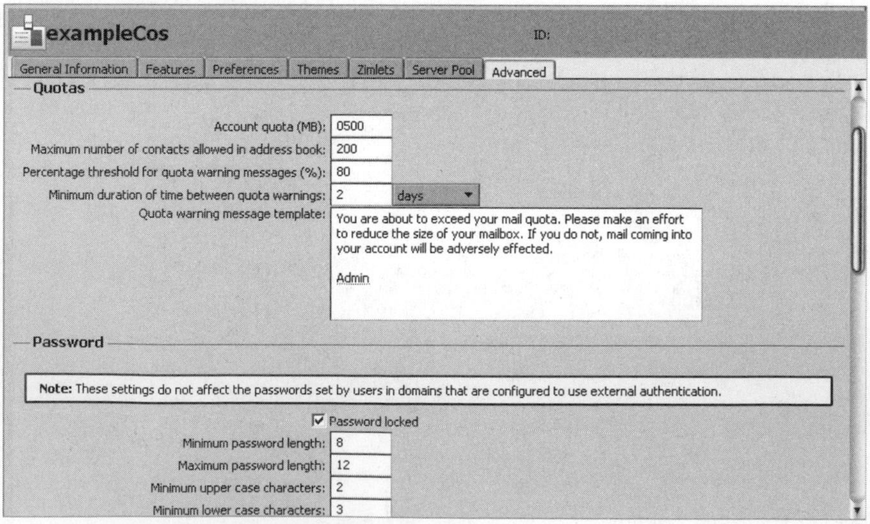

Figure 15-13. *Settings in the Advanced tab*

We have put some limits on our users here. In addition to the 500MB mailbox limit, users can have only 200 contacts in the address book and will receive a message when their account reaches 80% capacity every 2 days. We have also specified a minimum password length of 8 characters, and you can see that we have defined that they should at least contain two uppercase and three lowercase letters. There are other similar options for password control that you can't see in Figure 15-13; one of these is password aging, which we set to 90 days. You can set other options in the Advanced tab like e-mail retention. With this option, you can set universally how long you keep trash and spam messages, which can help reduce space on your host.

Now that we have a Class of Service defined, we can save it using the Save button and use it when we create our users or assign it to existing users. Let's move on to creating some users. You can create users two ways: one at a time or several at a time using the bulk provisioning method.

■**Note** The `zmprov` command technically provides a third way to create users. We will be covering this command in the "zmprov: The Third Way" sidebar later in this chapter.

Adding New Users

We will now work with our user accounts. We start by clicking Accounts in the left-hand menu. The main screen now has a list of our current users in it, as you can see in Figure 15-14.

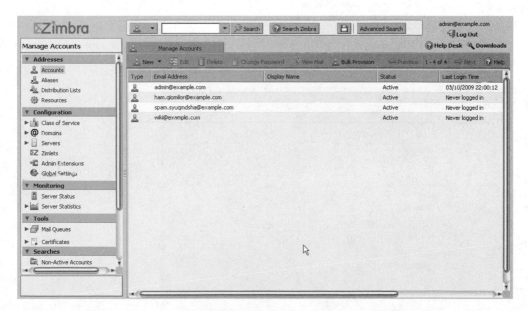

Figure 15-14. *Selecting Accounts from the console*

Figure 15-14 shows we already have four users: admin, ham.qiomilor, spam.syuqmdsha, and wiki. These are system-supplied accounts. The admin account, which is the user we are currently signed in as, has advanced privileges to administer Zimbra. The ham and spam users are for the spam filtering service. Zimbra will use these two accounts to help categorize incoming mail into spam (annoying mail) and ham (good mail). As you can see, these two account names have a dot (.) followed by a random set of characters. Zimbra does this so that the addresses can't be guessed by spammers and used to reduce the effectiveness of your filtering capabilities. Zimbra uses SpamAssassin as the spam filter.

■**Note** Read about how SpamAssassin works in detail in Chapter 10.

The wiki user is used by the Documents component of the Zimbra server, and we will be explaining this in the "Using Zimbra" section a little later on.

Now we will add some users. As mentioned previously, Zimbra allows you to add one user at a time or several users at once through bulk provision. In the console, we can add multiple accounts using the Bulk Provision button. Clicking it will present a dialog asking for the location of a CSV file (CSV is short for comma-separated values). Zimbra's bulk provision feature allows you to assign a mail address, a display name, and a password for each user. Our CSV file looks like the following:

```
jsmith@example.com,Jane Smith,somepassword
bsingh@example.com,Bev Singh,somepassword
ataylor@example.com,Angela Taylor,somepassword
```

We have saved these details to a file called users.txt. In Figure 15-15, you can see that we have already browsed to the location of the file and are ready to click Next.

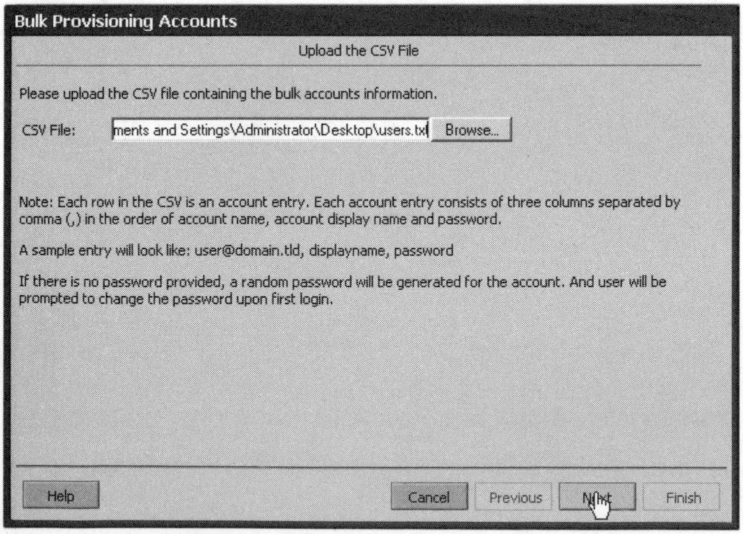

Figure 15-15. *Adding the users.txt CSV for bulk provisioning*

When we click Next, we are then shown the details we are about to enter. We are going to add the users listed in our CSV file, as shown in Figure 15-16; this gives us a chance to confirm the details are correct.

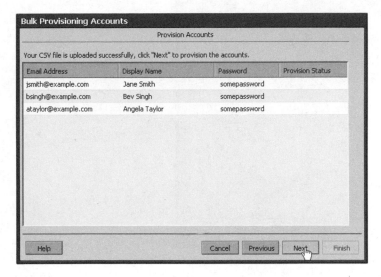

Figure 15-16. *Confirming the user details before adding them*

When we click the Next button, our provisioning will commence, and we will be presented with a confirmation window detailing the accounts added and their completion status. Ours have all completed successfully, as you can see in Figure 15-17.

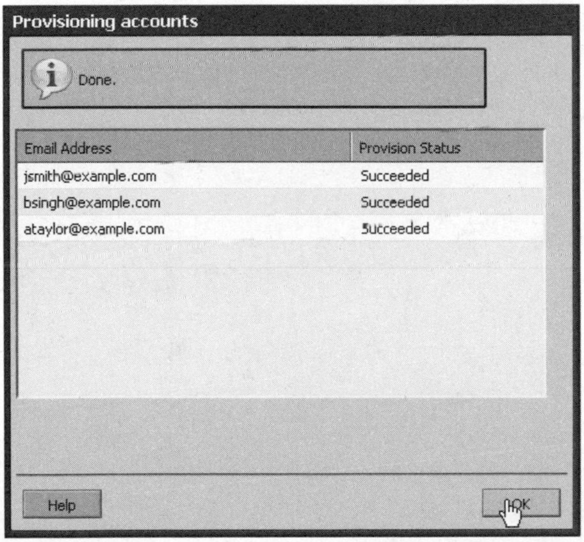

Figure 15-17. *Our users are now provisioned.*

Now to complete the process, we are shown a final pop-up window giving us a summary of our actions, as in Figure 15-18.

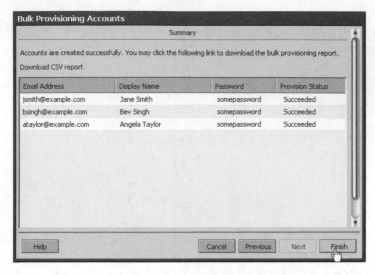

Figure 15-18. *Summary of the bulk provisioning process*

Next, we are going to show you how to add an individual user to a host. Start by selecting the New button in the Accounts window, as shown in Figure 15-19.

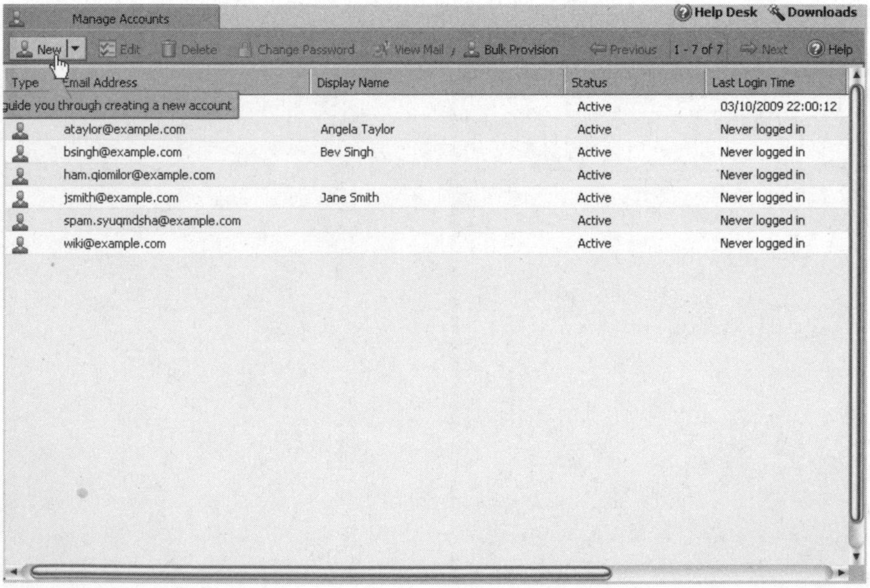

Figure 15-19. *Adding a single user*

We are adding the user Jim Bob. We add the details for our new user, such as his account name, what he uses to log in to Zimbra with, and his first and last names, as shown in

Figure 15-20. The canonical address is shown in the From field when the e-mail is sent from this user. We will add an e-mail alias for this name shortly. You can also see that we have specified the CoS for the user as being `examplecos`. The Class of Service field will automatically look up any available CoS values.

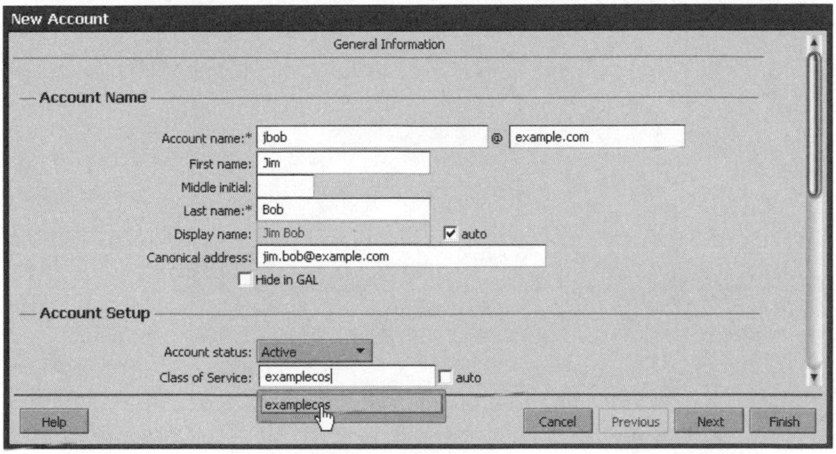

Figure 15-20. *Adding the account details of our user*

Next are the user's contact details. You can see what we entered for our user in Figure 15-21.

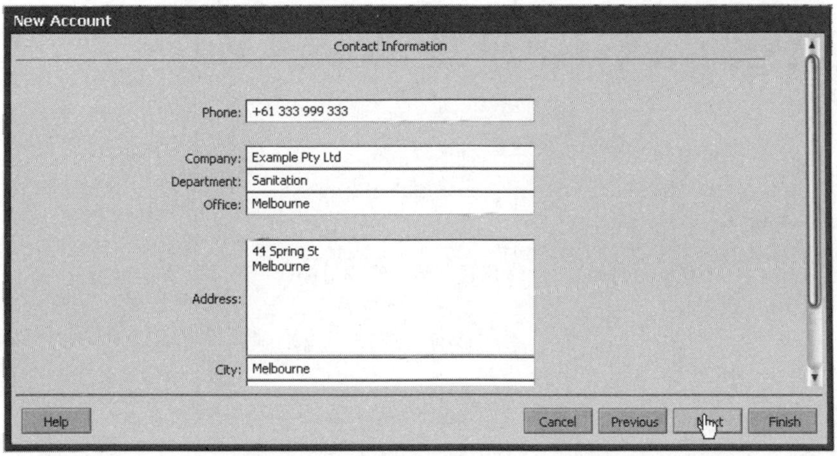

Figure 15-21. *General contact details*

Next, we need to add the alias we mentioned earlier for our new user. We will add the aliases `jim.bob@example.com` and `jimmy.bob@example.com`. Mail aliases are used to allow multiple e-mail addresses to be attached to a user account. Now our user can receive mail addressed to `jim.bob@example.com`, `jimmy.bob@example.com`, and `jbob@example.com`. You can see this in Figure 15-22.

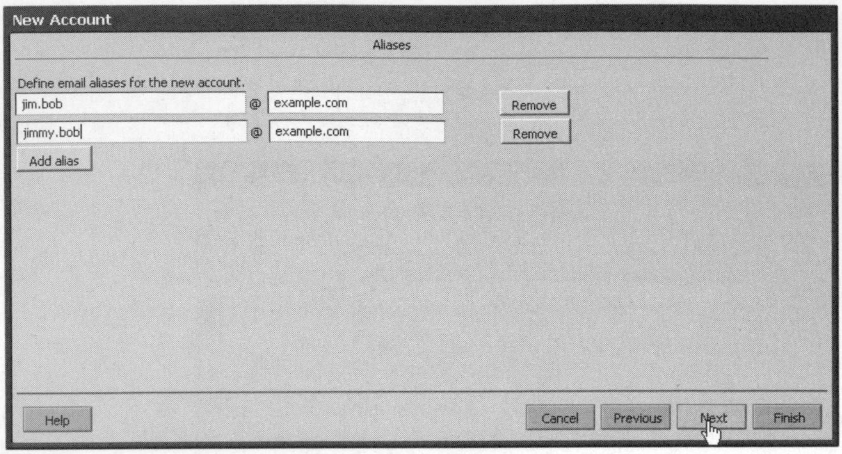

Figure 15-22. *User mail aliases*

We can now set up any forwarding addresses. When a user has signed in to his accounts, he can set up a forwarding address of his own if the Allow the user to specify a forwarding address check box option is selected. This also allows you to forward mail destined for your new user's account to another address if you so wish. You also have the option to sneakily forward mail to another address that the user will not be aware of. This can be used to watch correspondence sent to the user. We require neither of these options and have left them unchecked, as you can see in Figure 15-23.

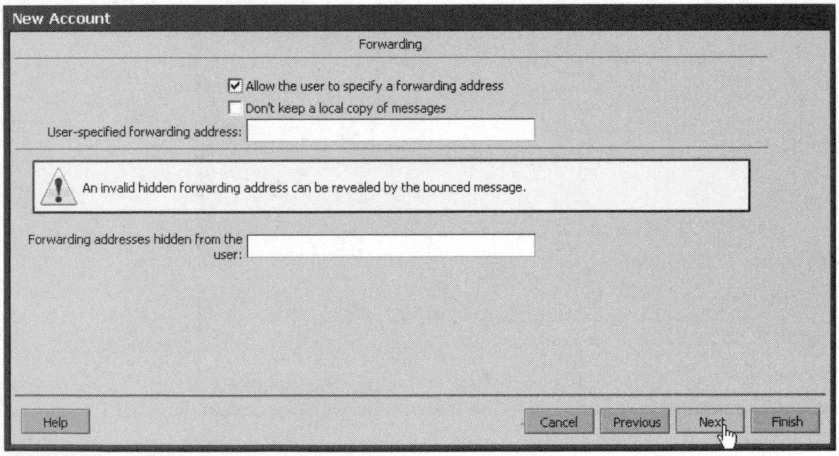

Figure 15-23. *Forwarding addresses*

We click Finish now, and the rest of the details are automatically filled in for us by our `examplecos` CoS. Our new user will now be created and appear in the Accounts window along with the other accounts we have created.

ZMPROV: THE THIRD WAY

We mentioned earlier in this chapter that there is technically a third way to bulk provision user accounts. Using the zmprov command, you can add many users at once, including their CoS setting as well as any other particular setting you require.

```
zmprov ca jsmith@example.com password displayName 'Jane Smith' ➡
zimbraCOS 5e9069c4-4e3b-466e-b64c-03ca442e0247
```

Here we have used zmprov with the ca option to create accounts. We have given our new user, jsmith@example.com, a password of "password" and a display name of Jane Smith. We have also added her to the examplecos CoS by specifying ZimbraCOS, which can be found in details of the examplecos in the Administration Console or by using the following:

```
$ zmprov gc examplecos |grep zimbraId
zimbraId: 5e9069c4-4e3b-466e-b64c-03ca442e0247
```

So to create many accounts at once, use a script that includes the following:

```
#!/bin/bash
zmprov ca bsingh@example.com password displayName 'Bevan Singh' ➡
zimbraCOSId 5e9069c4-4e3b-466e-b64c-03ca442e0247
zmprov ca jsmith@example.com password displayName 'Jane Smith' ➡
zimbraCOSId 5e9069c4-4e3b-466e-b64c-03ca442e0247
zmprov ca ataylor@example.com password displayName 'Angela Taylor' ➡
zimbraCOSId 5e9069c4-4e3b-466e-b64c-03ca442e0247
```

By adding these lines to a script, like users.sh, and then running it as the zimbra user, you will add the three users to the examplecos CoS. For more information on using the zmprov command, please read http://www.zimbra.com/docs/os/latest/administration_guide/A_app-command-line.13.2.html.

Aliases and Distribution Lists

Under the Accounts menu is the Aliases menu. Clicking the Aliases menu allows us to see the two aliases we created for Jim Bob. Here we can add new or manipulate existing aliases. You can see the two new aliases we created in Figure 15-24.

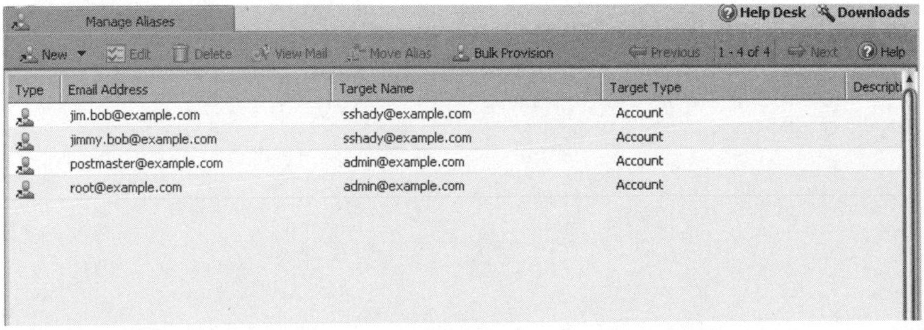

Type	Email Address	Target Name	Target Type	Descripti
👤	jim.bob@example.com	sshady@example.com	Account	
👤	jimmy.bob@example.com	sshady@example.com	Account	
👤	postmaster@example.com	admin@example.com	Account	
👤	root@example.com	admin@example.com	Account	

Figure 15-24. *The new aliases we have created*

Currently the `root` and `postmaster` e-mail addresses are aliased to the `admin` user. The `root` and the `postmaster` addresses are important addresses for host and Internet communications. The hosts will use the `root@example.com` address to send alert messages, and the `postmaster@example.com` address is used for correspondence by various Internet services. You may wish to change these to point to an account that is more appropriate for handling these messages; otherwise, you will have to remember to sign in to the `admin` account from time to time to read the mail there.

We are now going to add two distribution lists. Distribution lists are ways of grouping more than one e-mail address together under another e-mail address, much like aliases for multiple user addresses. We will create one list, called `allstaff`, to serve as a way of messaging all the staff we have. The other, called `melboffice`, will be used only for messaging those in the Melbourne office. You can create any distribution list you like as long as it has a unique name. You could have a list named `sales` for all the sales staff, business managers, executives, and so on to allow you to contact your company's business units. To create a distribution list, you start by clicking Distribution Lists, and then click the New button, as you see in Figure 15-25.

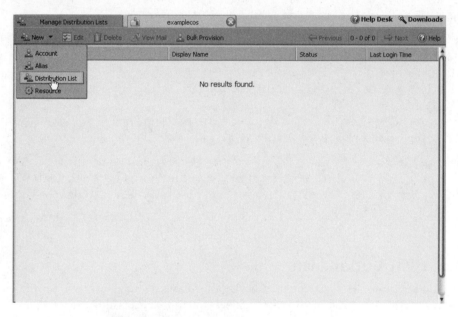

Figure 15-25. *Creating a new distribution list*

You create a list by assigning a unique name to your group (the e-mail address cannot already exist in your mail domain). We will create a distribution list called `allstaff@example.com`, and in Figure 15-26 you can see the details we have used to create it.

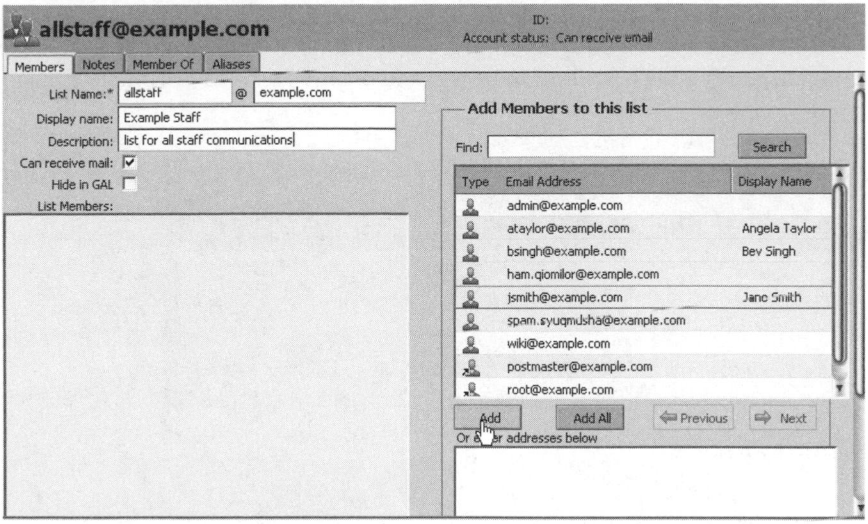

Figure 15-26. *Adding users to our list*

You assign members to your lists in one of two ways: by typing their addresses in manually in the Or enter addresses below box or by using the search tool. Clicking the Search button with an empty search field will return all the available users. You can see in Figure 15-26 we have selected the users we wish to assign to this group. We do not wish to add any system users like the ham, spam, or wiki accounts. When you have highlighted the accounts you wish to add to the distribution list, click the Add button. This moves the users over to the List Members section, as shown in Figure 15-27.

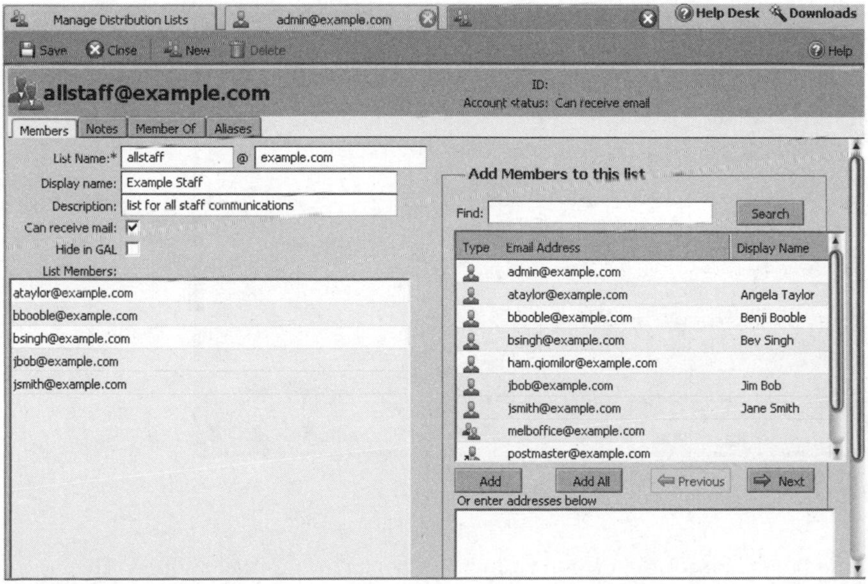

Figure 15-27. *Member list*

In more complex scenarios, you can add distribution lists to other distribution lists and create aliases for your lists. When you click Save, your distribution list is saved, and you can view your lists by again clicking the Distribution Lists menu; Figure 15-28 shows our distributions lists displayed.

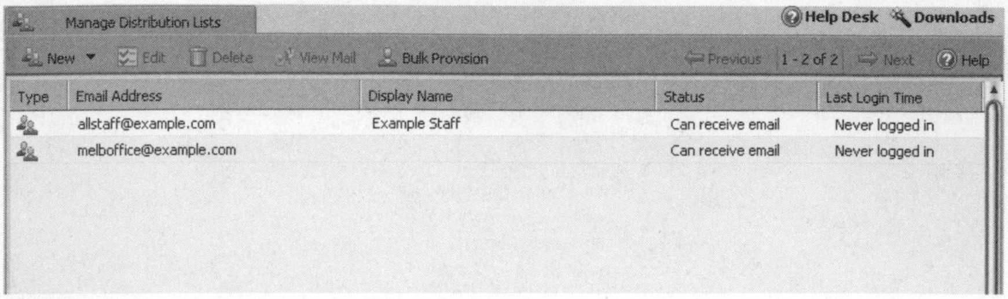

Figure 15-28. *Our distribution lists*

Adding Resources

Not only can you have user accounts, aliases, and distribution lists, you can also have resources. Resources are things you may want to track the use of, like rooms, projectors, and any other shared items in your company that someone might need to check out. In our calendar, which we will show you later in the "Using Zimbra" section, we can ask people to attend meetings. When we schedule a meeting, we can also book resources like a room or a projector so that people can track who has what and when.

We are going to show you how to create a room resource. We select the Resources menu, which will bring up a list of all available resources that presently exist. We then click the New button to bring up the New Resource window, as shown in Figure 15-29.

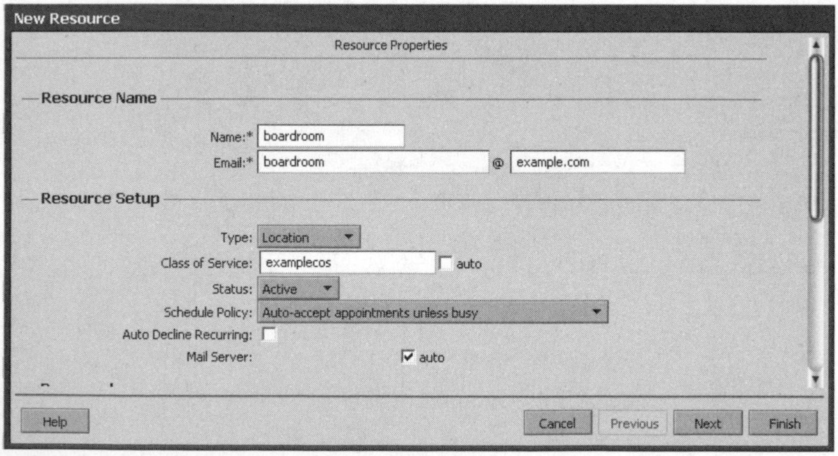

Figure 15-29. *Adding a new room resource*

We have named the resource boardroom, and it too has its own e-mail address. The type of resource is Location. The other option you have here is Equipment, which shares the examplecos CoS. The status is Active, and it is set to Auto-accept appointments unless busy.

The other options are Accept all appointments and Manually accept or decline appointments, where another user will control this acceptance.

When we click Next, we are given the opportunity to add more details to this resource. In Figure 15-30, you can see we have added a contact name and details for the resource, as well as details of the room itself.

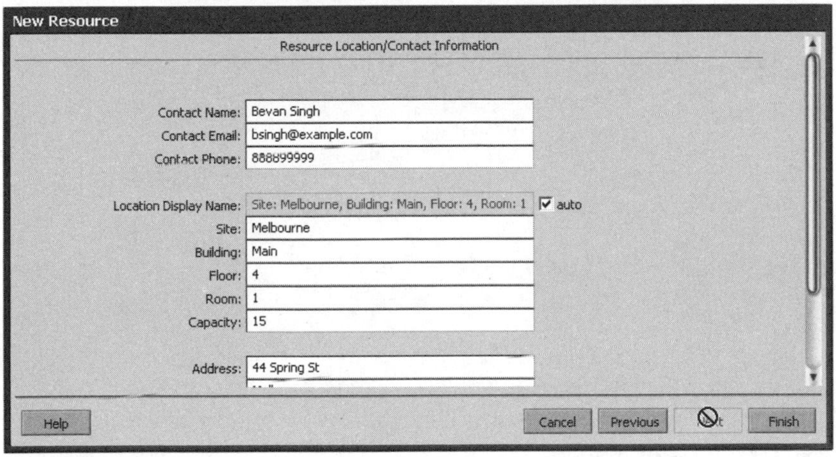

Figure 15-30. *Contact and location details for the resource*

When we are happy with the details, we can click the Finish button. You can now see that we have created our resource location, and we also have an equipment resource we created earlier using the same process (see Figure 15-31).

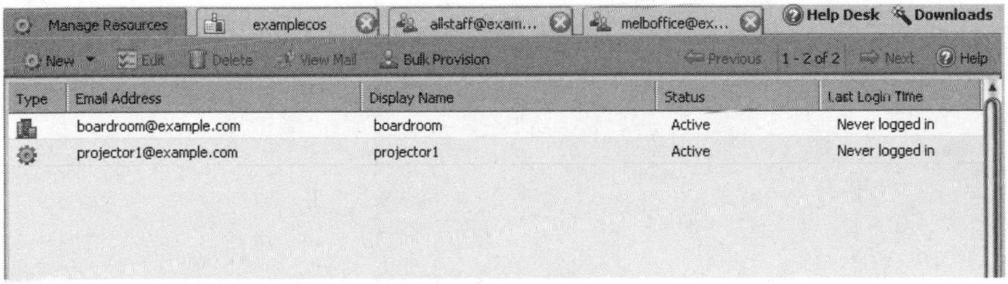

Figure 15-31. *Our available resources*

Now that we have added our user accounts, aliases, distribution lists, and resources, we can begin to use our Zimbra server. Before we do, we would like to show some of the other aspects of the Administration Console, starting with managing our Zimlets.

Adding Zimlets

As we have already mentioned, Zimlets are add-on programs or scripts that provide extra functionality to our Zimbra server. These are generally created and maintained by the Zimbra user base community. We will show you how to add a Zimlet via the Administration Console.

You'll find the collection of Zimlets from the Zimbra website here: `http://gallery.zimbra.com/`. You can download a Zimlet to your desktop and then you use the Zimlets menu to deploy them to your server. Figure 15-32 shows the Zimlets window.

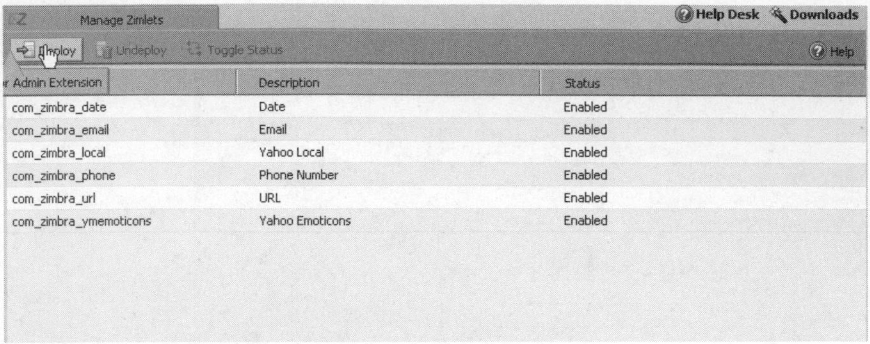

Figure 15-32. *The Zimlets window*

We have chosen to deploy the `emailquotes` Zimlet. We have already downloaded the `com_zimbra_emailquotes` file to our desktop. Now we click the Deploy button and browse to find our file, as you can see in Figure 15-33.

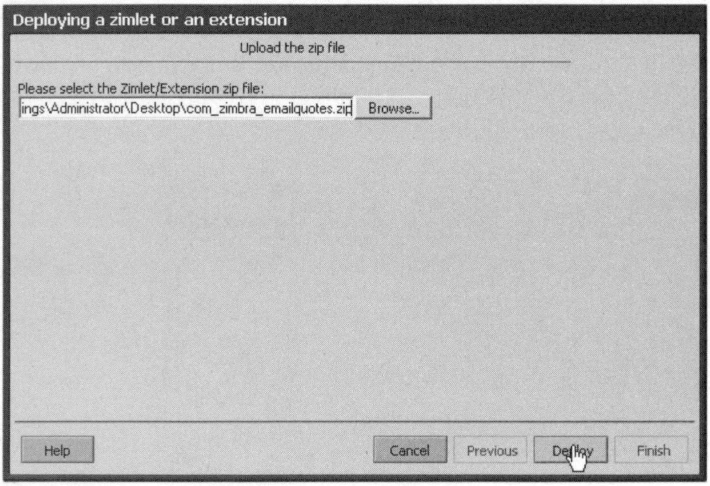

Figure 15-33. *Locating a Zimlet*

The next step is to click the Deploy button. This will begin installing the Zimlet and displaying the progress of the installation. You will see a completion message if all went well, as we did when the installation was finished (see Figure 15-34); if not, you will get an error message indicating the problem.

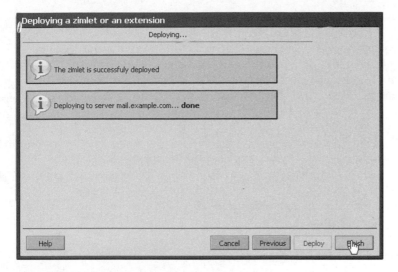

Figure 15-34. *Zimlet installation complete*

Now that we have installed our Zimlet, we can add it to our examplecos CoS to make it available to all the users we added (see Figure 15-35).

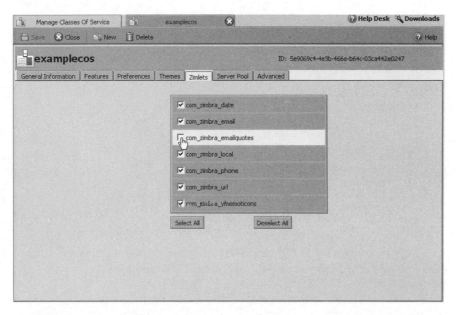

Figure 15-35. *Adding our Zimlet to our CoS*

We will show you how to use the `emailquotes` Zimlet in the "Using Our Zimlets" section later in this chapter.

You can also use the same process to add Admin Extensions. Admin Extensions are like Zimlets but are made available to the Administration Console. The bulk upload we did earlier is an example of the Admin Extensions that can be created. Now that we have completed this step, we will show you how to add your own SSL certificate to your Zimbra installation.

Adding an SSL Certificate

Whenever you can, you should try to make your communications as secure as possible. For this example, we wish to encrypt all web traffic for our Zimbra service. We are now going to show you how to create a certificate request and then install the certificate in the Zimbra server. First, we click the Certificates menu. In Figure 15-36, you can see that the next step is to click the Install Certificate button.

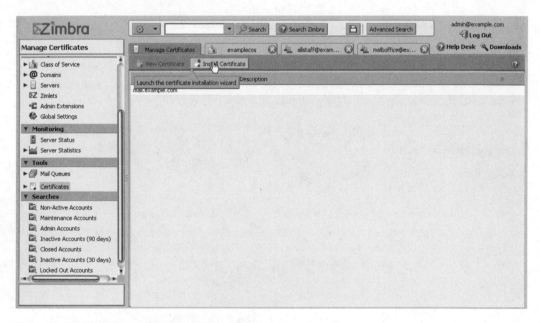

Figure 15-36. *The SSL certificate window*

This brings up the window you see in Figure 15-37, through which we select the server we wish to work on. We select the only option available to us, mail.example.com.

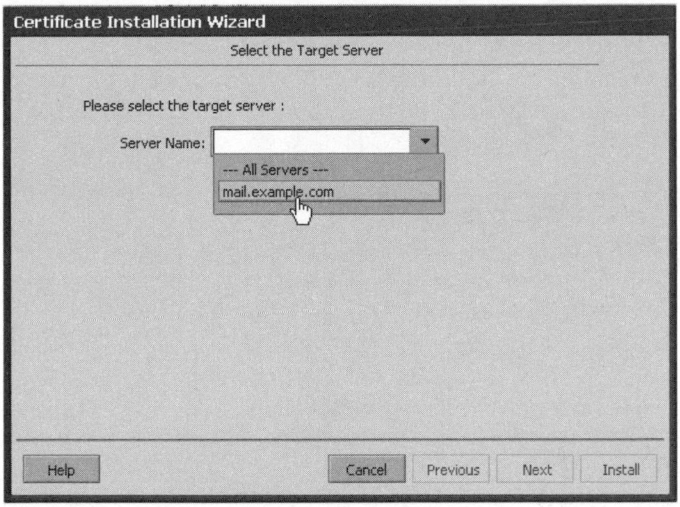

Figure 15-37. *Selecting the target server*

Next, we are presented with a set of installation options, as shown in Figure 15-38. This window allows you to install a self-signed certificate, create a CSR, or install a certificate you have received from a commercial organization. In this case, we are going to create a CSR so we can sign it with our own Certificate Authority, which we created in Chapter 10. We select the Generate the CSR for the commercial certificate authoriser option, even though we are signing the certificate ourselves.

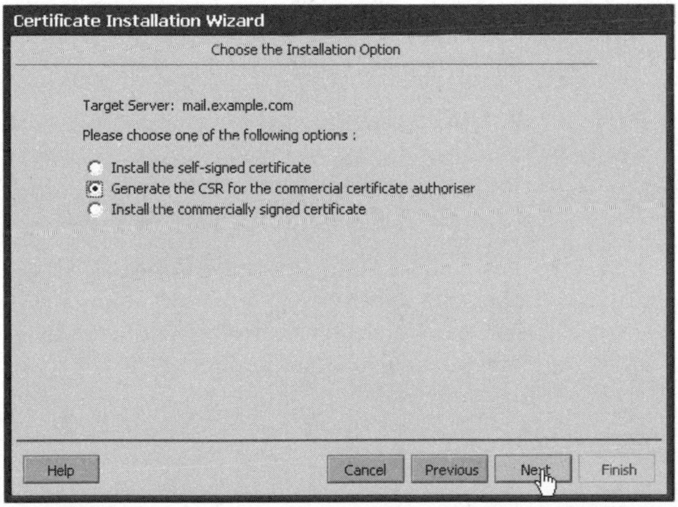

Figure 15-38. *Selecting the option to generate a CSR*

We are now asked to fill out the details required to generate our CSR. The required fields for us here are Common Name and Organisation Name. Common Name is the name of the host, and the Organisation Name is required by our Certificate Authority to sign our certificate. The other details are appropriate to our host. Figure 15-39 shows how we have filled out the fields in this window.

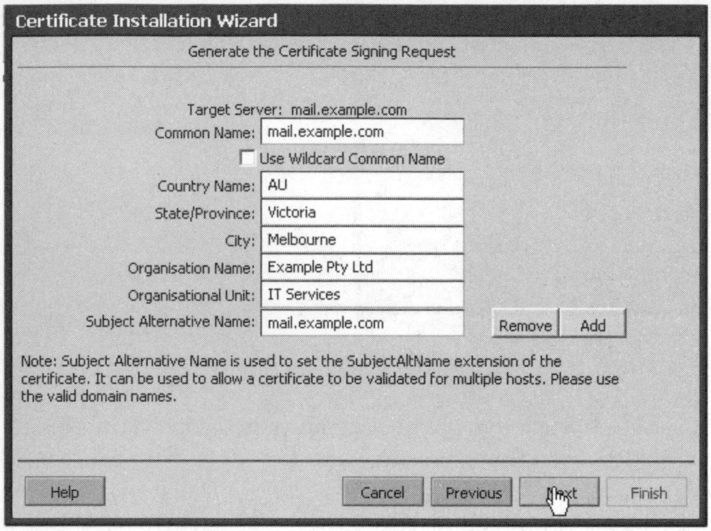

Figure 15-39. *CSR details*

We save the CSR to a new file. If we were getting a commercial organization to sign the CSR, we would send the CSR file to them. In our situation, we will sign our certificate as follows: we first copy our certificate to our host with the Certificate Authority and we issue these commands:

```
$ cd /etc/CA
$ sudo openssl ca -out /root/mail.example.com.cert -config ./openssl.cnf ➥
-infiles /root/current.csr
```

We then need to enter the passphrase for the CA and sign the certificate. Once this is done, we can now add the certificate to our Zimbra mail server. In Figure 15-40, you can see that we have navigated back to where we can choose to install our certificate. We did this by selecting Install Certificate and choosing the target server, mail.example.com.

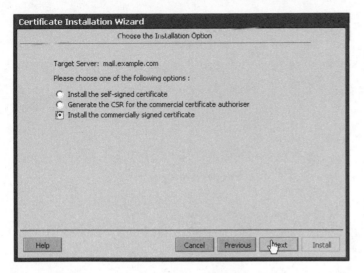

Figure 15-40. *Selecting the option to install our certificate*

We are now asked to browse for the location of our certificate and root CA (see Figure 15-41).

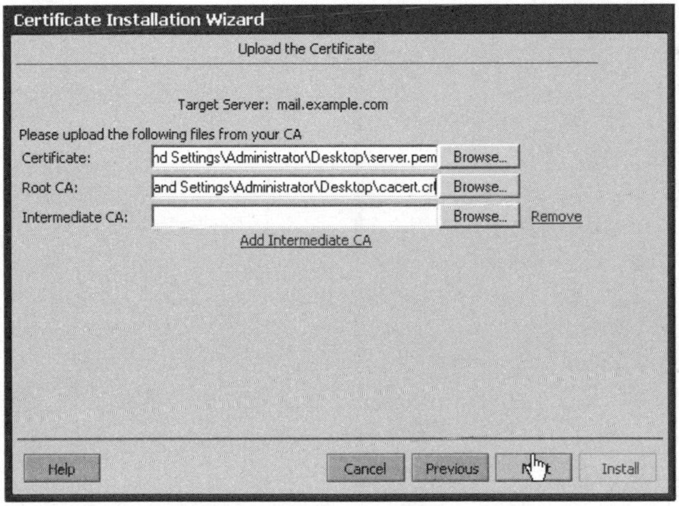

Figure 15-41. *Browsing for the location of the certificate and root CA*

As shown in Figure 15-42, we are now given the opportunity to review the details of our certificate.

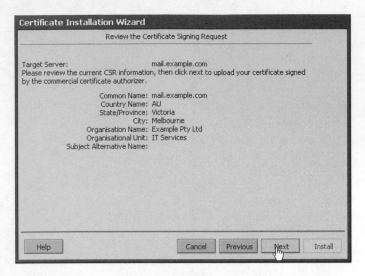

Figure 15-42. *Confirming the certificate details*

Clicking Next will bring us to the window that installs the certificate (see Figure 15-43).

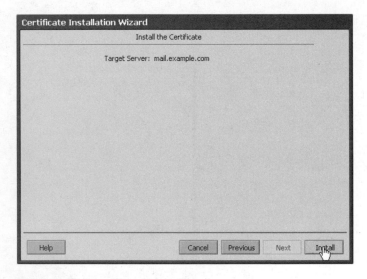

Figure 15-43. *Installing the certificate*

Next, we are given confirmation that our certificate has been installed correctly (see Figure 15-44).

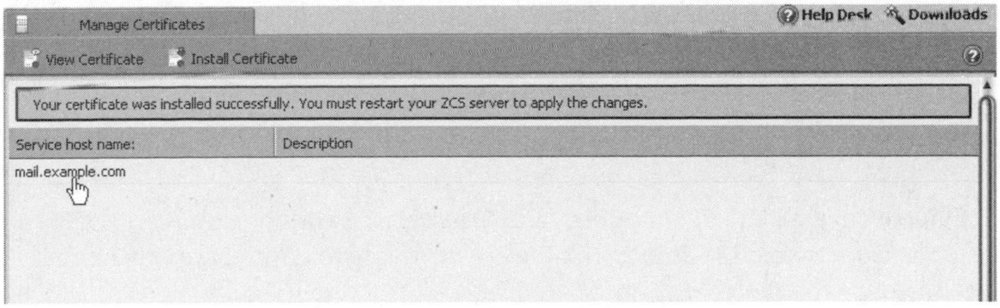

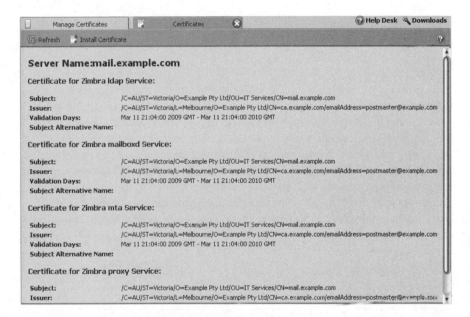

Figure 15-44. *Certificate installation successful*

Last of all, we are able to view our newly installed certificate by highlighting it and then clicking View Certificate; you can see the results that occur when we do so in Figure 15-45.

Figure 15-45. *Viewing the installed certificate*

Now that the certificate is installed, we need to turn on HTTPS sessions using the Zimbra command zmtlsctl, which controls the use of HTTPS. Using this command, you can choose the http, https, or both methods to specify a protocol for connecting to your Zimbra server's web interface. We are going to use https only, so we issue the following from the command line on our mail server. Make sure you are the zimbra user before issuing the zmtlsctl command.

```
zimbra@mail:~$ zmtlsctl https
Setting tls mode to https
Updating /opt/zimbra/mailboxd/etc/jetty.xml.in...done.
Updating /opt/zimbra/jetty/etc/zimbra.web.xml.in...done.
Updating /opt/zimbra/jetty/etc/zimbraAdmin.web.xml.in...done.
Updating PROTOCOL MODE in /opt/zimbra/mailboxd/etc/zimbra.web.xml.in...done.
Rewriting config files for webxml and mailboxd...done.
```

```
Updating /opt/zimbra/cyrus-sasl/etc/saslauthd.conf.in...done.
Rewriting config files for cyrus-sasl...done.
Setting ldap config zimbraMailMode https for mail.example.com...done.
zimbra@mail:~$  zmcontrol stop
zimbra@mail:~$  zmcontrol start
```

You can see that we have set the TLS mode to our https service and then stopped and started the service using the zmcontrol command. We are now able to connect to our Zimbra host using HTTPS only.

■**Tip** Wherever possible, and especially when using any website requiring username and password valida-tion, you should use the highest security protocols you can. This is our reason for selecting HTTPS over HTTP in this example.

Global Settings

In the Global Settings section of the Administration Console, you view and manage further settings for your server. You can define the attachments accepted by your server, the MTA settings for your Postfix server, and IMAP/POP and antivirus and spam settings. Here are the changes that we have made for our server, which might be of importance to you as well.

Figure 15-46 presents the General Information settings. You can see the limit to the results returned by the global address list (GAL) is set to 100, the default. This may need to be higher or lower if your organization is a large one and you have problems with the performance of your LDAP server. Also, notice that there is a limit on the size of files that can be uploaded into the Briefcase. The Briefcase is a shareable user space in which you can put documents. This allows you to have access to documents remotely.

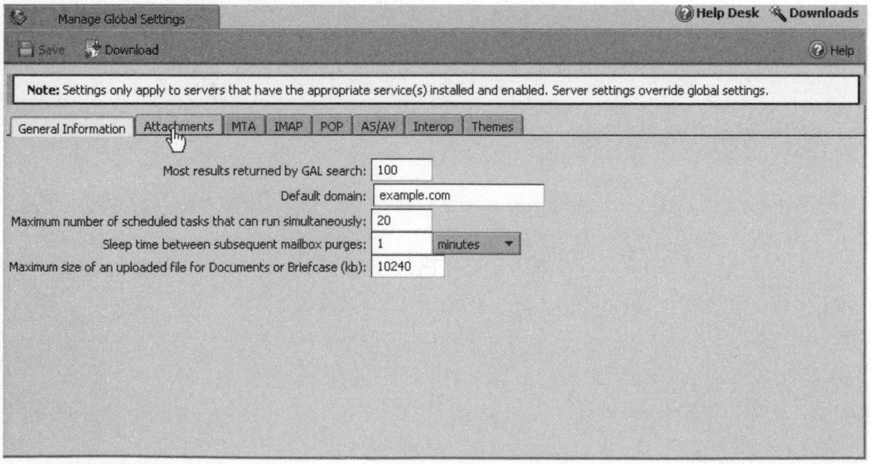

Figure 15-46. *General Information tab in the Global Settings area of the console*

Next, we set the attachments that we will accept via the Attachments tab, shown in Figure 15-47. Here you can exclude attachments ending in a particular extension, such as .exe or .js. This helps to protect your users from malicious attachments. Here you can also override the CoS settings for viewing attachments. The figure shows we have excluded all possible extensions of files available to us. You can add any extension you wish, using the New extension field at the bottom.

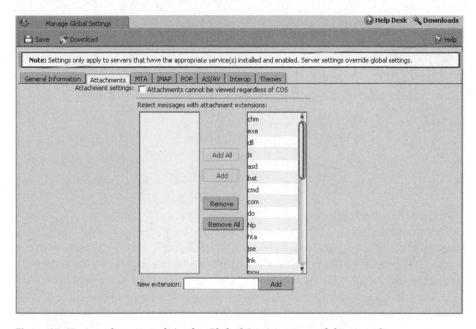

Figure 15-47. *Attachments tab in the Global Settings area of the console*

In the MTA tab, you set the configuration details for your Postfix server. It is here you can set options like specifying a relay MTA, which allows you to send all mail via a perimeter MTA. The perimeter MTA hides your internal mail servers from direct public access and can also do preliminary mail scanning to prevent malicious attacks to your primary mail servers.

It is also here that you can set a maximum message size and other MTA details. You can see some of the details we have set in Figure 15-48.

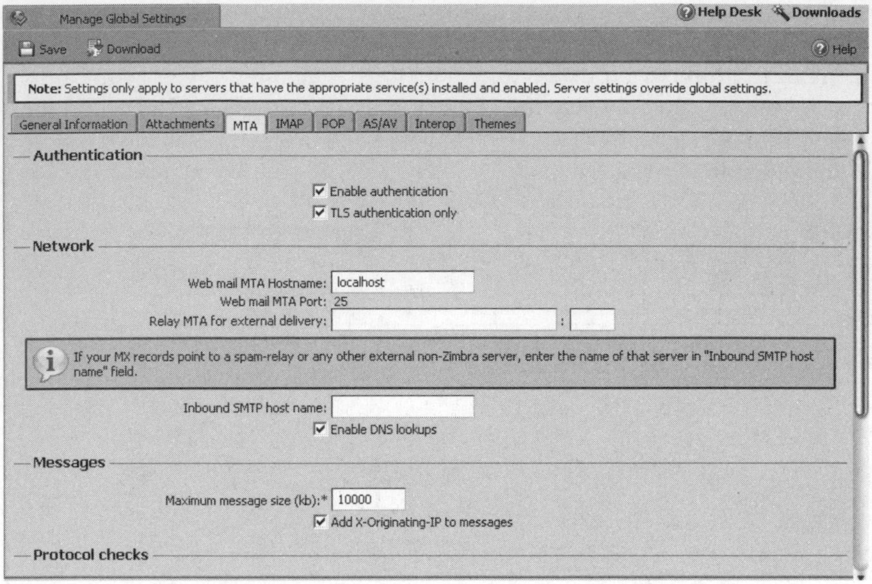

Figure 15-48. *MTA tab in the Global Settings area of the console*

In the IMAP and POP tabs, we have disabled the IMAP and POP services. In Chapter 10, recall that we showed you how to configure POP and IMAP, protocols used by e-mail clients like Microsoft Outlook or Thunderbird to connect to your mail server and retrieve mail.

We have decided not to start these services because we want everyone to use the web interface. If you take a look at these tabs, you will notice that you have simple Enable IMAP services and Enable POP services check box options that will turn the services on or off. Any changes here will require a restart to take effect.

Next is the AS/AV tab. AS/AV is short for antispam/antivirus. In Figure 15-49, notice that we have set the Subject prefix to SPAM:, as well as specified percentages in the Kill percent and Tag percent fields. Your spam filter rates possible spam on a percentage of certainty. If it is 75% certain that an e-mail you are receiving is spam, the spam filter will kill it, moving it to a quarantine area of the mail server. If the spam filter is 33% certain the e-mail is spam, it will allow the message to pass to its intended recipient but will tag it with the Subject prefix SPAM:, and it will be up to the recipient to decide whether the e-mail is spam or not.

You might be in the position where you have an existing Microsoft Exchange server already on your network with a group of users in your organization already using it. The Interop tab allows you to add the details of the Microsoft Exchange server. In this scenario, users on the MS Exchange server and users on the Zimbra server are able to schedule calendar events together by exchanging free/busy information.

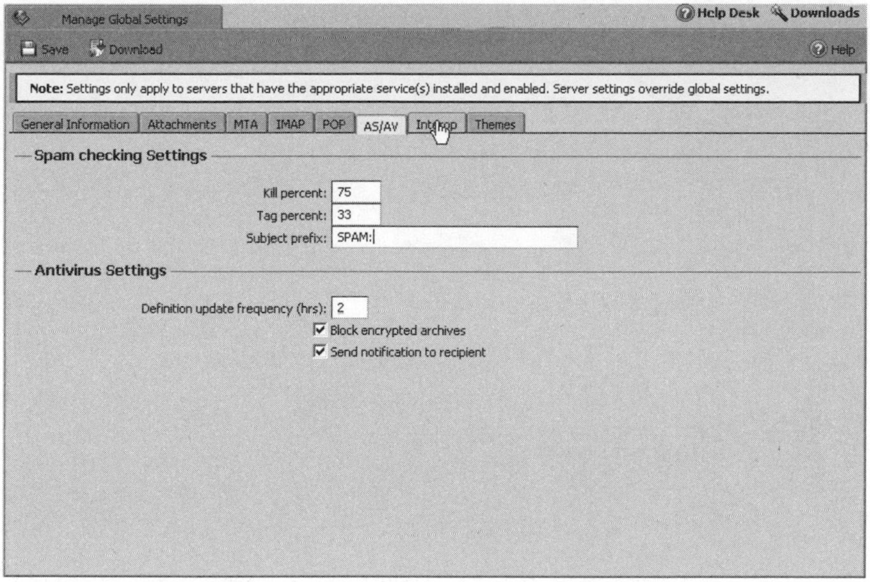

Figure 15-49. *AS/AV tab in the Global Settings area of the console*

The last tab in the Global Settings section is Themes. Options on this tab allow you to change the color of your foreground, background, and so on.

It should be noted that the changes here in Global Settings section can be overridden by the settings in the Servers section. Also, some changes in the Global Settings section require a restart of the Zimbra service before they take effect. Zimbra provides easy-to-understand informational notes in their Administration Console, and we urge you to read them for more details.

Monitoring Zimbra

The Zimbra Administration Console also provides the ability to monitor some details of your mail server. The Server Statistics window, shown in Figure 15-50, presents the types of statistics that are available to you. You can view message counts, message volumes, and antispam/antivirus activity over some predefined periods to time through this window.

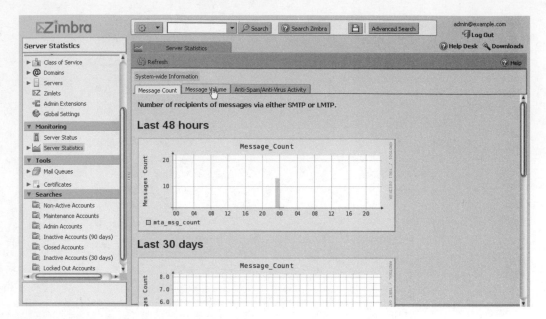

Figure 15-50. *Server Statistics window*

This window also allows you to see what is going on with your mail queues. Mail queues give an indication of the actual performance of your mail host and the ability to clear any troubling messages that you might have. Troubling messages might be a bounce-back message generated by a spam e-mail or a message that someone is trying to send large e-mails. Figure 15-51 shows the mail queues Deferred, Incoming, Active, Corrupt, and Held, which are the queues you would expect to find in a normal Postfix installation. High counts usually point to a problem you should investigate further.

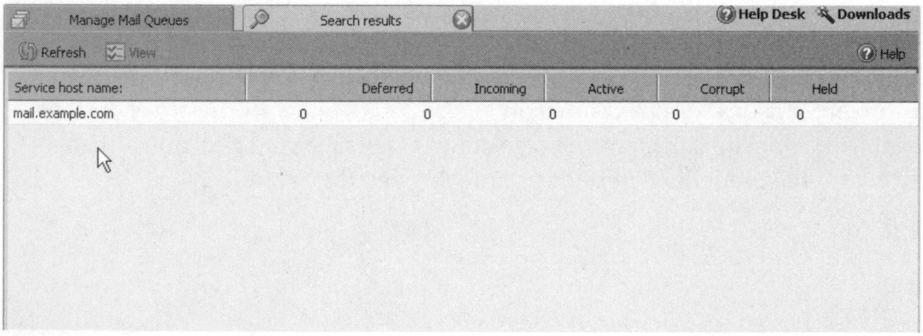

Service host name:	Deferred	Incoming	Active	Corrupt	Held
mail.example.com	0	0	0	0	0

Figure 15-51. *Mail queues*

Note We discussed the Postfix mail server and mail queues in Chapter 10.

This completes our overview of the Administration Console for the Zimbra server.

■**Note** A good resource for configuring Zimbra, apart from the *ZCS Administrator's Guide*, can be found at the following web page: `http://wiki.zimbra.com/index.php?title=Main_Page`.

Let's now look at using the web interface that Zimbra provides.

Using Zimbra

The Zimbra web interface works as comprehensive mail client, allowing your user base to access mail, contacts, a calendar, and documents from one web application. The quality and performance of this product, compared to its costly rivals, will certainly make many small business users happy.

■**Tip** Remember that Zimbra has a free desktop client that performs similarly to the web interface.

The web client can use advanced features provided by Ajax or a more standard HTML offering. The Ajax client allows for more advanced presentation and is a bit more resource hungry than the standard HTML client. Remote users might like to use the standard HTML version if they need better performance. People using PDAs or mobile devices might like to use the Mobile mode that is also available.

■**Note** For more information on Ajax, read the article at `http://en.wikipedia.org/wiki/Ajax_(programming)`.

We access our Zimbra mail server via the following URL: `https://mail.example.com`. Figure 15-52 shows the different modes that are available. The Default mode is set in the Creating a Class of Service section of the Preferences tab. In the `examplecos` CoS, we have set the mode to Standard HTML, which allows for better performance.

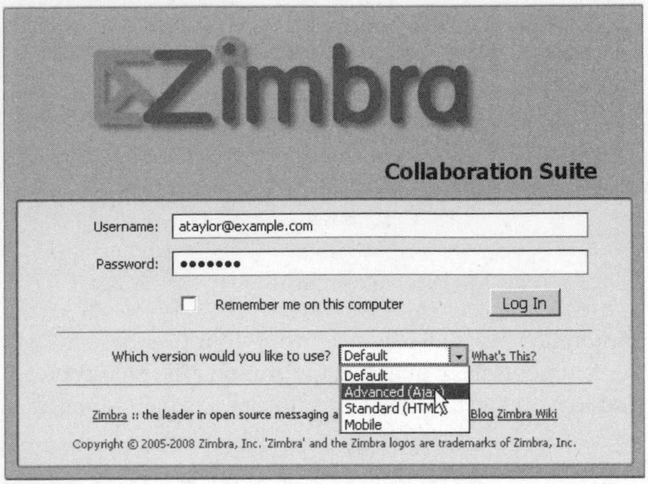

Figure 15-52. *Login for our Zimbra web client*

In Figure 15-52, you can see that the ataylor user is using the username and password we have provided, and she has selected to use the Advanced (Ajax) web client.

Using E-Mail

Choosing the Advanced (Ajax) mode opens up a user web space like the one shown in Figure 15-53. On the left you have the typical navigation panel, and along the top of main panel you have the tabbed navigation of Zimbra features and action buttons available to the feature you are working on. Changing the feature in the tabbed navigation will change the panel on the left and the action buttons available to it. In this case, we are working on the Mail feature, and you can see that we have selected to create a new e-mail.

We will demonstrate sending an e-mail to ourselves to show how an e-mail is sent and received. As you can see in Figure 15-54, the e-mail window is very standard. You add addresses, a subject, and a message body. You can also add attachments, as is typical in e-mail clients. The address field will automatically try to complete e-mail addresses it finds in your Global Address List.

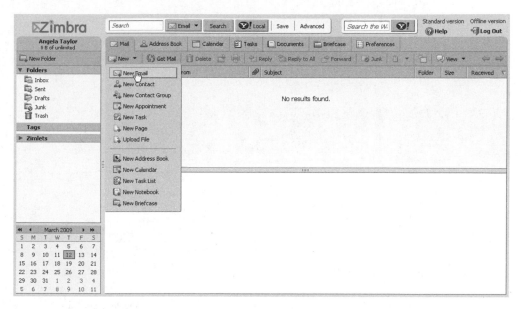

Figure 15-53. *Using the Mail feature*

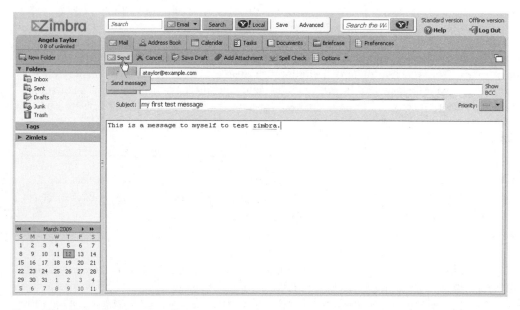

Figure 15-54. *Sending an e-mail*

When we click Send, the e-mail is whisked away and delivered back to our mailbox. In Figure 15-55, you can see that the mail message has been delivered to our inbox. The message window shows the inbox listing and the preview pane. When you double-click a message, the preview pane becomes larger. You can manage your mail messages with the usual Reply, Reply to all, Forward, and Print options you expect in your e-mail client.

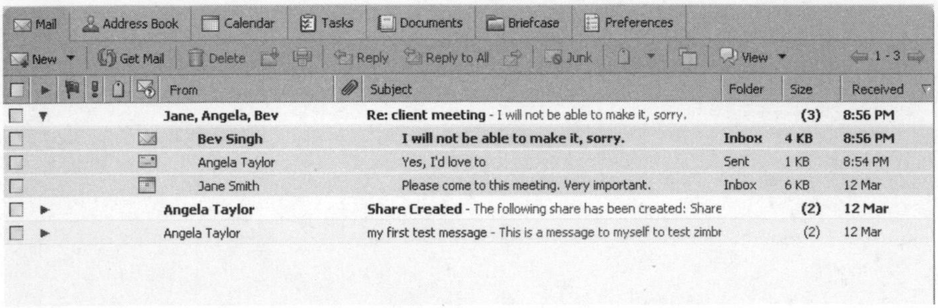

Figure 15-55. *Messages by conversation*

One of the things you may not be familiar with is the concept of messages displayed by conversation. When you receive an e-mail from someone, it is considered the start of a conversation. If you reply to the e-mail, the reply is automatically pinned below the original mail. Any other replies are pinned below that, and so on. You can see what we mean in Figure 15-55.

This figure shows that the client meeting message conversation has been expanded, as indicated by the little down arrow on the left-hand side of the message window. The original message, from Jane Smith, is an invitation to a meeting. Angela Taylor has responded positively to that message, and Bevan Singh has said he can't make it. This forms a conversation based upon the original e-mail. The next unrelated e-mail message would create a new conversation.

■Tip Grouping messages by conversation is kind of like using predictive text on mobile devices: some people love it, and some people hate it. You can change whether messages are grouped by conversation in the CoS or in the individual user's preferences settings.

The other concept that might be unfamiliar is tags, which are used to quickly group different mail message conversations together. It is a similar concept to folders, but tags can group messages across folders. Say you get a lot of appointment requests; you could have a tag called appointments that you use on all such e-mails. You can then store the actual e-mails in the folder that suits the business unit to which they relate. This way you can quickly see all your appointments across all your folders quickly and easily. In Figure 15-56, we have added a tag named my appointments. We have tagged the client meeting appointment with it and stored the actual e-mail in the sales folder. Now we can quickly view all our appointment e-mails by clicking the my appointments tag.

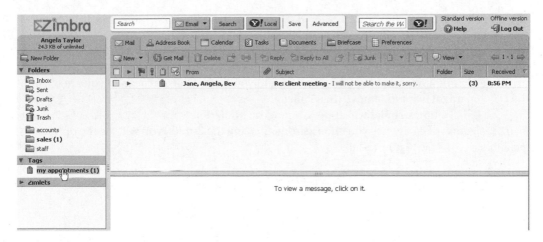

Figure 15-56. *Grouping messages by tags*

Tagging works throughout many of the features provided by Zimbra.

Using Our Zimlets

As we have already mentioned, Zimlets provide additional functionality to your Zimbra server. They are usually written by community members and shared with other Zimbra users. Notice the Zimlets section in the left-hand navigational panel. Expanding the menu displays any Zimlets currently available; Figure 15-57 shows that we have two Zimlets on our Zimbra server.

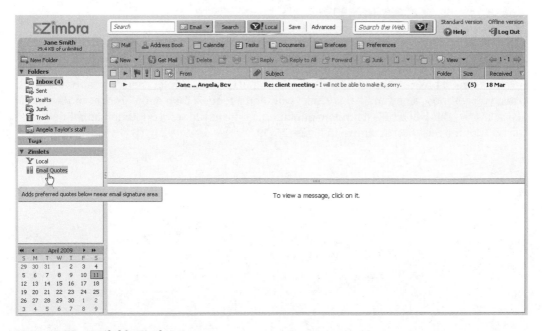

Figure 15-57. *Available Zimlets*

The Local Zimlet is provided by Yahoo!, the new owners of Zimbra, and is meant to show you local maps of your area. You might be disappointed with this feature if you live in some remote city like Melbourne, Australia. The resolution provided by Yahoo! Maps for countries outside the US is what you'd see from about 30,000 feet. Compare the detail of, say, Tokyo, population 21 million, to that of Elko, Nevada, and you'll see what we mean. If you are outside the US, you might want to remove this Zimlet.

The Email Quotes Zimlet will append a random quotation from `http://www.quotedb.com` from a selection of categories you choose from. Clicking the Zimlet, you will see the options available to you (see Figure 15-58).

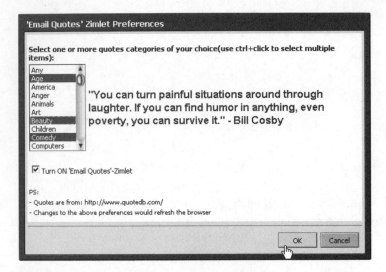

Figure 15-58. *Configuring the Email Quotes Zimlet*

You can select multiple quote categories using your mouse and Shift or Ctrl button, and turn this Zimlet on or off through the Turn ON 'Email Quotes'-Zimlet check box option. Now when you compose a new mail, this Zimlet will send a request for a quote from `http://www.quotedb.com`. This will return a random quotation, and you will see a quotation appended to the body of the message, as shown in Figure 15-59.

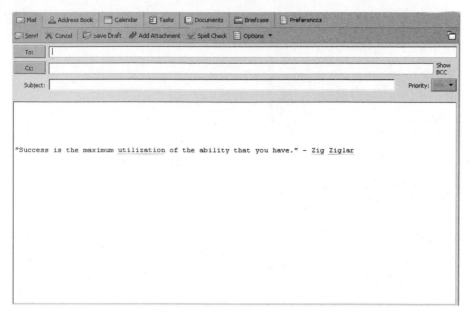

Figure 15-59. *The Email Quotes Zimlet appending a quote to the body of an e-mail*

This may not be the most professional way of communicating with your business clients, but it does demonstrate what a Zimlet is. Following are some of the Zimlets that may be of greater benefit to you:

- *Salesforce.com*: `http://gallery.zimbra.com/gallery.php?act=viewProd&productId=18`

- *Webex Zimlet*: `http://gallery.zimbra.com/gallery.php?act=viewProd&productId=51`

- *Dimdim Web Meeting*: `http://gallery.zimbra.com/gallery.` `php?act=viewProd&productId=77`

- *Asterix PBX Integration Zimlet*: `http://gallery.zimbra.com/gallery.` `php?act=viewProd&productId=94`

Also, we recommend taking the Zimlet tour provided by Zimbra for a good demonstration of the capabilities of Zimlets: `http://www.zimbra.com/demos/zimbra_zimlets.html`.

Sharing Folders, Address Books, Documents, and More

One thing that makes the Zimbra server a collaborative server is the ability to share folders, address books, calendars, and documents with other users of our Zimbra server. Sharing things in Zimbra is done through the same process no matter what is being shared. Sharing an e-mail folder between people in the office is very easy to do. Angela Taylor has decided to share the staff folder with others in company. How does she do it?

First, she creates the folder staff using the New Folder link above the Inbox frame on the left of the screen. To share it, she right-clicks the staff folder and selects Share Folder. This brings up the window shown in Figure 15-60, Share Properties, through which the user can specify options for the shared folder.

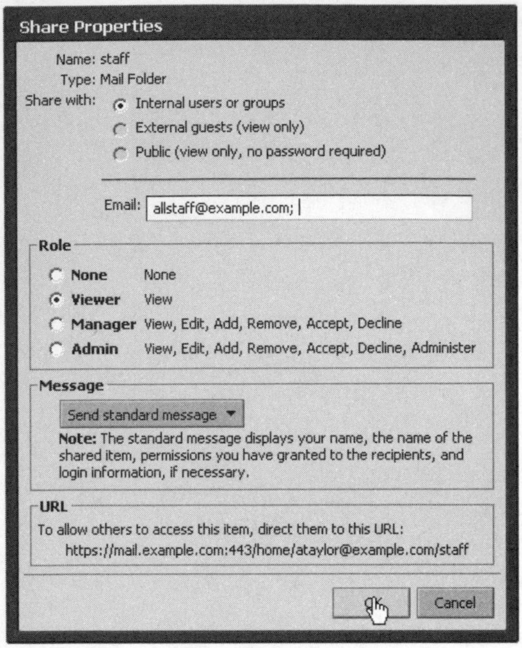

Figure 15-60. *Sharing folders*

With mail folders, you are limited to sharing only with internal users or groups. The role defines the access rights of the users you are sharing with. In this example, we are letting people view e-mail in our directory only through the View role. This is the basic level of sharing. If you wish to allow people to interact further with mail in the folder, you can assign them either the Manager or Admin role.

This window also allows you to send a standard message to users you are inviting to share the folder or make your own by choosing an option from the Message section. We have chosen to share this directory with the distribution group allstaff@example.com, which means that everyone in our company will be able to accept this shared folder and view the messages placed in it. This can be a way of distributing e-mails across your company quickly and easily by placing any e-mail you receive in the staff directory.

On clicking OK, everyone on the distribution list will have the opportunity to accept or decline the shared folder. In Figure 15-61, notice that Bev Singh, who is on the allstaff distribution list, has received his e-mail and is about to accept the share.

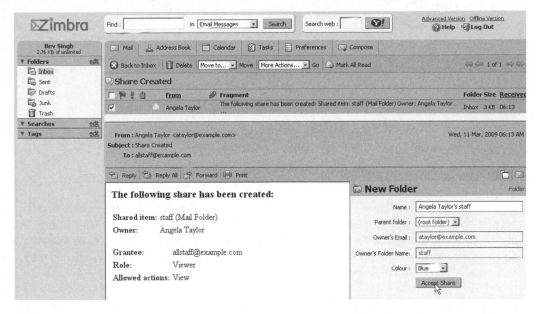

Figure 15-61. *Accepting the shared folder*

After accepting the share, the folder is created under Bev's inbox. Sharing everything else in Zimbra follows the same process. Zimbra's sharing capabilities allow you to do the following, among other things:

- Create a new address book called major clients and share it with sales staff.

- Share a calendar among your local work group to coordinate your meetings and events.

- Have private calendars that no one else can see, or allow people to see when you are free or busy.

- Share documents with others in your work group or other areas of the company.

- Allow users external to your company to see some documents.

From these suggested uses, you can see that you can share nearly everything in Zimbra with others in your business groups.

Next, we'll show you how to create a calendar, share that calendar, and create an appointment. First, navigate to the Calendar tab and click New Calendar to bring up a dialog box that allows you to create a new calendar (see Figure 15-62). The options in this dialog allow you to exclude the new calendar from reporting whether you are free or busy, synchronize appointments from a remote calendar, and specify a color and name for the calendar. In the figure, you can see that we are going to create a calendar called work group.

Figure 15-62. *Creating a calendar*

After clicking OK, select the new calendar, right-click, and select Share to begin the process of sharing your calendar. In our case, we want to share our calendar with our Melbourne office staff. We will allow our staff to manage the calendar, which means they will be able to add appointments, accept appointments, and so on. Figure 15-63 shows the way we created this share.

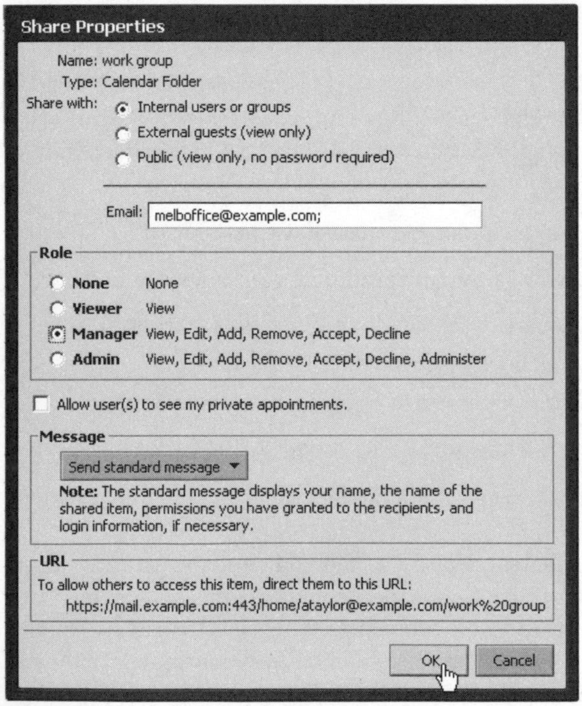

Figure 15-63. *Sharing our calendar*

Now everyone on the melboffice distribution list will receive an e-mail asking them to accept the shared calendar. We are going to create an appointment for 9 a.m. Thursday morning and invite everyone in the Melbourne office to it. To do so, we first highlight the appropriate block of time, as shown in Figure 15-64.

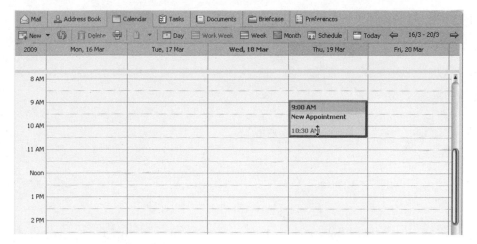

Figure 15-64. *Blocking time*

Next, the QuickAdd Appointment window pops up. Clicking the More detail button makes several tabs available for creating our meeting, as shown in Figure 15-65.

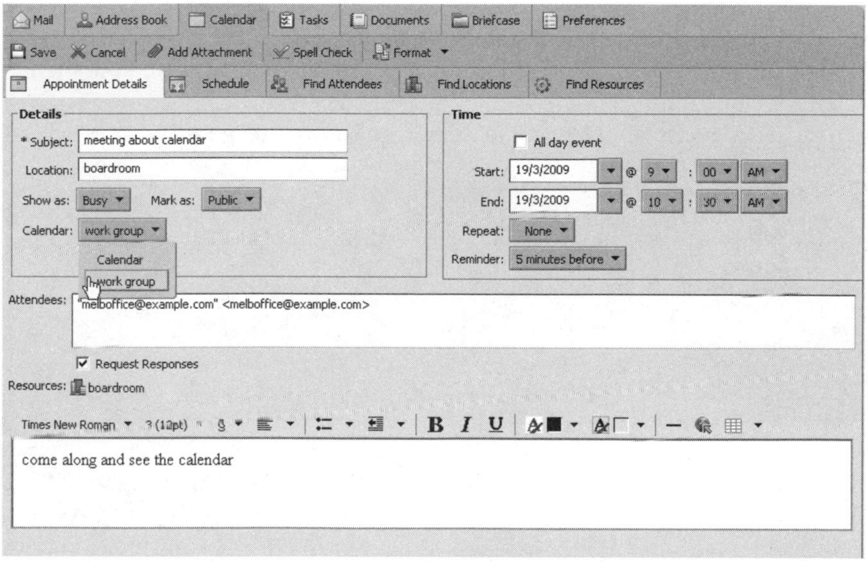

Figure 15-65. *Creating the appointment*

You can see that we have created a subject titled "meeting about calendar," booked the boardroom resource, and invited everyone in the `melboffice` distribution group, taking care to select the work group calendar. We then save the appointment, which will appear as a block of time, as shown in Figure 15-66, in the color of the calendar.

Figure 15-66. *Appointment created*

We can now move that block, extend it, or delete it, and it will be mirrored in everyone's calendar.

Next to the Calendar tab is the Tasks tab. Here you can create and share tasks, like personal task lists or shared task lists. It has some basic workflow and time management features that can come in handy for tracking the progress of tasks that have been assigned. Sharing these tasks follows the same process you have already seen for sharing folders and calendars in Zimbra.

We now want to show you the Documents tab of the Zimbra server. Here you can create documents that you can share within your organization or indeed the world in a comprehensive wiki-like system.

Navigating to the Documents tab takes you to the screen shown in Figure 15-67.

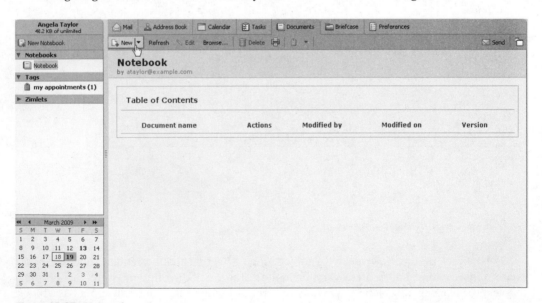

Figure 15-67. *Using documents*

As you can see by looking in the left panel, you can group your work into notebooks. Each notebook you create can be shared with people in your organization or with anyone outside your organization if you like, and herein lies the power of this tool: the documents you store here could include company FAQs, user documentation, or any other useful information users should have access to.

We will show you how to create a new page in an existing notebook. Selecting New brings up an editing window through which you create your new document. For the purposes of this demonstration, we'll create a quick FAQ, as shown in Figure 15-68.

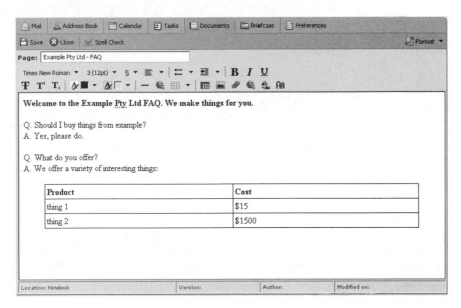

Figure 15-68. *Creating a FAQ document*

As you might gather, it is very easy to create a document in Zimbra, and, unlike many wikis, you don't have to learn any additional syntax. You can use formatting styles and create tables and spreadsheets very easily and quickly. Once done, you save the document and go back to the TOC of your notebook, as shown in Figure 15-69.

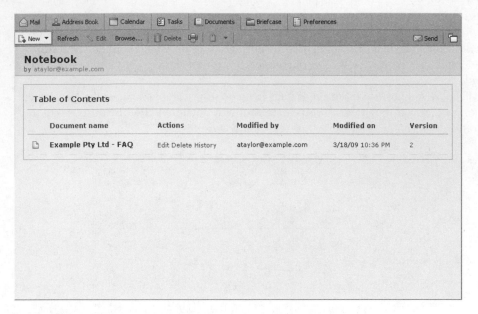

Figure 15-69. *The TOC of our notebook*

Now you have a notebook and a TOC that describes the documents it holds. If you care to look at the detail of the page we have created, you will see that it contains version information and modification details. You can use this for many of your company's internal or external documents. A right-click of the notebook will display the sharing options available to you.

The last thing we wish to show you is the Briefcase feature. This is used to store documents that you might have on your desktop so you can retrieve them easily from anywhere. Figure 15-70 shows that we have a Briefcase we are about to share. In the Briefcase is a Word document.

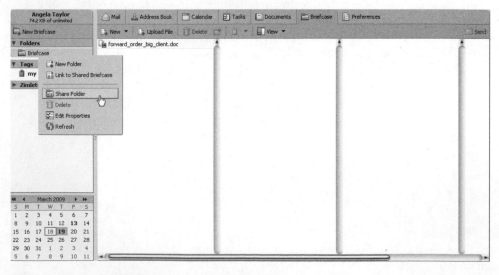

Figure 15-70. *Our Briefcase*

You can create as many Briefcases as you like and share them with whomever you like in your organization. One neat feature of the Briefcase: clicking a document in your Briefcase allows you to send a link to the document in an e-mail.

Migrating from an Existing E-Mail Service

Chances are your organization already has an e-mail system, and you want to migrate your users' existing e-mail to the new Zimbra server. How you achieve this depends on the e-mail system you are migrating from. Zimbra provides two migration tools for download from the Administration Console. You can see them in Figure 15-71.

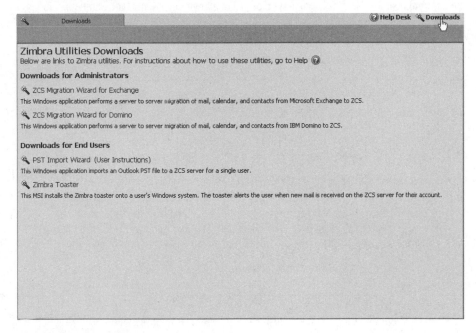

Figure 15-71. *Migration tools*

Inside the Administration Console, on the right-hand side you will see a Downloads link that provides these downloads. There is one for Microsoft Exchange and one for IBM Domino. The other two downloads are for end users: one allows migration of PST files (the Microsoft Outlook files that store your e-mail) into Zimbra, and the other provides alerts when new mail arrives to the end user's Zimbra account.

Zimbra provides documentation for migrating from MS Exchange to Zimbra here: `http://www.zimbra.com/docs/os/latest/migration_wizard_for_exchange_installation_guide/`.

Those who have an alternative IMAP server that they wish to migrate to Zimbra can use the imapsync tool. The Zimbra wiki provides some detailed documentation on how to achieve this sort of migration here: `http://wiki.zimbra.com/index.php?title=User_Migration`.

The imapsync tool allows you to migrate mail between almost any IMAP server. You use this tool to connect to one IMAP server and then transfer the e-mail from one account to an account on the Zimbra server. Users must first be provisioned on the Zimbra server. You can download the imapsync tool from here: `http://freshmeat.net/projects/imapsync/`.

Ubuntu provides imapsync from online repositories, so you only have to issue `aptitude` to install it.

```
$ sudo aptitude install imapsync
```

Red Hat RHEL hosts require you to download the imapsync package from the Freshmeat website and install all of the required dependencies (see the `INSTALL` file for a list of the required dependencies). CentOS and Fedora provide imapsync via Yum repositories at RPM-Forge (`https://rpmforge.net`).

■**Tip** When transferring mail from another mail server, or to just allow bigger e-mail attachments, you may have to increase the default mail attachment size. You can do that by issuing following command as the `zimbra` user:

```
$ zmprov mcf zimbraMtaMaxMessageSize 50000000
```

You could use the imapsync tool as follows:

```
$ imapsync --host1 orig.imap.host  --user1 username --passfile1 /etc/password ➥
 --host2 mail.example.com --user2 username --passfile2 /etc/password
```

Using the `imapsync` command, we specify the IMAP host we wish to migrate e-mail from, provisioning the username and password for a user on that IMAP host. We then specify the details of the Zimbra host we are migrating to, giving the username and password we expect on that host. The `--passfile1` and `--passfile2` options are used to specify a file with a password in it for that username. This file should be securely stored on the host using 600 permissions.

■**Note** You can also batch up the migration if you have several users you wish to migrate with large amounts of e-mail. See the User Migration wiki page for more details: `http://wiki.zimbra.com/index.php?title=Main_Page`.

Summary

By now you likely see the advantages of having a collaboration service such as Zimbra. Zimbra is not the only collaboration server on the market, but we consider it to be an easy-to-use and fully featured collaboration server.

In this chapter, we have shown you how to do the following:

- Install and configure the Zimbra server.

- Add user accounts, distribution lists, and resources to the Zimbra server.

- Send e-mail using the Zimbra web client.

- Share items like folders, calendars, documents, and address books, using the Zimbra web client.

- Create calendars and calendar events, and invite people to attend.

- Create documents.

- Use the `Briefcase` feature.

- Migrate user accounts from one e-mail system to Zimbra.

In the next chapter, we will show you the open source alternative to Active Directory, OpenLDAP, and explain directory services.

CHAPTER 16

■■■

Directory Services

By Dennis Matotek

Directory services are widespread throughout major computer networks. An LDAP directory is an example of this type of service. LDAP directories are special databases that usually contain usernames, passwords, common names, e-mail addresses, business addresses, and other attributes. Organizations first used directory services to facilitate the distribution of address books and user information. Since that time, directory services have grown to take on roles as the central repositories for all user information and authentication services. Applications are now being developed with the ability to authenticate against directory services, further enhancing their importance within an organization.

In this chapter, we are going to show you how to install and configure an OpenLDAP server. We are also going to talk about extending your OpenLDAP directory server by adding your own schema. We will show you how to design the access control lists to secure your installation, as well as how to manage your LDAP server via command-line tools and a web-based GUI. Finally, you'll see how to integrate your LDAP server with your existing network and applications, including the ability to implement single sign-on services, Apache web authentication, and web-based application authentication.

Directory services implementations can be complicated. While installation is very simple, they are often very intricate to configure securely. OpenLDAP does not have a commercially supported version, but even the simplest question to the OpenLDAP mailing list is regularly answered by senior engineers and designers of the project (which is an enormous help and absolute credit to their dedication). That said, you would be well served by purchasing a book dedicated to the subject before you begin your installation to further your understanding of this software. We would like to recommend to you the following:

- *Deploying OpenLDAP* by Tom Jackiewicz (Apress, 2004)

- *Mastering OpenLDAP: Configuring, Securing and Integrating Directory Services* by Matt Butcher (Packt Publishing, 2007)

■**Tip** The OpenLDAP website also contains a very good administration guide and FAQ at `http://www.openldap.org`.

What Is LDAP?

LDAP, which stands for Lightweight Directory Access Protocol, is used to access X.500-based directory services derived from the Directory Access Protocol (DAP). X.500 is a set of protocols that outline how user information should be stored and how that information should be accessed. LDAP resulted from the Directory Access Protocol not having TCP/IP capabilities.

■**Note** For more information on the X.500 OSI protocol, please see `http://en.wikipedia.org/wiki/X.500`.

Several common types of directory services exist, and they are all derived from the X.500 DAP OSI model. Examples of these are Microsoft's Active Directory, Red Hat's Directory Services, and Sun's Directory Server Enterprise Edition. In this chapter, we will be concentrating on the commonly used and very robust OpenLDAP server. OpenLDAP was forked off from the original project originally designed by the University of Michigan and now continues on through the work of a community of engineers and developers from the OpenLDAP project (`http://www.openldap.org/project/`).

The X.500 DAP OSI model describes some fundamental concepts to which LDAP complies. First, you need to have a single Directory Information Tree (DIT). This is a hierarchical organization of entries. Each of these entries requires a distinguished name (DN). The DN of an entry is made up of the relative distinguished name (RDN) and the ancestor entries that it belongs to. Figure 16-1 shows the basic relationships between DIT, DN, and RDN.

The DIT is the directory tree, and in this case it has the root DN of `dc=com`. There are several ways to define your root and main branches. Some people choose a layout based on their DNS domains, as we have here, and some people use geographic locations, such as `o=US`, `o=AU`, or `o=DE`, as their root. In our case, we choose to use the DNS domain name naming standard as we are not overly concerned about the geographic locations of our organization. We can always introduce the `LocalityName` attribute further down the tree if we wish to, as we have with the `compB` branch where we specify a locality of `l=Amsterdam`. Some thought should be given to how you want to lay out your directory structure, but ultimately you want it to be as simple and easy to understand as possible.

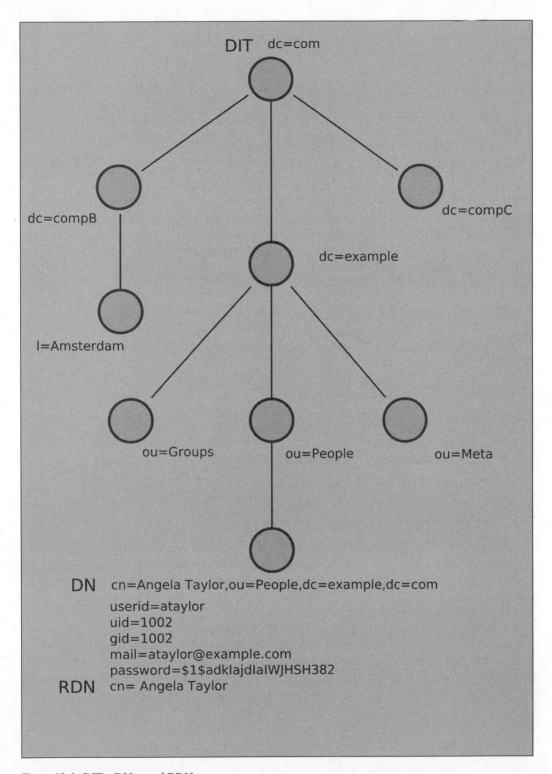

Figure 16-1. *DITs, DNs, and RDNs*

■Tip It is important to define a standard way of naming your branches and describing your organization now and stick to it.

The branches are used to organize your information into logical groups. These logical groups are called *organizational units* and represented as ou. You can group whatever you like together, but the main organizational units you will normally see in your LDAP tree are People, Groups, and Machines. You store everything to do with your people under ou=People, your user groups under ou=Groups, and your nonhuman assets under ou=Machines (also commonly named ou=Hosts). Organizational units can hold other organizational units and can be as complicated as you want them to be, although we again recommend simpler as better when it comes to designing your DIT.

The DN is a unique entry under the root, which is made up of the RDN and its ancestors. You can see in Figure 16-1 that we have a DN of cn=Angela Taylor,ou=People,dc=example, dc=com. It is made up of the RDN cn=Angela Taylor and the ancestors of ou=People, dc=example, and dc=com. Likewise, ou=People,dc=example,dc=com is also a DN for the People organizational unit, and ou=People is an RDN of it.

Each DN entry is made up of classes and attributes that describe that entry. The object classes describe what attributes must be present or are allowed to be present. The classes may support other classes in order to provide extended attributes to them. These attributes are described by the RDN value. Classes and attributes must be defined in a schema and must be unique.

A *schema* is set of definitions that describe the data that can be stored in the directory server. Schemas are used to describe the syntax and matching rules for an available class and attribute definitions. If you find your organization is not properly described by the available schema files, you can create your own schema file for your company if you wish. Once you have created your schema file, you then include it in your OpenLDAP configuration files.

It is common for organizations to require certain attributes to describe your users or your internal systems that are not provided in the schema files supplied. In this case, you will make your own classes and attributes in your own schema file. When creating your schema file, you must remember to make the names for your object classes and attributes unique.

It is good practice to add a prefix to all your created attributes and classes to make sure they are unique. For instance, we could define an "active:" attribute for our example company as exampleActive. We could then use exampleActive to enable and disable entries by setting it to TRUE or FALSE.

Here's how this would look in an LDAP entry:

```
dn: uid=user1,ou=People,dc=example,dc=com
uid: user1
exampleActive: TRUE
```

Once this attribute is added to an entry in LDAP, we can use filters to search for all instances of exampleActive = TRUE in our LDAP directory, which would speed up the results for active users. This is just an example of how you can use your own schema definitions; there may be other ways to achieve the same outcome.

By default, OpenLDAP uses the Berkeley Database (originally referred to as Berkeley DB, and then Sleepycat DB, it is now owned by Oracle and carries its original name). It is extremely fast and scalable, with databases holding millions of records. It is optimized for reading, searching, and browsing. OpenLDAP can use other databases as the back end if you desire.

Different directory servers are available to use if you are not satisfied with OpenLDAP. Red Hat has its own directory server that is free in Fedora but available by subscription with RHEL. Active Directory from Microsoft is another LDAP server, as are Sun's free Directory Server Enterprise Edition and Novell's eDirectory.

General Considerations

Ubuntu and Red Hat offer different releases of OpenLDAP. Ubuntu uses a recent 2.4 release, and Red Hat issues a 2.3 release. Both are considered stable and secure, but the 2.4 release has some improvements. Following are the differences between the releases as taken from the OpenLDAP changelog.

OpenLDAP 2.3 (released June 2005) functional enhancements and improved scalability:

- Access control extensions including "don't disclose on error" provisions
- Configuration back end (cn-config)
- Password policy overlay (work in progress)
- Sync provider overlay
- Delta-syncrepl support
- LDAP v3 extensions:
  - ManageDIT extensions (work in progress)
  - Component matching (experimental)

OpenLDAP 2.4 (released October 2007) functional enhancements and improved scalability:

- Updated slapd dispatcher

- MirrorMode and MultiMaster replication

- Proxy sync replication

- Expanded monitoring

- Multiple new overlays

- Expanded documentation

- New socket back end (experimental)

- LDAP v3 extensions:

  - LDAP chaining operation support

  - LDAP don't use copy control support

  - LDAP dynamic directory services (RFC 2589)

You may not understand all these features at this stage, but you don't need to in order to get OpenLDAP working. Depending on the purpose of your LDAP installation, however, you may wish to choose the Ubuntu offering over the Red Hat release, as it has newer features than the Red Hat one.

■**Note** Fedora also has the most recent version of OpenLDAP.

If you were seeking support for MultiMaster replication capabilities (i.e., the ability to have more than one LDAP master directory service), you should choose the Ubuntu offering. MultiMaster enhances redundancy of your LDAP installation.

You can also make use of overlays. Overlays give OpenLDAP advanced functionality to alter or extend the normal LDAP behavior. Overlays such as the ppolicy overlay enable password controls that are not provided in the base code of OpenLDAP. The ppolicy overlay allows you to set things like password aging and minimum character length.

You will also need to decide what kind of authentication methods you are going to support in your organization. OpenLDAP supports two authentication methods, simple and SASL. The simple method has three modes of operation:

- *Anonymous*: No username or password is supplied.

- *Unauthenticated*: A username is supplied but no password.

- *Username/Password authentication*: A valid username and password must be provided.

Of the SASL method, the *OpenLDAP Administrator's Guide* says you need an existing working Cyrus SASL installation to provide the SASL mechanism. This is not entirely true, depending on the mechanism of SASL you wish to implement. You can set up PLAIN/LOGIN and DIGESTMD5 mechanisms pretty easily. However, you must have Cyrus SASL installed. SASL provides the following mechanisms:

- PLAIN/LOGIN

- DIGESTMD5

- GSSAPI (Kerberos v5)

- EXTERNAL (X.509 public/private key authentication)

■ **Note** SASL (PLAIN/LOGIN, DIGESTMD5) requires cleartext passwords to be used in the `userPasswd` attribute. Whether this is good or not for security is heavily debated. One side of the argument goes something like this: "Once I access your database, I've got access to all your passwords." The counter to this is, "If you've got access to my database, the game is over anyway. At least I'm not sending passwords over the wire."

You can read more about these different authentication methods at the following pages in the *OpenLDAP Administrator's Guide*:

- `http://www.openldap.org/doc/admin24/security.html#Authentication%20Methods`

- `http://www.openldap.org/doc/admin24/sasl.html`

Implementation

Before we show you how to install the OpenLDAP server on our example system, we need to go over a few details of the implementation:

- We are not installing this OpenLDAP server on a host that has a Zimbra mail server already installed. This is because Zimbra provides its own OpenLDAP server and will conflict with the one we are about to install.

- We will set a CNAME in our DNS that will point ldap.example.com to the `headoffice.example.com` record or define some other DNS A record to the host on which we are installing our LDAP server. See Chapter 9 for instructions on DNS.

- We are not using any replication of our directory service. Replication is where we can have more than one LDAP server on our network sharing all or part of our LDAP data and answering client requests. It takes additional configuration to enable this.

Let's view just one piece of our network. Suppose that we have a web server on our network, and we want to make sure only people from a certain group within our organization are able to access it. Normally, we would need to add a complicated login mechanism to our website, have some kind of user database to store the information, and so on. With our Apache web server, we can use the Apache LDAP module to get our web server to use an LDAP server to authenticate requests. Without this authentication, the website will not be accessible. We can also have other services authenticating against our OpenLDAP directory server. In Figure 16-2, you can see how we would authenticate our web servers.

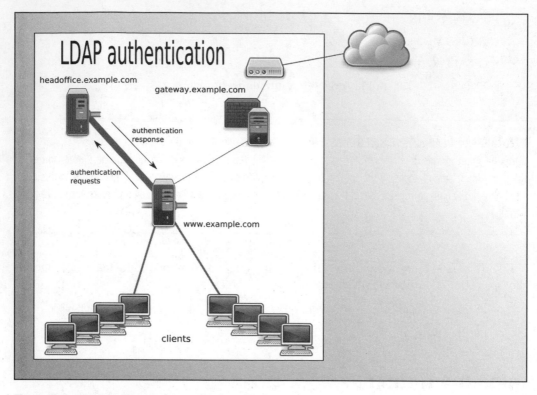

Figure 16-2. *LDAP authentication of web services*

Figure 16-2 presents a simple diagram showing a web server using LDAP to authenticate our desktop or Internet clients to web services. (The LDAP service and the web service can be on the same host if you do not have the necessary hardware resources.) When a request is received by a website, the user making the request requires validation before access is granted. An authentication request is sent to the LDAP service on headoffice.example.com. If the user is validated, the LDAP server sends the response to the web service, and the user can access the site.

Many of the services that we have described in this book can be made to use an LDAP service. This allows you to centralize your authentication services on the one host, reducing complexity, increasing authentication security, and providing a central repository for all your staff details.

We are going to show you how to set up both your LDAP service and authentication for an Apache web service.

Installation

OpenLDAP is available on both Red Hat and Ubuntu via their online repositories. Again, for OpenLDAP, subtle differences exist between the two distributions, and we'll detail these next.

Red Hat Installation Guide

We will now take you through the installation of an OpenLDAP server on our Red Hat host. The binaries are available from the Red Hat network, and you can install them via the yum command or via the Package Manager GUI. We will install them via the yum command as follows:

```
$ sudo yum install openldap openldap-clients openldap-servers
openldap-servers-overlays
```

This installs the necessary files for configuring, running, and managing the LDAP server. The openldap package installs the base packages required to allow the host to integrate with the OpenLDAP server. The openldap-clients package installs the tools to manage and query the LDAP server. The openldap-servers package installs the necessary files to run an OpenLDAP server. The openldap-servers-overlays provides the extended functionality mentioned earlier.

The configuration files for OpenLDAP are stored in /etc/openldap/:

```
$ sudo ls -l /etc/openldap/
total 40
drwxr-xr-x 2 root root 4096 Nov  6 18:57 cacerts
-rw-r----- 1 root ldap  921 Nov  6 18:56 DB_CONFIG.example
-rw-r--r-- 1 root root  327 Sep 14 09:10 ldap.conf
drwxr-xr-x 3 root root 4096 Mar 11 06:02 schema
-rw-r----- 1 root ldap 3731 Nov  6 18:57 slapd.conf
```

The configuration file specifically for the configuration of LDAP clients is /etc/openldap/ldap.conf. This is usually managed on Red Hat hosts by the system-auth-config utility, which will fill in the details as required.

Ubuntu Installation Guide

To install OpenLDAP on an Ubuntu host, we require the ldap-utils package and the slapd package to be installed. The following command will install these packages:

```
$ sudo aptitude install ldap-utils slapd
```

When you issue this command, the slapd package will ask you to provide a password for your root LDAP user. You can enter your password and proceed with the installation. If you do not wish to supply one, you can just press the Enter key twice (we will show you how to create a password in the upcoming "Configuration" section). Once installed, the ldap-utils package will install the files needed to manage and search your LDAP directory. The slapd package installs the necessary files to run and configure your LDAP directory. The client configuration packages are auth-client-config (PAM and NSS profile switcher) and ldap-auth-client (metapackage for LDAP authentication along with ldap-auth-config).

Configuration

We now want to give you a look at the main configuration file for OpenLDAP, slapd.conf. We are going to show you how to safely configure an LDAP directory service. In our example, we'll do this from our Ubuntu host; some of the directory paths will be different for Red Hat. For Red Hat hosts, the configuration directory is called /etc/openldap instead of /etc/ldap, which is for Ubuntu hosts. Both distributions store the databases in /var/lib/ldap.

```
# Global Directives:

# Schema and objectClass definitions
include         /etc/ldap/schema/core.schema
include         /etc/ldap/schema/cosine.schema
include         /etc/ldap/schema/nis.schema
include         /etc/ldap/schema/inetorgperson.schema
include         /etc/ldap/schema/ppolicy.schema
include         /etc/ldap/schema/example.com.schema
```

Let's begin by looking at the first include statements. OpenLDAP uses the include statement followed by a file name to read that file into its configuration. Here we are including the common schema files provided by OpenLDAP plus the example.com.schema file, which we will use to introduce our own attributes for our own special needs. We will show you more about this schema in the "Creating a Schema" section.

```
pidfile         /var/run/slapd/slapd.pid
argsfile        /var/run/slapd/slapd.args
```

Next is the pidfile location and the location of a file that will contain the arguments that the slapd server was started with. For example, the argsfile will contain this information:

```
jsmith@ldap:/etc/ldap$ cat /var/run/slapd/slapd.args
/usr/sbin/slapd -h ldap://ldap.example.com ldaps://ldap.example.com ➥
-g openldap -u openldap -f /etc/ldap/slapd.conf
```

The log level is important to help debug your installation. To be honest, to the new user it can be very confusing as to what is being reported. However, the logging level is additive, and you can get finer-grained detail in the logs. In a production environment, we recommend setting this value to 0 and, if you wish to, using the audit overlay to monitor what is happening to your installation.

```
Loglevel        480
```

We set our logging level to 480. This will show search filters, configuration file processing, access controls, and connection information in our logs. Table 16-1 lists the available logging levels.

Table 16-1. *Additive Logging Levels*

Level	Description
-1	Turns on all debugging information. Useful for finding out where your LDAP server is failing before you make your logging level more fine-grained.
0	Turns all debugging off. Recommended for production mode.
1	(0x1 trace) Traces function calls.
2	(0x2 packets) Debugs packet handling.
4	(0x4 args) Provides heavy trace debugging (function args).
8	(0x8 conns) Provides connection management.
16	(0x10 BER) Prints out packets sent and received.
32	(0x20 filter) Provides search filter processing.
64	(0x40 config) Provides configuration file processing.
128	(0x80 ACL) Provides access control list processing.
256	(0x100 stats) Provides connections, LDAP operations, and results (recommended).
512	(0x200 stats2) Indicates stats log entries sent.
1024	(0x400 shell) Prints communication with shell back ends.
2048	(0x800 parse) Parses entries.
16384	(0x4000 sync) Provides LDAPSync replication.
32768	(0x8000 none) Logs only messages at whatever log level is set.

As mentioned, the Loglevel setting is additive, meaning you can enable more logging by adding the values of the things you wish to log. As you may have already worked out, our Loglevel of 480 comprises the level 32 (search filter), 64 (configuration processing), 128 (access control list processing), and 256 (connections and LDAP operations results). This is a good setting while we are setting up our LDAP service, as it provides a nice level of information. If we get stuck, we can change the Loglevel to -1 to turn on debugging, which turns on all logging features. Also remember that in a production environment, you would normally want to have the Loglevel set at 0. You can also list the hexadecimal numbers on one line to achieve the same result; in this case, we would set the log level to Loglevel 0x20 0x40 0x80 0x100.

Next, we have the modules section. Modules are added to the configuration to provide access to certain functionality.

```
# Where the dynamically loaded modules are stored
modulepath      /usr/lib/ldap
moduleload      back_hdb
moduleload      ppolicy.la
```

Here we are declaring the path in which to find our modules, modulepath /usr/lib/ldap. Next, we declare the modules that we wish to load: back_hdb, which is the hierarchical Berkeley Database we are going to use, and ppolicy. The ppolicy module allows us to have greater control of the passwords in our database via password expiry and other password control features.

```
# The maximum number of entries that is returned for a search operation
sizelimit 500
tool-threads 1
```

We can declare the maximum number of results that are returned from a search. This is set to 500 (the default). If you do not wish to have a limit, you can choose unlimit here. The tool-threads directive tells the slapd daemon to use only one CPU to run indexes on. If you have more than one CPU, you can set this to a higher number, but not higher than the number of CPUs you have. Other performance settings can be turned on including threads, timelimits, and socket buffers.

Next, we can configure the TLS settings. TLS, or Transport Layer Security, is used for encrypting communications between our server and its clients.

```
TLSCACertificateFile /etc/ssl/certs/ca-bundle.crt
TLSCertificateFile /etc/ssl/certs/ldap.pem
TLSCertificateKeyFile /etc/ssl/certs/ldap.key
TLSVerifyClient never
```

Here we create a certificate file from our private key and add the details. The issuing certificate file is added to the ca-bundle.crt file. We also specify never for TLSVerifyClient as we do not wish to verify the certificate presented by a particular client in our instance.

Next is the second part of our security measures, the security strength factor, or ssf. Here we can define the minimum security strength we allow for our connections and specify higher-security-strength communications for more sensitive roles. The security line here describes the factors of security we require for certain connection types:

```
security ssf=1 update_ssf=112 simple_bind=56
```

The ssf=1 setting describes the overall security strength factor we require for our service. The update_ssf=112 setting describes the overall security strength required for directory updates, and the simple_bind=56 setting is the required security factor for simple_bind operations. The ssf values are as follows:

- 0 (zero) implies no protection.

- 1 implies integrity protection only.

- 56 allows DES or other weak ciphers.

- 112 allows triple DES and other strong ciphers.

- 128 allows RC4, Blowfish, and other modern strong ciphers.

The default is 0. This manages the strength of security mechanisms, such as SSL, that are used to make connections to your directory service. You can combine them in your access control lists to control what those connections can access, depending on the security strength of the connection. We will explain this concept further in the "Access Control Lists" section later in this chapter.

We are now going to declare the back-end database that will hold our DIT. There are several options here. Normally, you will choose between either bdb or hdb for the database, as these are the defaults. The other types you can choose from (ldap, ldif, metadirectory, perl, etc.) are used for proxying your LDAP server.

■Note For more information on the choices for back-end databases available to you, please see the online documentation: http://www.openldap.org/doc/admin24/backends.html.

```
backend         hdb
database        hdb
```

We have chosen the Ubuntu default for our database type, hdb. The common choices are bdb and hdb. These types both refer to the Oracle Berkeley DB, which as mentioned previously was originally developed and designed by Berkeley University (hence the name) and was also formerly known as Sleepycat DB. The two databases take identical commands and differ only in that one has a hierarchical layout (hdb). This allows for subtree renames, subtrees being the branches from the root of the DIT.

The database directive marks the start of a new database instance declaration. We can declare more than one database instance. The next detail we require is the top of the DIT and a user to have full access to it, like a root user.

```
suffix          "dc=example,dc=com"
rootdn          "cn=admin,dc=example,dc=com"
rootpw          {SSHA}4Tx/MG/x4/mKCf7OheEohw+axXV61Jg+
```

The suffix directs queries for dc=example,dc=com to this database instance. You can have more than one suffix declared here. rootdn is the root user, who has full access to database; the password is declared in rootpw. You can create a password using the slappasswd command as follows:

```
$ sudo slappasswd
```

The password that is printed can then be copied and pasted to rootpw in slapd.conf. The next directive is where we will hold the database workspace.

```
directory       "/var/lib/ldap"
```

This directory must be writable by the user who runs the slapd daemon; for Ubuntu this user is openldap, and for Red Hat the user is ldap.

Next, we have an overlay declaration. An overlay, as previously mentioned, provides certain additional functionality not normally supplied by the OpenLDAP server. In this case, we are declaring the ppolicy overlay.

```
overlay ppolicy
ppolicy_default "cn=default,ou=Policies,dc=example,dc=com"
ppolicy_use_lockout
```

The ppolicy overlay provides certain functions that allow you to better control password security on your LDAP server. OpenLDAP itself provides no password management features, such as password expiry and password history. This overlay allows you to declare a policy or associate different policies with different parts of the DIT tree. Here we declare a default policy with the DN cn=default,ou=Policies,dc=example,dc=com. We also declare that we wish to use the lockout feature of the ppolicy. This allows us to send a message back to the requesting client if it is locked out. This can provide information to attackers who will then know whether a username exists or not, so you might wish to turn this off.

We will add further to the ppolicy overlay when we load our LDIFs into the OpenLDAP database in the "Password Policy Overlay" section.

■**Note** LDIF is the file format for declaring the contents of your LDAP database. You will see how to use the client tools to create and use these LDIF files in the "LDIFs and Adding Users" section.

You also have to declare the performance tunings you wish to give your database. Use dbconfig to set various aspects of your database in your DB_CONFIG file if there isn't a file already present when slapd is started. If the file exists, any new settings here will be ignored, and you should directly edit the DB_CONFIG file, which will be in the /var/lib/ldap directory.

```
dbconfig set_cachesize 0 5242880 0
dbconfig set_lk_max_objects 1500
dbconfig set_lk_max_locks 1500
dbconfig set_lk_max_lockers 1500
```

Our database tuning parameters here provide for 512MB of in-memory cache through the set_cachesize setting. The syntax of set_cachesize is the size in gigabytes (0), followed by bytes (5242880), and the number of cache segments to use (0). The other dbconfig settings are standard defaults, for Ubuntu anyway.

■**Note** You can read more about dbconfig settings here: http://www.oracle.com/technology/ documentation/berkeley-db/db/ref/toc.html.

Next, we can set our indexes. Indexes are used to speed up searches on the database.

```
index          objectClass eq
index          cn sub
index          exampleActive pres,eq
index          uid,uidNumber pres,eq
```

As a rule, you should index what your clients are commonly going to search for. An e-mail client's address book may search for the common name, or cn, when it looks for people's names to populate its address book entries. In such a case, you would want to have an index of the cn attribute optimized for substrings, sub. Table 16-2 lists the common types of indexes available.

Table 16-2. *Common Index Types*

Type	Description
sub	Useful for optimizing string searches that contain wildcards like cn=Jane*
eq	Useful for optimizing searches for exact strings like sn=Smith
pres	Useful for optimizing searches for object classes or attributes, like objectclass=person
approx	Useful for optimizing searches for sounds-like searches, like sn~=Smi*

Other index types are available, and you can read about them on the slapd.conf man page. We wish to index the objectclass, cn, and uid, which we know will be commonly searched when users try to authenticate.

Other performance-related settings for the Berkeley DB are lastmod and checkpoint.

```
lastmod      on
checkpoint   512 30
```

The checkpoint directive tells the slapd daemon to flush the buffer to disk and write a checkpoint to the transaction log. This directive indicates we want this checkpoint process to be performed whenever the transaction log gets to be 512K in size or every time 30 minutes have elapsed. The lastmod on directive records the last modification in an RDN, cn=Lastmod,dc=example,dc=com. The DN of the object modified, the type of modification, and when it was modified are recorded.

We declare where to look for our access control list using the include statement. We will discuss the access control lists and how to use them in the "Access Control Lists" section shortly.

```
include /etc/ldap/access.example.com
```

We then create another database by using the database directive. The config type of database is used to store our slapd configuration. With this we can make changes to our LDAP database without having to restart the server.

```
#########################################
database config
rootdn cn=admin,cn=config
rootpw {SSHA}4Tx/MG/x4/mKCf7OheEohw+axXV61Jg+
```

This database requires a rootDN and a password. The config database is created when we start our slapd daemon from the slapd.conf file and any other included files. The directives here in slapd.conf are converted into LDIF format files in the slapd.d directory in the configuration directory: /etc/ldap or /etc/openldap depending on your distribution. It allows you to use the LDAP tools to manage the database.

■**Note** You can read more about the configuration engine database here: http://www.openldap.org/doc/admin24/slapdconf2.html.

We are not ready to start our LDAP server yet. First we are going to create the extra files that we have previously specified in our slapd.conf file. We need to create the schema file example.com.schema and the access control list file access.example.com.

Creating a Schema

In our slapd.conf file, we declared that we want to add a schema file called example.com.schema. In this schema file, we will include a simple class and attribute that we will use to indicate whether a user account is active or not. First let's look at how to declare an object in the schema. The following appears in the core.schema file in the schema directory:

```
objectclass ( 1.3.6.1.4.1.1466.344 NAME 'dcObject'
  DESC 'RFC2247: domain component object'
  SUP top AUXILIARY MUST dc )
```

This is one of the main object classes that will be included in the DIT. We need to declare what type of entity we are using, and so we start with objectclass (*detail*). Whitespace is important when declaring your objects and attributes. The number you see, 1.3.6.1.4.1.1466.344, is the private enterprise number (PEN), or Object Identifier (OID), which is a unique series of numbers for indentifying objects; if you are familiar with SNMP, you should recognize this.

■**Note** You can register for your own OID or PEN at the Internet Assigned Numbers Authority (IANA) website: http://pen.iana.org/pen/PenApplication.page.

Then we give that object class a name, dcObject, and a description. The next line tells you that this will inherit the object class SUP top. The AUXILIARY indicates the type of object class and the MUST dc says that if this object is declared in the directory server, the attribute dc must also be added.

■**Note** The full detail of declaring object classes is contained in this RFC: http://www.rfc-editor.org/rfc/rfc4512.txt. A quick explanation on extending your schemas can be found here: http://www.openldap.org/doc/admin24/schema.html.

Let's take a look at our own schema file, /etc/ldap/schema/example.com.schema.

```
# $Id$

attributetype ( 1.1.3.10 NAME 'exampleActive'
  DESC 'Example User Active'
  EQUALITY booleanMatch
  SYNTAX 1.3.6.1.4.1.1466.115.121.1.7 )

objectclass ( 1.1.1.2 NAME 'exampleClient'
  SUP top AUXILIARY
  DESC 'Example.com User objectclass'
  MAY ( exampleActive ))
```

In these two schema objects, we have two OIDs, which we made up. These might conflict with other existing schema files. We would like to avoid this, so we would normally apply for our own PEN. We'll pretend we did so and that we received an OID of 1.3.6.1.4.1.111111, where 1.3.6.1.4.1 is the IANA *arc*, or node, and the 111111 is the special number that distinguishes our company from other companies. We can now use our OID in place of the ones in the preceding schema.

■**Caution** As we mentioned, we have made up the 1.3.6.1.4.1.111111 OID for the purpose of this demonstration. Please do not make up numbers or use this OID in your production environment. You should really get your own PEN; otherwise, you risk having conflicts and things breaking. For more information on OIDs and LDAP, please also view the following: `http://www.zytrax.com/books/ldap/apa/oid.html`.

```
attributetype ( 1.3.6.1.4.1.111111.3.1.1 NAME 'exampleActive'
  DESC 'Example User Active'
  SINGLE-VALUE
  EQUALITY booleanMatch
  SYNTAX 1.3.6.1.4.1.1466.115.121.1.7 )

objectclass ( 1.3.6.1.4.1.111111.3.2.1 NAME 'exampleClient' SUP top AUXILIARY
  DESC 'Example.com User objectclass'
  MAY ( exampleActive ))
```

Once you have a PEN or an OID, you can divide it into useful segments (also called nodes or arcs). Generally, you can use an OID for not only LDAP schema objects, but also SNMP MIBs. As you can see, we have branched off 1.3.6.1.4.1.111111.3 for our LDAP schema definitions. Under that, we will place all our object class definitions under 1.3.6.1.4.1.111111.3.2 and our attributes under 1.3.6.1.4.1.111111.3.1.

■**Note** Assigning 1.3.6.1.4.1.111111.3.1 and 1.3.6.1.4.1.111111.3.2 to LDAP classes and attributes is completely arbitrary. You can choose whatever numbering scheme you desire.

We set the `exampleActive` attribute to be a Boolean match, meaning it can represent either true or false. Setting this attribute to TRUE will mean that our account is active. Setting it to FALSE will mean the account is not active. We can index this attribute, which will again speed up our searches. This is why we set the following in our `slapd.conf` earlier:

```
index      exampleActive pres,eq
```

The `exampleClient` object class defines that we may have the `exampleActive` attribute present (as indicated by MAY) when we include that object class in our DN entry. If we wanted to enforce its presence, we can specify MUST instead. The object class is of type AUXILIARY and has the superclass, defined by SUP top. The default object type is STRUCTURAL. You must have one STRUCTURAL object class in your entries, and you cannot have two STRUCTURAL object classes pointing to the same parent or superior class.

■**Note** For an explanation of this problem, please read the following: `http://www.linuxlaboratory. org/?q=node/44`. The RFC that describes the LDAP schema files can be found at `http://www. rfc-editor.org/rfc/rfc4512.txt`.

We will use the example.com.schema file when we declare our users in the "LDIF and Adding Users" section of this chapter.

Access Control Lists

Every connection that accesses your LDAP server has to be given specific access to various parts of the tree if you want it to be secure. You can specify from where you accept connections, the level of security, or the encryption that connection must have to gain access, right down to the branch or attribute that you allow access to. You also have several levels of access that you can then grant to the requesting connection: manage, write, read, search, and auth.

We have included our configuration in our slapd.conf file with the following instruction:

```
include /etc/ldap/access.example.com
```

In its most basic form, access is given using the following syntax:

```
access to what [ by who [ access ] [ control ] ]+
```

what is an entity in the LDAP database, *who* is the client requesting the information, and *access* is the level of access you wish that client to have on it. *control* specifies how the list is processed after this entry and is optional.

In the following simple example, we give read access to everything in our DIT:

```
access to *
        by * read stop
```

You can use the wildcard * to allow general unrestricted access. The access control here indicates any user has read access to anything. Next is a control statement that tells slapd to stop processing any other directives. Order is important in your access control list, with directives of a higher order being processed before those of a lower order. When you give a privilege or access level, it implies all the previous ones. For example, read access automatically grants the preceding disclose, auth, compare, search access levels, including read access rights. Table 16-3 lists the access levels you can assign to a request for access to an entity.

Table 16-3. *Access Privileges*

Access	Privileges
none	Allows no access at all
disclose	Allows no access but returns an error
auth	Enables bind operations (authenticate)
compare	Allows you to compare the entity
search	Allows you to search that part of the DIT
read	Allows read access
write	Allows write access
manage	Allows all access and the ability to delete entities

When you choose none, you are denying all access to the entity without returning an error to the requestor. This helps prevent information leakage of what is and what isn't in your DIT. The disclose access, unlike none, will return an error to the requesting client.

Looking further at requesting access to an entity, you need to know who is requesting the access. There can be more than one *who* declaration, each using certain keywords. These keywords can be combined with a *style* qualifier, which can be something like regex or exact. The regex style refers to a regular expression that can be used to match various parts of a DN. It is more costly in processing your access control list.

■**Tip** See the *OpenLDAP Administrator's Guide* for tips on using regular expressions: `http://www.` `openldap.org/doc/admin24/access-control.html#Tips%20for%20using%20regular%20` `expressions%20in%20Access%20Control.`

It is always less costly, in processing terms, yet more precise to describe exactly what you would like to give access to and to whom. For example:

```
access to dn.subtree=ou=People,dc=example,dc=com
      by dn.exact="cn=admin,ou=meta,dc=example,dc=com" read
```

Here we are again granting read access to everything under the organizational unit People. We are being specific and defining that this access only be granted to the DN cn=admin,ou=meta, dc=example,dc=com.

Defining what to grant access to can get tricky. Several standard methods are available for granting access. You can use the following:

```
dn.base
dn.one
dn.subtree
dn.children
```

To explain how these relate to the objects we are working on, we will borrow an example from the *OpenLDAP Administrator's Guide*. Imagine we have the following lists:

```
0: dc=example,dc=com
1: cn=Manager,dc=example,dc=com
2: ou=people,dc=example,dc=com
3: uid=jsmith,ou=people,dc=example,dc=com
4: cn=addresses,uid=jsmith,ou=people,dc=example,dc=com
5: uid=ataylor,ou=people,dc=example,dc=com
```

When we try to work on parts of the DIT, we can declare the scope of our pattern matches.

```
dn.base="ou=people,dc=example,dc=com" match 2;
dn.one="ou=people,dc=example,dc=com" match 3, and 5;
dn.subtree="ou=people,dc=example,dc=com" match 2, 3, 4, and 5; and
dn.children="ou=people,dc=example,dc=com" match 3, 4, and 5.
```

Declaring the right scope will capture the right part of the DIT tree. As you can see, the scope dn.base will just reference the level of the declared tree, ou=people,dc=example,dc=com. The scope of dn.one will act on the immediate part of the tree after ou=people,dc=example,dc=com.

The dn.subtree scope will act on everything under ou=people,dc=example,dc=com and itself, whereas dn.children will work on everything under ou=people,dc=example,dc=com.

■**Note** You can read more about who you are giving access to here: http://www.openldap.org/doc/ admin24/access-control.html#Who%20to%20grant%20access%20to.

In LDAP, you can use filters, which are a means of weeding out undesirable data and leaving behind the exact results you want. In access control lists, you can use filters to be more specific about what you are granting access to. Take a look at the following line:

```
access to dn.subtree="ou=people,dc=example,dc=com" attrs="userPassword"
      by dn.exact="cn=admin,ou=meta,dc=example,dc=com" write
      by * none
```

In this example, we have declared we would like this to apply to everything under and including ou=people,dc=example,dc=com and to any attribute called userPassword that might be found under there. In this case, the attribute userPassword is the filter. We are giving the admin user write access to the userPassword, and everything will be silently refused.

The man pages are excellent resources for further information on access control lists, and the *OpenLDAP Administrator's Guide* is also very good: http://www.openldap.org/doc/admin24/ access-control.html.

We'll now take you through the access control list we are going to use in our example.com LDAP DIT. First we are defining access to our password information. As we have previously mentioned, the access control lists are read and implemented top to bottom. It is important to keep the sensitive access control lists at the top so that they are not overridden by a higher entry.

```
access to attrs=userPassword,shadowLastChange,entry
          by ssf=128 dn.exact="cn=webadmin,ou=meta,dc=example,dc=com" auth
          by ssf=128 anonymous auth
          by ssf=128 self write
```

In this section, we have restricted access to the users' password information, stored in the attributes userPassword, shadowLastChange throughout the DIT, but generally in the ou=People,dc=example,dc=com branch. We are going to allow only the administrators to have special access. The webadmin user will be used to bind to our LDAP server from our web server so that our web users can authenticate. We only allow access to these attributes by connections with a security strength factor equal to or greater than 128.

■**Note** We mentioned security strength factors earlier. You can use other options to restrict access to your attributes, like specifying a peername or domain from which to accept connections. For more information on this and access control lists in general, please see http://www.openldap.org/doc/admin24/ access-control.html.

We are granting anonymous auth access, that is, clients need not bind to our LDAP server to authenticate. This is important for single sign-on services, which we will explain later on in the "Single Sign-On" section of this chapter. We also give users the ability to change their own password details by allowing self write access.

As we have said, order is important. When an access request comes into your LDAP host, the access control list is parsed, and if a match is found, access is either granted or denied. You can speed your access requests by putting your access control list in order of most requested access to least. You want all those common requests to be toward the top of your access control list and the less common requests closer to the bottom. Assume for this example some *meta users* will have access to various parts of our directory server, and that these users will have the most commonly requested access requests. That is why we have our access controls dealing with the *meta users* group toward the top of the list just below our user passwords entry.

The branch ou=meta holds the users who control access to our directory server. We don't always require a client to bind to our directory server, but sometimes we want them to, such as when we are performing web authentication. You have already seen that we have granted access to the user password entries to webadmin. Now we are declaring the ability of those DNs to see their own information:

```
access to dn.subtree="ou=meta,dc=example,dc=com"
        by group.exact="cn=admins,ou=Groups,dc=example,dc=com" write
        by self read
```

We allow write access to this organizational unit by the cn=admins group, in which we will put our system administrator users, and read access by the meta users themselves. This prevents the users defined under the ou=meta organizational unit from being able to change any of their own entries, and this gives greater security to those users.

Next, we grant access to everything under the ou=People branch, bearing in mind that we have already defined access to the user password attributes earlier in the access control list. The earlier access definition will override any access we detail here for the previously defined attributes. The administrator accounts require at least read access, and we have given the admins group write access. We will want the admins group to also change details from time to time. The webadmin user just requires read access only. We give read access to the entry itself with the self keyword.

```
access to dn.subtree="ou=People,dc=example,dc=com"
        by dn.exact="cn=webadmin,ou=meta,dc=example,dc=com" read
        by group.exact="cn=admins,ou=Groups,dc=example,dc=com" write
        by self read
```

You may have different requirements in your network, and it is quite common to have the self access as write instead. This setting will give the users the ability to change their own attribute details that define their personal information, whereas read access does not.

In the following code, we grant access to the ou=Groups branch where we will hold all our group information:

```
access to dn.subtree="ou=Groups,dc=example,dc=com"
        by dn.exact="cn=webadmin,ou=meta,dc=example,dc=com" read
        by group.exact="cn=admins,ou=Groups,dc=example,dc=com" write
        by users read
```

As you can see, this is similar to the ou=People branch with the same administrator accounts having the same access. However, we have allowed authenticated users the ability to read the groups by specifying users read.

Next, we have the ou=Hosts organizational unit. Some people name this unit machines, but the choice is yours. It will hold all your host information, IP addresses, locations, and so forth. We have used the scope of subtree, and there is minimal write access granted to everything except the cn=admins group.

```
access to dn.subtree="ou=Hosts,dc=example.com"
        by group.exact="cn=admins,ou=Groups,dc=example,dc=com" write
        by anonymous read
```

Here the cn=admins group will require write access. We give anonymous clients, clients that have not made a bind connection (giving a username and password), read access. Various applications make use of the ou=Hosts organizational unit including such applications as Samba.

The final rule we will have is a blanket denial rule. This will enforce the rejection of all other access. This is basically superfluous, as anything not granted explicit access will be denied; however, it shows the end of your access control list set and prevents any access control lists that might be present below it being read in by mistake.

```
access to * by * none stop
```

The wildcards here match everything, meaning that any access sort is denied, and all further processing is stopped by the stop option in the control field. Other processing controls available are break and continue.

The break control option will, on a match, stop further processing in that access control group and jump to the next. The continue option, after a match, will continue processing further down the access control group, allowing for incremental privileges to be granted. The stop option just immediately stops any further processing and is the default control.

Our complete access control list can be seen in Listing 16-1.

Listing 16-1. *The Complete Access Control List*

```
access to attrs=userPassword,shadowLastChange,entry
        by ssf=128 dn.exact="cn=webadmin,ou=meta,dc=example,dc=com" auth
        by ssf=128 anonymous auth
        by ssf=128 self write

access to dn.subtree="ou=meta,dc=example,dc=com"
        by dn.exact="cn=webadmin,ou=meta,dc=example,dc=com" read
        by group.exact="cn=admins,ou=Groups,dc=example,dc=com" write
        by self read

access to dn.subtree="ou=People,dc=example,dc=com"
        by dn.exact="cn=webadmin,ou=meta,dc=example,dc=com" read
        by group.exact="cn=admins,ou=Groups,dc=example,dc=com" write
        by self write
        by users read
```

```
access to dn.subtree="ou=Groups,dc=example,dc=com"
        by dn.exact="cn=webadmin,ou=meta,dc=example,dc=com" read
        by group.exact="cn=admins,ou=Groups,dc=example,dc=com" write
        by anonymous read

access to dn.subtree="ou=Hosts,dc=example.com"
        by group.exact="cn=admins,ou=Groups,dc=example,dc=com" write
        by dn.exact="cn=webadmin,ou=meta,dc=example,dc=com" search

access to *
        by * none
```

With these files in place, we can now try to start our LDAP server.

Starting the slapd Daemon

You can run your slapd daemon in two ways: with the slapd.d configuration engine or without it. As mentioned previously, the configuration engine enables the LDAP configuration to be changed on the fly using standard LDAP syntax and commands. Both ways are supported, but running without the configuration engine will eventually be deprecated, so we recommend starting slapd with it. You will need to start your service manually to create the slapd.d configuration engine. To start and create slapd.d, issue the following command:

```
$ sudo mkdir /etc/ldap/slapd.d
```

On Red Hat, you need to create the directory in /etc/openldap. You then perform the following command, after changing to the configuration directory (/etc/openldap or /etc/ldap):

```
$ sudo slapd -f slapd.conf -F slapd.d -u openldap -g openldap -d -1
```

You will notice that this is being run in the foreground, and you can see whether there are any problems when it tries to start. This is achieved with the -d -1 option, where -1 is the log level that turns on full debugging. For Red Hat hosts, you would use -u ldap -g ldap for the user that runs OpenLDAP instead of -u openldap, which is for Ubuntu hosts. -f slapd.conf points to the configuration file, and F points to the slapd.d directory, which will hold the LDIF files for your configuration engine.

When your slapd instance starts, you will see that the slapd.d directory now contains several files and directories. These files contain the LDAP settings you have specified in slapd.conf and other included files in an LDIF file format.

■**Note** LDIF file formats are described in RFC 2849: http://www.ietf.org/rfc/rfc2849.txt.

LDIFs are composed of the basic form of an entry like the following:

```
# comment
dn: <distinguished name>
<attrdesc>: <attrvalue>
<attrdesc>: <attrvalue>
   <blank line>
```

Let's view one of the ones that we have created under the slapd.d directory:

```
cat /etc/ldap/slapd.d/cn\=config.ldif
dn: cn=config
objectClass: olcGlobal
cn: config
olcConfigFile: /etc/ldap/slapd.conf
olcConfigDir: slapd.d
olcArgsFile: /var/run/slapd/slapd.args
olcAttributeOptions: lang-
olcAuthzPolicy: none
olcConcurrency: 0
olcConnMaxPending: 100
olcConnMaxPendingAuth: 1000
olcGentleHUP: FALSE
```

You can see that it is made up of the distinguished name, dn: cn=config, and then several and attribute descriptions and their values. This enables us to use the LDAP tools, like ldapmodify, to change the configuration of our OpenLDAP server without restarting our server.

■**Note** You can see more about managing the configuration of your OpenLDAP server here: https://
help.ubuntu.com/8.10/serverguide/C/openldap-server.html.

Like other services running on your host, the state of these services, whether they are running or not, is controlled by the scripts in /etc/init.d. You can manually start or stop an LDAP server service using the following on Red Hat:

```
$ sudo /sbin/service ldap start|stop
```

Or using the invoke-rc.d command on Ubuntu:

```
$ sudo /usr/sbin/invoke-rc.d slapd start|stop
```

Once the service is started, you can tail the logs to confirm it started successfully. You can also use the logs to monitor and solve problems with your access requests.

Setting Up Your LDAP Client

Ubuntu and Red Hat both use the `ldap.conf` file to configure systemwide LDAP defaults for clients. Applications that use the OpenLDAP libraries will use these files to get the LDAP details. You will find Ubuntu's file in the directory `/etc/ldap` and Red Hat's in `/etc/openldap`.

■**Note** It is important that you don't get this confused with the `nss_ldap` file, which is also called `ldap.conf` and can be found here on both distributions: `/etc/ldap.conf`.

You will need to edit your `ldap.conf` file by adding the following lines of text. In our case, we are going to cheat a little and not worry about setting up client SSL certificates for our LDAP clients. If this host was being used to replicate our LDAP server, we would definitely ensure that both server and client had SSL verification enabled. Check the man page for `ldap.conf` for details.

```
URI ldap://ldap.example.com/
BASE dc=example,dc=com
TLS_CACERT /etc/ssl/certs/ca-bundle.crt
TLS_REQCERT allow
```

The `URI` points to our LDAP server. The `BASE` is the default base DN for LDAP operations. `TLS_CACERT` points to our CA certificate file, which will contain our example.com CA certificate. The `allow` we specify in the `TLS_REQCERT` field means that we will try to verify the certificate, and if it happens to be a bad one, we proceed anyway with the connection. Other options are `demand`, which means that if no certificate is provided or the certificate is bad, the session stops immediately (this is the default); `try`, which means the connection will continue if no certificate is provided, but if a bad certificate is provided, the connection is stopped immediately; and `never`, which means your host will not request or check the server certificate before establishing the connection.

If you were looking at a Red Hat host, you would most likely find your SSL CA certificate in the `/etc/pki/tls/certs` directory.

LDAP Management and Tools

So how do you manage entries with LDAP? Several tools are available for just this purpose. Using the command line, you can add entries from text files, search for existing entries, and delete entries. The text files are required to be in a format called LDIF. The format of the LDIF file is

```
dn: <dn entry>
objectclass: <objectclass to be included>
attribute: <attribute value described in an objectclass>
```

It is generally a good idea to create separate LDIF files for the different sections you are dealing with. For example, everything under ou=People,dc=example,dc=com can be in people. ldif and everything under ou=Groups,dc=example,dc=com can be in groups.ldif. Alternatively, for fresh LDAP servers, you can have all your entries in the one file, but be wary that in LDAP servers with existing entries, you will get errors if you try to add an existing entry again. You can use the # symbol at the start of each line of an entry to comment out that entry in your LDIF file in such cases. LDIF files can be used by the LDAP tools by using the -f *filename* option that we will detail in the following sections.

The other way to manage entries is to use one of the many GUI tools that are available. We will show how to install and configure a web-based GUI in the "LDAP Account Manager: Web-Based GUI" section.

LDIFs and Adding Users

At the very top of the DIT sits the rootDN. The DIT starts with the declaration of the dcObject class. The following is a snippet of the LDIF text file we will use to populate our LDAP server:

```
dn: dc=example,dc=com
objectclass: dcObject
dc: example
```

This declares that we are going to create the rootDN dc=example,dc=com. According to the dcObject object class in the core.schema we declared in the slapd.conf earlier, we must include the dc attribute. Let's look at the object class declaration from the core.schema file.

```
objectclass ( 1.3.6.1.4.1.1466.344 NAME 'dcObject'
        DESC 'RFC2247: domain component object'
        SUP top AUXILIARY MUST dc )
```

You can see how we use the preceding object class in the declaration of the dn: dc=example, dc=com. We specify the dc attribute as we are directed to use, indicated by the MUST clause in the object definition. We will add this entry when we add our users in the next section. This should be the first entry you add to your LDAP server.

Next, we want to set up the users in our organization, so we will now declare our People organizational unit. We could separate this section into a new file for our people entries if we wished.

```
dn: ou=People,dc=example,dc=com
objectclass: organizationalUnit
ou: People
```

You can see that the LDIF format requires the declaration of the DN, followed by the object classes we wish to use, and the attributes. Each declaration should be separated by a blank line. The order of declaration is also important; you can't create a user in ou=People,dc=hitwise,dc=com until that organizational unit is created. The object class organizationalUnit requires that we declare the ou attribute as we have here, ou: People.

Now we are going to add a user, jsmith:

```
dn: uid=jsmith,ou=People,dc=example,dc=com
objectclass: top
objectclass: person
```

```
objectclass: posixAccount
objectclass: exampleClient
cn: Jane Smith
sn: Smith
uid: jsmith
uidNumber: 1000
gidNumber: 1000
exampleActive: TRUE
homeDirectory: /home/jsmith
userPassword: {SHA}IOq+XWSw4hZ5boNPUtYfOLcDMvw=
```

So let's look at the DN first. You can see that we declare our DN using the uid attribute. We could have used a couple variations here other than uid=jsmith: cn=Jane Smith or mail=jane. smith@example.com. Which of these you end up using on your system depends on what you think will be best for your server (keeping indexes in mind). Next, we have to declare the object class top and person. It is optional to include the posixAccount and exampleClient object classes. The top object class, a superclass, is required to provide the other object classes. The person object class provides the sn (surname) and cn (common name) attributes. The object class posixAccount will provide the attributes useful for Unix/Linux hosts such as userPassword, uid, uidNumber, gidNumber, and homeDirectory. exampleClient provides the exampleActive attributes, which we can use to activate and deactivate our users. Please note that the attribute value for Boolean attributes like exampleActive must be uppercase.

We'll now add Groups as an organizationalUnit so that we can make use of groups to manage access to our users. Again, we can create a new LDIF text file for our groups.

```
dn: ou=Groups,dc=example,dc=com
objectclass: top
objectclass: organizationalUnit
ou: Groups
```

You can see that creating the organizational unit for Groups is very similar to the way we declared the People organizational unit earlier. As required by the schema definition, we have used and declared the ou attribute to name our DN. Next, we declare the group admins that we will use to group our administrators.

```
dn: cn=admins,ou=Groups,dc=example,dc=com
objectclass: top
objectclass: groupOfNames
cn: admins
member: uid=ataylor,ou=People,dc=example,dc=com
```

We declare a group list with the groupOfNames object class, which allows us to just add members. We could have also used the posixGroup object class, which would allow us to use gidNumbers as well. We can add as many members to the group as we like by adding member: *DN* on a separate line.

Now we can look at adding our details to the LDAP database. To do so, we will use the ldapadd tool that comes with OpenLDAP.

Adding Users from LDIF Files

The LDAP tools all share a common set of options that you can provide to connect to your LDAP server. The OpenLDAP client tools can be used to connect to other LDAP servers provided by other software manufacturers. Table 16-4 lists the common options that are available to most LDAP tools.

Table 16-4. *Common LDAP Tool Options*

Option	Description
-x	Performs a simple bind.
-v	Specifies verbose output.
-W	Prompts for a password.
-f	Points to an input file, which can be a different type under a different tool context.
-D	Specifies the DN to bind as. This DN must have proper access rights to work on the entries.
-Z	Tries using TLS to make the LDAP connection. -ZZ indicates that use of TLS must be successful before continuing with the connection.
-Y	Specifies the SASL authentication mechanism to connect to your LDAP server. You must have SASL configured to use this option.
-X	Specifies the SASL authzid, or the requested authorization ID for a SASL bind.
-U	Specifies the SASL authcid, or the authentication ID for a SASL bind.
-b	Specifies the base DN. Instead of querying the whole tree, you can specify a base to start from, like ou=People,dc=example,dc=com.
-s	Indicates the scope of the search query. Can be either base, one, sub, or children.

Some of the options we have shown in Table 16-4 will not be available to all LDAP tools. The syntax of the LDAP tool commands usually looks like this:

ldaptool <options> filter entry

There are several LDAP tools available. The main ones are ldapadd, ldapmodify, ldapsearch, and ldapdelete, and as we said, they all share some or all of the common options shown previously. For the exact options available, please refer to the man pages for those tools.

Adding users to our LDAP server is very easy now that we have created our LDIF file. Let's look at the complete LDIF file. As we have mentioned, we need to add the dc entry, or the top level of our DIT, at the top of this file.

```
$ sudo cat users.ldif
dn: dc=example,dc=com
objectclass: dcObject
dc: example

dn: ou=People,dc=example,dc=com
objectclass: organizationalUnit
ou: People
```

```
dn: uid=jsmith,ou=People,dc=example,dc=com
objectclass: top
objectclass: person
objectclass: posixAccount
objectclass: exampleClient
cn: Jane Smith
sn: Smith
uid: jsmith
uidNumber: 1000
gidNumber: 1000
exampleActive: TRUE
homeDirectory: /home/jsmith
userPassword: {SHA}IOq+XWSw4hZ5boNPUtYfOLcDMvw=

dn: uid=ataylor,ou=People,dc=example,dc=com
objectclass: top
objectclass: person
objectclass: posixAccount
objectclass: exampleClient
cn: Angela Taylor
sn: Taylor
uid: ataylor
uidNumber: 1002
gidNumber: 1000
exampleActive: TRUE
homeDirectory: /home/ataylor
userPassword: {SHA}IOq+XWSw4hZ5boNPUtYfOLcDMvw=

dn: ou=meta,dc=example,dc=com
objectclass: organizationalUnit
objectclass: top
ou: meta

dn: cn=webadmin,ou=meta,dc=example,dc=com
objectClass: organizationalRole
objectclass: simpleSecurityObject
userPassword: {SHA}IOq+XWSw4hZ5boNPUtYfOLcDMvw=

dn: ou=Groups,dc=example,dc=com
objectclass: top
objectclass: organizationalUnit
ou: Groups

dn: cn=staff,ou=Groups,dc=example,dc=com
objectclass: top
objectclass: posixGroup
gidNumber: 1000
cn: staff
```

```
dn: cn=admins,ou=Groups,dc=example,dc=com
objectclass: top
objectclass: groupOfNames
cn: admins
member: uid=ataylor,ou=People,dc=example,dc=com

dn: ou=Hosts,dc=example,dc=com
objectclass: top
objectclass: organizationalUnit
ou: Hosts
```

We are now going to add our users using the file users.ldif. The ldapadd tool is very versatile and takes many options. The way we will use it is as follows:

```
$ ldapadd -xWv -D cn=admin,dc=example,dc=com -h ldap.example.com -Z -f users.ldif
```

The ldapadd command can use the SASL authentication method or the simple method. -x will make ldapadd use the simple method. -W tells ldapadd that we want to be prompted for a password. -v is to be verbose in its information. When you specify -D, you give the username you wish to bind with. In this case, we are using the cn=admin,dc=example,dc=com user, and as you may remember, this is the rootDN we added to the slapd.conf file earlier. The -h switch is the hostname, ldap.example.com. -Z tells the command to use STARTTLS, or make a TLS connection to the LDAP host, but if you have TLS already set in /etc/ldap/ldap.conf or /etc/openldap/ldap.conf, your command will fail. Finally, -f indicates the file we wish to use to add our users, users.ldif.

The options you use here are the same for all the other LDAP tools; see the man page for more details. When you issue this command, you will get something like this:

```
jsmith@ldap:/etc/ldap$ ldapadd -xWv -D cn=admin,dc=example,dc=com ➥
-h ldap.example.com -Z -f users.ldif
ldap_initialize( ldap://ldap.example.com )
Enter LDAP Password:
add objectclass:
        top
        person
        exampleClient
        posixAccount
add cn:
        Jane Smith
add sn:
        Smith
add uid:
        jsmith
add uidNumber:
        1000
add gidNumber:
        1000
add exampleActive:
        TRUE
```

```
add homeDirectory:
        /home/jsmith
add userPassword:
        {SHA}IOq+XWSw4hZ5boNPUtYfOLcDMvw=
adding new entry "uid=jsmith,ou=People,dc=example,dc=com"
modify complete
```

If successful, you will see a "Modify complete" message. If something goes wrong, you receive an error message.

Searching Your LDAP Tree

Now that we have some entries in our LDAP database, we can search it to make sure we can return useful information. Let's look at ways we can search our LDAP directory.

```
$ ldapsearch -xvW -h ldap.example.com -Z \
-D uid=ataylor,ou=People,dc=example,dc=com \
-b ou=People,dc=example,dc=com -s sub \
'(&(&(objectclass=person)(uid=jsmith))(exampleActive=TRUE))' cn
```

The arguments we use for the search are similar to the ones we use for the ldapadd command. We first specify that we are performing a simple bind with verbose output, and we wish to be prompted for a password, -xvW. -h declares the host we wish to connect to, and -Z says try to make a connection using TLS (a -ZZ would mean to confirm that the TLS connection was successful before proceeding). Angela Taylor is a user that we have put in cn=admins,ou =Groups,dc=example,dc=com; remember that we have given write access to all entries under ou=People,dc=example,dc=com through our access control list. We have just added the user Jane Smith to our LDAP directory, and we will conduct a search to look at her details.

In our ldapsearch command, you can see we include a filter to make use of indexes and to reduce our search response time. We know that all user entries have the object class person. As we explained, in our slapd.conf file all object classes are indexed, so choosing one that you know is in the entity you are looking for will speed your searches. The uid attributes are also indexed, so we also want to filter on the uid of the entry we are looking for. Our search filter looks like (&(&(objectclass=person)(uid=jsmith))(exampleActive=TRUE)), which means to filter on the object class person AND on uid=jsmith AND that the account is active, as indicated by exampleActive=TRUE. The & operator indicates that we are searching for one AND the other. We can also use the | symbol to indicate we wish to search for one OR the other.

We specify the base of the DIT tree we wish to start searching from, -b ou=People, dc=example,dc=com, and the scope of our search is -s sub, or everything under it. And finally, we are searching for Jane's common name, or cn. The results of this search will look like the following:

```
ldap_initialize( ldap://ldap.example.com )
filter: (&(&(objectclass=person)(uid=jsmith))(exampleActive=TRUE))requesting: cn
# extended LDIF
#
# LDAPv3
# base <ou=People,dc=example,dc=com> with scope subtree
```

```
# filter: (&(&(objectclass=person)(uid=jsmith))(exampleActive=TRUE))
# requesting: cn
#

# jsmith, People, example.com
dn: uid=jsmith,ou=People,dc=example,dc=com
cn: Jane Smith

# search result
search: 3
result: 0 Success

# numResponses: 2
# numEntries: 1
```

Here you can see that we have returned the DN we were looking for and the common name for that entry. Next, let's look at deleting entries.

Deleting Entries from Your LDAP Directory

The other thing you are going to want to do often is delete entries in your LDAP directory. To delete entries, use the ldapdelete command. Again, this takes the same arguments as ldapadd and ldapsearch. For deleting more than one entry, you can input a text file, or you can delete entries individually. Assume we have the following entries in a new users.ldif file, and we want to delete them:

```
uid=jbob,ou=People,dc=example,dc=com
uid=tbird,ou=People,dc=example,dc=com
```

We can now add these two entries to a file called deluser.ldif and then run the ldapdelete command with the -f argument as follows:

```
ldapdelete -xvW -D uid=ataylor,ou=People,dc=example,dc=com \
-h ldap.example.com -Z -f deluser.ldif
ldap_initialize( ldap://ldap.example.com )
deleting entry "uid=jbob,ou=People,dc=example,dc=com"
deleting entry "uid=tbird,ou=People,dc=example,dc=com"
```

As a result, these entries are no longer in our directory and have been deleted.

■**Note** OpenLDAP is case insensitive, meaning that uid=jsmith,ou=People,dc=example,dc=com is treated the same as uid=jSmith,ou=people,dc=example,dc=com. Trying to add two Jane Smiths, one with a lowercase *s* and one with an uppercase *S*, will return a duplicate error.

Password Policy Overlay

Setting the password policy overlay allows us greater control over password aging and change history. Overlays, as explained earlier, provide extra functionality for your OpenLDAP server. We want to set our password aging to 7776000 (90 days in seconds) and our password history to 3, meaning we will store the previous three passwords supplied by users so they can't keep using the same one. The password will have to have a minimum of eight characters.

Recall that we have included the policy by specifying the following in the slapd.conf file:

```
moduleload      ppolicy.la
overlay ppolicy
ppolicy_default "cn=default,ou=Policies,dc=example,dc=com"
ppolicy_use_lockout
```

We now have to define the policy. To do that, we will need to add the following LDIF to our LDAP server:

```
dn: cn=default,ou=policies,dc=example,dc=com
objectClass: top
objectClass: device
objectClass: pwdPolicy
cn: default
pwdAttribute: 2.5.4.35
pwdMaxAge: 7776000
pwdExpireWarning: 6912000
pwdInHistory: 3
pwdCheckQuality: 1
pwdMinLength: 8
pwdMaxFailure: 4
pwdLockout: TRUE
pwdLockoutDuration: 1920
pwdGraceAuthNLimit: 0
pwdFailureCountInterval: 0
pwdMustChange: TRUE
pwdAllowUserChange: TRUE
pwdSafeModify: FALSE
```

■**Caution** Be warned, there is a horrible error in the documentation for this policy. It says that you should use the attribute userPassword for pwdAttribute. This will fail, and you will be incredibly frustrated trying to find a solution to this problem. You should use the numeric ID for the objectIdentifierMatch rule instead.

We have now added the password policy to our LDAP server, and it has some basic settings like password age (90 days in seconds), and passwords in history (3). This overlay will now make all password accounts comply with the password policy.

■**Note** Full details of the meanings of the attributes can be found at `http://linux.die.net/man/5/ slapo-ppolicy` or in the `man` page.

Testing Your Access Control Lists

From time to time, you will run into permission issues because of incorrectly functioning access control lists. There is a tool you can use to test your ACLs called `slapacl`. This tool tests access to attributes and object classes by the DN you wish to grant access to. For example, if we want to make sure that the DN `cn=webadmin,ou=meta,dc=example,dc=com`, the user we use to bind our web services during authentication, has `auth` access to the `userPassword` attribute of our user Angela Taylor, we would issue the following:

```
sudo slapacl -f /etc/ldap/slapd.conf \
  -b uid=ataylor,ou=People,dc=example,dc=com \
  -D cn=webadmin,ou=meta,dc=example,dc=com \
  -v userPassword/auth
```

The `slapacl` command requires `sudo` access. You need to specify the `slapd.conf` file you wish to test against with `-f /etc/ldap/slapd.conf` on an Ubuntu host; on a Red Hat host, you would need to use the `/etc/openldap/slapd.conf` file. `-b uid=ataylor,ou=People,dc=example, dc=com` is the DN we wish to test our access on. `-D cn=webadmin,ou=meta,dc=example,dc=com` is the DN that we wish to confirm has `auth` access to the DN of `uid=ataylor,ou=People, dc=example,dc=com`. We specify the attribute and authentication level we wish to test, in this case the attribute `userPassword` against the access `auth`. As you know, we need at least `auth` access for the DN `cn=webadmin,ou=meta,dc=example,dc=com` to authenticate with `userPassword`. If we are successful, we will get the following result:

```
authcDN: "cn=webadmin,ou=meta,dc=example,dc=com"
auth access to userPassword: ALLOWED
```

This confirms that the line in our access control list is working as we expect.

```
access to attrs=userPassword,shadowLastChange,sambaNTPassword,sambaLMPassword
        by dn.exact="cn=webadmin,ou=meta,dc=example,dc=com" auth
```

We'll test to see whether we can get write access to the same attribute to confirm that our access control list doesn't have a security hole in it.

```
sudo slapacl -f /etc/ldap/slapd.conf \
  -b uid=ataylor,ou=People,dc=example,dc=com \
  -D cn=webadmin,ou=meta,dc=example,dc=com \
  -v userPassword/write
 authcDN: "cn=webadmin,ou=meta,dc=example,dc=com"
write access to uid: DENIED
```

This is as we expect: we should be denied everything but auth access and below. You can also pass in other options that allow you to test access against such things as peernames and ssf.

One of the other useful ways to figure out what is going on with your access control lists, which can be incredibly trying, is to have the following in your access control list while you are testing:

```
access to * by * search
```

You combine this with the following logging settings in your slapd.conf file, your logfile and loglevel:

```
loglevel        416
logfile         /var/log/ldap.log
```

This will show the search filter and the access control list processing as well as connection management and configuration file processing. When a request comes in, it will produce output like the following:

```
slapd[29981]: conn=0 op=2 SRCH base="ou=people,dc=example,dc=com" scope=2 deref=3 ➥
filter="(&(objectClass=*)(uid=ataylor))"
slapd[29981]: conn=0 op=2 SRCH attr=uid
slapd[29981]: => access_allowed: search access to "ou=People,dc=example,dc=com" ➥
"entry" requested
slapd[29981]: => dn: [2] ou=meta,dc=example,dc=com
slapd[29981]: => dn: [3] ou=people,dc=example,dc=com
slapd[29981]: => acl_get: [3] matched
slapd[29981]: => acl_get: [3] attr entry
slapd[29981]: => acl_mask: access to entry "ou=People,dc=example,dc=com", attr ➥
"entry" requested
slapd[29981]: => acl_mask: to all values by "cn=webadmin,ou=meta,➥
dc=example,dc=com", (=0)
slapd[29981]: <= check a_dn_pat: cn=webadmin,ou=meta,dc=example,dc=com
slapd[29981]: <= acl_mask: [1] applying read(=rscxd) (stop)
slapd[29981]: <= acl_mask: [1] mask: read(=rscxd)
slapd[29981]: => slap_access_allowed: search access granted by read(=rscxd)
slapd[29981]: => access_allowed: search access granted by read(=rscxd)
```

The first line shows the search string of the request, SRCH base="ou=people,dc=exam ple,dc=com" scope=2 deref=3 filter="(&(objectClass=*)(uid=ataylor))". The output also shows the user making the request, cn=webadmin,ou=meta,dc=example,dc=com. You can see the process of the request for access to search ou=People,dc=example,dc=com and then the final acceptance for the search, because webadmin has read access to everything under ou=People,dc=example,dc=com.

With a combination of logs, the slapacl and ldapsearch tools, and the very useful OpenLDAP mailing list, you can achieve very intricate access control lists. Let's look at the other tools you can use to manage your LDAP servers, including the ldapsearch tool we just mentioned.

Backing Up Your LDAP Directory

Text-based files are great for building or restoring your LDAP directory. Once your directory is implemented, we suggest that you set up a script that might regularly output your LDAP database into a text file and save it. In Chapter 13, we introduced you to the Bacula backup server and showed you how to use the Client Run Before Job and the Client Run After Job options when we backed up our MySQL database. You can do a similar thing with the LDAP database, as shown in Listing 16-2.

Listing 16-2. *slapcat LDIF Dump*

```
#!/bin/bash

case $1 in
 start)
    slapcat -b dc=example,dc=com -l /var/lib/ldap/backup.ldif
      if [ $? -eq 0 ] ; then
        echo "backup successful"
      else
        echo "backup failed"
        exit 1;
      fi
 ;;

 stop)
    if [ -e /var/lib/ldap/backup.ldif ] ; then
       rm -f /var/lib/ldap/backup.ldif
         if [ $? -eq 0 ] ; then
           echo "removal of file successful"
         else
           echo "failed to remove file"
           exit 1;
         fi

   fi
 ;;
esac
exit 0
```

To get a perfect backup, you would want to stop the OpenLDAP directory server before you run the command in Listing 16-2; however, this is not always possible, and hot backups are preferable over no backups at all.

You use the slapcat command to dump the LDAP database to a file on disk using the Client Run Before Job script. You then get Bacula to back it up; Bacula can delete it by running the Client Run After Job script (see Listing 16-3).

Listing 16-3. *The Job Definition for Bacula Backup Service*

```
Job {
  Name = ldap.example.com
  Client = ldap-fd
  Enabled = yes
  JobDefs = "DefaultLinux"
  Client Run Before Job = "/usr/local/bin/ldap_backup start"
  Client Run After Job = "/usr/local/bin/ldap_backup stop"
}
```

This is based on the proviso that you have your LDAP backup script installed in `/usr/local/bin` on your ldap.example.com host.

Restoring your LDAP database is then simply a matter of restoring the file on your host and running the `slapadd` command with the following parameters (OpenLDAP should be shut down for this process):

```
$ slapadd -b dc=example,dc=com -f /etc/ldap/slapd.conf -l restored.ldif.backup.file
```

Here we have restored our LDAP database to how it was when we performed the last save. Because LDAP has no write-ahead logs, you cannot replay your most recent updates to your LDAP directory server like you can in a fully featured transactional relational database, so regular backups are important. We suggest at minimum you make backups nightly.

Managing your directory server via text files can get tiresome. Luckily, we have a solution if you're one of those who prefer a web-based GUI to do all the fiddly work for you, and we'll discuss this next.

LDAP Account Manager: Web-Based GUI

Several tools are available to manage your LDAP directories. We have decided to focus on one of them in this book, LDAP Account Manager (LAM). This is a web-based GUI that can take some of the administrative pain away from updating text files. It is available in two versions: a free version and an enterprise version that requires a fee. If you discover you do not like using this tool, you might want to try some of the others that exist, such as the following:

- *Luma*: http://luma.sourceforge.net/

- *GQ*: http://sourceforge.net/projects/gqclient/

- *phpldapAdmin*: http://phpldapadmin.sourceforge.net/

We chose to show you LAM because it is designed not only to manage LDAP, but also to provision user accounts. It allows you to create users based on templates that are easy to follow. It is also flexible enough to allow you to integrate your Samba user administration if you choose to do so.

Installation and Configuration

LAM is available for download with Ubuntu from its online repositories. To install it, you issue the following:

```
$ sudo aptitude install php5-mhash ldap-account-manager
```

For Red Hat hosts using RHEL, you have to download the Fedora RPMs from the Source-Forge website (`http://lam.sourceforge.net/download/index.htm`) and then use `rpm -ivh` to install them.

On Fedora hosts, LAM should be available from the online Yum repository. The Red Hat installation puts all the LAM files under `/var/www/html/lam`. All the configuration files are installed under `/var/www/html/lam/config`.

To install LAM, you will need a version of PHP installed on your host higher or equal to 5.1. You also need to edit your `php.ini` file and set the memory limit to 64MB as follows. You will find the `php.ini` file in `/etc/php5/apache2/php.ini` on Ubuntu and in `/etc/php.ini` for Red Hat hosts.

```
memory_limit = 64M
```

LAM is fairly easy to configure. On Ubuntu, some configuration files are installed into `/etc/ldap-account-manager`. You will find an example configuration for your Apache web server and the configuration file, `/etc/ldap-account-manager/config.cfg`, containing the default username and password for your LAM installation.

```
$ sudo vi /etc/ldap-account-manager/config.cfg
# password to add/delete/rename configuration profiles
password: somepassword

# default profile, without ".conf"
default: lam
```

In the `config.cfg` file, you can see we have set our own password to `somepassword` (cleartext, so be careful with your ownership and permissions). We also need to change the following file to add our own LDAP directory details. First, we make a copy of the file `/var/lib/ldap-account-manager/config/lam.conf`. We then make the changes in bold to the `/var/lib/ldap-account-manager/config/lam.conf` file.

```
$ sudo vi /var/lib/ldap-account-manager/config/lam.conf
# LDAP Account Manager configuration

# server address (e.g. ldap://localhost:389 or ldaps://localhost:636)
ServerURL: ldaps://ldap.example.com

# list of users who are allowed to use LDAP Account Manager
Admins: cn=admin,dc=example,dc=com

# password to change these preferences via webfrontend
Passwd: somepassword
```

```
# suffix of tree view
treesuffix: dc=example,dc=com

# maximum number of rows to show in user/group/host lists
maxlistentries: 30

# default language (a line from config/language)
defaultLanguage: en_GB.utf8:UTF-8:English (Great Britain)

# Number of minutes LAM caches LDAP searches.
cachetimeout: 5

# Module settings
modules: posixAccount_minUID: 1000
modules: posixAccount_maxUID: 30000
modules: posixAccount_minMachine: 50000
modules: posixAccount_maxMachine: 60000
modules: posixGroup_minGID: 1000
modules: posixGroup_maxGID: 20000
modules: posixGroup_pwdHash: SSHA
modules: posixAccount_pwdHash: SSHA
```

In the first section of this file, we add the details for our LDAP directory including the connection details, tree information, Posix UID, GID, and machine numbers.

```
# List of active account types.
activeTypes: user,group,host

types: suffix_user: ou=People,dc=example,dc=com
types: attr_user: #uid;#givenName;#sn;#uidNumber;#gidNumber
types: modules_user: person,posixAccount,shadowAccount,exampleClient

types: suffix_group: ou=Groups,dc=example,dc=com
types: attr_group: #cn;#gidNumber;#memberUID;#description
types: modules_group: posixGroup

types: suffix_host: ou=Hosts,dc=example,dc=com
types: attr_host: #cn;#description;#uidNumber;#gidNumber
types: modules_host: account,posixAccount

# Access rights for home directories
scriptRights: 750
```

In the last section of the file, we detail the account types we wish to enable in the activeTypes section and the LDAP branches that house these. The LAM administration tool will use these details to create the user accounts for us in our LDAP server.

In the original lam.conf file, references are available that will enable you to administer Samba user account information as well. Include these where appropriate if you want to do so.

Adding the Apache Virtual Host for LAM

We are going to add an Apache virtual host to our web server to host our LAM site. In Chapter 11, we showed you how to set up an Apache virtual host. The web service can run on any host; it does not have to be on the same host as the LDAP server, but in our example, this will be the case. We have chosen to house this site on our host with the IP address 192.168.0.1 and DNS name of ldap.example.com, also known as headoffice.example.com.

■**Note** Our headoffice.example.com host may now be overloaded with secure virtual hosts (https), and we may have to choose a nonstandard port, like 8443, to run our ldap.example.com website. Alternatively, we could run it on a completely different host.

On our Ubuntu host, we will have the following configuration: the main sections of this virtual host have been provided by the LAM package and can be found in /etc/ldap-account-manager/apache.conf. We have installed it in /etc/apache2/sites-available and have added the virtual host detail. On Red Hat, we would include the file in the /etc/httpd/conf.d/ directory.

```
$ sudo vi  /etc/apache2/sites-available/ldap.example.com
<VirtualHost 192.168.0.1:443>

  ServerName ldap.example.com

  DocumentRoot /var/www/sites/lam

  SSLEngine on
  SSLCertificateFile /etc/ssl/certs/ldap.pem
  SSLCertificateKeyFile /etc/ssl/certs/ldap.pem

  LogFormat "%v %l %u %t \"%r\" %>s %b" comonvhost
  CustomLog /var/log/apache2/ldap.example.com/access.log comonvhost
  ErrorLog /var/log/apache2/ldap.example.com/error.log
  Loglevel debug

Alias /lam /usr/share/ldap-account-manager

<Directory /usr/share/ldap-account-manager>
   Options +FollowSymLinks
   AllowOverride All
   Order allow,deny
   Allow from all
   DirectoryIndex index.html
</Directory>
```

```
<Directory /var/lib/ldap-account-manager/tmp>
   Options -Indexes
</Directory>

<Directory /var/lib/ldap-account-manager/sess>
   Options -Indexes
   Order allow,deny
   Deny from all
</Directory>

<Directory /var/lib/ldap-account-manager/config>
   Options -Indexes
   Order allow,deny
   Deny from all
</Directory>

<Directory /usr/share/ldap-account-manager/lib>
   Options -Indexes
    <Files ~ .*>
      Order allow,deny
      Deny from all
    </Files>
    <Files ~ fpdf.php>
      Order allow,deny
      Allow from all
    </Files>
</Directory>

<Directory /usr/share/ldap-account-manager/lib/font>
   Options -Indexes
   Order allow,deny
   Deny from all
</Directory>
</VirtualHost>
```

The virtual host is enclosed between the <VirtualHost> </VirtualHost> tags. In the /etc/apache/httpd.conf file, the following needs to be added:

```
NamedVirtualHost 192.168.0.10:80
```

On Red Hat hosts, this would be placed in the /etc/httpd/conf.d/httpd.conf file. Next, we start the Apache web server and point our browser at http://ldap.example.com. We are now presented with the login page for the LAM configuration tool, as shown in Figure 16-3.

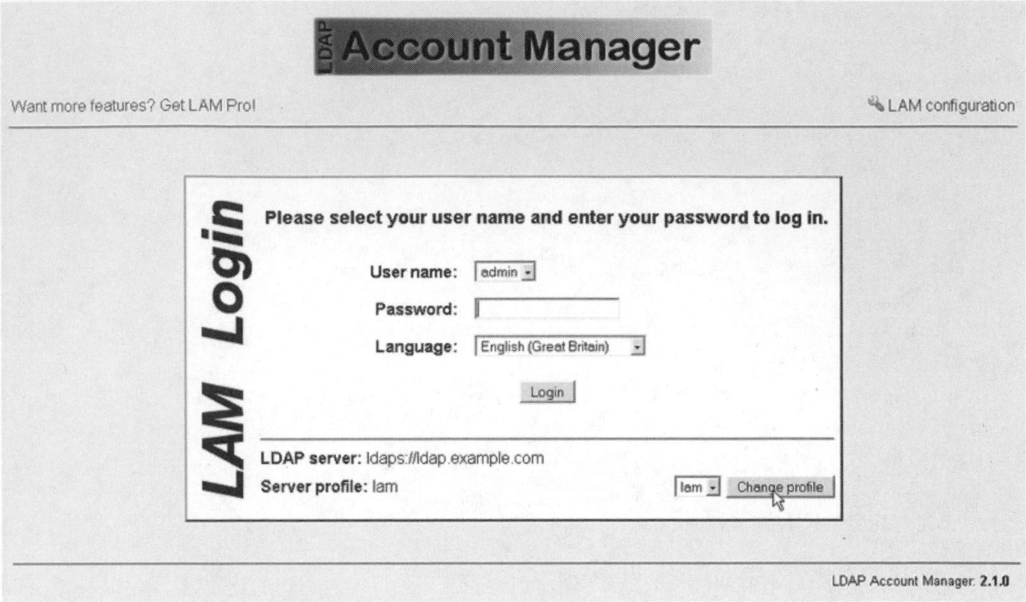

Figure 16-3. *LAM login page*

In the top right notice the LAM configuration link. This is used to perform general maintenance on the LAM configuration tool. On the login page, you will be asked for the password you have added to /etc/ldap-account-manager/config.cfg. Here you can change the general login settings as well as the password for your manager.

The admin user you can see in Figure 16-3 refers to the rootDN we specified in the /var/ lib/ldap-account-manager/config/lam.conf. When we enter the password for our rootDN, we are presented with the users we have already configured, as shown in Figure 16-4.

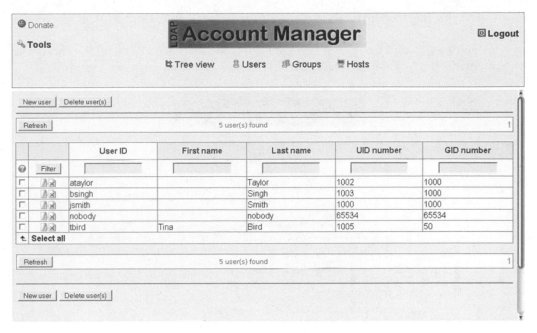

Figure 16-4. *Front page of the LAM web GUI*

We are now going to create a new user using the standard profile. Profiles serve as templates for creating users. We start by clicking the New User button to bring up the page shown in Figure 16-5.

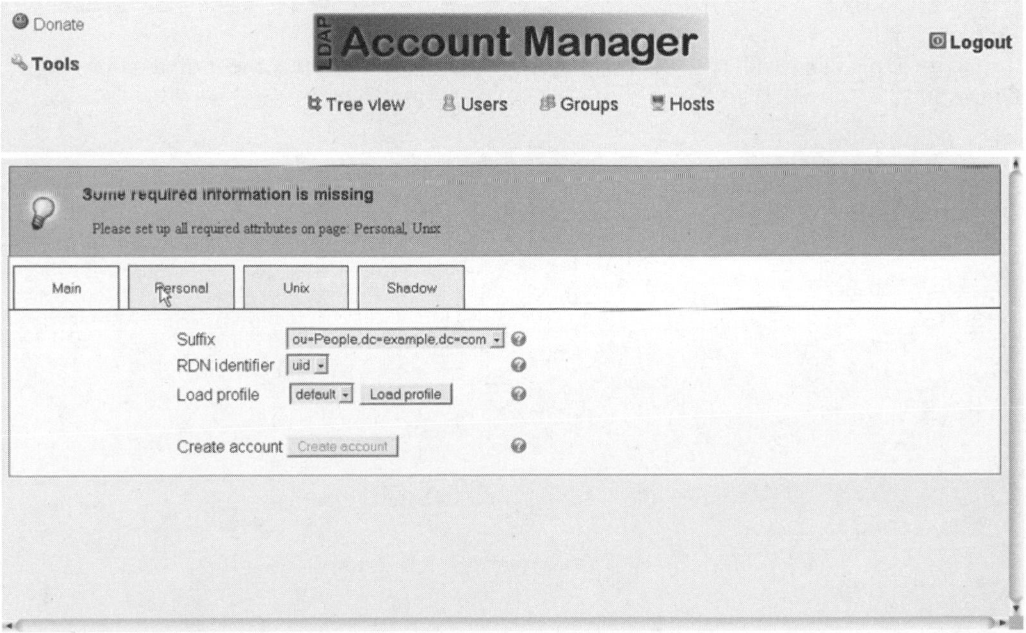

Figure 16-5. *Creating a new user*

You can see that the suffix is set to ou=People,dc=example,dc=com and the RDN identifier to uid.

We now need to click the Personal tab and fill out the details required there. The only details we will enter in the Personal tab are first name, last name, and description (see Figure 16-6).

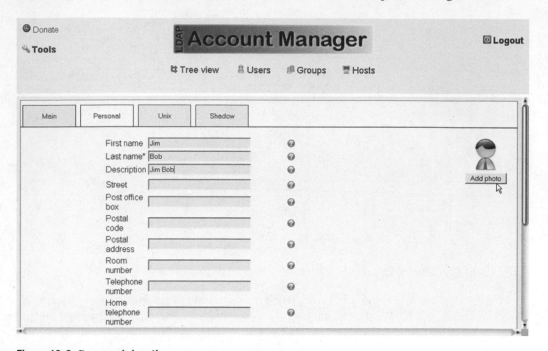

Figure 16-6. *Personal details*

In the Unix tab, we fill in the details required to add a Unix/Linux account, as shown in Figure 16-7.

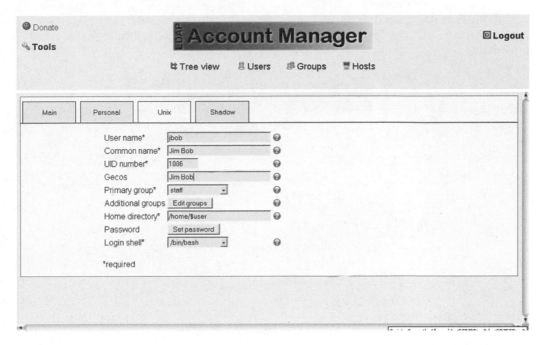

Figure 16-7. *Unix/Linux details*

In the Shadow tab, we will leave the defaults as is. You can see these defaults in Figure 16-8.

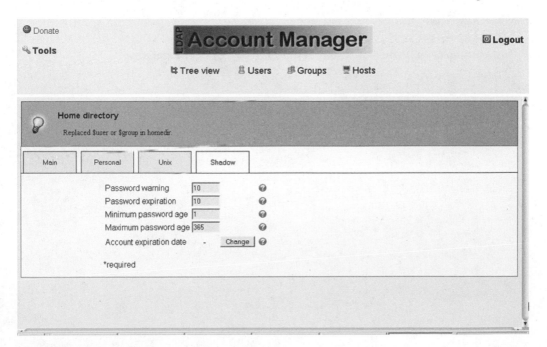

Figure 16-8. *Shadow details*

To finish creating our user, we go back to the Main tab and click the Create Account button. We then see a confirmation screen like the one in Figure 16-9 indicating a successful operation.

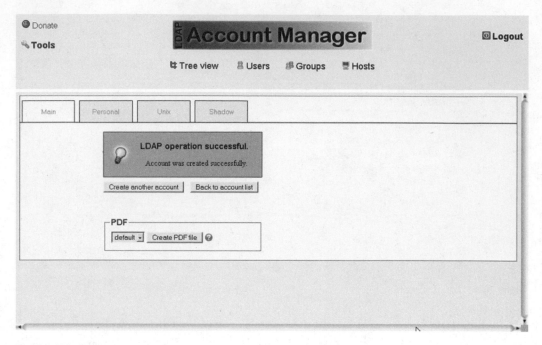

Figure 16-9. *New user created*

As you can see in Figure 16-10, our new user, jbob, has been created.

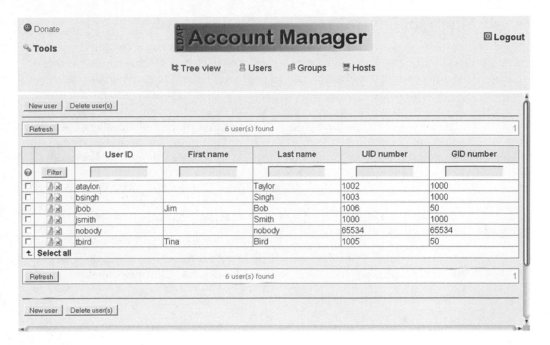

Figure 16-10. *LDAP user created*

You can use LAM to add and remove group and host entries in your LDAP directory, which we will leave you to explore further on your own. Remember, LAM is not the only LDAP management tool. If you do not like this LDAP management client for managing your LDAP service, we suggest you try one of the other clients we mentioned earlier.

Integration with Other Services

The main aim of deploying an LDAP server is to be able to integrate different services that require authentication with a single authentication service. We wish to use the same usernames and passwords across as many of our services as possible. This provides us with the ability to better manage user administration and allows us to set common password management policies across all our services, which provides greater security.

Our first step will be to centralize our Linux authentication so that all our Linux desktops and servers share the same authentication credentials. Next, we will show how to add LDAP authentication to web services. Lastly, we will show how a web-based application can use LDAP for its authentication services as well.

Single Sign-On: Centralized Linux Authentication

We are now going to show you how to centralize your user accounts on your Linux hosts. Having several Linux hosts with several user accounts on each can become cumbersome to manage. Passwords can get out of sync, and you might not remove users when they leave your company from all your hosts, creating potential security risks. To simplify this kind of user management, you could centralize your authentication service by pointing your Linux hosts to your LDAP server. To show you how to do that, we will first go through installing the necessary software and then examine the files used in the configuration. The good thing is that you should be able to use the authentication tools provided by your distribution to configure the necessary files that make single sign-on work.

On Ubuntu, you need these packages installed:

```
$ sudo aptitude install libpam-ldap libnss-ldap nss-updatedb libnss-db ➥
ldap-auth-config libpam-cracklib
```

When you install `ldap-auth-config`, you will be asked a series of questions to set up your LDAP authentication service on your client. You can also use the following command:

```
$ sudo dpkg-reconfigure ldap-auth-config
```

The `ldap-auth-config` tool will configure your settings so that you can then use LDAP to authenticate your host.

We are allowing `debconf` (Debian configuration manager) to control the settings for the LDAP server in the future, as you can see in Figure 16-11.

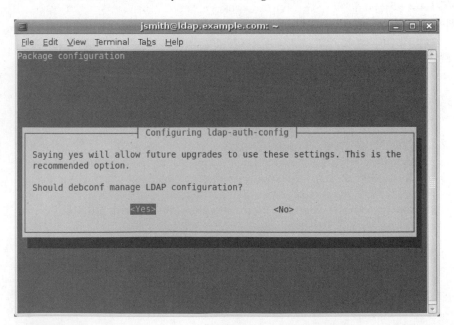

Figure 16-11. *Allowing debconf to manage LDAP configuration*

We now set the URI for our LDAP host, as shown in Figure 16-12.

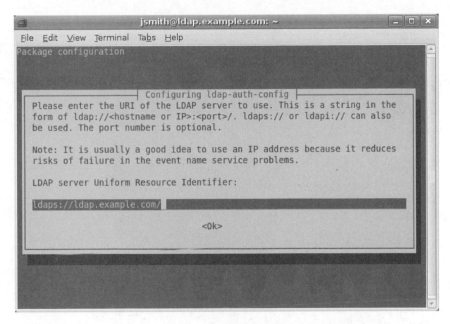

Figure 16-12. *Setting the URI for our LDAP host*

Figure 16-13 shows the base from which all searches will begin on the LDAP service.

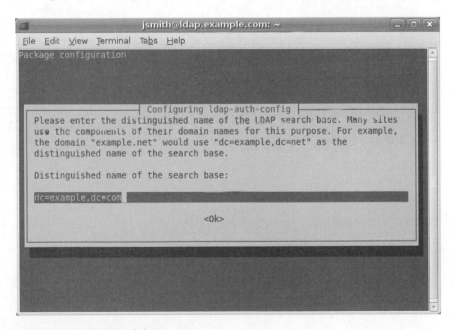

Figure 16-13. *The search base*

In the next screen, we select version 3 for the LDAP version to use in this case, as version 2 is deprecated (see Figure 16-14).

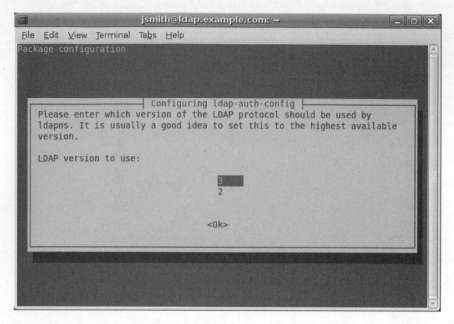

Figure 16-14. *Choosing the LDAP version*

You can allow your host to change passwords on your LDAP server, if that is your wish (see Figure 16-15). There is a security concern here in that a password file containing the root password for your LDAP server is on the client. This is something that we would not normally allow, but will do so here so you can see the rest of the tool.

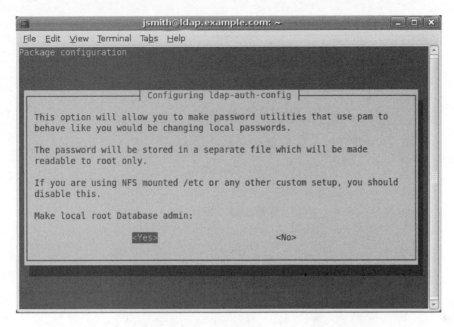

Figure 16-15. *Allowing passwords to be changed*

In the next screen, which you can see in Figure 16-16, we are asked whether we are required to authenticate with the LDAP service before we can authenticate our individual clients (authenticating with a separate common DN across all clients). We will choose No as we don't require authentication in this example.

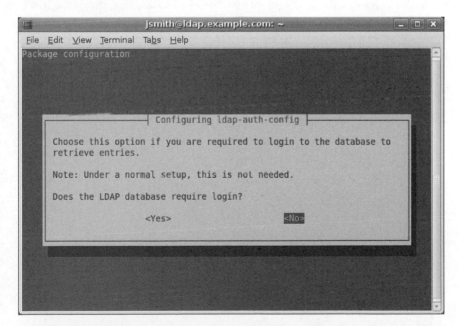

Figure 16-16. *Specifying whether we need to bind to the LDAP server before we authenticate*

In the next screen, we are asked to specify a user who has the ability to change passwords on our LDAP directory service (see Figure 16-17). This relates to the selection we made previously and is the also part of the security concern we spoke of.

Figure 16-17. *The user for changing passwords*

Next, we are required to provide the password for our root account, as shown in Figure 16-18. As you can see, the screen shows a message indicating the file will only be read by the local root account, but this is still a security concern if this host is compromised.

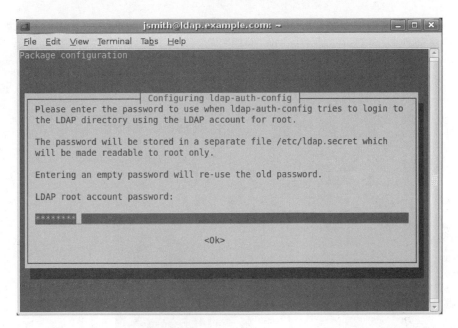

Figure 16-18. *The password for the root account*

The screen in Figure 16-19 shows the various crypt choices, or encryption mechanisms, available for our passwords and contains information that is used in the following screen, shown in Figure 16-20.

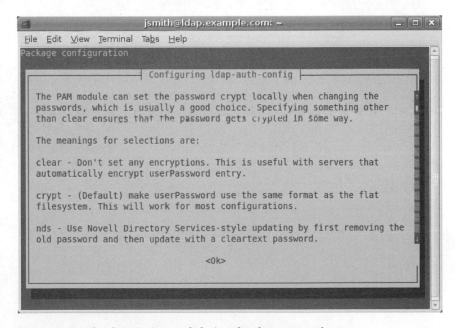

Figure 16-19. *The description and choices for the password crypt*

■Tip You can get a better understanding of encryption on Linux/Unix here: `http://en.wikipedia.org/`
`wiki/Crypt_(Unix)`.

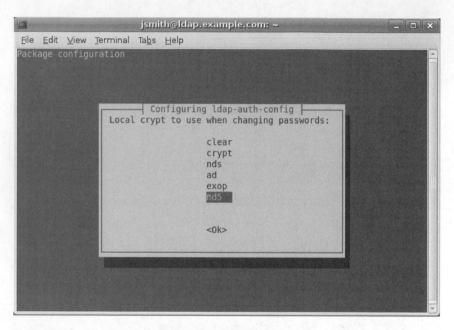

Figure 16-20. *We have chosen the MD5 crypt.*

The MD5 (`md5`) crypt is the most common crypt used in Linux hosts. Other choices here
include the AD server (`ad`) and Novell's eDirectory Server (`nds`) if you have such infrastructure.

On Red Hat, we need to install the following packages:

```
$ sudo yum install nss_ldap system-config-authentication
```

We will use the `system-config-authentication` tool to set up authenticating with our LDAP
service. On the desktop, we can select System ➤ Administration ➤ Authentication or run the
following command from the command line:

```
$ sudo system-config-authentication
```

In the dialog that appears, shown in Figure 16-21, we use the User Information tab to
specify information LDAP provides about the users for our host. We can allow just the user
information to come from LDAP but the authentication to come from some other service.
Here we have enabled LDAP support by clicking the appropriate check box.

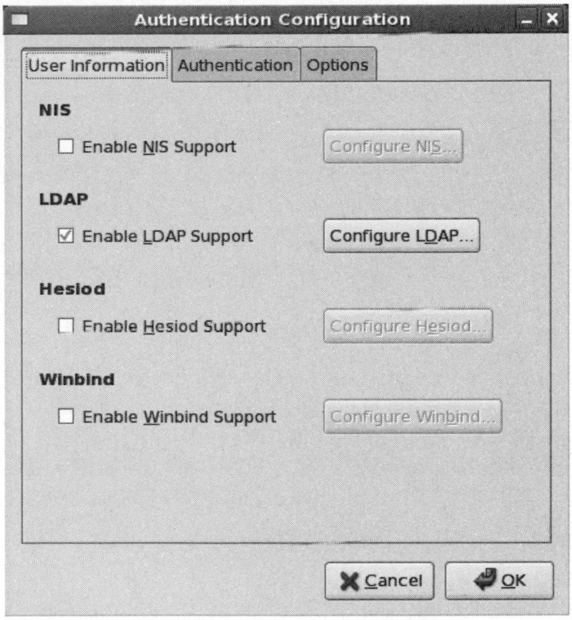

Figure 16-21. *Authentication Configuration dialog—User Information tab*

Next, we click the Configure LDAP button to bring up the LDAP Settings dialog shown in Figure 16-22.

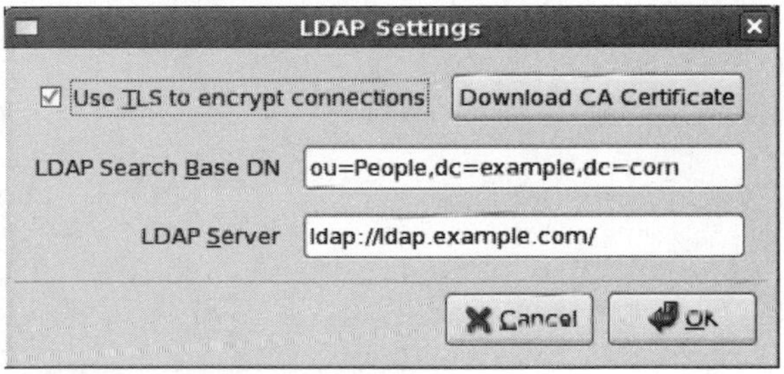

Figure 16-22. *LDAP configuration*

Here we have defined the details of our LDAP service. This should be very familiar to you now. We have indicated that we wish to use TLS to encrypt connections, and because of this, we are next asked for the URL of our CA certificate (see Figure 16-23).

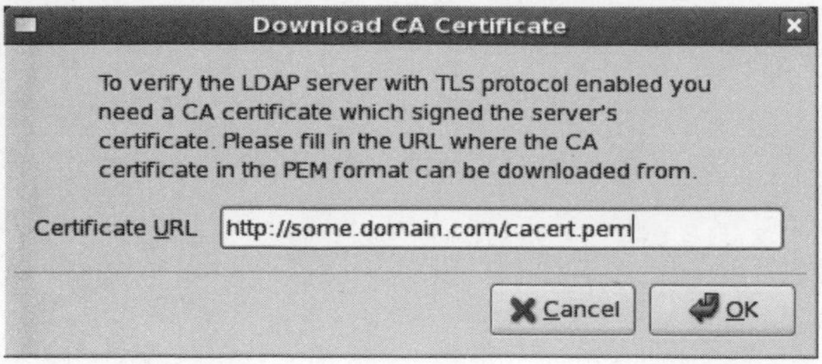

Figure 16-23. *URL where the CA certificate can be downloaded*

You may or may not have the CA certificate on a web host somewhere from which you can quickly download it and have the tool install it for you. If the CA you are using is already on your local file system, you can edit the `/etc/ldap.conf` file manually to tell PAM where to find it:

```
tls_cacertfile /etc/pki/tls/certs/ca-bundle.cert
```

It should be the same file you have defined in the `/etc/ldap/ldap.conf` or `/etc/openldap/ldap.conf` files, depending on your distribution.

In the Authentication tab, shown in Figure 16-24, we set LDAP as our authentication service. This is the same process as we used when specifying our user information, and the details are already filled out.

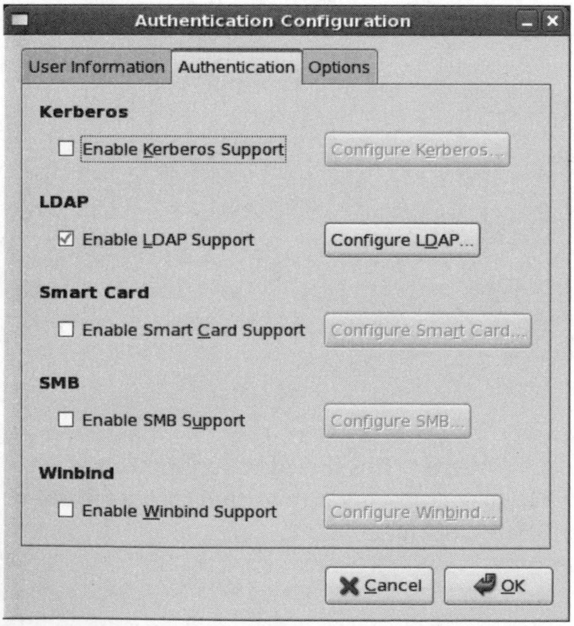

Figure 16-24. *Authentication Configuration dialog—Authentication tab*

On the Options tab, shown in Figure 16-25, we set the options for our LDAP service. As we did with our Ubuntu host, we choose MD5 to crypt our password, we specify that local authorization is sufficient for local users (allowing local users to authentication without LDAP support), and we specify to create the user's home directories when a user first logs in.

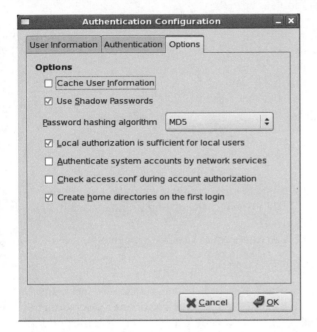

Figure 16-25. *Authentication Configuration dialog—Options tab*

How PAM Works

As explained in Chapter 4, Linux can use Pluggable Authentication Modules (PAM) to authenticate services against your LDAP service. PAM provides authentication, authorization, and password-changing abilities for hosts against LDAP servers. PAM is configured via the files located in the /etc/pam.d directory. As described in Chapter 4, the main PAM file on your Red Hat host is the /etc/pam.d/system-auth file. Listing 16-4 shows an example of the settings required to establish LDAP authentication on your host.

Listing 16-4. *PAM Settings for* system-auth *on Red Hat*

```
auth        required        pam_env.so
auth        sufficient      pam_unix.so nullok try_first_pass
auth        requisite       pam_succeed_if.so uid >= 500 quiet
auth        sufficient      pam_ldap.so use_first_pass
auth        required        pam_deny.so

account     required        pam_unix.so broken_shadow
account     sufficient      pam_localuser.so
account     sufficient      pam_succeed_if.so uid < 500 quiet
account     [default=bad success=ok user_unknown=ignore]  pam_ldap.so
account     required        pam_permit.so
```

```
password    requisite      pam_cracklib.so try_first_pass retry=3
password    sufficient     pam_unix.so md5 shadow nullok try_first_pass use_authtok
password    sufficient     pam_ldap.so use_authtok
password    required       pam_deny.so

session     optional       pam_keyinit.so revoke
session     required       pam_limits.so
session     optional       pam_mkhomedir.so
session     [success=1 ➥
            default=ignore] pam_succeed_if.so service in crond quiet ➥
use_uid
session     required       pam_unix.so
session     optional       pam_ldap.so
```

This file is generated for you, and you should not have to alter it yourself unless there is a good reason. You can see from Listing 16-4 that the file is made up of four independent management groups: auth, account, password, and session.

Take a look at the following line, which is an example of the auth management group:

```
auth        sufficient     pam_ldap.so use_first_pass
```

This group authenticates the user usually by some password challenge-response mechanism. The sufficient control value says that if this module is successful, consider the user authenticated. pam_ldap.so is the PAM shared object to be used. Lastly, use_first_pass is the optional syntax that says instead of asking for your password again, use the first one provided by one of the higher modules in the stack.

On Ubuntu hosts, the corresponding files are common-auth, common-password, common-session, and common-account in the /etc/pam.d directory.

■**Note** You can read more about PAM in the *System Administrator's Guide* here: http://www.kernel.org/pub/linux/libs/pam/Linux-PAM-html/Linux-PAM_SAG.html.

The other file central to PAM authenticating against an LDAP service is /etc/nsswitch.conf. This file requires the passwd, group, and shadow keywords to have these values:

```
passwd: files ldap
group: files ldap
shadow: files ldap
```

These tell PAM what authentication databases to use and the order in which to use them. So when we are looking for information we would normally find in /etc/passwd, we would first use the files on the host and then use LDAP. The same goes for group and shadow. The PAM and nsswitch.conf files should be configured for you by the authentication configuration tools provided by your distribution.

The next major file we need to look at is /etc/ldap.conf. You need to set the details in your /etc/ldap.conf file, which is the file the PAM LDAP module will refer to on your host. Your Linux host can use many different types of authentication service types—LDAP, NIS, and even Active Directory. The /etc/ldap.conf file defines the settings for your LDAP service such as those for attribute mapping.

■**Note** Mapping of attributes is done when the authentication service requires a certain attribute that is not normally provided with OpenLDAP, say, an attribute required by a NIS server. Take a look here at how to integrate Linux with Active Directory for an example of what we are describing: http://www.linux.com/articles/40983.

Your /etc/ldap.conf file will normally contain many possible settings you can use to authenticate your host. Listing 16-5 shows the basic settings used to achieve authentication for our LDAP service.

Listing 16-5. */etc/ldap.conf*

```
base dc=example,dc=com
uri ldap://ldap.example.com/

scope sub
timelimit 120
bind_timelimit 120
idle_timelimit 3600

pam_filter exampleActive=TRUE

tls_cacertfile /etc/pki/tls/certs/ca-bundle.crt
ssl start_tls
tls_cacertdir /etc/pki/tls/certs
pam_password md5
```

Again, you can see that we need to set the base of our LDAP DIT, which is ou=People, dc=example,dc=com. uri ldap is our LDAP host. The scope, bind timelimit, and idle timelimit settings are all defaults, but these could be adjusted to suit your environment. The pam filter can be a logical AND or OR search filter like the following: (&(uid=<username>) (exampleActive=TRUE)). This search filter will speed up directory searches by searching over the indexed exampleActive attribute and provides simple protection from unauthorized access by inactive user accounts. Next, we set the SSL details. tls cacertfile and tls cacertdir point to directories on a Red Hat host. On Ubuntu, they would be in the /etc/ssl/certs directory.

Now to test whether you can access your user accounts on your LDAP authenticated host, you can use either the id tool or the getent passwd tool.

The id tool prints the user's identity and will query the existing user databases or files for the details. Pick a user that doesn't have a local account on your host and do the following:

```
$ id bsingh
uid=1003(bsingh) gid=1000(staff) groups=1000(staff)
```

The other way is to use getent passwd, which will get entries from the administrative database like so:

```
$ getent passwd
<snip>
openldap:x:117:128:OpenLDAP Server Account,,,:/var/lib/ldap:/bin/false
bacula:x:118:129:Bacula:/var/lib/bacula:/bin/false
nobody :x!:65534:65534:nobody:/dev/null:
jsmith :*:1000:1000:Jane Smith:/home/jsmith:
bsingh:*:1003:1000:Bevan Singh:/home/bsingh:
ataylor:*:1002:1000:Angela Taylor:/home/ataylor:
jbob:*:1004:1000:Jim Bob:/home/jbob:
```

Here you can see an abbreviated list of the results returned. The accounts openldap and bacula are local user accounts. The accounts from nobody to jbob are provided by our LDAP server.

The next thing to do is to sign into the host using one of the accounts. A simple way to test this is to use SSH:

```
# ssh jbob@localhost
jbob@localhost's password:
Linux ldap.example.com 2.6.24-23-server #1 SMP Mon Jan 26 00:55:21 UTC 2009 i686

The programs included with the Ubuntu system are free software;
the exact distribution terms for each program are described in the
individual files in /usr/share/doc/*/copyright.

Ubuntu comes with ABSOLUTELY NO WARRANTY, to the extent permitted by
applicable law.

To access official Ubuntu documentation, please visit:
http://help.ubuntu.com/
Last login: Fri May  1 01:05:46 2009 from localhost.localdomain
$
```

In this example, user jbob has used SSH to log in to localhost, even though this user does not have an account on that host. We can now use jbob or any other valid user account in our LDAP server to sign in to our LDAP-aware hosts.

LDAP and Apache Authentication

Let's now look at how we get our web server to use our LDAP server to authenticate clients. When clients try to access the `https://ldap.example.com` website, they will be required to enter their LDAP username and password before they gain access. We will do two things to our web server to achieve this: make all our communications with our web server secure by enabling SSL on our web host, and add the LDAP details to the ldap.example.com virtual host.

■Note Chapter 11 discussed Apache virtual hosts.

We will assume this is being run from the ldap.example.com host and that there is no other Apache service running on it. First, on our Ubuntu host, we add the following to our `/etc/apache2/httpd.conf` file:

```
LDAPTrustedGlobalCert CA_BASE64 /etc/ssl/certs/ldap.pem
LDAPTrustedMode TLS
LDAPVerifyServerCert Off

NamedVirtualHost 192.168.0.1:80
NamedVirtualHost 192.168.0.1:443
```

■Note Again, you can add these directives to the `/etc/httpd/conf.d/httpd.conf` file (which you will need to create) on Red Hat hosts, or put this at the top of the virtual host file.

Next, let's examine the changes we will make to our ldap.example.com virtual host file:

```
$ sudo vi  /etc/apache2/sites-available/ldap.example.com

<VirtualHost 192.168.0.1:443>

  ServerName ldap.example.com

  DocumentRoot /var/www/sites/lam

  SSLEngine on
  SSLCertificateFile /etc/ssl/certs/ldap.pem
  SSLCertificateKeyFile /etc/ssl/certs/ldap.pem
```

```
    LogFormat "%v %l %u %t \"%r\" %>s %b" comonvhost
    CustomLog /var/log/apache2/vh_access.log comonvhost
    ErrorLog /var/log/apache2/vh_error.log
    Loglevel debug

Alias /lam /usr/share/ldap-account-manager

<Directory /usr/share/ldap-account-manager>
    Options +FollowSymLinks
    AllowOverride All
    Order allow,deny
    Allow from all
    AuthType Basic
    AuthName "LDAP example.com"
    AuthBasicProvider ldap
    AuthzLDAPAuthoritative on
    AuthLDAPURL ldap://ldap.example.com/ou=people,dc=example,dc=com?uid?sub
    AuthLDAPBindDN cn=webadmin,ou=meta,dc=example,dc=com
    AuthLDAPBindPassword Zf3If7Ay
    Require valid-user
    Require ldap-group cn=admins,ou=Groups,dc=example,dc=com
    DirectoryIndex index.html
</Directory>
...
<snip>
...
</VirtualHost>
```

■Note On Red Hat hosts, this file can be found in /etc/httpd/conf.d/vhost.conf, depending on how you manage your virtual hosts on Red Hat.

We have added the following to allow LDAP authentication with our web server:

```
LDAPTrustedGlobalCert CA_BASE64 /etc/ssl/certs/ldap.pem
LDAPTrustedMode TLS
LDAPVerifyServerCert Off
```

Here we have set the certificate file and the mode, and declined to verify the server certificate. LDAPTrustedMode TLS will make all LDAP connections use the TLS security transport. These directives must remain outside the <VirtualHost> tags. Inside the <VirtualHost> tags, we require the following:

```
AuthType Basic
AuthName "LDAP example.com"
AuthBasicProvider ldap
AuthzLDAPAuthoritative on
```

```
AuthLDAPURL ldap://ldap.example.com/ou=people,dc=example,dc=com?uid?sub
AuthLDAPBindDN cn=webadmin,ou=meta,dc=example,dc=com
AuthLDAPBindPassword Zf3If7Ay
Require valid-user
Require ldap-group cn=admins,ou=Groups,dc=example,dc=com
```

We have set `AuthType` to `Basic` and the `AuthName` to `LDAP example.com`. `AuthType` defines the method of authentication, and you have a choice between `Basic` and `Digest`. LDAP authentication requires `Basic`. `AuthName` is the name in the authentication window that pops up.

`AuthBasicProvider ldap` defines the server we are going to use, in this case the LDAP server, to provide our authentication mechanism. We indicate that we want the LDAP server to be the authoritative service to accept or decline access by specifying `AuthzLDAPAuthoritative on`. Next is the LDAP URL we are going to use for our authentication service, `AuthLDAPURL ldap://ldap.example.com/ou=people,dc=example,dc=com?uid?sub`. It specifies the base of our searches, `ou=People,dc=example,dc=com`, the attribute we are interested in, `uid`, and the scope of our searches, `sub`. Here you can now see where we are using the `cn=webadmin,ou=meta,dc=example,dc=com` meta account, which will bind to our LDAP server with the password also provided.

Finally, we specify that we require a `valid-user`, and the authenticating user must also belong to the LDAP group `cn=admin,ou=Groups,dc=example,dc=com`.

Note To find out more on LDAP and Apache authentication, read the following: `http://httpd.apache.org/docs/2.2/mod/mod_ldap.html`.

Before we proceed, we will need to make sure that the modules are added to our web host, and on Ubuntu we would do the following:

```
$ sudo a2enmod authnz_ldap
$ sudo a2enmod ssl
```

For Red Hat, we need to make sure the following lines in the /etc/http/conf/httpd.conf are present and that the package mod_ssl is installed:

```
LoadModule auth_basic_module modules/mod_auth_basic.so
LoadModule ldap_module modules/mod_ldap.so
LoadModule ssl_module modules/mod_ssl.so
LoadModule authnz_ldap_module modules/mod_authnz_ldap.so
```

We can start the web service on Ubuntu by issuing the following command:

```
$ sudo /usr/sbin/invoke-rc.d apache2 restart
```

And for a Red Hat host:

```
$ sudo /sbin/service httpd restart
```

We use our web browser now to connect to the LAM web GUI at the following address: `https://ldap.example.com/lam`.

In Figure 16-26, you can see the authentication challenge provided by Apache. We have entered the uid of ataylor, whom we know is a member of the cn=admins,ou=Groups,dc=example, dc=com group, which is required by our Apache configuration.

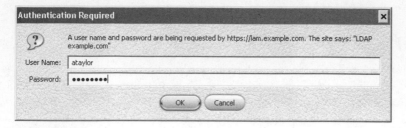

Figure 16-26. *The Apache request for username and password*

The following should appear in the Apache logs:

```
[Sun Apr 05 16:31:23 2009] [info] Initial (No.1) HTTPS request received for ➡
child 3 (server ldap.example.com:443)
[Sun Apr 05 16:31:23 2009] [debug] mod_authnz_ldap.c(377): [client 192.168.0.2] ➡
[1807] auth_ldap authenticate: using URL ➡
ldap://ldap.example.com/ou=people,dc=example,dc=com?uid?sub, ➡
referer: https://ldap.example.com/lam/templates/login.php
[Sun Apr 05 16:31:23 2009] [debug] mod_authnz_ldap.c(474): [client 192.168.0.2] ➡
[1807] auth_ldap authenticate: accepting ataylor, referer: ➡
https://ldap.example.com/lam/templates/login.php
[Sun Apr 05 16:31:23 2009] [debug] mod_authnz_ldap.c(715): [client 192.168.0.2] ➡
[1807] auth_ldap authorise: require group: testing for group membership in ➡
"cn=admins,ou=Groups,dc=example,dc=com", referer: ➡
https://ldap.example.com/lam/templates/login.php
[Sun Apr 05 16:31:23 2009] [debug] mod_authnz_ldap.c(721): [client 192.168.0.2] ➡
[1807] auth_ldap authorise: require group: testing for member: uid=ataylor, ➡
ou=People,dc=example,dc=com (cn=admins,ou=Groups,dc=example,dc=com), referer: ➡
https://ldap.example.com/lam/templates/login.php
[Sun Apr 05 16:31:23 2009] [debug] mod_authnz_ldap.c(730): [client 192.168.0.2] ➡
[1807] auth_ldap authorise: require group: authorisation successful (attribute ➡
member) [Comparison true (cached)][Compare True], referer: ➡
https://ldap.example.com/lam/templates/login.php
```

This shows that the LDAP server is authenticating our request using the username ataylor and testing that this user is a member of the cn=admin,ou=Groups,dc=example, dc=com group. This level of detail is provided by the debug logging option in the virtual host LogLevel directive.

LDAP Integration with KnowledgeTree DMS

As we mentioned at the start of the chapter, several applications now use LDAP to provide authentication services. One of these is the DMS application we introduced to you in Chapter 12. We will quickly show you how you can set your LDAP details in such an application.

We will have to make sure our DMS host can talk to our LDAP server. To test this, from the command line, we run the following:

```
ldapsearch -xvW -D cn=webadmin,ou=meta,dc=example,dc=com -Z ➡
-h ldap.example.com -b ou=People,dc=example,dc=com uid
```

If you try this for your DMS host and you get a response, your host can talk to the LDAP server. If not, you may need to correct some problems. First, make sure that the /etc/ldap/ ldap.conf (Ubuntu) or /etc/openldap/ldap.conf (Red Hat) file has the correct information. These files are the local configuration files for the LDAP clients. The following, based on our example, shows the details you will need:

```
URI ldap://ldap.example.com
BASE dc=example,dc=com
TLS_REQCERT allow
```

You need to make sure that the ldap.conf file is copied to *web-root*/ *knowledgetree-installation*/common/etc/openldap, where *web-root* is the location you have installed your KnowledgeTree DMS. In our case, it is installed in /data/web/DMS/ common/etc/openldap.

Assume that we have logged in and have navigated to the DMS Administration tab. We will need to be a DMS administrator to do this. We will now try to add a new authentication source (see Figure 16-27).

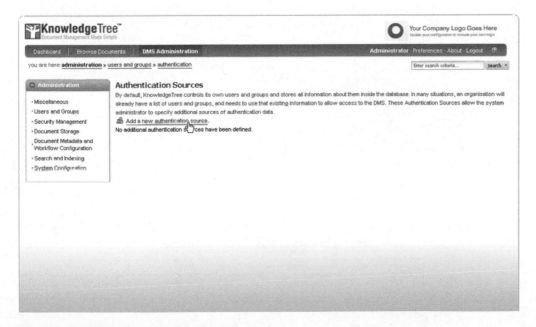

Figure 16-27. *Adding a new authentication source*

This brings up the screen shown in Figure 16-28, where we declare the type of authentication source we wish to choose.

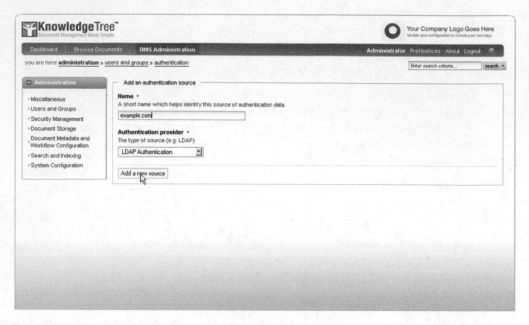

Figure 16-28. *Choosing LDAP authentication*

The Name setting is something with which to identify the authentication service, and we also specify the authentication provider here. We click Add a new source to go to the next screen, shown in Figure 16-29.

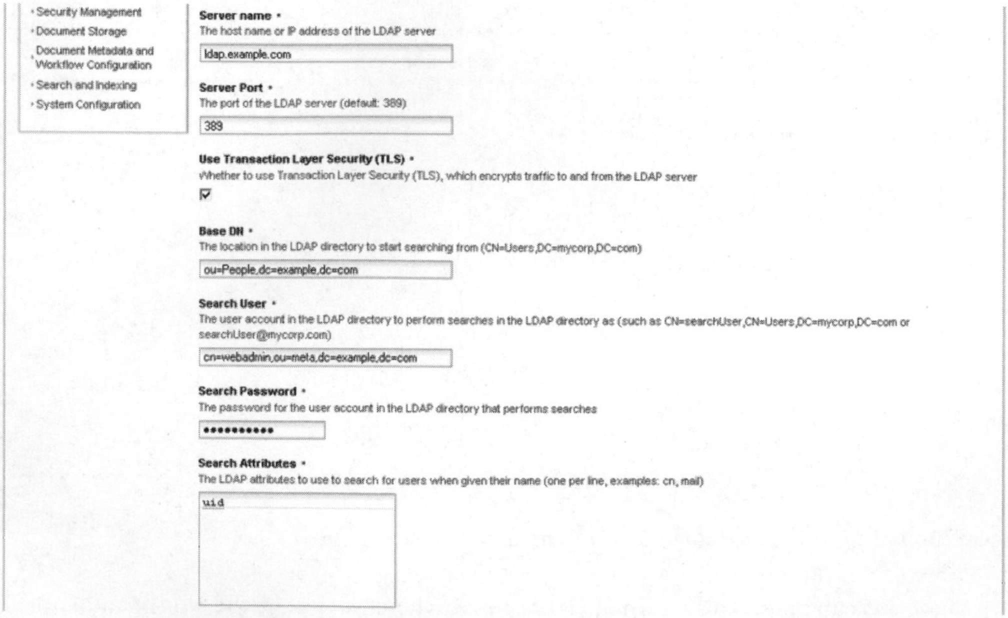

Figure 16-29. *LDAP details*

We define the server name (ldap.example.com) and server port (389), and select TLS encryption. The Base DN setting is ou=People,dc=example,dc=com. We have a user that we use to authentication our web services, and we specify that here also, cn=webadmin,ou=meta, dc=example,dc=com, as well as the password. We also specify the search attribute, uid, as we know this is indexed and the quickest way to find our users. We filter on the object class person (not shown in Figure 16-29), as we know that is a common object class for our users. We save these details and then are presented with the summary shown in Figure 16-30.

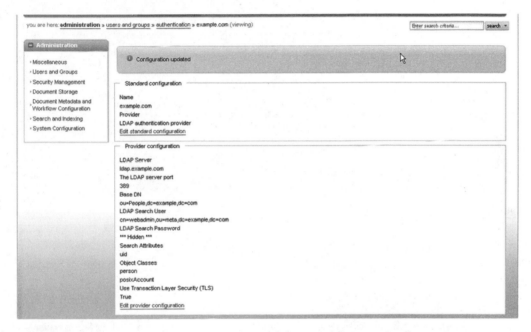

Figure 16-30. *Summary of our authentication service*

Now we can go to our User Management screen and click the Add from source button in the Add a user from an authentication source section, as shown in Figure 16-31.

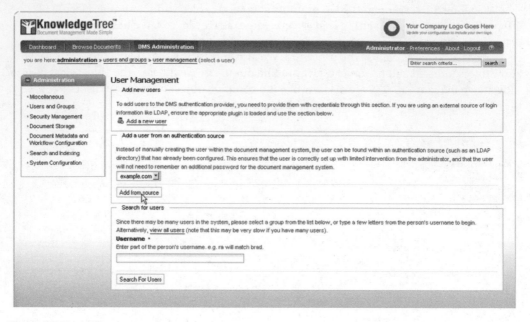

Figure 16-31. *Adding a user from source*

Next, we search for a user in our LDAP directory server or do a mass import. We will search for the user jbob, as shown in Figure 16-32.

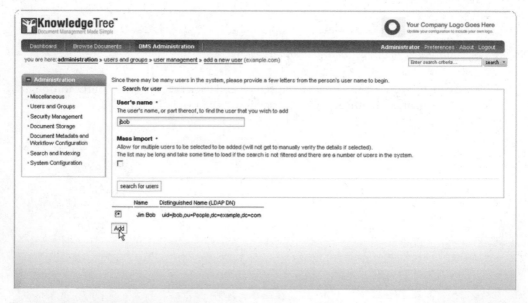

Figure 16-32. *Adding the user Jim Bob*

Here we have searched for our user, and our user has been returned. All we have to do now is add Jim Bob and work with him like we would a normal user.

■**Tip** After you have completed all your setup and testing, you should remember to change the `Loglevel` setting in `slapd.conf` to `0` and restart your `slapd` service for production use.

Summary

In this chapter, we discussed what a directory server is and how the entries are organized in the Directory Information Tree. We showed you how to configure and install an OpenLDAP directory server and populate it with user accounts and management accounts. We discussed schemas, indexes, and access control lists. We showed you how to use the various client tools provided by OpenLDAP to query and manage the LDAP server. You can now set up a web GUI to manage your LDAP directory and integrate LDAP into your network and existing applications.

You should now be able to do the following:

- Install and configure OpenLDAP on Ubuntu and Red Hat hosts.

- Understand and configure access control lists.

- Query and manage your LDAP directory.

- Install and configure the LAM web GUI.

- Set up single sign-on for Linux to LDAP.

- Configure Apache web server to use LDAP authentication to authenticate client access.

- Integrate OpenLDAP with KnowledgeTree DMS.

Directory services, as we have said, can play a central part in your network, and there are many things about this topic we have not even touched on in this chapter. We recommend that you purchase a book dedicated to the subject, read the online documentation at `http://www.openldap.org`, and use the mailing lists to help you further your knowledge in this area.

In the next chapter, you will read about performance monitoring and optimization.

## CHAPTER 17

Performance Monitoring and Optimization

By Peter Lieverdink

Now that your host is providing you services, it is important that it continue to do so. As your business grows, so will the workload on your servers. In this chapter, we will show you how to monitor resources such as disk space and processor and RAM usage. This will help you identify performance bottlenecks and make better use of the resources you have.

A small amount of tuning can alleviate the need to purchase additional hardware, so monitoring performance can help you save money as well as time.

Basic Health Checks

In this section, we look at some basic tools that help you determine the status of your hosts.

CPU Usage

When applications are running slow, the first thing you should check is whether the system is in fact busy doing anything. The quickest way to find out is via the uptime command, as shown in Listing 17-1.

Listing 17-1. *The uptime Command*

```
$ uptime
12:51:04 up 116 days,  7:09,  3 users,  load average: 0.01, 0.07, 0.02
```

This command prints a very short overview of the system status, including the current time, the amount of time the system has been on (or up), the number of logged-in users, and three numbers representing the systems workload.

In our example, the system was last booted 116 days, 7 hours, and 9 minutes ago. If you lose connectivity with a remote server, this allows you to easily determine whether the system was rebooted once you can log back in.

The number of logged-in users is the total number of current logins via the terminal console, in X, and via SSH. If you are logged in twice, you will be counted as two users. Users connected to a service like Samba or Apache are not counted here.

Finally, the system load is displayed in three numbers. These numbers form an index that indicates the average ratio of work scheduled to be done by a CPU versus the work actually being done, over the past 1-minute, 5-minute, and 15-minute periods.

A load of 1.00 means the amount of work being scheduled is identical to the amount of work a CPU can handle. Confusingly, if a host contains multiple CPUs, the load for each CPU is added to create a total; on a host with four CPU cores, a load of 4.00 means the same as a load of 1.00 on a single core system.

In our example, the average workload over the past minute was about 1%. Some extra tasks were running and probably completed a few minutes ago, as the average workload over the past 5 minutes was 7%.

Though these numbers should by no means be taken as gospel, they do provide a quick way to check whether a system is likely to be healthy or not. If the system load is 6.00 on a host with eight CPU cores, a lot of tasks may have just finished running. If the load is 60, a problem exists.

This problem can be that the host is running a few processes that monopolize the CPU, not allowing other processes enough cycles. We'll show you how to find these processes with the top utility a bit later on. Alternatively, your host might be trying to run far more processes than it can cope with, again not leaving enough CPU cycles for any of them. This may happen if a badly written application or daemon keeps spawning copies of itself. See the "Fork Bomb" sidebar for more information. We'll show you how to prevent this using the ulimit command later on.

Finally, it's possible that a process is waiting for the host to perform a task that cannot be interrupted, such as moving data to or from disk. If this task must be completed before the process can continue, the process is said to be in uninterruptible sleep. It will count toward a higher load average, but won't actually be using the CPU. We'll show you how to check how much the disk is being used in the "Advanced Tools" section a bit later.

FORK BOMB

We explained in Chapter 5 that when a daemon or service runs in the background, it forks a child process and makes init the parent process, while the original process exits. It's perfectly possible for a misbehaving application to do the wrong thing and keep forking child processes, rather than exiting. This is called a *fork bomb*.

A fork bomb creates new copies of itself as fast as the host will allow. One process creates two, two create two more, four lead to eight, etc., thus starving other processes of resources such as CPU cycles and, eventually, RAM.

Memory Usage

Another cause of reduced performance is excessive memory use. If a task starts using a lot of memory, the host will be forced to free up memory for it by putting other tasks into swap memory. Accessing swap memory, which after all is just a piece of disk that is used as if it were memory, is very slow compared to accessing RAM.

■**Note** A 32-bit operating system can generally only access up to 2- or 4GiB of RAM, depending on the BIOS and kernel. We recommend installing a 64-bit version of Linux on server hosts, so this limitation disappears.

You can quickly check how much RAM and swap memory a host is using via the free command. We'll pass it the -m option so it displays the sizes in megabytes, not kilobytes, as in Listing 17-2.

Listing 17-2. *The free Command*

```
$ free -m
             total       used       free     shared    buffers     cached
Mem:           503        147        356          0         17         56
-/+ buffers/cache:         72        430
Swap:          223          0        223
```

This listing gives you an instant overview of whether the system is running low on available memory. The first line tells you the status of RAM use. The total is the amount of RAM that is available to this host. This is then divided into RAM that is in use and RAM that is free.

The shared column is no longer used, but still displayed so that tools that depend on this output format don't break.

The buffers column tells you the amount of memory the kernel is using to act as a disk write buffer. This buffer allows applications to write data quickly and have the kernel deal with writing it to disk in the background. Data can also be read from this buffer, providing an additional speed increase. The last column, cached, tells you how much memory the kernel is using as a cache—much like Squid—to have access to information quickly.

Both the buffer and cache are resized as needed. If an application needs more RAM, the kernel will free up part of the cache or buffer space and reallocate the memory.

The second line again displays the used and free memory, but these totals do not include the buffer and cache, so they give more of an indication of how much RAM is actually being used by programs.

Finally, the last line tells us how much swap space the host is using. Over time, this number will rise slightly, as services that aren't being used can be parked in swap space by the kernel. Doing this allows it to reclaim the otherwise idle RAM and use it as buffer or cache.

This means that having your host use swap space is not necessarily a bad thing. However, if all memory and all swap space are in use, there is obviously a problem.

■**Note** On Windows, it might be desirable to make sure that a host has free memory available to run applications, but on Linux this is not the case. Free memory means wasted memory, as it is not being utilized, not even as buffer or cache.

We'll show you how to find out how much memory individual tasks are using in the "Advanced Tools" section.

Disk Space

The other finite resources a computer system has are disk space and disk speed. Generally speaking, a system won't slow down when a disk becomes full, but services may crash and cause your users grief, so it pays to keep an eye on usage and make more storage available when needed.

We'll show you how to check for disk speed problems in the next section.

■**Note** We covered the df and du tools for checking available and used disk space in Chapter 8.

Logs

Finally, if something untoward has occurred with an application or the kernel, you'll likely find a log entry in your system or kernel log. You will of course want to restart any service that crashed, but checking the logs for the cause of the problem will help you prevent the same thing from happening again.

If the log daemon itself has stopped, you can still check the kernel log buffer via the dmesg command.

■**Note** We will cover logging in detail in Chapter 18.

Advanced Tools

The basic tools give you a quick overview, but don't provide any information to help you determine the cause of a problem, if there is one. To this end, we'll show you some tools that can help you pinpoint bottlenecks.

CPU and Memory Use

To list details about currently running tasks, Linux provides the top utility. This is similar to the Task Manager you may be used to from Windows, but it runs in a terminal window, as shown in Figure 17-1. It provides a sortable and configurable listing of running processes and threads on the host.

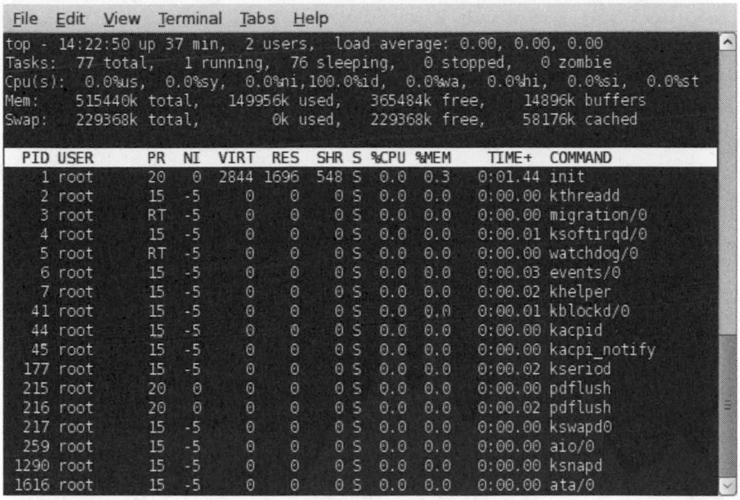

Figure 17-1. *The top utility*

The top of the output gives you a few header lines, which includes the information from uptime, as well as some aggregated data from the free and vmstat commands, which we'll discuss in the "Swap Space Use" and "Disk Access" sections a bit later on. You can toggle these headers on and off. The L key toggles the display of the load average line. You can toggle the task summary via the T key and memory information via M.

The rest of the display consists of several columns of information about running processes and threads. The columns you see here are shown by default, but you can enable or disable others as well. We've listed their headers and meaning in Table 17-1.

Table 17-1. *top Column headers*

Header	Meaning
PID	Tasks process ID. This unique identifier allows you to manipulate a task.
USER	The user name of the tasks owner, the account it runs as
PR	The task priority.
NI	The task niceness, an indication of how willing this task is to yield CPU cycles to other tasks. A lower or negative niceness means a high priority.
VIRT	The total amount of memory used by the task, including shared and swap memory.
RES	The total amount of physical memory used by the task, excluding swap memory.
SHR	The amount of shared memory used by the task. This memory is usually allocated by libraries and also usable by other tasks.
S	Task status. This indicates whether a task is running (R), sleeping (D or S), stopped (T), or zombie (Z).
%CPU	Percentage of available CPU cycles this task has used since the last screen update.
%MEM	Percentage of available RAM used by this task.
TIME+	Total CPU time the task has used since it started.
COMMAND	The name of the task being monitored.

You can obtain full descriptions for these and all other available fields in the man top manual page.

By default, the tasks are displayed in descending order and sorted by status. This means that if a task is either stopped or a zombie—i.e., it has a problem—it will be displayed at the top of the list. Read the "Zombies: Undead Tasks" sidebar to find out what a zombie process is.

To make the sorting more useful for checking on CPU usage, though, we will need to sort the %CPU column. We can choose a column to sort by pressing the F key, which brings up a list of available columns, as shown in Figure 17-2.

```
File  Edit  View  Terminal  Tabs  Help
Current Sort Field:  W  for window 1:Def
Select sort field via field letter, type any other key to return

  a: PID      = Process Id           * W: S        = Process Status
  b: PPID     = Parent Process Pid     x: COMMAND   = Command name/line
  c: RUSER    = Real user name         y: WCHAN     = Sleeping in Function
  d: UID      = User Id                z: Flags     = Task Flags <sched.h>
  e: USER     = User Name
  f: GROUP    = Group Name           Note1:
  g: TTY      = Controlling Tty        If a selected sort field can't be
  h: PR       = Priority               shown due to screen width or your
  i: NI       = Nice value             field order, the '<' and '>' keys
  j: P        = Last used cpu (SMP)    will be unavailable until a field
  k: %CPU     = CPU usage              within viewable range is chosen.
  l: TIME     = CPU Time
  m: TIME+    = CPU Time, hundredths Note2:
  n: %MEM     = Memory usage (RES)    ·Field sorting uses internal values,
  o: VIRT     = Virtual Image (kb)     not those in column display.  Thus,
  p: SWAP     = Swapped size (kb)      the TTY & WCHAN fields will violate
  q: RES      = Resident size (kb)     strict ASCII collating sequence.
  r: CODE     = Code size (kb)         (shame on you if WCHAN is chosen)
  s: DATA     = Data+Stack size (kb)
  t: SHR      = Shared Mem size (kb)
  u: nFLT     = Page Fault count
  v: nDRT     = Dirty Pages count
```

Figure 17-2. *Choosing a sort field*

We can press k to make the %CPU column our sort field, and then press Enter to go back to the task list. All processes are now sorted by the amount of CPU cycles they use, so if a process is running amok, you'll be able to spot it easily.

ZOMBIES: UNDEAD TASKS

Apart from the init process, every task on a Linux host is controlled by a parent process, and it reports its status back to this parent when it completes execution.

Sometimes things go wrong, though, and a parent process might crash, leaving a completed child waiting to report its status. If this happens, the child process turns into a zombie—a dead (completed) task without a controller. Usually such processes will become unstuck all by themselves and exit after a short time.

You can read more about zombies at http://en.wikipedia.org/wiki/Zombie_process.

You can also quickly change sort columns via the < and > keys, which shift the sort columns to the left and right, respectively. Press R to toggle between ascending and descending sort order.

If you want to list resources not shown by default, you can add columns to the display as well. Press F to access a listing of all available resource columns, as shown in Figure 17-3.

```
File  Edit  View  Terminal  Tabs  Help
Current Fields: AEHIOQTWKNMbcdfgjplrsuvyzX  for window 1:Def
Toggle fields via field letter, type any other key to return

* A: PID        = Process Id           v: nDRT      = Dirty Pages count
* E: USER       = User Name            y: WCHAN     = Sleeping in Function
* H: PR         = Priority             z: Flags     = Task Flags <sched.h>
* I: NI         = Nice value         * X: COMMAND   = Command name/line
* O: VIRT       = Virtual Image (kb)
* Q: RES        = Resident size (kb)   Flags field:
* T: SHR        = Shared Mem size (kb)    0x00000001  PF_ALIGNWARN
* W: S          = Process Status          0x00000002  PF_STARTING
* K: %CPU       = CPU usage               0x00000004  PF_EXITING
* N: %MEM       = Memory usage (RES)      0x00000040  PF_FORKNOEXEC
* M: TIME+      = CPU Time, hundredths     0x00000100  PF_SUPERPRIV
  b: PPID       = Parent Process Pid       0x00000200  PF_DUMPCORE
  c: RUSER      = Real user name           0x00000400  PF_SIGNALED
  d: UID        = User Id                  0x00000800  PF_MEMALLOC
  f: GROUP      = Group Name               0x00002000  PF_FREE_PAGES (2.5)
  g: TTY        = Controlling Tty          0x00008000  debug flag (2.5)
  j: P          = Last used cpu (SMP)      0x00024000  special threads (2.5)
  p: SWAP       = Swapped size (kb)        0x001D0000  special states (2.5)
  l: TIME       = CPU Time                 0x00100000  PF_USEDFPU (thru 2.4)
  r: CODE       = Code size (kb)
  s: DATA       = Data+Stack size (kb)
  u: nFLT       = Page Fault count
```

Figure 17-3. *Adding columns*

When you've chosen the fields you want to display, press Enter to go back to the task list.

■**Note** It is possible to select more fields than will fit onscreen. If this happens, you will need to unselect some other fields to make space.

Many more display options are available in top, and you can find them on the help menu. Press ? to access it. When you have customized the way top displays information to your liking, you can save the configuration by pressing W. This will write the settings to a file called .toprc in your home directory.

If you find a misbehaving task, you can use top to quit it. To do this, press k and enter the PID of the task in question. You will then be asked for the signal to send to the process. The signal to make a process terminate normally is 15. If this doesn't work, you might want to try sending signal 3, which is a bit sterner, or signal 9, which is akin to axe-murdering the process.

To find out more about signals, read the "Killing Is Not Always Murder" sidebar.

■**Note** You need to be the process owner or root user to be allowed to send signals to a process.

KILLING IS NOT ALWAYS MURDER

Though the act of sending signals to processes is called *killing* and is usually done via the `kill` command, it won't necessarily quit the process. It uses a facility in the kernel to send processes a signal.

Provided services have been designed to listen for this signal, they can be made to perform an action. Most commonly used is signal 1—also known as HUP. This signal causes most services to reload their configuration files, removing the need to stop and restart them.

If you want an application or process to quit, you can ask it to do so by sending it the TERM or QUIT signal, which are 15 and 3, respectively. A task that is ignoring polite requests to stop may be forced to via the 9, or KILL, signal.

You can read more about signals and what they do in the `man 7 signal` manual page.

If a process is using too much CPU time but should not be killed, you can try making it nicer, lowering its priority. This means it will yield more easily to other processes, allowing them to use some of the CPU cycles that were assigned to it. You can change process niceness by pressing the R key. `top` will ask you for the process ID, and then the new niceness value.

Unless you run `top` as `root` or via `sudo`, you can only make processes nicer. You cannot raise their priority, only lower it.

When done, press Q to quit `top`.

■**Note** You can also use the `renice` utility to change niceness and priority without using `top`. For instance, to change the niceness of process 8612, you would run `renice +5 8612`.

Gnome System Monitor

On Red Hat, and Ubuntu when running Gnome, you also have access to a graphical tool to display process and system information. This tool is called `gnome-system-monitor`, and you can start it via System ➤ Administration ➤ System Monitor, as shown in Figure 17-4.

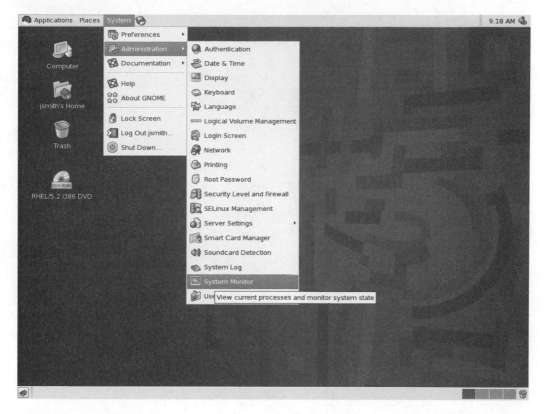

Figure 17-4. *Starting* gnome-system-monitor

This tool looks much more like the task manager on Windows and provides most of the same functionality that top does. It will start and show you the Resources tab by default, as shown in Figure 17-5.

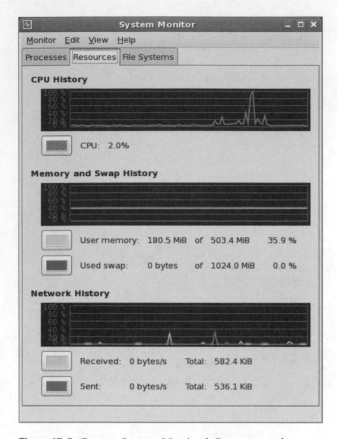

Figure 17-5. *Gnome System Monitor's Resources tab*

This view shows you the same information that is available in the headers in `top`, but also displays a graph with usage information from the last minute or so. This gives you a convenient overview of whether the system is running low on a particular resource.

To view the list of running tasks, switch to the Processes tab, as shown in Figure 17-6.

This provides you with the list of running processes. You are able to sort by different columns, by clicking the appropriate column header. Not all available columns are shown by default, but you can add or remove them. Choose Edit ➤ Preferences to open the System Monitor Preferences dialog, as shown in Figure 17-7.

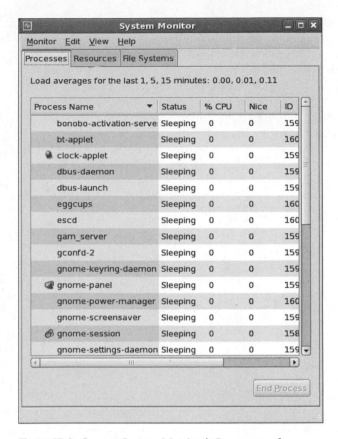

Figure 17-6. *Gnome System Monitor's Processes tab*

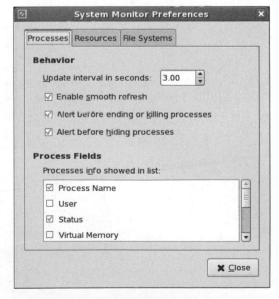

Figure 17-7. *System Monitor Preferences dialog*

To have a field displayed in the listing, just select its check box in the Process Fields listing. On this panel, you are also able to configure the process list update interval and whether or not the system monitor will warn you when you are about to kill a process. It's a good idea to let it, to help you prevent accidentally killing processes.

On the Resources tab you are able to change the update interval of the graphs and their background and grid colors. Finally, the File Systems tab allows you to specify how often the file system information is updated and whether or not to include "special" file systems like /proc and /sys in the listing. When done, close the System Monitor Preferences dialog.

Only processes owned by your user account will be shown in the process list, but you can switch this to have Gnome System Monitor display all processes on the system by selecting View ➤ All Processes, as shown in Figure 17-8.

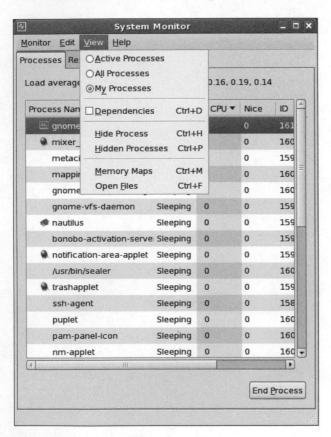

Figure 17-8. *Changing view options*

Finally, to terminate any misbehaving processes, you can select either End or Kill from the Edit menu. You can also right-click the process in the listing, as shown in Figure 17-9.

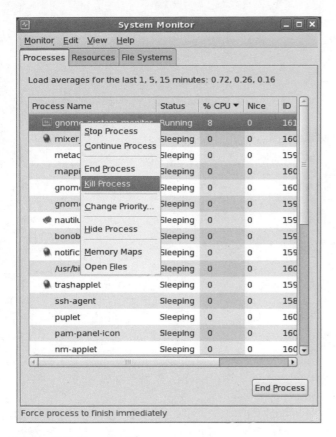

Figure 17-9. *Terminating a process*

Select End or Kill from the pop-up menu, and you will be asked to confirm the action, as shown in Figure 17-10.

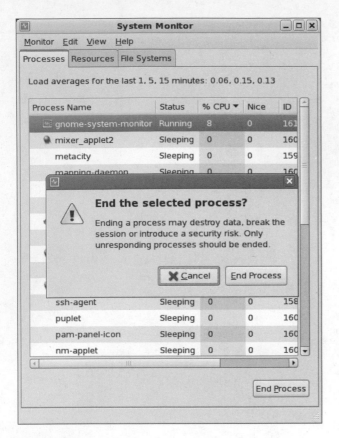

Figure 17-10. *Confirming process termination*

■**Note** Unless you run Gnome System Monitor as the `root` user, you will not be able to terminate any processes but your own.

In the pop-up menu and under the Edit menu you'll have the option to list open files. Choosing this will give you a listing of all files that are currently opened and in use by the process. This is similar to the output from the `lsof` command, which we covered in Chapter 8.

Swap Space Use

A lot of swap space in use may indicate the system is running low on memory. You can check whether this is the case via the `vmstat` utility. You normally want to tell this utility to print information every few seconds so you can spot any trends. Pass the `-n` option to prevent the headers from being reprinted and tell it to redisplay statistics every 5 seconds, as shown in Listing 17-3. Press Ctrl+C to quit `vmstat`.

Listing 17-3. *vmstat Output, Swap Activity*

```
$ vmstat -n 5,
procs -----------memory---------- ---swap-- -----io---- -system-- ----cpu----
 r  b   swpd   free   buff  cache   si   so    bi    bo   in   cs us sy id wa
 1  0      0  61404  13016 1518468   0    0    16    10    5    2  2  1 97  0
 0  0      0  60568  13040 1519388   0    0   154    87 3383 8453  6  1 91  1
 0  0      0  59484  13048 1520416   0    0   214    30 3416 13056  8  3 88  2
 0  0      0  53384  13060 1522088   0    0   335     1 3432 14855 10  3 86  1
 1  0      0  52416  13068 1522944   0    0   159    71 3383 15334 10  3 87  0
```

This rather impressive jumble of numbers gives us an indication of how much data is moving through the system. Each line consists of sets of numbers in six groups, which provide information on processes, memory, swap, input/output, system, and CPU.

Reduced performance due to excessive swap space usage will show up in two of these groups: swap and cpu.

The si and so columns in the swap group display the amount of swap memory that is being read from (si—swap in) and written to (so—swap out) your swap space. The wa column in the cpu group tells you the percentage of time the CPU is waiting for data—and thus not processing instructions.

If a host is spending most of its CPU cycles moving applications from and to swap space, the si and so column values will be high. The actual values will depend on the amount of swapping that is occurring and the speed of your swap device. The wa column will usually display values in the high 90s as well, indicating the CPU is waiting for an application or data to be retrieved from swap space.

You can solve this problem by using top to find out whether an application is using too much RAM and changing its configuration to use less.

■**Note** top itself is fairly resource hungry, so if a system is unresponsive and under extremely heavy load, it might be easier and quicker to reboot it than to wait for top to start.

In our example, the host is not using any swap space, and the CPU spends most of its time idle, indicating a light workload.

Disk Access

The vmstat utility will also give us information on how much data is being read from and written to disk. We've highlighted the bi (blocks in) and bo (blocks out) columns in the io group in Listing 17-4. By passing a second number as parameter, we've told vmstat to quit after 5 intervals.

Listing 17-4. *vmstat Output, I/O Activity*

```
$ vmstat 5 5
procs -----------memory---------- ---swap-- -----io---- -system-- ----cpu----
 r  b   swpd   free   buff  cache   si   so    bi    bo    in   cs us sy id wa
 1  0      0  61404  13016 1518468   0    0    16    10     5    2  2  1 97  0
 0  0      0  60568  13040 1519388   0    0   154    87  3383 8453  6  1 91  1
 0  0      0  59484  13048 1520416   0    0   214    30  3416 13056  8  3 88  2
 0  0      0  53384  13060 1522088   0    0   335     1  3432 14855 10  3 86  1
 1  0      0  52416  13068 1522944   0    0   159    71  3383 15334 10  3 87  0
```

These two numbers tell you exactly how many blocks of data are being read from (bi) and written to (bo) your disks during each interval. In our case, the system is reading more data from disk than it is writing back, but both numbers are low. Because the block size on our disks is 4K, this means they aren't very heavily loaded.

What constitutes a heavy load will depend on the block size and the speed of the disks. If a large file is being written, this number will go up for the duration of the write operation, but drop down again later.

You can get an idea of what your host is capable of by checking the numbers you get when creating a large file on an otherwise idle system. Run a dd command to create a 1GiB file containing only zeroes in the background, while running vmstat simultaneously, as shown in Listing 17-5.

Listing 17-5. *Checking Disk I/O Performance*

```
$ dd if=/dev/zero of=./largefile bs=1M count=1024 &
[1] 21835
$ vmstat 5 5
procs -----------memory---------- ---swap-- -----io---- -system-- ----cpu----
 r  b   swpd   free   buff  cache   si   so    bi    bo    in   cs us sy id wa
 1  1   5140  96056  96392 1598024   0    0     4    13    31   10  4  1 95  0
 2  0   5156  96512  54536 1655212   0    0     0 76164   737 3203  3 18 46 33
 0  5   5168 101772  53736 1667252   0    0     0 73152   717 3054  3 18 35 44
 0  0   5168 129984  51520 1677972   0    0    15 24598   532 1793  2  7 59 33
 0  0   5168 129984  51528 1677976   0    0     0    22   295 1196  2  0 98  0
1024+0 records in
1024+0 records out
1073741824 bytes (1.1 GB) copied, 13.1767 s, 81.5 MB/s
[1]+  Done                    dd if=/dev/zero of=./largefile bs=1M count=1024
$ rm ./largefile
```

The bo column is low for the first run, as the file data is still in the kernel buffer. At the next interval, however, you can see it spike to over 76,000 blocks. Keep in mind that this is over 5 seconds, though, so we can calculate the peak write rate on this particular host to be around 15,000 blocks per second.

If you notice degraded performance and vmstat shows a bo value that is up near the maximum rate the system could manage when you tested it for a long time, you have an application or service that is trying very hard to write a lot of data. This usually indicates a problem, so you should find out which application is the culprit and rectify the problem.

We'll come back to how you can get notifications when system performance degrades when we cover Nagios in Chapter 18.

Continuous Performance Monitoring

Now that you have the basic tools to diagnose where a performance bottleneck is, we will show you how to automate ongoing monitoring. This will give you access to longer-term performance and resource usage data, which in turn allows you to make a better determination on whether and when to upgrade hardware or migrate services to other hosts.

SNMP

Continuous performance monitoring is done via a protocol called Simple Network Management Protocol (SNMP). A host that is to be monitored typically runs an SNMP server, also known as an *agent*, which gathers performance statistics on an on-going basis. This agent can be queried by clients, which collect, process, and display the performance data.

Let's start by installing and configuring the SNMP agent and utilities. On Red Hat they are provided by the `net-snmp` and `net-snmp-utils` packages:

```
$ sudo yum install net-snmp net-snmp-utils
```

And on Ubuntu by the `snmpd` and `snmp` packages:

```
$ sudo apt-get install snmpd snmp
```

After installation, you need to change the configuration file so you are able to access more system performance information. An SNMP agent has three levels of access to resources, and the level of access is determined by the community name you use to connect. This community name effectively functions as a username and password at once, so it is wise to choose one that is not easily guessable, as system information might otherwise be disclosed to third parties.

Start by making sure the agent listens only on the local Internet network interface. On Ubuntu this is the default behavior, but on Red Hat you need to override the default parameters that are defined in `/etc/init.d/snmpd`. You can do this by creating a file called `/etc/snmp/snmpd.options` and adding in the options you want. This file will be sourced by the startup script, and your settings will override the defaults.

All you need to do is copy the default options from the `init` script to your new file and append the address you need the server to listen on, which in this example is 127.0.0.1, as shown in Listing 17-6.

Listing 17-6. `/etc/snmp/snmpd.options` *on Red Hat*

```
# Override the default daemon options.
#
OPTIONS="-Lsd -Lf /dev/null -p /var/run/snmpd.pid -a 127.0.0.1"
```

On Ubuntu, these options are defined by the `SNMPDOPTS` variable in `/etc/default/snmpd`.

■**Caution** You should make sure that Internet-facing machines are protected by a firewall and that the SNMP server is not needlessly listening for requests on external interfaces. The SNMP protocol uses UDP port 161.

Next, you need to configure a community name to use and grant it read-only access to all system variables. This is done in /etc/snmp/snmpd.conf on both Red Hat and Ubuntu.

First, you must define a community name and map this to an internal security name. In our example, Ubuntu has a configuration that is very nearly suitable for us, so we'll modify that to suit our needs. We can then also apply this configuration to a Red Hat host.

Listing 17-7 contains the configuration directives that map community names to internal security names.

Listing 17-7. *Default Community Mappings*

```
# First, map the community name (COMMUNITY) into a security name
# (local and mynetwork, depending on where the request is coming
# from):
#       sec.name  source           community
com2sec paranoid  default          public
#com2sec readonly  default          public
#com2sec readwrite default          private
```

We don't need the paranoid name, so we can comment it out. We'll use the readonly security name, as that is already configured to allow us access to all available information. We'll uncomment it, and then to provide some security, change the associated community name. We'll use axs4snmp in our example. Listing 17-8 shows the modified configuration snippet.

Listing 17-8. *Customized Community Mappings*

```
# First, map the community name (COMMUNITY) into a security name
# (local and mynetwork, depending on where the request is coming
# from):
#       sec.name  source           community
#com2sec paranoid  default          public
com2sec readonly  default          axs4snmp
#com2sec readwrite default          private
```

We don't need to change the group mappings on Ubuntu, but we've listed them in Listing 17-9 so we can make use of this configuration on Red Hat. Since the paranoid and readwrite security names are now undefined in our configuration, we don't need to worry about commenting their group mappings. We will use only the MyROGroup group.

Listing 17-9. *Default Group Mappings*

```
# Second, map the security names into group names:
#                sec.model  sec.name
group MyROSystem v1         paranoid
```

```
group MyROSystem v2c       paranoid
group MyROSystem usm       paranoid
group MyROGroup v1         readonly
group MyROGroup v2c        readonly
group MyROGroup usm        readonly
group MyRWGroup v1         readwrite
group MyRWGroup v2c        readwrite
group MyRWGroup usm        readwrite
```

Which information about a host is provided by an SNMP agent is not defined by snmpd itself, but by Management Information Bases (MIBs). These MIBs describe the information that is available for a host and make it available in a tree structure. Each item of information that can be retrieved (or set, if the agent was configured to allow this) is called an Object Identifier (OID). The MIBs used by snmpd are defined in /usr/share/snmp.

■**Note** You can read more about MIBs and OIDs at http://en.wikipedia.org/wiki/Simple_Network_
Management_Protocol#Management_Information_Bases_.28MIBs.29.

The amount and type of host information that may be retrieved by a client is defined by a view. Each view that is defined specifies a name for the view and the part of the OID tree that may be accessed. Listing 17-10 defines a view called all that provides access to all variables under .1 and a view called system that provides access to all variables under the .iso.org.dod. internet.mgmt.mib-2.system OID.

Listing 17-10. *Defining Views*

```
# Third, create a view for us to let the groups have rights to:
#           incl/excl subtree                       mask
view all     included  .1                           80
view system included  .iso.org.dod.internet.mgmt.mib-2.system
```

Next, you need to define access levels, which specify which groups can access specific views. Listing 17-11 shows the default configuration from Ubuntu, which is fine for our purposes. The MyROGroup group has read access to the all view.

Listing 17-11. *Default Access Configuration*

```
# Finally, grant the 2 groups access to the 1 view with different
# write permissions:
#               context sec.model sec.level match  read    write notif
access MyROSystem ""     any       noauth    exact  system none  none
access MyROGroup ""      any       noauth    exact  all    none  none
access MyRWGroup ""      any       noauth    exact  all    all   none
```

Those are the only changes you need to make to the configuration file in order to be able to retrieve performance and statistical information from the agent. However, you can also define some location and contact information that will make it easier to identify a host when you query it later.

You can set the `syslocation` and `syscontact` variables in a third configuration file, `/etc/snmp/snmpd.local.conf`, as shown in Listing 17-12.

Listing 17-12. *snmpd.local.conf*

```
# Set host specific information
syslocation Melbourne, Australia
syscontact Hostmaster <hostmaster@example.com>
```

You can now restart the SNMP server with `sudo service snmpd` restart on Red Hat or `sudo invoke-rc.d snmpd` restart on Ubuntu.

■**Tip** SNMP configuration can be somewhat of a black art. To quickly start using `snmpd`, create a single read-only community via `echo 'rocommunity xs4snmp default' | sudo tee /etc/snmp/snmpd.conf`. This will overwrite the existing configuration file.

Both Red Hat and Ubuntu also ship an SNMP configuration wizard called `snmpconf`. This wizard allows you to generate configuration files by answering questions about your host. If you find the configuration we've described in the preceding text is not suitable, you may want to create a custom one using this wizard.

Cacti

Now you have the SNMP agent gathering information, but you're not doing anything with those statistics yet. In this section, we'll show you how to put those statistics to use via Cacti, a web-based application that collects data from various sources and produces graphs, making it easy to spot trends.

In our examples, we'll use a web host called cacti.example.com to access statistics. To start, create a DNS CNAME or A entry on your DNS server and the required configuration directives and files for Apache. However, do not create the final `html` directory when creating directories in `/srv/www` on the file system. Be sure to add `index.php` to the list of default home page files on Red Hat.

■**Note** We covered managing DNS in Chapter 9 and creating virtual web hosts in Chapter 11.

Installation on Ubuntu

Cacti is available from the package system on Ubuntu, so you can install it via `sudo apt-get install cacti`. When asked what kind of web server you will use, select None, as shown in Figure 17-11.

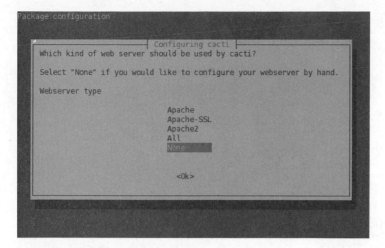

Figure 17-11. *Cacti configuration*

The package will now be installed. When done, you will be asked some questions to help it configure its database—Cacti stores data in MySQL. Using the dbconfig-common framework to manage the configuration means these settings will be automatically applied in the event of an update, so choose Yes, as shown in Figure 17-12.

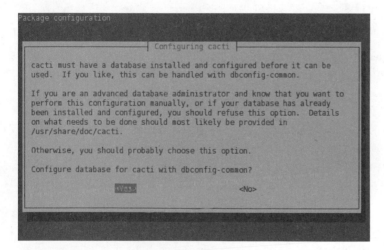

Figure 17-12. *Specifying to use dbconfig-common*

You will now be asked to enter the MySQL root user's password so a MySQL account can be created for Cacti. Next, you need to choose a password for this Cacti account. We'll leave the field blank so a secure password is generated automatically, as shown in Figure 17-13.

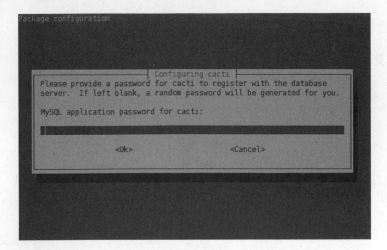

Figure 17-13. *Generating a password*

After you press Enter to accept this default, the MySQL user will be created and a database called `cacti` will be created and populated with tables.

You now need to change the `html` directory on your virtual host to instead point at the version of cacti that was installed by the package system. You can do this via a symbolic link. In our case, we issue the following:

```
$ sudo ln -s /usr/share/cacti/site /srv/www/cacti.example.com/html
```

Because Apache is allowed to follow symbolic links, it will serve the packaged version of Cacti when you visit your virtual host.

■**Tip** Most packaged web applications on Ubuntu install their site contents to a directory in `/usr/share`. Use `dpkg -L package` to find out the precise location so you can use these on your own virtual hosting setup.

Installation on Red Hat

On Red Hat, Cacti is not available directly, but after you add SNMP support to PHP, you can download and install the required packages from the Fedora EPEL repository.

```
$ sudo yum install php-snmp
$ sudo rpm -Uvh ➥
http://download.fedora.redhat.com/pub/epel/5/i386/rrdtool-1.2.27-3.el5.i386.rpm ➥
http://download.fedora.redhat.com/pub/epel/5/i386/cacti-0.8.7b-1.el5.noarch.rpm
```

Or you can add the EPEL repository to your host and then install packages from that repository. Add the EPEL repository, if it's not already added to your Yum configuration, by installing the epel-release RPM.

```
$ sudo rpm -Uvh ➥
http://download.fedora.redhat.com/pub/epel/5/i386/epel-release-5-3.noarch.rpm
```

You can then install the package via yum.

```
$ sudo yum install cacti
```

■**Note** A Cacti RPM package is also available from RPMForge.

The Cacti package will install an Apache configuration snippet that makes it available at the /cacti subdirectory on all virtual hosts. This is not what you want, so disable the snippet by renaming it.

```
$ sudo mv /etc/http/conf.d/cacti.conf /etc/http/conf.d/cacti.conf.disabled
```

Before you can serve the content of the Cacti package, you need to change the SELinux context so Apache is permitted to access it.

```
$ sudo chcon -R httpd_sys_content_t /usr/share/cacti
```

And then you can link the html directory on your virtual host to the version of Cacti that was installed by the package system.

```
$ sudo ln -s /usr/share/cacti /srv/www/cacti.example.com/html
```

Because Apache is allowed to follow symbolic links, it will serve the packaged version of Cacti when you visit your virtual host.

■**Tip** Most packaged web applications on Red Hat install their site contents to a directory in /usr/share. Use rpm -ql package to find out the precise location so you can use these on your own virtual hosting setup.

Finally, because Cacti uses MySQL to store its data, you need to create a MySQL user and database and enter these details into the configuration file.

```
mysql> CREATE DATABASE `cacti`;
Query OK, 1 row affected (0.00 sec)

mysql> GRANT ALL PRIVILEGES ON cacti.* TO `cacti`@`localhost` ➥
    IDENTIFIED BY 'secret';
Query OK, 0 rows affected (0.12 sec)
```

You can now enter these values into the Cacti configuration file at /etc/cacti/db.php, as shown in Listing 17-13.

Listing 17-13. *Cacti Configuration File*

```
/* make sure these values refect your actual database/host/user/password */
$database_type = "mysql";
$database_default = "cacti";
$database_hostname = "localhost";
$database_username = "cacti";
$database_password = "secret";
$database_port = "3306";
```

Finally, you need to enable the Cacti poller, which is a small utility that runs via cron every 5 minutes to collect data from all configured hosts. The package has installed the file /etc/cron.d/cacti for you, and all you need to do is remove the comment in front of the command, as in Listing 17-14.

Listing 17-14. *Cacti Poller Cron Entry*

```
*/5 * * * *    cacti    /usr/bin/php /usr/share/cacti/poller.php > /dev/null 2>&1
```

Cacti Configuration

You can complete installation by visiting your new virtual host. When you access it, you will be redirected to the /install/ subdirectory, where you can read installation and upgrade information, as well as the GPL license. If you agree to the license terms, click Next to begin installation.

On the next screen, Cacti tells you the database settings you've entered and allows you to select whether you're doing a new install or whether you're upgrading a previous version, as shown in Figure 17-14.

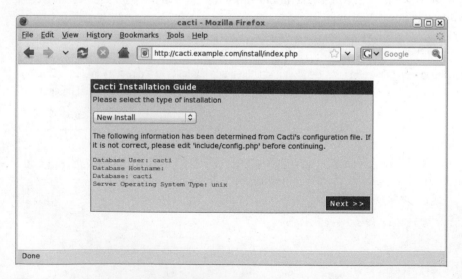

Figure 17-14. *Choosing an installation type*

On the next screen, shown in Figure 17-15, you'll see Cacti has detected all the command-line tools it needs to collect data and generate graphs. You can manually change these paths if you wish, but the defaults will suit us fine.

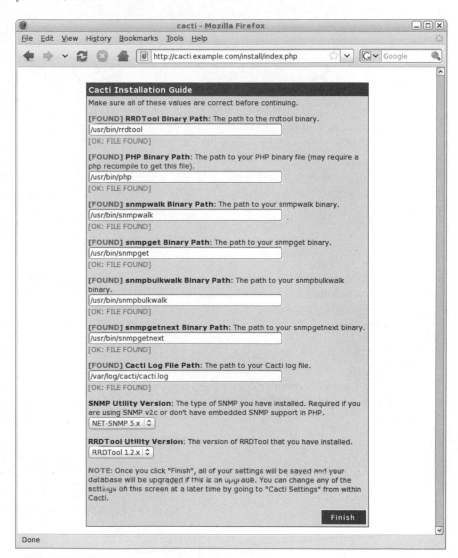

Figure 17-15. *Helper application locations*

Click Finish to accept these values and log in to Cacti. A user called admin was created when you installed, as shown in Figure 17-16, and the default password for this user is admin.

Figure 17-16. *The first Cacti login*

After the first login, you will be prompted to change the default password. Choose something secure and not easily guessable. If a third party gains access to your Cacti installation, that person will be able to obtain potentially useful information about your network and hosts.

Adding Hosts to Cacti

Now that you're logged in, you can tell Cacti about your agents, or hosts, so it can start collecting and graphing data. In Cacti-speak these are called *devices*.

On the main console, as shown in Figure 17-17, click Create devices.

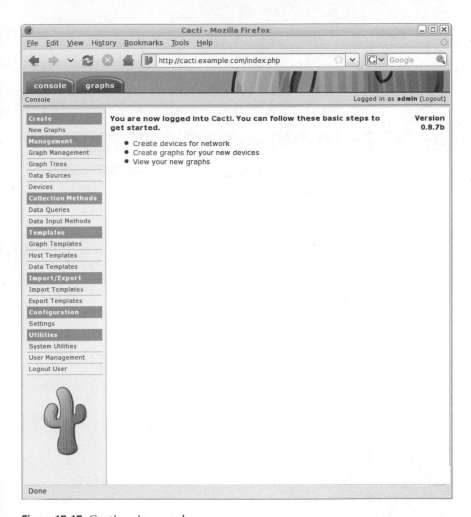

Figure 17-17. *Cacti main console*

As you can see in Figure 17-18, the local host was added automatically during installation, and it's already collecting data. Create a new device by clicking Add in the top-right corner.

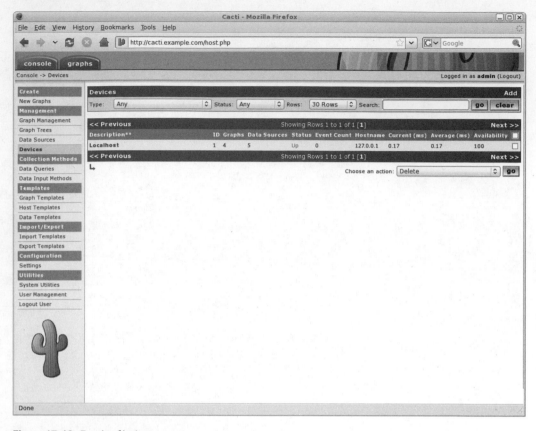

Figure 17-18. *Device listing*

On the device setup screen, shown in Figure 17-19, enter a description and the hostname or address for the device to add. Since you'll use SNMP to query the host, set the template to Generic SNMP-enabled host.

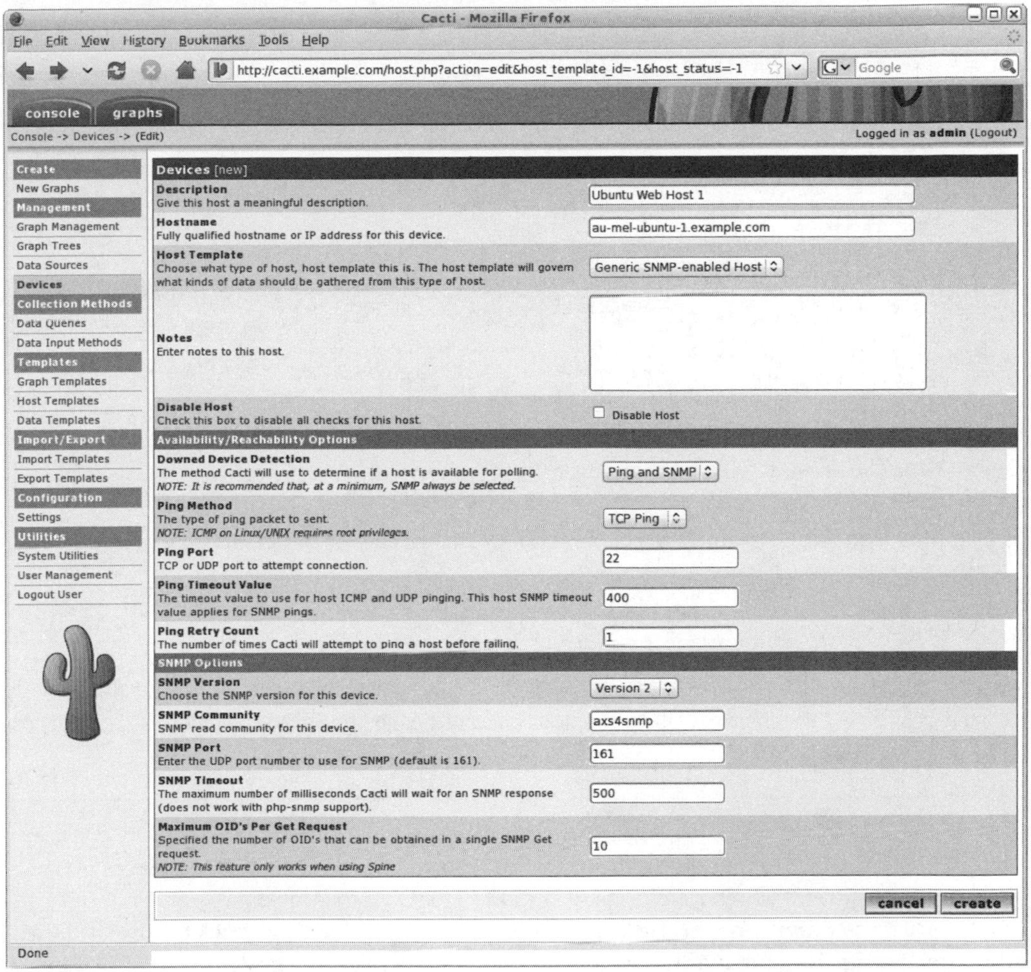

Figure 17-19. *Adding a new device*

Next, choose Version 2 as the SNMP version to use. This will allow you to change the Downed Device Detection option to SNMP and PING and set the ping type to TCP and the ping port to 22.

By setting the Downed Device Detection option as instructed, the host will be marked as down if Cacti is unable to make an SNMP connection and is unable to connect to the listed TCP port. Under SNMP options, set the SNMP community to axs4snmp. You can leave the other fields at their default values.

Click Create to add the device to Cacti. You will be returned to the device details page, but if all went well, you should have some output from the SNMP agent near the top of the screen, as you can see in Figure 17-20.

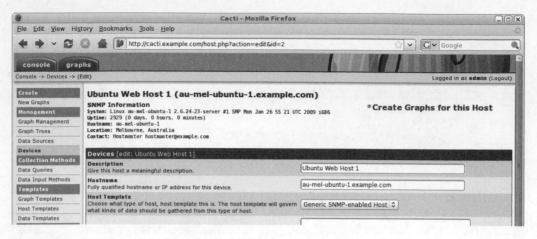

Figure 17-20. *The device was created successfully.*

Of note is that the uptime listed is the time the SNMP agent has been running, not the host uptime.

■**Tip** If you see an SNMP error, check that the Cacti host can connect to the remote SNMP agent. For instance, you can use the `snmpwalk` utility by providing it with a protocol version, community string, and host name, in this case `snmpwalk -v2c -c axs4snmp au-mel-ubuntu-1.example.com`.

Cacti can now gather data from the agent, but you still need to tell it which pieces of data you want to graph and which graphs you want to be created from this data.

Click Create Graphs for this Host and on the next page select the check box behind the eth0 interface line. Set the graph type to In/Out Bytes with Total Bandwidth, as shown in Figure 17-21, and then click Create.

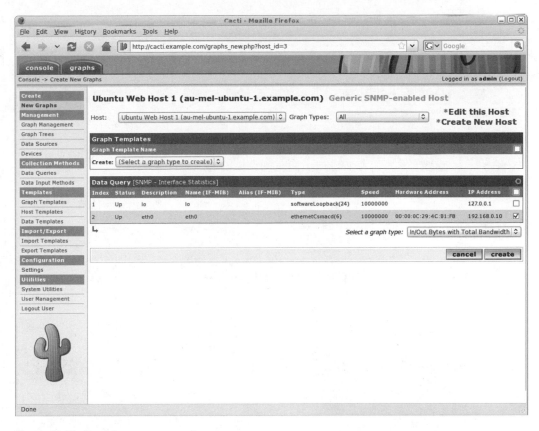

Figure 17-21. *Creating a new graph*

The same page will reload, but the eth0 line is grayed out to indicate this graph already exists.

Before you can view this graph, you need to add it to a graph tree. A *graph tree* is simply a hierarchy of hosts or graphs that allows you to display graphs grouped by type or host.

Select Graph Trees from the left-hand menu, click Default Tree, and then click Add.

On this page, select where on the tree you want the item you're adding to be displayed. We'll add it to the [root], but you can add it under a different tree or header as well. The tree item we're adding is a host, and the host is Ubuntu Web Host 1, as shown in Figure 17-22. You can leave the Graph Grouping Style on its default value. When done, click Create.

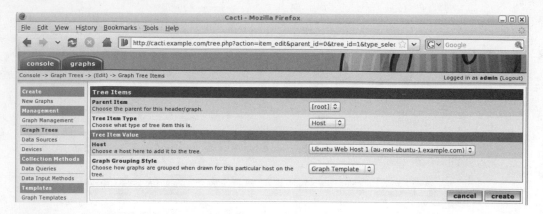

Figure 17-22. *Adding an item to a graph tree*

Now that you've added a graph, it's time to view it! Click the large blue graphs tab at the top of the page and select Ubuntu Web Host 1 in the tree. You're treated to the beginnings of a network traffic graph, as you can see in Figure 17-23.

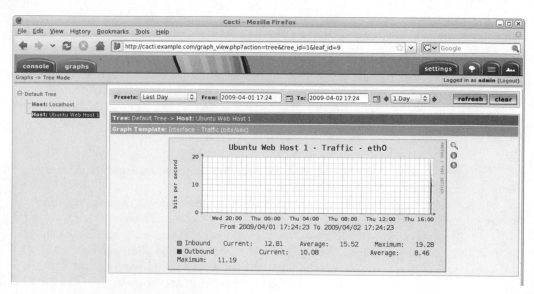

Figure 17-23. *The new network traffic graph*

If you click the graph image itself, you'll be taken to a page that shows four graphs, each with a different time interval. This allows you to monitor daily as well as extremely long-term trends.

When you click the magnifying glass next to a graph, your mouse cursor will change, and you are able to select an area of the graph. After you make your selection, the graph will zoom in to display only the selected area.

Try adding some more graphs. Click the blue console tab, followed by Devices in the left-hand menu, and then click Ubuntu Web Host 1 followed by Create Graphs for this Host.

Select Host MIB – Logged in Users from the list of Graph Templates and click Create. You will be asked to choose a color for the graph legend, as shown in Figure 17-24.

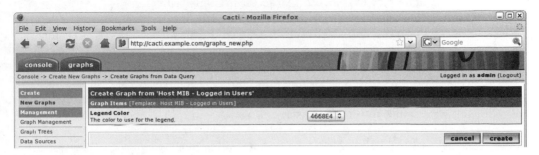

Figure 17-24. *Choosing a color*

If you don't like the default option, select a new color and click Create. You'll be returned to the graph creation screen, but at the top of the page you'll see a status message to let you know the new graph has been created.

Because you've already added the entire host to the graph tree, any new graphs you add to a host will be added to the graph tree as well.

It would also be nice to keep an eye on the number of processes on the host and CPU and memory usage, as well as the load average, so add these graphs to the host as well. If you jump back to the graphs listing, you'll see the graphs you just created appear to be broken. This is because the poller has not yet had time to collect this data. After at most ten minutes—the poller will have run twice by then—there will be data, so the graphs will be created.

Settings and Defaults

So that you don't need to change the Device Down Detection method and the SNMP community for each device you add, you can change the defaults via the Settings link under Configuration in the left-hand menu.

On the General tab, you can customize logging and SNMP defaults. Change the default to Version 2 and set the SNMP community name you picked earlier, and then click Save to store the new values. The Paths tab allows you to change the locations of the helper utilities you saw when you first configured Cacti. Unless these paths change, there is no need to modify anything on this screen.

Next is the Poller tab. This tab allows you to tell Cacti which poller you have configured for data gathering. In our case, we use cmd.php via cron, which is run every 5 minutes. If you decide to change that interval, you should tell Cacti here. On this tab, you can also change the Device Down Detection method. Set it to PING and SNMP, and use the TCP ping method to port 22.

■**Note** If Cacti needs to access remote SNMP agents, these agents need to be configured to listen on an accessible network interface, and their host firewall should permit access via a rule like
-A Firewall-eth0-INPUT -p udp -m state --state NEW -s 192.168.0.1 --dport 161 -j ACCEPT.

The Graph Export tab allows you to tell Cacti to send generated graphs to a remote directory or host. This enables you to include them on an externally accessible system status page, for instance, without needing to grant external access to Cacti itself.

If you want to change the way Cacti displays graphs or the font sizes on the graphs themselves, you can do that on the Visual tab. The final tab, Authentication, allows you to configure Cacti for use with an external authentication source like Apache htpasswd authentication or an external LDAP server, as long as LDAP support for PHP is installed.

If you choose to keep using built-in authentication, you can manage users via the User Management page accessible through the Utilities menu. To create a new user, click the Add link in the top-right corner and choose a username and password. The check boxes on the bottom half of the page allow you to grant separate permissions to each user.

We've shown you how to set up Cacti for basic monitoring, but it is designed to allow you to download and install additional graph templates to monitor additional devices and services. If you have a device for which a template is not available, you can also define new ones from within Cacti.

You can read more about Cacti at `http://www.cacti.net/`, and more data-gathering scripts and templates are available from `http://cacti.net/additional_scripts.php` as well as the Cacti forums at `http://forums.cacti.net/`.

■**Note** Alternative monitoring solutions include MRTG (`http://oss.oetiker.ch/mrtg/`) and Munin (`http://munin.projects.linpro.no/`).

Performance Optimization

When your host was installed, it was set up with defaults that offer reasonable performance for most configurations. However, since each host is different, you can usually tweak settings to make the configuration more optimal for a specific workload.

In this section, we'll show you some tips and tricks that should help speed up your host for most server-related tasks.

RECOMPILING FOR SPEED?

Some people might suggest that a good way to speed up your host is by recompiling your kernel and disabling functionality you don't need. While this may improve the speed with which your system will boot, it is unlikely to change the speed with which the kernel runs. After all, the code that is no longer present was never executed while it was in the kernel anyway.

Your new kernel will use slightly less RAM, but by compiling optional drivers as modules, they can be prevented from loading even without recompiling the kernel. For instance, if you do not use IPv6 networking, you can prevent the `ipv6` kernel module from loading by adding `blacklist ipv6` to the `/etc/modprobe.d/blacklist` file.

The same generally goes for applications. Disabling functionality will reduce the memory footprint, but not usually produce a measurable speed increase. For applications such as Apache or PHP, you can easily disable unused modules to reduce the amount of RAM that is used. Keep in mind that it might be cheaper to purchase additional RAM for a host than to spend hours tweaking configurations.

Recompiling Anyway?

If you've decided to compile your own kernel anyway, the first step is to obtain the source. You can always download the latest stable kernel source tarball from `http://www.kernel.org`. A good location to unpack it is `/usr/src`, where it will be made available systemwide.

Next, you should read the README file that ships with the kernel and ensure your system meets the minimum requirements for the kernel you will be building. You will need to ensure you've installed the CGU C compiler and all required development libraries. This includes libraries needed by the utilities that help you configure your kernel. The following table lists which library packages are required for each of the three most popular ways of configuring the kernel source:

Distribution	menuconfig	xconfig	gconfig
Red Hat	ncurses-devel	qt4-devel	gtk2-devel
Ubuntu	libncurses5-dev	libqt4-dev	libgtk2.0-dev

Next, configure the kernel source by running your preferred configuration utility. For a command-line system, use `make menuconfig`. For a KDE-based interface, you can use `make xconfig`, and for Gnome, use `make gconfig`. You should ensure you enable drivers and required options for all hardware and functionality you need. If you forget any, your kernel may not be able to boot your system.

On Red Hat, you can now make the build scripts generate an RPM file containing the new kernel and its modules via `make rpm`. On Ubuntu, you need to first install the `fakeroot` and `kernel-package` packages. Once that is done, you can generate a DEB package of the kernel via `fakeroot make-kpkg --revision=myhostname.1 --initrd kernel-image`.

Each of these methods will give you a kernel package that you can then install.

Caveats

Keep in mind that by not using a distribution kernel, you need to take care to compile and install a newer kernel if and when bugs or vulnerabilities that affect you are found. If you install a new piece of hardware, you may also need to reconfigure and compile a new kernel in order to include the appropriate driver.

Resource Limits

Linux allows you to enforce resource limits on users via the `ulimit` command. This is actually a built-in function of the bash shell. Any limits you set via this command apply only to the current shell and the processes it starts.

To report current limits, run `ulimit` with the `-a` option, as shown in Listing 17-15.

Listing 17-15. *Reporting Current Limits*

```
$ ulimit -a
core file size          (blocks, -c) 0
data seg size           (kbytes, -d) unlimited
scheduling priority             (-e) 0
```

```
file size              (blocks, -f) unlimited
pending signals             (-i) 16384
max locked memory      (kbytes, -l) 32
max memory size        (kbytes, -m) unlimited
open files                  (-n) 1024
pipe size         (512 bytes, -p) 8
POSIX message queues   (bytes, -q) 819200
real-time priority          (-r) 0
stack size             (kbytes, -s) 10240
cpu time              (seconds, -t) unlimited
max user processes          (-u) 16384
virtual memory         (kbytes, -v) unlimited
file locks                  (-x) unlimited
```

To prevent a fork bomb from being run by this shell user, you can change the maximum number of running processes, for instance, from 16384 to 1, using the -u option. If you then try to run a new process, the system will prevent you from doing so.

```
$ ulimit -u 1
$ ls
bash: fork: Resource temporarily unavailable
```

You receive an error to indicate the shell could not fork the command you tried to run.

■**Caution** If you are logged in via SSH or X, you will already have several running processes.

The other useful limits are the maximum memory size, which can be set via the -m option, and the number of open files, which you set via -n. You can obtain a full listing of options and their functions in the ulimit section of the man bash page.

Setting Limits for All Users

The ulimit command sets limits for the current shell, so you can add limits via /etc/profile or /etc/bashrc for users who log in. However, most daemons don't use shells, so adding limits to the shell configuration files won't have any effect.

You can instead use the limits module for PAM. This module is invoked when a user creates a new process, and it sets limits that you can define in /etc/security/limits.conf. This file defines both soft and hard limits for users and groups. We've included the sample limits.conf from Red Hat in Listing 17-16.

Listing 17-16. *Sample* limits.conf *File*

```
#<domain>       <type>   <item>        <value>
#*              soft     core          0
#*              hard     rss           10000
#@student       hard     nproc         20
```

```
#@faculty      soft    nproc          20
#@faculty      hard    nproc          50
#ftp           hard    nproc          0
#@student      -       maxlogins      4
```

Each line specifies a domain that the limit applies to. This domain can be a wildcard, a username, or a group name. Next comes the limit type, which can be either soft or hard. A hard limit can only be set by the root user, and when a user or process tries to break this limit, the system will prevent this. The soft limit can be adjusted by the user using the ulimit command, but it can only be increased to the value of the hard limit.

Next is the resource that is being limited. A full listing of available resources is included in the sample file, and it also available on the man limits.conf page. Last on each line is the value that the limit should be set to.

In the case of the sample file, the faculty group is allowed to run 20 concurrent processes according to their soft limit. However, any member of this group is allowed to change that limit to any value up to 50, but no higher than that.

sysctl and the proc File System

We briefly mentioned the proc file system in Chapter 8 as a way to obtain system information directly from the kernel. It also provides a way to tweak a running kernel to improve system performance. To this end, you can change values in virtual files under the /proc/sys directory.

The virtual files are grouped in subdirectories, based on the parts of the system they affect, as listed in Table 17-2.

Table 17-2. /proc/sys Subdirectories

Directory	Used By
abi	System emulation (e.g., running 32-bit applications on a 64-bit host).
debug	This is an empty directory, not used.
dev	Device-specific information.
fs	File system settings and tuning.
kernel	Kernel settings and tuning.
net	Network settings and tuning.
sunrpc	Sun Remote Procedure Call (NFS) settings.
vm	Memory, buffer, and cache settings and tuning.

We won't go into detail on every single file, but we'll give you an idea of the kinds of tweaking that can be done.

Each of the virtual files contains one or more values that can be read via cat or the sysctl utility. To read a value, pass its key as parameter to sysctl. The key is the full path to the file, with /proc/sys/ removed and the slashes optionally replaced with full stops. For instance, to check how likely your host is to use swap memory, you can check the contents of the /proc/sys/vm/swappiness file via sysctl vm.swappiness.

This particular value is an indication of how likely the kernel is to move information from RAM into swap space after it hasn't been used for a while. The higher the number, the more likely this is. The value in this case can range from 0 to 100, with 60 being the default. If you wanted to ensure your host is less likely to use swap memory, you could set the value to 20 instead via the sysctl utility and the -w option. You would need to then pass the key whose value you want to change and the new value.

```
$ sudo sysctl -w vm.swappiness=20
vm.swappiness = 20
```

Another example is the number of files and directories that can be open at any single moment on the system. This is defined in /proc/sys/fs/file-max, and you can read the value via the command sysctl fs.file-max. To increase the maximum number of open files to half a million, run sudo sysctl -w fs.file-max=500000.

■**Caution** Changing kernel variables in the proc file system can have not only a positive impact, but also a large adverse impact on system performance. We recommend you do not change anything unless you have a good reason to.

When the system is rebooted, these variables are reset to their default values. To make them persist, you can add an appropriate entry in the /etc/sysctl.conf file. When the system boots, all settings in this file are applied to the system via the sysctl -p command.

A comprehensive list of available variables, with documentation, is available in the Documentation/sysctl directory in the Linux kernel source. You can view it online at http://www.mjmwired.net/kernel/Documentation/sysctl/.

Storage Devices

In Chapter 8 you saw that in the event of a disk failure, the kernel needs to rebuild the raid array once a replacement disk is added. This task generates a lot of I/O and can degrade performance of other services that the machine may be providing. Alternatively, you might want to give priority to the rebuild process, at the expense of services.

While a rebuild occurs, the kernel keeps the rebuild speed between a set minimum and maximum value. We can change these numbers via the speed_min_limit and speed_max_limit entries in the /proc/sys/dev/raid directory.

A more acceptable minimum speed would be 20,000K per second per disk, and you can set it using sysctl.

```
$ sudo sysctl -w dev.raid.speed_limit_min=20000
```

Setting the minimum too high will adversely affect performance of the system, so make sure you set this number lower than the maximum throughput the system can handle, divided by the number of disks in your raid array.

The maximum, which can be changed by setting the dev.raid.speed_limit_max variable, is fairly high already. If you want a raid rebuild to have less of a performance impact, at the cost of a longer wait, you can lower this number.

To make these changes permanent, add these key-value pairs to /etc/sysctl.conf.

File System Tweaks

Each time a file or directory is accessed, even if it's only for reading, its last accessed time-stamp (or atime) needs to be updated and written to the disk. Unless you need this timestamp, you can speed up disk access by telling your host to not update these.

You simply add the `noatime` option to the `options` field in the `/etc/fstab` file for each file system on which you want to enable this option.

```
UUID=f87a71b8-a323-4e8e-acc9-efb0758a0642    /    ext3    defaults,➡
errors=remount-ro,noatime    0    1
```

This will enable the option the next time the file system is mounted. To make it active immediately, you can remount the file system using the `mount` command.

```
$ sudo mount -o remount,noatime /
```

■**Caution** Some applications use the atime value, and mounting a file system with the `noatime` option may break these applications.

In addition to mount options, file systems themselves provide some features that may improve performance; these vary depending on what a particular file system is used for. The main one of these is `dir_index`, and it applies to the ext2, ext3, and ext4 file systems. Enabling this feature causes the file system to create internal indexes that speed up access to directories containing a large number of files or subdirectories. You can use the `tune2fs` utility to check whether it's enabled.

```
$sudo tune2fs -l /dev/md0 | grep features
Filesystem features: has_journal resize_inode dir_index filetype needs_recovery ➡
    sparse_super large_file
```

In this case it's on, but if it wasn't, you could use `tune2fs` to enable it.

```
sudo tune2fs -O dir_index /dev/md0
```

Alternatively, features can be turned off by prefixing their name with a caret.

```
sudo tune2fs -O ^dir_index /dev/md0
```

Table 17-3 lists the most useful options for improving file system performance.

Table 17-3. *Must-Have File System Features for ext2, ext3, and ext4*

Feature	File System	Provides
dir_index	ext2, ext3, ext4	Faster access to directories containing many files
extents	ext4	Capability to reserve contiguous blocks of disk space
has_journal	ext3, ext4	Journaled file system, providing fast error recovery
sparse_super	ext2, ext3, ext4	Reduced number of backup superblocks, saving space
uninit_bg	ext4	Capability to create a list of unused inodes, so they may be skipped by fsck

By ensuring these options are set on the appropriate file systems, you can get the most out of them. After you change a file system feature, tune2fs will usually notify you that e2fsck needs to be run. This is because some of these options require data structures on the disk to be changed. You need to ensure the affected partitions are unmounted before you run e2fsck on them.

You can set which options should be enabled on the various ext file systems by changing the defaults in the /etc/mke2fs.conf file.

Summary

In this chapter, we've shown you simple tools that allow you to easily determine the basic health of a running host. You've learned how to

- Check CPU usage.

- Check memory and swap space usage.

We've also introduced more advanced system monitoring concepts and tools such as SNMP and Cacti, which will help you monitor resource usage and performance on an ongoing basis. You learned how to

- Install and configure SNMP.

- Install and configure Cacti.

- Use Cacti to monitor the health of your hosts.

In the next chapter, you'll see how to configure some monitoring of your hosts and services. We'll also show you how to configure logging and monitor the logs for unusual or suspicious activity.

■■■

Logging and Monitoring

By James Turnbull

Throughout this book, we've talked about logging and monitoring and their value in trouble-shooting your applications and services. In the first section of this chapter, we're going to look at how logs work on the Linux operating system and how to make use of that data. We'll look at how to store, aggregate, analyze, send alerts on, and rotate log entries and logs. We'll also look at some tools to make it easier to interact with your logs.

In the second section of this chapter, we'll show how you can use an open source tool called Nagios to monitor the applications and services we've introduced. Nagios allows you to define your hosts and the services that run on them. You can then ensure these hosts are up and that your services are functioning correctly. If they are not functioning, your monitoring system can then notify you about what has gone wrong. This process can greatly speed up the time it takes to identify and fix issues.

Logging

You've seen throughout the book that many applications and tools log data about their actions and status. This data usually ends up in the /var/log directory in a variety of files. However, this data isn't usually directly placed in these files by these applications. Instead, Linux uses a daemon called syslog to perform this logging.

Applications output data to the syslog daemon with log entries in a special format that the daemon can parse. The daemon then takes the log entries and can perform a variety of actions with them, including writing them out to a file.

You've seen a few syslog entries earlier in this book. Let's look at a syslog line now:

```
Feb 11 08:14:02 au-mel-ubuntu-1 syslogd 1.5.0#2ubuntu6: restart.
```

A syslog entry is constructed of a date, the name of the host that logged the entry, and the log data itself. Here we've shown a restart of the syslog daemon: syslogd 1.5.0#2ubuntu6: restart.

Syslog is the ubiquitous Unix format for logging. It is present on all flavors of Linux and indeed on almost all flavors of Unix. You can add it using third-party tools to Windows systems, and most network devices such as firewalls, routers, and switches are capable of generating syslog messages. This results in the syslog format being the closest thing to a universal logging standard that exists.

■Tip RFC 3164 documents the core syslog functionality, and you can read it at `http://www.ietf.org/rfc/rfc3164.txt`.

The syslog format is used by a variety of tools that vary in function and complexity and are generally all collectively called `syslog` daemons. These daemons include the basic syslog tool as well as more advanced variants such as syslog-NG (the NG means Next Generation) and rsyslog.

We will cover the basic syslog tool because it is the default on both Red Hat and Ubuntu. It also lays down the groundwork for understanding how logging works on Linux systems.

The syslog utility is designed to generate, process, and store meaningful event notification messages that provide the information required for administrators to manage their systems. Syslog is both a series of programs and libraries, including `syslogd`, the `syslog` daemon, and a communications protocol.

The most frequently used component of syslog is the `syslogd` daemon. This daemon runs on your system from startup and listens for messages from your operating system and applications. It is important to note that the `syslogd` daemon is a passive tool. It merely waits for input from devices or programs. It does not go out and actively gather messages.

■Note Syslog also uses another daemon, `klogd`. The Kernel Log daemon specifically collects messages from the kernel. This daemon is present on both Red Hat and Ubuntu and starts by default when your host starts.

The next major portion of the syslog tools is the syslog communications protocol. With this protocol it is possible to send your log data across a network to a remote system where another `syslog` daemon can collect and centralize your logs.

■Tip Syslog traffic is usually transmitted via UDP on port 514.

Configuring Syslog

The `syslog` daemon is controlled by a configuration file located in `/etc` called `syslog.conf`. This file contains the information about what devices and programs `syslogd` is listening for, where that information is to be stored, and what actions are to be taken when that information is received.

You can see the default `syslog.conf` configuration file from Ubuntu here:

```
# /etc/syslog.conf    Configuration file for syslogd.
#For more information see syslog.conf(5)
#manpage.
```

```
# First some standard logfiles.  Log by facility.

auth,authpriv.*                         /var/log/auth.log
*.*;auth,authpriv.none                  -/var/log/syslog
#cron.*                                 /var/log/cron.log
daemon.*                                -/var/log/daemon.log
kern.*                                  -/var/log/kern.log
lpr.*                                   -/var/log/lpr.log
mail.*                                  -/var/log/mail.log
user.*                                  -/var/log/user.log

# Logging for the mail system.  Split it up so that
# it is easy to write scripts to parse these files.
#
mail.info                               -/var/log/mail.info
mail.warning                            -/var/log/mail.warn
mail.err                                /var/log/mail.err

# Logging for INN news system
#
news.crit                               /var/log/news/news.crit
news.err                                /var/log/news/news.err
news.notice                             -/var/log/news/news.notice

# Some 'catch-all' logfiles.
#
*.=debug;\
auth,authpriv.none;\
news.none;mail.none                     -/var/log/debug
*.=info;*.=notice;*.=warning;\
auth,authpriv.none;\
cron,daemon.none;\
mail,news.none                          -/var/log/messages

# Emergencies are sent to everybody logged in.
#
*.emerg                                 *

# I like to have messages displayed on the console, but only on a
# virtual console I usually leave idle.
#
#daemon,mail.*;\
#news.=crit;news.=err;news.=notice;\
#*.=debug;*.=info;\
#*.=notice;*.=warning                   /dev/tty8

# The named pipe /dev/xconsole is for the 'xconsole' utility.  To
```

```
# use it, you must invoke 'xconsole' with the '-file' option:
#
#     $ xconsole -file /dev/xconsole [...]
#
# NOTE: adjust the list below, or you'll go crazy if you have a
# reasonably busy site..
#
daemon.*;mail.*;\
news.err;\
*.=debug;*.=info;\
*.=notice;*.=warning                        |/dev/xconsole
```

As you've discovered, both Red Hat and Ubuntu all store their log files in the /var/log directory but use different file names to store different types of log entries; for example, you saw in Chapter 10 (and you can see in the preceding syslog.conf configuration file) that Ubuntu stores mail-related syslog entries in the mail.log file. On Red Hat, however, mail-related syslog entries are written to the maillog file. You can check your host's syslog.conf configuration file to determine where the information you want will be written.

Each line in the syslog.conf file is structured into two fields, a selector field and an action field, which are separated by spaces or a tab. You can see an example of a line in Listing 18-1.

Listing 18-1. *syslog.conf Syntax*

```
mail.info                         -/var/log/mail.info
```

This example shows a selector, mail.info, together with the action /var/log/mail.info. The selector specifies a facility and a priority, separated by a period. Facilities tell you the source of log messages; for example, the mail facility is used for log messages related to mail services such as Postfix. A number of facilities are available, and we'll look at each in the next section. Each application specifies the facility it will use for its log entries.

The priority, in this case info, tells syslog the importance of the message being sent. A range of priorities are available, and we'll explain each shortly. Again, applications choose the priority of each message when they send them to syslog.

The action tells syslog what to do with the message; generally this means writing it to a file. In Listing 18-1, all messages from the mail facility with the info priority will be written to the file /var/log/mail.log.

Facilities

The facility identifies the source of the syslog message. Some operating system daemons and other common application daemons have standard facilities attached to them. The mail and kern facilities are two good examples, being mail-related event notification messages and all kernel-related messages, respectively.

Other processes and daemons that do not have a specified facility can use the local facilities, which range from local0 to local7. Table 18-1 lists all syslog facilities.

■**Tip** On Red Hat systems, the local7 is often used for boot messages, and these are directed to /var/log/boot.log.

Table 18-1. *Syslog Facilities on Linux*

Facility	Purpose
auth	Security-related messages
auth-priv	Access control messages
cron	Cron-related messages
daemon	Daemons and process messages
kern	Kernel messages
local0–local7	Reserved for locally defined messages
lpr	Spooling (printing) subsystem messages
mail	Mail-related messages
mark	Time-stamped messages generated by syslogd
news	Network news–related messages (for example, Usenet)
syslog	Syslog-related messages
user	The default facility when no facility is specified
uucp	UUCP-related messages

■**Note** The mark facility is a special case. It is used by the time-stamped messages that syslogd generates when you use the -m (minutes) flag. You can find more on this in the "Starting and Configuring the syslog Daemon" section.

There are also two special facilities: *, a wildcard that indicates all facilities, and none, which negates a facility selection.

You can see the wildcard selector in Listing 18-2.

Listing 18-2. *syslog.conf * Wildcard Selector*

```
*.emerg                          /dev/console
```

This will send all messages of the emerg priority, regardless of facility, to the console (this is another potential action that syslog can perform).

You can use the none wildcard selector to not select messages from a particular facility. The example shown in Listing 18-3 will tell syslog to not log any kernel messages to the file /var/log/messages.

Listing 18-3. *syslog.conf none Wildcard Selector*

```
kern.none                          /var/log/messages
```

Priorities

Priorities are organized in an escalating scale of importance. They are debug, info, notice, warning, err, crit, alert, and emerg. Each priority selector applies to the priority stated and all higher priorities, so uucp.err indicates all uucp facility messages of err, crit, alert, and emerg priorities.

As with facilities, you can use the wildcard selectors * and none. Additionally, you can use two other modifiers: = and !. The = modifier indicates that only one priority is selected; for example, cron.=crit indicates that only cron facility messages of crit priority are to be selected. The ! modifier has a negative effect; for example, cron.!crit selects all cron facility messages except those of crit *or higher priority*. You can also combine the two modifiers to create the opposite effect of the = modifier so that cron.!=crit selects all cron facility messages except those of crit priority. Only one priority and one priority wildcard can be listed per selector.

Actions

Actions tell the syslogd what to do with the event notification messages it receives. Syslog can perform five potential actions:

- Logging to a file

- Logging to a device

- Logging to a named pipe

- Logging to a specific user or the console

- Sending logs to another host

Listing 18-4 shows examples of the first four actions syslogd can take, including logging to a file, device file, named pipes, and the console or a user's screen.

Listing 18-4. *File, Device, and Named Pipe Actions*

```
cron.err      /var/log/cron
auth.!=emerg  /dev/lpr1
news.=notice  |/tmp/pipe
auth-priv     root,bob
```

In the first line all cron messages of err priority and higher are logged to the file /var/log/cron.

■**Note** When logging to files, syslogd allows you to add a hyphen (-) to the front of the file name like this: -/var/log/auth. This tells syslog to not sync the file after writing to it. This is designed to speed up the process of writing to the log. But it can also mean that if your system crashes between write attempts, you will lose data.

The second line has all auth messages except those of emerg priority being sent to a local printer lpr1.

The third sends all news messages of notice or greater priority to a named pipe called /tmp/pipe.

■Note Sending to a named pipe allows you to send syslog data to other applications; for example, you use named pipes to collect log messages and pass them to a log correlation engine or a database.

The fourth and last line sends all auth-priv messages to the users root and bob if they are logged in.

There is one last action you can perform, sending logs to another host, as you can see in Listing 18-5.

Listing 18-5. *Logging to a Remote System*

```
mail       @headoffice.example.com
```

In this example, all mail messages are sent to the host headoffice.example.com.

To send all logs we'd use this syntax:

```
*.*        @headoffice.example.com
```

Syslog uses UDP port 514 to transmit log messages. This assumes the syslog daemon on the remote host has been configured to receive logs and that you have suitable firewall rules in place to receive the log entries, for example:

```
-A Firewall-eth0-INPUT -p udp -m state --state NEW -s 192.168.0.254--dport 514 ➥
-j ACCEPT
```

Here we've created a firewall rule that allows the host to receive syslog data from the host 192.168.0.254 on UDP port 514.

Combining Multiple Selectors

You can also combine multiple selectors in your syslog.conf file, allowing for more sophisticated selections and filtering. For example, you can list multiple facilities separated by commas in a selector (see Listing 18-6).

Listing 18-6. *Multiple Facilities*

```
auth,auth-priv.crit                    /var/log/auth
```

This sends all auth messages and all auth-priv messages with a priority of crit or higher to the file /var/log/auth.

You cannot do this with priorities, though. If you want to list multiple priorities, you need to list multiple selectors separated by semicolons, as shown in Listing 18-7.

Listing 18-7. *Multiple Priorities*

```
auth;auth-priv.debug;auth-priv.!=emerg              /var/log/auth
```

This example shows you how to send all `auth` messages and all `auth-priv` messages with a priority of `debug` or higher, excluding `auth-priv` messages of `emerg` priority to the file `/var/log/auth`.

■**Tip** Just remember with multiple selectors that filtering works from left to right; `syslogd` will process the line starting from the selectors on the left and moving to the right of each succeeding selector. With this in mind, place the broader filters at the left, and narrow the filtering criteria as you move to the right.

You can also use multiple lines to send messages to more than one location, as shown in Listing 18-8.

Listing 18-8. *Logging to Multiple Places*

```
auth                               /var/log/auth
auth.crit                          bob
auth.emerg                         /dev/console
```

Here all `auth` messages are logged to `/var/log/auth` as previously, but `auth` messages of `crit` or higher priority are also sent to user `bob`, if he is logged in. Those of `emerg` priority are also sent to the console.

Starting and Configuring the syslog Daemon

The `syslogd` daemon and its sister process, the `klogd` daemon, are usually both started when your system boots up. On Red Hat this is done via the `syslog` init script that starts `syslogd` and `klogd`. On Ubuntu, the `syslog` daemon is started by the `sysklogd` init script.

On both Red Hat and Ubuntu, you can customize `syslogd`'s options using the `/etc/sysconfig/syslog` and the `/etc/default/syslogd` files, respectively. We're going to look at several of these options.

We discussed `mark` facility messages earlier. These are timestamps that are generated at specified intervals in your logs that look something like this:

```
Feb 24 21:46:05 au-mel-ubuntu-1 -- MARK -
```

They are useful, among other reasons, for acting as markers for programs parsing your log files. These timestamps are generated using the `-m mins` option when you start `syslogd`. To generate a `mark` message every 10 minutes, you would add the `-m 10` option to either the `/etc/sysconfig/syslog` or `/etc/default/syslogd` file. Here, we've added it to the `/etc/default/syslogd` file:

```
# Top configuration file for syslogd
#
# Full documentation of possible arguments are found in the man page
```

```
# syslogd(8).
#
# For remote UDP logging use SYSLOGD="-r"
#
SYSLOGD="-m 10"
```

Remember that mark is a facility in its own right, and you can direct its output to a particular file or destination:

```
mark      /var/log/messages
```

Here all mark facility messages will be directed to /var/log/messages. By default, the syslogd daemons on Red Hat and Ubuntu start with the -m option set to 0 that disables mark messages.

Lastly, we will look at the -r option, which allows syslogd to receive messages from external sources on UDP port 514. If syslogd is started with the -r option, it will listen on UDP port 514 for incoming syslog messages. It will put these messages into the appropriate log files on your host.

You can see this enabled in the /etc/sysconfig/syslog file on a Red Hat host.

```
# Options to syslogd
# -m 0 disables 'MARK' messages.
# -r enables logging from remote machines
# -x disables DNS lookups on messages recieved with -r
# See syslogd(8) for more details
SYSLOGD_OPTIONS="-m 0 -r"
# Options to klogd
# -2 prints all kernel oops messages twice; once for klogd to decode, and
#    once for processing with 'ksymoops'
# -x disables all klogd processing of oops messages entirely
# See klogd(8) for more details
KLOGD_OPTIONS="-x"
#
SYSLOG_UMASK=077
# set this to a umask value to use for all log files as in umask(1).
# By default, all permissions are removed for "group" and "other".
```

By default most syslogd daemons start without -r enabled, and you will have to specifically enable this option to get syslogd to listen.

Opening syslogd to your network can be a dangerous thing. The syslogd daemon is not selective about where it receives messages from: there are no access controls, and any system on your network can log to the syslogd port. This opens your machine to the risk of a DoS attack or a rogue program flooding your system with messages and using all the space in your log partition.

If you are going to use syslogd for remote logging, you have a couple of ways to make your installation more secure. The most obvious threat to syslogd daemons are DoS attacks in which your system is flooded with messages that could completely fill your disks. If your logs are located in the root partition, your system can potentially crash. To reduce the risk of this potential crash, we recommend you store your logs on a nonroot (non-/) partition. This means that even if all the space on your disk is consumed, the system will not crash.

The second way to secure your syslogd for remote logging is to ensure your firewall rules allow connections only from those systems that will be sending their logging data to you. Do not open your syslog daemon to all incoming traffic! Use an appropriate firewall rule, for example the rule we created earlier:

```
-A Firewall-eth0-INPUT -p udp -m state --state NEW -s 192.168.0.254--dport 514 ➥
-j ACCEPT
```

Testing Logging with logger

Present on both Red Hat and Ubuntu, logger is a useful command-line tool to test your logging configuration.

```
$ logger -p mail.info "This is a test message for facility mail and priority info"
```

This would write the message "This is a test message for facility mail and priority info" to your syslog daemon and into whatever destination you have configured for messages with a facility of mail and a priority of info.

As you can see, the -p parameter allows you to specify a facility and priority combination, and then the test message is contained in quotation marks.

We often use logger inside bash scripts to generate multiple messages for testing purposes. The script in Listing 18-9 generates a syslog message for every facility and priority combination.

Listing 18-9. *Log Testing bash Script*

```
#!/bin/bash

for f in
{auth,authpriv,cron,daemon,kern,lpr,mail,mark,news,syslog,user,uucp,local0,local1,➥
local2,local3,local4,local5,local6,local7}

  do
    for p in {debug,info,notice,warning,err,crit,alert,emerg}
  do
    logger -p $f.$p "Test syslog messages from facility $f with priority $p"
  done
  done
exit 0
```

You can also use logger to pipe a growing file into syslog.

```
$ tail -f /tmp/logfile | logger -p daemon.info
```

Here we've tailed the file /tmp/logfile into the logger command. Each line in the file would be written to the daemon facility with a priority of info.

Log Management and Rotation

An important part of managing your logging environment is controlling the volume of your log files and keeping your log files to a manageable size. To do this, you can rotate your logs.

Log rotation is the process of periodically copying the log file and usually adding a suffix like the date or an incrementing number. The syslog daemon then logs to a new file. You would usually keep rotated log files for a fixed period, for example, a week or a month.

Let's look at an example. We've got the /var/log/mail.log file. We could rotate this file daily and keep the rotated files for seven days. The log rotation process would kick off at a time we specified, copy the existing mail.log file to mail.log.1, for example, and then create an empty mail.log file. The log rotation process would also increment; if a mail.log.1 file existed, this file would be renamed to mail.log.2, and so on. If there were a mail.log.7 file, this file would be deleted and the mail.log.6 file incremented to mail.log.7.

Log rotation can be quite complicated to manually manage, so we recommend you use the logrotate tool. Both Red Hat and Ubuntu come with the logrotate tool, and it is usually installed and configured for you already. The default configuration handles most typical log files from applications installed on the host.

The logrotate command is simple to configure and relies on crontab to run on a scheduled basis. The base logrotate configuration is located in /etc/logrotate.conf, and you can see a typical file in Listing 18-10.

Listing 18-10. *logrotate.conf*

```
#log rotation
weekly
# keep old logs
rotate 4
#create new logs
create
#include .d files
include /etc/logrotate.d
```

This simple file contains the global options that logrotate uses to handle log files. In this example, all logs files rotate weekly, logs are rotated four times before they are deleted, new log files are created, and the logrotate tool checks the logrotate.d directory for any new logrotate files. You can use other options, some of which are shown in Table 18-2. You can delve into the logrotate man file for other options.

Table 18-2. *logrotate.conf Options*

Option	Description
daily	Logs are rotated on a daily basis.
weekly	Logs are rotated on a weekly basis.
monthly	Logs are rotated on a monthly basis.
compress	Old log files are compressed with gzip.
create mode owner group	New log files are created with a mode in octal form of 0700 and the owner and group (the opposite is nocreate).

Continued

Table 18-2. *Continued*

Option	Description
ifempty	The log file is rotated even if it is empty.
include directory or filename	The contents of the listed file and directory to be processed by logrotate are included.
mail address	When a log is rotated out of existence, it is mailed to address.
nomail	The last log is not mailed to any address.
missingok	If the log file is missing, it is skipped and logrotate moves on to the next without issuing an error message.
nomissingok	If the log file is missing, an error message is issued (the default behavior).
rotate count	The log files are rotated count times before they are removed. If count is 0, old log files are removed, not rotated.
size size[M,k]	Log files are rotated when they get bigger than the maximum size; M indicates size in megabytes, and k indicates size in kilobytes.
sharedscripts	Prescripts and postscripts can be run for each log file being rotated. If a log file definition consists of a collection of log files (for example, /var/log/samba/*), and sharedscripts is set, then the prescript/postscripts are run only once. The opposite is nosharedscripts.

Listing 18-10 shows the last command, include, which principally drives logrotate.

The logrotate.d directory included in Listing 18-10 holds a collection of files that tell logrotate how to handle your various log files.

You can also define additional directories and files and include them in the logrotate.conf file to suit your environment. Most distributions, however, use the logrotate.d directory and come with a number of predefined files in this directory to handle common log rotations such as mail, cron, and syslog messages. We recommend you add any new log rotation files here.

■**Note** Many packages will also add log rotation files to this directory when installed.

Listing 18-11 shows you one of these files.

Listing 18-11. *Red Hat syslog logrotate File*

```
/var/log/messages /var/log/secure /var/log/maillog /var/log/spooler ➥
/var/log/boot.log /var/log/cron
{
daily
rotate 7
sharedscripts
postrotate
    /bin/kill -HUP 'cat /var/run/syslogd.pid 2> /dev/null' 2> /dev/null || true
endscript
}
```

Inside these files you can override most of the global options in logrotate.conf to customize your log rotation for individual files or directories. Listing 18-11 first lists all the files to be rotated. This could also include directories using the syntax /path/to/log/files/*.

Then enclosed in { } are any options for this particular set of files. In this example, we have overridden the global logging options to rotate these files on a daily basis and keep seven rotations of the log files.

Next, we run a script. You can run scripts using the prerotate command, which runs the script prior to rotating any logs, or using postrotate, which runs the script after rotating the log file(s).

Listing 18-11 shows a script that restarts the syslog daemon after the log file(s) have been rotated. As the option sharedscripts is enabled, the script will be run only once no matter how many individual log files are rotated. The script statement is terminated with the endscript option.

So how does logrotate run? By default on both Red Hat and Ubuntu, cron runs logrotate at scheduled times. You can also manually run it on the command line.

If running on the command line, logrotate defaults to a configuration file of /etc/logrotate.conf. You can override this configuration file as you can see on the following line:

```
$ sudo logrotate /etc/logrotate2.conf
```

The logrotate command also has several command-line options to use, as shown in Table 18-3.

Table 18-3. *logrotate Command-Line Options*

Option	Description
-d	Debug mode in which no changes will be made to log files; it will output the results of what it may have rotated. Implies verbose mode also.
-v	Verbose mode.
-f	Forces a log rotation even if not required.

By default on most systems, logrotate is run on a daily basis by cron, and this is the model we recommend you use.

Log Analysis and Correlation

Now you have all of these log files, what can you do with them? Well, logs are useful for two purposes:

- To identify when something has gone wrong
- To help diagnose the problem when something has gone wrong

To achieve the first objective, you need a tool that will identify particular log messages and alert you to their presence. This process is called *log analysis and correlation*, and it is often considered a black art. But we're going to introduce you to a tool called SEC, which will make log analysis and correlation a simple part of your daily monitoring routine.

The first thing to remember is that analysis and correlation are two very different things. *Analysis* is the study of constituent parts and their interrelationships in making up a whole. As a system administer, the best analysis tool available is you. System administrators learn the patterns of their hosts' operations and can often detect a problem far sooner than automated monitoring or alerting systems have done on the same problem.

There are two problems with this model though. The first is that you cannot be everywhere at once. The second is that the growing volume of the data collected by the systems can become overwhelming.

This is where correlation comes in. *Correlation* is best defined as the act of detecting relationships between data. You set up tools to collect your data, filter the "wheat from the chaff," and then correlate that remaining data to put the right pieces of information in front of you so you can provide an accurate analysis.

Properly set up and managed tools can sort through the constant stream of data from the daily operations of your hosts. They can detect the relationships between that data and either put those pieces together into a coherent whole or provide you with the right pieces to allow you to put that analysis together for yourself.

But you have to ensure those tools are the right tools and are configured to look for the right things so you can rely on them to tell you that something is wrong and that you need to intervene.

The first stage of building such an automated log-monitoring system is to make sure you are collecting the right things and putting them in the right place. Make lists of all your applications, devices, and hosts and where they log. The second stage is bringing together all that information and working out what you really want to know. Make lists of the critical messages that are important to you and your hosts.

Group those lists into priority listings; some messages you may want to be paged for, others can go via e-mail, and some may trigger automated processes or generate attempts at self-recovery such as restarting a process.

The third stage is implementing your log correlation and analysis, including configuring your correlation tools and designing the required responses. Make sure you carefully document each message, the response to the message, and any special information that relates to this message.

Introducing SEC

SEC, or the Simple Event Correlator, is the most powerful open source log correlation tool available. SEC utilizes Perl regular expressions to find the messages that are important to running your system out of the huge volume of log traffic most Linux systems generate. It can find a single message or match pairs of related messages; for example, it can find matching messages that indicate when a user has logged on and off a system. SEC can also keep count of messages it receives and act only if it receives a number of messages exceeding a threshold that you can define. SEC can also react to the messages it receives by performing actions such as running a shell script. These actions can include the content of the messages. For example, it is possible to run a shell script as a SEC action and use some or all of the message content as a variable to be inputted into that shell script.

REGULAR EXPRESSIONS

As a result of SEC's reliance on Perl regular expressions, you need to get comfortable with using them. They initially can look a little scary, but they are in fact really easy to learn and use. A regular expression is a simple technique used to identify a string of text or numbers that interests you from a larger collection of data. A simple use might be to match the word *cat* whenever it appears. Using a regular expression, you could match the word when it appears on its own or as part of another word (e.g., *cat*egory).

There are several varieties of regular expressions, and different programming languages have slightly different syntax. The Perl programming language's regular expressions syntax is widely used and easy to learn. You can start with the Perl documentation on regular expressions, which is excellent. Try http:// www.perldoc.com/perl5.6.1/pod/perlre.html and http://www.perldoc.com/perl5.8.0/ pod/perlretut.html. Some excellent books on regular expressions are available such as *Mastering Regular Expressions* by Jeffery Friedl (O'Reilly, 2006). You can also find lots of other resources online such as the following:

- http://www.regextester.com/: An online testing tool that allows you to test your regular expressions

- http://www.troubleshooters.com/codecorn/littperl/perlreg.htm: A tutorial

- http://www.cs.tut.fi/~jkorpela/perl/regexp.html: A tutorial

- http://www.quanetic.com/Regex: A regular expression tester

- http://www.perlfect.com/articles/regextutor.shtml: A regular expression interactive tutorial

Seeing all this functionality, you may think SEC is overkill for your requirements, but the ability to expand your event correlation capabilities far outweighs the cost of implementation. In our experience, it is critical in a logging environment to avoid having to make compromises in monitoring that could cause you to potentially miss vital messages. The functionality richness of SEC should be able to cover all your current and future event correlation needs.

Because of SEC's complexity, it is impossible to completely cover all its features within this chapter, so we will avoid discussing some of the more advanced features of SEC, most notably contexts. SEC's full implementation and variables could easily occupy a book in their own right. We will get you started with SEC by showing you how to install it, how to get it running, how to point your logs to SEC, and how to set up some basic message-matching rules; then we will point you to the resources you will need to fully enable SEC within your own environment.

■**Tip** A good place to start learning more about SEC is the mailing list maintained at the SourceForge site for SEC. You can subscribe to the mailing list and read its archives at http://lists.sourceforge.net/ lists/listinfo/simple-evcorr-users. SEC's author Risto Vaarandi is a regular, active, and helpful participant to this list, and the archives of the list contain many useful examples of SEC rules to help you.

Installing SEC

You can install SEC from a package or via the SEC website. On Ubuntu, the required package is called sec.

```
$ sudo  aptitude install sec
```

On Red Hat, the SEC application has been packaged by the EPEL project (which provides additional packages for Red Hat Enterprise Linux), and you can download and install it using RPM.

```
$ sudo rpm -Uvh http://download.fedora.redhat.com/pub/epel/5/i386/➥
sec-2.4.1-1.el5.noarch.rpm
```

■**Note** You can also add the EPEL repository to your host and install the package via yum using the instructions at http://fedoraproject.org/wiki/EPEL/FAQ#How_can_I_install_the_packages_ from_the_EPEL_software_repository.3F.

You can also download SEC from its home page at http://kodu.neti.ee/~risto/sec/ in the Download section, for example:

```
$ wget http://prdownloads.sourceforge.net/simple-evcorr/sec-2.5.0.tar.gz
```

Installing SEC from this download is a simple process. We first unpack the archive file and change into the resulting directory.

```
$ tar -zxf sec-2.5.0.tar.gz
$ cd sec-2.5.0
```

Inside the archive is the engine of the SEC tool, a Perl script called sec.pl. Copy the sec.pl script to a directory in your path, and make it executable and owned by the root user.

```
$ sudo cp sel.pl /usr/local/bin/sec.pl
$ sudo chmod 0755 /usr/local/bin/sec.pl
$ sudo chown root:root /usr/local/bin/sec.pl
```

SEC also comes with a comprehensive man page that you should also install by issuing the following:

```
$ sudo cp sec.pl.man /usr/local/share/man/man8
$ sudo chown root:root /usr/local/share/man/man8/sec.pl.man
```

Running SEC

You start SEC from the command line by running the sec binary (or the sec.pl script if you've installed it from source), or you can start it via an init script.

On both Ubuntu and Red Hat, the init script installed by the package is called sec. You'll need to configure each a little to get SEC started.

Running SEC on Red Hat

On Red Hat, we need to review the /etc/sysconfig/sec file.

```
# Because SEC usage varies so widely from user to user, it is configured by
# default to not run.  Please read 'sec --help' for valid options to use in
# this configuration directive, or use the sample defaults included below.
#
# If you would like to run multiple instances of sec in order to track more
# than one log file, you can use also use $SEC_OPTIONS as an array.
#
# Also, please don't forget to read the sec man page or look at the
# configuration options for /etc/sec/.
#
# Default:
#
# SEC_ARGS="-detach -conf=/etc/sec/*.sec -input=/var/log/messages ➥
-log=/var/log/sec -intevents -pid=/var/run/sec.pid"
#
# For Multiple instances of SEC, use something like:
#
# SEC_ARGS[0]="-detach -conf=/etc/sec/sys/*.sec -input=/var/log/messages ➥
-log=/var/log/sec -intevents -pid=/var/run/sec.sys.pid"
#
# SEC_ARGS[1]="-detach -conf=/etc/sec/mail/*.sec -input=/var/log/messages➥
 -log=/var/log/sec -intevents -pid=/var/run/sec.mail.pid"
```

In this file, we need to tell sec what startup options to use. The easiest way is to use the default SEC_ARGS line already specified in the file. To do so, we uncomment it:

```
SEC_ARGS="-detach -conf=/etc/sec/*.sec -input=/var/log/messages -log=/var/log/sec ➥
-intevents -pid=/var/run/sec.pid"
```

Let's look at this line. Each option will be passed to SEC. The -detach option runs SEC as a daemon. The -conf option loads SEC configuration, which in this case are the rules we're going to use to match specific log entries. On Red Hat, SEC will load all files with a suffix of .sec located in the /etc/sec directory.

The -input option tells SEC which files to monitor for syslog log entries. In our example line, we're only looking at the /var/log/messages file. You can specify a file glob or multiple -input options to specify more files. For example, to specify all files with a suffix of .log, you would issue the following:

```
-input *.log
```

Or to specify multiple files:

```
-input=/var/log/messages -input=/var/log/secure
```

The -log option tells SEC where to log its output to, and the -intevents option generates start, stop, and restart log events for the SEC application itself.

Lastly, the -pid option specifies where the sec daemon's PID should be written.

We could then enable SEC to run at boot like so:

```
$ sudo chkconfig --level 35 sec on
$ sudo chkconfig --add sec
```

■**Note** Currently we don't have any rules, so SEC won't do anything when it starts.

Running SEC on Ubuntu

On Ubuntu, the 8.04 LTS release of SEC lacks a few amenities, such as an `init` script. The `sec` package for the next Ubuntu version contains what we need, so we're going to get the `/etc/default/sec` and `/etc/init.d/sec` files from this later release. To do this, we're going to download part of the later release:

```
$ cd /tmp
$ wget http://archive.ubuntu.com/ubuntu/pool/universe/s/sec/sec_2.4.2-1.diff.gz
$ gunzip sec_2.4.2-1.diff.gz
$ patch -p1 < 2.4.2-1.diff
$ cp debian/sec.default /etc/default/sec
$ cp debian/sec.init /etc/init.d/sec
```

First, we change into the `/tmp` directory. We then download one of the files that builds the `sec` package and use the `gunzip` command to uncompress it. The `patch` command is a special tool that performs a form of find and replace on files. In this case, it creates a number of files used in the Ubuntu install package in a directory called `debian`, including the `sec.default` and `sec.init` files that we're going to use. Lastly, we copy the files to the right places with the right names.

■**Note** We've also included these files in the source code for this book.

Now we have the files we need to adjust the `/etc/default/sec` configuration file.

```
#Defaults for sec
RUN_DAEMON="no"
DAEMON_ARGS="-conf=/etc/sec.conf -input=/var/log/syslog -pid=/var/run/sec.pid ➥
-detach -syslog=daemon"
```

First, we need to enable the `sec` daemon by changing the `RUN_DAEMON` option to yes.

```
RUN_DAEMON="yes"
```

Next, we need to update the arguments we're going to pass to the `sec` daemon. We're going to update the `DAEMON_ARGS` line to the following:

```
DAEMON_ARGS="-detach -conf=/etc/sec/*.sec -input=/var/log/syslog ➥
-input=/var/log/daemon.log -input=/var/log/messages -input=/var/log/auth.log ➥
-input=/var/log/user.log -pid=/var/run/sec.pid -syslog=daemon"
```

The first option, -detach, runs SEC in daemon mode. The next option, -conf, loads SEC's configuration, in our case all rules from files suffixed with .sec, in the /etc/sec directory. Let's quickly create that directory now:

```
$ sudo mkdir /etc/sec
```

For the moment we have no rules, so SEC will load without doing anything.

The -input options tell SEC which files to monitor for syslog messages. We've specified a few of the key files used to output logging data, for example, /var/log/syslog and /var/log/daemon.log.

Lastly, the -pid and -log options tell SEC to write its PID file to /var/run/sec.pid and to output its own log entries to /var/log/sec.log.

We can now tell Ubuntu to start SEC when we boot.

```
$ sudo update-rc.d sec defaults
```

SEC Command-Line Options

SEC has some additional command-line options to control its behavior and configuration. Table 18-4 covers some of the important ones.

Table 18-4. *SEC Command-Line Options*

Option	Description
-input=file pattern[=context]	This indicates the input sources for SEC, which can be files, named pipes, or standard input. You can have multiple input statements on your command line. The optional context option will set up a context. Contexts help you to write rules that match events from specific input sources. Note that we do not cover contexts in this chapter.
-pid=pidfile	This specifies a file to store the process ID of SEC. You must use this if you want a PID file.
-quoting and -noquoting	If quoting is turned on, all strings provided to external shell commands by SEC will be put inside quotes to escape them. The default is not to quote.
-tail and -notail	These tell SEC what to do with files. If -notail is set, SEC will read any input sources and then exit when it reaches the end of the file or source. If -tail is set, SEC will jump to the end of the input source and wait for additional input as if you had issued the tail -f command. The default is -tail.
-fromstart and -nofromstart	These flags are used in combination with -tail. When -fromstart is enabled, it will force SEC to process input files from start to finish, and then go into tail mode and wait for additional input. These options obviously have no effect if -notail is set. The default option is -nofromstart.

Continued

Table 18-4. *Continued*

Option	Description
-detach and -nodetach	If you add -detach to the command line, SEC will daemon-ize. The default is -nodetach, which has SEC running in the controlling terminal.
-testonly and -notestonly	If the -testonly option is specified, SEC will exit immediately after parsing the configuration file(s) for any errors. If the configuration file does not contain any errors, SEC will exit with an exit code of 0; otherwise, it exits with an exit code of 1. The default is -notestonly.

You can read about additional SEC options on time-outs in input sources in the SEC man page.

Using SEC

Now we're going to demonstrate how to create some simple SEC rules so you get an under-standing of how they work. Each SEC configuration file contains a series of rule statements. Each rule statement consists of a series of pairs of keys and values separated by an equals (=) sign. Each line has one key and value pair, as in this example:

```
type=Single
```

Multiple rules can be stored in a file, and each rule is separated by a blank line.

■Note You can use the backslash (\) symbol to continue a key-value pair onto the next line, and you can specify a comment using the pound, or #, symbol.

SEC works very simply. It monitors the input files we've specified using the -input option and watches for new log messages. When a new message is received, it scans its list of rules for any that might match the message. If it finds a matching rule for that message, it performs whatever action the rule specifies, for example, mails a message to a system administrator, runs a script, or the like. If the message doesn't match, SEC discards it, does nothing, and waits for further new messages.

■Note SEC just reads your log files. It doesn't change or delete any log entries.

Building SEC Rules

Let's look now at an example of a rule statement to better understand how SEC and SEC rules work. We're going to take a syslog message and use SEC to alert when it is received. We're going to employ the message generated when the su command is used to change to the root user. We want to issue an alert on this because no one should be using the root user; as responsible system administrators, we only use the sudo command. Let's look at an example of our message:

```
Feb 15 22:29:34 au-mel-rhel-1 su: pam_unix(su-l:session): session opened for user ➥
root by jsmith(uid=500)
```

This message is logged to the /var/log/secure file on Red Hat and the /var/log/auth.log file on Ubuntu. So we need SEC to monitor these files on our respective distributions using the -input configuration option. On Red Hat:

```
-input /var/log/secure
```

And on Ubuntu:

```
-input /var/log/auth.log
```

First, we'll create a file to hold our new rule, security.sec in the /etc/sec directory. When we start SEC, this file and the rules contained it in will be loaded.

```
$ sudo touch /etc/sec/security.sec
```

So we then create a rule in this file that will match this message and tell us what we need to know. You can see a simple rule in Listing 18-12.

Listing 18-12. *A SEC Rule Statement*

```
type=Single
continue=TakeNext
ptype=regexp
pattern=session opened for user root by (\w+)
desc=Root user login by $1 - is this authorised?
action=shellcmd /bin/echo '$0' | /bin/mail -s "%s" root@example.com
```

Let's discuss this example line by line. The first line indicates the type of SEC rule that is being used. In Listing 18-12 we have used the simplest rule, called Single, which simply finds a message and then executes an action.

■**Note** A number of different rule types exist, and we'll discuss them in this section.

The second line in Listing 18-12 is optional. The continue line has three potential options, TakeNext, DontCont, and GoTo. The first option, TakeNext, tells SEC that even if the log entry matches this rule, it should keep searching through the file for other rules that may match the entry.

The second option, DontCont, tells SEC that if the log entry matches this rule, it should stop there and not try to match the entry against any additional rules. This means that a log entry will be checked against every single rule in your configuration file until it finds a rule it matches that has a continue setting of DontCont. This is useful when some messages may be relevant to more than one rule in your configuration file. An example of when you could use this is if a message has more than one implication or purpose. For example, a user login message may be used to record user login statistics, but you may also want to be e-mailed if the root user logs on. You would use one rule to record the user statistics that has a continue option of TakeNext. After processing this rule, the message would be checked against the other rules in the configuration file and picked up by the rule that e-mails you if the root user logged on.

The last option, GoTo, tells SEC to pass the log entry to a specific rule that must exist in the current file.

Note If you omit the continue option from the rule statement, SEC defaults to DontCont and will stop when a rule matches a log entry.

The next two lines in the rule statement allow SEC to match particular events. The first is ptype, or pattern type. The pattern type tells SEC how to interpret the information on the next line, the pattern line. You can use the pattern types shown in Table 18-5.

Table 18-5. *SEC Pattern Types*

Pattern Type	Description
RegExp[*number*]	Indicates a Perl regular expression.
SubStr[*number*]	Indicates a substring.
PerlFunc	Calls a Perl function.
NRegExp[*number*]	Represents a negated regular expression. The results of the pattern match are negated.
NSubStr[*number*]	Represents a negated substring. The results of the pattern match are negated.
NPerlFunc	Calls a Perl function, with the results being negated.

Note The *number* portion after the pattern type tells SEC to compare the rule against the last *number* of log entries. If you leave *number* blank, then SEC defaults to 1, which is the last log entry received.

We're going to focus on the SubStr and RegExp pattern types. The SubStr pattern type matches a string of data, for example:

```
ptype=SubStr
pattern= dhclient: No DHCPOFFERS received.
```

This matches the message dhclient: No DHCPOFFERS received. and does not allow any regular expressions.

Listing 18-12 used a standard regexp pattern type that tells SEC to interpret the pattern line as a Perl regular expression.

■**Note** For the other pattern types, see the SEC man page.

The fourth line in Listing 18-12, `pattern`, shows the pattern itself. In this example, it is a regular expression. This regular expression would match any message that consisted of the string `session opened for user root by (\w+)`.

The (`\w+`) is a regular expression; it tells SEC to grab any word that follows by in our string; in this case, it'll match the name of the user who has opened the session as the `root` user.

We have placed part of the regular expression, [`\w+`], in parentheses. In a regular expression, the content of anything in the `pattern` line that you place in parentheses becomes a variable available to use in SEC.

In this instance, (`\w+`) becomes the variable $1; any subsequent data enclosed in parentheses would become $2, then $3, and so on. So if the message being tested against this rule is as follows:

```
su: pam_unix(su-1:session): session opened for user root by jsmith(uid=500)
```

the message would be matched, and the variable $1 would be assigned a content of `jsmith`.

■**Tip** Another special variable, $0, is reserved for the content of the log entry or entries the rule is being tested against. In this example, the variable $0 would contain the input line `su: pam_unix(su-1:session): session opened for user root by jsmith(uid=500)`.

The fifth line in Listing 18-12 shows the `desc` key-value pair. This is a textual description of the event being matched. Inside this description you can use any variables defined in the pattern, for example, the $1 we defined earlier in the `pattern` line.

Thus, the `desc` for Listing 18-12 is `Root user login by $1 - is this authorized?`. Using the message data in the previous paragraph, this would result in a description of `Root user login by jsmith - is this authorized?`. You will note that we have used the variable, $1, that we defined in the `pattern` line in the `desc` line.

■**Tip** The final constructed description is also available to you in SEC as the %s variable.

The fifth and last line in Listing 18-12 shows the `action` key-value pair. This line tells SEC what to do if the rule matches an incoming log entry.

In the `action` line, in addition to any variables defined in the pattern (the $0 variable and the %s variable indicating the `desc` line), you also have access to two other internal variables: %t, a timestamp that is equivalent to the result of the `date` command, and %u, a numeric timestamp that is equivalent to the result of the `time` command.

■**Note** SEC assumes that a blank line or comment is the end of the current rule statement, so only add comments or blank lines at the start or end of a rule statement.

Now you have seen your first SEC rule. This rule just scrapes the surface of what SEC is capable of doing.

Let's look at another example to show you what else SEC is capable of doing. Listing 18-13 uses the `SingleWithThreshold` rule type to identify repeated `sshd` failed login attempts.

Listing 18-13. *Using the `SingleWithThreshold` Rule Type*

```
type=SingleWithThreshold
ptype=regexp
pattern=(\w+)\s+sshd\[\d+\]\:\s+Failed password for (\w+) from (\d+.\d+.\d+.\d+) ➥
port \d+ \w+\d+
desc=User $2 logging in from IP $3 to host $1 failed to enter the correct password
thresh=3
window=60
action=write /var/log/badpassword.log %s
```

With this rule, we are looking to match variations on the following log entry:

```
Feb 15 23:23:13 au-mel-rhel-1 sshd[738]: Failed password for jsmith from ➥
192.168.1.10 port 44328 ssh2
```

The rule type we are using to do this is called `SingleWithThreshold`. This rule type matches log entries and keeps counts of how many are matched within a particular window of time. The window is specified using the `window` option and is expressed in seconds. In Listing 18-13, it is set to 60 seconds. The window starts counting when SEC first matches a message against that rule.

SEC then compares the number of matches to a threshold, which you can see defined in Listing 18-13 using the `thresh` option as three matches. If the number of matches reaches the threshold within the window of time, the `action` line is performed.

In Listing 18-13, the action we have specified is to write the contents of the `desc` line to the specified file, `/var/log/sshdbruteforce.log`, using the `write` action. The `write` action can write to a file, to a named pipe, or to standard output.

■**Tip** Another thing you could do is add a firewall rule blocking that IP address from SSH.

So what other rule types are available to you? Well, SEC has a large collection of possible rules that are capable of complicated event correlation. You can see a list of all the other available rule types in Table 18-6.

Table 18-6. *SEC Rule Types*

Rule Type	Description
`SingleWithScript`	Matches an event, executes a script, and then, depending on the exit value of the script, executes a further action.
`SingleWithSuppress`	Matches an event, executes an action immediately, and then ignores any further matching events for *x* seconds.
`Pair`	Has a paired set of matches. It matches an initial event and executes an action immediately. It ignores any following matching events until it finds the paired event and executes another action.
`PairWithWindow`	Also has a paired set of matches. When it matches an initial event, it waits for *x* seconds for the paired event to arrive. If the paired event arrives within the given window, it executes an action. If the paired event does not arrive within the given window, it executes a different action.
`SingleWithThreshold`	Counts up matching events during *x1* seconds and if more than a threshold of *t1* events is exceeded, it executes an action. Any additional events during that *x1* seconds are ignored.
`SingleWith2Thresholds`	Counts up matching events during *x* seconds, and if more than the threshold of *t1* events is exceeded, it executes an action. It then starts to count matching events again, and if the number during *x2* seconds drops below the threshold of *t2*, it executes another action.
`Suppress`	Suppresses any matching events. You can use this to exclude any events from being matched by later rules. This is useful for removing high-volume, low-informational content messages that would otherwise clog SEC.
`Jump`	Submits matching events to another rule set.
`Options`	Sets options for a rule set.
`Calendar`	Executes an action at a specific time.

So how do you use some of these other rule types? Let's look at some additional examples. Specifically, Listing 18-14 demonstrates using the `Pair` rule type.

Listing 18-14. *Using the* `Pair` *Rule Type*

```
type=Pair
ptype=regexp
pattern=(\w+\s+\d+\s+\d\d:\d\d:\d\d)\s+(\w+)\s+su\(pam_unix\)(\[\d+\])\:\s+session ➥
opened for user root by (\w+)\(\w+\=\d+\)
desc=User $4 has succeeded in an su to root at $1 on system $2. Do you trust ➥
user $4?
action=shellcmd /bin/echo '%s' | /bin/mail -s "SU Session Open Warning" ➥
root@example.com
ptype2=regexp
pattern2=(\w+\s+\d+\s+\d\d:\d\d:\d\d)\s+$2\s+su\(pam_unix\) $3\:\s+session closed ➥
for user root
desc2=Potentially mischievous user %4 has closed their su session at %1 on system %2
action2=shellcmd /bin/echo '%s' | /bin/mail -s "SU Session Close Warning" ➥
root@example.com
```

In this example, we are using `Pair` to detect whenever somebody used the `su` command to become `root` on a system and then monitor the log file for when that person closed that `su` session. So, we will be looking to match variations of the following two log entries:

```
Feb 15 22:29:34  au-mel-rhel-1  su(pam_unix)[17354]: session opened for ➥
user root by jsmith(uid=500)
Feb 15 23:56:45 au-mel-rhel-1  su(pam_unix)[17354]: session closed for user root
```

The rule type we will use for this is `Pair`, which is designed to detect a matching pair of log entries. You could also use the `PairWithWindow` rule type, which is designed to find a matching pair of log entries within a particular time window much like the `SingleWithThreshold` rule type you saw in Listing 18-13.

With the `Pair` rule types, you actually define two sets of pattern type and pattern, description, and action items. This is because you are matching two log entries. The second set of items are suffixed with the number 2 and referred to as `ptype2` and `pattern2`, and so on, to differentiate them from the first set.

The first set of items is used when the first log entry is matched; for example, the `action` line is executed when the log entry is matched. The second set of items is used if the second log entry is matched; for example, the `action2` line is executed when the second log entry is matched.

For the first set of pattern type and pattern, we have used a regular expression pattern type. Inside the pattern we have also defined a number of elements of the log entry we are seeking to match as variables: the hostname on which the `su` session took place, the user who used the `su` command, the time the session opened and closed, and the process ID that issued the `su` command.

You can then see that we have used some of these variables in the `desc` and `action` lines. The `action` we are using in Listing 18-14 is called `shellcmd` to execute a shell command when a log entry is matched.

The second pattern type will also be a regular expression. In this pattern, how do you know whether the log entry indicating the end of the `su` session is related to the original log entry opening the `su` session? Well, SEC can use variables from the first pattern line, `pattern`, and these variables can form part of the regular expression being matched in the second pattern line, `pattern2`.

In the first `pattern` line, we defined the hostname of the system the `su` session was taking place on as `$2` and the process ID of the session as `$3`. If you refer to those variables in the `pattern2` line, SEC knows you are referring to variables defined in the first `pattern` line. You use the hostname and process ID to match the incoming log entry against the first log entry.

But this raises another question. How does SEC tell the difference between the variables defined in the two pattern lines when you use them in the `desc2` line, for example? Well, variables for the first `pattern` line, if you want to use them again in the `desc2` or `action2` lines, are prefixed by `%`, and variables from the second `pattern` line are prefixed with `$`. You can see we have used the `$4` variable defined in the first `pattern` line in the `desc2` line by calling it `%4`.

Another useful rule type is `Suppress`. Listing 18-15 shows an example of a `Suppress` rule.

Listing 18-15. *Using the Suppress Rule Type*

```
type=Suppress
ptype=regexp
pattern=\w+\s+syslogd\[\d+\]\:\s+STATS: dropped \d+
```

Listing 18-15 is designed to suppress the following log entry:

```
Feb 15 21:19:23  syslogd[22565]: STATS: dropped 0
```

The Suppress rule type simply consists of the rule type, a pattern type, and a pattern to match. Event suppression is especially useful for stopping SEC processing events you know have no value. You can specify a series of Suppress rules at the start of your configuration file to stop SEC unnecessarily processing unimportant messages. Be careful to be sure you are not suppressing a useful message, and be especially careful not to make your regular expressions too broad, which could suppress messages you need to see from getting through.

Suppress rules are also a place where you could use the pattern type of Substr. Let's rewrite Listing 18-15 using a substring instead of a regular expression:

```
type=Suppress
ptype=substr
pattern=This message is to be suppressed.
```

To match a log entry to a substring rule, the content of the pattern line must exactly match the content of the log entry. If required in a substring, you can use the backslash constructs \t, \n, \r, or \s to indicate any tabulation, newlines, carriage returns, or space characters.

Tip As special characters are indicated with a backslash in Perl, if you need to use a backslash in a substring or regular expression, you must escape it. For instance, in Perl \\ denotes a backslash.

The Suppress rule type is not the only type of rule that allows you to suppress messages. You can also use the SingleWithSuppress rule type. This rule type is designed to match a single log entry, execute an action, and then suppress any other log entries that match the rule for a fixed period defined using the window line.

This is designed to allow you to enable message compression. Message compression is useful where multiple instances of a log entry are generated, but you need to be notified or have an action performed for only the first matched log entry. You can compress 100 messages to one response or action instead of each of the messages generating 100 individual responses or actions.

Listing 18-16 shows an example of the SingleWithSuppress rule type.

Listing 18-16. *Using the SingleWithSuppress Rule Type*

```
type=SingleWithSuppress
ptype=RegExp
pattern=(\S+): Table overflow [0-9]+ of [0-9]+ in Table (\S+)
desc=Please check for a table overflow in $2
action=shellcmd notify.sh "%s"
window=600
```

Listing 18-16 uses a regular expression to check for a table overflow message generated by a database. We know this message can be generated hundreds of times in a short period, so we use the `SingleWithSuppress` rule to match only the first log entry and notify a user about the error message.

If additional log entries are matched to this rule within the next 600 seconds (as defined using the `window` line), they are suppressed, and no action is performed. If the log entry appears again more than 600 seconds after the first log entry was matched, another action is generated, and all further matching log entries would be suppressed for another 600 seconds. This, for example, could be because the original problem has not been fixed and another notification is needed.

Within the last few examples, you have seen only a couple of SEC's possible actions, `write` and `shellcmd`. Within SEC, additional possible actions are available. Table 18-7 describes some of the key ones. You can view other actions in the SEC man page.

Table 18-7. *SEC Actions*

Action	Description
`assign %letter [text]`	This assigns the content of *text* to a user-defined *%letter* variable. You can use other % variables in your *text*, like those variables defined in your pattern. If you do not provide any *text*, the value of the variable %s is used.
`event [time] [event text]`	After *time* seconds, a event with the content of *event text* is created. SEC treats the *event text* string exactly like a log entry and compares it to all rules. If you do not specify any *event text*, the value of the %s variable is used. If you specify 0 as *time* or omit the value altogether, it will be created immediately.
`logonly`	The event description is logged to the SEC log file.
`none`	This takes no action.
`spawn shellcmd`	This is identical to the `shellcmd` action, but any standard output from `shellcmd` is inputted to SEC as if it were a log entry and matched against the rules. This is done by generating an event 0 *output line* to each line from standard output. Be careful that the `shellcmd` command being spawned does not output a large volume of data or an endless loop, as SEC will process these results first and thus become locked.

You can put more than one action on an `action` line by separating them with a semicolon. You can see this in the next line:

```
action=shellcmd notify.sh "%s"; write /var/log/output.log %s
```

Here we have combined the `shellcmd` and `write` actions.

Listing 18-17 shows one final example, the `Calendar` rule type. The `Calendar` rule type is constructed differently than the other rule types are constructed.

Listing 18-17. *Using the Calendar Rule Type*

```
type=Calendar
time=1-59 * * * *
desc=This is an important message SEC needs to check
action=shellcmd purge.sh
```

The Calendar rule type uses a special line called time. The time line uses the standard crontab format of five fields, separated by whitespace; those fields are minutes, hours, days of the month, months of the year, and weekdays. You can use the Calendar rule type to schedule events or kick off log-related processes. We often use Calendar events to schedule the clearing and management of files used during the logging process or to initiate a logging report.

Troubleshooting SEC

The examples in this chapter should have provided you with the grounding to start writing your own SEC rules. For further information and assistance with writing SEC rules, check the SEC FAQ and the examples at http://kodu.neti.ee/~risto/sec/FAQ.html and http://kodu.neti.ee/~risto/sec/examples.html, respectively.

Also available in the Red Hat package is a collection of example rules that are installed into the /etc/sec/examples directory. These examples create a regular report that uses the Calendar type, showing specific log entries. We've also included those examples in the source code for this book as well. Have a look at the 001_init.sec file to get started.

Also, as mentioned earlier, the SEC mailing list at http://www.estpak.ee/~risto/sec/#mailinglist is an excellent source of assistance and information.

Monitoring

Once you have all your applications and services running, you need to have some mechanism available to monitor them. This ensures your host lets you know when important events occur, such as when disk space runs out on a host or when a service unexpectedly stops.

In the IT world, this monitoring mechanism is called *enterprise monitoring*. Like the other applications and tools we've introduced you to in this book, a number of open source tools are available that can perform this monitoring, for example:

- Hyperic (http://www.hyperic.com/)
- M/Monit (http://mmonit.com/)
- Nagios (http://www.nagios.org)
- OpenNMS (http://www.opennms.org/)
- Zenoss (http://zenoss.com/)
- Zabbix (http://www.zabbix.com/)

Probably the most well-known of these is Nagios (pronounced as you can hear at http://community.nagios.org/2007/02/20/nagios-pronunciation/comment-page-1/), which we'll take a closer look at next.

Introducing Nagios

Nagios is a popular GPL-licensed monitoring tool that allows you to monitor infrastructure, applications, and even environmental characteristics like power and air conditioning. It comes with a simple web console that gives you a visual view of the state of your hosts and services. You can see an example console screen in Figure 18-1.

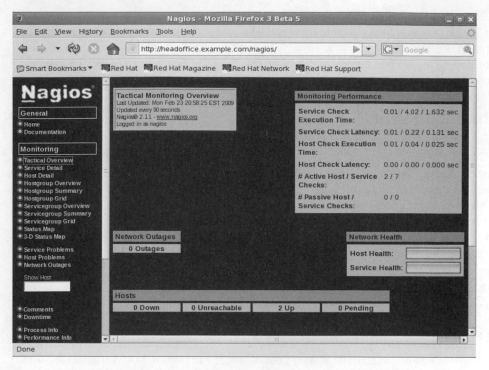

Figure 18-1. *An example console*

We're going to introduce you to Nagios and how to use it to monitor your hosts and services. We're going to show you how to set up some basic monitoring for your host and for some of the services we've introduced you to earlier in the book.

For this book, we'll look at version 2 of Nagios—it is packed full of features and functions. Nagios, however, is too complex to explain completely in this single chapter. Luckily, Nagios is very well documented, and you can find the documentation for version 2 at http://nagios. sourceforge.net/docs/2_0/ (and for version 3 at http://nagios.sourceforge.net/docs/3_0/).

■**Note** A number of books cover Nagios configuration including *Pro Nagios 2.0*, written by one of the author's of this book, James Turnbull (Apress, 2006). You can find additional books at http://www.nagios.org/propaganda/books/.

Nagios is capable of monitoring a wide variety of hosts and services on a number of platforms including Linux, BSD, Solaris, and even Windows (see http://nagios.sourceforge.net/docs/3_0/monitoring-windows.html for instructions on monitoring on Windows).

Nagios runs as a daemon and monitors the services on your hosts and their state. It can monitor to confirm both that a service is running and is performing appropriately. For example, if we were to monitor that a host is active using an ICMP ping (which we discussed in Chapter 6), we could configure it to alert if it can't contact the host or if responses take longer than a specified time to return.

To do this monitoring, you tell Nagios about your hosts and services by defining them as objects in the Nagios configuration. Each host is defined to Nagios, and then the services that run on that host are defined.

You also tell Nagios how you are going to monitor each host and service by defining commands. Each service uses particular commands to check its status, and each command specifies the binary or script used to check the status of a service.

■**Note** You will also define commands to send notifications, for example, to generate an e-mail when a service check fails.

To make creating commands easier, Nagios comes with a collection of *plug-ins*, which are binaries designed to check specific services; for example, Nagios has a plug-in called check_icmp that uses IMCP ping requests to confirm a host is active.

Nagios can query services on the local host as well as remote hosts. This querying is done either directly to the host (for example, connecting to the SMTP server on port 25 and testing you can receive e-mail) or via an agent installed on the host, which returns results to the monitoring host.

In addition to monitoring hosts and services, Nagios has a variety of other useful functions, including the following:

- An escalation model allows alerts to be escalated if a host or service does not recover or is not fixed (see http://nagios.sourceforge.net/docs/2_0/escalations.html).

- You have the ability to specify event handlers that can be triggered when a host or service fails. Event handlers can perform tasks like restarting services or deleting temporary files in an effort to automatically recover a host or service (see http://nagios.sourceforge.net/docs/2_0/eventhandlers.html).

- You can specify parent-child relationships and dependencies between hosts and services; for example, if a router is down, you can indicate you don't want Nagios to bother to check hosts behind that router because they won't be contactable (see http://nagios.sourceforge.net/docs/2_0/dependencies.html).

- You can design a distributed monitoring environment where there are redundant monitoring servers or where checks are distributed over multiple sites or locations (see http://nagios.sourceforge.net/docs/2_0/distributed.html and http://nagios.sourceforge.net/docs/2_0/redundancy.html).

Installing Nagios

Nagios is easy to install, and packages are available for both Red Hat and Ubuntu.

Installing Nagios on Red Hat

On Red Hat, we need to install a few packages starting with the libtool-ltdl package.

```
$ sudo yum install libtool-ltdl
```

We also need the `Perl-Net-SNMP`, `fping`, `nagios`, and `nagios-plugins` packages. To get these, we're going to install an additional repository, RPMForge, by installing an RPM package to enable the repository.

```
$ wget http://packages.sw.be/rpmforge-release/rpmforge-release-↦
0.3.6-1.el5.rf.i386.rpm
$ sudo rpm -Uvh rpmforge-release-0.3.6-1.el5.rf.i386.rpm
```

■**Note** You can find instructions and downloads for a variety of distributions at `https://rpmrepo.org/RPMforge/Using`.

Now we can use the `yum` command to install the required packages:

```
$ sudo yum install libtool-ltdl Perl-Net-SNMP fping nagios nagios-plugins
```

Installing Nagios on Ubuntu

On Ubuntu, we install the `nagios2` and `nagios-plugins` packages.

```
$ sudo apt-get install nagios2 nagios-plugins
```

This will install Nagios version 2 and all the required supporting packages including the Nagios plug-ins.

■**Tip** On Ubuntu 8.10, the next version of Nagios, version 3, is packaged, and you will need to install the `nagios3` package to use it. Nagios 3 has a number of updates and new features and you can read about them at `http://nagios.sourceforge.net/docs/3_0/whatsnew.html`.

Starting Nagios

On both Red Hat and Ubuntu, we start and stop Nagios with a standard `init` script. On Red Hat, this script is called `nagios`.

```
$ sudo service /etc/init.d/nagios start
```

The `nagios` daemon logs to the `/var/log/nagios/nagios.log` log file. You can confirm that the daemon has successfully started, or if it has not, you will see any errors in this file.

On Ubuntu, this service is called `nagios2`.

```
$ sudo invoke-rc.d nagios2 start
```

The daemon on Ubuntu logs to the `/var/log/nagios2/nagios.log` log file.

Nagios Configuration

We're going to quickly walk you through how to configure Nagios. In simple terms, the steps for configuring Nagios are as follows:

1. Create definitions for the hosts you wish to monitor.

2. Create definitions for the services you wish to monitor on your hosts.

3. Create commands to monitor your services.

4. Tell Nagios when you want them monitored.

5. Tell Nagios who should be told if a check fails.

6. Tell Nagios how people should be informed if a check fails—e-mail, IM, SMS, etc.

Nagios configuration is made up of objects. You define the host you wish to monitor as a host object and each service you wish to monitor as a service object. A variety of other object types also exist, such as time-period objects for monitoring periods and contact objects to tell Nagios whom to notify when something occurs.

We're going to show you how to configure your hosts in Nagios and then how to configure a variety of types of services. Along the way, we'll show you a variety of the other elements in Nagios configuration.

Nagios configuration on Red Hat is stored in /etc/nagios and on Ubuntu in /etc/nagios2. Nagios configuration files are suffixed with .cfg, and the main configuration file for Nagios is called nagios.cfg.

Both Red Hat and Ubuntu come with some sample configuration to help you get started with Nagios. On Red Hat, the /etc/nagios/localhost.cfg configuration file contains some basic configurations for your local host and some services on it. On Ubuntu, a much more extensive collection of configurations is available in the /etc/nagios2/conf.d and /etc/nagios-plugins/config directories.

Nagios also has a mode that enables you to check your configuration for errors prior to running the daemon. This is useful to confirm you don't have any errors.

On Red Hat, we would run the following:

```
$ sudo nagios -v /etc/nagios/nagios.cfg
```

and on Ubuntu:

```
$ sudo nagios2 -v /etc/nagios2/nagios.cfg
```

The -v option checks that all configuration is correct and if so outputs a statistical report showing the number of configuration objects defined.

■**Note** After changing Nagios configuration, you need to restart the daemon for the new configuration to be parsed.

The nagios.cfg File

The nagios.cfg configuration file contains the base configuration for your Nagios installation. Each option in this file is in the form of an option-value pair. For example, the location of the Nagios log file is specified using the log_file option; on Red Hat, this would be done as follows:

```
log_file=/var/log/nagios/nagios.log
```

This is usually the first option in your nagios.cfg file followed by the cfg_file and cfg_dir options that specify the location of your object configuration files. The cfg_file option allows you to specify an individual file that contains Nagios object configuration, for example:

```
cfg_file=/etc/nagios/localhost.cfg
```

You can specify multiple files; indeed, many people specify each object type in a separate file to organize them.

```
cfg_file=/etc/nagios/hosts.cfg
cfg_file=/etc/nagios/services.cfg
cfg_file=/etc/nagios/contacts.cfg
...
```

■**Note** It's a good idea to put your files into a *version control system (VCS)*, like Subversion. Such systems track your files and the changes to them. They are commonly used by programmers to track source code and used more and more by system administrators to track configuration files. You can read about version control at http://en.wikipedia.org/wiki/Revision_control and Subversion at http://svnbook.red-bean.com/.

The cfg_dir option specifies a directory. Nagios will load any file in this directory with a suffix of .cfg, for example:

```
cfg_dir=/etc/nagios2/conf.d
```

The nagios.cfg file contains a number of other useful options, some of which you can see in Table 18-8.

Table 18-8. *nagios.cfg Configuration File Options*

Option	Description
resource_file	A separate configuration file used to hold system variables such as paths and passwords.
nagios_user	The user to run Nagios as. This defaults to nagios.
nagios_group	The group to run Nagios as. This defaults to nagios.
log_rotation_method	When to rotate logs. Values are n for no rotation, h for hourly, d for daily, w for weekly, and m for monthly.
log_archive_path	The directory to store archived, rotated log files.
use_syslog	Whether to log Nagios output to syslog. This defaults to 1 for syslog logging. Set to 0 for no syslog logging.

You can also turn on and off checking of hosts and services and the sending of alerts at a global level on the nagios.cfg configuration file. For a full list of the available options, see http://nagios.sourceforge.net/docs/2_0/configmain.html.

Host Configuration

Let's start examining Nagios's configuration by opening Red Hat's /etc/nagios/localhost.cfg configuration file and having a look at its contents, starting with a host object definition.

■**Note** We've included both the Red Hat and Ubuntu sample configuration files with the source code for this chapter.

We're going to start with the host object definition in the file that you can see in Listing 18-18.

Listing 18-18. *A Host Object*

```
define host{
        use                     linux-server            ; Name of host template to use
                ; This host definition will inherit all variables that are defined
                ; in (or inherited by) the linux-server host template definition.
        host_name               localhost
        alias                   localhost
        address                 127.0.0.1
        }
```

You can see that an object definition starts with define, the type of object to define, in our case a host object, and the definition, which is enclosed in { } curly braces. Inside the definition are the attributes of the object defined by a series of key-value statements, separated by spaces. Our host object definition has four attributes: use, host_name, alias, and address.

■**Tip** Some attributes are mandatory for certain object definitions, meaning you must specify the attribute and a value for them. In the Nagios documentation, these values are specified in red at http://nagios. sourceforge.net/docs/2_0/xodtemplate.html.

The use attribute tells our host object to refer to a template. A template is a technique Nagios uses to populate an object definition with values that might be the same across many objects. For example, host objects will share many of the same attributes and characteristics. Rather than specify every single attribute in each host object definition, you can instead refer to a template. Nagios then creates the host object with all the attributes in the host definition plus those attributes in the template. We'll look at the additional attributes defined in the linux-server template in Listing 18-19 in a moment.

In this case, the rest of the attributes of our host object define its identity. The host_name attribute defines the name of the host object. This name must be unique. You can only have one host object called localhost or headoffice.example.com. Nagios also makes the host_name attribute available as a macro called $HOSTNAME$.

■**Note** Macros allow Nagios to imbed information about hosts and services in other object definitions, most specifically the commands Nagios uses to check services and send notifications. You'll see more macros later in this chapter; in the meantime, you can see a full list of these macros at http://nagios.sourceforge.net/docs/2_0/macros.html.

The alias attribute is another name for the object; in this case, we've used an alias of localhost. This alias is usually used as a longer description of the host and is also available as a macro called $HOSTALIAS$.

The last attribute, address, provides the IP address of the host; in this case we're monitoring our local host, 127.0.0.1. This IP address must be contactable by Nagios to allow monitoring to take place. It is also available as the macro $HOSTADDRESS$.

■**Note** You can also specify the fully qualified domain name of the host, but this requires that your DNS is working and can resolve the hostname. If your DNS fails, your Nagios checks may also fail. We recommend using the IP address as the value of this attribute.

Now let's see what additional attributes are provided by our linux-server template. In Listing 18-19, you can see the linux-server host object template.

Listing 18-19. *A Host Object Template*

```
define host{
        name                            linux-server    ; The name of this host ➥
template
        use                             generic-host    ; This template inherits ➥
other values from the generic-host template
        check_period                    24x7            ; By default, Linux hosts ➥
are checked round the clock
        max_check_attempts              10              ; Check each Linux host 10 ➥
times (max)
        check_command                   check-host-alive ; Default command to check➥
 Linux hosts
        notification_period             workhours       ; Linux admins hate to be ➥
woken up, so we only notify during the day
                                                        ; Note that the ➥
```

```
notification_period variable is being overridden from
                                               ; the value that is ➡
inherited from the generic-host template!
        notification_interval          120          ; Resend notification every➡
2 hours
        notification_options           d,u,r        ; Only send notifications ➡
for specific host states
        contact_groups                 admins       ; Notifications ➡
get sent to the admins by default
        register                       0            ; DONT REGISTER THIS ➡
DEFINITION - ITS NOT A REAL HOST, JUST A TEMPLATE!
        }
```

You can see we've defined a lot more attributes in our template. First, we define what sort of object this is a template for, in our case a host object. Next, using the name attribute, we give our template a name that must be unique. You can't have two templates named linux-server.

The next attribute is one you've seen before, use, and it allows us to specify a template that this template in turn inherits from. Confused? Simply put, Nagios allows you to chain templates together. This enables you to build quite complex template models that minimize the amount of typing needed to define your monitoring environment. We'll also look at the generic-host template in a moment.

■**Tip** What if you define the same attribute in multiple templates—which attribute value is used? Nagios inherits downward: the last reference to an attribute is the one that is used. For example, if the attribute check_period is defined in the templates generic-host and linux-server and in the host object definition for localhost, its value in the localhost object is the value used.

The next three attributes in Listing 18-19, check_period, max_check_attempts, and check_command, are all related.

The first attribute, check_period, tell Nagios when to check the host. In our case, we've specified a time period called 24x7. We also need to define this time period in our Nagios configuration.

```
define timeperiod{
        timeperiod_name 24x7
        alias          24 Hours A Day, 7 Days A Week
        sunday         00:00-24:00
        monday         00:00-24:00
        tuesday        00:00-24:00
        wednesday      00:00-24:00
        thursday       00:00-24:00
        friday         00:00-24:00
        saturday       00:00-24:00
        }
```

This is a simple time-period definition, which has a `timeperiod_name`, in our case 24x7, and an `alias` description. We've then defined each day of the week and the times during those days that we want the time period to cover. In this time-period definition, we're defining every day of the week and 24 hours a day.

To not cover a particular day, you simply don't specify it. The times are specified in 24-hour time, and you can specify multiple ranges, for example:

```
sunday      00:00-02:00,17:00-19:00
```

Here our time period is Sunday from midnight to 2 a.m. and 5 p.m. to 7 p.m.

Time periods are used in number of places in Nagios, but most commonly they specify when hosts and services should be checked and when notifications (messages generated when hosts and services fail or vary from their required state) should be sent.

The next attribute, `max_check_attempts`, specifies the number of times Nagios checks a host or service before determining that there is a problem.

The last attribute, `check_command`, tells Nagios what command to use to check the host's status, in this case `check-host-alive`.

This is one of the commands we discussed earlier. Let's look at it now.

```
define command{
        command_name    check-host-alive
        command_line    $USER1$/check_ping -H $HOSTADDRESS$ -w 3000.0,80% ➡
-c 5000.0,100% -p 1
        }
```

Commands are defined just like other objects. They are named with the `command_name` attribute, and the actual command to be executed is specified via the `command_line` attribute. In this case, we've specified the following line:

```
$USER1$/check_ping -H $HOSTADDRESS$ -w 3000.0,80% -c 5000.0,100% -p 1
```

The first part of the command, `$USER1$` is another Nagios macro. The `$USERx$` macros are configuration variables, usually configured in a file called `resource.cfg` (or another file specified in the `nagios.cfg` configuration file using the `resource_file` configuration option). In this example, the value of the `$USER1$` macro is the directory that contains the Nagios plug-ins:

```
$USER1$=/usr/lib/nagios/plugins
```

The next part of the command is the Nagios plug-in the command will employ, `check_ping`, which uses ICMP pings to check the status of your host.

■Note This assumes your host's firewall is configured to accept ICMP pings, as we discussed in Chapter 6.

In this command, you can see the use of one of Nagios' macros, `$HOSTADDRESS$`, that you learned earlier contains the IP address of the host. Whenever a host executes the check command, its address replaces the macro. This allows the same command to be used by multiple host objects. The macro is specified as the value of the `-H` option, which specifies the host to ping.

■**Note** You can get the help text from most Nagios plug-ins by running the command with the --help option. You can also run most Nagios plug-ins on the command line to see how they work, their command-line options, and what results they return.

The next two options, -w and -c, specify the thresholds for this check. If these thresholds are broken, Nagios will update the status of the host or service.

Hosts and services have different statuses. A host can be in the UP, DOWN, or UNREACHABLE state, and a service can be in the UP, WARNING, CRITICAL, or UNKNOWN state.

■**Note** The UNREACHABLE status is used when dependencies and parent-child relationships have been configured, and a host is not available because a parent or host it depends on is not available.

The plug-ins themselves though only return the WARNING, CRITICAL, and UNKNOWN states (the UNKNOWN state is generally set when a plug-in fails to run or an error is returned rather than a valid status). When these plug-ins are run for a host, Nagios interprets and converts these statuses into the appropriate UP and DOWN statuses, as you can see in Table 18-9.

Table 18-9. *Nagios Plug-in Status Conversions*

Plug-in Status	Host Status	Status Description
OK	UP	The host is up.
WARNING	UP or DOWN	The host could be up or down but by default is up. (See http://nagios.sourceforge.net/docs/2_0/configmain.html#use_aggressive_host_checking.)
UNKNOWN	DOWN	The host is down.
CRITICAL	DOWN	The host is down.

■**Note** This host state is also available to Nagios as a macro called $HOSTSTATE$.

The -w and -c options take two values: the round-trip time in milliseconds and the percentage of successful pings needed not to break the threshold. So, if the -w threshold is broken, the WARNING status is generated, and Nagios will mark the host as UP. However, if the -c threshold is broken, the CRITICAL status is generated, and Nagios will mark the host as DOWN. A notification will usually then be generated. The last option on our command line, -p, specifies the number of pings to send.

■Note In addition to the status returned by a plug-in, for example, WARNING or CRITICAL, you will also get some output describing that state, which you can use in notifications or display in the console. For example, the check_ping plug-in returns PING OK - Packet loss = 0%, RTA = 3.98 ms. This output is also available as a macro called $HOSTOUTPUT$ for hosts and $SERVICEOUTPUT$ for service checks.

The next attribute in Listing 18-19 is the notification_period. This differs slightly from the check period. While checks occur during the check_period, in our case the 24x7 period, notifications (the alerts that get generated when a status changes) will get sent only during the workhours time period:

```
define timeperiod{
        timeperiod_name workhours
        alias           "Normal" Working Hours
        monday          09:00-17:00
        tuesday         09:00-17:00
        wednesday       09:00-17:00
        thursday        09:00-17:00
        friday          09:00-17:00
        }
```

You can see that the workhours time period is 9 a.m. to 5 p.m., rather than 24 hours every day of the week as specified by our 24x7 check period.

The next attribute, notification_interval, configures how often Nagios will resend notifications if the status of the host doesn't change; here it's every 120 minutes, or 2 hours.

The notification_options attribute specifies when Nagios should send a notification. Here it is set to d, u, and r, which means Nagios will send notifications when the host is DOWN (d) or UNREACHABLE (u). The last option, r, sends a notification if the host has recovered (i.e., gone from a DOWN or UNREACHABLE state to an UP state).

The next attribute, contact_groups, tells Nagios whom to notify when a notification is generated. In our case, the value of this is admins, which refers to a contactgroup object. Contact groups are collections of contacts, which are the people you want to notify, for example, yourself or another system administrator, when a notification is generated. A contactgroup object looks like this:

```
define contactgroup{
        contactgroup_name       admins
        alias                   Nagios Administrators
        members                 nagios-admin
        }
```

A contact group has a name defined via the contactgroup_name attribute, a description provided by the alias attribute, and a list of the contacts in that group, specified using the members attribute. In this case, the only member of the contact group is nagios-admin, which you can see here:

```
define contact{
        contact_name                    nagios-admin
```

```
alias                            Nagios Admin
service_notification_period      24x7
host_notification_period         24x7
service_notification_options     w,u,c,r
host_notification_options        d,r
service_notification_commands    notify-by-email
host_notification_commands       host-notify-by-email
email                            nagios-admin@localhost
}
```

Contacts are very simple to define. Each has a name provided via the contact_name attribute and an alias.

For each contact, we specify when they should receive notifications and what notifications they should receive.

For specifying when to receive notifications, we use service_notification_period and the host_notification_period. In our case, the nagios-admin contact will receive notifications during the 24x7 time period you saw earlier, or in real terms 24 hours every day of the week, for both hosts and services.

For specifying which notifications, we use the service_notification_options and the host_notification_options attributes. For services, the nagios-admin contact will receive WARNING, UNKNOWN, or CRITICAL as indicated by the w, u, and c options, respectively; the r option means it will also receive recovery notifications. For hosts, the contact will only receive DOWN (d) and recovery (r) notifications.

The service_notification_commands and host_notification_commands attributes specify the commands Nagios uses to send the notifications. You can specify multiple commands by separating each with a comma. These commands are defined just like the commands used to check your hosts and services. Let's look at one of these commands, notify-by-email.

```
define command{
        command_name    host-notify-by-email
        command_line    /usr/bin/printf "%b" "***** Nagios 2.11 ➥
*****\n\nNotification Type: $NOTIFICATIONTYPE$\nHost: ➥
$HOSTNAME$\nState: $HOSTSTATE$\nAddress: $HOSTADDRESS$\nInfo: ➥
$HOSTOUTPUT$\n\nDate/Time: $LONGDATFTIME$\n" | /bin/mail -s ➥
"Host $HOSTSTATE$ alert for $HOSTNAME$!" $CONTACTEMAIL$
        }
```

Like the previous command you saw, a name is provided with the command_name attribute and the actual command to be executed by the command_line attribute. In this case, we're printing some text including a number of macros to the /bin/mail binary.

This would send an e-mail to any required contacts notifying them of the change in status. For example, if Nagios was monitoring our gateway.example.com host and a check of this host failed, a notification much like this would be generated:

```
***** Nagios 2.11 *****

Notification Type: PROBLEM
Host: gateway.example.com
State: DOWN
```

```
Address: 192.168.0.254
Info: PING CRITICAL - Packet loss = 100%

Date/Time: Fri Feb 13 00:30:28 EST 2009
```

■**Tip** Nagios can issue alerts through more than just e-mail. Indeed, Nagios can issue alerts to anything you can build an alert command for, for example, via SNMP, instant messaging like Jabber, a pager, or even a ticketing system like OTRS or Trac. See the notification documentation at `http://nagios.sourceforge. net/docs/2_0/notifications.html` for more details.

Table 18-10 provides a list of the macros used in our notification command.

Table 18-10. *Macros in the Notification Command*

Macro	Description
$NOTIFICATIONTYPE$	The type of notification; for example, PROBLEM, for an issue, or RECOVERY, if the host has recovered
$HOSTNAME$	The name of the host you are being notified about
$HOSTSTATE$	The current host state, for example UP or DOWN
$HOSTADDRESS$	The IP address of the host
$HOSTOUTPUT$	Text output from the command used to check the host's status
$LONGDATETIME$$	The date and time in long format (e.g., Fri Feb 13 00:30:28 EST 2009)
$CONTACTEMAIL$	The e-mail address of the contact to be e-mailed

■**Note** You can see a full list of macros and where you can use them at `http://nagios.sourceforge. net/docs/2_0/macros.html`.

Back to our contact definition, you can see the last attribute, email, which specifies an e-mail address for notifications to be sent to, which you've seen is available as the $CONTACTEMAIL$ macro.

Back to our template, you can see the last attribute in our Listing 18-19 template is register. This attribute is what tells Nagios that this is a template rather than a real host definition; when register is set to 0, Nagios doesn't try to create the host object, instead ignores it. The default setting for register is 1, which means any object definition that doesn't explicitly specify register 0 will be assumed to be a real host object and will be monitored by Nagios.

So now let's take a very quick look at the parent template, generic-host, shown in Listing 18-20.

Listing 18-20. *The generic-host Template*

```
define host{
        name                            generic-host  ; The name of this host template
        notifications_enabled           1             ; Host notifications are enabled
        event_handler_enabled           1             ; Host event handler is enabled
        flap_detection_enabled          1             ; Flap detection is enabled
        failure_prediction_enabled      1             ; Failure prediction is enabled
        process_perf_data               1             ; Process performance data
        retain_status_information       1             ; Retain status information ➡
across program restarts
        retain_nonstatus_information    1             ; Retain non-status ➡
information across program restarts
        notification_period             24x7          ; Send host notifications ➡
at any time
        register                        0             ; DONT REGISTER THIS ➡
DEFINITION - ITS NOT A REAL HOST, JUST A TEMPLATE!
        }
```

■**Note** We're not going to explain these options in any detail here; you can see read about them at
http://nagios.sourceforge.net/docs/2_0/xodtemplate.html#host.

You would define your own hosts in the same way as we've shown here. For example, our
gateway.example.com host would be defined like so:

```
define host{
        use                     linux-server            ; Name of host template to use
                ; This host definition will inherit all variables that are defined
                ; in (or inherited by) the linux-server host template definition
        host_name               gateway.example.com
        alias                   gateway.example.com
        address                 192.168.0.254
        }
```

■**Tip** Don't forget you need to restart Nagios after adding any new configuration.

Here we've defined a host object for gateway.example.com and specified we're going to use
the host templates we've just explored. We've specified its internal IP address, 192.168.0.254,
and Nagios will use this address to try to monitor the host via ICMP. The firewall on our
gateway.example.com host would have to allow ICMP packets to ensure monitoring is possible.

■**Note** There are several other object definitions related to host monitoring that we haven't looked at that allow you to group hosts together, enable dependencies between hosts, and provide similar functionality. You can see a full list of object types and their attributes at `http://nagios.sourceforge.net/docs/2_0/ xodtemplate.html`.

Service Configuration

Now that you know something about host objects, we're going to examine a service object. Services are defined using the service-type object and are linked to their underlying host. For example, based on our existing configuration examples, Listing 18-21 shows a service that checks the disk space of our root partition.

Listing 18-21. *A Service Definition*

```
define service{
        use                             local-service  ; Name of service template to use
        host_name                       localhost
        service_description             Root Partition
        check_command                   check_local_disk!20%!10%!/
        }
```

Our service definition is simple. The use attribute specifies a template our service is going to use. The host_name attribute specifies what host the service runs on, in our case localhost. The service_description describes the service. Lastly, the check_command attribute specifies the command that the service uses to check the status of whatever is being monitored. This check_command is slightly different; after the command we want to use you can see a string:

`!20%!10%!/`

This string is made up of variables we're passing to the command definition, each variable value prefixed with an exclamation mark (!). So here we are passing the values 20%, 10%, and / to the command. This allows us to reuse a command for multiple services, as you'll see in a moment.

Let's take a quick look at the check_local_disk command:

```
define command{
        command_name    check_local_disk
        command_line    $USER1$/check_disk -w $ARG1$ -c $ARG2$ -p $ARG3$
        }
```

Like our previous command, with command_line we've specified the $USER1$ macro to give us the path to the plug-in being executed. That plug-in is check_disk, which checks the status of a local disk.

You can also see the -w and -c options—which we told you earlier set the threshold values for the WARNING and CRITICAL statuses. Lastly, we have the -p option, which specifies the disk partition we're monitoring. In this command, however, the value of each option is $ARGx$: $ARG1$, $ARG2$, and $ARG3$, respectively. Each of these arguments represents one of the arguments we passed in our check_command attribute in Listing 18-21, so our command_line in fact looks like the following:

```
command_line    $USER1$/check_disk -w 20% -c 10% -p /
```

This results in a WARNING status being generated when only 20% of disk space is available and a CRITICAL status being generated when 10% of disk space is free, both statuses applying to the root file system, or /.

To create a service that monitors disks on another partition, for example /var, we would create a service like the following:

```
define service{
        use                     local-service   ; Name of service template to use
        host_name               localhost
        service_description Var Partition
        check_command           check_local_disk!20%!10%!/var
        }
```

Before we discuss some other services, let's take a quick look at the local-service template our service is using.

```
define service{
        name                    local-service   ; The name of this service template
        use                     generic-service ; Inherit default ➡
values from the generic-service definition
        check_period            24x7                    ; The service can be ➡
checked at any time of the day
        max_check_attempts      4                       ; Re-check the ➡
service up to 4 times in order to determine its final (hard) state
        normal_check_interval   5                       ; Check the service ➡
every 5 minutes under normal conditions
        retry_check_interval    1                       ; Re-check the ➡
service every minute until a hard state can be determined
        contact_groups          admins                  ; Notifications ➡
get sent out to everyone in the 'admins' group
        notification_options    w,u,c,r                 ; Send ➡
notifications about warning, unknown, critical, and recovery events
        notification_interval   60                      ; Renotify about ➡
service problems every hour
        notification_period     24x7                    ; Notifications ➡
can be sent out at any time
        register                0                       ; DON'T REGISTER ➡
DEFINITION - ITS NOT A REAL SERVICE, JUST A TEMPLATE!
        }
```

The service template, local-service, is similar to previous templates you've seen but with some additional attributes. The first of these new attributes, normal_check_interval, specifies how often Nagios should check the service is OK, in this case every 5 minutes. The second new attribute, retry_check_interval, is related. If, when checking the service, Nagios discovers the service is not OK, it retries the check the number of times specified in the max_check_attempts attribute. This is done before it marks the service as not OK. During this retry period, instead of checking once every 5 minutes as specified in `normal_check_interval`, the check is made every 1 minute as specified in `retry_check_interval`.

■**Note** Nagios has the concepts of *soft* and *hard* states. When a check fails, we've discovered Nagios checks it the number of times specified by `max_check_attempts`. Until Nagios exhausts all its check attempts, the host or service is marked as a soft fail state. When the check attempts are exhausted and a notification is generated, the host or service is now in a hard fail state. This soft fail mode means that if a host or service has temporarily failed and then recovers, you don't get a notification, thereby reducing the number of potential false positive alerts from your monitoring system. You can read more about this at `http://nagios.sourceforge.net/docs/2_0/statetypes.html`.

Note that this template also has a parent template, `generic-service`, which we're not going to discuss in detail. The options used in that template are explained at `http://nagios.sourceforge.net/docs/2_0/xodtemplate.html#service`.

■**Note** Nagios tries to be smart about monitoring and usually doesn't check hosts for their status unless a service running on that host has an issue. If a service on a host fails, Nagios usually schedules a check of the underlying host, too. You can read more about this at `http://nagios.sourceforge.net/docs/2_0/checkscheduling.html#host_checks`.

Let's look at another service definition, this one to monitor a network-based service, in Listing 18-22.

Listing 18-22. *A Network-Based Service Definition*

```
define service{
        use                     local-service  ; Name of service template to use
        host_name               gateway.example.com
        service_description     Check SMTP
        check_command           check_smtp!25
        }
```

In Listing 18-22, we have a new service, called Check SMTP, that uses our `local-service` template and a `check_command` of `check_smtp!25`. This passes the value 25 to a command called `check_smtp`. Let's look at that command now:

```
define command{
        command_name    check_smtp
        command_line    $USER1$/check_smtp -H $HOSTADDRESS$ -p $ARG1$
        }
```

Here we have a command that runs a plug-in called check_smtp. It accepts the $HOSTADDRESS$ macro, which is the IP address of the SMTP server we wish to check. The -p option specifies the port (the plug-in defaults to port 25), and we pass in this value as the $ARG1$ macro.

You can see a service alert generated by this service from the nagios.log log file here:

```
[1235270465] SERVICE ALERT: gateway.example.com;Check SMTP;CRITICAL;HARD;4;➥
CRITICAL - Socket timeout after 10 seconds
```

The nagios.log entry specifies the Unix epoch time (1235270465, or Sunday 22 Feb 13:41:05 2009), the type of alert, the host and service, and the nature of the alert including the output from the plug-in.

■**Note** You can convert epoch time online at http://www.epochconverter.com/.

REMOTE MONITORING

So far you've only seen how to monitor services on a local host, such as our local disk, or services that are accessible via the network, such as SMTP, IMAP, or SSH. Nagios can also monitor services on remote hosts that aren't exposed to the network. Nagios comes with a variety of instructions on how to monitor a variety of such remote hosts, but two of the principal mechanisms are NRPE and the check_by_ssh plug-in (read the FAQ entry at http://www.nagios.org/faqs/viewfaq.php?faq_id=59).

NRPE is a tool that allows you to execute the Nagios plug-ins on remote hosts and get the results back to the nagios daemon. You can find the NRPE documentation at http://nagios.sourceforge.net/docs/nrpe/NRPE.pdf.

The check_by_ssh plug-in, which we've shown you in this chapter, allows you to log in to a remote host by SSH, execute a command, and return results.

You'll find more information on monitoring methods in the following documentation:

- *Monitoring using SNMP*: http://nagios.sourceforge.net/docs/3_0/monitoring-routers.html

- *Monitoring Linux/Unix*: http://nagios.sourceforge.net/docs/3_0/monitoring-linux.html

- *Monitoring Windows*: http://nagios.sourceforge.net/docs/3_0/monitoring-windows.html

Simple Remote Monitoring

You can create a variety of network-based services using Nagios plug-ins, but what if you want to monitor services that aren't network facing or on the local host? One of the methods to do this is a special plug-in called check_by_ssh (for others see the "Remote Monitoring" sidebar).

The check_by_ssh plug-in uses SSH to connect to a remote host and execute a command. So to make use of the plug-in, you have an SSH daemon running on the remote host, and any intervening firewalls have to allow SSH access to and from the host.

You also need to use key-based authentication between the hosts because Nagios has no capability to input a password when checking the service. So we're going to start by creating a key to use between our Nagios server and the remote host.

■Note We introduced key-based SSH authentication in Chapter 9.

To create this key, we need to be logged in as a user who runs Nagios, usually `nagios`. We can do this using the `su` command.

```
$ sudo su - nagios
```

We then use the `ssh-keygen` command to generate a key:

```
nagios$ ssh-keygen  -t dsa
Generating public/private dsa key pair.
Enter file in which to save the key (/var/log/nagios/.ssh/id_dsa):
Created directory '/var/log/nagios/.ssh'.
Enter passphrase (empty for no passphrase):
Enter same passphrase again:
Your identification has been saved in /var/log/nagios/.ssh/id_dsa.
Your public key has been saved in /var/log/nagios/.ssh/id_dsa.pub.
The key fingerprint is:
41:32:dd:36:e4:cc:2a:7e:5e:01:10:00:b6:99:5f:b1 nagios@au-mel-rhel-1.example.com
```

We use the `-t dsa` option to create a DSA key. We are prompted to enter a location for the key, usually in the `.ssh` directory under the home directory of the `nagios` user—in this case, `/var/log/nagios/.ssh`. The private key is in the `id_dsa` file, and the public key is in the `id_dsa.pub` file. Instead of entering a passphrase for the key, we press Enter to specify an empty passphrase, because we need the connection to be made without a passphrase or password prompt.

We then need to copy the public key, `id_dsa.pub`, to the remote host and store it in the `authorized_keys` file for the user we're going to connect to. If you are following along with this example, you should create a user on the remote host and specify a password for it. In our case, we do so on the remote gateway.example.com host as follows:

```
gateway$ sudo useradd nagios
gateway$ sudo passwd nagios
```

We also need to create the `.ssh` directory on the remote host and protect it.

```
gateway$ mkdir /home/nagios/.ssh
gateway$ chmod 0700 /home/nagios/.ssh
```

We can then copy the file:

```
nagios$ scp .ssh/id_dsa.pub nagios@gateway.example.com:~/.ssh/authorized_keys
```

If this succeeds, we should now be able to SSH from the Nagios server to the gateway host without requiring a password.

```
nagios$ ssh nagios@gateway.example.com
```

We now configure Nagios to use this connection to check services. The `check_by_ssh` plug-in also relies on having the command to be executed installed on the remote host. This command is usually a Nagios plug-in, and hence the easiest way to do this is to install the Nagios plug-in package on the remote host. On Red Hat, we issue the following:

```
gateway$ sudo yum install nagios-plugins
```

Or on Ubuntu:

```
gateway$ sudo apt-get install nagios-plugins
```

We can then define a command that uses the check_by_ssh plug-in to monitor a service on the remote host. For example, to monitor the load on a remote host, we could use the following command:

```
define command {
        command_name    check_load_ssh
        command_line    $USER1$/check_by_ssh -H $HOSTADDRESS$ -l nagios ➥
-C "/usr/lib/nagios/plugins/check_load -w $ARG1$ -c $ARG2$"
}
```

We call our command check_load_ssh. The command_line specifies that we're executing the check_by_ssh plug-in and connecting to the host specified by the -H option.

The -l option specifies the name of the user we want to connect to on the remote host; here we're using the nagios user we just created.

The -C specifies the command we want to run on the remote host. In this case, we're running another, locally installed, Nagios plug-in called check_load and passing two arguments to it as the values of the -w and -c (WARNING and CRITICAL) thresholds.

■**Tip** The check_by_ssh command can do a whole lot more. Run it with the --help option to see all its capabilities.

Once we have our command, we can then define a service that uses it, like so:

```
define service {
        use                     local-service           ; check current ➥
load on machine
        service_description     Current Load
        check_command           check_ssh_load!5.0,4.0,3.0!10.0,6.0,4.0
}
```

Our service, called Current Load, executes the check_ssh_load command and passes two arguments, which specify the average load over 1, 5, and 15 minute intervals required to trigger a WARNING or CRITICAL status.

■**Note** We discussed load in Chapter 17.

This is a simple example of how to perform remote monitoring; it is not ideal (the key-based SSH connection could be a security vulnerability), but it is the fastest and simplest method. For more complicated environments, the NRPE server and corresponding command is usually a better approach.

■**Note** As with hosts, we haven't covered all of the available functionality for services. You can also group services together, make them dependent on each other, and perform a variety of other useful tricks with them. We recommend you read the available Nagios documentation and many of the other useful resources out there for more information.

Nagios Plug-Ins

You can choose from a large collection of plug-ins to create services and commands to check them. You can see a partial list of the available plug-ins in Table 18-11.

Table 18-11. *Nagios Plug-Ins*

Plug-In	Description
check_ntp	Checks the status of an NTP service
check_swap	Checks your swap
check_ifstatus	Checks the status of network interfaces
check_tcp	Checks the status of a TCP-based network service
check_by_ssh	Checks the status of a service via SSH
check_imap	Checks the status of an IMAP service
check_clamd	Checks the status of a ClamAV daemon
check_udp	Checks the status of a UDP-based network service
check_dig	Checks the DNS status via dig
check_ping	Checks the status of a host via ICMP
check_simap	Checks the status of an IMAP service
check_nagios	Checks the status of the Nagios process
check_snmp	Checks via SNMP
check_http	Checks the status of a web server
check_ssh	Checks the status of an sshd service

This is a small selection of the available plug-ins, but it should give you a good basis for creating appropriate checks for your environment. Most Nagios plug-ins are very simple and self-explanatory. Almost all of them provide the --help option to display their function and options.

Other plug-ins outside of the Nagios plug-in pack are also available. For example, you can find a huge collection of such plug-ins at http://www.nagiosexchange.org/cgi-bin/page.cgi?d=1.

■**Note** You can also find some useful add-ons at `http://www.nagios.org/download/addons/`.

You can develop your own plug-ins, if required. Some simple guidelines and examples for such development are located at `http://nagios.sourceforge.net/docs/2_0/plugins.html#howto`.

Setting Up the Nagios Console

Now that you understand how hosts and services can be defined, you can create your own hosts and services to supplement the examples provided with both distributions. Once you have created these hosts and services, it is useful to have a console to view them in. Nagios comes with a fully functional web-based console, and we're going to show you how to set it up.

■**Tip** Alternatives to the Nagios console are also available. You can see a good list of these at `http://www.nagiosexchange.org/cgi-bin/page.cgi?g=Utilities%2FGUI%2Findex.html;d=1`.

The Nagios console can run inside the Apache web server we demonstrated in Chapter 11. Both Red Hat and Ubuntu include default installations of the web console. On Red Hat, you can find the Apache configuration for Nagios at `/etc/httpd/conf.d/nagios.conf`; on Ubuntu, it's at `/etc/apache2/conf.d/nagios2.conf`.

Red Hat situates the console in a web service directory of `/nagios` and Ubuntu in a directory of `/nagios2`. If your web server is running, browsing to `http://headoffice.example.com/nagios/` and `http://headoffice.example.com/nagios2/` (replacing the hostname with the name of your Nagios host) on Red Hat and Ubuntu, respectively, should display your console.

■**Note** You can use what you learned in Chapter 11 to move your Nagios console to a virtual host or another location.

Console Authentication

To protect against people making malicious use of your Nagios console, the web server has some basic authentication. Nagios uses Apache's basic HTTP authentication to protect the console. When you open the console, you will be prompted for a username and password, as you can see in Figure 18-2.

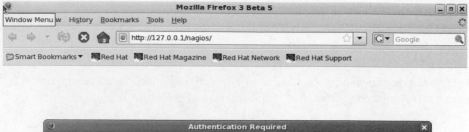

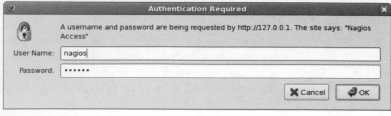

Figure 18-2. *Nagios authentication*

Apache basic authentication is configured by specifying a file holding usernames and passwords to the web server. This file is then queried by websites that are secured by basic authentication.

■Caution This is authentication with an emphasis on basic, however. Apache basic authentication uses very simply encrypted passwords that are easy to intercept and decrypt. To ensure better protection of your Nagios console, you should consider enabling SSL for it.

Let's look inside our Nagios Apache configuration for the location of our password file. On Red Hat, inside our /etc/httpd/conf.d/nagios.conf file, we find the following:

```
AuthName "Nagios Access"
AuthType Basic
AuthUserFile /etc/nagios/htpasswd.users
Require valid-user
```

On Ubuntu, in the /etc/apache2/conf.d/nagios2.conf file we have

```
AuthName "Nagios Access"
AuthType Basic
AuthUserFile /etc/nagios2/htpasswd.users
Require valid-user
```

The AuthName and AuthType directives enable basic authentication. The AuthUserFile specifies the location of the password file, /etc/nagios/htpasswd.users on Red Hat and /etc/nagios2/htpasswd.users on Ubuntu. This is the file we need to add our users to. The Require valid-user directive indicates that only users specified in this file can log into the console.

Once you've found where your authentication file needs to be, you need to create the file to hold your users and passwords. On Red Hat, you do this using a command called htpasswd; on Ubuntu, the command to use is htpasswd2.

Listing 18-23 shows this command in action.

Listing 18-23. *Using the* htpasswd *Command*

```
$ sudo htpasswd -c /etc/nagios/htpasswd.users jsmith
New password:
Re-type new password:
Adding password for user jsmith
```

The htpasswd command has two variables: the location of the file that holds our user-names and passwords, and the username of the user. We also use a command-line switch, -c. The -c switch is used when you first create a password file. After that you can drop this switch and merely specify the file and the user to be added.

In Listing 18-23, we create a new password file with the -c option that will be called htpasswd.users and located at /etc/nagios. We specify the user we're adding, jsmith, and are prompted for a password and then a verification of the entered password. Both passwords must match. If they do, the command will be successful, and the user will be added to the specified password file.

We can then use this username and password to sign in to the Nagios console and display the console screen, as you can see in Figure 18-3.

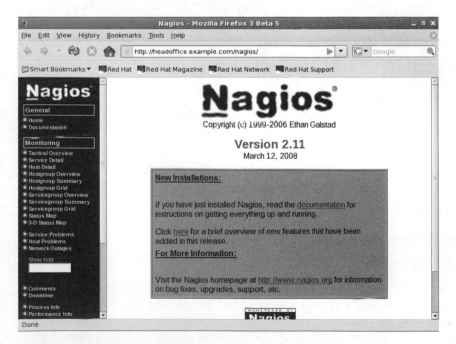

Figure 18-3. *The Nagios console*

Once we have users and passwords created, we can sign on to the console, but we also need to configure what access each user has. This is done by editing a configuration file called cgi.cfg, located in the /etc/nagios directory on Red Hat and in the /etc/nagios2 directory on Ubuntu.

Nagios has two types of users on the console: authenticated users and authenticated contacts. Both types of users need a username and password to sign on to the console. Authenticated users have their access specified in the cgi.cfg configuration file. Authenticated contacts are authenticated users, the username of each of which matches the name of a Nagios contact.

Hence, if the username jsmith, for example, matches the name of a contact, the value of the contact_name directive, this authenticated user becomes an authenticated contact.

So what's the difference? Authenticated users are granted some generic rights to view the web console. Authenticated contacts are granted further rights to view and manipulate the hosts and services for which they are contacts.

Let's look at the cgi.cfg file. The first directive in the cgi.cfg file is called use_authentication. It controls whether authentication is enabled for the Nagios web console and whether Nagios will use the authentication credentials provided from the web server. The directive looks like this:

```
use_authentication=1
```

A setting of 1, which is the default, enables authentication, and a setting of 0 disables it.

Authorization for particular functions on the console is provided by a series of directives in the cgi.cfg file that take lists of users, separated by commas, as options. For example:

```
authorized_for_all_services=jsmith,nagiosadmin
```

The authorized_for_all_services directive controls who can view services on the console, and we've specified that the users jsmith and nagiosadmin have this access.

Table 18-12 contains the full list of possible authorization directives and describes each one.

Table 18-12. *Authorization Directives*

Directive	Description
authorized_for_system_information	Users who can access the Nagios process information
authorized_for_configuration_information	Users who can see all configuration information
authorized_for_system_commands	Users who can issue commands through the web console
authorized_for_all_services	Users who are authorized to all services
authorized_for_all_hosts	Users who are authorized to all hosts
authorized_for_all_service_commands	Users who can issue service-related external commands
authorized_for_all_host_commands	Users who can issue host-related external commands

The first directive in Table 18-12, authorized_for_system_information, provides access to view information about the Nagios process and the server, such as when the process started and what settings are set on the server.

The second directive, authorized_for_configuration_information, provides authorization to view all configuration information, the object definitions, for your monitoring environment.

This includes the configuration of your hosts, services, contacts, and commands, as well as all other object types.

The third directive, `authorized_for_system_commands`, controls who has access to start, stop, or restart the Nagios process from the web console.

The next two directives, `authorized_for_all_services` and `authorized_for_all_hosts`, control which users can view all service and host information on the web console. Remember, authenticated contacts can view the information about the hosts and services for which they are contacts.

The last two directives in Table 18-12, `authorized_for_all_service_commands` and `authorized_for_all_host_commands`, allow you to specify users who are authorized to issue external commands to services and hosts, respectively. This allows you to perform actions such as disabling active checks of the host or service, or enabling or disabling notifications for the host or service.

■**Note** By default, all of the authorization directives are commented out in the `cgi.cfg` file. You will need to uncomment them and add any required users to the directives.

If you wish to specify that all users have access to a particular function, use the * symbol:

`authorized_for_all_services=*`

This directive setting would provide all authenticated users with access to view information about all services defined on the Nagios server. The * symbol will work for all authorization directives.

As we mentioned earlier, in addition to any authorization granted to them, users who are also contacts have access to the hosts and services for which they are contacts. For services, this access includes

- Viewing of service status

- Viewing of service configuration

- Ability to view service history and notifications

- Ability to issue commands to the service (start and stop checking, for example)

For hosts, this access includes

- Viewing of host status

- Viewing of host configuration

- Ability to view host history and notifications

- Ability to issue commands to the host (start and stop checking, for example)

Authenticated contacts that have access to a particular host because they are a contact for that host also have the same access to all the services on that host just as if they were a contact for those services. For example, if you are an authenticated contact for the blah host, you are able to view the status, configuration, service history, and notifications as well as issue commands to all the services defined on that host.

Console Functions

The Nagios console provides not only an interface through which to view your hosts and services, but also the ability to control how they are monitored. We're going to walk you through a few of the screens available in the console, but we recommend you have a look yourself at the views, graphs, lists, and controls available on the console.

For a summary of the status of your environment, the best view is the Tactical Monitoring Overview screen, which you can see in Figure 18-4.

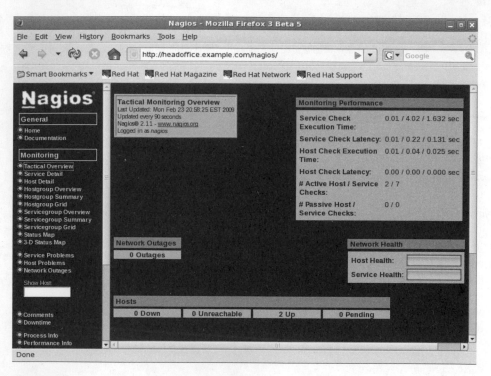

Figure 18-4. *The Tactical Monitoring Overview screen*

This screen displays the current status of the Nagios server and a summary of your host and service statuses. It is reached by clicking the Tactical Monitoring Overview link in the left-hand menu.

To see your hosts and services in more detail, the Host Detail and Service Detail links in the left-hand menu display a full list of the hosts and services being monitored. You can see the Service Detail screen in Figure 18-5.

Figure 18-6 shows the Host Detail screen.

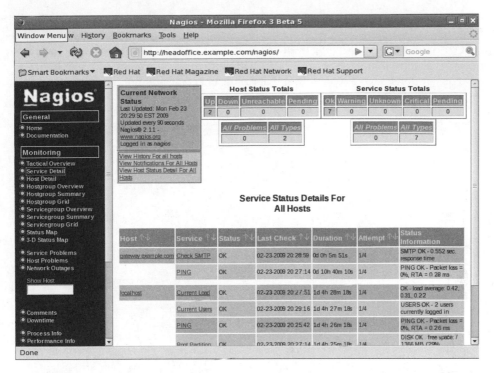

Figure 18-5. *The Service Detail screen*

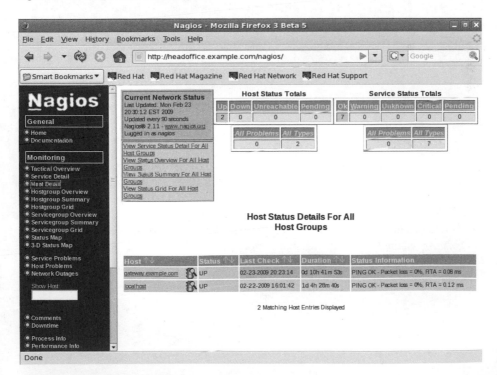

Figure 18-6. *The Host Detail screen*

On both these screens, you can click the hosts and services to drill down into their status and configuration.

The last console screen we're going to show you in Figure 18-7 is the Process Info screen, which displays the status of the Nagios process and its configuration. You can also configure a variety of Nagios options, such as enabling and disabling checking and notifications, through this screen.

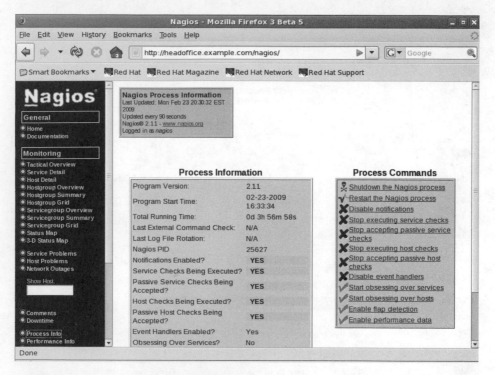

Figure 18-7. *The Nagios Process Info screen*

Troubleshooting Nagios

Lots of resources are available to help you with Nagios including websites, forums, and books, such as *Pro Nagios 2.0* by James Turnbull, one of the authors of this book (Apress, 2006).

You can find a number of support options, including commercial support, at http://www.nagios.org/support/; comprehensive documentation at http://www.nagios.org/docs/; and an FAQ for Nagios at http://www.nagios.org/faqs/. You can also subscribe to the active and helpful mailing list available at http://www.nagios.org/support/mailinglists.php, as well as check out the Nagios forum and wiki, both at http://community.nagios.org/wiki/index.php/Main_Page.

Summary

In this chapter, you've learned about logging and monitoring and how to make them work for you. You've discovered how syslog works and how to make the most out of your `syslog` daemon. You've also learned how to search your log data using SEC to find the log entries that are important to manage your environment.

In addition, the chapter explored Nagios, an enterprise monitoring tool. You've seen how to install and configure Nagios. You've also discovered how to configure your hosts and services and the supporting configuration needed to monitor your environment.

In the next chapter, we'll discuss provisioning hosts and show you how to manage your configuration with automated configuration tools.

CHAPTER 19

■ ■ ■

Configuration Management

By James Turnbull

In this chapter, we're going to look at two facets of configuration management:

- Automated provisioning and installation of new hosts
- Automated management of your configuration including files, users, and packages

The first process we're going to examine, automated provisioning or installation of new hosts, is sometimes called *bootstrapping*. In the Red Hat world, bootstrapping is often referred to as *kickstarting* (after the Kickstart tool used to perform it). On Ubuntu and Debian, the process is called *preseeding*.

Provisioning is a way of automatically installing a distribution to a host. When we first looked at installing distributions in Chapter 2, we demonstrated how to do it manually. You inserted a DVD and followed the onscreen prompts to install your distribution. Automated provisioning is a way of installing a distribution without being prompted by the configuration questions. This makes provisioning quick and simple, and it also has the advantage of ensuring every build is identical.

■**Tip** You can use provisioning for both server hosts and desktop hosts. Not only is it a quick way of building (or rebuilding) server hosts, but it can also be a quick way to automatically install desktops for your users

---

The second process we're going to examine is configuration management and automation. By now you've seen that you can accumulate a lot of installed packages, users, configuration files, and other settings. Your environment can quickly get complicated and difficult to manage if you don't take steps to control and automate it. Configuration management allows you to centralize your configuration, document it, and automate it. This allows you to manage and control changes to your environment and protects you against accidental or malicious configuration changes.

Both provisioning and configuration management are particularly useful if you have deployed a lot of hosts, but they are also useful in smaller environments, to save time and effort in managing your hosts.

Provisioning

We've talked a little about what provisioning is, but how you go about it varies between distributions. We are going to explain how to automatically provision both Red Hat and Ubuntu hosts.

Provisioning is usually a two-stage process:

1. Boot your host and send it the files required for installation.

2. Automate the installation steps.

The process starts with a host booting up. Remember in Chapter 5 when we told you about the boot sequence? On many hosts, you can configure that boot sequence to look in alternative places to get its boot instructions, for example, boot from a DVD or a USB stick. In addition to these methods, you can also get your boot instructions from a network source.

The technology behind this boot process is called Preboot Execution Environment (PXE). A network boot server is hence called a PXE boot (pronounced "pixie") server. The host that we intend to build uses a network query to find a PXE boot server, usually a network query to a DHCP server, that might offer it the files required to boot and then transfers those files to the host using a file transfer protocol called Trivial File Transfer Protocol (TFTP).

■**Note** You can read more about PXE at `http://en.wikipedia.org/wiki/Preboot_Execution_Environment`.

Once this initial boot takes place, your provisioning process continues by installing a prepackaged version of your distribution, usually with a series of automated scripted responses to the various configuration questions you are prompted for when installing.

■**Note** We're using network-based provisioning to create our hosts rather than any of the alternatives, such as CD or DVD. This is because we believe network-based provisioning is the simplest, easiest, and most efficient way to automatically build hosts.

In this chapter, we're going to introduce you to some useful tools. For Red Hat provisioning, we're going to look at Cobbler, an automated build framework. Cobbler also makes use of Red Hat's installation automation tool, Kickstart. For Ubuntu, we're going to show you how to set up a network boot server and also how to use Kickstart (supplemented with some elements of Ubuntu's Preseed provisioning tool) to build your hosts.

Provisioning with Red Hat Cobbler

Red Hat has a variety of tools for provisioning hosts, ranging from the most basic, Kickstart, which automates installations, to full-featured GUI management tools for host configuration such as Cobbler (https://fedorahosted.org/cobbler/), Spacewalk (http://www.redhat.com/spacewalk/), and Genome (http://genome.et.redhat.com/).

We're going to look at a combination of two tools:

- *Kickstart*: An installation automation tool
- *Cobbler*: A provisioning server that provides a PXE boot server

We'll take you through the process of creating a Cobbler server and a build to install. Later in this chapter, we'll show you how to configure Kickstart to automate your configuration and installation options.

Installing Cobbler

Let's start by installing Cobbler on your host. To run Cobbler, you need some prerequisite packages:

```
$ sudo yum install yum-utils createrepo dhcp tftp-server httpd
```

Here we've installed some additional Yum utilities and the createrepo package, which assist in repository management. We've also installed some additional packages Cobbler uses: the DHCP daemon, a TFTP server, and the Apache web server. You may already have these packages installed, in which case Yum will skip them.

■**Note** We talk about DHCP in Chapter 9 and Apache in Chapter 11.

You next need to install the latest version of Cobbler and another required package, python-cheetah, which assists with Kickstart configuration. You can download and install these packages from the Fedora EPEL repository.

```
$ sudo rpm  Uvh http://download.fedora.redhat.com/pub/epel/5/i386/cobbler-1.4.1-➥
1.el5.noarch.rpm http://download.fedora.redhat.com/pub/epel/5/i386/➥
python-cheetah-2.0.1-1.el5.i386.rpm
```

Or you can add the EPEL repository to your host and then install packages from that repository. You add the EPEL repository, if it's not already added to your Yum configuration, by adding the epel-release RPM.

```
$ sudo rpm -Uvh http://download.fedora.redhat.com/pub/epel/5/i386/➥
epel-release-5-3.noarch.rpm
```

You can then install the cobbler package.

```
$ sudo yum install cobbler
```

Configuring Cobbler

After you've installed the required packages, you need to configure Cobbler. Cobbler comes with a very handy check function that tells you what needs to be done to configure it. To see what needs to be done, run the following:

```
$ sudo cobbler check
The following potential problems were detected:
#0: The 'server' field in /etc/cobbler/settings must be set to something other than➥
 localhost, or kickstarting features will not work.  This should be a resolvable ➥
hostname or IP for the boot server as reachable by all machines that will use it.
#1: For PXE to be functional, the 'next_server' field in /etc/cobbler/settings must➥
 be set to something other than 127.0.0.1, and should match the IP of the boot ➥
server on the PXE network.
#2: service cobblerd is not running
#3: change 'disable' to 'no' in /etc/xinetd.d/tftp
#4: since iptables may be running, ensure 69, 80, 25150, and 25151 are unblocked
#5: fencing tools were not found, and are required to use the (optional) power ➥
management features. install cman to use them
```

You can see there are a few things you need to do to get Cobbler running. Let's work through each of these issues.

First, you configure the /etc/cobbler/settings file. You need to update two fields in this file, server and next_server. You need to replace the existing values (usually 127.0.0.1) with the IP address of your host, so a PXE-booted host can find your Cobbler host. In our case, we specify the following:

```
server 192.168.0.1
next_server 192.168.0.0.1
```

To update Cobbler's configuration, you then run this:

```
$ sudo cobbler sync
```

■**Note** You need to run the $ sudo cobbler sync command anytime you change the /etc/cobbler/ settings file. Common errors include leaving trailing spaces after options in the settings file. Make sure you delete any extra spaces from the file.

You also need to configure a DHCP server (like the one we introduced in Chapter 9). You have two choices here: you can get Cobbler to manage your existing DHCP server or you can tell your existing DHCP server to point to Cobbler.

Cobbler Managing Your DHCP

If you want to enable Cobbler to manage your DHCP server, then you need to enable another option in the /etc/cobbler/settings file:

```
manage_dhcp: 1
```

You also need to update a template file that Cobbler will use to configure your DHCP server, /etc/cobbler/dhcp.template. Listing 19-1 shows an example of this file.

Listing 19-1. *The /etc/cobbler/dhcp.template File*

```
# ********************************************************************
# Cobbler managed dhcpd.conf file
#
# generated from cobbler dhcp.conf template ($date)
# Do NOT make changes to /etc/dhcpd.conf. Instead, make your changes
# in /etc/cobbler/dhcp.template, as /etc/dhcpd.conf will be
# overwritten.
#
# ********************************************************************

allow booting;
allow bootp;

ddns-update-style interim;
ddns-ttl 3600;
default-lease-time 600;
max-lease-time 7200;
log-facility local7;

ignore client-updates;
set vendorclass = option vendor-class-identifier;

key dynamic-update-key {
    algorithm hmac-md5;
    secret "3PDRnypPtzJqpbQvbw/B7bhPuHqpUeOSdi95Z4Ez/IzhS61dzcK6MJ6CdFHkkegp➥
TN1kmXOM6GggRNE24aPmOw==";
}

zone 0.168.192.in-addr.arpa. {
    key dynamic-update-key;
    primary 192.168.0.1;
}

zone example.com. {
    key dynamic-update-key;
    primary 192.168.0.1;
}

subnet 192.168.0.0 netmask 255.255.255.0 {
    option routers 192.168.0.254;
    option domain-name "example.com";
    option domain-name-servers 192.168.0.1;
    option broadcast-address 192.168.0.255;
```

```
next-server  $next_server;
filename "/pxelinux.0";
group "static" {
    use-host-decl-names on;
    host au-mel-rhel-1 {
        hardware ethernet 00:16:3E:15:3C:C2;
        fixed-address au-mel-rhel-1.example.com;
    }
}
pool {
    range 192.168.0.101 192.168.0.150;
    deny unknown clients;
}
pool {
    range 192.168.0.151 192.168.0.200;
    allow unknown clients;
    default-lease-time 7200;
    max-lease-time 21600;
}
}
```

If you have an existing DHCP server with a configuration, you should update this template to reflect that configuration. You can see we've adjusted the template in Listing 19-1 to reflect the DHCP configuration we used in Chapter 9. We've added two settings:

```
allow booting;
allow bootp;
```

These two options tell the DHCP server to respond to queries from hosts who request network boots.

The other two important settings to note in Listing 19-1 are the `next-server` and `filename` configuration options. The `next-server` option is set to `$next_server`. This value will be replaced by the IP address we just configured in the `next_server` option in the `/etc/cobbler/settings` file. This tells our DHCP server where to route hosts who request a net boot.

The `filename` option is set to `/pxelinux.0`, which is the name of the boot file PXE-booted hosts should look for to start their boot process. We'll set up this file shortly.

Now, after changing these files, you need to run the following command:

```
$ sudo cobbler sync
```

■**Caution** If you have an existing DHCP server, this template will *overwrite* its configuration by overwriting the `/etc/dhcpd.conf` configuration file. Only do this if you are sure you know what you are doing, and make a copy of your existing `/etc/dhcpd.conf` file *before* running the command.

Cobbler Not Managing Your DHCP

If you don't want Cobbler to manage your DHCP, then you just need to adjust your existing DHCP configuration file, /etc/dhcpd.conf, to add the next-server and filename options. Let's update the relevant portions of the configuration we created in Chapter 9 with this option, as shown in Listing 19-2.

Listing 19-2. *Existing dhcpd.conf Configuration File*

```
allow booting;
allow bootp;

subnet 192.168.0.0 netmask 255.255.255.0 {
    option routers 192.168.0.254;
    option domain-name "example.com";
    option domain-name-servers 192.168.0.1;
    option broadcast-address 192.168.0.255;
    filename "/pxelinux.0";
    next-server 192.168.0.1;
    group "static" {
        use-host-decl-names on;
        host au-mel-rhel-1 {
            hardware ethernet 00:16:3E:15:3C:C2;
            fixed-address au-mel-rhel-1.example.com;
        }
    }
    pool {
        range 192.168.0.101 192.168.0.150;
        deny unknown clients;
    }
    pool {
        range 192.168.0.151 192.168.0.200;
        allow unknown clients;
        default-lease-time 7200;
        max-lease-time 21600;
    }
}
```

You can see we've added two options to the start of the DHCP section:

```
allow booting;
allow bootp;
```

These two options tell the DHCP server to respond to queries from booting clients.
We've also added the next-server option to our subnet definition.

```
next-server 192.168.0.1
```

The `next-server` option tells DHCP where to send hosts who request a PXE network boot. We need to specify the IP address of our Cobbler server.

Lastly, we've added the `filename` option, set to `/pxelinux.0`, which is the name of the boot file PXE-booted hosts should look for to start their boot process. We'll set up this file shortly.

■**Tip** After configuring your DHCP server, you will need to restart the Cobbler server for the new configuration to be applied.

Starting Cobbler and Apache

Next, you need to start the Cobbler daemon:

```
$ sudo service cobblerd start
```

You also need to ensure the Apache web server is started:

```
$ sudo service httpd start
```

Configuring TFTP

Once the daemon is started, you need to enable your TFTP server to send your boot file to the host to be installed. To do this, you edit the `/etc/xinet.d/tftp` file to enable a TFTP server. Inside this file find this line:

```
disable = yes
```

and change it to this:

```
disable = no
```

Next, you enable the TFTP server like so:

```
$ sudo chkconfig tftp on
```

■**Note** You don't need to start the service because it runs under the `xinetd` service that is already running. If you run the `chkconfig --list` command, you can see the `xinetd` services at the end of the listing, and you can also see that the `tftp` service is enabled.

You need to ensure your hosts can connect to the Cobbler server through your firewall by opening some required ports, 69, 80, 25150, and 25151, for example, by creating `iptables` rules such as the following:

```
-A Firewall-eth0-INPUT -s 192.168.0.0/24 -p udp -m state --state NEW --dport 69 -j ➥
ACCEPT
-A Firewall-eth0-INPUT -p tcp -m state --state NEW --dport 80 -j ACCEPT
-A Firewall-eth0-INPUT -s 192.168.0.0/24 -p tcp -m state --state NEW --dport 25150 ➥
-j ACCEPT
```

```
-A Firewall-eth0-INPUT -s 192.168.0.0/24 -p tcp -m state --state NEW --dport 25151 ➥
-j ACCEPT
```

These rules allow access for any host on the 192.168.0.0/24 subnet to the boot server on
the appropriate ports. You can find more information on firewall rules in Chapter 6.

Using Cobbler

Once you've configured Cobbler, you can start to make use of it. Cobbler allows you to specify
a distribution you'd like to build hosts with, imports that distribution's files, and then creates a
profile. You can then build hosts using this distribution and profile.

Let's start by creating our first profile using the import command.

```
$ sudo cobbler import --mirror=/media/cdrom --name=RHEL5 --arch=i386
```

You issue the cobbler command with the import option. The --mirror option specifies
the source of the distribution you want to package—in our case, we have used our DVD drive,
/media/cdrom, and have assumed our distribution CD or DVD is mounted on this drive.

You can also specify an online repository, for example:

```
$ sudo  cobbler import --mirror=rsync://ftp.iinet.net.au/pub/fedora/linux/releases/➥
10/Fedora/i386/ --name=Fedora10 --arch=i386
```

Here we've specified a Fedora 10 build available via rsync (a type of simple file transfer).
Cobbler will download the required files and create a distribution and a profile for our Fedora
10 build.

■**Tip** You will need sufficient disk space on your host to copy whatever distributions you want to keep. For
example, for the RHEL 5 build, you will need about 3GB of space.

Cobbler will run the import process and then return you to the prompt. Depending on the
performance of your host (and, if you are importing over the network, the speed of your connection), this may take some time.

The last two options in our import, --name and --arch, are the name of the profile we want
to create (e.g., RHEL5) and the architecture (e.g., i386, x86_64, etc.) of the distribution being
imported. Cobbler can usually detect this, but it is safer to specify it. The architecture will then
be suffixed to the name of the profile you are creating (e.g., RHEL5-i386).

After you've created your distribution and profile, you can see it in Cobbler using the report
option, as shown in Listing 19-3.

Listing 19-3. *A Cobbler Report*

```
$ sudo cobbler report
distro             : RHEL5-i386
architecture       : i386
breed              : redhat
created            : Tue Feb 24 21:46:33 2009
```

```
comment               : rhel5.2
initrd                : /var/www/cobbler/ks_mirror/RHEL5/images/pxeboot/initrd.img
kernel                : /var/www/cobbler/ks_mirror/RHEL5/images/pxeboot/vmlinuz
kernel options        : {}
ks metadata           : {'tree': 'http://@@http_server@@/cblr/links/RHEL5-i386'}
tree build time       : Thu May  1 09:23:47 2008
modified              : Tue Feb 24 21:52:03 2009
mgmt classes          : []
os version            : rhel5
owners                : ['admin']
post kernel options   : {}
redhat mgmt key       : <<inherit>>
template files        : {}
profile               : RHEL5-i386
distro                : RHEL5-i386
comment               :
created               : Tue Feb 24 21:46:33 2009
dhcp tag              : default
enable menu           : True
kernel options        : {}
kickstart             : /var/lib/cobbler/kickstarts/sample.ks
ks metadata           : {}
mgmt classes          : []
modified              : Tue Feb 24 21:46:33 2009
name servers          : []
owners                : ['admin']
post kernel options   : {}
redhat mgmt key       : <<inherit>>
repos                 : []
server                : <<inherit>>
template_files        : {}
virt bridge           : xenbr0
virt cpus             : 1
virt file size        : 5
virt path             :
virt ram              : 512
virt type             : qemu
```

This option displays all the distributions and their profiles currently imported into Cobbler.

■**Note** You may see more than one distribution and profile created from importing a distribution. For example, importing RHEL 5 will add the vanilla RHEL 5 distribution and the Xen (which is a type of virtualization we discuss in Chapter 20) version of RHEL 5.

Listing 19-3 shows our vanilla RHEL 5 distribution and the profile we created, RHEL5-i386. Most of the information in Listing 19-3 isn't overly important to us, but we do need to make note of the kickstart option, which has a value of /var/lib/cobbler/kickstarts/sample.ks. This Kickstart file will automate any build of a distribution; we'll look at it in more detail later in this chapter.

You can change what Kickstart file this profile uses (or edit other profile values) by editing your profile using the cobbler profile command. You can also list all the profiles by using the cobbler profile list command.

```
$ sudo cobbler profile edit --name=RHEL5-i386 --kickstart=/var/lib/cobbler/➥
kickstarts/custom.ks
```

Here we've edited the RHEL5-i386 profile to use the Kickstart file /var/lib/cobbler/kickstarts/custom.ks.

You can also remove a profile using the remove command or copy one using the copy command.

```
$ sudo cobbler profile copy --name=RHEL5-i386 --newname=RHEL5-i386-new
$ sudo cobbler profile remove --name=RHEL5-i386-new
```

The first command will copy the RHEL5-386 profile to RHEL5-i386-new, and the second command will delete the RHEL5-i386-new profile and its files.

■**Note** You can see the other options you can edit on your profile by looking at the cobbler command's man page.

Building a Host with Cobbler

Now that you've added a profile and a distribution, you can boot a host and install your distribution. Choose a host (or virtual machine) you wish to build and reboot it. Your host may automatically search for a boot device on your network, but more likely you will need to adjust its BIOS settings to adjust the boot order. In order to boot from Cobbler, you need to specify that your host boots from the network first.

When your host boots, it will request an IP address from the network and get an answer from your DHCP server, as you can see in Figure 19-1.

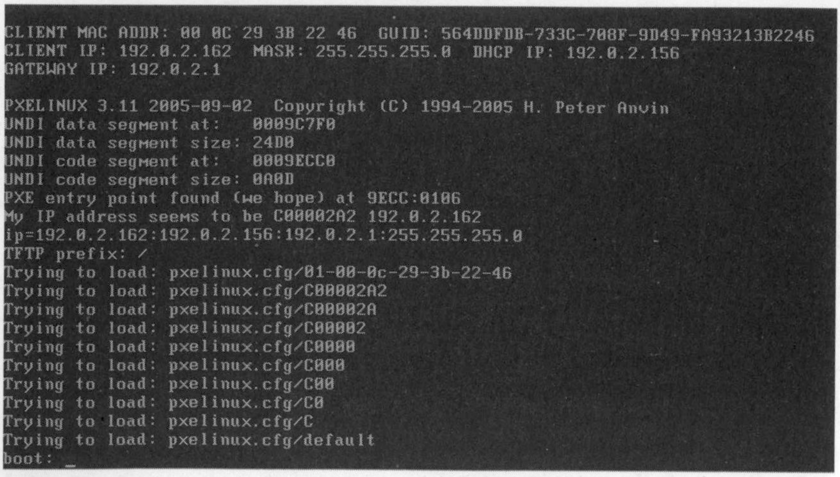

CLIENT MAC ADDR: 00 0C 29 3B 22 46 GUID: 564DDFDB-733C-708F-9D49-FA93213B2246
CLIENT IP: 192.0.2.162 MASK: 255.255.255.0 DHCP IP: 192.0.2.156
GATEWAY IP: 192.0.2.1
PXELINUX 3.11 2005-09-02 Copyright (C) 1994-2005 H. Peter Anvin
UNDI data segment at: 0009C7F0
UNDI data segment size: 24D0
UNDI code segment at: 0009ECC0
UNDI code segment size: 0A0D
PXE entry point found (we hope) at 9ECC:0106
My IP address seems to be C00002A2 192.0.2.162
ip=192.0.2.162:192.0.2.156:192.0.2.1:255.255.255.0
TFTP prefix: /
Trying to load: pxelinux.cfg/01-00-0c-29-3b-22-46
Trying to load: pxelinux.cfg/C00002A2
Trying to load: pxelinux.cfg/C00002A
Trying to load: pxelinux.cfg/C00002
Trying to load: pxelinux.cfg/C0000
Trying to load: pxelinux.cfg/C000
Trying to load: pxelinux.cfg/C00
Trying to load: pxelinux.cfg/C0
Trying to load: pxelinux.cfg/C
Trying to load: pxelinux.cfg/default
boot: _

Figure 19-1. *Network boot*

Your host will boot to a command line appropriately called `boot:`. From here, you can launch the Cobbler menu by typing **menu**. You can see an example of this menu in Figure 19-2.

Cobbler | http://cobbler.et.redhat.com
(local)
RHEL5-i386
rescue-RHEL5-i386
Press [Tab] to edit options
Automatic boot in 7 seconds...

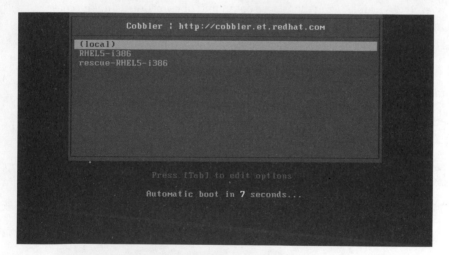

Figure 19-2. *The Cobbler menu*

From this menu, you can select the profile you'd like to install (e.g., `RHEL5-i386`). If you don't select a profile to be installed, Cobbler will automatically launch the first item on the menu, `(local)`, which continues the boot process on the local host.

■ **Note** If you don't have an operating system installed on this host, this boot process will obviously fail.

If you've selected a profile, then this profile will start the installation process using the instructions contained in the associated Kickstart file. If you are watching your installation process, you will see the installation screens progress—all without requiring input from you to continue or select options.

Using Cobbler, you can also specify configuration options for particular hosts. You don't need to do this, but it is useful if you have a specific role in mind for a host and want to specify a particular profile or Kickstart configuration. To do this, you add hosts to Cobbler, identifying them via their MAC or IP addresses, using the `system` command.

```
$ sudo cobbler system add --name=gateway.example.com --mac=00:0C:29:3B:22:46➡
--profile=RHEL5-i386 --kickstart=gateway.ks
```

Here we've added a system named gateway.example.com with the specified MAC address.

■**Note** You can usually see your MAC address during the network boot process, or you can often find it printed on a label on your network card.

The new host uses the `RHEL5-i386` profile and a Kickstart file called `gateway.ks`. If a host with the appropriate MAC address connects to our Cobbler host, then Cobbler will use these configuration settings to provision the host.

You can list the configured hosts using the `list` and `report` options.

```
$ sudo cobbler system list
gateway.example.com
```

A full listing of the gateway.example.com system definition can be seen using the `report` option.

```
$ sudo cobbler system report –name=gateway.example.com
```

We can also delete a system using the `remove` command:

```
$ sudo cobbler system remove --name=gateway.example.com
```

■**Note** You can read about additional Cobbler capabilities on the `cobbler` command's man page.

Cobbler Web Interface

Cobbler also has a simple web interface you can use to manage some of its options. It's pretty simple at this stage, and the command-line interface is much more fully featured, but it is available if you wish to implement it. You can find instructions at `https://fedorahosted.org/cobbler/wiki/CobblerWebInterface`.

Troubleshooting Cobbler

You can troubleshoot the network boot process by monitoring elements on your host, including your log files, and by using a network monitoring tool like the `tcpdump` or `tshark` command.

You can start by monitoring the output of the DHCP process by looking at the `/var/log/messages` log files. Cobbler also logs to the `/var/log/cobbler/cobbler.log` file and the files contained the `kickstep` and `syslog` directories also under `/var/log/cobbler`.

You can also monitor the network traffic passing between your booting host and the boot server. You can use a variety of network monitoring tools for this:

```
$ sudo tcpdump port tftp
```

Cobbler has a wiki page available that contains documentation at `https://fedorahosted.org/cobbler/wiki/UserDocs`. The documentation includes some useful tips for troubleshooting at `https://fedorahosted.org/cobbler/wiki/UserDocs#Troubleshooting`. The Cobbler community also has a mailing list at `https://fedorahosted.org/mailman/listinfo/cobbler` and an active IRC channel on Freenode at #cobbler.

Provisioning with Ubuntu

Like Red Hat, Ubuntu can automatically provision hosts, but it lacks a server solution like Cobbler. In order to achieve the same result on Ubuntu as on Red Hat, you will have to do a little more manual configuration of your Ubuntu host to network boot your hosts.

■**Note** Ubuntu can automate the installation process using a tool called Preseed. Ubuntu, however, also supports Kickstart. We're going to show you how to use a combination of Kickstart and Preseed to automate your installation in the next section.

COBBLER ON UBUNTU

Cobbler is also supported on Ubuntu; however, there are currently no packages built for Ubuntu. If you want to use Cobbler for Ubuntu, you can build it from source using the instructions at `https://fedorahosted.org/cobbler/wiki/DownloadInstructions` or create a package using the instructions in Chapter 7.

Installing Packages

We're going to start by setting up a PXE boot server on Ubuntu and installing some packages. You will need to install a TFTP server (to transfer the files to your target host) and the `inetutils-inetd` package to run the TFTP server. If it is not already installed on your host, you will need to install a DHCP server using the `dhcp3-server` package. Lastly, to deliver the distribution's files to the host to be built, we'll use the Apache web server. If you don't have Apache installed, you'll need to install the `apache2` package.

```
$ sudo apt-get install inetutils-inetd tftpd-hpa dhcp3-server apache2
```

■**Note** We show how to configure DHCP in Chapter 9.

Configuring the DHCP Server

Next, you need to configure your DHCP server. If you already have a DHCP server configured, we recommend updating the configuration to specify a PXE boot server for your existing DHCP ranges; otherwise you'll need to configure DHCP to provide addresses in an appropriate range to provision hosts. For example, you could create a DHCP range for provisioning hosts.

To configure our Ubuntu DHCP server, we update the /etc/dhcp3/dhcpd.conf configuration file. We add the required configuration to the example configuration we created in Chapter 9, as shown in Listing 19-4.

Listing 19-4. *Ubuntu Example DHCP Server Configuration*

```
allow booting;
allow bootp;
ddns-update-style interim;
ddns-ttl 3600;
default-lease-time 600;
max-lease-time 7200;
log-facility local7;

key dynamic-update-key {
    algorithm hmac-md5;
    secret "3PDRnypPtzJqpbQvbw/B7bhPuHqpUeOSdi95Z4Ez/IzhS61dzcK6MJ6CdFHkkegp➥
TN1kmXOM6GggRNE24aPmOw==";
}

zone 0.168.192.in-addr.arpa. {
    key dynamic-update-key;
    primary 192.168.0.1;
}

zone example.com. {
    key dynamic-update-key;
    primary 192.168.0.1;
}

subnet 192.168.0.0 netmask 255.255.255.0 {
    filename "pxelinux.0";
    next-server 192.168.0.1;
    option routers 192.168.0.254;
    option domain-name "example.com";
    option domain-name-servers 192.168.0.1;
    option broadcast-address 192.168.0.255;
    group "static" {
```

```
        use-host-decl-names on;
        host au-mel-rhel-1 {
            hardware ethernet 00:16:3E:15:3C:C2;
            fixed-address au-mel-rhel-1.example.com;
        }
    }
    pool {
        range 192.168.0.101 192.168.0.150;
        deny unknown clients;
    }
    pool {
        range 192.168.0.151 192.168.0.200;
        allow unknown clients;
        default-lease-time 7200;
        max-lease-time 21600;
    }
}
```

Here we add the `allow` directive for `bootp` and `booting`, which tells the DHCP server to accept network boot requests at the top of our file. In the `subnet` directive, we add two options, `filename` and `next-server`.

The `filename` option specifies the name of the file that the DHCP server will deliver to the host that wishes to net boot. This file contains the initial instructions to boot the host, and you should specify `pxelinux.0` here. We'll install this file shortly.

The `next-server` option tells our net-booting host the server from which to retrieve the boot files. You should specify the IP address of the PXE boot server.

■Tip After changing your DHCP configuration, you will need to restart the DHCP service.

Configure the TFTP Server

We installed the `tftp-hpa` package that contains the TFTP server. We now need to configure this server so it can transfer our boot files to the target host. To do this, we edit the `/etc/default/tftp-hpa` file:

```
#Defaults for tftpd-hpa
RUN_DAEMON="yes"
OPTIONS="-l -s /var/lib/tftpboot"
```

In the preceding code, we enable the `RUN_DAEMON` option by setting it to yes. Notice the `OPTIONS` line that specifies the `-l` and `-s` options. The `-l` option runs the daemon in stand-alone listen mode. The `tftpd` service usually runs under `inetd`, which is a type of daemon manager; the `-l` option tells it to run like a normal daemon. The `-s` option tells the daemon the location of our boot files, here `/var/lib/tftpboot`. This is where we'll store our boot files.

Once we've configured the `tftpd-hpa` package, we need to restart the `tftpd-hpa` service.

```
$ invoke-rc.d tftpd-hpa restart
```

Installing the Boot Files

You now need to install the files required to boot your host. These files will be installed into the /var/lib/tftpboot directory. Ubuntu comes with a collection of boot and kernel files specifically designed for network booting. These are available in the install/netboot directory on your Ubuntu media:

```
$ sudo cp -r /media/cdrom/install/netboot/* /var/lib/tftpboot/
```

or you can download them from the Ubuntu online repositories.

```
$ cd /tmp
$ lftp -c "open http://archive.ubuntu.com/ubuntu/dists/hardy/main/installer-i386/➥
current/images/; mirror netboot/"
$ mv netboot/* /var/lib/tftpboot
$ rm -fr netboot
```

Here we used the lftp command to copy the contents of the netboot directory for the Ubuntu 8.04 or Hardy release to our /tmp directory. We then moved the contents of this directory to the /var/lib/tftpboot directory.

■**Note** The lftp command is a more sophisticated version of the FTP file transfer command. To see how it works, refer to its man page.

Configuring the PXE Boot Loader

Now that you have the network boot files, you can configure the boot loader for your environment. Let's look at the contents of the /var/lib/tftpboot directory.

```
boot.img.gz
mini.iso
netboot.tar.gz
pxelinux.0 -> ubuntu-installer/i386/pxelinux.0
pxelinux.cfg -> ubuntu-installer/i386/pxelinux.cfg
ubuntu-installer
```

The directory contains five files (two of which are symlinked) and a directory called ubuntu-installer. The pxelinux.0 (which we configured in our DHCP server's filename option), boot.img.gz, and netboot.tar.gz files will do the initial boot of our host. The mini.iso file is an ISO (burnable to CD) image of the boot files. If you don't use network-based provisioning, you can burn this image to a CD and use it to boot and perform a minimal installation. The pxelinux.cfg directory contains the configuration files used by PXE to select what boot image to load (we'll adjust this for our environment shortly), and the ubuntu-installer directory contains files required for our PXE boot.

If you look in the pxelinux.cfg directory, you'll find a single file called default. This is the default configuration file used when booting hosts. Let's look at its contents:

```
DISPLAY ubuntu-installer/i386/boot-screens/boot.txt

F1 ubuntu-installer/i386/boot-screens/f1.txt
F2 ubuntu-installer/i386/boot-screens/f2.txt
F3 ubuntu-installer/i386/boot-screens/f3.txt
F4 ubuntu-installer/i386/boot-screens/f4.txt
F5 ubuntu-installer/i386/boot-screens/f5.txt
F6 ubuntu-installer/i386/boot-screens/f6.txt
F7 ubuntu-installer/i386/boot-screens/f7.txt
F8 ubuntu-installer/i386/boot-screens/f8.txt
F9 ubuntu-installer/i386/boot-screens/f9.txt
F0 ubuntu-installer/i386/boot-screens/f10.txt


DEFAULT install

LABEL install
    kernel ubuntu-installer/i386/linux
    append ks=http://192.0.2.161/ks.cfg vga=normal initrd=ubuntu-installer/i386/➥
initrd.gz --
LABEL linux
    kernel ubuntu-installer/i386/linux
    append vga=normal initrd=ubuntu-installer/i386/initrd.gz --
LABEL cli
    kernel ubuntu-installer/i386/linux
    append tasks=standard pkgsel/language-pack-patterns= pkgsel/install-language-➥
support=false vga=normal initrd=ubuntu-installer/i386/initrd.gz --

LABEL expert
    kernel ubuntu-installer/i386/linux
    append priority=low vga=normal initrd=ubuntu-installer/i386/initrd.gz --
LABEL cli-expert
    kernel ubuntu-installer/i386/linux
    append tasks=standard pkgsel/language-pack-patterns= pkgsel/install-language-➥
support=false priority=low vga=normal initrd=ubuntu-installer/i386/initrd.gz --

LABEL rescue
    kernel ubuntu-installer/i386/linux
    append vga=normal initrd=ubuntu-installer/i386/initrd.gz rescue/enable=true --

PROMPT 0
TIMEOUT 0
```

The file specifies our boot environment, first by specifying the text that will be displayed when our host boots, via the DISPLAY option, and when each function key is pressed (the F1 to F0 options). It then uses the LABEL option to specify the various types of boots that we can perform. The DEFAULT option specifies the default boot label, in our case install.

Each label specifies the kernel to load and the options to pass to that kernel.

■**Tip** You can find documentation on the boot options at `https://help.ubuntu.com/community/` `BootOptions`.

Lastly, the `PROMPT` and `TIMEOUT` options control how our boot sequence will operate. The `PROMPT` option, if set to 1, will wait at the boot prompt (see Figure 19-3) until a boot label is selected.

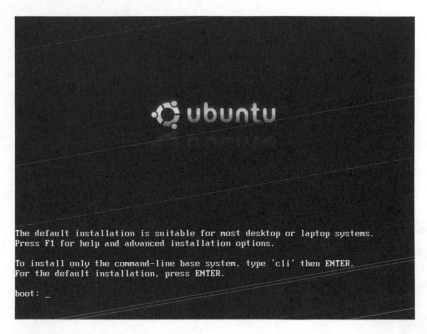

The default installation is suitable for most desktop or laptop systems.
Press F1 for help and advanced installation options.

To install only the command-line base system, type 'cli' then ENTER.
For the default installation, press ENTER.

boot: _

Figure 19-3. *The Ubuntu boot prompt*

If the `PROMPT` option is set to 0, then the default boot option will be immediately taken without waiting for a keypress. The `TIMEOUT` specifies how long in seconds it will wait at the boot prompt for that selection. If no option is selected before the timeout expires, then the default label will be booted. If you want your host to automatically boot and install, then you should set the `PROMPT` value to 0.

Rather than using the default configuration option, you can specify individual files in this directory for the specific host you wish to boot and build. To do this, create a file name using the target host's MAC address. For example, if your host's MAC address is 00:0A:E4:2E:A6:42, you could create a file called `000AE42EA642` by copying the default file and editing it. When the host with this MAC address requests a network boot, this configuration file will be used rather than the `default` file.

Configuring Apache for Provisioning

Next, you need to add the contents of the distribution you'd like to install to a directory and enable access via the Apache web server. After the boot process, these distribution files will be used to install your new host.

To do this, copy the files from the Ubuntu media by creating a directory called `ubuntu` under the `/var/www` directory and copying the contents of the Ubuntu installation media to it.

```
$ sudo mkdir /var/www/ubuntu
$ sudo cp -r /media/cdrom/* /var/www/ubuntu/
```

You can achieve the same result by directly mounting the CD or DVD. Using the `mount` command, use the `--bind` option to make the mounted CD or DVD available in the `/var/www/ubuntu` directory. This means you don't need to install the files onto your PXE boot host. The following command mounts whatever CD or DVD is mounted at `/media/cdrom` again at `/var/www/ubuntu`.

```
$ sudo mount --bind /media/cdrom/ /var/www/ubuntu/
```

The Apache web server should then serve these files out via HTTP. In our Kickstart configuration file, we'll tell the host how to find these files when it wants to install our distribution.

■**Note** We talk about how to configure and run Apache in Chapter 11.

Firewall Configuration

You also need to ensure your firewall is configured to allow the required access for network booting. To do this, you need to have port 69 open for the TFTP server and port 80 open for HTTP traffic. The following are some appropriate `iptables` rules:

```
-A Firewall-eth0-INPUT -s 192.168.0.0/24 -p udp -m state --state NEW --dport 69 ➡
-j ACCEPT
-A Firewall-eth0-INPUT -p tcp -m state --state NEW --dport 80 -j ACCEPT
```

These rules allow access for any host on the 192.168.0.0/24 subnet to the boot server on the appropriate ports. You can read more about firewall rules in Chapter 6.

Specifying the Kickstart File

To finish this configuration, you'll create and specify a Kickstart file to automate the actual installation process. You'll store this file in `/var/www/ubuntu` and make it available via the Apache web server, just like your distribution's installation files. Let's create a file now:

```
$ sudo touch /var/www/ubuntu/ks.cfg
```

We created a file called `ks.cfg` in the `/var/www/ubuntu` directory.

■**Note** If you mounted a DVD directory (as described previously), storing the `ks.cfg` file in the `/var/www/` `ubuntu` directory won't work, and you'll need to locate the file elsewhere (e.g., by creating another directory and placing it there).

Let's now edit the `ks.cfg` file to include some very basic configuration.

```
install
url --url http://192.168.0.1/ubuntu/
```

Our example file has two Kickstart options, `install` and `url`. The `install` option tells Kickstart to install rather than the alternative, `upgrade`, which upgrades an existing installation. The `url` option tells Kickstart where to find the files required to install the distribution; these are the files we are serving out via our Apache web server.

■**Note** When you boot a host with this example file, the installation starts, but since you haven't specified any answers to installation questions, you still need to answer each question. You'll add to this file in the next section and answer the required questions.

To use our `ks.cfg` configuration file, we need to tell our boot server where to find it. We do this by adding an additional option to one or more labels in our PXE configuration file, for example, `/var/lib/tftpboot/pxelinux.cfg/default`. Let's look at the install label from the default file:

```
LABEL install
    kernel ubuntu-installer/i386/linux
    append ks=http://192.168.0.1/ubuntu/ks.cfg vga=normal➥
initrd=ubuntu-installer/i386/initrd.gz --
```

You can see we've added the `ks` option to our kernel boot options. The `ks` option tells the boot server where to find our Kickstart file, in our case via HTTP at `http://192.168.0.1/ubuntu/ks.cfg`.

Network Booting an Ubuntu Host

You have set up your Ubuntu boot server and specified your distribution's installation files, and now you can boot and install hosts. To do this, you'll configure your host to boot from the network, usually using the appropriate BIOS setting.

The booting host will attempt to acquire an IP address from your DHCP server. If it gets an IP address, then it will request boot instructions. The DHCP server will provide the `pxelinux.0` file and direct the booting host to the PXE server. The PXE server will provide the appropriate boot files and display the Ubuntu boot screen, as shown in Figure 19-4.

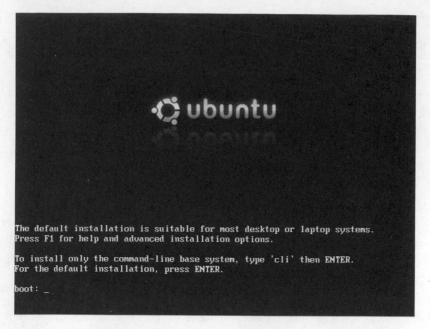

Figure 19-4. *The Ubuntu boot screen*

After bootup, the Kickstart configuration file will be retrieved and the installation process will be initiated. We'll look at automating that process in the next section.

Troubleshooting Ubuntu Network Booting

Troubleshooting the network boot process requires monitoring several elements on your host, including your log files, and using a network monitoring tool like the tcpdump or tshark command.

Let's start by monitoring the output of the DHCP process by looking at /var/log/daemon.log. You can also monitor the network traffic passing between your booting host and the boot server using a variety of network monitoring tools:

```
$ sudo tshark port tftp
Capturing on eth0
  0.000000  192.168.0.1 -> 192.168.0.161  TFTP Read Request, File: pxelinux.0\000, ➥
Transfer type: octet\000
  0.126924  192.168.0.1 -> 192.168.0.161  TFTP Read Request, File: pxelinux.0\000, ➥
Transfer type: octet\000
  0.238396  192.168.0.1 -> 192.168.0.161  TFTP Read Request, File: ➥
pxelinux.cfg/564ddfdb-733c-708f-9d49-fa93213b2246\000, Transfer type: octet\000
  0.242177  192.168.0.1 -> 192.168.0.161  TFTP Read Request, File: ➥
pxelinux.cfg/01-00-0c-29-3b-22-46\000, Transfer type: octet\000
  0.244886  192.168.0.1 -> 192.168.0.161  TFTP Read Request, ➥
File: pxelinux.cfg/C00002A4\000, Transfer type: octet\000
  0.246654  192.168.0.1 -> 192.168.0.161  TFTP Read Request, ➥
File: pxelinux.cfg/C00002A\000, Transfer type: octet\000
```

```
    0.248279  192.168.0.1 -> 192.168.0.161  TFTP Read Request, File: ➥
pxelinux.cfg/C00002\000, Transfer type: octet\000
    0.289393  192.168.0.1 -> 192.168.0.161  TFTP Read Request, File: ➥
 pxelinux.cfg/C0000\000, Transfer type: octet\000
    0.306368  192.168.0.1 -> 192.168.0.161  TFTP Read Request, File: ➥
pxelinux.cfg/C000\000, Transfer type: octet\000
    0.311124  192.168.0.1 -> 192.168.0.161  TFTP Read Request, File: ➥
pxelinux.cfg/C00\000, Transfer type: octet\000
    0.315184  192.168.0.1 -> 192.168.0.161  TFTP Read Request, File: ➥
pxelinux.cfg/C0\000, Transfer type: octet\000
    0.318966  192.168.0.1 -> 192.168.0.161  TFTP Read Request, File: ➥
pxelinux.cfg/C\000, Transfer type: octet\000
    0.333135  192.168.0.1 -> 192.168.0.161  TFTP Read Request, File: ➥
pxelinux.cfg/default\000, Transfer type: octet\000
    0.355684  192.168.0.1 -> 192.168.0.161  TFTP Read Request, File: ➥
ubuntu-installer/i386/boot-screens/boot.txt\000, Transfer type: octet\000
    0.361184  192.168.0.1 -> 192.168.0.161  TFTP Read Request, File: ➥
ubuntu-installer/i386/boot-screens/splash.rle\000, Transfer type: octet\000
```

Here we used the `tshark` command (installed via the `tshark` package) to monitor all traffic on port 69 (the TFTP port). You can see the request for the `pxelinux.0` file and our `pxelinux.cfg/default` configuration file, and finally the display of the Ubuntu boot screen.

■**Note** You can find more information about network booting at `https://help.ubuntu.com/8.04/ installation-guide/i386/install-methods.html`.

Kickstart and Preseed

On Red Hat, the language used to automatically install your host is called Kickstart. On Ubuntu, it is called Preseed. Kickstart, however, is also supported on Ubuntu in a form called Kickseed. The current Kickseed support can't configure Ubuntu completely, but helpfully it can also use selected Preseed directives to address any gaps. For simplicity's sake and because it's an easier language to use, we're going to show you how to use Kickstart to automate your installation for both Red Hat and Ubuntu. Where something isn't supported on Ubuntu, we'll show you how to use Preseed to configure it.

■**Note** Kickstart support for Ubuntu is growing regularly. The 8.10 and the Jaunty release (i.e., the future 9.04 release) will enhance this support further.

A Kickstart configuration file contains the instructions required to automate the installation process. It's a simple scripted process for most installation options, but it can be extended to do some complex configuration. Kickstart is heavily used on Red Hat, and more recently on

Ubuntu, so it's well documented. You can find detailed documentation for Kickstart on RHEL 5 at https://www.redhat.com/docs/en-US/Red_Hat_Enterprise_Linux/5/html/Installation_Guide/ch-kickstart2.html. This manual is also useful for provisioning Ubuntu hosts, as it uses many of the same directives. Again, when a particular directive isn't supported in Ubuntu, we'll provide you with the Preseed equivalent.

You can find documentation on Preseed and its directives at https://help.ubuntu.com/8.04/installation-guide/i386/appendix-preseed.html. We'll work with a few of these directives later in this section.

You've already seen how to specify Kickstart files to your provisioning environments, using both Cobbler on Red Hat and the PXE boot configuration on Ubuntu. Let's start by looking at some of the contents of a simple Kickstart file in Listing 19-5.

Listing 19-5. *A Kickstart File*

```
install
# System authorization information
auth  --useshadow  --enablemd5
# System bootloader configuration
bootloader --location=mbr
# Partition clearing information
clearpart --all --initlabel
# Use text mode install
text
```

Listing 19-5 shows a list of configuration directives starting with the install option, which dictates the behavior of the installation process by performing an installation. The alternative is upgrade, which automates an upgrade of a host.

You can then see configuration directives with options, for example, auth --useshadow --enablemd5, which tell Kickstart how to answer particular installation questions. The auth statement has the values --useshadow and --enablemd5 here, which enable shadow passwords and use of MD5, respectively.

The option that follows, bootloader with a value of --location=mbr, tells Kickstart to install the boot loader into the MBR. Next is the directive clearpart, which clears all partitions on the host and creates default labels for them. The final option, text, specifies we should use text-based installation as opposed to the GUI.

■**Tip** You can use Kickstart to upgrade hosts as well as install them. If you have an existing host, you can network boot from a new version of your operating system and use a Kickstart file to script and upgrade.

There are too many directives to discuss them individually, so we show you in Table 19-1 the directives that must be specified and some of the other major directives that you may find useful.

Table 19-1. *Required Kickstart Directives*

Directive	Description
auth	Configures authentication.
bootloader	Configures the boot loader.
keyboard	Configures the keyboard type.
lang	Configures the language on the host.
part	Configures partitions. This is required for installation, but not if upgrading.
rootpw	Specifies the password of the root user.
timezone	Specifies the time zone the host is in.

You can also find a useful list of the available directives with explanations at `http://www.redhat.com/docs/manuals/enterprise/RHEL-5-manual/Installation_Guide-en-US/s1-kickstart2-options.html`.

■**Tip** If you are on Red Hat, you can see an example Kickstart file that was created when you installed your host in the `/root/anaconda-ks.cfg` file. This will show you how your current host is built and can be used as an example to build similar hosts.

Installation Source

You've already seen the `install` and `upgrade` directives that specify the behavior of the installation. You can also specify the source of your installation files. In the Ubuntu provisioning section, you saw the `url` directive, which tells Kickstart to look for its installation files at an HTTP URL (e.g., `http://192.168.0.1/ubuntu`).

```
url --url http://192.168.0.1/ubuntu/
```

For Cobbler, we define a variable to specify the location of our installation source.

```
url --url=$tree
```

The `url` directive can also be used to specify an FTP server:

```
url --url ftp://jsmith:passsword@192.168.0.1/ubuntu
```

We can specify some alternative sources, including `cdrom`, when installing from a locally mounted CD or DVD and hard drive to install from a local partition.

```
harddrive --dir=/ubuntu --partition=/installsource
```

Keyboard, Language, and Time Zone

The next snippet we're going to show you configures our keyboard, language, and time zone.

```
# System keyboard
keyboard us
# System language
lang en_AU
# System timezone
timezone  Australia/Melbourne
```

Here we've specified us as the value for the keyboard directive to indicate a US keyboard. We've specified our language as en_AU (English Australian) and our time zone as Australia/Melbourne.

■**Tip** The keyboard, language, and time zone options are identical on Red Hat and Ubuntu.

Managing Users

You can also set the root user's password with the Kickstart rootpw directive.

```
rootpw --iscrypted $1$V.rhw$VUj.euMxoV9WkcQSanpGiO
```

The rootpw directive is a required Kickstart option for all Kickstart files. It can take either a plain-text value or an encrypted value for the root user's password when the --iscrtypted option is specified. You can create this encrypted password using the grub-md5-crypt command like so:

```
$ grub-md5-crypt
Password:
Retype password:
$1$V.rhw$VUj.euMxoV9WkcQSanpGiO
```

Specify the password you'd like to be encrypted and then retype it when prompted. You should then cut and paste the encrypted password into the Kickstart file.

On Ubuntu, the rootpw directive defaults to the --disabled option, in keeping with Ubuntu's approach of disabling the root user.

```
rootpw --disabled
```

■**Note** The --disabled option is not available on Red Hat hosts.

On Ubuntu, Kickstart can also create a new user with the user directive.

```
user jsmith --fullname "John Smith" --password password
```

The preceding code creates a new user called jsmith, with a full name of John Smith and a password of *password*. By adding the --iscrypted option, you can add a user with an encrypted password. We would create our encrypted password as we did with the rootpw directive.

Firewall and Network

On Red Hat, you can configure your host's initial firewall and network configuration.

```
# Firewall configuration
firewall --enabled --http --ssh --smtp
# SELinux configuration
selinux --disabled
```

Here we enabled the firewall with the `firewall` option and allowed access via HTTP, SSH, and SMTP. (You can disable the firewall with the `--disabled` option.) We also disabled SELinux using the `selinux --disabled` option.

Ubuntu cannot change firewall configuration through either Kickstart or Preseed, so you should just set this value as follows:

```
firewall --disabled
```

On both Red Hat and Ubuntu, you can configure your network connections with Kickstart like so:

```
# Network information
network --bootproto=static --device=eth0 --gateway=192.168.0.254 ➥
--ip=192.168.0.1 --nameserver=192.168.0.1 --netmask=255.255.255.0 --onboot=on
```

You can also specify network configuration for one or more interfaces using the `network` option. You can see we've set the various options required to configure the eth0 interface. You can also specify DHCP, for example:

```
network --bootproto=dhcp --device=eth0 --onboot=on
```

On Red Hat with Cobbler, if you're working with a specific host (one created with the `cobbler system` command), you can pass specific network configuration values to the Cobbler system configuration.

```
$ sudo cobbler system edit --name=gateway.example.com --mac=00:0C:29:3B:22:46➥
--profile=RHEL5 --interface=0 --ip=192.168.0.1 --subnet=255.255.255.0 --➥
gateway=192.168.0.254 --hostname=gateway --static=1
```

Here we've specified the `edit` command to change an existing Cobbler-defined system and passed network configuration values to our system. This would define a static network configuration for interface eth0. We specify that the configuration is static using the `--static=1` option; we would specify `--static=0` for a DHCP configuration. The interface to be configured is specified using the `--interface=0` option.

Then, instead of specifying a `network` line, in our Kickstart file we specify what Cobbler calls a *snippet*.

```
$SNIPPET('network_config')
```

When building your host, Cobbler passes the network configuration you've specified to this snippet and a template it contains. This is then converted into the appropriate `network` line and your host is configured.

■**Tip** This snippet is a simple use of Cobbler's snippet system. You can define a variety of other actions using snippets, and you can see a selection of these in the `/var/lib/cobbler/snippets` directory, including the `network_config` snippet we used in this section. You can see how to use these snippets in the `sample.ks` file, and you can find instructions on how to make use of templates and snippets at `https://fedorahosted.org/cobbler/wiki/KickstartTemplating` and `https://fedorahosted.org/cobbler/wiki/KickstartSnippets`.

Disks and Partitions

You've already seen one option Kickstart uses to configure disks and partitions, `clearpart`, which clears the partitions on the host. You can then use the `part` option to configure partitions on the host like so:

```
# Partition clearing information
clearpart --all --initlabel
part /boot --asprimary --bytes-per-inode=4096 --fstype="ext3" --size=150
part / --asprimary --bytes-per-inode=4096 --fstype="ext3" --size=4000
part swap --bytes-per-inode=4096 --fstype="swap" --size=512
```

■**Note** On Red Hat, you can create a similar configuration just by specifying the `autopart` option. The `autopart` option automatically creates three partitions. The first partition is a 1GB or larger root (/) partition, the second is a swap partition, and the third is an appropriate boot partition for the architecture. One or more of the default partition sizes can be redefined with the `part` directive.

You use the `part` option to create specific partitions. In the preceding code, we first created two partitions, /boot and /, both ext3. We specified a size of 150MB for the /boot partition and a size of 4000MB (or 4GB) for the / or root partition. We also created a swap partition with a size of 512MB.

Using Kickstart on Red Hat, we can create software RAID configurations, for example:

```
part raid.01 --asprimary --bytes-per-inode=4096 --fstype="raid" --grow --ondisk=sda ➥
--size=1
part raid.02 --asprimary --bytes-per-inode=4096 --fstype="raid" --grow --ondisk=sdb ➥
--size=1
part raid.03 --asprimary --bytes-per-inode=4096 --fstype="raid" --grow --ondisk=sdc ➥
--size=1
part raid.04 --asprimary --bytes-per-inode=4096 --fstype="raid" --grow --ondisk=sdd ➥
--size=1
part raid.05 --asprimary --bytes-per-inode=4096 --fstype="raid" --grow --ondisk=sde ➥
--size=1
raid / --bytes-per-inode=4096 --device=md0 --fstype="ext3" --level=5 raid.01 raid.02 ➥
raid.03 raid.04 raid.05
```

We specified five RAID disks, and each disk uses its entire contents as indicated by the `--grow` option. The respective disk to be used is specified with the `--ondisk` option, here ranging from sda to sde. Lastly, we used the `raid` option to specify the md0 RAID disk as the / or root partition.

■**Caution** On Ubuntu, Kickstart doesn't support RAID, although Preseed does partially. In version 8.04 of Ubuntu Preseed, RAID support is largely experimental and we don't recommend you provision and configure hosts with RAID configurations using it.

You can also create partitions using LVM during an automated installation. On Red Hat, for example, you would create them like so:

```
part /boot --fstype ext3 --size=150
part swap --size=1024
part pv1 --size=1 --grow
volgroup vg_root pv1
logvol  /  --vgname=vg_root  --size=81920 --name=lv_root
```

In the preceding sample, we created a 150MB boot partition, a 1GB swap partition, and a physical volume called pv1 on the remainder of the disk, using the `--grow` option to fill the rest of the disk. We then created an 80GB LVM logical volume called vg_root.

On Ubuntu, you can use the `preseed` directive to use Preseed to configure LVM inside your Kickstart file.

```
preseed --owner d-i partman-auto/method string lvm
preseed --owner d-i partman-lvm/device_remove_lvm boolean true
preseed --owner d-i partman-lvm/confirm boolean true
preseed --owner d-i partman-auto/choose_recipe select atomic
preseed --owner d-i partman/confirm_write_new_label boolean true
preseed --owner d-i partman/choose_partition select finish
preseed --owner d-i partman/confirm boolean true
```

The `preseed` directive is very simple and is a way of including Preseed directives in your Kickstart configuration. The directive is structured as follows:

```
preseed --owner owner key/sub-key value
```

The first part, `preseed`, tells Kickstart you are using a Preseed directive. The `--owner` option tells Preseed which application or function the directive belongs to—for example, `d-i` indicates that the Preseed directive belongs to the Debian installer.

■**Note** If you don't specify an `--owner` option, Preseed defaults to a value of `d-i`.

The key/subkey values specify the Preseed option to set; these values are structured as a collection of keys with a series of subkeys beneath each key. For example, the partman key contains all the Preseed options for configuring partitions. Here, underneath this key, you can see the confirm and confirm_write_new_label subkeys.

```
partman/confirm
partman/confirm_write_new_label
```

The type field contains the type of the value, for example, a string or a Boolean entry. The value field contains the actual value of the setting.

Let's apply Kickstart's preseed directive to our LVM configuration. We first select the LVM partitioning method:

```
preseed --owner d-i partman-auto/method string lvm
```

Then we remove any existing LVM devices using the device_remove_lvm directive and skip the confirmation message using the confirm directive.

```
preseed --owner d-i partman-lvm/device_remove_lvm boolean true
preseed --owner d-i partman-lvm/confirm boolean true
```

We then choose our partitioning method, in this case atomic, using the partman/choose_recipe key.

```
preseed --owner d-i partman-auto/choose_recipe select atomic
```

The atomic method creates all files in one partition, the recommended default for Ubuntu installations. Instead of atomic, we could specify home for a separate /home partition, and multi for separate /home, /usr, /var, and /tmp partitions.

We next tell Kickstart to automatically finish and write the LVM configuration.

```
preseed --owner d-i partman/choose_partition select finish
preseed --owner d-i partman/confirm boolean true
```

■**Tip** Support for native Kickstart—not using the preseed directive—for LVM configuration will be available in Ubuntu release 9.04.

You can also customize the exact disk and partition configuration using recipes you can read about at https://help.ubuntu.com/8.04/installation-guide/i386/preseed-contents.html.

■**Note** We discuss partitioning, software RAID, and LVM in Chapter 8.

Package Management

Using Kickstart, you can specify the packages you wish to install. On Red Hat, you specify a section starting with %packages and then the list of package groups or packages you wish to install.

```
%packages
@ Administration Tools
@ Server Configuration Tools
@ System Tools
@ Text-based Internet
dhcp
```

We specify an at symbol (@), a space, and then the name of the package group we wish to install, for example, Administration Tools. We can also specify individual packages by listing them by name without the @ symbol and space, as we have here with the dhcp package.

Ubuntu uses a similar setup:

```
%packages
@ kubuntu-desktop
dhcp-client
```

Here we've installed the Kubuntu-Desktop package group and the dhcp-client package.

■**Note** We discuss package groups in Chapter 7.

Installation Behavior

You can configure some of the behavior of the installation process, for example:

```
# Run the Setup Agent on first boot
firstboot –disable
# Skip installation key
key --skip
# Reboot after installation
reboot
```

Both the firstboot and key directives are specific to Red Hat and are not relevant on Ubuntu. The firstboot directive specifies whether the postinstallation menus that normally run on your first boot are enabled. Use --enable to have the menus run or --disable to skip them. The key directive controls entering a Red Hat installation key; use the --skip option to skip the entry screen.

RED HAT INSTALLATION KEYS

Kickstart also supports specifying Red Hat installation keys in your build (as discussed in Chapter 2). To do so, add the following values to your Kickstart file.

```
# RHEL Install Key
key $getVar('rhel_key', '--skip')
```

You can then specify some Kickstart metadata using the Cobbler system command for each host like so:

```
$ sudo cobbler system edit --name=00:0C:29:3B:22:46 ➥
--ksmeta="rhel_key=4ea373203ae2bd77"
```

You replace the key, 4ea373203ae2bd77, with your installation key for that host. If you don't specify a key, Kickstart will use the --skip option to skip the application of an installation key.

The reboot directive tells Kickstart to reboot the host after installation. You can also specify the shutdown directive to tell the host to shut down after installation.

Pre- and Postinstallation

You can run scripts before and after Kickstart installs your host. The prerun scripts run after the Kickstart configuration file has been parsed, but before your host is configured. Any prerun script is specified at the end of the Kickstart file and prefixed with the line %pre.

The postrun scripts are triggered after your configuration is complete and your host is installed. They should also be specified at the end of the Kickstart file and prefixed by a %post line. This is the %post section from our sample.ks configuration file:

```
%post
$SNIPPET('post_install_kernel_options')
$SNIPPET('post_install_network_config')
$SNIPPET('redhat_register')
```

Here we've specified three postrun Cobbler snippets that configure kernel and network options and register the host with Red Hat (as we are using RHN).

This postrun scripting space is useful to run any required setup applications or scripts.

Kickstart Configurator

Also available to create Kickstart files is the GUI-based Kickstart Configurator (see http://www.redhat.com/docs/manuals/enterprise/RHEL-5-manual/Installation_Guide-en-US/ch-redhat-config-kickstart.html). You can install this application using the system-config-kickstart package on Red Hat:

```
$ sudo yum install system-config-kickstart
```

On Ubuntu, you would use the following:

```
$ sudo apt-get install system-config-kickstart
```

You can then launch Kickstart Configurator from the Applications ➤ System Tools ➤ Kickstart menu or via the following:

```
$ system-config-kickstart
```

Figure 19-5 shows the application's interface.

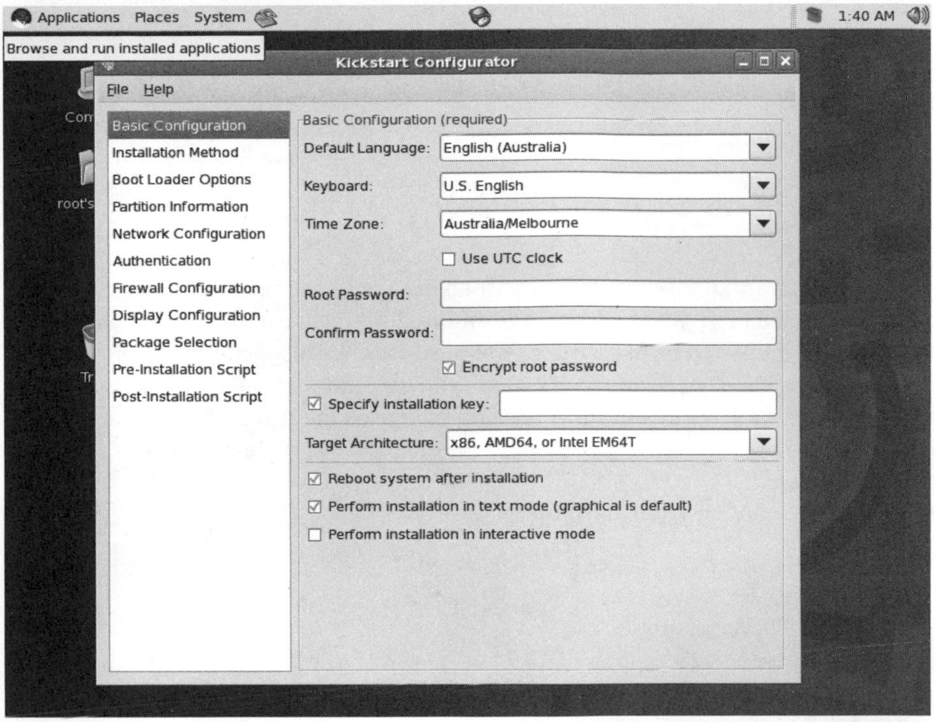

Figure 19-5. *The Kickstart Configurator interface*

Using Kickstart Configurator is often an easy way to quickly create simple Kickstart configurations if you don't wish to edit them on the command line.

Complete Kickstart Configurations

You've seen snippets of Kickstart (and some Preseed) configurations thus far. Let's now look at complete examples for both Red Hat and Ubuntu.

First up is a complete example for Red Hat:

```
install
reboot
url --url=$tree
key --skip
firstboot --disable
auth --enablemd5 --useshadow
bootloader --loader=mbr
keyboard us
```

```
lang en_AU
timezone  Australia/Melbourne
rootpw --iscrypted $1$V.rhw$VUj.euMxoV9WkcQSanpGiO
firewall --enabled --http --ssh --smtp
selinux --disabled
network --bootproto=dhcp --device=eth0 --onboot=on
clearpart --all –initlabel
autopart
%packages
@ Administration Tools
@ Server Configuration Tools
@ System Tools
@ Text-based Internet
dhcp
```

Here we created a very simple installation script. We're performing an installation and rebooting after the installation. We configured the required values like the keyboard, language, and time zone, and we created a password for the root user. We also enabled the firewall including access to the HTTP, SSH, and SMTP ports, and we requested a DHCP address for the eth0 interface. We cleared any existing partitions and then used the autopart directive to automatically partition the first disk on the host. Lastly, we installed a series of package groups as well as the dhcp package.

Here's a complete configuration on Ubuntu:

```
install
reboot
url --url http://192.0.2.161/ubuntu/
auth --useshadow --enablemd5
bootloader --location=mbr
keyboard us
lang en_AU
timezone  Australia/Melbourne
rootpw --disabled
user jsmith --fullname "John Smith" --password password
selinux --disabled
firewall --disabled
network --bootproto=dhcp --device=eth0 --onboot=on
preseed --owner d-i partman-auto/method string lvm
preseed --owner d-i partman-lvm/device_remove_lvm boolean true
preseed --owner d-i partman-lvm/confirm boolean true
preseed --owner d-i partman-auto/choose_recipe select atomic
preseed --owner d-i partman/confirm_write_new_label boolean true
preseed --owner d-i partman/choose_partition select finish
preseed --owner d-i partman/confirm boolean true
%packages
@ kubuntu-desktop
dhcp-client
```

Our Ubuntu configuration is very similar to our Red Hat configuration, but it's customized to suit the distribution—for example, we disabled the root user using the rootpw directive. You can also see where we used the preseed directive to directly specify some Preseed options to automatically configure LVM on our host.

■**Note** Both of the complete Kickstart files presented in this section are available with the source code for this book, which you can find in the Source Code area of the Apress website (http://www.apress.com).

Configuration Management

We've shown you throughout this book that configuring a Linux server includes quite a few tasks, for example, configuring hosts; creating users; and managing applications, daemons, and services. These tasks can be repeated many times in the life cycle of one host in order to add new configurations or remedy a configuration that has changed through error, entropy, or development. They can also be time-consuming and are generally not an effective use of time and effort.

The usual first response to this issue is to try to automate the tasks, which leads to the development of custom-built scripts and applications. Very few scripts developed in this ad hoc manner are ever published, documented, or reused, so the same tool is developed over and over again. These scripts also tend not to scale well, and they often require frequent maintenance.

Configuration management tools can automate these tasks efficiently and allow a consistent and repeatable life cycle for your hosts. We're going to show you how to use one of these tools, Puppet, to automate your configuration.

Introducing Puppet

Puppet (http://reductivelabs.com/) is an open source configuration management tool that relies on a client/server deployment model. It is licensed using the GPLv2 license. We're going to give you an overview of Puppet and how to use it to configure your environment and your hosts.

When using Puppet, central servers, called Puppet *masters*, are installed and configured. Client software is then installed on the target hosts, called *puppets* or *nodes*, that you wish to manage. Configuration is defined on the Puppet master, compiled, and then applied to the Puppet clients when they connect.

To provide client/server connectivity, Puppet uses XML-RPC web services running over HTTPS on TCP port 8140. To provide security, the sessions are encrypted and authenticated with internally generated self-signed certificates. Each Puppet client generates a self-signed certificate that is then validated and authorized on the Puppet master.

Thereafter, each client contacts the server—by default every 30 minutes, but this interval is customizable—to confirm that its configuration is up to date. If a new configuration is available or the configuration has changed, it is recompiled and then applied to the client. If required, a configuration update can also be triggered from the server, forcing configuration down to the client. If any existing configuration has varied on the client, it is corrected with the original configuration from the server. The results of any activity are logged and transmitted to the server.

At the heart of how Puppet works is a language that allows you to articulate and express your configuration. Your configuration components are organized into entities called *resources*, which in turn can be grouped together in *collections*. Resources consist of the following:

- Type

- Title

- Attributes

Listing 19-6 shows an example of a simple resource.

Listing 19-6. *A Puppet Resource*

```
file { "/etc/passwd":
     owner => "root",
     group => "root",
     mode => 0644,
}
```

The resource in Listing 19-6 is a file type resource. The file resource configures the attributes of files under management. In this case, it configures the /etc/passwd file and sets its owner and group to the root user and its permissions to 0644.

The resource type tells Puppet what kind of resource you are managing—for example, the user and file types are used for managing user and file operations on your nodes, respectively. Puppet comes with a number of resource types by default, including types to manage files, services, packages, cron jobs, and file systems, among others.

■**Tip** You can see a full list of the built-in resource types at http://reductivelabs.com/trac/puppet/wiki/TypeReference. You can also develop your own types in the Ruby programming language.

The resource's title identifies it to Puppet. Each title is made up of the name of the resource type (e.g., file) and the name of the resource (e.g., /etc/passwd). These two values are combined to make the resource's title (e.g., File["/etc/passwd"]).

■**Note** In a resource title, the name of the resource type is capitalized (File), and the name of the resource is encapsulated in block brackets and double quotes (["/etc/passwd"]).

Here the name, /etc/passwd, also tells Puppet the path of the file to be managed. Each resource managed by Puppet must be unique—for example, there can be only one resource called File["/etc/passwd"].

The attributes of a resource describe the configuration details being managed, such as defining a particular user and the attributes of that user (e.g., the groups the user belongs to or the location of the user's home directory). In Listing 19-6, we are managing the owner, group, and mode (or permissions) attributes of the file. Each attribute is separated from its value with the => symbols and is terminated with a comma.

Puppet also uses the concept of collections, which allow you to group together many resources. For example, an application such as Apache is made up of a package, a service, and a number of configuration files. In Puppet, each of these components would be represented as a resource (or resources) and then collected together and applied to a node. We'll look at some of these collection types later in this chapter.

Installing Puppet

Let's start by installing Puppet. For Puppet, the client and server installations are slightly different, and we'll show you how to install each.

Red Hat Installation

On Red Hat, on both servers and clients, you need to install some prerequisites, including the Ruby programming language.

```
$ sudo yum install ruby ruby-shadow
```

Next, you'll add the EPEL repository to your host and then install a number of packages from that repository. You can add the EPEL repository, if it's not already added to your Yum configuration, by adding the epel-release RPM.

```
$ sudo rpm -Uvh http://download.fedora.redhat.com/pub/epel/5/i386/➥
epel-release-5-3.noarch.rpm
```

On the server or master, you install the puppet, puppet-master, and facter packages from the EPEL repository.

```
$ sudo yum install puppet puppet-server facter
```

The puppet package contains the client, the puppet-master package contains the server, and the facter package contains a system inventory tool called Facter. Facter gathers information or facts about your hosts that is used to help customize your Puppet configuration.

On the client, you need to install only the puppet and facter packages.

```
$ sudo yum install puppet facter
```

Ubuntu Installation

On Ubuntu, the required packages are puppet, puppetmaster, and facter. The puppet package contains the Puppet client, the puppetmaster package contains the master, and the facter package contains the Facter system inventory tool.

On the server or master, you need to install this:

```
$ sudo apt-get install puppet puppetmaster facter
```

On the client, you need the following:

```
$ sudo apt-get install puppet facter
```

■Note Installing the `puppet`, `puppetmaster`, and `facter` packages will also install some prerequisite packages.

Configuring Puppet

We'll start configuring Puppet by setting up our Puppet master. Our configuration, including our *manifests* (the files containing our host configuration), will be located under the /etc/ puppet directory. Puppet's principal configuration file is located at /etc/puppet/puppet.conf.

We're going to store our actual configuration in a directory called `manifests` under the /etc/puppet directory. This directory is created when the Puppet packages are installed. The manifests directory needs to contain a file called site.pp that is the root of our configuration. Let's create that now.

```
$ sudo touch /etc/puppet/manifests/site.pp
```

■Note Manifest files containing configuration have a suffix of .pp.

We're also going to create three more directories, `classes`, `nodes`, and `files`, that will hold additional configuration files.

```
$ sudo mkdir /etc/puppet/manifests/{classes,files,nodes}
```

The `files` directory will hold any files we want to send to our managed clients. The `nodes` directory will contain definitions of our clients or nodes. The `classes` directory will contain our classes. *Classes* are collections of resources—for example, an Apache class containing all the resources needed to configure Apache.

We'll continue our configuration by defining these new directories in our site.pp file, as shown in Listing 19-7.

Listing 19-7. *The* site.pp *File*

```
import "nodes/*.pp"
import "classes/*.pp"

$puppetserver = "puppet.example.com"
```

The `import` statement tells Puppet to load all files with a suffix of .pp in both the `nodes` and `classes` directories into Puppet. The $puppetserver statement sets a variable. In Puppet, configuration statements starting with a dollar sign ($) are variables and can be used to specify values in a Puppet configuration.

In Listing 19-7, we've created a variable that contains the fully qualified domain name of our Puppet server, enclosed in double quotes.

■**Note** You can find quoting rules for Puppet at `http://reductivelabs.com/trac/puppet/wiki/` `LanguageTutorial#quoting`.

We recommend you create a DNS CNAME for your Puppet host (e.g., puppet.example.com), or add it to your `/etc/hosts` file:

```
# /etc/hosts
127.0.0.1 localhost
192.168.0.1 au-mel-ubuntu-1 au-mel-ubuntu-1.example.com puppet puppet.example.com
```

■**Note** We cover how to create CNAMEs in Chapter 9.

We also need to specify the fully qualified domain name in our `/etc/puppet/puppet.conf` configuration file. The configuration file is divided into sections, and each section configures a particular element of Puppet. For example, the [puppetd] section configures the Puppet client, and the [puppetmasterd] section configures the Puppet master or server. We're going to add only one entry, certname, to this file to get started. We'll add the certname value to the [puppetmasterd] section (if the section doesn't already exist in your file, then create the section).

```
[puppetmasterd]
certname=puppet.example.com
```

■**Note** Replace puppet.example.com with the fully qualified domain name of your host.

Adding the certname option addresses a bug with the Ruby SSL code present on many Ubuntu and Red Hat hosts. You can read more about the precise bug at `http://reductivelabs.com/trac/` `puppet/wiki/RubySSL-2007-006`.

Setting Up Puppet File Serving

In addition to configuring a variety of resources, Puppet can also serve out files—for example, it can deliver configuration files to a node. This file server is configured via the `/etc/puppet/` `fileserver.conf` configuration file. You can see a sample of this file in Listing 19-8.

Listing 19-8. *The* `fileserver.conf` *Configuration File*

```
[files]
  path /etc/puppet/manifests/files
  allow 192.168.0.0/24
  allow 127.0.0.1
```

File server configuration is very simple. We specify a file share—in our case called `files`—and enclose it in square brackets [ ]. Next, we specify the `path` for the file share, which here is the directory we created earlier, `/etc/puppet/manifests/files`. We can then specify `allow` and/or `deny` statements to control access to our file share. Here we've allowed access to the file share from anyone in the 192.168.0.0/24 subnet and from the localhost, 127.0.0.1.

■**Tip** You can read more about file serving at `http://reductivelabs.com/trac/puppet/wiki/FileServingConfiguration`.

Puppet Firewall Configuration

The Puppet master runs on TCP port 8140. This port needs to be open on your master's firewall, and your client must be able to route and connect to the master. To do this, you need to have some appropriate firewall rules on your master, such as the following:

```
-A Firewall-eth0-INPUT -p tcp -m state --state NEW --dport 8140 -j ACCEPT
```

The preceding line allows access from everywhere to TCP port 8140.

Starting Puppet Server

The Puppet master can be started via an `init` script. On Red Hat, we run the `init` script with the `service` command like so:

```
$ sudo service puppetmaster start
```

On Ubuntu, we run it using the `invoke-rc.d` command.

```
$ sudo invoke-rc.d puppetmaster start
```

■**Note** Output from the daemon can be seen in `/var/log/messages` on Red Hat hosts and `/var/log/daemon.log` on Ubuntu hosts.

Connecting Our First Client

Once you have the Puppet master configured and started, you can configure and initiate your first client. On the client, as we mentioned earlier, you need to install the `puppet` and `facter` packages using your distribution's package management system. We're going to install a client on the gateway.example.com host and then connect to our puppet.example.com host. This installation will also create a `/etc/puppet` directory with a `puppet.conf` configuration file.

When connecting our client, we first want to run the Puppet client from the command line rather than as a service. This will allow us to see what is going on when we connect. The Puppet client binary is called `puppetd`, and you can see a connection to the master initiated in Listing 19-9.

Listing 19-9. *Puppet Client Connection to the Puppet Master*

```
gateway$ puppetd --server=puppet.example.com --no-daemonize --verbose
info: Creating a new certificate request for gateway.example.com
info: Creating a new SSL key at /var/lib/puppet/ssl/private_keys/gateway.example.com➡
.pem
warning: peer certificate won't be verified in this SSL session
notice: Did not receive certificate
```

In Listing 19-9, we executed the puppetd binary with a number of options. The first option, --server, specifies the name or address of the Puppet master to connect to. We can also specify this in the main section of the /etc/puppet/puppet.conf configuration file on the client.

```
[main]
server=puppet.example.com
```

The --no-daemonize option runs the Puppet client in the foreground and prevents it from running as a daemon, which is the default behavior. The --verbose option enables verbose output from the client.

■**Tip** The --debug option provides further output that is useful for troubleshooting.

In Listing 19-9, you can see the output from our connection. The client has created a certificate signing request and a private key to secure our connection. Puppet uses SSL certificates to authenticate connections between the master and the client. The client is now waiting for the master to sign its certificate and enable the connection. At this point, the client is still running and awaiting the signed certificate. It will continue to check for a signed certificate every two minutes until it receives one or is canceled (using Ctrl+C or the like).

■**Note** You can change the time the Puppet client will wait using the --waitforcert option. You can specify a time in seconds or 0 to not wait for a certificate.

Now on the master, we need to sign the certificate. We do this using the puppetca binary.

```
puppet$ puppetca --list
gateway.example.com
```

■**Tip** You can find a full list of the binaries that come with Puppet at http://reductivelabs.com/trac/puppet/wiki/PuppetExecutables.

The --list option displays all the certificates waiting to be signed. We can then sign our certificate using the --sign option.

```
puppet$ puppetca --sign gateway.example.com
Signed gateway.example.com
```

Note You can sign all waiting certificates with the puppetca --sign --all command.

On the client, two minutes after we've signed our certificate, we should see the following entries:

```
notice: Got signed certificate
notice: Starting Puppet client version 0.24.7
err: Could not retrieve catalog: Could not find default node or by name with➥
'gateway.example.com, gateway' on node gateway.example.com
```

The client is now authenticated with the master, but we have another message present:

```
err: Could not retrieve catalog: Could not find default node or by name with➥
'gateway.example.com, gateway' on node gateway.example.com
```

The client has connected, but because we don't have anything configured for the client, we received an error message.

Caution It is important that the time is accurate on your master and client. SSL connections rely on the clock on hosts being correct. If the clocks are incorrect, then your connection may fail with an error, indicating that your certificates are not trusted. You can use NTP, which we discuss in Chapter 9, to ensure your host's clocks are accurate.

Creating Our First Configuration

Now our client has connected and we're going to add some configuration for it. On the Puppet master, we need to add a node definition and some configuration to apply to our client.

We'll start with the node configuration. To do this, we're going to create a file called gateway.example.com.pp in our /etc/puppet/manifests/nodes/ directory. You can see the contents of this file in Listing 19-10.

Listing 19-10. *Our Node Configuration*

```
node "gateway.example.com" {
    include sudo
}
```

The node directive defines a node or client configuration to Puppet. Each client needs a node directive, and inside the node you define the configuration that applies to the client. You specify the client name, enclosed in double quotes, and then you specify the configuration that applies to it inside curly braces { }.

■**Note** You can also specify a special node called `default`. If no node definition exists, then the contents of this node are applied to the client.

You can specify multiple clients in a node directive by separating each with a comma like so:

```
node "gateway.example.com", "headoffice.example.com" {
    include sudo
}
```

■**Note** At this stage, you can't specify nodes with wildcards (e.g., `*.example.com`). Puppet, however, does have an inheritance model in which you can have one node inherit values from another node. You can read about node inheritance at `http://reductivelabs.com/trac/puppet/wiki/LanguageTutorial#nodes`.

Inside our node definition you can see the `include` directive. The `include` directive adds classes (collections of resources) to our client's configuration. In this case, we're adding a class called `sudo`. You can include multiple classes by using multiple `include` directives or separating each class with commas.

```
include sudo,sshd
```

Let's add this class to our Puppet configuration. We're going to create a file called `sudo.pp` in the `/etc/puppet/manifests/classes` directory. You can see its contents in Listing 19-11.

Listing 19-11. *The sudo Class*

```
class sudo {
    package { sudo:
        ensure => present,
    }

    file { "/etc/sudoers":
        source => "puppet://$puppetserver/files/etc/sudoers",
        owner => "root",
        group => "root",
        mode => 0440,
    }
}
```

VERSION CONTROL

As your configuration gets more complicated, you should consider adding it to a version control system such as Subversion. A version control system allows you to record and track changes to files, and is commonly used by software developers. For configuration management, version control allows you to track changes to your configuration. This is highly useful if you need to revert to a previously known state or make changes without impacting your running configuration.

You can find information about how to use Subversion at `http://svnbook.red-bean.com/` and some specific ideas about how to use it with Puppet at `http://reductivelabs.com/trac/puppet/wiki/VersionControlPuppet`.

You can see we've added a `class` directive and called it `sudo`. The contents of our class are specified between the curly braces.

We've specified two resources inside our class, a `package` resource and a `file` resource. The package resource, `Package["sudo"]`, specifies that the package `sudo` must be installed using the attribute `ensure` and setting its value to `present`. To remove the package, we would set the `ensure` attribute to `absent`. If we wanted to ensure that the `sudo` package was always up to date, we would specify a value of `latest` for the `ensure` attribute like so:

```
package { sudo:
    ensure => latest,
}
```

On every Puppet run, the client will now check that the currently installed version of the `sudo` package is the latest. If it is the latest version, then Puppet will do nothing; if a later version is available, then Puppet will install it.

To manage your packages, Puppet uses the default package manager. For example, on Red Hat it will use `yum` and on Debian it will use `aptitude` to install, remove, or update your package. This is one of the more convenient features of Puppet—you specify the `package` resource, and Puppet detects the appropriate package manager to use and installs the required package. You don't need to do anything else or even understand how the package manager works.

■**Note** We've discovered that Puppet calls the various items it can configure *types*, for example, the `package` type. The code that interacts with a particular operating system (e.g., the code that interacts with the Yum package manager) is called a *provider*. Each type may have multiple providers. For example, the `package` type has providers for Yum, Aptitude, up2date, Ruby Gems, ports, portage, rug, and OSX DMG files, among many other package managers. The `package` providers allow Puppet to configure packages on a wide variety of Unix operating systems and Linux distributions.

Next, we've specified a file resource, `File["/etc/sudoers"]`. You've seen some of the attributes of this resource before: the `owner`, `group`, and `mode` attributes. The `source` attribute allows Puppet to retrieve a file from the Puppet file server and deliver it to the client. The value of this attribute is the name of the Puppet file server and the location and name of the file to retrieve.

```
puppet://$puppetserver/files/etc/sudoers
```

Let's break down this value. The `puppet://` part specifies that Puppet will use the Puppet file server protocol to retrieve the file.

■**Note** Currently this is the only protocol available. In future versions of Puppet, the file server will support other protocols, such as HTTP or rsync. This support is expected in versions after 0.25.0.

The `$puppetserver` variable contains the hostname of our Puppet server. We created this variable and placed it in our `site.pp` file earlier. Instead of the variable, you can specify the hostname of the file server here.

```
puppet://puppet.example.com/files/etc/sudoers
```

The next portion of our `source` value specifies the file share and the specific file to serve. Here the share is `files`, which we created earlier in our `fileserver.conf` file, and the specific file to load is `/etc/sudoers`. This assumes the file `sudoers` is in the directory `/etc/puppet/manifests/files/etc/sudoers`. Let's copy a `sudoers` file there now. We'll use the default `sudoers` file on our host.

```
puppet$ mkdir -p /etc/puppet/manifests/files/etc/
puppet$ cp /etc/sudoers /etc/puppet/manifests/files/etc/sudoers
```

CREATING A PUPPET CONFIGURATION

The best way to convert your existing configuration to Puppet is to start small. Choose a function or application, such as `sudo` or the SSH daemon, and convert its configuration management from manual to managed with Puppet. When these functions are stable, add additional components to your Puppet configuration. A good way to approach this task is to classify your hosts by their functions. For example, our gateway.example.com host runs a number of services such as Apache, Postfix, and OpenVPN, so a logical first step would be to configure these services and then slowly add the additional functions also supported on this host.

Applying Our First Configuration

We've created our first configuration and we're going to apply it on our client. Back on the gateway.example.com host, we run the Puppet client again, as shown in Listing 19-12.

Listing 19-12. *Applying Our First Configuration*

```
gateway$ puppetd --server=puppet.example.com --no-daemonize --verbose
notice: Starting Puppet client version 0.24.7
info: Caching catalog at /var/lib/puppet/localconfig.yaml
notice: Starting catalog run
info: Filebucket[/var/lib/puppet/clientbucket]: ➥
```

```
Adding /etc/sudoers(a8ae43fcf346af54d473b13b17d6d037)
notice: //Node[gateway.example.com]/sudo/File[/etc/sudoers]: Filebucketed to  with ➡
sum a8ae43fcf346af54d473b13b17d6d037
notice: //Node[gateway.example.com]/sudo/File[/etc/sudoers]/source: replacing from ➡
source puppet://puppet.example.com/files/sudoers with contents ➡
{md5}7255bc94cd66fc3416f991aed81ab447
notice: //Node[gateway.example.com]/sudo/File[/etc/sudoers]/mode: mode changed '640' ➡
to '440'
notice: Finished catalog run in 3.52 seconds
```

Tip Puppet logs to the /var/log/messages file on Red Hat and the /var/log/daemon.log file on Ubuntu.

In Listing 19-12, we've run the Puppet client, puppetd, and connected to the master. We can see a catalog run commence on our client. In Puppet, the combined configuration to be applied to a host is a catalog and the process of applying it is called a *run*.

Tip You can find a glossary of Puppet terminology at http://reductivelabs.com/trac/puppet/wiki/GlossaryOfTerms.

In the first step of our run, we see a line describing a filebucket. The filebucket is a special type used to back up files, and you'll note we didn't specify this type. Puppet automatically backs up files that are going to be changed or replaced (in this case, our host already has an /etc/sudoers file and we're going to replace it with our new file from the Puppet master). Here Puppet will copy the file to a directory on the client, usually underneath /var/lib/puppet/clientbucket. This means if we want to get this file back, we can manually retrieve it.

Tip Puppet can also back up the file to our master using the filebucket type. See http://reductivelabs.com/trac/puppet/wiki/TypeReference#filebucket.

After backing up the file, Puppet copies the new /etc/sudoers file from the master.

Tip Puppet also has a testing mode called noop. In this mode, Puppet doesn't update your configuration but merely tells you what it would have done. This is very useful for testing your configuration prior to applying it. You can run the Puppet client in noop mode by using the --noop option with the puppetd command.

Lastly, Puppet has changed the permissions of the new file to 0440. But why didn't Puppet change the owner and group of the file, too? Well, in this case, the file is already owned by the root user and belongs to the root group, so Puppet changes nothing. Puppet will make changes on the client only if something needs to be changed. If your current configuration is correct, then Puppet will not do anything.

So that's it. Puppet has configured our client. If the Puppet client was now running as a daemon, it would wait 30 minutes (by default) and then connect to the master again to check if the configuration has changed on our client or if a new configuration is available from the master. We can adjust this run interval using the `runinterval` option in the `/etc/puppet/puppet.conf` configuration file.

```
[puppetd]
runinterval=3600
```

Here we've adjusted the run interval to 3600 seconds, or 60 minutes.

PUPPET BEST PRACTICES

Puppet configuration can get quite complex. One of Puppet's users, Stanford University, has written a best practices guide that offers some advice about how to configure Puppet. The Puppet Best Practices guide is available at `http://reductivelabs.com/trac/puppet/wiki/PuppetBestPractice`. Remember, this document contains only guidelines, and the information within may not completely suit your environment.

Specifying Configuration for Multiple Hosts

We've barely scratched the surface of Puppet's configuration capabilities, so let's look at extending our current configuration to multiple clients or nodes. We'll demonstrate how to differentiate configuration on two clients and apply slightly different configuration to each.

To implement this differentiation, we're going to use Puppet's partner tool, Facter. Facter is a system inventory tool that returns facts about your hosts. We can run Facter from the command line using the `facter` binary to see what it knows about our gateway.example.com client.

```
gateway$ sudo facter
architecture => i386
domain => example.com
facterversion => 1.5.2
fqdn => gateway.example.com
hardwareisa => i686
hardwaremodel => i686
hostname => gateway
id => root
interfaces => eth0,eth1
ipaddress => 192.168.0.254
ipaddress_eth0 => 192.168.0.254
ipaddress_eth1 => 10.0.2.155
kernel => Linux
kernelrelease => 2.6.18-92.el5
```

```
kernelversion => 2.6.18
operatingsystem => RedHat
operatingsystemrelease => 5
...
```

We've shown you a small selection of the facts available in Facter, but you can see that it knows a lot about our host, including its name, network information, operating system, and even the release of the operating system.

So how is this useful to Puppet? Well, each of these facts is available to Puppet as a variable. Puppet runs Facter prior to applying any configuration, collects the client's facts, and then sends them to the Puppet master for use in configuring the client. For example, the hostname fact is available in our Puppet configuration as the variable $hostname. Let's look at an example in Listing 19-13.

MORE ABOUT FACTER

Facter supports adding facts via environment variables. Any environment variable on your client that is prefixed with FACTER (e.g., FACTER_LOCATION) will be available as the variable $location in your Puppet configuration. You can read more about this at http://reductivelabs.com/trac/puppet/wiki/FrequentlyAskedQuestions#can-i-access-environmental-variables-with-facter.

Facter is also highly extensible. With a small amount of Ruby code, you can add your own facts, for example, information customized to your environment. You can read about how to add these custom facts at http://reductivelabs.com/trac/puppet/wiki/AddingFacts.

Listing 19-13. *Using Facts*

```
class sudo {
    package { sudo:
        ensure => present,
    }

    file { "/etc/sudoers":
        source => "puppet://$puppetserver/files/$hostname/etc/sudoers",
        owner => "root",
        group => "root",
        mode => 0440,
    }
}
```

You can see the sudo class we previously defined with one small change in the source attribute of the File["/etc/sudoers"] resource.

```
puppet://$puppetserver/files/$hostname/etc/sudoers
```

We've added the $hostname variable to the source attribute's value. Now instead of looking for the file in the /etc/puppet/manifests/files/etc/ directory, it will look in the /etc/puppet/manifests/files/$hostname/etc directory. When the client connects, the $hostname variable will be replaced with the hostname of the client connecting—for example, if the gateway host connected, then the source attribute would become /etc/puppet/manifests/files/gateway/ etc. We can now have a different sudoers file for particular clients; for instance, we could have the following:

```
/etc/puppet/manifests/files/gateway/etc/sudoers
/etc/puppet/manifests/files/headoffice/etc/sudoers
```

Depending on which client connected, they would get a file appropriate to them. But this isn't the only use for facts. We can also use facts to determine how to configure a particular node, as shown in Listing 19-14.

Listing 19-14. *A Fact in a Case Statement*

```
node default {

    case $operatingsystem
        redhat:  { include redhat  } # include the redhat class
        ubuntu  { include ubuntu } # include the ubuntu class
        default: { include generic } # include the generic class
    }
}
```

Here we created our default node definition, which is the node configuration used for all nodes that don't explicitly have a node defined. Inside this node definition, we used a feature of the Puppet language, a case statement. The case statement, a concept common to many programming languages, specifies a result based on the value of a variable—in this case, the $operatingsystem fact, which contains the name of the operating system running on the client (e.g., redhat for Red Hat or ubuntu for Ubuntu).

■Tip Puppet has two other types of conditionals: selectors and if/else clauses. You can read about these at http://reductivelabs.com/trac/puppet/wiki/LanguageTutorial#conditionals.

In Listing 19-14, if the value of the $operatingsystem is redhat, then the redhat class is included on this client. If the value is ubuntu, then the ubuntu class is included. The last value, default, is the behavior if the value does not match either redhat or ubuntu. In this case, the generic class is applied to the client.

In a case statement, we can also specify multiple values by separating each with a comma like so:

```
case $operatingsystem
    redhat,centos:  { include redhat  } # include the redhat class
    ubuntu,debian  { include ubuntu } # include the ubuntu class
    default: { include generic } # include the generic class
}
```

Now if the value is redhat or centos, then the redhat class would be included, and if the value is ubuntu or debian, then the ubuntu class would be included.

We've used another Puppet conditional, a selector, in Listing 19-15.

Listing 19-15. *A Selector*

```
service { "sshdaemon":
    name => $operatingsystem ? {
        redhat => "sshd",
        ubuntu => "ssh",
        default => "ssh",
    }
    ensure => running,
```

In Listing 19-15, we introduced a new type, service, that manages services on hosts. We've titled our service resource sshdaemon, but we've used another attribute called name to specify the name that will be used to start or stop the service on the client. We've used a Puppet language construct called a *selector*, combined with the $operatingsystem fact, to specify the name attribute. This is because on each operating system we've specified, the SSH daemon is called something different. For example, on Red Hat the SSH daemon's init script is called sshd, while on Ubuntu it is called ssh.

The name attribute uses the value of the $operatingsystem fact to specify what the daemon will be called on each distribution. Puppet, in turn, uses this to determine what service to start or stop. So if the value of the $operatingsystem fact is redhat, then the service resource will use the name sshd to manage the SSH daemon. The default value is used when the value of the $operatingsystem is neither redhat nor ubuntu.

Lastly, the ensure attribute has been set to running to ensure the service will be started. We could set the ensure attribute to stopped to ensure it is not started.

■**Note** The Puppet language has a lot of useful features. You can find a full tutorial of the language at http://reductivelabs.com/trac/puppet/wiki/LanguageTutorial.

Relating Resources

Resources in Puppet also have the concept of *relationships*. For example, a service resource can be connected to the package that installs it. Using this, we could trigger a restart of the service when a new version of the package is installed. This allows us to do some useful things. Consider the simple example in Listing 19-16.

Listing 19-16. *Requiring Resources*

```
class ssh {
    service { "sshdaemon":
        name => $operatingsystem ? {
            redhat => "sshd",
            ubuntu => "ssh",
```

```
            default => "ssh",
        },
        ensure => running,
        require => File["/etc/ssh/sshd_config"],
    }

    file { "/etc/ssh/sshd_config":
        path    => "/etc/ssh/sshd_config",
        owner   => root,
        group   => root,
        mode    => 644,
        source  => "puppet://$puppetserver/files/etc/ssh/sshd_config",
        notify  => Service[sshdaemon],
    }
}
```

Listing 19-16 shows a new class called ssh, which contains the service resource we created in Listing 19-15. We have created a file resource to manage the /etc/ssh/sshd_config
file. You've seen almost all the attributes in these resources except require in the service
resource and notify in the file resource. These are not, however, normal attributes—they are
called *metaparameters*. Let's look at each metaparameter and see what it does.

The require metaparameter allows you to build a relationship to one or more resources.
Any resource you specify in the require metaparameter will be configured *before* this resource,
hence Puppet will process and configure the File["/etc/ssh/sshd_config"] resource before
the Service["sshdaemon"] resource. This approach ensures that the appropriate configuration
file is installed prior to starting the SSH daemon service. You could do a similar thing with a
package resource.

```
class httpd {
    package { "httpd":
        ensure => present,
    }

    service { "httpd":
        ensure => running,
        enabled => true,
        require => Package["httpd"],
    }
}
```

Here the package resource, Package["httpd"], must be installed before the
Service["httpd"] service can be started.

■Tip We've also added the enabled attribute to the Service["http"] resource. When set to true, this
attribute ensures our service starts when the host boots (similar to using the chkconfig or update-rc.d
command).

We've also specified another metaparameter, this one called `notify`, in Listing 19-16. This metaparameter has been added to the `File["/etc/ssh/sshd_config"]` resource. The `notify` metaparameter tells other resources about changes and updates to a resource. In this case, if the `File["/etc/ssh/sshd_config"]` resource is changed (e.g., if the configuration file is updated), then Puppet will notify the `Service["sshdaemon"]` resource, causing it to be run and thus restarting the SSH daemon service.

■**Tip** Two other relationships you can construct are subscribe and before. You can see both of these at `http://reductivelabs.com/trac/puppet/wiki/TypeReference#metaparameters` and also read about other available metaparameters you may find useful.

Using Templates

In addition to retrieving files from the Puppet file server, you can also make use of a template function to apply specific values inside those files to configure a service or application. Puppet templates use a Ruby template language called ERB (see `http://www.ruby-doc.org/stdlib/libdoc/erb/rdoc/`). It's very simple to use, as you can see in Listing 19-17.

Listing 19-17. *Using Templates*

```
file { "/etc/ssh/sshd_config":
        path    => "/etc/ssh/sshd_config",
        owner   => root,
        group   => root,
        mode    => 644,
        content => template("/etc/ssh/sshd_config.erb"),
        notify  => Service[sshdaemon],
    }
```

In Listing 19-17, we used the same `File["/etc/ssh/sshd_config"]` resource we created earlier, but we exchanged the `source` attribute for the `content` attribute. With the `content` attribute, rather than a file being retrieved from the Puppet file server, the contents of the file are populated from this attribute. The contents of the file can be specified in a string like so:

```
content => "this is the content of a file",
```

Or, as Listing 19-17 shows, we can use a special Puppet function called `template`. To use the template function, we specify a template file, and Puppet populates any ERB code inside the template with appropriate values. Listing 19-18 shows a very simple template.

Listing 19-18. *sshd_config Template*

```
Port 22
Protocol 2
ListenAddress <%= ipaddress_eth0 %>
```

```
SyslogFacility AUTHPRIV
PermitRootLogin no
PasswordAuthentication no
ChallengeResponseAuthentication no
GSSAPIAuthentication yes
GSSAPICleanupCredentials yes
UsePAM yes
X11Forwarding yes
Banner /etc/motd
```

We've only used one piece of ERB in Listing 19-18, to specify the ListenAddress of our SSH daemon, <%= ipaddress_eth0 %>. The <%= *value* %> syntax is how you specify variables in a template. Here we specified that Puppet should set the ListenAddress to the value of the $ipaddress_eth0 variable. This variable is, in turn, the value of the ipaddress_eth0 fact, which contains the IP address of the eth0 interface.

When we now connect a client that applies the File["/etc/ssh/sshd_config"] resource, the value of the ipaddress_eth0 fact on the client will be added to the template and then applied on the client in the /etc/ssh/sshd_config file.

You can perform a wide variety of functions in an ERB template—more than just specifying variables, including basic Ruby expressions. You can read about how to use templates in more detail at http://reductivelabs.com/trac/puppet/wiki/PuppetTemplating, and you can see another example of a typical template at http://reductivelabs.com/trac/puppet/wiki/Recipes/ResolvConf.

Puppet looks for templates in a directory specified by the templatedir configuration option. This option usually defaults to /var/lib/puppet/templates. We're going to override this to put our templates with the rest of our manifests and configuration. In the puppet.conf configuration file on the Puppet master, we add the following:

```
[puppetmasterd]
templatedir=/etc/puppet/manifests/templates
```

The template specified in Listing 19-17 is now located at /etc/puppet/manifests/templates/etc/ssh/sshd_config.

PUPPET AND PROVISIONING

You can also combine Puppet with your provisioning environment and boot servers. You can find instructions on how to combine Puppet with both Cobbler and Ubuntu Preseed at http://reductivelabs.com/trac/puppet/wiki/BootstrappingWithPuppet.

Definitions

You've already seen one type of Puppet collection: a class. There is another type of collection: the definition or define directive. *Definitions* are used for a configuration that has multiple instances on a client. The best way to think about a definition is as a reusable snippet of configuration that you can call with arguments.

This reuse is also the key difference between classes and definitions. Classes contain single instances of resources—for example, a class could contain a package resource that defined the httpd package. This package will exist only once on a node and hence is installed, removed, or managed using a class. But some configurations exist multiple times on your clients—for example, the httpd server may have multiple virtual hosts defined. You could then create a definition to configure virtual hosts and pass in appropriate arguments to configure each. As long as each set of arguments is different, Puppet will configure the new virtual host every time the definition is evaluated.

A definition is created by using the define directive, specifying a title for the definition and then listing any arguments in brackets. The definition itself is specified next and is enclosed in curly braces. Listing 19-19 contains a definition that runs a script to configure a new virtual host.

Listing 19-19. *Definition*

```
define new_vhost ( $ipaddress, $domain ) {
        exec { "/usr/sbin/create_vhost --vhost $title --ip $ipaddress --domain ➥
$domain":
        }
}

new_vhost { vhost1:
        ip => "192.0.2.155",
        domainname => "vhost1.example.com"
}
```

In Listing 19-19, we created a definition called new_vhost that has arguments of the variables $ipaddress and $domain. Inside the definition, we used the exec resource type (this is another type; it executes an external script). We specified three variables, $title and the previously mentioned $ipaddress and $domain variables, in the script defined in the exec resource type.

■**Note** The $title variable is available in all resources and contains the title of the resource.

On the next lines, we have actually called the new_vhost definition. We call it much like we define a resource type. We specify the name of the definition being called, the title, which in this case is vhost1 (which is also the value of the $title variable). We then specify the remaining variables to be passed to the definition in the same format as we would specify attributes in a resource.

If we use this definition, we'll see a log message on the client much like the following:

```
notice://new_vhost[vhost1]/Exec[/usr/sbin/create_vhost --vhost vhost1 --ip➥
192.0.2.155 --domain vhost1.example.com]/returns: executed successfully
```

■Tip You also saw a definition being used in a recipe, `http://reductivelabs.com/trac/puppet/wiki/Recipes/ResolvConf`, that we linked to earlier.

More Puppet

We've barely touched on Puppet in this chapter—there's a lot more to see. In the sections that follow, we'll describe some of the topics we haven't covered that you can explore further to make the best use of Puppet.

Modules

You've already seen two collections of resources, classes and definitions, but Puppet has another, more complex type of collection called a *module*. You can combine collections of classes, definitions, templates, files, and resources into modules. Modules are portable collections of configuration; for example, a module might contain all the resources required to configure Postfix or Apache.

You can read about how to use modules at `http://reductivelabs.com/trac/puppet/wiki/PuppetModules`. Also on this page are links to a huge number of user-contributed modules. Someone else has almost certainly written a module to configure a service or application you may want, and in many cases you can just download and reuse these modules to save having to write ones yourself.

You can read about how to create your own modules and how they are structured at `http://reductivelabs.com/trac/puppet/wiki/ModuleOrganisation`.

Functions

Puppet also has a collection of functions. *Functions* are useful commands that can be run on the Puppet master to perform actions. You've already seen two functions: `template`, which we used to create a template configuration file, and `include`, which we used to specify the classes for our nodes. There are a number of other functions, including the `generate` function that calls external commands and returns the result, and the `notice` function that logs messages on the master and is useful for testing a configuration.

You can see a full list of functions at `http://reductivelabs.com/trac/puppet/wiki/FunctionReference` and find some documentation on how to write your own functions at `http://reductivelabs.com/trac/puppet/wiki/WritingYourOwnFunctions`.

Reports

Puppet has the ability to report on events that have occurred on your nodes or clients. Reporting is pretty basic right now; you can see the current reports at `http://reductivelabs.com/trac/puppet/wiki/ReportReference`. You can also find some examples of how to use reports and build your own custom reports at `http://reductivelabs.com/trac/puppet/wiki/ReportsAndReporting`.

External Nodes

As you might imagine, when you begin to have a lot of nodes your configuration can become quite complex. If it becomes cumbersome to define all your nodes and their configuration in manifests, then you can use a feature known as *external nodes* to better scale this. External nodes allow you to store your nodes and their configuration in an external source. For example, you can store node information in a database or an LDAP directory. You can read more about external and LDAP nodes at http://reductivelabs.com/trac/puppet/wiki/ExternalNodes and http://reductivelabs.com/trac/puppet/wiki/LDAPNodes, respectively.

Environments

One of Puppet's most useful features is support for the concept of environments. *Environments* allow you to specify configuration for particular environments—for example, you might have development, test, and production environments. Puppet allows you to maintain parallel sets of configuration for each environment and apply them to different clients.

This is a powerful mechanism for catering for a variety of scenarios—for example, creating a development ➤ testing ➤ production life cycle for managing custom-designed infrastructure and applications. You can also use environments to maintain separate sets of configuration for sites or security zones—for example, separate configuration for Demilitarized Zones (DMZs) and the internal network.

You can read about environments at http://reductivelabs.com/trac/puppet/wiki/ UsingMultipleEnvironments.

Documenting Your Configuration

A bane of many system administrators is documentation, both needing to write it and needing to keep it up to date. Puppet has some useful built-in tools that allow you to document your configuration manifests and modules. By running the puppetdoc binary, you can have Puppet scan your manifests and configuration and generate documentation in HTML, among other formats. You can read about manifest documentation at http://reductivelabs.com/trac/ puppet/wiki/PuppetManifestDocumentation.

SCALING PUPPET

The default Puppet master uses an internal web server called Webrick. Generally this web server supports only a small number of clients, usually 30 to 50. To scale Puppet beyond this number of clients, you need to make use of the alternative web server, Mongrel. You can read about Puppet scalability at http://reductivelabs.com/ trac/puppet/wiki/PuppetScalability and http://reductivelabs.com/trac/puppet/wiki/ UsingMongrel.

Troubleshooting Puppet

Puppet has a big and helpful community as well as extensive documentation. In addition, one of the authors of this book, James Turnbull, has written a book specifically about Puppet called *Pulling Strings with Puppet* (Apress, 2008). In addition to the book, you can see Puppet's wiki at http://reductivelabs.com/trac/puppet/wiki. It includes a lot of useful resources such as the following reference pages:

- *Configuration Reference*: http://reductivelabs.com/trac/puppet/wiki/TypeReference
- *Type Reference*: http://reductivelabs.com/trac/puppet/wiki/TypeReference
- *Report Reference*: http://reductivelabs.com/trac/puppet/wiki/ReportReference
- *Function Reference*: http://reductivelabs.com/trac/puppet/wiki/FunctionReference

Also helpful on the wiki are the following resources:

- *Language Tutorial*: http://reductivelabs.com/trac/puppet/wiki/LanguageTutorial
- *Getting Started guide*: http://reductivelabs.com/trac/puppet/wiki/GettingStarted
- *FAQ*: http://reductivelabs.com/trac/puppet/wiki/FrequentlyAskedQuestions

In addition, you can find details of Puppet's mailing lists, the #puppet IRC channel, and a variety of other resources, including the ticketing system at http://reductivelabs.com/trac/puppet/wiki/GettingHelp.

Summary

In this chapter, we've introduced you to some simple provisioning tools that make the process of building and installing your hosts quick and easy. You've learned how to do the following:

- Configure a network boot infrastructure.
- Automatically boot a host with a chosen operating system.
- Install a chosen operating system and automatically answer the installation questions.

We've also introduced a configuration management tool, Puppet, that will help you consistently and accurately manage your environment. You've learned how to do the following:

- Install Puppet.
- Configure Puppet.
- Use Puppet to manage the configuration of your hosts.
- Use the more advanced features of Puppet.

In the next chapter, we'll demonstrate how you make can use of virtualization and virtual servers to deploy your infrastructure cheaply and efficiently.

CHAPTER 20

■ ■ ■

Virtualization

By Sander van Vugt

If you need to run more than one instance of an operating system, you can buy a server for every instance you need. In the past, this was quite a common solution. Nowadays, it's a better idea to buy one or a few powerful servers and use virtualization on these servers. *Virtualization* allows you to run several instances of operating systems on the same hardware. You can use virtualization to optimize the usage of your servers, and you can even use it to create test machines on your desktop. In this chapter, you'll learn what virtualization has to offer and how to install it on your Linux computer.

Virtualization Solutions

Dozens of virtualization solutions are available. In a Linux server environment, there are only a few that really matter:

- VirtualBox
- VMware
- Xen
- KVM
- OpenVZ

In the subsequent sections, you'll find a short description of each of these.

VirtualBox

VirtualBox is used as an application that you install on your computer, and it supports Windows as well as Linux host operating systems. VirtualBox is developed as a desktop virtualization solution, which means that it is a perfect option if you need to work on test machines for whatever reason, without the requirement to take these test machines in production. VirtualBox is available as an open source solution, so you can use and install it for free. Later in this chapter, we'll cover how to install VirtualBox on your computer and how to create virtual machines using VirtualBox.

VMware

In the early 1990s, VMware reinvented virtualization and took it to Intel-based computer architecture. The company started with a product that is now called VMware Workstation, an advanced solution that allows you to create virtual machines on top of a host operating system. Later, several products were added to the VMware product line. Because of the commercial nature of the VMware products, we won't explain how to install and work with them, but as VMware is a major player in the virtualization market, you do need to be aware of the different products that the company has to offer. Currently there are three of them:

- *VMware Workstation*: This is the perfect solution for training and development environments. With VMware Workstation, you can create virtual machines, but you can also save the state of a virtual machine to a snapshot. Working with snapshots allows you to easily revert to the original state of a virtual machine at any moment in time (provided that you have created a snapshot of that virtual machine). VMware Workstation is a proprietary commercial product.

- *VMware Server*: Originally, VMware Server was developed as a low-end virtualization solution for servers. Like VMware Workstation, it runs as an application from a host operating system. The most important difference between VMware Server and VMware Workstation is in the management interface. The VMware Server management interface makes it easier to manage several servers running VMware Server software. VMware Server is available as a free download from `http://www.vmware.com`.

- *VMware ESX*: The big hit from VMware is VMware ESX, an enterprise virtualization solution that runs as a hypervisor that is tightly integrated in a tuned version of Red Hat Linux. This solution is highly tuned and optimized to offer virtualization solutions for servers, but still it is a hypervisor that runs on top of a small host operating system. That means that all instructions generated by the virtual machine have to be captured and translated so that they can be handled by the hardware in your computer. VMware offers add-on products (available for separate purchase) to ESX that make it even easier to use virtual machines in an enterprise environment. There is, for example, VMware High Availability (HA), which makes sure that virtual machines are migrated to another host computer if a VMware host goes down. Another popular solution is VMotion, a product that allows you to migrate a virtual machine from one server to another server without downtime. You can find more information on VMware ESX at the VMware website, `http://www.vmware.com`.

Xen

Xen was developed at the University of Cambridge as a completely new approach to virtualization. The uniqueness of Xen is in the distinction between two different modes of virtualization. The new approach in virtualization that was invented by the founders of the Xen project is known as *paravirtualization*. In paravirtualization, the difference between the host and guest machines is eliminated.

In a paravirtual environment, the computer starts a hypervisor when it boots. On top of the hypervisor, the Domain 0 (also referred to as *Dom0*) machine is started. This is a special machine that has some specific tasks with regard to hardware access. Dom0 makes sure that there are no two virtual machines accessing hardware simultaneously. The main issue in paravirtualization is that the virtual machines do access hardware directly, without any translation that has to be performed by the host operating system. There is a condition to use paravirtualization, though: the virtual machines have to use a tuned kernel. That means you can't use just any operating system in paravirtualization. For instance, older Windows versions cannot benefit from the advantages that paravirtualization has to offer.

Apart from paravirtualization, Xen also offers *full virtualization*. In full virtualization, Dom0 functions as a host operating system, capturing the instructions generated by the virtual machines and translating them to the hypervisor layer. To minimize the performance impact of this approach, in full virtualization you need special virtualization support on the CPU. This support is shown as the VMX feature on Intel CPUs.

You can check if your CPU has this support by displaying the contents of the /proc/cpuinfo file. Listing 20-1 shows the contents of this file on a server that has virtualization support. You can see the VMX feature listed among the flags.

Listing 20-1. *Checking /proc/cpuinfo for CPU Virtualization Support*

```
processor       : 3
vendor_id       : GenuineIntel
cpu family      : 6
model           : 15
model name      : Intel(R) Xeon(R) CPU         X3230  @ 2.66GHz
stepping        : 11
cpu MHz         : 2666.844
cache size      : 4096 KB
physical id     : 0
siblings        : 1
core id         : 3
cpu cores       : 1
fpu             : yes
fpu_exception   : yes
cpuid level     : 10
wp              : yes
flags           : fpu de tsc msr pae mce cx8 apic sep mtrr mca cmov pat pse36
  clflush dts acpi mmx fxsr sse sse2 ss ht tm syscall nx lm constant_tsc pni monitor
  ds_cpl vmx est tm2 cx16 xtpr lahf_lm
bogomips        : 5335.56
clflush size    : 64
cache_alignment : 64
address sizes   : 36 bits physical, 48 bits virtual
power management:
```

No matter how you look at it, when using virtualization in full virtualization mode, you will suffer some performance loss. To compensate for this performance loss, some vendors offer a commercial driver pack. Novell, for instance, offers the Novell Virtualization Driver Pack, which contains some drivers that allow the storage and network adapters in your virtual machines to be used in paravirtual mode. Since these are specifically the adapters that are used most intensively, you can greatly benefit from such a solution to get optimized performance in a full virtual environment. Figure 20-1 gives a schematic overview of the Xen virtualization solution.

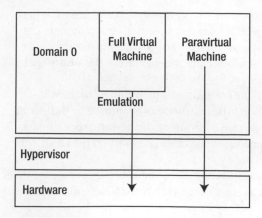

Figure 20-1. *Schematic overview of the Xen virtualization approach*

With regard to Xen, there is some confusion about who owns it. Originally, Xen was founded at the University of Cambridge (see http://www.cl.cam.ac.uk/research/srg/netos/xen/). The founders of Xen created it as an open source project so that other software and hardware companies could provide their input in the Xen project as well. But the founders of Xen also started their own company with the name XenSource.

In 2007, Citrix purchased XenSource. Based on the technology that came from XenSource, Citrix now offers Xen Server, a Citrix-branded product that comes with specific Citrix management tools. Apart from this product, there are still several Linux versions of Xen. Some Linux vendors have switched from Xen to KVM (see the next section), but Novell, for instance, still uses Xen as the default virtualization stack in its products. So in short, the founders of Xen now work for Citrix, but the Xen hypervisor still is and will always be an open source project.

KVM

The last virtualization solution that is highly relevant for Linux environments is KVM. KVM works in a similar way to Xen, but with a major difference. Where Xen is a complex product that uses its own hypervisor, KVM is just one kernel module that loads into an existing Linux kernel. The major benefit of this approach is that it makes virtualization a lot easier. No specific hypervisor is needed anymore, and apart from that, it is just one kernel module. This addresses one of the most important disadvantages of Xen: it is complex. Since in KVM you are dealing with one kernel module only, KVM makes virtualization a lot less complex. Currently, KVM is the default virtualization solution in both Red Hat and Ubuntu Server products.

OpenVZ

OpenVZ is a virtualization solution that uses a *container-based* approach, meaning that the host operating system boots a common kernel. From the host operating system, containers are used. You can compare these container environments to a chroot environment where an application runs in its own jail. In OpenVZ it's not an application, but a complete virtual machine that runs in this jail. Because the virtual machine needs to communicate to the host operating system directly, in an OpenVZ environment you can install only Linux virtual machines.

Working with VirtualBox

If you are a consultant, a trainer, or a developer, and the most important thing you want to do with virtual machines is test them, VirtualBox may be the solution for you. VirtualBox installs as an application on all major Linux distributions, and it allows you to create virtual machines. It performs well, even if performance was not the most important design goal when VirtualBox was created. In this section, you'll learn how to install VirtualBox and how to create a virtual machine in VirtualBox.

Installing VirtualBox

■**Note** VirtualBox is not something that you would typically install on a Linux server. It's a product that you would use on your Linux desktop, to show Linux servers to your customers. Therefore, in this section you won't find specific instructions on how to install VirtualBox on Ubuntu Server or Red Hat Enterprise Linux. Instead, I give you generic instructions that help you install it on almost any Linux distribution.

Most distributions don't include VirtualBox in their default repositories. Therefore, the best approach is to download and install the packages yourself. The following procedure describes how to do that. To make installation easier, make sure the following packages are installed before you begin:

- Qt 4.3 or later

- SDL 1.2.7 or later (look for libsdl)

- Kernel sources

1. Most distributions know the open source version of VirtualBox right from the repositories. To install it, use the package manager. You can do that by using the following command:

   ```
   yum install virtualbox-ose
   ```

   If you are using Ubuntu to install Virtual Box, use the following:

   ```
   apt-get install virtualbox-ose
   ```

2. After installing the software, make sure your user account is a member of the group vboxusers. Normally this group has GID 1000, but you should check in /etc/group if this is the case on your machine. The next command assumes that vboxusers has GID 1000 and you want to make the user linda a member of this group:

   ```
   groupmod -A linda vboxusers
   ```

3. For USB support, you have to change the line that loads the USB file system in /etc/fstab as well. The line that you get by default is

   ```
   usbfs       /proc/bus/usb     usbfs     noauto     0 0
   ```

Change it to the following:

```
usbfs       /proc/bus/usb       usbfs       mode=0644,gid=1000     0 0
```

4. At this point, you are ready to restart your computer, which will activate all changes.

Creating Virtual Machines with VirtualBox

Once you have rebooted your computer, you can now launch VirtualBox. Even if it has installed an icon in the graphical desktop on your computer, for a first launch it is better to open a console window and type the `VirtualBox` command, using your current user account. This permits you to see errors (if any) when starting the application.

If all goes well, you'll now see the VirtualBox Registration form, as shown in Figure 20-2. You have to register, providing your name and e-mail address, but if you don't want to get mail from VirtualBox in your inbox, don't forget to select the option "Please do not use this information to contact me."

Figure 20-2. *Before using VirtualBox, you have to register.*

At this point, you'll see the VirtualBox main window. It's time to start installing a virtual operating system using the following procedure.

■**Tip** When working with virtual operating systems, it's a good idea to create ISO files of your installation media on your computer's local hard drive. You can use `dd` to do that. For instance, the following command copies the content of the CD that actually is in `/dev/cdrom` to an ISO file with the name `/winxpsp.iso`: `dd if=/dev/cdrom of=/winxpsp2.iso`.

---

1. From the VirtualBox main window, click New. This opens a wizard that helps you create a virtual machine. From this wizard, click Next.

2. Type the name you want to assign to the virtual machine. Also select the OS Type that you are going to use in the virtual machine, and then click Next to continue (see Figure 20-3).

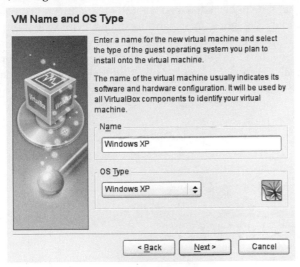

Figure 20-3. *Assigning a name to the virtual machine and selecting the operating system*

3. Specify the amount of RAM you want to use for this virtual machine and click Next. The wizard will automatically see how much RAM you have installed in your computer, thus making it impossible to grant too much RAM to a virtual machine (see Figure 20-4).

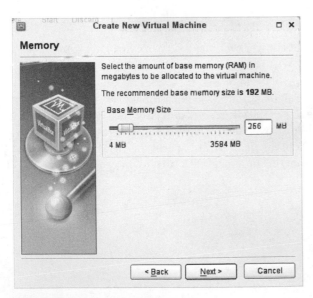

Figure 20-4. *Using the sliding bar to set the amount of RAM assigned to the virtual machine*

4. Next, the installer wants to know about the hard disk your virtual machine is going to use. At this point, you probably don't yet have a hard disk. Create it now, using the New button, which will start the Create New Virtual Disk Wizard. From this wizard, click Next to start. It asks you what type of hard disk you want to create. If you just want to try VirtualBox, select the option "Dynamically expanding image." This will use minimal disk space and is fast also. If you are creating a virtual machine and you're sure that you're going to use it for a long time, it's better to select the "Fixed-size image" option. Since it won't be fragmented, a fixed-size image is faster, but it also takes much longer to create. In Figure 20-5, we've selected "Dynamically expanding image."

Figure 20-5. *For fast access, select the "Dynamically expanding image" option.*

5. At this point, you need to provide a name that is used for the image file and a disk size. If you just want to test, the default size of 10GB will probably be enough. If not, use the sliding bar to increase the size of the virtual disk and click Next. In the next and last screen of the wizard, you see an overview of your selections. From this overview, click Finish. This brings you back to the main wizard, where the virtual disk file you've just created is now selected. From this interface, click Next to proceed (see Figure 20-6).

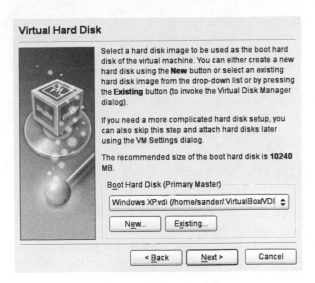

Figure 20-6. *Back in the main wizard, click Next to proceed.*

6. On the last window of the Create Virtual Machine Wizard, click Finish to return to the VirtualBox main screen. You'll see your virtual machine, which is now almost ready for use. You still need to specify what you want to do with the optical drive, though. Especially if you want to install a new operating system, you need to specify what to use as the CD or DVD (see Figure 20-7).

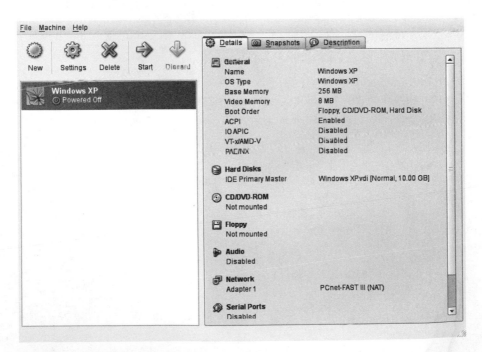

Figure 20-7. *Specifying what to use as the CD or DVD*

7. Click the CD/DVD-ROM link now and select the option Mount CD/DVD Drive. Next, select ISO Image File and click the Browse button. This brings you to an interface where you can browse the file system and look for the ISO file you want to use. After selecting the file from the VirtualBox main window, click Start to start the virtual machine. Assuming that you've selected the installation medium for the operating system that you want to install, this will start the installation of the virtual operating system. Proceed with the installation as usual.

Installing Virtual Machines with Xen

In the preceding section, you installed a virtual machine using VirtualBox. VirtualBox offers an easy-to-use solution that doesn't require you to start a specific kernel. This is not true for Xen; to work with Xen, you need a specific Xen hypervisor. In this section, you'll learn how to prepare your computer for usage of Xen. We assume that you've already installed all Xen packages manually. On Red Hat Enterprise, the installer does this on installation of the operating system when you select the Virtualization installation pattern.

To install Xen on a server that has already been installed, on Red Hat you can use sudo yum install xen kernel-xen virt-manager to install all the required packages. On Ubuntu Server you can do the same using sudo aptitude install ubuntu-xen-server.

Preparing Your Computer for Xen Usage

To use Xen, you need a special kernel. If you have installed all Xen packages on your distribution already, you need to make sure that your computer boots this specific Xen kernel. Sure, you can select it manually when your computer boots, but it is more convenient to configure GRUB to load the Xen kernel automatically. The following procedure describes how to do this:

1. Log in as root and activate the directory /boot/grub.

2. From this directory, open the grub.conf file in your favorite editor. Listing 20-2 gives an example of the contents of this file on a computer that has the Xen kernel installed.

Listing 20-2. *GRUB Configuration File on a Computer with the Xen Kernel Installed*

```
HKG:/boot/grub # cat menu.lst
default 1
timeout 8
gfxmenu (hd0,0)/message

title normal kernel
    root (hd0,0)
    kernel /vmlinuz-2.6.16.60-0.21-smp root=/dev/disk/by-id/scsi\
      -35000c5000ebacfc3-part3 vga=0x317    resume=/dev/sda2 splash=silent\
      showopts
    initrd /initrd-2.6.16.60-0.21-smp

title XEN
    root (hd0,0)
```

```
kernel /xen.gz
module /vmlinuz-2.6.16.60-0.21-xen root=/dev/disk/by-id/scsi\
    -35000c5000ebacfc3-part3 vga=0x317    resume=/dev/sda2 splash=silent\
    showopts
module /initrd-2.6.16.60-0.21-xen
```

As you can see, the example configuration file in Listing 20-2 has two sections. Make sure that section 2 is selected to be started as the default. You can do this by using the `default 1` line in the main part of the GRUB configuration.

3. Restart your server to boot the Xen kernel.

Creating Xen Virtual Machines

In a Xen environment, you can use a very convenient tool, Virtual Machine Manager, to create and manage virtual machines. Apart from that, you can use some command-line tools as well. As creating virtual machines from the command line is cumbersome, you definitely want to create them using Virtual Machine Manager from a graphical user environment. The following procedure shows you how this works.

1. Run the command `virt-manager` to start Virtual Machine Manager. Figure 20-8 shows the interface that appears.

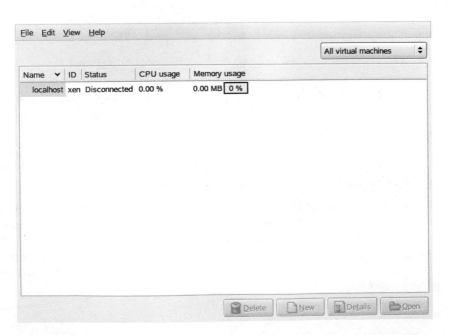

Figure 20-8. *The Virtual Machine Manager interface*

2. Double-click the line that reads localhost xen. This gives you a list of all the virtual machines that already exist on your computer. After you double-click the localhost line, you can click New to start creating a new virtual machine (see Figure 20-9).

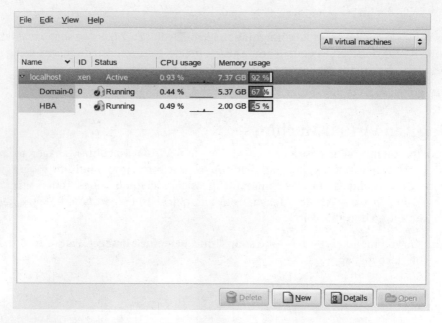

Figure 20-9. *Double-clicking the localhost line to add a new virtual machine*

3. Click New to start creating a new virtual machine. This starts a small wizard from which you can enter all parameters that are required to create virtual machines. From this wizard, click Forward.

4. You are now asked to enter a name for the system that you want to create. Anything is fine, as long as you can recognize later what this system is used for. Make sure that there are no spaces in the system name you are using.

5. Now you have to enter what kind of virtualization you want to use. If your operating system supports it, Paravirtualized is the best solution (see Figure 20-10). If the guest operating system does not support that (this is the case for Windows operating systems), Fully Virtualized will be your only option. To be able to install a virtual machine using full virtualization, make sure that the virtualization feature is enabled in the BIOS of your computer.

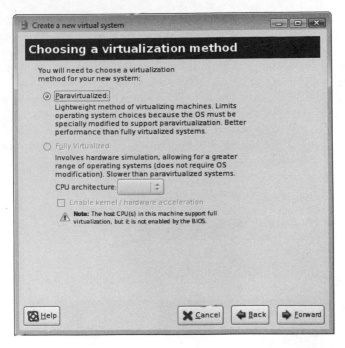

Figure 20-10. *If your operating system supports it, Paravirtualized is the best choice.*

6. You have to specify where Xen can find the installation files. Installation from local media is not supported by default, so enter the address of the repositories on an installation server that you have available for this (see Figure 20-11).

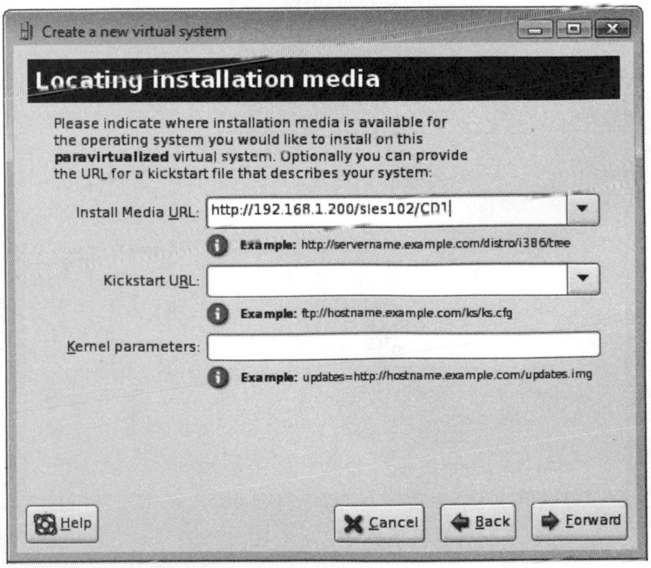

Figure 20-11. *Entering the address of the installation source*

7. You need to specify what you want to use as the storage back end for the virtual hard disk that you are going to assign to the virtual machine (see Figure 20-12). If you want to create a simple setup, use a disk file. For better performance, however, we recommend putting the hard disk on a partition or logical volume on the guest operating system. To keep it simple, in this chapter, we'll show how to install the virtual machine using a file as the storage back end. By default, this file will be 4000MB, which is a decent size for a small test machine. However, you might want to increase the size of this file, and if so, make sure that you select the option to allocate all disk space for the file now, as this will make sure that the file is allocated as contiguous disk space and that prevents fragmentation.

Figure 20-12. *Selecting the Simple File option to create the storage back end*

8. At this point, you need to configure networking. The default choice is to have your virtual machine work on a virtual network that it shares with the host only. For production purposes, this is not a very good idea. Select the "Shared physical device" option now and keep all defaults for networking (see Figure 20-13). When you select this option, the network card of the virtual host is bridged on the network and the virtual host will have full access to the entire network.

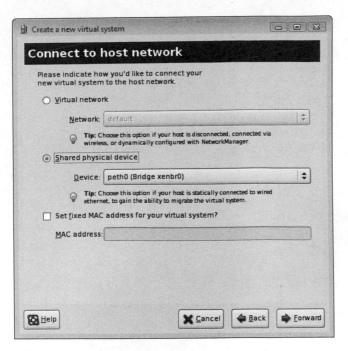

Figure 20-13. *Changing virtual networking to use the "Shared physical device" option*

9. You need to specify what you want to do with the memory assignment for the virtual machine (see Figure 20-14). Because you can dynamically adjust memory that is available to a virtual machine, you'll have to specify a maximum memory assignment and a default memory assignment. We recommend setting the maximum assignment considerably higher than the default memory assignment, which gives you the option of dynamically increasing the amount of available memory later without bringing down the virtual machine.

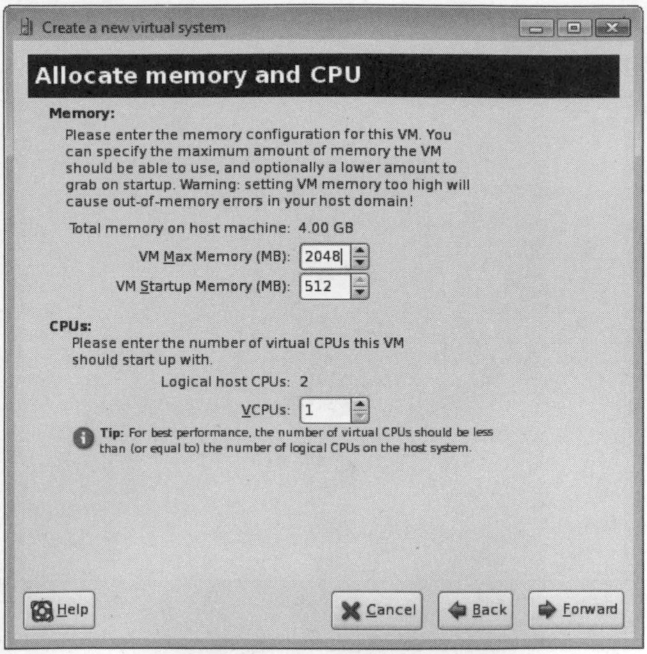

Figure 20-14. *Allocating virtual machine memory and CPU*

10. At this point, you'll see an overview of all your settings so far. From this overview, click Finish to start installing the virtual machine.

You now have your Xen virtual machine installed. Given the parameters used in the preceding procedure, you have created a disk file that is used as the storage back end, as well as a configuration file. This configuration file needs some more attention.

When creating a virtual machine in Xen, two configuration files are created for this virtual machine. In this example, we created a virtual machine with the name sles10. We want to have a look at the SUSE Linux Enterprise server from Novell, and for testing purposes, building a virtual machine is an excellent solution for that. Since we are using version 10 of SUSE Linux Enterprise Server 10, the name of this virtual machine is going to be sles10. This creates virtual machine configuration files with the names /etc/xen/vm/sles10 and /etc/xen/vm/sles10.xml. At the moment this was written, the latter file is not used at all. The former file is used, and it contains the complete configuration of the virtual machine. Listing 20-3 shows its contents.

Listing 20-3. *Contents of the Virtual Machine Configuration File*

```
HKG:~ # cat /etc/xen/vm/sles10
name="sles10"
uuid="cbadcde6-f744-3dae-e3d8-f4c6a364fe85"
memory=512
vcpus=4
on_poweroff="destroy"
on_reboot="restart"
on_crash="destroy"
```

```
localtime=0
builder="linux"
bootloader="/usr/lib/xen/boot/domUloader.py"
bootargs="--entry=xvda2:/boot/vmlinuz-xen,/boot/initrd-xen"
extra=" "
disk=[ 'file:/var/lib/xen/images/sles10/disk0,xvda,w',
  'file:/isos/sles102.iso,xvdb:cdrom,r', ]
vif=[ 'mac=00:16:3e:6b:d0:a4', ]
vfb=['type=vnc,vncunused=1']
```

If you look well enough to the settings used in the configuration file, you can recognize some of the settings that you've used while installing the virtual machine with Virtual Machine Manager. The following is a short explanation of the parameters you see in this file:

- name: The name of the virtual machine.

- uuid: A Universal Unique Identifier (UUID) assigned to the virtual machine.

- memory: The amount of RAM currently assigned to the virtual machine.

- vcpus: The number of virtual CPUs assigned to the virtual machine.

- on_poweroff: Defines what happens if you shut down the physical machine where the virtual machine currently is active. The setting destroy means that the virtual machine will be shut off.

- on_reboot: Defines what happens when the physical machine where the virtual machine currently is running reboots.

- on_crash: Defines what happens when the physical machine where the virtual machine currently is running crashes.

- localtime: Use 0 if your virtual machine uses UTC; use 1 if your virtual machine uses local time.

- builder: Indicates what operating system was used when creating this virtual machine.

- bootloader: This is the alternative to GRUB for the virtual machine. Virtual machines don't have their own boot loader but use the program mentioned here as an alternative to a boot loader.

- bootargs: Passes additional arguments to the boot loader specified in the previous argument.

- extra: Assigns additional options to the boot loader.

- disk: Specifies what to use as the storage back end for the virtual disks. In this example, you see file for both of the disk devices. On occasion, you will see phy, which refers to a physical device.

- vif: Specifies the MAC address and other properties for the virtual network card.

- vfb: Indicates in what way access to this virtual machine is allowed (if it is allowed). The default setting used in this example grants VNC access to the virtual machine.

Managing the Xen Virtual Machine

There are two interfaces for managing virtual machines. Some basic management tasks can be performed from Virtual Machine Manager. For advanced options, you'll have to use the xm command. Both are discussed in the sections that follow.

Managing Virtual Machines with Virtual Machine Manager

To manage a Xen virtual machine, some limited options are offered from the Virtual Machine Manager interface. You can access these options, which are mostly related to hardware management, by selecting the virtual machine from the Virtual Machine Manager main interface. When selecting this option, by default you can see an indicator that shows information about current CPU and memory usage (see Figure 20-15).

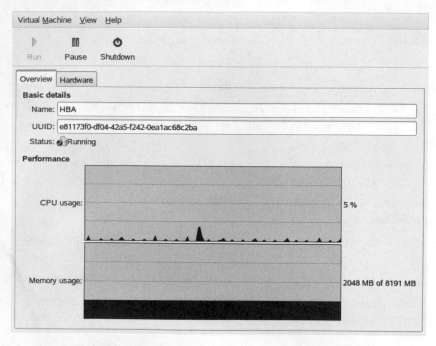

Figure 20-15. *The Overview window of the virtual machine*

If you select the Hardware tab, you'll see the hardware settings that are assigned currently to the virtual machine. Especially if you're using a paravirtualized machine, you have some very cool options available. For instance, you can change the number of CPUs or amount of memory currently assigned to the virtual machine, without having to restart it. To change the amount of memory that is currently assigned, select Memory on the Hardware tab. This will show you the current memory allocation. Enter the new memory allocation value and next click Apply to change the memory assignment (see Figure 20-16). Your virtual machine will pick this up immediately.

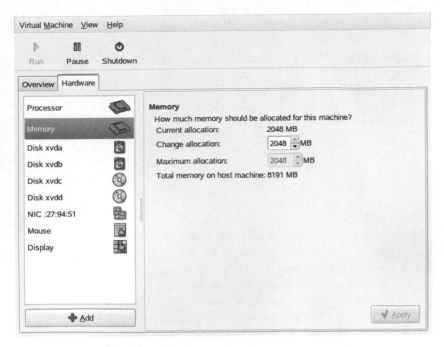

Figure 20-16. *Changing the memory allocation on a paravirtualized virtual machine*

From the Hardware overview in Virtual Machine Manager, you can add new hardware as well. Not all settings will be written to the configuration file immediately, though, and that means that for some settings you'll have to restart the virtual machine. Currently from this interface, you can assign new storage devices, network cards, and graphics devices. After you click the Add button, a wizard opens to guide you through the process of adding the hardware.

Managing Virtual Machines with the xm Command

Virtual Machine Manager offers some basic management options. If you want to unleash the complete power of the virtual machine management interface, you'll need the xm command. This command can work with many different arguments to tell the hypervisor exactly what you want to do with a virtual machine. As you can see in Listing 20-4, the xm help command gives a complete overview of all available options. For each of these options, you can get help from the command line as well, by using xm <option> help to show more usage information.

Listing 20-4. *Showing a Complete List of All Available xm Options*

```
HKG:~ # xm help
Usage: xm <subcommand> [args]

Control, list, and manipulate Xen guest instances.

xm full list of subcommands:

    console             Attach to <Domain>'s console.
    create              Create a domain based on <ConfigFile>.
    new                 Adds a domain to Xend domain management
    delete              Remove a domain from Xend domain management.
    destroy             Terminate a domain immediately.
    domid               Convert a domain name to domain id.
    domname             Convert a domain id to domain name.
    dump-core           Dump core for a specific domain.
    list                List information about all/some domains.
    mem-max             Set the maximum amount reservation for a domain.
    mem-set             Set the current memory usage for a domain.
    migrate             Migrate a domain to another machine.
    pause               Pause execution of a domain.
    reboot              Reboot a domain.
    rename              Rename a domain.
    restore             Restore a domain from a saved state.
    resume              Resume a Xend managed domain
    save                Save a domain state to restore later.
    shutdown            Shutdown a domain.
    start               Start a Xend managed domain
    suspend             Suspend a Xend managed domain
    sysrq               Send a sysrq to a domain.
    trigger             Send a trigger to a domain.
    top                 Monitor a host and the domains in real time.
    unpause             Unpause a paused domain.
    uptime              Print uptime for all/some domains.
    vcpu-list           List the VCPUs for all/some domains.
    vcpu-pin            Set which CPUs a VCPU can use.
    vcpu-set            Set the number of active VCPUs for allowed for
                        the domain.
    debug-keys          Send debug keys to Xen.
    dmesg               Read and/or clear Xend's message buffer.
    info                Get information about Xen host.
    log                 Print Xend log
    serve               Proxy Xend XMLRPC over stdio.
    sched-credit        Get/set credit scheduler parameters.
    sched-sedf          Get/set EDF parameters.
    block-attach        Create a new virtual block device.
    block-detach        Destroy a domain's virtual block device.
```

```
block-list          List virtual block devices for a domain.
block-configure     Change block device configuration
network-attach      Create a new virtual network device.
network-detach      Destroy a domain's virtual network device.
network-list        List virtual network interfaces for a domain.
vtpm-list           List virtual TPM devices.
vnet-list           List Vnets.
vnet-create         Create a vnet from ConfigFile.
vnet-delete         Delete a Vnet.
labels              List <type> labels for (active) policy.
addlabel            Add security label to domain.
rmlabel             Remove a security label from domain.
getlabel            Show security label for domain or resource.
dry-run             Test if a domain can access its resources.
resources           Show info for each labeled resource.
dumppolicy          Print hypervisor ACM state information.
setpolicy           Set the policy of the system.
resetpolicy         Set the policy of the system to the default
                    policy.
getpolicy           Get the policy of the system.
shell               Launch an interactive shell.
```

```
<Domain> can either be the Domain Name or Id.
For more help on 'xm' see the xm(1) man page.
For more help on 'xm create' see the xmdomain.cfg(5)  man page.
```

When working with the xm command, the most important command is xm list, which provides a list of all virtual machines that currently exist on your computer. Since almost all other xm commands need the ID or name of these virtual machines, you should always start with xm list. Listing 20-5 shows an example of the result of this command.

Listing 20-5. *Using xm list for a List of All Virtual Machines*

```
HKG:~ # xm list
Name                        ID    Mem VCPUs      State   Time(s)
Domain 0                     0   5497    4       r-----   9253.3
HBA                          1   2048    4       -b----  69064.1
sles10                       4    512    4       -b----    107.8
```

As you can see in Listing 20-5, for every machine the name, ID, memory assignment, number of allocated virtual CPUs, operational time, and current state are displayed. You'll see two states most of the time: a machine can be active, which means it has been doing something while you used the xm list command, or it can have the state of blocking, which means it was waiting for I/O when you used the command.

In case the information that xm list shows you doesn't give enough details, you can use xm top. Listing 20-6 shows the result of this command.

Listing 20-6. *Using xm top to See What Virtual Machines Are Doing*

```
HKG:~ # xm top
xentop - 20:20:20    Xen 3.2.0_16718_14-0.4
3 domains: 1 running, 2 blocked, 0 paused, 0 crashed, 0 dying, 0 shutdown
Mem: 8387960k total, 8383208k used, 4752k free    CPUs: 4 @ 2666MHz
      NAME  STATE   CPU(sec) CPU(%)    MEM(k) MEM(%)  MAXMEM(k) MAXMEM(%) VCPUS
   NETS NETTX(k) NETRX(k) VBDS    VBD_OO   VBD_RD   VBD_WR SSID
   Domain-0 -----r      9267    0.0   5628928   67.1   no limit      n/a      4
      0        0       0   0        0        0        0 2148573580
        HBA --b---     69078    0.0   2097152   25.0    2097152     25.0      4
      1 87381755 207537763    4        3 20436185 52349866 2148573580
   sles10 --b---        108    0.0    524288    6.3     524288      6.3      4
      1        3     1653    2        0    34211    20867 2148573580




   Delay  Networks  vBds  VCPUs  Repeat header  Sort order  Quit
```

As with the top utility in Linux, xm top shows you exactly what the virtual machines are doing. The command refreshes its status information every five seconds, allowing you to see changes occurring on your virtual machines. You should notice that the output of xm top is shown in two lines for every virtual machine. The network-related information that xm top shows is especially helpful—the NETS parameter displays the number of virtual network interfaces that the machine uses, and the NETTX and NETRX parameters give information about the number of blocks that these network cards have transmitted and received. In the example in Listing 20-6, you can see that the virtual machine HBA is by far the most active machine on the network.

If a physical machine has a problem, you may occasionally need to pull the power plug to switch it off immediately. You can do something similar using the xm command: xm destroy. This command is always followed by the name or the ID of the virtual machine. For instance, the command xm destroy 4 would immediately switch off the machine with ID 4 as shown by xm list. No worries—nothing really is destroyed, and you can easily switch the virtual machine on again by using the command xm start sles10.

Automatically Starting Xen Virtual Machines

When your physical machine has to restart, you probably want the virtual machines that were hosted by it to be restarted automatically as well. It's not too difficult to accomplish this, and the following procedure describes how it works.

1. Make sure that the xendomains service is started automatically. You can do this by adding this service to your runlevel. For instance, the command chkconfig --add xendomains works for this.

2. Create a directory with the name /etc/xen/vm/auto, using `mkdir /etc/xen/vm/auto`.

3. Find out which configuration file from /etc/xen/vm is used to start this virtual machine. For instance, to automatically start the virtual machine that has its configuration in the file sles10, as discussed before, you would use the sles10 file. Copy this file to the directory /etc/xen/auto that you've just created.

Xen offers many more features than the ones we discussed here. Consult the documentation that comes with your distribution for more information.

Installing Virtual Machines with KVM

If your CPU supports virtualization, KVM-based virtualization is the easiest to use—you just have to load a kernel module, and that's all. In this section, you'll learn how to prepare your machine as a KVM virtualization host, and then you'll learn how to install Windows and Ubuntu as virtualized operating systems in the KVM-virtualized environment. As Ubuntu Server was the first enterprise Linux distribution that started using KVM, we're using Ubuntu Server as the example operating system in this section.

■**Caution** When using virtualization, it's a very good idea to differentiate between the host operating system and the others. The host operating system is the first operating system that your server boots. It also has some very specific responsibilities for the other operating systems, such as managing access to drivers and managing the virtual machines themselves. To make sure that it can perform these tasks in the most efficient way, don't run any services (other than virtualization services) in the host operating system!

Preparing Your Server for KVM Virtualization: Networking

On a server where virtualization is used, you can have more virtual machines than you have network boards. Therefore, a solution needs to be implemented for the virtual machines to share network boards in your server. To make this possible, you need to create a virtual network bridge, and if you want it all to work smoothly, it's better to do this before you configure the first virtual machine.

Before starting, make sure that the bridge-utils package is installed. Next, to create the bridge, you need to redefine the contents of the /etc/network/interface file, as in the example shown in Listing 20-7. The code is meant to replace all content that you currently have in this file.

Listing 20-7. *Creating a Network Bridge*

```
auto lo
iface lo inet loopback

auto br0
iface br0 inet static
    address 192.168.1.99
    network 192.168.1.0
```

```
netmask 255.255.255.0
broadcast 192.168.1.255
gateway 192.168.1.254
bridge_ports eth0
bridge_fd 0
bridge_hello 2
bridge_maxage 12
bridge_stop off
```

This configuration file makes sure that when you reboot your server or restart your network, a device with the name br0 is created to replace the eth0 device. This device really works as a virtual bridge, with the network cards in all virtual machines assigned to it. However, this device is meant to use the physical eth0 as its physical back end, as specified by the line bridge_ports eth0. After creating the configuration file in this way, use sudo invoke-rc.d networking restart to restart your network. Your network is now ready to handle KVM virtual machines.

Setting Up KVM on Ubuntu Server

Perform the following steps to set up your server for virtualization (the procedure described here is supported on Ubuntu Server 8.04 and later).

1. Install all software necessary (the KVM and QEMU packages) for KVM virtualization. As root, use the command apt-get install kvm qemu libvirt-bin.

2. After installing these software packages, make sure that the kvm kernel module is loaded. Use lsmod to determine if this is the case (lsmod | grep kvm), and if the module is not loaded, install it using modprobe kvm.

■Tip Are you getting the "Operation is not supported" message while loading the kernel module? If so, you have the wrong CPU. Either upgrade your CPU to one that offers virtualization support or use Xen as your virtualization solution with an operating system that supports paravirtualization.

Next, you have to do some additional preparation that involves setting up the libvirt tools you will use to create virtual machines. First, you need to add the user account you want to use for KVM management purposes to the libvirtd group. You can do this using the sudo adduser <username> libvirtd command, replacing <username> with the name of the user whose account you want to use.

And that's it! Your Ubuntu Server is now ready for the installation and operation of guest operating systems. The next section describes how to install Windows as a guest operating system.

Installing Windows As a Guest Operating System on KVM

Before installing Windows as your first guest operating system, you should ask yourself exactly what you want to do with the virtualized machines. Is your server running in a data center, and are you accomplishing all tasks (including installation of the virtual machines) remotely? If so, you can run it without a GUI using the graphical interface on your workstation. If, on the other hand, you want to be able to manage the virtual machine(s) from the physical server itself, it's a good idea to install a GUI on your server. The procedure described in this section assumes that you do have some graphical interface that can be used to display the Windows installation interface.

1. To install Windows as a virtualized operating system, you first need to set up storage. The simplest way of trying out virtualization is by using a disk image file. You can create this by using dd or qemu-img, as in the following command that creates an 8GB disk image file with the name windows.img in the directory /var/lib/virt (make sure to create this directory before creating the image file!).

```
sudo dd if=/dev/zero of=/var/lib/virt/windows.img bs=1M count=8192
```

2. Now that you've created the disk image file, you can use the kvm command to install Windows. Make sure that the Windows installation CD is in the drive (or use an ISO file), and run the following command to start the installation, creating a Windows virtual machine with a total of 512MB of RAM. This command uses the windows.img disk file that you just created. Want to use an ISO file instead of a physical CD-ROM? Just replace /dev/cdrom by a complete path to the ISO file.

```
kvm -m 512 -cdrom /dev/cdrom -boot d windows.img
```

■**Tip** Is the kvm command complaining about the lack of support for virtualization on your CPU? You probably haven't switched on virtualization support in your system BIOS yet. Restart your machine, enter the system BIOS, and make sure that virtualization support is on. Typically, you'll find this in the Advanced section of your BIOS configuration, and the option that you are looking for has a name like vm, vt, or just virtualization.

---

3. This opens a QEMU window, in which you'll see the Windows installer loading. Complete the Windows installation from this interface.

4. Once the installation of virtualized Windows is finished, you can run it in the same way you installed it. Use the kvm command again, but omit the option -boot d, which ensures that you're booting from CD-ROM first. The following command runs an installed instance of Windows that is on the windows.img file:

```
kvm  -m 512 -cdrom /dev/cdrom windows.img
```

You now have your virtualized Windows machine. That was easy, wasn't it? Next, we'll have a look at how to install Ubuntu as a guest on top of your Ubuntu Server virtualization host.

Installing Ubuntu Server As a Guest Operating System on KVM

After reading the previous section about installing Windows as a guest operating system in KVM, you probably can already guess how to install an instance of virtualized Ubuntu. Fundamentally, there are no differences between installing Windows and installing Ubuntu: you create a virtual disk and install Ubuntu Server on that. Make sure that you have an ISO file of the Ubuntu installation media, and proceed as follows:

1. Create the disk file:

   ```
   dd if=/dev/zero of=/var/lib/virt/ubuntu.img bs=1M count=4096
   ```

2. Use the kvm command to start the installation from the Ubuntu ISO file:

   ```
   kvm  -m 256 -cdrom /isos/ubuntu.iso -boot d /var/lib/virt/ubuntu.img
   ```

■**Tip** Are you having problems installing Ubuntu or another Linux distribution as a guest operating system? The graphical menu that most boot loaders display nowadays before starting the installation could be the reason. Try a nongraphical installation program such as the Ubuntu net boot mini.iso file instead. This will help you install any Linux distribution without problems.

---

3. Install Ubuntu Server as if it was a "normal" server.

4. Boot the virtual Ubuntu Server you've just installed with the following command, and you're done:

   ```
   kvm -m 256 ubuntu.img
   ```

Managing KVM Virtual Machines with Virtual Manager

If you don't like starting and installing your virtual machines using the kvm command (or even with an enhancement to this command, like virt-install: sudo apt-get install python-virtinstall), virtual-manager may be the solution for you. This graphical utility provides an easy solution to creating and managing virtual machines. It does have a disadvantage, though: it needs an X server to run. That doesn't mean that you have to install the graphical environment locally on your server—you can run virt-manager from a workstation as well. For instance, from a workstation, establish an SSH session with your server and start virt-manager that way. That will give you all the benefits of the graphical virtual machine management tools without the hassle of installing a GUI on your server. As an alternative, you can also use a boot parameter to tell virt-manager it has to get its information from another machine. For instance, the following command connects to somenode.example. com and allows you to manage virtual machines on that node:

```
virt-manager -c qemu+ssh://somenode.example.com/system
```

In case you want to start virt-manager to create virtual machines on the local host, use the following:

```
virt-manager -c qemu:///system
```

In the following procedure, you'll learn how to create a virtual machine using virt-manager.

1. Start virt-manager. In this example, we assume you have established an SSH session with a remote server, so you can type **virt-manager -c qemu:///system** to start the virt-manager session. Alternatively, from the KVM interface, you can use the File ➤ Connect option to connect to QEMU on localhost. This will show you an interface, as in Figure 20-17.

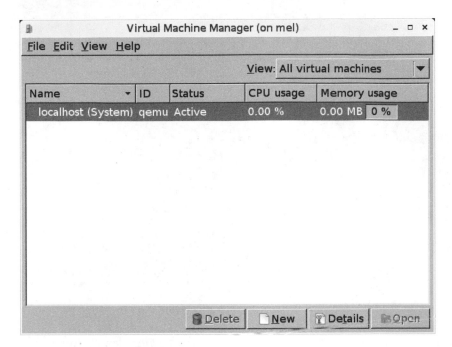

Figure 20-17. *Virtual Machine Manager*

2. Select the localhost line and click New to start creating a new virtual machine. This brings you to the first step of a wizard interface. Click Forward in this interface.

3. Enter the name of the system that you want to create. For instance, if you want to install a Windows XP test machine, WinXP might be a good idea. Next, click Forward to proceed.

4. The utility asks you what kind of virtualization you want to use. In KVM, you can only use the Fully Virtualized option that is shown; the Paravirtualized option is usable in Xen virtualization only (see Figure 20-18).

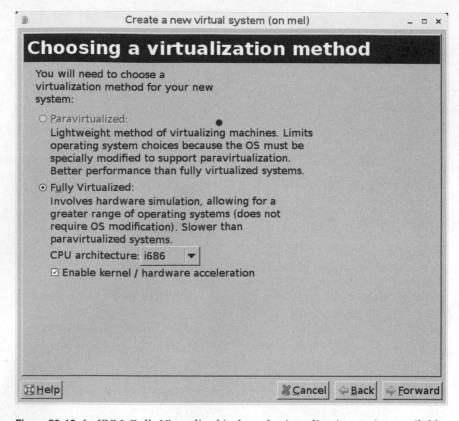

Figure 20-18. *In KVM, Fully Virtualized is the only virtualization option available.*

5. Now you need to specify how to start the installation. If, for example, you have an ISO image to install from, browse to the path where the installer can find the ISO image (see Figure 20-19). Also make sure to select the OS Type and OS Variant you want to install.

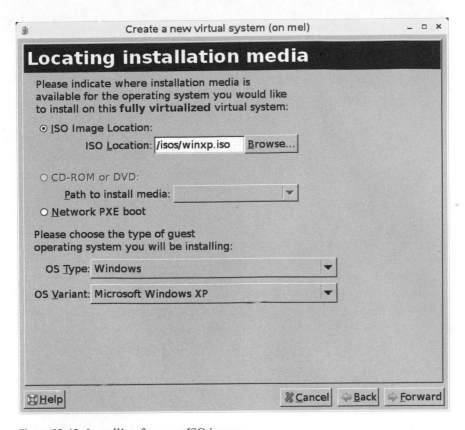

Figure 20-19. *Installing from an ISO image*

6. In the following window, you indicate what you want to install to (see Figure 20-20). For best performance, it is a good idea to give every virtual machine a dedicated partition or LVM logical volume. If you can't do that, you can install to a file. The installation interface will create this virtual disk file automatically for you.

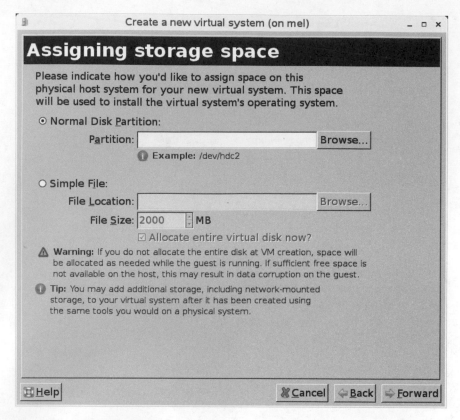

Figure 20-20. *Using a partition or LVM logical volume as the storage back end*

7. Select the networking method that you want to use. The most flexible way is to create a virtual network. In this configuration, which will always work, a network bridge is created as described earlier in this network. If your server has a fixed IP address, you can also choose to assign a second IP address to the network interface by selecting the "Shared physical device" option. After making your choice, click Forward to proceed.

8. Now enter the amount of RAM and number of CPUs you want to give to your virtual machine and click Forward (see Figure 20-21).

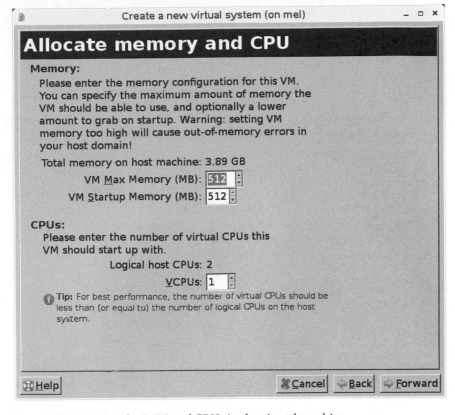

Figure 20-21. *Setting the RAM and CPUs in the virtual machine*

9. In the last screen the installation wizard shows you, you'll see an overview of the installation settings that are going to be used. Happy with that? Click Forward to start the installation of the virtual operating system. Once the installation is complete, you'll see that the new virtual machine is added to the `virt-manager` interface, and you'll be able to manage it from there.

Virtualization with OpenVZ

The virtualization approach in OpenVZ is completely different from the Xen and KVM approaches. As mentioned previously, OpenVZ offers a container-based approach, meaning that multiple isolated containers are created on a physical server. In these containers, the administrator can create the virtual machine. Every virtual machine runs completely isolated and therefore secure from the other virtual machines that run in other containers. Compared to other virtualization techniques, OpenVZ has a limitation, though: the host as well as all the virtual guest operating systems must run Linux. You can run different Linux distributions as a virtual guest. OpenVZ is also the basis of Parallels Virtuozzo Containers, a commercial virtualization solution that is used in exactly the same way.

The major benefit of this approach is performance, combined with security. In OpenVZ, it's just Linux talking to Linux, so no complex translation needs to be done. At the same time, the solution is also secure, because the containers act like environments that are isolated from one another.

Installation

You can run OpenVZ on both Red Hat and Debian. Currently, installation on Ubuntu is not supported. The following procedure takes you through an installation of OpenVZ on Red Hat–based systems. This procedure supports installation using Yum as well as installation with RPM packages; the procedure in this section describes how to install OpenVZ using Yum. For performance reasons, we strongly advise that you run OpenVZ on 64-bit hardware and a 64-bit operating system. The procedure presented here assumes that you are installing on a 64-bit OS.

1. There is a repository file available for OpenVZ. Before starting the installation, download it and put it in the /etc/yum.repos.d directory. You can download the repository file using the following wget command:

   ```
   wget http://download.openvz.org/openvz.repo
   ```

   Following this command, you should also import the GPG key that belongs to the repository, as follows:

   ```
   rpm --import http://download.openvz.org/RPM-GPG-Key-OpenVZ
   ```

2. Now you need to install the OpenVZ kernel. Different kernels are available, and the type of kernel that you select depends on the hardware you are using and the number of containers you are going to create. First, there is the SMP kernel, which you would use in a symmetric multiprocessor environment. It supports up to 4GB of RAM and a maximum of 10 to 20 containers. Next is the entnosplit kernel, which uses the Physical Address Extension (PAE) and supports a maximum of up to 64GB of RAM and 10 to 30 containers. Then there is the enterprise kernel, which also supports SMP and PAE and is the best choice to handle lots of containers, over 20 to 30 at the same time. When using OpenVZ on a 32-bit operating system, it is important that you choose the right kernel. If you are using a 64-bit operating system, the SMP kernel fits all needs, as in 64-bit there no longer is a 4GB RAM limitation that you need to overcome using PAE. Assuming that you are using 64-bit, use the following command to install this kernel:

   ```
   yum install ovzkernel-smp
   ```

   At this point, the OpenVZ kernel is installed and automatically added to your GRUB configuration. After a reboot, the OpenVZ kernel starts automatically.

3. Before restarting, you need to tune a couple of sysctl parameters. You can do that by making sure all the parameters shown in Listing 20-8 are in your /etc/sysctl.conf file.

Listing 20-8. *Required Optimization Parameters in /etc/sysctl.conf*

```
net.ipv4.ip_forward = 1
net.ipv6.conf.default.forwarding = 1
net.ipv6.conf.all.forwarding = 1
net.ipv4.conf.default.proxy_arp = 0
```

```
net.ipv4.conf.all.rp_filter = 1
kernel.sysrq = 1
net.ipv4.conf.default.send_redirects = 1
net.ipv4.conf.all.send_redirects = 0
```

4. Next, you must make sure that SELinux is off. You can do that by putting the following value in the /etc/sysconfig/selinux file:

```
SELINUX=disabled
```

5. You need to install the OpenVZ tools. To do this, use the following command:

```
yum install vzctl vzquota
```

6. If you are planning to use IP addresses in the virtual machines that are from a different IP address range than the IP address of the host machine, you next need to edit the /etc/vz/vz.conf file and make sure that it contains the following:

```
NEIGHBOUR_DEVS=all
```

7. At this point, you can restart your computer, which will activate the OpenVZ kernel.

Creating OpenVZ Virtual Machines

To create an OpenVZ virtual machine, you need a template for the virtual operating system that you want to create. Templates are available for all major Linux distributions, and you can download a list of templates from http://wiki.openvz.org/Download/template/precreated. For instance, if you wanted to use a CentOS 5 virtual machine, you would download the CentOS 5 template with the following commands:

```
cd /vz/template/cache
wget http://download.openvz.org/template/precreated/contrib/
    centos-5-i386-default.tar.gz
```

Once the template is downloaded, you can use it to start one or more virtual machines. To start a virtual machine based on the template you have just downloaded, use the following command:

```
vzctl create 150 --ostemplate centos-5-i386 default --config vps.basic
```

Here, vzctl is the master command that allows you to create and manage virtual machines. Like the ip command, vzctl is used with subcommands, of which create allows you to create a new virtual machine. Each virtual machine gets its own unique ID. It might be a good idea to use the last part of the IP address for this unique ID (150 in this example). Next, you need to specify which template to use. The template basically contains a bare, basic file that you need to fill with its own configuration. The --config option makes sure that a configuration file is created for this virtual machine. You will find the configuration file in the directory /etc/vz/conf. Every virtual machine gets its own configuration file. To manage the virtual machine, you can edit this file directly, but you can also pass different parameters on the command line to change the properties of the virtual machine.

When you create a virtual machine in this way, it will not restart automatically when you reboot your computer. To make sure that also happens, use the following command:

```
vzctl set 150 --onboot yes --save
```

Next, you can start entering the other parameters that you want to use in the virtual machine. This includes at least the IP configuration, which you can set with the following commands. Change the parameters used in these commands to match your current configuration:

```
vzctl set 150 --hostname nuuk.example.com --save
vzctl set 150 --ipadd 192.168.1.150 --save
vzctl set 150 --nameserver 193.79.237.39 --save
```

At this point, you have created a fairly decent basic configuration, which is stored in /etc/vz/conf/150.conf (given that this example used 150 as the ID of the virtual machine). Listing 20-9 shows what this file looks like at this point.

Listing 20-9. *Virtual Machine Configuration Written to a Configuration File*

```
[root@centos conf]# cat 150.conf
# Copyright (C) 2000-2008, Parallels, Inc. All rights reserved.
#
# This program is free software; you can redistribute it and/or modify
# it under the terms of the GNU General Public License as published by
# the Free Software Foundation; either version 2 of the License, or
# (at your option) any later version.
#
# This program is distributed in the hope that it will be useful,
# but WITHOUT ANY WARRANTY; without even the implied warranty of
# MERCHANTABILITY or FITNESS FOR A PARTICULAR PURPOSE.  See the
# GNU General Public License for more details.
#
# You should have received a copy of the GNU General Public License
# along with this program; if not, write to the Free Software
# Foundation, Inc., 59 Temple Place, Suite 330, Boston, MA  02111-1307  USA
#

ONBOOT="yes"

# UBC parameters (in form of barrier:limit)
KMEMSIZE="14372700:14790164"
LOCKEDPAGES="256:256"
PRIVVMPAGES="65536:69632"
SHMPAGES="21504:21504"
NUMPROC="240:240"
PHYSPAGES="0:9223372036854775807"
VMGUARPAGES="33792:9223372036854775807"
OOMGUARPAGES="26112:9223372036854775807"
NUMTCPSOCK="360:360"
```

```
NUMFLOCK="188:206"
NUMPTY="16:16"
NUMSIGINFO="256:256"
TCPSNDBUF="1720320:2703360"
TCPRCVBUF="1720320:2703360"
OTHERSOCKBUF="1126080:2097152"
DGRAMRCVBUF="262144:262144"
NUMOTHERSOCK="360:360"
DCACHESIZE="3409920:3624960"
NUMFILE="9312:9312"
AVNUMPROC="180:180"
NUMIPTENT="128:128"

# Disk quota parameters (in form of softlimit:hardlimit)
DISKSPACE="1048576:1153024"
DISKINODES="200000:220000"
QUOTATIME="0"

# CPU fair sheduler parameter
CPUUNITS="1000"

VE_ROOT="/vz/root/$VEID"
VE_PRIVATE="/vz/private/$VEID"
OSTEMPLATE="centos-5-i386-default"
ORIGIN_SAMPLE="vps.basic"
HOSTNAME="nuuk.example.com"
IP_ADDRESS="192.168.1.150"
NAMESERVER="193.79.237.39"
```

Now that you have created the virtual machine configuration, it's time to start the machine, using the following command:

```
vzctl start 150
```

Next, make sure to set the root password:

```
vzctl exec 150 passwd
```

The passwd will prompt you to set the root password, just as the passwd command will do this when used from the command line.

At this point, the virtual container is ready for usage. You can now contact it by using SSH or directly from the console of the host operating system by entering the following:

```
vzctl enter 150
```

If you have accessed the virtual container using vzctl enter, you can quit it by typing **exit**.

Basic OpenVZ Virtual Machine Management

Now that the virtual machine is up and running, it's time to have a look at some of the commands that you can use to manage it. As you'll see, those commands look a lot like the commands that you would use to manage a Xen virtual machine. First, you probably want to see a list of all the virtual machines that currently are available. You can get this list by using the command vzlist -a:

```
[root@centos conf]# vzlist -a
    CTID      NPROC STATUS  IP_ADDR        HOSTNAME
    150          19 running 192.168.1.150  nuuk.example.com
```

As you can see, this command shows you the current status of each of your virtual machines (just one machine is running in this example). Based on this information, you can stop a virtual machine (vzctl stop 150), restart it (vzctl restart 150), or completely delete it from the host machines hard drive (vzctl destroy 150). The last command works only if you have first stopped the virtual machine.

Summary

In this chapter, you learned how to work with virtualization in a Linux environment. We discussed three different methods to apply a virtualization solution. We first covered VirtualBox, which is useful for demonstration purposes where convenience is the most important need and performance is not as important. Next, we demonstrated how to configure Xen and KVM-based virtual environments on your computer. This information helps you in setting up virtualization and thus using server resources more efficiently in your network. The last part of this chapter discussed how to deploy OpenVZ in your environment. OpenVZ has a completely different approach to virtualization, as it works with the concept of virtual containers.

Index

You Need the Companion eBook

Your purchase of this book entitles you to buy the companion PDF-version eBook for only $10. Take the weightless companion with you anywhere.

We believe this Apress title will prove so indispensable that you'll want to carry it with you everywhere, which is why we are offering the companion eBook (in PDF format) for $10 to customers who purchase this book now. Convenient and fully searchable, the PDF version of any content-rich, page-heavy Apress book makes a valuable addition to your programming library. You can easily find and copy code—or perform examples by quickly toggling between instructions and the application. Even simultaneously tackling a donut, diet soda, and complex code becomes simplified with hands-free eBooks!

Once you purchase your book, getting the $10 companion eBook is simple:

❶ Visit **www.apress.com/promo/tendollars/**.

❷ Complete a basic registration form to receive a randomly generated question about this title.

❸ Answer the question correctly in 60 seconds, and you will receive a promotional code to redeem for the $10.00 eBook.

2855 TELEGRAPH AVENUE | SUITE 600 | BERKELEY, CA 94705